DISCOVER NEW PEDAGOGY

Throughout the text, new pedagogy enhances student learning. These new learning aids include:

- Three distinct competitive challenge boxes—Competing by Meeting Stakeholders' Needs (new to this edition), Competing through Globalization, and Competing through High-Performance Work Systems—provide excellent real-business examples to underscore key concepts throughout the text.
- Updated boxed material, chapter openings, and legal and research findings are found throughout.
- The end-of-chapter cases are all new in the third edition. Managing People: From the Pages of *Business Week* looks at incidents at real companies as reported by *Business Week* and encourages students to critically evaluate the problem and apply the chapter concepts.
- Web exercises at the end of each chapter give students the opportunity to see how the Web can be used for HR management.

Human Resource Management

Gaining a Competitive Advantage

Third Edition

Human Resource Management

Gaining a Competitive Advantage

Third Edition

Raymond A. Noe
The Ohio State University

John R. Hollenbeck
Michigan State University

Barry Gerhart
Vanderbilt University

Patrick M. Wright
Cornell University

Boston Burr Ridge, IL Dubuque, IA Madison, WI New York San Francisco St. Louis
Bangkok Bogotá Caracas Lisbon London Madrid
Mexico City Milan New Delhi Seoul Singapore Sydney Taipei Toronto

McGraw-Hill Higher Education

A Division of The ***McGraw-Hill*** *Companies*

HUMAN RESOURCE MANAGEMENT:
GAINING A COMPETITIVE ADVANTAGE

The book is printed on acid-free paper.

domestic 3 4 5 6 7 8 9 0 DOW/DOW 9 0 9 8 7 6 5 4 3 2 1 0
international 2 3 4 5 6 7 8 9 0 DOW/DOW 9 0 9 8 7 6 5 4 3 2 1 0

ISBN 0-07-228518-4

Vice president/Editor-in-chief: *Michael W. Junior*
Publisher: *Craig S. Beytien*
Senior sponsoring editor: *John E. Biernat*
Developmental editor: *Christine Scheid*
Marketing manager: *Ellen Cleary*
Project manager: *Karen J. Nelson*
Manager, new book production: *Melonie Salvati*
Designer: *Jennifer McQueen Hollingsworth*
Cover image: *© J. F. Martin/SIS*
Senior photo research coordinator: *Keri Johnson*
Supplement coordinator: *Matthew Perry*
Compositor: *ElectraGraphics, Inc.*
Typeface: *10.5/12 Goudy*
Printer: *R. R. Donnelley & Sons Company*

Library of Congress Cataloging-in-Publication Data

Human resource management : gaining a competitive advantage / Raymond A. Noe . . . [et al.]. — 3rd ed.
p. cm.
Includes index.
ISBN 0-07-228518-4 (alk. paper)
1. Personnel management—United States. I. Noe, Raymond A.
HF5549.2.U5H8 2000
658.3—dc21 99-24620

INTERNATIONAL EDITION

When ordering the title, use ISBN 0-07-116972-5

http://www.mhhe.com

To my parents, Raymond and Mildred,
my wife, Ann, and my children, Ray, Tim, and Melissa

—R. A. N.

To my parents, Harold and Elizabeth, my wife, Patty,
and my children, Jennifer, Marie,
Timothy, and Jeffrey

—J. R. H.

To my parents, Robert and Shirley, my wife, Heather,
and my children, Chris and Annie

—B. G.

To my parents, Patricia and Paul, my wife,
Mary, and my son, Michael

—P. M. W.

Preface

To grow and thrive in today's competitive environment, organizations must deal with several major challenges. First, they must provide "value." Traditionally, the concept of value has been considered a function of finance or accounting. However, we believe that how human resources are managed is crucial to the long-term value of a company and ultimately to its survival. Our definition of *value* includes not only profits but employee growth and satisfaction, additional employment opportunities, protection of the environment, and contributions to community programs.

Since the publication of the first edition of *Human Resource Management: Gaining a Competitive Advantage,* value has become even more critical. Organizations' resources are stretched tighter than ever, and allocating those resources wisely is imperative. For that reason, all functions in an organization must work together to contribute wherever they can; and all functions, particularly human resources, are increasingly being scrutinized for the value they add.

We believe that all aspects of human resource management—including how companies interact with the environment; acquire, prepare, develop, and compensate human resources; and design and measure work—can help companies meet their competitive challenges and create value. Meeting challenges is necessary to create value and to gain a competitive advantage.

The Competitive Challenges

The challenges organizations face today can be grouped into three categories:

- **The global challenge.** Increasingly, organizations are finding that to survive they must compete with organizations around the world. Companies must both defend their domestic markets from foreign competitors and broaden their scope to encompass global markets. Recent threats to and successes of U.S. businesses have proven that globalization is a continuing challenge.
- **The meeting stakeholders' needs challenge.** Key to success in today's business environment is to simultaneously meet investor or financial needs and those of other stakeholders including customers, employees, and the community. Companies are challenged to reach financial objectives through meeting customer needs and employee needs. Innovation, cost reduction, and quality objectives which relate directly to the financial success or failure of the firm are influenced by human resource management practices. Forward-looking businesses are capitalizing on the strengths of a diverse workforce. Businesses are realizing the advantages they have in attracting, retaining, and motivating employees through ethical and responsible actions. Successful companies have human resource management practices that motivate and reward employees to provide high quality products and services.
- **The high-performance work systems challenge.** Using new technologies such as computer-aided manufacturing, virtual reality, expert systems, and the Internet

can provide companies with an edge. New technologies can result in employees' "working smarter" as well as providing higher-quality products and services to customers. However, companies that have seen the greatest gains from new technology have human resource practices that support the use of technology. The design of work, training programs, and reward systems often need to be reconfigured to support employees' use of new technology. Thus, the three links of high-performance work systems are (1) human resources and their capabilities, (2) new technology and its opportunities, and (3) efficient work structures and policies that allow employees and technology to interact. The strength of each of these links determines an organization's competitiveness.

We believe that organizations must successfully deal with these challenges to create and maintain value, and the key to facing these challenges is a motivated, well-trained, and committed work force.

The Changing Role of the Human Resource Function

The human resource (HR) profession and practices have undergone substantial change and redefinition. Many articles written in both the academic and practitioner literature have been critical of the traditional HR function. Unfortunately, in many organizations HR services are not providing value but instead are mired down in managing trivial administrative tasks. Where this is true, HR departments can be replaced with new technology or outsourced to a vendor who can provide higher-quality services at a lower cost. While this recommendation is indeed somewhat extreme (and threatening to both HR practitioners and those who teach human resource management!), it does demonstrate that companies need to ensure that their HR functions are creating value for the firm.

Technology should be used where appropriate to automate routine activities, and managers should concentrate on HR activities that can add substantial value to the company. Consider employee benefits: Technology is available to automate the process by which employees enroll in benefits programs and to keep detailed records of benefits usage. This use of technology frees up time for the manager to focus on activities that can create value for the firm (e.g., how to control health care costs and reduce workers' compensation claims).

Although the importance of some HR departments is being debated, everyone agrees on the need to successfully manage human resources for a company to maximize its competitiveness. Three themes emerge from our conversations with managers and our review of research on HR practices. First, in today's flatter organizations, managers themselves are becoming more responsible for HR practices. Second, most managers believe that their HR departments are not well respected because of a perceived lack of competence, business sense, and contact with operations. Third, many managers believe that for HR practices to be effective they need to be related to the strategic direction of the business. This text emphasizes how HR practices can and should contribute to business goals and help to improve product and service quality and effectiveness.

Our intent is to provide students with the background to be successful HR professionals, to manage human resources effectively, and to be knowledgeable consumers of HR products. Managers must be able to identify effective HR practices to purchase these services from a consultant, to work with the HR department, or to design and implement them personally. The text emphasizes how a manager can more effectively manage human resources and highlights important issues in current HR practice.

We think this book represents a valuable approach to teaching human resource management for several reasons:

- The text draws from the diverse research, teaching, and consulting experiences of four authors. They have taught human resource management to undergraduates, traditional day M.B.A. students as a required and elective course, and more experienced managers and professional employees in weekend and evening M.B.A. programs. The teamwork approach gives a depth and breadth to the coverage that is not found in other texts.
- Human resource management is viewed as critical to the success of a business. The text emphasizes how the HR function, as well as the management of human resources, can help companies gain a competitive advantage.
- The book discusses current issues such as work-force diversity, organizational flexibility, the quality movement, work design, and retention and separation of employees, all of which have a major impact on business and HR practice.
- Strategic human resource management is introduced early in the book, and integrated throughout the text.
- Examples of how new technologies are being used to improve the efficiency and effectiveness of HR practices are provided throughout the text.

Changes in the Third Edition

In the swiftly changing business environment, currency is vital. Based on the comments of the reviewer of the second edition of the text we have made several improvements. Several important changes in the third edition of *Human Resource Management: Gaining a Competitive Advantage* maintain the text's competitive edge:

- Each chapter has been thoroughly updated to reflect the most recent academic research findings and new best company practices. New examples have been added throughout the text in each chapter.
- New chapter-opening vignettes are provided. Many of the companies illustrated have been recognized for their strong HR practices. For example, SAS Institute, whose HR practices are described in the opening for Chapter 10, was recently ranked third in *Fortune Magazine*'s 1999 annual survey of best companies to work for in America. Many companies illustrated have also had to deal with difficult human resource management issues. For example, the opening vignette of Chapter 2, "Strategic Human Resource Management," describes the problems that Delta Air Lines faced when they had to downsize to survive.
- New boxed features provide the most current real-world examples possible.
- A new box titled "Competing by Meeting Stakeholders' Needs" replaces the second edition's "Competing through Quality" and "Competing through Social Responsibility" boxes. This box continues to emphasize social responsibility and quality but from a broader perspective than found in previous editions. This new box better reflects the continuous challenge that companies face of how to meet the needs of multiple stakeholders, including shareholders, employees, and the community. The box shows examples of how companies have realized financial goals through meeting customer, employee, and community needs. For example, the

"Competing by Meeting Stakeholders Needs" box in Chapter 13, "Employee Benefits," show how the Big Three automakers are seeking to improve the quality of health care given to their employees and at the same time reduce benefit costs by devising a common report card for rating health care quality.
- The end-of-chapter cases have been replaced with cases from *Business Week* (see "Managing People: From the Pages of *Business Week*.") These cases provide real incidents that companies have faced as reported in *Business Week*. Detailed information about the company and the incident described are provided. The case questions require students to critically evaluate the problem presented and apply chapter content. We provide World Wide Web home page addresses for the companies discussed in the cases so that students and instructors can obtain additional information about each company's history, products and services, finances, and latest news releases.
- We reduced the number of Chapters from 19 to 16 to provide comprehensive but succinct coverage of HRM topics.

There are several changes in content, focus, and placement of the chapters found in this edition:

- In the second edition of the text, Chapter 2 was "Global Issues in Human Resources Management." The chapter covering this topic is now positioned toward the end of the text (Chapter 15) not to de-emphasize its importance, but to present it after students have been introduced to HRM practices so they can better understand how cultural and economic factors influence the effectiveness of HRM practices in different countries. Global issues continue to be emphasized throughout the text with the "Competing through Globalization" box.
- Chapter 5, "Human Resource Planning and Recruitment," covers how companies can develop and leverage labor market problems (e.g., excess or shortage of human resources) into opportunities to gain a competitive advantage. The chapter emphasizes how to develop and implement a human resource plan as well as how to recruit employees to meet human resource needs. This chapter represents a natural merger of Chapters 9 and 10 from the second edition.
- Chapter 10, "Employee Separation and Retention," covers effective HRM practices for retaining and separating employees. This chapter replaces Chapter 8, "Work Attitudes and Job Withdrawal," found in the second edition which provided a narrower and limited discussion of separation and retention issues. Given the high costs associated with losing valuable employees and keeping poor performers, many companies face the challenge of how to satisfy and motivate employees in order to increase innovation, efficiency, and product and service quality. The chapter focuses on the management of turnover, employee dismissal, how to measure and monitor employee morale, and effectively use data from employee attitude surveys.
- The last chapter of the text, Chapter 16, "Strategically Managing the HR Function," helps students revisit the idea of strategic human resource management discussed in Chapter 2 after they have been exposed to a wide range of HR practices. The chapter helps the student think strategically through emphasizing how HRM practices and the HR function can be configured to help the company reach business goals. The chapter emphasizes how by taking the customer's perspective the HR function can increase its effectiveness and contribute to the company's competitive advantage. We discuss the use of benchmarking, process reengineering, and a change model to ensure that HR practices are appropriate and effective.

- Chapter 9, "Employee Development," discusses important career and development issues that were presented in two chapters in the second edition of the text. The chapter now focuses on employee development and career management strategies that are employee-driven based on changes in the psychological contract that have occurred in the workplace.
- The videos and video cases have been updated to reflect current company information and competitiveness.
- Resources on the World Wide Web related to selection, training, recruiting, legal issues, quality, compensation, and labor force issues are provided throughout the text. These addresses give students and instructors access to the latest developments in human resource management and the ability to talk to experts in a particular HR practice area.

Organization

Human Resource Management: Gaining a Competitive Advantage includes an introductory chapter (Chapter 1) and five parts.

Chapter 1 provides a detailed discussion of the global, stakeholder, and work system challenges that influence companies' abilities to successfully meet the needs of shareholders, customers, employees, and other stakeholders. We discuss how the management of human resources can help companies meet the competitive challenges.

Part I includes a discussion of the environmental forces that companies face in attempting to capitalize on their human resources as a means to gain competitive advantage. The environmental forces include the strategic direction of the business, the legal environment, and the type of work performed and physical arrangement of the work.

A key focus of the strategic human resource management chapter is highlighting the role that staffing, performance management, training and development, and compensation play in different types of business strategies. A key focus of the legal chapter is enhancing managers' understanding of laws related to sexual harassment, affirmative action, and accommodations for disabled employees. The various types of discrimination and ways they have been interpreted by the courts are discussed. The chapter on analysis and design of work emphasizes how work systems can improve company competitiveness by alleviating job stress, and improving employee motivation and satisfaction with their jobs.

Part II deals with the acquisition and preparation of human resources including human resource planning and recruitment, selection, and training. The human resource planning chapter illustrates the process of developing a human resource plan. Also, the strengths and weaknesses of staffing options such as outsourcing, use of contingent workers, and downsizing are discussed. Strategies for recruiting talented employees are emphasized. The selection chapter emphasizes ways to minimize errors in employee selection and placement to improve the company's competitive position. Selection method standards such as validity and reliability are discussed in easily understandable terms without compromising the technical complexity of these issues. The chapter discusses selection methods such as interviews and various types of tests (including personality, honesty, and drug tests) and compares them on measures of validity, reliability, utility, and legality. The chapter on work attitudes identifies work attitudes (e.g., job satisfaction) that can influence company productivity and competitiveness. Interventions that can help managers maximize employee productivity and satisfaction to avoid withdrawal behaviors such as absenteeism are discussed.

We discuss the components of effective training systems and the manager's role in determining employees' readiness for training, creating a positive learning environment, and ensuring training is used on the job. The advantages and disadvantages of different training methods are described, such as virtual reality and distance learning. These new training methods have emerged as technology has developed.

Part III explores how companies can determine the value of employees and capitalize on their talents through retention and development strategies. The performance management chapter examines the strengths and weaknesses of performance management methods that use ratings, objectives, or behaviors. The chapter on retention and separation discusses how managers can maximize employee productivity and satisfaction to avoid absenteeism and turnover. The use of assessment, job experiences, formal courses, and mentoring relationships to develop employees is discussed.

Part IV covers rewarding and compensating human resources, including designing pay structures, recognizing individual contributions, and providing benefits. Here we explore how managers should decide the pay rate for different jobs, given the company's compensation strategy and the worth of jobs. The advantages and disadvantages of merit pay, gainsharing, and skill-based pay are discussed. The benefits chapter highlights the different types of employer-provided benefits and discusses how benefit costs can be contained. International comparisons of compensation and benefit practices are provided.

Part V covers special topics in human resource management, including labor–management relations, international HRM, and managing the HR function. The collective bargaining and labor relations chapter focuses on traditional issues in labor management relations, such as union structure and membership, the organizing process, and contract negotiations; it also discusses new union agendas and less adversarial approaches to labor–management relations. Social and political changes, such as introduction of the euro currency in the European Community, are discussed in the chapter on global human resource management. Selecting, preparing, and rewarding employees for foreign assignments are also discussed. The text concludes with a chapter that emphasizes how HR practices should be aligned to help the company meet its business objectives. The chapter emphasizes that the HR function needs to have a customer focus to be effective.

Video cases at the end of each part integrate the concepts presented. These cases are intended to give students practice dealing with real HR issues that companies are facing.

Features Designed to Aid Learning

Human Resource Management provides several features designed to aid learning:

- Learning objectives at the beginning of each chapter inform students about what they should know about managing human resources when they read the chapter.
- A chapter-opening vignette presents a real business problem or issue that provides background for the issues discussed in the chapter.
- "Competing through Globalization," "Competing by Meeting Stakeholders' Needs," and "Competing through High-Performance Work Systems" boxes in the chapters highlight how companies have gained a competitive advantage through effective human resource management practices designed to meet global, stakeholder (including customers, employees, shareholders, and community) and work system

challenges. The examples are drawn from a wide spectrum of businesses in different sectors of the economy, such as manufacturing, health care, service, and sales.

For example, the "Competing by Meeting Shareholders' Needs" box in Chapter 5, "Human Resource Planning and Recruitment," details the recruiting efforts that Shoney's and Denny's restaurant chains undertook to increase the diversity of their workforce and to eliminate their names being synonymous with racism resulting from how they treated their employees and customers.

In Chapter 8, the "Competing through Globalization," box shows how performance management practices may not generalize across countries. For example, at the Thai office of Singapore Airlines, managers resisted giving employees negative feedback because of their fear that this would cause them negative consequences in their life after death.

The "Competing through High-Performance Work Systems" box in Chapter 11 shows how technology is making salary data more easily accessible to employees and managers. Both employees and HR managers are using Web-based salary surveys to insure that salaries are equitable with external market salary rates.

- Important terms used in human resource management are boldfaced in each chapter.
- In-text examples feature companies from the service, retail, and manufacturing sectors of the economy.
- Discussion questions at the end of each chapter help students learn the concepts presented in the chapter and understand potential applications of the chapter material.
- Cases from the pages of *Business Week* present business problems related to the management of human resources. The cases give students the opportunity to immediately apply what they have learned in the chapter.
- All chapters include end-of-chapter exercises that require the student to use the World Wide Web. This helps the student understand the value of the Web for managing human resources.
- End-of-part video cases provide examples of companies that have used human resource management practices to gain a competitive advantage. The 12- to 15-minute videos contain conversations with managers and employees and footage of the operations of the business. The video cases and accompanying questions challenge students to view human resource issues and problems from multiple perspectives. References to World Wide Web sites help students and instructors find additional company information for classroom use.
- An end-of-book glossary defines key terms used in human resource management.
- Name and subject indexes at the end of the book aid in finding topics and key people and companies.
- State-of-the-art use of design and color make the book more readable for students and enhance learning.

Instructor Materials

- **Instructor's Manual, Transparency Masters, PowerPoint Slides.** Amit Shah of Frostburg State University is revising the *Instructor's Manual* and PowerPoint slides. The *Instructor's Manual* contains a lecture outline and notes, answers to the discussion questions, additional discussion questions and exercises, teaching suggestions, term paper and project topics, answers to the end-of-chapter case questions, and video case notes and answers. Transparency masters are included at the back of the *Instructor's Manual*. Some contain completely new material, some are drawn from key figures and tables in the text. There are 10 to 15 PowerPoint slides for each chapter. Five new slides for each chapter have been developed for the third edition.

- **Test Bank.** Authored by Nicholas Mathys of DePaul University, the *Test Bank* contains 25 true/false, 50 multiple-choice, and 10 essay questions per chapter, for a total of more than 1,600 questions. Questions are graded by level of difficulty, and text page references where answers can be found are provided. The test bank has been revised for the third edition.
- **Computerized Testing Program.** Available through McGraw-Hill, this test generator allows instructors to add and edit questions, create up to 99 different versions of the test, and more.
- **Videos.** The end-of-part videos can be used to generate in-class discussion and draw students' interest. A wide variety of company settings gives the videos broad appeal. All video cases have been updated or completely revised to reflect the most current company information.

Acknowledgments

Although this book enters its third edition it is important to acknowledge those who started it all. The first edition of this book would not have been possible if not for the entrepreneurial spirit of two individuals. Bill Schoof, president of Austen Press, gave us the resources and had the confidence that four unproven textbook writers could provide a new perspective for teaching human resource management. John Weimeister, our editor, provided us with valuable marketing information, coordinated all of the book reviews, helped us in making major decisions regarding the book, and made writing this book an enjoyable process. Although we miss working with John and Bill, they remain good friends and great examples of how to create good author relations. We were fortunate, however, to have the opportunity in the third edition to work with two very talented and hard-working Irwin editors, John Biernat and Christine Scheid. John and Christine have provided us with the expertise, encouragement and latitude needed to enhance the third edition of the book. Christine had the unenviable task of reminding four busy authors to meet deadlines and submit all of the chapter material. Ellen Cleary, marketing manager, deserves kudos for her ideas and efforts in creating excitement (and adoptions!) for the text. Amit Shah of Frostburg State University wrote a first class *Instructor's Manual*. Nicholas Mathys of DePaul University developed high-quality test questions for the *Test Bank*. Also, many thanks to the students who helped class-test the *Test Bank* questions.

Thanks to the editorial staff at Irwin McGraw-Hill. Karen Nelson made heroic efforts to follow our "cut and pastes" and placement of new material for the third edition. Thanks for your patience! Also, thanks to Bruce MacLean of MacLean Media for the videos, especially the custom footage for Part III.

We would like to thank the professors who gave of their time to review the text in full, and the many helpful comments and suggestions they shared with us:

Alison Barber
Michigan State University

Rober Figler
University of Akron

Bob Graham
Sacred Heart University

John Hannon
Purdue University

Ken Kovach
University of Maryland

Nick Mathys
DePaul University

Mark Roehling
Cornell University

Cynthia Sutton
Indiana University–South Bend

Steve Thomas
Southwest Missouri State University

Dan Turban
University of Missouri–Columbia

We would like to also acknowledge the contributions of those who assisted us on the second edition, including more than 250 survey respondents. Susan Raynis, Clarkson University, took the time to give us helpful suggestions early in the project. And special thanks to those who participated in the focus groups and manuscript reviews for previous editions:

Richard Arvey
University of Minnesota

Alison Barber
Michigan State University

Ron Beaulieu
Central Michigan University

Chris Berger
Purdue University

Sarah Bowman
Idaho State University

Charles Braun
University of Kentucky

Georgia Chao
Michigan State University

Michael Crant
University of Notre Dame

John Delery
Texas A & M University

Tom Dougherty
University of Missouri

Cynthia Fukami
University of Denver

Dan Gallagher
James Madison University

Donald G. Gardner
University of Colorado at Colorado Springs

Terri Griffith
University of Arizona

Bob Hatfield
Indiana University

Rob Heneman
Ohio State University

Wayne Hockwater
Florida State University

Denise Tanguay Hoyer
Eastern Michigan University

Natalie J. Hunter
Portland State University

Gwen Jones
State University of New York at Albany

Marianne Koch
University of Oregon

Tom Kolenko
Kennesaw State College

Larry Mainstone
Valparaiso University

Nicholas Mathys
DePaul University

Cheri Ostroff
Arizona State University

Robert Paul
Kansas State University

Sam Rabinowitz
Rutgers University

Katherine Ready
University of Wisconsin

Mike Ritchie
University of South Carolina

Josh Schwarz
Miami University, Ohio

Christina Shalley
University of Arizona

Richard Simpson
University of Utah

Scott Snell
Pennsylvania State University

Charles Vance
Loyola Marymount University

Raymond A. Noe
John R. Hollenbeck
Barry Gerhart
Patrick M. Wright
July 1999

About the Authors

Raymond A. Noe is the Robert and Ann Hoyt Professor of Management at The Ohio State University. He was previously a professor in the Department of Management at Michigan State University and the Industrial Relations Center of the Carlson School of Management, University of Minnesota. He received his BS in psychology from The Ohio State University and his MA and PhD in psychology from Michigan State University. Professor Noe conducts research and teaches undergraduate as well as MBA and PhD students in human resource management, managerial skills, quantitative methods, human resource information systems, training, employee development, and organizational behavior. He has published articles in the *Academy of Management Journal, Academy of Management Review, Journal of Applied Psychology, Journal of Vocational Behavior,* and *Personnel Psychology*. Professor Noe is currently on the editorial boards of several journals including *Personnel Psychology, Journal of Business and Psychology,* and *Journal of Training Research* and *Journal of Organizational Behavior*. Professor Noe has received awards for his teaching and research excellence, including the Herbert G. Heneman Distinguished Teaching Award in 1991 and the Ernest J. McCormick Award for Distinguished Early Career Contribution from the Society for Industrial and Organizational Psychology in 1993. He is also a fellow of the Society for Industrial and Organizational Psychology.

John R. Hollenbeck is Professor of Management at the Eli Broad Graduate School of Business Administration at Michigan State University. He received his PhD in management and organizational behavior from New York University in 1984. Professor Hollenbeck is the editor of *Personnel Psychology* and has served on the editorial boards of *Academy of Management Journal, Organizational Behavior and Human Decision Processes,* the *Journal of Management,* and the *Journal of Applied Psychology*. Professor Hollenbeck has been recognized for both his research and teaching. He was the first recipient of the Ernest J. McCormick Award for Distinguished Early Career Contributions to the field of Industrial and Organizational Psychology in 1992 and was the 1987 Teacher-Scholar Award winner at Michigan State University. Dr. Hollenbeck's research focuses on self-regulation theories of work motivation, employee separation and acquisition processes, and team decision making and performance.

Barry Gerhart is the Frances Hampton Currey Professor of Organization Studies at the Owen School of Management, Vanderbilt University. He was previously Associate Professor and Chairman of the Department of Human Resource Studies, School of Industrial and Labor Relations at Cornell University. He received his BS in psychology from Bowling Green State University in 1979 and his PhD in industrial relations from the University of Wisconsin–Madison in 1985. His research is in the areas of compensation/rewards, staffing, and employee attitudes. Professor Gerhart has worked with a variety of organizations, including TRW, Corning, and Bausch &

Lomb. His work has appeared in the *Academy of Management Journal*, *Industrial Relations*, *Industrial and Labor Relations Review*, *Journal of Applied Psychology*, *Personnel Psychology*, and *Handbook of Industrial and Organizational Psychology*, and he has served on the editorial boards of the *Academy of Management Journal*, *Industrial and Labor Relations Review*, and the *Journal of Applied Psychology*. He was a corecipient of the 1991 Scholarly Achievement Award, Human Resources Division, Academy of Management.

Patrick M. Wright is Associate Professor in the School of Industrial and Labor Relations at Cornell University. He was formerly Associate Professor of Management and Coordinator of the Master of Science in Human Resource Management program in the College of Business Administration and Graduate School of Business at Texas A & M University. He holds a BA in psychology from Wheaton College and an MBA and a PhD in organizational behavior/human resource management from Michigan State University. He teaches, conducts research, and consults in the areas of personnel selection, employee motivation, and strategic human resource management. His research articles have appeared in journals such as the *Academy of Management Journal*, *Journal of Applied Psychology*, *Organizational Behavior and Human Decision Processes*, *Journal of Management*, and *Human Resource Management Review*. He has served on the editorial boards of *Journal of Applied Psychology* and *Journal of Management* and also serves as an ad hoc reviewer for *Organizational Behavior and Human Decision Processes*, *Academy of Management Journal*, and *Academy of Management Review*. In addition, he has consulted for a number of organizations, including Whirlpool Corporation, Amoco Oil Company, and the North Carolina State Government.

Brief Contents

Contents

PART I
The Human Resource Environment 39

CHAPTER

Human Resource Management: Gaining a Competitive Advantage

OBJECTIVES

After reading this chapter, you should be able to

1. Discuss the roles and activities of a company's human resource function.
2. Discuss the competitive challenges influencing U.S. companies.
3. Discuss how human resource practices affect a company's balanced scorecard.
4. Discuss what companies should do to be competitive in the global marketplace.
5. Identify the characteristics of the work force and how they influence human resource management practices.
6. Discuss human resource practices that support high-performance work systems.
7. Provide a brief description of human resource management practices.

Texas Instruments: Human Resource Excellence

ENTER THE WORLD OF BUSINESS

Texas Instruments (TI), a global semiconductor company, is the world's leading designer and supplier of digital signal processing solutions. TI's businesses also include materials and controls, educational and productivity solutions, and digital imaging. TI is headquartered in Dallas, Texas, with 36,000 employees working in design centers, manufacturing sites, or sales offices in more than 129 locations around the world. TI's goal is to become a premier electronics company using a strategy of value, growth, and improved financial stability. TI's HR function has always been seen as a great asset to the business and has been recognized as "leading-edge" in the HR field. However, not until recently, according to the vice president of human resources at Texas Instruments, has the human resources department evolved from a group that provided great support to the businesses to a group that has started partnering with line management and beginning to understand business priorities. The HR function has started to take a leadership position on issues that affect the strategic direction of the business. The important role that HR plays in Texas Instruments' success is seen by the vice president's place on TI's Strategy Leadership Team with the Chief Operating Officer and the Chief Executive Officer. The vice president has helped the company recognize the need to develop technical capabilities in its employees to make sure long-term business strategies are successful. Each of TI's businesses' effectiveness is evaluated in three categories: business success, financial improvements, and people issues.

TI is involved in several initiatives to ensure that HR contributes to the business strategy. One of TI's three business priorities is improving employee development. Employee development is necessary to ensure that talent is available when needed. To develop talent, each TI employee must create a personal development plan in collaboration with his or her supervisor. The personal development plan is based on employees' examinations of where they want to be in their careers and where they are today. To meet their career needs, employees are encouraged to enroll in courses as well as to consider moves within the company to other departments or other product areas. Besides contributing to employee satisfaction, development plans help to ensure that TI has the talent needed for management positions (a process know as succession planning). High-performing employees are given time periods in which they are expected to move to new positions. The idea is to ensure that the company never has to fill a position with an employee who is not quite talented enough.

In addition to the development plan, TI emphasizes employee recruiting to attract employees needed for TI to meet its business needs. TI has created an Internet recruiting page designed to help attract top people. The web site includes useful job hunting advice such as how to develop a resumé and how to write a cover letter, as well as information about careers at TI. The site also includes a survey that job seekers complete (the "Fit Check") that helps them understand the match between TI's work culture and their needs. The Fit Check helps job seekers decide if TI is an employer they want to pursue. TI has devoted many resources to develop the site because it believes that the more prepared the job seekers are for job hunting, the easier the job will be for TI recruiters.

Other important HR issues address diversity and ethics. TI has developed diversity networks and mentoring programs to make TI a multicultural work force. TI also encourages ethical decision making in line with TI's three primary values (integrity, innovation, and commitment). Communications from HR help employees understand TI's ethical requirements. For example, recent topics on TI's electronic newsletter have included appropriate use of the Internet, the possible conflicts of "moonlighting" (holding two jobs), and the company's policy on offering and receiving business gifts.

SOURCE: G. Flynn, "Texas Instruments Engineers a Holistic HR," *Workforce* (February 1998), pp. 30–35, www.ti.com Texas Instruments' web site. Used with permission.

Introduction

Texas Instruments' (TIs') success illustrates the key role human resource management (HRM) plays in determining the effectiveness and competitiveness of U.S. businesses. **Competitiveness** refers to the company's ability to maintain and gain market share in its industry. TI's HRM practices have helped the company gain a **competitive advantage** over its competitors. That is, TI's human resource practices have helped the company provide services its customers value. The value of a product or service is determined by its quality and how closely the product fits customer needs.

Competitiveness is related to company effectiveness, which is determined by whether the company satisfies the needs of stakeholders (groups affected by business practices). Important stakeholders include stockholders, who want a return on their investment; customers, who want a high-quality product or service; and employees, who desire interesting work and reasonable compensation for their services. The community, which wants the company to contribute to activities and projects and minimize pollution of the environment, is also an important stakeholder. Companies that do not meet stakeholders' needs are unlikely to have a competitive advantage over other firms in their industry.

Human resource management (HRM) refers to the policies, practices, and systems that influence employees' behavior, attitudes, and performance. Many companies refer to HRM as involving "people practices." Figure 1.1 emphasizes that there are several important HRM practices. The strategy underlying these practices needs to be considered to maximize their influence on company performance. As the figure shows, HRM practices include determining human resource needs (HR planning), attracting potential employees (recruiting), choosing employees (selection), teaching employees how to perform their job and preparing them for the future (training and development), rewarding employees (compensation), evaluating their performance (performance management), and creating a positive work environment (employee relations). Texas Instruments' HRM practices discussed in this chapter's opening highlighted that effective HRM practices are developed and used to support business goals and objectives. That is, effective HRM practices are strategic! Effective HRM practices have been shown to relate to company performance by contributing to employee and customer satisfaction, innovation, productivity, and development of a favorable reputation in the firm's community.[1] The potential role of HRM in company performance has only recently been recognized.

Many companies have human resource management departments. However, human

FIGURE 1.1
Human Resource Management Practices

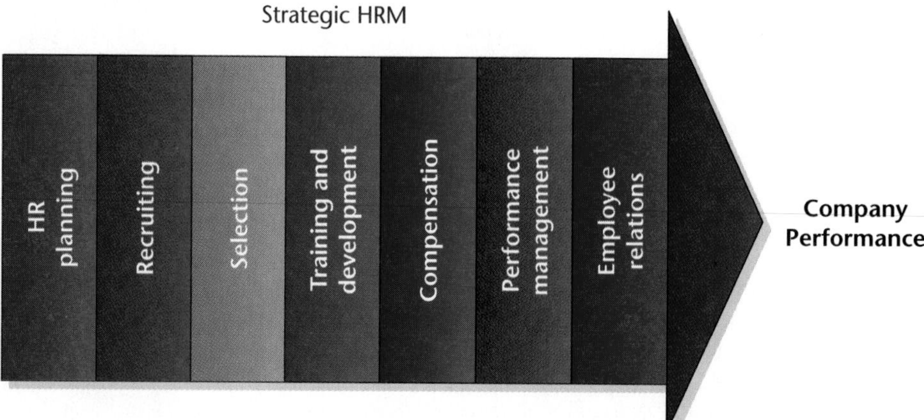

resource management is not just a functional responsibility! Managers participate in HRM practices on a daily basis. We begin by discussing the roles and skills that a human resource management department and/or managers need for any company to be competitive. The second section of the chapter identifies the competitive challenges that U.S. companies are currently facing that influence their ability to meet the needs of shareholders, customers, employees, and other stakeholders. We discuss how these competitive challenges are influencing HRM practices. The chapter concludes by highlighting the HRM practices covered in this book and the ways they help companies deal with the competitive challenges.

What Activities Do HR Departments Perform?

Only recently have companies looked at HRM practices as a means to contribute to profitability, quality, and other business goals through enhancing and supporting business operations.

Table 1.1 shows the activities of human resource departments. Since 1978, the average ratio of HR department staff to total number of employees has been 1.0 for every 100 employees served by the department. Expenditures for HR departments have been relatively stable over the past few years. The median HR department expenditure per employee from 1994 to 1995 was $823, with education and government organizations spending the least ($352) and transportation, communications, and utility companies the most ($1,320). As with other business functions, HR expenditures relative to operating costs have been fairly stable over the past few years.

Activities that the HR department is solely responsible for include outplacement, labor law compliance, record keeping, testing, unemployment compensation, and some aspects of benefits administration. The human resource department is most likely to collaborate with other company functions on employment interviewing, performance management and discipline, and efforts to improve quality and productivity. Large companies are more likely than small companies to employ HR specialists, with benefits spe-

TABLE 1.1
Activities of HR Departments

Employment and recruiting	Interviewing, recruiting, testing, temporary labor coordination
Training and development	Orientation–performance management skills training, productivity enhancement
Compensation	Wage and salary administration, job descriptions, executive compensation, incentive pay, job evaluation
Benefits	Insurance, vacation–leave administration, retirement plans, profit sharing, stock plans
Employee services	Employee assistance programs, relocation services, outplacement services
Employee and community relations	Attitude surveys, labor relations, publications, labor law compliance, discipline
Personnel records	Information systems, records
Health and safety	Safety inspection, drug testing, health, wellness
Strategic planning	International human resources, forecasting, planning, mergers and acquisitions

SOURCE: Based on SHRM–BNA Survey No. 60, "Human Resource Activities, Budgets and Staffs: 1994–95." Bulletin to Management, Bureau of National Affairs Policy and Practice Series, June 29, 1995. Washington, DC: Bureau of National Affairs.

TABLE 1.2
The Changing Role of Human Resources

	CURRENT	5–7 YEARS AGO
Maintaining records	15%	22%
Auditing and controlling	12	19
HR service provider	31	35
Product development	19	14
Strategic business partner	22	11

SOURCE: Based on a 1996 study by the Center for Effective Organizations, University of Southern California, and the Human Resource Planning Society.

cialists being the most prevalent. Other common specializations include recruitment, compensation, and training and development.[2]

The HR function is in transition from an administrative function to a strategic business partnership.[3] Table 1.2 shows that the percentage of time human resource departments are devoting to administrative roles such as maintaining records, auditing and controlling, and providing services has decreased. Advances in technology such as development of the Intranet have decreased the role of human resources in maintaining records by allowing HR services to be offered on a self-service basis at substantially less cost than traditional face-to-face services.[4] **Self-service** refers to giving employees control of HR transactions. Self-service also fits with the changing psychological contract—employees are expected to take greater responsibility for their own careers. Self-service is being used for a wide range of HR services including training course catalogs and course enrollment, benefits enrollment and inquiries, and attitude surveys. For example, at Richmond, Virginia-based LandAmerican Financial Group (a 4,000-employee company that processes title insurance), the company has self-service for address changes, benefits, enrollment and taxes, company policy information, and internal job postings. Besides reducing costs, the self-service system has helped to shape employee perceptions that HR is a progressive department.

Outsourcing of the administrative role has also occurred. **Outsourcing** refers to the practice of having another company (known as a vendor, third-party provider, or consultant) provide services. Many companies have outsourced payroll administration. Outsourcing is also being used for benefits administration, training, selection, and recruiting employees.

Other roles such as practice development and strategic business partnering have increased. One of the most comprehensive studies ever conducted regarding HRM concluded that "human resources is being transformed from a specialized, stand-alone function to a broad corporate competency in which human resources and line managers build partnerships to gain competitive advantage and achieve overall business goals."[5] There is an increase in managers in charge of the human resource function being included on high-level committees that are shaping the strategic direction of the company. These managers report directly to the CEO, president, or board of directors and they are being asked to propose solutions to business problems.

For example, the vice president–relationship leader of human resources for Corporate Services at American Express spends considerable time during his work day on HR projects supporting business initiatives.[6] He spends two hours reviewing service delivery and drivers of employee satisfaction. Service delivery and drivers of employee satisfaction are inherent in a Corporate Services vision statement know as "The Stand." (Three goals of "The Stand" include making people successful, inspiring customer loyalty, and continually transforming industries. Assessment of Corporate Services' progress toward reaching

TABLE 1.3 Questions Used to Determine if Human Resources Are Playing a Strategic Role in the Business

1. What is HR doing to provide value-added services to internal clients?
2. What can the HR department add to the bottom line?
3. How are you measuring the effectiveness of HR?
4. How can we reinvest in employees?
5. What HR strategy will we use to get the business from point A to point B?
6. What makes an employee want to stay at our company?
7. How are we going to invest in HR so that we have a better HR department than our competitors?
8. From an HR perspective, what should we be doing to improve our marketplace position?
9. What's the best change we can make to prepare for the future?

SOURCE: Excerpted A. Halcrow, "Survey Shows HR in Transition," *Workforce* (June 1988), p. 74. Used with permission.

these goals is determined by an annual employee survey.) Issues discussed in the two-hour meeting include how "The Stand" relates to competencies and behaviors as well as team training effectiveness, with a review of the current reward structure. Later in the day, he mentors a new director–relationship leader who supports government services and the corporate purchasing card group. (American Express services more than 1 million federal employees who use the Government Card when they travel.) He conducts an orientation with her that includes emphasizing the need to spend time to (1) understand the various government services business and (2) gain an understanding of the key HR challenges and start to develop an effective working relationship.

Table 1.3 provides several questions that managers can use to determine if HR is playing a strategic role in the business. If these questions have not been considered, it is highly unlikely that (1) the company is prepared to deal with competitive challenges and (2) human resources are being used to help a company gain competitive advantage! We will discuss strategic human resource management in more detail in Chapter 2.

What Skills Do HR Professionals Need?

Figure 1.2 shows the roles and competencies that are needed by HR professionals. Each of the quadrants corresponds to HR roles listed on the outside of the figure. Within each quadrant the competencies needed to be successful in the role are included. The roles and examples of the competencies needed to effectively manage human resources in the future are shown on the right side of Figure 1.2. These competencies include developing new HR practices and partnering with managers to align these practices with the business strategy, managing change, and representing employees' concerns to senior management as well as increasing employees' contributions to the company through training and identifying technologies and designing processes to increase efficiencies and lower costs.[7] The single biggest challenge for HR managers is to shift their focus from current operations to strategies for the future.[8] Another important challenge is to prepare non-HR managers to develop and implement human resource practices (e.g., performance management).

The roles and competency related to administration and control are included in the left half of Figure 1.2. The role of HR in administration and control will decrease because technology increasingly is being used to manage personnel records and provide employees with access to information regarding programs and services. However, to ef-

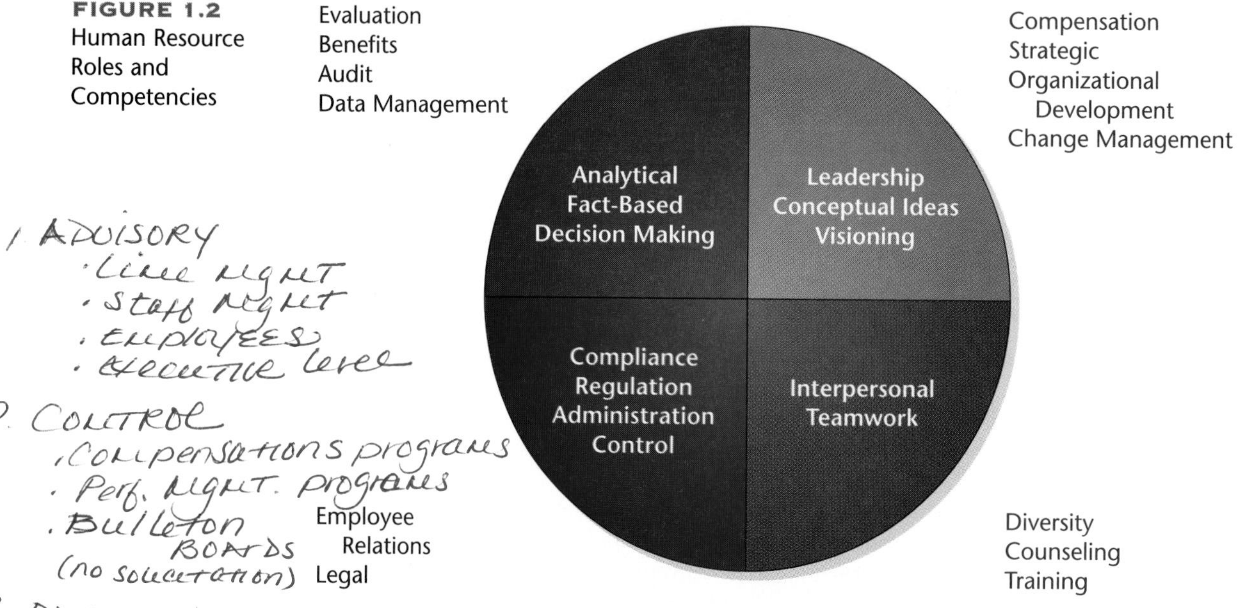

FIGURE 1.2 Human Resource Roles and Competencies

SOURCE: Adapted from "The Changing Human Resource Function," *The Conference Board,* 1990 (New York: The Conference Board Inc.), p. 11.

fectively manage human resources, analytical skills will be needed to measure and evaluate the effectiveness of HR practices.

Why has the importance of human resource management increased over the past 10 years? HRM is seen by managers as the most important lever for companies to gain a competitive advantage over both domestic and foreign competitors. We believe this is because HRM practices are directly related to companies' success in meeting competitive challenges. In the next section we discuss each of these challenges and their implications for HRM.

Competitive Challenges Influencing Human Resource Management

Three competitive challenges that companies will face in the next decade will increase the importance of human resource management practices: the global challenge, the challenge of meeting stakeholders' needs, and the high-performance work system challenge. These three challenges are shown in Figure 1.3.

THE GLOBAL CHALLENGE

We are in the midst of a global restructuring of the world's markets. Companies are finding that to survive, they must compete in international markets as well as fend off foreign corporations' attempts to gain ground at home. To meet these challenges, U.S. businesses must develop global markets, use their practices to improve global competitiveness, and better prepare employees for global assignments.

DEVELOPMENT OF GLOBAL MARKETS. Anecdotal evidence suggests that the most admired and successful companies in the world have not only created multinational corporations, but have created organizations with work forces and corporate cultures that reflect the characteristics of the global markets in which they operate.[9] Ex-

FIGURE 1.3 Competitive Challenges Influencing U.S. Companies

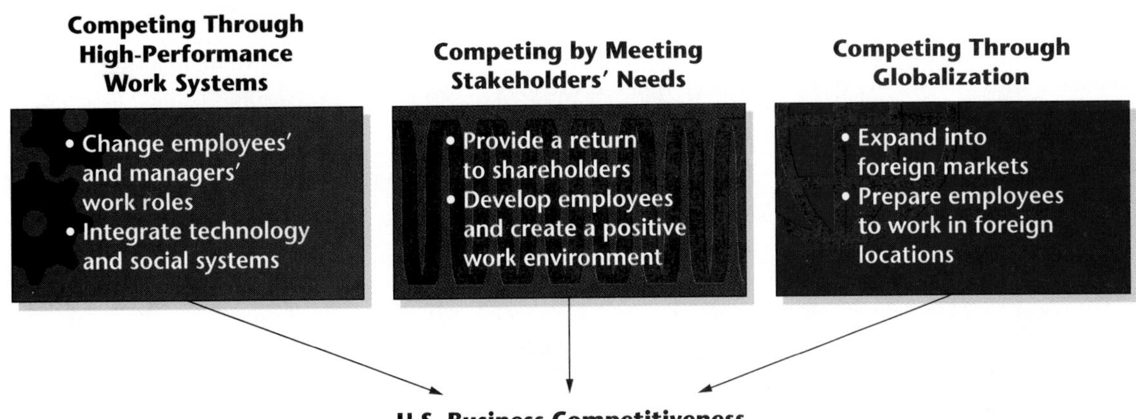

amples of these companies include General Electric, Coca-Cola, Microsoft, Walt Disney, Intel, Toyota Motors, ABB Asea Brown Boveri, and Hewlett-Packard.

These companies' key priorities include traditional business objectives such as customer focus and innovation. However, a distinguishing characteristic is that these companies believe that people are their most important asset. (See the "Competing through Globalization" box.) Believing that employees are the key to success translates into human resource practices including rewarding employee performance, measuring employee satisfaction, using an intensive employee selection process, promotion from within, and investing in employee development.

Many of the former communist nations of Europe and Asia appear to represent enormous opportunities for international business. Under communist rule, these countries were closed to Western businesses. Now, they present potential business opportunities. China, with a population of over 1 billion, represents a huge market for goods and services. And in Latin America, governments are selling state-owned businesses to private investors and foreign investment is welcome. This is not to say that developing these markets will be easy. Political instability, poor infrastructure (roads, communications), and poor economies make the risks involved in doing global business quite high.

Despite the risks, many U.S. competitors are willing to take these risks and are realizing high returns. They are reacting decisively to global changes and are positioning themselves to be active participants in those areas of the world that are expected to grow most rapidly. For example, ABB Asea Brown Boveri AG (Europe's largest engineering company and a competitor to General Electric) was one of the first western companies to react to the Asian monetary crisis.[10] With over 219,000 employees worldwide, ABB was considered a global company well before the Asian monetary crisis. But to capitalize on the crisis, the company underwent a massive restructuring plan involving layoffs in Europe and North America and production shifts to low-cost countries in Asia. The company also did away with its regional reporting structure and moved to organize its businesses along global lines. ABB hopes to beat its rivals by capitalizing on Asia's low production costs, which are half of European costs.

Training is an HR practice that has an important role in ABB's global business success. One of the biggest problems that ABB has to overcome is resistance to the idea that Asian countries can match the standards of European or North American factories and complete work on time. Plant managers at its electrical motor facility in Shanghai, China, have been trained on ABB quality standards by ABB employees on assignment in China (employees known as expatriates).

Successfully Brewing Global Operations

Lawrence Maltz signed an agreement with Starbucks Coffee International of Seattle to open Starbucks coffee franchises in Beijing, China. Maltz is a former executive with Starbucks who through his new joint venture, the Beijing Mei Da Coffee Company, has been distributing Starbucks coffee to Beijing hotels. Mei Da is now in charge of recruiting and training managers for the coffee shops. This is a major concern of foreign investors in China as the demand for local managers exceeds the available supply.

Mei Da built a list of managerial job candidates using job fairs, help-wanted ads, and headhunters. The goal was to find potential managers from the ranks of employees contributing to the success of American-style restaurants in Beijing such as Hard Rock Cafe and T.G.I. Friday's. Mei Da is finding that Starbucks is an attractive employer for several reasons. First, young Beijingers associate the company with the pop-culture scene in Seattle, where Starbucks Coffee is headquartered. Starbucks is also an attractive employer because of the company culture and opportunities for career and personal development. In traditional state-owned companies in China, rules and regulations provide little room for employee creativity and autonomy at work.

COMPETING THROUGH GLOBALIZATION

One attraction of the Starbucks culture is that employees are casual and respect one another. This contrasts with many joint ventures in China in which local nationals trained as managers are not trusted. They are not expected to share their opinions or question higher-level managers from the United States. As one managerial recruit stated, "People are looking for a good working environment where they can learn, and they are looking for dignity."

To maximize the chances that the new manager recruits will be successful and stay with Starbucks, considerable time and money are invested in training. To train the new recruits, they are sent to Tacoma, Washington, to learn the corporate culture and the secrets of brewing dozens of fancy coffees. This ensures that Starbucks' reputation for high-quality coffee will be maintained in its China operations. The U.S. training also helps to sell recruits on staying with the company. The success of the Starbucks brand in the United States strengthens recruits' confidence that their future will be satisfying with the company. This is important in China because managers with experience in a Western company will receive plenty of offers from other employers.

SOURCE: J Lee-Young, "Starbucks Expansion in China Is Slated," *The Wall Street Journal* (October 5, 1998), p. B13c. Reprinted with permission.

COMPETITIVENESS IN GLOBAL MARKETS THROUGH HRM PRACTICES. Despite the growth of the U.S. economy over the past 30 years, the United States has experienced a relative decline in the world economy, reflecting the faster economic growth of other countries.[11] For example, over the past three decades, U.S. dominance in export markets has been challenged by Japan, Germany, and a number of newly industrialized countries including South Korea and Taiwan. But the relative decline of the United States is not necessarily cause for concern—the relative decline reflects the growing world economy. Economic forecasts show a rapid rise in world output accounted for by countries such as China, Thailand, and Indonesia and a decline in the share enjoyed by industrialized countries such as Britain and the United States.[12] If these projections are correct, this suggests that there will be a dramatic shift in the world economy. Today's developing nations may account for over 60 percent of the world economy by 2020, while the United States and other countries that currently account for over 50 percent of economic activity will account for only about 38 percent!

European countries are taking steps to strengthen their competitive positions by developing a single currency. The **euro** is a single currency that will initially include 11 European Union countries: Austria, Belgium, Finland, France, Germany, Ireland, Italy, Luxembourg, the Netherlands, Portugal, and Spain.[13] The single currency is expected to strengthen the competitiveness of this block of countries. The euro bloc of countries rivals the United States in gross domestic product and population. For European businesses, the euro is seen as a way to cut costs and encourage cross-border mergers.

While many large firms such as Exxon, Ford, and Procter & Gamble are already multinational corporations that span the globe, many medium-sized and small businesses are becoming increasingly involved in international business. To be successful in the global marketplace, the challenge for all businesses—regardless of size—is to understand cultural differences and to invest in human resources. Traditionally, U.S. business has attempted to improve productivity by cutting investment in human resources while competitors in Japan, Germany, and elsewhere have invested heavily in employee training and work redesign. Consider the experience of General Electric (GE), a company known for satisfying shareholders and employees. GE purchased a majority interest in Tungsram, a manufacturer of lighting products in Hungary.[14] Tungsram was attractive to GE because of its low wage rates and the possibility of using the company to export lighting products to Western Europe. GE transferred some of its best managerial talent to Tungsram. However, GE ran into many problems. The Hungarians expected higher Western-style wage rates, not low wages. Americans wanted strong sales and marketing functions that would service customers, while the Hungarians believed these would take care of themselves. The American managers found the workers to lack motivation. The Hungarian employees believed the American managers were pushy. To turn the Tungsram plant around, GE had to invest an additional $400 million in new plant and equipment and in retraining employees. GE also had to lay off half of the work force!

To compete in the world economy, U.S. companies need to put greater effort into selecting and retaining talented employees, employee training and development, and dismantling traditional bureaucratic structures that limit employees' ability to be innovative and creative.[15]

PREPARING EMPLOYEES FOR INTERNATIONAL ASSIGNMENTS. Besides taking steps to ensure that employees are better used, U.S. companies must do a better job of preparing employees and their families for overseas assignments. The failure rate for expatriates (U.S. employees sent to work abroad) is higher than that for European and Japanese expatriates.[16] U.S. companies must carefully select employees to work abroad based on their ability to understand and respect the cultural and business norms of the host country, their language skills, and their technical ability. (In Chapter 7, "Training," we discuss effective cross-cultural training practices.) Additionally, U.S. companies must be willing to train and develop foreign employees to win foreign business. Several companies (e.g., Boeing, CSX Corporation) bring foreign workers to the United States for training and then return them to their home country.[17] For example, Boeing brings workers from India and Poland to the United States. They return to their home country with needed knowledge in aircraft design and manufacturing.

THE CHALLENGE OF MEETING STAKEHOLDERS' NEEDS

As we mentioned earlier, company effectiveness and competitiveness are determined by whether the company satisfies the needs of stakeholders. Stakeholders include stockholders (who want a return on their investment), customers (who want a high-quality product or service), and employees (who desire interesting work and reasonable compensation for their services). The community, which wants the company to contribute to activities and projects and minimize pollution of the environment, is also an important stakeholder.

Flexible Compensation Builds Employee, Customer, and Shareholder Satisfaction

Owens–Corning (the Toledo, Ohio, construction materials manufacturer) was experiencing poor sales and litigation for products that contained asbestos. This hindered both cash flow and employee morale. The company also had costly benefits and compensation programs that created an entitlement mentality among employees. Compensation was loosely linked to company performance. Medical benefits were the same for all employees regardless of their age or needs.

A new CEO decided to overhaul the company's goals and vision as a way to make the company more competitive. The CEO decided that besides sales goals, the company needed new core values. The values he emphasized included customer satisfaction, individual dignity, and meeting shareholder value. As a result, HR created a new compensation and benefits package that was in line with the values and would help Owens–Corning meet the sales goals.

The principles behind the new compensation and development plan, know as "Rewards and Resources," were to conserve cash, reduce fixed costs, provide employees with flexibility in their choices, and encourage employee stock ownership. "Rewards" relate to what employees receive for good job performance. "Resources" relate to employees' opportunities to save and make investments. "Rewards and Resources" is linked to company performance. There are several elements of the program. A global stock plan provides each employee with an annual bonus in stock (which depends on company performance), and each employee has the option to buy additional stock. A profit-sharing plan was developed that is based on company performance. Employees' retirement benefits were converted into a cash balance. The account has a guaranteed interest rate. The company credits the account with 2 percent of pay each year and additional monies based on age and years of service. Finally, the plan gives benefit choices to employees. Employees can decide what type and how much coverage they want in medical and dental care, life insurance, disability, vacations, and health care and dependent care spending accounts.

The program has contributed to bottom-line results and boosted employee satisfaction. Many other companies are looking to model their compensation and benefits plans based on "Rewards and Resources."

SOURCE: C.M. Solomon, Adapted from "Using Cash Drives Strategic Change," *Workforce* (February 1998), pp. 78–81. Used with permission.

THE BALANCED SCORECARD: MEASURING PERFORMANCE TO STAKEHOLDERS. The *balanced scorecard* gives managers an indication of the performance of a company based on the degree to which stakeholder needs are satisfied. The **balanced scorecard** gives managers the opportunity to look at the company from the perspective of internal and external customers, employees, and shareholders.[18] The balanced scorecard is important because it brings together most of the features that a company needs to focus on to be competitive. These include being customer-focused, improving quality, emphasizing teamwork, reducing new product and service development times, and managing for the long term.

The balance scorecard differs from traditional measures of company performance by emphasizing that the critical indicators chosen are based on the company's business strategy and competitive demands. Companies need to customize their balanced scorecard based on different market situations, products, and competitive environments.

Using the balanced scorecard to manage human resources. Communicating the scorecard to employees gives them a framework that helps them see the goals and strategies of the company, how these goals and strategies are measured, and how they influence the critical indicators. For example, Chase Manhattan Bank used the balanced scorecard to change the behavior of customer service representatives.[19] Before the company implemented the scorecard, if a customer requested a change in a service the bank provided to her, the representative would have simply met the customer's need. Based on knowledge of the scorecard, the customer service representative might now ask the customer if she is interested in the bank's other services such as financial planning, mortgages, loans, or insurance.

The balanced scorecard should be used to (1) link human resource management activities to the company's business strategy and (2) evaluate the extent to which the human resource function is helping the company meet its strategic objectives. Measures of human resource practices primarily relate to productivity, people, and process.[20] Productivity measures involve determining output per employee (such as revenue per employee). Measuring people includes assessing employees' behavior, attitudes, or knowledge. Process measures focus on assessing employees' satisfaction with *people systems* within the company. People systems can include the performance management system, the compensation and benefits system, and the development system. The "Competing by Meeting Stakeholders' Needs" box shows how people systems can contribute to competitive advantage. For HR activities to contribute to a company's competitive advantage, managers need to consider the questions shown in Table 1.4 and be able to answer them!

For example, consider Rockwater, a global engineering and construction company. Rockwater's balanced scorecard included critical indicators that could be directly influenced by human resource management practices.[21] One critical success indicator from the internal business perspective was a safety incident index. Innovation and learning included number of employee suggestions, a staff attitude survey, and revenue per employee. These critical indicators were used to direct the development of specific human resource management practices. To drive both product and service innovation and improvements in operations, the company believed that a supportive climate was necessary. The attitude survey and number of employee suggestions were used to measure the extent to which a positive work climate was created. Employee safety was seen as important because projects could be delayed and budget projection could be exceeded as a result of injuries and lost workdays. Revenue per employee measured the outcome of employee training programs.

MEETING CUSTOMER NEEDS FOR QUALITY. One major reason U.S. companies have failed to maintain industry leadership and increase exports relative to their major world competitors has been the decline in customers' perceptions of the quality of U.S. products. But how is quality defined? There is no universal definition of *quality*. The major differences relate to whether customer, product, or manufacturing process is emphasized. For example, quality expert W. Edwards Deming emphasized how well a

TABLE 1.4 The Balanced Scorecard

PERSPECTIVE	QUESTIONS ANSWERED	EXAMPLES OF CRITICAL INDICATORS
Customer	How do customers see us?	Time, quality, performance, service, cost
Internal	What must we excel at?	Processes that influence customer satisfaction, availability of information on service and/or manufacturing processes
Innovation and learning	Can we continue to improve and create value?	Improve operating efficiency, launch new products, continuous improvement, empowering of work force
Financial	How do we look to shareholders?	Profitability, growth, shareholder value

TABLE 1.5
Principles of Total Quality Management

1. Customer focus
2. Focus on process as well as results
3. Prevention versus inspection
4. Use of employees' expertise
5. Fact-based decision making
6. Feedback

SOURCE: Adapted from J.R. Jablonski, *Implementing Total Quality Management: An Overview* (San Diego: Pfeiffer & Company, 1991). Used by permission.

product or service meets the customer's needs. Philip Crosby's approach emphasizes how well the service or manufacturing process meets engineering standards.

Traditionally, U.S. companies have tried to manage quality by evaluating products after they have been manufactured or repairing them after they have been delivered—a "fix it if it's wrong" approach. However, world competitors such as Japan have emphasized an approach in which quality is designed into a product or service rather than relying on inspection to spot defects or mistakes. This can be considered a "get it right the first time" approach, a part of the total quality management system. **Total quality management (TQM)** can be defined as a "cooperative form of doing business that relies on the talents and capabilities of both labor and management to continually improve quality and productivity using work teams."[22] Although there are several approaches to TQM (e.g., those of Deming, Crosby, and Joseph Juran), these approaches share some common principles. Table 1.5 illustrates the six basic principles of TQM.

The TQM movement has caused a shift in management philosophy: How human resource issues are handled plays a key role in whether quality is achieved and, ultimately, in the success of a company.[23] Table 1.6 contrasts the HRM practices in companies recognized for successfully implementing TQM with traditional HRM practices. To ensure the success of TQM, companies need to create an environment that supports innovation, creativity, and risk taking to meet customer demands. Participative problem solving, involving managers, employees, and customers, should be used. Finally, communication between managers and employees concerning customer needs, development opportunities, and resources needs to be enhanced.

Several rewards have been established to recognize companies for quality, such as the Malcolm Baldrige National Quality Award and ISO 9000. **ISO 9000** quality standards were developed by the International Organization for Standardization, an organization in Geneva, Switzerland.[24] These standards were initially developed for companies in the European Community, but they have been adopted as national quality standards in nearly 100 countries including Austria, Switzerland, Norway, Japan, and Australia. ISO 9000 is the name of a family of standards (ISO 9001, ISO 9002) that includes 20 requirements for dealing with issues such as how to establish quality standards and document work processes. Companies are free to develop their own quality process to meet the standards. ISO 9001 is the most comprehensive standard because it covers product or service design and development, manufacturing, installation, and customer service. (ISO 9002 does not include design and development.) ISO 9000 certification is being used as a standard for companies wanting to be competitive both locally and globally. For example, U.S. companies hoping to win contracts from European Community customers need to have ISO 9000 certification. The "Big Three" U.S. automakers (GM, Ford, and Daimler) have developed a more rigorous version of ISO 9000 standards (QS-9000) that they are applying to their own operations as well as those of their suppliers. Suppliers need to meet QS-9000 standards to be major suppliers of parts and services to the Big Three.

TABLE 1.6 HRM Practices in Total Quality Companies

In companies that successfully implemented TQM, the corporate climate emphasized collective and cross-functional work, coaching and enabling employees, customer satisfaction, and quality, rather than the traditional emphasis on individualism, hierarchy, and profit.

HUMAN RESOURCE CHARACTERISTICS	TRADITIONAL MODEL	TOTAL QUALITY MODEL
Communications	Top-down	Top-down Horizontal, lateral Multidirectional
Voice and involvement	Employment-at-will Suggestion systems	Due process Quality circles Attitude surveys
Job design	Efficiency Productivity Standard procedures Narrow span of control Specific job descriptions	Quality Customization Innovation Wide span of control Autonomous work teams Empowerment
Training	Job-related skills Functional, technical	Broad range of skills Cross-functional Diagnostic, problem solving
	Productivity	Productivity and quality
Performance measurement and evaluation	Individual goals Supervisory review	Team goals Customer, peer, and supervisory review
	Emphasize financial performance	Emphasize quality and service
Rewards	Competition for individual merit increases and benefits	Team and group-based rewards Financial rewards, financial and nonfinancial recognition
Health and safety	Treat problems	Prevent problems Safety programs Wellness programs Employee assistance programs
Selection and promotion	Selection by manager	Selection by peers
Career development	Narrow job skills Promotion based on individual accomplishment	Problem-solving skills Promotion based on group facilitation
	Linear career path	Horizontal career path

SOURCE: R. Blackburn and B. Rosen, "Total Quality and Human Resources Management: Lessons Learned from Baldrige Award–Winning Companies," *Academy of Management Executive* 7 (1993), pp. 49–65. Used by permission.

The **Malcolm Baldrige National Quality Award** was established in 1987 by President Ronald Reagan to promote quality awareness, to recognize quality achievements of U.S. companies, and to publicize successful quality strategies.[25] To become eligible for the Baldrige award, companies must complete a detailed application that consists of basic information about the company (such as location, markets, and products) as well as an in-depth presentation of how the firm addresses specific criteria related to quality improvement. The ISO 9000 standards are similar to those for the Baldrige award. The Baldrige award criteria are shown in Table 1.7. A board of examiners composed of quality experts from industry, academia, and professional societies evaluates the company's application and also conducts site visits. Each Baldrige award applicant receives written feedback summarizing the company's strengths and needs for improvement. A maximum of two awards per year are given to firms in three categories: manufacturing companies, service companies, and small businesses.

Examining the criteria in Table 1.7, we see a recognition of the role that human re-

TABLE 1.7 Categories and Point Values for the Malcolm Baldrige National Quality Award Examination

Category	Points
Leadership The way senior executives create and sustain corporate citizenship, customer focus, clear values, and expectations and promote quality and performance excellence	**110**
Information and Analysis Management and effectiveness of the use of data and information to support customer-driven performance and market excellence	**80**
Strategic Planning The way the company sets strategic direction, how it determines plan requirements, and how plan requirements relate to customer and operational performance requirements	**80**
Human Resource Focus Company's efforts to develop and utilize the work force and to maintain an environment conducive to a high-performance organization (participation, continuous improvement, and personal and organizational growth)	**100**
Process Management Process design and control, including customer-focused design, product and service delivery, support services, and supply management	**100**
Business Results Company's performance and improvement in key business areas (customer satisfaction, financial indicators, human resources, suppliers and partners, and operations)	**450**
Customer and Market Focus Company's knowledge of the customer, customer service systems, responsiveness to customer, customer satisfaction	**80**
Total Points	**1,000**

SOURCE: Based on Malcolm Baldrige National Quality Award 1997 Award Criteria (Gaithersburg, MD: National Institute of Standards and Technology, 1997); "Overview of the Criteria for Performance Excellence," see www.quality.nist.gov.

sources can play in improving companies' competitiveness. Human resources is recognized as an important criterion as well as evaluated as part of business results. To attain total quality, managers must ensure that technological innovations are made and adopted, but more critical is how the people who are responsible for quality are managed.[26] Clearly, to be recognized as leaders in product or service quality, U.S. companies must effectively use their human resources.

We see one example of human resource management's role in improving quality at Trident Precision Manufacturing Inc. in Webster, New York.[27] Trident's customers were happy with its products, which ranged from metal brackets to machines that sort X-rays. But HR problems were occurring. Turnover was high with many employees quitting within months of joining the company. Trident had no quality process so products often reached the end of the assembly process with major defects and had to be completely rebuilt.

After attending a presentation on quality management, the senior research team realized that a major reason for the turnover and quality problems was that the firm failed to value employees. As a result, the management team developed a new management strategy focusing on five key business drivers: supplier partnerships, operational performance, customer satisfaction, shareholder value, and employee satisfaction. One of the first things the company did was implement a training course on TQM tools. The course included training on basic problem solving, quality improvements, just-in-time manufacturing, and interpersonal communications skills. The training has had a major impact on the business. Employees made more than 2,200 suggestions for how to improve

Trident's processes. (A full 98 percent have been implemented!) To raise employee satisfaction, Trident reviewed its recruiting processes as well as work culture. Investigation of the recruiting processes revealed that managers were not systematically evaluating job applicants. Basically, they were hiring anyone interested in a job at Trident! This resulted in hiring employees who lacked the necessary skills. People also were leaving Trident because they felt the company was not listening to employees' ideas.

As a result of this investigation, management has changed the recruiting process and the company culture. A successful job candidate must complete a series of interviews conducted by HR, senior managers, and members of the team he will be working with. Management has given employees the freedom and responsibility to identify problems and fix them before products are passed down to the next step in the assembly process. This change in the culture has positively impacted the "bottom line" and gained national recognition for the company. Turnover has dropped from 41 to 3.5 percent in the past ten years. Turnover in 1997 was 1 percent for employees with five or more years tenure in the company. Product defects came to 3 percent in 1988; the firm was defect-free in 1997. Two years ago the company won the Malcolm Baldrige Quality Award.

Some argue that the popularity of the Baldrige award has caused managers to devote too much time to completing the rigorous evaluation process and too little time to concentrating on promoting quality within the company.[28] Also, along with the recognition of winning the award comes the need to devote time speaking to companies in the United States and abroad about the organization's quality-improvement process. However, many companies use the Baldrige application process as a guide for managers to evaluate their own operations rather than as a strict set of rules to follow. For example, Solectron Corporation, an electronic assembly and contract manufacturing service business, used the Baldrige application process as a means to define its quality process and as a way to evaluate all departments' quality progress. The application process provided the company with a means to move toward continuous improvement.[29]

The Baldrige award appears to be having a positive impact on the quality of products and services produced by U.S. companies. A study of 20 companies that were among the highest-scoring applicants for the Baldrige award suggests that TQM results in overall improvement in corporate performance (including better employee relations and increased productivity, customer satisfaction, and market share).[30] One important finding of the study was that none of the companies it included realized positive benefits immediately. Those companies that realized benefits from TQM took a well-planned approach in implementing the program. Increasing employee participation in improving product and service quality takes time.

COMPOSITION OF THE LABOR FORCE. Company performance on the balanced scorecard is influenced by the characteristics of its labor force or current employees. The labor force of current employees is often referred to as the **internal labor force.** Employers identify and select new employees from the external labor market through recruiting and selection practices. The **external labor market** includes persons actively seeking employment. As a result, the skills and motivation of a company's internal labor force are influenced by the composition of the available labor market (the external labor market). The skills and motivation of a company's internal labor force determine the need for training and development practices and the effectiveness of the company's compensation and reward systems.

Competition for talented persons in the external labor market also affects the composition of a company's internal labor market. For example, when unemployment rates are low, many companies are unable to find employees they need to fill jobs. AMR Corporation (owner of American Airlines) has experienced a shortage of travel reservation agents.[31] As a result, AMR is developing courses with high schools in the Dallas, Texas area. AMR provides the high school with its Sabre reservation system, which students use in their curriculum. Approximately 20 percent of the students who studied the system have been hired by American Airlines, while other students are using the system in other travel-related jobs. Boeing, the airplane manufacturer, is heavily involved in teaching and recruiting in schools. For example, Boeing trains students to work in its manufacturing plants for two summers. As a result of that experience, the student is expected to be offered full-time employment after graduation.[32]

The Bureau of Labor Statistics, a part of the U.S. Department of Labor, tracks changes in the composition of the U.S. labor force and projects employment trends.[33] Over the 1996–2006 period, the labor force is projected to increase by 15 million from 134 million to 149 million workers. This is an increase of 11 percent, less than the 14 percent increase between 1986 and 1996. The composition of the labor force will change because of shifts in the U.S. population. The youth labor force (ages 16 to 24) is expected to grow more rapidly than the overall labor force for the first time in 25 years. The labor force aged 45 to 64 will grow faster than any other age group as the baby-boom generation (born from 1946 to 1964) continues to age. An aging work force means that employers will increasingly face issues such as career plateauing, retirement planning, and retraining of older workers to avoid skill obsolescence. Companies will struggle with how to control the rising costs of benefits and health care. Growth in the youth labor force suggests that employers will have to find ways to attract, train, and retain younger employees. (Consider the strategies used by AMR Corporation and Boeing discussed earlier.)

As Figure 1.4 shows, the U.S. work force is becoming increasingly diverse. It is projected that by 2006 the work force will be 72 percent white, 11 percent black, 12 percent Hispanic, and 5 percent Asian and other minorities. Labor force participation of women in all age groups is expected to increase, while men's participation rates are expected to continue to decline for all age groups under 45 years. The Asian and other labor force and Hispanic labor force are projected to increase faster than other groups because of immigration and higher-than-average birth rates.

Immigration is an important factor contributing to the diversity of the work force. Immigrants will likely account for an additional 1 million persons in the work force each year through 2006.[34] About 70 percent of these new workers will be Hispanics and Asians. There is considerable disagreement regarding the impact of immigration on employment prospects for U.S.-born workers and the U.S. economy. The U.S. economy has benefited by acquiring talented, intelligent workers from other countries, but it is

FIGURE 1.4
Changes in the U.S. Work Force, 1996 and 2006

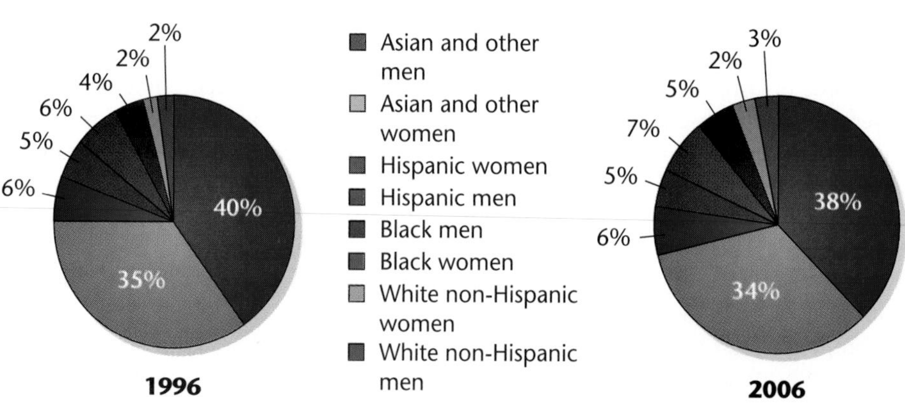

SOURCE: Bureau of Labor Statistics, "BLS Releases New 1996–2006 Employment Projections," www.bls.gov/new.release/ecopro.nws.htm. Numbers rounded to nearest percentage may not add to 100%.

unclear whether an influx of skilled workers from other countries results in lower wages or increased unemployment for U.S.-born employees. Immigrants who enter the United States illegally (from formerly communist countries, for example) tend to have less education and depend more on the welfare system than those who enter legally.[35]

The heterogeneous composition of the work force challenges companies to create HRM practices that ensure that the talents, skills, and values of all employees are fully utilized to help deliver high-quality products and services.

STRUCTURE OF THE ECONOMY. The competition for labor is affected by the structure of the economy. The structure of the economy is influenced by the growth and decline of industries, jobs, and occupations. Competition for labor is also influenced by the number of persons available for full-time work as well as the availability of alternative work schedules (e.g., part-time work).

Job growth is expected for employees at all levels of education and training. However, average growth is expected to be greatest for occupations requiring at least an associates degree rather than for occupations requiring less training. Professional specialty and service occupations are expected to account for 46 percent of the total job growth between 1996 and 2006.[36] Of all occupations, professional specialty occupations (e.g., engineering, science, law, teaching) are expected to grow the fastest between 1996 and 2006. Professional specialty occupations will add approximately 5 million jobs. These occupations require advanced education and are rewarded with high earnings. Growth in service occupations is the next-fastest-growing group with an expected addition of approximately 4.6 million jobs.

The expected growth of jobs in the service sector has important implications for HRM. Research shows that employee perceptions of HRM practices are positively related to customer evaluation of service quality. The more positive the employee perceptions of HRM practices (e.g., providing feedback, adequate training), the greater the customers' evaluation of service quality.[37] This suggests that to maximize customer service, companies in the service sector should consider creating both a positive experience for the customer and progressive HRM policies.

Other groups that are projected to grow faster than average are executive, administrative, and managerial occupations, technical and related support occupations, and marketing and sales occupations. Note that professional specialty occupations and service occupations differ on both the amount of education required for the job and expected earnings. Professional specialty occupations require more education and have greater earnings potential than do service jobs.[38]

Table 1.8 lists occupations that are projected to have the largest job growths or declines. Occupations that involve contact between people and are not too affected by new technologies are expected to have average or above-average growth rates. These jobs include insurance adjusters, investigators, and collectors as well as hotel desk clerks, clerical supervisors and managers, and teacher aides and education assistants. Technological advances, industry employment demands, and company restructuring are responsible for the declining occupations.

Retail will continue to be a source of jobs for unskilled workers.[39] Technology has made it possible for employees with low reading and math skills to perform customer transactions by replacing numerical key pads on point-of-sale terminals with pictures of products and menu items.

SKILL DEFICIENCIES. It is expected that the supply of individuals with the necessary education and training will not meet the demands of jobs in the U.S. economy.[40] Most new jobs created in the next decade will require higher levels of reading and writing skills (e.g., skills in reading journals and financial reports as well as writing business

TABLE 1.8 Projected Employment Demands of Occupations to 2006

LARGEST JOB GROWTH	LARGEST JOB DECLINE
1. Cashiers	1. Sewing machine operators
2. Systems analysts	2. Farmers
3. General managers and top executives	3. Bookkeeping, accounting, and auditing clerks
4. Registered nurses	4. Typists
5. Retail salespersons	5. Secretaries (except legal and medical)
6. Truck drivers	6. Cleaners and servants (private household)
7. Home health aides	7. Computer operators (except peripheral equipment)
8. Teacher aides and educational assistants	8. Farm workers
9. Nurse's aides, orderlies, and attendants	9. Duplicating, mail, and other office machine workers
10. Receptionists and information clerks	10. Welfare eligibility workers and interviewers

SOURCE: Based on G.T. Silvestri, "Occupational Employment Projections to 2006," *Monthly Labor Review* (November 1997), pp. 78, 80.

letters and reports).[41] Bureau of Labor Statistics projections suggest that the most rapid rate of growth will be among jobs requiring technical skills. These occupations and craft jobs often do not require a four-year college degree but instead rely on postsecondary education, such as that obtained from technical schools.

Two problems are evident as we examine skills: new entrants to the work force who come from diverse backgrounds and the current labor force. New entrants to the labor force often arrive without the skills needed for success. In the United States, a large proportion of the population has only fourth- to eighth-grade literacy levels. Literacy includes reading ability as well as the ability to understand and use printed information in all life activities. Compared to most other countries, the United States has a greater concentration of adults who score at the lowest literacy levels (including prose, document, and quantitative literacy categories).[42] And achievement levels of U.S. youth vary more widely than those in other countries. Although college attendance rates are high, the high school dropout rate is close to 15 percent. This rate is especially high among Hispanics (approximately 43 percent). Persons with only fourth- to eighth-grade literacy levels may make up as much as 65 percent of the entry-level work force in the year 2010.[43] This means that many new entrants to the labor market will not have the education needed to qualify for on-the-job or postsecondary training needed for available jobs. One reason for the poor educational preparation of U.S. youth is that employers do not reward educational achievement in math and science for youths who are seeking careers in fields other than medicine, science, and engineering.[44]

One estimate is that 27 million adults in the United States lack the basic writing, reading, and computational skills needed to perform well in the workplace.[45] In 1991 and 1998, The National Association of Manufacturing (NAM) conducted studies to determine the skills deficiencies of entry-level job applicants and current employees.[46] Over 4,000 NAM member firms chosen at random were surveyed. Similar skill deficiencies were found in both surveys. NAM members reported that job applicants have inadequate technical (62 percent), reading or writing (33 percent), oral communications (22 percent), and math skills (22 percent). Sixty percent of the manufacturers surveyed reported that their current employees possess deficiencies in basic math, writing, and comprehension skills. The skills gap has decreased manufacturers' competitiveness because it makes it hard for them to upgrade technology, reorganize work, and empower employees, which are key elements in high-performance work systems.

The skills gap has also caused manufacturers to delay adding new businesses. The labor shortages that many companies are experiencing due to low unemployment rates are made even worse by the lack of qualified job applicants. More than 25 percent of manufacturers typically reject over 75 percent of job applicants because they are unqualified. This is especially a problem for small businesses in research and development, construction, and manufacturing, which report that the scarcity of suitable workers is challenging their growth.[47] Small businesses rely heavily on the labor market to find skilled employees because they cannot afford to invest in training.

A joint research project between the American Society for Training and Development and the U.S. Department of Labor identified six types of skills besides academic skills (reading, writing, arithmetic) that U.S. employers say are basic to success in the workplace.[48] These skills include influence skills, interpersonal skills, communications skills, adaptability, personal management skills, and knowing how to learn. The study found that knowing how to learn served as the foundation for the other skills. Knowing how to learn is critical because the workplace demands that employees understand their work and the way it fits into the mission of the entire organization, that employees be able to innovate to improve product and service quality, and that they stay up to date with advances in technology.

The implications of the changing labor market for managing human resources are far-reaching. Because labor market growth will be primarily in female and minority populations, U.S. companies will have to ensure that employees and human resource management systems are free of bias to capitalize on the perspectives and values that women and minorities can contribute to improving product quality, customer service, product development, and market share. Increasing levels of employment in the service sector of the economy suggest that HRM practices in these companies need to ensure that customer service is rewarded and improved. Finally, both the U.S. government and the private sector are taking steps to combat skill deficiencies. The U.S. Congress passed the Workforce Investment Act of 1998 to facilitate business and government partnerships in education and training.[49] Companies are implementing remedial education programs to deal with skill deficiencies and are beginning to support training and lifelong learning and education beyond job-related skills (e.g., general equivalency degree programs and technical skills programs). The 1998 NAM study found that about 50 percent of manufacturers report investing 2 percent or more of company payroll dollars to train shop floor and hourly workers compared to an average of less than .5 percent in 1991!

Employers are investing in school-to-work programs. **School-to-work** programs include basic-skills training and joint training ventures with universities, community colleges, and high schools. For example, Rockwell International Corporation (which has an automobile brake component plant in York, South Carolina) helped to design blueprint-reading and metric system courses at a neighboring technical college. During their summer break, college professors worked at Intel Corporation plants in Oregon to better understand the type of work their students might perform. As a result, colleges in 10 states revised their curriculums.[50]

CHANGES IN THE EMPLOYMENT CONTRACT AND PLACE OF WORK. The **contingent work force,** which includes temporary, part-time, and self-employed workers, is growing. This work force was estimated to include about 32 million persons in 1994, and the use of temporary workers has doubled since 1990.[51] The increase in the number of contingent workers is occurring for several reasons.[52] Erosion of the traditional employment contract—lifetime employment for dedicated service—has occurred. Companies can no longer guarantee their employees job security. Many companies have reduced the number of full-time employees to lower associated labor costs and give the organization the flexibility to contract for skills when needed. Companies that use contingent employees from temporary agencies and contract firms are likely to experience a reduction in the administrative and financial burden associated with human resource management because the agencies take care of selecting, training, and compensating the workers.

Contingent work is also attractive from the worker's perspective. Many employees have decided to work on a contingent basis as a result of interests, values, and needs. Employees who have lost their jobs may take on temporary work while they are seeking full-time employment. Other employees are contingent workers so they can attend to raising young children or care for a sick family member. Still other contingent employees use temporary employment as a way to identify potential full-time employers that would satisfy their needs.

The use of contingent employees places a burden on managers to be able to identify when and how many contingent employees are needed—that is, on human resource planning. (Human resource planning is discussed in Chapter 5.) Managers also have to consider which jobs are critical to the business and therefore should be filled by full-time employees. Employee morale may suffer when full-time employees are replaced with contingent workers.

More work is being done outside the traditional office or factory. Such work is called **distributed work** and includes work done at home, on the road, or anywhere a person can connect to the office or peers using communications technology.[53] More than 21 million persons did some work at home as their primary job in 1997.[54] The overall number of persons doing job-related work at home did not grow dramatically between 1991 and 1997, but the number of wage-and-salary workers doing paid work at home did. More than half of those working at home were wage-and-salary workers who were not paid for their time worked at home. Close to 90 percent were in white-collar occupations including sales and administrative support and managers. All major industry groups except mining had significant numbers of workers doing paid work at home. Some estimates project that by 2005 about 25 percent of the labor force will be engaged in distributed work. Distributed work has important implications for managing human resources. Employees will need to be trained in using communication technologies to share data, text, and ideas with peers, managers, and customers. Companies may need to learn to use new types of employee evaluation to fairly and accurately assess performance.

EMPLOYEE VALUES. Because the work force is predicted to become more diverse in terms of age, ethnicity, and racial background, it is unlikely that one set of values will characterize all employees.[55] For example, "baby busters" (employees born between 1965 and 1975) value unexpected rewards for work accomplishments, opportunities to learn new things, praise, recognition, and time with the manager. "Traditionalists," employees born between 1925 and 1945, tend to be uncomfortable challenging the status quo and authority. They value income and employment security.

All employees, however, value several aspects of work regardless of their background. Employees view work as a means to self-fulfillment—that is, a means to more fully use their skills and abilities, meet their interests, and allow them to live a desirable lifestyle.[56] One report indicated that employees who are given opportunities to fully use and develop their skills, receive greater job responsibilities, believe the promotion system is fair, and have a trustworthy manager who represents the employee's best interests are more committed to their companies.[57] Fostering these values requires companies to develop HRM practices that provide more opportunity for individual contribution and entrepreneurship.[58] Because many employees place more value on the quality of nonwork activities and family life than on pay and production, employees will demand more flexible work policies that allow them to choose work hours and locations where work is performed.

Managing cultural diversity involves many different activities, including creating an organizational culture that values diversity, ensuring that HRM systems are bias-free, facilitating higher career involvement of women, promoting knowledge and acceptance of cultural differences, ensuring involvement in education both within and outside the company, and dealing with employees' resistance to diversity.[59] Table 1.9 presents ways that managing cultural diversity can provide a competitive advantage. Traditionally, in many U.S. companies the costs of poorly managing cultural diversity were viewed mainly as increased legal fees associated with discrimination cases. However, as Table 1.9 illustrates, the implications of successfully managing the diverse work force of the next decade go beyond legal concerns. How diversity issues are managed has implications for creativity, problem solving, retaining good employees, and developing markets for the firm's products and services. To successfully manage a diverse work force, managers must develop a new set of skills, including

1. Communicating effectively with employees from a wide variety of cultural backgrounds.
2. Coaching and developing employees of different ages, educational backgrounds, ethnicity, physical ability, and race.
3. Providing performance feedback that is based on objective outcomes rather than val-

TABLE 1.9
How Managing Cultural Diversity Can Provide Competitive Advantage

1. Cost argument	As organizations become more diverse, the cost of a poor job in integrating workers will increase. Those who handle this well will thus create cost advantages over those who don't.
2. Resource-acquisition argument	Companies develop reputations on favorability as prospective employers for women and ethnic minorities. Those with the best reputations for managing diversity will win the competition for the best personnel. As the labor pool shrinks and changes composition, this edge will become increasingly important.
3. Marketing argument	For multinational organizations, the insight and cultural sensitivity that members with roots in other countries bring to the marketing effort should improve these efforts in important ways. The same rationale applies to marketing to subpopulations within domestic operations.
4. Creativity argument	Diversity of perspectives and less emphasis on conformity to norms of the past (which characterize the modern approach to management of diversity) should improve the level of creativity.
5. Problem-solving argument	Heterogeneity in decisions and problem-solving groups potentially produces better decisions through a wider range of perspectives and more thorough critical analysis of issues.
6. System flexibility argument	An implication of the multicultural model for managing diversity is that the system will become less determinant, less standardized, and therefore more fluid. The increased fluidity should create greater flexibility to react to environmental changes (i.e., reactions should be faster and cost less).

SOURCE: T.H. Cox and S. Blake, "Managing Cultural Diversity: Implications for Organizational Competitiveness," *Academy of Management Executive* 5 (1991), p. 47. Used with permission.

ues and stereotypes that work against women, minorities, and handicapped persons by prejudging these persons' abilities and talents.

4. Creating a work environment that makes it comfortable for employees of all backgrounds to be creative and innovative.[60]

Many U.S. companies have already made a commitment to ensuring that diversity in their work force is recognized and effectively used for competitive advantage. The Seattle Times Company, a newspaper publisher, has taken an approach that emphasizes making sure its product does not reflect erroneous racial stereotypes as well as ensuring that stereotypes do not affect the way employees are treated. The company has formed a diversity committee made up of reporters, editors, and photographers who meet regularly to evaluate the paper's content and educate the rest of the newsroom staff about diversity issues. The company also conducts content audits, which involve evaluating the frequency of women and minorities in photographs and their appearance in positive or neutral situations.[61] Many other companies (e.g., Honeywell, Procter & Gamble, Wang) are currently involved in diversity training efforts using role plays, videotapes, and experiential exercises, which focus on understanding cultural differences, communication styles, and the ways stereotypes influence behavior toward persons with different characteristics.

The bottom line is that to gain a competitive advantage in the next decade, companies must harness the power of the diverse work force. These practices are needed not only to meet employee needs but to reduce turnover costs and ensure that customers receive the best service possible. The implication of diversity for HR practices will be highlighted throughout this book. For example, from a staffing perspective, it is important to ensure that tests used to select employees are not biased against minority groups. From a work design perspective, employees need flexible schedules that allow them to meet nonwork needs. From a training perspective, it is clear that all employees need to be made aware of the potential damaging effects of stereotypes. From a compensation perspective, new benefits such as eldercare and daycare need to be included in reward systems to accommodate the needs of a diverse work force.

LEGISLATION AND LITIGATION. Five main areas of the legal environment have influenced human resource management over the past 25 years.[62] These areas include equal employment opportunity legislation, employee safety and health, employee pay and benefits, employee privacy, and job security.

Legislation in these areas will continue to have a major impact on practices. For example, considerable debate surrounds affirmative action.[63] Affirmative action was created in 1965 by Executive Order 11246. (We discuss affirmative action further in Chapter 3.) The order not only prohibited discrimination but obligated companies to make sure women and minorities were not excluded from recruitment and training practices. The intent of affirmative action was for companies to take positive steps to ensure that discrimination would not occur. Affirmative action has evolved from posting notices that declare that a company won't discriminate to monitoring job candidate pools to ensure that women and minorities are included. Some companies have even identified numerical goals (called targets) to ensure minority representation. The U.S. Supreme Court will ultimately determine whether affirmative action is necessary (and in what form) to ensure that women and minorities have access to jobs and training programs or whether it is reverse discrimination, as some contend.

Also, there will likely be continued discussion of whether to add sexual orientation as a protected class under the Civil Rights Act of 1991. (A protected class is a characteristic that is illegal to use for making employment decisions.) Several state and city statutes include sexual orientation as a protected class.

Employers and the courts continue to struggle with identifying what constitutes religious discrimination. Employers are being asked to juggle the demands of workers who want to express their faith with those who find such expressions offensive.[64]

The increased use of and access to electronic databases by employees and employers suggest that in the near future legislation will be needed to protect employee privacy rights. Currently, there is no federal legislation outlining how employee databases should be used to protect privacy and confidentiality.

A final area of litigation that will continue to have a major influence on HRM practices involves job security. As companies are forced to close plants and lay off employees because of restructuring, technology changes, or financial crisis, the number of cases dealing with the illegal discharge of employees has increased. The issue of what constitutes employment at will—that is, employment that can be terminated at any time without notice—will be debated. Employers' work rules, recruitment practices, and performance evaluation systems will need to be revised to ensure that these systems do not falsely communicate employment agreements the company does not intend to honor (e.g., lifetime employment).

ETHICAL CONSIDERATIONS. Many decisions related to the management of human resources are characterized by uncertainty. Ethics can be considered the fundamental principles by which employees and companies interact.[65] These principles should be considered in making business decisions and interacting with clients and customers. Recent surveys suggest that the general public and managers do not have positive perceptions of the ethical conduct of U.S. businesses. For example, in a survey conducted by *The Wall Street Journal*, 4 out of 10 executives reported they were asked to behave unethically.[66]

As a result of unfavorable perceptions of U.S. business practices and an increased concern for better serving the customer, U.S. companies are becoming more aware of the need for all representatives of the company to act responsibly.[67] They have an interest in the way their employees behave because customer, government agency, and vendor perceptions of the company play an important role in maintaining the relationships necessary to sell products and services.

Ethical, successful companies can be characterized by four principles.[68] First, in their relationship with customers, vendors, and clients, these companies emphasize mutual benefits. Second, employees assume responsibility for the actions of the company. Third, they have a sense of purpose or vision the employees value and use in their day-to-day work. Finally, they emphasize fairness; that is, another person's interests count as much as their own.

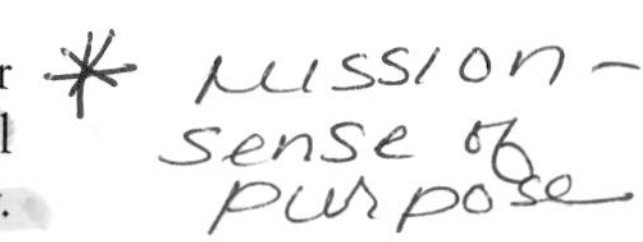

In the chapter opening we briefly discussed how Texas Instruments was emphasizing ethics as part of its strategy for conducting business. Besides addressing ethics issues in the *TI News*, a weekly electronic newsletter, TI is taking other actions.[69] At many TI locations "subject experts" are available to speak directly with employees. For example, if an employee is concerned about an ethical issue involving safety or an environmental issue, he can directly speak to a subject expert. The subject expert's phone number and e-mail address appear in easy-to-read pamphlets on everyday ethical and legal issues found at TI locations. To complement the subject experts, TI is developing a web site devoted exclusively to articles, policies, and procedures that deal with ethics. Employees can also directly access a toll-free hotline number where ethic questions are answered by professionals from TIs' ethics department. Employees can also contact the ethics department staff using a secure e-mail system.

There are basically three standards that human resource managers must satisfy for these practices to be considered ethical.[70] First, human resource practices must result in the greatest good for the largest number of people. Second, employment practices must

respect basic human rights of privacy, due process, consent, and free speech. Third, managers must treat employees and customers equitably and fairly. Throughout the book we will highlight ethical dilemmas in human resource management practices.

THE HIGH-PERFORMANCE WORK SYSTEM CHALLENGE

For U.S. companies to compete with foreign competitors, they will have to learn to better utilize employees' talents and skills and new technology. The challenge that companies face is how to integrate technology and structure to gain a competitive advantage—that is, competing through **high-performance work systems.** High-performance work systems maximize the fit between the company's social system (employees) and its technical system.[71]

Technological advances in manufacturing, transportation, telecommunications, and microprocessors are changing the way work is performed, managers' and employees' roles, and organizational structure. Technology also has made human resource information bases more available and accessible and created a need to develop HRM practices that integrate technology with people.

CHANGE IN EMPLOYEES' WORK ROLES AND SKILL REQUIREMENTS.

New technology causes changes in basic-skill requirements and work roles and often results in combining jobs.[72] For example, computer-integrated manufacturing uses robots and computers to automate the manufacturing process. The computer allows the production of different products that meet market demands simply by reprogramming the computer. As a result, laborer, material handler, operator–assembler, and maintenance jobs may be merged into one position. Computer-integrated manufacturing requires employees to monitor equipment and troubleshoot problems with sophisticated equipment, share information with other employees, and understand the interaction between components of the manufacturing process.[73]

Technology is often a means to achieve product diversification and customization. As a result, employees need job-specific product knowledge and basic learning skills to keep up with product development and design improvements. To customize products and services, employees must have the ability to listen and communicate with customers. Interpersonal skills, such as negotiation and conflict management, and problem-solving skills are more important than physical strength, coordination, and fine-motor skills, which were previously required for many manufacturing and service jobs.

INCREASE IN THE USE OF TEAMS TO PERFORM WORK. As the information needed to improve product quality and customer service becomes more available to employees at the point of sale or point of production because of advances in microprocessing systems, employees are expected to make more decisions concerning how their jobs are performed. One of the most popular methods of increasing employee responsibility and control is work teams. Work teams involve employees with various skills, who interact to assemble a product or provide a service. Work teams frequently assume many of the activities usually reserved for managers, such as selecting new team members, planning work schedules, and coordinating activities with customers and other units within the firm. Work teams also perform inspection and quality-control activities while the product or service is being completed, an important component for achieving total quality.

Besides the potential motivational advantages of work teams, labor costs can also be realized for companies adopting teams. A number of companies are reorganizing assembly operations—abandoning the assembly line in favor of hybrid operations combining mass production with jobs in which employees perform multiple tasks, use many skills, control the pace of work, and assemble the entire final product.[74] One example of this type of teamwork is Compaq Computer's assembly cells. In manufacturing sites in Scotland and Texas, computers are built by four-person teams. One person assembles parts, another builds components, and two people assemble the computer unit. The new teams helped raise labor productivity 51 percent.

CHANGES IN THE NATURE OF MANAGERIAL WORK. To gain the maximum benefit from the introduction of new technology in the workplace, managers must be able to move away from the "military model" of management, which emphasizes controlling, planning, and coordinating activities, and instead focus on creating work conditions that facilitate employee creativity and innovation. Because of advances in technology, information is more readily accessible to employees at all levels of the company, and decision making increasingly is decentralized. As a result, it is difficult, and certainly not effective, for managers to attempt to directly control interactions between work teams or between work teams and customers.

The manager's job will increasingly be to empower employees. Empowerment means giving employees responsibility and authority to make decisions regarding all aspects of product development or customer service.[75] Employees are then held accountable for products and services and, in return, share the rewards and failures that result. For empowerment to be successful, managers must serve in a linking and coordinating role.[76] The linking role involves representing employees (or teams) by ensuring that adequate resources are provided to perform the work (external linking), facilitating interactions across departments (informal linking), and ensuring that employees are updated on important issues and cooperate with each other through sharing of information and resources (internal linking). In addition, managers who successfully perform the internal linking role must be available and willing to help employees deal with problems daily.

Although strong interpersonal skills and communications skills are required by both managers and employees, managers have to either be able to provide answers to technical issues or, more likely, be able to refer employees to persons within or outside the firm who can provide insight into technical problems. This means that managers have to be more aware of various resources available within the company and the community.

CHANGES IN COMPANY STRUCTURE. The traditional design of U.S. companies emphasizes efficiency, decision making by managers, and dissemination of information from the top of the company to lower levels. However, this structure will not be effective in the work environment of the next decade, in which personal computers will give employees immediate access to information needed to complete customer orders or modify product lines. The box "Competing through High-Performance Work Systems" highlights GE Fanuc's adaptive high-involvement organizational structure. In the adaptive organizational structure, employees are in a constant state of learning and performance improvement. Employees are free to move wherever they are needed in the company. The adaptive organization is characterized by a core set of values or vital vision that drives all organizational efforts.[77] Previously established boundaries between managers and employees, employees and customers, employees and vendors, and the various functions within the company are abandoned. Employees, managers, vendors, customers, and suppliers work together to improve service and product quality and to create new products and services. Line employees are trained in multiple jobs, communicate directly with suppliers and customers, and interact frequently with engineers, quality experts, and employees from other functions.

Top-Grade Material and Work Systems Mean World-Class Excellence

COMPETING THROUGH HIGH-PERFORMANCE WORK SYSTEMS

GE Fanuc Automation North America, a joint venture between General Electric Company and FANUC Ltd. of Japan, has developed a high-involvement work force. Based in Charlottesville, Virginia, the joint venture employs 1,500 people. The reputation of the company is based on its excellence in automation control, research and development practices, and manufacturing facilities. The goal of the company is to improve customers' productivity with the best industrial automation technology, reliability, and services worldwide. Recognition of the company's commitment to quality is reflected in its being one of the first U.S. firms to become a certified ISO 9000 manufacturer.

GE Fanuc Automation achieved its reputation and recognition for quality as a result of the use of high-performance work practices. Central to its practices is the idea that employees closest to the work have the best improvement ideas. As a result, employees must be encouraged to voice their opinions and make changes.

How does the company use high-performance work practices? The facility has three layers of management and over 40 work teams set their own goals and measure success factors based on the overall business goals. Each team spends at least one hour per week measuring the goals and discussing new ways to be effective. To ensure team effectiveness, all employees receive more than 100 hours of training. Employees are also guaranteed that they will never lose their jobs due to an idea developed by the teams. Managers (known as coaches) are evaluated based on their support of the teams. Each functional team within the business has a dedicated HR manager who helps the team develop its strategies, accompanies the team on sales calls, and does whatever she can to help the team.

SOURCE: Based on G. Flynn, "HR Leaders Stay Close to the Line," *Workforce* (February 1997), p. 53; GE Fanuc Corporate Profile, "World Class Excellence," Internet address www.ge.com/gemis/gefanuc.

INCREASED AVAILABILITY OF INFORMATION BASES RELATED TO THE COMPANY'S HUMAN RESOURCES. Improvements in technology related to microcomputers and software have also had a major impact on the use of information for managing human resources. Traditionally, computers had been used in human resources only for compensation and benefits—for example, administering payroll. However, new advances in microchips have made it possible to store large quantities of data on personal computers and to perform statistical analyses that were once only possible with large mainframe computers. A **human resource information system (HRIS)** is a system used to acquire, store, manipulate, analyze, retrieve, and distribute information related to the company's human resources.[78] From the manager's perspective, an HRIS can be used to support strategic decision making, to avoid litigation, to evaluate programs or policies, or to support daily operating concerns.

Traditionally, HR software applications have been developed in response to record-keeping requirements dictated by legislation. As a result, most companies have HRISs that track payroll and benefits information in response to compliance requirements of legislation such as the Comprehensive Omnibus Budget Reconciliation Act, which requires group health plans to offer health benefits to former employees who have either retired or been terminated. Similarly, the large majority of companies also have HRIS applications related to applicant tracking and adverse impact analysis in response to Title VII of the Civil Rights Act.

However, certain trends suggest that performance management, succession planning, and training and employee-development applications are becoming increasingly important. For example, projections of the level of skills that will be available in the future work force suggest that math and reading competencies will be below the level required by new jobs. Changing technology can easily make the skills of technical employees obsolete. To meet internal and external customers' demands, work teams consisting of employees from different functional areas with different skills will have to be assembled. These trends demand that employees' skills and competencies be monitored carefully. Complicating this need for information is the fact that many employees are geographically dispersed across several locations within the same city or country, or across countries. In response to these needs companies have implemented global human resource management systems. Northern Telecom Limited (a Canadian telecommunications company that has facilities in 90 countries, including the United Kingdom, China, and the United States) needed access to information on employees located worldwide. The company has created a central database built on a common set of core elements. Anyone with authorization can view employee records from around the globe. Head count, salary, and recruiting data is continually updated as changes are made from around the world. Although the system is customized to specific country needs, several common data fields and elements are used globally. Northern Telecom's system has enabled managers from around the world to obtain up-to-date employee data to meet customer needs and address internal staffing issues.[79]

COMPETITIVENESS IN HIGH-PERFORMANCE WORK SYSTEMS. Unfortunately, many managers have tended to consider technological and structural innovations as independent of each other. That is, because of immediate demands for productivity, service, and short-term profitability, many managers tend to implement a new technology (e.g., networked computer system) or a new work design (e.g., service teams organized by product) without considering how a new technology might influence the efficiency or effectiveness of the way work is organized.[80] Without integrating technology and structure, maximized production and service will not be attained.

Human resource management practices that support high-performance work systems are shown in Table 1.10. The HR practices involved include employee selection, performance management, training, work design, and compensation. These practices are designed to provide employees with skills, incentives, knowledge, and autonomy. Research studies suggest that high-performance work practices are usually associated with increases in productivity and long-term financial performance.[81] Research also suggests that it is

TABLE 1.10
How HR Practices Support High-Performance Work Systems

- Teams are used to perform work.
- Employees participate in the selection process.
- Employees receive formal performance feedback and are actively involved in the performance-improvement process.
- Ongoing training is emphasized and rewarded.
- Employees' rewards and compensation relate to the company's financial performance.
- Equipment and work processes are structured to encourage maximum flexibility and interaction among employees.
- Employees participate in planning changes in equipment, layout, and work methods.
- Work design allows employees to use a variety of skills.
- Employees understand how their jobs contribute to the finished product or service.

SOURCE: Based on J.A. Neal and C.L. Tromley, "From Incremental Change to Retrofit: Creating High Performance Work Systems," *Academy of Management Executive* 9 (1995), pp. 42–54; M.A. Huselid, "The Impact of Human Resource Management Practices on Turnover, Productivity, and Corporate Financial Performance," *Academy of Management Journal* 38 (1995), pp. 635–72.

FIGURE 1.5 Relationship between HR Philosophy and Practices

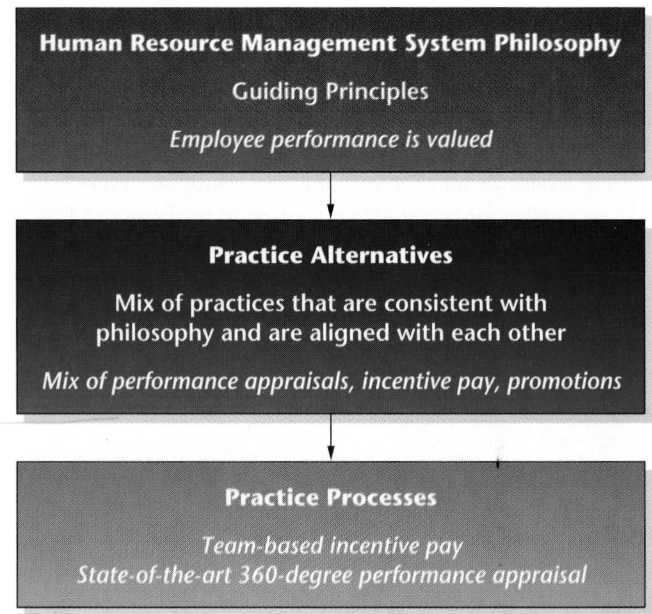

SOURCE: Based on B. Becker and B. Gerhart, "The Impact of Human Resource Management on Organizational Performance: Progress and Prospects," *Academy of Management Journal* 39 (1996), p. 786. Reprinted with permission.

more effective to improve HR practices as a whole, rather than focus on one or two isolated practices (such as the pay system or selection system).[82] There may be a best HR system, but whatever the company does, the practices must be aligned with each other and be consistent with the system if they are to have a positive effect on company performance.[83] We will discuss this alignment in more detail in Chapters 2 and 16. Figure 1.5 illustrates the relationship needed between the HR system, policies, and practices.

Owens–Corning Fiberglass is a good example of the holistic approach needed for high-performance work practices to be effective. Owens–Corning Fiberglass introduced new technology and integrated it with HRM practices to create a competitive advantage. The renovation of the Jackson, Tennessee, plant involved automation and a new glass-making recipe. To meet environmental standards the plant uses a new blend of materials that do not produce air pollution. The plant also includes ergonomic devices that let workers complete a wide variety of tasks (e.g., open rail doors and lift heavy machinery). Self-managed work teams were introduced for the first time in Owens–Corning operations. The selection process included tests designed to measure employees' ability to learn and get along with others. Cross-training of all team members will occur so that they have the complete set of skills needed in the fiberglass-making process. Has all of the investment in new human resource practices and technology paid off? The plant is an industry leader in fiberglass production.[84]

Meeting Competitive Challenges through HRM Practices

We have discussed the global, stakeholder, and high-performance work system challenges U.S. companies are facing. We have emphasized that management of human resources plays a critical role in determining companies' success in meeting the chal-

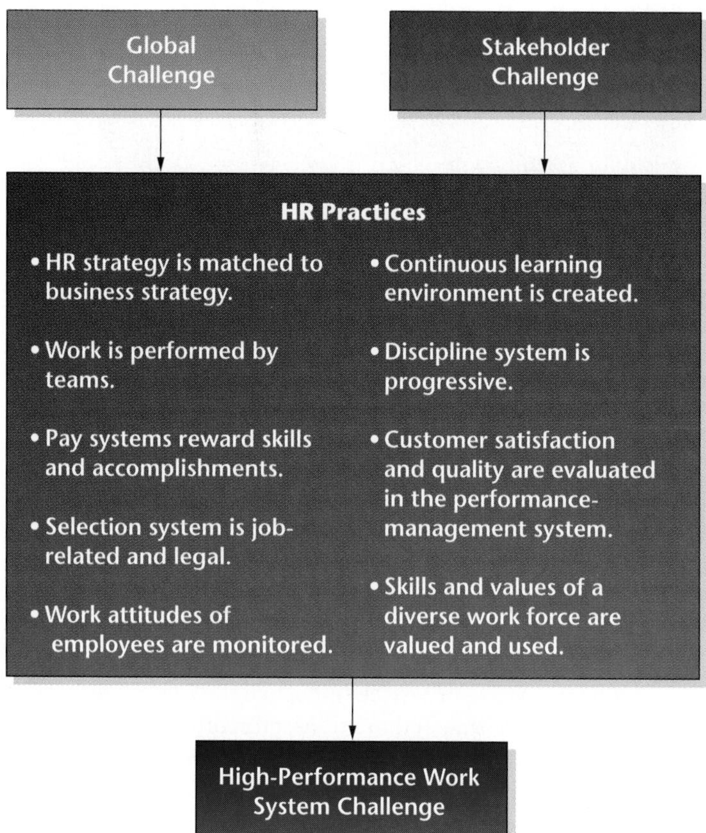

FIGURE 1.6
Examples of How HR Practices Can Help Companies Meet the Competitive Challenges

lenges. HRM practices have not traditionally been seen as providing economic value to the company. Economic value is usually associated with equipment, technology, and facilities. However, HRM practices have been shown to be valuable.[85] Compensation, staffing, training and development, performance management, and other HRM practices are investments that directly affect employees' motivation and ability to provide products and services that are valued by customers. Research has shown that companies that attempt to increase their competitiveness by investing in new technology and becoming involved in the quality movement also make investments in state-of-the-art staffing, training, and compensation practices.[86] Figure 1.6 shows examples of human resource practices that help companies deal with the three challenges. For example, to meet stakeholder needs, companies need to identify through their selection processes whether prospective employees value customer relations and have the levels of interpersonal skills necessary to work with fellow employees in teams. To meet all three challenges, companies need to capitalize on the diversity of values, abilities, and perspectives that employees bring to the workplace.

HRM practices that help companies deal with the three competitive challenges can be grouped into the four dimensions shown in Figure 1.7. These dimensions include the human resource environment, acquiring and preparing human resources, assessment and development of human resources, and compensating human resources. In addition, some companies have special issues related to labor management relations, international human resource management, and managing the human resource function.

FIGURE 1.7
Major Dimensions of HRM Practices Contributing to Company Competitiveness

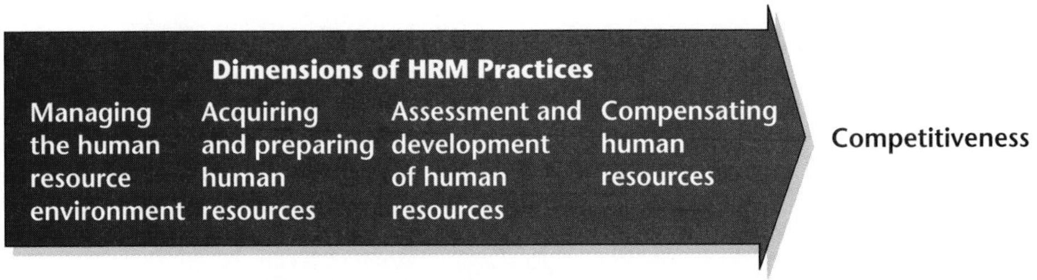

Dimensions of HRM Practices

Managing the human resource environment | Acquiring and preparing human resources | Assessment and development of human resources | Compensating human resources → **Competitiveness**

MANAGING THE HUMAN RESOURCE ENVIRONMENT

Managing internal and external environmental factors allows employees to make the greatest possible contribution to company productivity and competitiveness. Creating a positive environment for human resources involves

- Linking HRM practices to the company's business objectives—that is, strategic human resource management.
- Ensuring that HRM practices comply with federal, state, and local laws.
- Designing work that is motivational and satisfactory to the employee as well as maximizes customer service, quality, and productivity.

ACQUIRING AND PREPARING HUMAN RESOURCES

Customer needs for new products or services influence the number and type of employees businesses need to be successful. Terminations, promotions, and retirements also influence human resource requirements. Managers need to predict the number and type of employees who are needed to meet customer demands for products and services. Managers must also identify current or potential employees who can successfully deliver products and services. This area of human resource management deals with

- Identifying human resource requirements—that is, human resource planning, recruiting employees, selecting employees.
- Training employees to have the skills needed to perform their jobs.

ASSESSMENT AND DEVELOPMENT OF HUMAN RESOURCES

Managers need to ensure that employees have the necessary skills to perform current and future jobs. As we discussed earlier, because of new technology and the quality movement, many companies are redesigning work so that it is performed by teams. As a result, managers and employees may need to develop new skills to be successful in a team environment. Companies need to create a work environment that supports employees' work and nonwork activities. This area of human resource management deals with

- Measuring employees' performance.
- Preparing employees for future work roles and identifying employees' work interests, goals, values, and other career issues.
- Creating an employment relationship and work environment that benefits both the company and the employee.

COMPENSATING HUMAN RESOURCES

Besides interesting work, pay and benefits are the most important incentives that companies can offer employees in exchange for contributing to productivity, quality, and customer service. Also, pay and benefits are used to reward employees' membership in the company and attract new employees. The positive influence of new work designs, new technology, and the quality movement on productivity can be damaged if employees are not satisfied with the level of pay and benefits or believe pay and benefits are unfairly distributed. This area of human resource management deals with

- Creating pay systems.
- Rewarding employee contributions.
- Providing employees with benefits.

SPECIAL ISSUES

In some companies, employees are represented by a labor union. Managing human resources in a union environment requires knowledge of specific laws, contract administration, and the collective bargaining process.

Many companies are globally expanding their business through joint ventures, merger, and acquisitions, and by establishing new operations. Successful global expansion depends on the extent to which HRM practices are aligned with cultural factors as well as management of employees sent to work in another country. Human resource management practices must contribute to organizational effectiveness.

Human resource management practices of both managers and the human resource function must be aligned and contribute to the company's strategic goals. The final chapter of the book deals with how to effectively integrate human resources practices.

Organization of This Book

The topics in this book are organized according to the four areas of human resource management and special issues. Table 1.11 lists the chapters covered in the book.

The content of each chapter is based on academic research and examples of effective company practices. Each chapter includes examples of how the human resource management practice covered in the chapter helps a company gain a competitive advantage by addressing global, stakeholder, or high-performance work system challenges.

TABLE 1.11
Topics Covered in This Book

I The Human Resource Environment
- 2 Strategic Human Resource Management
- 3 The Legal Environment: Equal Employment Opportunity and Safety
- 4 The Analysis and Design of Work

II Acquisition and Preparation of Human Resources
- 5 Human Resource Planning and Recruitment
- 6 Selection and Placement
- 7 Training

III Assessment and Development of Human Resources
- 8 Performance Management
- 9 Employee Development
- 10 Employee Separation and Retention

IV Compensating Human Resources
- 11 Pay Structure Decisions
- 12 Recognizing Employee Contributions with Pay
- 13 Employee Benefits

V Special Topics in Human Resource Management
- 14 Collective Bargaining and Labor Relations
- 15 Managing Human Resources Globally
- 16 Strategically Managing the HR Function

DISCUSSION QUESTIONS

1. Traditionally, human resource management practices were developed and administered by the company's human resource department. Line managers are now playing a major role in developing and implementing HR practices. Why do you think non-HR managers are becoming more involved in developing and implementing HR practices?
2. Staffing, training, compensation, and performance management are important HRM functions. How can each of these functions help companies deal with meeting stakeholders' needs? High-performance work system challenges? Global challenges?
3. This book covers four human resource management practice areas: managing the human resource environment, acquiring and preparing human resources, assessment and development of human resources, and compensating human resources. Which area do you believe contributes most to helping a company gain a competitive advantage? Which area do you believe contributes the least? Why?
4. What is the balanced scorecard? Identify the four perspectives included in the balanced scorecard. How can HRM practices influence the four perspectives?
5. Is HRM becoming more strategic? Explain your answer.
6. Explain the implications of each of the following labor force trends for HRM: (1) aging work force, (2) diverse work force, (3) skill deficiencies.
7. What role do HRM practices play in a business decision to expand internationally?
8. Is business emphasis on quality a fad? Why or why not? What might a quality goal and high-performance work systems have in common in terms of HRM practices?
9. What disadvantages might result from outsourcing HRM practices? From employee self-service? From increased manager involvement in designing and using HR practices?

WEB EXERCISE

In this chapter we discuss three competitive challenges that companies face (global, managing stakeholders, and high-performance work systems). Go to the Society for Human Resource Management (SHRM) home page on the Web. The SHRM is an important professional society for human resource management. The address is www.shrm.org. Here you will find current articles related to HR issues. SHRM also publishes *HR Magazine*, a business magazine for human resources. Articles regarding a variety of HR topics are available online at www.workforceonline.com.

QUESTIONS

1. How are companies dealing with the competitive challenges? Use web resources to find an article that relates to how a company is dealing with the competitive challenges. Either click on "HR News On-line" on the SHRM home page or go to www.workforceonline.com.
2. Summarize the main topic of the article.
3. Identify how it relates to one of the competitive challenges discussed in the chapter.

MANAGING PEOPLE: FROM THE PAGES OF "BUSINESS WEEK"

BusinessWeek Daimler Has to Steer the Chrysler Merger

When Chrysler Corp. and Daimler Benz announced their megamerger—the largest international corporate marriage in history—it looked to be further evidence that globalization cannot be stopped. But unlike fluid flows of money and technology across borders, the links between companies of different nationalities can be quite brittle. Remember how Renault was unable to hang on to American Motors or how Matsushita had to disgorge Universal Studios? Unless tough decisions are quickly made to overcome deeply ingrained differences of strategy and culture, global combinations can easily fall apart. Indeed, the survival of Daimler Chrysler is already at risk.

The new company will face massive challenges. Daimler Chrysler will still be only the fifth-largest car company, behind General Motors, Ford, Toyota, and Volkswagen. Its product line, ranging from an $11,000 Dodge to a $130,000 Mercedes, could foster a confused image and culture. The German corporate governance system in which labor and banks hold board seats in order to take a longer-term view could collide with the obsession of American shareholders with immediate returns. Compensation philosophies could be irreconcilable: Just compare Chrysler Chairman and CEO Robert J. Eaton's 1997 pay package of $16 million with that of Daimler chief Jurgen E. Schrempp's $1.9 million. And politically explosive decisions are sure to arise about how to apportion layoffs between America and Germany when downsizing occurs because of the overcapacity in the global auto industry.

To make this deal work, Daimler—which has been subtly identified by both parties as the controlling partner despite all the talk about this being "a merger of equals"—needs to take complete charge, quickly and decisively. But in public statements, both Eaton and Schrempp have gone to great lengths to underline the "evolutionary" process of integrating the two companies. This slow-fuse approach—joint CEOs for a few years; headquarters in both Stuttgart and Detroit; separate operations for engineering, manufacturing, and marketing—could unleash powerful centrifugal forces among competing departments.

In fact, Daimler ought to study another set of deals involving a high-profile takeover by an admired foreign company of prized American assets: Sony Corp.'s acquisition of both CBS Records Inc. and Columbia Pictures in the late 1980s. Sony started off mistakenly thinking that it could oversee its freewheeling American companies from afar and with a light touch. It failed to put its own strong management structure in the U.S. It neglected to build links between Sony's American subsidiaries on the two coasts. It lost control of expenses, and by 1994, Sony was forced to take a $2.7 billion write-off.

But lessons were learned. The following year a new president, Nobuyuki Idei, put the Sony stamp on its U.S. operations. He replaced top management in America with highly professional U.S. executives, such as Howard Stringer, former president of CBS Broadcast Group, who supported Sony's tradition of teamwork and its goals of integrating its operations in the U.S. and around the world. Top Japanese executives were placed in New York and Los Angeles. Idei came to the U.S. once a month to oversee the business and to network with such American counterparts as Bill Gates and Andy Grove.

Sony went from a loss of $1.8 billion in 1995 to a pretax profit of $3.4 billion in 1997, helped in part by its enormous success with computer video games. A leader in the U.S.-based digital revolution, Sony has even marshaled the resources of its music subsidiary in New York, its movie business in Los Angeles, and its electronics expertise in Tokyo to produce European movies in local languages out of Germany.

Sony and Daimler are in different businesses, of course, and no one blueprint applies to all big international mergers. But the most successful global companies, such as Nestle, ABB Asea Brown Boveri, and General Electric, have put their unambiguous imprint on all their operations by imposing one strong corporate culture with central management for the most critical functions. Someone must articulate overall philosophy and values and establish companywide investment priorities. Someone must set financial and operational performance requirements, compensation policies, and development paths for senior executives. Unless Daimler takes charge of these kinds of tasks immediately, don't be surprised if the deal comes unwound. Announcing a big global merger is nothing compared to making it succeed.

QUESTIONS

1. One way to expand business globally is to merge with another company to create a powerful international corporation. The challenge of mergers is to unite two different companies with distinct business processes, strategies, and cultures. Mergers are even more challenging when they involve companies from different countries (such as the Chrysler–Daimler Benz merger). Executives need to review operational, financial, and people processes to develop a common set of rules, practices, and procedures for the "new" company. What HRM issues do Chrysler Corporation and Daimler Benz have to resolve to make the merger successful?
2. How might Chrysler and Daimler Benz decide which HRM practices to adopt companywide (globally)?

SOURCE: Jeffrey E. Garten, "Daimler Has to Steer the Chrysler Merger," *Business Week*, July 20, 1998.

NOTES

1. A.S. Tsui and L.R. Gomez-Mejia, "Evaluating Human Resource Effectiveness," in *Human Resource Management: Evolving Rules and Responsibilities*, ed. L. Dyer (Washington, DC: BNA Books, 1988), pp. 1187–227; M.A. Hitt, B.W. Keats, and S.M. DeMarie, "Navigating in the New Competitive Landscape: Building Strategic Flexibility and Competitive Advantage in the 21st Century," *Academy of Management Executive* 12, no. 4 (1998), pp. 22–42; J.T. Delaney and M.A. Huselid, "The Impact of Human Resource Management Practices on Perceptions of Organizational Performance," *Academy of Management Journal* 39 (1996), pp. 949–69.
2. SHRM-BNA Survey No. 60, "Human Resources Activities, Budgets, and Staffs: 1994–95." Bulletin to Management, Bureau of National Affairs Policy and Practice Series, June 29, 1995 (Washington, DC: Bureau of National Affairs).
3. A. Halcrow, "Survey Shows HR in Transition," *Workforce* (June 1988), pp. 73–80; J. Laabs, "Why HR Can't Win Today," *Workforce* (May 1998), pp. 62–74.
4. S. Greengard, "Building a Self-Service Culture That Works," *Workforce* (July 1998), pp. 60–64.
5. Towers Perrin, *Priorities for Competitive Advantage: An IBM Study Conducted by Towers Perrin*, 1992.
6. B.P. Sunoo, "A Day in the Life of John Harvey: Positioning HR for the Fast Track," *Workforce* (June 1988), pp. 64, 66, 68.
7. D. Ulrich, "A New Mandate for Human Resources," *Harvard Business Review* (January–February 1998), pp. 124–34.

8. Perrin, *Priorities*, p. 6.
9. J. Kahn, "The World's Most Admired Companies," *Fortune* (October 26, 1998), pp. 206–26; A. Fisher, "The World's Most Admired Companies," *Fortune* (October 27, 1997), p. 232.
10. C. Fleming and L. Lopez, "No Boundaries," *The Wall Street Journal* (September 9, 1998), p. R16.
11. C. Hill, *International Business* (Burr Ridge, IL: Irwin/McGraw-Hill, 1997).
12. "War of the Worlds," *The Economist* (October 1, 1994), pp. 3–4.
13. D. Aalund, "What's the Euro?" *The Wall Street Journal* (September 28, 1998), p. R6.
14. J. Perlez, "GE Finds Tough Going in Hungary," *The New York Times* (July 25, 1994), pp. C1, C3.
15. K. Roberts, E.E. Kossek, and C. Ozeki, "Managing the Global Workforce: Challenges and Strategies," *Academy of Management Executive* 12 (1988), no. 4, pp. 93–106.
16. R.L. Tung, "Expatriate Assignments: Enhancing Success and Minimizing Failure," *Academy of Management Executive* 1 (1987), pp. 117–26.
17. G.P. Zachary, "Stalled U.S. Workers' Objections Grow as More of Their Jobs Shift Overseas," *The Wall Street Journal*, October 9, 1995, pp. A2, A9.
18. R.S. Kaplan and D.P. Norton, "The Balanced Scorecard—Measures That Drive Performance," *Harvard Business Review* (January–February 1992), pp. 71–79; R.S. Kaplan and D.P. Norton, "Putting the Balanced Scorecard to Work," *Harvard Business Review* (September–October 1993), pp. 134–47.
19. M. Gendron, "Using the Balanced Scorecard," *Harvard Business Review* (October 1997), pp. 3–5.
20. D. Ulrich, "Measuring Human Resources: An Overview of Practice and a Prescription for Results," *Human Resource Management* 36 (1997), pp. 303–20.
21. Kaplan and Norton, "Putting the Balanced Scorecard to Work."
22. J.R. Jablonski, *Implementing Total Quality Management: An Overview* (San Diego: Pfeiffer & Company, 1991).
23. R.L. Dodson, "Speeding the Way to Total Quality," *Training and Development Journal* 45, no. 6 (1991), pp. 35–42.
24. S.L. Jackson, "What You Should Know about ISO 9000," *Training* (May 1992), pp. 48–52; Bureau of Business Practices, *Profile of ISO 9000* (Boston: Allyn & Bacon, 1992); "ISO 9000 International Standards for Quality Assurance," *Design Matters* (July 1995): http//www.best.com/~ISO9000/att/ISONet.html/.
25. U.S. Dept. of Commerce, *1997 Application Guidelines: Malcolm Baldrige National Quality Award* (Gaithersburg, MD: National Institute of Science and Technology, 1997).
26. K.F. Fisher and J.F. Spillane, "Quality and Competitiveness," *Training and Development Journal* 45 (1991), pp. 19–22, 24.
27. J.J. Laabs, "Quality Drives Trident's Success," *Workforce* (February 1998), pp. 44–49.
28. J. Main, "Is the Baldrige Overblown?" *Fortune*, July 1, 1991, pp. 62–64.
29. Conference Board, *People Practices in Baldrige Companies* (Report 1093-94-RR) (New York: The Conference Board, 1994), pp. 38–40.
30. General Accounting Office, *Management Practices: U.S. Companies Improve Performance through Quality Efforts* (GAO/NSIAD–91–190)(Washington, DC: U.S. General Accounting Office, 1991).
31. B. Copple and L. Lee, "Labor Squeeze Forces Corporate America Back to High School," *The Wall Street Journal* (July 22, 1998), pp. A1, A9.
32. Ibid.
33. H.N. Fullerton, "Labor Force 2006: Slowing Down and Changing Composition," *Monthly Labor Review* (November 1997), pp. 23–28. Also see the Bureau of Labor Statistics employment projections on the Web at www.bls.gov/news.release/ecopro.nws.htm.
34. M. Cohen, *Labor Shortages as America Approaches the Twenty-first Century* (Ann Arbor: University of Michigan Press, 1995); "Human Resources and Their Skills," in *The Changing Nature of Work*, ed. A. Howard (San Francisco: Jossey-Bass, 1995), pp. 211–22; H. Fullerton, "Another Look at the Labor Force," *Monthly Labor Review* (November 1993), pp. 31–40.
35. M. Mandel, "It's Really Two Immigrant Economies," *Business Week*, June 20, 1994, pp. 74–78.
36. G.T. Silvestri, "Occupational Employment Projections to 2006," *Monthly Labor Review* (November 1997), pp. 58–83.
37. B. Schneider and D.E. Bowen, "The Service Organization: Human Resource Management Is Crucial," *Organizational Dynamics* (Spring 1993), pp. 39–52; B. Schneider, S.K. Gunnabon, and K. Niles-Jolly, "Creating the Culture and Climate of Success," *Organizational Dynamics* (Summer 1994), pp. 17–29.
38. U.S. Department of Labor, "BLS Releases New 1996–2006 Employment Projections."
39. A. Saveri, "The Realignment of Workers and Work in the 1990s," in *New Directions in Career Planning and the Workplace*, ed. J. M. Kummerow (Palo Alto, CA: Consulting Psychologists Press, 1991), pp. 117–53.
40. A.P. Carnevale, L.J. Gainer, and A.S. Meltzer, *Workplace Basics: The Essential Skills Employers Want* (San Francisco: Jossey-Bass, 1990).
41. W.B. Johnston, *Workforce 2000* (Indianapolis: Hudson Institute, 1987); U.S. Dept. of Labor, *Opportunity 2000* (Washington, DC: U.S. Government Printing Office, 1987).
42. The Condition of Education 1996, "International Comparisons of Adult Literacy." From web site http:nces.ed.gov/pubsold/ce96/c9621a01.html.
43. I.S. Kirsch and A. Junglebutt, *Literacy: Profiles of Amer-*

ica's National Assessment of Educational Process (Princeton, NJ: Educational Testing Service, 1991).
44. J.H. Bishop, "Employment Testing and Incentives to Learn," *Journal of Vocational Behavior* 33 (1988), pp. 404–23.
45. E.E. Gordon, J. Ponitcell, and R.R. Morgan, "Back to Basics," *Training and Development Journal* (August 1989), pp. 73–76.
46. National Association of Manufacturers, Center for Workforce Success, and Grant Thornton LLP, "The Skills Gap" (Washington, DC: National Association of Manufacturing Publications Center, 1998).
47. S. Mehta, "Companies Plan More Hires but Worry That Qualified Labor Pool Is Shrinking," *The Wall Street Journal*, August 2, 1995, p. B3.
48. Carnevale, Gainer, and Meltzer, *Workplace Basics*.
49. The Workforce Investment Act of 1998, "Preliminary Analysis of the Act," August 5, 1998. Available at web address www.naepdc.org/issues/archive8-5.htm.
50. "Work Week," *The Wall Street Journal*, October 3, 1995, p. A1.
51. J. Alley, "The Temp Biz Boom: Why It Is Good," *Fortune*, October 16, 1995, pp. 53, 55; Jarratt and Coates, "Employee Development and Job Creation."
52. P. Brotherton, "Stuff to Suit," *HR Magazine* (December 1995), pp. 50–55.
53. Ibid.
54. Bureau of Labor Statistics, "Work at Home in 1997," Internet address www.bls.gov/news.release/homey.nws.htm.
55. C.M. Solomon, "Managing the Baby Busters," *Personnel Journal* (March 1992), pp. 52–59.
56. B. Wooldridge and J. Wester, "The Turbulent Environment of Public Personnel Administration: Responding to the Challenge of the Changing Workplace of the Twenty-first Century," *Public Personnel Management* 20 (1991), pp. 207–24; J. Laabs, "The New Loyalty: Grasp It. Earn It. Keep It," *Workforce* (November 1998), pp. 34–39.
57. "Employee Dissatisfaction on Rise in Last 10 Years, New Report Says," *Employee Relations Weekly* (Washington, DC: Bureau of National Affairs, 1986).
58. D.T. Hall and J. Richter, "Career Gridlock: Baby Boomers Hit the Wall," *The Executive* 4 (1990), pp. 7–22.
59. T.H. Cox and S. Blake, "Managing Cultural Diversity: Implications for Organizational Competitiveness," *The Executive* 5 (1991), pp. 45–56.
60. M. Loden and J.B. Rosener, *Workforce America!* (Homewood, IL: Business One Irwin, 1991).
61. D. Anfuso, "Awareness Efforts Put Diversity in the News," *Personnel Journal* (January 1995), p. 76.
62. J. Ledvinka and V.G. Scarpello, *Federal Regulation of Personnel and Human Resource Management*, 2d ed. (Boston: PWS-Kent, 1991).
63. C.M. Solomon, "Affirmative Action: What You Need to Know," *Personnel Journal* 74 (1995), pp. 56–67; F. Bloch, "Affirmative Action Hasn't Helped Blacks," *The Wall Street Journal*, March 1, 1995.
64. M.A. Jacobs, "Courts Wrestle with Religion in Workplace," *The Wall Street Journal*, October 10, 1995, p. B1.
65. M. Pastin, *The Hard Problems of Management: Gaining the Ethics Edge* (San Francisco: Jossey-Bass, 1986).
66. R. Ricklees, "Ethics in America," *The Wall Street Journal*, October 31–November 3, 1983, p. 33.
67. C. Lee, "Ethics Training: Facing the Tough Questions," *Training*, March 31, 1986, pp. 33, 38–41.
68. Pastin, *Hard Problems of Management*.
69. G. Flynn, "Texas Instruments Engineers a Holistic HR."
70. G.F. Cavanaugh, D. Moberg, and M. Velasquez, "The Ethics of Organizational Politics," *Academy of Management Review* 6 (1981), pp. 363–74.
71. J.A. Neal and C.L. Tromley, "From Incremental Change to Retrofit: Creating High Performance Work Systems," *Academy of Management Executive* 9 (1995), pp. 42–54.
72. P. Choate and P. Linger, *The High-Flex Society* (New York: Knopf, 1986); P.B. Doeringer, *Turbulence in the American Workplace* (New York: Oxford University Press, 1991).
73. K. Miller, *Retraining the American Work Force* (Reading, MA: Addison-Wesley, 1989).
74. M. Williams, "Some Plants Tear Out Long Assembly Lines, Switch to Craft Work," *The Wall Street Journal*, October 24, 1994, pp. A1, A4.
75. T.J. Atchison, "The Employment Relationship: Untied or Re-tied," *Academy of Management Executive* 5 (1991), pp. 52–62.
76. D. McCann and C. Margerison, "Managing High Performance Teams," *Training and Development Journal* (November 1989), pp. 52–60; S. Sheman, "Secrets of HP's 'Muddled' Team," *Fortune*, March 18, 1996, pp. 116–20.
77. T. Peters, "Restoring American Competitiveness: Looking for New Models of Organizations," *The Executive* 2 (1988), pp. 103–10.
78. M.J. Kavanaugh, H.G. Guetal, and S.I. Tannenbaum, *Human Resource Information Systems: Development and Application* (Boston: PWS-Kent, 1990).
79. S. Greengard, "When HRMS Goes Global: Managing the Data Highway," *Personnel Journal* (June 1995), pp. 91–106.
80. R.N. Ashkenas, "Beyond the Fads: How Leaders Drive Change with Results," *Human Resource Planning* 17 (1994), pp. 25–44.
81. M.A. Huselid, "The Impact of Human Resource Management Practices on Turnover, Productivity, and Corporate Financial Performance," *Academy of Management Journal* 38 (1995), pp. 635–72; U.S. Dept. of Labor, *High Performance Work Practices and Firm Performance* (Washington, DC: U.S. Government Printing Office, 1993).
82. B. Becker and M.A. Huselid, "High Performance Work

Systems and Firm Performance: A Synthesis of Research and Managerial Implications," in *Research in Personnel and Human Resource Management* 16, ed. G.R. Ferris (Stamford, CT: JAI Press, 1998), pp. 53–101.
83. B. Becker and B. Gerhart, "The Impact of Human Resource Management on Organizational Performance: Progress and Prospects," *Academy of Management Journal* 39 (1996), pp. 779–801.
84. F. Bleakley, "How an Outdated Plant Was Made New," *The Wall Street Journal*, November 10, 1994, pp. B1, B11.
85. W.F. Cascio, *Costing Human Resources: The Financial Impact of Behavior in Organizations*, 3d ed. (Boston: PWS-Kent, 1991).
86. S.A. Snell and J.W. Dean, "Integrated Manufacturing and Human Resource Management: A Human Capital Perspective," *Academy of Management Journal* 35 (1992), pp. 467–504; M.A. Youndt, S. Snell, J.W. Dean Jr., and D.P. Lepak, "Human Resource Management, Manufacturing Strategy, and Firm Performance," *Academy of Management Journal* 39 (1996), pp. 836–66; Delaney and Huselid, "The Impact of Human Resource Practices."

PART I
The Human Resource Environment

Strategic Human Resource Management

OBJECTIVES

After reading this chapter, you should be able to:

1. Describe the differences between strategy formulation and strategy implementation.
2. List the components of the strategic management process.
3. Discuss the role of the HR function in strategy formulation.
4. Describe the linkages between HR and strategy formulation.
5. Discuss the more popular typologies of generic strategies and the various HR practices associated with each.
6. Describe the different HR issues and practices associated with various directional strategies.
7. List the competencies the HR executive needs to become a strategic partner in the company.

Strategy and HR at Delta Air Lines

ENTER THE WORLD OF BUSINESS

In 1994, top executives at Delta Air Lines faced a crucial strategic decision. Delta, which had established an unrivaled reputation within the industry for having highly committed employees who delivered the highest quality customer service, had lost over $10 per share for two straight years. A large portion of its financial trouble was due to the $491 million acquisition of Pan Am in 1991, which was followed by the Gulf war (driving up fuel costs) and the early 90s recession (causing people to fly less). Its cost per available seat mile (what it costs to fly one passenger one mile) was 9.26 cents, among the highest in the industry. In addition, it was threatened by new discount competitors with significantly lower costs—in particular, Valujet, which flew out of Delta's Atlanta hub. How could Delta survive and thrive in such an environment? Determining the strategy for doing so was the top executives' challenge.

Chairman and Chief Executive Officer Ron Allen embarked upon the "Leadership 7.5" strategy, whose goal was to reduce the cost per available seat mile to 7.5 cents, comparable with Southwest Airlines. To implement this strategy required a significant downsizing over the following three years, trimming 11,458 people from its 69,555-employee work force (the latter number representing an 8 percent reduction from two years earlier). Many experienced customer service representatives were laid off and replaced with lower-paid, inexperienced, part-time workers. Cleaning service of planes as well as baggage handling were outsourced, resulting in layoffs of long-term Delta employees. The numbers of maintenance workers and flight attendants were reduced substantially.

The results of the strategy were mixed as financial performance improved but operational performance plummeted. Since it began its cost cutting, its stock price more than doubled in just over two years and its debt was upgraded. On the other hand, customer complaints about dirty airplanes rose from 219 in 1993 to 358 in 1994 and 634 in 1995. On-time performance was so bad that passengers joked that Delta stands for "Doesn't Ever Leave The Airport." Delta slipped from fourth to seventh among the top 10 carriers in baggage handling. Employee morale hit an all-time low, and unions were beginning to make headway toward organizing some of Delta's employee groups. In 1996, CEO Allen was quoted as saying, "This has tested our people. There have been some morale problems. But so be it. You go back to the question of survival, and it makes the decision very easy."

Shortly after, employees began donning cynical "SO BE IT" buttons. Delta's board saw union organizers stirring blue-collar discontent, employee morale destroyed, the customer service reputation in near shambles, and senior managers exiting the company in droves. Less than one year later, Allen was fired despite Delta's financial turnaround. His firing was "not because the company was going broke, but because its spirit was broken."

SOURCE: M. Brannigan and E. De Lisser, "Cost Cutting at Delta Raises the Stock Price but Lowers the Service," *The Wall Street Journal*, June 20, 1996, pp. A1, A8; M. Brannigan and J. White, "So Be It: Why Delta Air Lines Decided It Was Time for CEO to Take Off," *The Wall Street Journal*, May 30, 1997, p. A1.

Introduction

As the Delta example just illustrated, business organizations exist in an environment of competition. They have a number of resources at their disposal that they can use to compete with other companies. These resources are physical (e.g., plant, equipment, technology, and geographic location), organizational (e.g., the structure, planning, controlling, and coordinating systems, and group relations), and human (e.g., the experience, skill, and intelligence of employees). It is these resources under the control of the company that provide it with competitive advantage.[1]

The goal of strategic management in an organization is to deploy and allocate resources in a way that provides it with a competitive advantage. As you can see, two of the three classes of resources (organizational and human) are directly tied to the human resource function. As Chapter 1 pointed out, the role of human resource management is to ensure that a company's human resources provide it with a competitive advantage. Chapter 1 also pointed out some of the major competitive challenges that companies face today. These challenges require companies to take a proactive, strategic approach in the marketplace.

To be maximally effective, the HRM function must be integrally involved in the company's strategic management process.[2] This means that human resource managers should (1) have input into the strategic plan, both in terms of people-related issues and in terms of the ability of the human resource pool to implement particular strategic alternatives, (2) have specific knowledge of the organization's strategic goals, (3) know what types of employee skills, behaviors, and attitudes are needed to support the strategic plan, and (4) develop programs to ensure that employees have those skills, behaviors, and attitudes.

We begin this chapter by discussing the concept of strategy and by depicting the strategic management process. Then we discuss the levels of integration between the HRM function and the strategic management process in strategy formulation. Next we review some of the more common strategic models and, within the context of these models, discuss the various types of employee skills, behaviors, and attitudes, and the ways human resource practices aid in implementing the strategic plan. Finally, we discuss the new competencies needed by HR executives to fulfill the strategic role of HR.

What Is Strategic Management?

Many authors have noted that, in today's competitive market, organizations must engage in strategic planning to survive and prosper. *Strategy* comes from the Greek word *strategos*, which has its roots in military language. It refers to a general's grand design behind a war or battle. In fact, *Webster's New American Dictionary* defines *strategy* as the "skillful employment and coordination of tactics" and as "artful planning and management."

Strategic management is a process, an approach to addressing the competitive challenges an organization faces. It can be thought of as managing the "pattern or plan that integrates an organization's major goals, policies, and action sequences into a cohesive whole."[3] These strategies can be either the generic approach to competing or the specific adjustments and actions taken to deal with a particular situation.

First, business organizations engage in generic strategies that often fit into some strategic type. One example is "cost, differentiation, or focus."[4] Another is "defender, analyzer, prospector, or reactor."[5] Different organizations within the same industry often have different generic strategies. These generic strategy types describe the consistent way the company attempts to position itself relative to competitors.

However, a generic strategy is only a small part of the strategic management process.

Thus, the second aspect of strategic management is the process of developing strategies for achieving the company's goals in light of its current environment. Thus, business organizations engage in generic strategies, but they also make choices about such things as how to scare off competitors, how to keep competitors weaker, how to react to and influence pending legislation, how to deal with various stakeholders and special-interest groups, how to lower production costs, how to raise revenues, what technology to implement, and how many and what types of people to employ. Each of these decisions may present competitive challenges that have to be considered.

Thus, strategic management is more than a collection of strategic types. It is a process for analyzing a company's competitive situation, developing the company's strategic goals, and devising a plan of action and allocation of resources (human, organizational, and physical) that will increase the likelihood of achieving those goals. This kind of strategic approach should be emphasized in human resource management. Thus, HR managers should be trained to identify the competitive issues the company faces with regard to human resources and think strategically about how to respond.

Strategic human resource management (SHRM) can be thought of as "the pattern of planned human resource deployments and activities intended to enable an organization to achieve its goals."[6] For example, many firms have developed integrated manufacturing systems such as advanced manufacturing technology, just-in-time inventory control, and total quality management in an effort to increase their competitive position. However, these systems must be run by people. SHRM in these cases entails assessing the employee skills required to run these systems and engaging in HR practices, such as selection and training, that develop these skills in employees.[7] To take a strategic approach to HRM, we must first have an understanding of the role of HRM in the strategic management process.

COMPONENTS OF THE STRATEGIC MANAGEMENT PROCESS

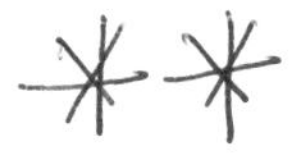

The strategic management process has two distinct yet interdependent phases: strategy formulation and strategy implementation. During **strategy formulation** the strategic planning groups decide on a strategic direction by defining the company's mission and goals, its external opportunities and threats, and its internal strengths and weaknesses. They then generate various strategic alternatives and compare those alternatives' ability to achieve the company's mission and goals. During **strategy implementation,** the organization follows through on the strategy that has been chosen. This consists of structuring the organization, allocating resources, ensuring that the firm has skilled employees in place, and developing reward systems that align employee behavior with the organization's strategic goals. Both of these strategic management phases must be performed effectively. It is important to note that this process does not happen sequentially. As we will discuss later with regard to emergent strategies, this process entails a constant cycling of information and decision making. Figure 2.1 presents the strategic management process.

In recent years organizations have recognized that the success of the strategic management process depends largely on the extent to which the HR function is involved.[8]

LINKAGE BETWEEN HR AND THE STRATEGIC MANAGEMENT PROCESS

The strategic choice really consists of answering questions about competition—i.e., how the firm will compete to achieve its missions and goals. These decisions consist of addressing the issues of where to compete, how to compete, and with what to compete, which are described in the accompanying display. While these decisions are all impor-

FIGURE 2.1
A Model of the Strategic Management Process

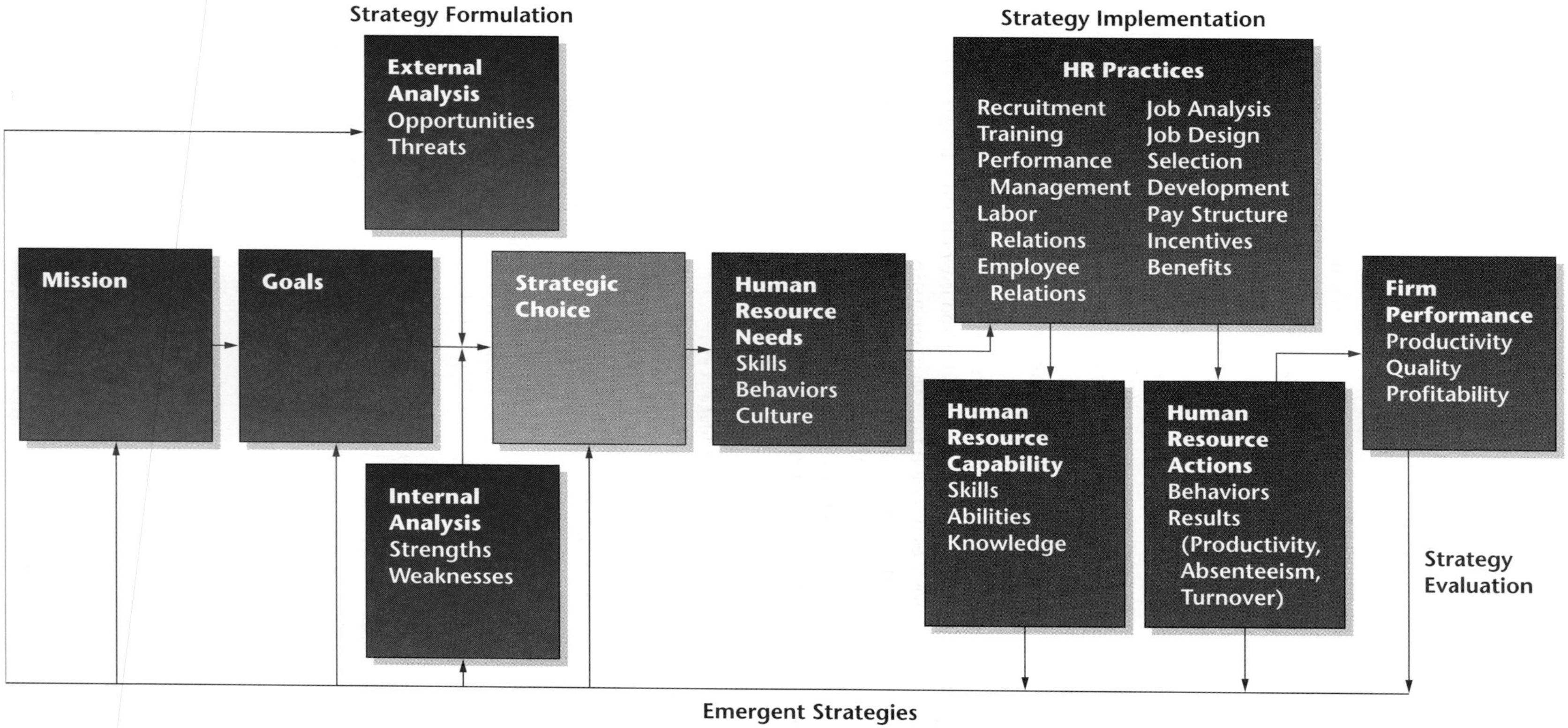

Strategy Formulation

External Analysis
Opportunities
Threats

Mission

Goals

Strategic Choice

Internal Analysis
Strengths
Weaknesses

Human Resource Needs
Skills
Behaviors
Culture

Strategy Implementation

HR Practices
Recruitment
Training
Performance Management
Labor Relations
Employee Relations
Job Analysis
Job Design
Selection
Development
Pay Structure
Incentives
Benefits

Human Resource Capability
Skills
Abilities
Knowledge

Human Resource Actions
Behaviors
Results (Productivity, Absenteeism, Turnover)

Firm Performance
Productivity
Quality
Profitability

Strategy Evaluation

Emergent Strategies

1. Where to compete?
   In what market or markets (industries, products, etc.) will we compete?
2. How to compete?
   On what criterion or differentiating characteristic(s) will we compete? Cost? Quality? Reliability? Delivery?
3. With what will we compete?
   What resources will allow us to beat our competition?
   How will we acquire, develop, and deploy those resources to compete?

FIGURE 2A
Strategy—Decisions about Competition

tant, strategic decision makers often pay less attention to the "with what will we compete" issue, resulting in poor strategic decisions. For example, PepsiCo in the 1980s acquired the fast food chains of Kentucky Fried Chicken, Taco Bell, and Pizza Hut ("where to compete" decisions) in an effort to increase its customer base. However, it failed to adequately recognize the differences between its existing work force (mostly professionals) and that of the fast food industry (lower-skilled people and high schoolers) as well as its ability to manage such a work force. This was one reason that PepsiCo, in 1998, spun off the fast food chains. In essence, it had made a decision about where to compete without fully understanding what resources it would take to compete in that market.

Boeing illustrates how failing to address the "with what" issue resulted in problems in its "how to compete" decisions. The aerospace firm's consumer products division recently got into a price war with Airbus Industrie, forcing it to move away from its traditional customer service strategy toward emphasizing cost reduction.[9] The strategy was a success on the sales end as Boeing received large numbers of orders for aircraft from firms such as Delta, Continental, Southwest, and Singapore Airline. However, it had recently gone through a large work force reduction (thus, it didn't have enough people to fill the orders) and did not have the production technology to enable the necessary increase in productivity. The result of this failure to address "with what will we compete" in making a decision about how to compete resulted in the firm's inability to meet delivery deadlines and the ensuing penalties it had to pay to its customers.

ROLE OF HR IN STRATEGY FORMULATION

As the preceding examples illustrate, often the "with what will we compete" questions present ideal avenues for HR to influence the strategic management process. This might be either through limiting strategic options or through forcing thoughtfulness among the executive team regarding how and at what cost the firm might gain or develop the human resources (people) necessary for such a strategy to be successful. For example, HR executives at PepsiCo could have noted that the firm had no expertise in managing the work force of fast food restaurants. The limiting role would have been for these executives to argue against the acquisition because of this lack of resources. On the other hand, they might have influenced the decision by educating top executives as to the costs (of hiring, training, etc.) associated with gaining people who had the right skills to manage such a work force.

A firm's strategic management decision making process usually takes place at its top levels, with a strategic planning group consisting of the chief executive officer, the chief financial officer, the president, and various vice presidents. However, each component of the process involves people-related business issues. Therefore, the HR function needs to be involved in each of those components. One recent study of 115 strategic business

FIGURE 2.2
Linkages of Strategic Planning and HRM

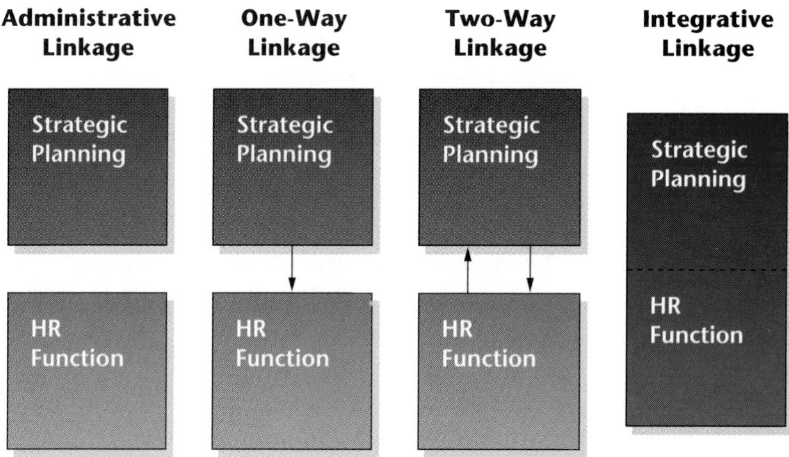

SOURCE: Adapted form K. Golden and V. Ramanujam, "Between a Dream and a Nightmare: On the Integration of the Human Resource Function and the Strategic Business Planning Process," *Human Resource Management* 24 (1985), pp. 429–51.

units within Fortune 500 corporations found that between 49 and 69 percent of the companies had some link between HRM and the strategic planning process.[10] However, the level of linkage varied, and it is important to understand these different levels.

Four levels of integration seem to exist between the HR function and the strategic management function: administrative linkage, one-way linkage, two-way linkage, and integrative linkage.[11] These levels of linkage will be discussed in relation to the different components of strategic management. The linkages are illustrated in Figure 2.2.

ADMINISTRATIVE LINKAGE. In administrative linkage (the lowest level of integration), the HR function's attention is focused on day-to-day activities. The HR executive has no time or opportunity to take a strategic outlook toward HR issues. The company's strategic business planning function exists without any input from the HR department. Thus, in this level of integration, the HR department is completely divorced from any component of the strategic management process in both strategy formulation and strategy implementation. The department simply engages in administrative work unrelated to the company's core business needs.

ONE-WAY LINKAGE. In one-way linkage, the firm's strategic business planning function develops the strategic plan and then informs the HR function of the plan. Many believe this level of integration constitutes strategic HRM—that is, the role of the HR function is to design systems and/or programs that implement the strategic plan. Although one-way linkage does recognize the importance of human resources in implementing the strategic plan, it precludes the company from considering human resource issues while formulating the strategic plan. This level of integration often leads to strategic plans that the company cannot successfully implement.

TWO-WAY LINKAGE. Two-way linkage does allow for consideration of human resource issues during the strategy formulation process. This integration occurs in three sequential steps. First, the strategic planning team informs the HR function of the various strategies the company is considering. Then, HR executives analyze the human resource implications of the various strategies, presenting the results of this analysis to the strategic planning team. Finally, after the strategic decision has been made, the strategic plan is passed on to the HR executive, who develops programs to implement it. The strategic planning function and the HR function are interdependent in two-way linkage.

INTEGRATIVE LINKAGE. Integrative linkage is dynamic and multifaceted, based on continuing rather than sequential interaction. In most cases, the HR executive is an integral member of the senior management team. Rather than an iterative process of information exchange, companies with integrative linkage have their HR functions built right into the strategy formulation and implementation processes. It is this role that we will discuss throughout the rest of this chapter.

Thus, in strategic HRM, the HR function is involved in both strategy formulation and strategy implementation. The HR executive provides the strategic planners with information about the company's human resource capabilities, and these capabilities are usually a direct function of the HR practices. This information about human resource capabilities helps top managers choose the best strategy, since they can consider how well each strategic alternative would be implemented. Once the strategic choice has been determined, the role of HR changes to the development and alignment of HR practices that will provide the company with employees having the necessary skills to implement the strategy. In addition, HR practices must be designed to elicit actions from employees in the company. In the next two sections of this chapter, we show how HR can provide a competitive advantage in the strategic management process.

Strategy Formulation

Five major components of the strategic management process are relevant to strategy formulation.[12] These components are depicted in Figure 2.3. The first component is the organization's mission. The mission is a statement of the organization's reason for being; it usually specifies the customers served, the needs satisfied and/or the values received

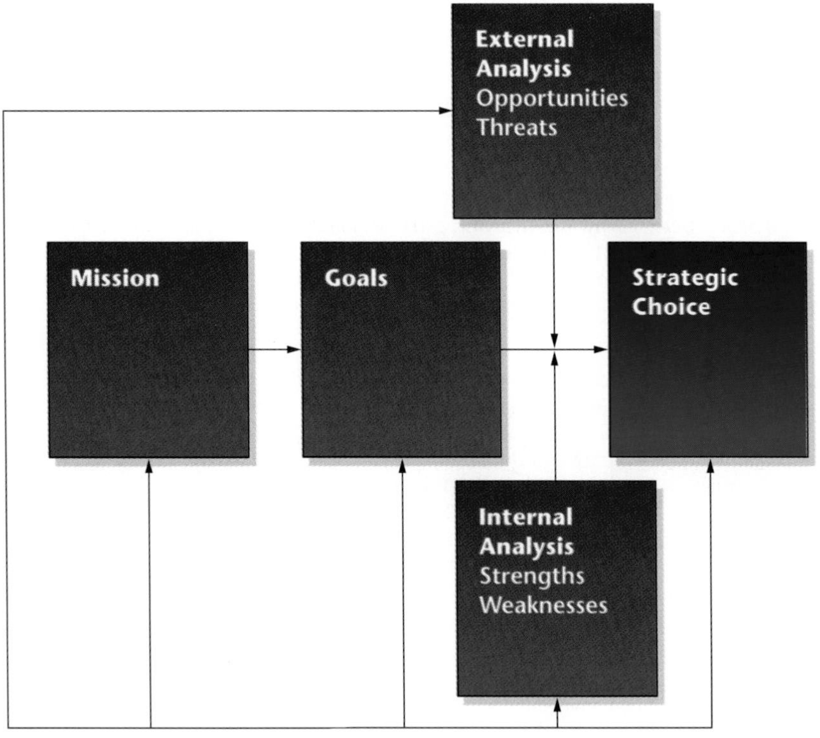

SOURCE: Adapted from K. Golden and V. Ramamijan, "Between a Dream and a Nightmare. *Human Resource Management,* 1985, pp. 429–451. Reprinted with permission.

FIGURE 2.3
Strategy Formulation

by the customers, and the technology used. The mission statement is often accompanied by a statement of a company's vision and/or values. For example, Table 2.1 illustrates the mission, vision, and values of Amoco Corporation.

An organization's **goals** are what it hopes to achieve in the medium- to long-term future; they reflect how the mission will be operationalized. The overarching goal of most profit-making companies in the United States is to maximize stockholder wealth. But companies have to set other long-term goals in order to maximize stockholder wealth. For example, among Digital Equipment Corporation's goals is to be one of the leading personal computer makers.

External analysis consists of examining the organization's operating environment to identify the strategic opportunities and threats. Examples of opportunities are customer markets that are not being served, technological advances that can aid the company, and labor pools that have not been tapped. Threats include potential labor shortages, new competitors entering the market, pending legislation that might adversely affect the company, and competitors' technological innovations.

Internal analysis attempts to identify the organization's strengths and weaknesses. It focuses on the quantity and quality of resources available to the organization—financial, capital, technological, and human resources. Organizations have to honestly and accurately assess each resource to decide whether it is a strength or a weakness.

External analysis and internal analysis combined constitute what has come to be called the SWOT (strengths, weaknesses, opportunities, threats) analysis. After going through the SWOT analysis, the strategic planning team has at its disposal all the information it needs to generate a number of strategic alternatives. The strategic managers compare these alternatives' ability to attain the organization's strategic goals; then they make their **strategic choice.** The strategic choice is the organization's strategy; it describes the ways the organization will attempt to fulfill its mission and achieve its long-term goals.

Many of the opportunities and threats in the external environment are people-

TABLE 2.1
Amoco Corporation's Mission, Vision, and Values

Our Mission

Amoco Corporation is a worldwide integrated petroleum and chemical company. We find and develop petroleum resources and provide quality products and services for our customers. We conduct our business responsibly to achieve a superior financial return, balanced with long-term growth, to benefit shareholders and fulfill our commitment to the community and the environment.

Our Vision

Amoco will be a global business enterprise, recognized throughout the world as preeminent by employees, customers, competitors, investors and the public. We will be the standard by which other businesses measure their performance. Our hallmarks will be the innovation, initiative and teamwork of our people, and our ability to anticipate and effectively respond to change, and to create opportunity.

Our Values

Integrity
People
Technology
Environment, Health and Safety
Business Relationships
Progress

SOURCE: Amoco corporation, 1994 Annual Report.

related. With fewer and fewer highly qualified individuals entering the labor market, organizations are beginning to compete not just for customers but for employees. It is HR's role to keep close tabs on the external environment for human resource—related opportunities and threats, especially those directly related to the HR function: potential labor shortages, competitor wage rates, government regulations affecting employment, and so on. For example, as discussed in Chapter 1, U.S. companies are finding that more and more high school graduates lack the basic skills needed to work, which is one source of the "human capital shortage."[13] However, not recognizing this environmental threat, many companies have encouraged the exit of older, more skilled workers while hiring less skilled younger workers who require basic-skills training.[14]

An analysis of a company's internal strengths and weaknesses also requires input from the HR function. Today, companies are increasingly realizing that their human resources are one of their most important assets. In fact, one estimate is that over one-third of the total growth in U.S. GNP between 1943 and 1990 was the result of increases in human capital. Failure to consider the strengths and weaknesses of the company's work force may result in its choosing strategies it is not capable of pursuing.[15] However, some research has demonstrated that few companies have achieved this level of linkage.[16] For example, one company chose a strategy of cost reduction through technological improvements. It built a plant designed around a computer-integrated manufacturing system with statistical process controls. Though this choice may seem like a good one, the company soon learned otherwise. It discovered that its employees could not operate the new equipment because 25 percent of the work force was functionally illiterate.[17]

Thus, with an integrative linkage, strategic planners consider all the people-related business issues before making a strategic choice. These issues are identified with regard to the mission, goals, opportunities, threats, strengths, and weaknesses, leading the strategic planning team to make a more intelligent strategic choice. While this process does not guarantee success, companies that address these issues are more likely to make a choice that will ultimately succeed. Table 2.2 gives examples of HR's role in strategic planning.

Recent research has supported the need to have HR executives integrally involved in strategy formulation. One study of U.S. petrochemical refineries found that the level of HR involvement was positively related to the refinery manager's evaluation of the effectiveness of the HR function.[18] A second study of manufacturing firms found that HR involvement was highest when top managers viewed employees as a strategic asset and associated with reduced turnover.[19] However, both studies found that HR involvement was unrelated to operating unit financial performance.

DELTA AIR LINES AND HR'S ROLE IN STRATEGY FORMULATION. Returning to the story of Delta's Leadership 7.5 strategy discussed at the opening of this chapter, how might an HR executive have influenced the decision to adopt the strategy? She could have pointed out that Delta had one source of sustainable competitive advantage (one that provided value, was rare, and was impossible or costly for its competitors to imitate):[20] its highly committed work force which delivered the highest level of customer service in the industry.[21] In fact, Delta employees were so committed to the airline, that in the 1980s the employees pitched in and brought the airline a new airplane. Thus, the limiting role would have been to point out the sheer idiocy of throwing away its one source of sustainable competitive advantage.

However, one lesson for all business decision makers is to never say no unless one can present a better alternative. Thus, an HR executive could have proposed an alternative strategy that would have reduced cost without sacrificing its work force. For ex-

TABLE 2.2
Examples of the Role of HR in Strategic Management

Philip Morris Companies Inc: Hamish Maxwell, Former Chairman and CEO

"At Philip Morris, we are results-oriented and a people-sensitive company. Our senior human resource executive reports to me, is a member of the Corporate Planning Committee, and is actively involved in setting the strategic direction of the business. With the size and complexity of the company increased as a result of the recent acquisition of Kraft, strategic planning has and must continue to take the impact of people management issues into account. I expect that this role will strengthen."

AT&T: Robert E. Allen, CEO

"At the time of the government break-up, AT&T had a domestic work force, a reputation for lifelong employment, and a history of predictability. Since 1984, however, we have trimmed about 70,000 jobs in the United States, increased our presence overseas, while at the same time enlightened our people about the topsy-turvy, unpredictable global marketplace. Throughout the past five years, the human resource department at AT&T has been a linch pin."

Dow Chemical U.S.A.: Keith R. McKennon, Former President

"To succeed in today's dynamic environment, we must be good at preparing our people for change—in the marketplace and in the work force. A diverse team of Dow people must be recruited, trained, and mobilized to assure those skills that will best meet customer needs. To do this, we will tie our human resource plans ever more closely to capital planning and the strategic thrusts of our businesses."

Shell Oil Company: F. H. Richardson, Former CEO

"The process of human resource management is an integral part of our company's strategic planning efforts. Key business plans, as well as the external environment, are considered in light of human resource implications. The process includes strategic evaluation sessions focusing on human resource issues."

Amoco Corporation: Richard M. Morrow, Former Chairman

"Amoco's strategic planning process focuses primarily on the financial and operating information required to meet the corporation's short- and long-term goals. The human resource function utilizes this data and the established goals to assess the people needs of the organization and develop appropriate plans to recruit, develop, motivate, and retain the people required. The final process is the integration of the operating, financial, and human resources components into the corporation's strategic plan."

Chrysler Motors Corporation: Robert A. Lutz, President and COO

"At Chrysler, we see the role of human resources as twofold—to provide leadership and programs that contribute importantly to the direction and performance of the corporation, and to promote a participative work environment that results in enhanced employee job satisfaction and the production of quality goods and services."

SOURCE: "A Shared Mindset" by David Ulrich and Arthur Yeung, *HR Magazine*, March 1989, pp. 38–45. Reprinted with permission of *HR Magazine*. Published by the Society for Human Resource Management, Alexandria, VA.

ample, a work force that buys a plane would certainly be willing to generate ways for the airline to run more efficiently. They might also have ideas regarding how to make any necessary work force reductions and perhaps would be willing to take temporary pay cuts to help the firm get back on its feet. This would be an example of a strategy that sought to deploy rather than destroy the firm's source of competitive advantage. The "Competing by Meeting Stakeholders' Needs" box illustrates how Sears was able to use its people to create a competitive advantage.

Research has indicated that few companies have fully integrated HR into the strategy formulation process.[22] As we've mentioned before, companies are beginning to recognize that in an intensely competitive environment, managing human resources

Sears Harnesses the Power of People

In 1992 Sears, Roebuck, and Company faced the worst year in its history, losing $3.9 billion on sales of $52.3 billion. With a vast majority of the loss coming from its merchandising group, clearly Sears had lost its focus (having diversified into insurance, financial services, brokerage, and real estate) and was characterized by a dinosaur culture. Arthur Martinez took over as the head of the merchandising group and sought to recreate one of America's best known institutions. Such a task entailed getting managers in the firm to understand how and why its people are its most important asset.

Early on, managerial task groups were assigned to examine and report on what constituted "world-class status" with regard to customers, employees, financial performance, innovation, and values. From this process came Sears' vision of becoming a "compelling place to work, shop, and invest" and its values of "passion for the customer, our people add value, and performance leadership."

Such vision and values, while intuitively appealing, may have not been worth the paper they were printed on had they not been backed up by important measurement systems. Sears worked with a group of statisticians and tested their business model. They found that a 5-unit increase in employee attitude (i.e., achieving a compelling place to work) results in a 1.3-unit increase in customer impression (i.e., finding Sears a compelling place to shop), which drives a .5 percent increase in revenue.

So, how can a firm drive employee attitudes? Sears spent significant time in the development and communication of learning maps (visual representations that provide information and encourage employees to think about the industry and company they work for). These maps were used to educate employees to the dynamics of the industry and Sears' position within it. In addition, Sears set out to change the behavior of leaders through creating a leadership model that integrated the vision and values.

The results have been profound. Sears estimates that its emphasis on the new business model resulted in an increase of $200 billion in revenues in 1997.

SOURCE: A. Rucci, S. Kirn, and R. Quinn, "The Employee–Customer–Profit Chain at Sears," *Harvard Business Review*, January–February 1998, pp. 82–97.

strategically can provide a competitive advantage. Thus, companies at the administrative linkage level will either become more integrated or face extinction. In addition, companies will move toward becoming integratively linked in an effort to manage human resources strategically.

It is of utmost importance that all people-related business issues be considered during the strategy formulation process. These issues are identified in the HR function. Mechanisms or structures for integrating the HR function into strategy formulation may help the strategic planning team make the most effective strategic choice. Once that strategic choice is determined, HR must take an active role in implementing it. This role will be discussed in the next section.

Strategy Implementation

Once an organization has gone through the process of strategy formulation and made its strategic choice, it has to execute that strategy—make it come to life in its day-to-day workings. The strategy a company pursues dictates certain HR needs. For a company to have a good strategy foundation, certain tasks must be accomplished in pursuit of the company's goals, individuals must possess certain skills to perform those tasks, and these individuals must be motivated to perform their skills effectively.

The basic premise behind strategy implementation is that "an organization has a variety of structural forms and organizational processes to choose from when implementing a given strategy," and these choices make an economic difference.[23] Five important variables determine success in strategy implementation: organizational structure; task design; the selection, training, and development of people; reward systems; and types of information and information systems. (See Figure 2.4.)

As we see in Figure 2.4, HRM has primary responsibility for three of the five implementation variables: task, people, and reward systems. In addition, HRM can also directly affect the two remaining variables: structure and information and decision processes. First, for the strategy to be successfully implemented, the tasks must be designed and grouped into jobs in a way that is efficient and effective.[24] In Chapter 6 we will examine how this can be done through the processes of job analysis and job design. Second, the HR function must ensure that the organization is staffed with people who have the necessary knowledge, skill, and ability to perform their part in implementing the strategy. This goal is achieved primarily through recruitment, selection and placement, training, development, and career management—topics covered in Chapters 5, 6, 7, and 9. In addition, the HR function must develop performance management and reward systems that lead employees to work for and support the strategic plan. The specific types of performance management systems are covered in Chapter 8, and the many issues involved in developing reward systems are discussed in Chapters 11 through 13. In other words, the role of the HR function becomes one of (1) ensuring that the company has the proper number of employees with the levels and types of skills required by the strategic plan[25] and (2) developing "control" systems that ensure that those employees are acting in ways that promote the achievement of the goals specified in the strategic plan.[26]

How does the HR function do this? As Figure 2.5 shows, it is through administering HR practices: job analysis/design, recruitment, selection systems, training and development programs, performance management systems, reward systems, and labor relations programs. The details of each of these HR practices are the focus of the rest of this book. However, at this point it is important to present a general overview of the HR practices and their role in strategy implementation. We will then discuss the various strategies companies pursue and the types of HR systems congruent with those strategies. First, we focus on how the strategic types are implemented; then we discuss the HR practices associated with various directional strategies.

FIGURE 2.4 Variables to Be Considered in Strategy Implementation

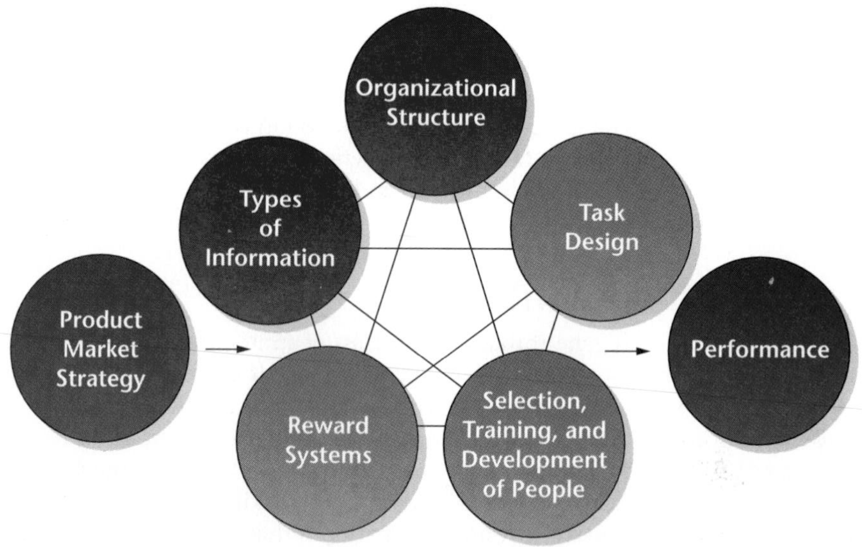

FIGURE 2.5
Strategy Implementation

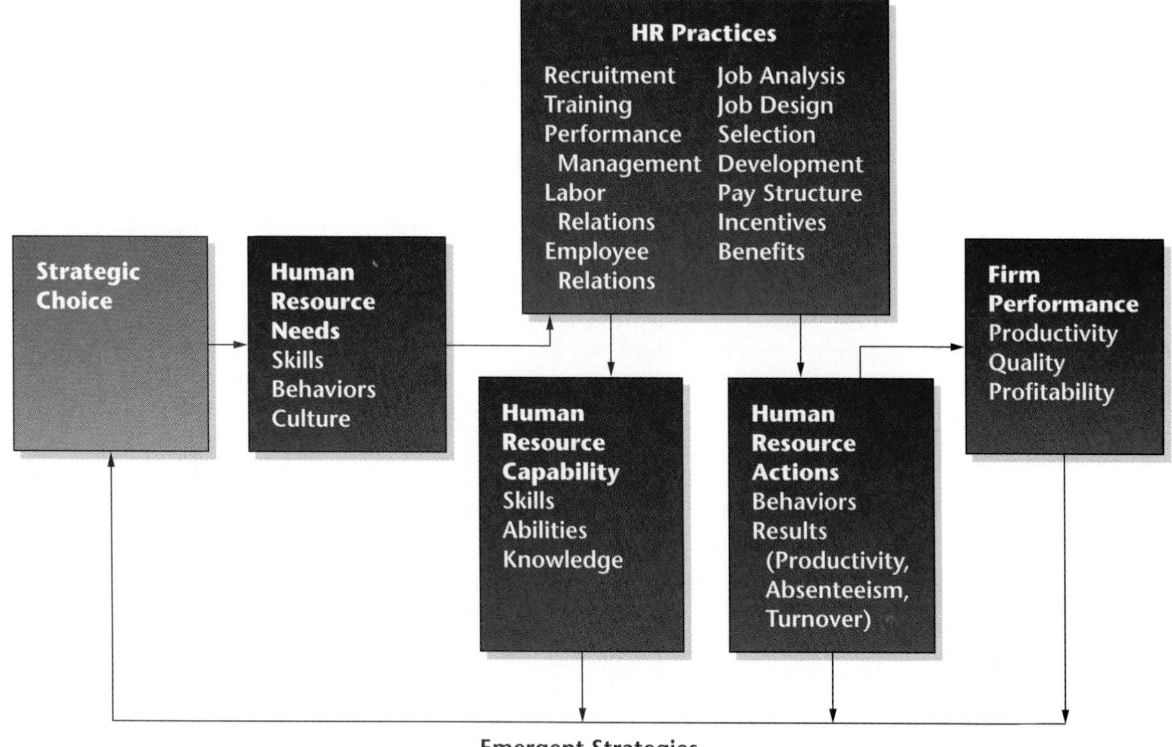

HR PRACTICES

The HR function can be thought of as having six menus of HR practices from which companies can choose the ones that are most appropriate to implementing the strategy. Each of these menus refers to a particular functional area of HRM: job analysis/design, recruitment/selection, training and development, performance management, pay structure/incentives/benefits, and labor/employee relations.[27] These menus are presented in Table 2.3.

JOB ANALYSIS AND DESIGN. Companies produce a given product or service (or set of products or services), and the manufacture of these products requires that a number of tasks be performed. These tasks are grouped together to form jobs. **Job analysis** is the process of getting detailed information about jobs. **Job design** deals with making decisions about what tasks should be grouped into a particular job. The way that jobs are designed should have an important tie to the strategy of an organization, because the strategy requires either new and different tasks or different ways of performing the same tasks. In addition, because many strategies entail the introduction of new technologies, this impacts the way that work is performed.[28]

In general, jobs can vary from having a narrow range of tasks (most of which are simplified and require a limited range of skills) to having a broad array of complex tasks requiring multiple skills. In the past, the narrow design of jobs has been used to increase efficiency, while the broad design of jobs has been associated with efforts to increase innovation. However, with the advent of total quality management methods and a vari-

TABLE 2.3
Menu of HR Practice Options

	Job Analysis and Design	
Few tasks	⟷	Many tasks
Simple tasks	⟷	Complex tasks
Few skills required	⟷	Many skills required
Specific job descriptions	⟷	General job descriptions
	Recruitment and Selection	
External sources	⟷	Internal sources
Limited socialization	⟷	Extensive socialization
Assessment of specific skills	⟷	Assessment of general skills
Narrow career paths	⟷	Broad career paths
	Training and Development	
Focus on current job skills	⟷	Focus on future job skills
Individual orientation	⟷	Group orientation
Train few employees	⟷	Train all employees
Spontaneous, unplanned	⟷	Planned, systematic
	Performance Management	
Behavioral criteria	⟷	Results criteria
Developmental orientation	⟷	Administrative orientation
Short-term criteria	⟷	Long-term criteria
Individual orientation	⟷	Group orientation
	Pay Structure, Incentives, and Benefits	
Pay weighted toward salary and benefits	⟷	Pay weighted toward incentives
Short-term incentives	⟷	Long-term incentives
Emphasis on internal equity	⟷	Emphasis on external equity
Individual incentives	⟷	Group incentives
	Labor and Employee Relations	
Collective bargaining	⟷	Individual bargaining
Top-down decision making	⟷	Participation in decision making
Formal due process	⟷	No due process
View employees as expense	⟷	View employees as assets

SOURCE: Adapted from Randall S. Schuler and Susan F. Jackson, "Linking Competitive Strategies with Human Resource Management Practices," *Academy of Management Executive* 1 (1987), pp. 207–19; and Cynthia Fisher, Lyle Schoenfeldt, and Ben Shaw, *Human Resource Management,* 2d ed. (Boston: Houghton Mifflin, 1992).

ety of employee involvement programs such as quality circles, many jobs are moving toward the broader end of the spectrum.[29]

EMPLOYEE RECRUITMENT AND SELECTION. **Recruitment** is the process through which the organization seeks applicants for potential employment. **Selection** refers to the process by which it attempts to identify applicants with the necessary knowledge, skills, abilities, and other characteristics that will help the company achieve its goals. Companies engaging in different strategies need different types and numbers of employees. Thus, the strategy a company is pursuing will have a direct impact on the types of employees that it seeks to recruit and select.[30]

EMPLOYEE TRAINING AND DEVELOPMENT. A number of skills are instilled in employees through training and development. **Training** refers to a planned effort to facilitate the learning of job-related knowledge, skills, and behavior by employees. **Development** involves acquiring knowledge, skills, and behavior that improve employees' ability to meet the challenges of a variety of existing jobs or jobs that do not yet exist. Changes in strategies often require changes in the types, levels, and mixes of skills. Thus, the acquisition of strategy-related skills is an essential element of the implementation of strategy.

For example, many companies have recently emphasized quality in their products, engaging in total quality management programs. These programs require extensive training of all employees in the TQM philosophy, methods, and often other skills that ensure quality.[31]

Through recruitment, selection, training, and development, companies can obtain a pool of human resources capable of implementing a given strategy.[32]

PERFORMANCE MANAGEMENT. **Performance management** is used to ensure that employees' activities and outcomes are congruent with the organization's objectives. It entails specifying those activities and outcomes that will result in the firm's successfully implementing the strategy. For example, companies that are "steady state" (i.e., not diversified) tend to have evaluation systems that call for subjective performance assessments of managers. This stems from the fact that those above the first-level managers in the hierarchy have extensive knowledge about how the work should be performed. On the other hand, diversified companies are more likely to use quantitative measures of performance to evaluate managers because top managers have less knowledge about how work should be performed by those below them in the hierarchy.[33]

Similarly, executives who have extensive knowledge of the behaviors that lead to effective performance use performance management systems that focus on the behaviors of their subordinate managers. However, when executives are unclear about the specific behaviors that lead to effective performance, they tend to focus on evaluating the objective performance results of their subordinate managers.[34]

PAY STRUCTURE, INCENTIVES, AND BENEFITS. The pay system has an important role in implementing strategies. First, a high level of pay and/or benefits relative to that of competitors can ensure that the company attracts and retains high-quality employees, but this might have a negative impact on the company's overall labor costs.[35] Second, by tying pay to performance, the company can elicit specific activities and levels of performance from employees.

In a study of how compensation practices are tied to strategies, researchers examined 33 high-tech and 72 traditional companies. They classified them by whether they were in a growth stage (greater than 20 percent inflation-adjusted increases in annual sales) or a maturity stage. They found that high-tech companies in the growth stage used compensation systems that were highly geared toward incentive pay, with a lower percentage of total pay devoted to salary and benefits. On the other hand, compensation systems among mature companies (both high-tech and traditional) devoted a lower percentage of total pay to incentives and a high percentage to benefits.[36]

LABOR AND EMPLOYEE RELATIONS. Whether companies are unionized or not, the general approach to relations with employees can strongly affect their potential for gaining competitive advantage. In the late 1970s Chrysler Corporation was faced with bankruptcy. Lee Iacocca, the new president of Chrysler, asked the union for wage and work-rule concessions in an effort to turn the company around. The union agreed to the concessions, in return receiving profit sharing and a representative on the board. Within only a few years, the relationship with and support from the union allowed Chrysler to pull itself out of bankruptcy to record profitability.[37]

Companies can choose to treat employees as an asset that requires investment of resources or as an expense to be minimized.[38] They have to make choices about how much employees can and should participate in decision making, what rights employees have, and what the company's responsibility is to them. The approach a company takes in making these decisions can result in it either successfully achieving its short- and long-term goals or ceasing to exist.

Recent research has begun to examine how companies develop sets of HR practices that maximize performance and productivity. For example, one study of automobile assembly plants around the world found that plants that exhibited both high productivity and high quality used "HR best practices," such as heavy emphasis on recruitment and hiring, compensation tied to performance, low levels of status differentiation, high levels of training for both new and experienced employees, and the use of employee participation through structures such as work teams and problem-solving groups.[39] Another study found that HR systems composed of selection testing, training, contingent pay, performance appraisal, attitude surveys, employee participation, and information sharing resulted in higher levels of productivity and corporate financial performance, as well as lower employee turnover.[40]

STRATEGIC TYPES

As we previously discussed, companies can be classified by the generic strategies they pursue. It is important to note that these generic "strategies" are not what we mean by a strategic plan. They are merely similarities in the ways companies seek to compete in their industries. Various typologies have been offered, but we will focus on the two generic strategies proposed by Porter: cost and differentiation.[41]

According to Michael Porter of Harvard, competitive advantage stems from a company's being able to create value in its production process. Value can be created in one of two ways. First, value can be created by reducing costs. Second, value can be created by differentiating a product or service in such a way that it allows the company to charge a premium price relative to its competitors. This leads to two basic strategies. According to Porter, the "overall cost leadership" strategy focuses on becoming the lowest-cost producer in an industry. This strategy is achieved by constructing efficient large-scale facilities, by reducing costs through capitalizing on the experience curve, and by controlling overhead costs and costs in such areas as research and development, service, sales force, and advertising. This strategy provides above-average returns within an industry, and it tends to bar other firms' entry into the industry, since the firm can lower its prices below competitors' costs. For example, IBM-clone computer manufacturers like AST, Dell, and Compaq have captured an increased share of the personal computer market by offering personal computers at lower cost than IBM and Apple.

The "differentiation" strategy, according to Porter, attempts to create the impression that the company's product or service is different from that of others in the industry. The perceived differentiation can come from creating a brand image, from technology, from offering unique features, or from unique customer service. If a company succeeds in differentiating its product, it will achieve above-average returns, and the differentiation may protect it from price sensitivity. For example, IBM has consistently emphasized its brand image and its reputation for superior service while charging a higher price for its computers.

A Cost Strategy That May Cost Children Their Health

When we think of the negative aspects of a cost strategy, we think about the obvious, visible ramifications: potential layoffs, longer hours for workers who survive cutbacks, frozen wages, the image of a "leaner, meaner" organization. Sometimes, however, there are hidden consequences; in fact, they may be hidden thousands of miles away from where we actually buy certain products.

In an effort to revive an economy (and an image) that has been choked by drug money, Colombia has been offering a new export: cut flowers, exported around the world. Flower growing is big business: Britain buys $50 million worth of carnations each year. Other flowers grown on Colombian farms include roses and lilies.

Unfortunately, the flower business is not as innocent as it sounds. To produce and ship flowers as cheaply as possible, the farms employ children, paying them about half the minimum wage. (Children earn 60,000 pesos per month, as opposed to the 118,000 required by law.) The children's work hours are illegal as well. They are supposed to work only four hours per day (at the same pay rate as adults); in reality, they work much longer, for much less pay. By their own and their employers' accounts, they are also productive; the farms "like to employ children because we have small hands and can work fast," explains one young worker.

But perhaps the worst consequence of this strategy is its effect on the children's health. They are often sick. Indeed, many of the children, who are fleeing drug-infested environments in the cities where they live, are suffering from the effects of another drug: pesticide. "I get dizzy and faint. My stomach hurts," complains one teenage girl. When this girl and her co-workers fall ill, they receive no health care or pay; they are considered temporary workers, and their contracts do not include medical benefits.

Although the Colombian Ministry has banned several types of pesticides (many of which were already banned in Europe and the United States), the farms continue to use them, and the children are exposed to them daily. "When they are eight or nine, we see children mixing pesticides in the tanks without gloves, masks, or any protection. We may not see the effects until 5 to 20 years later, when they can no longer move their hands," warns Dr. Gabriel Rueda, who works with an independent social-welfare group in Bogota. "Many farms use very dangerous organochlorides, which are prohibited in many countries." These pesticides contain toxins that can cause miscarriages, malformed fetuses, paralysis, and cancer, among other conditions.

As information about Colombia's child workers reaches the general public, and as competing flower growers from Russia and Japan enter the market, Colombian flower growers have grown concerned about their image. The Association of Colombian Flower Growers likes to encourage visitors to tour certain farms. But many farms are neither monitored nor toured by outsiders. (One farm, near Santa Cruz, stations armed guards near the gates and has wrapped barbed wire around its perimeters.) It is unclear whether flower buyers around the world will, in fact, respond to Colombia growers by refusing to buy their products. David Knight, manager of Interflora Flowers in Britain, says, "The Colombian government has good intentions, but it's a question of mechanics. We are aware that conditions are awful in some farms and good in others." The farms will most likely be forced to change their strategy, for a strategy that thrives on the abuse of its workers is ultimately doomed to failure. The competition will find a better way to grow and sell flowers.

SOURCE: Jocasta Shakespeare, "The Observer," London, July 9, 1995, as reported in *World Press Review,* October 1995, pp. 42–43.

HR NEEDS IN STRATEGIC TYPES

While all of the strategic types require competent people in a generic sense, each of the strategies also requires different types of employees with different types of behaviors and attitudes. As we noted earlier in Figure 2.1, different strategies require employees with specific skills and also require these employees to exhibit different "role behaviors."[42] **Role behaviors** are the behaviors required of an individual in her role as a job holder in a social work environment. These role behaviors vary on a number of dimensions. Additionally, different role behaviors are required by the different strategies. For example, companies engaged in a cost strategy require employees to have a high concern for quantity and a short-term focus, to be comfortable with stability, and to be risk averse. These employees are expected to exhibit role behaviors that are relatively repetitive and performed independently or autonomously. (See the "Competing by Meeting Stakeholders' Needs" box.)

Thus, companies engaged in cost strategies, because of the focus on efficient production, tend to specifically define the skills they require and invest in training employees in these skill areas. They also rely on behavioral performance management systems with a large performance-based compensation component. These companies promote internally and develop internally consistent pay systems with high pay differentials between superiors and subordinates. They seek efficiency through worker participation, soliciting employees' ideas on how to achieve more efficient production.

On the other hand, employees in companies with a differentiation strategy need to be highly creative and cooperative; to have only a moderate concern for quantity, a long-term focus, and a tolerance for ambiguity; and to be risk takers. Employees in these companies are expected to exhibit role behaviors that include cooperating with others, developing new ideas, and taking a balanced approach to process and results.

Thus, differentiation companies will seek to generate more creativity through broadly defined jobs with general job descriptions. They may recruit more from outside, engage in limited socialization of newcomers, and provide broader career paths. Training and development activities focus on cooperation. The compensation system is geared toward external equity, as it is heavily driven by recruiting needs. These companies develop results-based performance management system and divisional–corporate performance evaluations to encourage risk taking on the part of managers.[43]

A recent study of HR practice among steel minimills in the United States found that mills pursuing different strategies used different systems of HR practices. Mills seeking cost leadership tended to use control-oriented HR systems that were characterized by high centralization, low participation, low training, low wages, low benefits, and highly contingent pay, whereas differentiator mills used "commitment" HR systems, characterized as the opposite on each of those dimensions.[44] A later study from the same sample revealed that the mills with the commitment systems had higher productivity, lower scrap rates, and lower employee turnover than those with the control systems.

DIRECTIONAL STRATEGIES

As discussed earlier in this chapter, strategic typologies are useful for classifying the ways different organizations seek to compete within an industry. However, it is also necessary to understand how increasing size (growth) or decreasing it (downsizing) affects the HR function. For example, the top management team might decide that they need to invest more in product development or to diversify as a means for growth. With these types of strategies, it is more useful for the HR function to aid in evaluating the feasibility of the various alternatives and to develop programs that support the strategic choice.

Companies have used five possible categories of directional strategies to meet objectives.[45] Strategies emphasizing market share or operating costs are considered "concentration" strategies. With this type of strategy, a company is attempting to focus on what it does best within its established markets and can be thought of as "sticking to its knitting." Strategies focusing on market development, product development, innovation, or joint ventures make up the "internal growth" strategy. Companies with an internal growth strategy are channeling their resources toward building upon existing strengths.

Those attempting to integrate vertically or horizontally or to diversify are exhibiting an "external growth" strategy, usually through mergers or acquisitions. This strategy attempts to expand a company's resources or to strengthen its market position through acquiring or creating new businesses. Finally, a "divestment," or downsizing, strategy is one made up of retrenchment, divestitures, or liquidation. These strategies are observed among companies facing serious economic difficulties and seeking to pare down their operations. The human resource implications of each of these strategies are quite different.

CONCENTRATION STRATEGIES. Concentration strategies require that the company maintain the current skills that exist in the organization. This requires that training programs provide a means of keeping those skills sharp among people in the organization and that compensation programs focus on retaining people who have those skills. Appraisals in this strategy tend to be more behavioral because the environment is more certain, and the behaviors necessary for effective performance tend to be established through extensive experience.

INTERNAL GROWTH STRATEGIES. Internal growth strategies present unique staffing problems. Growth requires that a company constantly hire, transfer, and promote individuals, and expansion into different markets may change the necessary skills that prospective employees must have. In addition, appraisals often consist of a combination of behaviors and results. The behavioral appraisal emphasis stems from the knowledge of effective behaviors in a particular product market, and the results appraisals focus on achieving growth goals. Compensation packages are heavily weighted toward incentives for achieving growth goals. Training needs differ depending on the way the company attempts to grow internally. For example, if the organization seeks to expand its markets, training will focus on knowledge of each market, particularly when the company is expanding into international markets. On the other hand, when the company is seeking innovation or product development, training will be of a more technical nature, as well as focusing on interpersonal skills such as team building. Joint ventures require extensive training in conflict-resolution techniques because of the problems associated with combining people from two distinct organizational cultures.

MERGERS AND ACQUISITIONS. Increasingly we see both consolidation within industries and mergers across industries. For example, British Petroleum's recent agreement to acquire Amoco Oil represents a consolidation, or reduction in number of firms within the industry. On the other hand, Citicorp's merger with Traveller's Group to form Citigroup represents firms from different industries (pure financial services and insurance) combining to change the dynamics within both. Whatever the type, one thing is for sure—mergers and acquisitions are on the increase, and HR needs to be involved.

According to a report by the Conference Board, "people issues" may be one of the major reasons that mergers do not always live up to expectations. Some companies now heavily weigh firm cultures before embarking on a merger or acquisition. For example, prior to acquiring ValueRx, executives at Express Scripts, Inc., interviewed senior executives and middle managers at the potential target firm in order to get a sense of its culture.[46] In spite of this, less than one-third of the HR executives surveyed said that they had a major influence in how mergers are planned, yet 80 percent of them said that people issues have a significant impact after the deals are finalized.[47]

In addition to the desirability of HR playing a role in evaluating a merger opportunity, HR certainly has a role in the actual implementation of a merger or acquisition. Training in conflict resolution is also necessary when companies engage in an external growth strategy. All the options for external growth consist of acquiring or developing

Cultures Clash in Global Mergers

Going global can bring size and synergy, but it can also generate heat and heartache, as illustrated by the 1995 merger of Upjohn and Pharmacia. The merger looked like a marriage made in heaven with two second-tier pharmaceutical firms joining hands to take on the giants. Upjohn (located in Kalamazoo, Michigan) had $3.5 billion in sales, but its growth prospects were anemic due to a lack of breakthrough products in the pipeline. Pharmacia (based in Stockholm, Sweden, and having operations in Italy) was of similar size. Almost completely complementary to Upjohn, it had a strong menu of growth drugs, but limited distribution capability in the United States. Upjohn needed Pharmacia's breakthrough drugs and Pharmacia needed Upjohn's U.S. distribution capability.

However, the merger has been anything but a success, and the culture clash is the culprit. For example, everyone in Europe knows that Swedes take off for vacation during the entire month of July and Italians take the entire month of August off.

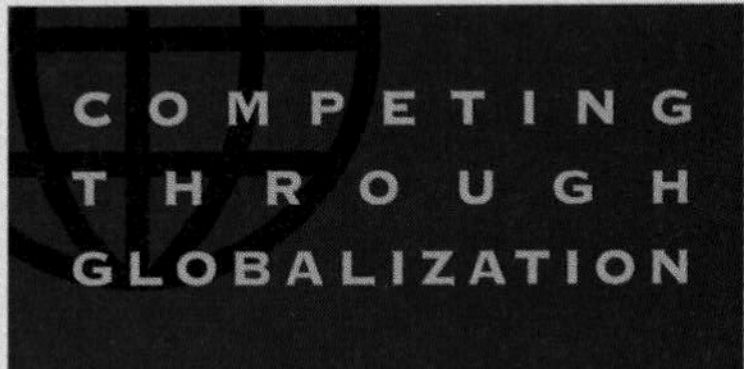

However, Upjohn employees were Americans, not Europeans. Thus, they went about scheduling a series of meetings for July and August only to have to cancel them because their colleagues were on vacation. In addition, Swedes were annoyed with having to write detailed monthly reports for the Americans, while the Americans were put off by the Europeans' opposition to Upjohn's policy of drug and alcohol testing.

While it is too early to rule the merger a failure, no one disputes that it has not yet met expectations. Costs related to the merger are $200 million higher than projected and the firm's stock has floundered on Wall Street. "There was probably an underappreciation . . . of these cultural differences," says Art Atkinson, former director for clinical research and development.

SOURCE: R. Frank and T. Burton, "Culture Clash Causes Anxiety for Pharmacia and Upjohn, Inc.," *Wall Street Journal Interact*. 3 February 4, 1997.

new businesses, and these businesses often have distinct cultures. Thus, many HR programs face problems in integrating and standardizing practices across the company's businesses. The relative value of standardizing practices across businesses must be weighed against the unique environmental requirements of each business and the extent of desired integration of the two firms. For example, with regard to pay practices, a company may desire a consistent internal wage structure to maintain employee perceptions of equity in the larger organization. In a recent new business developed by IBM, the employees pressured the company to maintain the same wage structure as IBM's main operation. However, some businesses may function in environments where pay practices are driven heavily by market forces. Requiring these businesses to adhere to pay practices in other environments may result in an ineffective wage structure. The Globalization box presents an example of what can happen when firms with both different organizational and societal cultures merge.

DOWNSIZING. Of increasing importance to organizations in today's competitive environment is HRM's role in downsizing or "rightsizing." The number of organizations undergoing downsizing has increased significantly. In fact, from 1988 to 1993, 1.4 million executives, managers, and administrators have been laid off during downsizing, compared with only 782,000 in the period from 1976 to 1981.[48] Table 2.4 lists some major company downsizings as well as statements from the companies' annual reports about the reasons behind the downsizing.

In spite of the increasing frequency of downsizing, research reveals that it is far from universally successful for achieving the goals of increased productivity and increased profitability. For example, Table 2.5 illustrates the results of a survey conducted by the American Management Association indicating that only about one-third of the com-

TABLE 2.4
Company Downsizings and Reasons Given

COMPANY	ANNUAL REPORT STATEMENT	TRANSLATION IN LAYOFFS
Sears	"Our dramatic downsizing certainly attracted a lot of attention over the last 18 months."	50,000
IBM	"Shortly after I [CEO Louis Gerstner] joined the company, I set as my highest priority to right-size the company as quickly as we could."	35,000
Boeing	"Boeing continues to take the steps necessary to adjust to the market downturn."	28,000
Kodak	"The fundamentals show that we are making real progress in reducing our cost base."	12,000
GE	"[Our] plan includes explicit programs that will result in the closing, downsizing and streamlining of certain production, service and administrative facilities worldwide."	10,000

SOURCE: "Bumstead, You're Downsized!" *Time* (April 1994): 143(16), p. 22. Reprinted by permission.

panies that went through downsizings actually achieved their goal of increased productivity. Another survey by the AMA found that over two-thirds of the companies that downsize repeat the effort a year later.[49] Also, research by the consulting firm Mitchell & Company found that companies that downsized during the 1980s lagged the industry average stock price in 1991.[50] Thus, it is important to understand the best ways of managing downsizings, particularly from the standpoint of the HR function's role.

Downsizing presents a number of challenges and opportunities for HRM. In terms of challenges, the HR function must "surgically" reduce the work force by cutting only the workers who are less valuable in their performance. Achieving this is difficult because the best workers are most able (and often willing) to find alternative employment and may leave voluntarily prior to any layoff. For example, in 1992 General Motors and the United Auto Workers agreed to an early retirement program for individuals between the ages of 51 and 65 who have been employed for 10 or more years. The program entails providing those who agree to retire with their full pension benefits, even if they obtain employment elsewhere, and as much as $13,000 toward the purchase of a GM car.[51]

Early retirement programs, although humane, essentially reduce the work force with a "grenade" approach. This type of reduction does not distinguish between good and poor performers but rather eliminates an entire group of employees. In fact, recent research indicates that when companies downsize by offering early retirement programs, they usually end up rehiring to replace essential talent within a year. Often the company does not achieve its cost-cutting goals because it spends 50 to 150 percent of the departing employee's salary in hiring and retraining new workers.[52]

Another HR challenge is to boost the morale of employees who remain after the reduction. This is discussed in greater detail in Chapter 5. Survivors may feel guilt over keeping their jobs when their friends have been laid off, or they may envy their friends who have retired with attractive severance and pension benefits. Their reduced satisfaction with and commitment to the organization may interfere with work performance. Thus, the HR function must maintain open communication with remaining employees to build their trust and commitment. Thus, all employees should be informed of the purpose of the downsizing, the costs to be cut, the duration of the downsizing, and the strategies to be pursued, rather than withholding information.[53] In addition, companies going through downsizing often develop compensation programs that tie the individual's compensation to the company's success. Employee ownership programs often result from downsizing, and gainsharing plans such as the Scanlon plan (discussed in Chapter 12) originated in companies facing economic difficulties.

TABLE 2.5
Effects of Downsizing on Desired Outcomes

DESIRED OUTCOME	PERCENTAGE THAT ACHIEVED DESIRED RESULT
Reduced expenses	46%
Increased profits	32
Improved cash flow	24
Increased productivity	22
Increased return on investment	21
Increased competitive advantage	19
Reduced bureaucracy	17
Improved decision making	14
Increased customer satisfaction	14
Increased sales	13
Increased market share	12
Improved product quality	9
Technological advances	9
Increased innovation	7
Avoidance of a takeover	6

SOURCE: *The Wall Street Journal,* June 6, 1991, p. B1. Reprinted by permission of *The Wall Street Journal,*

In spite of these challenges, downsizing provides opportunities for HRM. First, it often allows the company to "get rid of dead wood" and make way for fresh ideas. In addition, downsizing is often a unique opportunity to change an organization's culture. In firms characterized by antagonistic labor–management relations, downsizing can force the parties to cooperate and to develop new, positive relationships.[54] Finally, downsizing can demonstrate to top-management decision makers the value of the company's human resources to its ultimate success. The role of HRM is to effectively manage the process in a way that makes this value undeniable. We discuss the implications of downsizing as a labor force management strategy in Chapter 5.

DELTA AIR LINES AND HR'S ROLE IN STRATEGY IMPLEMENTATION. As was described in the opening vignette, HR issues were significant components to Delta's Leadership 7.5 strategy. While the effectiveness of the strategy has already been questioned, HR seemed to play a significant role in its implementation. Since labor costs are the largest single controllable cost for an airline, significant cost reductions had to have HR implications. Thus, costs were cut approximately $1.6 billion through work force reductions. These reductions were achieved through buyouts, early retirement, extended leaves, and layoffs. In many cases, experienced, highly paid, long-term Delta employees were replaced by less experienced, but also much lower paid employees, either full-time, part-time, or contract. For example, cleaning of the airplanes prior to this strategy was performed in-house by employees earning $7.80 an hour to start, with full benefits and travel privileges. This allowed Delta to often hire college graduates who were willing to take on such jobs to get a foot in the door at Delta. These employees were replaced with outside contractors, who received lower wages, few benefits, and no travel privileges, resulting in much lower labor costs. However, the downside was that Delta soon faced "smelly lavatories, soiled carpets, sticky tray tables and littered seat pockets."[55]

The negative outcomes of the strategy in terms of employee morale, customer service, and operational performance have been discussed. A vast majority of these stemmed from the strategy itself, but one wonders if the same strategy might have been implemented differently with less negative impact. For example, significant communications with employees regarding the need for restructuring might have provided more legitimacy to the downsizing effort. In addition, seeking to provide outplacement services to laid-off employees might have eased their transition out of the firm. HR might have developed programs aimed at boosting the morale of Delta's survivors. However, it is unlikely that such measures would have had a significant positive influence given the severity of the cuts. Again, it highlights the strategic importance of HR having an impact on the strategy formulation as well as implementation processes if people are to be deployed as a source of competitive advantage.

STRATEGY EVALUATION AND CONTROL

A final component to the strategic management process is that of strategy evaluation and control. Thus far we have focused on the planning and implementation of strategy. However, it is extremely important for the firm to constantly monitor the effectiveness of both the strategy and the implementation process. This monitoring makes it possible for the company to identify problem areas and either revise existing structures and strategies or devise new ones. In this process we see emergent strategies appear as well as the critical nature of human resources in competitive advantage.

THE ROLE OF HUMAN RESOURCES IN PROVIDING STRATEGIC COMPETITIVE ADVANTAGE

Thus far we have presented the strategic management process as including a step-by-step procedure by which HR issues are raised prior to deciding on a strategy and then HR practices are developed to implement that strategy. However, we must note that human resources can provide a strategic competitive advantage in two additional ways: through emergent strategies and through enhancing competitiveness. (See the "Competing through High-Performance Work Systems" box.)

EMERGENT STRATEGIES. Having discussed the process of strategic management, we also must distinguish between intended strategies and emergent strategies. Most people think of strategies as being proactive, rational decisions aimed toward some predetermined goal. The view of strategy we have presented thus far in the chapter focuses on intended strategies. *Intended strategies* are the result of the rational decision-making process used by top-level managers as they develop a strategic plan. This is consistent with the definition of *strategy* as "the pattern or plan that integrates an organization's major goals, policies, and action sequences into a cohesive whole."[56] The idea of emergent strategies is evidenced by the feedback loop in Figure 2.1.

Most strategies that companies espouse are intended strategies. For example, when Compaq was founded, the company had its strategy summarized in its name, an amalgam of the words *computer, compact,* and *quality*. Thus, the intended strategy was to build compact portable computers that were completely free of any defect, and all of the company's efforts were directed toward implementing that strategy. Following that strategy allowed Compaq to become one of the fastest-growing companies in the world, commanding 20 percent of the world market in 1991. In 1992 Compaq's performance began to falter again, sparking new CEO Eckhard Pfieffer to change Compaq's strategy to one focused on being a low-cost producer. This strategic change resulted in Compaq becoming the leading PC maker in the world in 1994.[57]

Emergent strategies, on the other hand, consist of the strategies that evolve from the grass roots of the organization and can be thought of as what organizations actually do, as opposed to what they intend to do. Strategy can also be thought of as "a pattern in a stream of decisions or actions."[58] For example, when Honda Motor Company first en-

Motorola's Strategy Uses All Its Resources

When Motorola embarks on a project, the organization employs every resource it has to plan and implement its strategy. In a high-technology field in which products, customers' needs, markets, and technology itself are constantly changing, Motorola and companies like it need to rely on internal and external growth strategies, as well as intended and emergent strategies. To complete these strategies, they must rely on people—their technical skill, motivation, and innovative ways of thinking.

We can view a microcosm of Motorola's use of high-performance work systems (teamwork, empowerment, training, and education development of new technology, and so forth) to move its strategy forward in its new Harvard, Illinois, location. One reason Motorola chose this location for a $100 million plant was the concentration of qualified workers. (The company normally hires only one in 10 applicants. Here, 65 percent of the applicants were hired.) Another reason for the choice of location was its proximity to a nearby cellular subscriber operation. (Employees from the existing operation were recruited to help employees at the new plant get things up and running.) The size of the lot—300 acres—was another factor. (Motorola can expand the plant if necessary.) All these considerations were part of the intended strategy.

Motorola's strategy does not stop at its own doors. At Harvard, the organization has reached out to the schools, focusing just as hard on the quality of education and training of future workers as it does on the development and manufacture of its products. With its Learning Leadership Teams, Motorola conducts meetings and programs to help teachers and administrators develop curricula that will launch students into a rapidly changing 21st century, preparing them to compete and succeed at their jobs. Teams of teachers then work with students, who also complete learning projects in teams. "Our message to our employees is that schools have to change, and we have to help them change." Not every educator greeted this encroachment with enthusiasm. "At first, what we were thinking was, Don't tell us what to do," says Fred Schroeder, assistant superintendent for the state's fourth-largest school district. "[But] we started talking with them and found out that their value orientation is not to criticize but to help."

COMPETING THROUGH HIGH-PERFORMANCE WORK SYSTEMS

Motorola also reaches out to its suppliers, working closely with them and insisting on striving for the highest quality. Motorola actually acts as a partner to its suppliers, providing training at its own Motorola University. "They are very demanding in terms of their quality standards and what they expect from suppliers, but they help you to become a better company," notes John Krehbeil, president of Molex. "They help educate your organization in a number of different areas." The establishment of Motolora University was part of the strategy of former chairman Robert Galvin. "In starting Motorola University, Bob Galvin realized he had to continually reinvest in the company," explains James Schwarz, president of Omni Circuits Inc.

Motorola is the undisputed technological leader in cellular communications, and there are some solid reasons for this. First, its strategy is always forward-thinking. "I think it's their commitment to research and development," observes Joe Fristenksy, a telecommunications industry analyst for Frost & Sullivan in California. Second, the organization's emergent strategy compares favorably with its intended strategy; Motorola actually does what it says it is going to do. "While other people are dreaming about, 'Well, maybe we can do this,' they look over, and Motorola is already halfway there. They get ahead of everybody else, which forces the rest of the pack to play catch-up," says Fristenksy. Third, quality is a driving force, not only in the development and production of its products but in the development of its people (employees, suppliers, and students in the community). "They're never happy; they're never satisfied. They always have to get better," says Schwarz.

Critics may charge that some of Motorola's strategy is paternalistic, designed to give the organization as much control as possible over people who are part of its environment. But the fact remains that Motorola relies heavily on the way its people function in a high-performance work system to maintain its competitive advantage in the market. Having the technology to produce the new generation of digital cellular communications is not of great value unless people understand the ways it will change their world.

SOURCE: John Rondy, "Makeover by Motorola," *Illinois Business*, 3d quarter 1995, pp. 41–49. Reprinted by permission.

tered the U.S. market with its 250 cc and 305 cc motorcycles in 1959, it believed that no market existed for its smaller, 50 cc, bike. However, the sales on the larger motorcycles were sluggish, and Japanese executives running errands around Los Angeles on Honda 50s attracted a lot of attention, including that of a buyer with Sears, Roebuck. Honda found a previously undiscovered market as well as a new distribution outlet (general retailers) that it had not planned on. This emergent strategy resulted in Honda having a 50 percent market share by 1964.[59]

The distinction between intended and emergent strategies has important implications for human resource management. The new focus on strategic HRM has tended to focus primarily on intended strategies. Thus, HRM's role has been seen as identifying for top management the people-related business issues relevant to strategy formulation and then developing HR systems that aid in the implementation of the strategic plan.

However, most emergent strategies are identified by those lower in the organizational hierarchy. It is often the rank-and-file employees who provide ideas for new markets, new products, and new strategies. HRM plays an important role in facilitating communication throughout the organization, and it is this communication that allows for effective emergent strategies to make their way up to top management. This fact led Philip Caldwell, Ford's chairman in the early 1980s, to state, "It's stupid to deny yourself the intellectual capability and constructive attitude of tens of thousands of workers."[60]

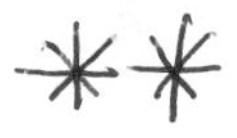

ENHANCING FIRM COMPETITIVENESS. A related way in which human resources can be a source of competitive advantage is through developing a human capital pool that provides the company with the unique ability to adapt to an ever-changing environment. Recently, managers have become interested in the idea of a "learning organization," in which people continually expand their capacity to achieve the results they desire.[61] This requires the company to be in a constant state of learning through monitoring the environment, assimilating information, making decisions, and flexibly restructuring to compete in that environment. Characteristics of learning organizations are discussed in Chapter 9. Companies that develop such learning capability have a competitive advantage. Although certain organizational information-processing systems can be an aid, ultimately the people (human capital) who make up the company provide the raw materials in a learning organization.

Thus, the role of human resources in competitive advantage should continue to increase because of the fast-paced change characterizing today's business environment. It is becoming increasingly clear that even as U.S. automakers have increased the quality of their cars to compete with the Japanese, these competitors have developed such flexible and adaptable manufacturing systems that they can respond to customer needs more quickly.[62] This flexibility of the manufacturing process allows the emergent strategy to come directly from the marketplace by determining and responding to the exact mix of customer desires. It requires, however, that the company have people in place who have the skills to similarly adapt quickly.[63] As George Walker, president of Delta Wire, stated, "Anyone can come in and buy machines like I have. The difference is the knowledge of your workers."[64] This statement exemplifies the increasing importance of human resources in developing and maintaining competitive advantage.[65]

STRATEGIC HUMAN RESOURCE EXECUTIVES

For a reader who is just getting his first glimpse of the HR function, it is impossible to portray what a vastly different role HR must play today compared to 20 or even 10 years ago. As noted earlier, HR has traditionally played a largely administrative role—simply processing paperwork plus developing and administering hiring, training, appraisal, compensation, and benefits systems—and all of this has been unrelated to the strategic direction of the firm. In the early 1980s HR took on more of a one-way linkage role, helping to implement strategy. Now, strategic decision makers are realizing the importance of people issues and so are calling for HR to become the "source of people expertise" in the firm.[66] This requires that they possess and use their knowledge of how people can and do play a role in competitive advantage as well as the policies, programs, and practices that can leverage the firm's people as a source of competitive advantage. This leads to an entirely new set of competencies for today's strategic HR executive.

In the future, HR professionals will need four basic competencies to become partners in the strategic management process.[67] (See Figure 2.6.) First, they will need to have "business competence"—knowing the company's business and understanding its economic financial capabilities. This calls for making logical decisions that support the company's strategic plan based on the most accurate information possible. Because in almost all companies the effectiveness of decisions must be evaluated in terms of dollar values, the HR executive must be able to calculate the costs and benefits of each alternative in terms of its dollar impact.[68] In addition, it requires that the nonmonetary impact be considered. The HR executive must be fully capable of identifying the social and ethical issues attached to its HR practices.

Second, HR professionals will need "professional–technical knowledge" of state-of-the-art HR practices in areas such as staffing, development, rewards, organizational design, and communication. New selection techniques, performance appraisal methods, training programs, and incentive plans are constantly being developed. Some of these programs can provide value, while others may be no more than the products of today's HR equivalent of snake oil. The HR executive must be able to critically evaluate the new techniques offered as state-of-the-art HR programs and use only those that will benefit the company.

Third, they must be skilled in the "management of change processes," such as diagnosing problems, implementing organizational changes, and evaluating results. Every time a company changes its strategy even in a minor way, the entire company has to change. These changes result in conflict, resistance, and confusion among the people

FIGURE 2.6
Human Resource Competencies

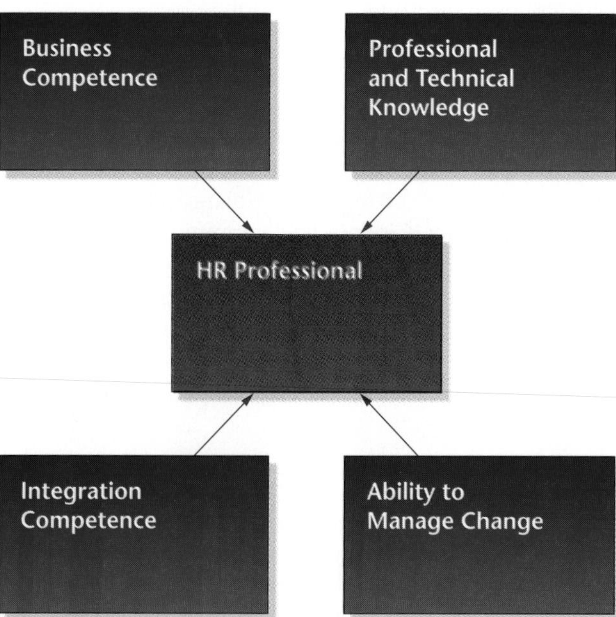

who must implement the new plans or programs. The HR executive must have the skills to oversee the change in a way that ensures its success. In fact, one survey of Fortune 500 companies found that 87 percent of the companies had their organization development/change function as part of the HR department.[69]

Finally, these professionals must also have "integration competence," meaning the ability to integrate the three other competencies to increase the company's value. This requires that, although specialist knowledge is necessary, a generalist perspective must be taken in making decisions. This entails seeing how all the functions within the HR area fit together to be effective and recognizing that changes in any one part of the HR package are likely to require changes in other parts of the package. For example, a health care company in central Texas was attempting to fill a position in the X-ray department. It was able to identify qualified candidates for the position, but none of the candidates accepted the offer. It was not until the company examined its total package (pay, benefits, promotion opportunities, etc.) and changed the composition of the package that it was able to fill the position.

The new strategic role for HR presents both opportunities and challenges. HR has the chance to profoundly impact the way organizations compete through people. On the other hand, with this opportunity comes serious responsibility and accountability. HR functions of the future must consist of individuals who view themselves as business people who happen to work in an HR function, rather than HR people who happen to work in a business.

SUMMARY

A strategic approach to human resource management seeks to proactively provide a competitive advantage through the company's most important asset: its human resources. The HR function needs to be integrally involved in the formulation of strategy to identify the people-related business issues the company faces. Once the strategy has been determined, HRM has a profound impact on the implementation of the plan by developing and aligning HR practices that ensure that the company has motivated employees with the necessary skills. Finally, the emerging strategic role of the HR function requires that HR professionals in the future develop business, professional–technical, change management, and integration competencies. As you will see more clearly in later chapters, this strategic approach requires more than simply developing a valid selection procedure or state-of-the-art performance management systems. Only through these competencies can the HR professional take a strategic approach to human resource management.

DISCUSSION QUESTIONS

1. Pick one of your university's major sports teams (e.g., football or basketball). How would you characterize that team's generic strategy? How does the composition of the team members (in terms of size, speed, ability, etc.) relate to that strategy? What are the strengths and weaknesses of the team? How do those dictate the team's generic strategy and its approach to a particular game?
2. Do you think that it is easier to tie human resources to the strategic management process in large or in small organizations? Why?
3. Consider some of the organizations you have been affiliated with. What are some examples of human resource practices that were consistent with that organization's strategy? What are examples of practices that were inconsistent with its strategy?
4. How can strategic management within the HR department ensure that HR plays an effective role in the company's strategic management process?
5. What types of specific skills (e.g., knowledge of financial accounting methods) do you think HR professionals will need to have the business, professional–technical, change management, and integrative competencies necessary in the future? Where can you seek to develop each of these skills?
6. What are some of the key environmental variables that you see changing in the business world today? What impact will those changes have on the HR function in organizations?

WEB EXERCISE

This chapter emphasized that for companies to gain a competitive advantage they must integrate HRM into the company's business strategy. Go to Allied-Signal's home page at www.alliedsignal.com.

1. What types of businesses is the company involved in?
2. What is the company's growth and productivity strategy?
3. What are the implications of the company's growth and productivity strategy for how the company manages its human resource? Make sure you describe the implications for recruitment and selection, training, performance management, and compensation.

MANAGING PEOPLE: FROM THE PAGES OF "BUSINESS WEEK"

BusinessWeek Unisys Aims for the Top of the Tree

The faces around him said it all. When Lawrence A. Weinbach took the top job at ailing Unisys Corp. in the fall of 1997, he quickly noticed that no one in the halls of the Blue Bell (Pa.) computer company smiled. In fact, many employees didn't even look him in the eye. And when Weinbach went out to visit big customers, most asked the same uneasy question: "Is Unisys viable?" Says Weinbach: "Nobody thought this company had a future."

These days, there's little worry about Unisys' survival. One year after his arrival, Weinbach, 58, has slashed the company's staggering debt load by nearly $1 billion, to a more manageable $1.3 billion. That has helped the company turn in strong earnings all year long. On Oct. 15, Unisys announced that profits nearly doubled in the third quarter, to $96 million on $1.8 billion in sales. And the stock has more than doubled, to 25⅞ since Weinbach's arrival.

Not bad for the first year on the job. But Weinbach's next year will be an even bigger test. He wants to build the company's services business—expected to hit $5 billion this year—into a high-octane profit engine, focusing on areas where Unisys has proven expertise—such as financial services and telecommunications. The trouble is, Weinbach faces a delicate balancing act: He has to rev up the services side as he copes with the expected decline of the company's traditional mainframe business, which still generates about 60% of the company's earnings. "The challenge is to do this and be perceived as a top-tier [services] player," says Merrill Lynch & Co. analyst Steven M. Milunovich. "They are still viewed as a second-tier computer company." Concedes Weinbach: "Are we there yet? No. But we are on our way."

Certainly Weinbach is not used to playing in the second tier. An accountant by training, he previously had a 36-year career at accounting and consulting giant Andersen Worldwide. Chief executive for his last eight years there, he upped revenues from $3.4 billion to $11.3 billion. But with Andersen's mandatory retirement age of 62 five years away, Weinbach decided to start a second career. "The challenge of coming into a turnaround and seeing if we could get [Unisys] to come alive was very enticing," he says.

At Unisys, Weinbach quickly moved to impose financial discipline on the company's erratic information services business. That unit focuses on a variety of services including the design and installation of sophisticated document imaging, voice-messaging, or customer-information systems for companies like Norwest Financial, the consumer-finance business of Norwest Corp. Those businesses, together with the company's networking and maintenance-service group, are expected to generate 67% of Unisys' $7.2 billion in annual revenues this year. But the service unit contributes just 39% of the company's operating income. One reason: Unisys bid so aggressively to win some contracts that a number of them, including one to manage the health insurance system for Florida state employees, were money losers.

Indeed, the information service group racked up losses of $400 million in 1995 and 1996 alone. Now, before a bid is made, the proposal gets a stringent internal review by executives who don't receive commissions on the deal. And Weinbach says Unisys won't be chasing huge outsourcing deals, in part because profits on such projects are slim.

Where Weinbach is scrambling after new business is in midsize service deals that can help the company build up its Internet expertise. A Unisys package called Cool ICE, for example, is the software glue that helps customers create electronic commerce applications that link their databases to Web sites. Although coming off a small customer base, sales are up 300% this year. Unisys also is hawking another program, FBA Navigator, a system for managing customer information at retail banks that allows banks to send personally tailored marketing pitches to customers over the Web.

Products like Navigator are part of another scheme to drive service revenue. Weinbach calls it repeatable solutions. These are predesigned systems that are developed to meet the needs of industries such as publishing, telecommunications, and transportation, which can then be tailored—using Unisys experts—to fit the specific requirements of individual customers and any number of hardware platforms.

Unisys, for instance, offers daily newspapers a system called Hermes. Developed in Europe in the 1970s, Hermes manages the flow of everything from archived stories and photos to the newspaper's daily content and layout. It has caught fire in the last three years, with a total of 100 newspapers now using the system—33 signed up in 1998 alone—including Rupert Murdoch's News International PLC, publisher of London's *The Sun*. "Their key was they were successful in Europe with customers that were happy with them," says Bill Hack, publishing systems director at Philadelphia Newspapers Inc., which is rolling out Hermes at its *Philadelphia Inquirer* and *Philadelphia Daily News* operations. So far, the midsize-service effort is paying off. In the first nine months of this year, total service revenue rose 17%, to $3.5 billion, generating operating income of $221 million, compared with just $86 million in the year-earlier period. And more than 25% of orders in services this year are from new clients.

While Weinbach says services are the future of Unisys, he isn't turning his back on hardware. Instead, he's zeroing in on high-end servers and mainframes. Earlier this year, he outsourced the production of low-end servers and personal computers to Hewlett-Packard Co. That's allowing the company to target much of its $300 million research and development budget on a new generation of high-end services. The new machines—the first line will be ready by mid-1999—will run Microsoft Corp.'s Windows NT operating system as well as other operating systems and use new-generation Intel Corp. chips.

That bet isn't without risks. Right now NT is the hot ticket among corporate users, but it isn't viewed as reliable enough to handle the high volume, mission-critical functions typically run on mainframes. Unisys is betting that, by partnering with Microsoft, the two companies can boost NT to handle those tasks for industries such as financial services. If the new hardware delivers, Unisys will be set to exploit the hot market for NT software and services. "The risk is that making NT industrial-strength takes longer and is more difficult than they currently project," says analyst Charles C. Burns of technology researcher Giga Information Group Inc.

None of Weinbach's ambitious plans will flourish, however, if he isn't able to overhaul the company's stodgy old mainframe image. That holds Unisys back in everything from recruiting to being considered a serious candidate for topflight contracts. A new ad campaign—costing $20 million in the fourth quarter alone—is aimed at blowing away that image. With its showcasing of hip young professionals who are so obsessed with their jobs that their heads are actually computer screens, the ads are a break from Unisys' traditional pitch.

Weinbach also is raising the bar on training. He's planning to roll out "Unisys University," a technical and management training program, in January of 1999 to keep employees up on technical issues and build a pool of experts. He reinstated a matching contribution from the company in employee 401(k) programs—cut during lean years— and started a program in which employees can buy Unisys stock at a discount. Now, employee turnover is down from 14% in 1996 to about 9% in the first quarter of this year. "We were concerned about morale and support at the company," says George F. Thomas, director of information systems at New York Clearing House Assn., a big Unisys mainframe customer. "Now you can see a turnaround in attitude."

There's still a lot of room for improvement, though. One senior executive at the company says some infighting continues between the hardware and services teams on issues like financial resources and manpower. Weinbach knows those units need to coordinate sales and service efforts better, so earlier this year he created one sales group to handle the company's 200 largest accounts. "We are trying to change the culture of this company," Weinbach says. If he can do that, Unisys may be able to focus on prospering instead of survival.

QUESTIONS

1. Describe the change in strategy and/or the major strategic thrusts taking place under Lawrence Weinbach at Unisys.
2. What are the implications of these strategic business issues for people issues (culture, competencies, critical behaviors, etc.)?
3. How can HR play a role in executing this strategy?

SOURCE: "Unisys Aims for the Top of the Tree," *Business Week*, November 9, 1998.

NOTES

1. J. Barney, "Firm Resources and Sustained Competitive Advantage," *Journal of Management* 17 (1991), pp. 99–120.
2. L. Dyer, "Strategic Human Resource Management and Planning," in *Research in Personnel and Human Resources Management*, ed. K. Rowland and G. Ferris (Greenwich, CT: JAI Press, 1985), pp. 1–30.
3. J. Quinn, *Strategies for Change: Logical Incrementalism* (Homewood, IL: Richard D. Irwin, 1980).
4. M. Porter, *Competitive Strategy: Techniques for Analyzing Industries and Competitors* (New York: Free Press, 1980).
5. R. Miles and C. Snow, *Organizational Strategy, Structure, and Process* (New York: McGraw-Hill, 1978).
6. P. Wright and G. McMahan, "Theoretical Perspectives for Strategic Human Resource Management," *Journal of Management* 18 (1992), pp. 295–320.
7. S. Snell and J. Dean, "Integrated Manufacturing and Human Resource Management: A Human Capital Per-

spective," *Academy of Management Journal* 35 (1992), pp. 467–504.

8. J. Butler, G. Ferris, and N. Napier, *Strategy and Human Resource Management* (Cincinnati, OH: Southwestern Publishing Co., 1991).
9. F. Biddle and J. Helyar, "Behind Boeing's Woes: Chunky Assembly Line, Price War with Airbus," *The Wall Street Journal*, April 24, 1998, pp. A1, A16.
10. K. Martell and S. Carroll, "How Strategic Is HRM?" *Human Resource Management* 34 (1995), pp. 253–67.
11. K. Golden and V. Ramanujam, "Between a Dream and a Nightmare: On the Integration of the Human Resource Function and the Strategic Business Planning Process," *Human Resource Management* 24 (1985), pp. 429–51.
12. C. Hill and G. Jones, *Strategic Management Theory: An Integrated Approach* (Boston: Houghton Mifflin, 1989).
13. W. Johnston and A. Packer, *Workforce 2000: Work and Workers for the Twenty-first Century* (Indianapolis, IN: Hudson Institute, 1987).
14. "Labor Letter," *The Wall Street Journal*, December 15, 1992, p. A1.
15. P. Wright, G. McMahan, and A. McWilliams, "Human Resources and Sustained Competitive Advantage: A Resource–Based Perspective," *International Journal of Human Resource Management* 5 (1994), pp. 301–26.
16. P. Buller, "Successful Partnerships: HR and Strategic Planning at Eight Top Firms," *Organizational Dynamics* 17 (1988), pp. 27–42.
17. M. Hitt, R. Hoskisson, and J. Harrison, "Strategic Competitiveness in the 1990s: Challenges and Opportunities for U.S. Executives," *The Executive* 5 (May 1991), pp. 7–22.
18. P. Wright, G. McMahan, B. McCormick, and S. Sherman, *Strategy, Core Competence, and HR Involvement as Determinants of HR Effectiveness and Refinery Performance*. Paper presented at the 1996 International Federation of Scholarly Associations in Management, Paris, France.
19. N. Bennett, D. Ketchen, and E. Schultz, *Antecedents and Consequences of Human Resource Integration with Strategic Decision Making*. Paper presented at the 1995 Academy of Management Meeting, Vancouver, BC, Canada.
20. J. Barney and P. Wright, "On Becoming a Strategic Partner: The Role of Human Resources in Gaining Competitive Advantage," *Human Resource Management* 37, no. 1 (1998), pp. 31–46.
21. Brannigan and White, "So Be It."
22. Golden and Ramanujam, "Between a Dream and a Nightmare."
23. J. Galbraith and R. Kazanjian, *Strategy Implementation: Structure, Systems, and Process* (St. Paul, MN: West Publishing, 1986).
24. B. Schneider and A. Konz, "Strategic Job Analysis," *Human Resource Management* 27 (1989), pp. 51–64.
25. P. Wright and S. Snell, "Toward an Integrative View of Strategic Human Resource Management," *Human Resource Management Review* 1 (1991), pp. 203–25.
26. S. Snell, "Control Theory in Strategic Human Resource Management: The Mediating Effect of Administrative Information," *Academy of Management Journal* 35 (1992), pp. 292–327.
27. R. Schuler, "Personnel and Human Resource Management Choices and Organizational Strategy," in *Readings in Personnel and Human Resource Management*, 3d ed., ed. R. Schuler, S. Youngblood, and V. Huber (St. Paul, MN: West Publishing, 1988).
28. J. Dean and S. Snell, "Integrated Manufacturing and Job Design: Moderating Effects of Organizational Inertia," *Academy of Management Journal* 34 (1991), pp. 776–804.
29. E. Lawler, *The Ultimate Advantage: Creating the High Involvement Organization* (San Francisco: Jossey-Bass, 1992).
30. J. Olian and S. Rynes, "Organizational Staffing: Integrating Practice with Strategy," *Industrial Relations* 23 (1984), pp. 170–83.
31. G. Smith, "Quality: Small and Midsize Companies Seize the Challenge—Not a Moment Too Soon," *Business Week*, November 30, 1992, pp. 66–75.
32. J. Kerr and E. Jackofsky, "Aligning Managers with Strategies: Management Development versus Selection," *Strategic Management Journal* 10 (1989), pp. 157–70.
33. J. Kerr, "Strategic Control through Performance Appraisal and Rewards," *Human Resource Planning* 11 (1988), pp. 215–23.
34. S. Snell, "Control Theory in Strategic Human Resource Management."
35. B. Gerhart and G. Milkovich, "Employee Compensation: Research and Practice," in *Handbook of Industrial and Organizational Psychology*, 2d ed., ed. M. Dunnette and L. Hough (Palo Alto, CA: Consulting Psychologists Press, 1992), pp. 481–569.
36. D. Balkin and L. Gomez-Mejia, "Toward a Contingency Theory of Compensation Strategy," *Strategic Management Journal* 8 (1987), pp. 169–82.
37. A. Taylor, "U.S. Cars Come Back," *Fortune*, November 16, 1992, pp. 52, 85.
38. S. Cronshaw and R. Alexander, "One Answer to the Demand for Accountability: Selection Utility as an Investment Decision," *Organizational Behavior and Human Decision Processes* 35 (1986), pp. 102–18.
39. P. MacDuffie, "Human Resource Bundles and Manufacturing Performance: Organizational Logic and Flexible Production Systems in the World Auto Industry," *Industrial and Labor Relations Review* 48 (1995), pp. 197–221; P. McGraw, "A Hard Drive to the Top," *U.S. News and World Report* 118 (1995), pp. 43–44.
40. M. Huselid, "The Impact of Human Resource Management Practices on Turnover, Productivity, and Corporate Financial Performance," *Academy of Management Journal* 38 (1995), pp. 635–72.

41. M. Porter, *Competitive Advantage* (New York: Free Press, 1985).
42. R. Schuler and S. Jackson, "Linking Competitive Strategies with Human Resource Management Practices," *Academy of Management Executive* 1 (1987), pp. 207–19.
43. R. Miles and C. Snow, "Designing Strategic Human Resource Management Systems," *Organizational Dynamics* 13, no. 1 (1984), pp. 36–52.
44. J. Arthur, "The Link between Business Strategy and Industrial Relations Systems in American Steel Mini-Mills," *Industrial and Labor Relations Review* 45 (1992), pp. 488–506.
45. A. Thompson and A. Strickland, *Strategy Formulation and Implementation: Tasks of the General Manager,* 3d ed. (Plano, TX: BPI, 1986).
46. G. Fairclough, "Business Bulletin," *The Wall Street Journal*, March 5, 1998, p. A1. October 2, 1997, p. A1.
47. P. Sebastian, "Business Bulletin," *The Wall Street Journal*.
48. J.S. Champy, *Reengineering Management: The Mandate for New Leadership* (New York: Harper Business, 1995).
49. S. Pearlstein, "Corporate Cutback Yet to Pay Off," *Washington Post*, January 4, 1994, p. B6.
50. K. Cameron, "Guest Editor's Note: Investigating Organizational Downsizing—Fundamental Issues," *Human Resource Management* 33 (1994), pp. 183–88.
51. N. Templin, "UAW to Unveil Pact on Slashing GM's Payroll," *The Wall Street Journal*, December 15, 1992, p. A3.
52. J. Lopez, "Managing: Early-Retirement Offers Lead to Renewed Hiring," *The Wall Street Journal*, January 26, 1993, p. B1.
53. A. Church, "Organizational Downsizing: What Is the Role of the Practitioner?" *The Industrial–Organizational Psychologist* 33, no. 1 (1995), pp. 63–74.
54. N. Templin, "A Decisive Response to Crisis Brought Ford Enhanced Productivity," *The Wall Street Journal*, December 15, 1992, p. A1.
55. Brannigan and De Lisser, "Cost Cutting at Delta."
56. J. Quinn, *Strategies for Change*.
57. H. Mintzberg, "Patterns in Strategy Formulation," *Management Science* 24 (1978), pp. 934–48.
58. R. Pascale, "Perspectives on Strategy: The Real Story behind Honda's Success," *California Management Review* 26 (1984), pp. 47–72.
59. N. Templin, "A Decisive Response to Crisis."
60. P. Senge, *The Fifth Discipline* (New York: Doubleday, 1990).
61. T. Stewart, "Brace for Japan's Hot New Strategy," *Fortune*, September 21, 1992, pp. 62–76.
62. C. Snow and S. Snell, *Staffing as Strategy*, vol. 4 of *Personnel Selection* (San Francisco: Jossey-Bass, 1992).
63. T. Batten, "Education Key to Prosperity—Report," *Houston Chronicle*, September 7, 1992, p. 1B.
64. P. Wright, "Human Resources as a Competitive Weapon," *Applied Advances in Strategic Management* 2 (1991), pp. 91–122.
65. G. McMahan, University of Texas at Arlington, *Personal Communications*.
66. G. McMahan and R. Woodman, "The Current Practice of Organization Development within the Firm: A Survey of Large Industrial Corporations," *Group and Organization Studies* 17 (1992), pp. 117–34.
67. D. Ulrich and A. Yeung, "A Shared Mindset," *Personnel Administrator*, March 1989, pp. 38–45.
68. G. Jones and P. Wright, "An Economic Approach to Conceptualizing the Utility of Human Resource Management Practices," *Research in Personnel/Human Resources* 10 (1992), pp. 271–99.
69. R. Schuler and J. Walker, "Human Resources Strategy: Focusing on Issues and Actions," *Organizational Dynamics* (Summer 1990), pp. 5–19.

CHAPTER

The Legal Environment: Equal Employment Opportunity and Safety

OBJECTIVES

After reading this chapter, you should be able to

1. Identify the three branches of government and the role each plays in influencing the legal environment of human resource management.
2. List the major federal laws that require equal employment opportunity and the protections provided by each of these laws.
3. Discuss the roles, responsibilities, and requirements of the federal agencies responsible for enforcing equal employment opportunity laws.
4. Identify the four theories of discrimination under Title VII of the Civil Rights Act and apply these theories to different discrimination situations.
5. Identify behavior that constitutes sexual harassment and list things that an organization can do to eliminate or minimize it.
6. Discuss the legal issues involved with preferential treatment programs.
7. Identify the major provisions of the Occupational Safety and Health Act (1970) and the rights of employees that are guaranteed by this act.

Competitive Advantage at Home Depot?

ENTER THE WORLD OF BUSINESS

Home Depot is a large home products firm mainly selling home repair products and equipment for the "do-it-yourselfer." Founded 20 years ago, it now boasts 100,000 employees and 504 warehouse-style stores. The firm's phenomenal growth has come from a strategy of providing superior service to its customers. The company prides itself on hiring people who are knowledgeable about home repair and who are able to teach customers how to do home repairs on their own. This strategy has resulted in Home Depot gaining a competitive advantage.

However, recently, some are calling into question the means for gaining such an advantage. In Home Depot's growth, a statistical anomaly has emerged. Approximately 70 percent of the merchandise employees (those directly involved in selling lumber, electrical supplies, hardware, etc.) are male, while approximately 70 percent of the operations employees (cashiers, accountants, back office staff, etc.) are female. This has resulted in a lawsuit against Home Depot on behalf of 17,000 current and former female employees as well as up to 200,000 rejected applicants.

Home Depot explains this disparity by noting that most women job applicants have experience as cashiers so they are placed in cashier positions, whereas male applicants express an interest or aptitude for crafts such as carpentry or plumbing. The plaintiffs' lawyers argue that Home Depot is guilty of reinforcing gender stereotypes and that hiring managers wrongly assume "that the presence of masculine traits among women and feminine traits among men is rare."

To avoid such lawsuits in the future, Home Depot could simply hire by quota, ensuring that there is an equal distribution of male and female employees across all job categories, something that Home Depot alleges would destroy its competitive advantage. Says its lawyer, "It will ultimately make Home Depot no different from the competitors it beat in the marketplace."

SOURCE: M. Boot, "For Plaintiffs' Lawyers, There's No Place Like Home Depot," *The Wall Street Journal*, interactive edition, February 12, 1997.

Introduction

In the opening chapter, we discussed the environment of the HR function, and we noted that several environmental factors affect an organization's HRM function. One is the legal environment, particularly the laws affecting the management of people. As the troubles at Home Depot indicate, legal issues can cause serious problems for a company's success and survival. In this chapter, we first present an overview of the U.S. legal system, noting the different legislative bodies, regulatory agencies, and judicial bodies that determine the legality of certain HRM practices. We then discuss the major laws and executive orders that govern these practices.

One point to make clear at the outset is that managers often want a list of "dos and don'ts" that will keep them out of legal trouble. They rely on rules such as "Don't ever ask a female applicant if she is married" without understanding the "why" behind these rules. Clearly, there are certain practices that are illegal or inadvisable, and this chapter will provide some valuable tips for avoiding discrimination lawsuits. However, such lists are not compatible with a strategic approach to HRM and are certainly not the route to developing a competitive advantage. They are simply mechanical reactions to the situations. Our goal is to provide an understanding of how the legislative, regulatory, and judicial systems work to define equal employment opportunity law. Armed with this understanding, a manager is better prepared to manage people within the limits imposed by the legal system. Doing so effectively is a source of competitive advantage.

The Legal System in the United States

The foundation for the U.S. legal system is set forth in the U.S. Constitution, which affects HRM in two ways. First, it delineates a citizen's constitutional rights, on which the government cannot impinge.[1] Most individuals are aware of the Bill of Rights, the first 10 amendments to the Constitution, but other amendments, such as the Fourteenth Amendment, also influence HR practices. The Fourteenth Amendment, called the *equal protection clause*, states that all individuals are entitled to equal protection under the law.

Second, the Constitution established three major governing bodies: the legislative, executive, and judicial branches. The Constitution explicitly defines the roles and responsibilities of each of these branches. Each branch has its own areas of authority, but these areas have often overlapped, and the borders between the branches are often blurred.

LEGISLATIVE BRANCH

The legislative branch of the federal government consists of the House of Representatives and the Senate. These bodies develop laws that govern many HR activities. Most of the laws stem from a perceived societal need. For example, during the civil rights movement of the early 1960s, the legislative branch moved to ensure that various minority groups received equal opportunities in many areas of life. One of these areas was employment, and thus Congress enacted Title VII of the Civil Rights Act. Similar perceived societal needs have brought about labor laws such as the Occupational Safety and Health Act, the Employee Retirement Income Security Act, the Age Discrimination in Employment Act, and, more recently, the Americans with Disabilities Act of 1990 and the Civil Rights Act of 1991.

EXECUTIVE BRANCH

The executive branch consists of the president of the United States and the many regulatory agencies the president oversees. Although the legislative branch passes the laws, the executive branch affects these laws in many ways. First, the president can propose bills to Congress that, if passed, would become laws. Second, the president has the power to veto any law passed by Congress, thus ensuring that few laws are passed without presidential approval—which allows the president to influence how laws are written.

Third, the regulatory agencies, under the authority of the president, have responsibility for enforcing the laws. Thus, a president can influence what types of violations are pursued. For example, many laws affecting employment discrimination are enforced by the Equal Employment Opportunity Commission under the Department of Justice. During President Jimmy Carter's administration, the Department of Justice brought a lawsuit against Birmingham, Alabama's, fire department for not having enough black firefighters. This suit resulted in a consent decree that required blacks to receive preferential treatment in hiring and promotion decisions. Two years later, during Ronald Reagan's administration, the Department of Justice sided with white firefighters in a lawsuit against the city of Birmingham, alleging that the preferential treatment required by the consent decree discriminated against white firefighters.[2]

Fourth, the president can issue executive orders, which sometimes regulate the activities of organizations that have contracts with the federal government. For example, Executive Order 11246, signed by President Lyndon Johnson, required all federal contractors and subcontractors to engage in affirmative action programs designed to hire and promote women and minorities within their organizations. Fifth, the president can influence the Supreme Court to interpret laws in certain ways. When particularly sensitive cases come before the Court, the attorney general, representing the executive branch, argues for certain preferred outcomes. For example, one recent court case involved a white female schoolteacher who was laid off from her job in favor of retaining a black schoolteacher with equal seniority and performance with the reason given as "diversity." The white woman filed a lawsuit in federal court and the Bush administration filed a brief on her behalf, arguing that diversity was not a legitimate reason to use race in decision making. She won in federal court, and the school district appealed. The Clinton administration, having been elected in the meantime, filed a brief on behalf of the school district, arguing that diversity was a legitimate defense.

Finally, the president appoints all the judges in the federal judicial system, subject to approval from the legislative branch. This affects the interpretation of many laws.

JUDICIAL BRANCH

The judicial branch consists of the federal court system, which is made up of three levels. The first level consists of the U.S. District Courts and quasi-judicial administrative agencies. The district courts hear cases involving alleged violations of federal laws. The quasi-judicial agencies, such as the National Labor Relations Board (or NLRB, which is actually an arm of the executive branch, but serves a judicial function), hear cases regarding their particular jurisdictions (in the NLRB's case, disputes between unions and management). If neither party to a suit is satisfied with the decision of the court at this level, the parties can appeal the decision to the U.S. Courts of Appeals. These courts were originally set up to ease the Supreme Court's case load, so appeals generally go from the federal trial level to one of the 13 appellate courts before they can be heard by the highest level, the Supreme Court. The Supreme Court must grant certiorari before hearing an appealed case. However, this is not usually granted unless two appellate

Germany Sends Vietnamese Workers Home

Laws governing employment opportunities for minorities differ from country to country, just as does the definition of the term *minority*. Each country deals with the hiring of immigrants and other minorities differently. Ultimately, employment opportunity laws are designed to create a competitive advantage for the country in the world marketplace, and the way minorities are integrated into a country's work force affects its competitiveness.

In unified Germany, Vietnamese residents who are part of the work force—or who would like to be—are facing deportation under a new law. During the next five years, Germany plans to expel 40,000 Vietnamese contract workers who were originally hired by the East German government and never awarded permanent residency or immigration status (along with other Vietnamese who are living illegally in the country). In a country whose economy was once considered a world power, there are now too many workers, too few jobs, and too much debt (taken on from the former East Germany). So the government has decided it must send these particular non-Germans home. (A few years ago, just after East and West Germany were unified, the new government offered its Vietnamese contract workers a stipend of $2,000 each and a ticket home; 50,000 of them accepted the offer. But there are still 100,000 Vietnamese in Germany.)

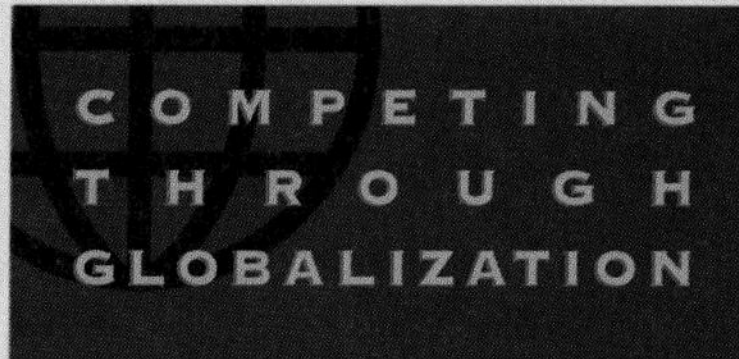

Because of the Holocaust of World War II, Germany has an especially public—and painful—history with minorities. Ironically, government officials claim that, because of a resurgence of neo-Nazi attitudes in Germany, they want to prevent problems by sending these foreigners back to their native land. Interior Minister Manfred Kanther explains that the new policy is "the only guarantee against the abuses of uncontrollable movements of immigrants in the future and against popular discontent turning to radical political forces."

"The people are afraid," responds Son Vu Van, director of a Vietnamese counseling service. "They are afraid to talk. They are afraid they will be expelled."

Germany has cracked down on far-rightists who espouse neo-Nazi philosophies. But the concurrent tightening of immigration laws and the dissolution of constitutional guarantees of asylum do seem to support the far right's desire to close Germany's doors. It remains to be seen whether these moves will affect Germany's competitiveness in the global market. Logic suggests that as the Internet and other components of worldwide information and communications technology break more and more boundaries, and as work forces around the world become more and more diverse to compete, a country that becomes more restrictive and exclusive will fall far behind its competitors.

SOURCE: Alan Cowell, "Berlin: Bad Dream for Vietnamese," *International Herald Tribune*, October 16, 1995, p. 7.

courts have come to differing decisions on the same point of law or if the case deals with an important interpretation of constitutional law.

The Supreme Court serves as the court of final appeal. Decisions made by the Supreme Court are binding; they can be overturned only through legislation. For example, Congress, dissatisfied with the Supreme Court's decisions in certain cases such as *Wards Cove Packing v. Atonio,* overturned those decisions through the Civil Rights Act of 1991.[3]

Having described the legal system that affects the management of HR, we now explore some major laws that regulate HR activities, particularly equal employment opportunity laws. We first discuss the major laws that mandate equal employment opportunity in the United States. Then we examine the agencies involved in enforcing these laws. This leads us into an examination of the four theories of discrimination, with a discussion of some relevant court cases. Finally, we explore some equal employment opportunity issues facing today's managers.

Equal Employment Opportunity

Equal employment opportunity (EEO) refers to the government's attempt to ensure that all individuals have an equal chance for employment, regardless of race, color, religion, sex, or national origin. To accomplish this, the federal government has used constitutional amendments, legislation, and executive orders, as well as the court decisions that interpret these laws. [However, equal employment laws are not the same in all countries. (See the "Competing through Globalization" box.)] The major EEO laws we discuss are summarized in Table 3.1.

TABLE 3.1 Summary of Major EEO Laws and Regulations 

ACT	REQUIREMENTS	COVERS	ENFORCEMENT AGENCY
Thirteenth Amendment	Abolished slavery	All individuals	Court system
Fourteenth Amendment	Provides equal protection for all citizens and requires due process in state action	State actions (e.g., decisions of government organizations)	Court system
Civil Rights Acts (CRAs) of 1866 and 1871 (as amended)	Grant all citizens the right to make, perform, modify, and terminate contracts and enjoy all benefits, terms, and conditions of the contractual relationship	All individuals	Court system
Equal Pay Act of 1963	Requires that men and women performing equal jobs receive equal pay	Employers engaged in interstate commerce	EEOC
Title VII of CRA	Forbids discrimination based on race, color, religion, sex, or national origin	Employers with 15 or more employees working 20 or more weeks per year; labor unions; and employment agencies	EEOC
Age Discrimination in Employment Act of 1967	Prohibits discrimination in employment against individuals 40 years of age and older	Employers with 15 or more employees working 20 or more weeks per year; labor unions; employment agencies; federal government	EEOC
Rehabilitation Act of 1973	Requires affirmative action in the employment of individuals with disabilities	Government agencies; federal contractors and subcontractors with contracts greater than $2,500	OFCCP
Americans with Disabilities Act of 1990	Prohibits discrimination against individuals with disabilities	Employers with more than 15 employees	EEOC
Executive Order 11246	Requires affirmative action in hiring women and minorities	Federal contractors and subcontractors with contracts greater than $10,000	OFCCP
Civil Rights Act of 1991	Prohibits discrimination (same as Title VII)	Same as Title VII, plus applies Section 1981 to employment discrimination cases	EEOC

CONSTITUTIONAL AMENDMENTS

THIRTEENTH AMENDMENT. The Thirteenth Amendment of the Constitution abolished slavery in the United States. Though one might be hard-pressed to cite an example of race-based slavery today, the Thirteenth Amendment has been applied in cases where the discrimination involved the "badges" (symbols) and "incidents" of slavery.

FOURTEENTH AMENDMENT. The Fourteenth Amendment forbids the state from taking life, liberty, or property without due process of law and prevents the states from denying the equal protection of the laws. Passed immediately after the Civil War, this amendment originally applied only to discrimination against blacks. It was soon broadened to protect other groups such as aliens and Asian-Americans, and more recently it has been applied to the protection of whites in allegations of reverse discrimination. In *Bakke v. California Board of Regents*, Alan Bakke alleged that he had been discriminated against in the selection of entrants to the University of California at Davis medical school.[4] The university had set aside 16 of the available 100 places for "disadvantaged" applicants who were members of racial minority groups. Under this quota system, Bakke was able to compete for only 84 positions, whereas a minority applicant was able to compete for all 100. The court ruled in favor of Bakke, noting that this quota system had violated white individuals' right to equal protection under the law.

One important point regarding the Fourteenth Amendment is that it is applicable only to "state actions." This means that only the decisions or actions of the government or of private groups whose activities are deemed state actions can be construed as violations of the Fourteenth Amendment. Thus, one could file a claim under the Fourteenth Amendment if one were fired from a state university (a government organization) but not if one were fired by a private employer.

CONGRESSIONAL LEGISLATION

THE RECONSTRUCTION CIVIL RIGHTS ACTS (1866 AND 1871). The Thirteenth Amendment eradicated slavery in the United States, and the Reconstruction Civil Rights Acts were attempts to further this goal. The Civil Rights Act passed in 1866 was later broken into two statutes. Section 1982 granted all persons the same property rights as white citizens. Section 1981 granted other rights, including the right to enter into and enforce contracts. Courts have interpreted Section 1981 as granting individuals the right to make and enforce employment contracts. The Civil Rights Act of 1871 granted all citizens the right to sue in federal court if they felt they had been deprived of some civil right. Although these laws might seem outdated, they are still used because they allow the plaintiff to recover both compensatory and punitive damages.

In fact, these laws came to the forefront in a Supreme Court case: *Patterson v. McClean Credit Union*.[5] The plaintiff had filed a discrimination complaint under Section 1981 for racial harassment. After being hired by McClean Credit Union, Patterson failed to receive any promotions or pay raises while she was employed there. She was also told that "blacks work slower than whites." Thus, she had grounds for discrimination and filed suit under Section 1981, arguing that she had been discriminated against in the making and enforcement of an employment contract. The Supreme Court ruled that this situation did not fall under Section 1981 because it did not involve the making and enforcement of contracts. However, the Civil Rights Act of 1991 amended this act to include the making, performance, modification, and termination of contracts, as well as all benefits, privileges, terms, and conditions of the contractual relationship.

THE EQUAL PAY ACT OF 1963. The Equal Pay Act, an amendment to the Fair Labor Standards Act, requires that men and women in the same organization who are doing equal work must be paid equally. The act defines *equal* in terms of skill, effort, responsibility, and working conditions. However, the act allows for reasons why men and women performing the same job might be paid differently. If the pay differences are the result of differences in seniority, merit, quantity or quality of production, or any factor other than sex (e.g., shift differentials or training programs), then differences are legally allowable.

TITLE VII OF THE CIVIL RIGHTS ACT OF 1964. This is the major legislation regulating equal employment opportunity in the United States. It was a direct result of the civil rights movement of the early 1960s, led by such individuals as Dr. Martin Luther King, Jr. It was Dr. King's philosophy that people should be "judged by the content of their character, and not the color of their skin." To ensure that employment opportunities would be based on one's character or ability rather than on their race, Congress wrote and passed Title VII, which President Lyndon Johnson signed into law.

Title VII states that it is illegal for an employer to "(1) fail or refuse to hire or discharge any individual, or otherwise discriminate against any individual with respect to his compensation, terms, conditions, or privileges of employment because of such individual's race, color, religion, sex, or national origin, or (2) to limit, segregate, or classify his employees or applicants for employment in any way that would deprive or tend to deprive any individual of employment opportunities or otherwise adversely affect his status as an employee because of such individual's race, color, religion, sex, or national origin." The act applies to organizations with 15 or more employees working 20 or more weeks a year that are involved in interstate commerce, as well as state and local governments, employment agencies, and labor organizations.

AGE DISCRIMINATION IN EMPLOYMENT ACT (ADEA). Passed in 1967 and amended in 1986, this act prohibits discrimination against employees over the age of 40. The act almost exactly mirrors Title VII in terms of its substantive provisions and the procedures to be followed in pursuing a case.[6] As with Title VII, the EEOC is responsible for enforcing this act.

The ADEA was designed to protect older employees when a firm reduces its work force through layoffs. By targeting older employees, who tend to have higher pay, a firm can substantially cut labor costs. Recently, firms have often offered early retirement incentives, a possible violation of the act because of the focus on older employees. Early retirement incentives require employees to sign an agreement waiving their rights to sue under the ADEA. Courts have tended to uphold the use of early retirement incentives and waivers as long as the individuals were not coerced into signing the agreements, the agreements were presented in a way that the employees could understand, and the employees were given enough time to make a decision.[7]

However, age discrimination complaints make up a large percentage of the complaints filed with the Equal Employment Opportunity Commission, and the number of complaints continues to grow whenever the economy is slow. For example, as we see in Figure 3.1, the cases increased during the early 1990s when many firms were downsizing, but the number of cases has decreased since then as the economy has been expanding. This often stems from firms seeking to lay off older (and thus higher-paid) employees when they are downsizing. In addition, these cases can be costly. Most cases are settled out of court, but these settlements run from between $50,000 and $400,000 per employee.[8] In one recent case Schering–Plough fired 35-year employee Fred Maiorino after he twice failed to accept an early retirement offer made to all sales representatives.

FIGURE 3.1
Age Discrimination Complaints, 1991–97

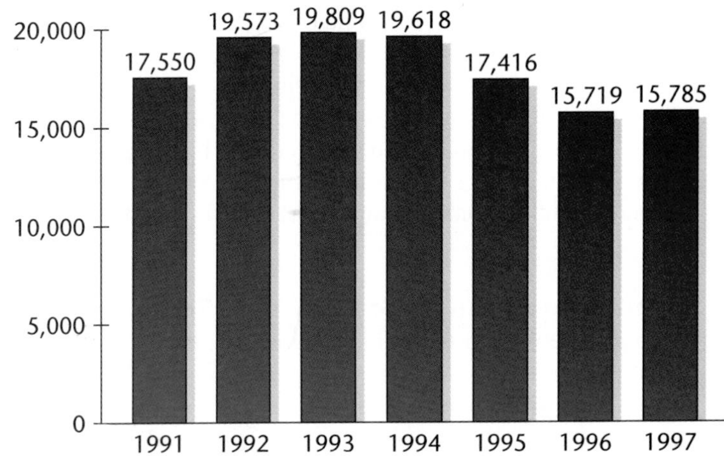

SOURCE: Equal Employment Opportunity Commission.

After hearing testimony that Maiorino's boss had plastered his file with negative paperwork aimed at firing him, rather than trying to help him improve his performance, the jurors unanimously decided he had been discriminated against because of his age. They awarded him $435,000 in compensatory damages and $8 million in punitive damages.[9]

THE VOCATIONAL REHABILITATION ACT OF 1973. This act covers executive agencies and contractors and subcontractors that receive more than $2,500 annually from the federal government. It requires them to engage in affirmative action for individuals with disabilities. Congress designed this act to encourage employers to actively recruit qualified individuals with disabilities and to make reasonable accommodations to allow them to become active members of the labor market. The Employment Standards Administration of the Department of Labor enforces this act.

VIETNAM ERA VETERAN'S READJUSTMENT ACT OF 1974. Similar to the Rehabilitation Act, this act requires federal contractors and subcontractors to take affirmative action toward employing Vietnam veterans (those serving between August 5, 1964, and May 7, 1975). The Office of Federal Contract Compliance Procedures, discussed later in this chapter, has authority to enforce this act.

CIVIL RIGHTS ACT OF 1991. The Civil Rights Act of 1991 (CRA 1991) amends Title VII of the Civil Rights Act of 1964, Section 1981 of the Civil Rights Act of 1866, the Americans with Disabilities Act, and the Age Discrimination in Employment Act of 1967. One major change in EEO law under CRA 1991 has been the addition of compensatory and punitive damages in cases of discrimination under Title VII and the Americans with Disabilities Act. Before CRA 1991, Title VII limited damage claims to equitable relief such as back pay, lost benefits, front pay in some cases, and attorney's fees and costs. CRA 1991 allows compensatory and punitive damages when intentional or reckless discrimination is proven. Compensatory damages include such things as future pecuniary loss, emotional pain, suffering, and loss of enjoyment of life. Punitive damages are meant to discourage employers from discriminating by providing for payments to the plaintiff beyond the actual damages suffered.

Recognizing that one or a few discrimination cases could put an organization out of business, thus adversely affecting many innocent employees, Congress has put limits on the amount of punitive damages. Table 3.2 depicts these limits. As can be seen, damages range from $50,000 to $300,000 per violation, depending upon the size of the or-

EMPLOYER SIZE	DAMAGE LIMIT
14 to 100 employees	$ 50,000
101 to 200 employees	100,000
201 to 500 employees	200,000
More than 500 employees	300,000

TABLE 3.2 Maximum Punitive Damages Allowed under the Civil Rights Act of 1991

ganization. Punitive damages are available only if the employer intentionally discriminated against the plaintiff(s) or if the employer discriminated with malice or reckless indifference to the employee's federally protected rights. These damages are excluded for an employment practice held to be unlawful because of its disparate impact.[10]

The addition of damages to CRA 1991 has had two immediate effects. First, by increasing the potential payoff for a successful discrimination suit, it has increased the number of suits filed against businesses. Second, organizations are now more likely to grant all employees an equal opportunity for employment, regardless of their race, gender, religion, or national origin. Many organizations have felt the need to make the composition of their work force mirror the general population to avoid costly lawsuits. This act adds a financial incentive for doing so.

AMERICANS WITH DISABILITIES ACT (ADA) OF 1990. One of the most far-reaching acts concerning the management of human resources is the Americans with Disabilities Act. This act protects individuals with disabilities from being discriminated against in the workplace. It prohibits discrimination based on disability in all employment practices such as job application procedures, hiring, firing, promotions, compensation, and training—in addition to other employment activities such as advertising, recruitment, tenure, layoff, leave, and fringe benefits. Because this act is so new, we will cover its various stipulations individually.

ADA defines a disability as a physical or mental impairment that substantially limits one or more major life activities, a record of having such an impairment, or being regarded as having such an impairment. The first part of the definition refers to individuals who have serious disabilities—such as epilepsy, blindness, deafness, or paralysis—that affect their ability to perform major life activities such as walking, seeing, performing manual tasks, learning, caring for oneself, and working. The second part refers to individuals who have a history of disability, such as someone who has had cancer but is currently in remission, someone with a history of mental illness, and someone with a history of heart disease. The third part of the definition, "being regarded as having a disability," refers, for example, to an individual who is severely disfigured and is denied employment because an employer fears negative reactions from others.[11]

Thus, ADA covers specific physiological disabilities such as cosmetic disfigurement and anatomical loss affecting the neurological, musculoskeletal, sensory, respiratory, cardiovascular, reproductive, digestive, genitourinary, hemic, or lymphatic systems. In addition, it covers mental and psychological disorders such as mental retardation, organic brain syndrome, emotional or mental illness, and learning disabilities. However, conditions such as obesity, substance abuse, eye and hair color, and lefthandedness are not covered.[12]

EXECUTIVE ORDERS

Executive orders are directives issued and amended unilaterally by the president. These orders do not require congressional approval, yet they have the force of law. Two executive orders directly affect HRM.

EXECUTIVE ORDER 11246. President Johnson issued this executive order, which prohibits discrimination based on race, color, religion, sex, and national origin. Unlike Title VII, this order applies only to federal contractors and subcontractors. Employers receiving more than $10,000 from the federal government must take affirmative action to ensure against discrimination, and those with contracts greater than $50,000 must develop a written affirmative action plan for each of their establishments within 120 days of the beginning of the contract. The Office of Federal Contract Compliance Procedures enforces this executive order.

EXECUTIVE ORDER 11478. President Richard M. Nixon issued this order, which requires the federal government to base all its employment policies on merit and fitness, and specifies that race, color, sex, religion, and national origin should not be considered. (The U.S. Office of Personnel Management is in charge of this.) The order also extends to all contractors and subcontractors doing $10,000 worth of business with the federal government. (The relevant government agencies have the responsibility to ensure that the contractors and subcontractors comply with the order.)

Enforcement of Equal Employment Opportunity

As discussed previously, the executive branch of the federal government bears most of the responsibility for enforcing all EEO laws passed by the legislative branch. In addition, the executive branch must enforce the executive orders issued by the president. The two agencies responsible for the enforcement of the laws and executive orders are the Equal Employment Opportunity Commission and the Office of Federal Contract Compliance Procedures, respectively.

EQUAL EMPLOYMENT OPPORTUNITY COMMISSION (EEOC)

A division of the Department of Justice, the EEOC is responsible for enforcing most of the EEO laws, such as Title VII, the Equal Pay Act, and the Americans with Disabilities Act. The EEOC has three major responsibilities: investigating and resolving discrimination complaints, gathering information, and issuing guidelines.

INVESTIGATION AND RESOLUTION. Individuals who feel they have been discriminated against must file a complaint with the EEOC or a similar state agency within 180 days of the incident. Failure to file a complaint within the 180 days results in the case's being dismissed immediately, with certain exceptions, such as the enactment of a seniority system that has an intentionally discriminatory purpose.

Once the complaint is filed, the EEOC takes responsibility for investigating the claim of discrimination. The complainant must give the EEOC 60 days to investigate the complaint. If the EEOC either does not believe the complaint to be valid or fails to complete the investigation, the complainant may sue in federal court. If the EEOC determines that discrimination has taken place, its representatives will attempt to provide a reconciliation between the two parties without burdening the court system with a lawsuit. Sometimes, the EEOC enters into a consent decree with the discriminating organization. This decree is an agreement between the agency and the organization that the organization will cease certain discriminatory practices and possibly institute additional affirmative action practices to rectify its history of discrimination.

If the EEOC cannot come to an agreement with the organization, there are two options. First, it can issue a "right to sue" letter to the alleged victim, which certifies that the agency has investigated and found validity in the victim's allegations. Second, although less likely, the agency may aid the alleged victim in bringing suit in federal court.

INFORMATION GATHERING. The EEOC also plays a role in monitoring the hiring practices of organizations. Each year, organizations with 100 or more employees must file a report (EEO-1) with the EEOC that provides the number of women and minorities employed in nine different job categories. The EEOC computer analyzes these reports to identify patterns of discrimination that can then be attacked through class-action suits.

ISSUANCE OF GUIDELINES. A third responsibility of the EEOC is to issue guidelines that help employers determine when their decisions are violations of the laws enforced by the EEOC. These guidelines are not laws themselves, but the courts give great deference to them when hearing employment discrimination cases.

For example, the *Uniform Guidelines on Employee Selection Procedures* is a set of guidelines issued by the EEOC, the Department of Labor, the Department of Justice, and the U.S. Civil Service Commission.[13] This document provides guidance on the ways an organization should develop and administer selection systems so as not to violate Title VII. The courts often refer to the *Uniform Guidelines* to determine whether a company has engaged in discriminatory conduct or to determine the validity of the procedures it used to validate a selection system. Another example: Since the passage of the ADA, employers have been somewhat confused about the act's implications for their hiring procedures. Therefore, the EEOC issued guidelines in the *Federal Register* that provided more detailed information regarding what the agency will consider legal and illegal employment practices concerning disabled individuals. Although companies are well advised to follow these guidelines, it is possible that courts will interpret the ADA differently from the EEOC. Thus, through the issuance of guidelines the EEOC provides employers with directions for making employment decisions that do not conflict with existing laws.

OFFICE OF FEDERAL CONTRACT COMPLIANCE PROCEDURES (OFCCP)

The OFCCP is the agency responsible for enforcing the executive orders that cover companies doing business with the federal government. Businesses with contracts for more than $50,000 cannot discriminate in employment based on race, color, religion, national origin, or sex, and they must have a written affirmative action plan on file.

These plans have three basic components.[14] First, the utilization analysis is a comparison of the race, sex, and ethnic composition of the employer's work force with that of the available labor supply. For each job group, the employer must identify the percentage of its work force with that characteristic (e.g., female) and identify the percentage of workers in the relevant labor market with that characteristic. If the percentage in the employer's work force is much less than the percentage in the comparison group, then that minority group is considered to be "underutilized."

Second, the employer must develop specific **goals and timetables** for achieving balance in the work force concerning these characteristics (particularly where underutilization exists). Goals and timetables specify the percentage of women and minorities that the employer seeks to have in each job group and the date by which that percentage is to be attained. These are not to be viewed as quotas. Quotas entail setting aside a specific number of positions to be filled only by members of the protected class. Goals and timetables are much more flexible, requiring only that the employer have specific goals and take steps toward the achievement of those goals. In fact, one study that examined companies with the goal of increasing black employment found that only 10 percent of them actually achieved their goals. Although this may sound discouragingly low, it is important to note that these companies increased their black employment more than companies that set no such goals.[15]

Third, employers with federal contracts must develop a list of **action steps** they will take toward attaining their goals to reduce underutilization. The company's CEO must make it clear to the entire organization that the company is committed to reducing underutilization, and all management levels must be involved in the planning process. For example, organizations can communicate job openings to women and minorities through publishing the company's affirmative action policy, recruiting at predominantly female or minority schools, participating in programs designed to increase employment opportunities for underemployed groups, and removing unnecessary barriers to employment. Organizations must also take affirmative steps toward hiring Vietnam veterans and individuals with disabilities.

The OFCCP annually audits government contractors to ensure that they have been actively pursuing the goals in their plans. These audits consist of (1) examining the company's affirmative action plan and (2) conducting on-site visits to examine how individual employees perceive the company's affirmative action policies. If the OFCCP finds that the contractors or subcontractors are not complying with the executive order, then its representatives may notify the EEOC (if there is evidence that Title VII has been violated), advise the Department of Justice to institute criminal proceedings, request that the Secretary of Labor cancel or suspend any current contracts, and forbid the firm from bidding on future contracts. This last penalty, called *debarment*, is the OFCCP's most potent weapon.

Having discussed the major laws defining equal employment opportunity and the agencies that enforce these laws, we now discuss the various types of discrimination and the ways these forms of discrimination have been interpreted by the courts in a number of cases.

Types of Discrimination

How would you know if you had been discriminated against? Assume that you have applied for a job and were not hired. How do you know if the organization decided not to hire you because you are unqualified, because you are less qualified than the individual ultimately hired, or simply because the person in charge of the hiring decision "didn't like your type"? Discrimination is a multifaceted issue. It is often not easy to determine the extent to which unfair discrimination affects an employer's decisions.

Legal scholars have identified three theories of discrimination: disparate treatment, disparate impact, and reasonable accommodation. In addition, there is protection for those participating in discrimination cases or opposing discriminatory actions. In the act, these theories are stated in very general terms. However, the court system has defined and delineated these theories through the cases brought before it. A comparison of the theories of discrimination is given in Table 3.3.

DISPARATE TREATMENT

Disparate treatment exists when individuals in similar situations are treated differently and the different treatment is based on the individual's race, color, religion, sex, national origin, age, or disability status. If two people with the same qualifications apply for a job and the employer decides whom to hire based on one individual's race, the individual not hired is a victim of disparate treatment. Under the disparate treatment the

TABLE 3.3 Comparison of Discrimination Theories

TYPES OF DISCRIMINATION	DISPARATE TREATMENT	DISPARATE IMPACT	REASONABLE ACCOMMODATION
Show intent?	Yes	No	Yes
Prima facie case	Individual is member of a protected group, was qualified for the job, and was turned down for the job, and the job remained open	Statistical disparity in the effects of a facially neutral employment practice	Individual has a belief or disability, provided the employer with notice (request to accommodate), and was adversely affected by a failure to be accommodated
Employer's defense	Produce a legitimate, nondiscriminatory reason for the employment decision or show bona fide occupational qualification (BFOQ)	Prove that the employment practice bears a manifest relationship with job performance	Job-relatedness and business necessity, undue hardship, or direct threat to health or safety
Plaintiff's rebuttal	Reason offered was merely a "pretext" for discrimination	Alternative procedures exist that meet the employer's goal without having disparate impact	
Monetary damages	Compensatory and punitive damages	Equitable relief (e.g., back pay)	Compensatory and punitive damages (if discrimination was intentional or employer failed to show good faith efforts to accommodate)

plaintiff must prove that there was a discriminatory motive—that is, that the employer *intended* to discriminate.

Whenever individuals are treated differently because of their race, sex, and so on, there is disparate treatment. For example, if a company fails to hire women with school-age children (assuming the women will be frequently absent) but hires men with school-age children, the applicants are being treated differently based on sex. Another example would be an employer who checks the references and investigates the conviction records of minority applicants but does not do so for white applicants. Why are managers advised not to ask about marital status? Because in most cases, a manager will either ask only the female applicants or, if the manager asks both males and females, he or she will make different assumptions about females (e.g., "She will have to move if her husband gets a job elsewhere") and males (e.g., "He's very stable"). In all these examples, notice that (1) people are being treated differently and (2) there is an actual intent to treat them differently.[16]

To understand how disparate treatment is applied in the law, let's look at how an actual court case, filed under disparate treatment, would proceed.

THE PLAINTIFF'S BURDEN. As in any legal case, the plaintiff has the burden of proving that the defendant has committed an illegal act. This is the idea of a "prima facie" case. In a disparate treatment case, the plaintiff meets the prima facie burden by showing four things:

1. The plaintiff belongs to a protected group.
2. The plaintiff applied for and was qualified for the job.

3. Despite possessing the qualifications, the plaintiff was rejected.
4. After the plaintiff was rejected, the position remained open and the employer continued to seek applicants with similar qualifications, or the position was filled by someone with similar qualifications.

Although these four things may seem easy to prove, it is important to note that what the court is trying to do is rule out the most obvious reasons for rejecting the plaintiff's claim (i.e., the plaintiff did not apply or was not qualified, or the position was already filled or had been eliminated). If these alternative explanations are ruled out, the court assumes that the hiring decision was based on a discriminatory motive.

THE DEFENDANT'S REBUTTAL. Once the plaintiff has made the prima facie case for discrimination, the burden shifts to the defendant. The burden is different depending upon whether the prima facie case presents only circumstantial evidence (i.e., there is no direct evidence of discrimination such as a formal policy to discriminate, but rather discriminatory intent must be inferred) or direct evidence (i.e., a formal policy of discrimination for some perceived legitimate reason). In cases of circumstantial evidence, the defendant simply must produce a legitimate, nondiscriminatory reason, such as that, although the plaintiff was qualified, the individual hired was more qualified.

However, in cases where direct evidence exists, such as a formal policy of only hiring women for waitress jobs because the business is aimed at catering to male customers (see the Hooters example in the "Competing by Meeting Stakeholders' Needs" box), then the defendant is more likely to offer a different defense. This defense argues that for this job, a factor such as race, sex, or religion was a **bona fide occupational qualification (BFOQ).** For example, if one were hiring an individual to hand out towels in a women's locker room, being a woman might be a BFOQ. However, there are very few cases in which race or sex qualify as a BFOQ, and in these cases it must be a necessary, rather than simply a preferred, characteristic of the job.

UAW v. Johnson Controls, Inc., illustrates the difficulty in using a BFOQ as a defense.[17] Johnson Controls, a manufacturer of car batteries, had instituted a "fetal protection" policy that excluded women of childbearing age from a number of jobs in which they would be exposed to lead, which can cause birth defects in children. The company argued that sex was a BFOQ essential to maintaining a safe workplace. The Supreme Court did not uphold the company's policy, arguing that BFOQs are limited to policies that are directly related to a worker's ability to do the job.

THE PLAINTIFF'S REBUTTAL. If the defendant provides a legitimate, nondiscriminatory reason for its employment decision, the burden shifts back to the plaintiff. The plaintiff must now show that the reason offered by the defendant was not in fact the reason for its decision but merely a "pretext" or excuse for its actual discriminatory decision. This could entail providing evidence that white applicants with very similar qualifications to the plaintiff have often been hired while black applicants with very similar qualifications were all rejected. To illustrate disparate treatment, let's look at the first major case dealing with disparate treatment, *McDonnell Douglas Corp. v. Green*.

McDonnell Douglas Corp. v. Green. This Supreme Court case was the first to delineate the four criteria for a prima facie case of discrimination. From 1956 to 1964, Green had been an employee at McDonnell Douglas, a manufacturing plant in St. Louis, Missouri, that employed about 30,000 people. In 1964, he was laid off during a general work force reduction. While unemployed, he participated in some activities that the company undoubtedly frowned upon: a "lock-in," where he and others placed a chain and padlock on the front door of a building to prevent the employees from leaving; and a

Between a Rock and a Hard Place at Hooters

The Equal Employment Opportunity Commission came after Hooters, the $300-million-a-year restaurant chain known for its scantily clad waitresses. But Hooters fought back.

The EEOC charged that Hooters illegally discriminates against men in hiring for its waitress jobs. It brought the action not because of any male complaints filed with the agency but rather because of an October 22, 1991, charge brought by EEOC Commissioner Ricky Silberman. The EEOC regulations allow for any commissioner to bring a charge, and then the agency seeks out supporting evidence for the charge. In fact, there is evidence that the charge was leveled not because of a concern to protect men from discrimination but in an effort to break up the chain for other reasons. According to one former high-ranking EEOC official, "The women attorneys [at the EEOC] are hot to do this case because they want to bust up a sexist restaurant chain."

The agency demanded that Hooters hire male waiters, provide sensitivity training to employees, establish a scholarship fund to enhance job opportunities for men, and set up a $22 million fund to compensate male victims of sex discrimination. The $22 million figure is arrived at by assuming that half of all waitpersons at Hooters should have been men. The EEOC also demanded that Hooters place quarter-page advertisements in a number of city newspapers inviting any male who applied for employment at Hooters since 1983 to file a claim.

Hooters not only rejected the settlement offer but also set out on a public relations blitz aimed at disparaging the EEOC. It has spent between $750,000 and $1 million on full-page advertisements in two national newspapers featuring a hairy man in a blond wig, tank top, and shorts asking, "What's wrong with this picture?" The company defends its hiring of only women for waitress positions as a bona fide occupational qualification. Hooters lawyer Patricia Casey wrote to the EEOC, stating, "The business of Hooters is predominantly the provision of entertainment, diversion, and amusement based on the sex appeal of the Hooters girls." The waitresses wear uniforms of short shorts and tight T-shirts or tank tops designed to tempt and titillate. In addition, Casey wrote, "The girls are expected to enhance the titillation by their interaction with customers. They are to flirt, cajole, and tease the patrons." Hooters employee Meghan O'Malley-Bernard observed at a rally in support of Hooters, "I could lose my job, and 10,000 other Hooters girls could lose their jobs."

SOURCE: D. Kunde, "Hooters Faces Sex Bias Charges," *Dallas Morning News*, November 16, 1995, pp. 1–2D; J. Bovard, "The EEOC's War on Hooters," *The Wall Street Journal*, November 17, 1995, p. A14. For more information on Hooters, see the Hooters home page on the World Wide Web at http://www.hooters.com.

"stall-in," where a group of employees stalled their cars at the gates of the plant so that no one could enter or leave the parking lot. About three weeks after the lock-in, McDonnell Douglas advertised for qualified mechanics, Green's trade, and he reapplied. When the company rejected his application, he sued, arguing that the company didn't hire him because of his race and because of his persistent involvement in the civil rights movement.

In making his prima facie case, Green had no problem showing that he was a member of a protected group, that he had applied for and was qualified for the job (having already worked in the job), that he was rejected, and that the company continued to advertise the position. The company's defense was that the plaintiff was not hired because he participated in the lock-in and the stall-in. In other words, the company was merely refusing to hire a troublemaker.

The plaintiff responded that the company's stated reason for not hiring him was a pretext for discrimination. He pointed out that white employees who had participated in the same activities (the lock-in and stall-in) were rehired, whereas he was not. The court found in favor of the plaintiff.

This case illustrates how similarly situated individuals (white and black) can be treated differently (whites were hired back while blacks were not) and the differences in treatment can be based on race. As we discuss later, most plaintiffs bring cases of sexual harassment under this theory of discrimination, sexual harassment being a situation where individuals are treated differently because of their sex.

MIXED-MOTIVE CASES. In a mixed-motive case, the defendant acknowledges that some discriminatory motive existed but argues that the same hiring decision would have been reached even without the discriminatory motive. In *Hopkins v. Price Waterhouse*, Elizabeth Hopkins was an accountant who had applied for partnership in her firm. Although she had brought in a large amount of business and had received high praise from her clients, she was turned down for a partnership on two separate occasions. In her performance reviews, she had been told to adopt more feminine dress and speech and received many other comments that suggested gender-based stereotypes. In court, the company admitted that a sex-based stereotype existed but argued that it would have come to the same decision (i.e., not promoted Hopkins) even if the stereotype had not existed.

One of the main questions that came out of this case was, Who has the burden of proof? Does the plaintiff have to prove that a different decision would have been made (i.e., that Hopkins would have been promoted) in the absence of the discriminatory motive? Or does the defendant have to prove that the same decision would have been made?

According to CRA 1991, if the plaintiff demonstrates that race, sex, color, religion, or national origin was a motivating factor for any employment practice, the prima facie burden has been met, and the burden of proof is on the employer to demonstrate that the same decision would have been made even if the discriminatory motive had not been present. If the employer can do this, the plaintiff cannot collect compensatory or punitive damages. However, the court may order the employer to quit using the discriminatory motive in its future employment decisions.

DISPARATE IMPACT

The second type of discrimination is called **disparate impact.** It occurs when a facially neutral employment practice disproportionately excludes a protected group from employment opportunities. A facially neutral employment practice is one that lacks obvious discriminatory content yet affects one group to a greater extent than other groups, such as an employment test. Although the Supreme Court inferred disparate impact from Title VII in the *Griggs v. Duke Power* case, it has since been codified into the Civil Rights Act of 1991.

There is an important distinction between disparate impact and disparate treatment discrimination. For there to be discrimination under disparate treatment, there has to be intentional discrimination. Under disparate impact, intent is irrelevant. The important criterion is that the consequences of the employment practice are discriminatory.

For example, if, for some practical reason, you hired individuals based on their height, you may not have intended to discriminate against anyone, and yet using height would have a disproportionate impact on certain protected groups. Women tend to be shorter than men, so fewer women will be hired. Certain ethnic groups, such as those of Asian ancestry, also tend to be shorter than those of European ancestry. Thus, your facially neutral employment practice will have a disparate impact on certain protected groups.

This is not to imply that simply because a selection practice has disparate impact, it is necessarily illegal. Some characteristics (such as height) are not equally distributed across race and gender groups, and in some jobs, these characteristics may be related to successful performance in the job. However, the important question is whether the characteristic is related to successful performance on the job. To help you understand how disparate impact works, let's look at a court proceeding involving a disparate impact claim.

THE PLAINTIFF'S BURDEN. In a disparate impact case, the plaintiff must make the prima facie case by showing that the employment practice in question disproportionately affects a protected group relative to the majority group. To illustrate this theory, let's assume that you are a manager who has 60 positions to fill. Your applicant pool has 80 white and 40 black applicants. You use a test that selects 48 of the white and 12 of the black applicants. Is this a disparate impact? Two alternative quantitative analyses are often used to determine whether a test has adverse impact.

The **four-fifth's rule** states that a test has disparate impact if the hiring rate for the minority group is less than four–fifths (or 80 percent) of the hiring rate for the majority group. Applying this analysis to the preceding example, we would first calculate the hiring rates for each group:

$$\text{Whites} = 48/80 = 60\%$$

$$\text{Blacks} = 12/40 = 30\%$$

Then we would compare the hiring rate of the minority group (30%) with that of the majority group (60%). Using the four-fifths rule, we would determine that the test has adverse impact if the hiring rate of the minority group is less than 80% of the hiring rate of the majority group. **Because it is less (i.e., 30%/60% = 50%, which is less than 80%),** we would conclude that the test has adverse impact. The four-fifths rule is used as a rule of thumb by the EEOC in determining adverse impact.

The **standard deviation rule** uses actual probability distributions to determine adverse impact. This analysis uses the difference between the expected representation (or hiring rates) for minority groups and the actual representation (or hiring rate) to determine whether the difference between these two values is greater than would occur by chance. Thus, in our example, 33% (40 of 120) of the applicants were blacks, so one would expect 33% (20 of 60) of those hired to be black. However, only 12 black applicants were hired. To determine if the difference between the expected representation and the actual representation is greater than we would expect by chance, we calculate the standard deviation (which, you might remember from your statistics class, is the standard deviation in a binomial distribution):

$$\sqrt{\text{Number hired} \times \frac{\text{Number of minority applicants}}{\text{Number of total applicants}} \times \frac{\text{Number of nonminority applicants}}{\text{Number of total applicants}}}$$

or, in this case:

$$\sqrt{60 \times \frac{40}{120} \times \frac{80}{120}} = 3.6$$

If the difference between the actual representation and the expected representation (20 – 12 = 8 in this case) of blacks is greater than 2 standard deviations (2 × 3.6, = 7.2 in this case), we would conclude that the test had adverse impact against blacks, because we would expect this result less than 1 time in 20 if the test were equally difficult for both whites and blacks.

The *Wards Cove Packing Co. v. Atonio* case involved an interesting use of statistics. The plaintiffs showed that the jobs in the cannery (lower-paying jobs) were filled primarily with minority applicants (in this case, American Eskimos). However, only a small percentage of the noncannery jobs (those with higher pay) were filled by nonminorities. The plaintiffs argued that this statistical disparity in the racial makeup of the cannery and noncannery jobs was proof of discrimination. The federal district, appellate, and Supreme Courts all found for the defendant, stating that this disparity was not proof of discrimination.

Once the plaintiff has demonstrated adverse impact, he or she has met the burden of a prima facie case of discrimination.[18]

DEFENDANT'S REBUTTAL. According to CRA 1991, once the plaintiff has made a prima facie case, the burden of proof shifts to the defendant, who must show that the employment practice is a "business necessity." This is accomplished by showing that the practice bears a relationship with some legitimate employer goal. With respect to job selection, this relationship is demonstrated by showing the job relatedness of the test, usually by reporting a validity study of some type, to be discussed in Chapter 11. For now, suffice it to say that the employer shows that the test scores are significantly correlated with measures of job performance.

Measures of job performance used in validation studies can include such things as objective measures of output, supervisor ratings of job performance, and success in training.[19] Normally, performance-appraisal ratings are used, but these ratings must be valid for the court to accept the validation results. For example, in *Albermarle Paper v. Moody*, the employer demonstrated that the selection battery predicted performance (measured with supervisors' overall rankings of employees) in only some of the 13 occupational groups in which it was used. In this case, the court was especially critical of the supervisory ratings used as the measure of job performance. The court stated, "There is no way of knowing precisely what criteria of job performance the supervisors were considering."[20]

PLAINTIFF'S REBUTTAL. If the employer shows that the employment practice is the result of some business necessity, the plaintiff's last resort is to argue that there are other employment practices that could sufficiently meet the employer's goal, practices that would not have adverse impact. Thus, if a plaintiff can demonstrate that selection tests other than the one used by the employer exist, that they do not have adverse impact, and that they correlate with job performance as highly as the employer's test, then the defendant can be found guilty of discrimination. Many cases deal with standardized tests of cognitive ability, so it is important to examine alternatives to these tests that have less adverse impact while still meeting the employer's goal. At least two separate studies reviewing alternative selection devices such as interviews, biographical data, assessment centers, and work sample tests have concluded that none of them met both criteria.[21] Thus, it seems that when the employment practice in question is a standardized test of cognitive ability, plaintiffs will have a difficult time rebutting the defendant's rebuttal.

Griggs v. Duke Power. To illustrate how this process works, let's look at the *Griggs v. Duke Power* case.[22] Following the passage of Title VII, Duke Power instituted a new system for making selection and promotion decisions. The system required either a high school diploma or a passing score on two professionally developed tests (the Wonderlic Personnel Test and the Bennett Mechanical Comprehension Test). A passing score was set so that it would be equal to the national median for high school graduates who had taken the tests.

The plaintiffs met their prima facie burden showing that both the high school diploma requirement and the test battery had adverse impacts on blacks. According to the 1960 census, 34 percent of white males had high school diplomas, compared with only 12 percent of black males. Similarly, 58 percent of white males passed the test battery, whereas only 6 percent of blacks passed.

Duke Power was unable to defend its use of these employment practices. A company vice president testified that the company had not studied the relationship between these employment practices and the employees' ability to perform the job. In addition, employees already on the job who did not have high school diplomas and had never taken the tests were performing satisfactorily. Thus, Duke Power lost the case.

It is interesting to note that the court recognized that the company had not intended to discriminate, mentioning that the company was making special efforts to help undereducated employees through financing two-thirds of the cost of tuition for high school training. This illustrates the importance of the *consequences*, as opposed to the *motivation*, in determining discrimination under the disparate impact theory.

REASONABLE ACCOMMODATION

Reasonable accommodation presents a relatively new theory of discrimination. It began with regard to religious discrimination, but has recently been both expanded and popularized with the passage of the ADA. Reasonable accommodation differs from these two theories in that rather than simply requiring an employer to refrain from some action, reasonable accommodation places a special obligation on an employer to affirmatively *do* something to accommodate an individual's disability or religion. This theory is violated when an employer fails to make reasonable accommodation, where that is required, to a qualified person with a disability or to a person's religious observation and/or practices.

RELIGION AND ACCOMMODATION. Often individuals with strong religious beliefs find that some observations and practices of their religion come into direct conflict with their work duties. For example, some religions forbid individuals from working on the sabbath day when the employer schedules them for work. Others might have beliefs that preclude them from shaving, which might conflict with a company's dress code. Although Title VII forbids discrimination on the basis of religion just like race or sex, religion also receives special treatment requiring employers to exercise an affirmative duty to accommodate individuals' religious beliefs and practices. As Figure 3.2 shows, the number of religious discrimination charges has consistently increased over the past few years, jumping significantly in 1997.

In cases of religious discrimination, an employee's burden is to demonstrate that he

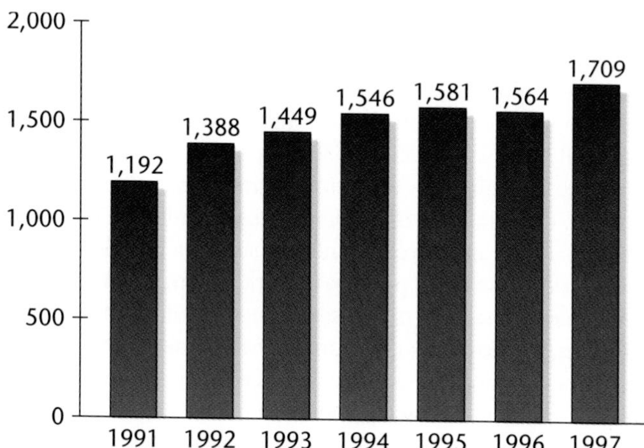

SOURCE: EEOC.

FIGURE 3.2 Religious Discrimination Complaints, 1991–1997

has a legitimate religious belief, that he provided the employer with notice of the need to accommodate his religious practice, and that adverse consequences occurred due to the employer's failure to accommodate. In such cases, the employer's major defense is to assert that to accommodate the employee would require an undue hardship.

Examples of reasonably accommodating a person's religious obligations might include redesigning work schedules (most often accommodating those who cannot work on their sabbath), providing alternate testing dates for applicants, not requiring union membership and/or payment of "charitable contributions" in lieu of union dues, or altering certain dress or grooming requirements. Note that while an employer is required to make a reasonable accommodation, it need not be the one that is offered by the employee.[23]

In one recent case, Wal-Mart agreed to settle with a former employee who alleged that he was forced to quit in 1993 after refusing to work on Sunday. Wal-Mart has agreed to pay the former employee unspecified damages, to instruct managers on employee's rights to have their religious beliefs accommodated, and to prepare a computer-based manual describing employees' rights and religious harassment.[24]

DISABILITY AND ACCOMMODATION. As previously discussed, ADA made discrimination against individuals with disabilities illegal. However, the act itself states that the employer is obligated not just to refrain from discriminating, but to take affirmative steps to accommodate individuals who are protected under the act.

Under disability claims, the plaintiff must show that she is a qualified applicant with a disability and that adverse action was taken by a covered entity. The employer's defense then depends upon whether the decision was made without regard to the disability or in light of the disability. For example, if the employer argues that the plaintiff is not qualified, then it has met the burden, and the question of reasonable accommodation becomes irrelevant.

If, however, the decision was made "in light of" the disability, then the question becomes one of whether the person could perform adequately with a reasonable accommodation. This leads to three potential defenses. First, the employer could allege job-relatedness or business necessity through demonstrating, for example, that it is using a test that assesses ability to perform essential job functions. However, then the question arises as to whether the applicant could perform the essential job functions with a reasonable accommodation. Second, the employer could claim an "undue hardship" to accommodate the individual. In essence, this argues that the accommodation necessary is an action requiring significant difficulty or expense. Finally, the employer could argue that the individual with the disability might pose a direct threat to his own or others' health or safety in the workplace. This requires examining the duration of the risk, the nature and severity of potential harm, the probability of the harm occurring, and the imminence of the potential harm.

What are some examples of reasonable accommodation with regard to disabilities? First is providing readily accessible facilities such as ramps and/or elevators for disabled individuals to enter the workplace. Second, job restructuring might include eliminating marginal tasks, shifting these tasks to other employees, redesigning job procedures, or altering work schedules. Third, an employer might reassign a disabled employee to a job with essential job functions she could perform. Fourth, an employer might accommodate applicants for employment who must take tests through providing alternative testing formats, providing readers, or providing additional time for taking the test. Fifth, readers, interpreters, or technology to offer reading assistance might be given to a disabled employee. Sixth, an employer could allow an employee to provide his own accommodation such as bringing a guide dog to work.[25] Note that most accommodations are inexpensive. A study by Sears Roebuck & Co. found that 69 percent of all accommodations cost

Abilitech Enables Disabled through Technology

As a social service agency, Abilitech, of Aston, PA, has for years trained people with disabilities for jobs in the computer field. Hoping to prepare disabled employees for challenging, high-paying jobs, Abilitech uses "adaptive technology" and extensive training in computer work. For example, for cerebral palsy victims with shaky hands, the agency places a shield on the computer's keyboard. The operator must place a finger through the appropriate hole in the shield in order to strike a key. This helps the operator avoid the frustration of hitting the wrong key or two keys at once. A special compact keyboard allows someone with muscular dystrophy to hit every key without ever moving her arms. A client with no arms learned how to operate the keyboard with his toes. Quadriplegic clients can work by talking to a computer that responds to their voice. Blind clients, such as Ellsworth Pierce, can work at a terminal with a mechanical voice that reads the screen to them. He says, "This has changed my life. Before I came here, the doors were closed."

Recently the company developed a profit-making division that sells commercial clients computer services such as systems analysis and computer programming. Seventy-five percent of the division's employees are disabled individuals who have taken the computer training offered by Abilitech and sometimes have overcome their particular physical limitations by using specially adapted computer equipment. Typically the employees earn between $20,000 and $40,000 per year, far more than most disabled people working as part of social welfare projects. The commercial division both brings jobs to disabled people and brings a commercial mentality to the agency. "The marketplace helps us keep our edge," says John F. Connolly Jr., Abilitech's president and chief executive.

COMPETING THROUGH HIGH-PERFORMANCE WORK SYSTEMS

While this commercial venture obviously benefits the disabled employees, how do the customers feel? "You can't beat the quality and the price, and they meet deadlines," says John Hirt, an information services manager at Elf AtoChem North America, Inc. "I like working with them because they are helping the disadvantaged," says Charles Schwab, sales and marketing vice president of MDC Industries Inc. "But if we just wanted to do good, we would make a donation."

SOURCE: R. Ricklefs, "Computer Trainer of Disabled Expands Its Commercial Reach," *The Wall Street Journal*, interactive edition, September 2, 1997.

nothing, 29 percent cost less than $1,000, and only 3 percent cost more than $1,000.[26] In addition, the "Competing through High-Performance Work Systems" box illustrates how accommodating disabled individuals can actually provide competitive advantage.

Retaliation for Participation and Opposition

Suppose that you overhear a supervisor in your workplace telling someone that he refuses to hire women because he knows they are just not cut out for the job. Believing this to be illegal discrimination, you face a dilemma. Should you come forward and report this statement? Or, if someone else files a lawsuit for gender discrimination, should you testify on behalf of the plaintiff? What happens if your employer threatens to fire you if you do anything?

Title VII of the Civil Rights Act of 1964 provides you with some protection. It states that employers cannot retaliate against employees for either "opposing" a perceived illegal employment practice or "participating in a proceeding" related to an alleged illegal employment practice. *Opposition* refers to expressing to someone through proper channels that you believe that an illegal employment act has taken place or is taking place. *Participation* refers to actually testifying in an investigation, hearing, or court proceeding regarding an illegal employment act. Clearly, the purpose of this provision is to protect employees from employers' threats and other forms of intimidation aimed at discouraging the employees from bringing to light acts they believe to be illegal.

These cases can be extremely costly for companies because they are alleging acts of intentional discrimination, and therefore plaintiffs are entitled to punitive damages. For example, a 41-year-old former Allstate employee who claimed that a company official told her that the company wanted a "younger and cuter" image recently was awarded $2.8 million in damages by an Oregon jury. The jury concluded that the employee was forced out of the company for opposing age discrimination against other employees.[27]

This does not mean that employees have an unlimited right to talk about how racist or sexist their employers are. The courts tend to frown on employees whose activities result in a poor public image for the company unless those employees had attempted to use the organization's internal channels—approaching one's manager, raising the issue with the HR department, and so on—before going public.

Current Issues Regarding Diversity and Equal Employment Opportunity

Because of recent changes in the labor market, most organizations' demographic compositions are becoming increasingly diverse. A study by the Hudson Institute projected that 85 percent of the new entrants into the U.S. labor force over the next decade will be females and minorities.[28] Integrating these groups into organizations made up predominantly of able-bodied white males will bring attention to important issues like sexual harassment, affirmative action, and the "reasonable accommodation" of employees with disabilities.

SEXUAL HARASSMENT

Clarence Thomas's Supreme Court confirmation hearings in 1991 brought the issue of sexual harassment into increased prominence. Anita Hill, one of Thomas's former employees, alleged that he had sexually harassed her while she was working under his supervision at the Department of Education and the Equal Employment Opportunity Commission. Although the allegations were never substantiated, the hearing made many people more aware of how often employees are sexually harassed in the workplace and, combined with other events, resulted in a tremendous increase in the number of sexual harassment complaints being filed with the EEOC, as we see in Figure 3.3. In ad-

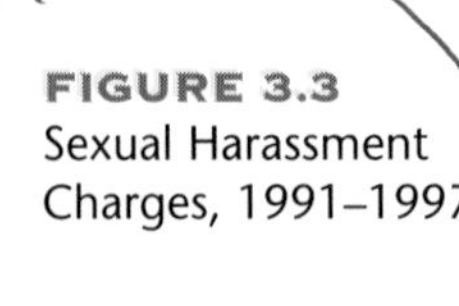

FIGURE 3.3
Sexual Harassment Charges, 1991–1997

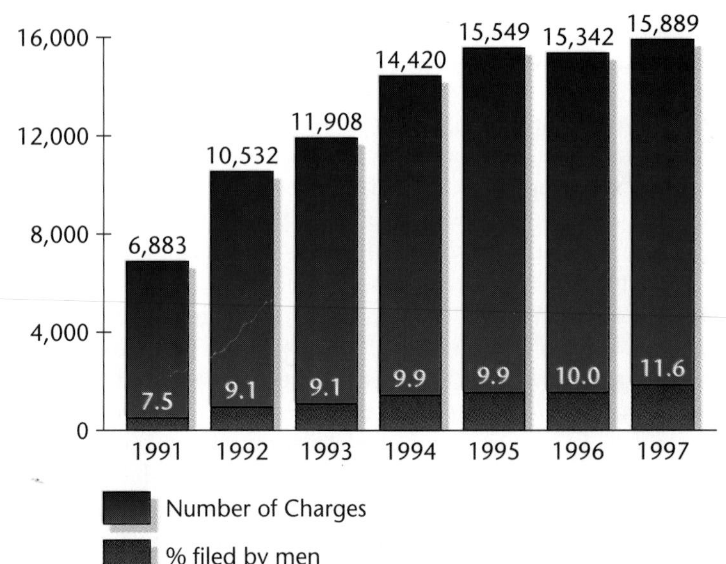

TABLE 3.4
EEOC Definition of Sexual Harassment

Unwelcome sexual advances, requests for sexual favors, and other verbal or physical contact of a sexual nature constitute sexual harassment when

1. Submission to such conduct is made either explicitly or implicitly a term of condition of an individual's employment,
2. Submission to or rejection of such conduct by an individual is used as the basis for employment decisions affecting such individual, or
3. Such conduct has the purpose or effect of unreasonably interfering with an individual's work performance or creating an intimidating, hostile, or offensive working environment.

SOURCE: EEOC guideline based on the Civil Rights Act of 1964, Title VII.

dition, after President Clinton took office and was faced with a sexual harassment lawsuit by Paula Corbin Jones for his alleged proposition to her in a Little Rock hotel room, the number of sexual harassment complaints took another jump from 1993 to 1994—again, potentially due to the tremendous amount of publicity regarding sexual harassment. Given all the publicity about President Clinton's affair with intern Monica Lewinsky and subsequent lying about it under oath in his deposition for the Paula Jones case and possibly before a grand jury (resulting in his impeachment), as well as his alleged groping of White House volunteer Kathleen Willey, we might expect to see another jump in the number of sexual harassment complaints from 1997 to 1998 and beyond.

Sexual harassment refers to unwelcome sexual advances. (See Table 3.4.) It can take place in two basic ways. "Quid pro quo" harassment occurs when some kind of benefit (or punishment) is made contingent upon the employee's submitting (or not submitting) to sexual advances. For example, a male manager tells his female secretary that if she submits to sex with him, he will help her get promoted, or he threatens to fire her if she fails to do so; these are clearly cases of quid pro quo sexual harassment.

The *Bundy v. Jackson* case illustrates quid pro quo sexual harassment.[29] Sandra Bundy was a personnel clerk with the District of Columbia Department of Corrections. She received repeated sexual propositions from Delbert Jackson, who was at the time a fellow employee (although he later became the director of the agency). She later began to receive propositions from two of her supervisors: Arthur Burton and James Gainey. When she raised the issue to their supervisor, Lawrence Swain, he dismissed her complaints, told her that "any man in his right mind would want to rape you," and asked her to begin a sexual relationship with him. When Bundy became eligible for a promotion, she was passed over because of her "inadequate work performance," although she had never been told that her work performance was unsatisfactory. The U.S. Court of Appeals found that Bundy had been discriminated against because of her sex, thereby extending the idea of discrimination to sexual harassment.

A more subtle, and possibly more pervasive, form of sexual harassment is "hostile working environment." This occurs when someone's behavior in the workplace creates an environment that makes it difficult for someone of a particular sex to work. Many plaintiffs in sexual harassment lawsuits have alleged that men ran their fingers through the plaintiffs' hair, made suggestive remarks, and physically assaulted them by touching their intimate body parts. Other examples include having pictures of naked women posted in the workplace, using offensive sexually explicit language, or using sex-related jokes or innuendoes in conversations.[30]

Note that these types of behaviors are actionable under Title VII because they treat individuals differently based on their sex. In addition, although most harassment cases involve male-on-female harassment, any individual can be harassed. For example, male employees at Jenny Craig recently alleged that they were sexually harassed, and a federal jury recently found that a male employee had been sexually harassed by his male boss.[31]

Inland Steel Faces Affirmative Action

The idea of affirmative action is easy to understand: to increase minority representation in the work force, hopefully at all levels of employment. (A company that achieves successful integration of minorities at all levels should also be more competitive than one that does not, because it draws from a larger labor pool.) The reality, however, is as complex as human relations itself.

Take, for example, Inland Steel Industries, Inc. (a large manufacturing corporation located in the Midwest), whose jobs—until recently—were held mostly by white men. Antidiscrimination laws, a changing population, and affirmative action—all facts of an employer's life—have changed the face of Inland Steel. Social responsibility lies in helping employees adjust to the diverse workplace, so that everyone views diversity as a positive thing. This is not an easy task when people believe their paychecks and career opportunities are at stake. But Inland Steel has been trying to face such a challenge.

A major problem in trying to apply affirmative action is that there is no textbook for doing so. Organizations must develop their own methods by trial and error. Also, people's perceptions of affirmative action—

what it is and how it will affect them—differ. For instance, one person might view affirmative action as applicable to all minorities as well as women. Another might view it as appropriate only to certain groups. Franklin Turner, a black male and a buyer for an Inland Steel subsidiary, claims, "Broadening the definition of *minority* has diluted it. It confuses the issue." He says that the promotion policy at his company places women (both white and black) ahead of black men. Instead of being a beneficiary of affirmative action, he sees himself as a victim.

Minorities, women, and white males get caught in a standoff. Consider these three different views by employees of the same company. Nathaniel Lott, a black male and a district sales rep for the same subsidiary, says, "Minorities are required to prove themselves to an extent not required of nonminorities." Paula Dent, a day-shift supervisor who is a black female, observes, "What I'm doing is not strictly on my own ability but is also filling a need of the company. . . . I felt I was qualified, but that doesn't always open doors. Sometimes the powers that be don't see the qualifications." Pat Goeringer, a second-shift supervisor who doesn't feel that affirmative action has neces-

There are three critical issues in these cases. First, the plaintiff cannot have "invited or incited" the advances. Often, the plaintiff's sexual history, whether she or he wears provocative clothing, and whether she or he engages in sexually explicit conversations are used to prove or disprove that the advance was unwelcome. However, in the absence of substantial evidence that the plaintiff invited the behavior, courts usually lean toward assuming that sexual advances do not belong in the workplace and thus are unwelcome. In *Meritor Savings Bank v. Vinson*, Michelle Vinson claimed that during the four years she worked at a bank she was continually harassed by the bank's vice president, who repeatedly asked her to have sex with him (she eventually agreed) and sexually assaulted her.[32] The Supreme Court ruled that the victim's voluntary participation in sexual relations was not the major issue, saying that the focus of the case was on whether the vice president's advances were unwelcome.

A second critical issue is that the harassment must have been severe enough to alter the terms, conditions, and privileges of employment. Although it has not yet been consistently applied, many courts have used the "reasonable woman" standard in determining the severity or pervasiveness of the harassment. This consists of assessing whether a reasonable woman, faced with the same situation, would have reacted similarly. The reasonable woman standard recognizes that behavior that might be considered appropriate by a man (e.g., off-color jokes) might not be considered appropriate by a woman.

The third issue is that the courts must determine whether the organization is liable for the actions of its employees. In doing so, the court usually examines two things.

sarily benefited her, comments, "I think white males have a right to complain about reverse discrimination, because they might get passed up. I think it's wrong to blame white males for everything that's gone wrong. . . . It's not fair."

Inland Steel started its affirmative action program after four black workers approached general manager Steve Bowsher, saying that they were tired of racist jokes and behavior by others on the job and that they felt they had been passed over for opportunities to advance. "I didn't have a clue," recalls Bowsher. "Hey, I'm a tall white person. The world was set up for me." But Bowsher listened and took action. He arranged classes for employees to discuss race and sex discrimination. He evaluated the pay that minority and female workers were receiving to make sure it was equal to that of white male workers. He banned racist and sexist jokes, pinup calendars on office walls, and company-paid country club memberships at clubs that practiced racial discrimination. Those who did not comply were fired. What were his reasons? "I've got to be the one to fix it because I have the power," he explains. Bowsher also actively recruits minorities for employment at Inland.

Fostering cooperation rather than suspicion among workers can only have a healthy effect on business. A company that has a unified (not homogenous) work force will be much more productive—and profitable—than one that is constantly dealing with the hostility of splinter groups. Inland Steel has created its own "textbook" rules for accomplishing this. First, support for affirmative action must come from top management. Second, affirmative action programs must be monitored, and managers must be made accountable for what happens. Third, a company must reach out to women and minorities if it wants to hire them. Just as important, it must provide training and guidance in their careers. Fourth, people must respect each other on the job, understanding their similarities and differences.

"[Affirmative action] is an ongoing journey because there are so many pieces," says Vivian Cosey, head of human resources at Inland's Ryerson Coil Processing plant. "It's not like learning an algebraic equation or even a foreign language." But it is a vital step toward gaining a competitive advantage.

SOURCE: Tim Jones, Janita Poe, and Stephen Franklin, "Progress and Problems of a Workplace Remedy," *Chicago Tribune*, September 3, 1995, pp. 1, 12; Janita Poe, Stephen Franklin, and Tim Jones, "True Equity Proves Elusive," *Chicago Tribune*, September 4, 1995, pp. 1, 6; Stephen Franklin, Tim Jones, and Janita Poe, "A Commitment to Action," *Chicago Tribune*, September 5, 1995, pp. 1, 8.

First, did the employer know about, or should he or she have known about, the harassment? Second, did the employer act to stop the behavior? If the employer knew about it and the behavior did not stop, the court usually decides that the employer did not act appropriately to stop it.

To ensure a workplace free from sexual harassment, there are some important steps that organizations can follow. First, the organization can develop a policy statement that makes it very clear that sexual harassment will not be tolerated in the workplace. Second, all employees, new and old, can be trained to identify inappropriate workplace behavior. Third, the organization can develop a mechanism for reporting sexual harassment that encourages people to speak out. Fourth, management can prepare to take prompt disciplinary action with those who commit sexual harassment as well as appropriate action to protect the victims of sexual harassment.[33]

AFFIRMATIVE ACTION AND REVERSE DISCRIMINATION

Few would argue that having a diverse work force in terms of race and gender is a desirable goal, if all individuals have the necessary qualifications. In fact, many organizations today are concerned with developing and managing diversity. (See the "Competing by Meeting Stakeholders' Needs" box.) To eliminate discrimination in the workplace, many organizations have affirmative action programs to increase minority representation. Affirmative action was originally conceived as a way of taking extra effort to attract and retain minority employees. This was normally done by extensively recruiting minorities on college campuses, advertising in minority-oriented publications, and providing educational and training opportunities to minorities.[34] However, over the years, many organizations have resorted to quotalike hiring to ensure that their work force composition mirrors that of the labor market. Sometimes these organizations act voluntarily; in other cases, the quotas are imposed by the courts or by the EEOC. Whatever the impetus for these hiring practices, many white and/or male individuals have fought against them, alleging what is called *reverse discrimination*.

An example of an imposed quota program is found at the fire department in Birmingham, Alabama. Having admitted a history of discriminating against blacks, the department entered into a consent decree with the EEOC to hold 50 percent of positions at all levels in the fire department open for minorities even though minorities made up only 28 percent of the relevant labor market. The result was that some white applicants were denied employment or promotion in favor of black applicants who scored lower on a selection battery. The federal court found that the city's use of the inflexible hiring formula violated federal civil rights law and the constitutional guarantee of equal protection. The appellate court agreed, and the Supreme Court refused to hear the case, thus making the decision final.

The entire issue of affirmative action should invoke considerable attention and debate over the next few years. While most individuals support the idea of diversity, few argue for the kinds of quotas that have to some extent resulted from the present legal climate. In fact, one recent survey revealed that only 16 percent of the respondents favored affirmative action with quotas, 46 percent favored it without quotas, and 28 percent opposed all affirmative action programs. One study found that people favor affirmative action when it is operationalized as recruitment, training, and attention to applicant qualifications but oppose it when it consists of discrimination, quotas, and preferential treatment.[35] Affirmative action and quotas constituted an important topic of debate for the 1996 presidential candidates, and there is reason to believe that some changes in the legal systems will be observed over the next few years.

OUTCOMES OF THE AMERICANS WITH DISABILITIES ACT

The ADA was passed with the laudable goals of providing employment opportunities for the truly disabled who, in the absence of legislation, were unable to find employment. Certainly, some individuals with disabilities have found employment as a result of its passage. However, as often occurs with legislation, the impact is not necessarily what was intended. First, there has been increased litigation. The EEOC reports that over 91,000 complaints have been filed since passage of the act. Approximately 50 percent of the complaints filed have been found to be without reasonable cause. For example, in July 1992 GTE Data Services fired an employee for stealing from other employees and bringing a loaded gun to work. The fired employee sued for reinstatement under ADA, claiming that he was the victim of a mental illness and thus should be considered disabled.[36]

A second problem is that the kinds of cases being filed are not what Congress intended to protect. Although the act was passed because of the belief that discrimination against individuals with disabilities occurred in the failure to hire them, 52.2 percent of the claims deal with firings, 28.9 percent with failure to make reasonable accommodation, and 12.5 percent with harassment. Only 9.4 percent of the complaints allege a failure to hire or rehire.[37] In addition, although the act was passed to protect people with major disabilities such as blindness, deafness, lost limbs, or paralysis, these

TABLE 3.5 Types of Complaints Filed Under ADA

	1992	1993	1994	1995	1996	1997	TOTAL
Number of complaints	1,048	15,274	18,859	19,798	18,046	18,108	91,133
% dealing with							
Back	20.8%	20.0%	19.4%	17.5%	16.1%	14.9%	17.5%
Emotional/psychiatric	9.1	9.9	12.4	13.2	15.0	15.3	13.2
Neurological	15.6	14.0	10.9	10.1	10.4	9.9	11.0
Extremities	5.3	4.2	9.3	10.8	11.1	10.6	9.3
Heart	4.6	5.2	4.3	3.7	3.5	3.7	4.0
Diabetes	5.2	3.5	3.5	3.5	3.7	3.7	3.6
Substance abuse	3.5	3.8	3.3	3.6	2.8	2.3	3.2
Hearing	4.8	3.2	3.0	2.7	2.6	2.8	2.8
Blood disorders	2.4	2.6	2.5	2.8	2.4	2.8	2.6
Vision	4.8	3.2	2.7	2.3	2.3	2.3	2.6
Cancer	3.0	2.7	2.4	2.1	2.2	2.5	2.4
Asthma	1.8	1.8	1.7	1.7	1.7	1.5	1.7

disabilities combined account for a small minority of the disabilities claimed. As we see in Table 3.5, the biggest disability category is "other," meaning that the plaintiff claims a disability that is not one of the 35 types of impairment listed in the EEOC charge data system. The second largest category is "back impairment," accounting for 17.5 percent of all charges, followed by mental-illness-related claims at 15.3 percent.

Finally, it does not appear that the act has had its anticipated impact on the employment of Americans with disabilities. According to the National Organization on Disability, a private group, only 31 percent of working-age Americans with disabilities were employed as of December 1993, compared with 33 percent in 1986, before the law was passed.

For these reasons, Congress is currently exploring the possibility of amending the act to more narrowly define the term *disability*.[38]

Employee Safety

Like equal employment opportunity, employee safety is regulated by both the federal and state governments. However, to fully maximize the safety and health of workers, employers need to go well beyond the letter of the law and embrace its spirit. With this in mind, we first spell out the specific protections guaranteed by federal legislation and then discuss various kinds of safety awareness programs that attempt to reinforce these standards.

THE OCCUPATIONAL SAFETY AND HEALTH ACT (OSHA)

Although concern for worker safety would seem to be a universal societal goal, the **Occupational Safety and Health Act of 1970 (OSHA)**—the most comprehensive legislation regarding worker safety—did not emerge in this country until the early 1970s. At that time, there were roughly 15,000 work-related fatalities every year.

OSHA authorized the federal government to establish and enforce occupational safety and health standards for all places of employment affecting interstate commerce. The responsibility for inspecting employers, applying the standards, and levying fines was assigned to the Department of Labor. The Department of Health was assigned responsibility for conducting research to determine the criteria for specific operations or occupations and for training employers to comply with the act. Much of this research is conducted by the National Institute for Occupational Safety and Health (NIOSH).

EMPLOYEE RIGHTS UNDER OSHA. The main provision of OSHA states that each employer has a general duty to furnish each employee a place of employment free from recognized hazards that cause or are likely to cause death or serious physical harm. This is referred to as the **general duty clause.** Some specific rights granted to workers under this act are listed in Table 3.6. The Department of Labor recognizes many specific types of hazards, and employers are required to comply with all the occupational safety and health standards published by NIOSH.

A recent example is the development of OSHA standards for occupational exposure to blood-borne pathogens such as the AIDS virus. These standards identify 24 affected industrial sectors, encompassing 500,000 establishments and 5.6 million workers. Among other features, these standards require employers to develop an exposure control plan (ECP). An ECP must include a list of jobs whose incumbents might be exposed to blood, methods for implementing precautions in these jobs, postexposure follow-up plans, and procedures for evaluating incidents in which workers are accidentally infected.

Although NIOSH publishes numerous standards, it is clearly not possible for regulators to anticipate all possible hazards that could occur in the workplace. Thus, the general duty clause requires employers to be constantly alert for potential sources of harm in the workplace (as defined by the standards of a reasonably prudent person) and to correct them. For example, managers at Amoco's Joliet, Illinois, plant realized that over the years some employees had created undocumented shortcuts and built them into their process for handling flammable materials. These changes appeared to be labor saving but created a problem; workers did not have uniform procedures for dealing with flammable products. This became an urgent issue because many of the experienced workers were reaching retirement age, and the plant was in danger of losing critical technical expertise. To solve this problem, the plant adopted a training program that met all the standards required by OSHA. That is, it conducted a needs analysis highlighting each task new employees had to learn and then documented these processes in written guidelines. New employees were given hands-on training with the new procedures and were then certified in writing by their supervisor. A computer tracking system was installed to monitor who was handling flammable materials, and this system immediately identified anyone who was not certified. The plant met requirements for both ISO 9000 standards and OSHA regulations and continues to use the same model for safety training in other areas of the plant.[39]

OSHA INSPECTIONS. OSHA inspections are conducted by specially trained agents of the Department of Labor called **compliance officers.** These inspections usually follow a tight "script." Typically, the compliance officer shows up unannounced. For ob-

TABLE 3.6
Rights Granted to Workers under the Occupational Safety and Health Act

Employees have the right to

1. Request an inspection.
2. Have a representative present at an inspection.
3. Have dangerous substances identified.
4. Be promptly informed about exposure to hazards and be given access to accurate records regarding exposures.
5. Have employer violations posted at the work site.

vious reasons, OSHA's regulations prohibit advance notice of inspections. The officer, after presenting her credentials, informs the employer of the reasons for the inspection and describes, in a general way, the procedures necessary to conduct the investigation.

There are four major components of an OSHA inspection. First, the compliance officer reviews the employer's records of deaths, injuries, and illnesses. OSHA requires this kind of record keeping from all firms with 11 or more full- or part-time employees. Second, the officer, typically accompanied by a representative of the employer (and perhaps by a representative of the employees), conducts a "walkaround" tour of the employer's premises. On this tour, the officer makes a note of any conditions he thinks violate specific published standards or the less specific general duty clause. The third component of the inspection, employee interviews, may take place during the tour. At this time, any person who is aware of a violation can bring it to the attention of the officer. Finally, there is a closing conference. Here, the compliance officer discusses his findings with the employer, noting any violations. The employer is given a reasonable time frame in which to correct these violations. If any violation represents imminent danger (i.e., could cause serious injury or death before being eliminated through the normal enforcement procedures), the officer may, through the Department of Labor, seek a restraining order from a U.S. District Court. Such an order compels the employer to correct the problem immediately.

CITATIONS AND PENALTIES. If a compliance officer believes that a violation has occurred, she issues a citation to the employer that specifies the exact practice or situation that violates the act. The employer is required to post this citation in a prominent place near the location of the violation—even if the employer intends to contest it. Nonserious violations may be assessed up to $1,000 for each incident, but this may be adjusted downward if the employer has no prior history of violations or if the employer has made a good-faith effort to comply with the act. Serious violations of the act or willful, repeated violations may be fined up to $10,000 per incident. Fines for safety violations are never levied against the employees themselves. The assumption is that safety is primarily the responsibility of the employer, who needs to work with employees to ensure that they engage in safe working procedures.

In addition to these civil penalties, criminal penalties may also be assessed for willful violations that result in the death of an employee. Fines can go as high as $20,000, and the employer or agents of the employer can be imprisoned. Criminal charges can also be brought against anyone who falsifies records that are subject to OSHA inspection or anyone who gives advance notice of an OSHA inspection without permission from the Department of Labor.

THE EFFECT OF OSHA. OSHA has been unquestionably successful in raising the level of awareness of occupational safety. Yet, legislation alone cannot solve all the problems of work-site safety. Indeed, the number of occupational illnesses increased fivefold between 1985 and 1990, according to a survey by the Bureau of Labor Statistics.[40] Many industrial accidents are a product of unsafe behaviors, not unsafe working conditions. Since the act does not directly regulate employee behavior, little behavior change can be expected unless employees are convinced of the standards' importance.[41] This has been recognized by labor leaders. For example, Lynn Williams, president of the United Steelworkers of America, has noted, "We can't count on government. We can't count on employers. We must rely on ourselves to bring about the safety and health of our workers."[42]

Since conforming to the statute alone does not necessarily guarantee safety, many employers go beyond the letter of the law. In the next section, we examine various kinds of employer-initiated safety awareness programs that comply with OSHA requirements and, in some cases, exceed them.

SAFETY AWARENESS PROGRAMS

Safety awareness programs go beyond compliance with OSHA and attempt to instill symbolic and substantive changes in the organization's emphasis on safety. These programs typically focus either on specific jobs and job elements or on specific types of injuries or disabilities. There are three primary components to a safety awareness program: identifying and communicating hazards, reinforcing safe practices, and promoting safety internationally.

IDENTIFYING AND COMMUNICATING JOB HAZARDS. Employees, supervisors, and other knowledgeable sources need to sit down and discuss potential problems related to safety. The Job Hazard Analysis Technique is one means of accomplishing this.[43] With this technique, each job is broken down into basic elements, and each of these is rated for its potential for harm or injury. If there is consensus that some job element has high hazard potential, this element is isolated and potential technological or behavioral changes are considered.

Another means of isolating unsafe job elements is to study past accidents. The **Technic of Operations Review (TOR)** is an analysis methodology that helps managers determine which specific element of a job led to a past incident.[44] The first step in a TOR analysis is to establish the facts surrounding the incident. To accomplish this, all members of the work group involved in the accident give their initial impressions of what happened. The group must then, through group discussion, reach a consensus on the single, systematic failure that most contributed to the incident as well as two or three major secondary factors that contributed to it.

An analysis of jobs at Burger King, for example, revealed that certain jobs required employees to walk across wet or slippery surfaces, which led to many falls. Specific corrective action was taken based on analysis of where people were falling and what conditions led to these falls. Now Burger King provides mats at critical locations and has generally upgraded its floor maintenance. The company also makes slip-resistant shoes available to employees in certain job categories.[45]

Communication of an employee's risk should take advantage of several media. Direct verbal supervisory contact is important for its saliency and immediacy. Written memos are important because they help establish a "paper trail" that can later document a history of concern regarding the job hazard. Posters, especially those placed near the hazard, serve as a constant reminder, reinforcing other messages.

In communicating risk, it is important to recognize two distinct audiences. Sometimes there are relatively young or inexperienced workers who need special attention. Research by the National Safety Council indicates that 40 percent of all accidents happen to individuals in the 20-to-29 age group and that 48 percent of all accidents happen to workers during their first year on the job.[46] The employer's primary concern with respect to this group is to inform them. However, the employer must not overlook experienced workers. Here the key concern is to remind them. Research indicates that long-term exposure and familiarity with a specific threat leads to complacency.[47] Experienced employees need retraining to jar them from complacency about the real dangers associated with their work. This is especially the case if the hazard in question poses a greater threat to older employees. For example, "falling off a ladder" is a greater threat to older workers than to younger ones. Over 20 percent of such falls lead to a fatality for workers in the 55 to 65 age group, compared with just 10 percent for all other workers.[48]

REINFORCING SAFE PRACTICES. One common technique for reinforcing safe practices is implementing a safety incentive program. Such a program rewards workers for their support and commitment to safety goals. Initially, programs are set up to focus on improving short-term monthly or quarterly goals or to encourage safety suggestions. These short-term goals are later expanded to include more wide-ranging long-term goals. Prizes are typically distributed in highly public forums (e.g., annual meetings or events). These prizes usually consist of merchandise rather than cash because merchandise represents a lasting symbol of achievement. A good deal of evidence suggests that such programs are effective in reducing injuries and their cost.[49]

Whereas the safety awareness programs just described focus primarily on the job, other programs focus on specific injuries or disabilities. Lower back disability (LBD), for example, is a major problem that afflicts many employees. LBD accounts for approximately 25 percent of all workdays lost, costing firms nearly $30 billion a year.[50] Human resource managers can take many steps to prevent LBD and rehabilitate those who are already afflicted. Eye injuries are another target of safety awareness programs. The National Society to Prevent Blindness estimates that 1,000 eye injuries occur every day in occupational settings.[51] A 10-step program to reduce eye injuries is outlined in Table 3.7. Similar guidelines can be found for everything from chemical burns to electrocution to injuries caused by boiler explosions.[52]

PROMOTING SAFETY INTERNATIONALLY. Given the increasing focus on international management, organizations also need to consider how to best ensure the safety of people regardless of the nation in which they operate. Cultural differences may make this more difficult than it seems. For example, a recent study examined the impact of one standardized corporationwide safety policy on employees in three different countries: the United States, France, and Argentina. The results of this study indicated that the same policy was interpreted differently because of cultural differences.

The individualistic, control-oriented culture of the United States stressed the role of top management in ensuring safety in a top-down fashion. However, this policy failed to work in Argentina, where the collectivist culture made employees feel that safety was everyone's joint concern; therefore, programs needed to be defined from the bottom up.[53]

TABLE 3.7
A 10-Step Program for Reducing Eye-Related Injuries

1. Conduct an eye-hazard job analysis.
2. Test all employees' vision to establish a baseline.
3. Select protective eyewear designed for specific operations.
4. Establish a 100 percent behavioral compliance program for eyewear.
5. Ensure that eyewear is properly fitted.
6. Train employees in emergency procedures.
7. Conduct ongoing education programs regarding eye care.
8. Continually review accident-prevention strategies.
9. Provide management support.
10. Establish written policies detailing sanctions and rewards for specific results.

SOURCE: T.W. Turrif, "NSPB Suggests 10-Step Program to Prevent Eye Injury," *Occupational Health and Safety* 60 (1991), pp. 62–66.

SUMMARY

Viewing employees as a source of competitive advantage results in dealing with them in ways that are ethical and legal as well as providing a safe workplace. An organization's legal environment—particularly the laws regarding equal employment opportunity and safety—has a particularly strong effect on its HRM function. HRM is concerned with the management of people, and government is concerned with protecting individuals. One of HRM's major challenges, therefore, is to perform its function within the legal constraints imposed by the government. Given the multimillion-dollar settlements resulting from violations of EEO laws (and the moral requirement to treat people fairly regardless of their gender or race), as well as the penalties for violating OSHA, HR and line managers need a good understanding of the legal requirements and prohibitions in order to manage their businesses in ways that are sound, both financially and ethically. Organizations that do so effectively will definitely have a competitive advantage.

DISCUSSION QUESTIONS

1. Disparate impact theory was originally created by the court in the Griggs case before finally being codified by Congress 20 years later in the Civil Rights Act of 1991. Given the system of law in the United States, from what branch of government should theories of discrimination develop?
2. Disparate impact analysis (the four-fifths rule, standard deviation analysis) is used in employment discrimination cases. The National Assessment of Education Progress conducted by the U.S. Department of Education found that among 21- to 25-year-olds, (a) 60 percent of whites, 40 percent of Hispanics, and 25 percent of blacks could locate information in a news article or almanac; (b) 25 percent of whites, 7 percent of Hispanics, and 3 percent of blacks could decipher a bus schedule; and (c) 44 percent of whites, 20 percent of Hispanics, and 8 percent of blacks could correctly determine the change they were due from the purchase of a two-item restaurant meal. Do these tasks (locating information in a news article, deciphering a bus schedule, and determining correct change) have adverse impact? What are the implications?
3. Many companies have dress codes that require men to wear suits and women to wear dresses. Is this discriminatory according to disparate treatment theory? Why?
4. Cognitive ability tests seem to be the most valid selection devices available for hiring employees, yet they also have adverse impact against blacks and Hispanics. Given the validity and adverse impact, and considering that race norming is illegal under CRA 1991, what would you say in response to a recommendation that such tests be used for hiring?
5. How might the reasonable accommodation requirement of ADA affect workers such as law enforcement officers and firefighters?
6. The reasonable woman standard recognizes that women have different ideas than men of what constitutes appropriate behavior. What are the implications of this distinction? Do you think it is a good or bad idea to make this distinction?
7. Employers' major complaint about ADA is that the costs of making reasonable accommodations will make them less competitive relative to other businesses (especially foreign ones) that do not face these requirements. Is this a legitimate concern? How should employers and society weigh the costs and benefits of ADA?
8. Many have suggested that OSHA penalties are too weak and misdirected (i.e., aimed at employers rather than employees) to have any significant impact on employee safety. Do you think that OSHA-related sanctions need to be strengthened, or are existing penalties sufficient? Defend your answer.

WEB EXERCISE

The Fair Measures Management Law Consulting Group provides training and legal services for managers, HR managers, business owners, and employees. Their web site has up-to-date information on court case decisions and legal interpretations of employment laws related to sexual harassment, wrongful termination, discrimination, and disability. Visit their web site at www.fairmeasures.com. Choose one of the legal areas to investigate (sexual harassment, wrongful termination, etc.). Click on the legal area. Find the most recent court decisions and interpretations for the area by clicking on the "What's New" articles. The articles are arranged by title. Click on any one of the article titles to view the article.

QUESTIONS

1. Read the article you have chosen.
2. Summarize its implications for HRM practices. Make sure you identify any new legal interpretations or changes in interpretations.

MANAGING PEOPLE: FROM THE PAGES OF "BUSINESS WEEK"

BusinessWeek Score One for the Disabled

Dorsey Ruley is that rare Chicago Bulls fan who has never leaped from his seat at a Michael Jordan moment. Not when Jordan returned in 1995 after a baseball sabbatical. Not even when Jordan led the team to its fourth championship and cried at the memory of his late father.

Emotional control has nothing to do with it. Ruley, 47, a product manager at Ameritech Corp., is a quadriplegic, bound to a wheelchair since 1982. During every one of those moments, all he saw was a sea of standing, clapping, stomping fans at Chicago's United Center.

Help may be on the way. A series of court judgments and settlements around the nation in recent months could force arena owners to improve seating for the disabled. The latest lawsuit to be resolved was in Portland, Oregon, where the Rose Garden will reopen for the NBA season—if there is one—with 101 newly elevated seats that allow average-size disabled people to see over the shoulders of average-size people in front of them. The past year also has brought resolution of disabilities-access lawsuits against arenas in Boston, Buffalo, Philadelphia, Broward County, Florida, and Washington.

For the better part of a decade, teams have been obsessed with maximizing stadium and arena revenues, building (or getting the public to build) facilities crammed with luxury suites and premium seating that target the corporate dollar. Yet often, these new stadiums have fewer seats than the facilities they replaced. Many teams would rather turn fans away than show empty areas—the better to create a sense of scarcity for game tickets. Fewer cheap seats also mean more elite audiences. Whether you call it good business or demographic cleansing, the games are less accessible to the disabled, the elderly, and fans on budgets.

The disabled have long been treated as a nuisance. Even in facilities built since 1992, when the Americans with Disabilities Act began requiring new arenas to reserve 1 percent of the seats for the disabled, they are shunted into so-called wheelchair ghettos in undesirable areas, usually in corners on the concourse level.

Arena officials contend that there just isn't much demand for wheelchair seats. Only 11 disabled people and nine companions held season tickets to Portland Trail Blazers games last season, and even with single-ticket purchases, the team doesn't sell all of its wheelchair seats, says J. Isaac, a Rose Garden senior vice president. "We've never had a situation since we opened the building [in 1995] when we had to turn away a wheelchair patron," he says.

The same goes at other arenas across the country. Only 25 percent of the wheelchair seats at new facilities are being used, says Kevin McGuire, a New York consultant who works on access issues. Says McGuire, "Just because you build something doesn't mean they'll come." That's why arena owners are lobbying to revise downward the ADA requirement of 1 percent. In January, the Access Board, which works with the Justice Dept. to implement the ADA, is expected to release new guidelines that could cut the required seating in half, McGuire says.

Disabled groups are certain to fight any adjustment. They argue that with baby boomers approaching their retirement years, 1 percent is a reasonable figure considering that the life of sports facilities is 20 to 30 years. Besides, they say, who wants to go to a game if they can't see the most exciting moments? Make arenas friendlier, and disabled attendance will spike up.

Not everyone is as dogged as Ruley, who has to take the freight elevator to and from the season-ticket holders' restaurant area at halftime. "You literally roll in with the garbage and roll out with the garbage," he says. That's not the kind of pick-and-roll he comes to see at a Bulls game.

DISCUSSION QUESTIONS

1. Do disabled individuals have a right to attend professional sporting events? Why or why not?
2. The owners argue that not enough disabled individuals come to the games to justify the amount of space (1%) mandated by the government to be set aside for them. Should the ability to exercise disabled individuals' rights be *paid for* by others? If so, at what point would you say that it becomes an unreasonable burden?
3. How should decisions like this be decided? By the courts? By the legislatures? By the owners? By the disabled?

SOURCE: "Score One for the Disabled." *Business Week*. November 19, 1998.

NOTES

1. J. Ledvinka, *Federal Regulation of Personnel and Human Resource Management* (Boston: Kent, 1982).
2. *Martin v. Wilks*, 49 FEP Cases 1641 (1989).
3. *Wards Cove Packing Co. v. Atonio*, FEPC 1519 (1989).
4. *Bakke v. Regents of the University of California*, 17 FEPC 1000 (1978).
5. *Patterson v. McLean Credit Union*, 49 FEPC 1814 (1987).
6. J. Friedman and G. Strickler, *The Law of Employment Discrimination: Cases and Materials*, 2d ed. (Mineola, NY: The Foundation Press, 1987).
7. "Labor Letter," *The Wall Street Journal*, August 25, 1987, p. 1.

8. J. Woo, "Ex-workers Hit Back with Age-Bias Suits," *The Wall Street Journal*, December 8, 1992, p. B1.
9. W. Carley, "Salesman's Treatment Raises Bias Questions at Schering–Plough," *The Wall Street Journal*, May 31, 1995, A1.
10. Special feature issue: "The New Civil Rights Act of 1991 and What It Means to Employers," *Employment Law Update* 6 (December 1991), pp. 1–12.
11. "ADA: The Final Regulations (Title I): A Lawyer's Dream/An Employer's Nightmare," *Employment Law Update* 16, no. 9 (1991), p. 1.
12. "ADA Supervisor Training Program: A Must for Any Supervisor Conducting a Legal Job Interview," *Employment Law Update* 7, no. 6 (1992), pp. 1–6.
13. Equal Employment Opportunity Commission, *Uniform Guidelines on Employee Selection Procedures*, Federal Register 43 (1978), pp. 38290–315.
14. Ledvinka, *Federal Regulation*.
15. R. Pear, "The Cabinet Searches for Consensus on Affirmative Action," *The New York Times*, October 27, 1985, p. E5.
16. *McDonnell Douglas v. Green*, 411 U.S. 972 (1973).
17. *UAW v. Johnson Controls, Inc.* (1991).
18. Special feature issue: "The New Civil Rights Act of 1991," pp. 1–6.
19. *Washington v. Davis*, 12 FEP 1415 (1976).
20. *Albermarle Paper Company v. Moody*, 10 FEP 1181 (1975).
21. R. Reilly and G. Chao, "Validity and Fairness of Some Alternative Employee Selection Procedures," *Personnel Psychology* 35 (1982), pp. 1–63; J. Hunter and R. Hunter, "Validity and Utility of Alternative Predictors of Job Performance," *Psychological Bulletin* 96 (1984), pp. 72–98.
22. *Griggs v. Duke Power Company*, 401 U.S. 424 (1971).
23. B. Lindeman and P. Grossman, *Employment Discrimination Law* (Washington, DC: BNA Books, 1996).
24. M. Jacobs, "Workers' Religious Beliefs May Get New Attention," *The Wall Street Journal*, August 22, 1995, pp. B1, B8.
25. Lindeman and Grossman, *Employment Discrimination Law*.
26. J. Reno and D. Thornburgh, "ADA—Not a Disabling Mandate," *The Wall Street Journal*, July 26, 1995, p. A12.
27. Woo, "Ex-workers Hit Back."
28. W. Johnston and A. Packer, *Workforce* 2000 (Indianapolis, IN: Hudson Institute, 1987).
29. *Bundy v. Jackson*, 641 F.2d 934, 24 FEP 1155 (D.C. Cir., 1981).
30. L.A. Graf and M. Hemmasi, "Risqué Humor: How It Really Affects the Workplace," *HR Magazine* (November 1995), pp. 64–69.
31. B. Carton, "At Jenny Craig, Men Are Ones Who Claim Sex Discrimination," *The Wall Street Journal*, November 29, 1995, p. A–1; "Male–on–Male Harassment Suit Won," *Houston Chronicle*, August 12, 1995, p. 21A.
32. *Meritor Savings Bank v. Vinson* (1986).
33. R. Paetzold and A. O'Leary-Kelly, "The Implications of U.S. Supreme Court and Circuit Court Decisions for Hostile Environment Sexual Harassment Cases," in *Sexual Harassment: Perspectives, Frontiers, and Strategies*, ed. M. Stockdale (Beverly Hills, CA: Sage); R. B. McAfee and D. L. Deadrick, "Teach Employees to Just Say 'No'!" *HR Magazine* (February 1996), pp. 586–89.
34. C. Murray, "The Legacy of the 60's," *Commentary* (July 1992), pp. 23–30.
35. D. Kravitz and J. Platania, "Attitudes and Beliefs about Affirmative Action: Effects of Target and of Respondent Sex and Ethnicity," *Journal of Applied Psychology* 78 (1993), pp. 928–38.
36. J. Mathews, "Rash of Unintended Lawsuits Follows Passage of Disabilities Act," *Houston Chronicle*, May 16, 1995, p. 15A.
37. C. Bell, "What the First ADA Cases Tell Us," *SHRM Legal Report* (Winter), pp. 4–7.
38. K. Mills, "Disabilities Act: A Help, or a Needless Hassle," *B/CS Eagle*, August 23, 1995, p. A7.
39. V. F. Estrada, "Are Your Factory Workers Know-It-All?" *Personnel Journal* (September 1995), pp. 128–34.
40. R. L. Simison, "Safety Last," *The Wall Street Journal*, March 18, 1986, p. 1.
41. J. Roughton, "Managing a Safety Program through Job Hazard Analysis," *Professional Safety* 37 (1992), pp. 28–31.
42. M. A. Verespec, "OSHA Reform Fails Again," *Industry Week*, November 2, 1992, p. 36.
43. R. G. Hallock and D. A. Weaver, "Controlling Losses and Enhancing Management Systems with TOR Analysis," *Professional Safety* 35 (1990), pp. 24–26.
44. H. Herbstman, "Controlling Losses the Burger King Way," *Risk Management* 37 (1990), pp. 22–30.
45. L. Bryan, "An Ounce of Prevention for Workplace Accidents," *Training and Development Journal* 44 (1990), pp. 101–2.
46. J. F. Mangan, "Hazard Communications: Safety in Knowledge," *Best's Review* 92 (1991), pp. 84–88.
47. T. Markus, "How to Set Up a Safety Awareness Program," *Supervision* 51 (1990), pp. 14–16.
48. J. Agnew and A. J. Saruda, "Age and Fatal Work-Related Falls," *Human Factors* 35 (1994), pp. 731–36.
49. R. King, "Active Safety Programs, Education Can Help Prevent Back Injuries," *Occupational Health and Safety* 60 (1991), pp. 49–52.
50. J. R. Hollenbeck, D. R. Ilgen, and S. M. Crampton, "Lower Back Disability in Occupational Settings: A Review of the Literature from a Human Resource Management View," *Personnel Psychology* 45 (1992), pp. 247–78.
51. T. W. Turriff, "NSPB Suggests 10-Step Program to Pre-

vent Eye Injury," *Occupational Health and Safety* 60 (1991), pp. 62–66.

52. D. Hanson, "Chemical Plant Safety: OSHA Rule Addresses Industry Concerns," *Chemical and Engineering News* 70 (1992), pp. 4–5; K. Broscheit and K. Sawyer, "Safety Exhibit Teaches Customers and Employees about Electricity," *Transmission and Distribution* 43 (1992), pp. 174–79; R. Schuch, "Good Training Is Key to Avoiding Boiler Explosions," *National Underwriter* 95 (1992), pp. 21–22.
53. M. Janssens, J. M. Brett, and F. J. Smith, "Confirmatory Cross-Cultural Research: Testing the Viability of a Corporation-wide Safety Policy," *Academy of Management Journal* 38 (1995), pp. 364–82.

CHAPTER

The Analysis and Design of Work

OBJECTIVES

After reading this chapter, you should be able to

1. Analyze a work-flow process, identifying the output, activities, and inputs in the production of a product or service.
2. Understand the importance of job analysis in strategic and human resource management.
3. Choose the right job analysis technique for a variety of human resource activities.
4. Identify the tasks performed and the skills required in a given job.
5. Understand the different approaches to job design.
6. Comprehend the trade-offs among the various approaches to designing jobs.

Teams and Levi's: A Poor Fit?

Throughout the 1990s an increasing number of organizations moved to team-based organizational structures where work is organized and assigned to groups rather than individuals. One of the first companies to start this trend was Chrysler, which used "cross-functional platform teams" to cut production time cycles and improve quality and customer satisfaction. Members of these cross-functional teams were taken from engineering, marketing, purchasing, production, and personnel units and assigned to specific projects. Because of the interdependence between these units when it comes to producing a winning automobile, having members of these units work together simultaneously rather than sequentially smoothed coordination patterns and spawned creativity.

ENTER THE WORLD OF BUSINESS

A number of organizations tried to mimic Chrysler's success by creating their own work teams, but the results have not always been so positive. For example, in the mid-1990s, Levi's directed its U.S. plants to abandon their individually structured production processes and replace them with team-oriented work designs. In the old piecework system, employees worked alone, performed a single, specialized task (e.g., attaching a zipper to a pair of jeans), and were paid according to the amount of work produced (e.g., zippers attached). In the new system, groups of 10 to 25 workers would share all the tasks that go into sewing together a pair of pants and then be paid according to the total number of trousers completed. The hope was that this change would make the work less boring, eliminate repetitive stress disorders like carpal tunnel syndrome, lower costs, and raise productivity.

By 1998, however, it was clear that these supposed benefits of team-based structures were not going to materialize at Levi's. In fact, if anything, this change in the nature of work had just the opposite effects. Instead of increased worker satisfaction, morale actually went down. The new system led to bitter fights between experienced, skilled workers who were formerly doing well with the individually based bonus system and slower, inexperienced workers who were holding the team back from its group goals. Efficiency, as measured by the quantity of pants produced per hour worked, dropped to 77 percent of preteam levels, while labor and overhead costs increased by 25 percent. In the end, whereas it formerly cost around $5 to stitch a pair of Dockers, with teams in place, the unit cost for the same pair of pants was $7.50.

Based on these figures, the team concept at Levi's was unofficially abandoned by most plant managers, who slowly, quietly, and without opposition from corporate levels returned to the old system—a system that seemed more in line with the company's original "rugged, individualistic" philosophy. As one plant manager noted, "We created a lot of anxiety and pain and suffering in our people, and for what?"

SOURCE: H. McCann, "Straight Talk in Teamland," *Wards Auto World* (February 1996), pp. 27–32; R.T. King, "Levi's Factory Workers Are Assigned to Teams, and Morale Takes a Hit," *The Wall Street Journal* (May 20, 1998), pp. A1, A6; S. Sherman, "Levi's: As Ye Sew, so Shall Ye Reap," (May 12, 1997), pp. 104–16.

Introduction

In Chapter 2, we discussed the processes of strategy formulation and strategy implementation. Strategy formulation is the process by which the company decides how it will compete in the marketplace; this is often the energizing and guiding force for everything it does. Strategy implementation is the way the strategic plan gets carried out in activities of organizational members. We noted that there are five important components in the strategy implementation process, three of which are directly related to the human resource management function and one of which we will discuss in this chapter: the task or job.[1]

Many of the central aspects of strategy formulation deal with how the work gets done, in terms of both individual job design as well as the design of organizational structures that link individual jobs to each other and the organization as a whole. The way a firm competes can have a profound impact on the ways jobs are designed and how they are linked via organizational structure. In turn, the fit between the company's structure and environment can have a major impact on the firm's competitive success.

For example, if a company wants to compete via a low-cost strategy, it needs to maximize efficiency. Efficiency is maximized by breaking jobs down into small, simple components that are executed repetitively by low-wage, low-skilled workers. Efficiency is also enhanced by eliminating any redundancy of support services, so that jobs are structured into functional clusters where everyone in the cluster is performing similar work. (Thus, all marketing people work together in a single unit, all engineering personnel work together in a single unit, etc.) People working together within these functional clusters learn a great deal about how the function can be used to leverage their skills into small amounts of increased efficiency via continuous, evolutionary improvements. This is the type of structure and job design that characterized Levi's in the early 1990s, and this type of design can be highly effective in stable, unchanging competitive environments.

On the other hand, if a company wants to compete via an innovation strategy, it needs to maximize flexibility. Flexibility is maximized by aggregating work into larger, holistic pieces that are executed by teams of higher-wage, higher-skilled workers. Flexibility is also enhanced by giving the units their own support systems and decision making authority to take advantage of local opportunities in regional or specialized product markets. People working together in these cross-functional clusters generate a greater number of creative and novel ideas that can be leveraged into more discontinuous, revolutionary improvements. This is the type of structure and job design that characterized Chrysler in the early 1990s, and this type of design can be highly effective in dynamic and changing competitive environments.

Thus, it should be clear from the outset of this chapter that there is no "one best way" to design jobs and structure organizations. The organization needs to create a fit between its environment, competitive strategy, and philosophy on the one hand, with its jobs and organizational design on the other. As the story that opened this chapter shows, Levi's, which had a fairly good fit among these dimensions in the early 1990s, evolved into a poorly fitting system by the end of the decade. The team-based structure of jobs that it developed was not ideally suited for its "rugged individualistic" philosophy of its workers or its relatively stable environment. It was also out of line with the need to compete on costs—which was especially salient in this time period because more and more of its competitors were moving jobs out of the United States into lower-wage countries.

This chapter discusses the analysis and design or work and, in doing so, lays out some considerations that go into making informed decisions about how to create and link jobs. The chapter is divided into three sections, the first of which deals with "big-picture" issues related to work-flow analysis and organizational structure. The remaining two sections deal with more specific, lower-level issues related to job analysis and job design.

The fields of job analysis and job design have extensive overlap, yet in the past they have been treated differently.[2] Job analysis has focused on analyzing existing jobs to gather information for other human resource management practices such as selection, training, performance appraisal, and compensation.[3] Job design, on the other hand, has focused on redesigning existing jobs to make them more efficient or more motivating to jobholders.[4] Thus, job design has had a more proactive orientation toward changing the job, whereas job analysis has had a passive, information gathering orientation. However, as we will show in this chapter, these two approaches are interrelated.

Work-Flow Analysis and Organization Structure

In the past, HR professionals and line managers have tended to analyze or design a particular job in isolation from the larger organizational context. Work-flow design is the process of analyzing the tasks necessary for the production of a product or service, prior to allocating and assigning these tasks to a particular job category or person. Only after we have a thorough understanding of work-flow design can we make informed decisions regarding how to initially bundle various tasks into discrete jobs that can be executed by a single person.

Organization structure refers to the relatively stable and formal network of vertical and horizontal interconnections among jobs that constitute the organization. Only after we have a thorough understanding of how one job relates to those above (supervisors), below (subordinates), and at the same level in different functional areas (marketing versus production), can we make informed decisions about how to redesign or improve jobs in a way that will benefit the entire organization.

Finally, both work-flow design and organization structure have to be understood in the context of how an organization has decided to compete. Both work-flow design and organization structure can be leveraged to gain competitive advantage for the firm, but how one does this depends on the firm's strategy and its competitive environment.

WORK-FLOW ANALYSIS

As we noted in Chapter 1, the institution of the Malcolm Baldrige National Quality award resulted in the development of many TQM programs in U.S. businesses. A theme common to nearly all quality programs is the need to identify clearly the outputs of work, to specify the quality standards for those outputs, and to analyze the processes and inputs necessary for producing outputs that meet the quality standards.[5] This conception of the work-flow process is useful for TQM because it provides a means for the manager to understand all the tasks required to produce a high-quality product as well as the skills necessary to perform those tasks. This work-flow process is depicted in Figure 4.1. In this section, we present an approach for analyzing the work process of a department as a means of examining jobs in the context of an organization.

ANALYZING WORK OUTPUTS

Every work unit—whether a department, team, or individual—seeks to produce some output that others can use. An output is the product of a work unit and is often an identifiable thing, such as a completed purchase order, an employment test, or a hot, juicy hamburger. However, an output can also be a service, such as the services provided by an airline that transports you to some destination, a housecleaning service that maintains your house, or a baby-sitter who watches over your children.

FIGURE 4.1
Developing a Work-Unit Activity Analysis

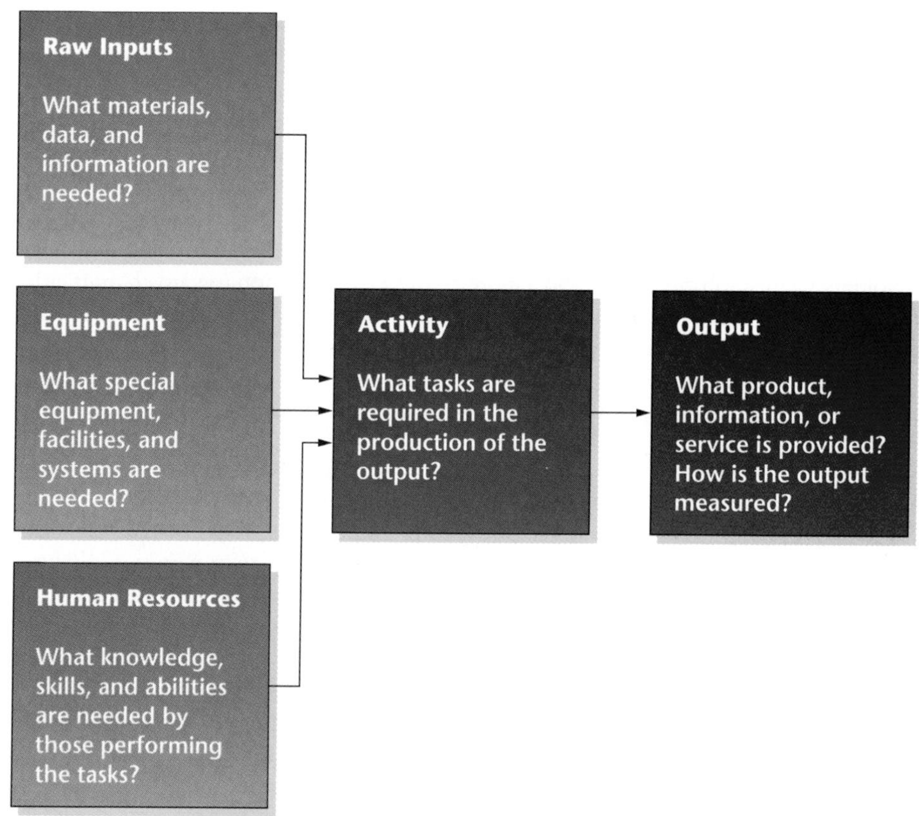

We often picture an organization only in terms of the product that it produces and then we focus on that product as the output. For example, we could easily identify the output of IBM as computers. However, to produce computers requires many work units, each generating a variety of outputs, and each of these work units has a number of individuals who generate some work output. Thus, an important determinant of the effectiveness of any organization is the efficiency and effectiveness with which it produces the many products within the various work units.

However, merely identifying an output or set of outputs is not sufficient. Once these outputs have been identified, it is necessary to specify the standards for the quantity or quality of these outputs. For example, a recently developed productivity improvement technique known as ProMES (productivity measurement and evaluation system) focuses attention on both identifying work-unit outputs and specifying the levels of required performance for different levels of effectiveness.[6] With ProMES, the members of a work unit identify each of the products (outputs) of the work unit for the various customers. They then evaluate the effectiveness of each level of products in the eyes of their customers.

The identification of work outputs has only recently gained attention among HR departments. As discussed in Chapter 2, HR executives have begun to understand the role of the HR department as they have attempted to analyze their customers inside the company and the products that those customers desire from the HR function.[7] This has resulted in HR managers' having a clearer understanding of the specific products that they supply to the company and allows them to focus on producing high-quality products. Without an understanding of the output of a work unit, any attempt at increasing work-unit effectiveness will be futile.

ANALYZING WORK PROCESSES

Once the outputs of the work unit have been identified, it is possible to examine the work processes used to generate the output. The work processes are the activities that members of a work unit engage in to produce a given output. Every process consists of operating procedures that specify how things should be done at each stage of the development of the product. These procedures include all the tasks that must be performed in the production of the output. The tasks are usually broken down into those performed by each person in the work unit.

Again, to design work systems that are maximally efficient, a manager needs to understand the processes required in the development of the products for that work unit. Often, as work loads increase within a work group, the group will grow by adding positions to meet these new requirements. However, when the work load lightens, members may take on tasks that do not relate to the work unit's product in an effort to appear busy. Without a clear understanding of the tasks necessary to the production of an output, it is difficult to determine whether the work unit has become overstaffed. Having a clear understanding of the tasks required allows the manager to specify which tasks are to be carried out by which individuals and eliminate tasks that are not necessary for the desired end. This ensures that the work group maintains a high level of productivity.

For example, Microsoft, currently the most successful computer software company in the world, strategically manages the design of the total work-flow process for competitive advantage. To maintain the sense of being an underdog, Microsoft deliberately understaffs its product teams in "small bands of people with a mission." This ensures both a lean organization and high levels of motivation.[8]

ANALYZING WORK INPUTS

The final stage in work-flow analysis is to identify the inputs used in the development of the work unit's product. For example, assume that you were assigned a paper titled "The Importance of Human Resources to Organizational Performance." The output of your work process will be a paper that you will turn in to the professor. To produce this paper, you must perform a number of tasks, such as conducting research, reading articles, and writing the paper. What, however, are the inputs? As shown in Figure 4.1, these inputs can be broken down into the raw materials, equipment, and human skills needed to perform the tasks. *Raw materials* consist of the materials that will be converted into the work unit's product. Thus, for your assignment, the raw materials would be the information available in the library regarding the various effects of human resources on organizational performance.

Equipment refers to the technology and machinery necessary to transform the raw materials into the product. As you attempt to develop your paper, you may go to the library and use the library computer-search system that provides you with a list of recent articles on the relationship between human resources and organizational performance. In addition, once you sit down to write, you will most likely have to use either a typewriter or, more likely in today's high-technology world, a word processor to put your thoughts on paper.

The final inputs in the work-flow process are the *human skills* and efforts necessary to perform the tasks. Many skills are required of you in producing your paper. For example, you need to have some knowledge of how to work the library computer-search facilities, you need some typing skill (or the phone number of a good typist), and you definitely need the ability to reason and write. Again, these skills are much more valuable for producing a high-quality product than are other skills such as being able to play the saxophone.

It is important to note that a flawed product can be caused by deficiencies at any phase in the production process. For example, if you fail to perform the task of spell-checking your paper before turning it in, you may receive a lower grade. Similarly, if you cannot obtain the best raw materials (i.e., you cannot find the right articles), do not use the proper equipment (e.g., the computer is down), or do not possess the necessary skills (you do not write well), your paper will receive less than the maximum grade.

Organization Structure

Whereas work-flow design provides a longitudinal overview of the dynamic relationships by which inputs are converted into outputs, organization structure provides a cross-sectional overview of the static relationships between individuals and units that create the outputs. Organization structure is typically displayed via organizational charts that convey both vertical reporting relationships and horizontal functional responsibilities.

DIMENSIONS OF STRUCTURE. Two of the most critical dimensions of organization structure are centralization and departmentation. **Centralization** refers to the degree to which decision making authority resides at the top of the organizational chart as opposed to being distributed throughout lower levels (i.e., authority is **decentralized**). Departmentation refers to the degree to which work units are grouped based upon functional similarity or on similarity of work flow.

FIGURE 4.2 The Functional Structure

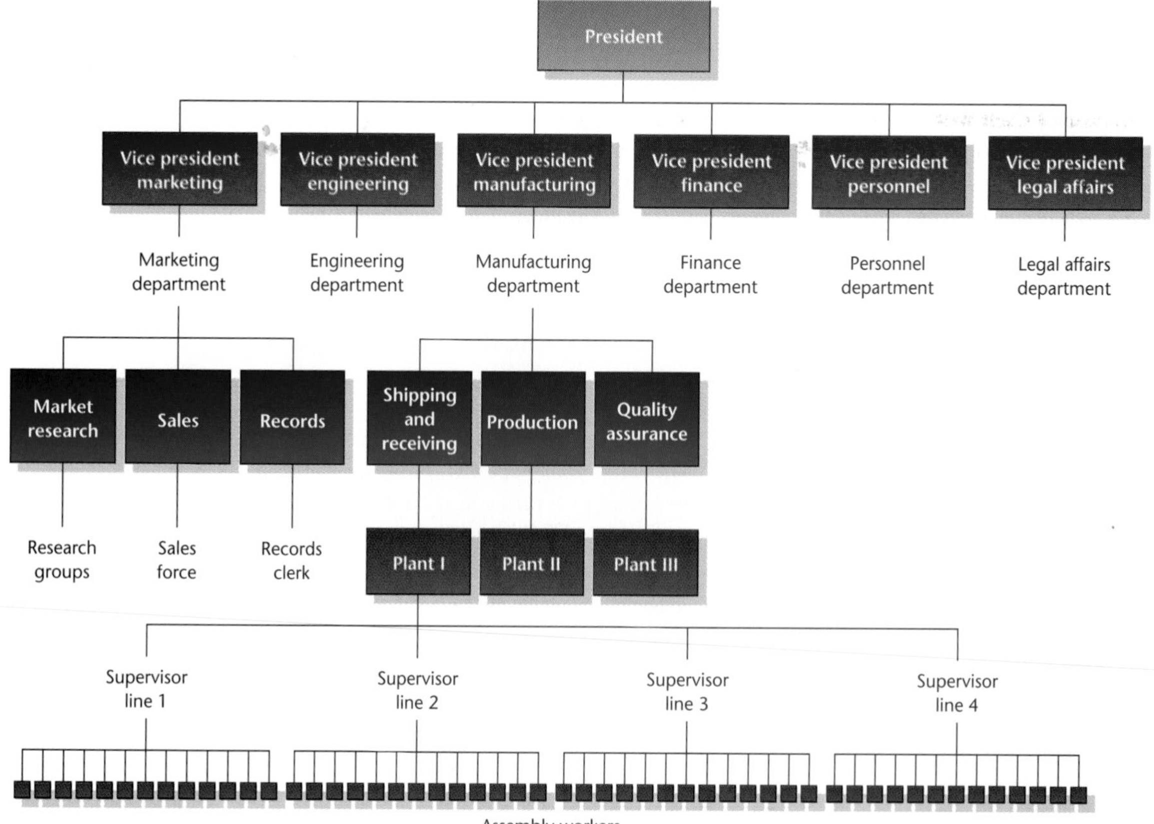

SOURCE: Adapted from John A. Wagner and John R. Hollenbeck. *Organizational Behavior: Securing Competitive Advantage* 3rd Edition. Prentice-Hall. Reprinted with permission.

For example, a school of business could be organized around functional similarity so that there would be a marketing department, a finance department, and an accounting department, and faculty within these specialized departments would each teach their area of expertise to all kinds of students. Alternatively, one could organize the same school around work-flow similarity, so that there would be an undergraduate unit, a graduate unit, and an executive development unit. Each of these units would have its own marketing, finance, and accounting professors who taught only their own respective students and not those of the other units.

STRUCTURAL CONFIGURATIONS. Although there are an infinite number of ways to combine centralization and departmentation, two common configurations of organization structure tend to emerge in organizations. The first type, referred to as a functional structure, is shown in Figure 4.2. A functional structure, as the name implies, employs a functional departmentation scheme with relatively high levels of centralization. High levels of centralization tend to go naturally with functional departmentation because individual units in the structures are so specialized that members of the unit may have a weak conceptualization of the overall organization mission. Thus, they tend to identify with their department and cannot always be relied on to make decisions that are in the best interests of the organization as a whole.

Alternatively, a second common configuration is a divisional structure, three examples of which are shown in Figures 4.3, 4.4, and 4.5. Divisional structures combine a work-flow departmentation scheme with relatively low levels of centralization. Units in these structures act almost like separate, self-sufficient, semi-autonomous organizations. The organization shown in Figure 4.3 is divisionally organized around different products, the organization shown in Figure 4.4 is divisionally organized around geographic regions, and the organization shown in Figure 4.5 is divisionally organized around different clients.

Because of their work-flow focus, their semi-autonomous nature, and their proximity to a homogeneous consumer base, divisional structures tend to be more flexible and innovative. They can detect and exploit opportunities in their respective consumer base faster than the more centralized functionally structured organizations. However, on the

FIGURE 4.3 Divisional Structure: Product Structure

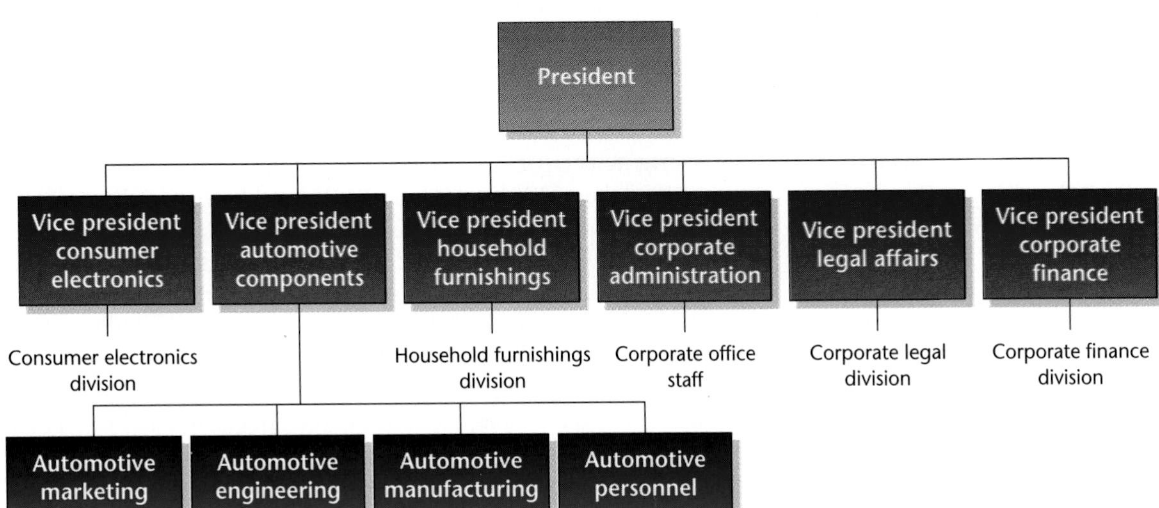

SOURCE: Adapted from John A. Wagner and John R. Hollenbeck. *Organizational Behavior: Securing Competitive Advantage* 3rd Edition. Prentice-Hall. Reprinted with permission.

FIGURE 4.4 Divisional Structure: Geographic Structure

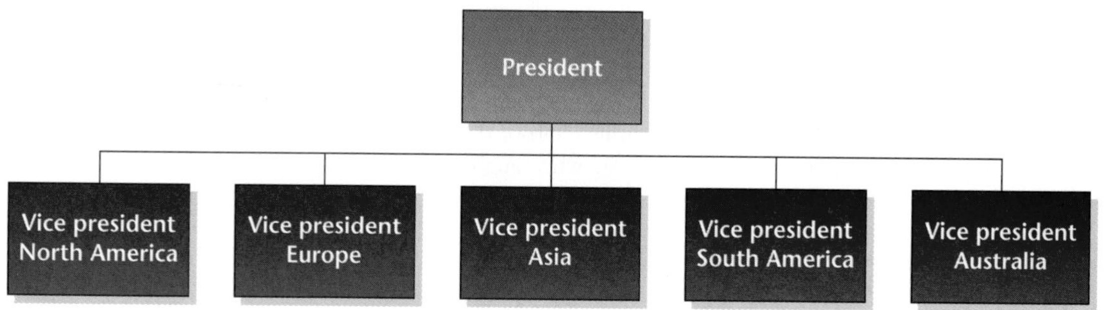

SOURCE: Adapted from John A. Wagner and John R. Hollenbeck. *Organizational Behavior: Securing Competitive Advantage* 3rd Edition. Prentice-Hall.

downside, divisional structures are not very efficient because of the redundancy associated with each group carrying its own functional specialists. Also, divisional structures can "self-cannibalize" if the gains achieved in one unit come at the expense of another unit (e.g., if sales in one General Motors unit like Oldsmobile come at the expense of another GM unit like Chevrolet).

Alternatively, functional structures are very efficient, with little redundancy across units, and provide little opportunity for self-cannibalization. However, these structures tend to be inflexible and insensitive to subtle differences across products, regions, or clients. Thus, in general, no one structure is always the best.

Functional structures are most appropriate in stable, predictable environments, where demand for resources can be well anticipated and coordination requirements between jobs can be refined and standardized over consistent repetitions of activity. This type of structure also helps support organizations that compete on cost, because efficiency is central to make this strategy work. This structure worked well for Levi's in the vignette that opened this chapter.

Divisional structures are most appropriate in unstable, unpredictable environments, where it is difficult to anticipate demands for resources, and coordination requirements between jobs are not consistent over time. This type of structure also helps support organizations that compete on differentiation or innovation, because flexible responsiveness is central to making this strategy work. This was the type of structure that worked well for Chrysler in the vignette opening this chapter but worked poorly when Levi's tried to import it into their context.

STRUCTURE AND THE NATURE OF JOBS. Finally, moving from big-picture issues to lower-level specifics, the type of organization structure also has implications for the design of jobs. Jobs in functional structures need to be narrow and highly specialized, and people need to work alone. Workers in these structures (even middle managers) tend to have little decision making authority or responsibility for managing coordination between themselves and others. Jobs in divisional structures need to be more holistic, with people working in teams that tend to have greater decision making authority.

In our next section, we cover specific approaches for analyzing and designing jobs. Whereas all of these approaches are viable, each focuses on a single, isolated job. These approaches do not necessarily consider how that single job fits into the overall work flow or structure of the organization. Thus, to use these techniques effectively, we have to have a good understanding of the organization as a whole. Without this big-picture appreciation, we might redesign a job in a way that might be good for that one job but out of line with the work flow, structure, or strategy of the organization.

FIGURE 4.5 Divisional Structure: Client Structure

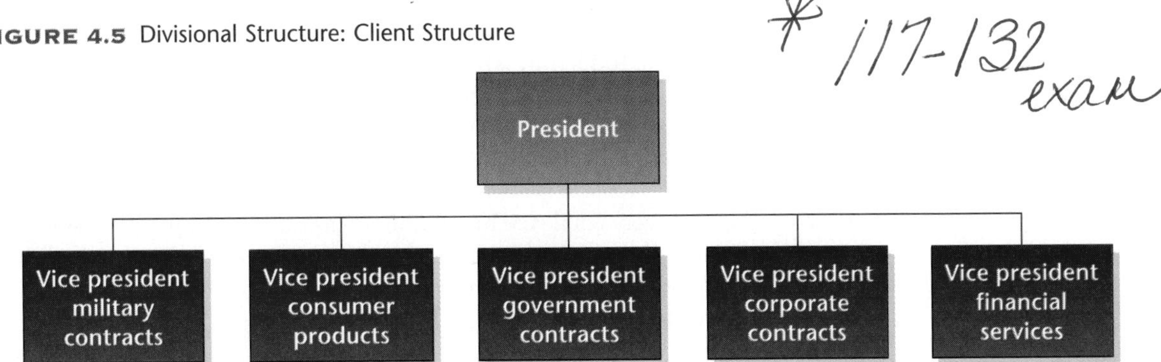

SOURCE: Adapted from John A. Wagner and John R. Hollenbeck. *Organizational Behavior: Securing Competitive Advantage* 3rd Edition. Prentice-Hall.

Job Analysis

Job analysis refers to the process of getting detailed information about jobs.[9] Job analysis has deep historical roots. For example, in his description of the "just" state, Socrates argued that society needed to recognize three things. First, there are individual differences in aptitudes for work, meaning that individuals differ in their abilities. Second, unique aptitude requirements exist for different occupations. Third, to achieve high-quality performance, society must attempt to place people in occupations that best suit their aptitudes. In other words, for society (or an organization) to succeed, it must have detailed information about the requirements of jobs (through job analysis) and it must ensure that a match exists between the job requirements and individuals' aptitudes (through selection).[10]

Whereas Socrates was concerned with the larger society, it is even more important for organizations to understand and match job requirements and people to achieve high-quality performance. This is particularly true in today's competitive marketplace. Thus, the information gained through job analysis is of utmost importance; it has great value to both human resource and line managers.

THE IMPORTANCE OF JOB ANALYSIS TO HR MANAGERS

Job analysis is such an important activity to HR managers that it has been called the building block of everything that personnel does.[11] This statement refers to the fact that almost every human resource program requires some type of information that is gleaned from job analysis: selection, performance appraisal, training and development, job evaluation, career planning, work redesign, and human resource planning.[12]

WORK REDESIGN. As previously discussed, job analysis and job design are interrelated. Often, a firm will seek to redesign work to make it more efficient or effective. To redesign the work, detailed information about the existing job(s) must be available. In addition, redesigning a job will, in fact, be similar to analyzing a job that does not yet exist.

HUMAN RESOURCE PLANNING. In human resource planning, planners analyze an organization's human resource needs in a dynamic environment and develop activities that enable a firm to adapt to change. This planning process requires accurate information about the levels of skill required in various jobs to ensure that enough individuals are available in the organization to meet the human resource needs of the strategic plan.[13]

SELECTION. Human resource selection deals with identifying the most qualified applicants for employment. To identify which applicants are most qualified, it is first necessary to determine the tasks that will be performed by the individual hired and the knowledge, skills, and abilities the individual must have to perform the job effectively. This information is gained through job analysis.[14]

TRAINING. Almost every employee hired by an organization will require some training in his job. Some training programs may be more extensive than others, but all require the trainer to have identified the tasks performed in the job to ensure that the training will prepare individuals to perform the job effectively.[15]

PERFORMANCE APPRAISAL. Performance appraisal deals with getting information about how well each employee is performing her job in order to reward those who are effective, improve the performance of those who are ineffective, or provide a written justification for why the poor performer should be disciplined. Through job analysis, the organization can identify the behaviors and results that distinguish effective performance from ineffective performance.[16]

CAREER PLANNING. Career planning entails matching an individual's skills and aspirations with opportunities that are or may become available in the organization. This matching process requires that those in charge of career planning know the skill requirements of the various jobs. This allows them to guide individuals into jobs in which they will succeed and be satisfied.

JOB EVALUATION. The process of job evaluation involves assessing the relative dollar-value of each job to the organization to set up internally equitable pay structures. If pay structures are not equitable, employees will be dissatisfied and quit, or they will not see the benefits of striving for promotions. To put dollar values on jobs, it is necessary to get information about different jobs to determine which jobs deserve higher pay than others.[17]

THE IMPORTANCE OF JOB ANALYSIS TO LINE MANAGERS

Job analysis is clearly important to the HR department's various activities, but it may not be as clear why it is important to line managers. There are many reasons. First, managers must have detailed information about all the jobs in their work group to understand the work-flow process. Earlier in this chapter, we noted the importance of understanding the work-flow process—specifically, identifying the tasks performed and the knowledge, skills, and abilities required to perform them. In addition, an understanding of this work-flow process is essential if a manager chooses to redesign certain aspects to increase efficiency or effectiveness.

Second, managers need to understand the job requirements to make intelligent hiring decisions. Very seldom do employees get hired by the human resource department without a manager's input. Managers will often interview prospective applicants and recommend who should receive a job offer. However, if the manager does not have a clear understanding of what tasks are performed on the job and the skills necessary to perform them, then the hiring decision may result in employees whom the manager "likes" but who are not capable of performing the job successfully.

Third, a manager is responsible for ensuring that each individual is performing his job satisfactorily (or better). This requires the manager to evaluate how well each person is performing and to provide feedback to those whose performance needs improvement. Again, this requires that the manager clearly understand the tasks required in every job.

JOB ANALYSIS INFORMATION

NATURE OF INFORMATION. Two types of information are most useful in job analysis: job descriptions and job specifications. A **job description** is a list of the tasks, duties, and responsibilities (TDRs) that the job entails. TDRs are observable actions. For example, a clerical job requires the jobholder to type. If you were to observe someone in that position over the course of a day, you would certainly see him typing at one time or another. When a manager attempts to evaluate job performance, it is most important to have detailed information about the work performed in the job (i.e., the TDRs). This makes it possible to determine how well an individual is meeting each job requirement. Table 4.1 shows a sample job description.

A **job specification** is a list of the knowledge, skills, abilities, and other characteristics (KSAOs) that an individual must have to perform the job. *Knowledge* refers to factual or procedural information that is necessary for successfully performing a task. A *skill* is an individual's level of proficiency at performing a particular task. *Ability* refers to a more general enduring capability that an individual possesses. Finally, other characteristics might be personality traits such as one's achievement motivation or persistence. Thus, KSAOs are characteristics about people that are not directly observable; they are observable only when individuals are carrying out the TDRs of the job. Thus, if someone applied for the clerical job discussed, you could not simply look at the individual to determine whether she possessed typing skills. However, if you were to observe that in-

TABLE 4.1
A Sample Job Description

Job Title: Maintenance Mechanic

General Description of Job: General maintenance and repair of all equipment used in the operations of a particular district. Includes the servicing of company vehicles, shop equipment, and machinery used on job sites.

1. *Essential Duty (40%): Maintenance of Equipment*
   Tasks: Keep a log of all maintenance performed on equipment. Replace parts and fluids according to maintenance schedule. Regularly check gauges and loads for deviances that may indicate problems with equipment. Perform nonroutine maintenance as required. May involve limited supervision and training of operators performing maintenance.
2. *Essential Duty (40%): Repair of Equipment*
   Tasks: Requires inspection of equipment and a recommendation that a piece be scrapped or repaired. If equipment is to be repaired, mechanic will take whatever steps are necessary to return the piece to working order. This may include a partial or total rebuilding of the piece using various hand tools and equipment. Will primarily involve the overhaul and troubleshooting of diesel engines and hydraulic equipment.
3. *Essential Duty (10%): Testing and Approval*
   Tasks: Ensure that all required maintenance and repair has been performed and that it was performed according to manufacturer specifications. Approve or reject equipment, as being ready for use on a job.
4. *Essential Duty (10%): Maintain Stock*
   Tasks: Maintain inventory of parts needed for the maintenance and repair of equipment. Responsible for ordering satisfactory parts and supplies at the lowest possible cost.

Nonessential Functions

Other duties as assigned.

Staying Alive on the Graveyard Shift: Beyond the Traditional KSAs

One area where it is difficult to balance the needs of employers, employees, and consumers is where there is a need to run operations 24 hours a day. For example, employers may have expensive equipment that for efficiency's sake cannot afford to lie idle overnight. In other cases, the need is generated by consumers who demand services around the clock, such as security or health care. The increased globalization of work also means that consumers or co-workers are sometimes in different time zones, which can generate nontraditional working hours.

When the job description entails working night shifts, the job specifications have to reflect this. Human beings are not nocturnal animals, so working at night is not a natural activity for most people. Virtually all of the body's functions are influenced by circadian rhythms regulated by an internal biological clock. This internal clock is in turn, influenced by patterns of sunlight and darkness, and when the two are not synchronized, bodily functions become impaired. Indeed, evidence suggests that people working the graveyard shift between 10 to 11 P.M. and 6 to 7 A.M. are more likely to have more health problems than other employees doing the same work. These problems include fatigue, sleeping disorders, depression, obesity, and increased risk of coronary disease. People who work at night have also been found to be more accident-prone and have higher absenteeism and turnover rates.

Fortunately, however, there seems to be wide variability in how people respond to this disruptive activity, and if this is taken into consideration when writing job specifications, some of these problems may be reduced. Research shows that people who are effective working at night tend to share a number of characteristics. First, they are "night owls," meaning that left on their own, they prefer to sleep late in the morning and stay up until very late at night. Second, they tend to be people who can sleep easily at different times of the day and, left to their own, take naps. Third, they exercise regularly, and hence do not compound the physical problems associated with night work with problems caused by inactive life-styles. Finally, effective shiftworkers either have a minimum of inflexible nonwork responsibilities (such as a large number of children) or have a dedicated support network that allows them to work irregular hours. Thus, when it comes to working the graveyard shift, worker health depends a great deal on developing the right job specifications, and dealing with nocturnality may be the most critical KSAO.

SOURCE: G. Koretz, "Perils of the Graveyard Shift: Poor Health and Low Productivity," *Business Week* (March 10, 1997), p. 22; C.R. Maiwald, J.L. Pierce, and J.W. Newstrom, "Workin' 8 P.M. to 8 A.M. and Lovin' Every Minute of It," *Workforce* (July 1997), pp. 30–36.

dividual type something, you could make an assessment of the level of typing skill the individual had. When a manager is attempting to fill a position, it is important to have accurate information about the characteristics a successful jobholder must have. This requires focusing on the KSAOs of each applicant.

SOURCES OF JOB ANALYSIS INFORMATION. In performing the job analysis, one question that often arises is, Who should make up the group of incumbents that are responsible for providing the job analysis information? Whatever job analysis method you choose, the process of job analysis entails obtaining information from people familiar with the job. We refer to these people as subject-matter experts because they are experts in their knowledge of the job.

In general, it will be useful for you to go to the job incumbent to get the most accurate information about what is actually done on the job. This is especially the case when it is difficult to monitor the person who does the job. As the "Competing through High-Performance Work Systems" box shows; this is becoming more and more prevalent with today's technology.

Telework

Prior to the Industrial Revolution, most people worked either close to or inside their own home. However, mass production technologies changed all this, separating work life from home life, as people began to travel to centrally located factories and offices. As we approach the new millennium, however, sky-rocketing office space prices combined with drastically reduced prices for portable electronic computing and communication devices seem ready to reverse this trend. The broad term for doing one's work away from a centrally located office is telework. Studies reveal that the cost savings from such programs can top $8,000 per employee annually. Not surprisingly, given these savings, the number of teleworkers has increased dramatically over the past few years. It has been estimated that over 10 million U.S. workers now fall under this heading.

For example, at IBM, a program was initiated where each teleworker was supplied with an IBM ThinkPad Notebook Computer with a modem, fax card, mobility software, and printer as well as an extra phone line for her home. Marketing employees were also supplied with cellular phones, alphanumeric pagers, facsimile machines, and personal copiers. All of these workers gave up dedicated office space at IBM headquarters and instead worked either in a small shared office space (allocated on a first-come/first-served basis), at home, or (better yet) at a customer's site. Because leases at different offices were up at different times, IBM could compare the effect of telework arrangements on a large number of outcomes, where the first workers whose jobs were converted were compared to workers doing the same work in a traditional office (whose lease had not yet expired).

COMPETING THROUGH HIGH-PERFORMANCE WORK SYSTEMS

The results of this experiment showed that productivity for teleworkers was significantly higher than for traditional workers, especially among women. Most of this came about by reducing wasted commuting time as well as eliminating distractions caused by working in a traditional office. Part of this productivity gain also resulted from the flexibility that allowed people to work when they were at their peak efficiency (late at night or early in the morning for some) and work around nonwork obligations (such as caring for a sick child). On the negative side, some teleworkers perceived that this type of arrangement hindered teamwork, felt isolated from informal networks of communication, and missed the mentoring opportunities that went along with traditional office work. Most interestingly, some teleworkers felt that the arrangements actually made it harder to balance home and work. Many had relied on time and distance to clearly differentiate when they were engaging in one role versus another (i.e., worker versus parent) and then struggled with this distinction when time and distance were removed. Thus, as we noted at the outset of this chapter, there is no one best way of designing work. Whereas telecommuting may have positive influences on some outcomes, it has negative effects on others.

SOURCE: M. Werner, "Working at Home—the Right Way to Be a Star in Your Bunny Slippers," *Fortune* (March 3, 1997), pp. 165–66; P. Coy, "Home Sweet Office," *Business Week* (April 6, 1998), p. 30; E.J. Hill, B.C. Miller, S.P. Weiner, and J. Colihan, "Influences of the Virtual Office on Aspects of Work and Work/Life Balance," *Personnel Psychology* 51 (1998), pp. 667–83.

However, particularly when the job analysis will be used for compensation purposes, incumbents might have an incentive to exaggerate their duties. Thus, you will also want to ask others familiar with the job, such as supervisors, to look over the information generated by the job incumbent. This serves as a check to determine whether what is being done is congruent with what is supposed to be done in the job. Although job incumbents and supervisors are the most obvious and frequently used sources of job analysis information, other sources can be helpful, particularly for service jobs.

It is important to understand the usefulness of different sources of job analysis information, because this information is only as good as the source. Research has revealed some interesting findings regarding various sources of job analysis information, particularly regarding job incumbents and supervisors.

One question is whether supervisors and incumbents agree in their job analysis ratings. Some research has demonstrated significant differences in the job analysis ratings provided from these two different sources.[18] However, other research has found greater agreement between supervisors and subordinates when rating general job duties than when rating specific tasks.[19] One conclusion that can be drawn from this research is that incumbents may provide the most accurate estimates of the actual time spent performing job tasks. However, supervisors may be a more accurate source of information about the importance of job duties.

Another question is whether a job incumbent's own performance level is related to the job analysis ratings. Although it is intuitively appealing to think that individuals who perform well in a job might give different ratings than individuals who do not perform well, the research has not borne this out. One frequently cited study compared the job analysis ratings of effective and ineffective managers and found that they tended to give the same ratings despite their performance level.[20] However, more recent research has also examined the relationship between job analysis and employee performance. In this research no differences were observed between high and low performers regarding the tasks and KSAOs generated, the ratings made regarding the time spent, or importance of the tasks.[21] However, differences have been observed in the types of critical incidents generated[22] and the ratings of the level of effectiveness of various incidents.[23] Thus, research at present seems inconclusive regarding the relationship between the performance level of the job analyst and the job analysis information she provides.

While the relationship between job analysis ratings and job performance is inconclusive, research has strongly demonstrated some demographic differences in job analysis information. One study found differences between males and females and between blacks and whites in the importance and time-spent ratings for a variety of tasks.[24] Similarly, another study observed minor differences between males and females and between blacks and whites in job analysis ratings. However, in this study larger differences in ratings were the result of the experience level of the job incumbent.[25] These research results imply that when conducting a job analysis, you should take steps to ensure that the incumbent group responsible for generating the job analysis information represents a variety of gender, racial, and experience-level categories.

JOB ANALYSIS METHODS

There are various methods for analyzing jobs and no "one best way." In this section, we will discuss three methods for analyzing jobs: the position analysis questionnaire, the task analysis inventory, and the job analysis system. Although most managers may not have time to use each of these techniques in the exact manner suggested, the three do provide some anchors for thinking about broad approaches, task-focused approaches, and person-oriented approaches to conducting job analysis.

POSITION ANALYSIS QUESTIONNAIRE (PAQ). We lead this section off with the PAQ because this is one of the broadest and most well-researched instruments for analyzing jobs. Moreover, its emphasis on inputs, processes, relationships, and outputs is consistent with the work flow analysis approach that we used in leading off this chapter (i.e., Figure 4.1).

The PAQ is a standardized job analysis questionnaire containing 194 items.[26] These items represent work behaviors, work conditions, and job characteristics that can be generalized across a wide variety of jobs. They are organized into six sections:

1. *Information input*—Where and how a worker gets information needed to perform the job.

2. *Mental processes*—The reasoning, decision making, planning, and information processing activities that are involved in performing the job.
3. *Work output*—The physical activities, tools, and devices used by the worker to perform the job.
4. *Relationships with other persons*—The relationships with other people required in performing the job.
5. *Job context*—The physical and social contexts where the work is performed.
6. *Other characteristics*—The activities, conditions, and characteristics other than those previously described that are relevant to the job.

The job analyst is asked to determine whether each item applies to the job being analyzed. The analyst then rates the item on six scales: extent of use, amount of time, importance to the job, possibility of occurrence, applicability, and special code (special rating scales used with a particular item). These ratings are submitted to the PAQ headquarters, where a computer program generates a report regarding the job's scores on the job dimensions.

Research has indicated that the PAQ measures 32 dimensions and 13 overall dimensions of jobs (listed in Table 4.2) and that a given job's scores on these dimensions can be very useful. The significant database has linked scores on certain dimensions to scores on subtests of the General Aptitude Test Battery (GATB). Thus, knowing the dimension scores provides some guidance regarding the types of abilities that are necessary to perform the job. Obviously, this technique provides information about the work performed in a format that allows for comparisons across jobs, whether those jobs are similar or dissimilar. Another advantage of the PAQ is that it covers the work context as well as inputs, outputs, and processes. As the "Competing through Globalization" box shows, the context in which work takes place has received a great deal of attention over the past few years among image-conscious organizations that have been damaged by charges of running overseas sweatshops.

In spite of its widespread use, the PAQ is not without problems. One problem is that to fill out the test, an employee needs the reading level of a college graduate; this disqualifies some job incumbents from the PAQ. In fact, it is recommended that only job analysts trained in how to use the PAQ should complete the questionnaire, rather than job incumbents or supervisors.[27] A second problem associated with the PAQ is that its general and standardized format leads to rather abstract characterizations of jobs. Thus, it does not lend itself well to describing the specific, concrete task activities that comprise the actual job. Thus, it is not ideal for developing job descriptions or redesigning jobs. Methods that do focus on this aspect of the work are needed if this is the goal.

TABLE 4.2
Overall Dimensions of the Position Analysis Questionnaire

Overall Dimensions
Decision/communication/general responsibilities
Clerical/related activities
Technical/related activities
Service/related activities
Regular day schedule versus other work schedules
Routine/repetitive work activities
Environmental awareness
General physical activities
Supervising/coordinating other personnel
Public/customer/related contact activities
Unpleasant/hazardous/demanding environment
Nontypical work schedules

Eliminating Sweatshops at Nike: Just Do It—but How?

Over the past decade, Nike has been one of the most profitable companies in the United States. However, at a time when the company's spokesperson, Michael Jordan, was bringing in over $10 million, the young, mostly women workers in its Indonesian plants were taking home only $2.23 a day. Moreover, working conditions in Nike's Serang plant, 50 miles west of Jakarta, were far from ideal. Hundreds of workers, some children, were crowded into vast sheds where they glued, stitched, pressed, and boxed 70 million pairs of shoes a year. Overtime was mandatory for most workers and severe forms of punishment were meted out to any worker who missed quantity or quality goals. Collusion between local management and government made organizing workers into unions both difficult and dangerous, and the high level of unemployment left workers powerless. Taken together, these labor practices helped keep costs so low and quality so high that a pair of running shoes that sell for $75 retail in the United States cost just $18.25 to manufacture.

With this type of cost and price structure, it is easy to see how Nike became so profitable. However, the ability to sustain these practices became an issue in 1996 when the U.S. media exposed these sweatshop conditions. As consumers became increasingly aware of how their sneakers were actually being made, some felt guilty, and human rights groups went so far as to organize boycotts of Nike products. Given the damage to Nike's image and future profitability, something had to be done.

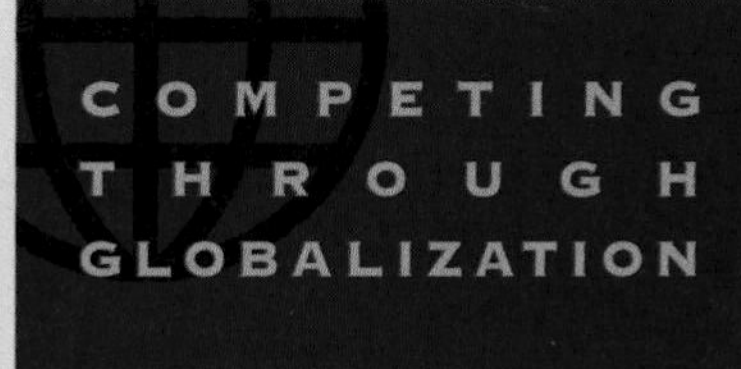

At first, Nike CEO Phillip Knight defended his operations, noting that Nike pays its workers no less than its rivals do and that these workers make more than minimum wage in the host countries. Critics countered that the level of pay was below the subsistence level and much lower than what is paid by other U.S. companies such as Coca-Cola, Gillete, and Goodyear.

To end this image problem once and for all, on May 12, 1998, Knight pledged to (a) raise the minimum worker age requirement, (b) adopt U.S.-style safety and health standards, and (c) allow human rights groups to help monitor working conditions in all foreign plants. He again showed his commitment to reform six months later by raising wages 22 percent to offset the currency devaluation that rocked Indonesia in the fall of 1998. Knight used both occasions to challenge his competitors to do the same, realizing that their failure to do so would put Nike at a competitive disadvantage. Although it is currently unclear how these competitors will respond, it is obvious that Nike is at least trying to establish its image as a trend setter in both footwear and working conditions in international locations.

SOURCE: M.L. Clifford, "Pangs of Conscience over Sweatshops," *Business Week*, July 29, 1996, p. 38; L. Himelstein, "Nike Hasn't Scrubbed Its Image Yet," *Business Week*, July 7, 1997, p. 44; A. Bernstein, "Nike Finally Does It," *Business Week*, May 25, 1998, p. 46; A. Bernstein, "A Floor under Foreign Factories," *Business Week*, November 2, 1998, pp. 126–27.

TASK ANALYSIS INVENTORY. The task analysis inventory refers to several different methods, each with slight variations. However, common to these approaches is the focus on analyzing all the tasks performed in the focal job. (It is not uncommon to have over 100 tasks.)

For example, the task inventory–CODAP method[28] entails asking subject matter experts (SMEs) to generate a list of the tasks performed in a job. Once this list has been developed, the SMEs rate each task on dimensions such as the relative amount of time spent on the task, the frequency of task performance, the relative importance of the task, the relative difficulty of the task, and whether the task can be learned on the job relatively quickly. These ratings are then subjected to the CODAP computer program that organizes the tasks into dimensions of similar tasks.

Task inventories focus on providing detailed information about the work performed in a given job. The detail of the information can be helpful in developing both selection exam plans and performance-appraisal criteria. Although a task inventory might

TABLE 4.3
Abilities Included in the Fleishman Job Analysis System

1. Oral comprehension	27. Arm–hand steadiness
2. Written comprehension	28. Manual dexterity
3. Oral expression	29. Finger dexterity
4. Written expression	30. Wrist–finger speed
5. Fluency of ideas	31. Speed of limb movement
6. Originality	32. Static strength
7. Memorization	33. Explosive strength
8. Problem sensitivity	34. Dynamic strength
9. Mathematical reasoning	35. Trunk strength
10. Number facility	36. Extent flexibility
11. Deductive reasoning	37. Dynamic flexibility
12. Inductive reasoning	38. Gross body coordination
13. Information ordering	39. Gross body equilibrium
14. Category flexibility	40. Stamina
15. Speed of closure	41. Near vision
16. Flexibility of closure	42. Far vision
17. Spatial orientation	43. Visual color discrimination
18. Visualization	44. Night vision
19. Perceptual speed	45. Peripheral vision
20. Selective attention	46. Depth perception
21. Time sharing	47. Glare sensitivity
22. Control precision	48. Hearing sensitivity
23. Multilimb coordination	49. Auditory attention
24. Response orientation	50. Sound localization
25. Rate control	51. Speech recognition
26. Reaction time	52. Speech clarity

indirectly suggest the types of KSAOs people might need to perform the job, these KSAOs do not come directly out of the process. Thus, other approaches that do put the focus squarely on the people requirement associated with jobs have been developed.

FLEISHMAN JOB ANALYSIS SYSTEM.[29] Another job analysis technique that elicits information about the worker's characteristics is the Fleishman Job Analysis System (FJAS). This approach defines *abilities* as enduring attributes of individuals that account for differences in performance. The system is based on a taxonomy of abilities that adequately represent all the dimensions relevant to work. This taxonomy includes 52 cognitive, psychomotor, physical, and sensory abilities, listed in Table 4.3.[30]

The actual FJAS scales consist of descriptions of the ability, followed by behavioral benchmark examples of the different levels of the ability along a seven-point scale. An example of the written comprehension ability scale from the FJAS is presented in Figure 4.6.

In using the job analysis technique, SMEs are presented with each of the 52 scales. These experts indicate the point on the scale that best represents the level of that ability required in a particular job. These ratings provide an accurate picture of the ability requirements of the job. Substantial research has shown the value of this general approach for human resource activities such as career development, selection, and training.[31]

FIGURE 4.6
Example of an Ability from the Fleischman Job Analysis System

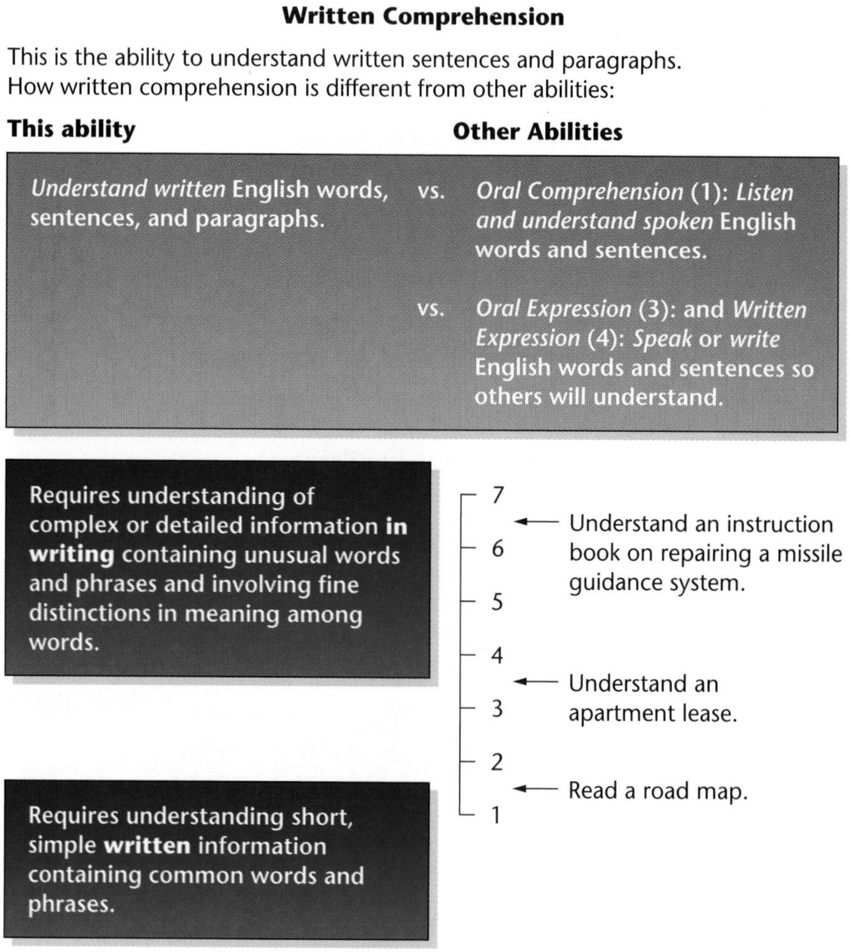

Written Comprehension

This is the ability to understand written sentences and paragraphs.
How written comprehension is different from other abilities:

This ability		Other Abilities
Understand written English words, sentences, and paragraphs.	vs.	*Oral Comprehension* (1): *Listen and understand spoken* English words and sentences.
	vs.	*Oral Expression* (3): and *Written Expression* (4): *Speak* or *write* English words and sentences so others will understand.

Requires understanding of complex or detailed information **in writing** containing unusual words and phrases and involving fine distinctions in meaning among words.

- 7
- ← Understand an instruction book on repairing a missile guidance system.
- 6
- 5
- 4
- ← Understand an apartment lease.
- 3
- 2
- ← Read a road map.
- 1

Requires understanding short, simple **written** information containing common words and phrases.

SOURCE: E.A. Fleishman and M. D. Mumford, "Evaluating Classifications of Job Behavior: A Construct Validation of the Ability Requirements Scales," *Personnel Psychology* 44 (1991), pp. 523–76. The complete set of ability requirement scales, along with instructions for their use, may be found in E.A. Fleishman, *Fleishman Job Analysis Survey* (F-JAS) (Palo Alto, CA: Consulting Psychologists Press, 1992). Used with permission.

DYNAMIC ELEMENTS OF JOB ANALYSIS

Although we tend to view jobs as static and stable, in fact, jobs tend to change and evolve over time. Those who occupy or manage the jobs often make minor, cumulative adjustments to the job that try to match either changing conditions in the environment or personal preferences for how to conduct the work.[32] Indeed, although there are numerous sources for error in the job analysis process,[33] the fact is that most inaccuracy is likely to result from job descriptions simply being outdated. For this reason, in addition to statically defining the job, the job analysis process must also detect changes in the nature of jobs.

For example, in today's world of rapidly changing products and markets, some people have begun to question whether the concept of the job is simply a social artifact that has outlived its usefulness. Indeed, many researchers and practitioners are pointing to a trend referred to as "dejobbing" in organizations. This trend consists of viewing organizations as a field of work needing to be done rather than a set of discrete jobs held by specific individuals. At Intel, for example, individuals are often first assigned to a project. That project changes over time with corresponding changes in the roles and requirements of the individual. Before that project is complete, the individual is assigned to an additional project or projects. Thus, besides having new responsibilities, the individual is required to work under a variety of team leaders, manage a variety of goals and timetables, and coordinate across various team locations and schedules of different team members. This requires that firms eliminate the traditional hierarchical arrangements in favor of more flexible and fluid structures and processes.

These "project-based" organizational structures require the type of broader understanding that comes from an analysis of work flows. Because the work can change so rapidly and it is impossible to rewrite job descriptions every week, it also illustrates the need for much more flexibility in the writing of job descriptions and specifications. However, legal requirements (as discussed in Chapter 3) may discourage firms from writing flexible job descriptions. Thus, firms seeking to use their employees as a source of competitive advantage must balance the need for flexibility with the need for legal documentation. This presents one of the major challenges faced by HR departments in the next decade, and rather than taking a passive job analytic approach, these types of changes really require an active approach to job design such as those discussed in our next section.

Job Design

So far we have approached the issue of managing work in a passive way, focusing only on understanding what gets done, the way it gets done, and the skills required to get it done. While this is necessary, it is a very static view of jobs, in that jobs must already exist and that they are already assumed to be structured in the one best way. However, a manager may often be faced with a situation in which the work unit does not yet exist, requiring jobs within the work unit to be designed from scratch. Sometimes work loads within an existing work unit are increased, or work group size is decreased while the same work load is required, a trend increasingly observed with the movement toward downsizing.[34] Finally, sometimes the work is not being performed in the most efficient manner. In these cases, a manager may decide to change the way that work is done in order for the work unit to perform more effectively and efficiently. This requires redesigning the existing jobs.

Job design is the process of defining the way work will be performed and the tasks that will be required in a given job. Job redesign refers to changing the tasks or the way work is performed in an existing job. To effectively design jobs, one must thoroughly understand the job as it exists (through job analysis) and its place in the larger work unit's work-flow process (work-flow analysis). Having a detailed knowledge of the tasks performed in the work unit and in the job, a manager then has many alternative ways to design a job. This can be done most effectively through understanding the trade-offs between certain design approaches.

Research has identified four basic approaches that have been used among the various disciplines (e.g., psychology, management, engineering, ergonomics) that have dealt with job design issues.[35] All jobs can be characterized in terms of how they fare according to each approach; thus, a manager needs to understand the trade-offs between emphasizing one approach over another. In the next section we discuss each of these approaches and examine the implications of each for the design of jobs. Table 4.4 displays how jobs are characterized along each of these dimensions.

MOTIVATIONAL APPROACH

The motivational approach to job design has its roots in the organizational psychology and management literatures. It focuses on the job characteristics that affect the psychological meaning and motivational potential, and it views attitudinal variables (such

TABLE 4.4
Characterizing Jobs on Different Dimensions of Job Design

The motivational job design approach

1. *Autonomy:* Does the job allow freedom, independence, or discretion in work scheduling, sequence, methods, procedures, quality control, and other types of decisions?
2. *Intrinsic job feedback:* Do the work activities themselves provide direct, clear information about the effectiveness (in terms of quality and quantity) of job performance?
3. *Extrinsic job feedback:* Do other people in the organization (such as managers and co-workers) provide information about the effectiveness (in terms of quality and quantity) of job performance?
4. *Social interaction:* Does the job provide for positive social interaction (such as teamwork or co-worker assistance)?
5. *Task/goal clarity:* Are the job duties, requirements, and goals clear and specific?
6. *Task variety:* Does the job have a variety of duties, tasks, and activities?
7. *Task identity:* Does the job require completion of a whole and identifiable piece of work? Does it give the incumbent a chance to do an entire piece of work from beginning to end?
8. *Ability/skill-level requirements:* Does the job require a high level of knowledge, skills, and abilities?
9. *Ability/skill variety:* Does the job require a variety of types of knowledge, skills, and abilities?
10. *Task significance:* Is the job significant and important compared with other jobs in the organization?
11. *Growth/learning:* Does the job allow opportunities for learning and growth in competence and proficiency?

The mechanistic job-design approach

1. *Job specialization:* Is the job highly specialized in terms of purpose and/or activity?
2. *Specialization of tools and procedures:* Are the tools, procedures, materials, etc., used on this job highly specialized in terms of purpose?
3. *Task simplification:* Are the tasks simple and uncomplicated?
4. *Single activities:* Does the job require the incumbent to do only one task at a time? Does it not require the incumbent to do multiple activities at one time or in very close succession?
5. *Job simplification:* Does the job require relatively little skill and training time?
6. *Repetition:* Does the job require performing the same activity or activities repeatedly?
7. *Spare time:* Is there very little spare time between activities on this job?
8. *Automation:* Are many of the activities of this job automated or assisted by automation?

continued

SOURCE: Reprinted by permission of publisher, from *Organizational Dynamics,* Winter 1987 ©1987. American Management Association, New York.

as satisfaction, intrinsic motivation, job involvement, and behavioral variables such as attendance and performance) as the most important outcomes of job design. The prescriptions of the motivational approach focus on increasing the complexity of jobs through such interventions as job enlargement, job enrichment, and the construction of jobs around sociotechnical systems.[36] Accordingly, a study of 213 different jobs found that the motivational attributes of jobs were positively related to the mental-ability requirements of workers in those jobs.[37]

An example of the motivational approach is Herzberg's Two-Factor theory, which argues that individuals are motivated more by intrinsic aspects of work such as the meaningfulness of the job content than by extrinsic characteristics such as pay.[38] Herzberg ar-

TABLE 4.4
Characterizing Jobs on Different Dimensions of Job Design *continued*

The biological job design approach

1. *Strength:* Does the job require fairly little muscular strength?
2. *Lifting:* Does the job require fairly little lifting, and/or is the lifting of very light weights?
3. *Endurance:* Does the job require fairly little muscular endurance?
4. *Seating:* Are the seating arrangements on the job adequate (with ample opportunities to sit, comfortable chairs, good postural support, etc.)?
5. *Size difference:* Does the workplace allow for all size differences between people in terms of clearance, reach, eye height, leg room, etc.?
6. *Wrist movement:* Does the job allow the wrists to remain straight, without excessive movement?
7. *Noise:* Is the workplace free from excessive noise?
8. *Climate:* Is the climate at the workplace comfortable in terms of temperature and humidity, and is it free of excessive dust and fumes?
9. *Work breaks:* Is there adequate time for work breaks given the demands of the job?
10. *Shift work:* Does the job not require shift work or excessive overtime?

The perceptual–motor job design approach

1. *Lighting:* Is the lighting in the workplace adequate and free from glare?
2. *Displays:* Are the displays, gauges, meters, and computerized equipment used on this job easy to read and understand?
3. *Programs:* Are the programs in the computerized equipment for this job easy to learn and use?
4. *Other equipment:* Is the other equipment (all types) used on this job easy to learn and use?
5. *Printed job materials:* Are the printed materials used on this job easy to read and interpret?
6. *Workplace layout:* Is the workplace laid out so that the employee can see and hear well enough to perform the job?
7. *Information input requirements:* Is the amount of attention needed to perform this job fairly minimal?
8. *Information-output requirements:* Is the amount of information that the employee must output on this job, in terms of both action and communication, fairly minimal?
9. *Information-processing requirements:* Is the amount of information that must be processed, in terms of thinking and problem solving, fairly minimal?
10. *Memory requirements:* Is the amount of information that must be remembered on this job fairly minimal?
11. *Stress:* Is there relatively little stress on this job?
12. *Boredom:* Are the chances of boredom on this job fairly small?

gued that the key to motivating employees was not through monetary incentives but through the redesign of jobs to make their work more meaningful.

A more complete model of how job design affects employee reactions is the "Job Characteristics Model."[39] According to this model, jobs can be described in terms of five characteristics. *Skill variety* is the extent to which the job requires a variety of skills to be used to carry out the tasks. *Task identity* is the degree to which a job requires completing a "whole" piece of work from beginning to end. *Task significance* is the extent to which the job has an important impact on the lives of other people. *Autonomy* is the degree to which the job allows an individual to make decisions about the way the work will be carried out. *Feedback* is the extent to which a person receives clear information about the effectiveness of his performance from the work itself.

These five job characteristics determine the motivating potential of a job by affecting the three critical psychological states of "experienced meaningfulness," "responsibility," and "knowledge of results." According to the model, when the core job characteristics (and thus the critical psychological states) are high, individuals will have a high level of internal work motivation. This is expected to result in higher quantity and quality of work as well as higher levels of job satisfaction.

Job design interventions emphasizing the motivational approach tend to focus on increasing the motivating potential of jobs. Much of the work on job enlargement (broadening the types of tasks performed), job enrichment (adding more decision-making authority to jobs), and self-managing work teams has its roots in the motivational approach to job design. While most of the research on these interventions has demonstrated that they increase employee satisfaction and performance quality, these interventions do not consistently result in increased quantity of performance.

MECHANISTIC APPROACH

The mechanistic approach has its roots in classical industrial engineering. The focus of the mechanistic approach is on identifying the simplest way to structure work that maximizes efficiency. This most often entails reducing the complexity of the work to provide more human resource efficiency—that is, making the work so simple that anyone can be trained quickly and easily to perform it. This approach focuses on designing jobs around the concepts of task specialization, skill simplification, and repetition.

Scientific management was one of the earliest and best-known statements of the mechanistic approach.[40] According to this approach, productivity could be maximized by taking a scientific approach to the process of designing jobs. Scientific management first sought to identify the "one best way" to perform the job. This entailed performing time-and-motion studies to identify the most efficient movements for workers to make. Once the best way to perform the work is identified, workers should be selected based on their ability to do the job, they should be trained in the standard "one best way" to perform the job, and they should be offered monetary incentives to motivate them to work at their highest capacity.

The scientific management approach was built upon in later years, resulting in a mechanistic approach that calls for jobs to be designed so that they are very simple and so that they lack any significant meaningfulness. By designing jobs in this way, the organization reduces its need for high-ability individuals and thus becomes less dependent on individual workers. Individuals are easily replaceable—that is, a new employee can be trained to perform the job quickly and inexpensively.

BIOLOGICAL APPROACH

The biological approach to job design comes primarily from the sciences of biomechanics (i.e., the study of body movements), work physiology, and occupational medicine, and it is usually referred to as ergonomics. **Ergonomics** is concerned with examining the interface between individuals' physiological characteristics and the physical work environment. The goal of this approach is to minimize the physical strain on the worker by structuring the physical work environment around the way the human body works. It thereby focuses on outcomes such as physical fatigue, aches and pains, and health complaints.

The biological approach has been applied in redesigning equipment used in jobs that are physically demanding. Such redesign is often aimed at reducing the physical demands of certain jobs so that anyone can perform them. In addition, many biological interventions focus on redesigning machines and technology, such as adjusting the height of the computer keyboard to minimize occupational illnesses (e.g., carpal tunnel syndrome). The design of chairs and desks to fit posture requirements is very important in many office jobs and is another example of the biological approach to job design. For example, one study found that having employees participate in an ergonomic redesign effort significantly reduced the number and severity of cumulative trauma disorders, lost production time, and restricted duty days.[41]

PERCEPTUAL–MOTOR APPROACH

The perceptual–motor approach to job design has its roots in the human-factors literature.[42] Whereas the biological approach focuses on physical capabilities and limitations, the perceptual–motor approach focuses on human mental capabilities and limitations. The goal is to design jobs in a way that ensures they do not exceed people's mental capabilities and limitations. This approach generally tries to improve reliability, safety, and user reactions by designing jobs in a way that reduces the information processing requirements of the job. In designing jobs, one looks at the capabilities of the least capable worker and then constructs job requirements that an individual of that ability level could meet. Similar to the mechanistic approach, this approach generally has the effect of decreasing the job's cognitive demands.

Jobs such as air traffic controller, oil refinery operator, and quality-control inspector require a large amount of information processing. Many clerical and assembly-line jobs, on the other hand, require very little information processing. However, in designing all jobs, managers need to be aware of the information processing requirements and ensure that these requirements do not exceed the capabilities of the least capable person who could potentially be performing the job.

TRADE-OFFS AMONG DIFFERENT APPROACHES TO JOB DESIGN

A recent stream of research has aimed at understanding the trade-offs and implications of these different job design strategies. Many authors have called for redesigning jobs according to the motivational approach so that the work becomes more psychologically meaningful. However, one study examined how the various approaches to job design are related to a variety of work outcomes. Table 4.5 summarizes their results. For example, in this study, job incumbents expressed higher satisfaction with jobs scoring high on motivational approach. Also, jobs scoring high on the biological approach were ones for which incumbents expressed lower physical requirements. Finally, the motivational and mechanistic approaches were negatively related, suggesting that designing jobs to maximize efficiency very likely results in a lower motivational component to those jobs.

Another recent study demonstrated that enlarging clerical jobs made workers more satisfied, less bored, more proficient at catching errors, and better at providing customer service. However, these enlarged jobs also had costs, such as higher training requirements, higher basic-skill requirements, and higher compensation requirements based on job-evaluation compensable factors.[43] Again, it is important to recognize the trade-off between the motivational value of jobs and the efficiency with which the jobs are performed.

Finally, research has examined how job design approaches relate to compensation. Starting from the assumption that job-evaluation (the process of determining the worth of jobs to organizations) links job design and market forces, researchers examined the relationship between job design approaches and both job evaluation results and pay. They found that jobs high on the motivational approach had higher job evaluation scores representing higher skill requirements and that these jobs had higher pay levels.

TABLE 4.5 Summary of Outcomes from the Job Design Approaches

JOB DESIGN APPROACH	POSITIVE OUTCOMES	NEGATIVE OUTCOMES
Motivational	Higher job satisfaction Higher motivation Greater job involvement Higher job performance Lower absenteeism	Increased training time Lower utilization levels Greater likelihood of error Greater chance of mental overload and stress
Mechanistic	Decreased training time Higher utilization levels Lower likelihood of error Less chance of mental overload and stress	Lower job satisfaction Lower motivation Higher absenteeism
Biological	Less physical effort Less physical fatigue Fewer health complaints Fewer medical incidents Lower absenteeism Higher job satisfaction	Higher financial costs because of changes in equipment or job environment
Perceptual–motor	Lower likelihood of error Lower likelihood of accidents Less chance of mental overload and stress Lower training time Higher utilization levels	Lower job satisfaction Lower motivation

SOURCE: Reprinted by permission of publisher, from *Organizational Dynamics,* Winter 1987 ©1987. American Management Association, New York. All rights reserved.

Jobs high on the mechanistic and perceptual–motor dimensions had lower skill requirements and correspondingly lower wage rates. Finally, jobs high on the biological dimension had lower physical requirements and had a weak positive relationship to wage rates. Thus, it seems reasonable to conclude that jobs redesigned to increase the motivating potential result in higher costs in terms of ability requirements, training, and compensation.[44]

To summarize, in designing jobs it is important to understand the trade-offs inherent in focusing on one particular approach to job design. Managers who seek to design jobs in a way that maximizes all the outcomes for jobholders and the organization need to be aware of these different approaches, understand the costs and benefits associated with each, and balance them appropriately to provide the organization with a competitive advantage.

SUMMARY

The analysis and design of work is one of the most important components to developing and maintaining a competitive advantage. Strategy implementation is virtually impossible without thorough attention devoted to work-flow analysis, job analysis, and job design. Managers need to understand the entire work-flow process in their work unit to ensure that the process maximizes efficiency and effectiveness. To understand this process, managers also must have clear, detailed information about the jobs that exist in the work unit, and the way to gain this information is through the job analysis process. Equipped with an understanding of the work-flow process and the existing job, managers can redesign jobs to ensure that the work unit is able to achieve its goals while individuals within the unit benefit on the various work–outcome dimensions such as motivation, satisfaction, safety, health, and achievement. This is one key to competitive advantage.

DISCUSSION QUESTIONS

1. Assume you are the manager of a fast food restaurant. What are the outputs of your work unit? What are the activities required to produce those outputs? What are the inputs?
2. Based on Question 1, consider the cashier's job. What are the outputs, activities, and inputs for that job?
3. Consider the "job" of college student. Perform a job analysis on this job. What are the tasks required in the job? What are the knowledge, skills, and abilities necessary to perform those tasks? What environmental trends or shocks (e.g., computers) might change the job, and how would that change the skill requirements?
4. Discuss how the following trends are changing the skill requirements for managerial jobs in the United States: (a) increasing use of computers, (b) increasing international competition, (c) increasing work–family conflicts.
5. Why is it important for a manager to be able to conduct a job analysis? What are the negative outcomes that would result from not understanding the jobs of those reporting to the manager?
6. What are the trade-offs between the different approaches to job design? Which approach do you think should be weighted most heavily when designing jobs?
7. For the cashier job in Question 2, which approach to job design was most influential in designing that job? In the context of the total work-flow process of the restaurant, how would you redesign the job to more heavily emphasize each of the other approaches?

WEB EXERCISE

The Center for Office Technology is a national group of employers, manufacturers, and associations dedicated to improving the office work environment. Visit the web site at www.cot.org. Review the information available on the home page. Click on the "1998 Outstanding Office Ergonomics Program Winners." The names of the two organizations who received this award are shown. Click on the name of one of the organizations to see the steps they took to improve the office environment.

QUESTIONS

1. What is ergonomics? Why is it important?
2. In this chapter we discuss four different job design dimensions: motivational, mechanistic, biological, and perceptual/motor. What steps did the company take to improve each of these job design dimensions?

MANAGING PEOPLE: FROM THE PAGES OF "BUSINESS WEEK"

BusinessWeek The New Factory Worker

Fred Price gropes his way downstairs in the dark, grabs a Danish, and races off to work at 4 A.M. Today is a special day for the 29-year-old North Carolina factory hand. On the job, he will schedule orders as usual for the tiny tool-and-die shop where he doubles as a supervisor when he's not bending metal himself. But at midday, test results are coming in from the state Labor Dept. in Raleigh. These aptitude exams for all 43 workers at Northeast Tool & Manufacturing Co., outside Charlotte, measure everything from math and mechanical skills to leadership and adaptability. And they come with a prescription. Now it appears that Price will have to pull back from the bird hunting a little and spend less time with the kids' go-cart. Like tens of thousands of factory workers across America, Fred Price is going back to school.

Growing up, Price liked to work with his hands more than his head. He would help his father fix the family's old Ford pickup, and once they rigged up a hydraulic log-splitter. In high school, he excelled in shop class but sat toward the back in English and math. These days, in an economy where even factory work increasingly is defined by blips on a computer screen, more schooling is the only road ahead. Northeast Tool, for one, will use the employee tests over the next several months to develop customized training for each worker. Some will enroll at a nearby community college. Others will take remote courses through computers set up at the plant. A few will attend afternoon classes with professors brought right into the mill. Price wants to pursue a two-year degree in metallurgy, even if it means putting in long hours on weekends. "Someday I hope to manage the plant," he says.

Until recently, Americans often divided ranks in high school between shop kids such as Price, who went on to industrial or service work, and college-bound students headed for white-collar or professional jobs. They parted ways at graduation and would move into distinct categories of manual and knowledge workers.

But over the past decade, thinned-out ranks of managers have been equipping factory workers with industrial robots and teaching them to use computer controls to operate massive steel casters and stamp presses. At the same time, managers are funneling reams of information through the computers, bringing employees into the data loop. Workers are trained to watch inventories, to know suppliers and customers, costs and prices. Knowledge that long separated brain workers from hand workers is now available via computer on the factory floor. At Northeast Tool, Rusty Arant, Fred Price's manager, points to a powerful computer he rigged up to a milling machine and says: "I crammed it with memory because I want these guys to be managing the business from the shop floor."

The trend toward high-skills manufacturing began in the mid-1980s with innovative companies such as Corning, Motorola, and Xerox. They replaced rote assembly-line work with an industrial vision that requires skilled and nimble workers to think while they work. In the 1990s, what was once the industrial avant-garde is now mainstream as its practices spread across the manufacturing sector. Large, old-line companies finally are learning the lesson that investments in training boost productivity, often at less cost than capital investments. And as the big guys push suppliers and subcontractors on quality, price, and just-in-time delivery, even little shops such as Northeast Tool see high skills as essential for competition.

The result is an intensifying transformation of the American factory. The ranks of manufacturers that put a majority of their workers through different types of training have doubled or tripled in the past decade, according to surveys of large companies by the University of California's Center for Effective Organizations. At the same time, the share of the country's 19 million factory workers with a year or two of college has jumped to 25 percent vs. 17 percent in 1985, according to the Bureau of Labor Statistics. An additional 19 percent have college diplomas today, up from 16 percent a decade ago. "There's a real rise in companies' willingness to invest in their workforces," says Pamela J. Tate, president of the Council for Adult & Experiential Learning, a Chicago consulting group.

This, investment, though, carries a none-too-subtle message for America's manufacturing workers: Hone your skills or risk being left behind. U.S. workers are being pushed to raise their technical savvy to the level of the best Japanese and German workers. At the same time, many are being asked to develop leadership skills and to take a role in managing that's rare in the top-down structures found in Asia and Europe.

Indeed, the old formula of company loyalty, a strong back, and showing up on time no longer guarantees job security, or even a decent paycheck. Today, industrial workers will thrive only if they use their wits and keep adding to their skills base. It's a rich irony: Millions of Americans who headed for the factory because they didn't like school, among other reasons, are now faced with a career-long dose of it. "It isn't whether you can hoist 100-pound sacks anymore," says Anthony Carnevale, a training expert at Educational Testing Service in Princeton, N.J. "Most of the work is mental."

Demanding as it is, the high-skills factory represents blue-collar America's best hope for retaining high wages in a world teeming with workers. Across the economy, in manufacturing and services alike, there has been a surge in demand for higher skills as employers reorganize work around new technologies and human capital-investments. Recently, the pressure for more capable workers has even begun to generate skills shortages in pockets around the country.

But many companies still need to catch up: Only 10 percent to 20 percent of large companies have adopted high-performance techniques, surveys show, including a third of large manufacturers, according to the National Association of Manufacturers. Others are actually going in the opposite direction. In industries as diverse as apparel making, telemarketing, and chicken processing, many employers continue to slice pay, avoid unions, and outsource work to lower-wage subcontractors. These trends have led to a growing inequality along skill and education lines, similar to the one cleaving society at large. So far, the net result has weighed more heavily downward, even in manufacturing, where average pay lagged inflation by 3 percent from 1989 to 1995, according to the BLS.

In this cutthroat environment, an individual worker's best chance of getting ahead now lies in advancing his or her skills whenever the opportunity arises. And plenty of workers are jumping at the chance. From downsized defense-industry hands in Long Beach, Calif., to white-smocked pharmaceutical workers in the Delaware Valley, they are studying for new factory jobs.

This even includes veterans in old-line smokestack companies. Take Adlai John Warner, 44, who put in 25 years at Acme Metal Inc., a specialty steelmaker outside Chicago. Warner always enjoyed learning and was quick with facts—quick enough to be given top security clearance as a U.S. Marine intelligence specialist in Vietnam. He had planned to attend college when he returned to Chicago after the war. Instead, he started a family and wound up making good money as a laborer at Acme.

Warner found the work tedious. Acme, like most other manufacturers, was organized for a low-skilled force and used Warner's body but not much of his brain. Even after he jumped a few rungs on the job ladder by apprenticing as a pipe fitter, the work required more endurance than thought. Warner describes long empty days of sitting around, waiting for pipe-fitting jobs, making time and a half with gobs of overtime. Despite pay that eventually reached $60,000 a year, the boredom prompted Warner to pursue a bachelor's degree in psychology at night at Chicago State University in the hopes of moving into human resources. He got his BA in 1978, but it never led anywhere.

Meanwhile, the world was closing in on Acme. Low-cost minimills and foreign mills threatened its niche in super-high-carbon steel, which is used in knife blades, tools, and critical machine parts. Its old equipment was falling apart. In 1994, management launched a $400 million redesign of the mill with a high-tech German caster—an audacious move for a $560 million company. But operation of the finicky caster, which converts molten steel into a two-inch–thick band, is fast and dangerous. If workers can't make quick decisions, they risk a "breakout," when hot liquid steel spills from the mold all over the machinery. To date, only minimill leader

Nucor Corp. and its offspring, Steel Dynamics Inc., with skilled and flexible workforces, have made money with the new technology.

In effect, Acme is betting the company on its workers' brains—and Warner has leaped at the opportunity. Last year, the company brought in scads of consultants to test those who volunteered among its 1,100 unionized ranks. They used an exhaustive battery of exams to look for reading, math, technical, and communication skills. Some workers weren't interested and took early retirement. About 750 were chosen to create an entirely new, team-oriented system. Warner qualified for an advanced job as a maintenance technician and last September promptly hit the books.

Acme set up classroom trailers next to the mill and brought in teachers from Detroit, Georgia, even Germany. The company paid Warner and 130 others to spend nine months, full-time, learning everything from metallurgy, math, and computers to a piece-by-piece study of the new machinery. The total cost to upgrade the workforce, including employee salaries, came to some $8 million, or just 2 percent of the amount Acme spent on the new caster. "We're being exposed to things we've never been exposed to before," says Warner appreciatively.

Warner and his colleagues also are involved in reinventing Acme's entire work system. In the spring, he and five other workers were selected to sit down with managers and consultants for weeks on end at a nearby Ramada Inn. There, they hung poster paper all over the walls and blackboards, marking up a scheme for the new workplace, from devising a pay system pegged to profits to redefining supervisors' roles. "The people working there have to make the decisions," says Anthony C. Capito, Acme's vice president for steel production. The new system, including the training received by Warner and his colleagues, will be put to the test when the new caster is brought on line this fall.

Workers at small manufacturers are facing similar tests. In 1985, when the then 18-year-old Fred Price landed his job at Northeast Tool, the job shop sold custom-made metal pieces primarily to local Carolina customers. Today, as regional markets meld into national and global ones, Northeast must boost quality enough to land contracts from the likes of BMW and Siemens. These companies want metal fashioned to precise tolerances that only statistical quality-control methods can achieve. Many demand that suppliers be certified to tough European standards, a goal Northeast is pursuing.

All this requires more training than Price, a high school graduate, had gained through work experience. For him, the payoff comes in getting a shot at advancement and improving his $15-an-hour pay. From manager Arant's perspective, there's no choice at all. Arant plans to use his higher-skilled workforce to bid for more lucrative business and expand. If he didn't, Northeast could fall behind, as Arant thinks some rivals may do. "They'll run the machines as long as they can and then close," he predicts.

Until recently, workers such as Price probably would have been out of luck. Northeast, a flyspeck of a company with annual revenues of less than $5 million, simply wouldn't have had the wherewithal to launch its ambitious training program. And many companies, large and small, were loath to invest too much in workers, only to lose them later. Now, though, more companies feel they can't afford not to train. And Northeast, like other small companies, has been able to tap into a growing network of local and state training initiatives. Often, these are cobbled together with regional or state development funds and community-college training programs.

As a result, Northeast is spending just $35,000 for its entire training plan. North Carolina has set up programs to assist small companies, helped out with staff advice, software, and access to the nearby community college. Such state programs are growing fast. "If we don't invest in higher skills, we relegate ourselves to low-wage jobs," says Eric Butler, president of Bay States Skills Corp., which coordinates training programs in Boston.

The education message rings so loudly today that some job-seekers actually target high-performance employers just to get the schooling. In fact, in the post–cold-war era, such companies are replacing military as a blue-collar training ground as a way to get some college education, or its equivalent, inexpensively. Many companies are willing to sink money into training if they feel confident the employee has the profile of a lifelong learner. "We look for people who want change, who don't see it as troublesome, but as an opportunity," says David P. Jones, an official of Aon Consulting, a Chicago firm that assists manufacturers in testing and hiring.

QUESTIONS

1. Examine the changes that have been made in Fred Price's job at Northeast Tool, and then compare these to the four types of job design approaches described earlier in this chapter. If we had before-and-after measures on each of the four approaches, which would have revealed the largest change in the content of the job and which would have revealed the least: motivational, mechanistic, biological, or perceptual–motor? Knowing what you do about the trade-offs for various changes in job design, what negative outcomes might we fear from the types of changes brought about at Northeast?
2. Technological changes, like the robotization of operations at Northeast Tool, can affect the structure of organizations, which in turn can change the level of skill requirements for workers. How did robotization affect the structure of Northeast Tool and the skill requirements for Fred Price's job? Can you think of other technological advancements that have resulted in the opposite effects on worker skill requirements (e.g., in the fast food or retail industries)? In what sense does the competitive strategy employed by the firm influence in which direction technology is likely to affect skill levels of workers?
3. As we will see throughout this text, globalization has widespread effects on human resource practices. To what extent were the changes in jobs that came about at North-

east Tool driven by factors outside the United States? If companies like Northeast Tool did not make these types of changes to compete, what other changes might they have had to make? If Fred Price was not willing to make the types of self-improvements he is making, what other types of changes might he have had to accept? What are the national implications of these kinds of changes, and how do these changes relate to the competitive advantage of nations like the United States?

SOURCE: S. Baker, "The New Factory Worker," *Business Week*, September 30, 1996.

NOTES

1. J. Galbraith and R. Kazanjian, *Strategy Implementation: Structure, Systems, and Process* (St. Paul, MN: West Publishing, 1986).
2. D. Ilgen and J. Hollenbeck, "The Structure of Work: Job Design and Roles," in *Handbook of Industrial & Organizational Psychology*, 2d ed., ed. M. Dunnette and L. Hough (Palo Alto, CA: Consulting Psychologists Press, 1991), pp. 165–208.
3. R. Harvey, "Job Analysis," in ibid., pp. 71–164.
4. R. Griffin, *Task Design: An Integrative Approach* (Glenview, IL: Scott Foresman, 1982).
5. B. Brocka and M.S. Brocka, *Quality Management: Implementing the Best Ideas of the Masters* (Homewood, IL: Business One Irwin, 1992).
6. R. Pritchard, D. Jones, P. Roth, K. Stuebing, and S. Ekeberg, "Effects of Group Feedback, Goal Setting, and Incentives on Organizational Productivity," *Journal of Applied Psychology* 73 (1988), pp. 337–60.
7. D. Bowen and E. Lawler, "Total Quality-Oriented Human Resources Management," *Organizational Dynamics* (1992), pp. 29–41.
8. M. Fefer, "Bill Gates' Next Challenge," *Fortune*, December 14, 1992, pp. 30–41.
9. E. McCormick, "Job and Task Analysis," in *Handbook of Industrial & Organizational Psychology*, ed. M. Dunnette (Chicago: Rand McNalley, 1976), pp. 651–96.
10. E. Primoff and S. Fine, "A History of Job Analysis," in *The Job Analysis Handbook for Business, Industry, and Government*, ed. S. Gael (New York: Wiley, 1988), pp. 14–29.
11. W. Cascio, *Applied Psychology in Personnel Management*, 4th ed. (Englewood Cliffs, NJ: Prentice-Hall, 1991).
12. P. Wright and K. Wexley, "How to Choose the Kind of Job Analysis You Really Need," *Personnel* (May 1985), pp. 51–55.
13. J. Walker, *Human Resource Strategy* (New York: McGraw-Hill, 1992).
14. R. Gatewood and H. Feild, *Human Resource Selection*, 2d ed. (Hinsdale, IL: Dryden, 1990).
15. I. Goldstein, *Training in Organizations*, 3d ed. (Pacific Grove, CA: Brooks/Cole, 1993).
16. K. Murphy and J. Cleveland, *Performance Appraisal: An Organizational Perspective* (Boston: Allyn & Bacon, 1991).
17. R. Harvey, L. Friedman, M. Hakel, and E. Cornelius, "Dimensionality of the Job Element Inventory (JEI): A Simplified Worker-Oriented Job-Analysis Questionnaire," *Journal of Applied Psychology* 73 (1988), pp. 639–46.
18. A. O'Reilly, "Skill Requirements: Supervisor–Subordinate Conflict," *Personnel Psychology* 26 (1973), pp. 75–80.
19. J. Hazel, J. Madden, and R. Christal, "Agreement between Worker–Supervisor Descriptions of the Worker's Job," *Journal of Industrial Psychology* 2 (1964), pp. 71–79.
20. K. Wexley and S. Silverman, "An Examination of Differences between Managerial Effectiveness and Response Patterns on a Structured Job-Analysis Questionnaire," *Journal of Applied Psychology* 63 (1978), pp. 646–49.
21. P. Conley and P. Sackett, "Effects of Using High- versus Low-Performing Job Incumbents as Sources of Job-Analysis Information," *Journal of Applied Psychology* 72 (1988), pp. 434–37.
22. W. Mullins and W. Kimbrough, "Group Composition as a Determinant of Job-Analysis Outcomes," *Journal of Applied Psychology* 73 (1988), pp. 657–64.
23. N. Hauenstein and R. Foti, "From Laboratory to Practice: Neglected Issues in Implementing Frame-of-Reference Rater Training," *Personnel Psychology* 42 (1989), pp. 359–78.
24. N. Schmitt and S. Cohen, "Internal Analysis of Task Ratings by Job Incumbents," *Journal of Applied Psychology* 74 (1989), pp. 96–104.
25. F. Landy and J. Vasey, "Job Analysis: The Composition of SME Samples," *Personnel Psychology* 44 (1991), pp. 27–50.
26. E. McCormick and R. Jeannerette, "The Position Analysis Questionnaire," in *The Job Analysis Handbook for Business, Industry, and Government*, pp. 880–901.
27. *PAQ Newsletter* (August 1989).
28. E. Primhoff, *How to Prepare and Conduct Job Element Examinations* (Washington, DC: U.S. Government Printing Office, 1975).
29. E. Fleishman and M. Reilly, *Handbook of Human Abilities* (Palo Alto, CA: Consulting Psychologists Press, 1992).
30. E. Fleishman and M. Mumford, "Ability Requirements Scales," in *The Job Analysis Handbook for Business, Industry, and Government*, pp. 917–935.
31. R. Christal, *The United States Air Force Occupational Research Project* (AFHRL-TR-73-75) (Lackland AFB, TX:

Air Force Human Resources Laboratory, Occupational Research Division, 1974).

32. M.K. Lindell, C.S. Clause, C.J. Brandt, and R.S. Landis, "Relationship between Organizational Context and Job Analysis Ratings," *Journal of Applied Psychology* 83 (1998), pp. 769–76.
33. F.P. Morgeson and M.A. Campion, "Social and Cognitive Sources of Potential Inaccuracy in Job Analysis," *Journal of Applied Psychology* 82 (1997), pp. 627–55.
34. K. Cameron, S. Freeman, and A. Mishra, "Best Practices in White Collar Downsizing: Managing Contradictions," *The Executive* 5 (1991), pp. 57–73.
35. M. Campion and P. Thayer, "Development and Field Evaluation of an Interdisciplinary Measure of Job Design," *Journal of Applied Psychology* 70 (1985), pp. 29–34.
36. R. Griffin and G. McMahan, "Motivation through Job Design," in *OB: The State of the Science*, ed. J. Greenberg (Hillsdale, NJ: Lawrence Erlbaum Associates, 1993).
37. M. Campion, "Ability Requirement Implications of Job Design: An Interdisciplinary Perspective," *Personnel Psychology* 42 (1989), pp. 1–24.
38. F. Herzberg, "One More Time: How Do You Motivate Employees?" *Harvard Business Review* 65 (1987), pp. 109–20.
39. R. Hackman and G. Oldham, *Work Redesign* (Boston: Addison-Wesley, 1980).
40. F. Taylor, *The Principles of Scientific Management* (New York: W.W. Norton, 1967) (originally published in 1911 by Harper & Brothers).
41. D. May and C. Schwoerer, "Employee Health by Design: Using Employee Involvement Teams in Ergonomic Job Redesign," *Personnel Psychology* 47 (1994), pp. 861–86.
42. W. Howell, "Human Factors in the Workplace," in *Handbook of Industrial & Organizational Psychology*, 2d ed., pp. 209–70.
43. M. Campion and C. McClelland, "Interdisciplinary Examination of the Costs and Benefits of Enlarged Jobs: A Job-Design Quasi-experiment," *Journal of Applied Psychology* 76 (1991), pp. 186–98.
44. M. Campion and C. Berger, "Conceptual Integration and Empirical Test of Job Design and Compensation Relationships," *Personnel Psychology* 43 (1990), pp. 525–53.

Southwest Airlines: Competing Through People

For some organizations, the slogan "focus on customers" is merely a slogan. At Southwest Airlines, however, it is a daily goal. For example, Southwest employees responded quickly to a customer complaint: Five students who commuted weekly to an out-of-state medical school notified Southwest that the most convenient flight got them to class 15 minutes late. To accommodate the students, Southwest moved

the departure time up by a quarter of an hour.

Southwest Airlines is an organization that has built its business and corporate culture around the tenets of total quality management. Focus on the customer, employee involvement and empowerment, and continuous improvement are not just buzz words to Southwest employees or to Herb Kelleher, CEO of Southwest Airlines in Dallas. In fact, Kelleher has even enlisted passengers in the effort to strengthen the customer-driven culture. Frequent fliers are asked to assist personnel managers in interviewing and selecting prospective flight attendants. Focus groups are used to help measure passenger response to new services and to help generate new ideas for improving current services. Additionally, the roughly 1,000 customers who write to the company every week generally get a personal response within four weeks. Southwest has been a frequent winner of the U.S. Department of Transportation's Triple Crown Award for best on-time performance, best baggage handling, and fewest customer complaints.

THE AIRLINE INDUSTRY

Southwest has been posting hefty profits in an industry that lost $4 billion between 1990 and 1993. Since the 1978 Airline Deregulation Act, constant fare wars and intense competition have contributed to a turbulent environment for the industry. Under deregulation, the government no longer dictates where a given airline will fly and which cities should have service. Rates and service are now determined through competitive forces. The impact on the industry has been tremendous. In 1991 alone, three carriers went through bankruptcy and liquidation, and in early 1992, TWA sought protection from its creditors. Very few airlines, such as Southwest, American, and Delta, have continued to grow into the 1990s.

In 1994, when industry earnings were only $100 million (on revenues of $54 billion), Southwest earned $179 million while spending an industry-low 7 cents a mile in operating costs. Southwest employing close to 26,000 employees, over the past ten years has grown revenues by 388% and net income by 1490%.

Both external factors, such as the price of jet fuel and the strength of the economy, and internal factors, including routing system designs, computerized reservation systems, and motivated, competent employees, help to determine success. The airline industry is capital intensive, with large expenditures for planes. In addition, carriers must provide superior customer service. Delayed flights, lost baggage, overbooked flights, cancellations, and unhelpful airline employees can quickly alienate an airline's passengers.

SOUTHWEST'S CORPORATE STRATEGY

Herb Kelleher has been the primary force in developing and maintaining a vision and strategy which have enabled Southwest Airlines to grow and maintain profitability. Created in the late 1960s as a low-fare, high-frequency, short-haul, point-to-point, single-class, noninterlining, fun-loving airline, it expands by "doing the same old thing at each new airport," Kelleher reports.

"Taking a different approach" is the Southwest way, which has allowed the airline to maintain growth even during periods of drastic change. Although reservations and ticketing are done in advance of a flight, seating occurs on a first-come, first-serve basis and is only one illustration of the company's nonconformist practices. Turnaround times are kept to an industry low of 15 minutes with the help of pilots and crew who clean and restock the planes. Refreshments are limited to soft drinks and peanuts, except on its longer flights when cookies and crackers are added to the menu. Southwest does not exchange tickets or baggage with other carriers. Kelleher has noted that if Southwest adopted an assigned seating and computerized, interlining reservation system, ground time would increase enough to necessitate the purchase of at least seven additional airplanes. At a cost of $25 million apiece, the impact on the fares customers pay would be high. Currently, Southwest charges significantly less than its competitors.

CORPORATE PHILOSOPHY, CULTURE, AND HRM PRACTICES

How does Southwest maintain its unique, cost-effective position? In an industry in which antagonistic labor-management relations are common, how does Southwest build cooperation with a work force that is 83 percent unionized? Led by Kelleher, the corporation has developed a culture that treats employees the same way it treats passengers—by paying attention, being responsive, and involving them in decisions.

According to Elizabeth Pedrick Sartain, vice-president of People (the company's top HRM person), Southwest's corporate culture makes the airline unique. "We feel this fun atmosphere builds a strong sense of community. It also counterbalances the stress of hard work and competition." As Kelleher has stated, "If you don't treat your own people well, they won't treat other people well." So, Southwest's focus is not only on the customer but on the employees, too.

At Southwest, the organizational culture includes a high value on flexibility of the work force. Employees take pride in their ability to get a plane ready to go in only 20 minutes, less than half the industry average. A cultural refrain is "Can't make money with the airplane sitting on the ground." Ramp agents unload baggage, clean the lavatories, carry out trash, and stock the plane with ice, drinks, and peanuts. Flight attendants prepare the cabin for the next flight, and pilots have been known to pitch in when they have time. Working hard is not just an obligation at Southwest; it is a source of pride. Ramp agent Mike Williams brags that in a conversation with an employee for another airline, the other man explained Southwest's fast turnaround by saying, in Williams's words, "The difference is that when one of [the other company's] planes lands, they work it, and when one of our planes lands, we *attack* it."

In addition to the high motivation and expectations for performance, evidence of the company culture can be seen in the recruitment and selection process. Southwest accepts applications for ground operations positions or as flight attendants all year round. Many of the applicants are Southwest customers who've seen recruitment ads like the one featuring Kelleher dressed as Elvis. In 1994, Southwest received more than 126,000 applications for a variety of positions; the People Department interviewed more than 35,000 individuals for 4,500 positions. The expanding company was off to an even faster start the next year; in the first two months of 1995, it hired 1,200 new employees. This large labor pool allows the company to hire employees who most closely fit a culture in which they are asked to use their own judgment and to go beyond "the job description."

Kelleher's philosophy of "fun in the workplace" can be seen in the amount of time devoted to employee recognition. When Southwest won the Triple Crown Award for the fifth year in a row, an airplane was dedicated to all employees. Their names were engraved on the outside of the overhead bins! Company parties can be triggered by many events, including the CEO's birthday, when employees dress in black. The annual company chili cook-off, Southwest's annual awards dinner, and the every Friday "Fun Day," when employees wear casual clothes or even costumes to work, illustrate the company credo that a sense of humor is a must and that relaxed people are productive people. Kevin Krone, area manager of marketing in the Detroit office, described efforts by the Detroit area airport employees to set up get-togethers to foster both fun and the commitment to the Southwest family that supports the airline's culture.

When a reporter asked about the amount of time and money spent on employee recognition, Kelleher replied that the company could save money if they didn't do it but that's like "cutting out your heart."

Employee involvement in decision making is another key tenet of organizational culture at Southwest. An active, informal suggestion system and all types of incentives (cash, merchandise, and travel passes) serve to reward employees for their ideas. Both teams and individuals are expected, as part of their role at Southwest, to contribute to the development of customer service improvements and cost savings.

Corporate responses to difficult issues are consistently formulated around the company philosophy. As the cost of benefits has risen, cost-conscious Southwest redesigned the employee benefits program into a flexible plan. However, the company went a step further a few years ago, when Sartain was director of benefits and compensation. She believed that for the effort to succeed and satisfy employees, communication was critical. After seeking the advice of more than 700 employees in seven different cities, a promotional program that parodied newspapers and morning news shows was presented. Horoscopes, advice columns, and advertisements all promoted the new program, BenefitsPlus. Employees found this format more fun and less intimidating than the traditional benefits brochure. In fact, the effort won Southwest first place in the 1990 Business Insurance Employee Benefits Communication Awards competition. More importantly, employees understand their benefits options and appreciate the willingness of their organization to communicate openly.

Many human resource practices have been designed to support the company culture. Compensation programs are designed to increase the connections between Southwest and its employees, who enjoy the benefits of a profit-sharing program. Southwest employees own roughly 11 percent of the company's outstanding stock. The company's union contracts have avoided overly restrictive work rules in order to support the efficient operation of the company. Part of the company credo is that employees need to be able (and want to be able) to step in wherever they are needed, regardless of job title or classification. Southwest has not laid off an employee since its founding in 1971; annual employee turnover, at 7 percent, is the industry's lowest. In 1998, pilots voted to keep the second half of a ten year contract that offers small pay increases but large stock options. Pilots will receive five 3% wage increases plus stock options exercisable at $8.89. This ten year agreement is unmatched in the airline industry. Also, in 1996 Kelleher voluntarily agreed to freeze his pay at its 1992 level through 1999 to match the pilots' wage freeze. Such shared sacrifice helps build morale and organizational commitment even further.

The combined focus on customers and employees has led to an increase in the diversity of Southwest's work force. To serve passengers in the southwestern United States more effectively, the company has been recruiting Spanish-speaking employees as well as offering a Spanish Berlitz course at a discount to current employees.

The employees of Southwest are actively involved in numerous community-based service projects at Ronald McDonald house and the Junior Olympics, among others. This commitment to service is encouraged and demonstrated within the organization, too. A catastrophe fund, initiated by employees, supports individual employees during personal crises. Departments frequently show appreciation to other departments by giving awards and parties.

Kelleher claims that it is hard for Southwest to expand through the purchase of other airlines because the difficulty of merging two corporate cultures, particularly when one is so strong, is too great. In fact, the company's recent difficulties in the Pacific Northwest bear this out. Its expansion into that market was accomplished through the purchase of Morris Air. But Southwest continues to compete. Southwest has expanded routes into the Northeast and East Coast including Providence and Manchester and Raleigh/Durham North Carolina. To help with the expansion, Southwest expects to purchase twenty new jets, increasing its capacity by 13% in 1999. Southwest is also considering U.S. transcontinental service as well as adding an international partner.

"We tell our people that we value inconsistency," Kelleher explains. "By that I mean that . . . I can't foresee all of the situations that will arise at the stations across our system. So what we tell our people is, 'Hey, we can't anticipate all of these things, *you* handle them the best way possible. *You* make a judgment and use *your* discretion; we trust you'll do the right thing.' If we think you've done something erroneous, we'll let you know—without criticism, without backbiting."

Employees offer a large number of what they consider to be "everyday examples" of ways they provide high-quality service to their customers. When a California customer service agent was approached by a harried man who needed to catch a flight to meet his vacationing family, the man wanted to check his dog onto the flight. Because Southwest does not fly animals, this could have caused him to miss the flight and his family. The service agent involved volunteered to take the dog home, care for it, and bring the dog back to meet the man two weeks later, upon his return. A torn-up back yard and a very appreciative customer were the outcomes.

DISCUSSION QUESTIONS

1. How has Southwest dealt with the competitive challenges in the airline industry today? Rank, in order of importance, the various human resource practices and business practices (such as the low-price strategy) that Southwest Airlines has developed to successfully meet its competitive challenges.
2. Do you think that Southwest's success is more a result of business practices, human resource practices, or the interaction between the two? Can good HR practices help a company be successful without good business practices?
3. How might a ground crew supervisor at Southwest describe her job, given the corporate culture and practices of this organization?
4. Which Southwest HRM strategies directly support total quality management?
5. What aspects of work life at Southwest do you think you would most enjoy and least enjoy? Why?
6. Would the HRM practices used at Southwest Airlines work in other organizations? Why or why not?

SOURCES: Scott McCartney, "Southwest Airlines Net Sets Record for 4th Quarter," *The New York Times*, January 26, 1996, A4; Brenda Paik Sunoo, "How Fun Flies at Southwest Airlines," *Personnel Journal*, June 1995, 62–73; Scott McCartney, "Salary for Chief of Southwest Air Rises after Four Years," *The Wall Street*

Journal, April 29, 1996, A24; "Southwest Air to Add Routes," *The Wall Street Journal*, April 4, 1996, C20; "Southwest Air to Add at Least One City before the Year Ends," *The Wall Street Journal*, May 17, 1996, C11; National Public Radio, "Morning Edition," June 30, 1994; J. Castelli, "Finding the Right Fit," *HRMagazine*, September 1990, 38–41; D. K. Henderson, "Southwest Luvs Passengers, Employees, Profits," *Air Transport World*, July 1991, 32–41; J. E. Hitchcock, "Southwest Airlines Renovates Benefits System," *HRMagazine*, July 1992, 54–56; C. A. Jaffe, "Moving Fast by Standing Still," *Nation's Business*, October 1991, 57–59; J. C. Quick, "Crafting an Organizational Culture: Herb's Hand at Southwest," *Organizational Dynamics*, 21 (1992): 45–56; R. S. Teitelbaum, "Southwest Airlines: Where Service Flies Right," *Fortune*, August 24, 1992, 115–116. Staff Reporter, "Southwest Pilots Vote to Keep Second Half of 10-Year Contract," *The Wall Street Journal*, September 21, 1998, A8: S. McCartney, "Southwest Puts New York on Map," *The Wall Street Journal*, October 4, 1998, B1–B4, S. Gruner, "Have Fun, Make Money," *Inc.*, May 1998, p. 123. S. McCartney, "Southwest Air Plans Service to Raleigh, Continuing Its Move Into East Coast," *The Wall Street Journal*, March 4, 1999, A4. For more information on Southwest Airlines, including the latest press releases, tour of a Boeing 737, or the most recent flight schedule, visit the Southwest Airlines home page on the World Wide Web at http://www.iflyswa.com.

PART II
Acquisition and Preparation of Human Resources

CHAPTER

Human Resource Planning and Recruitment

OBJECTIVES

After reading this chapter, you should be able to

1. Discuss how to align a company's strategic direction with its human resource planning.
2. Determine the labor demand of workers in various job categories.
3. Discuss the advantages and disadvantages of various ways of eliminating a labor surplus and avoiding a labor shortage.
4. Describe the various recruitment policies organizations adopt to make the job vacancies more attractive.
5. List the various sources from which job applicants can be drawn, their relative advantages and disadvantages, and the methods for evaluating them.
6. Explain the recruiter's role in the recruitment process, the limits the recruiter faces, and the opportunities available.

GE Medical: Lighting the Way through a Labor Shortage

ENTER THE WORLD OF BUSINESS

In the summer of 1998, the national unemployment rate in the United States dropped to 4.7 percent, its lowest level in over 25 years. For employers, this meant—despite a growing economy and increased demand for their products and services—an inability to meet this demand for their products and services because of a lack of qualified human resources. One survey of 300 financial, high-tech, manufacturing, and management consulting firms revealed that four out of five (80 percent) of these companies thought they could increase revenues if they could find the workers they need—some as much as 200 percent.

This widespread labor shortage can be seen in many industries. For example, at the low-skill end of the economy, HELP WANTED signs can be seen in almost every fast food restaurant, grocery store, and strip mall retailing outfit across the country. At the high-skill end of the economy, demand for engineering graduates has been so strong that unemployment rates for this group are estimated to be less than 1 percent. Indeed, the Information Technology Association of America estimates that 190,000 jobs stand vacant in this industry. With a large group of baby boomers approaching retirement age at the start of the new millennium, it seems unrealistic to think that labor shortages at the low-skill or high-skill end of the market are likely to go away soon.

While many employers complain about difficulties created by this unprecedented labor shortage, others see an opportunity to gain competitive advantage over their rivals. For example, General Electric Medical Systems not only has been able to fill all its high-tech vacancies, but at the same time has cut the cost of hiring by 20 percent, the time needed to fill a position by 30 percent, and the failure rate of new hires by 50 percent. GE Medical achieved this by applying many skills it already had in the area of procurement of wires, screws, and boards to the procurement of people. The process begins with a tight engineeringlike specification of the job requirements, followed by a quantitative analysis of the best performing source of recruits, such as internship programs and employee referrals.

To highlight the competitive aspect of the process, one favorite source of employee referrals is new employees who used to work for Motorola. These people are used to help recruit the best of their former coworkers, thus enhancing GE's ability to compete, while at the same time directly compromising the ability of their competitors. Similarly, Cisco Systems arranged its Website so that whenever anyone from rival 3Com visited, they were automatically greeted with: "Welcome to Cisco. Would you like a job?" This aggressive and innovative recruiting is a major component of Cisco's competitive strategy. Indeed, as Janet Skadden (director of human resources as Cisco) notes, the company is making its own products obsolete every 6 to 12 months. The same is true of HR.

SOURCE: R. MacDonald, "Help!" *Time,* June 22, 1998, pp. 67–72; R.E. Stross, "Employers Beg for Techie Help in the Valley," *Fortune,* July 21, 1997, pp. 98–102; S. Baker, "Calling All Nerds," *Business Week,* March 10, 1997, pp. 51–53; T.E. Stewart, "In Search of Elusive Tech Workers," *Fortune,* February 16, 1997, pp. 171–72; P. Nakache, "Cisco's Recruiting Edge," *Fortune,* January 12, 1999, pp. 275–76.

Introduction

As the opening vignette illustrates, employers do not exist in a vacuum. Two of the major ways that societal trends affect employers is through (1) consumer markets which affect the demand for goods and services, and (2) labor markets, which affect the supply of people to produce goods and services. In some cases, as we just saw, a shortage of labor will restrict growth during periods of high demand. In other cases, a surplus of labor will generate costs that cannot be recovered during periods of low product demand. Reconciling these two environmental forces is a challenge. Some firms will rise to this challenge and others will not, so here is another arena where one firm can gain a competitive advantage over another.

There are three keys to effectively utilizing labor markets to one's competitive advantage. First, companies must have a clear idea of their current configuration of human resources. In particular, they need to know the strengths and weaknesses of their present stock of employees. Second, organizations must have a plan as to where they are going in the future and be aware how their present configuration of human resources relates to the configuration that will be needed in the future. Third, where there are discrepancies between the present configuration and the configuration required for the future, organizations need programs that will address these discrepancies. Under conditions of a labor surplus, this may mean creating an effective downsizing intervention. Under conditions of a labor shortage, this may mean waging an effective recruitment campaign.

This chapter looks at tools and technologies that can be used to help an organization develop and implement effective strategies for leveraging labor market "problems" into opportunities to gain competitive advantage. In the first half of the chapter, we lay out the actual steps that go into developing and implementing a human resource plan. Through each section, we will focus especially on recent trends and practices (e.g., downsizing, employing temporary workers, outsourcing) that can have a major impact on the firm's bottom line results and overall reputation. In the second half of the chapter, we familiarize you with the process by which individuals find and choose jobs and the role of personnel recruitment in reaching these individuals and shaping their choices.

The Human Resource Planning Process

An overview of the human resource planning process is depicted in Figure 5.1. The process consists of forecasting, goal setting and strategic planning, and program implementation and evaluation. We will discuss each of these stages in the next sections of this chapter.

FORECASTING

The first step in the planning process is **forecasting,** as shown in the top portion of Figure 5.1. In personnel forecasting, the HR manager attempts to ascertain the supply of and demand for various types of human resources. The primary goal is to predict areas within the organization where there will be future labor shortages or surpluses.

Forecasting, on both the supply and demand sides, can be done using either statistical methods or judgmental methods. Statistical methods are excellent for capturing historic trends in a company's demand for labor, and under the right conditions they give predictions that are much more precise than those that could be achieved through subjective judgments of a human forecaster. On the other hand, many important events that occur in the labor market have no historical precedent; hence, statistical methods that work from historical trends are of little use in such cases. In these situations one

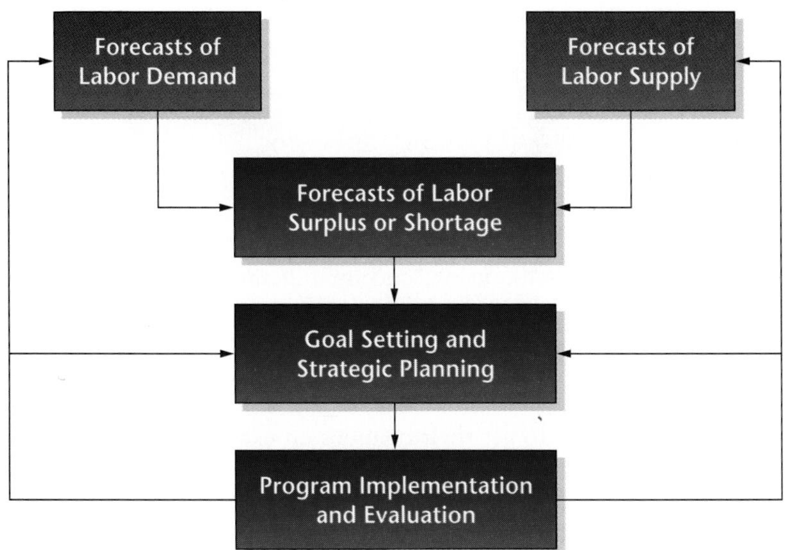

FIGURE 5.1 Overview of the Human Resource Planning Process

must rely on the pooled subjective judgments of experts, and their "best guesses" might be the only source from which to make inferences about the future. Typically, because of the complementary strengths and weaknesses of the two methods, companies that engage in human resource planning use a balanced approach that includes both statistical and judgmental components.

DETERMINING LABOR DEMAND. Typically, demand forecasts are developed around specific job categories or skill areas relevant to the organization's current and future state. Once the job categories or skills are identified, the planner needs to seek information that will help the planner predict whether the need for people with those skills or in that job category will increase or decrease in the future. Organizations differ in the sophistication with which such forecasts are derived.

At the most sophisticated level, an organization might have statistical models that predict labor demand for the next year given relatively objective statistics on leading indicators from the previous year. A **leading indicator** is an objective measure that accurately predicts future labor demand. For example, a manufacturer of automobile parts that sells its product primarily to the Big Three automakers would use several objective statistics on the Big Three automakers for one time period to predict how much demand there would be for the company's product at a later time period. As shown in Figure 5.2, inventory levels, sales levels, employment levels, and profits at the Big Three in one year might predict the demand for labor in the production assembler job category in the next year.

For example, using historical records, one might use multiple regression techniques to assess the best predictive model for estimating demand for production assemblers from information on sales levels, inventory levels, employment levels and profits at the Big Three. Since this is not a statistics book, a detailed explanation of regression techniques is beyond our scope. Rather, we will simply note here that this technique will convert information of the four or more leading indicators into a single predicted value for demand for production assemblers that is optimal—at least according to the historical data.

Statistical planning models are useful when there is a long, stable history that can be used to reliably detect relationships among variables. However, these models almost always have to be complemented by subjective judgments of people who have expertise

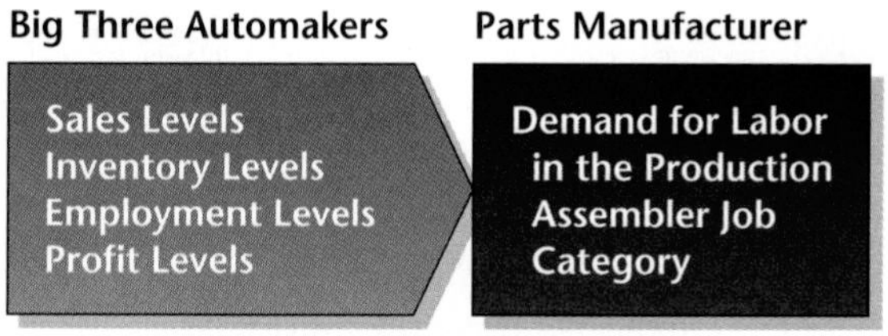

FIGURE 5.2
Leading Indicators of the Demand for Labor for a Hypothetical Auto Parts Manufacturer

Big Three Automakers	Parts Manufacturer
Sales Levels Inventory Levels Employment Levels Profit Levels	Demand for Labor in the Production Assembler Job Category

in the area. There are simply too many "once-in-a-lifetime" changes that have to be considered and that cannot be accurately captured in statistical models. For example, our small-parts manufacturer might learn that the leadership at one of the Big Three automakers changed and that the new leadership plans on closing 21 plants over the next 10 years. This event has no historical precedent, so the company might want to consult all its best managers to get their opinions on exactly how much this change would affect the demand for labor in different job categories.

DETERMINING LABOR SUPPLY. Once a company has projected labor demand, it needs to get an indicator of the firm's labor supply. Determining the internal labor supply calls for a detailed analysis of how many people are currently in various job categories (or who have specific skills) within the company. This analysis is then modified to reflect changes in the near future caused by retirements, promotions, transfers, voluntary turnovers, and terminations.

As in the case of labor demand, projections for labor supply can be derived either from historical statistical models or through judgmental techniques. One type of statistical procedure that can be employed for this purpose involves transitional matrices. **Transitional matrices** show the proportion (or number) of employees in different job categories at different times. Typically, these matrices show how people move in one year from one state (outside the organization) or job category to another state or job category.[1]

Table 5.1 shows a hypothetical transitional matrix for our parts manufacturer, focusing on seven job categories. Although these matrices look imposing at first, you will see that they are easy to read and use in determining the internal labor supply. A matrix like the one in this table can be read in two ways. First, we can read the rows to answer the question "Where did people in this job category in 1995 go by 1998?" For example, 70 percent of those in the clerical job category (row 7) in 1995 were still in this job category in 1998, and the remaining 30 percent had left the organization. For the production assembler job category (row 6), 80 percent of those in this position in 1995 were still there in 1998. Of the remaining 20 percent, half (i.e., 10 percent) were promoted to the production manager job category, and the other half (i.e., 10 percent) left the organization. Finally, 75 percent of those in the production manager job category in 1995 were still there in 1998, while 10 percent were promoted to assistant plant manager and 15 percent left the organization.

Reading these kinds of matrices across rows makes it clear that there is a career progression within this firm from production assembler to production manager to assistant plant manager. Although we have not discussed rows 1 through 3, it might also be noted that there is a similar career progression from sales apprentice to sales representative to sales manager. In this organization, the clerical category is not part of any career progression. That is, this job category does not feed any other job categories listed in Table 5.1.

A transitional matrix can also be read from top to bottom (i.e., the columns) to answer the question "Where did the people in this job category in 1998 come from (i.e., Where were they in 1995)?" Again, starting with the clerical job (column 7), 70 per-

TABLE 5.1
A Hypothetical Transitional Matrix for an Auto Parts Manufacturer

1995	1998 (1)	(2)	(3)	(4)	(5)	(6)	(7)	(8)
(1) Sales manager	.95							.05
(2) Sales representative	.05	.60						.35
(3) Sales apprentice		.20	.50					.30
(4) Assistant plant manager				.90	.05			.05
(5) Production manager				.10	.75			.15
(6) Production assembler					.10	.80		.10
(7) Clerical							.70	.30
(8) Not in organization	.00	.20	.50	.00	.10	.20	.30	

cent of the 1998 clerical positions were filled by people who were also in this position in 1995, and the remaining 30 percent were external hires (i.e., they were not part of the organization in 1995). In the production assembler job category (column 6), 80 percent of those occupying this job in 1998 occupied the same job in 1995, and the other 20 percent were external hires. The most diversely staffed job category seems to be that of production manager (column 5): 75 percent of those in this position in 1998 held the same position in 1995; however, 10 percent were former production assemblers who were promoted, 5 percent were former assistant plant managers who were demoted, and 10 percent were external hires who were not with the company in 1995.

Matrices such as these are extremely useful for charting historical trends in the company's supply of labor. More important, if conditions remain somewhat constant, they can also be used to plan for the future. For example, if we believe that we are going to have a surplus of labor in the production assembler job category in the next three years, we note that by simply initiating a freeze on external hires; the ranks of this position will be depleted by 20 percent on their own. Similarly, if we believe that we will have a labor shortage in the area of sales representatives, the matrix informs us that we may want to (1) decrease the amount of voluntary turnover in this position, since 35 percent of those in this category leave every three years, (2) speed the training of those in the sales apprentice job category so that they can be promoted more quickly than in the past, and/or (3) expand external recruitment of individuals for this job category, since the usual 20 percent of job incumbents drawn from this source may not be sufficient to meet future needs. As with labor demand, historical precedents for labor supply may not always be reliable indicators of future trends. Thus, statistical forecasts of labor supply also need to be complemented with judgmental methods.

DETERMINING LABOR SURPLUS OR SHORTAGE. Once forecasts for labor demand and supply are known, the planner can compare the figures to ascertain whether there will be a labor shortage or labor surplus for the respective job categories. Once this is determined, the organization can determine what it is going to do about these potential problems.

Japan's Matsushita Corporation provides a good example of the benefits of accurate forecasting. Because so many of Matsushita's revenues come from exported products, a leading indicator for its labor demand is the value of the Japanese yen against other currencies. There is a strong negative correlation between the yen and sales because when the value of the yen is high, Matsushita's products are more expensive. This depresses demand for its products and, of course, its demand for Japanese labor.

In 1988, Matsushita's planners anticipated that the price of the yen would rise 30 percent by 1994, leading them to conclude if they did nothing, they would wind up having an oversupply of Japanese labor. Therefore, rather than expanding in Japan, they decided to open "export centers" all over the world. The export centers designed and produced televisions and air conditioners in Malaysia, China, and the United States, and prices of these goods were unaffected by the rising yen. By 1995, it was clear that these projections about the yen were highly accurate, and Matsushita's export centers were doing booming business.[2] Meanwhile, other Japanese companies that failed to accurately predict what would happen with this valuable leading indicator had to lay off workers—an act almost unprecedented in Japan until that time.[3]

GOAL SETTING AND STRATEGIC PLANNING

The second step in the human resource planning process is goal setting and strategic planning, as shown in the middle of Figure 5.1. The purpose of setting specific quantitative goals is to focus attention on the problem and provide a benchmark for determining the relative success of any programs aimed at redressing a pending labor shortage or surplus. The goals should come directly from the analysis of labor supply and demand and should include a specific figure about what should happen with the job category or skill area and a specific timetable for when results should be achieved.

The auto parts manufacturer, for instance, might set a goal to reduce the number of individuals in the production assembler job category by 50 percent over the next three years. Similarly, the firm might set a goal to increase the number of individuals in the sales representative job category by 25 percent over the next three years.

Once these goals are established, the firm needs to choose from the many different strategies available for redressing labor shortages and surpluses. Table 5.2 shows some of the options for a human resource planner seeking to reduce a labor surplus. Table 5.3 shows some options available to the same planner intent on avoiding a labor shortage.

This stage is critical because the many options available to the planner differ widely in their expense, speed, effectiveness, amount of human suffering, and revocability (i.e., how easily the change can be undone). In the past decade, the typical organizational response to a surplus of labor has been downsizing, which is fast but high in human suffering. The typical organizational response to a labor shortage has been either hiring temporary employees or outsourcing, responses that are fast and high in revocability. Given the pervasiveness of these choices, we will devote special subsections of this chapter to each of these three options.

DOWNSIZING. We define **downsizing** as the planned elimination of large numbers of personnel designed to enhance organizational competitiveness. Many organizations adopted this strategic option in the late 1980s and early 1990s, especially in the United States. In fact, over 85 percent of the Fortune 1000 firms downsized between 1987 and 1998, resulting in more than 7 million permanent layoffs—an unprecedented figure in U.S. economic history. The jobs eliminated in these downsizing efforts should not be thought of as temporary losses due to business cycle downturns or a recession but as per-

TABLE 5.2
Options for Reducing an Expected Labor Surplus

OPTION	SPEED	HUMAN SUFFERING
1. Downsizing	Fast	High
2. Pay reductions	Fast	High
3. Demotions	Fast	High
4. Transfers	Fast	Moderate
5. Work sharing	Fast	Moderate
6. Retirement	Slow	Low
7. Natural attrition	Slow	Low
8. Retraining	Slow	Low

OPTION	SPEED	REVOCABILITY
1. Overtime	Fast	High
2. Temporary employees	Fast	High
3. Outsourcing	Fast	High
4. Retrained transfers	Slow	High
5. Turnover reductions	Slow	Moderate
6. New external hires	Slow	Low
7. Technological innovation	Slow	Low

TABLE 5.3
Options for Avoiding an Expected Labor Shortage

manent losses due to the changing competitive pressures faced by businesses today. In fact, in over 80 percent of the cases where downsizing took place, the organizations initiating the cutbacks were making a profit at the time.[4] For example, in 1998, General Electric Company set in motion a $2 billion restructuring program even though all of GE's divisions were generating double-digit return on investments.[5]

Rather than trying to stem current losses, the major reasons for most downsizing efforts dealt with promoting future competitiveness. Surveys indicate four major reasons that organizations engaged in downsizing. First, many organizations were looking to reduce costs, and since labor costs represent a big part of a company's total costs, this is an attractive place to start. For example, Union Carbide spent $70 million up front on a downsizing effort that resulted in $250 million a year in savings on salaries, wages, and benefits.

Second, in some organizations, closing outdated plants or introducing technological changes to old plants reduced the need for labor. For example, at Caterpillar, as a result of changes in the way the company employs information technology, it now needs only one shift of workers to turn out a volume of engines that would have required two shifts a few years ago. To appreciate this kind of trade-off, it is instructive to examine Caterpillar's old and new methods.

A few years ago, if a customer wanted to order an engine with particular features, it had to work with Caterpillar representatives to translate what it needed into Caterpillar part numbers. The representatives would then forward the order to a shop floor supervisor, who would relay the order to workers. Workers would then order the needed parts and assemble the tools required. Now, using a computer connected to a mainframe at Caterpillar's Peoria, Illinois, headquarters, customers can electronically order an engine with the desired specifications in plain English right over phone lines. Caterpillar's computer then translates that ordinary language into the company's internal language and then ships the order directly to the workers on the factory floor. While shop floor workers read the computer printouts to figure out what engine to produce next, the computer is already sending the same message to a computer-controlled monorail system and robots that bring the worker the necessary parts, the necessary tools, and instructions about what to do. By using up-to-date information technology, Caterpillar's enhanced productivity allows it to get twice as much work out of the same number of individuals.[6]

A third reason for downsizing was that many mergers and acquisitions reduced the need for bureaucratic overhead, displacing many managers and some professional staff members. For example, the threat of health care reform in the mid-1990s prevented many pharmaceutical companies from raising prices. To maintain profitability in the face of price stagnation, many firms pursued merger strategies so that they would have more products but fewer people. For example, Rouche Holding Ltd. purchased Syntex Corporation for $5.3 billion, acquiring all its products, but then cut the Syntex payroll from 10,000 people to 5,000.[7] Similarly, outside the pharmaceutical industry, the 1998

Global Turbulence Keeps Boeing Grounded

COMPETING THROUGH GLOBALIZATION

Although organizational reengineering and restructuring programs in the early 1990s led to the largest number of layoffs in U.S. history, the expansion of the economy and long-term bull market of the mid-1990s resulted in a steady reduction of downsizing programs. Indeed, whereas over 600,000 employees were laid off in 1993, layoffs dropped to just over 400,000 in 1995 and 300,000 in 1997. Just as it appeared that we were going to turn the corner on layoffs, however, the Asian economic crisis peaking in January 1998 threatened to reverse this trend, revealing the once hidden interdependencies of global product, financial, and labor markets.

Asia's labor market problems were ignited by a financial currency crisis that touched off bankruptcies, halted spending, and slowed growth throughout the region, where the number of job losses was staggering. Over 2 million workers were displaced in Indonesia, Thailand, and South Korea. These losses were made even more salient by the culture in many of these countries, which promoted lifetime job security. As one worker noted, "This may sound odd to foreigners, but layoffs and pains of restructuring are a whole new concept for Koreans."

Any hope among U.S. workers that this type of economic calamity could be contained within that region, however, were quickly dashed by experiences of companies like Boeing. Boeing, which had reduced its work force by over 35 percent between 1990 and 1995, went on a hiring binge that brought in over 40,000 new workers in 1997. Stuck with a backlog of orders, many insiders thought that Boeing had "overdownsized" to the point that it could not meet the growing demand for new aircraft production. Thus, the hiring surge was, if anything, overdue.

However, a large percentage of the new orders and growth in this industry were from Asia, and the devaluation of Asian currencies meant that they could no longer afford to purchase what had been ordered. Malaysian Airlines, for example, had $4 billion in orders and options for 13 Boeing 777s that had to be canceled because the airline was strapped to service its $3 billion debt. Similar problems caused canceled orders from Korean Airlines and Singapore Airlines. Boeing has since delayed launching the new 777 models, and in December 1997 announced it would cut its payroll by 12,000 people. Unlike their Asian counterparts, however, the displaced American workers will at least enter an otherwise strong labor market and—if nothing else—at least they are used to being laid off.

SOURCE: G. Koretz, "Will Downsizing Ever Let Up," *Business Week*, February 16, 1998, p. 26; M.L. Clifford, "Jobs Shock," *Business Week*, December 22, 1997, pp. 48–50; A. Bernstein, "Oops, That's Too Much Downsizing," *Business Week*, June 8, 1998, p. 38; B. Einhorn, "Clipped Wings for Airlines," *Business Week*, pp. 49–50; D. Greising, "It's the Best of Times—or Is It?" *Business Week*, January 12, 1998, pp. 36–38.

merger between First Union Corporation and CoreStates Financial Corporation created administrative efficiencies, but led to the elimination of 12,000 jobs.[8]

A fourth reason for downsizing was that, for economic reasons, many firms changed the location of where they did business. Some of this shift was from one area of the United States to another—in particular, many organizations moved from the Northeast, the Midwest, and California to the South and mountain regions of the West. (For example, Universal Studios moved many of its operations out of Los Angeles to Orlando, Florida, where the costs of producing television shows are over 40 percent less than in LA.)[9] Some of this shift was also due to jobs moving out of the United States altogether. In 1998, Fruit of the Loom, citing the high costs of American labor announced that it was going to cut 2,900 domestic jobs in the United States and move production to Mexico.[10] Indeed, as the "Competing through Globalization" box shows, international influences on labor markets are growing stronger with each passing year.

Although the jury is still out on whether these downsizing efforts have led to enhanced organizational effectiveness, some early indications are that the results have not lived up to expectations. A recent study of 52 Fortune 100 firms shows that most firms that announce a downsizing campaign show worse, rather than better, financial performance in the following years.[11]

There seem to be a number of reasons for the failure of most downsizing efforts to live up to expectations in terms of enhancing firm performance. First, although the initial cost savings are a short-term plus, the long-term effects of an improperly managed downsizing effort can be negative. For example, in the Rouche Holding–Syntex merger discussed earlier, most employees who left did so voluntarily, taking advantage of a lucrative severance package. This "parachute" gave employees two to three years of full compensation, depending on their job level. Many felt that this strategy led to turnover among the best, most marketable scientists and managers. One former Syntex scientist now asks, "What makes them think they can be successful scientifically and discover new drugs when they have lost most of their good discovery people?"[12]

Second, many downsizing campaigns wind up letting go of people who turn out to be irreplaceable assets. In fact, one survey indicated that in 80 percent of the cases, firms wind up replacing some of the very people who were let go. One senior manager of a Fortune 100 firm described a situation in which a bookkeeper making $9 an hour was let go, but then, when the company realized she knew many things about the company that no one else knew, hired her back as a consultant for $42 an hour.[13]

A third reason downsizing efforts often fail is that employees who survive the purges become narrow-minded, self-absorbed, and risk-averse. Motivation levels drop off, because any hope of future promotions—or even a future—with the company dies out. Many employees also start looking for alternative employment opportunities. The negative publicity associated with a downsizing campaign can also hurt the company's image in the labor market, making it more difficult to recruit employees at a later point in time. The key to avoiding this kind of reputational damage is to ensure that the need for the layoff is well explained and that procedures for implementing the layoff are fair.[14] Although this may seem to reflect common sense, organizations are often reluctant to provide this kind of information, especially if part of the reason for the layoff was top-level mismanagement.[15]

Although many of these problems with downsizing efforts can be reduced with better planning, this is hardly a panacea for increasing organizational competitiveness as we move into the new millennium. More judicious use of all the other avenues for eliminating a labor surplus (shown in Table 5.2) is needed, but because many of these take effect slowly, without better forecasting, organizations will be stuck with downsizing as their only viable option.

EARLY RETIREMENT PROGRAMS. Another popular means of reducing a labor surplus is to offer an early retirement program. As shown in Figure 5.3, the average age of the U.S. work force is increasing. But, although many baby boomers are approaching traditional retirement age, early indications are that this group has no intention of retiring any time soon.[16] Several forces fuel the drawing out of older workers' careers. First, the improved health of older people in general in combination with the decreased physical labor in many jobs has made working longer a viable option. Second, this option is attractive for many workers because they fear Social Security will be cut, and many have skimpy employer-sponsored pensions that may not be able to cover their expenses. Finally, age discrimination legislation and the outlawing of mandatory retirement ages have created constraints on organizations' ability to unilaterally deal with an aging work force.

Although an older work force has some clear advantages for employers in terms of experience and stability, it also poses problems. First, older workers are sometimes more costly than younger workers because of their higher seniority, higher medical costs, and higher pension contributions. When the value of the experience offsets these costs,

FIGURE 5.3
Aging of the U.S. Population, 2000–2020

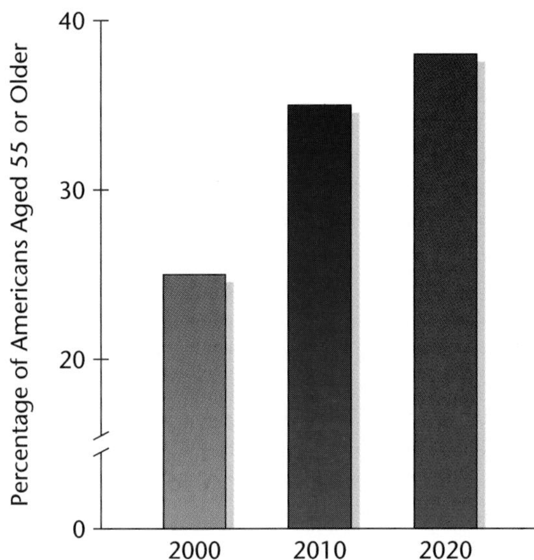

then employers are fine, but if it does not, it becomes difficult to pass these costs off to consumers. Second, since older workers typically occupy the best-paid jobs, they sometimes prevent the hiring or block the advancement of younger workers. This is frustrating for the younger workers and leaves the organization in a perilous position whenever the older workers do decide to retire.

For example, in the 20-year period between 1978 and 1997, Cummins Engine's Columbus plant did not hire a single new full-time person at its 2,800-employee plant. By the year 2000, almost all of its hourly workers will be old enough to retire, but there will be little if any experienced talent available to take their place. The company would like to bring in younger, cheaper workers, but its hands are tied by a no-layoff contract signed with the Diesel Workers Union and by poor performance in the product market (profits having dropped 29 percent in 1996).[17]

In the face of such demographic pressures, many employers try to induce voluntary attrition among their older workers through early retirement incentive programs. These programs come in an infinite variety. Depending on how lucrative they are, they meet with varied success. Although some research evidence suggests that these programs do induce attrition among lower-performing older workers,[18] to a large extent, such programs' success is contingent upon accurate forecasting. For example, at AT&T, CEO Mike Armstrong wanted to cut up to 11,000 managers between 1996 and 1999. However, by as early as 1997, 14,000 managers already opted for the package, and by 1998, AT&T went from having a labor surplus in this job category to having a severe labor shortage.[19]

EMPLOYING TEMPORARY WORKERS. While downsizing was the popular method for reducing a labor surplus, the 1990s saw hiring temporary workers and outsourcing as means of eliminating a labor shortage. Indeed, government estimates indicate that in 1997, there were close to 1 million people working in temporary job arrangements in the manufacturing sector alone, and 2.3 million across the entire economy.[20] Temporary employment affords firms the flexibility needed to operate efficiently in the face of swings in the demand for goods and services. Several other advantages with temporary employment arrangements need to be noted as well.

In addition to size flexibility, the use of temporary workers frees the firm from many administrative tasks and financial burdens associated with being the "employer of record." For example, the cost of benefits at McDonnell Douglas, including health care, pension, life insurance, workers' compensation, and unemployment insurance, accounted for 40 percent of payroll expenses in 1994. It is easy to understand why McDonnell Douglas's human resource plan raised the percentage of temporary workers from 4.3 percent in 1994 to 15 percent in 1996.

Second, small companies that cannot afford their own testing programs often get employees who have been tested by a temporary agency. For example, Cheryl Nelson (HR manager at Aligned Fiber Composites, a small manufacturer in Chatfield, Minnesota) notes that "we do not have a satisfactory means of testing employees in-house, so we turned to a temporary agency. We bring temporaries on for 90 days, and if they work out, and we can use them in permanent positions, we roll them on to our payroll." In fact, 17 percent of Aligned Fiber's permanent employees were once successful temporaries.[21]

Third, many temporary agencies train employees prior to sending them over to employers, which reduces training costs and eases the transition for both the temporary worker and the company. For example, when United Parcel Service (UPS) signed on with a temporary agency to supply data entry personnel, the agency designed a computer screen that simulated those used at UPS. A temporary worker would not be assigned to UPS unless he could achieve a certain keystroke level. Nike, the athletic shoe company, had a similar arrangement with an agency that provided workers who packed sneakers.[22]

Finally, because the temporary worker has little experience in the host firm, she brings an objective perspective to the organization's problems and procedures that is sometimes valuable. Also, since the temporary worker may have a great deal of experience in other firms, she can sometimes identify solutions to the host organization's problems that were confronted at a different firm. For example, one temporary worker at Lord, Abbett and Company, an investment firm in New York, suggested an efficient software program for managing portfolios that she had been trained with at a different firm. Thus, temporary employees can sometimes help employers to benchmark and improve their practices.

Certain disadvantages to employing temporary workers need to be overcome to effectively use this source of labor. For example, there is often tension between a firm's temporary employees and its full-time employees. Surveys indicate that 33 percent of full-time employees perceive the temporary help as a threat to their own job security. This can lead to low levels of cooperation and, in some cases, outright sabotage if not managed properly.

There are several keys to managing this problem. First, the organization needs to have bottomed out first in terms of any downsizing effort before it starts bringing in temporaries. A downsizing effort is almost like a death in the family for those employees who survive, and a decent time interval needs to exist before new temporary workers are introduced into this context. Without this time delay, there will be a perceived association between the downsizing effort (which was a threat) and the new temporary employees (who may be perceived by some as outsiders who have been hired to replace old friends). Any upswing in demand for labor after a downsizing effort should probably first be met by an expansion of overtime granted to core full-time employees. If this demand persists over time, one can be more sure that the upswing is not temporary and that there will be no need for future layoffs. The extended stretches of overtime will eventually tax the full-time employees, who will then be more receptive to the prospect of hiring temporary employees to help lessen their load.

Second, if the organization is concerned about the reactions of full-time workers to the temporaries, it may want to go out of its way to hire "nonthreatening" temporaries. For example, while most temporary workers want their temporary assignments to turn into full-time work (75 percent of those surveyed expressed this hope), not all do. Some prefer the freedom of temporary arrangements. These workers are the ideal temporaries for a firm with fearful full-time workers.

Firms can also create their own nonthreatening temporary pool staffed by full-time employees who move from unit to unit. For example, AT&T Universal Card Services in Jacksonville, Florida, created its own in-house temporary agency. These internal temporaries move from one department to another, depending on the demand for services. The company has created a special database that tracks each employee's past internal assignments, and this is used to check on the relevant experience of each such internal transfer.

Of course, in attempting to convince full-time employees that they are valued and not about to be replaced by temporary workers, the organization must not create the perception that temporary workers are second-class organizational citizens. As with managing the full-time employee concerns, there are several keys to managing the concerns of temporary employees. First, as far as possible, the organization should treat temporary employees the same way it treats full-time workers. For example, at Ford Motor Company in Detroit, temporary engineering employees were given the same memos, newsletters, and bulletins about the company as were regular employees, even though many of the projects they were working on had little to do with much of the organization's core business. Joe O'Hagan, principal engineer at Ford, notes, "We treated them as if they were an integral part of our team, and to be a part of our team, they had to know what everybody else knows. We worked to make sure they understood the big picture."[23]

HR staff can also prevent feelings of a two-tiered society by ensuring that the temporary agency provides benefits to the temporaries that are at least minimally comparable with those enjoyed by the full-time workers with whom they interact. For example, one temporary agency, MacTemps, provides its workers long-term health coverage, full disability insurance, and complete dental coverage. This not only reduces the benefit gap between the full-time and part-time workers but also helps attract the best part-time workers in the first place.

OUTSOURCING. Whereas a temporary employee can be brought in to manage a single job, in other cases a firm may be interested in getting a much broader set of services performed by an outside organization, and this is called **outsourcing.** For example, American Airlines established a contract with Johnson Controls Inc. to provide ticket agents for American's operations at 28 second-tier airports. In this case, cost control was the main reason—American paid its veteran agents at major airports $19 an hour plus benefits, the going market rate for this industry. Johnson Controls, on the other hand, pays the existing local market wage, only $8 an hour, for the 500 jobs that were handed over to it.

In other cases, outsourcing is driven by economies of scale that make it more efficient to hand over work to an outside agent. For example, several years ago Ford Motor Company had a unit that processed automobile financing applications. Now it hands this work over to Detroit-based MCN Corporation, which can do the same job with fewer people than Ford. MCN uses its seven giant mainframe computers and dedicated staff to process data for Ford (and over 25 other companies) with an efficiency that comes from a narrow focus on data entry and analysis, unfettered by the need to produce automobiles. APAC (a private telemarketing company in Cedar Rapids, Iowa) has a similar arrangement with Western Union, Compaq, Quill, Sears, and many other companies. APAC's specialty is answering the telephone, and its 4,000 operators take orders and provide information to customers of their clients. As Donald Gerryman, vice president of APAC, notes, "When you call our clients' 800 numbers, you get us."

Outsourcing is a logical choice when the firm simply does not have certain expertise and is not willing to invest the time and energy to develop it. For example, American

Express Financial Advisors (AEFA) has a leadership development division that provides training services to clients based on a detailed needs analysis. Sometimes this needs analysis turns up training requirements in areas where AEFA has no established curriculum. Where once the firm might have developed such curriculum for the client, now, to keep a more narrow focus, it launches a search for an outside supplier better able to meet this need. No new trainers are added to the AEFA payroll, and no costly curriculum development is initiated. As one manager notes, "There are just a lot of good programs out there, and we don't want to reinvent the wheel. . . . This allows us to keep ourselves very lean and focused."[24]

Outsourcing in the area of manufacturing often involves designing projects in the United States and then shipping manufacturing responsibilities overseas. Japanese and Korean firms, in particular, can often produce key components or even a finished product for 10 to 60 percent less than the cost on in-house manufacturing. For example, close to 50 percent of Chrysler's minicompact and subcompact cars are produced in Asia; Apple introduced a laptop computer produced by Sony; and Motorola set up equipment production centers in Hong Kong. Outsourcing in the service industry often means shipping data entry jobs overseas. Metropolitan Life Insurance has its medical claims analyzed in Ireland, where operating costs are about 35 percent less than in the United States. Typing mills in the Philippines are even more competitive, entering 10,000 characters for 50 cents; those in China will do the same for a mere 20 cents. Clearly, the labor supplies of countries like China, India, Jamaica, and those in Eastern Europe are creating an oversupply of labor for unskilled and low-skilled work.

Technological advancements in computer networking and transmission have speeded up the outsourcing process and have also helped it spread beyond manufacturing areas and low-skilled jobs. For example, firms that perform design engineering find that India is a fertile ground for outsourcing this type of work. India inherited a strong English-language school system from the days of British rule and has always emphasized mathematics in its school. Yet, Indian computer scientists earn only $1,300 a month on average, compared with $5,000 per month in the United States.[25] One survey of U.S. CEOs indicated that 42 percent of communication firms, 40 percent of computer manufacturers, and 37 percent of semiconductor companies rely on outsourcing to foreign firms, and most expect these percentages to grow to the 50 percent range by the late 1990s.[26]

Many are concerned that while this type of outsourcing may make good sense in the short term, its long-term implications for U.S. firms' competitiveness are negative. Although these firms may be reducing manufacturing costs, eventually they will find it more and more difficult to design products that can take advantage of innovations in technology. It is argued that outsourcing, if left unchecked, starts a downward spiral that prompts more and more outsourcing until the firm itself produces nothing of value. In the meantime, more and more U.S. workers get displaced. In the end, firms that do the manufacturing soon develop their own design teams and then become direct competitors with a substantial competitive advantage. For example, Toshiba once produced televisions for Sears and then introduced sets under its own brand name several years later. At that time, its marketing strategy was to simply say, "These televisions are exactly what you would get at Sears, but they cost less." Needless to say, Sears no longer produces televisions under its own brand name. Nationwide, whereas 100 percent of color television sets were manufactured by U.S. firms in 1960, by 1990 that share was down to 12 percent.[27]

OVERTIME AND EXPANDING WORKER HOURS. Companies facing a shortage of labor may be reluctant to hire new full-time or part-time employees. Under some conditions, these firms may have the option of trying to garner more hours out of the existing labor force. As Figure 5.4 shows, many employers opted for this strategy during

FIGURE 5.4
U.S. Factory Overtime Hours, 1990–97

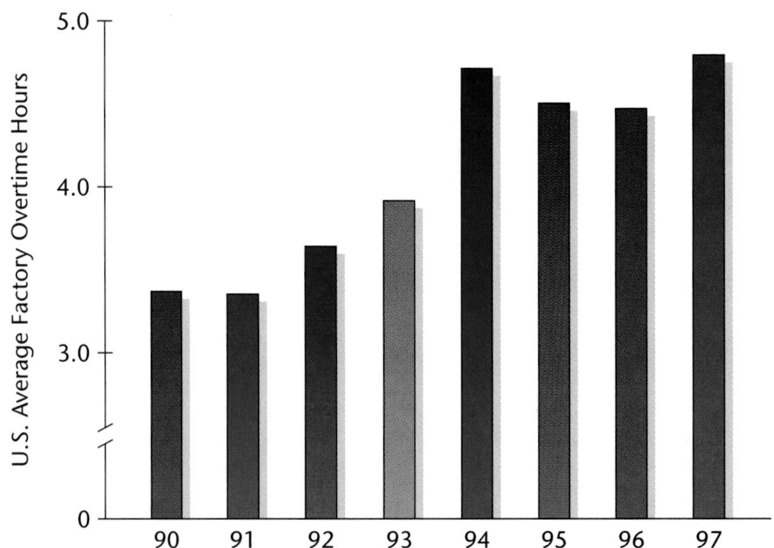

SOURCE: G. Koretz, "Overtime versus New Factories," *Business Week,* May 4, 1998, p. 34.

the 1990s. Indeed, 6 percent of the automobiles assembled in North America in 1997 resulted from overtime production. To put this in perspective, this is equivalent to the output of an additional four auto plants running on straight time.[28]

Despite having to pay workers time-and-a-half for overtime production, employers see this as preferable to hiring and training new employees—especially if they are afraid that current demand for products or services may not extend to the future. Also, for a short period of time at least, many workers enjoy the added compensation. However, over extended periods of time, employees experience stress and frustration from being overworked in this manner. Thus, it is not surprising that during the 1998 General Motor strikes, one of the employee demands was for the company to hire additional new workers.

PROGRAM IMPLEMENTATION AND EVALUATION

The programs developed in the strategic-choice stage of the process are put into practice in the program-implementation stage, shown at the bottom of Figure 5.1. A critical aspect of program implementation is to make sure that some individual is held accountable for achieving the stated goals and has the necessary authority and resources to accomplish this goal. It is also important to have regular progress reports on the implementation to be sure that all programs are in place by specified times and that the early returns from these programs are in line with projections.

The final step in the planning process is to evaluate the results. Of course, the most obvious evaluation involves checking whether the company has successfully avoided any potential labor shortages or surpluses. Although this bottom-line evaluation is critical, it is also important to go beyond it to see which of the specific parts of the planning process contributed to success or failure.

A good example of the type of diagnostic work that needs to be done can be seen in Bell Atlantic's recent failed downsizing effort. Convinced in 1994 that the company would need fewer workers, but facing a union (the Communication Workers of America) that was staunchly opposed to layoffs, Bell Atlantic developed a high-priced buyout plan. Any worker could take advantage of the buyout program, but they had do it before their contract expired in August 1998.

By June 1998 almost a third of its unionized work force (14,000 people) stood ready to take the company up on its offer. However, forecasts for product demand were grossly underestimated. Whereas Bell Atlantic forecasted lower demand for copper wiring, instead orders surged as many industrial and residential consumers added second lines for faxes and modems. The smaller work force could not keep up with demand, however. Stretching the hours of the remaining employees simply did not work in many traffic-congested metropolitan areas like New York City.

So, while many experienced employees were walking away with lucrative buyouts, Bell Atlantic had to replace them with inexperienced new hires amid a labor shortage in the overall U.S. economy. To avert disaster, the company had to offer a 25 percent hike in its already generous pension plan to any employee who would stay. The overall effect was to create an extravagant bonus system that rewarded employees for either staying or leaving.[29]

THE SPECIAL CASE OF AFFIRMATIVE ACTION PLANNING

We have argued that human resource planning is an important function that should be applied to an organization's entire labor force. It is also important to plan for various subgroups within the labor force. For example, affirmative action plans forecast and monitor the proportion of various protected group members, such as women and minorities, that are in various job categories and career tracks. The proportion of workers in these subgroups can then be compared with the proportion that each subgroup represents in the relevant labor market. This type of comparison is called a **work-force utilization review.** This process can be used to determine whether there are any subgroups whose proportion in the relevant labor market is substantially different from the proportion in the job category.

If such an analysis indicates that some group—for example, African Americans—makes up 35 percent of the relevant labor market for a job category but that this same group constitutes only 5 percent of the actual incumbents in that job category in that organization, then this is evidence of underutilization. Underutilization could come about because of problems in selection or from problems in internal movement, and this could be seen via transitional matrices discussed earlier in this chapter.

This kind of review is critical for many different reasons. First, many firms adopt "voluntary affirmative action programs" to make sure underutilization does not occur and to promote diversity. These efforts seem to be particularly needed at upper levels of management, where the underutilization of African Americans is most acute.[30] Second, companies might also engage in utilization reviews because they are legally required to do so. For example, if a company is a government contractor or subcontractor, Executive Order 11246 requires that such organizations maintain affirmative action programs. Third, affirmative action programs can be mandated by the courts as part of the settlement of discrimination complaints. Indeed, the new Civil Rights Act was largely supportive of these kind of court-ordered affirmative action plans.

Regardless of the motivation for adopting an affirmative action planning program, the steps required to execute such a plan are identical to the steps in the generic planning process discussed earlier in this chapter. That is, the company needs to assess current utilization patterns and then forecast how these are likely to change in the near future. If these analyses suggest that there is currently underutilization and if forecasts suggest that this problem is not likely to change, then the company may need to set goals and timetables for changing this situation. Certain strategic choices need to be made in the pursuit of these goals that might affect recruitment or selection practices, and then the success of these strategies has to be evaluated against the goals established earlier in the process.

The Human Resource Recruitment Process

As the first half of this chapter shows, it is difficult to always anticipate exactly how many (if any) new employees will have to be hired in a given year in a given job category. The role of human resource recruitment is to build a supply of potential new hires that the organization can draw on if the need arises. Thus, human resource recruitment is defined as any practice or activity carried on by the organization with the primary purpose of identifying and attracting potential employees.[31] It thus serves to create a buffer between planning and actual selection of new employees, which is the topic of our next chapter.

Recruitment activities are designed to affect (1) the number of people who apply for vacancies, (2) the type of people who apply for them, and/or (3) the likelihood that those applying for vacancies will accept positions if offered.[32] The goal of an organizational recruitment program is to ensure that the organization has a number of reasonably qualified applicants (who would find the job acceptable) to choose from when a vacancy occurs.

The goal of the recruiting is not simply to generate large numbers of applicants. If the process generates a sea of unqualified applicants, the organization will incur great expense in personnel selection (as discussed more fully in the next chapter), but few vacancies will actually be filled.

The goal of a personnel recruitment is not to finely discriminate among reasonably qualified applicants either. Recruiting new personnel and selecting new personnel are both complex processes. Each task is hard enough to accomplish successfully, even when one is well focused. Organizations explicitly trying to do both at the same time will probably not do either well. For example, research suggests that recruiters provide less information about the company when conducting dual-purpose interviews (interviews focused on both recruiting and selecting applicants).[33] Also, applicants apparently remember less information about the recruiting organization after dual-purpose interviews.[34]

Because of strategic differences among companies (see Chapter 2), the importance assigned to recruitment may differ.[35] In general, however, as shown in Figure 5.5, all companies have to make decisions in three areas of recruiting: (1) personnel policies, which affect the kinds of jobs the company has to offer, (2) recruitment sources used to solicit applicants, which affect the kinds of people who apply, and (3) the characteristics and behaviors of the recruiter, which affect the perceived fit between the applicant and the job.

FIGURE 5.5 Overview of the Individual Job Choice–Organizational Recruitment Process

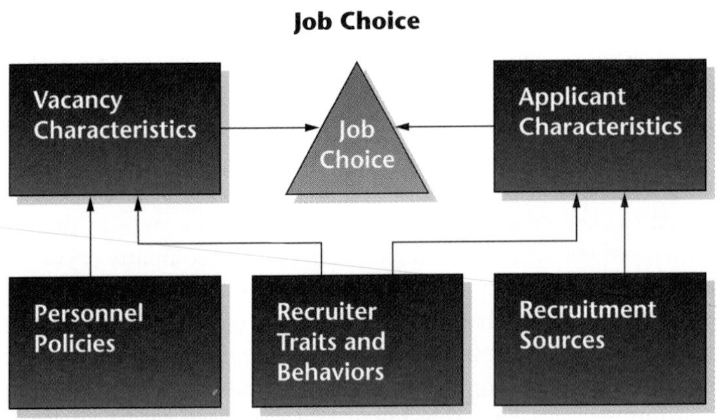

PERSONNEL POLICIES

Personnel policies is a generic term we use to refer to organizational decisions that affect the nature of the vacancies for which people are recruited. If the research on recruitment makes one thing clear, it is that characteristics of the vacancy are more important than recruiters or recruiting sources when it comes to predicting job choice.[36]

INTERNAL VERSUS EXTERNAL RECRUITING. One desirable feature of a vacancy is that it provides ample opportunity for advancement and promotion. One organizational policy that affects this is the degree to which the company "promotes from within"—that is, recruits for upper-level vacancies internally rather than externally. Indeed, a 1997 survey of MBA students found that this was their top consideration when evaluating a company.[37]

We discuss internal versus external recruiting both here and in "Recruitment Sources" later in this chapter because this policy affects the nature of both the job and the individuals who apply. For now, we focus on the effects that promote-from-within policies have on job characteristics, noting that such policies make it clear to applicants that there are opportunities for advancement within the company. These opportunities spring not just from the first vacancy but from the vacancy created when a person in the company fills that vacancy. For example, in a company with three levels of management, a vacancy at the third level that is filled from within may "trickle down," creating a vacancy at the second level; this, in turn, creates a vacancy at the first level.

McDonald's restaurants provide a good example of the virtues of promoting from within. Phil Hagans, an African American who was once a cook at a McDonald's, now owns two franchises thanks to a program that encourages low-income managers, regardless of race, to buy franchises. Hagans's restaurants not only turn a profit, they also perform a valuable social function by providing needed employment and work experience for many inner-city youths in the Houston area. In Hagans's view, programs such as this make McDonald's "the best company for African American entrepreneurs."[38] Other organizations cited as good companies for minorities are discussed in the "Competing by Meeting Stakeholders' Needs" box.

The retailing industry is an example of an entire sector of the economy that is increasingly being perceived as an area with good opportunities for internal advancement. This is especially the case for the superstores, such as Wal-Mart, Home Depot, and Target, where thousands of managers must be hired and promoted each year to run new outlets. Whereas the prestigious corporate giants in manufacturing and banking are cutting back personnel, Target chains hired 1,000 college graduates in the spring of 1996. In fact, as noted by Leonard Berry, director of the Center for Retailing, "These days, Wal-Mart and Kmart are two of the biggest recruiters on some college campuses." Applicants who used to shun retailing jobs are now attracted to them because of the opportunities for advancement. A new college graduate who goes to Target can have responsibility for 20 employees and an $8 million department just 12 weeks out of school. These trainees, if successful, can become managers of small stores in as little as three years. Some employees who started with Target at 24 years of age are regional senior vice presidents by the time they are 30.[39]

LEAD-THE-MARKET PAY STRATEGIES. Because pay is an important job characteristic for almost all applicants, companies that take a "lead-the-market" approach to pay—that is, a policy of paying higher-than-current market wages—have a distinct advantage in recruiting. Pay can also be used to make up for a job's less desirable features—for example, paying higher wages to employees who have to work midnight shifts. These kinds of specific shift differentials and other forms of more generic com-

Diversity: From Sinner to Saint in Nine Steps

In the early 1990s, Shoney's and Denny's restaurant chains were synonymous with racism in terms of how they treated both customers and employees. Their reputations were so bad that even late-night comics such as Jay Leno singled them out for ridicule ("They are serving something new at Denny's this year . . . African American customers.") It was no laughing matter, however, when in 1992 Shoney's paid out over $130 million to settle a class action suit brought by 20,000 African American employees, and Denny's paid out over $50 million in a similar class action suit filed by customers. Given this history, it was almost amazing that when *Fortune* came out with its inaugural list of "50 Best Companies for Blacks and Hispanics" in 1998, both Shoney's and Denny's made the top 15.

What does it take to make such a dramatic turnaround in managing diversity? To answer this question, it is instructive to look at the factors that went into the *Fortune* ranking system, because in an objective sense, this system quantifies some of the factors that minorities consider when evaluating how desirable it is to work for certain companies. Five of the nine factors that *Fortune* considers deal with minority representation at five different levels: the total work force, the board of directors, the 25 highest-paid officials, corporate officers, and managers. For example, in 1992 there was not a single African American, Hispanic, or Asian in top corporate management at Advantica, Denny's parent organization. However, by 1998, minorities accounted for over 30 percent of the top positions. Currently at Shoney's minorities constitute over 40 percent of the total labor force.

Two other factors that go into *Fortune's* rating system are the number of minorities hired within the past year and the number of diversity programs the company has in place. Denny's, for example, has teamed up with the NAACP's Fair Share Program, while Shoney's has partnered with the Southern Christian Leadership Conference in an effort to maintain yearly goals for minority hiring. These programs also target the last two criteria that go into the *Fortune* ranking system: the percentage of purchasing that goes to minority-owned suppliers and the amount of charitable giving to organizations that benefit minorities. Shoney's has increased direct purchases from minority suppliers from under $2 million in 1989 to over $36 million in 1997. Denny's (which had no contracts with minority vendors as recently as 1992) paid out over $125 million to such firms last year.

With all this focus on diversity, one might be concerned that these firms, along with the others listed among the Top 50, might lose their focus on the bottom line, but this does not seem to be the case. When *Fortune* compared the top 50 firms for diversity to the S&P 500, the top 50 outperformed the 500 by 12 percent over the previous three years and by 17 percent over the previous five. Thus, these firms seem to be meeting the needs of their employees, their customers, and their shareholders.

SOURCE: A. Faircloth, "Guess Who's Coming to Denny's?" *Fortune*, August 3, 1998, pp. 108–10; R. Johnson, "The 50 Best Companies for Asians, Blacks and Hispanics," *Fortune*, August 3, 1998, pp. 94–106; S. Branch, "What Blacks Think of Corporate America," *Fortune*, July 6, 1998, p. 140.

pensating differentials will be discussed in more detail in later chapters that focus on compensation strategies. We merely note here that "lead" policies make any given vacancy appear more attractive to applicants.

Increasingly, organizations that compete for applicants based on pay do so using pay forms other than wages and salary. For example, a 1997 survey indicates that close to 40 percent of employers used signing bonuses rather than higher wages to attract new hires, and up to 20 percent are providing lucrative stock option plans.[40] Bonuses and stock options are preferable for many employers because, unlike wages and salary, they tend not to compound over time and can be administered more flexibly.

EMPLOYMENT-AT-WILL POLICIES. Employment-at-will policies state that either party in the employment relationship can terminate that relationship at any time, regardless of cause. Companies that do not have employment-at-will provisions typically have extensive due process policies. Due process policies formally lay out the steps an employee can take to appeal a termination decision. Recent court decisions have increasingly eroded employers' rights to terminate employees with impunity.[41] To protect themselves from wrongful discharge suits, employers have been encouraged to state explicitly, in all formal recruiting documentation, that the employment is "at will."

Some authors have gone so far as to suggest that all mention of due process should be eliminated from company handbooks, personnel manuals, and recruiting brochures.[42] Although this may have some legal advantages, job security is an important feature to many job applicants. Organizational recruiting materials that emphasize due process, rights of appeal, and grievance mechanisms send a message that job security is high; employment-at-will policies suggest the opposite. Research indicates that job applicants find companies with due process policies more attractive than companies with employment-at-will policies.[43]

IMAGE ADVERTISING. Organizations often advertise specific vacancies (discussed later in "Recruitment Sources"). Sometimes, however, organizations advertise just to promote themselves as a good place to work in general.[44] Image advertising is particularly important for companies in highly competitive labor markets that perceive themselves as having a bad image.[45]

The challenge and responsibility associated with a job is an attractive characteristic for many people. Dow Chemical's $60 million television campaign in the early 1990s hammered home the message "Dow lets you do great things." This message was clearly aimed at affecting the general public's view of the nature of the work at Dow. It was also an attempt to offset recurring negative publicity resulting from controversies surrounding the production of napalm (1970s), Agent Orange (1980s), and faulty breast implants (1990s).[46] This negative publicity sometimes affected Dow's ability to recruit on college campuses. The U.S. Army's "Be all that you can be" campaign pursued a similar objective. These ads focused on the challenge associated with army jobs. They also attempted to offset certain negative attributes of the work, such as the fact that, in some of its jobs at certain times, other people are systematically trying to kill you.

Although the programs described here try to promote the employer in the labor market in general, other image advertising programs target specific groups within the overall labor market. For example, many large corporations with agricultural ties, such as DuPont and Cargill, struggle to attract minority applicants. Statistics indicate, for example, that Hispanics, Asians, and African Americans constitute a mere 4 percent, 3 percent, and 3 percent of all agriculture and food scientists, respectively. Lisa Barrios, a Mexican American who grew up in Chicago, typifies many urban minorities when she notes that "I assumed everything was just farming . . . if you didn't have a rural background, then you wouldn't be able to do it." After working at a special minority internship program at Monsanto's Hybritech unit in Indiana, however, Barrios changed her major from chemical engineering to agricultural engineering.[47]

RECRUITMENT SOURCES

The sources from which a company recruits potential employees are a critical aspect of its overall recruitment strategy. The total labor market is expansive; any single organization needs to draw from only a fraction of that total. The size and nature of the fraction that applies for an organization's vacancies will be affected by how (and to whom) the organization communicates its vacancies.[48] The type of person who is likely to respond to a job advertised on the Internet may be different from the type of person who responds to an ad in the classified section of a local newspaper. In this section, we examine the different sources from which recruits can be drawn, highlighting the advantages and disadvantages of each.

INTERNAL VERSUS EXTERNAL SOURCES. We discussed internal versus external sources of recruits earlier in this chapter and focused on the positive effects that internal recruiting can have on recruits' perceptions of job characteristics. We will now discuss this issue again, but with a focus on how using internal sources affects the kinds of people who are recruited.

In general, relying on internal sources offers a company several advantages.[49] First, it generates a sample of applicants who are well known to the firm. Second, these applicants are relatively knowledgeable about the company's vacancies, which minimizes the possibility of inflated expectations about the job. Third, it is generally cheaper and faster to fill vacancies internally.

For example, Inova Health Systems, a Virginia-based consortium of hospitals, originally centralized its human resource functions to cut recruitment costs. Prior to consolidation, Inova's many separate hospitals were all managing their own different recruitment and selection efforts. This not only led to duplication of efforts, but in many cases one Inova facility was competing with another for the very same applicants. Moreover, while no one facility had exorbitant costs, taken together they were spending $500,000 on recruitment advertising alone. The volume of applications (close to 30,000 a year) and the large numbers of interviews that needed to be conducted (over 3,000) added to these costs.

One part of the consolidation plan at Inova called for creating a database that contained all the existing personnel in one file, as well as an internal computer network for promoting interhospital communication. Once the new database was constructed, it became clear how many openings in one area could be filled by internal transfers and promotions from other areas that were experiencing a labor surplus. The vacancies were posted on the internal communication network, and then Inova employees were given first consideration when it came to interviewing. This policy enhanced the job satisfaction of current employees by increasing their chances of promotion and by enhancing the person–job fit via internal transfers. It also reduced the need for external hiring and the cost of generating and processing so many applications.[50]

With all these advantages, you might ask why any organization would ever employ external recruiting methods. There are several good reasons why organizations might decide to recruit externally.[51] First, for entry-level positions and perhaps even for some specialized upper-level positions, there may not be any internal recruits from which to draw. Second, bringing in outsiders may expose the organization to new ideas or new ways of doing business. Using only internal recruitment can result in a work force whose members all think alike and who therefore may be poorly suited to innovation.[52]

DIRECT APPLICANTS AND REFERRALS. Direct applicants are people who apply for a vacancy without prompting from the organization. Referrals are people who are prompted to apply by someone within the organization. These two sources of recruits share some characteristics that make them excellent sources from which to draw.

First, many direct applicants are to some extent already "sold" on the organization. Most of them have done some homework and concluded that there is enough fit between themselves and the vacancy to warrant their submitting an application. This process is called *self-selection*. When it works effectively, it takes a great deal of pressure off the organization's recruiting and selection systems. A form of aided self-selection occurs with referrals. Current employees (who are knowledgeable of both the vacancy and the person they are referring) do their homework and conclude that there is a fit between the person and the vacancy; they then sell the person on the job. Indeed, research shows that new hires that used at least one informal source reported having greater prehire knowledge of the organization than those who relied exclusively on formal recruitment sources. Those who report having multiple sources were even better, however, in terms of both prehire knowledge about the position and subsequent turnover. In fact, the turnover rate for applicants who came from multiple recruiting sources was half that of those recruited via campus interviews or newspaper advertisements.[53]

When one figures into these results the low costs of such sources, they clearly stand out as one of the best sources of new hires. Indeed, some employers even offer financial incentives to current employees for referring applicants who are accepted and perform acceptably on the job (e.g., stay 180 days).[54] Other companies play off their good reputations in the labor market to generate direct applications. For example, minorities constitute 26 percent of the 6,500 managerial and professional employees at Avon Products, and this enhances the firm's ability to recruit other minorities. As Al Smith, director of managing diversity at Avon, notes, "I get a lot of résumés from people of all cultures and ethnicities because Avon has a good reputation," and this precludes the need for expensive and sometimes unreliable outreach programs.[55]

Of course, referrals do not necessarily have to come just from current employees. The importance of good community relations to recruitment can be seen in the experience of Papa John's Pizza, which was rated number one on *Business Week*'s list of 100 Best Small Companies in America. Papa John's, one of the fastest-growing companies in the United States, once relied on classified ads to find drivers and store employees. This method was highly unreliable, however, because the company did not have the facilities to develop sophisticated tests of people's skills and attitudes. Store managers are now encouraged to make professional contacts within their communities, such as with the principal or guidance counselor at the local high school, leaders of church groups, and coaches in youth sports leagues. Store managers can then use these contacts to help generate referrals among promising young applicants. These community relationships help connect Papa John's to youths who have established good reputations in their community for reliability and trustworthiness. As one industry analyst notes, "I think the greatest advantage for Papa John's is recruitment. Once you get your feet wet recruiting that way, you can move on to bigger and better things."[56]

ADVERTISEMENTS IN NEWSPAPERS AND PERIODICALS. Advertisements to recruit personnel are ubiquitous, even though they typically generate less desirable recruits than direct applications or referrals—and do so at greater expense. However, since few employers can fill all their vacancies with direct applications and referrals, some form of advertising is usually needed. Moreover, an employer can take many steps to increase the effectiveness of this recruitment method.

The two most important questions to ask in designing a job advertisement are: What do we need to say? and To whom do we need to say it? With respect to the first question, many organizations fail to adequately communicate the specifics of the vacancy. Ideally, persons reading an ad should get enough information to evaluate the job and its requirements, allowing them to make a well-informed judgment regarding their qualifications. This could mean running long advertisements, which costs more. However, these additional costs should be evaluated against the costs of processing a huge number of applicants who are not reasonably qualified or who would not find the job acceptable once they learn more about it.

In terms of whom to reach with this message, the organization placing the advertisement has to decide which medium it will use. The classified section of local newspapers is the most common medium. It is a relatively inexpensive means of reaching a large number of people within a specified geographic area who are currently looking for work (or at least interested enough to be reading the classifieds). On the downside, this medium does not allow an organization to target skill levels very well. Typically, classified ads are read by many people who are either over- or underqualified for the position. Moreover, people who are not looking for work rarely read the classifieds, and thus this is not the right medium for luring people away from their current employers. Specially targeted journals and periodicals may be better than general newspapers at reaching a specific part of the overall labor market. In addition, employers are increasingly using television—particularly cable television—as a reasonably priced way of reaching people.[57]

PUBLIC EMPLOYMENT AGENCIES. The Social Security Act of 1935 requires that everyone receiving unemployment compensation be registered with a local state employment office. These state employment offices work with the U.S. Employment Service (USES) to try to ensure that unemployed individuals eventually get off state aid and back on employer payrolls. To accomplish this, agencies collect information from the unemployed about their skills and experiences.

With the passage of the Personal Responsibility and Work Opportunity Reconciliation Act of 1996, the pressure on welfare recipients to find jobs through either public employment agencies or other means has increased dramatically. This act sets a five-year limit on benefits and requires most people to land jobs in two years. It also provides incentives for organizations, in the form of federal tax credits, of up to $8,500 for each welfare recipient hired. Some credit this act with the 30 percent reduction in welfare rolls between 1994 and 1998.[58]

Employers can register their job vacancies with their local state employment office, and the agency will attempt to find someone suitable using its computerized inventory of local unemployed individuals. The agency makes referrals to the organization at no charge, and these individuals can be interviewed or tested by the employer for potential vacancies. Because of certain legislative mandates, state unemployment offices often have specialized "desks" for minorities, handicapped individuals, and Vietnam-era veterans. Thus, this is an excellent source for employers who feel they are currently underutilizing any of these subgroups.

PRIVATE EMPLOYMENT AGENCIES. Public employment agencies serve primarily the blue-collar labor market; private employment agencies perform much the same service for the white-collar labor market. Unlike public agencies, however, private employment agencies charge the organization for the referrals. Another difference between private and public employment agencies is that one doesn't have to be unemployed to use a private employment agency.

One special type of private employment agency is the so-called executive search firm (ESF). These agencies are often referred to as headhunters because, unlike the other sources we have examined, they operate almost exclusively with people who are currently employed. For example, when BMW sought to open its new U.S. plant, it used an executive search firm to help "liberate" Allen Kinzer and Edwin Buker from Honda. These two executives were vice presidents for Honda's U.S. operations, and BMW was looking to re-create Honda's success by recruiting them.[59]

Dealing with executive search firms is sometimes a sensitive process because executives may not want to advertise their availability for fear of their current employer's reaction. Thus, ESFs serve as an important confidentiality buffer between the employer and the recruit. ESFs are expensive to employ for both direct and indirect reasons. Directly, according to a 1997 survey, ESFs often charge one-third to half of the salary of the executive who is eventually placed.[60] Indirectly, employers who use ESFs wind up having to lure people not from unemployment but from jobs that they may be quite satisfied with. A company in a growing industry may have to offer as much as 50 percent more than the executive's current pay to prompt her to take the new job.[61]

COLLEGES AND UNIVERSITIES. Most colleges and universities have placement services that seek to help their graduates obtain employment. Indeed, on-campus interviewing is the most important source of recruits for entry-level professional and managerial vacancies.[62] Organizations tend to focus especially on colleges that have strong reputations in areas for which they have critical needs (chemical engineering, public accounting, etc.).[63]

For example, 3M has a five-part college recruiting strategy. First, the company concentrates its efforts on 25 to 30 selected universities, trying not to spread itself too thin. Second, it has a commitment to these selected universities and returns each year with new openings. Third, 3M uses a large number of line managers in its recruiting interviews, because they have a better real-world knowledge about the jobs and working conditions relative to more narrowly informed human resource staff. Fourth, the HR staff is used to coordinate the line managers' activities with the university's staff, making sure that the same person works with the same university year in and year out to achieve "continuity of contact." Finally, 3M strives for continuous improvement by frequently asking students they have recruited to give them feedback on the process and, where possible, to compare and contrast 3M's process with the process used by other firms recruiting at the same university.[64]

Many employers have found that to effectively compete for the best students, they need to do more than just sign prospective graduates up for interview slots. One of the best ways to establish a stronger presence on a campus is with a college internship program. For example, Dun & Bradstreet funds a summer intern program for minority M.B.A. students and often hires these interns for full-time positions when they graduate.[65] These kinds of programs allow an organization to get early access to potential applicants and to assess their capacities directly.

Another way of increasing one's presence on campus is to participate in university job fairs. In general, a job fair is a place where many employers gather for a short time to meet large numbers of potential job applicants. Although job fairs can be held anywhere (e.g., at a hotel or convention center), campuses are ideal locations because of the large number of well-educated, yet unemployed, individuals who live there. Job fairs are a rather inexpensive means of generating an on-campus presence and can even provide one-on-one dialogue with potential recruits—dialogue that could not be achieved through less interactive media like newspaper ads.

Finally, as more organizations attempt to compete on a global level, the ability to recruit individuals who will be successful both at home and abroad is a growing concern. Many organizations feel that college campuses are one of the best places to search for this type of transportable talent. Molex Inc., for example, is a U.S. technology firm with 8,000 employees—only 2,000 of whom live in the United States. Molex derives 70 percent of its $950 million in annual sales from outside the United States, and thus the majority of workers are either expatriates, local nationals, or foreign service employees. Three critical aspects of Molex's recruitment strategy are critical to its success in attaining an internationally talented work force.

First, Molex focuses on recruiting college students. As one manager at Molex states, "We have had more success molding younger people into this company and into overseas assignments than taking more experienced people who've worked for other companies." Second, Molex recruits many foreigners (especially MBA candidates) who are studying in the United States for assignments back in their native country. These individuals have the best of both worlds in terms of having a formal education in U.S. business practices and also understanding both the language and culture of their home

Recruiters: Taking a Ride on the Information Superhighway

"The entire world is at your fingertips," says Tim Johnson (manager or university relations for Advanced Micro Devices of Sunnyvale, California), speaking about the use of the Internet for recruiting human resources. Like many human resource professionals, Johnson is now using the Internet, the computer network that links over 3 million host computers, as well as online services such as CompuServe, Prodigy, and America Online to recruit personnel.

In the old days, college recruiting for Johnson was a grueling task. Setting up a job fair took hours to organize the display and get all the brochures and paperwork in order. Then there was the matter of meeting all the recruits, many of who were not qualified, and answering the same questions over and over again. There was also the travel time, hotel stay, and the piles of paperwork—all of which had to get done before he returned to his office, where his in-basket was often overflowing due to his absence. All in all, Johnson notes, "It isn't especially cost-effective or time-effective to hit the road, but it has been a necessity."

The information superhighway is making this type of recruiting less of a necessity. In the competition to be bigger, better, faster, and cheaper, many organizations find that online recruiting is a valuable weapon. Bigger applicant pools can be generated online because the organization's listing can be seen worldwide—not just in the local paper or in a single professional magazine. Organizations can also take advantage of accessing a large number of ready-made applications. For example, Career Mosaic includes more than 50,000 resumés that can be electronically searched for key terms, such as *MBA*, *finance*, and *fluent in Spanish*.

COMPETING THROUGH HIGH-PERFORMANCE WORK SYSTEMS

Better applicant pools are also generated for some types of high-tech jobs in that online applicants have already passed a test of computer literacy by accessing the ad. Fast response times too can be generated via online recruiting. Applicants interested in positions posted by Staples (the large office products retailer) can transmit their resumés right back over the lines that sent them the ad. Hence a process that would have taken six or seven days with newspaper ads and the U.S. mail now gets done in hours. Finally, online recruiting can be comparatively cheap. A one-week ad in the *Boston Globe*, for example, can cost $1,500 versus $75 for an add on E-Span.

While online recruiting may currently only supplement rather than replace much of the legwork associated with recruiting, its targeted use should be considered by today's human resource professional. As Tim Johnson notes from first-hand experience, "It's effective, it's efficient, it saves time and money. Online capabilities allow a greater level of sophistication, and that is increasingly important as everyone battles for a competitive edge."

SOURCE: M.L. Abramson, "Changing Jobs? Try the Net," *Fortune*, March 2, 1998, pp. 205–6; S. Greengard, "As HR Goes Online," *Personnel Journal*, July 1995, pp. 55–65; M. Loeb, "Getting Hired by Getting Wired," *Fortune*, November 13, 1995, p. 252.

country. Finally, when recruiting U.S. students, Molex requires that each person hired be fluent in both English and one other language. This commitment to multilingual competency can be seen at the national headquarters, where 15 different languages are spoken.[66]

ELECTRONIC RECRUITING. As we highlight in the "Competing through High-Performance Work Systems" box, many advantages of a typical job fair can now be gained without the need to place the recruiter and recruit in the same physical location. Computer recruitment networks and videoconferencing technologies allow employers to conduct searches that are widely distributed geographically, without ever leaving the home office. Within the past few years, the use of computer networks to recruit employees has expanded a great deal. Two of the most actively searched sites are CareerMosaic (careermosaic.com) with 70,000 job listings supplied free to job seekers, who can then post resumés for potential employers, and CareerPath (careerpath.com), with 250,000 jobs pulled from help-wanted sections of over 60 major newspapers.

TABLE 5.4
Hypothetical Yield Ratios for Five Recruitment Sources

	RECRUITING SOURCE				
	LOCAL UNIVERSITY	RENOWNED UNIVERSITY	EMPLOYEE REFERRALS	NEWSPAPER AD	EXECUTIVE SEARCH FIRMS
Resumés generated	200	400	50	500	20
Interview offers accepted	175	100	45	400	20
Yield ratio	87%	25%	90%	80%	100%
Applicants judged acceptable	100	95	40	50	19
Yield ratio	57%	95%	89%	12%	95%
Accept employment offers	90	10	35	25	15
Yield ratio	90%	11%	88%	50%	79%
Cumulative yield ratio	90/200 45%	10/400 3%	35/50 70%	25/500 5%	15/20 75%
Cost	$30,000	$50,000	$15,000	$20,000	$90,000
Cost per hire	$333	$5,000	$428	$800	$6,000

Another technological innovation in recruiting that eliminates travel requirements but allows for a more personal meeting between employer and applicant is videoconferencing.[67] Used mostly on college campuses, videoconferencing allows applicants and employers to meet each other technologically "face-to-face."

EVALUATING THE QUALITY OF A SOURCE. Because there are few rules about the quality of a given source for a given vacancy, it is generally a good idea for employers to monitor the quality of all their recruitment sources. One means of accomplishing this is to develop and compare yield ratios for each source.[68] Yield ratios express the percentage of applicants who successfully move from one stage of the recruitment and selection process to the next. Comparing yield ratios for different sources helps determine which is best or most efficient for the type of vacancy being investigated. Data on cost per hire is also useful in establishing the efficiency of a given source.

Table 5.4 shows hypothetical yield ratios and cost-per-hire data for five recruitment sources. For the job vacancies generated by this company, the best two sources of recruits are local universities and employee referral programs. Newspaper ads generate the largest number of recruits, but relatively few of these are qualified for the position. Recruiting at nationally renowned universities generates highly qualified applicants, but relatively few of them ultimately accept positions. Finally, executive search firms generate a small list of highly qualified, interested applicants, but this is an expensive source compared with other alternatives.

RECRUITERS

The last part of the model presented in Figure 5.5 that we will discuss is the recruiter. We consider the recruiter this late in the chapter to reinforce our earlier observation that the recruiter often gets involved late in the process. In many cases, by the time a recruiter meets some applicants, they have already made up their minds about what they desire in a job, what the current job has to offer, and their likelihood of receiving a job offer.[69]

Moreover, many applicants approach the recruiter with some degree of skepticism.

FIGURE 5.6
Relative Impact of the Recruiter on Various Recruitment Interview Outcomes

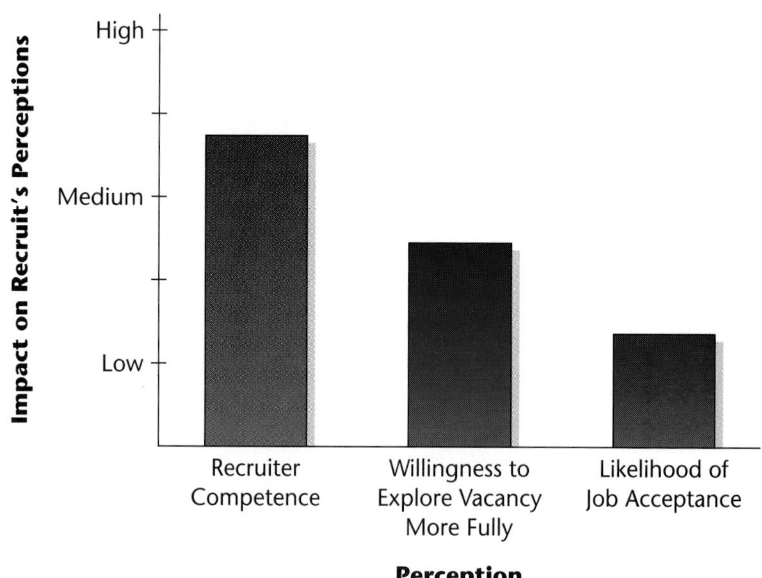

Knowing that it is the recruiter's job to sell them on a vacancy, some applicants may discount what the recruiter says relative to what they have heard from other sources (e.g., friends, magazine articles, professors). For these and other reasons, recruiters' characteristics and behaviors seem to have less impact on applicants' job choices than we might expect. Moreover, as shown in Figure 5.6, whatever impact a recruiter does have on an applicant lessens as we move from reaction criteria (i.e., how the applicant felt about the recruiter) toward job choice criteria (i.e., whether the applicant takes the job).[70]

RECRUITER'S FUNCTIONAL AREA. Most organizations must choose whether their recruiters are specialists in human resources or experts at particular jobs (e.g., supervisors or job incumbents). Some studies indicate that applicants find a job less attractive and the recruiter less credible when he is a personnel specialist.[71] This does not completely discount personnel specialists' role in recruiting, but it does indicate that such specialists need to take extra steps to ensure that applicants perceive them as knowledgeable and credible.

RECRUITER'S TRAITS. Two traits stand out when applicants' reactions to recruiters are examined. The first, which could be called "warmth," reflects the degree to which the recruiter seems to care about the applicant and is enthusiastic about her potential to contribute to the company. The second characteristic could be called "informativeness." In general, applicants respond more positively to recruiters who are perceived as warm and informative. These characteristics seem more important than such demographic characteristics as age, sex, or race, which have complex and inconsistent effects on applicant responses.[72]

RECRUITER'S REALISM. Perhaps the most well-researched aspect of recruiting deals with the level of realism that the recruiter incorporates into his message. Since the recruiter's job is to attract candidates, there is some pressure to exaggerate the positive features of the vacancy while downplaying the negative features. Applicants are highly sensitive to negative information. Research suggests that the highest-quality applicants may be less willing to pursue jobs when this type of information comes out.[73] On the other hand, if the recruiter goes too far in a positive direction, the candidate can be misled and lured into taking the job under false pretenses. This can lead to a serious case of unmet expectations and a high job-turnover rate.[74] In fact, unrealistic descriptions of a job may even lead new job incumbents to believe that the employer is deceitful.[75]

Many studies have looked at the capacity of "realistic job previews" to circumvent this problem and help minimize early job turnover. On the whole, the research suggests that the effect of realistic job previews on eventual turnover is weak and inconsistent.[76] Certainly, the idea that one can go overboard in selling a vacancy to a recruit has merit. However, the belief that informing people about the negative characteristics of the job will "inoculate" them to such characteristics seems unwarranted, based on the research conducted to date.[77] Thus, we return to the conclusion that an organization's decisions about personnel policies that directly affect the job's attributes (pay, security, advancement opportunities, and so on) will probably be more important than recruiter traits and behaviors in affecting job choice.

ENHANCING RECRUITER IMPACT. Although research suggests that recruiters do not have much influence on job choice, this does not mean recruiters cannot have an impact. Most recruiters receive little training.[78] Recent research has attempted to find conditions in which recruiters do make a difference. Based on this research, an organization can take several steps to increase the impact that recruiters have on those they recruit.

First, recruiters can provide timely feedback. Applicants react very negatively to delays in feedback, often making unwarranted attributions for the delays (e.g., the organization is uninterested in my application). Second, recruiters need to avoid behaviors that might convey the wrong organizational impression.[79] Table 5.5 lists quotes from ap-

TABLE 5.5 Quotes from Recruits Who Were Repelled by Recruiters

One firm I didn't think of talking to initially, but they called me and asked me to talk with them. So I did, and then the recruiter was very, very rude. Yes, very rude, and I've run into that a couple of times. (engineering graduate)

I had a very bad campus interview experience . . . the person who came was a last-minute fill-in. . . . I think he had a couple of "issues" and was very discourteous during the interview. He was one step away from yawning in my face. . . .The other thing he did was that he kept making these (nothing illegal, mind you) but he kept making these references to the fact that I had been out of my undergraduate and first graduate programs for more than 10 years now. (MBA with 10 years of experience)

________ has a management training program which the recruiter had gone through. She was talking about the great presentational skills that ________ teaches you, and the woman was barely literate. She was embarrassing. If that was the best they could do, I did not want any part of them. Also, ________ and ________'s recruiters appeared to have real attitude problems. I also thought they were chauvinistic. (arts undergraduate)

________ had a set schedule for me which they deviated from regularly. Times overlapped, and one person kept me too long, which pushed the whole day back. They almost seemed to be saying that it was my fault that I was late for the next one! I guess a lot of what they did just wasn't very professional. Even at the point when I was done, where most companies would have a cab pick you up, I was in the middle of a snowstorm in Chicago and they said, "You can get a cab downstairs." There weren't any cabs. I literally had to walk 12 or 14 blocks with my luggage, trying to find some way to get to the airport. They didn't book me a hotel for the night of the snowstorm so I had to sit in the airport for eight hours trying to get another flight. . . They wouldn't even reimburse me for the additional plane fare. (industrial relations graduate student)

The guy at the interview made a joke about how nice my nails were and how they were going to ruin them there due to all the tough work. (engineering undergraduate)

SOURCE: S.L. Rynes, R.D. Bretz, Jr., and B. Gerhart, "The Importance of Recruitment in Job Choice: A Different Way of Looking," *Personnel Psychology* 44 (1991), pp. 487–521.

plicants who felt that they had had extremely bad experiences with recruiters. Third, recruiting can be done in teams rather than by individuals. As we have seen, applicants tend to view line personnel (e.g., job incumbents and supervisors) as more credible than personnel specialists, so these kinds of recruiters should be part of any team. On the other hand, personnel specialists have knowledge that is not shared by line personnel (who may perceive recruiting as a small part of their "real" job), so they should be included as well.

SUMMARY

Human resource planning uses labor supply and demand forecasts to anticipate labor shortages and surpluses. It also entails programs that can be utilized to reduce a labor surplus (e.g., downsizing, early retirement programs) and eliminate a labor shortage (e.g., bringing in temporary workers, expanding overtime). When done well, human resource planning can enhance the success of the organization while minimizing the human suffering resulting from poorly anticipated labor surpluses or shortages. Human resource recruiting is a buffer activity that creates an applicant pool that the organization can draw from in the event of a labor shortage that is to be filled with new hires. Organizational recruitment programs affect applications through personnel policies (e.g., promote-from-within policies, due process provisions) that affect the attributes of the vacancies themselves. They can also impact the nature of people who apply for positions by using different recruitment sources (e.g., recruiting from universities versus advertising in newspapers). Finally, organizations can use recruiters to influence individuals' perceptions of jobs (e.g., eliminating misconceptions, clarifying uncertainties) or perceptions of themselves (e.g., changing their valences for various work outcomes).

DISCUSSION QUESTIONS

1. Discuss the effects that an impending labor shortage might have on the following three subfunctions of human resource management: selection and placement, training and career development, and compensation and benefits. Which subfunction might be most heavily impacted? In what ways might these groups develop joint cooperative programs to avert a labor shortage?
2. Discuss the costs and benefits associated with statistical versus judgmental forecasts for labor demand and labor supply. Under what conditions might either of these techniques be infeasible? Under what conditions might both be feasible, but one more desirable than the other?
3. Some companies have detailed affirmative action plans, complete with goals and timetables, for women and minorities, and yet have no formal human resource plan for the organization as a whole. Why might this be the case? If you were a human resource specialist interviewing with this company for an open position, what would this practice imply for the role of the human resource manager in that company?
4. Recruiting people for jobs that entail international assignments is increasingly important for many companies. Where might one go to look for individuals interested in these types of assignments? How might recruiting practices aimed at these people differ from those one might apply to the "average" recruit?
5. Discuss the relative merits of internal versus external recruitment. What types of business strategies might best be supported by recruiting externally, and what types might call for internal recruitment? What factors might lead a firm to decide to switch from internal to external recruitment or vice versa?

WEB EXERCISE

In this chapter we discussed how electronic recruiting using the Web can be used to identify and attract potential employees. Texas Instruments (TI) is using the Web not only to post job openings, but to provide potential job candidates with information about the company so they can decide if their values and the working conditions they want are a "match" with those available at Texas Instruments. Go to www.ti.com, TI's home page on the Web. Click on "Employment" and then click on "Why Work at T.I.?". Click on "Fit check". The "Fit check" is a questionnaire that TI designed for potential job applicants to determine whether they "fit" with TIs environment and culture.

QUESTIONS

1. Complete the "Fit check" as if you were interested in a job with TI.

2. What types of work environment characteristics and values are included in the "Fit check"?
3. If the "Fit check" indicates that a job candidate's interests and values do not match TIs should they still consider working at TI? Explain your answer. What are some of the problems that TI might experience if a "mismatched" employee is hired?

MANAGING PEOPLE: FROM THE PAGES OF "BUSINESS WEEK"

BusinessWeek Forget the Huddled Masses: Send Nerds

As a headhunter, George Van Derven has an unlikely connection: Russia's former state airline, Aeroflot. Not that Van Derven trades in pilots, flight mechanics, or surly Russian flight attendants. But in a former career, he sold a computerized reservation system to Aeroflot and came to know the talented programmers stashed in the back offices. When Aeroflot broke up into regional carriers in 1992, Van Derven promptly tapped its brain pool. Now, as president of Alternative Technology Resources Inc. in Sacramento, Van Derven is mining a rich lode of programming talent and busily dispatching it to understaffed computer departments throughout the Western world.

Other recruiters should be so lucky. High-tech headhunters for Andersen Consulting tramp through technical schools in Budapest and job fairs in Manila. At a recent training session for programmers in Holland, Microsoft Corp. hired bouncers to keep headhunters at bay. And a recruiter for IBM's Global Services Div., who is trying to hire 15,000 software hands this year alone, introduces himself as James R. Bunch, "as in bunch of jobs."

The Information Revolution is racing ahead of its vital raw material: brainpower. As demand explodes for computerized applications for everything from electronic commerce on the Internet to sorting out the Year 2000 glitch, companies are finding themselves strapped for programmers. In the U.S., alone, which accounts for two-thirds of the world's $300 billion market in software products and services, some 190,000 high-tech jobs stand open, most of them for programmers, according to the Information Technology Assn.

That's sending companies scouring the globe for talent—and lifting salaries skyward. A typical programmer's wages, now some $70,000, is jumping 13 percent a year, and far higher in the hottest niches, such as Java Internet software and SAP business applications. These days, $20,000 signing bonuses are commonplace and stock options are being handed out with as little fanfare as office supplies. If the pace keeps up, experts say, ballooning salaries could wind up damaging the global tech machine as margins are squeezed and investments postponed.

And relief is nowhere in sight. Experts predict the gap between computer-science students and expected demand won't ease for a decade, if then. Too many bright young people, especially in Europe and the U.S., consider programming geek work and choose other careers. In the U.S., the number of computer-science graduates has plummeted in the past decade or so, from 48,000 graduates in 1984 to an estimated 26,000 this year. "This is a real limiting factor to growth," says Avron Barr, a researcher at Stanford Computer Industry Project who is investigating the shortage.

Indeed, for high-tech companies, the dearth of programmers is the greatest threat to expansion in the coming year—far more menacing, they say, than an economic slump or competition in the marketplace. And it's not just a problem for tech companies. Plenty of others are desperate for the same talent. Auto makers from Tokyo to Detroit are packing more computing power into their cars and plants. Banks, brokerages, and phone companies are rushing to outdo each other with the zippiest online services, all requiring herds of nerds. Those that choose not to install the newest technology, says Owens Corning CIO Michael Radcliff, are "creating a competitive liability."

Of course, if you're willing to pay—or have the stock options to entice—you could be up to your propeller hats in programmers. In Silicon Valley, star programmers are swimming in stock options, driving Porsches, and buying homes in the pricey Los Altos hills. At Netscape Communications Corp., which plans to hire more than 1,000 programmers this year, employees receive up to $5,000 just for a successful referral and the pampered programmers are treated to onsite massages, teeth-cleanings, and laundry service. The company lines up their 49ers tickets and books their white-water rafting vacations. All this to keep them from succumbing to a stream of calls from headhunters. "Everybody's going crazy now trying to find these folks," says Margie Mader, Netscape's human-resources director.

How did the shortage get so bad? For years, tech companies had little reason to fret. In the early '90s, the industry snapped up hundreds of thousands of workers who were dropped into the job market when large corporations downsized—a source now running dry.

At the same time, the very act of writing software has not speeded up despite the computer revolution and the terabytes of information hurtling around the globe. Today, even the best of programmers painstakingly turns out some 10 lines of code a day. To whip up today's software programs—even a cellular telephone requires some 300,000 lines of code—takes armies of programmers laboriously writing away. Consider this: There are six million software programmers and counting in the world today, two million of them in the U.S. and one million in Japan. As an industrial model, it's akin to pre-Gutenberg monasteries with their legions of scribbling monks.

For years, global savants pooh-poohed the pending programmer crunch by pointing to India, which boasted a seemingly bottomless reserve of techies. India, they said, would be to software what Saudi Arabia was to oil. And true, with 50,000 programmers pouring out of schools every year—twice the American total—India is a valuable labor pool.

But with global technology bursting to $3 trillion this decade—four times higher than in the '80s—India's supply simply isn't enough. And no other plentiful source of software skills appears to be on the horizon. Russia has promise, but it's limited: Few of its programmers speak English or understand business applications. China is a possibility, but it's likely to employ most of its programmers over the next decade for its own massive development projects. "I had this one programmer from China," laments one official at Electronic Data Systems Corp. "I took him through the whole immigration process, got his papers. Then he got a better offer."

Naturally, in this world of predators, there's a pecking order. Sitting on top are the fast-growth companies with hot Internet technologies. They're magnets for talented programmers, and they can pad their offers with rich stock options. Service companies such as Andersen Consulting, IBM Global Services, and Ernst & Young, which are helping companies install systems worldwide, are forced to routinely dole out six-figure salaries to programmers with experience in business applications. They compete with countless body shops—outsourcing companies that pay as much as $300,000 for skilled programmers willing to live on the road.

At the bottom of the pile are the corporate tech departments throughout the world. Many are short on money and stock options. And if they install a popular system, bringing their staff up to date on something new from, say, Oracle Corp. or the German software giant SAP, their departments get raided in no time. Don Yates became familiar with SAP's leading software package for business while helping install the system in the early '90s at Royal LePage Ltd., a real estate company in Toronto. Within a year, the 18-person department was picked clean. "I was the last one to go," says Yates, who now makes three times as much money, some $150,000, as an itinerant programmer for EMI, a Pittsburgh-based company that rents out software talent.

No surprise, then, that companies are trying any tactic, including turning to the World Wide Web. Since the Net is where most programmers spend idle hours, growing numbers of recruiters are using it to chase them down. That's where Michael L. McNeal casts his global net. McNeal, human-resources chief at Cisco Systems Inc., needs to hire 1,000 people each quarter, many of them programmers. Like other recruiters, he buys ads on popular Web sites like the Dilbert page, which funnels traffic to Cisco's Web site. There, the company lists some 500 current job openings. Applicants in foreign countries can hit hot buttons to translate the page into Cantonese, Mandarin, Russian. And, by filling out a short questionnaire, they can create a resume and zap it to Cisco.

Cisco's Web page draws 500,000 job searches per month. This gives Cisco gobs of data about the job market, including which companies have interested employees. Armed with the best prospects, McNeal then turns to Cisco employees for help, asking them to call recruits, who speak the same language.

Like the others, Microsoft recruits on the Web and snaps up startups for talent—some 20 companies in 1996, alone. But to get its software up and running throughout the world, Microsoft relies on service companies, which are grossly understaffed. Microsoft calculates that its service partners are short 41,000 professionals trained to install Microsoft products. This is forcing the company to educate new recruits. With an effort known as Skills 2000, Microsoft is pushing into 350 schools and colleges around the world. It hammers out curricula that will produce more programmers, such as adding computer training in business schools.

A big part of the efforts is in Europe, a major market that has 18 million unemployed workers. Microsoft's solution is to invite jobless Europeans in 11 countries into free training programs. In the past year, 3,000 Europeans have gone through the program, with 98 percent of them landing jobs.

It's in this $170 billion market for global software services, including the Big Six consulting firms, IBM Global Services, Manpower, and many others, that demand for programmers is especially hot. This is because corporations need loads of help to link far-flung operations with the latest in E-mail networks, inventory control, and finance packages. "The productive sector of the economy is becoming absolutely dependent on software systems," says reengineering author Michael Hammer. "If SAP vanished, you couldn't buy a can of Coke."

In the finance capitals of London, Tokyo and Hong Kong, banks are installing vast new systems to adapt to Europe's single currency and Japan's financial deregulation. Meanwhile, they're working overtime to sort out the Year 2000 glitch, the dating problem companies face when the year of double zeroes rolls around. Mastech Corp., a Pittsburgh-based outsourcer, sent a handful of programmers a year ago to follow a Citibank contract from Singapore to London. Once in London, they found a wealth of other business and started importing more programmers from South Africa, Sri Lanka, India, and Australia. "We have 50 people now, and we'd hire another 50 today if we could find them," says country manager Guil Hastings.

As recruiters travel, they focus on regional specialties. The Russians are whizzes at math. India's university at Puna has a strong Japanese language program, which positions it well for Japan's Year 2000 work-load. South African programmers learned to cope during the years of the anti-apartheid boycott with a motley collection of jerry-rigged mainframes. This makes them especially adept at Year 2000 work, which is targeted toward aging mainframe software.

As for programmers, the world is their oyster. In a computer lab in Austin, Tex., Natalia Bogataya and her husband, Konstantin Bobovich, both Belorussians and products of Van

Derven's so-called Russian connection, labor away on a mainframe program. They've left their college-age children with relatives in Minsk and are debugging insurance software for Computer Sciences Corp. "We can't use our experience in our country," Bobovich explains, "and my wife said, 'Let's see America.'"

Why not? In today's fervid market, programmers can write their own tickets.

QUESTIONS

1. This case discusses the labor shortage associated with computer programmers that some fear will constrain worldwide economic growth as we enter the new millennium. What characteristics of the product demand market have led to the explosion in demand for programmers? What characteristics of the programming job have limited the number of people willing to develop the skills necessary to meet this demand? Which of the seven options this chapter listed for avoiding a labor shortage have been attempted by employers in this market? Which do you think will be most successful?
2. Some have argued that the shortage of programmers is partly due to employers that (a) tend to offer temporary employment arrangements rather than full-time ones to maintain flexibility, (b) discriminate against older programmers in favor of younger ones who will work longer hours, and (c) substitute low-paid immigrant workers for higher-wage American workers. To what extent does this seem to be true or false? To what extent can an actual or perceived labor shortage be created by employers because of their chosen business strategies?

SOURCE: "Forget the Huddled Masses: Send Nerds." *Business Week*, July 21, 1997.

NOTES

1. D.W. Jarrell, *Human Resource Planning: A Business Planning Approach* (Englewood Cliffs, NJ: Prentice-Hall, 1993).
2. B. Schlender, "Matsushita Shows How to Go Global," *Fortune*, July 11, 1994, pp. 159–66.
3. P. Smith, "Salariless Man," *The Economist*, September 16, 1995, p. 79.
4. W.F. Cascio, "Whither Industrial and Organizational Psychology in a Changing World of Work?" *American Psychologist* 50 (1995), pp. 928–39.
5. D. Greising, "It's the Best of Times—or Is It?" *Business Week*, January 12, 1998, pp. 35–38.
6. M. Magnet, "The Productivity Payoff Arrives," *Fortune*, July 27, 1994, pp. 79–84.
7. R.T. King, "Is Job Cutting by Drug Makers Bad Medicine?" *The Wall Street Journal*, August 23, 1995, pp. B1–B3.
8. Greising, "It's the Best of Times."
9. K. Labich, "The Geography of an Emerging America," *Fortune*, June 27, 1994, pp. 88–94.
10. Greising, "It's the Best of Times."
11. K.P. DeMeuse, P.A. Vanderheiden, and T.J. Bergmann, "Announced Layoffs: Their Effect on Corporate Financial Performance," *Human Resource Management* 33 (1994), pp. 509–30.
12. King, "Is Job Cutting by Drug Makers Bad Medicine?"
13. W.F. Cascio, "Downsizing: What Do We Know? What Have We Learned?" *Academy of Management Executive* 7 (1993), pp. 95–104.
14. D. Skarlicki, J.H. Ellard, and B.R.C. Kellin, "Third Party Perceptions of a Layoff: Procedural, Derogation, and Retributive Aspects of Justice," *Journal of Applied Psychology* 83 (1998), pp. 119–27.
15. R. Folger and D.P. Skarlicki, "When Tough Times Make Tough Bosses: Managerial Distancing as a Function of Layoff Blame," *Academy of Management Journal* 41 (1998), pp. 79–87.
16. R. Stodghill, "The Coming Job Bottleneck," *Business Week*, March 24, 1997, pp. 184–85.
17. Ibid.
18. S. Kim and D. Feldman, "Healthy, Wealthy, or Wise: Predicting Actual Acceptances of Early Retirement Incentives at Three Points in Time," *Personnel Psychology* 51 (1998), pp. 623–42.
19. P. Wechsler, "AT&T Managers Rush out the Door," *Business Week*, June 15, 1998, p. 53.
20. L. Schiff, "Manufacturing's Hidden Asset: Temporary Employees," *Fortune*, November 10, 1997, pp. 28–29.
21. S. Caudron, "Contingent Work Force Spurs HR Planning," *Personnel Journal* (July 1994), pp. 52–59.
22. G. Flynn, "Contingent Staffing Requires Serious Strategy," *Personnel Journal* (April 1995), pp. 50–58.
23. S. Caudron, "Are Your Temps Doing Their Best?" *Personnel Journal* (November 1995), pp. 32–38.
24. T. Cothran, "Outsourcing on the Inside Track," *Training* (May 1995), pp. 31–37.
25. K. Bradsher, "American Workers Watch as Jobs Go Overseas," *International Herald Tribune*, August 29, 1995, pp. C1–C2.
26. R.A. Bettis, S.P. Bradley, and G. Hamel, "Outsourcing and Industrial Decline," *Academy of Management Executive* 6 (1992), pp. 7–22.
27. Ibid.
28. G. Koretz, "Overtime versus New Factories," *Business Week*, May 4, 1998, p. 34.
29. A. Bernstein, "Bell Atlantic North Faces a Monstrous Labor Crunch," *Business Week*, June 8, 1998, p. 38.
30. G.N. Powell and D.A. Butterfield, "Effect of Race on

Promotions to Top Management in a Federal Department," *Academy of Management Journal* 40 (1997), pp. 112–28.

31. A.E. Barber, *Recruiting Employees* (Thousand Oaks, CA: Sage, 1998).
32. J.A. Breaugh, *Recruitment: Science and Practice* (Boston: PWS–Kent, 1992).
33. C.K. Stevens, "Antecedents of Interview Interactions, Interviewers' Ratings, and Applicants' Reactions," *Personnel Psychology* 51 (1998), pp. 55–85.
34. A.E. Barber, J.R. Hollenbeck, S.L. Tower, and J.M. Phillips, "The Effects of Interview Focus on Recruitment Effectiveness: A Field Experiment," *Journal of Applied Psychology* 79 (1994), pp. 886–96.
35. J.D. Olian and S.L. Rynes, "Organizational Staffing: Integrating Practice with Strategy," *Industrial Relations* 23 (1984), pp. 170–83.
36. G.T. Milkovich and J.M. Newman, *Compensation* (Homewood, IL: Richard D. Irwin, 1990).
37. S. Branch, "MBAs Are Hot Again and They Know It," *Fortune*, November 14, 1997, pp. 155–57.
38. J. Kaufman, "A McDonald's Owner Becomes a Role Model for Black Teenagers," *The Wall Street Journal*, August 23, 1995, p. A1.
39. K. Helliker, "Sold on the Job: Retailing Chains Offer a Lot of Opportunity, Young Managers Find," *The Wall Street Journal*, August 25, 1995, p. A1.
40. K. Clark, "Reasons to Worry about Rising Wages," *Fortune*, July 7, 1997, pp. 31–32.
41. M. Leonard, "Challenges to the Termination-at-Will Doctrine," *Personnel Administrator* 28 (1983), pp. 49–56.
42. C. Schowerer and B. Rosen, "Effects of Employment-at-Will Policies and Compensation Policies on Corporate Image and Job Pursuit Intentions," *Journal of Applied Psychology* 74 (1989), pp. 653–56.
43. M. Magnus, "Recruitment Ads at Work," *Personnel Journal* 64 (1985), pp. 42–63.
44. S.L. Rynes and A.E. Barber, "Applicant Attraction Strategies: An Organizational Perspective," *Academy of Management Review* 15 (1990), pp. 286–310.
45. Breaugh, *Recruitment*.
46. J. Bussey, "Dow Chemical Tries to Shed Tough Image and Court the Public," *The Wall Street Journal*, November 20, 1987, p. 1.
47. R. Thompson, "More Diversity in Agriculture: A Hard Row," *The Wall Street Journal*, September 19, 1995, p. B1.
48. M.A. Conrad and S.D. Ashworth, "Recruiting Source Effectiveness: A Meta-analysis and Re-examination of Two Rival Hypotheses" (paper presented at the annual meeting of the Society of Industrial/Organizational Psychology, Chicago, 1986).
49. Breaugh, *Recruitment*.
50. P. A. Savill, "HR at Inova Reengineers Recruitment Process," *Personnel Journal* (June 1995), pp. 109–14.
51. Breaugh, *Recruitment*.
52. R.S. Schuler and S.E. Jackson, "Linking Competitive Strategies with Human Resource Management Practices," *Academy of Management Executive* 1 (1987), pp. 207–19.
53. C.R. Williams, C.E. Labig, and T.H. Stone, "Recruitment Sources and Posthire Outcomes for Job Applicants and New Hires: A Test of Two Hypotheses," *Journal of Applied Psychology* 78 (1994), pp. 163–72.
54. A. Halcrow, "Employers Are Your Best Recruiters," *Personnel Journal* 67 (1988), pp. 42–49.
55. G. Flynn, "Do You Have the Right Approach to Diversity?" *Personnel Journal* (October 1995), pp. 68–75.
56. B.P. Sunoo, "Papa John's Rolls Out Hot HR Menu," *Personnel Journal* (September 1995), pp. 38–47.
57. Breaugh, *Recruitment*.
58. K.H. Hammonds, "Welfare to Work: A Good Start," *Business Week*, June 1, 1998, pp. 102–4.
59. J. Mitchell, "BMW Names 2 Honda Executives to Oversee New U.S. Assembly Plant," *The Wall Street Journal*, November 29, 1992, p. B4.
60. J. Reingold, "Casting for a Different Set of Characters," *Business Week*, December 8, 1997, pp. 38–39.
61. J. Greenwald, "Invasion of the Body Snatchers," *Time*, April 23, 1984, p. 41.
62. P. Smith, "Sources Used by Employers When Hiring College Grads," *Personnel Journal* (February 1995), p. 25.
63. J.W. Boudreau and S.L. Rynes, "Role of Recruitment in Staffing Utility Analysis," *Journal of Applied Psychology* 70 (1985), pp. 354–66.
64. D. Anfuso, "3M's Staffing Strategy Promotes Productivity and Pride," *Personnel Journal* (February 1995), pp. 28–34.
65. L. Winter, "Employers Go to School on Minority Recruiting," *The Wall Street Journal*, December 15, 1992, p. B1.
66. C.M Solomon, "Navigating Your Search for Global Talent," *Personnel Journal* (May 1995), p. 94–97.
67. K.O. Magnusen and K.G. Kroeck, "Video Conferencing Maximizes Recruiting," *HRMagazine*, August 1995, pp. 70–72.
68. R. Hawk, *The Recruitment Function* (New York: American Management Association, 1967).
69. C.K. Stevens, "Effects of Preinterview Beliefs on Applicants' Reactions to Campus Interviews," *Academy of Management Journal* 40 (1997), pp. 947–66.
70. C.D. Fisher, D.R. Ilgen, and W.D. Hoyer, "Source Credibility, Information Favorability, and Job Offer Acceptance," *Academy of Management Journal* 22 (1979), pp. 94–103; G.N. Powell, "Applicant Reactions to the Initial Employment Interview: Exploring Theoretical and Methodological Issues," *Personnel Psychology* 44 (1991), pp. 67–83; N. Schmitt and B.W. Coyle, "Applicant Decisions in the Employment Interview," *Journal of Applied Psychology* 61 (1976), pp. 184–92.

71. M.S. Taylor and T.J. Bergman, "Organizational Recruitment Activities and Applicants' Reactions at Different Stages of the Recruitment Process," *Personnel Psychology* 40 (1984), pp. 261–285; Fisher, Ilgen, and Hoyer, "Source Credibility."
72. L.M. Graves and G.N. Powell, "The Effect of Sex Similarity on Recruiters' Evaluations of Actual Applicants: A Test of the Similarity–Attraction Paradigm," *Personnel Psychology* 48 (1995), pp. 85–98.
73. R.D. Bretz and T.A. Judge, "Realistic Job Previews: A Test of the Adverse Self-Selection Hypothesis," *Journal of Applied Psychology* 83 (1998), pp. 330–37.
74. J.P. Wanous, *Organizational Entry: Recruitment, Selection and Socialization of Newcomers* (Reading, MA: Addison–Wesley, 1980).
75. P. Hom, R.W. Griffeth, L.E. Palich, and J.S. Bracker, "An Exploratory Investigation into Theoretical Mechanisms Underlying Realistic Job Previews," *Personnel Psychology* 51 (1998), pp. 421–51.
76. G.M. McEvoy and W.F. Cascio, "Strategies for Reducing Employee Turnover: A Meta-analysis," Journal of Applied Psychology 70 (1985), pp. 342–53; S.L. Premack and J.P. Wanous, "A Meta-analysis of Realistic Job Preview Experiments," *Journal of Applied Psychology* 70 (1985), pp. 706–19.
77. P.G. Irving and J.P. Meyer, "Reexamination of the Met-Expectations Hypothesis: A Longitudinal Analysis," *Journal of Applied Psychology* 79 (1995), pp. 937–49.
78. R.W. Walters, "It's Time We Become Pros," *Journal of College Placement* 12 (1985), pp. 30–33.
79. S.L. Rynes, R.D. Bretz, and B. Gerhart, "The Importance of Recruitment in Job Choice: A Different Way of Looking," *Personnel Psychology* 44 (1991), pp. 487–522.

6

CHAPTER

Selection and Placement

OBJECTIVES

After reading this chapter, you should be able to

1. Establish the basic scientific properties of personnel selection methods, including reliability, validity, and generalizability.
2. Discuss how the particular characteristics of a job, organization, or applicant affect the utility of any test.
3. Describe the government's role in personnel selection decisions, particularly in the areas of constitutional law, federal laws, executive orders, and judicial precedent.
4. List the common methods used in selecting human resources.
5. Describe the degree to which each of the common methods used in selecting human resources meets the demands of reliability, validity, generalizability, utility, and legality.

Microsoft: An Intelligent Approach to Personnel Selection

Bill Gates, co-founder of software giant Microsoft, is considered by many sources to be the richest man in the world, with a net worth estimated at over $40 billion. However, like many organizations, Microsoft started as a small firm and found an early niche by licensing its product (DOS operating system) to a much larger company (IBM). Microsoft grew quickly over the years, however, and the nature of who was hired during this growth period is one of the major factors that has led to its success. As one industry observer has noted, "The deliberate way in which Gates has fashioned an organization that prizes smart people is the single most important, and the most deliberately overlooked, aspect of Microsoft's success."

ENTER THE WORLD OF BUSINESS

General intelligence or cognitive ability is the central feature that Microsoft screens for in evaluating 120,000 job applicants yearly. Indeed, the goal of the entire selection and placement process is to find the smartest people and then place them in the jobs best suited to their talents. General intelligence is often valued more heavily than experience. In many cases, Microsoft has turned away applicants with long resumés in the area of software development. Instead, it is likely to raid major universities' math or physics departments to obtain people who are highly intelligent—even if they have little direct programming experience.

This emphasis on general reasoning and problem-solving ability in its personnel reflects the needs embodied in Microsoft's environment, its business strategy, and its culture. That is, the world of software development is changing constantly, so possession of yesterday's skills means less than the ability to develop new skills. Thus, Microsoft's strategy is to "outsmart" the competition in terms of both recognizing and then quickly adapting to changing conditions. This leads to an organizational culture where intellectual debate is vigorously promoted. Those who lack mental agility are not likely to ever feel comfortable within this culture—a culture some have labeled elitist or even arrogant.

Personnel selection and placement is seen as so central at Microsoft that (despite all his other pressing concerns), Gates makes himself available to both recruit and interview prospective job candidates. He feels that intelligence and creativity are reasonably innate so the company cannot do much to change people along these lines after they are hired. Gates has stated, "Take our 20 best people away, and I will tell you that Microsoft would become an unimportant company." This confirms the central role of people to both Microsoft's past success and its future competitive strategy.

SOURCE: A. Fisher, "The World's Most Admired Companies," *Fortune* (October 27, 1997), pp. 220–32; D. Seligman, "Brains in the Office," *Fortune* (January 13, 1997), p. 38; R.E. Stross, "Microsoft's Big Advantage—Hiring Only the Supersmart," *Fortune* (November 25, 1996), pp. 159–62.

Introduction

Any organization that intends to compete through people must take the utmost care with how it chooses organizational members. As one can see with Microsoft, personnel selection decisions made over the course of an organization's history are instrumental to its ability to survive, adapt, and grow. The competitive aspects of selection decisions become especially critical when organizations are confronted with tight labor markets or when competitors tap the same labor market. If one company systematically skims off the best applicants, the remaining companies must make do with what is left.

The purpose of this chapter is to familiarize you with ways to minimize errors in employee selection and placement and, in doing so, increase your company's competitive position. The chapter first focuses on five standards that should be met by any selection method. The chapter then evaluates several common selection methods according to those standards.

Selection Method Standards

Personnel selection is the process by which companies decide who will or will not be allowed into their organizations. Several generic standards should be met in any selection process. We focus on five: (1) reliability, (2) validity, (3) generalizability, (4) utility, and (5) legality. The first four build off each other, in the sense that the preceding standard is often necessary but not sufficient for the one that follows. This is less the case with legal standards. However, a thorough understanding of the first four standards helps us understand the rationale underlying many legal standards.

RELIABILITY

Much of the work in personnel selection involves measuring characteristics of people to determine who will be accepted for job openings. For example, we might be interested in applicants' physical characteristics (e.g., strength or endurance), their cognitive abilities (e.g., mathematical ability or verbal reasoning capacity), or aspects of their personality (e.g., their initiative or integrity). Whatever the specific focus, in the end we need to quantify people on these dimensions (i.e., assign numbers to them) so we can order them from high to low on the characteristic of interest. Once people are ordered in this way, we can then make decisions about whom to hire and whom to reject.

One key standard for any measuring device is its reliability. We define **reliability** as the degree to which a measure is free from random error.[1] If a measure of some supposedly stable characteristic such as intelligence is reliable, then the score a person receives based on that measure will be consistent over time and in different contexts.

TRUE SCORES AND THE RELIABILITY OF MEASUREMENT. Most measuring done in personnel selection deals with complex characteristics like intelligence, integrity, and leadership ability. However, to appreciate some of the complexities in measuring people, we will consider something concrete in discussing these concepts: the measurement of height. For example, if we were measuring an applicant's height, we might start by using a 12-inch ruler. Let's say the first person we measure turns out to be 6 feet 1 and 4/16 inches tall. It would not be surprising to find out that someone else measuring the same person a second time, perhaps an hour later, found this applicant's height to be 6 feet and 12/16 inches. The same applicant, measured a third time, maybe the next day, might be measured at 6 feet 1 and 8/16 inches tall.

As this example makes clear, even though the person's height is a stable characteristic, we get slightly different results each time he is assessed. This means that each time the person is assessed, we must be making slight errors. If a measurement device were perfectly reliable, there would be no errors of measurement. If we used a measure of height that was not as reliable as a ruler—for example, guessing someone's height after seeing her walk across the room—we might see a great deal of unreliability in the measure. Thus, reliability refers to the measuring instrument (a ruler versus a visual guess) rather than to the characteristic itself.

Because one never really knows the true score for the person being measured, there is no direct way to capture the "true" reliability of the measure. We can estimate reliability in several different ways, however, and since most of these rely on computing a correlation coefficient, we will briefly describe and illustrate this statistic.

The *correlation coefficient* is a measure of the degree to which two sets of numbers are related. The correlation coefficient expresses the strength of the relationship in numerical form. A perfect positive relationship (i.e., as one set of numbers goes up, so does the other) equals +1.0; a perfect negative relationship (i.e., as one goes up, the other goes down) equals –1.0. When there is no relationship between the sets of numbers, the correlation equals .00. Although the actual calculation of this statistic goes beyond the scope of this book (see any introductory statistics book or spreadsheet program), it will be useful for us to conceptually examine the nature of the correlation coefficient and what this means in personnel selection contexts.

When assessing the reliability of a measure, for example, we might be interested in knowing how scores on the measure at one time relate to scores on the same measure at another time. Obviously, if the characteristic we are measuring is supposedly stable (like intelligence or integrity) and the time lapse is short, this relationship should be strong. If it were weak, then the measure would be inconsistent—hence unreliable. This is what is called assessing *test–retest reliability*.

Plotting the two sets of numbers on a two-dimensional graph often helps us to appreciate the meaning of various levels of the correlation coefficient. Figure 6.1, for example, examines the relationship between student scholastic aptitude in one's junior and senior years in high school, where aptitude for college is measured in three ways: (1) via the scores on the Scholastic Aptitude Test (SAT), (2) via ratings from a high

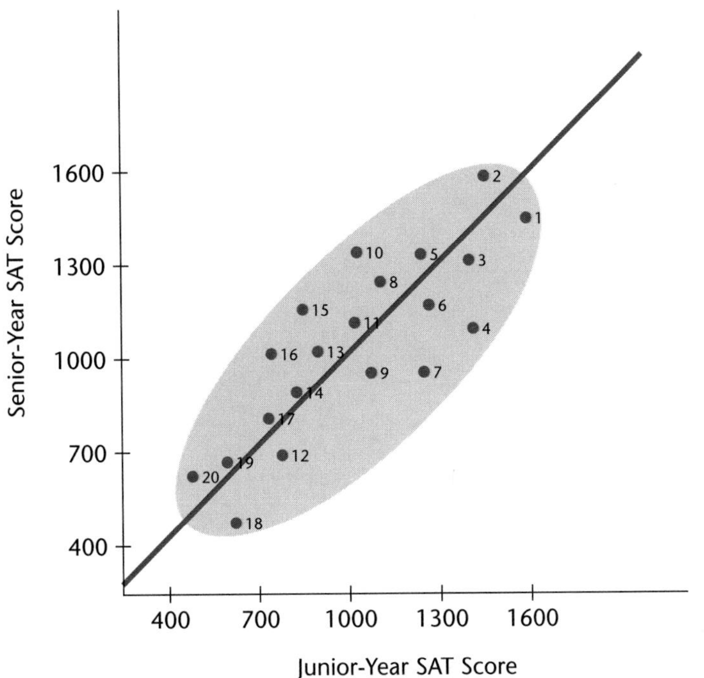

FIGURE 6.1A
Measurements of a Student's Aptitude

school counselor on a 1-to-100 scale, and (3) via tossing dice. In this plot, each X on the graphs represents a person whose scholastic aptitude is assessed twice (in the junior and senior years), so in Figure 6.1a, X_1 represents a person who scored 1580 on the SAT in the junior year and 1500 in the senior year; X_{20} represents a person who scored 480 in the junior year and 620 in the senior year.

Turning first to Figure 6.1a, it is clear that there is a very strong relationship between SAT scores across the two years. This relationship is not perfect in that the scores changed slightly from one year to the next, but not a great deal. Indeed, if there were a perfect 1.0 correlation, the plot would show a straight line proceeding at a 45-degree angle. The correlation coefficient for this set of data is in the .90 range. In this case, this .90 is considered the test–retest estimate of reliability.

Turning to Figure 6.1b, we see that the relationship between the high school counselor's ratings across the two years, while still positive, is not as strong. That is, the counselor's ratings of individual students' aptitudes for college are less consistent over the two years than their test scores. The correlation, and hence test–retest reliability, of this measure of aptitude is in the .50 range.

Finally, Figure 6.1c shows a worst-case scenario, where the students' aptitudes is assessed by tossing two six-sided dice. As you would expect, the random nature of the dice means that there is virtually no relationship between scores taken in one year and scores taken the next. Hence, in this instance, the correlation and test–retest estimate of reliability is .00. Although no one would seriously consider tossing dice to be a measure of aptitude, it is worth noting that research shows that overall ratings of job applicants' suitability for jobs based on unstructured interviews is very close to .00. Thus, one cannot assume a measure is reliable without actually checking this directly. Novices in measurement are often surprised at exactly how unreliable many human judgments turn out to be.

In addition to test–retest estimates, the consistency of multiple-items tests or scales can be assessed via *split-half reliability* estimates. For example, the SAT test has hundreds

FIGURE 6.1B

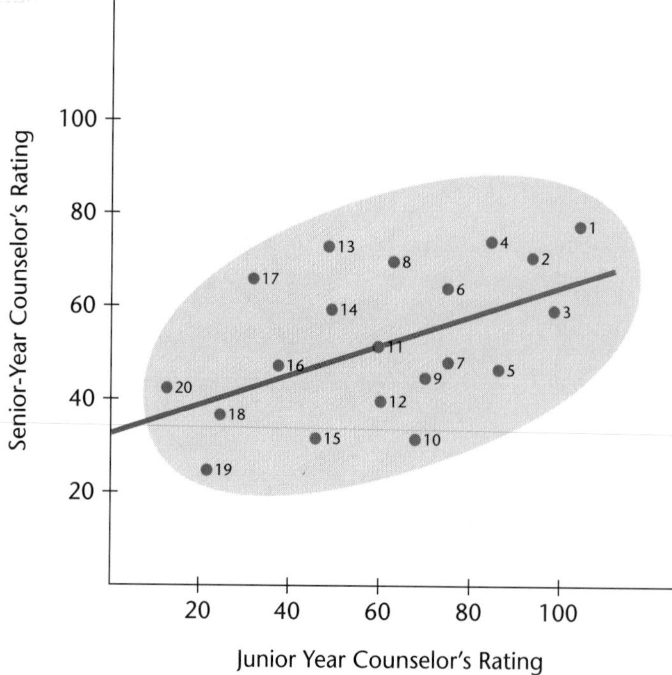

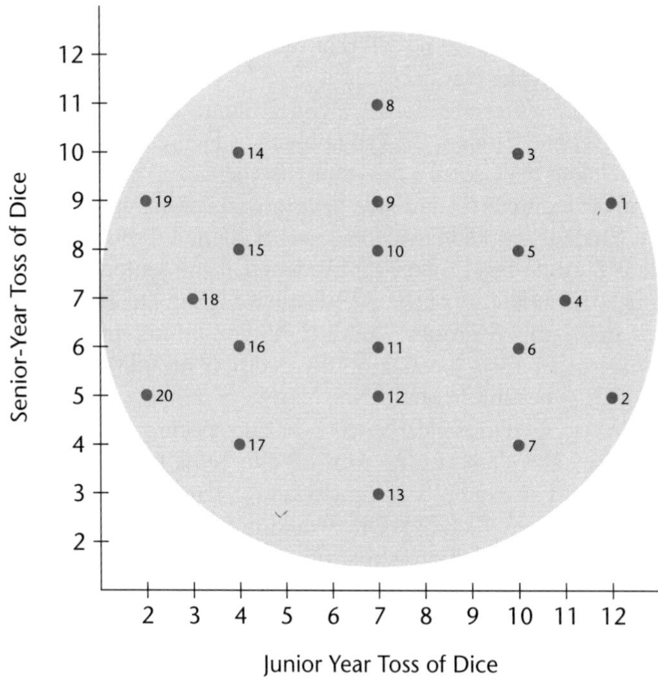

of questions. Via this method, one could take this test and break it up into two tests: one consisting of the odd-numbered items and one consisting of the even-numbered items. The correlation between these two halves of the test is referred to as the split-half reliability. If plotted, this would look very much like what we see in Figure 6.1a, except the horizontal axis would reflect scores on the odd-numbered items, and the vertical axis would reflect scores on the even-numbered items.

Finally, reliability can also be assessed via *inter-rater reliability* estimates. In this method, two different human judges rate the person on the dimension of interest, and we then correlate the separate opinions of the two judges. If plotted, this would look very much like what we see in Figure 6.1b, except the vertical axis would not reflect the counselor's rating at a different time. Instead, the vertical axis would reflect a different person's (e.g., a teacher's) ratings of the student taken at the same time as the counselor's rating.

STANDARDS FOR RELIABILITY. Regardless of what characteristic we are measuring, we want highly reliable measures. Thus, in the previous example, when it comes to measuring students' aptitudes for college, the SAT is more reliable than counselor ratings, which in turn are more reliable than tossing dice. But in an absolute sense, how high is high enough—.50, .70, .90? This is a difficult question to answer specifically because the required reliability depends in part on the nature of the decision being made about the people being measured.

For example, let's assume some college admissions officer was considering several students depicted in Figures 6.1a and 6.1b. Turning first to Figure 6.1b, assume the admissions officer was deciding between Student 1 (X_1) and Student 20 (X_{20}). For this decision, the .50 reliability of the ratings is high enough because the difference between the two students is so large that one would make the same decision for admission regardless of the year in which the rating was taken. That is, Student 1 (with scores of 100 and 80 in the junior and senior year, respectively) is always admitted and Student 20 (with scores of 12 and 42 for junior and senior years, respectively) is always rejected. Thus, although the ratings in this case are not all that reliable in an absolute sense, their reliability is high enough to make this decision.

On the other hand, let's assume the same college admissions officer was deciding between Student 1 (X_1) and Student 2 (X_2). Looking at Figure 6.1a, it is clear that even with the highly reliable SAT scores, the difference between these students is so small that one would make a different admission decision depending upon what year one obtained the score. Student 1 would be selected over Student 2 if the junior-year score was used, but Student 2 would be chosen over Student 1 if the senior-year score was used. Thus, even though the reliability of the SAT exam is high in an absolute sense, it is not high enough to make this decision. Under these conditions, the admissions officer needs to find some other basis for making the decision regarding these two students (e.g., high school GPA or rank in graduating class).

Although these two scenarios clearly show that no specific value of reliability is always acceptable, they also demonstrate why, all else being equal, the more reliable a measure is, the better. For example, turning again to Figures 6.1a and 6.1b, consider Student 9 (X_9) and Student 14 (X_{14}). One would not be able to make a decision between these two students based upon scholastic aptitude scores if assessed via counselor ratings, because the unreliability in the ratings is so large that scores across the two years conflict. That is, Student 9 has a higher rating than Student 14 in the junior year, but Student 14 has a higher rating than Student 9 in the senior year.

On the other hand, one would be able to base the decision of scholastic aptitude scores if assessed via the SAT, because the unreliability of the SAT scores is so low that scores across the two years point to the same conclusion. That is, Student 9's scores are always higher than Student 14's scores. Clearly, all else being equal, the more reliable the measure, the more likely it is that we can base decisions on the score differences that it reveals.

VALIDITY

We define **validity** as the extent to which performance on the measure is related to performance on the job. A measure must be reliable if it is to have any validity. On the other hand, we can reliably measure many characteristics (e.g., height) that may have no relationship to whether someone can perform a job. For this reason, reliability is a necessary but insufficient condition for validity.

CRITERION-RELATED VALIDATION. One way of establishing the validity of a selection method is to show that there is an empirical association between scores on the selection measure and scores for job performance. If there is a substantial correlation between test scores and job-performance scores, criterion-related validity has been established. For example, Figure 6.2 shows the relationship between 1998 scores on the Scholastic Aptitude Test (SAT) and 1999 freshman grade point average (GPA). In this example, there is roughly a .50 correlation between the SAT and GPA. This .50 is referred to as a *validity coefficient*. Note that we have used the correlation coefficient to assess both reliability and validity, which may seem somewhat confusing. The key distinction is that the correlation reflects a reliability estimate when we are attempting to assess the same characteristic twice (e.g., SAT scores in the junior and senior years), but the correlation coefficient reflects a validity coefficient when we are attempting to relate one characteristic (SAT) to performance on some task (GPA).

Criterion-related validity studies come in two varieties. **Predictive validation** seeks to establish an empirical relationship between test scores taken prior to being hired and eventual performance on the job. Predictive validation requires one to administer tests

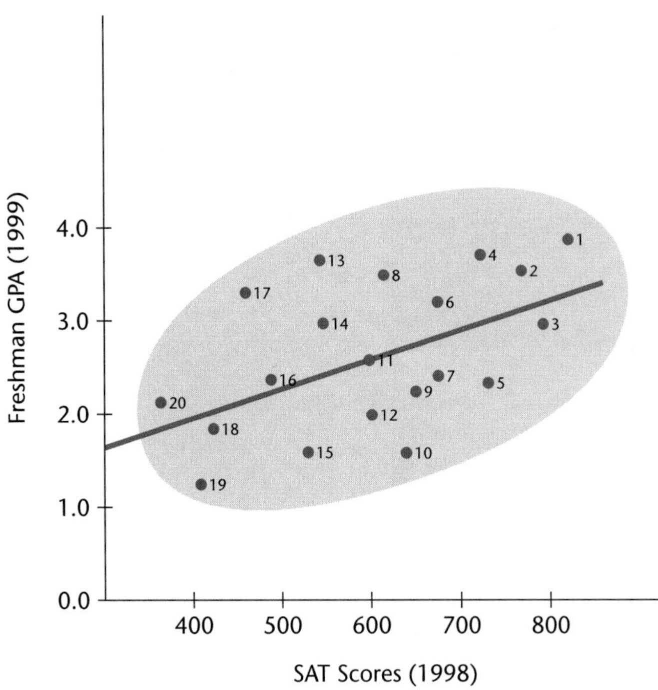

FIGURE 6.2 Relationship between 1998 SAT Scores and 1999 Freshman GPA

to job applicants and then wait for some time after test administration to see how a subset of those applicants (i.e., those who were actually hired) performed.

Because of the time and effort required to conduct a predictive validation study, many employers are tempted to use a different design. **Concurrent validation** assesses the validity of a test by administering it to people already on the job and then correlating test scores with existing measures of each person's performance. The logic behind this strategy is that if the best performers currently on the job perform better on the test than those who are currently struggling on the job, the test has validity. (Figure 6.3 compares the two types of validation study.)

Despite the extra effort and time needed for predictive validation, it is superior to concurrent validation for a number of reasons, First, job applicants (because they are seeking work) are typically more motivated to perform well on the tests than are current employees (who already have jobs). Second, current employees have learned many things on the job that job applicants have not yet learned. Therefore, the correlation between test scores and job performance for current employees may not be the same as the correlation between test scores and job performance for less knowledgeable job applicants. Third, current employees tend to be homogeneous—that is, similar to each other on many characteristics.[2] Thus, on many of the characteristics needed for success on the job, most current employees will show restriction in range. This restricted range makes it hard to detect a relationship between test scores and job-performance scores because few of the current employees will be very low on the characteristic you are trying to validate.

For example, if emotional stability is a characteristic required for a nursing career, it is quite likely that most nurses who have amassed five or six years' experience will score high on this characteristic. Yet to validate a test, you need both high test scorers (who should subsequently perform well on the job) and low test scorers (who should perform poorly on the job). Thus, while concurrent studies can sometimes help one anticipate the results of predictive studies, they do not serve as substitutes.[3]

Obviously, we would like our measures to be high in validity, but as with the relia-

FIGURE 6.3
Graphic Depiction of Concurrent and Predictive Validation Designs

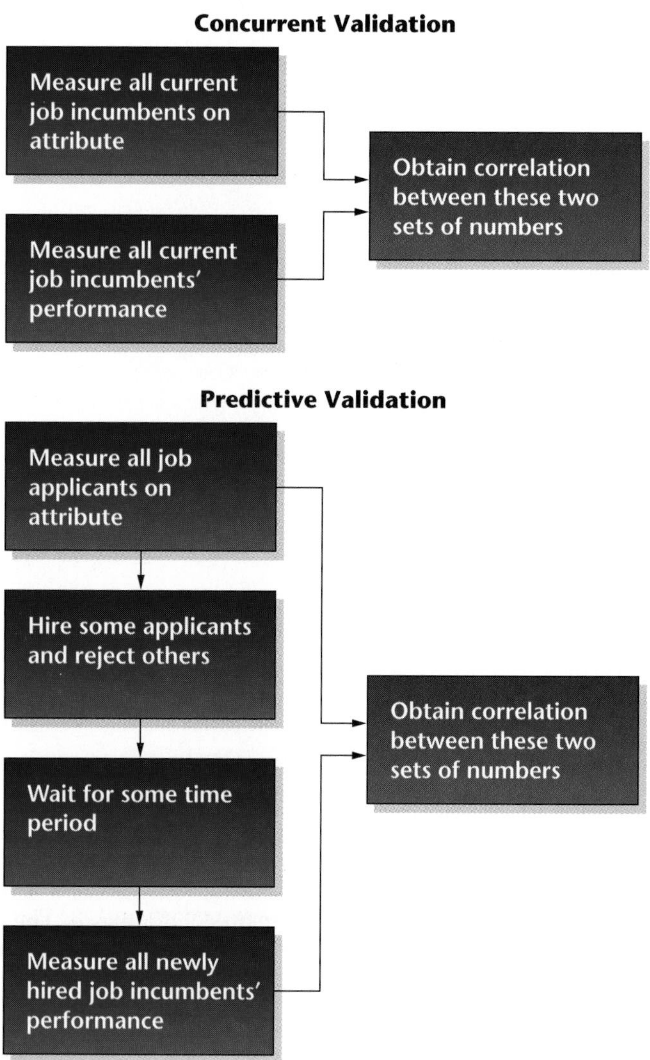

bility standard, we must also ask, how high is high enough? When trying to determine how much validity is enough, one typically has to turn to tests of statistical significance. A test of statistical significance answers the question, "How likely is it that a correlation of this size could have come about through luck or chance?"

Table 6.1 shows how big a correlation between a selection measure and a measure of job performance needs to be to achieve statistical significance at a level of .05 (i.e., there is only a 5 out of 100 chance that one could get a correlation this big by chance alone). While it is generally true that bigger correlations are better, the size of the sample on which the correlation is based plays a large role as well. Since many of the selection methods we examine in the second half of this chapter generate correlations in the .20s and .30s, we often need samples of 80 to 90 people.[4] A validation study with a small sample (e.g., 20 people) is almost doomed to failure from the start. Thus, many companies are too small to use a criterion-related validation strategy for most, if not all, of their jobs.

CONTENT VALIDATION. When sample sizes are small, an alternative test-validation strategy, content validation, can be used. **Content validation** is performed by

TABLE 6.1
Required Level of Correlation to Reach Statistical Significance as a Function of Sample Size

SAMPLE SIZE	REQUIRED CORRELATION
5	.75
10	.58
20	.42
40	.30
80	.21
100	.19

demonstrating that the items, questions, or problems posed by the test are a representative sample of the kinds of situations or problems that occur on the job.[5] A test that is content valid exposes the job applicant to situations that are likely to occur on the job, and then tests whether the applicant currently has sufficient knowledge, skill, or ability to handle such situations.

For example, one general contracting firm that constructed tract housing needed to hire one construction superintendent.[6] This job involved organizing, supervising, and inspecting the work of many subcontractors involved in the construction process. The tests developed for this position attempted to mirror the job. One test was a scrambled subcontractor test, where the applicant had to take a random list of subcontractors (roofing, plumbing, electrical, fencing, concrete, etc.) and put them in the correct order that each should appear on the site. A second test measured construction-error recognition. In this test, the applicant went into a shed that was specially constructed to have 25 common and expensive errors (e.g., faulty wiring, upside-down windows) and recorded whatever problems she could detect. Because the content of these tests so closely parallels the content of the job, one can safely make inferences from one to the other.

Although criterion-related validity is established by empirical means, content validity is achieved primarily through a process of expert judgement. One means of quantifying the degree of content validity is to use the content-validation ratio (CVR). To calculate this ratio, various individuals considered experts on the job are assembled. These people review each test (or item), and then categorize each test in terms of whether the skill or knowledge the test assesses is essential to the job. The content-validation ratio is then calculated from the formula

$$CVR = \frac{n_e - N/2}{N/2}$$

where n_e is the number of judges who rate the item "essential" and N is the number of judges. CVR equals 1.0 when all judges believe the item is essential and –1.0 when all judges believe it is nonessential. A CVR of .00 means there is complete disagreement on the degree to which the item is essential. Table 6.2 shows the level of CVR needed to achieve statistical significance as a function of the number of judges.[7]

The ability to use content validation in small sample settings makes it generally more applicable than criterion-related validation. However, content validation has two limitations.[8] First, one assumption behind content validation is that the person who is to be hired must have the knowledge, skills, or abilities at the time she is hired. Thus, it is not appropriate to use content validation in settings where the applicant is expected to learn the job in a formal training program conducted after selection.

Second, since subjective judgement plays such a large role in content validation, it is critical to minimize the amount of inference involved on the part of judges. Thus, the judges' ratings need to be made with respect to relatively concrete and observable behaviors (e.g., "applicant detects common construction errors" or "arranges optimal sub-

TABLE 6.2 Required Level of Content-Validation Ratio to Reach Statistical Significance as a Function of the Number of Judges

NUMBER OF JUDGES	REQUIRED CONTENT-VALIDATION RATIO
5	.99
8	.75
10	.62
15	.49
30	.33

contractor schedules"). Content validation would be inappropriate for assessing more abstract characteristics such as intelligence, leadership capacity, and integrity.

GENERALIZABILITY

Generalizability is defined as the degree to which the validity of a selection method established in one context extends to other contexts. There are three primary "contexts" over which we might like to generalize: different situations (i.e., jobs or organizations), different samples of people, and different time periods. Just as reliability is necessary but not sufficient for validity, validity is necessary but not sufficient for generalizability.

It was once believed, for example, that validity coefficients were situationally specific—that is, the level of correlation between test and performance varied as one went from one organization to another, even though the jobs studied seemed to be identical. Subsequent research has indicated that this is largely false. Rather, tests tend to show similar levels of correlation even across jobs that are only somewhat similar (at least for tests of intelligence and cognitive ability). Correlations with these kinds of tests change as one goes across widely different kinds of jobs, however. Specifically, the more complex the job, the higher the validity of many tests.[9]

It was also believed that tests showed differential subgroup validity, which meant that the validity coefficient for any test–job performance pair was different for people of different races or gender. This belief was also refuted by subsequent research, and, in general, one finds very similar levels of correlations across different groups of people.[10]

Because the evidence suggests that test validity often extends across situations and subgroups, *validity generalization* stands as an alternative for validating selection methods for companies that cannot employ criterion-related or content validation. Validity generalization is a three-step process. First, the company provides evidence from previous criterion-related validity studies conducted in other situations that shows that a specific test (e.g., a test of emotional stability) is a valid predictor for a specific job (e.g., nurse at a large hospital). Second, the company provides evidence from job analysis to document that the job it is trying to fill (nurse at a small hospital) is similar in all major respects to the job validated elsewhere (nurse at a large hospital). Finally, if the company can show that it uses a test that is the same as or similar to that used in the validated setting, then one can "generalize" the validity from the first context (large hospital) to the new context (small hospital).[11]

UTILITY

Utility is the degree to which the information provided by selection methods enhances the bottom-line effectiveness of the organization.[12] In general, the more reliable, valid, and generalizable the selection method is, the more utility it will have. On the other hand, many characteristics of particular selection contexts enhance or detract from the usefulness of given selection methods, even when reliability, validity, and generalizability are held constant.

Figures 6.4a and 6.4b, for example, show two different scenarios where the correla-

FIGURE 6.4A

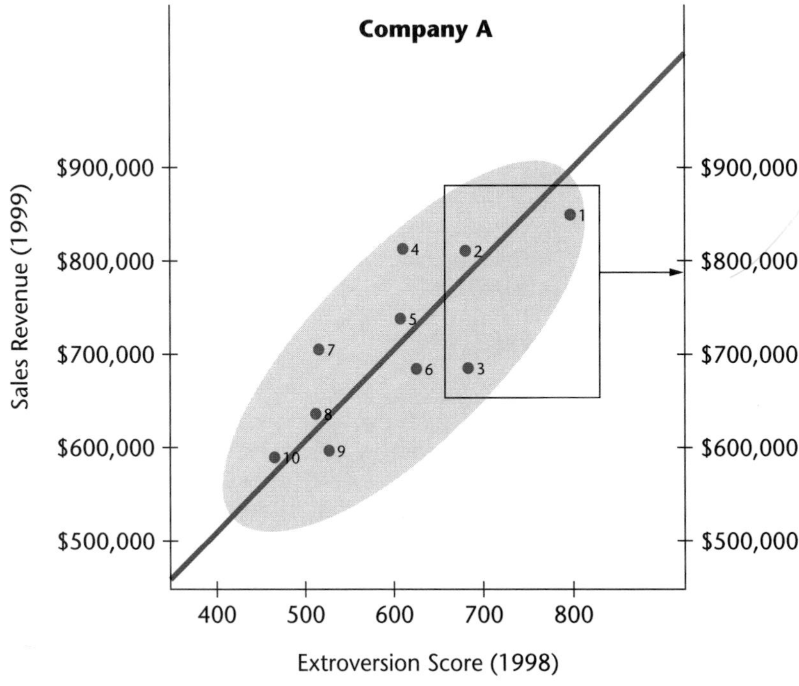

FIGURE 6.4B

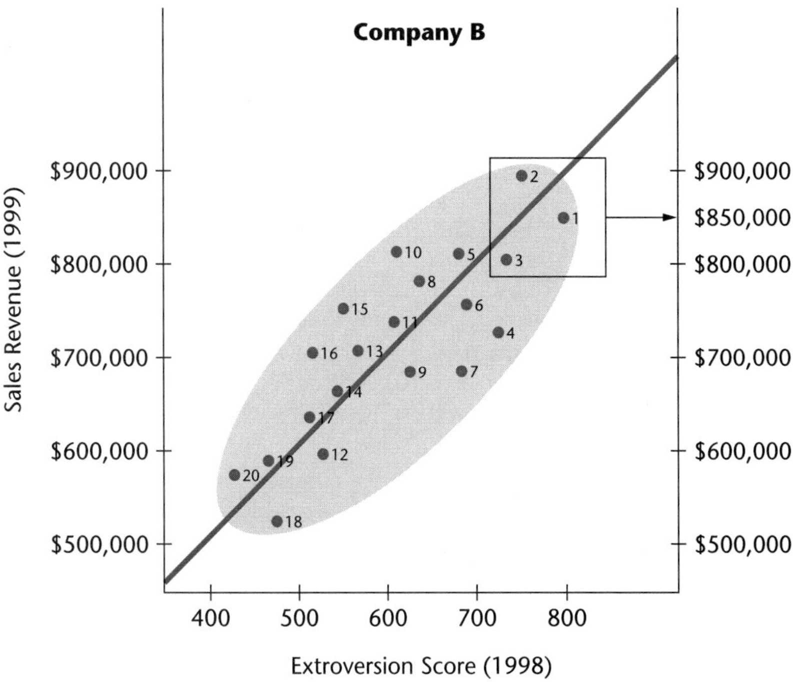

tion between a measure of extroversion and the amount of sales revenue generated by a sample of sales representatives is the same for two different companies: Company A and Company B. Although the correlation between the measure of extroversion and sales is the same, Company B derives much more utility or practical benefit from the measure. That is, as indicated by the arrows proceeding out of the boxes (which indicate the people selected), the average sales revenue of the three people selected by

Electronic HR—Eliminating the Paperwork

COMPETING THROUGH HIGH-PERFORMANCE WORK SYSTEMS

Human resource offices are filled with paper—often so full of paper that it is hard to find anything from the past or store anything for the future. Fortunately today's technology allows organizations to drastically cut down on the amount of paper needed to conduct personnel-related tasks. Many organizations are using this technological edge to reduce costs, speed the processing of tasks, and improve performance.

For example, when Mirage Resorts had to hire 9,600 workers for Bellagio, its new Las Vegas luxury resort scheduled to open in October 1998, it totally computerized the process. The process began with a newspaper ad that was e-mailed to several local papers. Applicants then called to schedule an appointment with an automated server using their touch-tone phones. When applicants arrived at their appointed times, they were greeted and taken to a computer terminal where they entered their responses to a 165-item application form and test presented on the computer. Responses to the application form were put into a database that could be searched by various department heads, who then scheduled interviews with promising candidates. These interviews were highly standardized and their results were also fed into the database, which was used for making decisions.

Although when this book went to press, it was still too early to tell how those decisions turned out, it is clear that the process for making the decision was a vast improvement over traditional methods. The entire process generated a pool of 75,000 applicants for a selection ratio of 13 percent (i.e., 9,600 hires/75,000 applicants). In terms of timing, it took just over five months to process all these applicants, compared to the nine months that Mirage experienced the last time it did a mass hiring effort such as this. Vice President Arte Nathan also estimates that the company saved $600,000 on paper, file space, and temporary help that would have been associated with a more traditional hiring procedure.

SOURCE: V. Frazee, "Go Paperless One Sheet at a Time," *Personnel Journal* (November, 1996), pp. 68–76; E.P. Gunn, "How Mirage Resorts Sifted 75,000 Applicants to Hire 9,600 in 24 Weeks," *Fortune* (October 12, 1998), p. 195.

Company B (Figure 6.4b) is $850,000 compared to $780,000 from the three people selected by Company A (Figure 6.4a).

The major difference between these two companies is that Company B generated twice as many applicants as Company A. This means that the selection ratio (the percentage of people selected relative to the total number of people tested) is quite low for Company B (3/20) relative to Company A (3/10). Thus, the people selected by Company B have higher amounts of extroversion than those selected by Company A; therefore, Company B takes better advantage of the relationship between extroversion and sales. Although this might be somewhat offset by the cost of recruiting and measuring 20 more people, this added cost is probably trivial relative to the difference in revenue shown in this example ($70,000). Thus, the utility of any test generally increases as the selection ratio gets lower, so long as the additional costs of recruiting and testing are not excessive.

Where the economic consequences to an organization of failure versus success on the job are great, testing has greater utility. For example, a test of sales ability might have greater utility for a company selling cars than for one selling candy. The sales difference between a "good" auto salesperson and an average one might be $100,000 a month, versus a difference of perhaps $2,000 a month for a good versus an average candy seller.

Finally, the utility of any selection procedure is also a function of how many people are tested and the cost of the testing. Obviously, as the number of people who have to be tested and the cost of the test increase, the utility of the testing process goes down. Fortunately, as the "Competing through High-Performance Work Systems" box shows, this cost can be reduced by aggressively employing new computer technologies.

LEGALITY

The final standard that any selection method should adhere to is **legality.** All selection methods should conform to existing laws and existing legal precedents. Many issues related to selecting employees safely under U.S. law were discussed generically in Chapter 3. Our treatment there was broad and dealt with legal aspects in all areas of human resource management. In this chapter, we will focus more narrowly on issues that relate directly to personnel selection, bypassing constitutional amendments and focusing more squarely on federal legislation and executive orders.

FEDERAL LEGISLATION. Three primary federal laws form the basis for a majority of the suits filed by job applicants. First, the Civil Rights Act of 1991 (discussed in Chapter 3), an extension of the Civil Rights Act of 1964, protects individuals from discrimination based on race, color, sex, religion, and national origin with respect to hiring as well as compensation and working conditions. The 1991 act differs from the 1964 act in three important areas.

First, it establishes employers' explicit obligation to establish the business necessity of any neutral-appearing selection method that has had adverse impact on groups specified by the law. This is typically done by showing that the test has significant criterion-related or content validity. Second, it allows the individual filing the complaint to have a jury decide whether he or she may recover punitive damages (in addition to lost wages and benefits) for emotional injuries caused by the discrimination.[13] This can generate large settlements, such as the one arrived at by Shoney Inc., where 18 African American employees were awarded $105 million to settle a racial discrimination suit.[14] Finally, it explicity prohibits the granting of preferential treatment to minority groups. For example, it specifically prohibits adjusting scores upward on tests just because someone is in a group with lower average scores (sometimes referred to as race norming). Adjusting scores in this way has been found to have a number of negative effects, not only on the attitudes of white males, but on the proposed beneficiaries of such preferential treatment. Research shows that when selection decisions are perceived as being based partially on group membership, it undermines the confidence and hurts the job performance of the women or minority group members the program was designed to help.[15]

The Age Discrimination in Employment Act of 1967 is also widely used in personnel selection. This act mirrors the Civil Rights Act of 1964 in its protections and, as amended in 1978, covers job applicants over the age of 40. The act does not protect younger workers (thus, there is never a case for "reverse discrimination" here), and like the most recent civil rights act, it allows for jury trials and punitive damages. This act makes almost all "mandatory retirement" programs illegal (i.e., company policies that dictate that everyone who reaches a set age must retire).

Litigation brought forward under this act surged by over 200 percent between 1991 and 1998. Two trends have combined to generate this increase: the general aging of the work force and recent attempts by organizations to downsize. Together, these trends have led to the displacement of many older workers who have brought age discrimination suits against their former employers. The long list of companies sued under this act includes CBS Inc., McDonnell Douglas, Northwest Airlines, and Disney.

Finally, the Americans with Disabilities Act (ADA) of 1991 protects individuals with physical and mental disabilities (or with a history of the same). It extends the Vocational Rehabilitation Act of 1973, requiring employers to make "reasonable accommodation" to disabled individuals whose handicaps may prevent them from performing essential functions of the job as currently designed. "Reasonable accommodation" could include restructuring jobs, modifying work schedules, making facilities accessible, providing readers, or modifying equipment.

Employers need not make accommodations that cause "undue hardship." In other words, if the accommodation is "unduly costly, extensive, substantially disruptive, or fundamentally alters the nature of the job," the employer need not comply. Undue hardship can also be established if the employer can show that hiring the applicant will result in a direct threat to the safety of that person or others he or she encounters on the job despite attempts at accommodation.

This act also restricts many preemployment inquiries.[16] For instance, it is legal to ask an applicant, "Can you meet the attendance requirements for this job?" but it is not legal to ask, "How many days did you miss work in your last job because you were sick?" because the latter question might reveal a disability. The ADA also prohibits tests that might reveal a psychological or physical disability. (These would fall under the heading of "illegal medical examinations.") If a manager is uncertain whether a test would be considered medical, she should review the test to determine whether it must be interpreted by a medical professional or whether the behavior or trait assessed by the test is so fundamental to the job that it can be interpreted by any line manager.

EXECUTIVE ORDERS. As noted in Chapter 3, the executive branch of the government also regulates hiring decisions through the use of executive orders. Executive Order 11246 parallels the protections provided by the Civil Rights Act of 1964 but goes beyond the 1964 act in two important ways. First, not only do the executive orders prohibit discrimination, they actually mandate that employers take affirmative action to hire qualified minority applicants. The executive orders also allow the government to suspend all business with a contractor while an investigation is being conducted (rather than waiting for an actual finding), which puts a great deal of pressure on employers to comply with these orders. Executive orders are monitored by the Office of Federal Contract Compliance Procedures (OFCCP), which issues guidelines (e.g., the Affirmative Action Program Guidelines published by the Bureau of National Affairs in 1983) to help companies comply.

Types of Selection Methods

The first half of this chapter laid out the five standards by which we can judge selection measures. In the second half of this chapter, we examine the common selection methods used in various organizations and discuss their advantages and disadvantages in terms of these standards.

INTERVIEWS

A selection interview has been defined as "a dialogue initiated by one or more persons to gather information and evaluate the qualifications of an applicant for employment."[17] The selection interview is the most widespread selection method employed in organizations.

Unfortunately, the long history of research on the employment interview suggests that, without proper care, it can be unreliable, low in validity,[18] and biased against a number of different groups.[19] Moreover, interviews are relatively costly because they require at least one person to interview another person, and these persons have to be brought to the same geographic location. Finally, in terms of legality, the subjectivity embodied in the process often makes applicants upset, particularly if they fail to get a job after being asked apparently irrelevant questions. The Supreme Court ruled in *Watson v. Fort Worth Bank and Trust* that subjective selection methods like the interview must be validated by traditional criterion-related or content-validation procedures.[20]

Fortunately, more recent research has pointed to a number of concrete steps that one can employ to increase the utility of the personnel selection interview.[21] First, HR staff should keep the interview structured, standardized, and focused on accomplishing a small number of goals. That is, they should plan to come out of each interview with quantitative ratings on a small number of dimensions that are observable (e.g., interpersonal style or ability to express oneself) and avoid ratings of abilities that may be better measured by tests (e.g., intelligence). In the words of one experienced interviewer for Johnson and Son Inc., "Gut feelings count, but the goal is controlled subjectivity."[22]

Second, ask questions dealing with specific situations that are likely to arise on the job, and use these to determine what the person is likely to do in that situation. These types of **situational interview** items come in two varieties, as shown in Table 6.3. Some items are "experience-based" and require the applicant to reveal an actual experience he or she had in the past when confronting the situation. Other items are "future-oriented" and ask what the person is likely to do when confronting a certain hypothetical situation in the future. Research suggests that these types of items can both show validity but that experience-based items often outperform future-oriented items.[23]

Ameritech Cellular Services uses these types of situational questions in its interview procedures. Interviewees answer questions that directly relate to past experiences and future behaviors. As James Reicks, director of human resources, notes, "We're shifting toward competency-based systems which really zero in on the attributes of a candidate. We're looking for specific examples of how they succeeded in previous jobs rather than examining their entire work history."[24]

It is also important to use multiple interviewers who are trained to avoid many of the subjective errors that can result when one human being is asked to rate another. That is, interviewers need to be made aware of their own biases, prejudices, and other personal features that may color their perceptions of others.[25] For example, at Levi Strauss, the human resource department makes sure women and minorities play a large role in interviewing job applicants to ensure their perspective is included.[26] Many employers

TABLE 6.3
Examples of Experience-Based and Future-Oriented Situational Interview Items

Experience-based	
Motivating employees:	"Think about an instance when you had to motivate an employee to perform a task that he or she disliked but that you needed to have done. How did you handle that situation?"
Resolving conflict:	"What was the biggest difference of opinion you ever had with a co-worker? How did you resolve that situation?"
Overcoming resistance to change:	"What was the hardest change you ever had to bring about in a past job, and what did you do to get the people around you to change their thoughts or behaviors?"
Future-oriented	
Motivating employees:	"Suppose you were working with an employee whom you knew greatly disliked performing a particular task. You needed to get this task completed, however, and this person was the only one available to do it. What would you do to motivate that person?"
Resolving conflict:	"Imagine that you and a co-worker disagree about the best way to handle an absenteeism problem with another member of your team. How would you resolve that situation?"
Overcoming resistance to change:	"Suppose you had an idea for change in work procedures that would enhance quality, but some members of your work group were hesitant to make the change. What would you do in that situation?"

are now videotaping interviews and then sending the tapes (rather than the applicants) around from place to place. This is seen by some as a cost-effective means of allowing numerous raters to evaluate the candidate under standard conditions.[27]

REFERENCES AND BIOGRAPHICAL DATA

Just as few employers would think of hiring someone without an interview, nearly all employers also use some method for getting background information on applicants before an interview. This information can be solicited from the people who know the candidate through reference checks.

The evidence on the reliability and validity of reference checks suggests that these are, at best, weak predictors of future success on the job.[28] The main reason for this low validity is that the evaluations supplied in most reference letters are so positive that it is hard to differentiate applicants. As Northwestern Bell's district manager of management employment notes, "They all say, 'This is the greatest individual the world has ever seen, the next president, at least.' . . . It isn't always accurate."[29]

This problem with reference letters has two causes. First, the applicant usually gets to choose who writes the letter and can thus choose only those writers who think the highest of her abilities. Second, since letter writers can never be sure who will read the letters, they may fear that supplying damaging information about someone could come back to haunt them. This fear is well placed. Over 10,000 such suits have been filed since 1983. In 70 percent of these cases, the recipient of the bad reference prevails, and the average award is over $500,000. (The record is $1.9 million.)[30]

Intuit Corporation, the Menlo Park, California, software company that produces *Quicken*, tries to get around these problems by requesting references in bulk—sometimes asking for as many as 12 letters of reference. The first two or three people listed invariably have nothing but positive things to say about the candidate, but, according to Sharyn Vacunich, staffing manager for Intuit, once you get beyond those people, you hear more than just positive things.[31]

The evidence on the utility of biographical information collected directly from job applicants is much more positive, especially for certain occupational categories such as clerical and sales jobs[32] and for particular outcomes like turnover.[33] The low cost of obtaining such information significantly enhances its utility, especially when the information is used in conjunction with a well-designed follow-up interview that complements, rather than duplicates, the biographical information bank.[34]

The biographical information form also provides a written document that the organization can verify via outside checks. For example, APCOA Inc. (a Cleveland-based company that operates parking facilities at 400 urban sites and 70 airports in 42 states) conducts a battery of checks. Depending on the position, this investigation can include driving records, credit history, criminal record, and education and employment verification. According to Bobbi Navarro, a human resource staff member at APCOA, "The perception is [that] a parking company would never spend the time and energy to do all this, but if you're committed to excellence, then it's absolutely necessary. The hiring process can set you apart from the competition, and nowadays, you have to know who the people are who work for you. the risk is just too great to ignore."[35] Indeed, as the "Competing by Meeting Stakeholders' Needs" box illustrates, this need to eliminate risk in hiring undesirable applicants has provided a boost to the private investigative services industry, which now tailors its products to corporate clientele.

In terms of legal concerns, it should be noted that asking certain questions is illegal regardless of their impact. There is substantial variation from state to state on what constitutes a legal versus an illegal inquiry. Consult the Fair Employment Practices Commission in your state to find out more.

Background Investigations: Protecting Employees and Customers

Under the legal doctrine of "negligent hiring," an employer can be held responsible for criminal acts perpetrated by employees. So for example, in 1997, the family of a person killed by a security guard at an apartment complex in Nevada successfully sued the guard's employer because it had failed to look into his past criminal background. Faced with this kind of pressure and a general unwillingness on the part of past employers to provide much information on former employees, more and more organizations are turning to private investigators to help collect information on potential hires.

Indeed, investigative services to corporate clients is one of the fast-growing industries in the United States, with revenues expected to exceed $4 billion by the year 2000—a fivefold increase since 1980. New players in this industry emerge each year, and four of the Big Six consulting firms began building large investigative divisions within the last two years. Technological changes that have made information gathering more affordable have accelerated this activity. Whereas many may see this as an invasion of privacy, few employers seem willing to weigh privacy higher than employee and customer safety.

For example, Bell South has conducted background checks on all new hires for the past 10 years. Jim Monk, the organization's security director, notes that up to 20 percent of applicants conceal activity that might warrant closer scrutiny for certain types of jobs. This might include a poor driving record for someone applying for a job that entails operating motor vehicles, bankruptcies or poor credit histories for people expected to handle large sums of money, or criminal convictions for people who may be sent out to work in or around people's homes. Thus, in an effort to protect the organization, its employees, and its customers, more and more organizations are doing some detective work prior to making any hiring decisions, with the need to protect applicants' privacy taking a back seat to these concerns.

SOURCE: E.A. Robinson, "Beware: Job Seekers Have No Secrets," *Fortune* (December 29, 1997), p. 285; K. Clark, "The Detectives," *Fortune* (April 14, 1997), pp. 123–26.

PHYSICAL ABILITY TESTS

Although automation and other advances in technology have eliminated or modified many physically demanding occupational tasks, many jobs still require certain physical abilities. In these cases, tests of physical abilities may be relevant not only to predicting performance but to predicting occupational injuries and disabilities as well.[36] There are seven classes of tests in this area: ones that evaluate (1) muscular tension, (2) muscular power, (3) muscular endurance, (4) cardiovascular endurance, (5) flexibility, (6) balance, and (7) coordination.[37]

The criterion-related validities for these kinds of tests for certain jobs are quite strong.[38] Unfortunately, these tests, particularly the strength tests, are likely to have an adverse impact on some applicants with disabilities and many female applicants. For example, roughly two-thirds of all males score higher than the highest-scoring female on muscular tension tests.[39]

There are two key questions to ask in deciding whether to use these kinds of tests. First, is the physical ability essential to performing the job and is it mentioned prominently enough in the job description? Neither the Civil Rights Act nor the ADA requires employers to hire individuals who cannot perform essential job functions, and both accept a written job description as evidence of the essential functions of the job.[40] Second, is there a probability that failure to adequately perform the job would result in some risk to the safety or health of the applicant, co-workers, or clients? The "direct threat" clause of the ADA makes it clear that adverse impact against those with disabilities is warranted under such conditions.

COGNITIVE ABILITY TESTS

Cognitive ability tests differentiate individuals on their mental rather than physical capacities. Cognitive ability has many different facets, although we will focus only on three dominant ones.[41] **Verbal comprehension** refers to a person's capacity to understand and use written and spoken language. **Quantitative ability** concerns the speed and accuracy with which one can solve arithmetic problems of all kinds. **Reasoning ability,** a broader concept, refers to a person's capacity to invent solutions to many diverse problems.

Some jobs require only one or two of these facets of cognitive ability. Under these conditions, maintaining the separation among the facets is appropriate. However, many jobs that are high in complexity require most, if not all, of the facets, and hence one general test is often as good as many tests of separate facets.[42] Highly reliable commercial tests measuring these kinds of abilities are widely available, and they are generally valid predictors of job performance. The validity of these kinds of tests is related to the complexity of the job, however, in that one sees higher criterion-related validation for complex jobs than for simple jobs.[43]

One of the major drawbacks to these tests is that they typically have adverse impact on African Americans. In the past, the difference between the means for blacks and whites meant that an average black would score at the 16th percentile of the distribution of white scores.[44] Indeed, the notion of race norming, alluded to earlier, was born of the desire to use these high-utility tests in a manner that avoided adverse impact. Fortunately, more recent data suggest that race differences in scores on cognitive ability tests have decreased significantly over the years.

PERSONALITY INVENTORIES

While ability tests attempt to categorize individuals relative to what they can do, personality measures tend to categorize individuals by what they are like. Two recent reviews of the personality literature independently arrived at five common aspects of personality.[45] We refer to these five major dimensions as the Big Five, and they include (1) extroversion, (2) adjustment, (3) agreeableness, (4) conscientiousness, and (5) inquisitiveness. Table 6.4 lists each of these with a corresponding list of adjectives that fit each dimension.

Although it is possible to find reliable, commercially available measures of each of these traits, the evidence for their validity and generalizability is low. Conscientiousness is one of the few factors that displays any validity across a number of different job categories, and many real-world managers rate this as one of the most important characteristics they look for in employees.[46] People high in conscientiousness show more stamina at work, which is helpful in many occupations. For example, at the highest levels of management, many CEOs of the largest companies—such as Herb Kelleher of Southwest Airlines, Tony O'Reilly of H.J. Heinz, and Wolfgang Schmitt of Rubbermaid—report working 80 to 90 hours a week and get by on as little as 5 to 6 hours of sleep each night.[47] Conscientiousness seems to be a particularly good predictor when

TABLE 6.4 The Five Major Dimensions of Personality Inventories

Dimension	Adjectives
1. Extroversion	Sociable, gregarious, assertive, talkative, expressive
2. Adjustment	Emotionally stable, nondepressed, secure, content
3. Agreeableness	Courteous, trusting, good-natured, tolerant, cooperative, forgiving
4. Conscientiousness	Dependable, organized, persevering, thorough, achievement-oriented
5. Inquisitiveness	Curious, imaginative, artistically sensitive, broad-minded, playful

teamed with tests of mental ability because there is a stronger relationship between this trait and performance when ability is high.[48]

Although conscientiousness is the only dimension of personality that seems to show predictive validity across all situations, there are contexts where other components of the Big Five relate to job performance. First, extroversion and agreeableness seem to be related to performance in jobs such as sales or management—it is easy to see why these types of attributes would be required for such jobs.[49] These two factors also seem to be predictive of performance in team contexts, although in many cases it is the score of the lowest team member that determines the whole group outcome. That is, one highly disagreeable, introverted, or unconscientious member can ruin an entire team.[50]

Finally, the validity for almost all of the Big Five factors in terms of predicting job performance also seems to be higher when the scores are not obtained from the applicant, but are instead taken from other people.[51] The lower validity associated with self-reports of personality can be traced to two factors. First, people sometimes lack insight into what their own personalities are actually like (or are perceived by others), so their scores are inaccurate or unreliable. Second, applicants can sometimes fake their responses to personality items, making themselves seem more conscientious, agreeable, and extroverted than they really are.[52]

WORK SAMPLES

Work-sample tests and job-performance tests attempt to simulate the job in miniaturized form. For example, many organizations use an "In-Basket" test when assessing people who are applying for managerial jobs. In an in-basket test, job candidates are asked to respond to memos that typify the problems confronted by those who already hold the job. The key in this and other forms of work-sample tests is the behavioral consistency between the requirements of the job and the requirements of the test.[53]

Work-sample tests tend to be job specific—that is, tailored individually to each different job in each organization. On the positive side, this has resulted in tests that demonstrate a high degree of criterion-related validity. In addition, the obvious parallels between the test and the job make content validity high. In general, this reduces the likelihood that rejected applicants will challenge the procedure through litigation. Available evidence also suggests that these tests are low in adverse impact.[54]

Finally, as shown in the "Competing through Globalization" box, work-sample tests, because they get directly at the ability to do the job, are particularly useful when hiring non-U.S. citizens, for whom background information may be hard to collect or interpret.

With all these advantages come two drawbacks. First, by their very nature the tests are job-specific, so generalizability is low. Second, partly because a new test has to be developed for each job and partly because of their nonstandardized formats, these tests are relatively expensive to develop. It is much more cost-effective to purchase a commercially available cognitive ability test that can be used for a number of different job categories within the company than to develop a test for each job. For this reason, some have rated the utility of cognitive ability tests higher than work-sample tests, despite the latter's higher criterion-related validity.[55]

In the area of managerial selection, work-sample tests are typically the cornerstone in assessment centers. Generically, the term *assessment center* is used to describe a wide variety of specific selection programs that employ multiple selection methods to rate either applicants or job incumbents on their managerial potential. Someone attending an assessment center would typically experience work-sample tests such as an in-basket test and several tests of more general abilities and personality. Because assessment centers employ multiple selection methods, their criterion-related validity tends to be quite

Hiring Foreign Nationals for U.S. Firms

Although the majority of firms in the United States hire U.S. citizens, the search for the world's best talent may require crossing the U.S. borders. This is increasingly common in industries such as software development, engineering, pharmaceuticals, and aerospace, where high-ability, low-cost talent can be found in Russia, India, Taiwan, Singapore, China, and Korea. However, hiring foreign nationals for U.S. firms is not as easy as you might think. There are a number of barriers to overcome when hiring non-U.S. citizens.

For example, documenting and verifying the credentials of foreign nationals is difficult. For example, if the applicant has attended a non-U.S. university, how does the institution and the degree awarded compare to what would be found in the United States? To get around overseas educational idiosyncrasies, some companies like Mobil Corporation conduct their own screening tests for basic skills in reading and math. Other companies—such as the Knowledge Company in Fairfax, Virginia—employ work-sample tests, where, for example, an applicant for an engineering job would be asked to submit drawings and plans for a certain product, which would be evaluated by experts.

Also, the typical criminal background check is difficult because, except for the most serious crimes, there is little information within the United States regarding crimes committed in other countries. Beyond this, the American Foreign Corrupt Practices

COMPETING THROUGH GLOBALIZATION

Act even bars U.S. entry of foreign businesspeople who might have bribed government officials in their home countries—even if that is not against the law in those countries.

Finally, even if one is able to obtain the necessary data for making an informed hiring decision with respect to a foreign national, the U.S. Department of Labor requires the employer to show that (1) the employment of this person will not adversely affect wages and working conditions of U.S. citizens who work in similar occupations and (2) no U.S. citizens are willing and able to do the work at that specific time.

Taken altogether, these and other hurdles associated with hiring foreign nationals make this a difficult though not impossible proposition. Since many companies are not able or willing to go through this effort, here is yet another area where one organization can gain competitive advantage over another. Indeed, as Texas Instruments' William Glickman notes, "If American firms are going to compete successfully in the years ahead, they must look everywhere for those with the best ability."

SOURCE: C.J. Bachler, "Global Inpats—Don't Let Them Surprise You," *Personnel Journal* (June 1996), pp. 54–65; R. Horn, "Give Me Your Huddled . . . High Tech Ph.D.s: Are High Skilled Foreigners Displacing U.S. Workers?" *Business Week* (November 6, 1995), pp. 161–62; S. Greengard, "Gain the Edge in the Knowledge Race," *Personnel Journal* (August 1996), pp. 52–56.

high. Indeed, research indicates that one of the best combinations of selection methods includes work-sample tests with a highly structured interview and a measure of general cognitive ability. The validity coefficient expected from such a combined battery often exceeds .60.[56]

HONESTY TESTS AND DRUG TESTS

Many problems that confront society also exist within organizations, which has led to two new kinds of tests: honesty tests and drug-use tests. Many companies formerly employed polygraph tests, or lie detectors, to evaluate job applicants, but this changed with the passage of the Polygraph Act in 1988. This act banned the use of polygraphs in employment screening for most organizations. However, it did not eliminate the problem of theft by employees. As a result, the paper-and-pencil honesty testing industry was born.

Paper-and-pencil honesty tests typically ask applicants directly about their attitudes

TABLE 6.5
Sample Items from a Typical Integrity Test

1. It's OK to take something from a company that is making too much profit.
2. Stealing is just a way of getting your fair share.
3. When a store overcharges its customers, it's OK to change price tags on merchandise.
4. If you could get into a movie without paying and not get caught, would you do it?
5. Is it OK to go around the law if you don't actually break it?

SOURCE: "T or F? Honesty Tests," p. 104. Reprinted with permission, *Inc.* magazine, February 1992.

toward theft or their past experiences with theft. Some sample items are shown in Table 6.5. Given the recent development of these tests, there is not a great deal of independent evidence (i.e., evidence not generated by those who publish and sell the tests) on their reliability and validity. A large-scale independent review of validity studies conducted by the publishers of many integrity tests suggests they can be predictive of both theft and other disruptive behaviors.[57] One of the few predictive studies conducted by someone other than a publisher of honesty tests also suggests that these tests predict theft in convenience store settings.[58] Another positive feature of these tests is that one does not see large differences attributable to race or sex so they are not likely to have adverse impact on these demographic groups.[59]

As is the case with measures of personality, some people are concerned that people confronting an honesty test can fake their way to a passing score. The evidence suggests that people instructed to fake their way to a high score (indicating honesty) can do so. However, it is not clear that this affects the validity of the predictions made using such tests. That is, it seems that despite this built-in bias, scores on the test still predict future theft. Thus, the effect of the faking bias is not large enough to detract from the test's validity.[60]

Although it is always a good rule to locally evaluate the reliability and validity of any selection method, because of the novelty of these kinds of measures this may be even more critical with honesty tests. For example, Nordstrom's, the large department store chain, uses the Reid Survey to screen for violent tendencies, drug use, and dishonesty. Originally, the test was only one of many factors that went into the final hiring decision, so there were some people hired who were not recommended by the Reid test. Follow-up studies showed that the turnover rate for those recommended by the Reid test was only 22 percent, compared with 44 percent of those who did not pass the test but were hired anyway. Since the test cost only $5 to administer, this represents a major cost saving in the stores using the test.[61]

As with theft, there is a growing perception of the problems caused by drug use among employees. Indeed, 79 percent of Fortune 1000 chief executives cited substance abuse as a significant problem in their organizations, and 50 percent of medium-size and large organizations test applicants for drug use.[62] Because the physical properties of drugs are invariant and subject to highly rigorous chemical testing, the reliability and validity of drug tests are very high.

The major controversies surrounding drug tests involve not their reliability and validity but also whether they represent an invasion of privacy, an unreasonable search and seizure, or a violation of due process. Urinalysis and blood tests are invasive procedures, and accusing someone of drug use is a serious matter. As with honesty testing, there has not been a great deal of legislation or litigation in this area to date; however, this might not be true in the future.

Employers considering the use of drug tests would be well advised to make sure that

TABLE 6.6
A Summary Table Evaluating Personnel Selection Methods

METHOD	RELIABILITY	VALIDITY	GENERALIZABILITY	UTILITY	LEGALITY
Interviews	Low when unstructured and when assessing nonobservable traits	Low if unstructured and nonbehavioral	Low	Low, especially because of expense	Low, because of subjectivity and potential interviewer bias; also lack of validity makes job-relatedness low
Reference checks	Low, especially when obtained from letters	Low because of lack of range in evaluations	Low	Low, although not expensive to obtain	Those writing letters may be concerned with charges of libel
Biographical information	High test–retest, especially for verifiable information	High criterion-related validity; low in content validity	Usually job-specific, but have been successfully developed for many job types	High; inexpensive way to collect vast amounts of potentially relevant data	May have adverse impact; thus often develop separate scoring keys based on sex or race
Physical ability tests	High	Moderate criterion-related validity; high content validity for some jobs	Low; only pertain to physically demanding jobs	Moderate for some physical jobs; may prevent expensive injuries and disability	Often have adverse impact on women and people with disabilities; need to establish job-relatedness
Cognitive ability tests	High	Moderate criterion-related validity; content validation inappropriate	High; predictive for most jobs, although best for complex jobs	High; low cost and wide application across diverse jobs in companies	Often have adverse impact on race, especially for African Americans, though decreasing over time
Personality inventories	High	Low criterion-related validity for most traits; content validation inappropriate	Low; few traits predictive for many jobs	Low, although inexpensive for jobs where specific traits are relevant	Low, because of cultural and sex differences on most traits, and low job-relatedness in general
Work-sample tests	High	High criterion and content validity	Usually job-specific, but have been successfully developed for many job types	High, despite the relatively high cost to develop	High, because of low adverse impact and high job-relatedness
Honesty tests	Insufficient independent evidence	Insufficient independent evidence	Insufficient independent evidence	Insufficient independent evidence	Insufficient history of litigation, but will undergo scrutiny
Drug tests	High	High	High	Expensive, but may yield high payoffs for health-related costs	May be challenged on invasion-of-privacy grounds

their drug-testing programs conform to some general rules. First, these tests should be administered systematically to all applicants applying for the same job. Second, testing seems more defensible for jobs that involve safety hazards associated with failure to perform. Test results should be reported back to the applicant, who should be allowed an avenue of appeal (and perhaps retesting). Tests should be conducted in an environment that is as unintrusive as possible, and results from those tests should be held in strict confidence. Finally, when testing current employees, the program should be part of a wider organizational program that provides rehabilitation counseling.[63]

SUMMARY

In this chapter, we examined the five critical standards with which all personnel selection methods should conform: reliability, validity, generalizability, utility, and legality. We also looked at nine different selection methods currently used in organizations and evaluated each with respect to these five standards. Table 6.6 summarizes these selection methods and can be used as a guide in deciding which test to use for a specific purpose. Although we discussed each type of test individually, it is important to note in closing that there is no need to use only one type of test for any one job. Indeed, managerial assessment centers use many different forms of tests over a two- or three-day period to learn as much as possible about candidates for important executive positions. As a result, highly accurate predictions are often made, and the validity associated with the judicious use of multiple tests is higher than for tests used in isolation.

DISCUSSION QUESTIONS

1. We examined nine different types of selection methods in this chapter. Assume that you were just rejected for a job based on one of these methods. Obviously, you might be disappointed and angry regardless of what method was used to make this decision, but can you think of two or three methods that might leave you most distressed? In general, why might the acceptability of the test to applicants be an important standard to add to the five we discussed in this chapter?
2. Videotaping applicants in interviews is becoming an increasingly popular means of getting multiple assessments of that individual from different perspectives. Can you think of some reasons why videotaping interviews might also be useful in evaluating the interviewer? What would you look for in an interviewer if you were evaluating one on videotape?
3. Distinguish between concurrent and predictive validation designs, discussing why the latter is preferred over the former. Examine each of the nine selection methods discussed in this chapter and determine which of these would have their validity most and least affected by the type of validation design employed.
4. Some have speculated that in addition to increasing the validity of decisions, employing rigorous selection methods has symbolic value for organizations. What message is sent to applicants about the organization through hiring practices, and how might this message be reinforced by recruitment programs that occur before selection and training programs that occur after selection?

WEB EXERCISE

Saville & Holdsworth (SHL) is an international human resource consulting firm that provides assessment solutions for companies. To learn more about SHL, visit their home page at www.shlusa.com. SHL has a web site for students. Go to www.shldirect.com/shldirect-forstudents/SHL-Direct-2.asp?. This site provides examples of test questions used by employers in the employee selection process. Click on "Practice Test and Feedback." Go to the bottom of the page and click on "Example Questions." Review each of the four categories of sample questions by clicking them on (verbal, numerical, diagrammatic, personality).

QUESTIONS

1. How would you validate verbal tests? numerical tests? diagrammatic tests? personality tests?
2. Why might job candidates question the validity of personality test items such as those you reviewed?

MANAGING PEOPLE: FROM THE PAGES OF "BUSINESS WEEK"

BusinessWeek It's Not Easy Making Pixie Dust

We are in the Utilidor—a series of tunnels below Disney World's Magic Kingdom theme park in Orlando. The tunnel complex is generally off-limits to outsiders, but not to 41 visiting managers whose companies have anted up $2,295 a head so they can learn about Walt Disney Co.'s approach to people management.

This underground city is a beehive of activity. Employees rush through the gray concrete tunnels, scrambling to put on costumes and assume their roles upstairs. Golf carts speed by with supplies. Makeup artists prepare an array of Cinderella and Snow White wigs.

Before coming to this 3½-day seminar, I was skeptical. The program sounded like little more than a dream junket: three nights at the resort's most elegant hotel, plus four-day passes to Disney's theme parks. Besides, I thought, what could any manager possibly learn at Disney World? By the end of the first day's activities, however, my note pad was brimming with ideas and lessons dished out by Disney staff.

My colleagues, most of them human-resource managers, take the program seriously. Most are facing a slew of challenges in need of Disney-style magic. A delivery manager at Anheuser–Busch Cos. is trying to make his drivers more responsive to retailers. Personnel managers at a fast-growing bagel chain in Florida worry about maintaining standards as they beef up the chain's ranks. And an employee trainer at South Africa's state-owned transportation conglomerate is looking for ways to streamline the company's hiring process.

Disney's reputation for cleanliness, attention to detail, and helpful employees is what has drawn them here. "Everyone knows how wonderful Disney is, so you figure they must be doing something right," says Kathleen Scappini, who works for Multi-Media in West Hartford, Conn. That "something right" is what Disney refers to as the "pixie-dust" formula, with four key ingredients—employee ***selection,*** training, support, and benefits. Our seminar, "Disney's Approach to People Management," promises to reveal how the company motivates employees.

Instructors, called facilitators, tell us that we cannot count on Tinkerbell. "The solutions are not complicated," assures Jeff Soluri, a Disney instructor. "It's attention to detail and hard-nosed business practices that produce the magic."

If there is pixie dust, it starts with the hiring process. One of the first activities is a field trip to Disney's "casting center," a Venetian-style castle where job candidates view a video before being interviewed. The short film informs job seekers about the company's strict appearance guidelines (one ring per hand and no tattoos, please) and the rigors of the work. By being blunt and detailed, Disney says, it's able to weed out incompatible candidates at the first crack.

The critical part of the process, though, is employee training. New hires, who average less than $10 an hour, are treated to a visual company history. They are told that they are not just employees but pivotal "cast members" in a "show." From street sweepers to monorail pilots, each cast member must go out of his way to make the resort seem unreal. No matter how tired workers are or how deeply guests may try their patience, they must never lose composure. To do so, the company tells its cast, is to risk alienating a guest, spoiling the illusion, and damaging Disney's standing in entertainment and American culture.

Between excursions, participants share what they have learned—and what they might use. Disney staffers with wireless microphones dart Oprah-like through a conference room seeking comments. They get plenty. John Lealos, the Anheuser-Busch manager, says he wants to incorporate more of an appreciative, team feel into his unit's corporate culture. "If we can get that kind of atmosphere at our company, the productivity will go up," he says. Hugo Strydom, the training manager at South Africa's Transmit Ltd., intends to use a Disney-style orientation to weed out weak candidates in a major hiring blitz.

QUESTIONS

1. This case reveals a great deal about what Disney looks for in a job applicant as well as what it does to get unsuitable job candidates to remove themselves from the process (i.e., realistic job previews). If you were called in as a consultant to help Disney with its personnel selection and placement process, what sorts of tests, measures, and methods that were covered in this chapter would you use to further screen job applicants?
2. If you wanted to prove to Disney that the tests, measures, and methods you introduced were actually helping it gain competitive advantage, what type of evidence would you collect, and how would you present this evidence?

SOURCE: Antonio Fins, "It's Not Easy Making Pixie Dust," *Business Week* (September 19, 1997).

NOTES

1. J. C. Nunnally, *Psychometric Theory* (New York: McGraw–Hill, 1978).
2. B. Schneider, "An Interactionist Perspective on Organizational Effectiveness," in *Organizational Effectiveness: A Comparison of Multiple Models*, ed. K.S. Cameron and D.A. Whetton (Orlando, FL: Academic Press, 1983), pp. 27–54.
3. N. Schmitt, R.Z. Gooding, R.A. Noe, and M. Kirsch,

"Meta-Analysis of Validity Studies Published between 1964 and 1982 and the Investigation of Study Characteristics," *Personnel Psychology* 37 (1984), pp. 407–22.

4. J. Cohen, *Statistical Power Analysis for the Behavioral Sciences* (New York: Academic Press, 1977).
5. C.H. Lawshe, "Inferences from Personnel Tests and Their Validity," *Journal of Applied Psychology* 70 (1985), pp. 237–38.
6. D.D. Robinson, "Content-Oriented Personnel Selection in a Small Business Setting," *Personnel Psychology* 34 (1981), pp. 77–87.
7. C.H. Lawshe, "A Quantitative Approach to Content Validity," *Personnel Psychology* 28 (1975), pp. 563–75.
8. P.R. Sackett, "Assessment Centers and Content Validity: Some Neglected Issues," *Personnel Psychology* 40 (1987), pp. 13–25.
9. F.L. Schmidt and J.E. Hunter, "The Future of Criterion-Related Validity," *Personnel Psychology* 33 (1980), pp. 41–60; F.L. Schmidt, J.E. Hunter, and K. Pearlman, "Task Differences as Moderators of Aptitude Test Validity: A Red Herring," *Journal of Applied Psychology* 66 (1982), pp. 166–85; R.L. Gutenberg, R.D. Arvey, H.G. Osburn, and R.P. Jeanneret, "Moderating Effects of Decision-Making/Information Processing Dimensions on Test Validities," *Journal of Applied Psychology* 68 (1983), pp. 600–8.
10. F.L. Schmidt, J.G. Berner, and J.E. Hunter, "Racial Differences in Validity of Employment Tests: Reality or Illusion," *Journal of Applied Psychology* 58 (1974), pp. 5–6.
11. Society for Industrial and Organizational Psychology, *Principles for the Validation and Use of Personnel Selection Procedures* (College Park, MD: University of Maryland Press, 1987).
12. J.W. Boudreau, "Utility Analysis for Decisions in Human Resource Management," in *Handbook of Industrial & Organizational Psychology*, ed. M.D. Dunnette and L.M. Hough (Palo Alto, CA: Consulting Psychologists Press, 1992).
13. K.F. Ebert, "New Civil Rights Act Invites Litigation," *Personnel Law Update* 6 (1991), p. 3.
14. R.J. Smith, "Shoney's to Set Aside $105 Million in Pact to Settle Racial Case," *The Wall Street Journal*, November 4, 1992, p. G12.
15. M.E. Heilman, W.S. Battle, C.E. Keller, and R.A. Lee, "Type of Affirmative Action Policy: A Determinant of Reactions to Sex-Based Preferential Selection," *Journal of Applied Psychology* 83 (1998), pp. 190–205.
16. B.S. Murphy, "EEOC Gives Guidance on Legal and Illegal Inquiries Under ADA," *Personnel Journal* (August 1994), p. 26.
17. R.L. Dipboye, *Selection Interviews: Process Perspectives* (Cincinnati, OH: South-Western Publishing, 1991).
18. J.E. Hunter and R. H. Hunter, "Validity and Utility of Alternative Predictors of Job Performance," *Psychological Bulletin* 96 (1984), pp. 72–98.
19. R. Pingitore, B.L. Dugoni, R.S. Tindale, and B. Spring, "Bias against Overweight Job Applicants in a Simulated Interview," *Journal of Applied Psychology* 79 (1994), pp. 909–17.
20. *Watson v. Fort Worth Bank and Trust*, 108 Supreme Court 2791 (1988).
21. M.A. McDaniel, D.L. Whetzel, F.L. Schmidt, and S.D. Maurer, "The Validity of Employment Interviews: A Comprehensive Review and Meta-Analysis," *Journal of Applied Psychology* 79 (1994), pp. 599–616; A.I. Huffcutt and W.A. Arthur, "Hunter and Hunter (1984) Revisited: Interview Validity for Entry-Level Jobs," *Journal of Applied Psychology* 79 (1994), pp. 184–90.
22. J. Solomon, "The New Job Interview: Show Thyself," *The Wall Street Journal*, December 4, 1989, p. B4.
23. M.A. Campion, J.E. Campion, and J.P. Hudson, "Structured Interviewing: A Note of Incremental Validity and Alternative Question Types," *Journal of Applied Psychology* 79 (1994), pp. 998–1002; E.D. Pulakos and N. Schmitt, "Experience-based and Situational Interview Questions: Studies of Validity," *Personnel Psychology* 48 (1995), pp. 289–308.
24. S. Greengard, "Are You Well Armed to Screen Applicants?" *Personnel Journal* (December 1995), pp. 84–95.
25. G. Stasser and W. Titus, "Effects of Information Load and Percentage of Shared Information on the Dissemination of Unshared Information during Group Discussion," *Journal of Personality and Social Psychology* 53 (1987), pp. 81–93.
26. A. Cuneo, "Diverse by Design," *Business Week*, June 6, 1992, p. 72.
27. T. Libby, "Surviving the Group Interview," *Forbes*, March 24, 1986, p. 190; Dipboye, *Selection Interviews*, p. 210.
28. Hunter and Hunter, "Validity and Utility."
29. L. McDonnell, "Interviews and Tests Counting More as Past Employers Clam Up," *Minneapolis Tribune*, May 3, 1981.
30. J.B. Copeland, "Revenge of the Fired," *Newsweek*, February 16, 1987, pp. 46–47.
31. Greengard, "Are You Well Armed to Screen Applicants?"
32. Hunter and Hunter, "Validity and Utility"; R.R. Reilly and G.T. Chao, "Validity and Fairness of Some Alternative Employee Selection Procedures," *Personnel Psychology* 35 (1982), pp. 1–62.
33. F.A. Mael and B.E. Ashforth, "Loyal from Day One: Biodata, Organizational Identification, and Turnover among Newcomers," *Personnel Psychology* 48 (1995), pp. 309–33.
34. T.W. Dougherty, D.B. Turban, and J.C. Callender, "Confirming First Impressions in the Employment Interview: A Field Study of Interviewer Behavior," *Journal of Applied Psychology* 79 (1994), pp. 659–65.
35. Greengard, "Are You Well Armed to Screen Applicants?"
36. J.R. Hollenbeck, D.R. Ilgen, and S.M. Crampton,

"Lower-Back Disability in Occupational Settings: A Human Resource Management View," *Personnel Psychology* 42 (1992), pp. 247–78.

37. J. Hogan, "Structure of Physical Performance in Occupational Tasks," *Journal of Applied Psychology* 76 (1991), pp. 495–507.
38. B. R. Blakely, M.A. Quinones, M.S. Crawford, and I.A. Jago, "The Validity of Isometric Strength Tests," *Personnel Psychology* 47 (1994), pp. 247–74.
39. J. Hogan, "Physical Abilities," in *Handbook of Industrial & Organizational Psychology*, 2d ed., ed. M.D. Dunnette and L.M. Hough (Palo Alto, CA: Consulting Psychologists Press, 1991).
40. Americans with Disabilities Act of 1990, S. 933, Public Law 101-336 (1990).
41. Nunnally, *Psychometric Theory*.
42. M.J. Ree, J.A. Earles, and M.S. Teachout, "Predicting Job Performance: Not Much More than g," *Journal of Applied Psychology* 79 (1994), pp. 518–24.
43. L.S. Gottfredson, "The g Factor in Employment," *Journal of Vocational Behavior* 29 (1986), pp. 293–96; Hunter and Hunter, "Validity and Utility"; Gutenberg et al., "Moderating Effects"; Schmidt, Berner, and Hunter, "Racial Differences in Validity."
44. A.R. Jenson, "g: Artifact or Reality?" *Journal of Vocational Behavior* 29 (1986), pp. 301–31.
45. M.R. Barrick and M.K. Mount, "The Big Five Personality Dimensions and Job Performance: A Meta-Analysis," *Personnel Psychology* 44 (1991), pp. 1–26; L.M. Hough, N.K. Eaton, M.D. Dunnette, J.D. Camp, and R.A. McCloy, "Criterion-Related Validities of Personality Constructs and the Effect of Response Distortion on Test Validities," *Journal of Applied Psychology* 75 (1990), pp. 467–76.
46. W.S. Dunn, M.K. Mount, M.R. Barrick, and D.S. Ones, "Relative Importance of Personality and General Mental Ability on Managers' Judgments of Applicant Qualifications," *Journal of Applied Psychology* 80 (1995), pp. 500–9.
47. L. Smith, "Stamina: Who Has It, Why You Need It and How You Get It," *Fortune*, November 28, 1994.
48. P.M. Wright, K.M. Kacmar, G.C. McMahan, and K. Deleeuw, "P = f(M × A): Cognitive Ability as a Moderator of the Relationship between Personality and Job Performance," *Journal of Management* 21 (1995), pp. 1129–39.
49. M. Mount, M.R. Barrick, and J.P. Strauss, "Validity of Observer Ratings of the Big Five Personality Factors," *Journal of Applied Psychology* 79 (1994), pp. 272–80.
50. M.R. Barrick, G.L. Stewart, M.J. Neubert, and M.K. Mount, "Relating Member Ability and Personality to Work Team Processes and Team Effectiveness," *Journal of Applied Psychology* 83 (1998), pp. 377–91; J.L. LePine, J.R. Hollenbeck, D.R. Ilgen, and J. Hedlund, "Effects of Individual Differences on the Performance of Hierarchical Decision Making Teams: Much More than g," *Journal of Applied Psychology* 82 (1997), pp. 803–11.
51. Mount, Barrick, and Strauss, "Validity of Observer Ratings."
52. J.G. Rosse, M.D. Stecher, J.L. Miller, and R.A. Levin, "The Impact of Response Distortion on Preemployment Personality Testing and Hiring Decisions," *Journal of Applied Psychology* 83 (1998), pp. 634–44.
53. P.F. Wernimont and J.P. Campbell, "Signs, Samples and Criteria," *Journal of Applied Psychology* 46 (1968), pp. 417–19.
54. Hunter and Hunter, "Validity and Utility"; W. Cascio and N. Phillips, "Performance Testing: A Rose among Thorns?" *Journal of Applied Psychology* 32 (1979), pp. 751–66; F.L. Schmidt, A. Greenthol, J.E. Hunter, J. Berner, and F. Seaton, "Job Sample vs. Paper-and-Pencil Trade and Technical Tests: Adverse Impact and Examiner Attitudes," *Personnel Psychology* 30 (1977), pp. 187–97.
55. Hunter and Hunter, "Validity and Utility."
56. F.L. Schmidt and J.E. Hunter, "The Validity and Utility of Selection Methods in Personnel Psychology: Practical and Theoretical Implications of 85 Years of Research Findings," *Psychological Bulletin* 124 (1998), pp. 262–74.
57. D.S. One, C. Viswesvaran, and F.L. Schmidt, "Comprehensive Meta-Analysis of Integrity Test Validities: Findings and Implications for Personnel Selection and Theories of Job Performance," *Journal of Applied Psychology* 78 (1993), pp. 679–703.
58. H.J. Bernardin and D.K. Cooke, "Validity of an Honesty Test in Predicting Theft among Convenience Store Employees," *Academy of Management Journal* 36 (1993), pp. 1097–1106.
59. D. S. Ones and C. Viswesvaran, "Gender, Age, and Race Differences on Overt Integrity Tests: Results across Four Large-Scale Job Applicant Data Sets," *Journal of Applied Psychology* 83 (1998), pp. 35–42.
60. M.R. Cunningham, D.T. Wong, and A.P. Barbee, "Self-Presentation Dynamics on Overt Integrity Tests: Experimental Studies of the Reid Report," *Journal of Applied Psychology* 79 (1994), pp. 643–58.
61. Greengard, "Are You Well Armed to Screen Applicants?"
62. M. Freudenheim, "Workers Substance Abuse Increasing, Survey Says," *The New York Times*, December 13, 1988, p. 2; J.P. Guthrie and J.D. Olian, "Drug and Alcohol Testing Programs: The Influence of Organizational Context and Objectives" (paper presented at the Fourth Annual Conference of the Society for Industrial/Organizational Psychology, Boston, 1989).
63. K.R. Murphy, G.C. Thornton, and D.H. Reynolds, "College Students' Attitudes toward Drug Testing Programs," *Personnel Psychology* 43 (1990), pp. 615–31.

CHAPTER 7 Training

OBJECTIVES

After reading this chapter, you should be able to

1. Discuss how training can help companies gain a competitive advantage.
2. Explain the role of the manager in identifying training needs and supporting use of training on-the-job.
3. Conduct a needs assessment.
4. Evaluate employees' readiness for training.
5. Discuss the strengths and weaknesses of presentation, hands-on, and group training methods.
6. Explain the potential advantages of new technologies for training.
7. Design a training session to maximize learning.
8. Choose an appropriate evaluation design based on training objectives and analysis of constraints.
9. Design a cross-cultural preparation program.
10. Develop a program for effectively managing diversity.

Advancing Medical Technology through Training

ENTER THE WORLD OF BUSINESS

Medtronic is a 12,000-employee Minneapolis, Minnesota-based company that specializes in developing and selling medical technology. Medtronic provides about half of the heart pacemakers in the world and also manufactures heart valves, angioplasty catheters, and blood-pumping devices. As in most companies, sales is a top priority. But sales at Medtronic relates to life and death. Salespeople just don't sell products. They must teach consumers (physicians) how to use the products. It is not uncommon for Medtronic salespeople to be advising physicians in the operating room while they are changing heart valves or installing a pacemaker into a patient!

Multimedia was first used at Medtronic for purely marketing purposes. Salespeople would use a laptop personal computer equipped with a CD player to show physicians the benefits and correct usage of heart valves. When the interactive program was introduced at a national sales meeting, demand for the CD exceeded supply. Salespeople went out and purchased laptop computers so that they could use the CD!

This created a training challenge for Medtronic. The sales staff had to learn to use the laptop PCs and understand how to use the interactive program. Classroom instruction, role playing, and a built-in tutorial were developed to teach salespeople how to use the PC and the CD program.

Medtronic is exploring expanding the use of multimedia for training as well as marketing. Currently, Medtronic extensively uses classroom-based training for salespeople. Although the product CDs are being used as a learning tool by helping to prepare the staff for sales presentations, the CDs are only one step the company is taking toward the goal of enhancing learning. The current manager of sales training is pushing for expanded use of multimedia training because it can cut salespeople's time in the classroom. The manager believes that multimedia training will increase the consistency and efficiency of training and provide salespeople with feedback regarding which dimensions of the product they "know." The current CD-based product programs work best for experienced salespeople who already are familiar with the product. New salespeople need feedback and help screens, both being available from multimedia applications. New salespeople need to be able to interact with the product at their own pace, so that they are comfortable explaining and demonstrating all aspects of the product to physicians. Salespeople's time is also in great demand. Multimedia provides accessibility to training wherever and whenever they can access their laptop computer. Multimedia can also help the entire sales force learn about new products as quickly as possible.

The next step in the process is convincing the marketing department that new multimedia products need to be developed so that they can be used for both marketing and training.

SOURCE: W. Webb, "High-Tech in the Heartland," *Training* (May 1997), pp. 51–56.

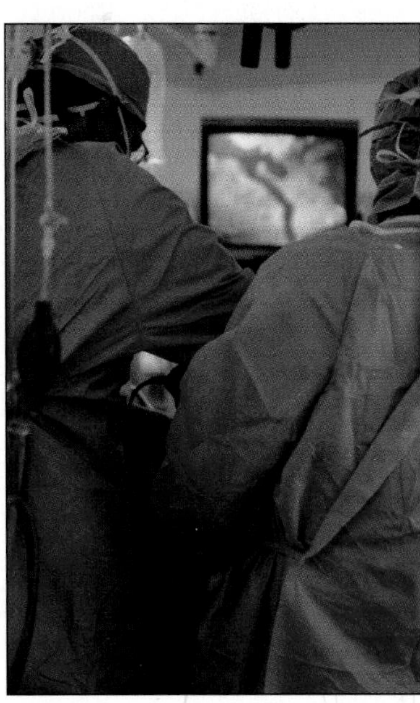

Introduction

The opening vignette on Medtronic illustrates how companies are considering using training to gain a competitive advantage. Typically, U.S. companies have not used training for this purpose. U.S. employers spend approximately $59 billion, or only slightly more than 1 to 2 percent of their payroll, on formal training activities.[1] Lack of investment in training is an often-cited reason why U.S. companies are losing market share to foreign competition. For example, whereas 66 percent of German workers are involved in apprenticeship training programs, only two-tenths of 1 percent of U.S. workers are involved in similar programs.[2] On average, U.S. firms spend about one-third of what their Japanese counterparts spend on worker training per year.[3] Even more sobering are statistics suggesting that only 16 percent of U.S. employees have ever received any training from their employers!

U.S. companies are starting to recognize the important role that training plays in improving productivity, quality, and competitiveness. For example, General Electric, U.S. Robotics, W.H. Brady, Texas Instruments, Andersen Consulting, and Federal Express have all made substantial financial investments in training. (These companies invest between 3 and 5 percent of their payroll in training.)[4]

Why do these companies and many others believe that investment in training can help them gain a competitive advantage? Training can

- Increase employees' knowledge of foreign competitors and cultures, which is critical for success in foreign markets.
- Help ensure that employees have the basic skills to work with new technology, such as robots and computer-assisted manufacturing processes.
- Help employees understand how to work effectively in teams to contribute to product and service quality.
- Ensure that the company's culture emphasizes innovation, creativity, and learning.
- Ensure employment security by providing new ways for employees to contribute to the company when their jobs change, their interests change, or their skills become obsolete.
- Prepare employees to accept and work more effectively with each other, particularly with minorities and women.[5]

High-Leverage Training Strategy: A Systematic Approach

In general, *training* refers to a planned effort by a company to facilitate employees' learning of job-related competencies. These competencies include knowledge, skills, or behaviors that are critical for successful job performance. The goal of training is for employees to master the knowledge, skill, and behaviors emphasized in training programs and to apply them to their day-to-day activities. Recently it has been acknowledged that to gain a competitive advantage, training has to involve more than just basic skill development.[6] Training is moving from a primary focus on teaching employees specific skills to a broader focus of creating and sharing knowledge.[7] That is, to use training to gain a competitive advantage, training should be viewed broadly as a way to create intellectual capital. Intellectual capital includes basic skills (skills needed to perform one's job), advanced skills (such as how to use technology to share information with other employees), an understanding of the customer or manufacturing system, and self-motivated creativity.

Keep in mind that traditionally most of the emphasis on training has been at the basic and advanced skill levels. But some estimate that soon up to 85 percent of the jobs in the United States and Europe will require extensive use of knowledge. This requires employees to share knowledge and creatively use it to modify a product or serve the customer, as well as to understand the service or product development system.

Many companies have adopted this broader perspective, which is known as high-leverage training. **High-leverage training** is linked to strategic business goals and objectives, uses an instructional design process to ensure that training is effective, and compares or benchmarks the company's training programs against training programs in other companies.[8]

High-leverage training practices also help to create working conditions that encourage continuous learning. **Continuous learning** requires employees to understand the entire work system including the relationships among their jobs, their work units, and the company. (Continuous learning is similar to the idea of system understanding mentioned earlier.)[9] Employees are expected to acquire new skills and knowledge, apply them on the job, and share this information with other employees. Managers take an active role in identifying training needs and help to ensure that employees use training in their work. To facilitate the sharing of knowledge, managers may use informational maps that show where knowledge lies within the company (for example, directories that list what a person does as well as the specialized knowledge she possesses) and use technology such as groupware or the Internet that allows employees in various business units to work simultaneously on problems and share information.[10]

High-leverage training practices are one characteristic of companies considered to be **learning organizations.** A learning organization is one whose employees are continuously attempting to learn new things and apply what they have learned to improve product or service quality. Improvements do not stop when formal training is completed.[11]

A learning organization is also a company that has an enhanced capacity to learn, adapt, and change. Training processes are carefully scrutinized and aligned with company goals.[12] In a learning organization, training is seen as one part of a system designed to create intellectual capital.

The essential features of a learning organization appear in Table 7.1. Note that the learning organization emphasizes that learning occurs not only at the individual-employee level (as we traditionally think of learning), but also at the group and organizational levels. The learning organization emphasizes system-level learning. **System-level learning** refers to the company's ability to preserve what is learned over time. That

TABLE 7.1
Key Features of a Learning Organization

FEATURE	DESCRIPTION
Continuous learning	Employees share learning with each other and use their jobs as a basis for applying and creating knowledge.
Knowledge generation and sharing	Systems are developed for creating, capturing, and sharing knowledge.
Critical systematic thinking	Employees are encouraged to think in new ways, see relationships and feedback loops, and test assumptions.
Learning culture	Learning is rewarded, promoted, and supported by manager and company objectives.
Encouragement of flexibility and experimentation	Employees are encouraged to take risks, innovate, explore new ideas, try new processes, and develop new products and services.
Valuing of employees	System and environment focus on ensuring the development and well-being of every employee.

SOURCE: Adapted from M.A. Gephart, V.J. Marsick, M.E. Van Buren, and M.S. Spiro, "Learning Organizations Come Alive," *Training and Development* 50 (1996), pp. 34–45. Reprinted with permission.

is, despite the fact that employees (and even divisions) of the company may no longer exist, their knowledge is still available. Two features of Table 7.1's learning organization relate directly to system-level learning. Continuous learning and knowledge generation encourage employees to share information with each other. How might this occur? There are several ways to create and share knowledge:

1. Use technology and software such as LOTUS Notes and e-mail, or create a company Intranet that allows people to store information and share it with others.
2. Publish directories that list what employees do, how they can be contacted, and the type of knowledge they have.[13]
3. Develop informational maps that identify where specific knowledge is stored in the company.
4. Create a chief information officer position for cataloging and facilitating the exchange of information in the company.
5. Require employees to give presentations to other employees about what they have learned from training programs they have attended.
6. Allow employees to take time off from work (e.g., sabbaticals) to acquire knowledge or study problems.
7. Create an online library of learning resources such as journals, technical manuals, training opportunities, and seminars.

For example, Arthur Andersen has created a knowledge system that allows consultants to form relationships with people working on similar projects.[14] The consultants are organized into communities of practice based on their competencies. The knowledge system allows the consultants to store and access information about clients, processes, and technical information. Through sharing information the consultants can develop new applications themselves and help other consultants at Andersen learn from their experiences.

Companies that are striving to become learning organizations also usually change the structure of the organization. The restructuring can involve organizing work by teams instead of an assembly line process, creating smaller business units or profit centers that are required to capture and share knowledge and make decisions as needed to improve customer service or product quality. For example, the *Calgary Herald* newspaper used teams of senior managers plus sales and editorial representatives to protect and expand its advertising revenue from home builders.[15] A competing paper in Calgary had launched an aggressive campaign to take some of this revenue away from the *Herald*. The traditional response would have been to look at the problem from strictly an advertising perspective (e.g., increase advertising sales pressure). Instead, using ideas from the multifunctional teams (e.g., a drawing among readership for a $250,000 home), revenues increased and readership of the *Herald's* "Homes" section increased. A beneficial side benefit was that reporters and sales people realized they could work together without compromising the values of their discipline.

In this chapter, we emphasize the conditions through which training practices can help companies gain competitive advantage and the role that managers can play in contributing to a high-leverage training effort and creating a learning organization.

Designing Effective Training Systems

One of the key characteristics of training systems that contribute to competitiveness is that they are designed according to the instructional design process.[16] **Instructional design process** refers to a systematic approach for developing training programs. Table 7.2 presents the six steps of this process, which emphasizes that effective training practices involve more than just choosing the most popular and colorful training method.

TABLE 7.2
Components of Instructional Design

1. Conducting needs assessment
   - Organizational analysis
   - Person analysis
   - Task analysis
2. Ensuring employees' readiness for training
   - Attitudes and motivation
   - Basic skills
3. Creating a learning environment
   - Identification of learning objectives and training outcomes
   - Meaningful material
   - Practice
   - Feedback
   - Observation of others
   - Administering and coordinating program
4. Ensuring transfer of training
   - Self-management strategies
   - Peer and manager support
5. Selecting training methods
   - Presentational methods
   - Hands-on methods
   - Group methods
6. Evaluating training programs
   - Identification of training outcomes and evaluation design
   - Cost–benefit analysis

Step 1 is to conduct a needs assessment, which is necessary to determine if training is needed. Step 2 involves ensuring that employees have the motivation and basic skills to master training content. Step 3 involves ensuring that the training session (or the learning environment) has the factors necessary for learning to occur. Step 4 involves ensuring that trainees apply the content of training to their jobs. This involves support from managers and peers for the use of training content on-the-job as well as getting the employee to understand how to take personal responsibility for skill improvement. Step 5 involves choosing a training method. As we shall see in this chapter, a variety of training methods are available ranging from traditional on-the-job training to use of new technologies such as the Internet. The key is to choose a training method that will provide the appropriate learning environment to achieve the training objectives. Step 6 involves evaluation—that is, determining whether training achieved the desired learning outcomes and/or financial objectives.

The first step in the instructional design process, **needs assessment,** refers to the process used to determine if training is necessary. Figure 7.1 shows the causes and outcomes resulting from needs assessment. As we see, there are many different "pressure points" that suggest that training is necessary. These pressure points include performance problems, new technology, internal or external customer requests for training, job redesign, new legislation, changes in customer preferences, new products, or employees' lack of basic skills. Note that these pressure points do not guarantee that training is the correct solution. Consider, for example, a delivery truck driver whose job is to deliver anesthetic gases to medical facilities. The driver mistakenly hooks up the supply line of a mild anesthetic to the supply line of a hospital's oxygen system, contaminating the hospital's oxygen supply. Why did the driver make this mistake, which is clearly a perfor-

FIGURE 7.1 The Needs Assessment Process

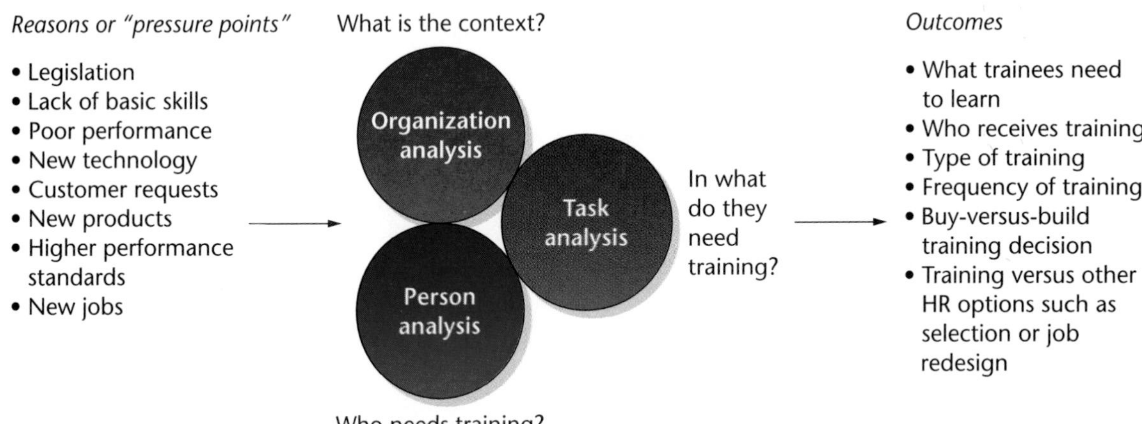

mance problem? The driver may have made this mistake because of a lack of knowledge about the appropriate line hookup for the anesthetic, anger over a requested salary increase that his manager recently denied, or mislabeled valves for connecting the gas supply. Only the lack of knowledge can be addressed by training. The other pressure points require addressing issues related to the consequence of good performance (pay system) or the design of the work environment.

Needs assessment typically involves organizational analysis, person analysis, and task analysis.[17] Organizational analysis involves considering the context in which training will occur. That is, **organizational analysis** involves determining the appropriateness of training, given the company's business strategy, its resources available for training, and support by managers and peers for training activities.

Person analysis helps to identify who needs training. **Person analysis** involves (1) determining whether performance deficiencies result from a lack of knowledge, skill, or ability (a training issue) or from a motivational or work-design problem, (2) identifying who needs training, and (3) determining employees' readiness for training. **Task analysis** includes identifying the important tasks and knowledge, skill, and behaviors that need to be emphasized in training for employees to complete their tasks.

In practice, organizational analysis, person analysis, and task analysis are usually not conducted in any specific order. However, because organizational analysis is concerned with identifying whether training fits with the company's strategic objectives and whether the company wants to devote time and money to training, it is usually conducted first. Person analysis and task analysis are often conducted at the same time because it is often difficult to determine whether performance deficiencies are a training problem without understanding the tasks and the work environment.

What outcomes result from a needs assessment? As shown in Figure 7.1, the needs assessment process results in information related to who needs training and what trainees need to learn, including the tasks in which they need to be trained plus knowledge, skill, behavior, or other job requirements. Needs assessment helps to determine whether the company will purchase training from a vendor or consultant or else develop training using internal resources.

ORGANIZATIONAL ANALYSIS

Managers need to consider three factors before choosing training as the solution to any pressure point: the company's strategic direction, the training resources available, and support of managers and peers for training activities.

SUPPORT OF MANAGERS AND PEERS. Various studies have found that peer and manager support for training is critical. The key factors to success are a positive attitude among peers and managers about participation in training activities; managers' and peers' willingness to provide information to trainees about how they can more effectively use knowledge, skills, or behaviors learned in training on the job; and the availability of opportunities for the trainees to use training content in their job.[18] If peers' and managers' attitudes and behaviors are not supportive, employees are not likely to apply training content to their jobs.

COMPANY STRATEGY. In Chapter 2, we discussed the importance of business strategy for a company to gain a competitive advantage. The plan or goal that the company chooses to achieve strategic objectives has a major impact on whether resources (money, trainers' time, program development) should be devoted to addressing a training pressure point.

Table 7.3 describes four business strategies—concentration, internal growth, external growth, and disinvestment—and highlights the implications of each for training practices.[19] Each strategy differs based on the goal of the business. A **concentration strategy** focuses on increasing market share, reducing costs, or creating and maintaining a market niche for products and services. Southwest Airlines has a concentration strategy. It focuses on providing short-haul, low-fare, high-frequency air transportation. It utilizes one type of aircraft (the Boeing 737), has no reserved seating, and serves no meals. This has enabled Southwest to keep costs low and revenues high. An **internal growth strategy** focuses on new market and product development, innovation, and joint ventures. For example, the merger between two auto companies, Daimler-Benz and Chrysler, created one company with strengths in the U.S. and international markets. An **external growth strategy** emphasizes acquiring vendors and suppliers or buying businesses that allows the company to expand into new markets. For example, General Electric, a manufacturer of lighting products and jet engines, acquired the National Broadcast Corporation (NBC), a television and communications company. A **disinvestment strategy** emphasizes liquidation and divestiture of businesses. For example, General Mills sold its restaurant businesses including Red Lobster.

Preliminary research suggests a link between business strategy and amount and type of training.[20] As shown in Table 7.3, training issues vary greatly from one strategy to another. For example, divesting companies need to train employees in job-search skills and focus on cross-training remaining employees who may find themselves in jobs with expanding responsibilities. Companies focusing on a market niche (a concentration strategy), need to emphasize skill currency and development of their existing work force.

It is important to identify the prevailing business strategy to ensure that the company is allocating enough of its budget to training activities, that employees are receiving training on relevant topics, and that employees are receiving the right amount of training.[21]

A good example of how a training function can contribute to business strategy is evident in the changes made by SunU, the training and development organization of Sun Microsystems, a manufacturer of computer workstations and workstation software.[22] SunU realigned its training philosophy and the types of training conducted to be more linked to the strategy of Sun Microsystems. Sun Microsystems was in a constantly evolving business due to new technologies, products, and product markets (an internal growth strategy). SunU found that its customers wanted training services that could be developed quickly, could train many people, and would not involve classroom training. Because of the internal growth strategy, Sun Microsystems was also interested in maintaining and improving the knowledge and competence of its current work force.

TABLE 7.3
Implications of Business Strategy for Training

STRATEGY	EMPHASIS	HOW ACHIEVED	KEY ISSUES	TRAINING IMPLICATIONS
Concentration	• Increase market share • Reduce operating costs • Create or maintain market niche	• Improve product quality • Productivity improvement or technical process innovation • Customize products or services	• Skill currency • Development of existing work force	• Team building • Cross-training • Specialized programs • Interpersonal skill training • On-the-job training
Internal growth	• Market development • Product development • Innovation • Joint ventures	• Market existing products/add distribution channels • Global market expansion • Modify existing products • Create new or different products • Expand through joint ownership	• Creating new jobs and tasks • Innovation	• Support or promote high-quality communication of product value • Cultural training • Help in development of organizational culture that values creative thinking and analysis • Technical competence in jobs • Manager training in feedback and communication • Conflict negotiation skills
External growth (acquisition)	• Horizontal integration • Vertical integration • Concentric diversification	• Acquire firms operating at same stage in product market chain (new market access) • Acquire businesses that can supply or buy products • Acquire firms that have nothing in common with acquiring firm	• Integration • Redundancy • Restructuring	• Determine capabilities of employees in acquired firms • Integrate training systems • Methods and procedures of combined firms • Team building
Disinvestment	• Retrenchment • Turnaround • Divestiture • Liquidation	• Reduce costs • Reduce assets • Generate revenue • Redefine goals • Sell off all assets	• Efficiency	• Motivation, goal setting, time management, stress management, cross-training • Leadership training • Interpersonal communications • Outplacement assistance • Job-search skills training

As a result of the need to better align the training function with the needs generated by the business strategy, SunU took several steps. First, SunU developed a new approach to determining the knowledge and skills that the employees needed to meet business goals. SunU identified several basic competencies (such as customer relations). A team of trainers at SunU constantly reviews these competencies and discusses them with key senior managers. For example, in the customer service competency, vice presidents and directors of sales and marketing are interviewed to identify training needs. As a result of this process SunU learned more about the business needs and was able to develop relevant training. To help deliver training quickly to a large number of trainees without relying on the classroom, SunU developed videoconferencing programs that allow training to be delivered simultaneously to several sites without requiring trainees to travel to a central location. To help maintain and improve the knowledge and abilities of its employees, SunU developed a desktop library that enables all employees to access CD-ROMs containing up-to-date information on technologies and products as well as profiles on customers and competitors.

TRAINING RESOURCES. It is necessary to identify whether the company has the budget, time, and expertise for training. For example, if the company is installing computer-based manufacturing equipment in one of its plants, it has three possible strategies for dealing with the need to have computer-literate employees. First, the company can decide that given its staff expertise and budget, it can use internal consultants to train all affected employees. Second, the company may decide that it is more cost-effective to identify employees who are computer-literate by using tests and work samples. Employees who fail the test or perform below standards on the work sample can be reassigned to other jobs. Choosing this strategy suggests that the company has decided to devote resources to selection and placement rather than training. Third, because it lacks time or expertise, the company may decide to purchase training from a consultant.

Many companies identify vendors and consultants who can provide training services by using requests for proposals.[23] A **request for proposal (RFP)** is a document that outlines for potential vendors and consultants the type of service the company is seeking, the type and number of references needed, the number of employees who need to be trained, funding for the project, the follow-up process used to determine level of satisfaction and service, expected date of completion of the project, and the date when proposals must be received by the company. The request for proposal may be mailed to potential consultants and vendors or posted on the company's Web site. The request for proposal is valuable because it provides a standard set of criteria against which all consultants will be evaluated. The RFP also helps eliminate the need to evaluate outside vendors who cannot provide the needed services.

Usually the RFP helps to identify several vendors who meet the criteria. The next step is to choose the preferred provider. Table 7.4 provides examples of questions to ask vendors.

When using a consultant or other outside vendor to provide training services, it is also important to consider the extent to which the training program will be customized based on the company's needs or whether the consultant is going to provide training services based on a generic framework that it applies to many different organizations. For example, Towers Perrin, a well-known, successful New York consulting firm, told

TABLE 7.4
Questions to Ask Vendors and Consultants

How much and what type of experience does your company have in designing and delivering training?
What are the qualifications and experiences of your staff?
Can you provide demonstrations or examples of training programs you have developed?
Would you provide references of clients for whom you worked?
What evidence do you have that your programs work?

SOURCE: Based on R. Zemke and J. Armstrong, "Evaluating Multimedia Developers," *Training* (November 1996), pp. 33–38. Adapted with permission. Lakewood Publications, Minneapolis, MN.

several clients that it would study their companies in detail and provide a customized diversity training program to fit their needs. However, six companies (including Nissan USA, Thompson Consumer Electronics, and Harris Bank) were given the same 18 recommendations (e.g., separate the concept of affirmative action from that of managing diversity)![24]

How long should you expect it would take a vendor or consultant to develop a training program? The answer is "It depends."[25] Some consultants estimate that development time ranges from 10 to 20 hours for each hour of instruction. Highly technical content requiring more frequent meeting with subject matter experts can add an additional 50 percent more time. For training programs using new technology (such as a CD-ROM) development time can range from 300 to 1,000 hours per hour of program time depending on how much animation, graphics, video, and audio are included, how much new content needs to be developed, the number of practice exercises and type of feedback to be provided to trainees, and the amount of "branches" to different instructional sequences.

PERSON ANALYSIS

Person analysis helps the manager identify whether training is appropriate and which employees need training. In certain situations, such as the introduction of a new technology or service, all employees may need training. However, when managers, customers, or employees identify a problem (usually as a result of a performance deficiency), it is often unclear whether training is the solution.

A major pressure point for training is poor or substandard performance—that is, there is a gap between employees' current performance and their expected performance. Poor performance is indicated by customer complaints, low performance ratings, or on-the-job incidents such as accidents and unsafe behavior. Another potential indicator of the need for training is if the job changes such that current performance levels need to be improved or employees must be able to complete new tasks.

Figure 7.2 shows the factors that influence employees' performance and learning. These factors include person characteristics, input, output, consequences, and feed-

FIGURE 7.2
Factors That Influence Employee Performance and Learning

Person Characteristics
- Ability and skill
- Attitudes and motivation

Input
- Understand need to perform
- Necessary resources (equipment, etc.)
- Interference from other job demands
- Opportunity to perform

Output
- Standard to judge successful performers

Consequences
- Positive consequences/incentives to perform
- Few negative consequences to perform

Feedback
- Frequent and specific feedback about how the job is performed

} Performance and Learning

SOURCE: G. Rummler, "In Search of the Holy Performance Grail," *Training and Development* (April 1996), pp. 26–31. Reprinted with permission.

back.[26] **Person characteristics** refer to the employees' knowledge, skill, ability, and attitudes. **Input** relates to the instructions that tell employees what, how, and when to perform. Input also refers to the support that the employees are given to help them perform. This support includes resources such as equipment, time, or budget. Support also includes feedback and reinforcement from managers and peers. **Output** refers to the job's performance standards. **Consequences** refer to the type of incentives that employees receive for performing well. **Feedback** refers to the information that employees receive while they are performing.

From a manager's perspective, to determine if training is needed, for any performance problem you need to analyze characteristics of the performer, input, output, consequences, and feedback. How might this be done? Based on the model in Figure 7.2, you should ask several questions to determine if training is the likely solution to a performance problem.[27] Assess whether

1. The performance problem is important and has the potential to cost the company a significant amount of money from lost productivity or customers.
2. Employees do not know how to perform effectively. Perhaps they received little or no previous training or the training was ineffective. (This problem is a characteristic of the person.)
3. Employees cannot demonstrate the correct knowledge or behavior. Perhaps they were trained but they infrequently or never used the training content (knowledge, skills, etc.) on the job. (This is an input problem.)
4. Performance expectations are clear (input) and there are no obstacles to performance such as faulty tools or equipment.
5. There are positive consequences for good performance, while poor performance is not rewarded. For example, if employees are dissatisfied with their compensation, their peers or a union may encourage them to slow down their pace of work. (This involves consequences.)
6. Employees receive timely, relevant, accurate, constructive, and specific feedback about their performance (a feedback issue).
7. Other solutions such as job redesign or transferring employees to other jobs are too expensive or unrealistic.

If employees lack the knowledge and skill to perform and the other factors are satisfactory, training is needed. If employees have the knowledge and skill to perform, but input, output, consequences, or feedback are inadequate, training may not be the best solution. For example, if poor performance results from faulty equipment, training cannot solve this problem, but repairing the equipment will! If poor performance results from lack of feedback, then employees may not need training, but their managers may need training on how to give performance feedback!

TASK ANALYSIS

Task analysis results in a description of work activities, including tasks performed by the employee and the knowledge, skills, and abilities required to successfully complete the tasks. A task is a statement of an employee's work activity in a specific job. There are four steps in task analysis:

1. Select the job(s) to be analyzed.
2. Develop a preliminary list of tasks performed on the job by interviewing and observing expert employees and their managers and talking with others who have performed a task analysis.
3. Validate or confirm the preliminary list of tasks. This involves having a group of

subject matter experts (job incumbents, managers, etc.) answer in a meeting or on a written survey several questions regarding the tasks. The types of questions that may be asked include the following: How frequently is the task performed? How much time is spent performing each task? How important or critical is the task for successful performance of the job? How difficult is the task to learn? Is performance of the task expected of entry-level employees?[28]

Table 7.5 presents a sample task analysis questionnaire. This information is used to determine which tasks will be focused on in the training program. The person or committee conducting the needs assessment must decide the level of ratings across dimensions that will determine that a task should be included in the training program. Tasks that are important, frequently performed, and of moderate-to-high levels of difficulty should be trained. Tasks that are not important and are infrequently performed will not be trained. It is difficult for managers and trainers to decide if tasks that are important, are performed infrequently, and require minimal difficulty should be included in training. Managers and trainers must determine whether important tasks—regardless of how frequently they are performed or their level of difficulty—will be included in training.

4. Once the tasks are identified, it is important to identify the knowledge, skills, or abilities necessary to successfully perform each task. This information can be collected using interviews and questionnaires. Information concerning basic skill and cognitive

TABLE 7.5
Sample Task Statement Questionnaire

Name Date
Position

Please rate each of the task statements according to three factors: the *importance* of the task for effective performance, how *frequently* the task is performed, and the degree of *difficulty* required to become effective in the task. Use the following scales in making your ratings.

Importance	*Frequency*
4 = Task is critical for effective performance.	4 = Task is performed once a day.
3 = Task is important but not critical for effective performance.	3 = Task is performed once a week.
2 = Task is of some importance for effective performance.	2 = Task is performed once every few months.
1 = Task is of no importance for task performance.	1 = Task is performed once or twice a year.
0 = Task is not performed.	0 = Task is not performed.

Difficulty

4 = Effective performance of the task requires extensive prior experience and/or training (12–18 months or longer).
3 = Effective performance of the task requires minimal prior experience and training (6–12 months).
2 = Effective performance of the task requires a brief period of prior training and experience (1–6 months).
1 = Effective performance of the task does not require specific prior training and/or experience.
0 = This task is not performed.

Task	*Importance*	*Frequency*	*Difficulty*
1. Ensuring maintenance on equipment, tools, and safety controls			
2. Monitoring employee performance			
3. Scheduling employees			
4. Using statistical software on the computer			
5. Monitoring changes made in processes using statistical methods			

ability requirements is critical for determining if certain levels of knowledge, skills, and abilities will be prerequisites for entrance to the training program (or job) or if supplementary training in underlying skills is needed. For training purposes, information concerning how difficult it is to learn the knowledge, skill, or ability is important—as is whether the knowledge, skill, or ability is expected to be acquired by the employee before taking the job.[29]

EXAMPLE OF A TASK ANALYSIS. Each of the four steps of a task analysis can be seen in this example from a utility company. Trainers were given the job of developing a training system in six months.[30] The purpose of the program was to identify tasks and knowledge, skills, abilities, and other considerations that would serve as the basis for training program objectives and lesson plans.

The first phase of the project involved identifying potential tasks for each job in the utility's electrical maintenance area. Procedures, equipment lists, and information provided by subject matter experts (SMEs) were used to generate the tasks. SMEs included managers, instructors, and senior technicians. The tasks were incorporated into a questionnaire administered to all technicians in the electrical maintenance department. The questionnaire included 550 tasks. Figure 7.3 shows sample items from the questionnaire for the electrical maintenance job. Technicians were asked to rate each task on importance, difficulty, and frequency of performance. The rating scale for frequency included zero. A zero rating indicated that the technician rating the task had never performed the task. Technicians who rated a task zero were asked not to evaluate the task's difficulty and importance.

Customized software was used to analyze the ratings collected via the questionnaire. The primary requirement used to determine whether a task required training was its importance rating. A task rated "very important" was identified as one requiring training

FIGURE 7.3 Sample Items from Task Analysis Questionnaires for the Electrical Maintenance Job

Job: Electrical Maintenance Worker

		Task Performance Ratings		
Task #s	**Task Description**	**Frequency of performance**	**Importance**	**Difficulty**
199-264	Replace a light bulb	0 1 2 3 4 5	0 1 2 3 4 5	0 1 2 3 4 5
199-265	Replace an electrical outlet	0 1 2 3 4 5	0 1 2 3 4 5	0 1 2 3 4 5
199-266	Install a light fixture	0 1 2 3 4 5	0 1 2 3 4 5	0 1 2 3 4 5
199-267	Replace a light switch	0 1 2 3 4 5	0 1 2 3 4 5	0 1 2 3 4 5
199-268	Install a new circuit breaker	0 1 2 3 4 5	0 1 2 3 4 5	0 1 2 3 4 5
		Frequency of performance 0=never 5=often	**Importance** 1=negligible 5=extremely high	**Difficulty** 1=easiest 5=most difficult

SOURCE: E.F. Holton III and C. Bailey, "Top to Bottom Curriculum Redesign," *Training & Development* (March 1995), pp. 40–44. Reprinted with permission. All rights reserved.

regardless of its frequency or difficulty. If a task was rated moderately important but difficult, it also was designated for training. Tasks rated unimportant, not difficult, and done infrequently were not designated for training.

The list of tasks designated for training were reviewed by the SMEs to determine if they accurately described job tasks. The result was a list of 487 tasks. For each of the 487 tasks, two SMEs identified the necessary knowledge, skills, abilities, and other factors required for performance. This included information on working conditions, cues that initiate the task's start and end, performance standards, safety considerations, and necessary tools and equipment. All data were reviewed by plant technicians and members of the training department. More than 14,000 knowledge, skill, ability, and other considerations were clustered into common areas. An identification code was assigned to each group that linked groups to task and knowledge, skill, ability, and other factors. These groups were then combined into clusters. The clusters represented qualification areas. That is, the task clusters related to linked tasks that the employees must be certified in to perform the job. The clusters were used to identify training lesson plans and course objectives. Trainers also reviewed the clusters to identify prerequisite skills for each cluster.

ENSURING EMPLOYEES' READINESS FOR TRAINING

The second step in the instructional design process is to evaluate whether employees are ready to learn. **Readiness for training** refers to whether (1) employees have the personal characteristics (ability, attitudes, beliefs, and motivation) necessary to learn program content and apply it on the job and (2) the work environment will facilitate learning and not interfere with performance.

Although managers are not often trainers, they play an important role in influencing employees' readiness for training. **Motivation to learn** is the desire of the trainee to learn the content of the training program.[31] Various research studies have shown that motivation is related to knowledge gain, behavior change, or skill acquisition in training programs.[32] Managers need to ensure that employees' motivation to learn is as high as possible. They can do this by ensuring employees' self-efficacy; understanding the benefits of training; being aware of training needs, career interests, and goals; understanding work environment characteristics; and ensuring employees' basic-skills levels. Managers should also consider input, output, consequences, and feedback since these factors influence motivation to learn.

SELF-EFFICACY. **Self-efficacy** is the employees' belief that they can successfully learn the content of the training program. The training environment is potentially threatening to many employees who may not have extensive educational experience or who have little experience in the particular area emphasized by the training program. For example, training employees to use equipment for computer-based manufacturing represents a potential threat, especially if employees are intimidated by new technologies and do not have confidence in their ability to master the skills needed to use a computer. Research has demonstrated that self-efficacy is related to performance in training programs.[33] Managers can increase employees' self-efficacy level by

1. Letting employees know that the purpose of training is to try to improve performance rather than to identify areas in which employees are incompetent.
2. Providing as much information as possible about the training program and purpose of training prior to the actual training.
3. Showing employees the training success of their peers who are now in similar jobs.
4. Providing employees with feedback that learning is under their control and they have the ability and the responsibility to overcome any learning difficulties they experience in the program.

UNDERSTANDING THE BENEFITS OR CONSEQUENCES OF TRAINING. Employees' motivation to learn can be enhanced by communicating to them the potential job-related, personal, and career benefits they may receive as a result of attending the training program. These benefits may include learning a more efficient way to perform a process or procedure, establishing contacts with other employees in the firm (e.g., networking), or increasing opportunities to pursue different career paths. The communication from the manager about potential benefits should be realistic. Unmet expectations about training programs have been shown to adversely affect motivation to learn.[34]

AWARENESS OF TRAINING NEEDS, CAREER INTERESTS, AND GOALS. To be motivated to learn in training programs, employees must be aware of their skill strengths and weaknesses and of the link between the training program and improvement of their weaknesses.[35] Managers should make sure that employees understand why they are asked to attend training programs, and they should communicate the link between training and improvement of skill weaknesses or knowledge deficiencies. This can be accomplished by sharing performance-appraisal information with the employee, holding career development discussions, or having the employee complete a self-evaluation of his or her skill strengths and weaknesses and career interests and goals.

If possible, employees need to be given a choice of what programs to attend and must perceive how actual training assignments are made to maximize motivation to learn. Several recent studies have suggested that giving trainees a choice regarding which programs to attend and then honoring those choices maximizes motivation to learn. Giving employees choices but not necessarily honoring them can have detrimental effects on motivation to learn.[36]

WORK ENVIRONMENT CHARACTERISTICS. Employees' perceptions of two characteristics of the work environment—situational constraints and social support—are critical determinants of motivation to learn. Situational constraints include lack of proper tools and equipment, materials and supplies, budgetary support, and time. *Social support* refers to managers' and peers' willingness to provide feedback and reinforcement.[37]

To ensure that the work environment enhances trainees' motivation to learn, managers need to

1. Provide materials, time, job-related information, and other work aids necessary for employees to use new skills or behavior before participating in training programs.
2. Speak positively about the company's training programs to employees.
3. Let employees know they are doing a good job when they are using content training in their work.
4. Encourage work-group members to involve each other in trying to use new skills on the job by soliciting feedback and sharing training experiences and situations in which training content was helpful.
5. Provide employees with time and opportunities to practice and apply new skills or behaviors to their work.

BASIC SKILLS. Employees' motivation to learn in training activities can also be influenced by the degree to which they have **basic skills**—cognitive ability and reading and writing skills needed to understand the content of training programs. Recent forecasts of the skill levels of the U.S. work force indicate that managers will likely have to work with employees who lack those skills.[38]

Managers need to conduct a literacy audit to determine employees' basic-skill levels. Table 7.6 shows the activities involved in conducting a literacy audit.

TABLE 7.6
Performing a Literacy Audit

Step 1. Observe employees to determine the basic skills they need to be successful in their job. Note the materials the employee uses on the job, the tasks performed, and the reading, writing, and computations completed by the employee.

Step 2. Collect all materials that are written and read on the job and identify computations that must be performed to determine the necessary level of basic-skill proficiency. Materials include bills, memos, and forms such as inventory lists and requisition sheets.

Step 3. Interview employees to determine the basic skills they believe are needed to do the job. Consider the basic-skill requirements of the job yourself.

Step 4. Determine whether employees have the basic skills needed to successfully perform the job. Combine the information gathered by observing and interviewing employees and evaluating materials they use on their jobs. Write a description of each job in terms of reading, writing, and computation skills needed to perform successfully.

Step 5. Develop or buy tests that ask questions relating specifically to the employee's job. Ask employees to complete the tests.

Step 6. Compare test results with the description of the basic skills required for the job (from step 5). If the level of employees' reading, writing, and computation skills does not match the basic skills required by the job, then a basic-skills problem exists.

SOURCE: U.S. Department of Education, U.S. Department of Labor. *The Bottom Line: Basic Skills in the Workplace* (Washington, DC: 1988), pp. 14–15.

Cognitive Ability. Research shows that cognitive ability influences learning and job performance. **Cognitive ability** includes three dimensions: verbal comprehension, quantitative ability, and reasoning ability.[39] Verbal comprehension refers to the person's capacity to understand and use written and spoken language. Quantitative ability refers to how fast and accurately a person can solve math problems. Reasoning ability refers to the person's capacity to invent solutions to problems. Research shows that cognitive ability is related to successful performance in all jobs.[40] The importance of cognitive ability for job success increases as the job becomes more complex.

For example, a supermarket cashier needs low to moderate levels of all three dimensions of cognitive ability to successfully perform her job. An emergency room physician needs higher levels of verbal comprehension, quantitative ability, and reasoning ability than the cashier. The supermarket cashier needs to understand denominations of money to give customers the correct amount of change. The cashier also needs to invent solutions to problems. (For example, how does the cashier deal with items that are not priced that the customer wants to purchase?) The cashier also needs to be able to understand and communicate with customers (verbal comprehension). The physician also needs quantitative ability, but at a higher level. For example, when dealing with an infant experiencing seizures in an emergency situation, the physician needs to be able to calculate the correct dosage of medicine (based on an adult dosage) to stop the seizures after considering the child's weight. The physician has to be able to quickly diagnose the situation and determine what actions (blood tests, X-rays, respiratory therapy) are necessary. The physician also needs to communicate clearly to the patient (or its parents) the treatment and recovery process.

Cognitive ability influences job performance and ability to learn in training programs. If trainees lack the cognitive ability level necessary to perform job tasks, they will not perform well. Also, trainees' level of cognitive ability can influence performance if they can learn in training programs.[41] Trainees with low levels of cognitive ability are more likely to fail to complete training or (at the end of training) receive low grades on tests to measure how much they have learned.

As discussed in Chapter 6, to identify employees without the cognitive ability to succeed on the job or in training programs, companies use paper-and-pencil cognitive ability tests. Determining a job's cognitive ability requirement is part of the task analysis process discussed later in this chapter.

Reading Ability. Lack of the appropriate reading level can impede performance and learning in training programs. Material used in training should be evaluated to ensure that its reading level does not exceed that required by the job. **Readability** refers to the difficulty level of written materials.[42] A readability assessment usually involves analysis of sentence length and word difficulty.

If trainees' reading level does not match the level needed for the training materials, four options are available. First, determine whether it is feasible to use video or on-the-job training, which involves learning by watching and practicing rather than by reading. Second, employees without the necessary reading level could be identified through reading tests and reassigned to other positions more congruent with their skill levels. Third, again using reading tests, identify employees who lack the necessary reading skills and provide them with remedial training. Fourth, determine whether the job can be redesigned to accommodate employees' reading levels. The fourth option is certainly most costly and least practical. Therefore, alternative training methods need to be considered or you can elect a nontraining option. Nontraining options include selecting employees for jobs and training opportunities on the basis of reading, computation, writing, and other basic skill requirements.

Many companies are finding that employees lack the basic skills needed to successfully complete training programs. For example, a training program for 1,800 hourly employees at Georgia-Pacific (a paper manufacturer) was ineffective.[43] Employees reported that they understood training content but once they left training and returned to their jobs, they couldn't successfully perform maintenance tasks. In trying to determine the cause of the failed training, employees' basic skills were tested. Tests revealed that many employees had difficulty reading and writing. As a result, they were unable to understand the materials used in training. This translated into reduced learning and poor job performance.

To help ensure that employees have the necessary basic skills needed to succeed in training, Georgia-Pacific developed a basic skills assessment and training program. The first step involved assessment (or measurement) of employees' basic skills. A test of reading and math skills was given to employees. People who scored at or above a ninth grade reading level were eligible to attend training programs. Those with literacy levels below ninth grade were counseled to attend basic skills training. Because Georgia-Pacific's primary concern was how to convince employees to attend training, the company had to establish trust with the employees. In general, employees who lack basic skills are embarrassed to admit they have difficulty and are afraid that their lack of literacy will cost them their jobs. To alleviate these fears, employees received confidential counseling about their test results, they were not required to start basic skills training immediately after the assessment, and the company did not put information regarding test results (pass or fail) in employees' personnel files.

A local community college supplied the basic skills training. Classes were set up close to Georgia-Pacific's plants so employees could attend classes before or after their work shifts. There was no charge for the classes. Now the work force has the necessary basic skills. To ensure that new employees do not lack basic skills, Georgia-Pacific has changed its hiring qualifications. The company does not accept applications from anyone who hasn't completed a specific 18-month schedule of courses at the community college.

CREATING A LEARNING ENVIRONMENT

Learning involves a permanent change in behavior. For employees to acquire knowledge and skills in the training program and apply this information in their jobs, the training program needs to include specific learning principles. Educational and industrial psychologists and instructional design specialists have identified several conditions under which employees learn best.[44] Table 7.7 shows the events that need to take place for learning to occur in the training program and their implications for instruction.

EMPLOYEES NEED TO KNOW WHY THEY SHOULD LEARN. Employees learn best when they understand the objective of the training program. The **objective** refers to the purpose and expected outcome of training activities. There may be objectives for each training session as well as overall objectives for the program. Training objectives based on the training needs analysis help employees understand why they need training. Objectives are also useful for identifying the types of training outcomes that should be measured to evaluate a training program's effectiveness.

A training objective has three components:

1. A statement of what the employee is expected to do (performance).
2. A statement of the quality or level of performance that is acceptable (criterion).
3. A statement of the conditions under which the trainee is expected to perform the desired outcome (conditions).[45]

For example, a training objective for a customer-service training program for retail salespersons might be "After training, the employee will be able to express concern [performance] to all irate customers by a brief (fewer than 10 words) apology, only after the

TABLE 7.7
Instructional Events and Their Implications for the Learning Environment

INSTRUCTIONAL EVENTS	IMPLICATIONS
Informing the learner of the lesson objective	Provide a demonstration of the performance to be expected. Indicate the kind of verbal question to be answered.
Presenting stimuli with distinctive features	Emphasize the features of the subject to be perceived. Use formatting and figures in text to emphasize features.
Limiting the amount to be learned	Chunk lengthier material. Provide a visual image of material to be learned. Provide practice and overlearning to aid the attainment of automatization.
Providing learning guidance	Provide verbal cues to proper combining sequence. Provide verbal links to a larger meaningful context. Use diagrams and models to show relationships among concepts.
Elaborating the amount to be learned	Vary the context and setting for presentation and recall of material. Relate newly learned material to previously learned information. Provide a variety of contexts and situations during practice.
Providing cues that are used in recall	Suggest cues that elicit the recall of material. Use familiar sounds or rhymes as cues.
Enhancing retention and learning transfer	Design the learning situation to share elements with the situation of use. Provide verbal links to additional complexes of information.
Providing feedback about performance correctness	Provide feedback on degree of accuracy and timing of performance. Confirm that original expectancies were met.

SOURCE: Adapted from R.M. Gagne, "Learning Processes and Instruction," *Training Research Journal* 1 (1995/96), pp. 17–28.

customer has stopped talking [criteria] and no matter how upset the customer is [conditions]."

Good training objectives provide a clear idea of what the trainees are expected to do at the end of training. Standards of satisfactory performance (e.g., speed, time constraints, products, reactions) that can be measured or evaluated should be included. Any resources (equipment, tools) that the trainees need to perform the action or behavior specified in the objective need to be described. The conditions under which performance of the objective is expected to occur also need to be described. These conditions can relate to the physical work setting (e.g., at night), mental stresses (e.g., an angry customer), or equipment failure (e.g., malfunctioning landing gear on an airplane).

EMPLOYEES NEED TO USE THEIR OWN EXPERIENCES AS A BASIS FOR LEARNING. Employees are more likely to learn when the training is linked to their current job experiences and tasks—that is, when it is meaningful to them.[46] To enhance the meaningfulness of training content, the message should be presented using concepts, terms, and examples familiar to trainees. For example, in a retail salesperson customer-service program, the meaningfulness of the material will be increased by using scenarios of unhappy customers actually encountered by salespersons in stores. Recent research indicates that besides linking training to current job experiences, learning can be enhanced by providing trainees with the opportunity to choose their practice strategy and other characteristics of the learning environment.[47]

EMPLOYEES NEED TO HAVE OPPORTUNITIES TO PRACTICE. **Practice** involves having the employee demonstrate the learned capability (e.g., cognitive strategy, verbal information) emphasized in the training objectives under the conditions and performance standards specified by the objective. For practice to be effective, it needs to actively involve the trainee, include overlearning (repeated practice), take the appropriate amount of time, and include the appropriate unit of learning (amount of material). Practice also needs to be relevant to the training objectives.

Learning will not occur if employees practice only by talking about what they are expected to do. For example, using the objective for the customer-service course previously discussed, practice would involve having trainees participate in role playing with unhappy customers (customers upset with poor service, poor merchandise, or exchange policies). Trainees need to continue to practice even if they have been able to perform the objective several times **(overlearning).** Overlearning helps the trainee become more comfortable using new knowledge and skills and increases the length of time the trainee will retain the knowledge, skill, or behavior.

Trainers need to be sure that instruction does not exceed employees' short-term and long-term memory capacities. As we noted earlier, research suggests that no more than four to five items can be attended to at one time. If a lengthy procedure or process is to be taught, instruction needs to be delivered in shorter sessions or chunks in order not to exceed memory limits.[48] Visual images are another way to reduce demands on memory. Finally, automatizing (making performance of a task so automatic that it requires little thought or attention to be performed) is another way to reduce memory demands. For example, it would be difficult for a jet engine mechanic to perform some of the later parts of a maintenance procedure unless the earlier steps (such as removing the cover of the turbines) have been automatized. The more automatization of a procedure that occurs, the more memory is freed up to concentrate on other learning and thinking. Automatization occurs through overlearning, that is, learners are provided with extra learning opportunities even after they have demonstrated that they can perform adequately.

It is also important to consider whether to have only one practice session or to use distributed (multiple) practice sessions. Distributed practice sessions have been shown to result in more efficient learning of skills than continuous practice.[49] With factual information, the less meaningful the material and the greater its length or difficulty, the better distributed practice sessions are for learning.

A final issue related to practice is how much of the training should be practiced at one time. One option is that all tasks or objectives should be practiced at the same time (whole practice). Another option is that an objective or task should be practiced individually as soon as each is introduced in the training program (part practice). It is probably best to employ both whole and part practice in a training session. Trainees should have the opportunity to practice individual skills or behaviors. If the skills or behaviors introduced in training are related to one another, the trainee should demonstrate all of them in a practice session after they are practiced individually.

For example, one objective of the customer-service training for retail salespersons is learning how to deal with an unhappy customer. Salespersons are likely to have to learn three key behaviors: (1) greeting disgruntled customers, (2) understanding their complaints, and then (3) identifying and taking appropriate action. Practice sessions should be held for each of the three behaviors (part practice). Then another practice session should be held so that trainees can practice all three skills together (whole practice). If trainees were only given the opportunity to practice the behaviors individually, it is unlikely that they would be able to deal with an unhappy customer.

For practice to be relevant to the training objectives, several conditions must be met.[50] Practice must be related to the training objectives. The trainer should identify what trainees will be doing when practicing the objectives (performance), the criteria for attainment of the objective, and the conditions under which they may perform. These conditions should be present in the practice session. Next, the trainer needs to consider the adequacy of the trainees' performance. That is, how will trainees know whether their performance meets performance standards? Will they see a model of desired performance? Will they be provided with a checklist or description of desired performance? Can the trainees decide if their performance meets standards, or will the trainer or a piece of equipment compare their performance with standards?

If trainees' performance does not meet standards, the trainer must also decide if they will understand what is wrong and how to fix it. That is, trainers need to consider if trainees can diagnose their performance and take corrective action or if they will need help from the trainer or a fellow trainee.

EMPLOYEES NEED FEEDBACK. **Feedback** is information about how well people are meeting the training objectives. To be effective, feedback should focus on specific behaviors and be provided as soon as possible after the trainees' behavior.[51] Also, positive trainee behavior should be verbally praised or reinforced. Videotape is a powerful tool for giving feedback. Trainers should view the videotape with trainees, provide specific information about how behaviors need to be modified, and praise trainee behaviors that meet objectives.

EMPLOYEES LEARN BY OBSERVING AND INTERACTING WITH OTHERS. According to social learning theory, people learn by observing and imitating the actions of models. For the model to be effective, the desired behaviors or skills need to be clearly specified, and the model should have characteristics (such as age or position) similar to the target audience.[52] After observing the model, trainees should have the opportunity to reproduce the skills or behavior shown by the model in practice sessions.

Communities of practice refer to groups of employees who work together, learn from each other, and develop a common understanding of how to get work accomplished.[53] The idea of communities of practice suggests that learning occurs on the job as a result of social interaction. Every company has naturally occurring communities of practice that develop as a result of relationships that employees develop to accomplish work. For example, Xerox needed to train service representatives as a result of merging three separate service departments into a single unit. Xerox trained the service reps by bringing them together in shared work spaces where they were in constant contact with each other. In this environment, the service representatives taught each other how to do their jobs and practiced their skills on customer calls. One representative described the experience as involving continuous learning through sharing information with other reps and hearing how other reps dealt with different types of service calls.

EMPLOYEES NEED THE TRAINING PROGRAM TO BE PROPERLY COORDINATED AND ARRANGED. Training coordination is one of several aspects of training administration. **Training administration** refers to coordinating activities before, during, and after the program.[54] Training administration involves

1. Communicating courses and programs to employees.
2. Enrolling employees in courses and programs.
3. Preparing and processing any pretraining materials such as readings or tests.
4. Preparing materials that will be used in instruction (e.g., copies of overheads, cases).
5. Arranging for the training facility and room.
6. Testing equipment that will be used in instruction.
7. Having backup equipment (e.g., paper copy of slides, an extra overhead projector bulb) should equipment fail.
8. Providing support during instruction.
9. Distributing evaluation materials (e.g., tests, reaction measures, surveys).
10. Facilitating communications between trainer and trainees during and after training (e.g., coordinating exchange of e-mail addresses).
11. Recording course completion in the trainees' training records or personnel files.

Good coordination ensures that trainees are not distracted by events (such as an uncomfortable room or poorly organized materials) that could interfere with learning. Activities before the program include communicating to trainees the purpose of the program, the place it will be held, the name of a person to contact if they have questions, and any preprogram work they are supposed to complete. Books, speakers, handouts, and videotapes need to be prepared. Any necessary arrangements to secure rooms and equipment (such as VCRs) should be made. The physical arrangement of the training room should complement the training technique. For example, it would be difficult for a team-building session to be effective if the seats could not be moved for group activities. If visual aids will be used, all trainees should be able to see them. Make sure that the room is physically comfortable with adequate lighting and ventilation. Trainees should be informed of starting and finishing times, break times, and location of bathrooms. Minimize distractions such as phone messages. If trainees will be asked to evaluate the program or take tests to determine what they have learned, allot time for this activity at the end of the program. Following the program, any credits or recording of the names of trainees who completed the program should be done. Handouts and other training materials should be stored or returned to the consultant. The end of the program is also a good time to consider how the program could be improved if it will be offered again.

Helping "Hard-Cores" Help Themselves

Marriott International Inc.'s Pathways to Independence program has resulted in jobs for 700 people during the 1990s. Marriott currently operates the program in several large cities such as New Orleans, Atlanta, and Los Angeles, and plans to expand the program to others including Cleveland, Baltimore, and Richmond, Virginia. Marriott helps find employment for persons who would otherwise be considered to be "hard-core unemployed." Now working for Marriott as hotel employees are persons formerly on welfare because they could not find and retain jobs due to problems ranging from dropping out of high school, drug addiction, and arrest records to emotional scarring from poor marital or family relationships. The six-week program consists of classroom training and work sessions in Marriott properties (e.g., hotels).

Marriott's Pathways program was developed not out of goodwill but as a way to attract employees to lower-paying jobs that were difficult to fill. The program costs about $5,000 per trainee and the government funds slightly over half the expenses. It costs approximately $900 to find a new employee to replace an employee who has left. If Marriott can keep the workers it trains two and one-half times longer than the average worker tenure, the training will pay for itself.

To qualify for the program, applicants must have a sixth grade reading level, pass a drug test, and demonstrate a desire to work. Less than 25 percent of the applicants are accepted into the program. Despite the rigorous selection process, program participants need both job skills and life management skills to succeed. Besides providing job skills, trainers have to build trainees' self-confidence and often help the employee deal with personal issues. For example, one Marriott trainer brought a pair of slacks and shoes to work for a trainee. She also made numerous phone calls to arrange child care for other trainees, and spent the afternoon visiting shelters and driving trainees to government

agencies. A key problem is how to prepare workers to budget their money and manage their first paycheck.

Once welfare recipients who complete the Pathways program become Marriott "associates" (employees), they are provided with a toll-free phone number where questions dealing with child care, finances, school systems, and domestic and substance abuse can be answered by trained counselors. Marriott created the service as a result of determining that its managers were spending up to 50 percent of their time counseling employees who had personal problems!

Approximately, 45 percent of the 700 Pathways participants remain with the company. Studies have shown that in some areas, such as Washington, D.C., Pathway trainees stay with the company longer than other employees. For example, one employee who had recently overcome an addiction to crack cocaine successfully completed training and received a job offer from a Residence Inn where she now serves as a housekeeper.

Training evaluation has helped Marriott to modify the program to increase the success rate of Pathway trainees. Analysis revealed that unreliable child care and drug abuse were primary causes of Pathway trainees' failing to complete training or leaving the company. Marriott is planning to use more rigorous criteria for welfare recipients to qualify for the program. Marriott plans to require trainees to have child care, transportation, and housing arrangements. It also plans to run background checks and to require participants to take drug tests before and during training.

SOURCE: Based on F. Jossi, "From Welfare to Work," *Training* (April 1997), pp. 45–50; D. Milbank, "Hiring Welfare People, Hotel Chain Finds Is Tough but Rewarding," *The Wall Street Journal* (October 31, 1996), pp. A1, A14; D. Milbank, "Marriott Tightens Job Program Screening," *The Wall Street Journal* (July 15, 1997), pp. A2, A12.

TRANSFER OF TRAINING

Transfer of training refers to the use of knowledge, skills, and behaviors learned in training on the job. As Figure 7.4 shows, transfer of training is influenced by the climate for transfer, manager support, peer support, opportunity to use learned capabilities, technology support, and self-management skills. As we discussed earlier, learning is influenced by the learning environment (e.g., meaningfulness of the material, opportuni-

FIGURE 7.4 Work Environment Characteristics Influencing Transfer of Training

ties for practice and feedback) and employees' readiness for training (e.g., self-efficacy, basic-skill level). If no learning occurs in the training program, transfer is unlikely.

CLIMATE FOR TRANSFER. One way to think about the work environment's influence on transfer of training is to consider the overall climate for transfer. **Climate for transfer** refers to trainees' perceptions about a wide variety of characteristics of the work environment that facilitate or inhibit use of trained skills or behavior. These characteristics include manager and peer support, opportunity to use skills, and the consequences for using learned capabilities.[55] Table 7.8 shows characteristics of a positive climate for transfer of training. Research has shown that transfer of training climate is significantly related to positive changes in managers' administrative and interpersonal behaviors following training.

MANAGER SUPPORT. Manager support refers to the degree to which trainees' managers (1) emphasize the importance of attending training programs and (2) stress the application of training content to the job. For example, trainers at the California Housing Partnership train project managers of rental housing on how to schedule complex tasks. Unfortunately, many trainees do not implement the scheduling system because when they return to their community agencies, their managers are not convinced that the scheduling system is worthwhile to use.[56] The Competing by Meeting Stakeholders' Needs box shows the importance of support for non-traditional employees.

The greater the level of manager support, the more likely that transfer of training will occur.[57] The basic level of support that a manager can provide is acceptance allowing trainees to attend training. The highest level of support is to participate in training as an instructor (teaching in the program). Managers who serve as instructors are more likely to provide many of the lower-level support functions such as reinforcing use of newly learned capabilities, discussing progress with trainees, and providing opportunities to practice. To maximize transfer of training, trainers need to achieve the highest level of support possible. Managers can also facilitate transfer through reinforcement (use of action plans). An **action plan** is a written document that includes the steps that the trainee and manager will take to ensure that training transfers to the job. The action plan identifies (1) specific projects or problems that the trainees will work on and (2) equipment or other resources that the manager will provide to help the trainee. The action plan includes a schedule of specific dates and times when the manager and trainee agree to meet to discuss the progress being made in using learned capabilities on the job.

TABLE 7.8
Characteristics of a Positive Climate for Transfer of Training

CHARACTERISTIC	EXAMPLE
Supervisors and co-workers encourage and set goals for trainees to use new skills and behaviors acquired in training.	Newly trained managers discuss how to apply their training on the job with their supervisors and other managers.
Task cues: Characteristics of a trainee's job prompt or remind him or her to use new skills and behaviors acquired in training.	The job of a newly trained manager is designed in such a way as to allow him or her to use the skills taught in training.
Feedback consequences: Supervisors support the application of new skills and behaviors acquired in training.	Supervisors notice newly trained managers who use their training.
Lack of punishment: Trainees are not openly discouraged from using new skills and behaviors acquired in training.	When newly trained managers fail to use their training, they are not reprimanded.
Extrinsic reinforcement consequences: Trainees receive extrinsic rewards for using new skills and behaviors acquired in training.	Newly trained managers who successfully use their training will receive a salary increase.
Intrinsic reinforcement consequences: Trainees receive intrinsic rewards for using new skills and behaviors acquired in training.	Supervisors and other managers appreciate newly trained managers who perform their job as taught in training.

SOURCE: Adapted from J.B. Tracey, S.I. Tannenbaum, and M.J. Kavanagh, "Applying Trained Skills on the Job: The Importance of the Work Environment," *Journal of Applied Psychology* 80 (1995). Copyright © 1995 by the American Psychological Association. Adapted with permission.

At a minimum, special sessions should be scheduled with managers to explain the purpose of the training and set expectations that they will encourage attendance at the training session, provide practice opportunities, reinforce use of training, and follow up with employees to determine the progress in using newly acquired capabilities.

PEER SUPPORT. Transfer of training can also be enhanced by creating a support network among the trainees.[58] A **support network** is a group of two or more trainees who agree to meet and discuss their progress in using learned capabilities on the job. This could involve face-to-face meetings or communications via electronic mail. Trainees could share successful experiences in using training content on the job. They can also discuss how they obtained resources needed to use training content or how they coped with a work environment that interfered with use of training content.

A newsletter might be written to show how trainees are dealing with transfer of training issues. Distributed to all trainees, the newsletter might feature interviews with trainees who were successful in using new skills. Managers may also provide trainees with a mentor—a more experienced employee who previously attended the same training program. The mentor may be a peer. The mentor can provide advice and support related to transfer of training issues (e.g., how to find opportunities to use the learned capabilities).

OPPORTUNITY TO USE LEARNED CAPABILITIES. Opportunity to use learned capabilities **(opportunity to perform)** refers to the extent to which the trainee is provided with or actively seeks experience with newly learned knowledge, skill, and behaviors from the training program. Opportunity to perform is influenced by both the work environment and trainee motivation. One way trainees have the opportunity to use learned capabilities is through assigned work experiences (e.g., problems, tasks) that require their use. The trainees' manager usually plays a key role in determining work assignments. Opportunity to perform is also influenced by the degree to which trainees take personal responsibility to actively seek out assignments that allow them to use newly acquired capabilities.

Opportunity to perform includes breadth, activity level, and task type.[59] *Breadth* includes the number of trained tasks performed on the job. *Activity level* is the number of times or the frequency with which trained tasks are performed on the job. *Task type* refers to the difficulty or criticality of the trained tasks that are actually performed on the job. Trainees who are given opportunities to use training content on the job are more likely to maintain learned capabilities than trainees given few opportunities.[60]

Opportunity to perform can be measured by asking former trainees to indicate (1) whether they perform a task, (2) how many times they perform the task, and (3) the extent to which they perform difficult and challenging tasks. Individuals who report low levels of opportunity to perform may be prime candidates for "refresher courses" (courses designed to let trainees practice and review training content). Refresher courses are necessary because these persons have likely experienced a decay in learned capabilities since they haven't had opportunities to perform. Low levels of opportunity to perform may also indicate that the work environment is interfering with using new skills. For example, the manager may not support training activities or give the employee the opportunity to perform tasks using skills emphasized in training. Finally, low levels of opportunity to perform may indicate that training content is not important for the employee's job.

TECHNOLOGICAL SUPPORT. **Electronic performance support systems** (EPSSs) are computer applications that can provide, as requested, skills training, information access, and expert advice.[61] EPSS systems may be used to enhance transfer of training by providing trainees with an electronic information source that they can refer to on an as-needed basis as they attempt to apply learned capabilities on the job.

For example, Atlanta-based poultry processor Cagle's Inc. uses EPSS for employees who maintain the chicken-processing machines.[62] Because the machines that measure and cut chickens are constantly increasing in sophistication, it is impossible to continually train technicians so that they know the equipment's details. However, technicians are trained on the basic procedures they need to know to maintain these types of machines. When the machines encounter a problem, the technicians rely on what they have learned in training as well as the EPSS system, which provides more detailed instructions about the repairs. The EPSS system also tells technicians the availability of parts and where in inventory to find replacement parts. The EPSS system consists of a postage–stamp size computer monitor attached to a visor that magnifies the screen. The monitor is attached to a three-pound computer about half the size of a portable compact disc player. Attached to the visor is a microphone that the technician uses to give verbal commands to the computer. The EPSS helps employees diagnose and fix the machines very quickly. This is important given that the plant processes more than 100,000 chickens a day and chicken is a perishable food product!

SELF-MANAGEMENT SKILLS. Training programs should prepare employees to self-manage their use of new skills and behaviors on the job.[63] Specifically, within the training program, trainees should be given the opportunity to set goals for using skills or behaviors on the job, identify conditions under which they might fail to use them, identify the positive and negative consequences of using them, and monitor their use of them. Also, trainees need to understand that it is natural to encounter difficulty in trying to use skills on the job; relapses into old behavior and skill patterns do not indicate that trainees should give up. Finally, because peers and supervisors on the job may be unable to provide rewards for using new behaviors or provide feedback automatically, trainees need to create their own reward system and ask peers and managers for feedback.

SELECTING TRAINING METHODS

A number of different methods can be used to help employees acquire new knowledge, skills, and behaviors. Figure 7.5 presents the most popular training methods based on a survey of companies conducted by Lakewood Publications, publishers of *Training* magazine. The survey results suggest that lectures and videotapes are the most frequently used training methods. Other frequently used methods include case studies and role plays. Companies are also beginning to use new technologies for training. As the figure shows, computer-based training using a CD-ROM is the most frequently used new technology.

Technology is having a major impact on the delivery of training programs. Surveys indicate that currently only 17 percent of training time involves the use of new technologies, but by 2005 35 percent of training time is expected to use new technologies such as Web-based training.[64] New technology is also influencing training administration and training support. Multimedia training (such as the CD-ROM) and virtual reality enable training environments to almost perfectly mimic the actual work setting. New technologies also allow trainees to see, feel, and hear how equipment as well as other persons respond to their behaviors. Interactive voice response and imaging systems makes it possible to have paperless enrollment in training and tracking of training records. Software is available to facilitate storage and sharing of intellectual capital (information and learned capabilities) between employees. Electronic performance support systems give employees access to information from experts on an as-needed basis.

New training technologies can result in lower delivery costs and flexibility in delivery.[65] For example, training delivered by an instructor at a central location requires employees to spend time away from their regular job and requires the company to incur travel costs for bringing employees to a central location. Lower delivery costs can be realized by using satellite-based training or distance learning in which training programs are transmitted via satellite to several locations. Also, use of CD-ROM or Web-based

FIGURE 7.5 Overview of the Use of Instructional Methods

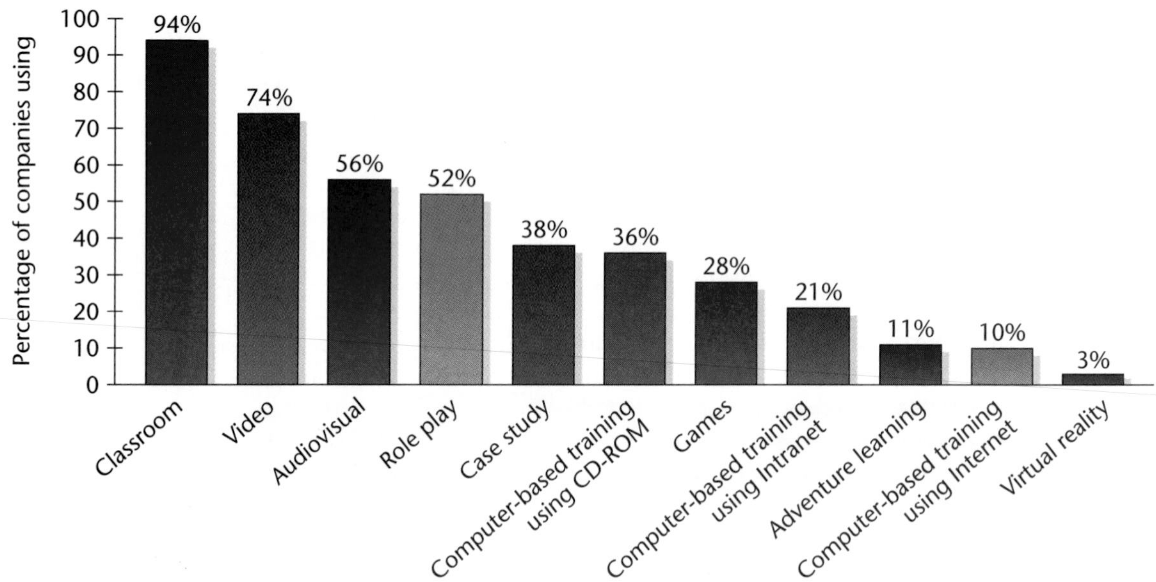

SOURCE: Based on "Industry Report 1997," *Training* (October 1997), p. 56. Adapted with permission.

training gives employees the flexibility to participate in training on a 24-hour basis at home or work through use of a personal computer. Linking training to personal computers also gives employees more responsibility for their own training. Such technology also includes characteristics that can enhance learning that often are not found in traditional instructor-led programs (e.g., immediate feedback, multiple practice opportunities, and opportunities for the employees to learn at their own pace).

However, having state-of-the-art instructional technology should not be the guiding force in choosing a training method. The specific instructional method used should be based on the training objectives. Instructional methods can be crudely grouped into three broad categories: presentation methods, hands-on methods, and group-building methods.[66]

PRESENTATION METHODS. **Presentation methods** refer to methods in which trainees are passive recipients of information. Presentation methods include traditional classroom instruction, distance learning, and audiovisual techniques. These are ideal for presenting new facts, information, different philosophies, and alternative problem-solving solutions or processes.

Classroom Instruction. Classroom instruction typically involves having the trainer lecture a group. In many cases, the lecture is supplemented with question-and-answer periods, discussion, or case studies. Classroom instruction remains a popular training method despite new technologies such as interactive video and computer-assisted instruction. Traditional classroom instruction is one of the least expensive, least time-consuming ways to present information on a specific topic to a large number of trainees. Also, the more active participation, job-related examples, and exercises that the instructor can build into traditional classroom instruction, the more likely trainees will learn and use the information presented on the job.

Distance Learning. Distance learning is used by geographically dispersed companies to provide information about new products, policies, or procedures, as well as skills training and expert lectures.[67] Distance learning features two-way communication between people. Distance learning includes simultaneous learning in which trainees attend training programs in which they can communicate with the trainer and other trainees at other locations. It includes audioconferencing, videoconferencing, and docuconferencing (which allows employees to collaborate on a shared document via computers). Distance learning also includes individualized personal-computer–based training.[68] Course materials and instruction may be distributed using the Internet or a CD-ROM. Trainees and trainers interact via e-mail, electronic bulletin boards, or conferencing systems.

Video teleconferencing usually includes a telephone link so that trainees viewing the presentation can call in questions and comments to the trainer. Also, satellite networks allow companies to link up with industry-specific and educational courses for which employees receive college credit and job certification. IBM, Digital Equipment, and Eastman Kodak are among the many firms that subscribe to the National Technological University, which broadcasts courses throughout the United States that technical employees need to obtain advanced degrees in engineering.[69]

An advantage of distance learning is that the company can save on travel costs. It also gives employees in geographically dispersed sites the opportunity to receive training from experts who would not otherwise be available to visit each location. For example, the research and development group at 3M found considerable cost savings by using videoconferencing to conduct an eight-week class on imaging technology that involved instructors from Europe and the United States.[70] Without videoconferencing the class would have cost $100,000, making it too expensive. With videoconferencing the course cost only $13,000.

The major disadvantage of distance learning is the potential for lack of interaction between the trainer and the audience. That's why a communications link between employees and the trainer is so important. Also, on-site instructors or facilitators should be available to answer questions and moderate question-and-answer sessions.

Audiovisual Techniques. **Audiovisual instruction** includes overheads, slides, and video. As Figure 7.5 shows, video is one of the most popular instructional method.[71] It has been used for improving communications skills, interviewing skills, and customer-service skills and for illustrating how procedures (e.g., welding) should be followed. Video is, however, rarely used alone. It is usually used in conjunction with lectures to show trainees real-life experiences and examples. For example, excerpts from the movie *Hoosiers* are often used to complement a lecture on the topic of leadership. In the movie, Gene Hackman plays a basketball coach in a rural Indiana high school. The coach successfully molds the team members' skills and develops their confidence. The team wins the Indiana state high school basketball championship against a larger school with better facilities and more talented players. Video is also a major component of behavior modeling and, naturally, interactive video instruction.

The use of video in training has a number of advantages. First, the trainer can review, slow down, or speed up the lesson, which gives him flexibility in customizing the session depending on trainees' expertise. Second, trainees can be exposed to equipment, problems, and events that cannot be easily demonstrated, such as equipment malfunctions, angry customers, or emergencies. Third, trainees are provided with consistent instruction. Program content is not affected by the interests and goals of a particular trainer. Fourth, videotaping trainees allows them to see and hear their own performance without the interpretation of the trainer. As a result, trainees cannot attribute poor performance to the bias of external evaluators such as the trainer or peers.

Most problems in video result from the creative approach used.[72] These problems include too much content for the trainee to learn, poor dialogue between the actors (which hinders the credibility and clarity of the message), overuse of humor or music, and drama that makes it confusing for the trainee to understand the important learning points emphasized in the video.

HANDS-ON METHODS. **Hands-on methods** refer to training methods that require the trainee to be actively involved in learning. Hands-on methods include on-the-job training, simulations, business games and case studies, behavior modeling, interactive video, and Web-based training. These methods are ideal for developing specific skills, understanding how skills and behaviors can be transferred to the job, experiencing all aspects of completing a task, and dealing with interpersonal issues that arise on the job.

On-the-Job Training (OJT). Companies spend between $90 billion and $180 billion annually on informal on-the-job training, compared with $30 billion on formal off-the-job training.[73] OJT can be useful for training newly hired employees, upgrading the skills of experienced employees when new technology is introduced, cross-training employees within a department or work unit, and orienting transferred or promoted employees to their new jobs. The basic philosophy of OJT is that employees learn through observing peers or managers performing the job and trying to imitate their behavior.

OJT takes various forms, including apprenticeships and self-directed training programs. Regardless of the specific type, effective OJT programs include the following characteristics:

1. A policy statement that describes the purpose of OJT and emphasizes the company's support for it.
2. A clear specification of who is accountable for conducting OJT. If managers conduct OJT, this is mentioned in their job descriptions and is part of their performance evaluation.
3. A thorough review of OJT practices (program content, types of jobs, length of program, cost savings) at other companies in similar industries.
4. Training of managers and peers in the principles of structured OJT.
5. Availability of lesson plans, checklists, procedure manuals, training manuals, learning contracts, and progress report forms for use by employees who conduct OJT.
6. Evaluation of employees' levels of basic skills (reading, computation, writing) before OJT.[74]

For example, Borden's Inc.'s North American Pasta Division's OJT program has many of these characteristics.[75] Not all managers and peers are used as trainers. Borden's invests in trainer selection, training, and rewards to ensure OJT's effectiveness. Employees and managers interested in being instructors are required to apply for the position. Those chosen as instructors are required to complete a demanding train-the-trainer course. The course involves classroom training as well as time on the manufacturing floor to learn how to operate machinery such as pasta machines and correctly teach other employees to use the equipment. Borden's also builds accountability into the OJT program. Trainees are responsible for completing a checklist requiring them to verify that the trainer helped them to learn the skills needed and used effective instructional techniques.

Self-directed learning involves having employees take responsibility for all aspects of learning—when it is conducted and who will be involved. For example, at Corning Glass, new engineering graduates participate in an OJT program called SMART (self-managed, awareness, responsibility, and technical competence).[76] Each employee is responsible for seeking the answers to a set of questions (e.g., "Under what conditions would a statistician be involved in the design of engineering experiments?") by visiting plants and research facilities and meeting with technical engineering experts and managers. After employees complete the questions, they are evaluated by a committee of peers who have already completed the SMART program. Evaluations have shown that the program cuts employees' start-up time in their new jobs from six weeks to three weeks. It is effective for a number of reasons. It encourages active involvement of the new employees in learning and allows flexibility in finding time for training. It has a peer-review evaluation component that motivates employees to complete the questions correctly. And, as a result of participating in the program, employees make contacts throughout the company and gain a better understanding of the technical and personal resources available within the company.

There are several advantages and disadvantages of self-directed learning.[77] It allows trainees to learn at their own pace and receive feedback about the learning performance. For the company, self-directed learning requires fewer trainers, reduces costs associated with travel and meeting rooms, and makes multiple-site training more realistic. Self-directed learning provides consistent training content that captures the knowledge of experts. Self-directed learning also makes it easier for shift employees to gain access to training materials. A major disadvantage of self-directed learning is that trainees must be willing and comfortable learning on their own. That is, trainees must be motivated to learn. From the company perspective, self-directed learning results in higher development costs, and development time is longer than with other types of training programs.

Self-directed learning will likely be more common in the future, as companies seek

World-Class Training Creates Exemplary Service in Exotic Locations

COMPETING THROUGH GLOBALIZATION

The Four Seasons Regent Hotel and Resorts is a luxury hotel operations and management group with 22,000 employees worldwide including approximately 13,000 in international locations. The Four Seasons faced the challenge of opening a new hotel and resort at Jambaran Bay, Bali.

Although there were more than 10,000 job applicants wanting to fill 580 jobs at the resort, none were able to speak English and many did not understand Western cuisine and customs. Traditional training methods used by the Four Seasons were ineffective because these programs were geared to young Americans with college educations who were familiar with the Four Seasons' corporate philosophy and operations. The native employees were gracious and hospitable. Their motivation to serve customers was high. However, they were unfamiliar with which foods are served at which meals (e.g., cereal is a breakfast food) and the finer points of serving Westerners, such as the fork goes on the left side of the plate. In fact, several trainees had never seen a hamburger or french fries! In addition to the need to understand Western culture, new employees lacked English language skills. This was critical because English was the official language of the hotel chain.

To address these training needs, the human resources staff created a self-directed learning center. The Self Access Learning Center emphasizes communication skills as well as English language skills. Its purpose is to teach skills and improve employees' confidence in their communications. The center includes video recorders, training modules, books, and magazines. Besides English, the center also teaches Japanese, (the language of 20 percent of hotel visitors) and provides training for foreign managers in Bahasa Indonesian, the native language of Indonesia. The training process begins by administering an English test to potential employees to gauge the level of English training they need. As employees complete each level of the training, they receive a monetary incentive.

How has the training paid dividends? Travel experts rated the Four Season Bali as one of the top hotels in the world. Business has increased steadily since the hotel opened, with guests from North America, Europe, Asia, Australia, and South America. As a result of the training, the Four Seasons is prepared for expansion. As the hotel industry expands in Asia, Four Seasons now has a trained and talented staff that can be used to meet human resource needs as new resorts are developed. Four Seasons learned that the company must combine the training needs of the local culture with the standards of the company's culture to create a successful international business.

SOURCE: Bassed on C.M. Solomon, "When Training Doesn't Translate," *Workforce* 76, no. 3 (1997), pp. 40–44. Used with permission.

to train staff flexibly, to take advantage of technology, and to encourage employees to be proactive in their learning rather than driven by the employer.[78] (See the "Competing through Globalization" box.)

Apprenticeship is a work-study training method with both on-the-job training and classroom training.[79] To qualify as a registered apprenticeship program under state or federal guidelines, at least 144 hours of classroom instruction and 2,000 hours, or one year, of on-the-job experience is required.[80] Apprenticeships can be sponsored by individual companies or by groups of companies cooperating with a union. The majority of apprenticeship programs are in the skilled trades, such as plumbing, carpentry, electrical work, and bricklaying.

Apprenticeship programs are more widely used in Western European countries (such as Germany and Denmark) than in the United States.[81] In these countries, apprenticeship is linked with employment, education, and training systems (i.e., it is a system that provides youths with the schooling needed to obtain work in the skill trades). The U.S. government is considering establishing a federally directed apprenticeship program to ease the school-to-work transition for youths who are not motivated or skilled enough to attend college. Such a program may help to alleviate the shortage of skilled workers that many manufacturers are experiencing.[82]

One of the major advantages of an apprenticeship program is that learners have the opportunity to earn pay while they learn. This is important because the programs can last for several years. (Learners' wages increase automatically as their skills improve.) Also, apprenticeships are usually effective learning experiences because they involve learning why and how a task is performed in classroom instruction provided by local trade schools, high schools, and community colleges. OJT involves assisting a certified tradesperson (a journeyman) at the work site.

One disadvantage of apprenticeship programs is that minorities' and women's access to these programs has been restricted because of unions' and employers' choice of men for entry-level jobs.[83] Another is that there is no guarantee jobs will be available when the program is completed.

For example, the German apprenticeship model has recently had its problems.[84] German businesses such as Siemens and Daimler Benz have been experiencing high wage and welfare costs so they are creating most new jobs outside the country. These firms want flexible workers who will upgrade their skills, rather than employees from the apprenticeship program who are well trained in just one trade or occupation. As a result, the availability of apprenticeships for trainees has declined.

Simulations. A simulation is a training method that represents a real-life situation, with trainees' decisions resulting in outcomes that mirror what would happen if the trainee were on the job. Simulations, which allow trainees to see the impact of their decisions in an artificial, risk-free environment, are used to teach production and process skills as well as management and interpersonal skills.

Simulators need to have identical elements to those found in the work environment. The simulator needs to respond exactly like the equipment would under the conditions and response given by the trainee. For this reason simulators are expensive to develop and need constant updating as new information about the work environment is obtained.

Simulators replicate the physical equipment that employees use on the job. For example, at Motorola's Programmable Automation Literacy Lab, employees who may never have worked with a computer or robot learn to operate them.[85] Before entering the lab, employees are given a two-hour introduction to factory automation, which introduces new concepts, vocabulary, and computer-assisted manufacturing. The simulator allows trainees to become familiar with the equipment by designing a product (a personalized memo holder). Also, trainees do not have to be afraid of the impact of wrong decisions; errors are not as costly as they would be if the trainees were using the equipment on an actual production line. Success in simple exercises with the robot and computer increases employees' confidence that they can work successfully in an automated manufacturing environment.

Simulations are also used to develop managerial skills. Looking Glass© is a simulation designed to develop both teamwork and individual management skills.[86] In this program, participants are assigned different roles in a glass company. On the basis of memos and correspondence, each participant interacts with other members of the management team over the course of six hours. Participants' behavior and interactions in solving the problems described in correspondence are recorded and evaluated. At the conclusion of the simulation, participants are given feedback regarding their performance.

A recent development in simulations is the use of virtual reality technology. **Virtual reality** is a computer-based technology that provides trainees with a three-dimensional learning experience. Using specialized equipment or viewing the virtual model on the computer screen, trainees move through the simulated environment and interact with its components.[87] For example, Motorola's advanced manufacturing courses for employees learning to run the Pager Robotic Assembly facility use virtual reality. Employees are fitted with a head-mount display that allows them to view the virtual world, which includes the actual lab space, robots, tools, and the assembly operation. The trainees hear and see the actual sounds and sights as if they were using the real equipment. Also, the equipment responds to the employees' actions (e.g., turning on a switch or dial).

Business Games and Case Studies. Situations that trainees study and discuss (case studies) and business games in which trainees must gather information, analyze it, and make decisions are primarily used for management skill development. Games stimulate learning because participants are actively involved and they mimic the competitive nature of business. The types of decisions that participants make in games include all aspects of management practice, including labor relations (e.g., agreement in contract negotiations), marketing (e.g., the price to charge for a new product), and finance (financing the purchase of new technology). For example, Market Share, part of a marketing management course at Nynex Corporation, requires participants to use strategic thinking such as competitive analysis to increase market share.[88] The playing board is divided into different segments representing the information industry (e.g., cable, radio). Teams of two or three players compete to gain market share by determining where the team will allocate its efforts and challenge opponents' market share.

Documentation on learning from games is anecdotal.[89] Games may give team members a quick start at developing a framework for information and help develop cohesive groups. For some groups (such as senior executives), games may be more meaningful training activities (because the game is realistic) than presentation techniques such as classroom instruction.

Cases may be especially appropriate for developing higher-order intellectual skills such as analysis, synthesis, and evaluation. These skills are often required by managers, physicians, and other professional employees. Cases also help trainees develop the willingness to take risks given uncertain outcomes, based on their analysis of the situation. To use cases effectively, the learning environment must give trainees the opportunity to prepare and discuss their case analyses. Also, face-to-face or electronic communication among trainees must be arranged. Because trainee involvement is critical for the effectiveness of the case method, learners must be willing and able to analyze the case and then communicate and defend their positions.

There are a number of available sources for preexisting cases. It is especially important to review preexisting cases to determine how meaningful they will be to the trainee. Preexisting cases on a wide variety of problems in business management (e.g., human resource management, operations, marketing, advertising) are available from Harvard Business School, The Darden Business School at the University of Virginia, McGraw-Hill publishing company, and various other sources.

Behavior Modeling. Research suggests that behavior modeling is one of the most effective techniques for teaching interpersonal skills.[90] Each training session, which typically lasts four hours, focuses on one interpersonal skill, such as coaching or communicating ideas. Each session includes a presentation of the rationale behind the key behaviors, a videotape of a model performing the key behaviors, practice opportunities using role playing, evaluation of a model's performance in the videotape, and a planning session devoted to understanding how the key behaviors can be used on the job. In the practice sessions, trainees are provided with feedback regarding how closely their behavior matches the key behaviors demonstrated by the model. The role playing and modeled performance are based on actual incidents in the employment setting in which the trainee needs to demonstrate success.

Interactive Video. Interactive video combines the advantages of video and computer-based instruction. Instruction is provided one-on-one to trainees via a monitor connected to a keyboard. Trainees use the keyboard or touch the monitor to interact with the program. Interactive video is used to teach technical procedures and interpersonal skills. The training program may be stored on a videodisc or compact disc (CD-ROM). For example, Federal Express's 25-disc interactive video curriculum includes courses related to customer etiquette, defensive driving, and delivery procedures.[91] As Federal Express discovered, interactive video has many advantages. First, training is individualized. Employees control what aspects of the training program they want to view. They can skip ahead when they feel competent, or they can review topics. Second, employees receive immediate feedback concerning their performance. Third, training is more convenient for both employers and employees. Regardless of employees' work schedules, they can have access to the equipment, which is located at their work site. From the employer's standpoint, the high cost of developing interactive video programs and purchasing the equipment is offset by the reduction in instructor costs and travel costs related to a central training location. At Federal Express, interactive video has made it possible to train 35,000 customer-contact employees in 650 locations nationwide, saving the company millions of dollars. Without interactive video, it would have been impossible for Federal Express to deliver consistent high-quality training. The main disadvantage of interactive video is the high cost of developing the courseware. This may be a particular problem for courses in which frequent updates are necessary.[92]

Web-Based Training. Web-based training refers to training that is delivered on public (Internet) or private (intranets) computer networks and displayed by a Web browser.[96] For example, Amdahl Corporation (a mainframe computer manufacturer) has set up an intranet.[94] Employees use Netscape to browse the Web along with a company-developed Web browser. Every department at Amdahl has its own Web home page. The home page describes what services the department provides. Many employees also have their own personal home pages. The training department home page includes a list of courses offered by the training department. The manufacturing department gives employees access to technical manuals via the intranet.

Web-based training supports virtual reality, animation, interactions, communications between trainees, and real-time audio and video.The sophistication of Web-based training varies. The simplest level facilitates communications between trainers and trainees. More complex uses of the Internet involve actual delivery of training. At the highest level, the Internet (or intranet) is used for both training and storage of intellectual capital, and trainees are very actively involved in learning. Sound, automation, and video are used in Web-based training. In addition, trainees are linked to other resources on the Web. They are also required to share information with other trainees and to deposit knowledge and insights gained from the training (such as potential applications of the training content) in a database that is accessible to other employees.

Web-based training has advantages similar to other multimedia methods. (See the "Competing through High-Performance Work Systems" box.) Advantages of Web-based training include the ability to deliver training to trainees anywhere in the world at any time, cost savings and efficiency in training administration, the use of self-directed, self-paced instruction, the ability to monitor trainees' performance, and controllable access to training.[95] Web-based training has several advantages from learning and cost perspectives. Web-based training allows the trainee to have complete control over the delivery of training, provides links to other resources, and allows the trainee to

New Training Technologies Are More than a Fad for GTE

GTE Telephone Operations is a subsidiary of the largest local access telephone company in the United States. Recently, the company has reconsidered the relationship between training and the company's business goals. As a result, the company has reduced the size of the education and training department by two-thirds and decided to use new technology to cut training costs and increase the benefits gained from training. The company's goal is that 50 percent of new training programs being developed use a technology-based approach.

GTE has utilized new technologies to streamline training enrollments as well as delivery of training content. An online database of courses was developed. This enables employees to quickly review training offerings to find courses that meet their needs. It also makes it easier for course offerings to be updated by the training staff. As a result of the introduction of a new national order collection system, education and training staff developed a computer program to simulate the new order-entry environment faced by employees who worked on collecting orders. Training was needed for all employees who worked on service orders including installers, maintenance technicians, salespersons, and engineers. The training simulation includes the actual order-entry screens that employees are required to complete. As the employee works through the simulation, it provides suggestions and online help. GTE staff also developed Web-based training and electronic support performance support systems. For training sites that may not yet have access to the corporate intranet, the staff developed low-cost portable links (local area network) that trainers and employees can use at any site to connect into the GTE intranet.

COMPETING THROUGH HIGH-PERFORMANCE WORK SYSTEMS

The company has realized several cost savings as well as learning advantages by using the new technology for training. The training can be quickly updated. Employees can access online help from the intranet as they serve customers. Also, they can access training from their own personal computers, reducing the time commitment and costs associated with traveling to a central training location. Employees can learn at their own pace and can review training materials at any time.

Despite the staff reductions, use of these technologies has helped the education and training group provide more than 2.5 million student hours a year! The new technology is not intended to eliminate the need for instructor-based training. Rather, at GTE the instructor's role is changing from being responsible for the delivery of training to serving more as a coach or mentor for trainees. New technologies are allowing GTE to better meet employees needs for quick access to training at any time.

SOURCE: Based on K. Rayl, "GTE's Training Goes High-Tech," *Workforce* 77, no. 4 (1998), pp. 36–40. Used with permission.

share information and communicate with other trainees and the trainer or to make "deposits" into databases. This sharing can occur before, during, or after training. Learner control, linking, and sharing facilitate learning and transfer of training because trainees are actively involved in learning and the material is directly related to current issues and problems the employee is facing. Web-based training also allows more than one person to access the training materials at the same time (asynchronous training). For example, at Xerox Management Institute, team members from the United States, Europe, and South America use the Web site (http://www.isim.com) to access study guides, discuss assignments with other students, and interact with the trainer.[96] Homework assignments are posted and addresses of other links that lead to additional information on topics are provided. These links, known as **hyperlinks,** allow a user to easily move from one Web page to another. Owens-Corning's learning resource home page has hyperlinks to all available forms of training information including CD-ROM, Web-based, and trainer-led programs. The site supports online registration for courses and allows assessment tools (such as quizzes) to be sent to the trainee, scored, and used to register trainees in appropriate courses.[97] At both Xerox and Owens-Corning, employees can access the classes on their own timetables. This has boosted employee participation and lowered training costs. Savings are realized by avoiding travel and lodging costs.

An additional advantage of Web-based training is ease of updating the training program using authoring language (such as html), which continues to become more user-friendly. Trainers can quickly make changes at low cost. These changes take effect as soon as they are made. Ease of changing program content is an advantage that Internet-based training has over a CD-ROM. To change a CD-ROM program requires that a new master CD be produced and copies made and distributed to trainees.

Effective Web-based training is grounded on a thorough needs assessment and complete learning objectives. Also, the site must use a combination of sound, words, and diagrams to ensure that it appeals to the learning preferences of the majority of users. The Web must create a learning environment through providing meaningful material, communicating objectives, and enabling trainees to practice and receive feedback. **Repurposing** refers to directly translating a training program that uses a traditional training method onto the Web. Web-based training that involves merely repurposing an ineffective training program based on lecture or another traditional training method will result in ineffective training! Unfortunately, in their haste to use Web-based training, many companies are repurposing bad training!

Allen Telecom Group's Web site provides a good example of the types of training administration tasks that can be handled by a Web site.[98] The training department can publish training bulletins, schedule classes, prepare class rosters, track attendance, track costs, and store and modify training records. Employees can access the site to review class offerings, access current schedules, register for classes, communicate with trainers, and generate their own personal training records.

Disadvantages include computer networks' inability to handle extensive video and audio (often referred to as the bandwidth problem), the need to control and bill users, and the difficulty of writing or revising training curricula based on a linear learning method (e.g., learn A first, then B, then C) to hypermedia. Hypermedia allow the user to decide the direction and order of learning.

GROUP-BUILDING METHODS. **Group-building methods** help trainees share ideas and experiences, build group or team identity, understand the dynamics of interpersonal relationships, and get to know their own strengths and weaknesses and those of their co-workers. Various training techniques are available to improve work-group or team performance, to establish a new team, and to improve interactions among different teams. All involve examination of feelings, perceptions, and beliefs about the functioning of the team; discussion; and development of plans to apply what was learned in training to the team's performance in the work setting.

Adventure Learning. **Adventure learning** focuses on the development of teamwork and leadership skills using structured outdoor activities.[99] Adventure learning appears to be best suited for developing skills related to group effectiveness such as self-awareness, problem solving, conflict management, and risk taking. Adventure learning may involve strenuous, challenging physical activities such as dogsledding or mountain climbing. It can also use structured individual and group outdoor activities such as climbing walls, going through rope courses, making trust falls (in which each trainee stands on a table and falls backward into the arms of fellow group members), climbing ladders, and traveling from one tower to another using a device attached to a wire that connects the two towers.

For example, a Chili's restaurant manager in adventure learning was required to scale a three-story-high wall.[100] About two-thirds away from the top of the wall the manager became very tired. She successfully reached the top of the wall using the advice and encouragement shouted from team members on the ground below. When asked to consider what she learned from the experience, she reported that the exercise made her realize that reaching personal success depends on other people. At her restaurant, everyone has to work together to make the customers happy.

For adventure learning programs to be successful, the exercises should be related to the types of skills that participants are expected to develop. Also, after the exercises, a skilled facilitator should lead a discussion about what happened in the exercise, what was learned, how what happened in the exercise relates to the job situation, and how to set goals and apply what was learned on the job.[101]

Does adventure learning work? Rigorous evaluations of the impact of adventure learning on productivity and performance have not been conducted. However, participants often report that they gained a greater understanding of themselves and the ways they interact with their co-workers. One of the keys to the success of an adventure learning program may be the insistence that whole work groups participate together so that group dynamics that inhibit effectiveness can emerge and be discussed.

The physically demanding nature of adventure learning and the requirement that trainees often have to touch each other in the exercises may increase the company's risk for negligence claims due to personal injury, intentional infliction of emotional distress, and invasion of privacy. Also, the Americans with Disabilities Act (discussed in Chapter 3) raises questions about requiring employees with disabilities to participate in physically demanding training experience.[102]

Team Training. Team training involves coordinating the performance of individuals who work together to achieve a common goal. Such training is an important issue when information must be shared and individuals affect the overall performance of the group. For example, in the military as well as the private sector (e.g., nuclear power plants, commercial airlines), much of the work is performed by crews, groups, or teams. Successful performance depends on coordination of individual activities to make decisions, team performance, and readiness to deal with potentially dangerous situations (e.g., an overheating nuclear reactor).

Team training strategies include cross-training and coordination training.[103] **Cross-training** involves having team members understand and practice each other's skills so that members are prepared to step in and take another member's place should he temporarily or permanently leave the team. **Coordination training** involves training the team in how to share information and decision making responsibilities to maximize team performance. Coordination training is especially important for commercial aviation and surgical teams who are in charge of monitoring different aspects of equipment and the environment, but must share information to make the most effective decision regarding patient care or aircraft safety and performance. **Team leader training** refers to training that the team manager or facilitator receives. This may involve training the manager how to resolve conflict within the team or help the team coordinate activities or other team skills.

Team training usually involves multiple methods. For example, a lecture or video may be used to disseminate knowledge regarding communication skills to trainees. Role plays or simulations may be used to give trainees the opportunity to put the communication skills emphasized in the lecture into practice. Boeing utilized team training to improve the effectiveness of teams used to design the Boeing 777.[104] At Boeing, 250 teams with 8 to 15 members each worked on the design of the aircraft. Team members included engineers with different specialties (e.g., design engineers, production engineers), reliability specialists, quality experts, and marketing professionals. This type of team is known as a concurrent engineering team because employees from all the business functions needed to design the aircraft work together at the same time. For concurrent engineering teams to be successful, team members must understand how the process or product they are working on fits with the finished product. Because each 777 aircraft contains millions of parts, it is important that they fly together!

Boeing's team training approach began with an extensive orientation for team members. The orientation emphasized how team members were supposed to work together. Following orientation, the teams were given their work assignments. Trainers helped the team work through issues and problems on an as-needed basis. That is, trainers were available to help the teams if the teams requested help. Trainers provided training in communication skills, conflict resolution, and leadership.

Research suggests that teams that are effective in training develop procedures to identify and resolve errors, coordinate information gathering, and reinforce each other.[105]

Action Learning. Action learning involves giving teams or work groups an actual problem, having them work on solving it and commit to an action plan, and holding them accountable for carrying out the plan.[106] Typically, action learning involves between 6 and 30 employees. It may also include customers and vendors. There are several variations on the composition of the group. In one variation, the group includes a single customer for the problem being dealt with. Sometimes the groups include cross-functional team members (i.e., members from different company departments) who all have a stake in the problem. Or the group may involve employees from multiple functions who all focus on their own functional problems, each contributing to helping solve the problems identified. For example, Whirlpool used action learning to deal with recovering overpaid duty on compressors that the company was importing from Brazil. Members of the procurement group formed a team that dealt with the problem of how to deal with what they would do to implement Whirlpool's strategies for cost reduction and inventory control. The team developed a process for recovering the duty, resulting in savings to Whirlpool of hundreds of thousands of dollars a year.

Action learning is a widespread training practice in Europe, but it is just starting to be used in the United States. Although action learning has not been formally evaluated, the process appears to maximize learning and transfer of training because it involves real-time problems that employees are facing. Also, action learning can be useful for identifying dysfunctional team dynamics that can get in the way of effective problem solving.

EVALUATING TRAINING PROGRAMS

Examining the outcomes of a program helps in evaluating its effectiveness. These outcomes should be related to the program objectives (discussed earlier), which help trainees understand the purpose of the program. **Training outcomes** can be categorized into five categories: cognitive outcomes, skill-based outcomes, affective outcomes, results and return on investment.[107]

COGNITIVE OUTCOMES. **Cognitive outcomes** are used to determine the degree to which trainees are familiar with principles, facts, techniques, procedures, or processes emphasized in the training program. Cognitive outcomes measure what knowledge trainees learned in the program. Typically, paper-and-pencil tests are used to assess cognitive outcomes.

SKILL-BASED OUTCOMES. **Skill-based outcomes** are used to assess the level of technical or motor skills and behaviors. Skill-based outcomes include acquisition or learning of skills (skill learning) and use of skills on the job (skill transfer). The extent to which trainees have learned skills can be evaluated by observing their performance in work samples such as simulators. Skill transfer is usually determined by observation. For example, a resident medical student may perform surgery while the surgeon carefully observes, giving advice and assistance as needed. Peers and managers may also be asked to rate trainees' behavior or skills based on their observations.

AFFECTIVE OUTCOMES. **Affective outcomes** include attitudes and motivation. One type of affective outcome is trainees' reactions toward the training program. **Reaction outcomes** refer to trainees' perceptions of the program including the facilities, trainers, and content. (Reaction outcomes are often referred to as a measure of "creature comfort.") This information is typically collected at the program's conclusion. Reactions are useful for identifying what trainees thought was successful and what inhibited learning.

Reaction outcomes are typically collected via a questionnaire completed by trainees. It usually asks questions like the following: "How satisfied are you with the training program?" "Did the session meet your personal expectations?" "How comfortable did you find the classroom?" Keep in mind that while reactions provide useful information, they usually only weakly relate to learning or transfer of training.

Other affective outcomes that might be collected in an evaluation include tolerance for diversity, motivation to learn, safety attitudes, and customer service orientation. Affective outcomes can be measured using surveys. The specific attitude of interest depends on the program objectives. For example, attitudes toward equal employment opportunity laws might be an appropriate outcome to use to evaluate a diversity training program.

RESULTS. **Results** are used to determine the training program's payoff for the company. Examples of results outcomes include reduced costs related to employee turnover or accidents, increased production, and improvements in product quality or customer service. For example, to evaluate a program designed to teach delivery van drivers safe driving practices, Federal Express tracked drivers' accidents and injuries over a 90-day period after they had completed the training program.[108]

RETURN ON INVESTMENT. **Return on investment (ROI)** refers to comparing the training's monetary benefits with the cost of the training. Training costs include direct and indirect costs.[109] **Direct costs** include salaries and benefits for all employees involved in training, including trainees, instructors, consultants, and employees who design the program; program material and supplies; equipment or classroom rentals or purchases; and travel costs. **Indirect costs** are not related directly to the design, development, or delivery of the training program. They include general office supplies, facilities, equipment, and related expenses; travel and expenses not directly billed to one program; training department management and staff salaries not related to any one program; and administrative and staff support salaries. **Benefits** refer to what of value the company gains from the training program.

Later in the chapter we will show a detailed example of how to determine the costs, benefits, and return on investment from a training program.

Which training outcomes measure is best? The answer depends on the training objectives. For example, if the instructional objectives identified business-related outcomes such as increased customer service or product quality, then results outcomes should be included in the evaluation. Both reaction and cognitive outcomes are usually collected before the trainees leave the training site. As a result, these measures do not help determine the extent to which trainees actually use the training content in their jobs (transfer of training). Skill-based, affective, and results outcomes measured following training can be used to determine transfer of training—that is, the extent to which training has resulted in a change in behavior, skill, or attitude or directly influenced objective measures related to company effectiveness (e.g., sales).

REASONS FOR EVALUATING TRAINING. Many companies are beginning to invest millions of dollars in training programs to help gain a competitive advantage. Firms with high-leverage training practices not only invest large sums of money into developing and administering training programs but also evaluate training programs. Why should training programs be evaluated?

1. To identify the program's strengths and weaknesses. This includes determining if the program is meeting the learning objectives, the quality of the learning environment, and if transfer of training to the job is occurring.
2. To assess whether the content, organization, and administration of the program (including the schedule, accommodations, trainers, and materials) contribute to learning and the use of training content on the job.
3. To identify which trainees benefited most or least from the program.
4. To gather data to assist in marketing programs through collecting information from participants about whether they would recommend the program to others, why they attended the program, and their level of satisfaction with the program. To determine the financial benefits and costs of the program.
5. To compare the costs and benefits of training versus non training investments (such as work redesign or a better employee selection system).
6. To compare the costs and benefits of different training programs to choose the best program.

Walgreen is a good example of a company that has reconsidered the role of training based on evaluation data. At Walgreen, a training course for new technicians was developed to replace on-the-job training they received from the pharmacists who hired them. This course involved 20 hours of classroom training and 20 hours of supervision on the job. Since the company has several thousand stores, large amounts of money and time were being invested in the training. As a result, the company decided to evaluate the program.

The evaluation consisted of comparing technicians who had completed the program with some who had not. Surveys asking questions about new employees' performance were sent to the pharmacists who supervised the technicians. Some questions related to speed of entering patient and drug data into the store computer and how often the technician offered customers generic drug substitutes. In comparing the two groups, the results showed that formally trained technicians were more efficient and wasted less of the pharmacist's time than those who received traditional on-the-job training. Sales in pharmacies with formally trained technicians exceeded sales in pharmacies with on-the-job–trained technicians by an average of $9,500 each year.[110]

EVALUATION DESIGNS. A number of different evaluation designs can be applied to training programs.

Pretest/Posttest with Comparison Group. In this method, a group of employees who receive training and a group who do not are compared. Outcome measures are collected from both groups before and after training. If improvement is greater for the training group than the comparison group, this provides evidence that training is responsible for the change.

Pretest/Posttest. This method is similar to the pretest/posttest comparison group design but has one major difference: No comparison group is used. The lack of a comparison group makes it difficult to rule out the effects of business conditions or other factors as explanations for changes. This design is often used by companies that want to evaluate a training program but are uncomfortable with excluding certain employees or that only intend to train a small group of employees.

Posttest Only. In this method, only training outcomes are collected. This design can be strengthened by adding a comparison group (which helps to rule out alternative explanations for changes). The posttest-only design is appropriate when trainees (and the comparison group, if one is used) can be expected to have similar levels of knowledge, behavior, or results outcomes (e.g., same number of sales, equal awareness of how to close a sale) prior to training.

Time Series. In the time-series method, training outcomes are collected at periodic intervals before and after training. (In the other evaluation designs we have discussed, training outcomes are collected only once before and after training.) A comparison group can also be used with a time-series design. One advantage of the time-series design is that it allows an analysis of the stability of training outcomes over time. This type of design is frequently used to evaluate training programs that focus on improving readily observable outcomes (such as accident rates, productivity, and absenteeism) that vary over time. For example, a time-series design was used to evaluate the extent to which a training program helped improve the number of safe work behaviors in a food manufacturing plant.[111] Observations of safe work behavior were made during 25 weeks. Training directed at increasing the number of safe behaviors was introduced after approximately five weeks. The number of safe acts observed varied across the observation period. However, the number of safe behaviors increased after the training program was conducted and remained stable across the observation period.

There is no one appropriate evaluation design. Several factors need to be considered in choosing an evaluation design:[112]

- Size of the training program.
- Purpose of training.
- Implications if a training program does not work.
- Company norms regarding evaluation.
- Costs of designing and conducting an evaluation.
- Need for speed in obtaining program effectiveness information.

For example, if a manager is interested in determining how much employees' communications skills have changed as a result of participating in a behavior-modeling training program, a pretest/posttest comparison group design is necessary. Trainees should be randomly assigned to training and no-training conditions. These evaluation design features give the manager a high degree of confidence that any communication skill change is the result of participating in the training program.[116] This type of evaluation design is also necessary if the manager wants to compare the effectiveness of two training programs.

Evaluation designs without pretesting or comparison groups are most appropriate in situations where the manager is interested in identifying whether a specific level of performance has been achieved (e.g., can employees who participated in behavior-modeling training adequately communicate their ideas?). In this situation the manager is not interested in determining how much change has occurred.

Arthur Andersen's evaluation strategy for a training course delivered to the company's tax professionals is a good example of how company norms regarding evaluation and the purpose of training influence the type of evaluation design chosen.[114] Arthur Andersen views training as an effective method for developing human resources. Training is expected to provide a good return on investment. The company used a combination of affective, cognitive, behavior, and results criteria to evaluate a five-week course designed to prepare tax professionals to understand state and local tax law. The course involved two weeks of self-study and three weeks of classroom work. A pretest/posttest comparison design was used. Before they took the course, trainees took a test to determine their knowledge of state and local tax laws and completed a survey designed to assess their self-confidence in preparing accurate tax returns. The evaluators also identified the trainees' (accountants') billable hours related to calculating state and local tax returns and the revenue generated by the activity. After the course, evaluators again identified billable hours and surveyed trainees' self-confidence. The results of the evaluation indicated that the accountants were spending more time doing state and local tax work. Also, the trained accountants produced more revenue doing state and local tax work than accountants who had not yet received the training (comparison group). There was also a significant improvement in the accountants' confidence following training, and they were more willing to promote their expertise in state and local tax preparation. Finally, after 15 months, the amount of revenue gained by the company more than offset the cost of training. On average, the increase in revenue for the trained tax accountants was more than 10 percent.

DETERMINING RETURN ON INVESTMENT. **Cost-benefit analysis** is the process of determining the economic benefits of a training program using accounting methods. Determining the economic benefits of training involves determining training costs and benefits. Training cost information is important for several reasons:

1. To understand total expenditures for training, including direct and indirect costs.
2. To compare the costs of alternative training programs.
3. To evaluate the proportion of money spent on training development, administration, and evaluation, as well as to compare monies spent on training for different groups of employees (e.g., exempt versus nonexempt).
4. To control costs.[115]

Determining Costs. Training costs include direct and indirect costs.[116] Direct costs include salaries and benefits for all employees involved in training, including trainees, instructors, consultants, and employees who design the program; program material and supplies; equipment or classroom rentals or purchases; and travel costs. Indirect costs are not related directly to the design, development, or delivery of the training program. They include general office supplies, facilities, equipment, and related expenses; travel and expenses not directly billed to one program; training department management and staff salaries not related to any one program; and administrative and staff support salaries.

One method for comparing costs of alternative training programs is the resource requirements model.[119] This model compares equipment, facilities, personnel, and materials costs across different stages of the training process (training design, implementation, needs assessment, development, and evaluation). Use of the resource requirements model can help determine overall differences in costs between training programs. Also, costs incurred at different stages of the training process can be compared across programs.

Determining Benefits. To identify the potential benefits of training, the company must review the original reasons that the training was conducted. For example, training may have been conducted to reduce production costs or overtime costs or to increase the amount of repeat business. A number of methods may be helpful in identifying the benefits of training:

1. Technical, academic, and practitioner literature summarizes the benefits that have been shown to relate to a specific training program.
2. Pilot training programs assess the benefits on a small group of trainees before a company commits more resources.

TABLE 7.9
Training Program Costs

Direct costs	
Instructor	$ 0
In-house instructor (12 days @ $125 per day)	1,500
Fringe benefits (25% of salary)	375
Travel expenses	0
Materials ($60 × 56 trainees)	3,360
Classroom space and audiovisual equipment (12 days @ $50 per day)	600
Refreshments ($4 per day × 3 days × 56 trainees)	672
Total direct costs	$ 6,507
Indirect costs	
Training management	$ 0
Clerical and administrative salaries	750
Fringe benefits (25% of salary)	187
Postage, shipping, and telephone	0
Pre- and posttraining learning materials ($4 × 56 trainees)	224
Total indirect costs	$ 1,161
Development costs	
Fee for program purchase	$ 3,600
Instructor training	
Registration fee	1,400
Travel and lodging	975
Salary	625
Benefits (25% of salary)	156
Total development costs	$ 6,756
Overhead costs	
General organizational support, top management time (10% of direct, indirect, and development costs)	$ 1,443
Total overhead costs	$ 1,443
Compensation for trainees	
Trainees' salaries and benefits (based on time away from job)	$16,969
Total training costs	$32,836
Cost per trainee	$ 587

TABLE 7.10
Determination of Training Benefits

OPERATIONAL RESULTS AREA	HOW MEASURED	RESULTS BEFORE TRAINING	RESULTS AFTER TRAINING	DIFFERENCES (+ OR −)	EXPRESSED IN
Quality of panels	Percentage rejected	2 percent rejected—1,440 panels per day	1.5 percent rejected—1,080 panels per day	.5 percent—360 panels	$720 per day $172,800 per year
Housekeeping	Visual inspection using 20-item checklist	10 defects (average)	2 defects (average)	8 defects	Not measurable in $
Preventable accidents	Number of accidents	24 per year	16 per year	8 per year	$48,000 per year
	Direct cost of accidents	$144,000 per year	$96,000 per year	$48,000 per year	

$$\text{ROI} = \frac{\text{Return}}{\text{Investment}} = \frac{\text{Operational results}}{\text{Training costs}} = \frac{\$220{,}800}{\$32{,}836} = 6.7$$

Total savings: $220,800

SOURCE: Adapted from D.G. Robinson and J. Robinson, "Training for Impact," *Training & Development Journal* (August 1989), pp. 30–42.

3. Observance of successful job performers can help a company determine what successful job performers do differently from unsuccessful job performers.[118]

Making the Analysis. A cost–benefit analysis is best explained by an example.[119] A wood plant produced panels that contractors used as building materials. The plant employed 300 workers, 48 supervisors, seven shift superintendents, and a plant manager. The business had three problems. First, 2 percent of the wood panels produced each day were rejected because of poor quality. Second, the production area was experiencing poor housekeeping, such as improperly stacked finished panels that would fall on employees. Third, the number of preventable accidents was higher than the industry average. To correct these problems, supervisors were trained in performance management and interpersonal skills related to quality problems and poor work habits of employees and in rewarding employees for performance improvement. The supervisors, shift superintendents, and plant manager attended training. Training was conducted in a hotel close to the plant. The training program was purchased from a consultant and used videotape. Also, the instructor for the program was a consultant. Costs were determined as shown in Table 7.9.

Benefits of the training were identified by considering why training was conducted (quality of panels, housekeeping, accidents). Table 7.10 shows how benefits were determined.

It is important to recognize that more sophisticated methods are available for determining the dollar value of training. For example, **utility analysis** assesses the dollar value of training based on estimates of the difference in job performance between trained and untrained employees, the number of individuals trained, the length of time a training program is expected to influence performance, and a measure of the variability in job performance in the untrained group of employees.[120] These methods require the use of a pretest/posttest design with a comparison group. Other types of economic analysis evaluate training as it benefits the firm or the government using direct and indirect training costs, government incentives paid for training, wage increases received by trainees as a result of completion of training, tax rates, and discount rates.[121]

Legal Issues

Certain training situations can make an employer vulnerable to legal actions.[122]

EMPLOYEE INJURY DURING A TRAINING ACTIVITY. On-the-job training and simulations often involve the use of work tools and equipment (e.g., welder, printing press) that could cause injury if incorrectly used. Workers' compensation laws in many states make employers responsible for paying employees' their salary and/or providing them with a financial settlement for injuries received during any employment-related activity such as training. Managers should ensure that employees are warned of potential dangers from incorrectly using equipment and that safety equipment is used.

EMPLOYEES OR OTHERS INJURED OUTSIDE A TRAINING SESSION. Managers should ensure that trainees have the necessary level of competence in knowledge, skills, and behaviors before they are allowed to operate equipment or interact with customers. Even if a company pays for training to be conducted by a vendor, it is still liable for injuries or damages resulting from the actions of poorly, incorrectly, or incompletely trained employees.

BREACH OF CONFIDENTIALITY OR DEFAMATION. Managers should ensure that information placed in employees' files regarding performance in training activities is accurate. Also, before discussing an employee's performance in training with other employees or using training performance information for promotion or salary decisions, managers should tell employees that training performance will be used in that manner.

REPRODUCING AND USING COPYRIGHTED MATERIAL IN TRAINING CLASSES WITHOUT PERMISSION. **Copyrights** protect the expression of an idea (e.g., a training manual for a software program) but not the ideas that the material contains (e.g., the use of help windows in the software program). Copyrights also prohibit others from creating a product based on the original work and from copying, broadcasting, or publishing the product without permission.

The use of videotapes, learning aids, manuals, and other copyrighted materials in training classes without obtaining permission from the owner of the material is illegal. Managers should ensure that all training materials are purchased from the vendor or consultant who developed them or that permission to reproduce materials has been obtained. For example, Wilson Learning Corporation—a major developer and distributor of training-related products—holds the copyright to its sales training materials. To use the product, clients must pay Wilson Learning a fee and agree to attend a training seminar to familiarize them with the materials.

EXCLUDING WOMEN, MINORITIES, AND OLDER EMPLOYEES FROM TRAINING PROGRAMS. Women, minorities, and older employees can be illegally excluded from training programs by not being made aware of opportunities for training or purposeful exclusion from enrolling in training programs. Managers and trainers must ensure that stereotypes do not influence (1) decisions about who to send to training programs or (2) to whom training opportunities are communicated. For example, stereotypes such as "older workers are resistant to change" and "women are not aggressive enough for managerial positions" may result in excluding qualified women and older workers from training programs.

NOT ENSURING EQUAL TREATMENT OF ALL EMPLOYEES WHILE IN TRAINING. Equal treatment of all trainees means that conditions of the learning environment such as opportunities for practice, feedback, and role playing are available for all trainees regardless of their background. Also, trainers should avoid jokes, stories, and props that might create a hostile learning environment.

REQUIRING EMPLOYEES TO ATTEND PROGRAMS THAT MIGHT BE OFFENSIVE. Allstate Insurance has been the focus of several religious discrimination lawsuits by insurance agents who found Scientology principles emphasized in agent training programs to be offensive and counter to their religious beliefs (e.g., employees who met their sales goals were not to be questioned no matter how they behaved, but persons who failed to meet their sales goals deserved to be harassed and treated poorly).[123]

REVEALING DISCRIMINATORY INFORMATION DURING A TRAINING SESSION. At Lucky Store Foods, a California supermarket chain, notes taken by a trainer during a diversity training program were used as evidence of discrimination.[124] In the training session supervisors were asked to verbalize their stereotypes. Some comments ("women cry more," "black women are aggressive") were derogatory toward women and minorities. The plaintiff in the case used the trainers notes as evidence that the company conducted the training session to avoid an investigation by the Equal Employment Opportunity Commission. The case was settled out of court.

NOT ACCOMMODATING TRAINEES WITH DISABILITIES. As we discussed in Chapter 3, the **Americans with Disabilities Act (ADA)** of 1990 prohibits individuals with disabilities from being discriminated against in the workplace.

In the context of training, **reasonable accommodation** refers to making training facilities readily accessible to and usable by individuals with disabilities. Reasonable accommodation may also include modifying instructional media, adjusting training policies, and providing trainees with readers or interpreters. Employers are not required to make reasonable accommodation if the person does not request them. Employers are also not required to make reasonable accommodation if persons are not qualified to participate in training programs (e.g., they lack the prerequisite certification or educational requirements).

One example of how the ADA might influence training activities involves adventure learning. Adventure learning experiences demand a high level of physical fitness. Employees who have a disability can not be required to attend adventure learning training programs.[125] If it does not cause an undue hardship, employees should be offered an alternative program for developing the learned capabilities emphasized in the adventure learning program.

It is impossible to give specific guidelines regarding the type of accommodations that trainers and managers should make to avoid violating the ADA. It is important to identify if the training is related to "essential" job functions. That is, are the tasks or knowledge, skills, and abilities that are the focus of training fundamental to the position? To the extent that the disability makes it difficult for the person to receive training necessary to complete essential job functions, managers must explore whether it is possible to make reasonable accommodations.

Cross-Cultural Preparation

As we mentioned in Chapter 1, companies today are challenged to expand globally. Because of the increase in global operations, employees often work outside their country of origin or work with employees from other countries. An **expatriate** works in a country other than his country of origin. For example, Microsoft is headquartered in the United States but has facilities around the world. To be effective, expatriates in the Microsoft Mexico operations in Mexico City must understand the region's business and social culture. Because of a growing pool of talented labor around the world, greater use of host-country nationals is occurring.[129] A key reason is that a host-country national can more easily understand the values and customs of the work force than an expatriate can. Also, training and transporting U.S. employees and their families to a foreign assignment and housing them there tend to be more expensive than hiring a host-country national. We discuss international human resource management in detail in Chapter 15. Here the focus is on understanding how to prepare employees for expatriate assignments.

Cross-cultural preparation involves educating employees (expatriates) and their families who are to be sent to a foreign country. To successfully conduct business in the global marketplace, employees must understand the business practices and the cultural norms of different countries.

STEPS IN CROSS-CULTURAL PREPARATION

To prepare employees for cross-cultural assignments, companies need to provide cross-cultural training. Most U.S. companies send employees overseas without any preparation. As a result, the number of employees who return home before completing their assignments is higher for U.S. companies than for European and Japanese companies.[127] U.S. companies lose more than $2 billion a year as a result of failed overseas assignments.

To be successful in overseas assignments, expatriates (employees on foreign assignments) need to be

1. Competent in their area of expertise.
2. Able to communicate verbally and nonverbally in the host country.
3. Flexible, tolerant of ambiguity, and sensitive to cultural differences.
4. Motivated to succeed, able to enjoy the challenge of working in other countries, and willing to learn about the host country's culture, language, and customs.
5. Supported by their families.[128]

One reason for U.S. expatriates' high failure rate is that companies place more emphasis on developing employees' technical skills than on preparing them to work in other cultures. Research suggests that the comfort of an expatriate's spouse and family is the most important determinant of whether the employee will complete the assignment.[129]

The key to a successful foreign assignment appears to be a combination of training and career management for the employee and his family. Foreign assignments involve three phases: predeparture, on-site, and repatriation (preparing to return home). Training is necessary in all three phases.

PREDEPARTURE PHASE. In the predeparture phase, employees need to receive language training and an orientation in the new country's culture and customs. It is critical that the family be included in the orientation programs.[130] Expatriates and their families need information about housing, schools, recreation, shopping, and health care facilities in the area where they will live. An expatriate also must discuss with her manager how the foreign assignment fits into her career plans and what type of position she can expect upon return.

Cross-cultural training methods range from presentational techniques, such as lectures that expatriates and their families attend on the customs and culture of the host country, to actual experiences in the home country in culturally diverse communities.[131] Experiential exercises, such as miniculture experiences, allow expatriates to spend time with a family in the United States from the ethnic group of the host country.

Research suggests that the degree of difference between the United States and the host country (cultural novelty), the amount of interaction with host country citizens and host nationals (interaction), and the familiarity with new job tasks and work environment (job novelty) all influence the "rigor" of the cross-cultural training method used.[132] Hands-on and group building methods are most effective (and most needed) in assignments with a high level of cultural and job novelty that require a good deal of interpersonal interaction with host nationals.

ON-SITE PHASE. On-site training involves continued orientation to the host country and its customs and cultures through formal programs or through a mentoring relationship. Expatriates and their families may be paired with an employee from the host country who helps them understand the new, unfamiliar work environment and community.[133]

REPATRIATION PHASE. **Repatriation** prepares expatriates for return to the parent company and country from the foreign assignment. Expatriates and their families are likely to experience high levels of stress and anxiety when they return because of the changes that have occurred since their departure. This shock can be reduced by providing expatriates with company newsletters and community newspapers and by ensuring that they receive personal and work-related mail from the United States while they are on foreign assignment. It is also not uncommon for employees and their families to have to readjust to a lower standard of living in the United States than they had in the foreign country, where they may have enjoyed maid service, a limousine, private schools, and clubs. Salary and other compensation arrangements should be worked out well before employees return from overseas assignments.

Aside from reentry shock, many expatriates decide to leave the company because the assignment they are given upon returning to the United States has less responsibility, challenge, and status than the foreign assignment.[134] As noted earlier, career planning discussions need to be held before the employees leave the United States to ensure that they understand the positions they will be eligible for upon repatriation.

Monsanto has a successful repatriation program. Monsanto is an agricultural, chemical, and pharmaceutical company with 50 expatriates and 35 international employees working in the United States. Preparation for repatriation begins before the employee leaves the United States. Employees and both their sending and receiving manager develop an agreement about their understanding of the assignment and how it fits into the company's business objectives. Expectations regarding the assignment and how the knowledge gained will be used when the employee returns are specified. Monsanto's program involves having expatriates share their experiences with American peers, superiors, and subordinates. The program also provides repatriating employees with a way to work through personal difficulties. After their return, expatriates meet with several colleagues of their choice for a debriefing segment. The debriefing segment includes a trained counselor who discusses all the important aspects of the repatriation and helps the employee understand what he is experiencing. The debriefing not only helps the returning expatriate but also helps educate peers and colleagues to better understand different cultural issues and business environments.[135]

Managing Work Force Diversity

The goals of diversity training are (1) to eliminate values, stereotypes, and managerial practices that inhibit employees' personal development and (2) therefore to allow employees to contribute to organizational goals regardless of their race, sexual orientation, gender, family status, religious orientation, or cultural background.[136] Because of Equal Opportunity Employment laws, companies have been forced to ensure that women and minorities were adequately represented in their labor force. That is, companies were focused on ensuring equal access to jobs. **Managing diversity** involves creating an environment that allows all employees to contribute to organizational goals and experience personal growth. This includes access to jobs as well as fair and positive treatment of all employees. This requires the company to develop employees so that they are comfortable working with others from a wide variety of ethnic, racial, and religious backgrounds.

As Chapter 1 said, management of diversity has been linked to innovation, improved productivity, and lower employee turnover and other costs related to human resources.[137]

MANAGING DIVERSITY THROUGH ADHERENCE TO LEGISLATION

One approach to managing diversity is through affirmative action policies and by making sure that human resource practices meet standards of equal employment opportunity laws.[138] This approach rarely results in changes in employees' values, stereotypes, and behaviors that inhibit productivity and personal development. Figure 7.6 shows the cycle of disillusionment resulting from managing diversity by relying solely on adherence to employment laws. The cycle begins when the company realizes that it must change policies regarding women and minorities because of legal pressure or a discrepancy between the number or percentage of women and minorities in the company's work force and the number available in the broader labor market. To address these concerns, a greater number of women and minorities are hired by the company. Managers see little need for additional action because women and minority employment rates reflect their availability in the labor market. However, as women and minorities gain experience in the company, they may become frustrated. Managers and co-workers may avoid providing coaching or performance feedback to women and minorities because they are uncomfortable interacting with individuals from different gender, ethnic, or racial backgrounds. Co-workers may express beliefs that women and minorities are employed only because they received special treatment (e.g., hiring standards were lowered).[139] As a result of their frustration, women and minorities may form support groups to voice their concerns to management. Because of the work atmosphere, women and minorities may fail to fully utilize their skills and leave the company.

MANAGING DIVERSITY THROUGH DIVERSITY TRAINING PROGRAMS

The preceding discussion is not to suggest that companies should be reluctant to engage in affirmative action or pursue equal opportunity employment practices. However, affirmative action without additional supporting strategies does not deal with issues of assimilating women and minorities into the work force. To successfully manage a diverse work force, companies need to ensure that

- Employees understand how their values and stereotypes influence their behavior toward others of different gender, ethnic, racial, or religious backgrounds.

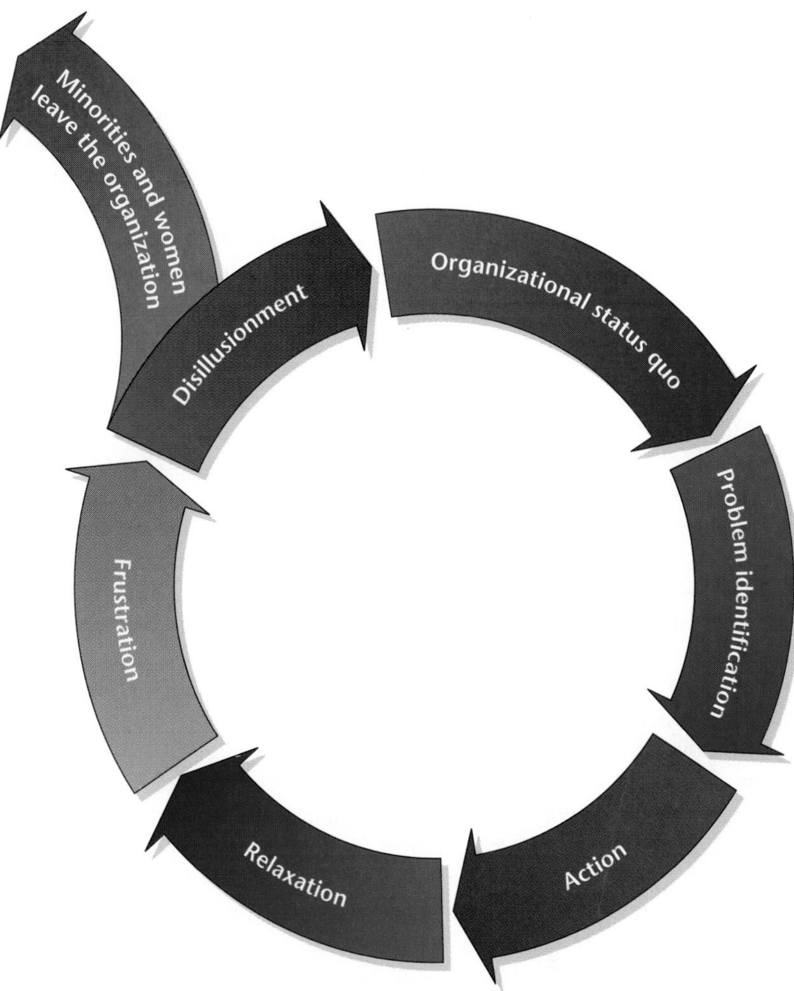

FIGURE 7.6 Cycle of Disillusionment Resulting from Managing Diversity through Adherence to Legislation

SOURCE: "Capitalizing on Global Diversity" by Cresencio Torres and Mary Bruxelles, *HR Magazine,* December 1992, pp. 30–33. Reprinted with the permission of *HR Magazine.* Published by the Society for Human Resource Management, Alexandria, VA.

- Employees gain an appreciation of cultural differences among themselves.
- Behaviors that isolate or intimidate minority group members improve.

This can be accomplished through diversity training programs. **Diversity training** refers to training designed to change employee attitudes about diversity and/or developing skills needed to work with a diverse work force. Diversity training programs differ according to whether attitude or behavior change is emphasized.[140]

ATTITUDE AWARENESS AND CHANGE PROGRAMS. Attitude awareness and change programs focus on increasing employees' awareness of differences in cultural and ethnic backgrounds, physical characteristics (e.g., disabilities), and personal characteristics that influence behavior toward others. The assumption underlying these programs is that, by increasing their awareness of stereotypes and beliefs, employees will be able to avoid negative stereotypes when interacting with employees of different backgrounds. The programs help employees consider the similarities and differences between cultural groups, examine their attitudes toward affirmative action, or analyze their beliefs about why minority employees are successful or unsuccessful in their jobs. Many of these programs use videotapes and experiential exercises to increase employees' awareness of the negative emotional and performance effects of stereotypes, values, and behaviors on minority group members. For example, 3M conducts workshops in which managers are asked to assess their attitudes toward stereotypical statements about race, age, and gender.[141] The participants select two stereotypes they hold and consider how these stereotypes affect their ability to manage. One of the most popular video training packages, Copeland Griggs Productions' "Valuing Diversity Training Program," involves three days of training that focus on managing differences, diversity in the workplace, and cross-cultural communications.

The attitude awareness and change approach has been criticized for several reasons.[142] First, by focusing on group differences, the program may communicate that certain stereotypes and attitudes are valid. For example, in diversity training a male manager may learn that women employees prefer to work by building consensus rather than by arguing until others agree with their point. He might conclude that the training has validated his stereotype. As a result, he will continue to fail to give women important job responsibilities that involve heated negotiations with customers or clients. Second, encouraging employees to share their attitudes, feelings, and stereotypes toward certain groups may cause employees to feel guilty, angry, and less likely to see the similarities among racial, ethnic, or gender groups and the advantages of working together.

BEHAVIOR-BASED PROGRAMS. **Behavior-based programs** focus on changing the organizational policies and individual behaviors that inhibit employees' personal growth and productivity.

One approach of these programs is to identify incidents that discourage employees from working up to their potential. Groups of employees are asked to identify specific promotion opportunities, sponsorship, training opportunities, or performance management practices that they believe were handled unfairly. Their views regarding how well the work environment and management practices value employee differences and provide equal opportunity may also be collected. Specific training programs may be developed to address the issues presented in the focus groups.

Another approach is to teach managers and employees basic rules of behavior in the workplace.[143] For example, managers and employees should learn that it is inappropriate to use statements and engage in behaviors that have negative racial, sexual, or cultural content. Companies that have focused on teaching rules and behavior have found that employees react less negatively to this type of training than to other diversity training approaches.

CHARACTERISTICS OF SUCCESSFUL DIVERSITY EFFORTS

Is a behavior-based or an attitude awareness and change program most effective? Increasing evidence shows that attitude awareness programs are ineffective and that one-time diversity training programs are unlikely to succeed. For example, R. R. Donnelley & Sons suspended its diversity awareness training program even though the company has spent more than $3 million on it as a result of a racial discrimination lawsuit.[144]

At various training sessions participants were encouraged to voice their concerns. Many said that they were experiencing difficulty in working effectively due to abuse and harassment. The managers attending the training disputed the concerns. Also, after training, an employee who applied for an open position was rejected, because, she was told she had been too honest in expressing her concerns during the diversity training session. Although R. R. Donnelley held many diversity training sessions, little progress was made in increasing the employment and promotion rates of women and minorities. Because of the low ratio of black employees to white employees, many black employees were asked to attend multiple training sessions to ensure diverse groups, which they resented. The company declined to release data requested by shareholders that it provided to the Equal Employment Opportunity Commission regarding female and minority representation in jobs throughout the company. The firm also failed to act on recommendations made by company-approved employee "diversity councils."

More generally, a survey of diversity training efforts found that

- The most common area addressed through diversity is the pervasiveness of stereotypes, assumptions, and biases.
- Fewer than one-third of the companies do any kind of long-term evaluation or follow-up. The most common indicators of success were reduced grievances and lawsuits, increased diversity in promotions and hiring, increased self-awareness of biases, and increased consultation of HR specialists on diversity-related issues.
- Most programs lasted only one day or less.
- Three-fourths of the survey respondents indicated that they believed the typical employee leaves diversity training with positive attitudes toward diversity. However, over 50 percent reported that the programs have no effect over the long term.

Table 7.11 shows the characteristics associated with the long-term success of diversity programs. It is critical that the diversity program be tied to business objectives. For example, cultural differences affect the type of skin cream consumers believe they need or the fragrance they may be attracted to. Understanding cultural differences is part of understanding the consumer (which is critical to the success of companies such as Avon). Top management support can be demonstrated by creating a structure to support the initiative.

Gannett is a $4 billion information and communication company that publishes *USA Today* plus daily and weekly newspapers in cities and communities throughout the United States and owns many radio and TV stations. Its diversity program incorporates numerous characteristics shown in Table 7.11. The commitment to diversity starts at the top of the company. The company's operating principles include guaranteeing respect for and fairness in dealing with employees and creating a work environment where opportunity is based on merit. The company's top executives report to the board of directors each year on progress in diversity and the report is shared with the rest of

TABLE 7.11 Characteristics Associated with Diversity Programs' Long-Term Success

- Top management provides resources, personally intervenes, and publicly advocates diversity.
- The program is structured.
- Capitalizing on a diverse work force is defined as a business objective.
- Capitalizing on a diverse work force is seen as necessary to generate revenue and profits.
- The program is evaluated.
- Manager involvement is mandatory.
- The program is seen as a culture change, not a one-shot program.
- Managers and demographic groups are not blamed for problems.
- Behaviors and skills needed to successfully interact with others are taught.
- Managers are rewarded on progress toward meeting diversity goals.

SOURCE: S. Rynes and B. Rosen, "What Makes Diversity Programs Work?" *HR Magazine* (October 1994), pp. 67–73; S. Rynes and B. Rosen, "A Field Survey of Factors Affecting the Adoption and Perceived Success of Diversity Training," *Personnel Psychology* 48 (1995), pp. 247–70; J. Gordon, "Different from What? Diversity as a Performance Issue," *Training* (May 1995), pp. 25–33.

the company. Gannett measures diversity efforts through a survey that measures the work climate for women and minority employees. Managers provide employees with the survey results and then work with them to address issues raised in the survey. Gannett offers many workshops addressing behavior change and awareness of attitudes. For example, a case approach is used in a program called "It Takes All Kinds." In this program, trainees discuss how they would handle situations such as a woman who wants to work at home or a minority group member who wants a position he is not qualified for. Gannett also extensively communicates regarding diversity efforts. Weekly and monthly articles about diversity efforts and successes are published in the company newspaper, newsletter, and employees magazine.

Gannett's diversity program has resulted in more women and minorities moving into the managerial level—23 percent of managers are women, 9 percent are minorities. Gannett has received numerous awards for its diversity efforts (e.g., the Catalyst award for corporations with distinguished records in the employment and advancement of women).[146]

Another important characteristic of diversity programs is that managers are rewarded for progress toward meeting diversity goals. Allstate Insurance Company surveys all 50,000 of its employees four times a year. The survey asks employees to evaluate how well the company is satisfying customers and employees. Several questions are used as a "diversity index." Employees are asked questions about the extent to which manager's racial or gender biases affect development opportunities, promotions, and service to customers. Twenty-five percent of a manager's yearly bonus is determined by how employees evaluate her on the diversity index.[147]

As you can see from this discussion, successful diversity programs involve more than just an effective training program. Top management support, diversity policies and practices, training and development, and administrative structures, such as conducting diversity surveys and evaluating managers' progress on diversity goals, are needed.[148]

Joint Union–Management Programs

To be more competitive, U.S. industries that have lost considerable market share to foreign competition (e.g., the auto industry) have developed joint union–management training. Both labor and management have been forced to accept new roles. Employees need to become involved in business planning and strategic decision making, and management needs to learn how to share power and allow worker participation in decision making.

The initial goal of these programs was to help displaced employees find new jobs by providing skill training and outplacement assistance. Currently, **joint union–management training programs** provide a wide range of services designed to help employees learn skills that are directly related to their job and also develop skills that are "portable"—that is, valuable to employers in other companies or industries.[149] Both employers and unions contribute money to run the programs and both oversee their operation. Major joint efforts involve the United Auto Workers with Ford and General Motors, the Communication Workers of America with U S WEST, and the United Steel Workers with 12 major steel companies.

The United Auto Workers–Ford Education Development and Training Program includes

- A Life/Education Planning Program that helps employees determine their career needs and interests and links them with resources in the community.
- An Education and Training Assistance Plan that assists employees in identifying appropriate courses at colleges and universities and provides tuition reimbursement.

- A Skills Enhancement Program providing counseling and assistance related to adult basic education, high school completion, general education development, and English as a second language.
- A College and University Options Program that makes both degree and nondegree college and technical training more accessible for employees. It provides workshops for employees, on-site course registration, classes at times that are convenient to employees, and credits for college-level knowledge.
- Targeted education, training, or counseling projects related to the specific educational or counseling needs of a specific location or segment of the work force.
- A Successful Retirement Planning Program offering preretirement planning to employees and their spouses.
- A Financial Education Program covering topics such as personal financial planning, investment, and insurance as well as wills and trusts.[150]

Yes, these programs are costly (General Motors has spent $1.6 billion jointly with the UAW since 1984) and employees may get trained in skills that are not directly related to their current jobs. But both labor and management believe that these programs improve the literacy levels of the work force and contribute to productivity. Both parties believe that encouraging lifelong learning is a key aspect of the work force being able to adapt to new technologies and global competition.

Socialization and Orientation

Organizational socialization is the process by which new employees are transformed into effective members of the company. As Table 7.12 shows, effective socialization involves being prepared to perform the job effectively, learning about the organization, and establishing work relationships. Socialization involves three phases: anticipatory socialization, encounter, and settling in.[151]

ANTICIPATORY SOCIALIZATION. Anticipatory socialization occurs before the individual joins the company. Through **anticipatory socialization,** expectations about the company, job, working conditions, and interpersonal relationships are developed. These expectations are developed through interactions with representatives of the company (e.g., recruiters, prospective peers, and managers) during the recruitment and selection process. The expectations are also based on prior work experiences in similar jobs.

Potential employees need to be provided with realistic job information. A **realistic**

TABLE 7.12 What Employees Should Learn and Develop through the Socialization Process

History	The company's traditions, customs, and myths; background of members
Company goals	Rules, values, or principles directing the company
Language	Slang and jargon unique to the company; professional technical language
Politics	How to gain information regarding the formal and informal work relationships and power structures in the company
People	Successful and satisfying work relationships with other employees
Performance proficiency	What needs to be learned; effectiveness in using and acquiring the knowledge, skills, and abilities needed for the job.

SOURCE: Based on G.T. Chao, A.M. O'Leary-Kelly, S. Wolf, H. Klein, and P.D. Gardner, "Organizational Socialization: Its Content and Consequences," *Journal of Applied Psychology* 79 (1994), pp. 730–43.

job preview provides accurate information about the attractive and unattractive aspects of the job, working conditions, company, and location to ensure that employees develop appropriate expectations. This information needs to be provided early in the recruiting and selection process. It is usually given in brochures, in videos, or by the company recruiter during an interview. Although research specifically investigating the influence of realistic job previews on employee turnover is weak and inconsistent, we do know that unmet expectations resulting from the recruitment and selection process have been shown to relate to dissatisfaction and turnover.[152] As we will see, employees' expectations about a job and a company may be formed by interactions with managers, peers, and recruiters rather than from specific messages about the job.

ENCOUNTER. The **encounter phase** occurs when the employee begins a new job. No matter how realistic the information they were provided during interviews and site visits, individuals beginning new jobs will experience shock and surprise.[153] Employees need to become familiar with job tasks, receive appropriate training, and understand company practices and procedures.

Challenging work plus cooperative and helpful managers and peers have been shown to enhance employees' learning a new job.[154] New employees view managers as an important source of information about their job and the company. Research evidence suggests that the nature and quality of the new employee's relationship with the manager has a significant impact on socialization.[155] In fact, the negative effects of unmet expectations can be reduced by the new employee having a high-quality relationship with her manager! Managers can help create a high-quality work relationship by helping the new employee understand her role, providing information about the company, and being understanding regarding the stresses and issues that the new employee is experiencing.

TABLE 7.13
Content of Orientation Programs

I. Company-level information
- Company overview (e.g., values, history, mission)
- Key policies and procedures
- Compensation
- Employee benefits and services
- Safety and accident prevention
- Employee and union relations
- Physical facilities
- Economic factors
- Customer relations

II. Department-level information
- Department functions and philosophy
- Job duties and responsibilities
- Policies, procedures, rules, and regulations
- Performance expectations
- Tour of department
- Introduction to department employees

III. Miscellaneous
- Community
- Housing
- Family adjustment

SOURCE: J.L. Schwarz and M.A. Weslowski, "Employee Orientation: What Employers Should Know," *The Journal of Contemporary Business Issues* (Fall 1995), p. 48. Used with permission.

SETTLING IN. In the settling-in phase, employees begin to feel comfortable with their job demands and social relationships. They begin to work on resolving work conflicts (e.g., too much work to do, conflicting demands of the job) and conflicts between work and nonwork activities. Employees are interested in the company's evaluation of their performance and in learning about potential career opportunities within the company.

Employees need to complete all three phases of the socialization process to fully contribute to the company. For example, employees who do not feel that they have established good working relationships with co-workers will likely spend time and energy worrying about relationships with other employees rather than being concerned with product development or customer service. Employees who experience successful socialization are more motivated, more committed to the company, and more satisfied with their jobs.[156]

Orientation programs play an important role in socializing employees. Orientation involves familiarizing new employees with company rules, policies, and procedures. Table 7.13 shows the content of orientation programs. Typically, a program includes information about the company, department in which the employee will be working, and community.

While the content of orientation programs is important, the process of orientation cannot be ignored. Too often, orientation programs consist of completing payroll forms and reviewing personnel policies with managers or human resource representatives. The new employee is a passive recipient of information. New employees have little opportunity to ask questions or interact with peers and their managers.

Effective orientation programs include active involvement of the new employee. Table 7.14 shows the characteristics of effective orientation programs. An important characteristic of effective orientation programs is that peers, managers, and senior co-workers are actively involved in helping new employees adjust to the work group.[157]

Before being assigned to their plant locations, new engineers at Pillsbury, for example, have a one-year headquarters assignment.[158] They are provided with a mentor (a senior engineer), who helps them understand the technical engineering resources available within the company. The mentor also helps them become familiar with the community and deal with relocation issues. New engineers attend seminars in which engineers from different divisions (e.g., frozen foods) explain the role of engineering. New employees also have the opportunity to meet key players in engineering management at Pillsbury.

Similarly, new employees and their managers are actively involved in the new orientation program at Corning Glass.[159] Corning Glass was experiencing turnover among its high-potential new employees. Employees were leaving the company because they felt the company had a sink-or-swim attitude toward new hires. As a result, Corning designed a new orientation process including

TABLE 7.14 Characteristics of Effective Orientation Programs

Employees are encouraged to ask questions.
Program includes information on both technical and social aspects of the job.
Orientation is the responsibility of the new employee's manager.
Debasing and embarrassing new employees are avoided.
Formal and informal interactions with managers and peers occur.
Programs involve relocation assistance (e.g., house hunting, information session on the community for employees and their spouses).
Employees are provided the information about the company's products, services, and customers.

- *Manager preparation*. Hiring managers are given guidelines and checklists that specify the steps they should take before and after the arrival of new employees.
- *Guided self-learning*. Managers are encouraged to spend the first two weeks orienting new employees to the job and the company rather than focusing on their regular job duties. Each new employee is provided with a workbook that requires him to learn about the company's customers, suppliers, objectives, and culture. It is up to the employee to decide how to complete the workbook questions (e.g., interviews, visits to the company resource center). The manager and employee jointly review the answers to the workbook questions. If the employee needs more information, the learning period is extended.
- *Organization acculturation*. During their first three months, employees attend seminars on Corning's philosophy, culture, and values.

Retention data suggest that the orientation program is a success. It has resulted in a 25 to 35 percent increase in retention of new employees in comparison with employees who did not take the new program.

Training and Pay Systems

Training is increasingly being linked to employees' compensation through the use of skill-based pay systems. (We discuss characteristics of skill-based pay systems in detail in Chapter 11, "Pay Structure Decisions.") In skill-based pay systems, employees' pay is based primarily on the knowledge and skills they possess rather than the knowledge and skills necessary to successfully perform their current job.

Skill-based pay systems have several implications for training systems. Since pay is directly tied to the amount of knowledge and skill employees have obtained, employees will be motivated to attend training programs. This means that the volume of training conducted, as well as training costs, will increase. Skill-based pay systems require continual evaluation of employees' skills and knowledge to ensure that employees are competent in the skills acquired in training programs.

SUMMARY

Technological innovations, new product markets, and a diverse work force have increased the need for companies to reexamine how their training practices contribute to learning. In this chapter we discussed a systematic approach to training, including needs assessment, design of the learning environment, consideration of employee readiness for training, and transfer-of-training issues. We reviewed numerous training methods and stressed that the key to successful training was to choose a method that would best accomplish the objectives of training. We also emphasized how training can contribute to effectiveness through establishing a link with the company's strategic direction and demonstrating through cost–benefit analysis how training contributes to profitability. Managing diversity and cross-cultural preparation are two training issues that are relevant given company needs to capitalize on a diverse work force and global markets.

DISCUSSION QUESTIONS

1. Noetron, a retail electronics store, recently invested a large amount of money to train sales staff to improve customer service. The skills emphasized in the program include how to greet customers, determine their needs, and demonstrate product conveniences. The company wants to know whether the program is effective. What outcomes should it collect? What type of evaluation design should it use?
2. "Melinda," bellowed Toran, "I've got a problem and you've got to solve it. I can't get people in this plant to work together as a team. As if I don't have enough trouble with the competition and delinquent accounts, now I have to put up with running a zoo. It's your responsibility to see that the staff gets along with each other. I want a human relations training proposal on my desk by Monday." How would you determine the need for human rela-

tions training? How would you determine whether you actually had a training problem? What else could be responsible?

3. Assume you are general manager of a small seafood company. Most training is unstructured and occurs on the job. Currently, more-senior fish cleaners are responsible for teaching new employees how to perform the job. Your company has been profitable, but recently wholesale fish dealers that buy your product have been complaining about the poor quality of your fresh fish. For example, some fillets have not had all the scales removed and abdomen parts remain attached to the fillets. You have decided to change the on-the-job training received by the fish cleaners. How will you modify the on-the-job training to improve the quality of the product delivered to the wholesalers?
4. A training needs analysis indicates that managers' productivity is inhibited because they are reluctant to delegate tasks to their subordinates. Suppose you had to decide between using adventure learning and interactive video for your training program. What are the strengths and weaknesses of each technique? Which would you choose? Why? What factors would influence your decision?
5. To improve product quality, a company is introducing a computer-assisted manufacturing process into one of its assembly plants. The new technology is likely to result in substantial modification of jobs. Employees will also be required to learn statistical process-control techniques. The new technology and push for quality will require employees to attend numerous training sessions. Over 50 percent of the employees who will be affected by the new technology completed their formal education over 10 years ago. Only about 5 percent of the company's employees have used the tuition reimbursement benefit. How should management maximize employees' readiness for training?
6. A training course was offered for maintenance employees in which trainees were supposed to learn how to repair and operate a new, complex electronics system. On the job, maintenance employees were typically told about a symptom experienced by the machine operator and were asked to locate the trouble. During training, the trainer would pose various problems for the maintenance employees to solve. He would point out a component on an electrical diagram and ask, "What would happen if this component was faulty?" Trainees would then trace the circuitry on a blueprint to uncover the symptoms that would appear as a result of the problem. You are receiving complaints about poor troubleshooting from maintenance foremen who supervise employees who have completed the program. The trainees are highly motivated and have the necessary prerequisites. What is the problem with the training course? What recommendations do you have for fixing this course?
7. What factors contribute to the effectiveness of Web training programs?

WEB EXERCISE

The Interactive Patient is a realistic interactive computer simulation of a patient's visit to a physician's office. The Interactive Patient is a Web-based training program used to train medical students at Marshall University and provide continuous education credits to practicing physicians.

Visit and review the Interactive Patient at http://nt.media.hku.hk/interactivepatient/medicus.htm.

Evaluate the program according to the conditions necessary for learning to occur.

a. What are the program's strengths and weaknesses?
b. How would you improve the program?

MANAGING PEOPLE: FROM THE PAGES OF "BUSINESS WEEK"

BusinessWeek Get Serious About Diversity Training

During the past decade, Corporate America has spent hundreds of millions of dollars trying to effect racial harmony. Why? In part, the legacy of the civil rights movement demanded such an effort. More than that, though, changing demographics made such an effort urgent. The Hudson Institute's 1987 Workforce 2000 report made that stunningly clear. Its conclusion: Minorities would make up more than half of net new entrants into the labor force by 2000.

That statistic got chief executives' attention. Ever since, Big Business has diligently sought to root out the racial biases, stereotypes, and discriminatory practices that might hurt performance or bring on costly civil rights litigation. In the process, a cottage industry of sorts known as diversity training has mushroomed.

Unfortunately, recent allegations of discriminatory behavior at Texaco Inc. confirm that the movement hasn't exactly spurred a new age of social enlightenment. Rather, senior executives' patronizing and disdainful taped references to black employees (using terminology they most likely learned during diversity courses) reflect the deep racial divide and distrust that linger in many companies across a broad range of industries.

Texaco has apologized. In the face of disastrous publicity and the threat of a government probe, Chairman and CEO Peter I. Bijur's words of atonement have sounded sincere. And the company has created a special board committee on diversity.

If history is any guide, though, those bromides won't do much good. Texaco, after all, has had a diversity training program for at least three years. Judging by the host of discrimination suits from employees in that time, the effort hasn't reduced racial tension. No surprise, says Taylor Cox Jr., an associate professor at the University of Michigan business school: "Most of the organizations that have invested in diversity training have not received a proper return on their investment."

Theoretically, making diversity initiatives work shouldn't be that difficult. During the past decade, corporations have shown a remarkable capacity to reinvent their work culture with total quality management, reengineering, and teamwork. In each program, companies have modified employee behavior—often overcoming strong resistance.

Solving race matters, of course, is trickier because it necessarily focuses attention on a specific group of employees. That creates the potential for resentment and greater division. Moreover, the capacity of employers to change the way people think and feel is limited at best. "It's hard to get inside peoples' heads and manage their attitudes," admits Patsy A. Randell, vice-president for corporate diversity at Honeywell Inc.

QUESTIONS

1. Why do diversity training programs fail?
2. Assume you are in charge of developing a diversity training program. Discuss the process you would use for developing the program. What activities would the program include?
3. How might you evaluate your program to determine if it is effective? Make sure you identify the outcomes you would collect and the evaluation design you recommend.

SOURCE: Ron Stodghill II, "Commentary: Get Serious about Diversity Training," *Business Week* (November 25, 1996).

NOTES

1. "Industry Report," *Training* (October 1997), pp. 33–76.
2. A.P. Carnevale, "Enhancing Skills in the New Economy," in *The Changing Nature of Work*, ed. A. Howard (San Francisco: Jossey–Bass, 1995), pp. 238–51; M. McCain, "Apprenticeship Lessons from Europe," *Training and Development* (November 1994), pp. 38–41; "Best-in-the-World Practices," *Training and Development* (June 1994), pp. 52–57.
3. *Chicago Tribune*, June 14, 1992, sec. 1, p. 18.
4. K. Kelly, "Motorola: Training for the Millennium," *Business Week*, March 28, 1994, pp. 158–62.
5. I.I. Goldstein and P. Gilliam, "Training Systems Issues in the Year 2000," *American Psychologist* 45 (1990), pp. 134–43.
6. J.B. Quinn, P. Anderson, and S. Finkelstein, "Leveraging Intellect," *Academy of Management Executive* 10 (1996), pp. 7–27.
7. T.T. Baldwin, C. Danielson, and W. Wiggenhorn, "The Evolution of Learning Strategies in Organizations: From Employee Development to Business Redefinition," *Academy of Management Executive* 11, pp. 47–58; J. J. Martocchio and T.T. Baldwin, "The Evolution of Strategic Organizational Training," in *Research in Personnel and Human Resource Management* 15, ed. G.R. Ferris (Greenwich, CT: JAI Press, 1997), pp. 1–46.
8. A.P. Carnevale, "America and the New Economy," *Training and Development Journal* (November 1990), pp. 31–52.
9. J.M. Rosow and R. Zager, *Training the Competitive Edge* (San Francisco: Jossey-Bass, 1988).
10. L. Thornburg, "Accounting for Knowledge," *HR Magazine* (October 1994), pp. 51–56; T.A. Stewart, "Mapping Corporate Brainpower," *Fortune* (October 30, 1995), p. 209.
11. D. Senge, "The Learning Organization Made Plain and Simple," *Training and Development Journal* (October 1991), pp. 37–44.
12. M.A. Gephart, V.J. Marsick, M.E. Van Buren, and M.S. Spiro, "Learning Organizations Come Alive," *Training and Development* 50 (1996), pp. 35–45; C.M. Solomon, "HR Facilitates the Learning Organization Concept," *Personnel Journal* (November 1994), pp. 56–66; T.A. Stewart, "Getting Real about Brainpower," *Fortune* (November 27, 1995), pp. 201–3; L. Thornburg, "Accounting for Knowledge," *HR Magazine* (October 1994), pp. 51–56.
13. Gephart, Marsick, Van Buren, and Spiro, "Learning Organizations Come Alive."
14. J.B. Quinn, P. Anderson, and S. Finkelstein, "Leveraging Intellect," *Academy of Management Executive* 10 (1996), pp. 7–27.
15. T. Gilbert, "Creating a Learning Newspaper," in *The Fifth Discipline Fieldbook*, ed. P.M. Senge, C. Roberts, R.B. Ross, B.J. Smith, and A. Kleiner (New York: Currency–Doubleday, 1994), pp. 474–78.
16. R. Noe, *Employee Training and Development* (Burr Ridge, IL: Irwin/McGraw–Hill, 1999).
17. I.L. Goldstein, E.P. Braverman, and H. Goldstein, "Needs Assessment," in *Developing Human Resources*, ed. K.N. Wexley (Washington, DC: Bureau of National Affairs, 1991), pp. 5–35 to 5–75.
18. J.Z. Rouillier and I.L. Goldstein, "Determinants of the

Climate for Transfer of Training" (presented at Society of Industrial/Organizational Psychology meetings, St. Louis, MO, 1991); J.S. Russell, J.R. Terborg, and M.L. Powers, "Organizational Performance and Organizational Level Training and Support," *Personnel Psychology* 38 (1985), pp. 849–63; H. Baumgartel, G.J. Sullivan, and L.E. Dunn, "How Organizational Climate and Personality Affect the Pay-off from Advanced Management Training Sessions," *Kansas Business Review* 5 (1978), pp. 1–10.

19. A.P. Carnevale, L.J. Gainer, and J. Villet, *Training in America* (San Francisco: Jossey-Bass, 1990); L.J. Gainer, "Making the Competitive Connection: Strategic Management and Training," *Training and Development* (September 1989), pp. s1–s30.
20. S. Raghuram and R.D. Arvey, "Business Strategy Links with Staffing and Training Practices," *Human Resource Planning* 17 (1994), pp. 55–73.
21. Carnevale, Gainer, and Villet, *Training in America*.
22. P.A. Smith, "Reinventing SunU," *Training and Development* (July 1994), pp. 23–27.
23. B. Gerber, "How to Buy Training Programs," *Training* (June 1989), pp. 59–68.
24. D.A. Blackmon, "Consultants' Advice on Diversity Was Anything but Diverse," *The Wall Street Journal* (March 11, 1997), pp. A1, A16.
25. R. Zemke and J. Armstrong, "How Long Does It Take? (The Sequel)," *Training* (May 1997), pp. 69–79.
26. G. Rummler, "In Search of the Holy Performance Grail," *Training and Development* (April 1996), pp. 26–31; D.G. Langdon, "Selecting Interventions," *Performance Improvement* 36 (1997), pp. 11–15.
27. R.F. Mager and P. Pipe, *Analyzing Performance Problems: Or You Really Oughta Wanna*, 2d ed. (Belmont, CA: Pittman Learning, 1984); A.P. Carnevale, L.J. Gainer, and A.S. Meltzer, *Workplace Basics Training Manual*, 1990 (San Francisco: Jossey-Bass, 1990); G. Rummler, "In Search of the Holy Performance Grail."
28. C.E. Schneier, J.P. Guthrie, and J.D. Olian, "A Practical Approach to Conducting and Using Training Needs Assessment," *Public Personnel Management* (Summer 1988), pp. 191–205.
29. I. Goldstein, "Training in Organizations," in *Handbook of Industrial/Organizational Psychology*, 2d ed., ed. M.D. Dunnette and L.M. Hough (Palo Alto, CA: Consulting Psychologists Press, 1991), vol. 2, pp. 507–619.
30. E.F. Holton III and C. Bailey, "Top-to-Bottom Curriculum Redesign," *Training and Development* (March 1995), pp. 40–44.
31. R.A. Noe, "Trainees' Attributes and Attitudes: Neglected Influences on Training Effectiveness," *Academy of Management Review* 11 (1986), pp. 736–49.
32. T.T. Baldwin, R.T. Magjuka, and B.T. Loher, "The Perils of Participation: Effects of Choice on Trainee Motivation and Learning," *Personnel Psychology* 44 (1991), pp. 51–66; S.I. Tannenbaum, J.E. Mathieu, E. Salas, and J.A. Cannon-Bowers, "Meeting Trainees' Expectations: The Influence of Training Fulfillment on the Development of Commitment, Self-Efficacy, and Motivation," *Journal of Applied Psychology* 76 (1991), pp. 759–69.
33. M.E. Gist, C. Schwoerer and B. Rosen, "Effects of Alternative Training Methods on Self-Efficacy and Performance in Computer Software Training," *Journal of Applied Psychology* 74 (1989), pp. 884–91; J. Martocchio and J. Dulebohn, "Performance Feedback Effects in Training: The Role of Perceived Controllability," *Personnel Psychology* 47 (1994), pp. 357–73; J. Martocchio, "Ability Conceptions and Learning," *Journal of Applied Psychology* 79 (1994), pp. 819–25.
34. W.D. Hicks and R.J. Klimoski, "Entry into Training Programs and Its Effects on Training Outcomes: A Field Experiment," *Academy of Management Journal* 30 (1987), pp. 542–52.
35. R.A. Noe and N. Schmitt, "The Influence of Trainee Attitudes on Training Effectiveness: Test of a Model," *Personnel Psychology* 39 (1986), pp. 497–523.
36. M.A. Quinones, "Pretraining Context Effects: Training Assignments as Feedback," *Journal of Applied Psychology* 80 (1995), pp. 226–38; Baldwin, Magjuka, and Loher, "The Perils of Participation.
37. L.H. Peters, E.J. O'Connor, and J.R. Eulberg, "Situational Constraints: Sources, Consequences, and Future Considerations," in *Research in Personnel and Human Resource Management*, ed. K.M. Rowland and G.R. Ferris (Greenwich, CT: JAI Press, 1985), vol 3, pp. 79–114; E.J. O'Connor, L.H. Peters, A. Pooyan, J. Weekley, B. Frank, and B. Erenkranz, "Situational Constraints Effects on Performance, Affective Reactions, and Turnover: A Field Replication and Extension," *Journal of Applied Psychology* 69 (1984), pp. 663–72; D.J. Cohen, "What Motivates Trainees?" *Training and Development Journal* (November 1990), pp. 91–93; Russell, Terborg, and Powers, "Organizational Performance."
38. A. P. Carnevale, "America and the New Economy," *Training and Development Journal* (November 1990), pp. 31–52.
39. J. Nunally, *Psychometric Theory* (New York: McGraw–Hill, 1978).
40. L. Gottsfredson, "The g Factor in Employment," *Journal of Vocational Behavior* 19 (1986), pp. 293–96.
41. M.J. Ree and J.A. Earles, "Predicting Training Success: Not Much More than g," *Personnel Psychology* 44 (1991), pp. 321–32.
42. D.R. Torrence and J.A. Torrence, "Training in the Face of Illiteracy," *Training and Development Journal* (August 1987), pp. 44–49.
43. M. Davis, "Getting Workers Back to the Basics," *Training and Development* (October 1997), pp. 14–15.
44. C.E. Schneier, "Training and Development Programs: What Learning Theory and Research Have to Offer,"

Personnel Journal (April 1974), pp. 288–93; M. Knowles, "Adult Learning," in *Training and Development Handbook*, 3d ed., ed. R.L. Craig (New York: McGraw-Hill, 1987), pp. 168–79; R. Zemke and S. Zemke, "30 Things We Know for Sure about Adult Learning," *Training* (June 1981), pp. 45–52; B.J. Smith and B.L. Delahaye, *How to Be an Effective Trainer*, 2d ed. (New York: Wiley, 1987).

45. B. Mager, *Preparing Instructional Objectives*, 2d ed. (Belmont, CA: Lake Publishing, 1984); B.J. Smith and B.L. Delahaye, *How to Be an Effective Trainer*, 2d ed. (New York: John Wiley and Sons, 1987).
46. K.A. Smith-Jentsch, F.G. Jentsch, S.C. Payne, and E. Salas, "Can Pre-training Experiences Explain Individual Differences in Learning?" *Journal of Applied Psychology* 81 (1996), pp. 110–16.
47. J.K. Ford, D.A. Weissbein, S.M. Guly, and E. Salas, "Relationship of Goal Orientation, Metacognitive Activity and Practice Strategies with Learning Outcomes and Transfer" *Journal of Applied Psychology*, 83 (1998), pp. 218–33.
48. J.C. Naylor and G.D. Briggs, "The Effects of Task Complexity and Task Organization on the Relative Efficiency of Part and Whole Training Methods," *Journal of Experimental Psychology* 65 (1963), pp. 217–24.
49. W. McGehee and P.W. Thayer, *Training in Business and Industry* (New York: Wiley, 1961).
50. R.M. Mager, *Making Instruction Work* (Belmont, CA: David Lake, 1988).
51. R.M. Gagne and K.L. Medsker, *The Condition of Learning* (Fort Worth, TX: Harcourt–Brace, 1996).
52. P.J. Decker and B.R. Nathan, *Behavior Modeling Training: Principles and Applications* (New York: Praeger, 1985).
53. D. Stamps, "Communities of Practice," *Training* (February 1997), pp. 35–42.
54. Smith and Delahaye, *How to Be an Effective Trainer;* M. Van Wart, N.J. Cayer, and S. Cook, *Handbook of Training and Development for the Public Sector* (San Francisco: Jossey–Bass, 1993)
55. J.B. Tracey, S.I. Tannenbaum, and M.J. Kavanaugh, "Applying Trained Skills on the Job: The Importance of the Work Environment," *Journal of Applied Psychology* 80 (1995), pp. 239–52; P.E. Tesluk, J.L. Farr, J.E. Mathieu, and R.J. Vance, "Generalization of Employee Involvement Training to the Job Setting: Individual and Situational Effects," *Personnel Psychology* 48 (1995), pp. 607–32; J.K. Ford, M.A. Quinones, D.J. Sego, and J.S. Sorra, "Factors Affecting the Opportunity to Perform Trained Tasks on the Job," *Personnel Psychology* 45 (1992), pp. 511–27.
56. A. Rossett, "That Was a Great Class, but . . . ," *Training and Development* (July 1997), pp. 19–24.
57. J.M. Cusimano, "Managers as Facilitators," *Training and Development* 50 (1996), pp. 31–33.
58. C.M. Petrini, ed., "Bringing It Back to Work," *Training and Development Journal* (December 1990), pp. 15–21.
59. Ford, Quinones, Sego, and Sorra, "Factors Affecting the Opportunity to Perform Trained Tasks on the Job."
60. Ibid.; M.A. Quinones, J.K. Ford, D.J. Sego, and E.M. Smith, "The Effects of Individual and Transfer Environment Characteristics on the Opportunity to Perform Trained Tasks," *Training Research Journal* 1 (1995/96), pp. 29–48.
61. G. Stevens and E. Stevens, "The Truth about EPSS," *Training and Development* 50 (1996), pp. 59–61.
62. "In Your Face EPSs," *Training* (April 1996), pp. 101–2.
63. R.D. Marx, "Relapse Prevention for Managerial Training: A Model for Maintenance of Behavior Change," *Academy of Management Review* 7 (1982), pp. 433–41; G.P. Latham and C.A. Frayne, "Self-Management Training for Increasing Job Attendance: A Follow-up and Replication," *Journal of Applied Psychology* 74 (1989), pp. 411–16.
64. "HRD Executives Forecast Tremendous Growth of Learning Technologies," in *National Report of Human Resources*, ed. D. Koehle (Alexandria, VA: American Society of Training and Development, November-December 1997), p. 3.
65. "Top Training Facilities," *Training* (March 1995), special section, H.; U. Gupta, "TV Seminars and CD-ROMs Train Workers," *The Wall Street Journal*, January 3, 1996, pp. B1, B6.
66. C. Lee, "Who Gets Trained in What?" *Training* (October 1991), pp. 47–59; W. Hannum, *The Application of Emerging Training Technology* (San Diego, CA: University Associates, 1990); B. Filipczak, "Make Room for Training," *Training* (October 1991), pp. 76–82; A.P. Carnevale, L.J. Gainer, and A.S. Meltzer, *Workplace Basics Training Manual* (San Francisco: Jossey-Bass, 1990).
67. Hannum, *Application of Emerging Training Technology;* "Putting the Distance into Distance Learning," *Training* (October 1995), pp. 111–18.
68. P.A. Galagan, "Think Performance: A Conversation with Gloria Gery," *Training and Development* (March 1994), pp. 47–51.
69. Rosow and Zager, *Training: The Competitive Edge*.
70. M. Nadeau, "Reach out and Touch Someone," *Personnel Journal* (May 1995), pp. 120–24; B. Filipczak and B. Leonard, "Distance Learning: Work & Training Overlap," *HR Magazine* (April 1996), pp. 40–48.
71. C. Lee, "Who Gets Trained in What?"; A.P. Carnevale, L.J. Gainer, and A.S. Meltzer, *Workplace Basics Training Manual* (San Francisco: Jossey-Bass, 1990).
72. R.B. Cohn, "How to Choose a Video Producer," *Training* (July 1996), pp. 58–61.
73. A.P. Carnevale, "The Learning Enterprise," *Training and Development Journal* (February 1989), pp. 26–37.
74. W.J. Rothwell and H.C. Kanzanas, "Planned OJT Is

Productive OJT," *Training and Development Journal* (October 1990), pp. 53–56.

75. B. Filipczak, "Who Owns Your OJT?" *Training* (December 1996), pp. 44–49.
76. D.B. Youst and L. Lipsett, "New Job Immersion without Drowning," *Training and Development Journal* (February 1989), pp. 73–75; G.M. Piskurich, *Self-Directed Learning* (San Francisco: Jossey-Bass, 1993).
77. G.M. Piskurich, "Self-Directed Learning," in *The ASTD Training and Development Handbook*, 4th ed., pp. 453–72; G.M. Piskurich, "Developing Self-Directed Learning," *Training and Development* (March 1994), pp. 31–36.
78. P. Warr and D. Bunce, "Trainee Characteristics and the Outcomes of Open Learning," *Personnel Psychology* 48 (1995), pp. 347–75.
79. R.W. Glover, *Apprenticeship Lessons from Abroad* (Columbus, OH: National Center for Research in Vocational Education, 1986).
80. Commerce Clearing House, Inc., *Orientation-Training* (Chicago, IL: Personnel Practices Communications, Commerce Clearing House, 1981), pp. 501–905.
81. McCain, "Apprenticeship Lessons from Europe."
82. R. Narisetti, "Manufacturers Decry a Shortage of Workers while Rejecting Many," *The Wall Street Journal*, September 8, 1995, pp. A1, A4.
83. *Eldredge v. Carpenters JATC* (1981). 27 Fair Employment Practices. Bureau of National Affairs, 479.
84. K.L. Miller and K.N. Anhalt, "Without Training, I Can't Start My Real Life," *Business Week* (September 16, 1996), p. 60.
85. A.F. Cheng, "Hands-on Learning at Motorola," *Training and Development Journal* (October 1990), pp. 34–35.
86. M.W. McCall Jr. and M.M. Lombardo, "Using Simulation for Leadership and Management Research," *Management Science* 28 (1982), pp. 533–49.
87. N. Adams, "Lessons from the Virtual World," *Training* (June 1995), pp. 45–48.
88. A. Richter, "Board Games for Managers," *Training and Development Journal* (July 1990), pp. 95–97.
89. M. Hequet, "Games That Teach," *Training* (July 1995), pp. 53–58.
90. G.P. Latham and L.M. Saari, "Application of Social Learning Theory to Training Supervisors through Behavior Modeling," *Journal of Applied Psychology* 64 (1979), pp. 239–46.
91. D. Filipowski, "How Federal Express Makes Your Package Its Most Important," *Personnel Journal* (February 1992), pp. 40–46.
92. Hannum, *Application of Emerging Training Technology*.
93. "What is Web-Based Training," World Wide Web site http://www.clark.net/pub/nractive/f1.html.
94. B. Filipczak, "An Internet of Your Very Own," in *Using Technology-Delivered Training*, ed. D. Zielinski (Minneapolis, MN: Lakewood, 1997), pp. 127–28.
95. D. Glener, "The Promise of Internet-Based Training," *Training and Development* (September 1996), pp. 57–58.
96. "The Real World of Intranet-Based Training, *Training with Multimedia* 2 (1996), pp. 1–5.
97. C. Pollack and R. Masters, "Using Internet Technologies to Enhance Training," *Performance Improvement* (February 1997), pp. 28–31.
98. "The Real World of Internet-Based Training."
99. R.J. Wagner, T.T. Baldwin, and C.C. Rowland, "Outdoor Training: Revolution or Fad?" *Training and Development Journal* (March 1991), pp. 51–57; C.J. Cantoni, "Learning the Ropes of Teamwork," *The Wall Street Journal*, October 2, 1995, p. A14.
100. C. Steinfeld, "Challenge Courses Can Build Strong Teams," *Training and Development* (April 1997), pp. 12–13.
101. P.F. Buller, J.R. Cragun, and G.M. McEvoy, "Getting the Most out of Outdoor Training," *Training and Development Journal* (March 1991), pp. 58–61.
102. C. Clements, R.J. Wagner, C.C. Roland, "The Ins and Outs of Experiential Training," *Training and Development* (February 1995), pp. 52–56.
103. Ibid.
104. P. Froiland, "Action Learning," *Training* (January 1994), pp. 27–34.
105. R.L. Oser, A. McCallum, E. Salas, and B.B. Morgan, Jr., "Toward a Definition of Teamwork: An Analysis of Critical Team Behaviors," Technical Report 89-004 (Orlando, FL.: Naval Training Research Center, 1989).
106. P. Froiland, "Action Learning," *Training* (January 1994), pp. 27–34.
107. K. Kraiger, J.K. Ford, and E. Salas, "Application of Cognitive, Skill-Based, and Affective Theories of Learning Outcomes to New Methods of Training Evaluation," *Journal of Applied Psychology* 78 (1993), pp. 311–28; J.J. Phillips, "ROI: The Search for Best Practices," *Training and Development* (February 1996), pp. 42–47; D.L. Kirkpatrick, "Evaluation of Training," in *Training and Development Handbook*, 2d ed., ed. R. L. Craig (New York: McGraw-Hill, 1976), pp. 18-1 to 18-27.
108. J.J. Phillips, "Was It the Training?" *Training and Development* (March 1996), pp. 28–32; Phillips, "ROI: The Search for Best Practices."
109. D.A. Grove and C. Ostroff, "Program Evaluation," in *Developing Human Resources*, ed. K.N. Wexley (Washington, DC: Bureau of National Affairs, 1991), pp. 5-185 to 5-220.
110. B. Gerber, "Does Your Training Make a Difference? Prove It!" *Training* (March 1995), pp. 27–34.
111. J. Komaki, K.D. Bardwick, and L.R. Scott, "A Behavioral Approach to Occupational Safety: Pinpointing and Reinforcing Safe Performance in a Food Manufacturing Plant," *Journal of Applied Psychology* 63 (1978), pp. 434–45.
112. A.P. Carnevale and E.R. Schulz, "Return on Invest-

ment: Accounting for Training," *Training and Development Journal* (July 1990), pp. S1–S32; P.R. Sackett and E.J. Mullen, "Beyond Formal Experimental Design: Toward an Expanded View of the Training Evaluation Process," *Personnel Psychology* 46 (in press), pp. 613–27; S.I. Tannenbaum and S.B. Woods, "Determining a Strategy for Evaluating Training: Operating within Organizational Constraints," *Human Resource Planning* 15 (1992), pp. 63–81; R.D. Arvey, S.E. Maxwell, and E. Salas, "The Relative Power of Training Evaluation Designs under Different Cost Configurations," *Journal of Applied Psychology* 77 (1992), pp. 155–60.

113. D.A. Grove and C.O. Ostroff, "Program Evaluation," in *Developing Human Resources*, ed. K.N. Wexley (Washington, DC: BNA Books, 1991), pp. 185–219.
114. B. Gerber, "Does Your Training Make a Difference? Prove It," *Training* (March 1995), pp. 27–34.
115. Carnevale and Schulz, "Return on Investment."
116. Ibid.; G. Kearsley, *Costs, Benefits, and Productivity in Training Systems* (Boston: Addison-Wesley, 1982).
117. Ibid.
118. D.G. Robinson and J. Robinson, "Training for Impact," *Training and Development Journal* (August 1989), pp. 30–42.
119. Ibid.
120. J.E. Matheiu and R.L. Leonard, "Applying Utility Analysis to a Training Program in Supervisory Skills: A Time-Based Approach," *Academy of Management Journal* 30 (1987), pp. 316–35; F.L. Schmidt, J.E. Hunter, and K. Pearlman, "Assessing the Economic Impact of Personnel Programs on Work-Force Productivity," *Personnel Psychology* 35 (1982), pp. 333–47; J.W. Boudreau, "Economic Considerations in Estimating the Utility of Human Resource Productivity Programs," *Personnel Psychology* 36 (1983), pp. 551–76.
121. U.E. Gattiker, "Firm and Taxpayer Returns from Training of Semiskilled Employees," *Academy of Management Journal* 38 (1995), pp. 1151–73.
122. J.K. McAfee and L.S. Cote, "Avoid Having Your Day in Court," *Training and Development Journal* (April 1985), pp. 56–60.
123. R. Sharpe, "In Whose Hands? Allstate and Scientology," *The Wall Street Journal* (March 22, 1995), pp. A1, A4.
124. Bureau of National Affairs, "Female Grocery Store Employees Prevail in Sex-Bias Suit against Lucky Stores," *BNAs Employee Relations Weekly* 10 (1992), pp. 927–38; *Stender v. Lucky Store Inc.*, DC Ncalifornia, No. c-88-1467, 8/18/92.
125. J. Sample and R. Hylton, "Falling Off a Log—and Landing in Court," *Training* (May 1996), pp. 67–69.
126. B. Ettorre, "Let's Hear It for Local Talent," *Management Review* (October 1994), p. 9; S. Franklin, "A New World Order for Business Strategy," *Chicago Tribune* (May 15, 1994): sec. 19, pp. 7–8.
127. R.L. Tung, "Selection and Training of Personnel for Overseas Assignments," *Columbia Journal of World Business* 16 (1981), pp. 18–78.
128. W.A. Arthur, Jr., and W. Bennett, Jr., "The International Assignee: The Relative Importance of Factors Perceived to Contribute to Success," *Personnel Psychology* 48 (1995), pp. 99–114; G.M. Spreitzer, M.W. McCall, Jr., and Joan D. Mahoney, "Early Identification of International Executive Potential," *Journal of Applied Psychology* 82 (1997), pp. 6–29.
129. J.S. Black and J.K. Stephens, "The Influence of the Spouse on American Expatriate Adjustment and Intent to Stay in Pacific Rim Overseas Assignments," *Journal of Management* 15 (1989), pp. 529–44.
130. E. Dunbar and A. Katcher, "Preparing Managers for Foreign Assignments," *Training and Development Journal* (September 1990), pp. 45–47.
131. J.S. Black and M. Mendenhall, "A Practical but Theory-Based Framework for Selecting Cross-Cultural Training Methods," in *Readings and Cases in International Human Resource Management*, ed. M. Mendenhall and G. Oddou (Boston: PWS–Kent, 1991), pp. 177–204.
132. S. Ronen, "Training the International Assignee," in *Training and Development in Organizations*, ed. I.L. Goldstein (San Francisco: Jossey-Bass, 1989), pp. 417–53.
133. P.R. Harris and R.T. Moran, *Managing Cultural Differences* (Houston: Gulf Publishing, 1991).
134. Ibid.
135. C.M. Solomon, "Repatriation: Up, Down, or Out?" *Personnel Journal* (January 1995), pp. 28–37; D.R. Briscoe, *International Human Resource Management* (Englewood Cliffs, NJ: Prentice-Hall, 1994).
136. S.E. Jackson and Associates, *Diversity in the Workplace: Human Resource Initiatives* (New York: Guilford Press, 1992).
137. T.C. Cox, *Cultural Diversity in Organizations* (San Francisco: Berrett–Kohler, 1993), pp. 24–27.
138. R.R. Thomas, "Managing Diversity: A Conceptual Framework," in *Diversity in the Workplace* (New York: Guilford Press), pp. 306–18.
139. M.E. Heilman, C.J. Block, and J.A. Lucas, "Presumed Incompetent? Stigmatization and Affirmative Action Efforts," *Journal of Applied Psychology* 77, pp. 536–44.
140. B. Gerber, "Managing Diversity," *Training* (July 1990), pp. 23–30; T. Diamante, C.L. Reid, and L. Ciylo, "Making the Right Training Moves," *HR Magazine* (March 1995), pp. 60–65.
141. C.M. Solomon, "The Corporate Response to Workforce Diversity," *Personnel Journal* (August 1989), pp. 43–53; A. Morrison, *The New Leaders: Guidelines on Leadership Diversity in America* (San Francisco: Jossey–Bass, 1992).
142. S.M. Paskoff, "Ending the Workplace Diversity Wars,"

Training (August 1996), pp. 43–47; H.B. Karp and N. Sutton, "Where Diversity Training Goes Wrong," *Training* (July 1993), pp. 30–34.

143. Paskoff, "Ending the Workplace Diversity Wars."
144. A. Markels, "Diversity Program Can Prove Divisive," *The Wall Street Journal* (January 30, 1997), pp. B1–B2; "R.R. Donnelley Curtails Diversity Training Moves," *The Wall Street Journal* (February 13, 1997), pp. B3.
145. S. Rynes and B. Rosen, "What Makes Diversity Programs Work?" *HR Magazine* (October 1994), pp. 67–73; S. Rynes and B. Rosen, "A Field Survey of Factors Affecting the Adoption and Perceived Success of Diversity Training," *Personnel Psychology* 48 (1995), pp. 247–70.
146. L.E. Wynter, "Allstate Rates Managers on Handling Diversity," *The Wall Street Journal* (November 1, 1997), p. B1.
147. Wynter, "Allstate." Also, see Gannett's home page at http://www.gannett.com, "Gannett's Basic Game Plan."
148. C.T. Schreiber, K.F. Price, and A. Morrison, "Workforce Diversity and the Glass Ceiling: Practices, Barriers, Possibilities," *Human Resource Planning* 16 (1994), pp. 51–69.
149. M. Hequet, "The Union Push for Lifelong Learning," *Training* (March 1994), pp. 26–31; S.J. Schurman, M.K. Hugentoble, and H. Stack, "Lessons from the UAW–GM Paid Education Leave Program," in *Joint Training Programs*, ed. L.A. Ferman, M. Hoyman, J. Cutcher-Gershenfeld, and E.J. Savoie (Ithaca, NY: ILR Press, 1991), pp. 71–94.
150. E.S. Tomasko and K.K. Dickinson, "The UAW–Ford Education Development and Training Program," in *Joint Training Programs*, pp. 55–70.
151. D.C. Feldman, "A Contingency Theory of Socialization," *Administrative Science Quarterly* 21 (1976), pp. 433–52; D.C. Feldman, "A Socialization Process That Helps New Recruits Succeed," *Personnel* 57 (1980), pp. 11–23; J.P. Wanous, A.E. Reichers, and S.D. Malik, "Organizational Socialization and Group Development: Toward an Integrative Perspective," *Academy of Management Review* 9 (1984), pp. 670–83; C.L. Adkins, "Previous Work Experience and Organizational Socialization: A Longitudinal Examination," *Academy of Management Journal* 38 (1995), pp. 839–62; E.W. Morrison, "Longitudinal Study of the Effects of Information Seeking on Newcomer Socialization," *Journal of Applied Psychology* 78 (1993), pp. 173–83.
152. G.M. McEnvoy and W.F. Cascio, "Strategies for Reducing Employee Turnover: A Meta-Analysis," *Journal of Applied Psychology* 70 (1985), pp. 342–53.
153. M.R. Louis, "Surprise and Sense Making: What Newcomers Experience in Entering Unfamiliar Organizational Settings," *Administrative Science Quarterly* 25 (1980), pp. 226–51.
154. R.F. Morrison and T.M. Brantner, "What Enhances or Inhibits Learning a New Job? A Basic Career Issue," *Journal of Applied Psychology* 77 (1992), pp. 926–40.
155. D.A. Major, S.W.J. Kozlowski, G.T. Chao, and P.D. Gardner, " A Longitudinal Investigation of Newcomer Expectations, Early Socialization Outcomes, and the Moderating Effect of Role Development Factors," *Journal of Applied Psychology* 80 (1995), pp. 418–31.
156. D.C. Feldman, *Managing Careers in Organizations* (Glenview, IL: Scott–Foresman, 1988).
157. Ibid; D. Reed-Mendenhall and C.W. Millard, "Orientation: A Training and Development Tool," *Personnel Administrator* 25, no. 8 (1980), pp. 42–44; M.R. Louis, B.Z. Posner, and G.H. Powell, "The Availability and Helpfulness of Socialization Practices," *Personnel Psychology* 36 (1983), pp. 857–66; C. Ostroff and S.W.J. Kozlowski, Jr., "Organizational Socialization as a Learning Process: The Role of Information Acquisition," *Personnel Psychology* 45 (1992), pp. 849–74; D.R. France and R.L. Jarvis, "Quick Starts for New Employees," *Training and Development* (October 1996), pp. 47–50.
158. Pillsbury engineering orientation program.
159. D.B. Youst and L. Lipsett, "New Job Immersion without Drowning," *Training and Development* (February 1989), pp. 73–75.

Job Search in Cyberspace

With the national unemployment rate the lowest in thirty years, many businesses from manufacturing to hotel chains are using nontraditional methods to attract and recruit potential employees. One new method that is being used to link employers and job seekers is the Internet. In less than three years the number of job postings on the Internet has grown from less than 15,000 to approximately one-half million. Large

and small companies such as Texas Instruments, Wendy's International, and Lockheed Martin are listing job openings on the Internet either on their own home pages or using specialized on-line services such as The Monster Board (www.monster.com) or Career Mosaic (www.careermosaic.com).

The Internet provides many advantages to both employers and job seekers. Corporate recruiters find that the process of finding qualified job candidates is falling from weeks and months to days. Compared to the process involved in placing a newspaper ad, job postings can be quickly submitted electronically with job candidates submitting resumes soon after. There is no limit on the length of the job description that companies can post which makes it easy to include all relevant job qualifications and describe in detail the working conditions and even the company culture. Another advantage of the Internet is the ability to access more people from a broader labor market (newspaper ads and job fairs are typically restricted to narrow geographic areas). From the job seekers vantage point, the Internet allows job searches to be conducted on a 24-hour basis without leaving home. Using key words and search engines, job seekers can type in the position they want and within seconds local and national job openings matching the key words are shown. Even for job seekers who may not have access to a computer at home, Internet access is growing. The U.S. Department of Labor is developing "Internet Access" zones in community colleges, universities, and public employment agencies. The number of public libraries and academic career centers with Internet access is growing.

Increased use of the Internet for recruiting has changed the way that job candidates prepare resumes. Because of the large volume of electronic resumes submitted for job openings, companies are using electronic scanning to sift through job candidates' resumes and identify those with the skills needed for the job. For example, Allied Signal receives over 100,000 resumes per year. Hiring managers search the resumes using key words that relate to the skills required for the job. The hiring manager can also tell the computer whether the skills are required or just desired. The electronic scanning systems look for key words or phrases on the resumes and present those to the manager. The electronic systems scan the resumes and identify resumes with the necessary qualifications. Many of these systems also indicate how much of the hiring manager's qualifications were found on the resume and rank the candidates from most desirable to least desirable.

Traditionally, job candidates worried about the appearance and layout of their resumes. With Internet job search and electronic scanning of resumes, description of skills and experiences is critical. Some job candidates try to beat the system by guessing which key words the computer is looking for and including those on the resume. This results in a resume full of snazzy buzz words and business jargon to describe skills and job experiences. Some counselors suggest including the words that the company uses in its job posting. For example, if you are going to present yourself as having human resource management experience it is probably best not to use the dated term "Personnel" to describe your experience. The companies who have developed the electronic scanners insist that preparing a scannable resume is no different than preparing a traditional-style resume. The obsession with finding "magic words" is a waste of time. The more skills and experiences provided, the more opportunities a candidate will have to match available positions.

While electronic scanning and Internet job posting are a different way of recruiting and choosing which job candidates to pursue, discrimination doesn't occur and job seekers are now never out of the running for jobs. A computer doesn't care whether a job candidate is a woman or a man. It allows employers to be more specific in identifying potential job candidates (a Harvard Business School graduate who once worked at Netscape, for example). Job seekers also remain in computerized resume pools for a long time after they apply for a job. For example, at Eli Lilly job candidate's resumes remain in the database for approximately one year. This means that when different human resource needs occur, a hiring manager using a new set of key words and qualifications, may choose a candidate who was rejected for an earlier position.

DISCUSSION QUESTIONS

1. What difficulties might companies have to deal with in using electronic job postings?
2. Do the roles of the hiring manager and the HR manager change when electronic recruiting is used? Explain.
3. What are the advantages and disadvantages of replacing human processing of resumes (e.g., hiring manager or HR reading resumes) with electronic processing of resumes?

Source: Based on A. Markels, "Job Hunting Takes Off in Cyberspace," *The Wall Street Journal*, September 20, 1996, B1 & B5; R. Johnson, "Some Employers Lift Hiring Standards Amid Labor Shortage, Weak Applicants," *Wall Street Journal*, February 17, 1999, pp. A2, A10; A. Starcke, "Recruitment Agenda: Internet Recruiting Shows Rapid Growth," *HR Magazine* (August 1996), pp. 61–66; E.P. Pollock, "Sir: Your Application for a Job Is Rejected; Sincerely, Hal 9000," *The Wall Street Journal*, August 30, 1998 A1, A12.

PART III
Assessment and Development of HR

8

CHAPTER

Performance Management

OBJECTIVES

After reading this chapter, you should be able to

1. Identify the major determinants of individual performance.
2. Discuss the three general purposes of performance management.
3. Identify the five criteria for effective performance management systems.
4. Discuss the four approaches to performance management, the specific techniques used in each approach, and the way these approaches compare with the criteria for effective performance management systems.
5. Choose the most effective approach to performance measurement for a given situation.
6. Discuss the advantages and disadvantages of the different sources of performance information.
7. Choose the most effective source(s) for performance information for any situation.
8. Distinguish types of rating errors and explain how to minimize each in a performance evaluation.
9. Identify the characteristics of a performance measurement system that follows legal guidelines.
10. Conduct an effective performance feedback session.

Ford Motors Rolls Out Performance-Based Buyout Plan

ENTER THE WORLD OF BUSINESS

Ford Motor Company plans to offer a generous buyout program targeted to poorly performing salaried employees or average-performing employees who have been evaluated as having "limited potential." Buyout programs typically include a lump sum payment of money based on the employee's years of service and salary level plus other incentives to persuade employees to voluntarily resign or retire early. Ford's buyout is generous compared to other companies'. Its buyout offer may include up to 12 months of pay and insurance benefits, a two-year paid lease on a used Ford vehicle, retraining or relocation money, cash bonus, and profit sharing. The buyout program comes at a time when Ford, General Motors, and Daimler-Chrysler face pressure from Wall Street and foreign competition to cut costs and increase worker productivity.

Employees are considered as having limited potential if they do not have the ability to advance in the company. Ford's managers are advised to tell candidates for the buyout program that they are not likely to be considered for promotion and future pay increases and bonuses will be limited. Although the program is voluntary, managers are advised to tell buyout candidates that management believes they should separate from the company. Ford wants 50 percent of the buyout acceptances to come from employees eligible to retire, 25% from employees with 11 to 29 years of service, and the remainder from employees with 1 to 10 years service.

Before a business reorganization in 1995, an employee or manager only had to get a good job performance rating from her boss to be eligible for advancement opportunities. Now with more work being performed in teams, an employee needs to be found to be a good performer by peers and customers, as well as the boss.

Several aspects of Ford's program are unique. First, the buyout program is targeted specifically to average and poor performers. Many companies offering buyout programs find that star performers leave as well as poor performers. Second, Ford's approach to the problem of dealing with poor performers is unique because most companies only try to get rid of poor performers. Average employees usually leave on their own for another job opportunity, due to spouse relocation, or as a result of their manager telling them they have limited opportunities to advance.

The buyout program has been greeted with resentment and caused anxiety among salaried employees. Salaried employees are just now becoming comfortable with the reorganization of the company. Also, many feel that Ford has been a paternalistic employer in that company policies took care of employees as if they were family members.

SOURCE. T. D. Schellhardt and S. K. Goo, "At Ford, Buyout Plan Has a Twist," *The Wall Street Journal* (July 22, 1998), pp. B1, B6; R. Konrad, "White-Collar Buyout Plan Focuses on 'Low Performers'," *Detroit Free Press* (July 15, 1998), pp. 1A, 7A.

Introduction

Companies that seek to gain competitive advantage through employees must be able to manage the behavior and results of all employees. The opening vignette illustrates that one of managers' most difficult challenges is how to convince poor performers to leave the company. In a unique use of performance appraisal information for administrative purposes, Ford Motors has decided to offer a generous buyout program targeted to poorly and average-performing employees. In this chapter we will discuss characteristics that performance appraisal systems need for administrative purposes such as this. For example, Ford must ensure that the system is job-related and the rationale for performance evaluations is well-documented.

Traditionally, the formal performance appraisal system has been viewed as the primary means for managing employee performance. Performance appraisal was an administrative duty performed by managers and primarily the responsibility of the human resource function. Managers view performance appraisal as an annual ritual—they quickly complete the form and use it to catalog all the negative information they have collected on an employee over the previous year. Because they may dislike confrontation and not feel that they know how to give effective evaluations, some managers spend as little time as possible giving employees feedback. Not surprisingly, most managers and employees dislike performance appraisals! The major reasons for this dislike include the lack of ongoing review, lack of employee involvement, and lack of recognition for good performance.[1]

We believe that performance appraisal is only one part of the broader process of performance management. We define **performance management** as the process through which managers ensure that employees' activities and outputs are congruent with the organization's goals. Performance management is central to gaining competitive advantage.

Our performance management system has three parts: defining performance, measuring performance, and feeding back performance information. First, a performance management system specifies which aspects of performance are relevant to the organization, primarily through *job analysis* (discussed in Chapter 4). Second, it measures those aspects of performance through **performance appraisal,** which is only one method for managing employee performance. Third, it provides feedback to employees through **performance feedback** sessions so that they can adjust their performance to the organization's goals. Performance feedback is also fulfilled through tying rewards to performance via the compensation system (e.g., merit increases or bonuses), a topic to be covered in Chapters 11 and 12.

In this chapter, we examine a variety of approaches to performance management. We begin with a model of the performance management process that helps us examine the system's purposes. Then we discuss specific approaches to performance management and the strengths and weaknesses of each. We also look at various sources of performance information. The errors resulting from subjective assessments of performance are presented, as well as the means for reducing those errors. Then we discuss some effective components to performance feedback. Finally, we address components of a legally defensible performance management system.

An Organizational Model of Performance Management

For many years, researchers in the field of HRM and industrial–organizational psychology focused on performance appraisal as a measurement technique.[2] The goal of these performance appraisal systems was to measure individual employee performance reliably and validly. This perspective, however, tended to ignore some very important influences on the performance management process. Thus, we begin this section by presenting the major purposes of performance management from an organizational rather than a measurement perspective. To do this, we need to understand the process of performance. Figure 8.1 depicts our process model of performance.

As the figure shows, individuals' attributes—their skills, abilities, and so on—are the raw materials of performance. For example, in a sales job, an organization wants someone who has good interpersonal skills and knowledge of the products. These raw materials are transformed into objective results through the employee's behavior. Employees can exhibit behaviors only if they have the necessary knowledge, skills, abilities, and other characteristics. Thus, employees with good product knowledge and interpersonal skills can talk about the advantage of various brands and can behave in a friendly, helpful manner (not that they necessarily display those behaviors, only that they *can* display them). On the other hand, employees with little product knowledge or interpersonal skills cannot effectively display those behaviors. The objective results are the measurable, tangible outputs of the work, and they are a consequence of the employee's or the work group's behavior. In our example, if a salesperson displays the correct behaviors, he will likely make a number of sales.

Another important component in our organizational model of the performance management system is the organization's strategy. The link between performance management and the organization's strategies and goals is often neglected. Chapter 2 pointed out that most companies pursue some type of strategy to attain their revenue,

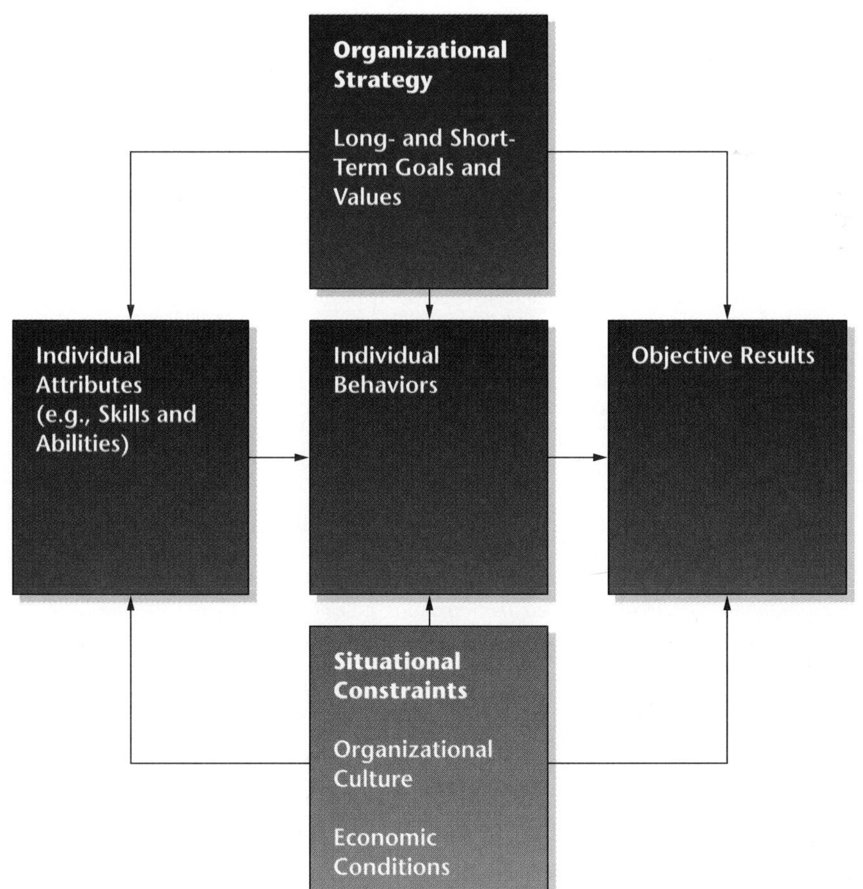

FIGURE 8.1 Model of Performance Management in Organizations

profit, and market-share goals. Divisions, departments, work groups, and individuals within the company must align their activities with these strategies and goals. If they are not aligned, then the likelihood of achieving the goals becomes small. How is this link made in organizations? Primarily by specifying what needs to be accomplished and what behaviors must be exhibited for the company's strategy to be implemented. This link is being recognized as necessary more and more often, through the increasing popularity of **performance planning and evaluation (PPE)** systems. PPE systems seek to tie the formal performance appraisal process to the company's strategies by specifying at the beginning of the evaluation period the types and level of performance that must be accomplished to achieve the strategy. Then at the end of the evaluation period, individuals and groups are evaluated based on how closely their actual performance met the performance plan. In an ideal world, performance management systems would ensure that all activities support the organization's strategic goals.

Finally, our model notes that situational constraints are always at work within the performance management system. As discussed previously, an employee may have the necessary skills and yet not exhibit the necessary behaviors. Sometimes the organizational culture discourages the employee from doing things that might be effective. Work-group norms often dictate what the group's members do and the results they produce. On the other hand, some people are simply not motivated to exhibit the right behaviors. This often occurs if the employees do not believe that their behaviors will be rewarded with pay raises, promotions, and so forth. Finally, people may be performing effective behaviors, and yet the right results do not follow. For example, an outstanding salesperson may not have a large dollar volume because the economy is bad and people are simply not buying.

Thus, as you can see in Figure 8.1, employees must have certain attributes to perform a set of behaviors and achieve some results. To gain competitive advantage, the attributes, behaviors, and results must be tied to the company's strategy. It is also important to note that constraints exist within the work environment that often preclude employees from performing. Table 8.1 provides recommendations for an effective performance management system. Regardless of the job or company, effective performance management systems measure performance criteria (e.g., behaviors, sales) as precisely as

TABLE 8.1
Recommendations for Designing an Effective Performance Management System

Strive for precision in defining and measuring performance.

Define performance with a focus on valued outcomes. Use outcomes that can be defined in terms of relative frequencies of behavior.

Include performance criteria that include various ways that employees can add value to a product or service (e.g., quantity, quality, timeliness, cost-effectiveness, interpersonal impact).

Include measures of work behaviors that add value above and beyond what is necessary to perform the job (e.g., assisting co-workers, taking the initiative to repair broken equipment).

Link performance dimensions to meeting internal and external customer requirements.

Internal customer definitions of performance should be linked to external customer satisfaction.

Measure and correct for the impact of situational constraints.

Monitor actual and perceived constraints through interviews, surveys, and observation.

SOURCE: Adapted from Exhibit 2.1 in H.J. Bernardin, C.M. Hagan, J.S. Kane, and P. Villanova, "Effective Performance Management: A Focus on Precision, Customers, and Situational Constraints," in *Performance Appraisal: State of the Art in Practice,* ed. J.W. Smither (San Francisco: Jossey–Bass, 1998), p. 56. Used by permission.

possible. Effective performance management systems also serve a strategic function by linking performance criteria to internal and external customer requirements. Effective performance management systems also include a process for changing the system based on the effects of situational constraints. We will next examine the purposes of performance management systems.

Purposes of Performance Management

The purposes of performance management systems are of three kinds: strategic, administrative, and developmental.

STRATEGIC PURPOSE

First and foremost, a performance management system should link employee activities with the organization's goals. One of the primary ways strategies are implemented is through defining the results, behaviors, and, to some extent, employee characteristics that are necessary for carrying out that strategy, and then developing measurement and feedback systems that will maximize the extent to which employees exhibit the characteristics, engage in the behaviors, and produce the results. To achieve this strategic purpose, the system must be flexible, because when goals and strategies change, the results, behaviors, and employee characteristics usually need to change correspondingly. However, performance management systems do not commonly achieve this purpose. A survey indicates that only 13 percent of the companies questioned were using their performance appraisal system to communicate company objectives.[3] In addition, surveys of HR practitioners regarding the purposes of performance appraisal suggest that most systems focus on administrative and developmental purposes.[4]

ADMINISTRATIVE PURPOSE

Organizations use performance management information (performance appraisals, in particular) in many administrative decisions: salary administration (pay raises), promotions, retention–termination, layoffs, and recognition of individual performance.[5] Despite the importance of these decisions, however, many managers, who are the source of the information, see the performance appraisal process only as a necessary evil they must go through to fulfill their job requirements. They feel uncomfortable evaluating others and feeding those evaluations back to the employees. Thus, they tend to rate everyone high or at least rate them the same, making the performance appraisal information relatively useless. For example, one manager stated, "There is really no getting around the fact that whenever I evaluate one of my people, I stop and think about the impact—the ramifications of my decisions on my relationship with the guy and his future here. . . . Call it being politically minded, or using managerial discretion, or fine-tuning the guy's ratings, but in the end, I've got to live with him, and I'm not going to rate a guy without thinking about the fallout."[6]

DEVELOPMENTAL PURPOSE

A third purpose of performance management is to develop employees who are effective at their jobs. When employees are not performing as well as they should, performance management seeks to improve their performance. The feedback given during a performance evaluation process often pinpoints the employee's weaknesses. Ideally, however, the performance management system identifies not only any deficient aspects of the employee's performance but also the causes of these deficiencies—for example, a skill deficiency, a motivational problem, or some obstacle holding the employee back.

Managers are often uncomfortable confronting employees with their performance weaknesses. Such confrontations, although necessary to the effectiveness of the work group, often strain everyday working relationships. Giving high ratings to all employees enables a manager to minimize such conflicts, but then the developmental purpose of the performance management system is not fully achieved.[7]

The purposes of an effective performance management system are to link employee activities with the organization's strategic goals, furnish valid and useful information for making administrative decisions about employees, and provide employees with useful developmental feedback. Fulfilling these three purposes is central to gaining competitive advantage through human resources. A vital step in performance management is to develop the measures by which performance will be evaluated. Thus, we next discuss the issues involved in developing and using different measures of performance.

Performance Measures Criteria

In Chapter 4 we discussed how, through job analysis, one can analyze the job to determine exactly what constitutes effective performance. Once the company has determined, through job analysis and design, what kind of performance it expects from its employees, it needs to develop ways to measure that performance. This section presents the criteria underlying job performance measures. Later sections discuss approaches to performance measurement, sources of information, and errors.

Although people differ about criteria to use to evaluate performance management systems, we believe that five stand out: strategic congruence, validity, reliability, acceptability, and specificity.

STRATEGIC CONGRUENCE

Strategic congruence is the extent to which the performance management system elicits job performance that is congruent with the organization's strategy, goals, and culture. If a company emphasizes customer service, then its performance management system should assess how well its employees are serving the company's customer. Strategic congruence emphasizes the need for the performance management system to provide guidance so that employees can contribute to the organization's success. This requires systems flexible enough to adapt to changes in the company's strategic posture.

Take, for example, a drug company whose business strategy is to penetrate the North American market for dermatology compounds.[8] To be successful the company needs to shorten the drug development cycle, attract and retain research and development talent, and maximize the effectiveness of research teams. These are core competencies of the business. Performance measures are linked directly to the core competencies. These include number of dermatology compound submissions to the Food and Drug Administration (FDA), number of compound approvals by the FDA, turnover of senior engineers, and team leadership and collaboration. The sources for information regarding these performance measures include FDA decisions, team member feedback on surveys, and turnover rates. Team and individual accountabilities are directly linked to the performance measures. For example, research teams' performance goals include FDA submission and approval of three compounds.

Most companies' appraisal systems remain constant over a long period of time and through a variety of strategic emphases. However, when a company's strategy changes, its employees' behavior needs to change too.[9] The fact that they often do not change may account for why many managers see performance appraisal systems as having little impact on a firm's effectiveness.

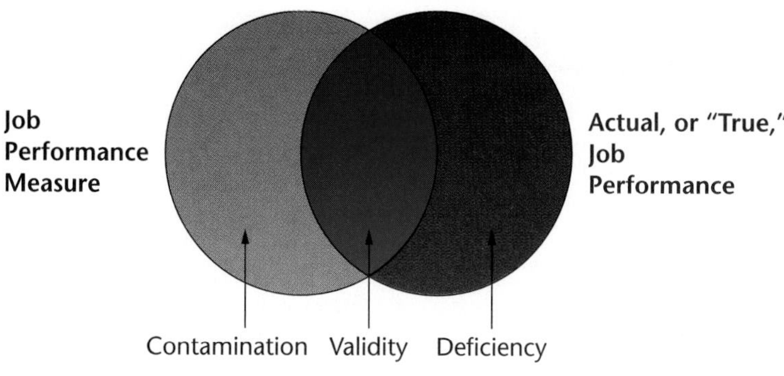

FIGURE 8.2
Contamination and Deficiency of a Job Performance Measure

VALIDITY

Validity is the extent to which the performance measure assesses all the relevant—and only the relevant—aspects of performance. This is often referred to as "content validity." For a performance measure to be valid, it must not be deficient or contaminated. As you can see from Figure 8.2, one of the circles represents "true" job performance—all of those aspects of performance relevant to being successful in the job. On the other hand, companies must use some measure of performance, such as a supervisory rating of performance on a set of dimensions or measures of the objective results on the job. Validity is concerned with maximizing the overlap between actual job performance and the measure of job performance (the green portion in the figure).

A performance measure is deficient if it does not measure all aspects of performance (the blue portion in the figure). An example is a system at a large university that assesses faculty members based more on research than teaching, thereby relatively ignoring a relevant aspect of performance.

A contaminated measure evaluates irrelevant aspects of performance or aspects that are not job related (the ochre portion in the figure). The performance measure should seek to minimize contamination, but its complete elimination is seldom possible. An example of a contaminated measure is the use of actual sales figures for evaluating salespersons across very different regional territories. Often sales are highly dependent upon the territory (e.g., number of potential customers, number of competitors, economic conditions) rather than the actual performance of the salesperson. A salesperson who works harder and better than others might not have the highest sales totals because the territory simply does not have as much sales potential as others. Thus, to use these figures alone would be to use a measure that is strongly affected by things beyond the control of the individual employee.

RELIABILITY

Reliability refers to the consistency of the performance measure. One important type of reliability is *interrater reliability:* the consistency among the individuals who evaluate the employee's performance. A performance measure has interrater reliability if two individuals give the same (or close to the same) evaluations of a person's job performance. Evidence seems to indicate that most subjective supervisory measures of job performance exhibit low reliability.[10] With some measures, the extent to which all the items rated are internally consistent is important (*internal consistency reliability*).

In addition, the measure should be reliable over time (*test–retest reliability*). A measure that results in drastically different ratings depending on the time at which the measures are taken lacks test–retest reliability. For example, if salespeople are evaluated

TABLE 8.2 Categories of Perceived Fairness and Implications for Performance Management Systems

FAIRNESS CATEGORY	IMPORTANCE FOR PERFORMANCE MANAGEMENT SYSTEM	IMPLICATION
Procedural Fairness	Development	• Give managers and employees opportunity to participate in development of system • Ensure consistent standards when evaluating different employees • Minimize rating errors and biases
Interpersonal Fairness	Use	• Timely and complete feedback • Allow employees to challenge the evaluation • Provide feedback in an atmosphere of respect and courtesy
Outcome Fairness	Outcomes	• Communicate expectations regarding performance evaluations and standards • Communicate expectations regarding rewards

SOURCE: Adapted from S.W. Gilliland and J.C. Langdon, "Creating Performance Management Systems That Promote Perceptions of Fairness," in *Performance Appraisal: State of the Art in Practice,* ed. J.W. Smither (San Francisco: Jossey–Bass, 1998), pp. 209–43. Used by permission.

based on their actual sales volume during a given month, it would be important to consider their consistency of monthly sales across time. What if an evaluator in a department store examined sales only during May? Employees in the lawn and garden department would have high sales volumes, but those in the men's clothing department would have somewhat low sales volumes. Clothing sales in May are traditionally lower than other months. One needs to measure performance consistently across time.

ACCEPTABILITY

Acceptability refers to whether the people who use the performance measure accept it. Many very elaborate performance measures are extremely valid and reliable, but they consume so much of managers' time that they refuse to use it. Alternatively, those being evaluated by a measure may not accept it.

Acceptability is affected by the extent to which employees believe the performance management system is fair. As Table 8.2 shows, there are three categories of perceived fairness: procedural, interpersonal, and outcome fairness. The table also shows specifically how the performance management system is developed, how the system is used, and how the outcomes linked to it affect perceptions of fairness. In developing and using a performance management system, managers should take the steps shown in the column labeled "Implications" in Table 8.2 to ensure that the system is perceived as fair. Research suggests that performance management systems that are perceived as unfair are likely to be legally challenged, used incorrectly, and decrease employee motivation to improve.[11]

SPECIFICITY

Specificity is the extent to which the performance measure gives specific guidance to employees about what is expected of them and how they can meet these expectations (see the "Competing Through High-Performance Work Systems" box). Specificity is relevant to both the strategic and developmental purposes of performance management. If a measure does not specify what an employee must do to help the company achieve its

A New Performance Appraisal System Is the Best Medicine

COMPETING THROUGH HIGH-PERFORMANCE WORK SYSTEMS

Rhone–Poulenc Rorer Inc. (RHR) is one of the world's top pharmaceutical companies. RHR operates in more than 60 countries with 6,000 employees in the United States and 28,000 worldwide. A new performance management system has been developed at the company. One goal of the system is to give managers a better way to communicate goals and expectations to employees. Another goal is to allow managers flexibility in rewarding employees. To design the system, HR managers at RHR conducted focus groups and held conversations with employees and line managers. They searched for best performance management practices by looking at systems used by other companies and sold by consulting firms.

The old performance management system allowed employees to equate their performance rating with a dollar value. When employees received their rating, they could determine how much the rating was worth in their annual salary increase. Under the old method, once employees heard the rating, they were not motivated to participate in the performance discussion. The new performance appraisal system eliminates the rating scale. The new system is designed to improve the performance feedback discussion. Eliminating the ratings is seen as a way to create more meaningful discussion between employees and their bosses. The company wants performance evaluations to focus more on development as well as to lead to more open and honest discussions.

RHR also revamped the appraisal form. The new appraisal form focuses on the company's key objectives, the day-to-day accountabilities of each position, and behaviors the company has identified as important for all positions including customer focus, teamwork, and people management skills. The new form allows managers to be more precise in setting and measuring performance objectives. Managers are expected to break down company business goals into clear objectives for each employee and track their progress.

As a result of the new performance management process, managers are able to make more meaningful increases in compensation to high-performing, average, and marginal employees. Managers review the salary budget, historical and current compensation data, and salary surveys of other companies in addition to each individual employee's performance. HR generalists support the process by consulting with managers and helping them create the best compensation scenario for employees. Managers can draw from salary increase monies, bonuses tied to RHR's financial performance, and stock options. The partnership between HR and managers ensures consistency and equity in how the system is used.

SOURCE: M. N. Martinez, "Rewards Given the Right Way," *HR Magazine* (May 1997), pp. 109–16. Reprinted with permission.

strategic goals, it becomes difficult for it to achieve its strategic purpose. Additionally, if the measure fails to point out an employee's performance problems, it is almost impossible for the employee to correct her performance.

Approaches to Measuring Performance

The model of performance management presented in Figure 8.1 shows that we can manage performance by focusing on employee attributes, behaviors, or results. In addition, we can measure performance in a relative way, making overall comparisons among individuals' performance. Finally, we can develop a performance measurement system that incorporates some variety of the preceding measures, as evidenced by the quality approach to measuring performance. Various techniques use a combination of these approaches. In this section, we explore these approaches to measuring and managing performance, discussing the techniques that are associated with each approach, and evaluating these approaches against the criteria of strategic congruence, validity, reliability, acceptability, and specificity.

THE COMPARATIVE APPROACH

The comparative approach to performance measurement consists of techniques that require the rater to compare an individual's performance with that of others. This approach usually uses some overall assessment of an individual's performance or worth, and seeks to develop some ranking of the individuals within a given work group. At least three techniques fall under the comparative approach: ranking, forced distribution, and paired comparison.

RANKING. Simple ranking requires managers to rank employees within their departments from highest performer to poorest performer (or best to worst). Alternation ranking, on the other hand, consists of a manager looking at a list of employees, deciding who is the best employee, and crossing that person's name off the list. From the remaining names, the manager decides who the worst employee is and crosses that name off the list—and so forth.

Ranking is one method of performance appraisal that has received some specific attention in the courts. In the *Albermarle v. Moody* case, the validation of the selection system was conducted using employee rankings as the measure of performance. The court actually stated, "There is no way of knowing precisely what criteria of job performance that supervisors were considering, whether each supervisor was considering the same criteria—or whether, indeed, any of the supervisors actually applied a focused and stable body of criteria of any kind."[12]

FORCED DISTRIBUTION. The *forced distribution* method also uses a ranking format, but employees are ranked in groups. This technique requires the manager to put certain percentages of employees into predetermined categories as depicted in Table 8.3. The example in the table shows how Merck combines the performance of the division with individual performance to recommend the distributions of employees that should fall into each category. For example, among poorly performing divisions (Not Acceptable), only 1 percent of employees should receive the highest rating (TF = Top 5 percent), whereas among top-performing divisions (Exceptional), 8 percent of employees should receive the highest rating. In some situations, the forced distribution method forces

TABLE 8.3
Proposed Guidelines for Targeted Distribution of Performance Ratings
Targeted Employee Rating Distribution, by Divisional Performance

		PERFORMANCE RATING FOR DIVISIONS				
PERFORMANCE RATING FOR EMPLOYEES	RATING TYPE	EX EXCEPTIONAL	WD WITH DISTINCTION	HS HIGH STANDARD	RI ROOM FOR IMPROVEMENT	NA NOT ACCEPTABLE
TF Top 5%	Relative	8%	6%	5%	2%	1%
TQ Top quintile	Relative	20%	17%	15%	12%	10%
OU Outstanding **VG** Very good **GD** Good	Absolute Absolute Absolute	71%	75%	75%	78%	79%
LF Lower 5% **NA** Not acceptable	Relative Absolute	1%	2%	5%	8%	10%
PR Progressing		Not Applicable				

SOURCE: Reprinted with permission of The Conference Board, New York City. Data supplied by Merck & Co.; chart by Kevin J. Murphy, University of Rochester.

managers to categorize employees based on distribution rules not on their performance. For example, even if a manager's employees are all above average performers, the manager is forced to rate some employees as "Not Acceptable."

PAIRED COMPARISON. The *paired-comparison* method requires managers to compare every employee with every other employee in the work group, giving an employee a score of 1 every time she is considered the higher performer. Once all the pairs have been compared, the manager computes the number of times each employee received the favorable decision (i.e., counts up the points), and this becomes the employee's performance score.

The paired-comparison method tends to be time-consuming for managers and will become more so as organizations become flatter with an increased span of control. For example, a manager with 10 employees must make 45 (i.e., 10 × 9/2) comparisons. However, if the group is increased to 15 employees, 105 comparisons must be made.

Evaluating the Comparative Approach. The comparative approach to performance measurement provides an effective tool when the major purpose of the system is to differentiate employee performance. These techniques virtually eliminate problems of leniency, central tendency, and strictness. This is especially valuable if the results of the measures are to be used in making administrative decisions such as pay raises and promotions. In addition, they are relatively easy to develop and in most cases easy to use; thus, they are often considered acceptable by the users.

One problem with these techniques, however, is their common failure to be linked to the strategic goals of the organization. While raters can make their ratings based on the extent to which individuals' performances support the strategy, this link is seldom made explicit. In addition, because of the subjective nature of the ratings, their actual validity and reliability depend on the raters themselves. Some firms seek to use multiple evaluators to reduce the biases of any individual, but most do not. At best, we could conclude that their reliability and validity are modest.

These techniques lack specificity for feedback purposes. Based only on their relative rankings, individuals are completely unaware of what they must do differently to improve their ranking. This puts a heavy burden on the manager to provide specific feedback beyond that of the rating instrument itself. Finally, many employees and managers are less likely to accept evaluations based on comparative approaches. Evaluations are dependent on how employee's performance is relative to other employees in a group, team, or department (normative standard) rather than to absolute standards of excellent, good, fair, and poor performance.

THE ATTRIBUTE APPROACH

The attribute approach to performance management focuses on the extent to which individuals have certain attributes (characteristics or traits) believed to be desirable for the company's success. The techniques that use this approach tend to define a set of traits—such as initiative, leadership, and competitiveness—and evaluate individuals on them.

GRAPHIC RATING SCALES. The most common form that the attribute approach to performance management takes is the *graphic rating scale*. Table 8.4 shows a graphic rating scale used in a manufacturing company. As you can see, a list of traits is evaluated by a five-point (or some other number of points) rating scale. The manager considers one employee at a time, circling the number that signifies how much of that trait the individual has. Graphic rating scales can provide the rater with a number of differ-

TABLE 8.4
Example of a Graphic Rating Scale

The following areas of performance are significant to most positions. Indicate your assessment of performance on each dimension by circling the appropriate rating

PERFORMANCE DIMENSION	RATING				
	DISTINGUISHED	EXCELLENT	COMMENDABLE	ADEQUATE	POOR
Knowledge	5	4	3	2	1
Communication	5	4	3	2	1
Judgment	5	4	3	2	1
Managerial skill	5	4	3	2	1
Quality performance	5	4	3	2	1
Teamwork	5	4	3	2	1
Interpersonal skills	5	4	3	2	1
Initiative	5	4	3	2	1
Creativity	5	4	3	2	1
Problem solving	5	4	3	2	1

ent points (a "discrete" scale) or with a continuum along which the rater simply places a check mark (a "continuous" scale).

The legal defensibility of graphic rating scales was questioned in the *Brito v. Zia* (1973) case. In this case, Spanish-speaking employees had been terminated as a result of their performance appraisals. These appraisals consisted of supervisors' rating subordinates on a number of undefined dimensions such as volume of work, quantity of work, job knowledge, dependability, and cooperation. The court criticized the subjective nature of these appraisals, and stated that the company should have presented empirical data demonstrating that the appraisal was significantly related to actual work behavior.

MIXED STANDARD SCALES. *Mixed standard scales* were developed as a means of getting around some of the problems with graphic rating scales. To create a mixed standard scale. We must define the relevant performance dimensions, and then develop statements representing good, average, and poor performance along each dimension. These statements are then mixed with the statements from other dimensions on the actual rating instrument. An example of a mixed standard scale is presented in Table 8.5.

As we see in the table, the rater is asked to complete the rating instrument by indicating whether the employee's performance is above (+), at (0), or below (–) the statement. A special scoring key is then used to score the employee's performance for each dimension. Thus, for example, if the employee's performance is above all three statements, she receives a 7. If the employee is below the good statement, at the average statement, and above the poor statement, a score of 4 is assessed. If the employee is below all three statements he is given a rating of 1. This scoring is applied to all the dimensions to determine an overall performance score.

Note that mixed standard scales were originally developed as trait-oriented scales. However, this same technique has been applied to instruments using behavioral rather than trait-oriented statements as a means of reducing rating errors in performance appraisal.[13]

Evaluating the Attribute Approach. Managers need to be aware that attribute-based performance methods are the most popular methods in organizations. They are quite easy to develop and are generalizable across a variety of jobs, strategies, and organizations. In addition, if much attention is devoted to identifying those attributes relevant

TABLE 8.5
An Example of a Mixed Standard Scale

Three traits being assessed:
- Initiative (INTV)
- Intelligence (INTG)
- Relations with others (RWO)

Levels of performance in statements:
- High (H)
- Medium (M)
- Low (L)

Instructions: Please indicate next to each statement whether the employee's performance is above (+), equal to (0), or below (–) the statement.

		Statement	Rating
INTV	H	1. This employee is a real self-starter. The employee always takes the initiative and his/her superior never has to prod this individual.	+
INTG	M	2. While perhaps this employee is not a genius, s/he is a lot more intelligent than many people I know.	+
RWO	L	3. This employee has a tendency to get into unnecessary conflicts with other people.	0
INTV	M	4. While generally this employee shows initiative, occasionally his/her superior must prod him/her to complete work.	+
INTG	L	5. Although this employee is slower than some in understanding things, and may take a bit longer in learning new things, s/he is of average intelligence.	+
RWO	H	6. This employee is on good terms with everyone. S/he can get along with people even when s/he does not agree with them.	–
INTV	L	7. This employee has a bit of a tendency to sit around and wait for directions.	+
INTG	H	8. This employee is extremely intelligent, and s/he learns very rapidly.	–
RWO	M	9. This employee gets along with most people. Only very occasionally does s/he have conflicts with others on the job, and these are likely to be minor.	–

Scoring Key:

STATEMENTS			SCORE
HIGH	MEDIUM	LOW	
+	+	+	7
0	+	+	6
–	+	+	5
–	0	+	4
–	–	+	3
–	–	0	2
–	–	–	1

Example score from preceding ratings:

	STATEMENTS			SCORE
	HIGH	MEDIUM	LOW	
Initiative	+	+	+	7
Intelligence	0	+	+	6
Relations with others	–	–	0	2

to job performance and carefully defining them on the rating instrument, they can be as reliable and valid as more elaborate measurement techniques.

However, these techniques fall short on several of the criteria for effective performance management. There is usually little strategic congruence between the techniques and the company's strategy. These methods are used because of the ease in developing them and because the same method (e.g., list of traits, comparisons) is generalizable across any organization and any strategy. In addition, these methods usually have very vague performance standards that are open to different interpretations by different raters. Because of this, different raters often provide extremely different ratings and rankings. The result is that both the validity and reliability of these methods are usually low.

Virtually none of these techniques provides any specific guidance on how an employee can support the company's goals or on what to do to correct performance deficiencies. In addition, when raters give feedback, these techniques tend to elicit defensiveness from employees. For example, how would you feel if you were told that on a five-point scale, you were rated a "2" in maturity? Certainly you might feel somewhat defensive and unwilling to accept that judgment, as well as any additional feedback. Also, being told you were rated a "2" in maturity doesn't tell you what you need to do to improve your rating.

THE BEHAVIORAL APPROACH

The behavioral approach to performance management attempts to define the behaviors an employee must exhibit to be effective in the job. The various techniques define those behaviors, and then require managers to assess the extent to which employees exhibit them. We discuss five techniques that rely on the behavioral approach.

CRITICAL INCIDENTS. The *critical incident* approach requires managers to keep a record of specific examples of effective and ineffective performance on the part of each employee. Here's an example of an incident described in the performance evaluation of an appliance repair person:

> A customer called in about a refrigerator that was not cooling and was making a clicking noise every few minutes. The technician prediagnosed the cause of the problem and checked his truck for the necessary parts. When he found he did not have them, he checked the parts out from inventory so that the customer's refrigerator would be repaired on his first visit and the customer would be satisfied promptly.

These incidents are used to give specific feedback to employees about what they do well and what they do poorly, and they can be tied to the company's strategy by focusing on incidents that best support that strategy. However, many managers resist having to keep a daily or weekly log of their employees' behavior. It is also often difficult to make comparisons among employees, since each incident is specific to that individual.

BEHAVIORALLY ANCHORED RATING SCALES (BARS). A *behaviorally anchored rating scale* (BARS) builds on the critical incidents approach. It is designed to specifically define performance dimensions by developing behavioral anchors associated with different levels of performance.[14] An example of BARS is presented in Figure 8.3. As you can see, the performance dimension has a number of examples of behaviors that indicate specific levels of performance along the dimension.

To develop BARS, we first gather a large number of critical incidents that represent effective and ineffective performance on the job. These incidents are classified into performance dimensions, and the ones that experts agree clearly represent a particular level of performance are used as behavioral examples (or anchors) to guide the rater. The manager's task is to consider an employee's performance along each dimension and determine where on the dimension the employee's performance fits using the behavioral anchors as guides. This rating becomes the employee's score for that dimension.

Behavioral anchors have advantages and disadvantages. One advantage is that they

FIGURE 8.3
Task-BARS Rating Dimension: Patrol Officer

Preparing for Duty

7 — Always early for work, gathers all necessary equipment to go to work, fully dressed, uses time before roll call to review previous shift's activities and any new bulletins, takes notes of previous shift's activity mentioned during roll call.

6 — Always early for work, gathers all necessary equipment to go to work, fully dressed, checks activity from previous shifts before going to roll call.

5 — Early for work, has all necessary equipment to go to work, fully dressed.

4 — On time, has all necessary equipment to go to work, fully dressed.

3 — Not fully dressed for roll call, does not have all necessary equipment.

2 — Late for roll call, does not check equipment or vehicle for damage or needed repairs, unable to go to work from roll call, has to go to locker, vehicle, or home to get necessary equipment.

1 — Late for roll call majority of period, does not check equipment or vehicle, does not have necessary equipment to go to work.

SOURCE: Adapted from R. Harvey, "Job Analysis," in *Handbook of Industrial & Organizational Psychology,* 2d ed., ed. M. Dunnette and L. Hough (Palo Alto, CA.: Consulting Psychologists Press, 1991), p.138.

can increase interrater reliability by providing a precise and complete definition of the performance dimension. A disadvantage is that they can bias information recall—that is, behavior that closely approximates the anchor is more easily recalled than other behavior.[15] Research has also demonstrated that managers and their subordinates do not make much of a distinction between BARS and trait scales.[16]

BEHAVIORAL OBSERVATION SCALES. A *behavioral observation scale (BOS)* is a variation of BARS. Like BARS, a BOS is developed from critical incidents.[17] However, a BOS differs from BARS in two basic ways. First, rather than discarding a large number of the behaviors that exemplify effective or ineffective performance, a BOS uses many of them to more specifically define all the behaviors that are necessary for effective performance (or that would be considered ineffective performance). Instead of using, say, 4 behaviors to define 4 levels of performance on a particular dimension, a BOS may use 15 behaviors. An example of a BOS is presented in Table 8.6.

A second difference is that rather than assessing which behavior best reflects an individual's performance, a BOS requires managers to rate the frequency with which the employee has exhibited each behavior during the rating period. These ratings are then averaged to compute an overall performance rating.

The major drawback of a BOS is that it may require more information than most managers can process or remember. A BOS can have 80 or more behaviors, and the manager must remember how frequently an employee exhibited each of these behaviors over a 6- or 12-month rating period. This is taxing enough with regard to one employee, but managers often must rate 10 or more employees.

A direct comparison of BOS, BARS, and graphic rating scales found that both managers and employees prefer BOS for differentiating good from poor performers, maintaining objectivity, providing feedback, suggesting training needs, and being easy to use among managers and subordinates.[18]

TABLE 8.6
An Example of a Behavioral Observation Scale (BOS) for Evaluating Job Performance

Overcoming Resistance to Change

(1) Describes the details of the change to subordinates.

Almost Never	1	2	3	4	5	Almost Always

(2) Explains why the change is necessary.

Almost Never	1	2	3	4	5	Almost Always

(3) Discusses how the change will affect the employee.

Almost Never	1	2	3	4	5	Almost Always

(4) Listens to the employee's concerns.

Almost Never	1	2	3	4	5	Almost Always

(5) Asks the employee for help in making the change work.

Almost Never	1	2	3	4	5	Almost Always

(6) If necessary, specifies the date for a follow-up meeting to respond to the employee's concerns.

Almost Never	1	2	3	4	5	Almost Always

Total = ________

Below Adequate	Adequate	Full	Excellent	Superior
6–10	11–15	16–20	21–25	26–30

Scores are set by management.

SOURCE: G. Latham and K. Wexley, *Increasing Productivity through Performance Appraisal,* p. 56. © 1994, 1981 Addison–Wesley Publishing Co., Inc. Reprinted by permission of Addison–Wesley Longman Publishing Company, Inc.

ORGANIZATIONAL BEHAVIOR MODIFICATION (OBM). *Organizational behavior modification* entails managing the behavior of employees through a formal system of behavioral feedback and reinforcement. This system builds on the behaviorist view of motivation, which holds that individuals' future behavior is determined by past behaviors that have been positively reinforced. The techniques vary, but most of them have four components. First, they define a set of key behaviors necessary for job performance. Second, they use a measurement system to assess whether these behaviors are exhibited. Third, the manager or consultant informs employees of those behaviors, perhaps even setting goals for how often the employees should exhibit those behaviors. Finally, feedback and reinforcement are provided to employees.[19]

OBM techniques have been used in a variety of settings. One technique, referred to as *behavior management,* was used to increase the performance of cleaning people in the hotel industry.[20] Housekeepers were asked to follow a 70-item behavioral checklist, checking off each behavior as they performed it. By providing feedback and reinforcement, management was able to increase housekeepers' performance, as Figure 8.4 shows. Similar results have been observed with respect to the frequency of safety behaviors in a processing plant.[21]

ASSESSMENT CENTERS. Although assessment centers are usually used for selection and promotion decisions, they have also been used as a way of measuring managerial performance.[22] At an assessment center, individuals usually perform a number of simulated tasks, such as leaderless group discussions, in-baskets, and role playing. Assessors observe the individuals' behavior and evaluate their skill or potential as managers. We discuss assessment centers more in Chapter 9.

The advantage of assessment centers is that they provide a somewhat objective measure of an individual's performance at managerial tasks. In addition, they provide specific performance feedback, and individualized developmental plans can be designed. For example, ARCO Oil & Gas Corporation sends its managers through assessment centers to identify their individual strengths and weaknesses and to create developmental action plans for each manager.

An interesting public-sector application of assessment centers is in the state govern-

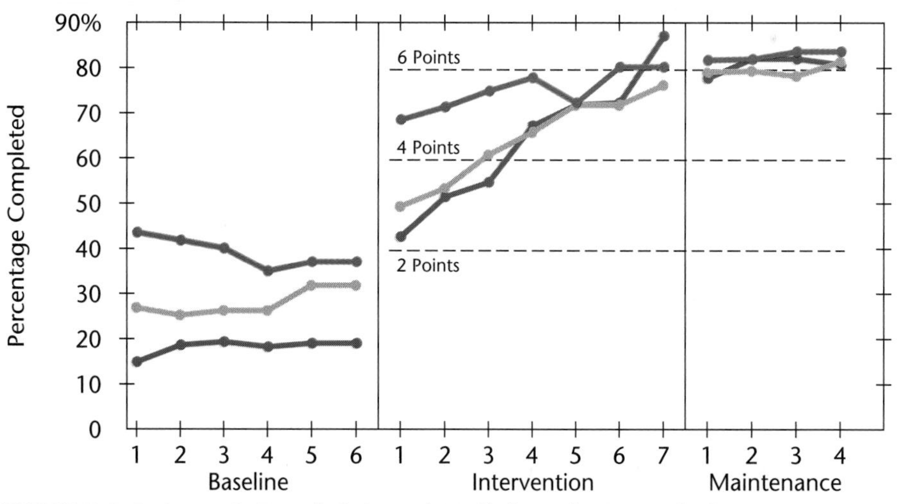

FIGURE 8.4 Increases in Productivity for Housekeepers as a Result of Behavior Management

SOURCE: D.C. Anderson, C. Crowell, S. Sponsel, M. Clarke, and J. Spence. "Behavior Management in the Public Accommodations Industry: A Three-Project Demonstration," *Journal of Organizational Behavior Modification* 4 (1983), p. 57. © 1982 The Haworth Press, Binghamton, New York. Reprinted with permission.

ment of North Carolina. Managers there can go through an assessment process to become "certified middle managers." This process includes an assessment center at the beginning of the certification program, from which an individualized developmental action plan is created. The developmental plan, implemented over approximately two years, consists of training programs and on-the-job developmental experiences. At the end of the two years, the manager attends the certification assessment center. Those who successfully meet the criteria set forth in the certification assessment center then become certified.

Evaluation of the Behavioral Approach. The behavioral approach can be very effective. It can link the company's strategy to the specific types of behavior necessary for implementing that strategy. It provides specific guidance and feedback for employees about the performance expected of them. Most of the techniques rely on in-depth job analysis, so the behaviors that are identified and measured are valid. Because those who will be using the system are involved in developing the measures, the acceptability is also often high. Finally, with a substantial investment in training raters, the techniques are reasonably reliable.

The major weaknesses have to do with the organizational context of the system. Although the behavioral approach can be closely tied to a company's strategy, the behaviors and measures must be constantly monitored and revised to ensure that they are still linked to the strategic focus. This approach also assumes that there is "one best way" to do the job and that the behaviors that constitute this best way can be identified. One study found that managers seek to control behaviors when they perceive a clear relationship between behaviors and results. When this link is not clear, they tend to rely on managing results.[23] The behavioral approach might be best suited to less complex jobs (where the best way to achieve results is somewhat clear) and least suited to complex jobs (where there are multiple ways, or behaviors, to achieve success).

THE RESULTS APPROACH

The results approach focuses on managing the objective, measurable results of a job or work group. This approach assumes that subjectivity can be eliminated from the measurement process and that results are the closest indicator of one's contribution to organizational effectiveness.[24] We will examine two performance management systems that use results: management by objectives and the productivity measurement and evaluation system.

MANAGEMENT BY OBJECTIVES (MBO). *Management by objectives (MBO)* is popular in both private and public organizations.[25] The original concept came from the accounting firm of Booz, Allen, and Hamilton and was called a "manager's letter." The process consisted of having all the subordinate managers write a letter to their superiors, detailing what their performance goals were for the coming year and how they planned to achieve them. Harold Smiddy applied and expanded this idea at General Electric in the 1950s, and Douglas McGregor has since developed it into a philosophy of management.[26]

In an MBO system, the top management team first defines the company's strategic goals for the coming year. These goals are passed on to the next layer of management, and these managers define the goals they must achieve for the company to reach its goals. This goal-setting process cascades down the organization so that all managers are setting goals that help the company achieve its goals.[27] These goals are used as the standards by which an individual's performance is evaluated.[28]

MBO systems have three common components.[29] One, they require specific, diffi-

Performance Management Practices May Not Directly Translate

COMPETING THROUGH GLOBALIZATION

Performance management approaches (behaviors, objectives, etc.) usually generalize across countries. To effectively manage performance in non-U.S. locations, companies need to change the way the methods are used including the behaviors that are rated, who is asked to perform the rating, and how feedback is provided. For example, National Rental Car uses a behaviorally based rating scale for customer service representatives. To measure the extent to which customer service representatives' behaviors are contributing to the strategic goal of improving customer service, behaviors such as smiling, making eye contact, greeting customers, and solving customer problems are evaluated. Depending on the country, appropriate behaviors need to be measured. For example, in Japan the angle of bowing as well as the proper back alignment and eye contact would be judged according to culturally defined standards. In Ghana and many other African nations, behaviors would be used that reflect loyalty and repaying of obligations as well as behaviors related to following regulations and procedures.

Besides taking into account cultural differences when identifying specific behaviors that should be evaluated, performance management systems should also be adapted to reflect cultural norms and values. For example, when working in rapidly changing markets, such as Southeast Asia, performance plans may need to be updated more frequently than annually. Ito–Yokado, the Japanese company that controls 7–Eleven convenience stores, has implemented technology into the cash registers that allows headquarters to monitor every time a sale is made and how often managers use analytical tools included in the system to track product sales. American managers have resisted the Japanese philosophy of discipline and control. They feel that managers know from experience how to stock shelves and make changes in product mix due to the weather or special events. Also, they resent being under surveillance by headquarters.

Although positive feedback is universally appreciated and valued, in the United States we are more used to direct feedback than employees in other countries. For example, in Mexico you need to provide positive feedback before focusing the discussion on behaviors the employee needs to improve. At the Thai office of Singapore Airlines, managers resisted giving negative feedback to employees because of their fear that this would cause them to have bad karma, and as a result, they would be reincarnated at a lower level in their next life. The airlines allowed them to adapt the feedback process to fit local cultures.

SOURCE: D. D. Davis, "International Performance Measurement and Management," in *Performance Appraisal: State of the Art in Practice*, ed. J. W. Smither (San Francisco: Jossey–Bass, 1998), pp. 95–131; L. S. Chee, "Singapore Airlines: Strategic Human Resource Initiatives," in *International Human Resource Management: Think Globally, Act Locally*, ed. D. Torrington (Upper Saddle River, NJ: Prentice Hall, 1994), pp. 143–59; M. Gowan, S. Ibarreche, and C. Lackey, "Doing the Right Things in Mexico," *Academy of Management Executive* 1996 (Vol. 10), pp. 74–81; N. Shirouzu and J. Bigness, "7–Eleven Operators Resist System to Monitor Managers," *The Wall Street Journal* (June 16, 1997), pp. B1, B5.

cult, objective goals. (An example of MBO-based goals used in a financial service firm is presented in Table 8.7.) Two, the goals are not usually set unilaterally by management but with the managers' and subordinates' participation. Three, the manager gives objective feedback throughout the rating period to monitor progress toward the goals.

Research on MBO has revealed two important findings regarding its effectiveness.[30] Of 70 studies examined, 68 showed productivity gains, while only 2 showed productivity losses, suggesting that MBO usually increases productivity. Also, productivity gains tend to be highest when there is substantial commitment to the MBO program from top management: an average increase of 56 percent when commitment was high, 33 percent when commitment was moderate, and 6 percent when commitment was low.

Clearly, MBO can have a very positive effect on an organization's performance. Considering the process through which goals are set (i.e., involvement of staff in setting objectives), it is also likely that MBO systems effectively link individual employee performance with the firm's strategic goals.

TABLE 8.7 An Example of a Management by Objectives (MBO) Measure of Job Performance

KEY RESULT AREA	OBJECTIVE	% COMPLETE	ACTUAL PERFORMANCE
Loan Portfolio Management	Increase portfolio value by 10% over the next 12 months	90	Increased portfolio value by 9% over the past 12 months
Sales	Generate fee income of $30,000 over the next 12 months	150	Generated fee income of $45,000 over the past 12 months

For example, Pier 1 Imports was able to give store managers and salespeople access to real-time sales totals and analyses, telling them exactly how they were doing compared with, say, the day before or the month before. Instead of creating a sweatshop atmosphere, as some critics worried, employees took the figures as a challenge. "The more information you give the associates, the more ownership they feel in the store's performance," says Dave Self, a regional manager for 33 Pier 1 stores.

Pier 1 employees agree. "It adds to the excitement," claims Alicia Winchell, an assistant manager. During the day, clerks at the store rotate their use of a backroom computer that gives them up-to-the-minute sales data. They learn not only how many items were sold and at what price but also how many people entered the store and the percentage of those who bought something. They know how many items are new and how many were imported from overseas. These figures help managers and sales staff create better value for customers, paying close attention to everyone who walks in the door. Paula Hankins, a store manager, spent a half hour one day helping an interior designer select some small decorations. The designer hadn't planned to spend $250 that day but said that Hankins "did a great job pointing out what I wanted."

Pier 1 management makes an important distinction about the data: They are an informational tool, not an instrument of discipline. If a store fails to meet a certain short-term goal, "It's not like they're blaming us for it," says employee Kim Smith. Results provide valuable insight into the whole performance management picture.[31]

PRODUCTIVITY MEASUREMENT AND EVALUATION SYSTEM (PROMES). The main goal of ProMES is to motivate employees to higher levels of productivity.[32] It is a means of measuring and feeding back productivity information to personnel.

ProMES consists of four steps. First, people in an organization identify the products, or the set of activities or objectives, the organization expects to accomplish. The organization's productivity depends on how well it produces these products. At a repair shop, for example, a product might be something like "quality of repair." Second, the staff defines indicators of the products. Indicators are measures of how well the products are being generated by the organization. Quality of repair could be indicated by (1) return rate (percentage of items returned that did not function immediately after repair) and (2) percentage of quality-control inspections passed. Third, the staff establishes the contingencies between the amount of the indicators and the level of evaluation associated with that amount. Fourth, a feedback system is developed that provides employees and work groups with information about their specific level of performance on each of the indicators. An overall productivity score can be computed by summing the effectiveness scores across the various indicators.

Because this technique is somewhat new, it has been applied in only a few situations. However, research thus far strongly suggests it is effective in increasing productivity. (Figure 8.5 illustrates the productivity gains in the repair shop described previously.)

The research also suggests the system is an effective feedback mechanism. However, users found it time-consuming to develop the initial system. Future research on ProMES needs to be conducted before drawing any firm conclusions, but the existing research indicates that this may be a useful performance management tool.

Evaluation of the Results Approach. One advantage of the results approach is that it minimizes subjectivity, relying on objective, quantifiable indicators of performance. Thus, it is usually highly acceptable to both managers and employees. Another advantage is that it links an individual's results with the organization's strategies and goals.

A disadvantage is that objective measurements can be both contaminated and deficient—contaminated because they are affected by things that are not under the employee's control, such as economic recessions, and deficient because not all the important aspects of job performance are amenable to objective measurement. Another disadvantage of the results approach is that individuals may focus only on aspects of their performance that are measured, neglecting those that are not. For example, if the large majority of employees goals relate to productivity it is unlikely they will be concerned with customer service. One study found that objective performance goals led to higher performance but that they also led to less helping of co-workers.[33] A final disadvantage is that, though results measures provide objective feedback, the feedback may not help employees learn how they need to change their behavior to increase their performance. If baseball players are in a hitting slump, simply telling them that their batting average is .190 may not motivate them to raise it. Feedback focusing on the exact behavior (e.g., taking one's eye off the ball, dropping one's shoulder) that needs to be changed would be more helpful.[34]

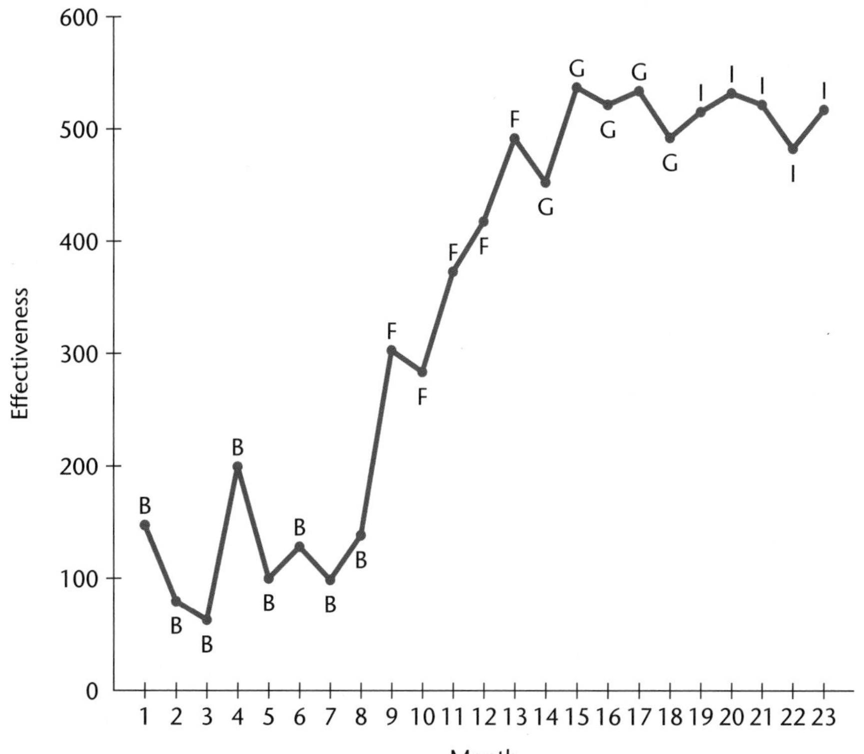

FIGURE 8.5
Increases in Productivity for a Repair Shop Using ProMES Measures

SOURCE: R. Pritchard, S. Jones, P. Roth, K. Stuebing, and S. Ekeberg, "The Evaluation of an Integrated Approach to Measuring Organizational Productivity," *Personnel Psychology* 42 (1989), pp. 69–115. Used by permission.

THE QUALITY APPROACH

Thus far we have examined the traditional approaches to measuring and evaluating employee performance. Two fundamental characteristics of the quality approach are a customer orientation and a prevention approach to errors. Improving customer satisfaction is the primary goal of the quality approach. Customers can be internal or external to the organization. A performance management system designed with a strong quality orientation can be expected to

- Emphasize an assessment of both person and system factors in the measurement system.
- Emphasize that managers and employees work together to solve performance problems.
- Involve both internal and external customers in setting standards and measuring performance.
- Use multiple sources to evaluate person and system factors.[35]

Based on this chapter's earlier discussion of the characteristics of an effective performance management system, it should be apparent to you that these characteristics are not just unique to the quality approach but are characteristics of an effective appraisal system!

Advocates of the quality approach believe that most U.S. companies' performance management systems are incompatible with the quality philosophy for a number of reasons:

1. Most existing systems measure performance in terms of quantity, not quality.
2. Employees are held accountable for good or bad results to which they contribute but do not completely control.
3. Companies do not share the financial rewards of successes with employees according to how much they have contributed to them.
4. Rewards are not connected to business results.[36]

Sales, profit margins, and behavioral ratings are often collected by managers to evaluate employees' performance. These are person-based outcomes. An assumption of using these types of outcomes is that the employee completely controls them. However, according to the quality approach, these types of outcomes should not be used to evaluate employees' performance because they do not have complete control over them (i.e., they are contaminated). For example, for salespersons, performance evaluations (and salary increases) are often based on attainment of a sales quota. It is assumed that salespersons' abilities and motivation are directly responsible for their performance. However, quality approach advocates argue that better determinants of whether a salesperson reaches the quota are "systems factors," (such as competitors' product price changes) and economic conditions (which are not under the salesperson's control).[37] Holding employees accountable for outcomes affected by systems factors is believed to result in dysfunctional behavior, such as falsifying sales reports, budgets, expense accounts, and other performance measures, as well as lowering employees' motivation for continuous improvement.

Quality advocates suggest that the major focus of performance evaluations should be to provide employees with feedback about areas in which they can improve. Two types of feedback are necessary: (1) subjective feedback from managers, peers, and customers about the personal qualities of the employee and (2) objective feedback based on the work process itself using statistical quality-control methods.

Performance feedback from managers, peers, and customers should be based on such dimensions as cooperation, attitude, initiative, and communication skills. Performance evaluation should include a discussion of the employee's career plans. The quality approach also strongly emphasizes that performance appraisal systems should avoid providing overall evaluations of employees (e.g., ratings such as excellent, good, poor). Categorizing employees is believed to encourage them to behave in ways that are expected based on their ratings. For example, "average" performers may not be motivated to improve their performance but rather may continue to perform at the expected level. Also, because employees do not have control over the quality of the system in which they work, employee performance evaluations should not be linked to compensation. Compensation rates should be based on prevailing market rates of pay, seniority, and business results, which are distributed equitably to all employees.

Statistical process control techniques are very important in the quality approach. These techniques provide employees with an objective tool to identify causes of problems and potential solutions. These techniques include process-flow analysis, cause-and-effect diagrams, Pareto charts, control charts, histograms, and scattergrams.

Process-flow analysis involves identifying each action and decision necessary to complete work, such as waiting on a customer or assembling a television set. Process-flow analysis is useful for identifying redundancy in processes that increase manufacturing or service time. For example, one business unit at Owens–Corning was able to confirm that customer orders were only error-free about 25 percent of the time (an unacceptable level of service). To improve the service level, the unit mapped out the process to identify bottlenecks and problem areas. As a result of the mapping process, one simple change (installing an 800-number for the fax machine) increased overall accuracy of orders as well as speed of transaction.[38]

In *cause-and-effect diagrams*, events or causes that result in undesirable outcomes are identified. Employees try to identify all possible causes of a problem. The feasibility of the causes is not evaluated, and as a result, cause-and-effect diagrams produce a large list of possible causes.

A *Pareto chart* is used to highlight the most important cause of a problem. In a Pareto chart, causes are listed in decreasing order of importance, where importance is usually defined as the frequency with which that cause resulted in a problem. The assumption of Pareto analysis is that the majority of problems are the result of a small number of causes. Figure 8.6 shows a Pareto chart listing the reasons managers give for not selecting current employees for a job vacancy.

Control charts involve collecting data at multiple points in time. By collecting data at different times, employees can identify what factors contribute to an outcome and when they tend to occur. Figure 8.7 shows the percentage of employees hired internally for a company for each quarter between 1993 and 1995. Internal hiring increased dramatically during the third quarter of 1994. The use of control charts helps employees understand the number of internal candidates who can be expected to be hired each year. Also, the control chart shows that the amount of internal hiring conducted during the third quarter of 1994 was much larger than normal.

Histograms are used for displaying distributions of large sets of data. Data are grouped into a smaller number of categories or classes. Histograms are useful for understanding the amount of variance between an outcome and the expected value or average outcome. Figure 8.8 is a histogram showing the number of days it took a company to fill nonexempt job vacancies. The histogram shows that most nonexempt jobs took from 17 to 21 days to fill, and the amount of time to fill nonexempt jobs ranged from 1 to 33 days. If an HR manager relied simply on data from personnel files on the number of days it took to fill nonexempt positions, it would be extremely difficult to understand the variation and average tendency in the amount of time to fill the positions.

Scattergrams show the relationship between two variables, events, or different pieces of data. Scattergrams help employees determine whether the relationship between two variables or events is positive, negative, or zero.

FIGURE 8.6
Pareto Chart

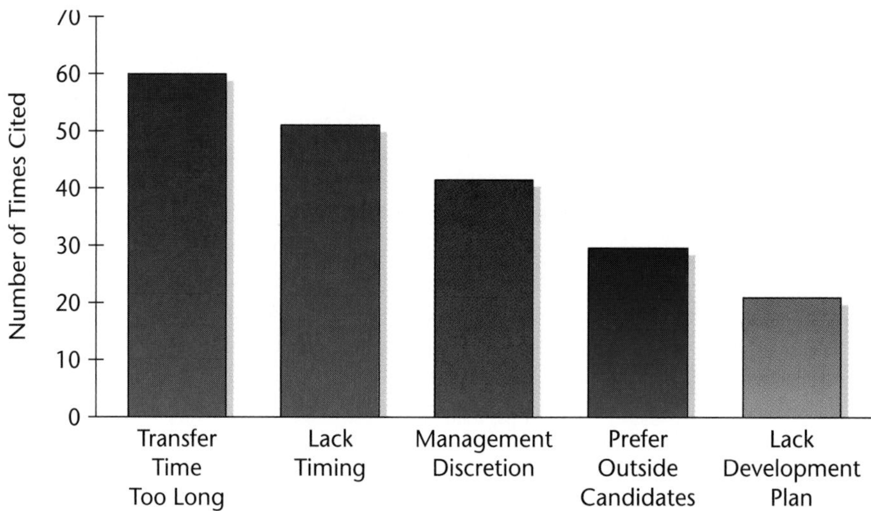

SOURCE: "Seven Basic Quality Tools" by Carla Carter, *HR Magazine*, January 1992, p. 83. Reprinted with permission of *HR Magazine*. Published by the Society for Human Resource Management, Alexandria, VA.

FIGURE 8.7
Control Chart

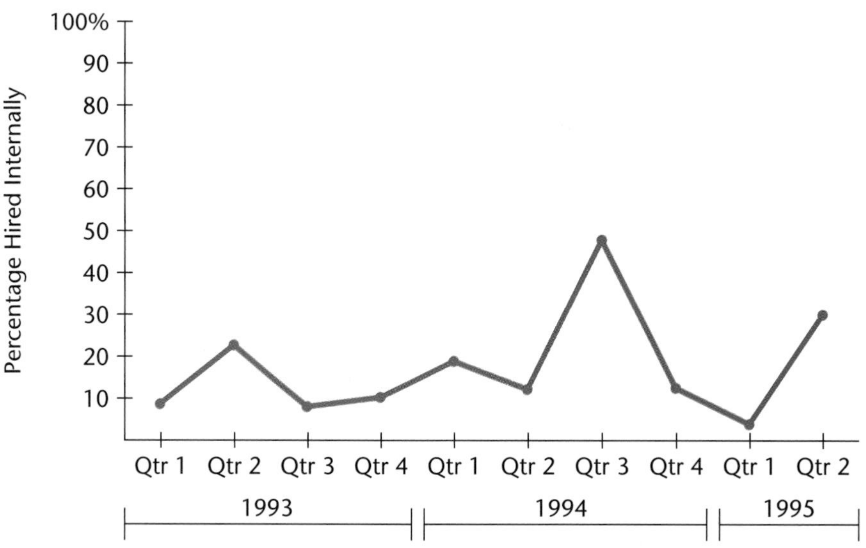

SOURCE: "Seven Basic Quality Tools" by Carla Carter, *HR Magazine*, January 1992, p. 82. Reprinted with permission of *HR Magazine*. Published by the Society for Human Resource Management, Alexandria, VA.

Evaluation of the Quality Approach. The quality approach relies primarily on a combination of the attribute and results approaches to performance measurement. However, traditional performance appraisal systems focus more on individual employee performance, while the quality approach adopts a systems-oriented focus.[39] Many companies may be unwilling to completely abandon their traditional performance management system because it serves as the basis for personnel selection validation, identification of

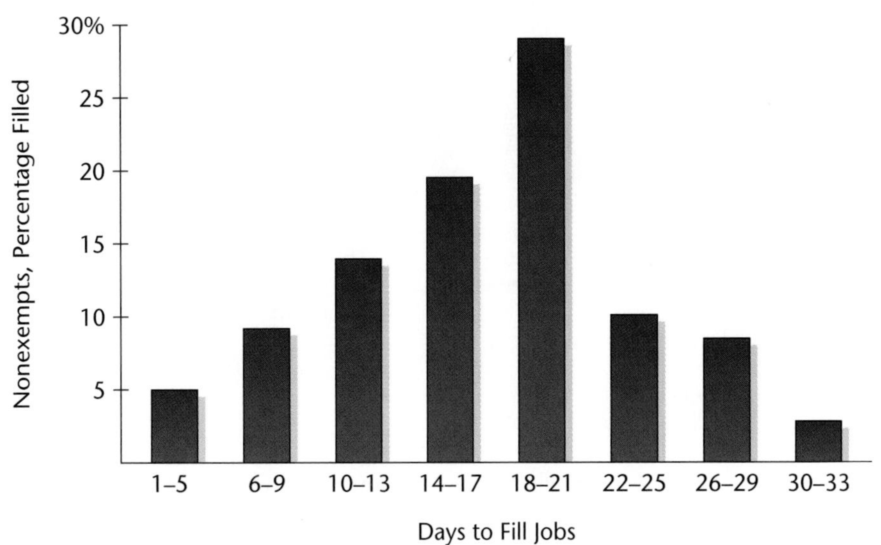

FIGURE 8.8
Histogram

SOURCE: "Seven Basic Quality Tools" by Carla Carter, *HR Magazine,* January 1992, p. 83. Reprinted with permission of *HR Magazine.* Published by the Society for Human Resource Management, Alexandria,VA.

training needs, or compensation decisions. Also, the quality approach advocates evaluation of personal traits (e.g., cooperation), which are difficult to relate to job performance unless the company has been structured into work teams.

In summary, organizations can take five approaches to measuring performance: comparative, attribute, behavioral, results, and quality. Table 8.8 summarizes the various approaches to measuring performance based on the criteria we set forth earlier and illustrates that each approach has strengths and weaknesses. As the quality approach illustrates, often the most effective way of measuring performance is to rely on a combination of two or more alternatives. For example, performance management systems in many companies evaluate the extent to which managers reach specific performance goals as well as evaluate their behavior. However, in most cases, the performance measures consist of some kind of ratings. These ratings must come from some source. The next section will discuss the various sources of performance information.

Choosing a Source for Performance Information

Whatever approach to performance management is used, it is necessary to decide whom to use as the source of the performance measures. Each source has specific strengths and weaknesses. We discuss five primary sources: managers, peers, subordinates, self, and customers.

MANAGERS

Managers are the most frequently used source of performance information. It is usually safe to assume that supervisors have extensive knowledge of the job requirements and that they have had adequate opportunity to observe their employees—in other words, that they have the ability to rate their employees. In addition, because supervisors have something to gain from the employees' high performance and something to lose from

TABLE 8.8
Evaluation of Approaches to Performance Measurement

	CRITERIA				
APPROACH	STRATEGIC CONGRUENCE	VALIDITY	RELIABILITY	ACCEPTABILITY	SPECIFICITY
Comparative	Poor, unless manager takes time to make link	Can be high if ratings are done carefully	Depends on rater, but usually no measure of agreement used	Moderate; easy to develop and use but resistance to normative standard	Very low
Attribute	Usually low; requires manager to make link	Usually low; can be fine if developed carefully	Usually low; can be improved by specific definitions of attributes	High; easy to develop and use	Very low
Behavioral	Can be quite high	Usually high; minimizes contamination and deficiency	Usually high	Moderate; difficult to develop, but accepted well for use	Very high
Results	Very high	Usually high; can be both contaminated and deficient	High; main problem can be test–retest—depends on timing of measure	High; usually developed with input from those to be evaluated	High regarding results, but low regarding behaviors necessary to achieve them
Quality	Very high	High, but can be both contaminated and deficient	High	High; usually developed with input from those to be evaluated	High regarding results, but low regarding behaviors necessary to achieve them

low performance, they have the motivation to make accurate ratings.[40] Finally, feedback from supervisors is strongly related to performance.[41]

Problems with using supervisors as the source of performance information can occur in particular situations. In some jobs, for example, the supervisor does not have an adequate opportunity to observe the employee performing his job duties. For example, in outside sales jobs, the supervisor does not have the opportunity to see the salesperson at work most of the time. This usually requires that the manager occasionally spend a day accompanying the salesperson on sales calls. However, on those occasions the employee will be on his best behavior, so there is no assurance that performance that day accurately reflects performance when the manager is not around.

Also, some supervisors may be so biased against a particular employee that to use her as the sole source of information would result in less-than-accurate measures for that individual. Favoritism is a fact of organizational life, but it is one that must be minimized as much as possible in the performance management process.[42] Thus, the performance evaluation system should seek to minimize the opportunities for favoritism to affect ratings. One way to do this is not to rely on only a supervisor's evaluation of an employee's performance.

While managers are the most frequently used source of performance information, it is ironic that upper level managers or chief executive officers whose decisions affect all of the company's shareholders, rarely receive performance evaluating. This situation is

Shareholders Get Larger Returns by Evaluating Top Dogs

Performance evaluations of CEOs are rare at most companies. However, many corporate board members and CEOs are recognizing their value. For example, Thomas Loarie (chairman and CEO of KeraVision Inc, a 12-year-old vision correction company in California) had an evaluation completed by the company's six directors. Mr. Loarie is well liked by the directors. But the evaluation was important because the company was at a critical point in the business. KeraVision is developing a new approach for treating common vision problems by reshaping the cornea by adding materials rather than cutting or removing tissue. The procedure has just been approved in Europe. It is still awaiting approval in the United States. KeraVision's net loss in 1997 was $19 million and it expects losses to continue. The future of the cornea procedure in the United States is uncertain because even if it is approved by the FDA, the company is unsure if consumers will be willing to pay for a procedure that is unlikely to be covered by medical insurance.

The six nonmanagement directors evaluate Mr. Loarie each August during a retreat that lasts two or three days. The process is separate from the process used to set his annual compensation. Directors use a 17-item questionnaire that focuses on four key areas: company performance, leadership, team building and management

succession, and leadership of external stakeholders such as customers.

In the appraisal, directors have criticized Mr. Loarie for providing unrealistically low projections of sales of the cornea procedure in Europe. The directors suggested that the projections may have resulted from Mr. Loarie failing to set high sales expectations for European managers. The board encouraged him to develop a management succession plan. (The company's founder was diagnosed with a terminal illness.) Mr. Loarie disagreed with the directors on this recommendation. He argued that it is impossible to develop a succession plan in such a small company. The board also rated him lower than he expected on involving its members. As a result of the appraisal, he has taken steps to get the board involved in setting the company's objectives. He has encouraged more interactions between senior managers and board members.

Although CEOs view appraisals such as Mr. Loarie's with anxiety, these appraisals are helpful in building an understanding with the board of directors. Such feedback is also useful for changing the CEO's strategy and policies, likely improving the bottom line. This translates into benefits for employees and shareholders alike!

SOURCE: T. D. Schellhardt, "Behind the Scenes at One CEO's Performance Review," *The Wall Street Journal* (April 27, 1998), pp. B1–B2. Reprinted by permission.

beginning to change as the "Competing by Meeting Stakeholders' Needs" box highlights.

PEERS

Another source of performance information is the employee's co-workers. Peers are an excellent source of information in a job such as law enforcement, where the supervisor does not always have the opportunity to observe the employee. Peers have expert knowledge of job requirements, and they often have the most opportunity to observe the employee in day-to-day activities. Peers also bring a different perspective to the evaluation process, which can be valuable in gaining an overall picture of the individual's performance. In fact, peers have been found to provide extremely valid assessments of performance in several different settings.[43]

One disadvantage of using peer ratings is the potential for friendship to bias ratings.[44] Little empirical evidence suggests that this is often a problem, however. Another disadvantage is that when the evaluations are made for administrative decisions, peers often find the situation of being both rater and ratee uncomfortable. When these ratings are used only for developmental purposes, however, peers react favorably.[45]

SUBORDINATES

Subordinates are an especially valuable source of performance information when managers are being evaluated. Subordinates often have the best opportunity to evaluate how well a manager treats employees. One recent study found that managers viewed receiving upward feedback more positively when receiving feedback from subordinates who were identified, but subordinates preferred to provide anonymous feedback. When subordinates were identified, they inflated their ratings of the manager.[46]

One problem with subordinate evaluations is that they give subordinates power over their managers, thus putting the manager in a difficult situation.[47] This can lead to managers' emphasizing employee satisfaction over productivity. However, this happens only when administrative decisions are made from these evaluations. As with peer evaluations, it is a good idea to use subordinate evaluations only for developmental purposes. To assure subordinates that they need not fear retribution from their managers, it is necessary to use anonymous evaluations and use at least three subordinates for each manager.

SELF

Although self-ratings are not often used as the sole source of performance information, they can still be valuable.[48] Obviously, individuals have extensive opportunities to observe their own behavior, and they usually have access to information regarding their results on the job.

One problem with self-ratings, however, is a tendency toward inflated assessments. This stems from two sources. One, if the ratings are going to be used for administrative decisions (e.g., pay raises), it is in the employees' interests to inflate their ratings. Two, there is ample evidence in the social psychology literature that individuals attribute their poor performance to external causes, such as a co-worker whom they think has not provided them with timely information. Although self-ratings are less inflated when supervisors provide frequent performance feedback, it is not advisable to use them for administrative purposes.[49] The best use of self-ratings is as a prelude to the performance feedback session to get employees thinking about their performance and to focus discussion on areas of disagreement.

CUSTOMERS

Service industries are expected to account for virtually all of job growth between 1996 and 2006.[50] As a result, we would expect many companies to be moving toward involving customers in their evaluation systems. One writer has defined *services* this way: "Services is something which can be bought and sold but which you cannot drop on your foot."[51] Because of the unique nature of services—the product is often produced and consumed on the spot—supervisors, peers, and subordinates often do not have the opportunity to observe employee behavior. Instead, the customer is often the only person present to observe the employee's performance and thus is the best source of performance information.

Many companies in service industries have moved toward customer evaluations of employee performance. Marriott Corporation provides a customer satisfaction card in every room and sends mail surveys to a random sample of customers after their stay in a Marriott hotel. Whirlpool's Consumer Services Division conducts both mail and telephone surveys of customers after factory service technicians have serviced their appliances. These surveys allow the company to evaluate an individual technician's customer-service behaviors while in the customer's home.

There are two situations when using customer evaluations of employee performance are appropriate.[52] The first is when an employee's job requires her to directly provide a

TABLE 8.9 Frequency of Observation for Various Sources of Performance Information

	SOURCE				
	SUPERVISOR	PEERS	SUBORDINATES	SELF	CUSTOMERS
Task					
Behaviors	Occasional	Frequent	Rare	Always	Frequent
Results	Frequent	Frequent	Occasional	Frequent	Frequent
Interpersonal					
Behaviors	Occasional	Frequent	Frequent	Always	Frequent
Results	Occasional	Frequent	Frequent	Frequent	Frequent

SOURCE: Adapted from K. Murphy and J. Cleveland, *Performance Appraisal: An Organizational Perspective* (Boston: Allyn & Bacon, 1991).

service to the customer or link the customer to other services within the company. Second, customer evaluations are appropriate when the company is interested in gathering information to determine what products and services the customer wants. That is, customer evaluations serve a strategic goal by integrating marketing strategies with human resource activities and policies. Customer evaluations collected for this purpose are useful for both evaluating the employee and helping to determine whether changes in other HR activities (e.g., training, compensation system) are needed to improve customer service.

The weakness of customer surveys is their expense. Printing, postage, phone, and labor can add up to hundreds of dollars for the evaluation of one individual. Thus, many companies conduct such evaluations only once a year for a short period of time.

In conclusion, the best source of performance information often depends on the particular job. One should choose the source or sources that provide the best opportunity to observe employee behavior and results. Table 8.9 summarizes this information for most jobs. Often, eliciting performance information from a variety of sources results in a performance management process that is accurate and effective. In fact, one recent popular trend in organizations is called *360-degree appraisals*.[53] This technique consists of having multiple raters (boss, peers, subordinates, customers) provide input into a manager's evaluation. The major advantage of the technique is that it provides a means for minimizing bias in an otherwise subjective evaluation technique. It has been used primarily for strategic and developmental purposes and is discussed in greater detail in Chapter 9.[54]

Rater Errors in Performance Measurement

Research consistently reveals that humans have tremendous limitations in processing information. Because we are so limited, we often use "heuristics," or simplifying mechanisms, to make judgments, whether they are judgments about investments or about people.[55] These heuristics, which appear often in subjective measures of performance, can lead to rater errors. Performance evaluations may also be purposefully distorted. We discuss rater errors and appraisal politics next.

SIMILAR TO ME. "Similar to me" is the error we make when we judge those who are similar to us more highly than those who are not. Research has demonstrated that this effect is strong, and when similarity is based on demographic characteristics such as race or sex, it can result in discriminatory decisions.[56] Most of us tend to think of ourselves as effective, and so if others are like us—in race, gender, background, attitudes, or beliefs—we assume that they too are effective.

CONTRAST. Contrast error occurs when we compare individuals with one another instead of against an objective standard. Consider a completely competent performer who works with a number of peers who are outstanding. If the competent employee receives lower-than-deserved ratings because of his outstanding colleagues, that is contrast error.

DISTRIBUTIONAL ERRORS. Distributional errors are the result of a rater's tendency to use only one part of the rating scale. *Leniency* occurs when a rater assigns high (lenient) ratings to all employees. *Strictness* occurs when a manager gives low ratings to all employees—that is, holds all employees to unreasonably high standards. *Central tendency* reflects that a manager rates all employees in the middle of the scale. These errors pose two problems. First, they make it difficult to distinguish among employees rated by the same rater. Second, they create problems in comparing the performance of individuals rated by different raters. If one rater is lenient and the other is strict, employees of the strict rater will receive significantly fewer rewards than those rated by the lenient rater.

HALO AND HORNS. These errors refer to a failure to distinguish among different aspects of performance. *Halo error* occurs when one positive performance aspect causes the rater to rate all other aspects of performance positively—for example, professors who are rated as outstanding researchers because they are known to be outstanding teachers. *Horns error* works in the opposite direction: One negative aspect results in the rater assigning low ratings to all the other aspects.

Halo and horns errors are a problem in that they preclude making the necessary distinctions between strong and weak performance. Halo error leads to employees believing that no aspects of their performance need improvement. Horns error leads to employees becoming frustrated and defensive.

REDUCING RATER ERRORS

Two approaches to reducing rating errors have been offered.[57] *Rater error training* attempts to make managers aware of rating errors and helps them develop strategies for minimizing those errors.[58] These programs consist of having the participants view videotaped vignettes designed to elicit rating errors such as "contrast." They then make their ratings and discuss how the error influenced the rating. Finally, they are given learning points regarding ways to avoid committing those errors. This approach has been shown to be effective for reducing errors, but there is evidence that reducing rating errors can also reduce accuracy.[59]

Rater accuracy training, also called *frame-of-reference training*, attempts to emphasize the multidimensional nature of performance and thoroughly familiarize raters with the actual content of various performance dimensions. This involves providing examples of performance for each dimension and then discussing the actual or "correct" level of performance that the example represents.[60] Accuracy training does seem to increase accuracy, provided that the training allows practice in making ratings and offers feedback about their accuracy.[61]

APPRAISAL POLITICS

Appraisal politics refer to evaluators purposefully distorting a rating to achieve personal or company goals. Research suggests that several factors promote appraisal politics. These factors are inherent in the appraisal system and the company culture. Appraisal politics are most likely to occur when raters are accountable to the employee being rated, there are competing rating goals, and a direct link exists between performance appraisal and highly desirable rewards. Also, appraisal politics are likely to occur if top executives tolerate distortion or are complacent toward it, and if distortion strategies are part of "company folklore" and are passed down from senior employees to new employees.

It is unlikely that appraisal politics can be completely eliminated. Unfortunately, there is little research on the best methods to eliminate appraisal politics. To minimize appraisal politics, managers should keep in mind the characteristics of a fair appraisal system shown in Table 8.2. In addition, managers should

- Train raters on the appropriate use of the process as discussed previously.
- Build top management support for the appraisal system and actively discourage distortion.
- Give raters some latitude to customize performance objectives and criteria for their ratees.
- Recognize employee accomplishments that are not self-promoted.
- Make sure constraints such as budget do not drive the process.
- Make sure that appraisal processes are consistent across the company.
- Foster a climate of openness to encourage employees to be honest about weaknesses.[62]

Performance Feedback

Once the expected performance has been defined and employees' performance has been measured, it is necessary to feed that performance information back to the employees so they can correct any deficiencies. The performance feedback process is complex and provokes anxiety for both the manager and the employee. Table 8.10 provides examples of feedback that managers have given employees. You be the judge as to these statements' effectiveness in improving employees' performance!

Few of us feel comfortable sitting in judgment of others. The thought of confronting others with what we perceive to be their deficiencies causes most of us to shake in our shoes. If giving negative feedback is painful, receiving it can be excruciating—thus the importance of the performance feedback process.

TABLE 8.10 Examples of Performance Feedback

Since my last report; this employee has reached rock bottom and has started to dig.
His men would follow him anywhere, but only out of morbid curiosity.
I would not allow this employee to breed.
This associate is really not so much of a "has-been," but more of "definitely won't-be."
Works well when under constant supervision and cornered like a rat in a trap.
When she opens her mouth, it seems that this is only to change whichever foot was previously in there.
He would be out of his depth in a parking-lot puddle.
This young lady has delusions of adequacy.
He sets low personal standards, then consistently fails to achieve them.
This employee should go far—and the sooner he starts, the better.
This employee is depriving a village somewhere of an idiot.

SOURCE: Yasha Harari, *The Daily Dose* (www.harari.org/index.html), July 22, 1997.

CHARACTERISTICS OF AN EFFECTIVE PERFORMANCE FEEDBACK PROCESS

If employees are not made aware of how their performance is not meeting expectations, their performance will almost certainly not improve. In fact, it may get worse. Effective managers provide specific performance feedback to employees in a way that elicits positive behavioral responses. The following process increases the potential for a successful performance feedback session.

FEEDBACK SHOULD BE GIVEN FREQUENTLY, NOT ONCE A YEAR. There are two reasons for this. First, managers have a responsibility to correct performance deficiencies immediately on becoming aware of them. If performance is subpar in January, waiting until December to appraise the performance could mean an 11-month productivity loss. Second, a major determinant of how effectively a feedback session goes is the extent to which the subordinate is not surprised by the evaluation. An easy rule to follow is that employees should receive such frequent performance feedback that they already know almost exactly what their formal evaluation will be.

CREATE THE RIGHT CONTEXT FOR THE DISCUSSION. Managers should choose a neutral location for the feedback session. The manager's office may not be the best place for a constructive feedback session because the employee may associate the office with unpleasant conversations. Managers should describe the meeting as an opportunity to discuss the role of the employee, the role of the manager, and the relationship between them. Managers should also acknowledge that they would like the meeting to be an open dialogue.

ASK THE EMPLOYEE TO RATE HIS PERFORMANCE BEFORE THE SESSION. Having employees complete a self-assessment before the feedback session can be very productive. It requires employees to think about their performance over the past rating period, and it encourages them to think about their weaknesses. Although self-ratings used for administrative decisions are often inflated, there is evidence that they may actually be lower than supervisors' ratings when done for developmental purposes. Another reason a self-assessment can be productive is that it can make the session go more smoothly by focusing discussion on areas where disagreement exists, resulting in a more efficient session. Finally, employees who have thought about past performance are more able to participate fully in the feedback session.

ENCOURAGE THE SUBORDINATE TO PARTICIPATE IN THE SESSION. Managers can take one of three approaches in performance feedback sessions. In the "tell-and-sell" approach, managers tell the employees how they have rated them and then justify these ratings. In the "tell-and-listen" approach, managers tell employees how they have rated them and then let the employees explain their side of the story. In the "problem-solving" approach, managers and employees work together to solve performance problems in an atmosphere of respect and encouragement. In spite of the research demonstrating the superiority of the problem-solving approach, most managers still rely on the tell-and-sell approach.[63]

When employees participate in the feedback session, they are consistently satisfied with the process. (Recall our discussion of fairness earlier in this chapter.) Participation includes allowing employees to voice their opinions of the evaluation, as well as discuss performance goals.[64] One study found that, other than satisfaction with one's supervisor, participation was the single most important predictor of satisfaction with the feedback session.[65]

RECOGNIZE EFFECTIVE PERFORMANCE THROUGH PRAISE. One usually thinks of performance feedback sessions as focusing on the employee's performance problems. This should never be the case. The purpose of the session is to give accurate performance feedback, which entails recognizing effective performance as well as poor performance. Praising effective performance provides reinforcement for that behavior. It also adds credibility to the feedback by making it clear that the manager is not just identifying performance problems.

FOCUS ON SOLVING PROBLEMS. A common mistake that managers make in providing performance feedback is to try to use the session as a chance to punish poor-performing employees by telling them how utterly lousy their performance is. This only reduces the employees' self-esteem and increases her defensiveness, neither of which will improve performance.

To improve poor performance, a manager must attempt to solve the problems causing it. This entails working with the employee to determine the actual cause and then agreeing on how to solve it. For example, a salesperson's failure to meet a sales goal may be the result of lack of a proper sales pitch, lack of product knowledge, or stolen sales by another salesperson. Each of these causes requires a different solution. Without a problem-solving approach, however, the correct solution might never be identified.

FOCUS FEEDBACK ON BEHAVIOR OR RESULTS, NOT ON THE PERSON. One of the most important things to do when giving negative feedback is to avoid questioning the employee's worth as a person. This is best accomplished by focusing the discussion on the employee's behaviors or results, not on the employee. To say, "You're screwing up! You're just not motivated!" will bring about more defensiveness and ill feelings than stating, "You did not meet the deadline that you agreed to because you spent too much time on another project."

MINIMIZE CRITICISM. Obviously, if an individual's performance is below standard, some criticism must take place. However, an effective manager should resist the temptation to reel off a litany of offenses. Having been confronted with the performance problem, an employee often agrees that a change is in order. However, if the manager continues to come up with more and more examples of low performance, the employee may get defensive.

AGREE TO SPECIFIC GOALS AND SET A DATE TO REVIEW PROGRESS. The importance of goal setting cannot be overemphasized. It is one of the most effective motivators of performance.[66] Research has demonstrated that it results in increased satisfaction, motivation to improve, and performance improvement.[67] Besides setting goals, the manager must also set a specific follow-up date to review the employee's performance toward the goal. This provides an added incentive for the employee to take the goal seriously and work toward achieving it.

Managing the Performance of Marginal Employees

As we emphasized in the previous discussion, employees need performance feedback to take actions to improve their current job performance. As we will discuss in Chapter 9, "Employee Development," performance feedback is also needed for employees to develop their knowledge and skills for the future. In addition to understanding how to effectively give employees performance feedback, managers need to be aware of what types of actions are likely to improve and maintain that performance. For example, giving performance feedback to marginal employees may not be sufficient for improving their performance. **Marginal employees** are those employees who are performing at a bare minimum level due to a lack of ability and/or motivation to perform well.[68]

Table 8.11 shows actions for the manager to take with four different types of employees. As the table highlights, managers need to take into account whether employees lack ability, motivation, or both in considering ways to improve performance. To determine an employee's level of ability, a manager should consider if she has the knowledge, skills, and abilities needed to perform effectively. Lack of ability may be an issue if an employee is new in a job or the job has recently changed. To determine employees' level of motivation, managers need to consider if employees are doing a job they want to do and if they feel they are being appropriately paid or rewarded. A sudden negative change in an employee's performance may indicate that he is experiencing personal problems.

Employees with high ability and motivation are likely good performers (*solid performers*). Table 8.11 emphasizes that managers should not ignore employees with high ability and high motivation. Managers should provide development opportunities to keep them satisfied and effective. Poor performance resulting from lack of ability but not motivation (i.e., *misdirected effort*) may be improved by skill development activities such as training or temporary assignments. Managers with employees who have the ability but lack motivation (*underutilizers*) need to consider actions that focus on interpersonal problems or incentives. These actions include making sure that incentives or rewards that the employee values are linked to performance and making counseling available to help employees deal with personal problems or career or job dissatisfaction. Chronic poor performance by employees with low ability and motivation (*deadwood*) indicates that outplacement or firing may be the best solution.

TABLE 8.11
Ways to Manage Employees' Performance

		ABILITY	
		HIGH	LOW
Motivation	High	Solid performers • Reward good performance • Identify development opportunities • Provide honest, direct feedback	Misdirected effort • Coaching • Frequent performance feedback • Goal setting • Training or temporary assignment for skill development • Restructured job assignment
	Low	Underutilizers • Give honest, direct feedback • Provide counseling • Use team building and conflict resolution • Link rewards to performance outcomes • Offer training for needed knowledge or skills • Stress management	Deadwood • Withholding pay increases • Demotion • Outplacement • Firing • Specific, direct feedback on performance problems

SOURCE: Based on M. London, *Job Feedback* (Mahwah, NJ: Lawrence Erlbaum Associates, 1997), pp. 96–97. Used by permission.

Developing and Implementing a System That Follows Legal Guidelines

We now discuss the legal issues and constraints affecting performance management. Because performance measures play a central role in such administrative decisions as promotions, pay raises, and discipline, employees who sue an organization over these decisions ultimately attack the measurement systems on which the decisions were made. Two types of cases have dominated: discrimination and unjust dismissal.

In discrimination suits, the plaintiff often alleges that the performance measurement system unjustly discriminated against the plaintiff because of race or gender. Many performance measures are subjective, and we have seen that individual biases can affect them, especially when those doing the measuring harbor racial or gender stereotypes.

In *Brito* v. *Zia*, the Supreme Court essentially equated performance measures with selection tests.[69] It ruled that the *Uniform Guidelines on Employee Selection Procedures* were applicable to evaluating the adequacy of a performance appraisal instrument. This ruling presents a challenge to those involved in developing performance measures, because a substantial body of research on race discrimination in performance rating has demonstrated that both white and black raters give higher ratings to members of their own racial group, even after rater training.[70] There is also evidence that the discriminatory biases in performance rating are worse when one group makes up a small percentage of the work group. When the vast majority of the group is male, females receive lower ratings; when the minority is male, males receive lower ratings.[71]

In the second type of suit, an unjust dismissal suit, the plaintiff claims that the dismissal was for reasons other than those the employer claims. For example, an employee who works for a defense contractor might blow the whistle on the company for defrauding the government. If the company fires the employee, claiming that she was performing poorly, she may argue that the firing was, in fact, because of blowing the whistle on the employer—in other words, that the dismissal was unjust. The court case will likely focus on the performance measurement system used as the basis for claiming the employee's performance was poor.

Because of the potential costs of discrimination and unjust dismissal suits, an organization needs to determine exactly what the courts consider a legally defensible performance management system. Based on reviews of court decisions dealing with performance management systems, we offer the following characteristics of a system that will withstand legal scrutiny.[72]

1. The system should be developed by conducting a valid job analysis that ascertains the important aspects of job performance.
2. The system should be based on either behaviors or results; evaluations of ambiguous traits should be avoided.
3. Raters should be trained in how to use the system rather than simply given the materials and left to interpret how to conduct the appraisal.
4. There should be some form of review by upper-level managers of all the performance ratings, and there should be a system for employees to appeal what they consider to be an unfair evaluation.
5. The organization should provide some form of performance counseling or corrective guidance to help poor performers improve their performance before being dismissed.
6. Multiple raters should be used, particularly if an employee's performance is unlikely to be seen by only one rating source such as manager or customer.

Use of Technology for Performance Management: Electronic Monitoring

Employees' performance ratings, disciplinary actions, and work-rule violations can be stored in electronic databases. Personal computers are also increasingly being used for monitoring the actual performance and productivity of service employees.[73] For example, at a General Electric customer service center, agents answer over 14,000 telephone inquiries per day. The agents' calls are recorded and reviewed to help the agent improve customer service. American Airlines also monitors calls to its reservation centers. Managers can hear what the agents tell customers and see what agents enter on their personal computer screens. One disadvantage of monitoring is that employees sometimes find it demoralizing, degrading, and stressful. To avoid the potential negative effect of performance monitoring, managers must communicate why employees are being monitored. Nonmanagement employees also need to be involved in monitoring and coaching less-experienced employees.

Legislation regarding computer monitoring may occur in the future. Both the U.S. House and Senate have considered legislation designed to protect employees' rights from being violated by computer monitoring (The Privacy for Consumers and Workers Act).

USING PERFORMANCE MANAGEMENT APPLICATIONS FOR DECISION MAKING

Performance management applications are available to help managers tailor performance problems.[74] Software is available to help the manager customize performance rating forms for each job. The manager determines the performance standard for each job and rates each employee according to the appropriate standards. The manager receives a report summarizing the employees' strengths and weaknesses. The report also provides information regarding how different the employee's performance was from the established standard.

Performance diagnosis applications ask the manager for information about performance problems (e.g., Has the employee been trained in he skills that caused the performance problem?) and the work environment (e.g., Does the employee work under time pressure?). The software analyzes the information and provides the manager with solutions to consider in dealing with the performance problem.

SUMMARY

Measuring and managing performance is a challenging enterprise and one of the keys to gaining competitive advantage. Performance management systems serve strategic, administrative, and developmental purposes—their importance cannot be overestimated. A performance measurement system should be evaluated against the criteria of strategic congruence, validity, reliability, acceptability, and specificity. Measured against these criteria, the comparative, attribute, behavioral, results, and quality approaches have different strengths and weaknesses. Thus, deciding which approach and which source of performance information are the best depends on the job in question. Effective managers need to be aware of the issues involved in determining the best method or combination of methods for their particular situations. In addition, once performance has been measured, a major component of a manager's job is to feed that performance information back to employees in a way that results in improved performance rather than defensiveness and decreased motivation. Managers should take action based on the causes for poor performance: ability, motivation, or both. Managers must be sure that their performance management system can meet legal scrutiny, especially if it is used to discipline or fire poor performers.

DISCUSSION QUESTIONS

1. What are examples of administrative decisions that might be made in managing the performance of professors? Developmental decisions?
2. What would you consider the strategy of your university (e.g., research, undergraduate teaching, graduate teaching, a combination)? How might the performance management system for faculty members fulfill its strategic purpose of eliciting the types of behaviors and results required by this strategy?
3. If you were developing a performance measurement system for faculty members, what types of attributes would you seek to measure? Behaviors? Results?
4. What sources of performance information would you use to evaluate faculty members' performance?
5. The performance of students is usually evaluated with an overall results measure of grade point average. How is this measure contaminated? How is it deficient? What other measures might you use to more adequately evaluate student performance?
6. Think of the last time that you had a conflict with another person, either at work or at school. Using the guidelines for performance feedback, how would you provide feedback to that person regarding his performance in a way that is effective?
7. Explain what fairness has to do with performance management.
8. Why might a manager intentionally distort appraisal results? What would you recommend to minimize this problem?
9. Can computer monitoring of performance ever be acceptable to employees? Explain.

WEB EXERCISE

Go to the Performance Appraisal and Management Resource Center at http://members.xoom.com/perform/index.htm. The purpose of this Web site is to educate managers and HR professionals so they can use performance management systems effectively. Click on "Articles, critiques, and new ideas." Here you will find articles that discuss how HR departments and management "screwup" performance management systems as well as critiques of systems (e.g., ranking systems) and new ideas for performance management.

1. Choose either an article, critique, or new idea from this Web site. Read the article.
2. Summarize the major points of the article you chose.
3. Critique the article. What assumptions are made in the article? Are the arguments in the article supported by the research discussed in this chapter? What are the potential practical implications of this article for performance management systems?

MANAGING PEOPLE: FROM THE PAGES OF "BUSINESS WEEK"

BusinessWeek In the Cockpit with TWA's Pilot-President

The passengers had boarded, the plane was fueled, and the cockpit had been checked. Yet the TWA jet sat idle at the gate in St. Louis, and Captain Bill Compton wasn't very happy. He clenched his jaw and got on the radio: "We need a tug." Minutes passed. No help arrived to push the plane away from the gate. In the race to get to San Francisco on time, Flight 177 had already fallen behind.

Unlike the thousands of other delays at airports across the country on that April day, however, this one would not go unnoticed by those higher up the ladder. Before a week had passed, TWA would analyze its entire operation at St. Louis to determine whether tug delays were common. It was all the doing of the pilot—who has a little bit of pull back at company headquarters.

In fact, William F. Compton, when he isn't out flying MD-80s, is the president of Trans World Airlines Inc. A pilot at the carrier for the past 30 years, he joined the company board as a union representative in 1993 and was picked to join management in a 1996 shake-up. Today, Compton is the only major airline executive whose voice you might hear over the intercom on your next flight. He's also the latest in a line of pilots-cum-managers at TWA that includes Charles A. Lindbergh and Howard Hughes.

"You get thousands of written reports telling you how things are going, but you get the best view from the shop floor," says the affable, white-haired 51-year-old. "My shop floor is the cockpit." So despite a work schedule that keeps Compton at the office until 11 most nights, he gets airborne for a couple of days a month. Each time, he comes back with a list of things that need improvement, and he fires off inquisitive e-mail to the company's vice presidents. Compton has had the white lines repainted on the St. Louis airport tarmac so that baggage trucks no longer get in the way of planes. And he fired a manager at another major airport when, four months after Compton had been there, bags were still routinely late being loaded onto planes.

Thanks largely to his leadership, TWA is in the midst of a dramatic operational turnaround. First as head of operations, and since his December 1997 promotion to president, Compton has overseen TWA's efforts to get its planes to their destinations on schedule. The strategy: On-time planes mean more business travelers, which means more revenue and more financing, which will allow TWA to invest in the newer planes needed to complete the turnaround.

So far, Flight 177 isn't much of an advertisement for the strategy—it's running 18 minutes late before it even leaves the gate. But Compton and the TWA management team have a better story to tell about the airline's performance generally. By rallying the carrier's 22,000 employees—the same people he has been eating dinner with in airport motels for years—Compton helped lift the airline's on-time ranking from dead last in 1996 to second in 1997. The percentage of Trans World's seats being filled is now the highest since airline deregulation in 1978, and on Apr. 22 TWA reported its best first quarter in a decade.

Of course, it still lost money—$54 million, including a noncash charge to issue stock to employees—and many challenges remain for the carrier. Consumers view it as a faded brand with a fleet full of old planes. Lingering uneasiness over the crash of Flight 800 has not helped. And if TWA's financial position is improving, it has a long way to go. Margins, as well as the average fares it collects from passengers, are near the bottom of the industry, in part because TWA attracts far fewer high-paying business passengers than any other major carrier. Though analysts expect it finally to turn a slim profit this year, its weak cash position, at $346 million, could leave it vulnerable in a slowdown. "This is one of the greatest environments for the airline business in a very long time, and TWA is not making any money. That's scary," says one big investor.

On top of all that, with the recently announced marketing alliance between American Airlines and USAirways and a pending one between United and Delta, TWA will have to overcome rivals with even more convenient schedules than before. Indeed, TWA's bid to survive will be a test of whether today's skies have room for anything but behemoths and low-fare carriers. "TWA did not provide a good product for north of a decade," concedes Compton, as Flight 177 breaks above the clouds and moves beyond the 10,000-foot ceiling under which all cockpit chatter must relate directly to the flight. "People don't come back in the blink of an eye."

Still, it's hard to deny the progress that Compton, CEO Gerald L. Gitner, and other executives have made in the 18 months since they took over. "TWA is working on all the things that need to get worked on," says Cameron Burr, president of Burr & Associates Inc., a New Canaan (Conn.) aerospace-investment firm that owns about 1 percent of TWA. With $500 million in new financing over the past six months, the carrier has freed itself from debt to Carl C. Icahn and no longer seems an imminent candidate for a spot next to Eastern Air Lines in the corporate dustbin.

The fight to save the company is, in many ways, a personal one for Compton. He has worked there since he was 21, and he even met his wife, a TWA flight attendant, through the company. As for his love affair with planes, that began in Peru where, as a child, Compton used to watch his father flying for a subsidiary of Pan American World Airlines Inc. "I'd sit out on the ramp in Lima and look at the DC-3—with only 20 seats, and it would only go 120 miles an hour—and I'd say, 'Now, look at this big airplane,'" Compton recalls as Flight 177 soars over the Rockies at 530 miles and hour. "I knew I wanted to be a pilot."

Compton's effort to improve TWA's operations began with a direct appeal to its employees. He wants them watching the carrier's on-time numbers as closely as he studies the St. Louis Cardinals' box scores.

Shortly after taking over, Gitner and Compton decided that reversing TWA's dismal on-time flight performance had to be their first priority. In early 1997, Compton chaired a group of employees that identified a dozen major reasons the flights were so often late. The culprits ranged from TWA's aging fleet—its older planes require frequent repairs that cause delays—to the fact that virtually any ground crew member was authorized to hold up a flight, no matter how trivial the reason. Careful always to talk about safety first—Flight 800 had crashed just months before—Compton traveled the country, convincing employees of the importance of a reliable schedule and gathering ideas on how to improve.

Now, employees receive daily reports about on-time performance—and only the station manager at each airport may hold up a flight. Moreover, departures are no longer delayed to ensure connections with incoming planes. While that may strand a few passengers, it gets hundreds more to their destinations on time by preventing the entire hub system from running late. But there's still work to be done. A tough winter in the St. Louis hub that caused many flights to be delayed has sent TWA back down to fifth place in on-time performance this year. "We had a good spurt, but now it's been more spotty," says Joe Chronic, current chairman of TWA's pilot union.

So every flight becomes a miniature battle to win back the confidence of travelers who grew fed up with missing meetings because of TWA. "It got to the point in 1995 and '96 where I wouldn't wear a TWA T-shirt in my neighborhood," says Compton with a laugh. "I was afraid I'd get rocks thrown at me." With Flight 177 on autopilot, he starts to chew on the same lunch that passengers are eating back in coach while bantering with his 34-year-old co-pilot, Joe Tersteeg, whom he had met just that day.

Employee relations are probably the trickiest part of Compton's new job. Only two years after he was serving as the pilots' appointed advocate, he finds himself as the executive whom management's labor negotiators report to. That has strained Compton's friendships with some pilots, they say—and the toughest test is yet to come. The company's negotiations with its unions, which began last fall, will not be easy. After 15 years of concessions to keep the company afloat, TWA employees are paid far less and have less generous benefits than their counterparts at other airlines. The maximum that a pilot of an MD-80 can earn, for example, is $103 for each hour spent in the air, vs. an industry average of $160. Flight attendants, who often wander up to the cockpit when Compton is flying to plead with the boss for a better contract, have it worse, earning in the mid-$20,000s even with seniority. TWA agrees its workers need a raise, though a fight is likely over how big it should be.

As Flight 177 approaches the Sierra Nevada range, it's easy to put such thorny issues aside and appreciate the joys of flying. There are no clouds, and the cockpit has a 180-degree view of the mountains that separate Nevada and California. The sun's glare reflects off lakes dozens of miles away. Best of all, gentler headwinds have helped make an on-time arrival start to seem possible. "This must be a nice change of pace from the stuff you deal with," co-pilot Tersteeg says. "This," Compton replies, "is like playing hooky."

Touchdown comes at 1:50 P.M. Even with a short wait on the runway, the plane taxies into the gate just five minutes behind its scheduled 1:52 arrival, qualifying it as "on time." Compton's day, of course, isn't over. He will head back to the crew hotel, call the office in St. Louis, answer mail from employees, and review revenue projections. After all, wind and air-traffic control may have allowed Flight 177 to land nearly on time, but 254 other TWA jets came in late that day. On each one, he worries there may be some passengers who have decided they're fed up with TWA.

QUESTIONS

1. What performance management approach (or combination of approaches) do you believe will be most effective in improving TWA's on-time flight performance? What approach would you use for pilots? For grounds crew (employees who service the planes)?
2. Advocates of the quality approach argue that systems factors (factors not under the employee's control that affect performance) need to be taken into account in performance management systems. What systems factors can affect on-time flight performance? Explain how you would control for systems factors in the performance management approach you recommended in your answer to question 1.

SOURCE: David Leonhardt, "In the Cockpit with TWA's Pilot-President," *Business Week* (May 11, 1998).

NOTES

1. C. Lee, "Performance Appraisal: Can We Manage Away the Curse?" *Training* (May 1996), pp. 44–49.
2. K. Murphy and J. Cleveland, *Performance Appraisal: An Organizational Perspective* (Boston: Allyn & Bacon, 1991).
3. Commerce Clearing House, *Performance Appraisal: What Three Companies Are Doing* (Chicago, IL: Commerce Clearing House, 1985).
4. J. Cleveland, K. Murphy, and R. Williams, "Multiple Uses of Performance Appraisal: Prevalence and Correlates," *Journal of Applied Psychology* 74 (1989), pp. 130–35.
5. Ibid.
6. C. Longenecker, "Behind the Mask: The Politics of Employee Appraisal," *Academy of Management Executive* 1 (1987), p. 183.
7. M. Beer, "Note on Performance Appraisal," in *Readings in Human Resource Management*, ed. M. Beer and B. Spector (New York: Free Press, 1985).
8. C.E. Schneier, D. G. Shaw, and R. W. Beatty, "Performance Measurement and Management: A Tool for Strategic Execution," *Human Resource Management* 30 (1991), pp. 279–301.
9. R. Schuler and S. Jackson, "Linking Competitive Strategies with Human Resource Practices," *Academy of Management Executive* 1 (1987), pp. 207–19.
10. L. King, J. Hunter, and F. Schmidt, "Halo in a Multidimensional Forced-Choice Performance Evaluation Scale," *Journal of Applied Psychology* 65 (1980), pp. 507–16.
11. B.R. Nathan, A.M. Mohrman, and J. Millman, "Interpersonal Relations as a Context for the Effects of Appraisal Interviews on Performance and Satisfaction: A Longitudinal Study," *Academy of Management Journal* 34 (1991), pp. 352–69; M.S. Taylor, K.B. Tracy, M.K. Renard, J.K. Harrison, and S.J. Carroll, "Due Process in Performance Appraisal: A Quasi-experiment in Procedural Justice," *Administrative Science Quarterly* 40 (1995), pp. 495–523; J.M. Werner and M.C. Bolino, "Explaining U.S. Courts of Appeals Decisions Involving Performance Appraisal: Accuracy, Fairness, and Validation," *Personnel Psychology* 50 (1997), pp. 1–24.
12. *Albermarle Paper Company v. Moody*, 10 FEP 1181 (1975).
13. F. Blanz and E. Ghiselli, "The Mixed Standard Scale: A New Rating System," *Personnel Psychology* 25 (1973), pp. 185–99; K. Murphy and J. Constans, "Behavioral Anchors as a Source of Bias in Rating," *Journal of Applied Psychology* 72 (1987), pp. 573–77.
14. P. Smith and L. Kendall, "Retranslation of Expectations: An Approach to the Construction of Unambiguous Anchors for Rating Scales," *Journal of Applied Psychology* 47 (1963), pp. 149–55.
15. Murphy and Constans, "Behavioral Anchors"; M. Piotrowski, J. Barnes-Farrel, and F. Esrig, "Behaviorally Anchored Bias: A Replication and Extension of Murphy and Constans," *Journal of Applied Psychology* 74 (1989), pp. 823–26.
16. U. Wiersma and G. Latham, "The Practicality of Behav-

ioral Observation Scales, Behavioral Expectation Scales, and Trait Scales," *Personnel Psychology* 39 (1986), pp. 619–28.
17. G. Latham and K. Wexley, *Increased Productivity through Performance Appraisal* (Boston: Addison-Wesley, 1981).
18. Wiersma and Latham, "The Practicality of Behavioral Observation Scales, Behavioral Expectation Scales, and Trait Scales."
19. D.C. Anderson, C. Crowell, J. Sucec, K. Gilligan, and M. Wikoff, "Behavior Management of Client Contacts in a Real Estate Brokerage: Getting Agents to Sell More," *Journal of Organizational Behavior Management* 4 (1983), pp. 67–96.
20. D.C. Anderson, C. Crowell, S. Sponsel, M. Clarke, and J. Brence, "Behavior Management in the Public Accommodations Industry: A Three-Project Demonstration," *Journal of Organizational Behavior Modification* 4 (1983), pp. 33–65.
21. J. Komaki, R. Collins, and P. Penn, "The Role of Performance Antecedents and Consequences in Work Motivation," *Journal of Applied Psychology* 67 (1982), pp. 334–40.
22. Latham and Wexley, *Increasing Productivity through Performance Appraisal*.
23. S. Snell, "Control Theory in Strategic Human Resource Management: The Mediating Effect of Administrative Information," *Academy of Management Journal* 35 (1992), pp. 292–327.
24. T. Patten, Jr., *A Manager's Guide to Performance Appraisal* (New York: Free Press, 1982).
25. M. O'Donnell and R. O'Donnell, "MBO—Is it Passe?" *Hospital and Health Services Administration* 28, no. 5 (1983), pp. 46–58; T. Poister and G. Streib, "Management Tools in Government: Trends over the Past Decade," *Public Administration Review* 49 (1989), pp. 240–48.
26. D. McGregor, "An Uneasy Look at Performance Appraisal," *Harvard Business Review* 35, no. 3 (1957), pp. 89–94.
27. E. Locke and G. Latham, *A Theory of Goal Setting and Task Performance* (Englewood Cliffs, NJ: Prentice-Hall, 1990).
28. S. Carroll and H. Tosi, *Management by Objectives* (New York: Macmillan, 1973).
29. G. Odiorne, *MBO II: A System of Managerial Leadership for the 80's* (Belmont, CA: Pitman Publishers, 1986).
30. R. Rodgers and J. Hunter, "Impact of Management by Objectives on Organizational Productivity," *Journal of Applied Psychology* 76 (1991), pp. 322–26.
31. Kevin Helliker, "Pressure at Pier 1: Beating Sales Numbers of Year Earlier Is a Storewide Obsession, *The Wall Street Journal*, December 7, 1995, pp. B1, B2.
32. R. Pritchard, S. Jones, P. Roth, K. Stuebing, and S. Ekeberg, "The Evaluation of an Integrated Approach to Measuring Organizational Productivity," *Personnel Psychology* 42 (1989), pp. 69–115.
33. P. Wright, J. George, S. Farnsworth, and G. McMahan, "Productivity and Extra-Role Behavior: The Effects of Goals and Incentives on Spontaneous Helping," *Journal of Applied Psychology* 78, no. 3 (1993), pp. 374–81.
34. Latham and Wexley, *Increasing Productivity through Performance Appraisal*.
35. R.L. Cardy, "Performance Appraisal in a Quality Context: A New Look at an Old Problem," in *Performance Appraisal: State of the Art in Practice*, ed. J.W. Smither (San Francisco: Jossey-Bass, 1998), pp. 132–62.
36. E.C. Huge, *Total Quality: An Executive's Guide for the 1990s* (Homewood, IL: Richard D. Irwin, 1990), see Chapter 5, "Measuring and Rewarding Performance," pp. 70–88; W.E. Deming, *Out of Crisis* (Cambridge, MA: MIT Center for Advanced Engineering Study, 1986).
37. M. Caroselli, *Total Quality Transformations* (Amherst, MA: Human Resource Development Press, 1991); Huge, *Total Quality*.
38. J.D. Cryer and R.B. Miller, *Statistics for Business: Data Analysis and Modeling* (Boston: PWS-Kent, 1991); C. Carter, "Seven Basic Quality Tools," *HR Magazine* (January 1992), pp. 81–83; D.K. Denton, "Process Mapping Trims Cycle Time," *HR Magazine* (February 1995), pp. 56–61.
39. D.E. Bowen and E.E. Lawler III, "Total Quality-Oriented Human Resource Management," *Organizational Dynamics* 21 (1992), pp. 29–41.
40. R. Heneman, K. Wexley, and M. Moore, "Performance Rating Accuracy: A Critical Review," *Journal of Business Research* 15 (1987), pp. 431–48.
41. T. Becker and R. Klimoski, "A Field Study of the Relationship between the Organizational Feedback Environment and Performance," *Personnel Psychology* 42 (1989), pp. 343–58.
42. L. Axline, "Performance Biased Evaluations," *Supervisory Management* (November 1991), p. 3.
43. K. Wexley and R. Klimoski, "Performance Appraisal: An Update," in *Research in Personnel and Human Resource Management* (vol. 2), ed. K. Rowland and G. Ferris (Greenwich, CT: JAI Press, 1984).
44. F. Landy and J. Farr, *The Measurement of Work Performance: Methods, Theory, and Applications* (New York: Academic Press, 1983).
45. G. McEvoy and P. Buller, "User Acceptance of Peer Appraisals in an Industrial Setting," *Personnel Psychology* 40 (1987), pp. 785–97.
46. D. Antonioni, "The Effects of Feedback Accountability on Upward Appraisal Ratings," *Personnel Psychology* 47 (1994), pp. 349–56.
47. Murphy and Cleveland, *Performance Appraisal*.
48. J. Bernardin and L. Klatt, "Managerial Appraisal Systems: Has Practice Caught Up with the State of the Art?" *Public Personnel Administrator* (November 1985), pp. 79–86.
49. R. Steel and N. Ovalle, "Self-Appraisal Based on Supervisor Feedback," *Personnel Psychology* 37 (1984), pp.

667–85; L.E. Atwater "The Advantages and Pitfalls of Self-Assessment in Organizations," in *Performance Appraisal: State of the Art in Practice*, pp. 331–65.

50. Bureau of Labor Statistics, *Employment and Earnings* (Washington, DC: U.S. Department of Labor, 1997).
51. E. Gummerson, "Lip Services—a Neglected Area of Service Marketing," *Journal of Services Marketing* 1 (1987), pp. 1–29.
52. Bernardin, Hagan, Kane, and Villanova, "Effective Performance Management: A Focus on Precision, Customers, and Situational Constraints." In *Performance Appraisal: State of the Art in Practice*, J.W. Smither, ed. (San Francisco: Jossey-Bass, 1998), pp. 3–48.
53. R. Hoffman, "Ten Reasons You Should Be Using 360-Degree Feedback," *HR Magazine* (April 1995), pp. 82–84.
54. S. Sherman, "How Tomorrow's Best Leaders Are Learning Their Stuff," *Fortune*, November 27, 1995, pp. 90–104; W.W. Tornow, M. London & Associates, *Maximizing the value of 360-Degree Feedback* (San Francisco: Jossey-Bass, 1998); D.A. Waldman, L.E. Atwater, and D. Antonioni, "Has 360 Degree Feedback Gone Amok?" *Academy of Management Executive* 12 (1988), pp. 86–94.
55. A. Tversky and D. Kahneman, "Availability: A Heuristic for Judging Frequency and Probability," *Cognitive Psychology* 5 (1973), pp. 207–32.
56. K. Wexley and W. Nemeroff, "Effects of Racial Prejudice, Race of Applicant, and Biographical Similarity on Interviewer Evaluations of Job Applicants," *Journal of Social and Behavioral Sciences* 20 (1974), pp. 66–78.
57. D. Smith, "Training Programs for Performance Appraisal: A Review," *Academy of Management Review* 11 (1986), pp. 22–40.
58. G. Latham, K. Wexley, and E. Pursell, "Training Managers to Minimize Rating Errors in the Observation of Behavior," *Journal of Applied Psychology* 60 (1975), pp. 550–55.
59. J. Bernardin and E. Pence, "Effects of Rater Training: Creating New Response Sets and Decreasing Accuracy," *Journal of Applied Psychology* 65 (1980), pp. 60–66.
60. E. Pulakos, "A Comparison of Rater Training Programs: Error Training and Accuracy Training," *Journal of Applied Psychology* 69 (1984), pp. 581–88.
61. W. Borman, "Job Behavior, Performance, and Effectiveness," in *Handbook of Industrial & Organizational Psychology*, 2d ed., ed. M. Dunnette and L. Hough (Palo Alto, CA: Consulting Psychologists Press, 1991), pp. 271–326.
62. S.W.J. Kozlowski, G.T. Chao, and R.F. Morrison, "Games Raters Play: Politics, Strategies, and Impression Management in Performance Appraisal," in *Performance Appraisal: State of the Art in Practice*, pp. 163–205.
63. K. Wexley, V. Singh, and G. Yukl, "Subordinate Participation in Three Types of Appraisal Interviews," *Journal of Applied Psychology* 58 (1973), pp. 54–57; K. Wexley, "Appraisal Interview," in *Performance Assessment*, ed. R.A. Berk (Baltimore: Johns Hopkins University Press, 1986), pp. 167–85.
64. D. Cederblom, "The Performance Appraisal Interview: A Review, Implications, and Suggestions," *Academy of Management Review* 7 (1982), pp. 219–27; B.D. Cawley, L.M. Keeping, and P.E. Levy, "Participation in the Performance Appraisal Process and Employee Reactions: A Meta-analytic Review of Field Investigations," *Journal of Applied Psychology* 83, no. 3 (1998), pp. 615–63.
65. W. Giles and K. Mossholder, "Employee Reactions to Contextual and Session Components of Performance Appraisal," *Journal of Applied Psychology* 75 (1990), pp. 371–77.
66. E. Locke and G. Latham, *A Theory of Goal Setting and Task Performance* (Englewood Cliffs, NJ: Prentice-Hall, 1990).
67. H. Klein, S. Snell, and K. Wexley, "A Systems Model of the Performance Appraisal Interview Process," *Industrial Relations* 26 (1987), pp. 267–80.
68. M. London and E.M. Mone, "Managing Marginal Performance in Organizations Striving for Excellence," in *Human Resource Dilemmas in Work Organizations: Strategies for Resolution*, ed. A.K. Korman (New York: Guilford, 1993), pp. 95–124.
69. *Brito v. Zia Co.*, 478 F.2d 1200 (10th. Cir. 1973).
70. K. Kraiger and J. Ford, "A Meta-Analysis of Ratee Race Effects in Performance Rating," *Journal of Applied Psychology* 70 (1985), pp. 56–65.
71. P. Sackett, C. DuBois, and A. Noe, "Tokenism in Performance Evaluation: The Effects of Work Groups Representation on Male–Female and White–Black Differences in Performance Ratings," *Journal of Applied Psychology* 76 (1991), pp. 263–67.
72. G. Barrett and M. Kernan, "Performance Appraisal and Terminations: A Review of Court Decisions since *Brito v. Zia* with Implications for Personnel Practices," *Personnel Psychology* 40 (1987), pp. 489–503; H. Feild and W. Holley, "The Relationship of Performance Appraisal System Characteristics to Verdicts in Selected Employment Discrimination Cases," *Academy of Management Journal* 25 (1982), pp. 392–406; J.M. Werner and M.C. Bolino, "Explaining U.S. Courts of Appeals Decisions Involving Performance Appraisal: Accuracy, Fairness, and Validation," *Personnel Psychology* 50 (1997), pp. 1–24.
73. S.E. Forrer and Z.B. Leibowitz, *Using Computers in Human Resources* (San Francisco: Jossey-Bass, 1991)
74. G. Bylinsky, "How Companies Spy on Employees," *Fortune*, November 4, 1991, pp. 131–40; T.L. Griffith, "Teaching Big Brother to Be a Team Player: Computer Monitoring and Quality," *Academy of Management Executive* (1993), pp. 73–80.

CHAPTER

Employee Development

OBJECTIVES

After reading this chapter, you should be able to

1. Discuss current trends in using formal education for development.
2. Relate how assessment of personality type, work behaviors, and job performance can be used for employee development.
3. Develop successful mentoring programs.
4. Explain how job experiences can be used for skill development.
5. Tell how to train managers to coach employees.
6. Discuss the steps in the development planning process.
7. Explain the employees' and company's responsibilities in the development planning process.
8. Discuss what companies are doing for management development issues including succession planning, melting the glass ceiling, and helping dysfunctional managers.

Jewel Food Stores' Development Program

ENTER THE WORLD OF BUSINESS

Jewel Food Stores, headquartered in the Chicago area, has supermarkets in Illinois, Indiana, Iowa, and Wisconsin. Employing approximately 3,000 employees, Jewel has a reputation for attracting employees with the potential for management positions and then developing their managerial talent. Jewel believes that the quality of the store managers relates to store performance. High-quality managers are necessary to create working conditions that motivate employees to provide high-quality customer service as well as a clean and pleasant shopping environment. This results in satisfied customers and employees. For example, many top-level managers of Toys "R" Us, Staples, and Kmart Super Centers all came from Jewel's development program.

How does Jewel develop managerial talent? Jewel recruits talent from local and regional colleges. In one program recruits are placed in an accelerated development program that prepares them for a management job within three to five years. In another program, recruits work directly under a senior manager in the company who oversees their training and development to ensure that they get the types of experience necessary for them to compete for store management positions. Besides relying on talent recruited from outside the company, Jewel identifies current employees who have the potential to successfully take on managerial responsibilities. Jewel provides financial support for these employees to get the education they need to prepare them for managerial work.

All of the programs include individual coaching with a psychologist who is available to work with employees and their managers to help improve on-the-job training and development.

SOURCE: E. Burton, "Jewel Food Stores: A Profile," from "Corporate Corner," Management and Education Division of the Academy of Management Newsletter 23 (March 1997), p. 9. Reprinted by permission.

Introduction

As the Jewel Food Stores example illustrates, management development is a key component of a company's employee development efforts. Traditionally, development has focused on management-level employees, while line employees received training designed to improve a specific set of skills needed for their current job. However, with the greater use of work teams and increased involvement of employees in all aspects of business, development is becoming ever more important for all employees. Why? Employee development is a necessary component of a company's efforts to improve quality, to meet the challenges of global competition and social change, and to incorporate technological advances and changes in work design. Increased globalization of product markets compels companies to help their employees understand cultures and customs that affect business practices. Because more of an employee's responsibilities are organized on a project or customer basis (rather than on a functional basis) and an increased use of work teams, employees need to develop a broader range of technical and interpersonal skills. Employees must also be able to perform roles traditionally reserved for managers. Legislation (such as the Civil Rights Act of 1991), labor market forces, and a company's social responsibility dictate that employers provide women and minorities with access to development activities that will prepare them for managerial positions. Because companies (and their employees) must constantly learn and change to meet customer needs and compete in new markets, the emphasis placed on both training and development has increased.

The chapter begins by discussing the relationship between development, training, and careers. Second, we look at development approaches. The development approaches include formal education, assessment, job experiences, and interpersonal relationships. The chapter emphasizes the types of skills, knowledge, and behaviors that are strengthened by each development method. Choosing a development approach is one part of the development planning process. Before one or multiple developmental approaches are used, the employee and the company must have an idea of the employee's development needs and the purpose of development. Identifying the needs and purpose of development is part of the development planning process. The third section of the chapter provides an overview of the steps of the development planning process. Employee and company responsibilities at each step of the process are emphasized. The chapter concludes with a discussion of special issues in employee development including succession planning, dealing with dysfunctional managers, and using development to help women and minorities move into upper-level management positions (referred to as melting the glass ceiling).

The Relationship Between Development, Training, and Careers

DEVELOPMENT AND TRAINING. Development refers to formal education, job experiences, relationships, and assessment of personality and abilities that help employees prepare for the future. Because it is future-oriented, it involves learning that is not necessarily related to the employee's current job.[1] Table 9.1 shows the differences between training and development. Traditionally, training is focused on helping employees' performance in their current jobs. Development helps prepare them for other positions in the company and increases their ability to move into jobs that may not yet exist.[2] Development also helps employees prepare for changes in their current job that may result from new technology, work designs, new customers, or new product markets. Chapter 7 emphasized the strategic role of training. It is important to note that as train-

TABLE 9.1
Comparison between Training and Development

	TRAINING	DEVELOPMENT
Focus	Current	Future
Use of work experiences	Low	High
Goal	Preparation for current job	Preparation for changes
Participation	Required	Voluntary

ing continues to become more strategic (i.e., related to business goals), the distinction between training and development will blur.

DEVELOPMENT AND CAREERS. Traditionally, careers have been described in various ways.[3] Careers have been described as a sequence of positions held within an occupation. For example, a university faculty member can hold assistant, associate, and full professor positions. A career has also been described in the context of mobility within an organization. For example, an engineer may begin her career as a staff engineer. As her expertise, experience, and performance increase, she may move through advisory engineering, senior engineering, and senior technical positions. Finally, a career has been described as a characteristic of the employee. Each employee's career consists of different jobs, positions, and experiences.

The new concept of the career is often referred to as a protean career.[4] A **protean career** is a career that is frequently changing based on both changes in the person's interests, abilities, and values and changes in the work environment. Compared to the traditional career, employees here take major responsibility for managing their careers. For example, an engineering employee may decide to take a sabbatical from her engineering position to work in management at the United Way Agency for a year. The purpose of this assignment could be to develop her managerial skills as well as help her personally evaluate if she likes managerial work more than engineering.

Changes in the psychological contract between employees and company have influenced the development of the protean career.[5] A **psychological contract** is the expectations that employers and employees have about each other. Traditionally, the psychological contract emphasized that the company would provide continued employment (job security) and advancement opportunities if the employee remained with the company and maintained a high level of job performance. Pay increases and status were linked directly to vertical movement in the company (promotions).

The protean career has several implications for employee development. The goal of the new career is psychological success. **Psychological success** is the feeling of pride and accomplishment that comes from achieving life goals that are not limited to achievements at work (e.g., raising a family, good physical health). Psychological success is more under the control of the employee than the traditional career goals, which were not only influenced by employee effort but were controlled by the availability of positions in the company. Psychological success is self-determined rather than solely determined through signals the employee receives from the company (e.g., salary increase, promotions). Psychological success appears to be especially prevalent among the new generation of persons entering the work force. The generation called Generation X is often unimpressed with status symbols, wants flexibility in doing job tasks, and desires meaning from its work.[6]

Employees need to develop new skills rather than rely on a static knowledge base. This has resulted from companies' need to be more responsive to customers' service and product demands. The types of knowledge that an employee needs to be successful have changed.[7] In the traditional career, "knowing how" (having the appropriate skills and knowledge to provide a service or produce a product) was critical. Although knowing how remains important, employees need to "know why" and "know whom." Knowing why refers to understanding the company's business and culture so that the employee can develop and apply knowledge and skills that can contribute to the business. Knowing whom refers to relationships that the employee may develop to contribute to company success. These relationships may include networking with vendors, suppliers, community members, customers, or industry experts. Learning to know whom and know why requires more than formal courses and training programs. Learning and development in the protean career are increasingly likely to involve relationships and job experiences rather than formal courses.

The emphasis on continuous learning and learning beyond knowing how as well as changes in the psychological contract are altering the direction and frequency of movement within careers (career pattern).[8]

Traditional career patterns consisted of a series of steps arranged in a linear hierarchy, with higher steps in the hierarchy related to increased authority, responsibility, and compensation. Expert career patterns involve a lifelong commitment to a field or specialization (e.g., law, medicine, management). These types of career patterns will not disappear. Rather, career patterns involving movement across specializations or disciplines (a spiral career pattern) will become more prevalent. These new career patterns mean that to develop employees (as well as for employees to take control of their own careers) will require providing them with the opportunity to (a) determine their interests, skill strengths, and weaknesses and (b) based on this information seek out appropriate development experiences that will likely involve job experiences and relationships as well as formal courses.

The most appropriate view of a career is that it is "boundaryless."[9] It may include movement across several employers or even different occupations. Statistics indicate that the average employment tenure for all American workers is only five years.[10] For example, Craig Matison, 33 years old, took a job with Cincinnati Bell Information System, a unit of Cincinnati Bell Corporation that manages billing for phone and cable companies.[11] Although he has been on the job only six months, he is already looking to make his next career move. Not wanting to stay on the technical career path, he regularly explores company databases for job postings, looking for sales and marketing opportunities within the company. A career may also involve identifying more with a job or profession than with the present employer. A career can also be considered boundaryless in the sense that career plans or goals are influenced by personal or family demands and values. Finally, *boundaryless* may refer to the fact that career success may not be tied to promotions. Rather, career success may be related to achieving goals that are personally meaningful to the employee rather than those set by parents, peers, or the company.

As this discussion shows, to retain and motivate employees companies need to provide a system to identify and meet employees' development needs. This is especially important to retain good performers and employees who have potential for managerial positions. This system is often known as a **career management** or **development planning system.** We will discuss these systems in detail later in the chapter.

Approaches to Employee Development

Four approaches are used to develop employees: formal education, assessment, job experiences, and interpersonal relationships.[12] Many companies use a combination of these approaches. For example, New York City–based Metropolitan Transportation Authority (MTA) found that it needed a system for developing employees for first-level management positions.[13] As a result, the Future Managers Program (FMP) was created.

The goal of the program was to develop first-level managers who understood the transportation business and operations. Employees in the FMP survive a rigorous selection process involving interviews and assessment centers. FMP uses assessment, courses, job experiences, and relationships to develop managers. The program combines classroom instruction with job rotation. Classroom instruction provides a learning foundation, while job rotation exposes employees to a wide variety of on-the-job experiences. Classtime is devoted to case study analysis, team building, and developing skills in problem solving, delegation, leadership, and communications. Working in groups, students must complete a project that involves real issues such as creating a customer service brochure in Chinese. Examples of assignments in the job rotation include working at Grand Central Terminal, working with the system road foreman, and working in the operations control center. Job rotation is to familiarize employees with different aspects of operations so they are prepared to move into a new area when positions become available.

Because future managers are often confronted with new situations, mentors are provided to help trainees understand the agency's culture and to answer their questions. The students receive continued feedback on their performance throughout the program based on supervisory and peer evaluations.

Does the program work? Although they are not guaranteed a job after completing the program, the majority of graduates have received jobs they targeted after graduation. The long-term success of the program will be determined by analyzing graduates' career progression in MTA.

Keep in mind that although the large majority of development activity is targeted at managers, all levels of employees may be involved in one or more development activity. For example, grocery store clerks usually receive performance appraisal feedback (a development activity related to assessment). As part of the appraisal process they are asked to complete an individual development plan outlining (1) how they plan to change their weaknesses and (2) their future plans (including positions or locations desired and education or experience needed). Next we explore each type of development approach.

FORMAL EDUCATION

Formal education programs include off-site and on-site programs designed specifically for the company's employees, short courses offered by consultants or universities, executive MBA programs, and university programs in which participants actually live at the university while taking classes. These programs may involve lectures by business experts, business games and simulations, adventure learning, and meetings with customers. Many companies (e.g., Motorola, IBM, GE, Metropolitan Financial, Dow) have training and development centers that offer one- or two-day seminars as well as week-long programs. For example, General Electric's Management Development Institute in Crotonville, New York, teaches courses in manufacturing and sales, marketing, and advanced management training.[14] Tuition ranges from $800 for a half-week conference to $14,000 for a four-week executive development course. Tuition is paid for by the employee's business unit. Figure 9.1 shows the types of development programs used at GE and their target audiences.

Table 9.2 shows the five largest institutions for executive education. There are several important trends in executive education. More and more companies and universities are using distance learning (which we discussed in Chapter 7) to reach executive audiences.[15] For example, Duke University's Fuqua School of Business is offering an electronic executive MBA program. Using their personal computers, students "attend" CD–ROM video lectures as well as traditional face-to-face lectures. They can download

FIGURE 9.1
Examples of Development Programs at General Electric

PROGRAM	DESCRIPTION	TARGET AUDIENCE	COURSES
Executive Development Sequence	Courses emphasize strategic thinking, leadership, cross-functional integration, competing globally, customer satisfaction.	Senior professionals and executives identified as high-potential	Manager Development Course Global Business Management Course Executive Development Course
Core Leadership Program	Courses develop functional expertise, business excellence, management of change.	Managers	Corporate Entry Leadership Conference Professional Development Course New Manager Development Course Experienced Manager Course
Professional Development Program	Courses emphasize preparation for specific career path.	New employees	Audit Staff Course Financial Management Program Human Resources Program Technical Leadership Program

SOURCE: Based on World Wide Web site http://www.ge.com/ibcrucl8.htm.

study aids and additional videos and audio programs. Students discuss lectures and work on team projects using computer bulletin boards, e-mail, and live chat rooms. They use the Internet to research specific companies and class topics. They also travel to Europe, China, and South America for classes and meetings with local business owners.

Another trend in executive education is for companies and the education provider (business school or other educational institution) to create short custom courses with the content designed specifically to meet the needs of the audience. For example, in the Global Leadership Program run by Columbia University's business school, executives work on real problems they face in their jobs. A manager for window maker Pella Corporation left the program with a plan for international sales![16]

The final important trend in executive education is to supplement formal courses from consultants or university faculty with other types of development activities. Avon Products' "Passport Program" is targeted at employees the company thinks can become general managers.[17] To learn Avon's global strategy, they meet for each session in a different country. The program brings a team of employees together for six-week periods spread over 18 months. Participants are provided with general background of a functional area by university faculty and consultants. Then, the team works with senior executives on a country project such as how to penetrate a new market. The team projects are presented to Avon's top managers.

Managers who attend the Center for Creative Leadership development program take psychological tests, receive feedback from managers, peers, and direct reports, participate in group building activities (like adventure learning discussed in Chapter 7), receive counseling, and set improvement goals and write development plans.[18]

Most companies consider the primary purpose of education programs to be providing the employee with job-specific skills.[19] Unfortunately, there has been little research on the effectiveness of formal education programs. In a study of Harvard University's Advanced Management Program, participants reported that they had acquired valuable knowledge from the program (e.g., how globalization affects a company's structure). They said the program broadened their perspectives on issues facing their companies, increased their self-confidence, and helped them learn new ways of thinking and looking at problems.[20]

TABLE 9.2
Five Largest Institutions for Executive Education

SCHOOL	ANNUAL REVENUE (MILLIONS)	FIVE-YEAR GROWTH	PERCENTAGE OF CUSTOMIZED PROGRAMS	NUMBER OF PROGRAMS
University of Pennsylvania, Wharton School (Philadelphia, Pennsylvania)	$25.0	257%	55%	100
IMD (Lausanne, Switzerland)	23.5	42	39	124
Harvard University Graduate School of Business (Boston, Massachusetts)	30.1	20	5	28
Administration Center for Creative Leadership (Greensboro, North Carolina)	23.7	57	34	28
University of Michigan (Ann Arbor, Michigan)	21.5	53	10	63

SOURCE: J. A. Byrne, "Virtual Business Schools," *Business Week* (October 23, 1995), p. 68.

ASSESSMENT

Assessment involves collecting information and providing feedback to employees about their behavior, communication style, or skills.[21] The employees, their peers, managers, and customers may be asked to provide information. Assessment is most frequently used to identify employees with managerial potential and to measure current managers' strengths and weaknesses. Assessment is also used to identify managers with the potential to move into higher-level executive positions, and it can be used with work teams to identify the strengths and weaknesses of individual team members and the decision processes or communication styles that inhibit the team's productivity.

Companies vary in the methods and the sources of information they use in developmental assessment. Many companies provide employees with performance appraisal information. Companies with sophisticated development systems use psychological tests to measure employees' skills, personality types, and communication styles. Self, peer, and managers' ratings of employees' interpersonal styles and behaviors may also be collected. Popular assessment tools include the Myers–Briggs Type Indicator, assessment center, benchmarks, performance appraisal, and 360-degree feedback system.

MYERS–BRIGGS TYPE INDICATOR®. **Myers–Briggs Type Indicator (MBTI)** is the most popular psychological test for employee development. As many as 2 million people take the MBTI in the United States each year. The test consists of more than 100 questions about how the person feels or prefers to behave in different situations (e.g., "Are you usually a good 'mixer' or rather quiet and reserved?"). The MBTI is based on the work of Carl Jung, a psychologist who believed that differences in individuals' behavior resulted from preferences in decision making, interpersonal communication, and information gathering. The MBTI identifies individuals' preference for energy (introversion versus extroversion), information gathering (sensing versus intuition), decision-making (thinking versus feeling), and life-style (judging versus perceiving).[22] The energy dimension determines where individuals gain interpersonal strength and vitality. Extroverts (E) gain energy through interpersonal relationships. Introverts (I) gain energy by focusing on personal thoughts and feelings. The information gathering preference relates to the actions individuals take when making decisions. Individuals with a Sensing (S) preference tend to gather facts and details. Intuitives (I) tend to focus less on facts and more on possibilities and relationships between ideas. Decision making style preferences differ based on the amount of consideration the person gives to others' feelings in making a decision. Individuals with a Thinking (T) preference tend to be very objective in making decisions. Individuals with a Feeling (F) preference tend to evaluate the impact of potential decisions on others and be more subjective in making a decision. The life-style preference reflects an individual's tendency to be flexible and adaptable. Individuals with a Judging (J) preference focus on goals, establish deadlines, and prefer to be conclusive. Individuals with a Perceiving (P) preference tend to enjoy surprises, like to change decisions, and dislike deadlines.

Sixteen unique personality types result from the combination of the four MBTI preferences. (See Table 9.3.) Each person has developed strengths and weaknesses as a result of using his preferences. For example, individuals who are Introverted, Sensing, Thinking, and Judging (known as ISTJs) tend to be serious, quiet, practical, orderly, and logical. These persons have the ability to organize tasks, be decisive, and follow through on plans and goals. ISTJs have several weaknesses because they have not used the opposite preferences: Extroversion, Intuition, Feeling, and Perceiving. Potential weaknesses for ISTJs include problems dealing with unexpected opportunities, appearing too task-oriented or impersonal to colleagues, and making overly quick decisions.

The MBTI is used for understanding such things as communication, motivation, teamwork, work styles, and leadership. For example, it can be used by salespeople or executives who want to become more effective at interpersonal communication by learning things about their own personality styles and the way they are perceived by others. The MBTI can help develop teams by matching team members with assignments that allow them to capitalize on their preferences and helping employees understand how the different preferences of team members can lead to useful problem solving.[23] For example, employees with an Intuitive preference can be assigned brainstorming tasks. Employees with a Sensing preference can be given the responsibility of evaluating ideas.

Research on the validity, reliability, and effectiveness of the MBTI is inconclusive.[24] People who take the MBTI find it a positive experience and say it helps them change their behavior. MBTI scores appear to be related to one's occupation. Analysis of managers' MBTI scores in the United States, England, Latin America, and Japan suggests that a large majority of all managers have certain personality types (ISTJ, INTJ, ESTJ, or ENTJ). However, MBTI scores are not necessarily stable over time. Studies in which the MBTI was administered at two different times found that as few as 24 percent of those who took the test were classified as the same type the second time.

The MBTI is a valuable tool for understanding communication styles and the ways people prefer to interact with others. Because it does not measure how well employees perform their preferred functions, it should not be used to appraise performance or evaluate employees' promotion potential. Furthermore, MBTI types should not be viewed as unchangeable personality patterns.

ASSESSMENT CENTER. The **assessment center** is a process in which multiple raters or evaluators (also known as assessors) evaluate employees' performance on a number of exercises.[25] An assessment center is usually held at an off-site location such as a conference center. From 6 to 12 employees usually participate at one time. Assessment centers are primarily used to identify if employees have the personality characteristics, administrative skills, and interpersonal skills needed for managerial jobs. They are also increasingly being used to determine if employees have the necessary skills to work in teams.

The types of exercises used in assessment centers include leaderless group discussions, interviews, in-baskets, and role plays.[26] In a **leaderless group discussion,** a team of five to seven employees is assigned a problem and must work together to solve it within a certain time period. The problem may involve buying and selling supplies,

TABLE 9.3
The 16 Personality Types Used in the Myers–Briggs Type Indicator Assessment

	SENSING TYPES (S)		INTUITIVE TYPES (N)	
	THINKING (T)	FEELING (F)	FEELING (F)	THINKING (T)
Introverts (I)				
Judging (J)	**ISTJ** Quiet, serious, earn success by thoroughness and dependability. Practical, matter-of-fact, realistic, and responsible. Decide logically what should be done and work toward it steadily, regardless of distractions. Take pleasure in making everything orderly and organized—their work, their home, their life. Value traditions and loyalty.	**ISFJ** Quiet, friendly, responsible, and conscientious. Committed and steady in meeting their obligations. Thorough, painstaking, and accurate. Loyal, considerate, notice and remember specifics about people who are important to them, concerned with how others feel. Strive to create an orderly and harmonious environment at work and at home.	**INFJ** Seek meaning and connection in ideas, relationships, and material possessions. Want to understand what motivates people and are insightful about others. Conscientious and committed to their firm values. Develop a clear vision about how best to serve the common good. Organized and decisive in implementing their vision.	**INTJ** Have original minds and great drive for implementing their ideas and achieving their goals. Quickly see patterns in external events and develop long-range explanatory perspectives. When committed, organize a job and carry it through. Skeptical and independent, have high standards of competence and performance—for themselves and others.
Perceiving (P)	**ISTP** Tolerant and flexible, quiet observers until a problem appears, then act quickly to find workable solutions. Analyze what makes things work and readily get through large amounts of data to isolate the core of practical problems. Interested in cause and effect, organize facts using logical principles, value efficiency.	**ISFP** Quiet, friendly, sensitive, and kind. Enjoy the present moment, what's going on around them. Like to have their own space and to work within their own time frame. Loyal and committed to their values and to people who are important to them. Dislike disagreements and conflicts, do not force their opinions or values on others.	**INFP** Idealistic, loyal to their values and to people who are important to them. Want an external life that is congruent with their values. Curious, quick to see possibilities, can be catalysts for implementing ideas. Seek to understand people and to help them fulfill their potential. Adaptable, flexible, and accepting unless a value is threatened.	**INTP** Seek to develop logical explanations for everything that interests them. Theoretical and abstract, interested more in ideas than in social interaction. Quiet, contained, flexible, and adaptable. Have unusual ability to focus in depth to solve problems in their area of interest. Skeptical, sometimes critical, always analytical.
Extraverts (E)				
Perceiving (P)	**ESTP** Flexible and tolerant, they take a pragmatic approach focused on immediate results. Theories and conceptual explanations bore them—they want to act energetically to solve the problem. Focus on the here-and-now, spontaneous, enjoy each moment that they can be active with others. Enjoy material comforts and style. Learn best through doing.	**ESFP** Outgoing, friendly, and accepting. Exuberant lovers of life, people, and material comforts. Enjoy working with others to make things happen. Bring common sense and a realistic approach to their work, and make work fun. Flexible and spontaneous, adapt readily to new people and environments. Learn best by trying a new skill with other people.	**ENFP** Warmly enthusiastic and imaginative. See life as full of possibilities. Make connections between events and information very quickly, and confidently proceed based on the patterns they see. Want a lot of affirmation from others, and readily give appreciation and support. Spontaneous and flexible, often rely on their ability to improvise and their verbal fluency.	**ENTP** Quick, ingenious, stimulating, alert, and outspoken. Resourceful in solving new and challenging problems. Adept at generating conceptual possibilities and then analyzing them strategically. Good at reading other people. Bored by routine, will seldom do the same thing the same way, apt to turn to one new interest after another.
Judging (J)	**ESTJ** Practical, realistic, matter-of-fact. Decisive, quickly move to implement decisions. Organize projects and people to get things done, focus on getting results in the most efficient way possible. Take care of routine details. Have a clear set of logical standards, systematically follow them and want others to also. Forceful in implementing their plans.	**ESFJ** Warmhearted, conscientious, and cooperative. Want harmony in their environment, work with determination to establish it. Like to work with others to complete tasks accurately and on time. Loyal, follow through even in small matters. Notice what others need in their day-by-day lives and try to provide it. Want to be appreciated for who they are and for what they contribute.	**ENFJ** Warm, empathetic, responsive, and responsible. Highly attuned to the emotions, needs, and motivations of others. Find potential in everyone, want to help others fulfill their potential. May act as catalysts for individual and group growth. Loyal, responsive to praise and criticism. Sociable, facilitate others in a group, and provide inspiring leadership.	**ENTJ** Frank, decisive, assume leadership readily. Quickly see illogical and inefficient procedures and policies, develop and implement comprehensive systems to solve organizational problems. Enjoy long-term planning and goal setting. Usually well informed, well read, enjoy expanding their knowledge and passing it on to others. Forceful in presenting their ideas.

SOURCE: Reproduced with special permission of the publisher, Consulting Psychologists Press, Inc., Palo Alto, CA 94303, from *Manual: A Guide to the Development and Use of the Myers–Briggs Type Indicator* by Isabel Briggs-Myers and Mary H. McCaulley.

nominating a subordinate for an award, or assembling a product. In the **interview,** employees may be asked to answer questions about their work and personal experiences, skill strengths and weaknesses, and career plans. An **in-basket** is a simulation of the administrative tasks of the manager's job. The exercise includes a variety of documents that may appear in the in-basket on a manager's desk. The participants are asked to read the materials and decide how to respond to them. Responses might include delegating tasks, scheduling meetings, writing replies, or completely ignoring the memo! **Role plays** refer to the participant taking the part or role of a manager or other employee. For example, an assessment center participant may be asked to take the role of a manager who has to give a negative performance review to a subordinate. The participant is provided with information regarding the subordinate's performance. The participant is asked to prepare for and actually hold a 45-minute meeting with the subordinate to discuss the performance problems. The role of the subordinate is played by a manager or other member of the assessment center design team or company. The assessment center might also include testing. Interest and aptitude tests may also be used to evaluate an employee's vocabulary, general mental ability, and reasoning skills. Personality tests may be used to determine if employees can get along with others, their tolerance for ambiguity, and other traits related to success as a manager.

The exercises in the assessment center are designed to measure employees' administrative and interpersonal skills. Skills that are typically measured include leadership, oral communication, written communication, judgment, organizational ability, and stress tolerance. Table 9.4 shows an example of the skills measured by the assessment center. As we see, each exercise gives participating employees the opportunity to demonstrate several different skills. For example, the exercise requiring scheduling to meet production demands evaluates employees' administrative and problem solving ability. The leaderless group discussion measures interpersonal skills such as sensitivity toward others, stress tolerance, and oral communications skills.

Managers are usually used as assessors. The managers are trained to look for employee behaviors that are related to the skills that will be assessed. Typically, each assessor is assigned to observe and record one or two employees' behaviors in each exercise. The

TABLE 9.4
Examples of Skills Measured by Assessment Center Exercises

	EXERCISES				
	IN-BASKET	SCHEDULING EXERCISE	LEADERLESS GROUP DISCUSSION	PERSONALITY TEST	ROLE PLAY
SKILLS					
Leadership (Dominance, coaching, influence, resourcefulness)	x		x	x	x
Problem solving (Judgment)	x	x	x		x
Interpersonal (Sensitivity, conflict resolution, cooperation, oral communication)			x	x	x
Administrative (Organizing, planning, written communications)	x	x	x		
Personal (Stress tolerance, confidence)			x	x	x

X indicates skill measured by exercise.

assessors review their notes and rate each employee's level of skills (for example, 5 = high level of leadership skills, 1 = low level of leadership skills). After all employees have completed the exercises, the assessors meet to discuss their observations of each employee. They compare their ratings and try to agree on each employee's rating for each of the skills.

As we mentioned in Chapter 6, research suggests that assessment center ratings are related to performance, salary level, and career advancement.[27] Assessment centers may also be useful for development purposes because employees who participate in the process receive feedback regarding their attitudes, skill strengths, and weaknesses.[28] In some organizations, such as Eastman Kodak, training courses and development activities related to the skills evaluated in the assessment center are available to employees.

BENCHMARKS. Benchmarks© is an instrument designed to measure the factors that are important to being a successful manager. The items measured by Benchmarks are based on research that examines the lessons executives learn at critical events in their careers.[29] This includes items that measure managers' skills in dealing with subordinates, acquiring resources, and creating a productive work climate. Table 9.5 shows the 16 skills and perspectives believed to be important for becoming a successful manager. These skills and perspectives have been shown to be related to performance evaluations, bosses' ratings of promotability, and actual promotions received.[30] To get a complete picture of managers' skills, the managers' supervisors, their peers, and the managers themselves all complete the instrument. A summary report presenting the self-ratings and ratings by others is provided to the manager, along with information

TABLE 9.5
Skills Related to Managerial Success

Resourcefulness	Can think strategically, engage in flexible problem solving behavior, and work effectively with higher management.
Doing whatever it takes	Has perseverance and focus in the face of obstacles.
Being a quick study	Quickly masters new technical and business knowledge.
Building and mending relationships	Knows how to build and maintain working relationships with co-workers and external parties.
Leading subordinates	Delegates to subordinates effectively, broadens their opportunities, and acts with fairness toward them.
Compassion and sensitivity	Shows genuine interest in others and sensitivity to subordinates' needs.
Straight forwardness and composure	Is honorable and steadfast
Setting a developmental climate	Provides a challenging climate to encourage subordinates' development.
Confronting problem subordinates	Acts decisively and fairly when dealing with problem subordinates.
Team orientation	Accomplishes tasks through managing others.
Balance between personal life and work	Balances work priorities with personal life so that neither is neglected.
Decisiveness	Prefers quick and approximate actions to slow and precise ones in many management situations.
Self-awareness	Has an accurate picture of strengths and weaknesses and is willing to improve.
Hiring talented staff	Hires talented people for his team.
Putting people at ease	Displays warmth and a good sense of humor.
Acting with flexibility	Can behave in ways that are often seen as opposites.

SOURCE: Adapted with permission from C.D. McCauley, M.M. Lombardo, and C.J. Usher, "Diagnosing Management Development Needs: An Instrument Based on How Managers Develop," *Journal of Management* 15 (1989), pp. 389–403.

about how the ratings compare with those of other managers. A development guide with examples of experiences that enhance each of the skills and how successful managers use the skills is also available.

PERFORMANCE APPRAISALS AND 360-DEGREE FEEDBACK SYSTEMS. As we mentioned in Chapter 8, **performance appraisal** is the process of measuring employees' performance. Performance appraisal information can be useful for employee development under certain conditions.[31] The appraisal system must provide specific information to employees about their performance problems and ways they can improve their performance. This includes providing a clear understanding of the differences between current performance and expected performance, identifying causes of the performance discrepancy, and developing action plans to improve performance. Managers must be trained in providing performance feedback and must provide that feedback often. Managers also need to monitor employees' progress in carrying out the action plan.

A recent trend in the use of performance appraisals for management development is the upward feedback and 360-degree feedback process. Dow Chemical, Hallmark, Honeywell, Raychem, and AT&T use this appraisal process. **Upward feedback** refers to the appraisal process that involves collecting subordinates' evaluations of managers' behaviors or skills. The 360-degree feedback process is a special case of the upward feedback process. In **360-degree feedback systems,** employees' behaviors or skills are evaluated not only by subordinates, but by peers, customers, their bosses, and themselves. The raters complete a questionnaire asking them to rate the person on a number of different dimensions. Table 9.6 provides an example of the type of skill and items used in a questionnaire designed for a 360-degree feedback system. Here "Communicating information and ideas" is the dimension of the manager's behavior being evaluated. Each of the five items relate to specific aspects of written and oral communications (e.g., clarity of messages). Typically, raters are asked to rate the degree to which each particular item is a strength or if development is needed.

The results of a 360-degree feedback system show the manager how she was rated on each item. The results also show how self-evaluations differ from evaluations from the other raters. Typically, managers are asked to review their results, seek clarification from the raters, and participate in development planning designed to set specific development goals based on the strengths and weaknesses identified.[32] Table 9.7 shows the type of activities involved in development planning using the 360-degree feedback process.[33]

The benefits of 360-degree feedback include collecting multiple perspectives of managers' performance, allowing the employee to compare his own personal evaluation with the views of others, and formalizing communications about behaviors and skills rated between employees and their internal and external customers. For example, Robert Allen, a high-level AT&T executive, now more freely airs his opinions in executive committee meetings based on the feedback he received from his subordinates as part of a 360-degree feedback system. Several studies have shown that performance improvement and behavior change occur as a result of participating in upward feedback and 360-degree feedback systems.[34]

TABLE 9.6
Sample Dimension and Items from a 360-Degree Feedback Instrument

Communicating information and ideas
Person makes points effectively to a resistant audience.
Person is skilled at public speaking.
Person is good at disseminating information to others.
Person has good writing skills.
Person writes understandable, easy-to-read memos.

TABLE 9.7
Activities in Development Planning

1. **Understand strengths and weaknesses.**
   Review ratings for strengths and weaknesses.
   Identify skills or behaviors where self and others' (manager, peer, customer) ratings agree and disagree.
2. **Identify a development goal.**
   Choose a skill or behavior to develop.
   Set a clear, specific goal with a specified outcome.
3. **Identify a process for recognizing goal accomplishment.**
4. **Identify strategies for reaching the development goal.**
   Establish strategies such as reading, job experiences, courses, and relationships.
   Establish strategies for receiving feedback on your progress.
   Establish strategies for receiving reinforcement for new skill or behavior.

Potential limitations of 360-degree feedback systems include the time demands placed on the raters to complete the evaluation, managers seeking to identify and punish raters who provided negative information, the need to have a facilitator to help interpret results, and companies' failure to provide ways that managers can act on the feedback they receive (e.g, development planning, meeting with raters, taking courses).

In effective 360-degree feedback systems, reliable or consistent ratings are provided, raters' confidentiality is maintained, the behaviors or skills assessed are job-related (valid), the system is easy to use, and managers receive and act on the feedback.[35]

New technology allows 360-degree questionnaires to be delivered electronically to the raters via their personal computers. This helps to increase the number of completed questionnaires returned, makes it easier to process the information, and makes it quicker to provide feedback reports to managers.

Regardless of the assessment method used, the information must be shared with the employee for development to occur. Along with the assessment information, the employee needs suggestions for correcting skill weaknesses and using skills already learned. These suggestions might be to participate in training courses or develop skills through new job experiences. Based on the assessment information and available development opportunities, employees should develop an action plan to guide their self-improvement efforts.

JOB EXPERIENCES

Most employee development occurs through job experiences.[36] **Job experiences** refer to relationships, problems, demands, tasks, or other features that employees face in their jobs. A major assumption of using job experiences for employee development is that development is most likely to occur when there is a mismatch between the employee's skills and past experiences and the skills required for the job. To be successful in their jobs, employees must stretch their skills—that is, they are forced to learn new skills, apply their skills and knowledge in a new way, and master new experiences.[37] As the "Competing through Globalization" box shows, to prepare employees to grow overseas business markets, companies are using international job experiences.

Most of what we know about development through job experiences comes from a series of studies conducted by the Center for Creative Leadership.[38] Executives were asked to identify key events in their careers that made a difference in their managerial styles and the lessons they learned from these experiences. The key events included those involving the job assignment (e.g., fix a failing operation), those involving interpersonal

Successful Penetration of World Markets Requires More than Just an Overseas Vacation

International assignments are increasingly being used to help companies grow overseas business markets and prepare employees to work in international locations and manage overseas operations. Take, for example, Edward Barrall, international human resource manager for Hines (a Houston, Texas, international real estate and property management company). Hines manages approximately $8 billion in real estate assets. Prior to joining Hines, Barrall worked in Moscow for a small import–export company. He was familiar with the culture and history of Eastern Europe and had mastered the Russian language. Based on Barrall's background, Hines sent him to Moscow to set up a new HR department from scratch. His job was to try to blend the company's culture and the Russian work force's culture. Barrall had to take Western management concepts and adapt them to the Russian legal and cultural environments. Barrall is now working at corporate headquarters in Houston as the new HR manager for international operations. Thanks to his experience in Russia, he has helped Hines to reduce costs by convincing overseas managers to adopt compensation and benefits programs rather than treat each employee individually.

Another example comes from General Electric's successful action learning programs to develop managers' global skills. (We discussed action learning in Chapter 7.) Teams of managers participate in the action learning process. GE's program begins with an assessment of leadership effectiveness. Managers are given feedback on how their leadership behaviors may be in sync with and counter to what is needed to be successful in a global environment. The next step involves giving the managers a challenging assignment in an international location. One assignment involved having the managers consider how GE might change the lighting market in Western Europe. These assignments require managers to visit the international location to conduct interviews and gather information. For example, for the Western Europe market, managers interviewed suppliers, customers, and vendors. The managers shared results of their research with other managers and then returned to the United States to present their recommendations to heads of business units. Besides using experience to change the managers' perceptions of what skills are necessary to be a global leader, after the presentations, follow-up meetings were held for the team members to discuss what they had learned and to evaluate how they functioned as teams. The action learning process ended with a meeting with Jack Welch, CEO of General Electric. Several ideas that the teams gained from the action learning experience were implemented.

COMPETING THROUGH GLOBALIZATION

SOURCE: J.J. Laabs, "Getting Ahead by Going Abroad," *Global Workforce* (January 1998), pp. 10–11; D. Dotlich and J.L. Noel, *Action Learning* (San Francisco: Jossey–Bass, 1998), pp. 84–87.

relationships (e.g., get along with supervisors), and the specific type of transition required (e.g., situations in which the executive did not have the necessary background). The job demands and what employees can learn from them are shown in Table 9.8.

One concern in the use of demanding job experiences for employee development is whether they are viewed as positive or negative stressors. Job experiences that are seen as positive stressors challenge employees to stimulate learning. Job challenges viewed as negative stressors create high levels of harmful stress for employees exposed to them. Recent research findings suggest that all of the job demands, with the exception of obstacles, are related to learning.[39] Managers reported that obstacles and job demands related to creating change were more likely to lead to negative stress than the other job demands. This suggests that companies should carefully weigh the potential negative consequences before placing employees in development assignments involving obstacles or creating change.

Although the research on development through job experiences has focused on executives and managers, line employees can also learn from job experiences. As we noted

TABLE 9.8
Job Demands and the Lessons Employees Learn from Them

Making transitions	*Unfamiliar responsibilities:* The manager must handle responsibilities that are new, very different, or much broader than previous ones.
	Proving yourself: The manager has added pressure to show others she can handle the job.
Creating change	*Developing new directions:* The manager is responsible for starting something new in the organization, making strategic changes in the business, carrying out a reorganization, or responding to rapid changes in the business environment.
	Inherited problems: The manager has to fix problems created by a former incumbent or take over problem employees.
	Reduction decisions: Decisions about shutting down operations or staff reductions have to be made.
	Problems with employees: Employees lack adequate experience, are incompetent, or are resistant.
Having high level of responsibility	*High stakes:* Clear deadlines, pressure from senior managers, high visibility, and responsibility for key decisions make success or failure in this job clearly evident.
	Managing business diversity: The scope of the job is large with responsibilities for multiple functions, groups, products, customers, or markets.
	Job overload: The sheer size of the job requires a large investment of time and energy.
	Handling external pressure: External factors that affect the business (e.g., negotiating with unions or government agencies; working in a foreign culture; coping with serious community problems) must be dealt with.
Being involved in nonauthority relationships	*Influencing without authority:* Getting the job done requires influencing peers, higher management, external parties, or other key people over whom the manager has no direct authority.
Facing obstacles	*Adverse business conditions:* The business unit or product line faces financial problems or difficult economic conditions.
	Lack of top management support: Senior management is reluctant to provide direction, support, or resources for current work or new projects.
	Lack of personal support: The manager is excluded from key networks and gets little support and encouragement from others.
	Difficult boss: The manager's opinions or management styles differ from those of the boss, or the boss has major shortcomings.

SOURCE: C. D. McCauley, L. J. Eastman, and J. Ohlott, "Linking Management Selection and Development through Stretch Assignments," *Human Resource Management* 84 (1995), pp. 93–115. Copyright © 1995 John Wiley and Sons, Inc. Reprinted by permission of John Wiley and Sons, Inc.

earlier, for a work team to be successful, its members now need the kinds of skills that only managers were once thought to need (e.g., dealing directly with customers, analyzing data to determine product quality, resolving conflict among team members). Besides the development that occurs when a team is formed, employees can further develop their skills by switching work roles within the team.

Figure 9.2 shows the various ways that job experiences can be used for employee development. These include enlarging the current job, job rotation, transfers, promotions, downward moves, and temporary assignments with other companies.

ENLARGING THE CURRENT JOB. **Job enlargement** refers to adding challenges or new responsibilities to employees' current jobs. This could include such activities as special project assignments, switching roles within a work team, or researching new ways to serve clients and customers. For example, an engineering employee may be asked to join a task force charged with developing new career paths for technical employees. Through this project work, the engineer may be asked to take leadership for

FIGURE 9.2
How Job Experiences Are Used for Employee Development

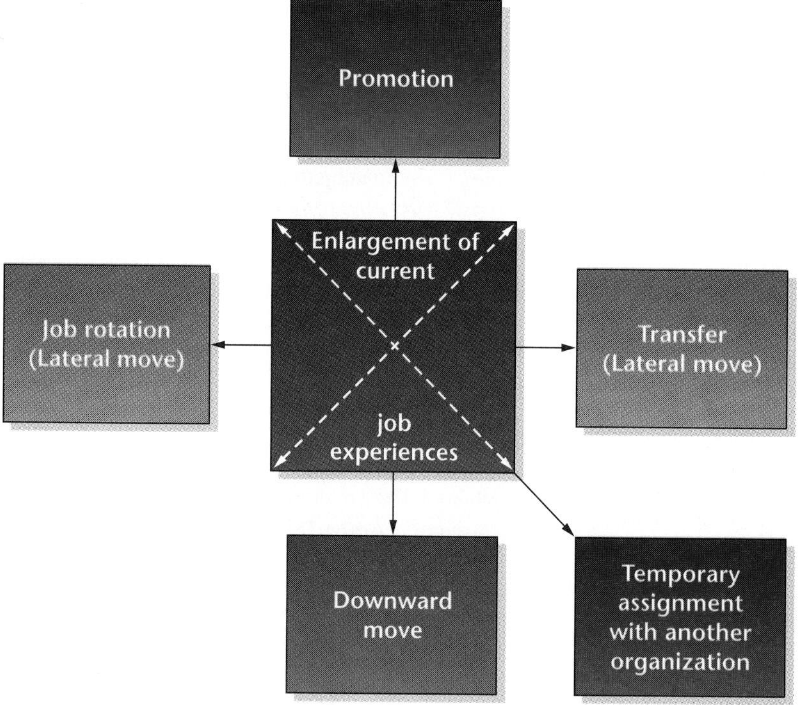

certain aspects of career path development (such as reviewing the company's career development process). As a result, the engineer has the opportunity not only to learn about the company's career development system, but to use leadership and organizational skills to help the task force reach its goals.

JOB ROTATION. **Job rotation** involves providing employees with a series of job assignments in various functional areas of the company or movement among jobs in a single functional area or department. For example, at McDonnell Douglas the job rotation program in finance is within the finance function because employees need to understand all aspects of budgeting. Greyhound Financial Corporation has a job rotation program known as muscle-building for high-potential executive managers.[40] Managers are put in departments where they will have to perform tasks different from those they have performed in the past. They maintain their titles and compensation levels while moving through the assignments, which vary in status. The time employees spend in each job varies depending on the assignment's purpose. In the Greyhound program, assignments last two years.

Job rotation helps employees gain an overall appreciation of the company's goals, increases their understanding of different company functions, develops a network of contacts, and improves their problem solving and decision making skills.[41] Job rotation has also been shown to be related to skill acquisition, salary growth, and promotion rates. But, there are several potential problems with job rotation for both the employee and the work unit. The rotation may create a short-term perspective on problems and solutions in rotating employees and their peers. Employees' satisfaction and motivation may be adversely affected because they find it difficult to develop functional specialties and they don't spend enough time in one position to receive a challenging assignment. Productivity losses and work load increases may be experienced by both the department gaining a rotating employee and the department losing the employee due to training demands and loss of a resource.

TABLE 9.9
Characteristics of Effective Job Rotation Systems

1. Job rotation is used to develop skills as well as give employees experience needed for managerial positions.
2. Employees understand specific skills that will be developed by rotation.
3. Job rotation is used for all levels and types of employees.
4. Job rotation is linked with the career management process so employees know the development needs addressed by each job assignment.
5. Benefits of rotation are maximized and costs are minimized through managing timing of rotations to reduce work load costs and help employees understand job rotation's role in their development plans.
6. All employees have equal opportunities for job rotation assignments regardless of their demographic group.

SOURCE: Based on L. Cheraskin and M. Campion, "Study Clarifies Job Rotation Benefits," *Personnel Journal* (November 1996), pp. 31–38. Used with permission of ACC Communications Inc.

The characteristics of effective job rotation systems are shown in Table 9.9. As we see, effective job rotation systems are linked to the company's training, development, and career management systems. Also, job rotation is used for all types of employees, not just those with managerial potential.

TRANSFERS, PROMOTIONS, AND DOWNWARD MOVES. Upward, lateral, and downward mobility is available for development purposes in most companies.[42] In a **transfer,** an employee is given a job assignment in a different area of the company. Transfers do not necessarily involve increased job responsibilities or increased compensation. They are likely lateral moves (a move to a job with similar responsibilities). **Promotions** are advancements into positions with greater challenges, more responsibility, and more authority than in the previous job. Promotions usually include pay increases.

Transfers may involve relocation within the United States or to another country. They can be stressful not only because the employee's work role changes, but if the employee is in a two-career family, the spouse must find new employment. Also, the family has to join a new community. Transfers disrupt employees' daily lives, interpersonal relationships, and work habits.[43] People have to find new housing, shopping, health care, and leisure facilities, and they may be many miles from the emotional support of friends and family. They also have to learn a new set of work norms and procedures, they must develop interpersonal relationships with their new managers and peers, and they are expected to be as productive in their new jobs as they were in their old jobs even though they may know very little about the products, services, processes, or employees for whom they are responsible.

Because transfers can be anxiety provoking, many companies have difficulty getting employees to accept them. Research has identified the employee characteristics associated with a willingness to accept transfers:[44] high career ambitions, a belief that one's future with the company is promising, and a belief that accepting a transfer is necessary for success in the company. Employees who are not married and not active in the community are generally most willing to accept transfers. Among married employees, the spouse's willingness to move is the most important influence on whether an employee will accept a transfer.

A **downward move** occurs when an employee is given a reduced level of responsibility and authority.[45] This may involve a move to another position at the same level, but with less authority and responsibility (lateral demotion), a temporary cross-functional move, or a demotion because of poor performance. Temporary cross-functional moves to lower-level positions, which give employees experience working in different functional areas, are most frequently used for employee development. For example, engineers who want to move into management often take lower-level positions (e.g., shift supervisor) to develop their management skills.

Because of the psychological and tangible rewards of promotions (e.g., increased feeling of self-worth, salary, and status in the company), employees are more willing to accept promotions than they are to accept lateral or downward moves. Promotions are more readily available when a company is profitable and growing. When a company is restructuring and/or experiencing stable or declining profits—especially if numerous employees are interested in promotions and the company tends to rely on the external labor market to staff higher-level positions—promotion opportunities may be limited.[46]

Unfortunately, many employees have difficulty associating transfers and downward moves with development. They see them as punishments rather than as opportunities to develop skills that will help them achieve long-term success with the company. Many employees decide to leave a company rather than accept a transfer. Companies need to successfully manage transfers not only because of the costs of replacing employees but because of the costs directly associated with them. For example, GTE spends approximately $60 million a year on home purchases and other relocation costs such as temporary housing and relocation allowances.[47] One challenge companies face is learning how to use transfers and downward moves as development opportunities—convincing employees that accepting these opportunities will result in long-term benefits for them.

To ensure that employees accept transfers, promotions, and downward moves as development opportunities, companies can provide

- Information about the content, challenges, and potential benefits of the new job and location.
- Involvement in the transfer decision by sending the employees to preview the new location and giving them information about the community.
- Clear performance objectives and early feedback about their job performance.
- A host at the new location to help them adjust to the new community and workplace.
- Information about how the job opportunity will affect their income, taxes, mortgage payments, and other expenses.
- Reimbursement and assistance in selling and purchasing or renting a place to live.
- An orientation program for the new location and job.
- Information on how the new job experiences will support the employee's career plans.
- Assistance for dependent family members including identifying schools and child care and elder care options.
- Help for the spouse in identifying and marketing her skills and finding employment.[48]

TEMPORARY ASSIGNMENTS WITH OTHER ORGANIZATIONS. Two companies can agree to exchange employees. First Chicago National Bank and Kodak participated in an employee exchange program so that the two companies could better understand each other's business and how to improve the services provided.[49] For example, an employee from First Chicago helped Kodak's business imaging division identify applications for compact disc technology. A Kodak employee helped First Chicago understand areas within the bank that could benefit from imaging technology.

Temporary assignments can include a **sabbatical** (a leave of absence from the company to renew or develop skills). Employees on sabbatical often receive full pay and benefits. Sabbaticals provide employees with the opportunity to get away from the day-to-day stresses of their jobs and acquire new skills and perspectives. Sabbaticals also allow employees more time for personal pursuits such as writing a book or spending more time with young children. Sabbaticals are common in a variety of industries ranging from consulting firms to the fast food industry.[50] For example, McDonald's Corporation offers an 8-week sabbatical to employees with 10 years of service and 16 weeks to those with 20 years of service. How employees spend their sabbaticals varies from company to company. Some employees may work for a nonprofit service agency, others may study at a college or university or travel and work on special projects in non-U.S. subsidiaries of the company.

INTERPERSONAL RELATIONSHIPS

Employees can also develop skills and increase their knowledge about the company and its customers by interacting with a more experienced organizational member. Mentoring and coaching are two types of interpersonal relationships that are used to develop employees.

MENTORING. A **mentor** is an experienced, productive senior employee who helps develop a less experienced employee (the protégé). Most mentoring relationships develop informally as a result of interests or values shared by the mentor and protégé. Research suggests that employees with certain personality characteristics (e.g., emotional stability, the ability to adapt their behavior based on the situation, high needs for power and achievement) are most likely to seek a mentor and be an attractive protégé for a mentor.[51]

Mentoring relationships can also develop as part of a planned company effort to bring together successful senior employees with less experienced employees.

Developing Successful Mentoring Programs. Although many mentoring relationships develop informally, one major advantage of formalized mentoring programs is that they ensure access to mentors for all employees, regardless of gender or race. An additional advantage is that participants in the mentoring relationship know what is expected of them.[52] One limitation of formal mentoring programs is that mentors may not be able to provide counseling and coaching in a relationship that has been artificially created.[53]

Table 9.10 presents the characteristics of a successful formal mentoring program.

TABLE 9.10
Characteristics of Successful Formal Mentoring Programs

1. Mentor and protégé participation is voluntary. Relationship can be ended at any time without fear of punishment.
2. Mentor–protégé matching process does not limit the ability of informal relationships to develop. For example, a mentor pool can be established to allow protégés to choose from a variety of qualified mentors.
3. Mentors are chosen on the basis of their past record in developing employees, willingness to serve as a mentor, and evidence of positive coaching, communication, and listening skills.
4. The purpose of the program is clearly understood. Projects and activities that the mentor and protégé are expected to complete are specified.
5. The length of the program is specified. Mentor and protégé are encouraged to pursue the relationship beyond the formal time period.
6. A minimum level of contact between the mentor and protégé is specified.
7. Protégés are encouraged to contact one another to discuss problems and share successes.
8. The mentor program is evaluated. Interviews with mentors and protégés are used to obtain immediate feedback regarding specific areas of dissatisfaction. Surveys are used to gather more detailed information regarding benefits received from participating in the program.
9. Employee development is rewarded, which signals managers that mentoring and other development activities are worth their time and effort.

Mentors should be chosen based on interpersonal and technical skills. They also need to be trained. For example, New York Hospital–Cornell Medical Center developed a mentoring program for housekeeping employees. Each mentor has between 5 and 10 protégés to meet with on a quarterly basis. To qualify as mentors employees have to receive outstanding performance evaluations, demonstrate strong interpersonal skills, and be able to perform basic cleaning tasks and essential duties of all housekeeping positions including safety procedures (such as handling infectious waste).

Mentors undergo a two-day training program that emphasizes communications skills. They are also taught how to convey information about the job and give directions effectively without criticizing employees.[54]

Benefits of Mentoring Relationships. Both mentors and protégés can benefit from a mentoring relationship. Research suggests that mentors provide career and psychosocial support to their protégés. **Career support** includes coaching, protection, sponsorship, and providing challenging assignments, exposure, and visibility. **Psychosocial support** includes serving as a friend and a role model, providing positive regard and acceptance, and creating an outlet for the protégé to talk about anxieties and fears. Additional benefits for the protégé include higher rates of promotion, higher salaries, and greater organizational influence.[55]

Mentoring relationships provide opportunities for mentors to develop their interpersonal skills and increase their feelings of self-esteem and worth to the organization. Mentors in the New York Hospital–Cornell Medical Center program receive a small financial reward ($1 per hour raise), but they support the program because they are recognized for helping less experienced employees. For individuals in technical fields such as engineering or health services, the protégé may help them gain knowledge about important new scientific developments in their field (and therefore prevent them from becoming technically obsolete).

Purposes of Mentoring Programs. Mentor programs are used to socialize new employees, to increase the likelihood of skill transfer from training to the work setting, and to provide opportunities for women and minorities to gain the exposure and skills needed to evolve into managerial positions. Consider the New York Hospital–Cornell Medical Center mentoring program we just discussed. The program is designed to help new employees more quickly learn housekeeping duties and understand the culture of the hospital. One benefit of the program is that new employees' performance deficiencies are more quickly corrected. Although the formal mentoring of new employees lasts only two weeks, mentors are available to provide support many months later.

At E. I. Du Pont de Nemours and Company's corporate headquarters, Steve Croft and Janet Graham have met at least once a month for the past seven years to share problems, information, and advice as part of Du Pont's mentoring program.[56] He is a planning manager in Du Pont's research division. She is an administrative assistant in the toxicology lab where Steve used to work. From a list of volunteers, mentees choose mentors (managers and executives) whose skills and experience they want to learn about. Croft, the mentor, has answered mentee Graham's questions about corporate programs and given her the opportunity to meet scientists and managers in the company. Graham has also learned more about the role of other departments in the company and budgetary priorities. Croft too has benefited from the relationship. He has learned about how management decisions affect employees. For example, when the toxicology lab was forced to begin to charge departments for its services (rather than being supported from the company's general fund), Croft learned about employees' reactions and anxieties from Graham.

Because of the lack of potential mentors, a formal reward system supporting mentoring, and belief that the quality of mentorships developed in a formal program is poorer than informal mentoring relationships, some companies have initiated group mentoring programs. In **group mentoring programs,** a successful senior employee is paired with a group of four to six less experienced protégés. One potential advantage of the mentoring group is that protégés can learn from each other as well as from a more experienced senior employee. The leader helps protégés understand the organization, guides them in analyzing their experiences, and helps them clarify career directions. Each member of the group may have specific assignments to complete or the group may work together on a problem or issue.[57]

COACHING. A **coach** is a peer or manager who works with an employee to motivate him, help him develop skills, and provide reinforcement and feedback. There are three roles that a coach can play.[58] Part of coaching may be one-on-one with an employee (e.g., giving him feedback). Another role is to help employees to learn for themselves. This involves helping them find experts who can assist them with their concerns and teaching them how to obtain feedback from others. Third, coaching may involve providing resources such as mentors, courses, or job experiences that the employee may not be able to gain access to without the coach's help. For example, at National Semiconductor, managers participate in a 360-degree feedback program. Each manager selects another manager as a coach. Both attend a coaching workshop that focuses on skills such as active listening. The workshop presents a coaching process that includes creating a contract outlining members' roles and expectations, discussing 360-degree feedback, and identifying specific improvement goals and a plan for achieving them. After each pair works alone for six to eight months, they evaluate their progress.

To develop coaching skills, training programs need to focus on four issues related to managers' reluctance to provide coaching.[59] First, managers may be reluctant to discuss performance issues even with a competent employee because they want to avoid confrontation. This is especially an issue when the manager is less of an expert than the employee. Second, managers may be better able to identify performance problems than to help employees solve them. Third, managers may also feel that the employee interprets coaching as criticism. Fourth, as companies downsize and operate with fewer employees, managers may feel that there is not enough time for coaching.

Career Management and Development Planning Systems

Companies' career management systems vary in the level of sophistication and the emphasis they place on the different components of the process. Steps and responsibilities in the career management system are shown in Figure 9.3.

SELF-ASSESSMENT. Self-assessment helps employees determine their interests, values, aptitudes, and behavioral tendencies. It often involves psychological tests such as the Myers–Briggs Inventory (described earlier in the chapter), the Strong–Campbell Interest Inventory, and the Self-Directed Search. The Strong–Campbell helps employees identify their occupational and job interests; the Self-Directed Search identifies employees' preferences for working in different type of environments (e.g., sales, counseling, landscaping). Tests may also help employees identify the relative values they place on work and leisure activities. Self-assessment can involve exercises such as the one in Table 9.11. This type of exercise helps an employee consider where she is now in her career, identify future plans, and gauge how her career fits with her current situation and available resources. In some companies, counselors assist employees in the self-assessment process and interpret the results of psychological tests.

FIGURE 9.3
Steps and Responsibilities in the Career Management Process

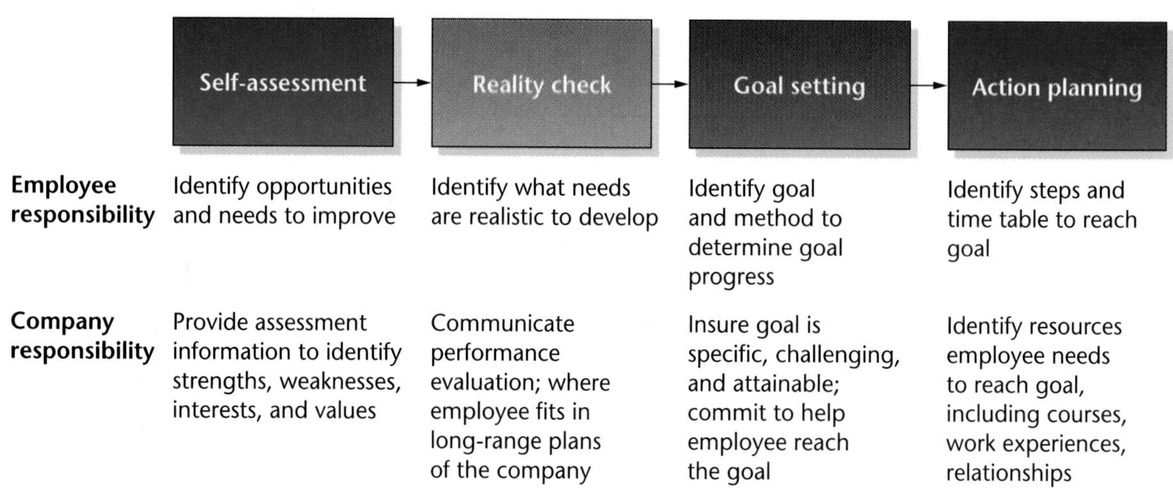

Through the assessment, a development need can be identified. This need can result from gaps between current skills and/or interests and the type of work or position the employee wants. For example, a branch manager at Wells Fargo Bank for 14 years enjoyed both working with computers and researching program development issues.[60] He was having difficulty in choosing whether to pursue further work experiences with computers or enter a new career in developing software applications. Psychological tests he completed as part of the company's career assessment program confirmed his strong interests in research and development. As a result, he began his own software design company.

REALITY CHECK. Employees receive information about how the company evaluates their skills and knowledge and where they fit into the company's plans (e.g., potential promotion opportunities, lateral moves). Usually, this information is provided by the employee's manager as part of the performance appraisal process. It is not uncommon in well-developed career management systems for the manager to hold separate performance appraisals and career development discussions. For example, in Coca-Cola USA's system, employees and managers have a separate meeting after the annual performance review to discuss the employee's career interests, strengths, and possible development activities.[61]

GOAL SETTING. Employees determine their short- and long-term career goals during this phase of the career planning process. These goals usually relate to desired positions (e.g., to become sales manager within three years), level of skill application (e.g., to use one's budgeting skills to improve the unit's cash flow problems), work setting (e.g., to move to corporate marketing within two years), or skill acquisition (e.g., to learn how to use the company's human resource information system). These goals are usually discussed with the manager and written into a development plan. A development plan is shown in Figure 9.4.

ACTION PLANNING. During this phase, employees determine how they will achieve their short- and long-term career goals. Action plans may involve any one or combination of development approaches discussed in the chapter (e.g., enrolling in courses and seminars, getting additional assessment, obtaining new job experiences, or

TABLE 9.11
Example of a Self-Assessment Exercise

ACTIVITY (PURPOSE)
Step 1: ***Where am I?*** **(Examine current position of life and career.)** Think about your life from past and present to the future. Draw a time line to represent important events.
Step 2: ***Who am I?*** **(Examine different roles.)** Using 3 × 5 cards, write down one answer per card to the question "Who am I?"
Step 3: ***Where would I like to be and what would I like to happen?*** **(This helps in future goal setting.)** Consider your life from present to future. Write an autobiography answering three questions: What do you want to have accomplished? What milestones do you want to achieve? What do you want to be remembered for?
Step 4: ***An ideal year in the future*** **(Identify resources needed.)** Consider a one-year period in the future. If you had unlimited resources, what would you do? What would the ideal environment look like? Does the ideal environment match step 3?
Step 5: ***An ideal job*** **(Create current goal.)** In the present, think about an ideal job for you with your available resources. Consider your role, resources, and type of training or education needed.
Step 6: ***Career by objective inventory*** **(Summarize current situation.)** • What gets you excited each day? • What do you do well? What are you known for? • What do you need to achieve your goals? • What could interfere with reaching your goals? • What should you do now to move toward reaching your goals? • What is your long-term career objective?

SOURCE: Based on J.E. McMahon and S.K. Merman, "Career Development," in *The ASTD Training and Development Handbook*, 4th ed., ed. R.L. Craig (New York: McGraw–Hill, 1996), pp. 679–97. Reproduced with permission.

finding a mentor or coach).[62] It is important to note that the development approach used is dependent on the needs and developmental goal.

EXAMPLE OF A CAREER MANAGEMENT SYSTEM. United Parcel Service's (UPS's) career development system illustrates the career planning process and the strategic role it can play in ensuring that staffing needs are met.[63] UPS has 285,000 employees in 185 nations and territories who are responsible for making sure that packages are picked up and delivered in a timely fashion. UPS was forced to deal with how to develop its managerial ranks which included 49,000 people worldwide. The task was to develop a management development system that would ensure that managers' skills were up to date and link the system to selection and training activities. As a result, UPS designed a career management process. The process starts with the manager identifying the skills, knowledge, and experience that the work team needs to meet current and anticipated business needs. Gaps between needs and relevant qualifications of the team are identified. The manager then identifies the development needs of each team member. Next, team members complete a series of exercises that help them with self-assessment, goal setting, and development planning. The manager and employee work together to create an individual development plan. In the discussion, the manager shares performance appraisal information and her analysis of team needs with the employee. That is, the manager provides a "reality check." The plan includes the employee's career goals and development actions that they will pursue during the next year. To en-

FIGURE 9.4
Career Development Plan

Development Needs—Current Position Specific knowledge and skills needed to improve or maintain satisfactory performance:
Development Needs—Future Position Specific knowledge and skills to get ready for next position: **Target Job:**
Development Activities Manager and employee will work together to implement the following actions:
Development Objectives: Behavior or results demonstrating development needs are being met:
Results
Date: **Employee's Signature:** **Manager's Signature:**

sure that the career management process helps with future staffing decisions, division wide career development meetings are held. Here managers report on the development needs and plans as well as their work teams' capabilities. Training and development managers attend to ensure that a realistic training plan is created. The process is repeated at higher levels of management. The ultimate result is a master plan with training activities and development plans that are coordinated among the functional areas.

Using the Intranet to Drive Development Planning

Technology such as the intranet facilitates the process of giving employees complete control over their development while enabling them to plan their development at their convenience! For example, Ford Motor Company in Detroit, Michigan, has recognized that to be successful, its employees must be trained and developed. To facilitate the development process, Ford created the "Personal Development Roadmap" (PDR), a Web-based resource available on the company intranet that allows marketing, sales, and service employees to take control of their personal and professional development. The PDR helps employees answer three questions: What skills do I have? What skills should I have? And how do I enhance my skills?

On an annual basis employees are asked to self-assess their current skills levels by completing an online profile. The PDR compares each employee's profile to the expected skill levels for the employee's job group. Following the self-assessment, the employee identifies the areas that he would like development to focus on. The PDR will recommend education (Ford Motor Company classes and seminars), exploration (activities outside of Ford Motor), and/or experiences (job assignments and other on-the-job opportunities) to help meet the employee's development needs. Employees can enroll in a suggested course offered by Ford Motor Company through the Web site. The PDR also helps the employee in creating an annual development plan that is related to attaining the development needs. Ford has identified specific leader behaviors (e.g., drive for results, innovation, desire to serve) that all salaried employees need for the company to become the leading marketing, sales, and service company. The PDR focuses on helping employees improve these leadership behaviors.

COMPETING THROUGH HIGH-PERFORMANCE WORK SYSTEMS

Although it is too early to evaluate the success of PDR, Ford Motor Company has developed the PDR to help employees continually improve their knowledge, skills, and abilities, to align their behavior with company goals and strategies, and to take responsibility for their own performance, progress, and development.

SOURCE: Ford Motor Company brochure "Personal Development Roadmap," 1998. Courtesy Ford Motor Company.

The UPS system includes all of the steps in the career management process. The most important feature of the system is the sharing of information about individual employees, districts, and functional development and training needs and capabilities. This use of information from employees, districts, and company functions, allows UPS to be better prepared to meet changing staffing needs and customer demands than many companies.

The "Competing through High Performance Work Systems" box gives an example of how companies are using new technology to give employees complete control of their career management. Several important design factors should be considered in the process of developing a career management system. (See Table 9.12.) Tying development of the system to business objectives and needs, top management support, and having managers and employees participate in building the system are especially important to helping overcome resistance to using the system.

EXAMPLE OF AN EMPLOYEE'S USE OF A CAREER MANAGEMENT SYSTEM. Robert Brown, a program manager in an information systems department, needs to increase his knowledge of available project management software. His performance appraisal indicated that only 60 percent of the projects he is working on are being approved due to incomplete information. (Assessment identified his development need.) As a result, Robert and his manager agree that his development goal is to increase his knowledge of available project management software, which can boost his effectiveness in project management. To raise his knowledge of project management software, Robert will read articles (formal education), meet with software vendors, and contact vendors' customers for their evaluations of the project management software they have used (job

TABLE 9.12
Design Factors of Effective Career Management Systems

1. System is positioned as a response to a business need.
2. Employees and managers participate in development of the system.
3. Employees are encouraged to take an active role in career management.
4. Evaluation is ongoing and used to improve the system.
5. Business units can customize the system for their own purposes (with some constraints).
6. Employees need access to career information sources (including advisors and positions available).
7. Senior management supports the career system.
8. Career management is linked to other human resource practices such as performance management, training, and recruiting systems.

SOURCE: Based on B. Baumann, J. Duncan, S.E. Former, and Z. Leibowitz, "Amoco Primes the Talent Pump," *Personnel Journal* (February 1996), pp. 79–84.

experiences). His manager will provide the names of customers to contact. Robert and his manager set six months as the target date for completion of these activities.

Special Issues in Employee Development

MELTING THE GLASS CEILING

A major development issue facing companies today is how to get women and minorities into upper-level management positions—how to break the **glass ceiling.** The glass ceiling is a barrier to advancement to the higher levels of the organization. This barrier may be due to stereotypes or company systems that adversely affect the development of women or minorities.[64] The glass ceiling is likely caused by lack of access to training programs, appropriate developmental job experiences, and developmental relationships (such as mentoring).[65] Research has found no gender differences in access to job experiences involving transitions or creating change.[66] However, male managers received significantly more assignments involving high levels of responsibility (high stakes, managing business diversity, handling external pressure) than female managers of similar ability and managerial level. Also, female managers reported experiencing more challenge due to lack of personal support (a type of job demand considered to be an obstacle that has been found to relate to harmful stress) than male managers. Managers making developmental assignments need to carefully consider whether gender biases or stereotypes are influencing the types of assignments given to women versus men.

The "Competing by Meeting Stakeholders' Needs" box shows the steps that Procter & Gamble is taking to melt the glass ceiling. Women and minorities often find it difficult to find mentors because of their lack of access to the "old boy network," managers' preference to interact with other managers of similar status rather than with line employees, and intentional exclusion by managers who have negative stereotypes about women's and minorities' abilities, motivation, and job preferences.[67] Potential mentors may view minorities and women as a threat to their job security because they believe affirmative action plans give those groups preferential treatment.

As part of their approach to managing diversity, many companies are using mentoring programs to ensure that women and minorities gain the skills and visibility needed to move into managerial positions. For example, Pacific Bell appointed a task force to study why there were relatively few promotions of minority managers and few structured programs to help managers improve their skills.[68] The task force found that support from an older mentor at some time in a manager's career was necessary for career advancement and skill development. As a result, Pacific Bell devised a development pro-

Selling Women on a Career at P&G

Procter & Gamble has successfully used its marketing strategy to sell its products to women. It had been less successful in bringing women into its management ranks. A study of employee turnover found that two of every three high-performing employees who left the company were women. Because P&G only promotes from within, retention of high performers is critical. Until recently, no women sat on P&G's executive committee and few executives were female.

To uncover the reasons for women's low retention rate and lack of movement into executive positions, P&G conducted interviews and surveys. P&G found that women felt their consensus-building management styles were not valued in the company's command-and-control culture, which favors quick, aggressive decision makers. Because career planning was not openly discussed at the company, women employees reported that they didn't know where they stood with the company. Employee opinion surveys revealed that a "lack of feeling valued" was a larger issue for women than for men. Women employees realized that to be successful, they needed to put in long hours. But they wanted flexible hours, not part-time work schedules that would slow their promotion.

P&G then created a task force to study the brand management career path, the major career path to executive-level management. The team set goals to lower the female turnover rate and achieve 40 percent women at

each level of brand management by the year 2005. The task force developed a mentoring program known as Mentor Up. In Mentor Up junior women mentor senior men on issues affecting women. Women were initially skeptical of the program, but gradually, as the relationships developed, women were comfortable providing male managers with their perspectives on what issues were important to them. The Mentor Up program helped male managers realize gender problems throughout the company. One manager learned through his mentor that a group of male managers excluded a female co-worker from attending a baseball game with ad agency employees. He confronted the men, who had not realized their mistake. In addition to Mentor Up, the task force repackaged family-friendly benefits and programs that were already offered by the company but many employees were unaware of. Also, the task force came up with an internal ad campaign to convince women they could succeed at P&G.

The task force effort has begun to show results. The turnover rate for women is now equal to that for men, and women's job satisfaction has improved 25 percent over its 1994 level. In 1996 the company's highest-ranking woman became the first woman on P&G's executive committee. Because women now represent 31 percent of general managers (an increase from just 5 percent in 1992), it is likely that a woman will soon be named to oversee one of the company's business units.

SOURCE: T. Parker-Pope, "Inside P&G, a Pitch to Keep Women Employees," *The Wall Street Journal* (September 9, 1998), pp. B1, B6. Reprinted by permission.

gram for minority managers. Besides working with their immediate supervisors to develop career goals, trainees work with executive mentors who are at least two levels above the trainees. The mentors have input into the development plan and meet frequently with the trainees. Pacific Bell received an award from the U.S. Department of Labor for its commitment to equal employment opportunity.

SUCCESSION PLANNING

Succession planning primarily involves the identification and tracking of high-potential employees. High-potential employees are those the company believes are capable of being successful in higher-level managerial positions such as general manager of a strategic business unit, functional director (e.g., director of marketing), or chief executive officer (CEO).[69] High-potential employees typically participate in fast-track development programs that involve education, executive mentoring and coaching, and rotation through job assignments.[70] Job assignments are based on the successful career paths of the managers whom the high-potential employees are being prepared to replace. High-potential employees may also receive special assignments, such as making presentations and serving on committees and task forces. The objectives of fast-track development programs are

- Developing future managers for midmanager to executive positions.
- Providing companies with a competitive advantage in attracting and recruiting talented employees.
- Helping retain managerial talent within the company.[71]

Research suggests that the development of high-potential employees involves three stages.[72] A large pool of employees may initially be identified as high-potential employees, but the numbers are reduced over time because of turnover, poor performance, or a personal choice not to strive for a higher-level position. In stage 1, high-potential employees are selected. Those who have completed elite academic programs (e.g., an MBA at Stanford) or who have been outstanding performers are identified. Psychological tests such as assessment centers may also be used.

In stage 2, high-potential employees receive development experiences. Those who succeed are the ones who continue to demonstrate good performance. A willingness to make sacrifices for the company is also necessary (e.g., accepting new assignments or relocating to a different region). Good oral and written communication skills, an ease in interpersonal relationships, and a talent for leadership are a must. In what is known as a tournament model of job transitions, high-potential employees who meet their senior managers' expectations in this stage are given the opportunity to advance into the next stage of the process.[73] Employees who do not meet the expectations are ineligible for higher-level managerial positions in the company.

To reach stage 3, high-potential employees usually have to be seen by top management as fitting into the company's culture and having the personality characteristics needed to successfully represent the company. These employees have the potential to occupy the company's top positions. In stage 3, the CEO becomes actively involved in developing the employees, who are exposed to the company's key personnel and are given a greater understanding of the company's culture. It is important to note that the development of high-potential employees is a slow process. Reaching stage 3 may take 15 to 20 years.

At American Greetings Corporation, headquartered in Cleveland, Ohio, the succession planning process involves several steps.[74] A four-person team that includes the senior vice president of human resources, the president, the chief executive officer, and the executive development director identifies high-potential candidates for the company's top three levels of management. On an ongoing basis, each committee member recommends four or five lower-level managers who show leadership potential. Each recommendation is challenged to demonstrate evidence (performance, experiences, etc.) that the nominees have high potential. The committee reviews each individual's set of competencies and compares them against standards that the company has determined are necessary for its leaders. The committee then identifies developmental tasks for any weaknesses in leadership capabilities. For example, if a high-potential employee lacks experience overseeing a project that has a major impact on the business, the employee is scheduled to receive an opportunity to become involved in a project of large scope when one becomes available. After completion of the project, the employee is required to brief the development committee on the results of the project.

Some companies' succession planning systems identify a small number of potential managers for each position. While this approach allows developed activities to be targeted to a select few highly talented managers, it also limits the company's ability to staff future managerial positions and may cause a talent drain. That is, high-potential employees who are not slotted on the short list for managerial positions may leave the company. Because American Greetings' approach to succession planning focuses on identifying and creating a large number of qualified leaders, it increases the likelihood that the company will have qualified leaders even if managerial responsibilities change in the future. This approach helps to build commitment among a large number of high-potential employees. This broader approach to succession planning also makes these high-potential employees more effective in their current positions.

DEVELOPING MANAGERS WITH DYSFUNCTIONAL BEHAVIORS

A number of studies have identified managerial behaviors that can cause an otherwise competent manager to be ineffective. These behaviors include insensitivity to others, inability to be a team player, arrogance, poor conflict management skills, inability to meet business objectives, and inability to change or adapt during a transition.[75] For example, a skilled manager who is interpersonally abrasive, aggressive, and an autocratic leader may find it difficult to motivate subordinates, may alienate internal and external customers, and may have trouble getting her ideas accepted by her superiors. These managers are in jeopardy of losing their jobs and have little chance of future advancement because of the dysfunctional behaviors. Typically, a combination of assessment, training, and counseling are used to help managers change the dysfunctional behavior.

One example of a program designed specifically to develop managers with dysfunctional behavior is the Individual Coaching for Effectiveness (ICE) program.[76] Although such programs' effectiveness needs to be further investigated, research suggests that managers' participation in them results in skill improvement and reduced likelihood of termination.[77] The ICE program includes diagnosis, coaching, and support activities. The program is tailored to the manager's needs. Clinical, counseling, or industrial–organizational psychologists are involved in all phases of the ICE program. They conduct the diagnosis, coach and counsel the manager, and develop action plans for implementing new skills on the job.

The first step in the ICE program, diagnosis, involves collecting information about the manager's personality, skills, and interests. Interviews with the manager, his supervisor, and colleagues as well as psychological tests are used to collect this information to determine whether the manager can actually change the dysfunctional behavior. For example, personality traits such as extreme defensiveness may make it difficult for the manager to change his behavior. If it is determined that the manager can benefit from the program, then specific developmental objectives tailored to his needs are set. The manager and his supervisor are typically involved in this process.

The coaching phase of the program first involves presenting the manager with information about the targeted skills or behavior. This may include information about principles of effective communication or teamwork, tolerance of individual differences in the workplace, or conducting effective meetings. The second step is for the manager to participate in behavior modeling training (discussed in Chapter 7). The manager also receives psychological counseling to overcome beliefs that may inhibit learning the desired behavior.

The support phase of the program involves creating conditions to ensure that the manager is able to use the new behaviors and skills acquired in the ICE program on the job. The supervisor is asked to provide feedback to the manager and the psychologist about progress made in using the new skills and behavior. The psychologist and manager identify situations in which the manager may tend to rely on dysfunctional behavior. The coach and manager also develop action plans that outline how the manager should try to use new behavior in daily work activities.

SUMMARY

This chapter emphasized the various development methods that companies use: formal education, assessment, job experiences, and interpersonal relationships. Most companies use one or more of these approaches to develop employees. Formal education involves enrolling employees in courses or seminars offered by the company or educational institutions. Assessment involves measuring the employee's performance, behavior, skills, or personality characteristics. Job experiences include job enlargement, rotating to a new job, promotions, or transfers. A more experienced, senior employee (a mentor) can be used to help employees better understand the company and gain exposure and visibility to key persons in the organization. Part of a manager's job responsibility may be to coach employees. Regardless of the development approaches used, employees should have a development plan to identify (1) the type of development needed, (2) development goals, (3) the best approach for development, and (4) whether development goals have been reached. For development plans to be effective, both the employee and the company have responsibilities that need to be completed.

DISCUSSION QUESTIONS

1. How could assessment be used to create a productive work team?
2. List and explain the characteristics of effective 360-degree feedback systems.
3. Why do companies develop formal mentoring programs? What are the potential benefits for the mentor? For the protégé?
4. Your boss is interested in hiring a consultant to help identify potential managers among current employees of a fast food restaurant. The manager's job is to help wait on customers and prepare food during busy times, oversee all aspects of restaurant operations (including scheduling, maintenance, on-the-job training, and food purchase), and help motivate employees to provide high-quality service. The manager is also responsible for resolving disputes that might occur between employees. The position involves working under stress and coordinating several activities at one time. She asks you to outline the type of assessment program you believe would do the best job of identifying employees who will be successful managers. What will you tell her?
5. Many employees are unwilling to relocate because they like their current community, and spouses and children prefer not to move. Yet employees need to develop new skills, strengthen skill weaknesses, and be exposed to new aspects of the business to prepare for management positions. How could an employee's current job be changed to develop management skills?
6. What is coaching? Is there one type of coaching? Explain.
7. Why are many managers reluctant to coach their employees?
8. Why should companies be interested in helping employees plan their careers? What benefits can companies gain? What are the risks?
9. What are the manager's role in a career management system? Which role do you think is most difficult for the typical manager? Which is the easiest role? List the reasons why managers might resist involvement in career management.

WEB EXERCISE

The Mentoring Institute Inc. is one of many companies that develop mentoring programs. Visit their Web site at www.mentor-u.com/. This site has information about different types of mentoring programs including orientation for new hires, career development, and developing executives and leaders. Review this site to answer the following questions.

1. Identify the similarities and differences between mentoring programs designed for orientation and mentoring programs designed for executives.
2. What types of benefits can companies expect from mentoring programs designed for career development?

MANAGING PEOPLE: FROM THE PAGES OF "BUSINESS WEEK"

BusinessWeek Wanted: A Few Good CEOs

There are few management issues of greater importance to companies, their investors, or their employees than who will lead a company in the future. The recent blowups underscore the imperative for CEOs and their boards to do a better job of preparing for succession. And as the generation of executives whose careers began in the postwar years hits retirement age, the issue will play out in record numbers: Of the 500 companies in the Standard and Poor's index, 17% have CEOs who are 63 or older. According to Bain & Co., that's up from only 10% in 1993.

For many companies it's a top of the mind concern. GE Chairman and CEO Jack Welch, who plans to retire when he turns 65, refuses to publicly discuss his much watched succession with U.S. reporters, but he recently told the French magazine *L'Expansion* that the issue has become "an obsession" for him. "It's on my mind constantly," said Welch. "Finding the right person is the most important thing that I can do for the company."

At GE there are roughly half a dozen senior candidates for Welch's job. But at the vast majority of corporations, there are far fewer, if any, logical internal successors. Just what would happen at these companies remains unknown, in part because passing the baton to a new leader is fraught with risk and emotion. In that area now, GE is in a rare position. It boasts such "bench strength" (a large number of managers who are prepared to take the CEO job) that the company has become a favorite poaching grounds for headhunters.

At other companies the CEO's contract has been extended past original retirement dates because of an uncertainty about succession. Shareholders need active and involved boards attuned to the leadership needs of their companies. The sudden demise or departure of a CEO should not become a messy melodrama leaving a company without leadership and investors without returns.

QUESTIONS

1. What recommendations would you have for identifying and preparing managers for CEO positions? Make sure you indicate the development approach(es) you would use as well as the succession planning process.
2. What are the advantages and disadvantages of publicly identifying a group of managers as high-potential managers?
3. What actions should companies take to ensure that women and minority managers have access to development opportunities needed to reach upper levels of management?

SOURCE: J.A. Byrne, J. Reingold, and R. Melcher, "Wanted: A Few Good CEOs," *Business Week* (August 11, 1997), pp. 64–70.

NOTES

1. M. London, *Managing the Training Enterprise* (San Francisco: Jossey–Bass, 1989).
2. R.W. Pace, P.C. Smith, and G.E. Mills, *Human Resource Development* (Englewood Cliffs, NJ: Prentice–Hall, 1991); W. Fitzgerald, "Training versus Development," *Training and Development Journal* (May 1992), pp. 81–84; R.A. Noe, S.L. Wilk, E.J. Mullen, and J.E. Wanek, "Employee Development: Issues in Construct Definition and Investigation of Antecedents," in *Improving Training Effectiveness in Work Organizations*, ed. J.K. Ford (Mahwah, NJ: Lawrence Erlbaum, 1997), pp. 153–89.
3. J. H. Greenhaus and G.A. Callanan, *Career Management*, 2d ed. (Fort Worth, TX: Dryden Press, 1994).
4. D.T. Hall, "Protean Careers of the 21st Century," *Academy of Management Executive* 11 (1996), pp. 8–16.
5. D.M. Rousseau, "Changing the Deal while Keeping the People," *Academy of Management Executive* 11 (1996), pp. 50–61; D.M. Rousseau and J.M. Parks, "The Contracts of Individuals and Organizations," in *Research in Organizational Behavior* 15, ed. L.L. Cummings and B.M. Staw (Greenwich, CT: JAI Press, 1992), pp. 1–47.
6. P. Sellers, "Don't Call Me a Slacker," *Fortune* (December 12, 1994), pp. 181–96.
7. M.B. Arthur, P.H. Claman, and R.J. DeFillippi, "Intelligent Enterprise, Intelligent Careers," *Academy of Management Executive* 9 (1995), pp. 7–20.
8. K.R. Brousseau, M.J. Driver, K. Eneroth, and R. Larsson, "Career Pandemonium: Realigning Organizations and Individuals," *Academy of Management Executive* 11 (1996), pp. 52–66.
9. M.B. Arthur, "The Boundaryless Career: A New Perspective of Organizational Inquiry," *Journal of Organization Behavior* 15 (1994), pp. 295–309; P.H. Mirvis and D.T. Hall, "Psychological Success and the Boundaryless Career," *Journal of Organization Behavior* 15 (1994), pp. 365–80.
10. B.P. Grossman and R.S. Blitzer, "Choreographing Careers," *Training and Development* (January 1992), pp. 67–69.
11. J.S. Lubin and J.B. White, "Throwing Off Angst, Workers Are Feeling in Control of Their Careers," *The Wall Street Journal* (1997), pp. A1, A6.
12. R.J. Campbell, "HR Development Strategies," in *Developing Human Resources*, ed. K.N. Wexley (Washington, DC: BNA Books, 1991), 5-1–5-34. Campbell, "HR Development Strategies"; M.A. Sheppeck and C.A. Rhodes, "Management Development: Revised Thinking in Light of New Events of Strategic Importance," *Human Resource Planning* 11, (1988) pp. 159–72; B. Keys and J. Wolf, "Management Education: Current Issues and Emerging Trends," *Journal of Management* 14 (1988), pp. 205–29; L.M. Saari, T.R. Johnson, S.D. McLaughlin, and D. Zimmerle, "A Survey of Management Training and Education Practices in U.S. Companies," *Personnel Psychology* 41 (1988), pp. 731–44.
13. K. Walter, "The MTA Travels Far with Its Future Managers Program," *Personnel Journal* (August 1995), pp. 68–72.
14. T.A. Stewart, "GE Keeps Those Ideas Coming," *Fortune* (August 12, 1991), pp. 41–49; N.M. Tichy, "GE's Cro-

tonville: A Staging Ground for a Corporate Revolution," *The Executive* 3 (1989), pp. 99–106.

15. J.A. Byrne, "Virtual Business Schools," *Business Week* (October 23, 1995), pp. 64–68; T. Bartlett, "The Hottest Campus on the Internet," *Business Week* (October 20, 1997), pp. 77–80.
16. J. Reingold, "Corporate America Goes to School," *Business Week* (October 20, 1997), pp. 66–72.
17. J. Reingold, "Corporate America Goes to School."
18. L. Bongiorno, "How'm I Doing," *Business Week* (October 23, 1995), pp. 72, 74.
19. T.A. Stewart, "GE Keeps Those Ideas Coming," *Fortune* (August 12, 1991), pp. 41–49.
20. G.P. Hollenbeck, "What Did You Learn in School? Studies of a University Executive Program," *Human Resource Planning* 14 (1991), pp. 247–60.
21. A. Howard and D.W. Bray, *Managerial Lives in Transition: Advancing Age and Changing Times* (New York: Guilford, 1988); J. Bolt, *Executive Development* (New York: Harper Business, 1989); J.R. Hinrichs and G.P. Hollenbeck, "Leadership Development," in *Developing Human Resources*, ed. K.N. Wexley (Washington, DC: BNA Books, 1991), pp. 5-221 to 5-237.
22. S.K. Hirsch, *MBTI Team Member's Guide* (Palo Alto, CA: Consulting Psychologists Press, 1992); A.L. Hammer, *Introduction to Type and Careers* (Palo Alto, CA: Consulting Psychologists Press, 1993).
23. A. Thorne and H. Gough, *Portraits of Type* (Palo Alto, CA: Consulting Psychologists Press, 1991).
24. D. Druckman and R.A. Bjork, eds. *In the Minds Eye: Enhancing Human Performance* (Washington, DC: National Academy Press, 1991); M.H. McCaulley, "The Myers–Briggs Type Indicator and Leadership," in *Measures of Leadership*, ed. K.E. Clark and M.B. Clark (West Orange, NJ: Leadership Library of America, 1990), pp. 381–418.
25. G.C. Thornton III and W.C. Byham, *Assessment Centers and Managerial Performance* (New York: Academic Press, 1982); L.F. Schoenfeldt and J.A. Steger, "Identification and Development of Management Talent," in *Research in Personnel and Human Resource Management*, ed. K.N. Rowland and G. Ferris (Greenwich, CT: JAI Press, 1989), vol. 7, pp. 151–81.
26. G.C. Thornton, III and W.C. Byham, *Assessment Centers and Managerial Performance* (New York: Academic Press, 1982).
27. B.B. Gaugler, D.B. Rosenthal, G.C. Thornton, III, and C. Bentson, "Metaanalysis of Assessment Center Validity," *Journal of Applied Psychology* 72 (1987), pp. 493–511; D. W. Bray, R. J. Campbell, and D. L. Grant, *Formative Years in Business: A Long-Term AT&T Study of Managerial Lives* (New York: Wiley, 1974).
28. R.G. Jones and M.D. Whitmore, "Evaluating Developmental Assessment Centers as Interventions," *Personnel Psychology* 48 (1995), pp. 377–88.
29. C.D. McCauley and M.M. Lombardo, "Benchmarks: An Instrument for Diagnosing Managerial Strengths and Weaknesses," in *Measures of Leadership*, pp. 535–45.
30. C.D. McCauley, M.M. Lombardo, and C.J. Usher, "Diagnosing Management Development Needs: An Instrument Based on How Managers Develop," *Journal of Management* 15 (1989), pp. 389–403.
31. S.B. Silverman, "Individual Development through Performance Appraisal," in *Developing Human Resources*, pp. 5-120 to 5-151.
32. J.S. Lublin, "Turning the Tables: Underlings Evaluate Bosses," *The Wall Street Journal* (October 4, 1994), pp. B1, B14; B. O'Reilly, "360 Feedback Can Change Your Life," *Fortune* (October 17, 1994), pp. 93–100; J.F. Milliman, R.A. Zawacki, C. Norman, L. Powell, and J. Kirksey, "Companies Evaluate Employees from All Perspectives," *Personnel Journal* (November 1994), pp. 99–103.
33. Center for Creative Leadership, *Skillscope for Managers: Development Planning Guide* (Greensboro, NC: Center for Creative Leadership, 1992); G. Yukl and R. Lepsinger, "360 Feedback," *Training* (December 1995), pp. 45–50.
34. L. Atwater, P. Roush, and A. Fischthal, "The Influence of Upward Feedback on Self- and Follower Ratings of Leadership," *Personnel Psychology* 48 (1995), pp. 35–59; J.F. Hazucha, S.A. Hezlett, and R.J. Schneider, "The Impact of 360-Degree Feedback on Management Skill Development," *Human Resource Management* 32 (1993), pp. 325–51; J.W. Smither, M. London, N. Vasilopoulos, R.R. Reilly, R.E. Millsap, and N. Salvemini, "An Examination of the Effects of an Upward Feedback Program over Time," *Personnel Psychology* 48 (1995), pp. 1–34.
35. D. Bracken, "Straight Talk about Multirater Feedback," *Training and Development* (September 1994), pp. 44–51.
36. M.W. McCall, Jr., M.M. Lombardo, and A.M. Morrison, *Lessons of Experience* (Lexington, MA: Lexington Books, 1988).
37. R.S. Snell, "Congenial Ways of Learning: So Near yet So Far," *Journal of Management Development* 9 (1990), pp. 17–23.
38. McCall, Lombardo, and Morrison, *Lessons of Experience*; M.W. McCall, "Developing Executives through Work Experiences," *Human Resource Planning* 11 (1988), pp. 1–11; M.N. Ruderman, P.J. Ohlott, and C.D. McCauley, "Assessing Opportunities for Leadership Development," in *Measures of Leadership*, pp. 547–62; C.D. McCauley, L.J. Estman, and P.J. Ohlott, "Linking Management Selection and Development through Stretch Assignments," *Human Resource Management* 34 (1995), pp. 93–115.
39. C.D. McCauley, M.N. Ruderman, P.J. Ohlott, and J.E. Morrow, "Assessing the Developmental Components of Managerial Jobs," *Journal of Applied Psychology* 79 (1994), pp. 544–60.
40. Management Development Report, Winter 1988–89

(Alexandria, VA: American Society for Training and Development, 1988–89); G.B. Northcraft, T.L. Griffith, and C.E. Shalley, "Building Top Management Muscle in a Slow Growth Environment: How Different Is Better at Greyhound Financial Corporation," *The Executive* 6 (1992), pp. 32–41.

41. M. London, *Developing Managers* (San Francisco: Jossey–Bass, 1985); M.A. Campion, L. Cheraskin, and M.J. Stevens, "Career-Related Antecedents and Outcomes of Job Rotation," *Academy of Management Journal* 37 (1994), pp. 1518–42; M. London, *Managing the Training Enterprise* (San Francisco: Jossey–Bass, 1989).
42. D.C. Feldman, *Managing Careers in Organizations* (Glenview, IL: Scott–Foresman, 1988).
43. J.M. Brett, L.K. Stroh, and A.H. Reilly, "Job Transfer," in *International Review of Industrial and Organizational Psychology: 1992,* ed. C.L. Cooper and I.T. Robinson (Chichester, England: John Wiley and Sons, 1992); D.C. Feldman and J.M. Brett, "Coping with New Jobs: A Comparative Study of New Hires and Job Changers," *Academy of Management Journal* 26 (1983), pp. 258–72.
44. R.A. Noe, B.D. Steffy, and A.E. Barber, "An Investigation of the Factors Influencing Employees' Willingness to Accept Mobility Opportunities," *Personnel Psychology* 41 (1988), pp. 559–80; S. Gould and L.E. Penley, "A Study of the Correlates of Willingness to Relocate," *Academy of Management Journal* 28 (1984), pp. 472–78; J. Landau and T.H. Hammer, "Clerical Employees' Perceptions of Intraorganizational Career Opportunities," *Academy of Management Journal* 29 (1986), pp. 385–405; R.P. Duncan and C.C. Perruci, "Dual Occupation Families and Migration," *American Sociological Review* 41 (1976), pp. 252–61; J.M. Brett and A.H. Reilly, "On the Road Again: Predicting the Job Transfer Decision," *Journal of Applied Psychology* 73 (1988), pp. 614–620.
45. D.T. Hall and L.A. Isabella, "Downward Moves and Career Development," *Organizational Dynamics* 14 (1985), pp. 5–23.
46. H.D. Dewirst, "Career Patterns: Mobility, Specialization, and Related Career Issues," in *Contemporary Career Development Issues,* ed. R. F. Morrison and J. Adams (Hillsdale, NJ: Lawrence Erlbaum, 1991), pp. 73–108.
47. N.C. Tompkins, "GTE Managers on the Move," *Personnel Journal* (August 1992), pp. 86–91.
48. J.M. Brett, "Job Transfer and Well-Being," *Journal of Applied Psychology* 67 (1992), pp. 450–63; F.J. Minor, L.A. Slade, and R.A. Myers, "Career Transitions in Changing Times," in *Contemporary Career Development Issues,* pp. 109–20; C.C. Pinder and K.G. Schroeder, "Time to Proficiency following Job Transfers," *Academy of Management Journal* 30 (1987), pp. 336–53; G. Flynn, "Heck No—We Won't Go!" *Personnel Journal* (March 1996), pp. 37–43.
49. D. Gunsch, "Customer Service Focus Prompts Employee Exchange," *Personnel Journal* (October 1992), pp. 32–38.
50. C.J. Bachler, "Workers Take Leave of Job Stress," *Personnel Journal* (January 1995), pp. 38–48.
51. D.B. Turban and T.W. Dougherty, "Role of Protege Personality in Receipt of Mentoring and Career Success," *Academy of Management Journal* 37 (1994), pp. 688–702; E.A. Fagenson, "Mentoring Who Needs It? A Comparison of Proteges and Nonproteges Needs for Power, Achievement, Affiliation, and Autonomy," Journal of Vocational Behavior 41 (1992), pp. 48–60.
52. A.H. Geiger, "Measures for Mentors," *Training and Development Journal* (February 1992), pp. 65–67.
53. K.E. Kram, *Mentoring at Work: Developmental Relationships in Organizational Life* (Glenview, IL: Scott–Foresman, 1985); L.L. Phillips-Jones, "Establishing a Formalized Mentoring Program," *Training and Development Journal* 2 (1983), pp. 38–42; K. Kram, "Phases of the Mentoring Relationship," *Academy of Management Journal* 26 (1983), pp. 608–25; G.T. Chao, P.M. Walz, and P.D. Gardner, "Formal and Informal Mentorships: A Comparison of Mentoring Functions and Contrasts with Nonmentored Counterparts," *Personnel Psychology* 45 (1992), pp. 619–36.
54. C.M. Solomon, "Hotel Breathes Life Into Hospital's Customer Service," *Personnel Journal* (October 1995), p. 120.
55. G.F. Dreher and R.A. Ash, "A Comparative Study of Mentoring among Men and Women in Managerial, Professional, and Technical Positions," *Journal of Applied Psychology* 75 (1990), pp. 539–46; J. L. Wilbur, "Does Mentoring Breed Success?" *Training and Development Journal* 41 (1987), pp. 38–41; R.A. Noe, "Mentoring Relationships for Employee Development," in *Applying Psychology in Business: The Handbook for Managers and Human Resource Professionals*, ed. J.W. Jones, B.D. Steffy, and D.W. Bray (Lexington, MA: Lexington Books, 1991), pp. 475–82; M.M. Fagh and K. Ayers, Jr., "Police Mentors," *FBI Law Enforcement Bulletin* (January 1985), pp. 8–13; K. Kram, "Phases of the Mentor Relationships," *Academy of Management Journal* 26 (1983), pp. 608–25; R.A. Noe, "An Investigation of the Determinants of Successful Assigned Mentoring Relationships," *Personnel Psychology* 41 (1988), pp. 457–79; B.J. Tepper, "Upward Maintenance Tactics in Supervisory Mentoring and Nonmentoring Relationships," *Academy of Management Journal* 38 (1995), pp. 1191–205; B.R. Ragins and T.A. Scandura, "Gender Differences in Expected Outcomes of Mentoring Relationships," *Academy of Management Journal* 37 (1994), pp. 957–71.
56. F. Jossi, "Mentoring in Changing Times," *Training* (August 1997), pp. 50–54.
57. B. Kaye and B. Jackson, "Mentoring: A Group Guide," *Training and Development* (April 1995), pp. 23–27.
58. D.B. Peterson and M.D. Hicks, *Leader as Coach* (Minneapolis, MN: Personnel Decisions, 1996).

59. R. Zemke, " The Corporate Coach," *Training* (December 1996), pp. 24–28.
60. Consulting Psychologists Press, "Wells Fargo Helps Employees Change Careers," *Strong Forum* 8, no. 1 (1991), p. 1.
61. L. Slavenski, "Career Development: A Systems Approach," *Training and Development Journal* (February 1987), pp. 56–60.
62. D.T. Jaffe and C.D. Scott, "Career Development for Empowerment in a Changing Work World," in *New Directions in Career Planning and the Workplace*, ed. J.M. Kummerow (Palo Alto, CA: Consulting Psychologists Press, 1991), pp. 33–60; L. Summers, "A Logical Approach to Development Planning," *Training and Development* 48 (1994), pp. 22–31; D.B. Peterson and M.D. Hicks, *Development First* (Minneapolis, MN: Personnel Decisions, 1995).
63. Z. Leibowitz, C. Schultz, H.D. Lea, and S.E. Forrer, "Shape Up and Ship Out," *Training and Development* (August 1995), pp. 39–42.
64. U.S. Dept. of Labor, *A Report on the Glass Ceiling Initiative* (Washington, DC: U.S. Dept. of Labor, 1991).
65. P.J. Ohlott, M.N. Ruderman, and C.D. McCauley, "Gender Differences in Managers' Developmental Job Experiences," *Academy of Management Journal* 37 (1994), pp. 46–67.
66. L.A. Mainiero, "Getting Anointed for Advancement: The Case of Executive Women," *Academy of Management Executive* 8 (1994), pp. 53–67; J.S. Lublin, "Women at Top Still Are Distant from CEO Jobs," *The Wall Street Journal* (February 28, 1995), pp. B1, B5; P. Tharenov, S. Latimer, and D. Conroy, "How Do You Make It to the Top? An Examination of Influences on Women's and Men's Managerial Advancement," *Academy of Management Journal* 37 (1994), pp. 899–931.
67. U.S. Dept. of Labor, *A Report on the Glass Ceiling Initiative;* R. A. Noe, "Women and Mentoring: A Review and Research Agenda," *Academy of Management Review* 13 (1988), pp. 65–78; B.R. Ragins and J.L. Cotton, "Easier Said than Done: Gender Differences in Perceived Barriers to Gaining a Mentor," *Academy of Management Journal* 34 (1991), pp. 939–51.
68. L. Roberson and N.C. Gutierrez, "Beyond Good Faith: Commitment to Recruiting Management Diversity at Pacific Bell," in *Diversity in the Workplace*, ed. S. Jackson & Associates (New York: Guilford Press, 1992), pp. 65–88.
69. C.B. Derr, C. Jones, and E.L. Toomey, "Managing High-Potential Employees: Current Practices in Thirty-Three U.S. Corporations," *Human Resource Management* 27 (1988), pp. 273–90.
70. H.S. Feild and S.G. Harris, "Entry-Level, Fast-Track Management Development Programs: Developmental Tactics and Perceived Program Effectiveness," *Human Resource Planning* 14 (1991), pp. 261–73.
71. Ibid.
72. Derr, Jones, and Toomey, "Managing High-Potential Employees"; K.M. Nowack, "The Secrets of Succession," *Training and Development* 48 (1994), pp. 49–54; J.S. Lublin, "An Overseas Stint Can Be a Ticket to the Top," *The Wall Street Journal* (January 29, 1996), pp. B1, B2.
73. Ibid.
74. S. Caudron, "Plan Today for an Unexpected Tomorrow," *Personnel Journal* (September 1996), pp. 40–45.
75. M.W. McCall, Jr., and M.M. Lombardo, "Off the Track: Why and How Successful Executives Get Derailed," Technical Report no. 21 (Greensboro, NC: Center for Creative Leadership, 1983); E.V. Veslor and J.B. Leslie, "Why Executives Derail: Perspectives Across Time and Cultures," *Academy of Management Executive* 9 (1995), pp. 62–72.
76. L.W. Hellervik, J.F. Hazucha, and R.J. Schneider, "Behavior Change: Models, Methods, and a Review of Evidence," in *Handbook of Industrial and Organizational Psychology*, 2d ed., ed. M.D. Dunnette and L.M. Hough (Palo Alto, CA: Consulting Psychologists Press, 1992), vol. 3, pp. 823–99.
77. D.B. Peterson, "Measuring and Evaluating Change in Executive and Managerial Development," (paper presented at the annual conference of the Society for Industrial and Organizational Psychology, Miami, 1990).

10 CHAPTER

Employee Separation and Retention

OBJECTIVES

After reading this chapter, you should be able to

1. Distinguish between involuntary and voluntary turnover, and discuss how each of these forms of turnover can be leveraged for competitive advantage.
2. List the major elements that contribute to perceptions of justice and how to apply these in organizational contexts involving discipline and dismissal.
3. Specify the relationship between job satisfaction and various forms of job withdrawal, and identify the major sources of job satisfaction in work contexts.
4. Design a survey feedback intervention program and use this to promote retention of key organizational personnel.

Programming Loyalty

ENTER THE WORLD OF BUSINESS

Because of its intangible nature, many organizations have struggled to understand and treat "knowledge" like all their other tangible assets. Nowhere is this more clear than in how some organizations treat personnel turnover. As Maury Hanigan, founder of Hanigan Consulting, notes, "If a $2,000 desktop computer disappears from an employee's desk, I guarantee there will be a six-week investigation—it will be a big deal. But if a $100,000 professional or executive with all kinds of expertise and client relationships gets poached by a competitor, there is no investigation. No one is called on the carpet for it."

This attitude does not characterize the SAS Institute, however. The SAS Institute is a privately held statistical software producer that manages and analyzes databases for more than 30,000 customer sites in over 120 countries. A large part of the programming work at SAS deals with taking data from numerous old and incompatible systems at the user's site and integrating it into the SAS system where it can be analyzed for trends and patterns. Because each user's needs and configuration are unique, establishing a long-term relationship between the customer and the SAS representative is essential for efficient, high-quality service.

Unfortunately, the high demand for computer programmers means that SAS must constantly battle other employers bent on stealing away its best employees. The fact that SAS has only a 4 percent rate of annual turnover in this ruthlessly competitive industry—where the norm is 20 percent—says a great deal about the company, its retention strategy, and its growth from a three-man operation in 1976 to a company estimated to be worth $5 billion today.

James Goodnight (the company's CEO and majority owner) states, "I like happy people." At first glance, it seems that the billionaire owner has given the employees a great deal to be happy about. Located on a spacious 200-acre campus, the company headquarters boasts private offices for each employee, a free clinic staffed by two doctors and six nurse practitioners, and a 35,000-square-foot recreation facility. The facilities host coffee break rooms stocked with free soft drinks, fruit, and candy. The subsidized lunch room includes a pianist who entertains daily.

However, equally important are the perks that Goodnight does not offer, because his goal is not so much happiness as it is loyalty. For example, SAS does not offer tuition reimbursement because of the belief that once degreed, employees might be more likely to leave. Instead, the company helps to subsidize an excellent private school for the children of employees, which makes the parents more likely to stay. Unlike other companies that compete for technical employees, SAS does not offer stock options for fear that enriched employees might launch ventures of their own. Instead, it offers subsidized housing and country club memberships in real estate developments owned by Goodnight—things that would be difficult for employees to replace if they were to leave. Finally, SAS is not the highest-paying employer in the industry, but instead offers a paternalistic orientation, whose value is not lost on its employees. As Jim Davis (program manager for data warehousing) notes, "I could make more money somewhere else, and about twice a month headhunters call, but money isn't everything. You're treated as family here."

SOURCE: S. Branch, "You Hired 'Em. But Can You Keep 'Em," *Fortune* (November 9, 1998), pp. 247–50; T.D. Schellhardt, "An Idyllic Workplace under a Tycoon's Thumb," *The Wall Street Journal* (November 23, 1998), p. B1; A. Bernstein, "We Want You to Stay. Really," *Business Week* (June 22, 1998), pp. 67–72.

Introduction

Every executive recognizes the need for satisfied, loyal customers. If the firm is publicly held, it is also safe to assume that every executive appreciates the need to have satisfied, loyal investors. Customers and investors provide the financial resources that allow the organization to survive. Not every executive understands the need to generate satisfaction and loyalty among employees, however. Yet, retention rates among employees are related to retention rates among both customers[1] and investors.[2] Since executives at many organizations have been slow to pick up on this linkage, this provides yet another area where one firm can gain a competitive advantage over others in the market. That is, as shown in the opening vignette, successful firms like SAS are able to convert employee satisfaction and loyalty, on the one hand, into customer and investor satisfaction and loyalty on the other.

In addition to holding on to key personnel, another hallmark of successful firms is their ability and willingness to dismiss employees who are engaging in counterproductive behavior. Indeed, it is somewhat ironic that one of the keys to retaining productive employees is ensuring that these people are not being made miserable by supervisors or co-workers who are engaging in unproductive, disruptive, or dangerous behavior. For example, as one manager recently said, "We didn't realize the full impact of keeping 'C' players. Not only do they have a minimal impact on the bottom line, they rarely know how to develop, coach, or motivate 'A' players. Consequently, they cause our good performers to leave the company."[3]

Thus, to compete effectively, organizations must take steps to ensure that good performers are motivated to stay with the organization, whereas chronicly low performers are allowed, encouraged, or, if necessary, forced to leave. Retaining top performers is not always easy, however. Recent developments have made this more difficult than ever. For example, the rash of layoffs and downsizings of the early and mid-1990s has reduced company loyalty. Couple this general attitude of mistrust with the tight labor markets characterizing the late 1990s, and we have a work force that is both willing and able to leave on a moment's notice. Similarly, the increased willingness of people to sue their employer, combined with an unprecedented level of violence in the workplace, has made discharging employees legally complicated and personally dangerous.

The purpose of this chapter (the last in Part III of this book) is to focus on employee separation and retention. The material presented in Part III's previous two chapters ("Performance Management" and "Employee Development") can be used to help establish who are the current effective performers as well as who is likely to respond well to future developmental opportunities. This chapter completes Part III by discussing what can be done to retain high-performing employees who warrant further development as well as managing the separation process for low-performing employees who have not responded well to developmental opportunities.

Since much of what needs to be done to retain employees involves compensation and benefits, this chapter also serves as a bridge to Part IV, which addresses these issues in more detail. The chapter is divided in two sections. The first examines **involuntary turnover,** that is, turnover initiated by the organization (often among people who would prefer to stay). The second deals with **voluntary turnover,** that is, turnover initiated by employees (often whom the company would prefer to keep). Although both types of turnover reflect employee separation, they are clearly different phenomena that need to be examined separately.[4]

Managing Involuntary Turnover

Despite a company's best efforts in the area of personnel selection, training, and design of compensation systems, some employees will occasionally fail to meet performance requirements or will violate company policies while on the job. When this happens, organizations need to invoke a discipline program that could ultimately lead to the individual's discharge. For a number of reasons, discharging employees can be a very difficult task that needs to be handled with the utmost care and attention to detail.

First, there are legal aspects to this decision that can have important repercussions for the organization. Historically, in the absence of a specified contract, either the employer or the employee could sever the employment relationship at any time. The severing of this relationship could be for "good cause," "no cause," or even "bad cause." Over time, this policy has been referred to as the **employment-at-will doctrine.** This employment-at-will doctrine has eroded significantly over time, however. Today employees who are fired sometimes sue their employers for wrongful discharge.

A wrongful discharge suit typically attempts to establish that the discharge either (1) violated an implied contract or covenant (i.e., the employer acted unfairly) or (2) violated public policy (i.e., the employee was terminated because he refused to do something illegal, unethical, or unsafe). Courts have been quite willing to listen to such cases, and employees win settlements over 70 percent of the time. The average award is more than $500,000, and the cost for mounting a defense can be anywhere from $50,000 to $250,000.[5] Thus, there is great financial risk associated with any termination decision.

In addition to the financial risks associated with a dismissal, there are issues related to personal safety. Although the fact that some former employees use the court system to get back at their former employer may be distressing, even more problematic are employees who respond to a termination decision with violence directed at the employer. Violence in the workplace has become a major organizational problem in the 1990s. Workplace homicide is the fastest growing form of murder in the United States—especially for women, for whom homicide is the leading cause of death in the workplace.[6]

Although any number of organizational actions or decisions may incite violence among employees, the "nothing else to lose" aspect of employee dismissal cases makes for a dangerous situation. Indeed, although the needs of investors, co-workers, and customers may dictate discharging a given employee, as the "Competing by Meeting Stakeholders' Needs" box shows, the person actually implementing the dismissal needs to consider safety as well.

Given the critical financial and personal risks associated with employee dismissal, it is easy to see why the development of a standardized, systematic approach to discipline and discharge is critical to all organizations. These decisions should not be left solely to the discretion of individual managers or supervisors. In the next section, we explore aspects of an effective discipline and discharge policy.

PRINCIPLES OF JUSTICE

In Chapter 8 ("Performance Management") we touched on the notion of justice, particularly as this relates to the notion of outcome justice, procedural justice, and interactional justice. There we noted that employees are more likely to respond positively to negative feedback regarding their performance if they perceive the appraisal process as being fair on these three dimensions. Obviously, if fairness is important with respect to

Managing Dismissal: Self-Preservation

On May 14, 1998, Bill Larson (director of human resources at Grace General Hospital in Winnipeg, Manitoba) met with one of the hospital's maintenance workers to regrettably inform him that he was being dismissed from the company. After the meeting, Larson noted to his co-workers that the meeting had gone well and that things were proceeding "appropriately." However, this view did not seem to be shared by the dismissed employee, who later that day walked into Larson's office and stabbed him to death with a hunting knife.

Far from being an isolated incident, the Larson killing reflects a new reality in the managing of human resources—specifically, the increased level of violence in society at large has spilled over to the workplace, where line managers and human resource personnel are more often than not the target of such violence. Indeed, according to the National Institute of Occupational Safety and Health, disgruntled employees are responsible for two homicides and 180 assaults a week. Since nothing makes an employee more disgruntled than being dismissed, the manner in which one holds such a dismissal event cannot be taken for granted.

Security specialists who have performed case studies of employee dismissal episodes that ended in violence suggest there are a number of steps one might take to minimize the risk inherent in this situation. First, in terms of setting up the meeting, one should conduct a threat assessment of the individual, trying to determine if the person poses a risk. For example, how central is the job or organization to this person's self-concept? Has this person made threats to co-workers or supervisors in the past? If a criminal background check was not performed when hiring the person, it may be a good idea to conduct one prior to firing them. Also, one should work closely with the company's Employee Assistance Program (EAP) to determine if the person has been or is receiving treatment for any mental disorders. Although EAPs are bound by confidentiality provisions, these can be waived if the person has made threats to do harm to specific individuals.

COMPETING BY MEETING STAKEHOLDERS' NEEDS

When it comes to running the meeting itself, archival data suggests that most companies like to conduct the meeting on Friday afternoon. However, Monday morning dismissals actually seem to be associated with less violent repercussions. Security personnel should be alerted to the upcoming meeting, but keep a low profile to prevent any escalation of the situation. The place where the meeting is held should be public. The presence of a third party is also beneficial. The tone of the meeting should do everything possible to show respect for the individual and give the person hope for the future (e.g., outplacement counseling). Finally, even if the meeting itself seems to go well, vigilance and monitoring must still be maintained, especially after "anniversaries" of the incident. In many cases, violence occurs months, even up to a year, after the dismissal. Although all this may seem a little extreme, as John Hopkins, president of CASE Management Associates EAP firm, notes, "denial and underpreparation are the common denominators of companies that have been involved with violent situations."

SOURCE: S. Caudron, "Target HR," *Workforce* (August 1998); pp. 45–52; G. Flynn, "Why Employees Are So Angry," *Workforce* (September 1998), pp. 26–32.

ongoing feedback, this is even more critical in the context of a final termination decision. Therefore, we will explore the three types of fairness perceptions in greater detail here, with an emphasis on how these need to be operationalized in effective discipline and discharge policies.[7] Indeed, a thorough understanding of these justice principles will make it clear why many organizations have enacted various policies regarding progressive discipline, Employee Assistance Programs (EAPs), alternative dispute resolution, and outplacement.

As we noted earlier in Chapter 8, **outcome fairness** refers to the judgment that people make with respect to the *outcomes received* relative to the outcomes received by other people with whom they identify (i.e., referent others). Clearly, a situation where

TABLE 10.1
Six Determinants of Procedural Justice

(1) **Consistency.** The procedures are applied consistently across time and other persons.
(2) **Bias Suppression.** The procedures are applied by a person who has no vested interest in the outcome or no prior prejudices regarding the individual.
(3) **Information Accuracy.** The procedure is based upon information that is perceived to be true.
(4) **Correctabilty.** The procedure has built-in safeguards that allow one to appeal mistakes or bad decisions.
(5) **Representativeness.** The procedure is informed by the concerns of all groups or stakeholders (co-workers, customers, owners) affected by the decision, including the individual being dismissed.
(6) **Ethicality.** The procedure is consistent with prevailing moral standards as they pertain to issues like invasion of privacy or deception.

TABLE 10.2
Four Determinants of Interactional Justice

(1) **Explanation.** Emphasize aspects of procedural fairness that justify the decision.
(2) **Social Sensitivity.** Treat the person with dignity and respect.
(3) **Consideration.** Listen to the person's concerns.
(4) **Empathy.** Identify with the person's feelings.

one person is losing his job while others are not is conducive to perceptions of outcome unfairness on the part of the discharged employee. The degree to which this potentially unfair act translates into the type of anger and resentment that might spawn retaliation in the form of violence or litigation, however, depends upon perceptions of procedural and interactional justice.[8]

Whereas outcome justice focuses on the ends, procedural and interactional justice focus on means. If methods and procedures used to arrive at and implement decisions that impact the employee negatively are seen as fair, the reaction is likely to be much more positive than if this is not the case. **Procedural justice** focuses specifically on the *methods used to determine the outcomes received.* Table 10.1 details six key principles that determine whether people perceive procedures as being fair. Even given all the negative ramifications of being dismissed from one's job, the person being dismissed may accept the decision with minimum anger if the procedures used at arriving at the decision are consistent, unbiased, accurate, correctable, representative, and ethical.

Whereas procedural justice deals with how a decision was made, **interactional justice** refers to the *interpersonal nature of how the outcomes were implemented.* Table 10.2 lists the four key determinants of interactional justice. When the decision is explained well and implemented in a fashion that is socially sensitive, considerate, and empathetic, this helps diffuse some of the resentment that might come about from a decision to discharge an employee.

PROGRESSIVE DISCIPLINE

Except in the most extreme cases, employees should generally not be terminated for a first offense. Rather, termination should come about at the end of a systematic discipline program. Effective discipline programs have two central components: documentation (which includes specific publication of work rules and job descriptions that should be in place prior to administering discipline) and progressive punitive measures. Thus, as shown in Table 10.3, punitive measures should be taken in steps of increasing

TABLE 10.3 An Example of a Progressive Discipline Program

OFFENSE FREQUENCY	ORGANIZATIONAL RESPONSE	DOCUMENTATION
First offense	Unofficial verbal warning	Witness present
Second offense	Official written warning	Document filed
Third offense	Second official warning, with threat of temporary suspension	Document filed
Fourth offense	Temporary suspension and "last chance notification"	Document filed
Fifth offense	Termination (with right to go to arbitration)	Document filed

magnitude, and only after having been clearly documented. This may start with an unofficial warning for the first offense, followed by a written reprimand for additional offenses. At some point, later offenses may lead to a temporary suspension. Before a company suspends an employee, it may even want to issue a "last chance notification," indicating that the next offense will result in termination. Such procedures may seem exasperatingly slow, and they may fail to meet one's emotional need for quick and satisfying retribution. In the end, however, when problem employees are discharged, the chance that they can prove they were discharged for poor cause has been minimized.

ALTERATIVE DISPUTE RESOLUTION

At various points in the discipline process, the individual or the organization might want to bring in outside parties to help resolve discrepancies or conflicts. As a last resort, the individual might invoke the legal system to resolve these types of conflicts, but in order to avoid this, more and more companies are turning to **alternative dispute resolution** (ADR) techniques that show promise in terms of resolving disputes in a timely, constructive, cost-effective manner.

Alternative dispute resolution can take on many different forms, but in general, ADR proceeds through the four stages shown in Table 10.4. Each stage reflects a somewhat broader involvement of different people, and the hope is that the conflict will be resolved at earlier steps. However, the last step may include binding arbitration, where an agreed upon neutral party resolves the conflict unilaterally if necessary.

Experience shows that ADR can be highly effective in terms of cost and time savings. For example, over a four-year period, one large company, Houston-based Brown and Root, found that legal fees dropped 90 percent after instituting ADR. Indeed, of the 2,000 disputes initiated by employees at that time, only 30 ever reached the binding arbitration stage. The cost savings are so large in some cases that employers—trying to convince skeptical employees to use the system—even provide financial assistance to hire attorneys. For example, Philip Morris provides aggrieved employees with up to $3,500 in financial assistance to help them prepare their case. In this way, they assure the employees that their rights are being respected and that they are getting a fair hearing in the process.[9]

Instead of providing this type of financial assistance, some other organizations force all employees to use the ADR system by treating it as a condition of employment. For example, Rockwell International requires all new employees to sign an agreement to pursue binding arbitration in the event of a dispute. As the "Competing through High-Performance Work Systems" box shows, however, this specific aspect of ADR has recently come under intense scrutiny.

While ADR is effective in dealing with problems related to performance and interpersonal differences in the workplace, many of the problems that lead an organization

TABLE 10.4
Stages in Alternative Dispute Resolution

Stage 1: Open door policy
The two people in conflict (e.g., supervisor and subordinate) attempt to arrive at a settlement together. If none can be reached, they proceed to

Stage 2: Peer review
A panel composed of representatives from the organization that are at the same level of those people in the dispute hears the case and attempts to help the parties arrive at a settlement. If none can be reached, they proceed to

Stage 3: Mediation
A neutral third party from outside the organization hears the case and, via a nonbinding process, tries to help the disputants arrive at a settlement. If none can be reached, the parties proceed to

Stage 4: Arbitration
A professional arbitrator from outside the organization hears the case, and resolves it unilaterally by rendering a specific decision or award. Most arbitrators are experienced employment attorneys or retired judges.

to want to terminate an individual's employment relate to drug or alcohol abuse. In these cases, the organization's discipline and dismissal program should also incorporate an employee assistance program. Due to the increased prevalence of EAPs' in organizations, we describe them in detail here.

EMPLOYEE ASSISTANCE PROGRAMS

Drug and alcohol abuse have been estimated to cost U.S. companies nearly $100 billion a year in lost productivity.[10] Although health care costs in general have risen sharply, treatment costs for mental and chemical dependency disorders appear to be rising even faster.[11] To lower these costs and to help get unproductive employees back on track, many employers are turning to EAPs.

An **EAP** is a referral service that supervisors or employees can use to seek professional treatment for various problems. EAPs began in the 1950s with a focus on treating alcoholism, but in the 1980s they expanded into drug treatment as well. EAPs continue to evolve, and many are now fully integrated into companies' overall health benefits plans, serving as gatekeepers for health care utilization—especially for mental health.[12] For example, when the Campbell Soup Company incorporated mental health treatment into its EAP in 1990, claims costs associated with psychiatrists decreased 28 percent in a single year.[13] This kind of program is frequently referred to as a carve-out plan. In carve-out plans, mental health and chemical dependency benefits are provided by a single vendor that has responsibility for all of the company's health benefits.

EAPs vary widely, but most share some basic elements. First, the programs are usually identified in official documents published by the employer (e.g., employee handbooks). Supervisors (and union representatives, where relevant) are trained to use the referral service for employees whom they suspect of having health-related problems. Employees are also trained to use the system to make self-referrals when necessary. Finally, costs and benefits of the programs (as measured in positive employee outcomes such as return-to-work rates) are evaluated, typically annually.

Given EAPs' wide range of options and evolving nature, we need to constantly analyze their effectiveness. For example, there is a current debate about the desirability of costly, intensive, inpatient alcoholism and substance abuse services over less costly outpatient care. Some fear that the lower initial costs of outpatient treatment might be offset by higher long-term costs because of relapse or other forms of failure. To settle this

Mandatory Arbitration: Constitutional Implications of Just-in-Time Justice

Like many recent graduates just out of business school, Mary Cremin was so excited about joining a firm—here Merrill Lynch, Pierce, Fenner and Smith Inc., that she failed to carefully read up on all the company's employment policies. When her employment was terminated in 1995 for what she perceived to be a discriminatory reason (having children), she tried to sue her employer, but was then surprised to learn that she was precluded from doing so by Merrill Lynch's mandatory arbitration policy. Stating that "I didn't know I signed away my constitutional rights," Cremin is now the lead plaintiff in a sexual discrimination class action suit aimed at striking down mandatory arbitration.

Many organizations began turning to alternative dispute resolution (ADR) programs in the late 1980s, when the rising incidence and cost of employee lawsuits, in terms of both time and money, prompted a search for quicker, cheaper forms of conflict resolution. ADR programs allow the employer to tap into computerized registrars of mediators and arbitrators who are managed by outside providers such as Resolute Systems Inc., JAMS/Endispute, and the American Arbitration Association. The disputants can do computer searches of potential mediators or arbitrators with various types of experience or expertise and then, when a "neutral" person acceptable to both parties is found, have their case heard outside a normal courtroom. Compared to the average time to have a civil case heard by a judge and perhaps jury (2.5 years), ADR programs are quick and less costly to invoke.

COMPETING THROUGH HIGH-PERFORMANCE WORK SYSTEMS

Moreover, in 1991, ADR programs got a major boost from the U.S. Supreme Court, which upheld the use of a signed contract of employment in which the employee agreed to follow mandatory arbitration procedures. In the intervening years, however, a strong backlash against mandatory arbitration has been gaining force across the country. For example, a federal judge in Boston refused to apply Merrill Lynch's policy in a sex discrimination suit by a broker prior to the Cremin case partly because arbitrators sided with brokerage firms in 93 out of 97 cases initiated by members of the New York Stock Exchange between 1993 and 1997.

Prompted by this and other cases at the U.S. Court of Appeals level, on March 2, 1998, the U.S. Supreme Court agreed to hear a case brought by a South Carolina longshoreman trying to break free of his employer's mandatory arbitration program with respect to a disability claim. If the court rules against the company, this would sharply limit the use of such policies. Many employers, seeing the writing on the wall, are not waiting for the results of this case to change their policies. For example, in November 1998, Smith Barney agreed to scale back its mandatory arbitration policy and instead rely more heavily on ADR programs that end in mediation or voluntary (rather than mandatory) arbitration.

SOURCE: D. Weimer, "Force into Arbitration? Not Any More," *Business Week* (March 16, 1998), pp. 31–35; M. Lee, "See You in Court—or Mediation," *Business Week* (October 12, 1998), pp. 34–36.

question for itself, General Electric performed an experiment at its plant in Lynn, Massachusetts. To evaluate the relative effectiveness of three possible treatment courses, GE researchers assessed the experiences of 227 workers who were randomly assigned to one of the three treatments: (1) compulsory hospitalization followed by participation in Alcoholics Anonymous (AA), (2) compulsory AA without hospitalization, or (3) the employee's choice of treatments (1) or (2).

The results of this study indicated that after two years, workers who received hospital care fared the best despite the fact that this option was chosen less often by the employees themselves.[14] A study of drug dependency has shown comparable results.[15] The message from these studies is clear: Although both employers (for cost reasons) and employees (for convenience reasons) may be attracted to short-term, low-cost treatments, everyone might be better served by focusing on long-term costs and well-being.

Another controversy surrounding EAPs is whether to establish an in-house EAP staffed with professionals who work for the company or employ an outside agency. The in-house approach is usually more cost-effective and offers employees rapid, convenient access to services. However, in-house plans run the risk of a loss of confidentiality. Indeed, lawsuits have been filed by employees who alleged that they suffered harm in the course of obtaining services from in-house EAPs.[16]

By adhering to certain guidelines, employers can minimize their liability while still benefiting from EAPs. First, the company should retain the services of qualified, experienced professionals and be able to document their qualifications objectively. Second, the company should not use overly coercive tactics in securing employees' participation in the EAP. This is easier said than done, and supervisors will likely require training in how to confront troubled personnel in a manner that makes them willing to seek help rather than become defensive. Third, companies should strive to keep EAP use confidential. For example, it is a good idea to keep EAP records separate from the rest of the human resource database system and strictly limit access to the EAP data. Fourth, employers should ensure that employees have the opportunity to provide feedback on the services received through their EAP. This allows the company to catch any problems while they are still isolated events rather than patterns of abuse.[17]

OUTPLACEMENT COUNSELING

The terminal nature of an employee discharge not only leaves the person angry, it also leads to confusion as to how to react and in a quandary regarding what happens next. If the person feels there is nothing to lose and nowhere else to turn, the potential for violence or litigation is higher than most organizations are willing to tolerate. Therefore, many organizations provide **outplacement counseling,** which tries to help dismissed employees manage the transition from one job to another.

Some organizations have their own in-house staff for conducting this counseling. In other companies, outside consultants are kept on a retainer basis to help with individual cases. Regardless, goals of outplacement programs are to help the former employee deal with the psychological issues associated with losing one's job (grief, depression, fear), while at the same time helping him find new employment.

Outplacement counseling is aimed at helping people realize that losing a job is not the end of the world and that other opportunities exist. Indeed, for many people, losing a job can be a critical learning experience that plants the seed for future success. For example, when John Morgridge was fired from his job as branch manager at Honeywell 20 years ago, it made him realize that his own assertiveness and need for independence were never going to cut it in a large, bureaucratic institution like Honeywell. Morgridge took his skills and went on to build computer network maker Cisco Systems, which is now worth over $1 billion.[18]

While this is a success story for Morgridge, the fact that a major corporation like Honeywell let his talent go certainly reflects a lost opportunity for the company. Retaining people who can make such contributions is a key to gaining and maintaining competitive advantage. The second half of this chapter is devoted to issues related to retention.

Managing Voluntary Turnover

In the vignette that opened this chapter, we discussed a number of reasons why employers are more concerned than ever about employee retention. We also showed how companies like SAS develop so much loyalty within their work force that key personnel resist lucrative offers from headhunters or competing firms. SAS is not alone in this concern. For example, in 1998, Ernst & Young actually created an "Office of Retention" which had its own separate budget and was charged with identifying a subset of people at all levels of the organization who were central to Ernst & Young's future, and doing what was necessary to keep them happy.[19]

In this section of the chapter, we will examine the job withdrawal process that characterizes voluntary employee turnover, and illustrate the central role that job satisfaction plays in this process. We will also discuss what aspects of job satisfaction seem most critical to retention and how to measure these facets. Finally we will show how survey–feedback interventions, designed around these measures, can be used to strategically manage the voluntary turnover process so that high performers are retained, while marginal performers are allowed to leave.

PROCESS OF JOB WITHDRAWAL

Job withdrawal is a set of behaviors that dissatisfied individuals enact to avoid the work situation. The right side of Figure 10.1 shows a model grouping the overall set of behaviors into three categories: behavior change, physical job withdrawal, and psychological job withdrawal.

We will present the various forms of withdrawal in a progression, as if individuals try the next category only if the preceding is either unsuccessful or impossible to implement. This theory of **progression of withdrawal** has a long history and many adherents.[20] Others have suggested that there is no tight progression in that any one of the categories can compensate for another and people choose the category that is most likely to redress the specific source of dissatisfaction.[21] Either way, the withdrawal behaviors are clearly related to one another, and they are all at least partially caused by job dissatisfaction.[22]

BEHAVIOR CHANGE. One might expect that an employee's first response to dissatisfaction would be to try to change the conditions that generate the dissatisfaction. This can lead to supervisor–subordinate confrontation, perhaps even conflict, as dissatisfied workers try to bring about changes in policy or upper-level personnel. Where employees are unionized, it can lead to an increased number of grievances being filed.[23] Where employees are not unionized, dissatisfaction can lead to the formation of a union. Research indicates that there is a very strong relationship between dissatisfaction with economic aspects of work and unionization activity.[24]

Even in organizations without unions, employees can initiate change through **whistle-blowing** (making grievances public by going to the media).[25] The damage that a single well-placed whistle-blower can do to an organization was revealed at Archer Daniels Midland (ADM). Top executive Mark Whitacre, working in cooperation with the FBI, taped many conversations that were later used to charge ADM with price fixing in one of the biggest antitrust cases in the 1990s.[26]

FIGURE 10.1
An Overall Model of the Job Dissatisfaction–Job Withdrawal Process

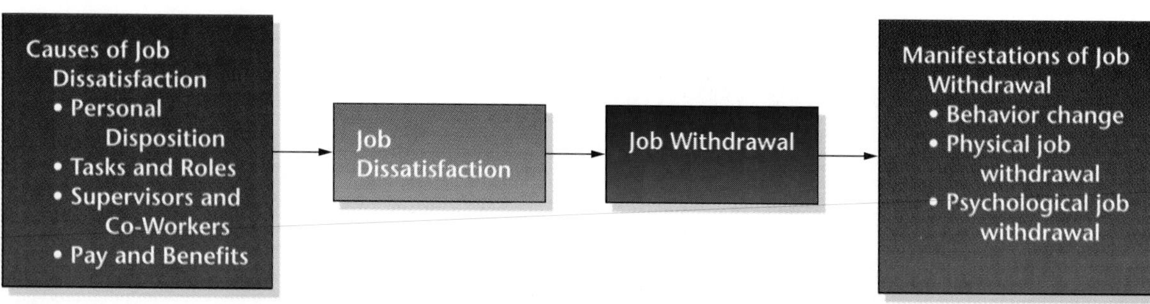

Employees can also sue their employers when the disputed policies relate to race, sex, safe working conditions, or any other aspect of employment regulated by state or federal laws. As we have seen, such suits are costly, both financially and in terms of the firm's image, regardless of whether the firm wins or loses. Most employers would prefer to avoid litigation altogether. Keeping a majority of their employees happy is one means of achieving this.

PHYSICAL JOB WITHDRAWAL. If the job conditions cannot be changed, a dissatisfied worker may be able to solve his problem by leaving the job. This could take the form of an internal transfer if the dissatisfaction is job-specific (e.g., the result of an unfair supervisor or unpleasant working conditions). On the other hand, if the source of the dissatisfaction relates to organizationwide policies (e.g., lack of job security or below-market pay levels), organizational turnover is likely.

In addition to the overall turnover rate, we need to be concerned with the nature of the turnover in terms of who is staying and who is leaving. For example, turnover rates among minorities at the managerial level are often two to three times that of white males, and this is often attributable to a perceived lack of opportunities for promotions. Indeed, Figure 10.2 shows the disparity in upper-level jobs for varying groups. Lawrence Perlman, CEO of Ceridian Corporation of Minneapolis, states, "The combination of women and people of color dropping out is really discouraging . . . it just isn't good business." To prevent this exodus, Ceridian set diversity goals for promotions and career enhancing experiences. Similar steps are being taken at Polaroid, Ameritech, Texaco, and Dow Chemical.[27]

As we just noted, many employees who would like to quit their jobs have to stay on if they have no other employment opportunities. Another way of physically removing oneself from the dissatisfying work is to be absent.[28] Like turnover, absenteeism is disruptive and costly to an organization. Absenteeism problems in organizations have been increasing lately, especially in the manufacturing industry. Research indicates a 3.5 percent increase in absenteeism in 1993 and a 4.1 percent increase in 1994 in the work force as a whole, with a 15 percent increase in 1994 in the manufacturing sector. It has been estimated that absenteeism costs organizations an average of $505 a day for large employers and $662 a day for employers with fewer than 100 employees.[29]

Short of missing the whole day, a dissatisfied employee may be late for work. Although not as disruptive as absenteeism, tardiness can be costly, and tardiness is related to job satisfaction.[30] Tardiness can be especially costly when companies are organized

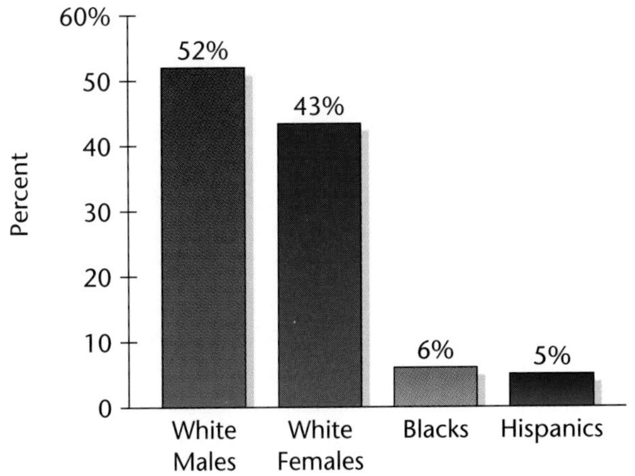

SOURCE: M. Galen, "Diversity: Beyond the Numbers Game," *Business Week* (August 14, 1995), pp. 60–61.

FIGURE 10.2 Percentage of Executive and Managerial Jobs Held by Various Subgroups around teams, because the tardy individual often creates difficulties that spill over and affect the other team members.

PSYCHOLOGICAL WITHDRAWAL. When dissatisfied employees are unable to change their situation or remove themselves physically from their jobs, they may psychologically disengage themselves from their jobs. Although they are physically on the job, their minds may be somewhere else.

This psychological disengagement can take several forms. First, if the primary dissatisfaction has to do with the job itself, the employee may display a very low level of job involvement. **Job involvement** is the degree to which people identify themselves with their jobs. People who are uninvolved with their jobs consider their work an unimportant aspect of their lives. For them, performing well or poorly on the job does not really affect their self-concept, which makes them harder to motivate.[31] Over time, job dissatisfaction leads to low job involvement.

A second form of psychological disengagement, which can occur when the dissatisfaction is with the employer as a whole, is a low level of organizational commitment. **Organizational commitment** is the degree to which an employee identifies with the organization and is willing to put forth effort on its behalf.[32] Individuals who have low organizational commitment are often just waiting for the first good opportunity to quit their jobs. In other words, they have developed a strong intention to leave the organization. In the meantime, like individuals with low job involvement, they are often difficult to motivate. Like job involvement, organizational commitment is strongly related to job satisfaction.

Organizational commitment has been attracting a great deal of attention recently. Most employers feel that the staffing policies of the 1980s and early 1990s may have killed company loyalty in the late 1990s.[33] To cope with global competition, deregulation, hostile takeovers, and unprecedented levels of corporate debt, many companies were forced to slash their labor costs through massive layoffs. As Rudy Oswald, chief economist for the AFL–CIO, noted, "Workers have a right to be upset and angry. They have been bought and sold and have seen their friends and relations fired and laid off in large numbers. There is little bond between employers and workers anymore."[34]

Surveys of American workers support Oswald's claim. When asked, "Compared with 10 years ago, are employees today more loyal or less loyal to their companies?" 63 percent said "less" while only 22 percent said "more." Half of those responding said it was likely they would change employers in the next five years. Thus, just as U.S. businesses are trying to inculcate a new sense of worker participation and involvement, many of their employees are showing reduced levels of commitment.

JOB SATISFACTION AND JOB WITHDRAWAL

As we see in Figure 10.1, the key driving force behind all the different forms of job withdrawal is **job satisfaction.** We will define job satisfaction as a pleasurable feeling that results from the perception that one's job fulfills or allows for the fulfillment of one's important job values.[35] This definition reflects three important aspects of job satisfaction. First, job satisfaction is a function of values, defined as "what a person consciously or unconsciously desires to obtain." Second, this definition emphasizes that different employees have different views of which values are important, and this is critical in determining the nature and degree of their job satisfaction. One person may value high pay above all else; another may value the opportunity to travel; another may value staying within a specific geographic region. The third important aspect of job satisfaction is perception. It is one's perception of one's present situation relative to one's values that matters. An individual's perceptions may not be a completely accurate reflection of reality, and different people may view the same situation differently.

In particular, people's perceptions are often strongly influenced by their frame of reference. A **frame of reference** is a standard point that serves as a comparison for other points and thus provides meaning. For example, an upper-level executive who offers a 6 percent salary increase to a lower-level manager might expect this to make the manager happy because inflation (the executive's frame of reference) is only 3 percent. The manager, on the other hand, might find the raise quite unsatisfactory because it is less than the 9 percent raise received by one of her colleagues who does similar work (the manager's frame of reference). A person's frame of reference often reflects her average past experience.[36] It may also reflect her perceptions or other peoples' experience (i.e., her reference group).[37] Thus, values, perceptions, and importance are the three components of job satisfaction. People will be satisfied with their jobs as long as they perceive that their jobs meet their important values.

SOURCES OF JOB DISSATISFACTION

Many aspects of people and organizations can cause dissatisfaction among employees. We will focus on the categories shown on the left side of Figure 10.1.

PERSONAL DISPOSITIONS. Because dissatisfaction is an emotion that ultimately resides within the person, it is not surprising that many who have studied these outcomes have focused on individual differences. **Negative affectivity** is a term used to describe a dispositional dimension that reflects pervasive individual differences in satisfaction with any and all aspects of life. Individuals who are high in negative affectivity report higher levels of aversive mood states, including anger, contempt, disgust, guilt, fear, and nervousness across all contexts (i.e., work and nonwork).[38]

People who are high in negative affectivity tend to focus extensively on the negative aspects of themselves and others.[39] They are also more likely, in a given situation, to experience significantly higher levels of distress than others—which implies that some people bring dissatisfaction with them to work. Research has shown that negative affectivity in early adolescence is predictive of overall job dissatisfaction in adulthood. There were also significant relationships between work attitudes measured over 5-year[40] and 10-year[41] periods even for workers who changed employers and/or occupations. Thus, these people may be relatively dissatisfied regardless of what steps the organization or the manager takes.

Although those low in negative affectivity generally report more job satisfaction than those who are high in it, when people who are generally low in negative affectivity do decide they are dissatisfied with their work, their behavioral reaction is much stronger. That is, research with nurses has shown that the relationship between job satisfaction and turnover is especially high for those low in negative affectivity. Relative to those with a positive outlook on life, people high in negative affectivity are more used to being dissatisfied and hold out less hope that finding a new job will lead to any better results.[42]

Although the causes of negative affectivity are not completely known, research that examined identical twins who were raised apart suggests that there may be a genetic component.[43] Thirty-four pairs of twins were measured for their general job satisfaction and their satisfaction with intrinsic and extrinsic aspects of the job. The researchers found a significant relationship between the ratings for each member of a pair, despite the fact that the twins were raised apart and worked at different jobs. Other research on genetic twins reared apart has shown similar effects on perceptions of the degree to which one's organization provides a supportive climate.[44]

This suggests the importance of personnel selection as a way of raising overall levels of employee satisfaction. Interviews should assess the degree to which any job applicant has a history of chronic dissatisfaction with his employment. If an applicant states that he was dissatisfied with his past six jobs, what makes the employer think he won't be dissatisfied with this one?

Finally, although the focus of this chapter is job dissatisfaction, we must recognize that dissatisfaction with other facets of life can spill over into the workplace. That is, a worker who is having problems with a spouse or family may attribute some of this negative affect to the job or organization. The National Institute of Mental Health (NIMH) estimates that clinical depression affects 17.6 million Americans, including 9 percent of all male workers and 17 percent of all female workers.

Although managers cannot be expected to become clinical psychologists, in their attempt to diagnose some work-related performance problems, the possibility of clinical depression should not be dismissed altogether, and employees can be advised to seek help from qualified professionals via a company-sponsored Employee Assistance Program. For example, NIMH runs a program called DART (Depression Awareness Recognition and Treatment), which provides educational materials and management training sessions for managers of large organizations, including AT&T, Sears, Pacific Bell, and Westinghouse. Eighty percent of those suffering depression can be managed with help; the Americans with Disabilities Act covers these individuals. "Reasonable accommodation" in these cases might include several weeks of leave to adjust to medication or perhaps altering work schedules to allow for therapy sessions. The gains achieved by early recognition and treatment can be substantial. A program similar to the DART program at First Chicago Bank dropped its behavioral health care costs from 15 percent of total medical plan costs to just 8 percent.[45]

TASKS AND ROLES. As a predictor of job dissatisfaction, nothing surpasses the nature of the task itself.[46] Many aspects of a task have been linked to dissatisfaction. Several elaborate theories relating task characteristics to worker reactions have been formulated and extensively tested. We discussed several of these in Chapter 4. In this section, we will focus on three primary aspects of tasks that affect job satisfaction: the complexity of the task, the degree of physical strain and exertion on the job, and the value the employee puts on the task.[47]

With a few exceptions, there is a strong positive relationship between task complexity and job satisfaction. That is, the boredom generated by simple, repetitive jobs that do not mentally challenge the worker leads to frustration and dissatisfaction.[48] Moreover, monotony at work has been shown to have a particularly strong negative effect on women relative to men. For example, one recent study of blue-collar workers in 32 manufacturing plants showed that increased repetitive activity at work led to absenteeism rates for women that were three times the rates for men.[49]

One intervention that employees themselves often introduce to low-complexity situations is to bring personal stereo headsets to work. Many supervisors disapprove of this practice, which can be understood in situations where employees need to interact with customers. However, in simple jobs with minimal customer contact (e.g., processing paperwork or data entry) the research actually suggests that personal stereo headsets can improve performance. For example, one study examined stereo headset use among workers in 32 jobs within a large retailing organization. The results indicated the stereo group outperformed a no-stereo control group on simple jobs (e.g., invoice processor) but performed worse than controls on jobs high in complexity (e.g., accountant).[50]

The second primary aspect of a task that affects job satisfaction is the degree to which the job involves physical strain and exertion.[51] This aspect is sometimes overlooked at a time when automation has removed much of the physical strain associated with jobs. Indeed, the fact that technology has aimed to lessen work-related physical exertion indicates that such exertion is almost universally considered undesirable. Nevertheless many jobs can still be characterized as physically demanding.

The third primary aspect is whether the object of the work promotes something valued by the worker. Over 1 million volunteer workers in the United States perform their jobs almost exclusively because of the meaning they attach to the work. Some of these jobs are even low in complexity and high in physical exertion. These volunteers view themselves as performing a worthwhile service, however, and this overrides the other two factors and increases satisfaction with the job. Similarly, several low-paying occupations (e.g., social services, religious orders) explicitly try to make up for pay deficiencies by appealing to the prospective employee's nonfinancial values. The Peace Corps, for example, attempts to recruit applicants by describing its work as "the toughest job you will ever love." Similar recruiting advertisements for Catholic priests mention that "the pay is low but the rewards are infinite."

One of the major interventions aimed at reducing job dissatisfaction is job enrichment, which explicitly focuses on the task as a source of dissatisfaction. **Job enrichment** refers to specific ways to add complexity and meaningfulness to a person's work. As the term suggests, this intervention is directed at jobs that are "impoverished" or boring because of their repetitive nature or low scope. Many job enrichment programs are based on the job characteristics theory discussed earlier in Chapter 4.

For example, at Xerox, work was once structured along four large functional units: manufacturing, research, marketing, and finance. Segmenting the work this way reduces the meaningfulness of many jobs. It also isolates workers from each other and distances them from customers. Thus, CEO Paul Allaire restructured the organization into separate product divisions that each did its own manufacturing, research, marketing, and finance. Dan Cholish, a veteran Xerox engineer, had been a "one-dimensional" engineer, but under the new system he has learned a little about manufacturing, finance, and marketing as he concentrates on customer needs. According to Cholish, "I've probably visited more customers in the last six months than I had in my last six years on my old assignment."[52]

As another example, at Motorola "total customer satisfaction" teams are given authority to make changes in production or any other work procedures, and then given bonuses tied to improved defect rates or cycle times. One team used basic industrial engineering techniques to analyze inventory and ultimately reduced average levels of supply from seven weeks to four weeks, saving the company $2.4 million. Such results often breed functional internal competition, since, as one team member noted, "Other workers were all jealous of our team." Internal competition can drive other teams to raise their standards of excellence, and greatly contribute to the organization's overall competitive advantage.[53]

Another task-based intervention is **job rotation.** This is a process of systematically moving a single individual from one job to another over the course of time. Although employees may not feel capable of putting up with the dissatisfying aspects of a particular job indefinitely, they often feel they can do so temporarily. Job rotation can do more than simply spread out the dissatisfying aspects of a particular job. It can increase work complexity for employees and provide valuable cross-training in jobs so that employees eventually understand many different jobs. This makes for a more flexible work force and increases workers' appreciation of the other tasks that have to be accomplished for the organization to complete its mission.[54]

In addition to the specific task performed by an individual, in the broader scheme of work, each person also has a "role" in the organization.[55] The person's **role** in the organization can be defined as the set of expected behaviors that both the person and other people who make up the social environment have for the person in that job. These expected behaviors include all the formal aspects of the job and usually much more as well. That is, co-workers, supervisors, and clients or customers have expectations for the person that go beyond what is formally described as the person's job. Expectations have a large impact on how the person responds to the work.

Three aspects of organizational roles stand out as significant influences on job satisfaction: role ambiguity, role conflict, and role overload. **Role ambiguity** refers to the level of uncertainty about what the organization expects from the employee in terms of what to do or how to do it. Ambiguity associated with work methods and scheduling are two of the most problematic forms of ambiguity, but by far, the most critical dimension in terms of predicting job satisfaction is ambiguity around performance criteria. Employees have strong needs to know precisely how they are going to be evaluated on the job—and when this is unclear, job satisfaction suffers.[56]

A second source of dissatisfaction is **role conflict,** recognition of incompatible or contradictory demands by the person who occupies the role. Role conflict occurs in many different forms. For example, a member of a cross-functional project team might have a project manager as well as a manager in her functional area who hold mutually exclusive expectations for the employee. Another form of role conflict occurs when the employee may be occupying more than one role at a time and the roles have incompatible expectations. Conflict between work roles and family roles, for example, is common in organizations.

This is especially a problem when employees are asked to take assignments overseas that are highly disruptive to other members of the family. Research shows that the inability to effectively manage this type of role conflict is the single biggest cause of expatriate turnover.[57] Many organizations try to minimize work–family conflict for both domestic and internationally placed employees through various forms of family-friendly benefits (e.g., company-sponsored day care or flextime).[58] We will deal with these types of programs in detail in Chapter 13 on employee benefits. For now, we will simply note that this type of conflict creates dissatisfaction among employees and can lead to problems in retention.

Dissatisfaction can also arise from **role overload,** a state in which too many expectations or demands are placed on the person (whereas **role underload** refers to the opposite problem). There can be either too much or too little task scope. Research on job stress has focused primarily on high-scope jobs (i.e., jobs that require the person to manage too many things). As we have noted, role overload seems to be an increasingly prevalent problem in today's organizations because of their emphasis on downsizing and cost cutting.[59]

Because role problems rank just behind job problems in creating job dissatisfaction, interventions that aim directly at role elements have been created. One such intervention, the role analysis technique shown in Figure 10.3, is designed to increase the communication and understanding of the various sets of role expectations that exist for a specific employee.[60]

In the **role analysis technique,** the role occupant and each member of the role occupant's role set (e.g., supervisors, co-workers, subordinates) are asked to write down their expectations for the role occupant. Then everybody is gathered together, and each person goes through his list. All the expectations are written out so that ambiguities can be removed and conflicts identified. Where there are conflicts, the group as a whole tries to decide how they should be resolved. When this is done throughout an organization, instances of overload and underload may be discovered, and role requirements may be traded off so that more balanced roles are developed.

SUPERVISORS AND CO-WORKERS. The two primary sets of people in an organization who affect job satisfaction are co-workers and supervisors. A person may be sat-

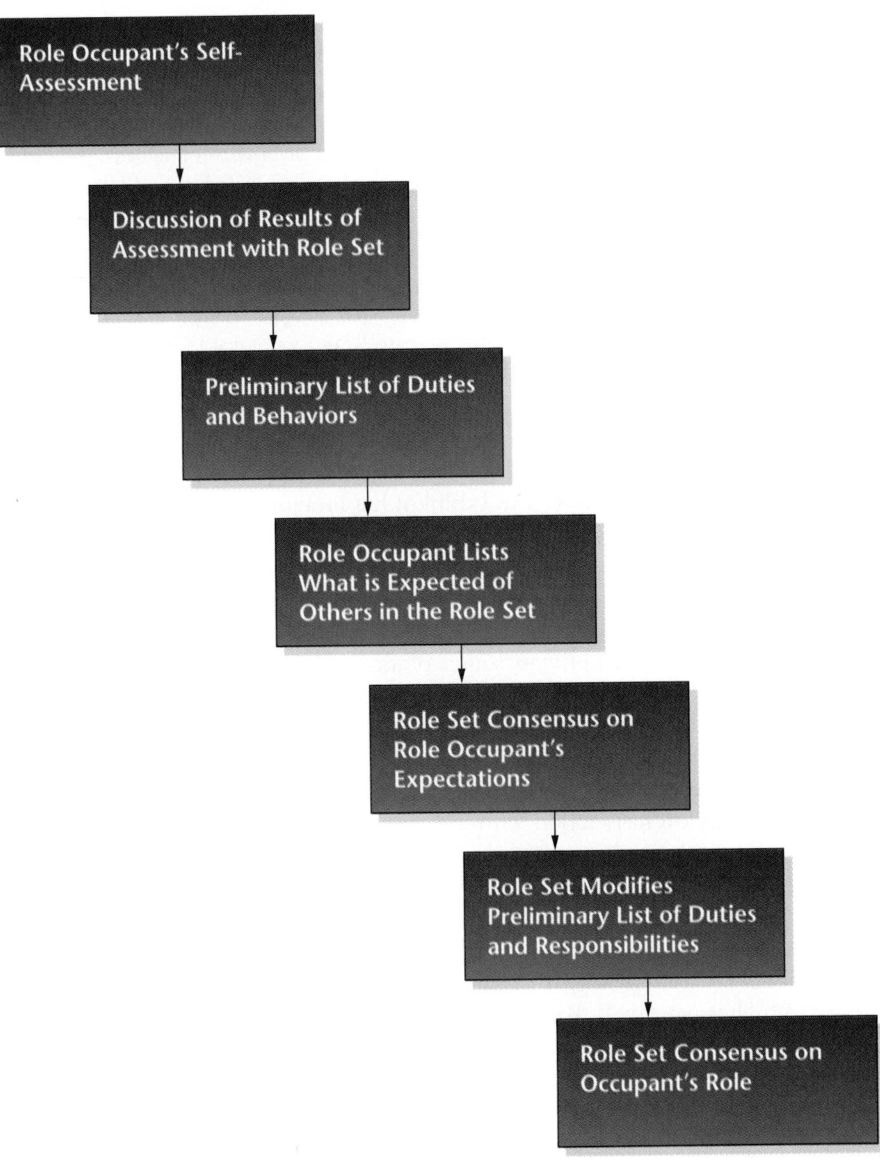

FIGURE 10.3
A Schematic Representation of the Role Analysis Technique

isfied with her supervisor and co-workers for one of three reasons. First, she may have many of the same values, attitudes, and philosophies that the co-workers and supervisors have. Most individuals find this very important. Indeed, many organizations try to foster a culture of shared values among employees. Even if one cannot generate a unifying culture throughout an entire organization, it is worth noting that increases in job satisfaction can be derived simply from congruence among supervisors and subordinates at one level.[61]

Second, the person may be satisfied with his supervisor and co-workers because they provide social support. Social support means the degree to which the person is surrounded by other people who are sympathetic and caring. Considerable research indicates that social support is a strong predictor of job satisfaction, whether the support comes from supervisors or co-workers.[62] Also, as we indicated earlier, fair interpersonal treatment in terms of interactional justice is also a strong predictor of job satisfaction and turnover.[63]

Third, one's supervisor or co-workers may help the person attain some valued outcome. For example, a new employee may be uncertain about what goals to pursue or what paths to take to achieve those goals. He will likely be satisfied with a supervisor or with co-workers who can help clarify those goals and paths.[64]

Because a supportive environment reduces dissatisfaction, many organizations foster team building both on and off the job (e.g., via softball or bowling leagues). The idea is that group cohesiveness and support for individual group members will be increased through exposure and joint efforts. Although management certainly cannot ensure that each stressed employee develops friends, it can make it easier for employees to interact—a necessary condition for developing friendship and rapport.

For example, American Airlines teamed up with the environmental group Nature Conservancy to sponsor a "Teamwork for Nature" day in several U.S. cities. Employee teams reported for cleanup duty and helped by gathering litter, pulling weeds, and constructing fences. Some teams even worked on more elaborate projects such as installing irrigation systems or controlling erosion problems. Flight attendant Jacqueline Grant noted, "The nice thing about it is every employee group, regardless of their job description, can participate in their own way. I think it has brought a lot of departments closer together."[65]

PAY AND BENEFITS. We should not discount the influence of the job incumbent, the job itself, and the surrounding people in terms of influencing job satisfaction, but for most people, work is their primary source of income and financial security. Pay is also seen as an indicator of status within the organization as well as in society at large. Thus, for some people, pay is a reflection of self-worth, so pay satisfaction takes on critical significance when it comes to retention. Indeed, the role of pay and benefits is so large that we will devote the entire next part of this book to these topics. Within this chapter, we will focus primarily on satisfaction with four aspects of pay (pay levels, pay raises, pay structure, and benefits) and how these are assessed within the organization. Methods for addressing these issues will be discussed in Part IV of this book.

One of the main dimensions of satisfaction with pay deals with pay levels, that is, the absolute amount of income associated with the job. Indeed, when it comes to retention, employees being recruited away from one organization by another are often lured with promises of higher pay levels. Benefits also make up a large portion of any worker's total compensation package. Hence, satisfaction with benefits is another important dimension of overall pay satisfaction. Because many individuals have a difficult time ascertaining the true dollar value of their benefits package, however, this dimension may not always be as salient to people as pay itself.

Whereas satisfaction with pay level and benefits reflects an interest in the absolute value of these dimensions, two other important aspects of pay satisfaction take on a more relative nature. Satisfaction with pay structure deals with how happy the person is with the manner in which pay within the organization is rank ordered across different job categories. A manager of a sales force, for example, might be satisfied with her overall pay, but if she discovers that due to sales commissions, some subordinate actually winds up with higher pay, then dissatisfaction with the structure of pay may result. Finally, relative to changes over time, satisfaction with raises also needs to be considered. People generally expect that their pay will increase over time, and to the extent that this expectation is not met, they may wind up dissatisfied with pay raises.

MEASURING AND MONITORING JOB SATISFACTION

Most attempts to measure job satisfaction rely on workers' self-reports. There is a vast amount of data on the reliability and validity of many existing scales as well as a wealth of data from companies that have used these scales, allowing for comparisons across firms. Established scales are excellent places to begin if employers wish to assess the satisfaction levels of their employees. An employer would be foolish to "reinvent the wheel" by generating its own versions of measures of these broad constructs. Of course, in some cases, organizations want to measure their employees' satisfaction with aspects of their work that are specific to that organization (e.g., satisfaction with one particular health plan versus another). In these situations, the organization may need to create its own scales, but this will be the exception rather than the rule.

One standardized, widely used measure of job satisfaction is the Job Descriptive Index (JDI). The JDI emphasizes various facets of satisfaction: pay, the work itself, supervision, co-workers, and promotions. Table 10.5 presents several items from the JDI scale. Other standardized scales emphasize overall satisfaction. Table 10.6 presents sample items from one of these measures. Finally, some scales avoid language altogether, relying on pictures. The faces scale in Figure 10.4 is an example of this type of measure.

Other scales exist for those who want to get even more specific about different facets of satisfaction. For example, although the JDI we just examined assesses satisfaction with pay, it does not break pay up into different dimensions.[66] The Pay Satisfaction Questionnaire (PSQ) focuses on these more specific dimensions (i.e., pay levels, benefits, pay structure, and pay raises). Thus this measure gives a more detailed view of exactly what aspects of pay are most or least satisfying.[67] Taking this even further, we can find scales that take just one of these dimensions—benefits—and then break this down even further into multiple facets of satisfaction with benefits.

Clearly, there is no end to the number of satisfaction facets that we might want to measure, but the key in operational contexts, where the main concern is retention, is making sure that scores on whatever measures taken truly relate to voluntary turnover among valued people. For example, satisfaction with co-workers might be low, but if this aspect of satisfaction is not too central to employees, it may not translate into voluntary turnover. Similarly, in an organization that bases raises on performance, low performers might report being dissatisfied with raises, but this may not reflect any operational problem. Indeed, the whole strategic purpose of many pay-for-performance plans

TABLE 10.5
Sample Items from a Standardized Job Satisfaction Scale (i.e., the JDI)

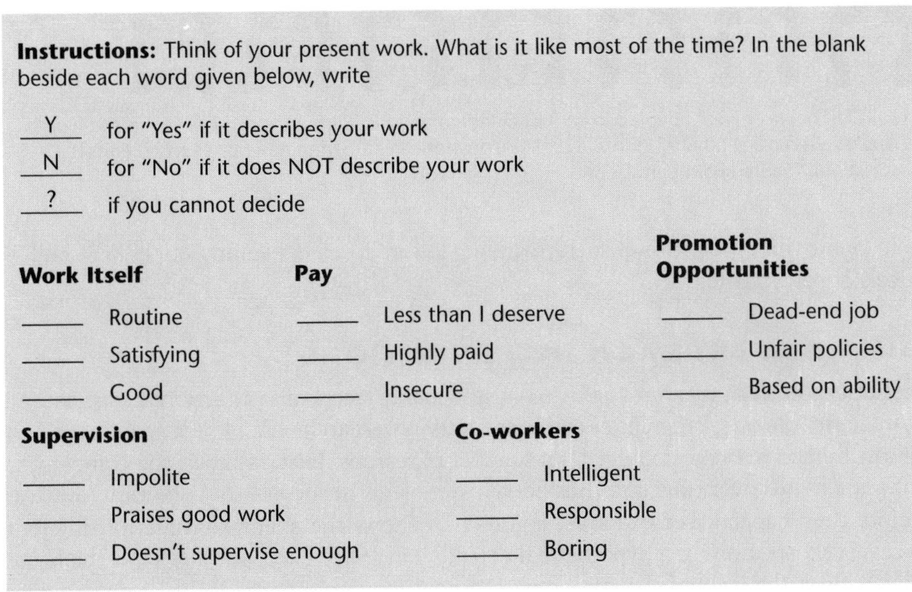

Instructions: Think of your present work. What is it like most of the time? In the blank beside each word given below, write

__Y__ for "Yes" if it describes your work
__N__ for "No" if it does NOT describe your work
__?__ if you cannot decide

Work Itself
_____ Routine
_____ Satisfying
_____ Good

Pay
_____ Less than I deserve
_____ Highly paid
_____ Insecure

Promotion Opportunities
_____ Dead-end job
_____ Unfair policies
_____ Based on ability

Supervision
_____ Impolite
_____ Praises good work
_____ Doesn't supervise enough

Co-workers
_____ Intelligent
_____ Responsible
_____ Boring

SOURCE: W.K. Balzar, D.C. Smith, D.E. Kravitz, S.E. Lovell, K.B. Paul, B.A. Reilly, and C.E. Reilly, *User's Manual for the Job Descriptive Index (JDI)* (Bowling Green, OH: Bowling Green State University, 1990).

TABLE 10.6
Sample Items from a Standardized Scale That Measures Overall Job Satisfaction

Instructions: Put a check beside the answer that you feel is most appropriate regarding your present job.

All in all, how satisfied are you with your job?

_____ Very satisfied
_____ Somewhat satisfied
_____ Not too satisfied
_____ Not at all satisfied

If a good friend of yours told you he or she was interested in working in a job like yours for your employer, would you recommend it to him or her?

_____ Strongly recommend this job
_____ Would have doubts about recommending this job
_____ Strongly advise against taking this job

Knowing what you know now, if you had to decide all over again to take the job you have now, what would you decide?

_____ Decide without hesitation to take the same job
_____ Would have some second thoughts about taking the same job
_____ Definitely decide not to take the same job

SOURCE: R.P. Quinn and G.L. Staines, *The 1977 Quality of Employment Survey* (Ann Arbor: Survey Research Center, Institute for Social Research, University of Michigan, 1979). Reprinted with permission.

FIGURE 10.4
Example of a Simplified, Nonverbal Measure of Job Satisfaction

Job Satisfaction from the Faces Scale
Consider all aspects of your job. Circle the face that best describes your feelings about your job in general.

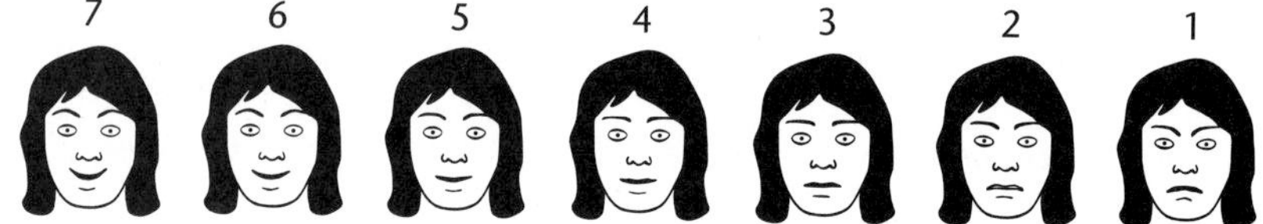

SOURCE: The faces were adapted from R.B. Dunham and J.B. Herman and published in the *Journal of Applied Psychology* 60 (1975), pp. 629–31. Copyright 1975 by the American Psychological Association. Adapted with permission.

is to create this type of dissatisfaction among low performers to motivate them to higher levels of performance.

SURVEY-FEEDBACK INTERVENTIONS

Regardless of what measures are used or how many facets of satisfaction are assessed, a systematic, ongoing program of **employee survey research** should be a prominent part of any human resource strategy for a number of reasons. First, it allows the company to monitor trends over time and thus prevent problems in the area of voluntary turnover before they happen. For example, Figure 10.5 shows the average profile for different facets of satisfaction for a hypothetical company in 1995, 1997, and 1999. As the figure makes clear, the level of satisfaction with promotion opportunities in this company has eroded over time, whereas the satisfaction with co-workers has improved. If there was a strong relationship between satisfaction with promotion opportunities and voluntary

FIGURE 10.5
Average Profile for Different Facets of Satisfaction Over Time

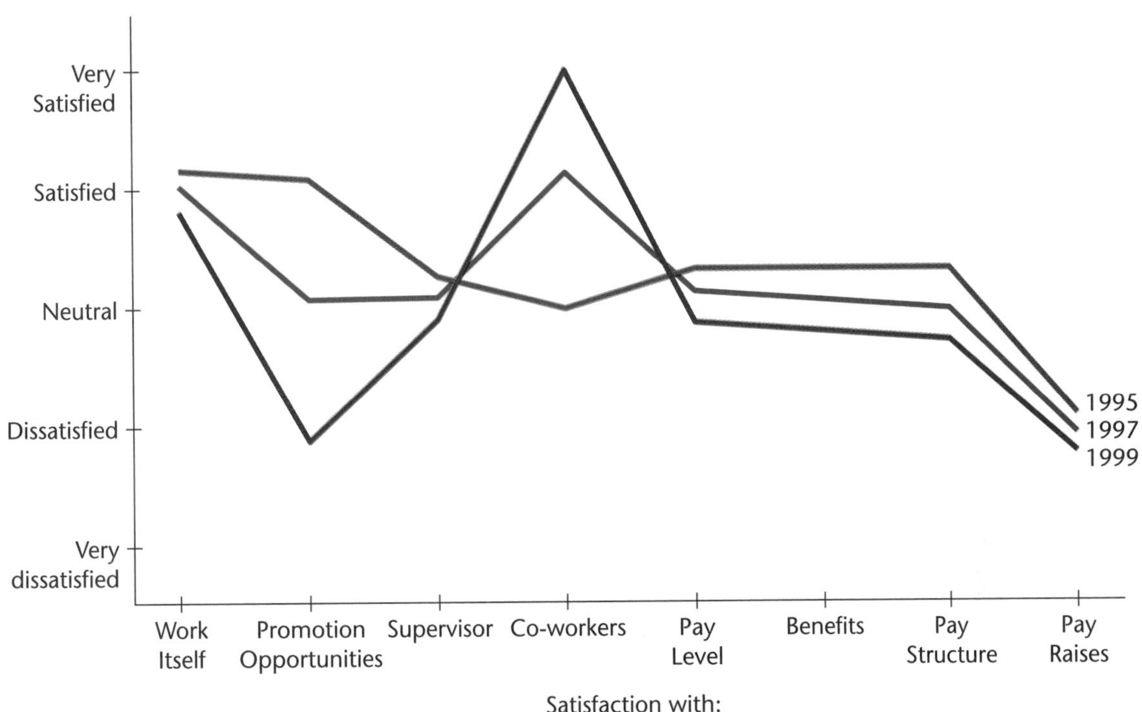

turnover among high performers, this would constitute a threat that the organization might need to address via some of the techniques discussed in our previous chapter, "Employee Development."

A second reason for engaging in an ongoing program of employee satisfaction surveys is that it provides a means of empirically assessing the impact of changes in policy (e.g., introduction of a new performance appraisal system) or personnel (e.g., introduction of a new CEO) on worker attitudes. For example, Figure 10.6 shows the average profile for different satisfaction facets for a hypothetical organization one year before and one year after a merger. An examination of the profile makes it clear that since the merger, satisfaction with supervision and pay structure have gone down dramatically, and this has not been offset by any increase in satisfaction along other dimensions. Again, this might point to the need for training programs for supervisors (like those discussed in Chapter 7) or changes in the job evaluation system (like those discussed in our upcoming Chapter 11).

Third, when these surveys incorporate standardized scales like the JDI or PSQ, they often allow the company to compare itself with others in the same industry along these dimensions. For example, Figure 10.7 shows the average profile for different satisfaction facets for a hypothetical organization and compares this to the industry average. Again, if we detect major differences between one organization and the industry as a whole (e.g., on overall pay levels), this might allow the company to react and change its policies before there is a mass exodus of people moving to the competition. Indeed, this kind of mass migration not only threatens firms, but (as the "Competing through Globalization" box shows) can destabilize an entire nation if the exodus is in a vital industry.

For example, according to Figure 10.7, the satisfaction with pay levels is low relative to the industry, but this is offset by higher-than-industry-averages satisfaction with benefits and the work itself. As we showed in Chapters 6 ("Selection and Placement"), the

FIGURE 10.6
Average Profile for Different Facets of Satisfaction Before and After a Major Event

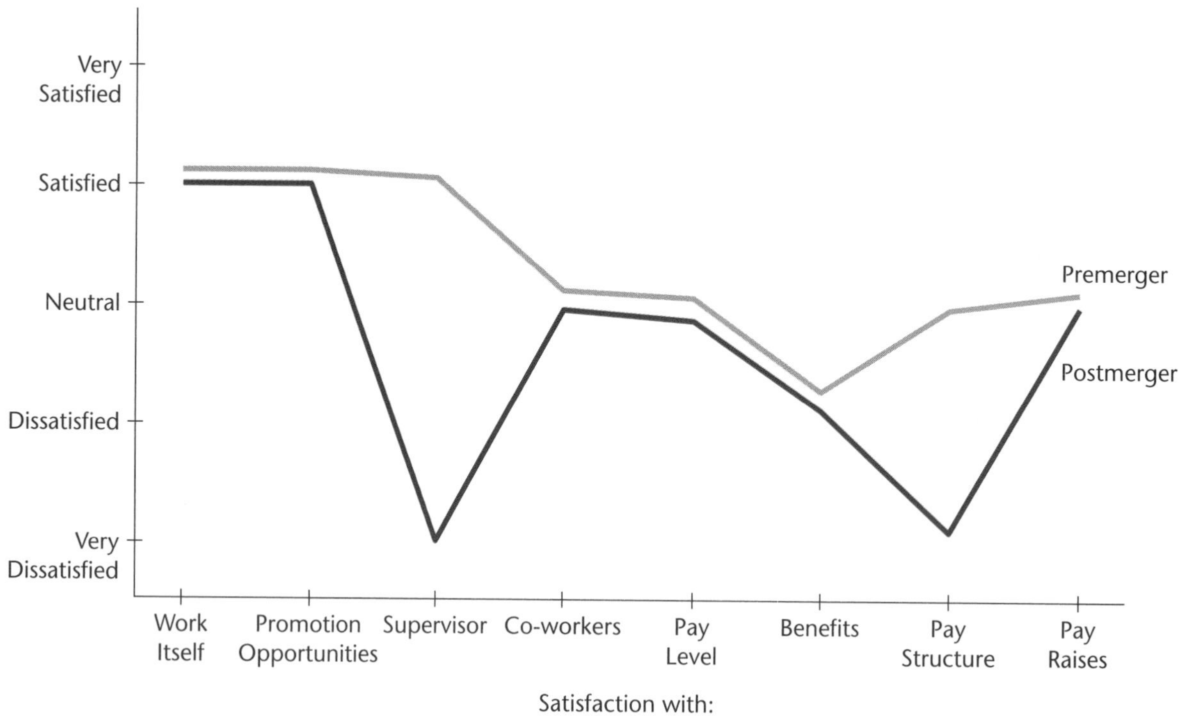

FIGURE 10.7
Average Profile for Different Facets of Satisfaction Versus the Industry Average

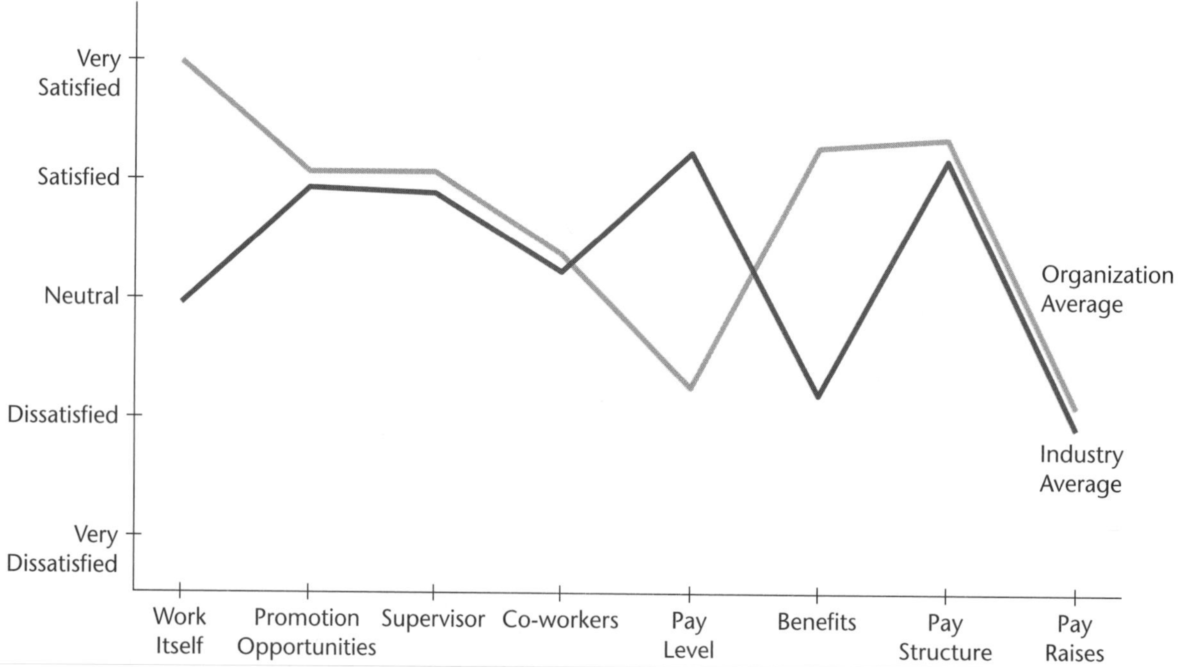

Vive les États Unis

The fires that drove the Industrial Age were fueled by coal, oil, and natural resources—and wars were fought over who would control such assets. As we move into the 21st century, the fuel that drives the new Information Age is knowledge and technological capacity, but many nations are surrendering these assets without even putting up a fight. Although the focus of this chapter is on firm-level competition plus leveraging the retention of top performers as a competitive strategy for organizations, the same issues hold true at the national level. France's recent experiences show this all too well.

For example, between 1991 and 1997, the number of French citizens registered with France's consulate in San Francisco quintupled to over 55,000. Although the Statue of Liberty welcomes the "poor, tired and huddled masses yearning to be free," the people fleeing France for the United States are young engineers, programmers and MBAs seeking to be entrepreneurs. In 1998 alone, 25 percent of France's graduates from elite universities left the country, and 77 percent of French youth report that they would work overseas, given the opportunity. This brain drain is a serious threat in a country already struggling with a 24 percent rate of unemployment, because these emigrés are the very people whom the nation needs to create new jobs and industries.

The factors driving this exodus mirror, at a national level, the very things we have noted that create dissatisfaction and intention to leave at the organizational level. For example, part of the issue is dissatisfaction with pay—a French business graduate earns less than half the salary of a new MBA in the United States. Another part of the issue is dissatisfaction with the amount of personal responsibility offered by the work itself. For example, Eric DiBenedetto knew that in France, it would be 15 years before he could assume any serious responsibilities. By contrast, after coming to the United States, the 32-year-old launched his own venture firm, Convergence Partners, and in no time had established a $60 million fund. Finally, another part of the problem deals with lack of respect in that French society still views entrepreneurs as shady wheeler-dealers and attempts to protect the general citizenry from them via tight government regulation.

Belatedly recognizing the problem, French authorities are only now starting to develop policies to stem the tide. However, many analysts think that these steps are too little, too late. For example, the government has offered to cut social security taxes on stock option gains for companies less than five years old, but not reduce the heavy federal tax on stock options in general. Similarly, minor changes in how the country taxes capital gains look more impressive on paper than in reality. DiBenedetto notes, "The French model is not working, and the gap between the U.S. and France is not closing, it's getting wider."

SOURCE: G. Edmondson, "Go West, Young Frenchman," *Business Week* (March 9, 1998), pp. 31–33; J. Smith, "A Brain Drain in France," *Business Week* (October 6, 1997), pp. 54–55.

organization might want to use this information to systematically screen people. That is, the fit between the person and the organization would be best if the company selected applicants who reported being most interested in the nature of the work itself and benefits, and rejected those applicants whose sole concern was with pay levels.

Within the organization, a systematic survey program also allows the company to check for differences between units and hence benchmark "best practices" that might be generalized across units. For example, Figure 10.8 shows the average profile for five different regional divisions of a hypothetical company. The figure shows that satisfaction with pay raises is much higher in one of the regions relative to the others. If the overall amount of money allocated to raises was equal through the entire company, this implies that the manner in which raises are allocated or communicated in the Midwest region might be something that the other regions should look into.

Finally, yearly surveys give employees a constructive outlet for voicing their concerns

FIGURE 10.8
Average Profile for Different Facets of Satisfaction for Different Regional Divisions

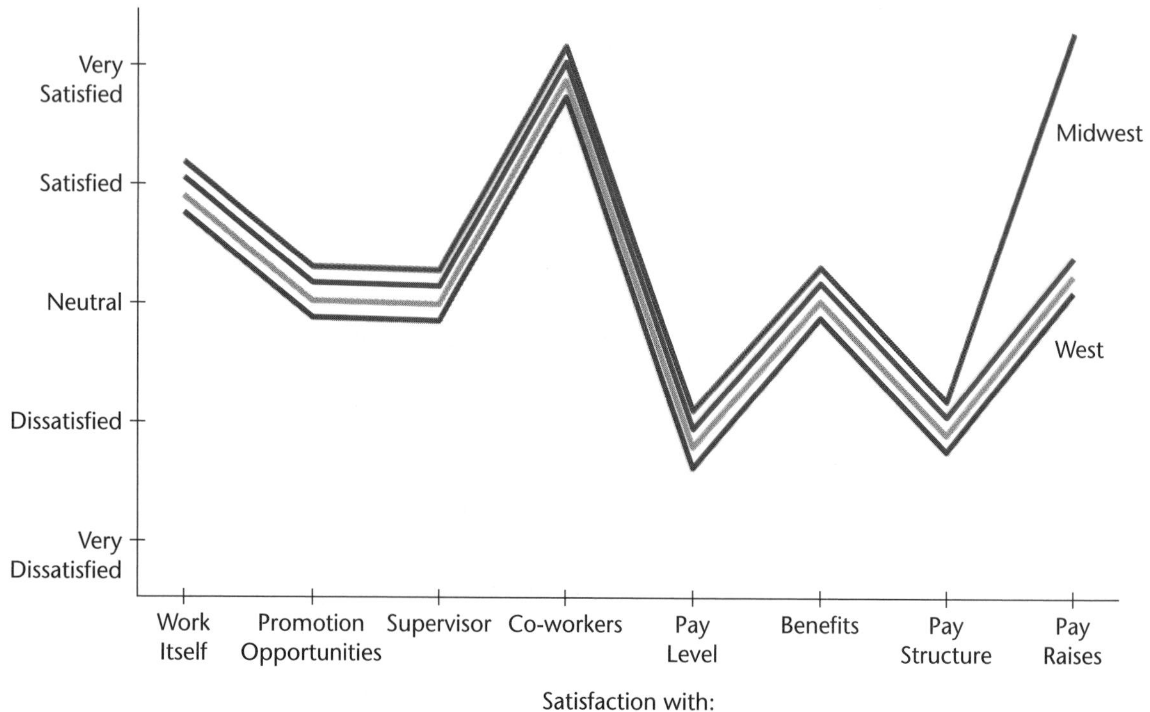

and frustrations. Employees' ability to handle dissatisfying work experiences is enhanced when they feel they have an opportunity to air their problems. Formalized opportunities to state complaints about one's work situation have been referred to as **voicing.**[68] Research has shown that voicing provides employees an active, constructive outlet for their work frustrations.[69] For example, a study of nurses indicated that providing such voicing mechanisms as an employee attitude survey and question-and-answer sessions between employees and management enhanced worker attitudes and cut turnover.[70] The value of voicing opportunities has been expressed well by Norman Plummer, president of Monitrex (a San Francisco-based health care provider): "If you don't provide an environment for open communication, you'll suffer through revolutions rather than evolutions."[71]

Obviously a great deal can be learned from employee satisfaction surveys. It is surprising that many companies conducting regular consumer satisfaction surveys fail to show the same concern for employee satisfaction. Retention is an issue involving both customers and employees, however, and—as we noted at the outset of this chapter—the two types of retention are substantially related. For example, sales agents at State Farm Insurance stay with the company for an average of 18 to 20 years—two to three times the average tenure in this industry. This kind of tenure allows the average State Farm agent to learn the job and develop long-term customer relations that cannot be matched by competitors who may lose half of their sales staff each year. State Farm also benefits from this experienced staff by systematically surveying its agents to get their views about where customer satisfaction is high, where it is low, and what can be done to improve service.[72] The result in terms of the bottom line is that State Farm achieves 40 percent higher sales per agent compared to the competition. In addition, as an indicator of quality of service, the retention rate among State Farm customers exceeds 95 percent.[73]

Although findings such as these are leading more and more companies to do such surveys, conducting an organizational opinion survey is not something that should be taken lightly. Especially in the beginning, surveys such as this often raise expectations. It is critical that the organization conducting the survey is ready to act on the results. For example, at Doctor's Hospital in Manteca, California, a survey of employees' opinions revealed dissatisfaction (defined as an "unfavorable" rating by at least 35 percent of the employees) in several areas. When these results were fed back to employees, each problem area was accompanied by a corresponding action plan so that people could see how the organization intended to address the problem. In the area of career development, for instance, the survey indicated that even though the hospital reimbursed 100 percent of employee expenses for tuition, it did so at the end of the semester, and the inability to pay the money up front prevented many from using this benefit. Based on these results, the hospital now provides tuition up front along with loans to help defray nontuition costs associated with taking a class (e.g., child care expenses). Thus, what was once a source of dissatisfaction for employees is now a source of satisfaction.[74]

SUMMARY

This chapter examined issues related to employee separation and retention. Involuntary turnover reflects a separation initiated by the organization, often when the individual would prefer to stay a member of the organization. Voluntary turnover reflects a separation initiated by the individual, often when the organization would prefer that the person stay a member. Organizations can gain competitive advantage by strategically managing the separation process so that involuntary turnover is implemented in a fashion that does not invite retaliation, and voluntary turnover among high performers is kept to a minimum. Retaliatory reactions to organizational discipline and dismissal decisions can be minimized by implementing these decisions in a manner that promotes feelings of procedural and interactive justice. Voluntary turnover can be minimized by measuring and monitoring employee levels of satisfaction with critical facets of job and organization, and then addressing any problems identified by such surveys.

DISCUSSION QUESTIONS

1. The discipline and discharge procedures described in this chapter are systematic but rather slow. In your opinion, are there some offenses that should lead to immediate dismissal, and, if so, how would you justify this to a court if you were sued for wrongful discharge?
2. Organizational turnover is generally considered a negative outcome, and many organizations spend a great deal of time and money trying to reduce it. What situations would indicate that an increase in turnover might be just what an organization needs? Given the difficulty of terminating employees, what organizational policies might promote the retention of high-performing workers but voluntary turnover among low performers?
3. Three popular interventions for enhancing worker satisfaction are job enrichment, job rotation, and role analysis. What are the critical differences between these interventions, and under what conditions might one be preferable to the others?
4. If off-the-job stress and dissatisfaction begin to create on-the-job problems, what are the rights and responsibilities of the human resource manager in helping the employee to overcome these problems? Are intrusions into such areas an invasion of privacy, a benevolent and altruistic employer practice, or simply a prudent financial step taken to protect the firm's investment?
5. Discuss the advantages of using published, standardized measures in employee attitude surveys. Do employers ever need to develop their own measures for such surveys? Where would one turn to learn about how to do this?

WEB EXERCISE

Visit www.expertss.com. This is the web site for Expert Survey Systems Inc, a company that provides employee attitude survey services to various companies. This web site provides information and resources on organizational surveys. Use this web site to answer the following questions.

1. Review the demo version of the 89 item Employee Opin-

ion Survey. What aspects of the work environment are measured on this survey. What suggestions might you have for improving this survey?

2. What are the strengths and weaknesses of using the telephone or voice technology to collect survey data?

3. What are some of the methods used to share survey results with employees? Identify strengths and weaknesses for each method.

MANAGING PEOPLE: FROM THE PAGES OF "BUSINESS WEEK"

BusinessWeek Low-Wage Lessons

At 5:30 A.M. the first workers arrive for the morning shift at the Marriott Hotel in downtown Chicago. They come from the farthest reaches of the metropolitan area and from all corners of the world: Bosnian refugees and born-in-America welfare moms, Chinese immigrants and black teenagers don their uniforms for the day. A few yards and a world removed from the crystal chandeliers and fresh flowers their guests see, a remarkable staff of hundreds whirs into motion.

Maria Martinez picks up her room-cleaning assignments. A Mexican immigrant, she takes citizenship classes at the hotel after work. Tommie Powell, onetime welfare dad and former factory worker from the city's North Side, heads to the basement and his job in the hotel's recycling operation. Arthur Seredyn, who arrived from Poland three years ago, scrubs out the swimming pool.

Their pay: about $7 an hour. That's typical for Marriott International Inc.'s 134,417 U.S. housekeepers, laundry workers, dishwashers, and other hourly staffers. It is, Marriott says, the wage that the labor market dictates. "If we pay wages in excess of the productive contribution of our people, we will become noncompetitive ourselves," says J.W. Marriott Jr., chairman of the nation's fourth-largest hotel company.

But a low-paid work force brings with it a host of problems: lack of education, poor work habits, inability to speak English, culture clashes, financial woes, inadequate child care, and domestic violence, for starters. People don't show up when they should; they leave without explanation. Every day in every hotel, such issues threaten employees' livelihoods—and the hotelier's.

The needs of low-wage employees once were easy to ignore. If a dishwasher quit, after all, there always was someone else happy to take the work. Not today, though. While the economy demands more and more highly educated workers, the need persists for more maids, meatpackers, and sewing-machine operators. Nearly 30 percent of all U.S. employees make $7.28 an hour or less, up from 23.5 percent in 1973, according to the Economic Policy Institute. At the same time, with employment running at a low 5.2 percent rate in September, companies are hard-pressed in many places to find new workers. "It's critical that we become more skilled at managing this workforce," says Donna Klein, Marriott's director of work-life programs.

Marriott International, with a small group of other low-wage employers, is coming to terms with this challenging, increasingly important group. Paying its U.S. workers a median rate of $7.40 an hour, including overtime, the hotelier resists offering the higher wages that would attract more qualified workers. It has waged often bitter battles, moreover, against attempts at unionization. Instead, it has embraced a host of informal and formal solutions—including employee stock options, a social-services referral network, day care, and welfare-to-work training classes—designed to keep workers on the job and keep guests satisfied.

On one level, these are predictable responses as employers try to avert pay raises amid signs of a labor crunch. "They'll do a host of things before putting money into people's pockets," says Harvard University economist Richard B. Freeman. And critics insist that Marriott simply is taking advantage of vulnerable workers who can't get jobs elsewhere. But while its approach may hark back in some ways to the paternalistic labor strategies of old company towns, it has also launched something new: an attempt to forge a more lasting, more productive relationship with lower-wage workers. Employers "have returned full circle to a social contract with employees," notes Faith A. Wohl, director of the U.S. General Service Administration's Office of Workplace Initiatives.

"A LOT OF BABYSITTING." Amid ever more intense competition, Marriott will thrive only if it can wring out bigger productivity gains and provide world-class service. Its human resources strategies win such results. Even without big pay hikes, Marriott employees often exhibit loyalty and even enthusiasm for their employer, and many feel they have a chance for advancement within the company. Analysts say its employee turnover rate is well below most rivals'.

There is a cost. Historically, it has been Marriott's hotel managers and supervisors who have helped solve workers' problems—playing social worker, in effect. "Many managers spend 15 percent of their time doing social work," explains Clifford J. Ehrlich, Marriott International's senior vice president for human resources. "That's time not spent dealing with customer issues." They counsel employees confronting family problems, juggle shifts to accommodate erratic child care, or lend them money to pay pressing bills. "It's frustrating," says one Chicago area manager. "These employees need a lot of babysitting."

Yet Marriott has forged unquestionably strong bonds with many employees. "Every day I put on this uniform, just like an NBA player," proudly proclaims Thong Lee, a bartender who has worked 16 years at the Seattle Marriott. Lee has never forgotten that his boss, Sandy Olson, shut down the hotel laundry where he used to work for a day so the entire staff could attend his mother's funeral. The gesture earned Lee's loyalty for life–though the stock options the company offers all employees haven't hurt, either. Lee, who learned all the English he knows from Marriott, now owns several rental properties funded by his Marriott stock and pay.

BIG EXPANSION. Now, Marriott is launching a range of corporate programs to alleviate the demands on local hotel managers—and to accommodate its aggressive growth plans. The chain expects to add 1,000 mostly franchised hotels by 2000, and managers who come aboard with franchisees may not buy into the social-worker role. At the same time, the ranks of Marriott managers have been thinned by about 5 percent in recent years. So new, institutionalized supports aim to replace the old one-on-one style. "Our philosophy hasn't change . . . but it's a more professional approach," says J.W. Marriott.

Pathways to Independence, for example, is a company-developed class on basic work skills for former welfare recipients, offered at hotels in 15 cities. In June, the company finished rolling out the Associate Resource Line, a national toll-free referral service that hooks up its workers with local social services. In December, it will start a program in Washington, D.C., and two other sites to teach workers how to become better parents and partners. And next year, with two other hotel groups, Marriott will inaugurate Atlanta's Inn for Children, a 24-hour subsidized child care center.

Marriott also has led 28 companies—including J.C. Penney, Hyatt International, McDonald's, ConAgra, and Levi Strauss—to study ways to improve management of low-wage employees. With the help of the Families and Work Institute, a nonprofit research outfit in Manhattan, the so-called Employer Group plans to share best practices, create the first comprehensive demographic profile of this work force, and advocate public policies that benefit low-wage workers—such as broader application of the Earned Income Tax Credit.

MISUNDERSTANDINGS. Yet companies and unions still know relatively little about low-wage workers and their needs. Marriott only began studying its hourly-wage work force in 1993, after realizing that child care benefits launched three years earlier had left many problems of this population unresolved. It immediately found that a quarter have some literacy problems—mostly difficulties speaking English. Overall, Marriott workers speak and read 65 different languages.

Language barriers in this massive Babel can disrupt hotel operations—and worse. William D. Fleet, human resources director at the Seattle Marriott, where employees speak 17 languages, once fired a Vietnamese kitchen worker for wrongly accusing a chef of assault. Only after another employee was attacked by a kitchen worker did Fleet figure out that the Vietnamese employee had used the word *chef* to refer to all kitchen workers with white uniforms. The misunderstanding had led to the firing of a good staffer and delayed the arrest of a dangerous one.

Marriott managers fear the inability to speak English also may get in the way of service. "People will do the things they do well and shy away from things that make them look foolish," says Fleet. That's why he instituted a comprehensive ESL program for staffers to take on company time. After all, workers who know English interact better with guests. Teresa Ortiz, a housekeeper at the downtown San Francisco Marriott, once took a couple to the service elevator because she didn't know how to tell them how to get to the 39th floor. (An ESL graduate now, she says proudly, "I can tell them.")

More than half of the Marriotts in the U.S. offer workers ESL classes—a relatively cheap and easy productivity device. Beyond language, however, looms the far greater challenge of managing epic cultural divides. Last year, with the help of a local refugee resettlement organization, the Des Moines Marriott hired 20 Bosnian immigrants to join a 60-member housekeeping staff. The Bosnians, who easily got legal status as refugees, helped plug the holes left by Mexican workers who fled after managers installed a new screening technique for uncovering illegal immigrants. After finding a handful of undocumented workers, Marriott watched its applicant pool of predominantly Mexican workers evaporate.

While the Bosnians came to the rescue, they brought other problems. New to America, they "don't have anybody" to help them here, says hotel services director Wanda Johnson. "You figure out their phone bills, enroll their kids in school, and set up doctors' appointments." More than that, their arrival was resented by remaining Mexican workers who still were being checked for immigration status. Managers had to keep the peace by reassuring them that the company was screening workers to comply with the law, not to dump them.

When managers can overcome cultural divides, they win commitment. Sara Redwell, an assistant general manager at the North Arlington Heights (Illinois) Courtyard Hotel, started working at Marriott 12 years ago at age 23 as a housekeeper after immigrating with her mother from Mexico. While taking ESL and other college classes, she was promoted to housekeeping manager in 1990 and, last year, to her present job. There, she supervises 20 employees, most of whom are Spanish-speaking. She mentors food server Elodia Lopez, a Mexican immigrant whom she would like to promote to restaurant supervisor, by teaching her a new English phrase every day. "What Marriott gave to me, I want to give to others," she says.

Can Marriott reproduce the same dedication with human resources systems sent down from headquarters? In some ways, such standardized programs could prove more effective. Marriott's Associate Resource Line is offered in more than 100 languages—more than any one manager could handle. So far, about 7,000 staffers have called and been assigned a social worker, who finds them local help. Marriott anticipates savings of five times its $2 million investment from reduced turnover, absenteeism, and tardiness.

Gladys Chacon, a single mother who is an accounting clerk at the Chicago Downtown Marriott, found child care last year for her six-year-old, Jazmine, through the resource line. "If I hadn't found good day care, I would have had to quit my job," she says. In her previous job at a grocery, she had to stay home many days when an unreliable sitter didn't show.

The Fatherhood Project, to be launched by the Families and Work Institute in December for Marriott in Washington, will teach male employees and spouses of female ones how to become better fathers—a benefit other companies offer primarily for white-collar staffers. Surveys show that women view a more involved partner as a key stress-reducer. "Less burnout at the workplace is the big payoff," says Marriott's Klein. Single fathers, such as Chicago recycling worker Tommie Powell, can take advantage of the program, too. "It's hard working full-time and having teenagers at home," says Powell, who has a 16-year-old daughter and 19-year-old son.

Powell and 600 other Marriott employees also have benefited from Pathways to Independence. The six-week program, which could serve as a model as welfare reform, takes hold, teaches business basics, such as showing up on time, and life lessons, such as self-esteem and personal financial management. One of the few companies with such a plan, Marriott works with federally funded local organizations to split the $5,500-per-person costs. By targeting welfare recipients, it harvests an overlooked labor pool—and Pathways graduates placed in Marriott jobs have a 13 percent turnover rate, far below the company's national average.

Sabrina McWhite, who took the Pathways course last year and then left welfare, works in the kitchen at the Metro Center Marriott in Washington and wants to become a chef. A high school graduate who dropped out of the University of the District of Columbia, McWhite credits Pathways for teaching her "how to manage money correctly, how to always have backup for child care," and other responsibilities. With a regular paycheck now, she has been able to buy her four-year-old daughter a special book bag. "I feel so good I could give it to her," she says.

Still, Marriott's critics keep asking, Why can't it simply pay higher wages? "Their hypocrisy stands out," says John W. Wilhelm, secretary–treasurer of the hotel workers' union. Marriott, which insists its pay is comparable to union wages, says it has always tried to treat workers fairly. "We hire people who have never had jobs before and give them a chance," says J.W. Marriott. That's largely true. But this isn't a story about altruism. Marriott's unusual approach to the low-wage dilemma is dictated by corporate self-interest: Helping workers can cut costs and lift productivity. And that goes right to the bottom line.

QUESTIONS

The vignette that opened this chapter dealt with retaining knowledge workers, that is, high-skilled managers and professionals who reflect an organization's high-priced talent. This end-of-chapter case focuses on the other end of the spectrum (low-wage, low-skill workers) and shows that retention of these employees is also a concern. After reading this article, reread the opening vignette and then answer the following questions:

1. In what ways are the issues that drive retention for low-skill workers similar to or different than the issues that drive retention among high-skill workers? Other than money, what inducements may mean more to low skill-workers relative to high-skill workers? What inducements mean the same to all workers?
2. Other than turnover, how might the responses of low-skill workers to dissatisfaction regarding the job or organization be different or similar to the responses of high-skill workers? If an organization wanted to monitor satisfaction levels among its employees, how might the nature of the monitoring program differ for high- versus low-skill workers?
3. All of the programs aimed at retaining low-skill workers described in this end-of-chapter reading cost money, and some of them cost a great deal of money. Why would these employers spend money in this way, as opposed to just raising wages and attracting a higher-skill labor force? In your opinion, are these programs a hypocritical response on the part of employers who will do anything to avoid raising wages, or are they a realistic response given the nature of this segment of the work force?

SOURCE: "Low-Wage Lessons," *Business Week*, November 11, 1996.

NOTES

1. M.L. Schmit and S.P. Allscheid, "Employee Attitudes and Customer Satisfaction: Making Theoretical and Empirical Connections," *Personnel Psychology* 48 (1995), pp. 521–36.
2. F. Reichheld, *The Loyalty Effect* (Cambridge, MA: Harvard Business School Press, 19).
3. S. Branch, "You Hired 'Em. But Can You Keep 'Em," *Fortune* (November 9, 1998), pp. 247–50.
4. J.D. Shaw, J.E. Delery, C.D. Jenkins, and N. Gupta, "An Organizational-Level Analysis of Voluntary Turnover," *Academy of Management Journal* 41 (1998), pp. 511–25.
5. J.B. Copeland, W. Turque, L. Wright, and D. Shapiro, "The Revenge of the Fired," *Newsweek*, February 16, 1987, pp. 46–47.
6. A.Q. Nomani, "Women Likelier to Face Violence in the Workplace," *The Wall Street Journal* (October 31, 1995), p. A16.
7. N.D. Cole and G.P. Latham, "Effects of Training in Procedural Justice on Perceptions of Disciplinary Fairness by Unionized Employees and Disciplinary Subject Matter Experts," *Journal of Applied Psychology* 82 (1997), pp. 699–705.

8. D.P. Skarlicki and R. Folger, "Retaliation in the Workplace: The Roles of Distributive, Procedural, and Interactional Justice," *Journal of Applied Psychology* 82 (1997), pp. 434–43.
9. S. Caudron, "Blowing the Whistle on Employee Disputes," *Workforce* (May 1997), pp. 50–57.
10. M. McGarvey, "The Challenge of Containing Health-Care Costs," *Financial Executive* 8 (1992), pp. 34–40.
11. B.B. Pflaum, "Seeking Sane Solutions: Managing Mental Health and Chemical Dependency Costs," *Employee Benefits Journal* 16 (1992), pp. 31–35.
12. J. Smith, "EAPs Evolve to Health Plan Gatekeeper," *Employee Benefit Plan Review* 46 (1992), pp. 18–19.
13. E. Stetzer, "Bringing Sanity to Mental Health," *Business Health* 10 (1992), p. 72.
14. S. Johnson, "Results, Relapse Rates Add to Cost of Non-Hospital Treatment," *Employee Benefit Plan Review* 46 (1992), pp. 15–16.
15. C. Mulcany, "Experts Eye Perils of Mental Health Cuts," *National Underwriter* 96 (1992), pp. 17–18.
16. G.C. Parliman and E.L. Edwards, "Employee Assistance Programs: An Employer's Guide to Emerging Liability Issues," *Employee Relations Law Journal* 17 (1992), pp. 593–601.
17. S.H. Milne, T.C. Blum, and P.M. Roman, "Factors Influencing Employees' Propensity to Use an Employee Assistance Program," *Personnel Psychology* 47 (1994), pp. 123–45.
18. J. Jones, "How to Bounce Back if You're Bounced Out," *Business Week* (January 27, 1998), pp. 22–23.
19. Branch, "You Hired 'Em."
20. D.W. Baruch, "Why They Terminate," *Journal of Consulting Psychology* 8 (1944), pp. 35–46; J.G. Rosse, "Relations among Lateness, Absence and Turnover: Is There a Progression of Withdrawal?" *Human Relations* 41 (1988), pp. 517–31.
21. C. Hulin, "Adaptation, Persistence and Commitment in Organizations," in *Handbook of Industrial & Organizational Psychology* 2nd ed., ed. M.D. Dunnette and L.M. Hough (Palo Alto, CA: Consulting Psychologists Press, 1991), pp. 443–50.
22. C. Hulin, M. Roznowski, and D. Hachiya, "Alternative Opportunities and Withdrawal Decisions," *Psychological Bulletin* 97 (1985), pp. 233–50.
23. C.E. Labig and I.B. Helburn, "Union and Management Policy Influences on Grievance Initiation," *Journal of Labor Research* 7 (1986), pp. 269–84.
24. C. Schreisheim, "Job Satisfaction, Attitudes towards Unions, and Voting in a Union Representation Election," *Journal of Applied Psychology* 63 (1978), pp. 548–52.
25. M.P. Miceli and J.P. Near, "Characteristics of Organizational Climate and Perceived Wrongdoing Associated with Whistle-Blowing Decisions," *Personnel Psychology* 38 (1985), pp. 525–44.
26. M. Whitacre, "My Life as a Corporate Mole for the FBI," *Fortune* (September 4, 1995).
27. M. Galen, "Diversity: Beyond the Numbers Game," *Business Week* (August 14, 1995), pp. 60–61.
28. R.D. Hackett and R.M. Guion, "A Re-evaluation of the Job Satisfaction–Absenteeism Relation," *Organizational Behavior and Human Decision Processes* 35 (1985), pp. 340–81.
29. J. Jones, "Absenteeism on Rise, at $505 an Employee," *Chicago Tribune*, August 29, 1995, p. 3.
30. J.G. Rosse and H.E. Miller, "Relationship between Absenteeism and Other Employee Behaviors," in *New Approaches to Understanding, Measuring, and Managing Employee Absence*, ed. P.S. Goodman and R.S. Atkin (San Francisco: Jossey–Bass, 1984).
31. R. Kanungo, *Work Alienation* (New York: Praeger Publishers, 1982).
32. R.T. Mowday, R.M. Steers, and L.W. Porter, "The Measurement of Organizational Commitment," *Journal of Vocational Behavior* 14 (1979), pp. 224–47.
33. J. Laabs, "The New Loyalty: Grasp It, Earn It, Keep It," *Workforce* (November 1998), pp. 34–39.
34. J. Castro, "Where Did All the Gung-ho Go?" *Time* (September 11, 1989), pp. 52–55.
35. E.A. Locke, "The Nature and Causes of Job Dissatisfaction," in *The Handbook of Industrial & Organizational Psychology*, ed. M.D. Dunnette (Chicago: Rand McNally, 1976), pp. 901–69.
36. J.W. Thibaut and H.H. Kelly, *The Social Psychology of Groups* (New York: Wiley, 1959).
37. J.S. Adams and W.B. Rosenbaum, "The Relationship between Worker Productivity to Cognitive Dissonance about Wage Inequities," *Journal of Applied Psychology* 46 (1962), pp. 161–64.
38. D. Watson, L.A. Clark, and A. Tellegen, "Development and Validation of Brief Measures of Positive and Negative Affect: The PANAS Scales," *Journal of Personality and Social Psychology* 54 (1988), pp. 1063–70.
39. T.A. Judge, E.A. Locke, C.C. Durham, and A.N. Kluger, "Dispositional Effects on Job and Life Satisfaction: The Role of Core Evaluations," *Journal of Applied Psychology* 83 (1998), pp. 17–34.
40. B.M. Staw, N.E. Bell, and J.A. Clausen, "The Dispositional Approach to Job Attitudes: A Lifetime Longitudinal Test," *Administrative Science Quarterly* 31 (1986), pp. 56–78; B.M. Staw and J. Ross, "Stability in the Midst of Change: A Dispositional Approach to Job Attitudes," *Journal of Applied Psychology* 70 (1985), pp. 469–80.
41. R.P. Steel and J.R. Rentsch, "The Dispositional Model of Job Attitudes Revisited: Findings of a 10-Year Study," *Journal of Applied Psychology* 82 (1997), pp. 873–79.
42. T.A. Judge, "Does Affective Disposition Moderate the Relationship between Job Satisfaction and Voluntary Turnover?" *Journal of Applied Psychology* 78 (1993), pp. 395–401.

43. R.D. Arvey, T.J. Bouchard, N.L. Segal, and L.M. Abraham, "Job Satisfaction: Genetic and Environmental Components," *Journal of Applied Psychology* 74 (1989), pp. 187–93.
44. S.L. Hershberger, P. Lichenstein, and S.S. Knox, "Genetic and Environmental Influences on Perceptions of Organizational Climate," *Journal of Applied Psychology* 79 (1994), pp. 24–33.
45. J. Vennochi, "When Depression Comes to Work," *Working Woman* (August 1995), pp. 43–51.
46. B.A. Gerhart, "How Important Are Dispositional Factors as Determinants of Job Satisfaction? Implications for Job Design and Other Personnel Programs," *Journal of Applied Psychology* 72 (1987), pp. 493–502.
47. E.F. Stone and H.G. Gueutal, "An Empirical Derivation of the Dimensions along which Characteristics of Jobs are Perceived," *Academy of Management Journal* 28 (1985), pp. 376–96.
48. L.W. Porter and R.M. Steers, "Organizational, Work and Personal Factors in Employee Absenteeism and Turnover," *Psychological Bulletin* 80 (1973), pp. 151–76.
49. S. Melamed, I. Ben-Avi, J. Luz, and M.S. Green, "Objective and Subjective Work Monotony: Effects on Job Satisfaction, Psychological Distress, and Absenteeism in Blue Collar Workers," *Journal of Applied Psychology* 80 (1995), pp. 29–42.
50. G.R. Oldham, A. Cummings, L.J. Mischel, J.M. Schmidtke, and J. Zhou, "Listen While You Work? Quasi-experimental Relations between Personal-Stereo Headset Use and Employee Work Responses," *Journal of Applied Psychology* 80 (1995), pp. 547–64.
51. Locke, "The Nature and Causes of Job Dissatisfaction."
52. L. Jones, "Xerox Is Rewriting the Book on Organization 'Architecture'," *Chicago Tribune*, December 29, 1992, pp. 3–1, 3–2.
53. G.C. Hill and K. Yamada, "Motorola Illustrates How an Aged Giant Can Remain Vibrant," *The Wall Street Journal*, December 9, 1992, p. A1.
54. J.R. Hackman and G.R. Oldham, "Motivation through the Design of Work," *Organizational Behavior and Human Performance* 16 (1976), pp. 250–79.
55. D.R. Ilgen and J.R. Hollenbeck, "The Structure of Work: Job Design and Roles," in *Handbook of Industrial & Organizational Psychology*, 2d ed.
56. J.A. Breaugh and J.P. Colihan, "Measuring Facets of Job Ambiguity: Construct Validity Evidence," *Journal of Applied Psychology* 79 (1994), pp. 191–201.
57. M.A. Shaffer and D.A. Harrison, "Expatriates' Psychological Withdrawal from Interpersonal Assignments: Work, Non-work, and Family Influences," *Personnel Psychology* 51 (1998), pp. 87–118.
58. P.M. Caligiuri, M.M. Hyland, A.S. Bross, and A. Joshi, "Testing a Theoretical Model for Examining the Relationship Between Family Adjustment and Expatriates' Work Adjustment," *Journal of Applied Psychology* 83 (1998), pp. 598–614.
59. T.J. Newton and R.S. Keenan, "Role Stress Reexamined: An Investigation of Role Stress Predictors," *Organizational Behavior and Human Decision Processes* 40 (1987), pp. 346–68.
60. I. Dayal and J. M. Thomas, "Operation KPE: Developing a New Organization," *Journal of Applied Behavioral Sciences* 4 (1968), pp. 473–506.
61. B.M. Meglino, E.C. Ravlin, and C.L. Adkins, "A Work Values Approach to Corporate Culture: A Field Test of the Value Congruence Process and Its Relationship to Individual Outcomes," *Journal of Applied Psychology* 74 (1989), pp. 424–33.
62. G.C. Ganster, M.R. Fusilier, and B.T. Mayes, "Role of Social Support in the Experience of Stress at Work," *Journal of Applied Psychology* 71 (1986), pp. 102–11.
63. M.A. Donovan, F. Drasgow, and L.J. Munson, "The Perceptions of Fair Interpersonal Treatment Scale: Development and Validation of a Measure of Interpersonal Treatment in the Workplace," *Journal of Applied Psychology* 83 (1998), pp. 683–92.
64. R.T. Keller, "A Test of the Path–Goal Theory of Leadership with Need for Clarity as a Moderator in Research and Development Organizations," *Journal of Applied Psychology* 74 (1989), pp. 208–12.
65. J. Lawrence, "American Airlines: A Profile in Employee Involvement," *Personnel Journal* (August 1992), p. 63.
66. H.G. Heneman and D.S. Schwab, "Pay Satisfaction: Its Multidimensional Nature and Measurement," *International Journal of Applied Psychology* 20 (1985), pp. 129–41.
67. T. Judge and T. Welbourne, "A Confirmatory Investigation of the Dimensionality of the Pay Satisfaction Questionnaire," *Journal of Applied Psychology* 79 (1994), pp. 461–66.
68. A.O. Hirshman, *Exit Voice and Loyalty* (Cambridge, MA: Harvard University Press, 1970).
69. D. Farrell, "Exit, Voice, Loyalty and Neglect as Responses to Job Dissatisfaction: A Multidimensional Scaling Study," *Academy of Management Journal* 26 (1983), pp. 596–607.
70. D.G. Spencer, "Employee Voice and Employee Retention," *Academy of Management Journal* 29 (1986), pp. 488–502.
71. B. Lambert, "Give Your Company a Check-up," *Personnel Journal* (September 1995), pp. 143–46.
72. B. Schneider, S.D. Ashworth, A.C. Higgs, and L. Carr, "Design, Validity and Use of Strategically-Focused Employee Attitude Surveys," *Personnel Psychology* 49 (1996), pp. 695–705.
73. M. Loeb, "Wouldn't It Be Good to Work for the Good Guys?" *Fortune* (October 14, 1996), pp. 223–24.
74. T. Gray, "A Hospital Takes Action on Employee Survey," *Personnel Journal* (March 1995), pp. 74–77.

Von Maur: Fashionable and Effective People Practices

Von Maur is a family-owned fashion department store. Von Maur stores have an open, spacious store design that allows a clear view of all departments from any point in the store. Antique furniture for customers to sit and relax on, fabric-covered walls, and a pianist playing popular music at a grand piano create a warm, classy, comfortable shopping atmosphere. It is the largest privately-held retail department store in Iowa. Besides locations in Iowa, the company has grown to a 14-store chain with locations in Illinois, Indiana, and Nebraska. Von Maur has served customers for over 125 years.

According to store manager, Kris Nikel, "Customer service is our single most important selling point. It is what sets us apart from the competition. As a company we have made it our goal to provide customers with the best possible shopping experience everytime they walk into the store. And the first step is making sure that the employees they encounter are the best. We put our employees to the test challenging them every day." Von Maur offers a challenging fast-paced environment for employees who desire to succeed. The company policy is to promote from within whenever possible. Von Maur hires people with the intention of promoting them based on their ability and interests.

Von Maur recognizes that the employee is the most important link to the customer. As a result, the company uses training and development to create a motivated and talented workforce. Von Maur's training program includes formal education, job experiences, interpersonal relationships, and assessment. Formal education is offered to employees in two forms—initial job training and an executive training program. Entry-level employees start with an initial associates training program. Associates Training lasts one week, training employees in all aspects of their jobs. Trainers utilize videos and manuals. Training needs of each employee are reviewed at 45 days, 90 days, and at regular intervals to insure that performance problems and skill and knowledge needs are met. The executive training program is designed for employees with a college degree who are interested in an executive-level position with the company. This program introduces the employees to all aspects of store operations including direct selling, corporate functions (personnel, finance, store management) operations, and merchandising.

At Von Maur, interpersonal relationships, or the Buddy System are used to help new associates gain actual sales floor experience, first through observation, and then by letting new associates handle situations themselves. The mentor or buddy is available to help new employees through unfamiliar situations and help them learn the nuances of a new job that can never be completely explained in formal training sessions. The Buddy System allows employees the chance to ask questions in a non-threatening atmosphere.

To complement the company's strong training emphasis, Von Maur has a strong performance management program. After 45 days new associates meet with their manager for a performance discussion. At this point the associates are seen as still learning and therefore are given lower sales goals than more experienced employees. After 90 days, the evaluation is more specific and employees are held more accountable for reaching sales goals. Another aspect of the performance management system, the company's Customer Service Improvement Program, involves each department manager meeting individually with each employee every month. At this meeting the manager chooses one area of the associate's performance to focus on. This becomes the area that the associate tries to improve over the next month-long period before the next evaluation.

Associates are also required to evaluate their own performance using a behavioral checklist. This checklist is used in their performance discussion with their manager and serves as a constant reminder of the areas they need to improve. Managers are not excluded from performance management. Four times a year, managers from all of the Von Maur stores travel to headquarters in Davenport, Iowa for training and performance review sessions.

Von Maur provides several incentive programs to recognize excellent performance. At weekly Heroics meetings, employees who have received special compliments for customer service are honored. Two programs (Pacesetters and All-Star) are designed to recognize employees who consistently demonstrate strong performance and commitment to superior customer service. Honored associates receive plaques, larger merchandise discounts, and cash bonuses.

In a business such as Von Maur's where customer service is the most important goal, strong employees are the most important asset. Through the integration of training, development, and performance management, Von Maur provides its employees with the tools they need to deal effectively with customers. These programs strengthen the company and make Von Maur an attractive employer.

DISCUSSION QUESTIONS

1. What are the potential advantages and disadvantages of the Buddy System used to train new associates?
2. Part of the Customer Service Improvement Program involves self-assessment. That is, associates are asked to rate their own performance. Do you think that this is a good idea? Explain.
3. How could Von Maur include customers in the performance management process? Should they? Why or why not?
4. What is the relationship between training and performance management at Von Maur? Do you think that this linkage is important? Explain.

Source: "Von Maur—The Ultimate Fashion Department Store" see www.vonmaur.com

PART IV
Compensation of Human Resources

11

CHAPTER

Pay Structure Decisions

OBJECTIVES

After reading this chapter, you should be able to

1. List the major decision areas and concepts in employee compensation management.
2. Describe the major administrative tools used to manage employee compensation.
3. Explain the importance of competitive labor-market and product-market forces in compensation decisions.
4. Discuss the significance of process issues such as communication in compensation management.
5. Describe new developments in the design of pay structures.
6. Explain where the United States stands from an international perspective on pay issues.
7. Explain the reasons for the controversy over executive pay.
8. Describe the regulatory framework for employee compensation.

Changing Pay to Support IBM's Turnaround

ENTER THE WORLD OF BUSINESS

A few years ago, IBM went from dominating its industry to a period of crisis. Its downfall was a result of many factors. It became sluggish in taking advantage of new technologies and lost touch with customers and the marketplace. Its cost structure was too high. More recently, however, IBM has reemerged as a highly successful company under Lou Gerstner's leadership. Although no one change can be singled out as being responsible for the turnaround, a major change had to do with the compensation system and how it, in turn, altered the culture of the company and the behaviors of individual employees. IBM's old compensation approach had four characteristics. First, it emphasized internal equity over external competitiveness. In other words, a marketing manager and a manufacturing manager might have been paid at the same level to prevent internal tensions regardless of whether the market pay rate for the two jobs was the same. Second, the system was highly bureaucratic, having over 5,000 job titles and 24 salary grades. Third, managers were given little discretion in how they allocated pay increases to their employees. Finally, most of an employee's pay came in the form of base salary, and very little was put at risk in the sense of being linked to profits or stock performance. Fundamental changes have been made in each of these four areas. Pay is now market-driven, focusing on external competitiveness. There are now only 1,200 jobs and 10 broad bands (in place of the 24 salary grades). This fits with IBM's desire to reduce bureaucracy and hierarchy and to push decisions to lower levels. The same logic led to a plan to decentralize decisions regarding pay to managers, giving them more freedom to recognize differences in individual performance. Merit pay increase budgets were decreased and the money was shifted to pay-at-risk programs that linked employees' pay to performance goals. Finally, like many other major companies, IBM has cut employment levels to reduce costs, going from over 400,000 employees early in the 1990s to roughly 250,000 today.

SOURCE: A.S. Richter, "Paying the People in Black at Big Blue," *Compensation and Benefits Review* (May-June 1998), pp. 51–59. Reprinted with permission.

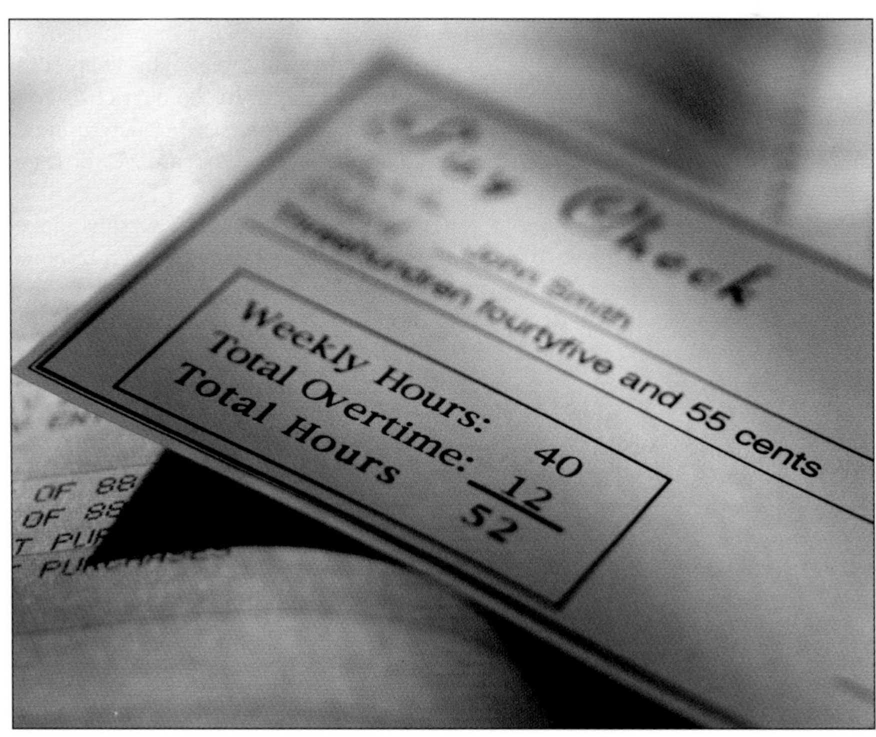

Introduction

From the employer's point of view, pay is a powerful tool for furthering the organization's strategic goals. First, pay has a major impact on employee attitudes and behaviors. It influences the kind of employees who are attracted to (and remain with) the organization, and it can be a powerful tool for aligning current employees' interests with those of the broader organization. Second, employee compensation is typically a significant organizational cost and thus requires close scrutiny. As Table 11.1 shows, total compensation (cash and benefits) averages 30.3 percent of revenues and varies both within and across industries, with the ratios of companies at the 90th percentile being approximately double those of companies at the 10th percentile in health care and manufacturing and five times larger in the insurance industry.

From the employees' point of view, policies having to do with wages, salaries, and other earnings have a major impact on their overall income and thus their standard of living. Both the level of pay and its seeming fairness compared with others' pay is important. Pay is also often considered a sign of status and success. Employees attach great importance to pay decisions when they evaluate their relationship with the organization. Therefore, pay decisions must be carefully managed and communicated.

Pay decisions can be broken into two major areas: pay structure and individual pay. In this chapter, we focus on **pay structure,** which in turn entails a consideration of pay level and job structure. **Pay level** is defined here as the average pay (including wages, salaries, and bonuses) of jobs in an organization. (Benefits could also be included, but these are discussed separately in Chapter 13.) **Job structure** refers to the relative pay of jobs in an organization. Consider the same two jobs in two different organizations. In Organization 1, jobs A and B are paid an annual average compensation of $40,000 and $60,000, respectively. In Organization 2, the pay rates are $45,000 and $55,000, respectively. Organizations 1 and 2 have the same pay level ($50,000), but the job structures (relative rates of pay) differ.

Both pay level and job structure are characteristics of organizations and reflect decisions about jobs rather than about individual employees. This chapter's focus is on why and how organizations attach pay policies to jobs. In the next chapter, we look within jobs to discuss the different approaches that can be used to determine the pay of individual employees as well as the advantages and disadvantages of these different approaches.

Why is the focus on jobs in developing a pay structure? As the number of employees in an organization increases, so too does the number of human resource management decisions. In determining compensation, for example, each employee must be assigned a rate of pay that is acceptable in terms of external, internal, and individual equity (defined later) and in terms of the employer's cost. Although each employee is unique and thus requires some degree of individualized treatment, standardizing the treatment of similar employees (e.g., those with similar jobs) can help greatly to make compensation administration and decision making more manageable and more equitable. Thus, pay

TABLE 11.1 Total Compensation as a Percentage of Revenues

INDUSTRY	PERCENTILE		
	10TH	50TH	90TH
Health care	35.7%	48.7%	61.6%
General manufacturing	13.9	22.2	36.6
Insurance	6.8	9.9	27.0
All industries	8.9	26.6	55.0

SOURCE: Saratoga Institute, *1997 Human Resource Financial Report* (Saratoga, CA, 1997). Reprinted with permission.

policies are often attached to particular jobs rather than tailored entirely to individual employees.

Equity Theory and Fairness

In discussing the consequences of pay decisions, it is useful to keep in mind that employees often evaluate their pay relative to that of other employees. Equity theory suggests that people evaluate the fairness of their situations by comparing them with those of other people.[1] According to the theory, a person (P) compares her own ratio of perceived outcomes O (e.g., pay, benefits, working conditions) to perceived inputs *I* (e.g., effort, ability, experience) to the ratio of a comparison other (o).

$$O_P/I_P <, >, \text{ or } = O_o/I_o?$$

If P's ratio (O_P/I_P) is smaller than the comparison other's ratio (O_o/I_o), underreward inequity results. If P's ratio is larger, overreward inequity results, although evidence suggests that this type of inequity is less likely to occur and less likely to be sustained because P may rationalize the situation by reevaluating her outcomes less favorably or inputs (i.e., self-worth) more favorably.[2]

The consequences of P's comparisons depend on whether equity is perceived. If equity is perceived, no change is expected in P's attitudes or behavior. In contrast, perceived inequity may cause P to restore equity. Some ways of restoring equity are counterproductive, including (1) reducing one's own inputs (e.g., not working as hard), (2) increasing one's outcomes (e.g., theft), (3) leaving the situation that generates perceived inequity (e.g., leaving the organization or refusing to work or cooperate with employees who are perceived as overrewarded).

Equity theory's main implication for managing employee compensation is that to an important extent, employees evaluate their pay by comparing it with what others get paid, and their work attitudes and behaviors are influenced by such comparisons. Another implication is that employee perceptions are what determine their evaluation. The fact that management believes its employees are paid well compared with those of other companies does not necessarily translate into employees' beliefs. Employees may have different information or make different comparisons than management.

Three types of employee social comparisons of pay are especially relevant in making pay-level and job-structure decisions. (See Table 11.2.) First, *external equity* pay comparisons focus on what employees in other organizations are paid for doing the same general job. Such comparisons are likely to influence the decisions of applicants to accept job offers as well as the attitudes and decisions of employees about whether to stay with an organization or take a job elsewhere. (See Chapters 5 and 10.) The organization's choice of pay level influences its employees' external pay comparisons and their consequences. A market pay survey is the major administrative tool organizations use in choosing a pay level.

TABLE 11.2 Pay Structure Concepts and Consequences

PAY STRUCTURE DECISION AREA	ADMINISTRATIVE TOOL	FOCUS OF EMPLOYEE PAY COMPARISONS	CONSEQUENCES OF EQUITY PERCEPTIONS
Pay level	Market pay surveys	External equity	External employee movement (attraction and retention of quality employees); labor costs; employee attitudes
Job structure	Job evaluation	Internal equity	Internal employee movement (promotion, transfer, job rotation); cooperation among employees; employee attitudes

Second, *internal equity* pay comparisons focus on what employees within the same organization, but in different jobs, are paid. Employees make comparisons with lower-level jobs, jobs at the same level (but perhaps in different skill areas or product divisions), and jobs at higher levels. Indeed, the opening vignette mentioned comparisons between employees in lower-paying jobs and those in the executive suite. These comparisons may influence general attitudes of employees; their willingness to transfer to other jobs within the organization; their willingness to accept promotions; their inclination to cooperate across jobs, functional areas, or product groups; and their commitment to the organization. The organization's choice of job structure influences its employees' internal comparisons and their consequences. Job evaluation is the major administrative tool organizations use to design job structures.

Third, employees make internal *equity* pay comparisons with others performing the same job. Such comparisons are most relevant to the following chapter, which focuses on using pay to recognize individual contributions and differences.

We now turn to ways to choose and develop pay levels and pay structures, the consequences of such choices, and the ways two administrative tools—market pay surveys and job evaluation—help in making pay decisions.

Developing Pay Levels

MARKET PRESSURES

Any organization faces two important competitive market challenges in deciding what to pay its employees: product-market competition and labor-market competition.

PRODUCT-MARKET COMPETITION. First, organizations must compete effectively in the product market. In other words, they must be able to sell their goods and services at a quantity and price that will bring a sufficient return on their investment. Organizations compete on multiple dimensions (e.g., quality, service), and price is one of the most important dimensions. An important influence on price is the cost of production.

An organization that has higher labor costs than its product-market competitors will have to charge higher average prices for products of similar quality. Thus, for example, if labor costs are 30 percent of revenues at Company A and Company B, but Company A has labor costs that are 20 percent higher than those of Company B, we would expect Company A to have product prices that are higher by (.30 × .20) = 6 percent. At some point, the higher price charged by Company A will contribute to a loss of its business to competing companies with lower prices (like Company B). One study, for example, found that in the early 1990s the wage and benefit cost to produce a small car was approximately $1,700 for Ford Motor, $1,800 for Chrysler, and $2,400 for General Motors.[3] Thus, if all other costs were equal, General Motors would have to sell the same quality car for $600 to $700 more than would Ford or Chrysler.

Therefore, *product-market competition* places an *upper bound* on labor costs and compensation. This upper bound is more constrictive when labor costs are a larger share of total costs and when demand for the product is affected by changes in price (i.e., demand is *elastic*). Although costs are only one part of the competitive equation (productivity is just as important), higher costs may result in a loss of business. In the absence of clear evidence on productivity differences, costs need to be closely monitored.

What components make up labor costs? A major component is the average cost per employee. This is made up of both direct payments (such as wages, salaries, and bonuses) and indirect payments (such as health insurance, social security, and unemployment compensation). A second major component of labor cost is the staffing level (number of employees). Not surprisingly, financially troubled organizations often seek to cut costs by focusing on one or both components. Staff reductions, hiring freezes, wages and salary freezes, and sharing benefits costs with employees are several ways of enhancing the organization's competitive position in the product market.

LABOR-MARKET COMPETITION. A second important competitive market challenge is *labor-market competition*. Essentially, labor-market competition is the amount an organization must pay to compete against other companies that hire similar employees. These labor-market competitors typically include not only companies that have similar products but also those in different product markets that hire similar types of employees. If an organization is not competitive in the labor market, it will fail to attract and retain employees of sufficient numbers and quality. For example, even if a computer manufacturer offers newly graduated electrical engineers the same pay as other computer manufacturers, if automobile manufacturers and other labor-market competitors offer salaries $5,000 higher, the computer company may not be able to hire enough qualified electrical engineers. Labor-market competition places a *lower bound* on pay levels.

EMPLOYEES AS A RESOURCE

Because organizations have to compete in the labor market, they should consider their employees not just as a cost but as a resource in which the organization has invested and from which it expects valuable returns. Although controlling costs has a direct effect on an organization's ability to compete in the product market, the organization's competitive position can be compromised if costs are kept low at the expense of employee productivity and quality. Having higher labor costs than your competitors is not necessarily bad if you also have the best and most effective work force, one that produces more products of better quality.

Pay policies and programs are one of the most important human resource tools for encouraging desired employee behaviors and discouraging undesired behaviors. Therefore, they must be evaluated, not just in terms of costs, but in terms of the returns they generate—how they attract, retain, and motivate a high-quality work force. For example, if the average revenue per employee in Company A is 20 percent higher than in Company B, it may not be important that the average pay in Company A is 10 percent higher than in Company B.

DECIDING WHAT TO PAY

Although organizations face important external labor- and product-market pressures in setting their pay levels, a range of discretion remains.[4] How large the range is depends on the particular competitive environment the organization faces. Where the range is broad, an important strategic decision is whether to pay above, at, or below the market average. The advantage of paying above the market average is the ability to attract and retain the top talent available, which can translate into a highly effective and productive work force. The disadvantage, however, is the added cost.

So, under what circumstances do the benefits of higher pay outweigh the higher costs? According to **efficiency wage theory,** one circumstance is when organizations have technologies or structures that depend on highly skilled employees. For example, organizations that emphasize decentralized decision making may need higher-caliber employees. Another circumstance where higher pay may be warranted is when an organization has difficulties observing and monitoring its employees' performance. It may therefore wish to provide an above-market pay rate to ensure the incentive to put forth maximum effort. The theory is that employees who are paid more than they would be paid elsewhere will be reluctant to "shirk" (i.e., not work hard) because they wish to retain their good job.[5]

MARKET PAY SURVEYS

As mentioned in Chapter 1, total quality management emphasizes the key importance of *benchmarking*, a procedure in which an organization compares its own practices against those of the competition. This notion is relevant in compensation management. Benchmarking against product-market and labor-market competitors is typically accomplished through the use of one or more pay surveys, which provide information on going rates of pay among competing organizations.

The use of pay surveys requires answers to several important questions:[6]

1. Which employers should be included in the survey? Ideally, they would be the key labor-market and product-market competitors.
2. Which jobs are included in the survey? Because only a sample of jobs is ordinarily used, care must be taken that the jobs are representative in terms of level, functional area, and product market. Also, the job content must be sufficiently similar.
3. If multiple surveys are used, how are all the rates of pay weighted and combined? Organizations often have to weight and combine pay rates because different surveys are often tailored toward particular employee groups (labor markets) or product markets. The organization must decide how much relative weight to give to its labor- and product-market competitors in setting pay.

Several factors come into play when deciding how to combine surveys.[7] Product-market comparisons that focus on labor costs are likely to deserve greater weight when (1) labor costs represent a large share of total costs, (2) product demand is elastic (i.e., it changes in response to product price changes), (3) the supply of labor is inelastic, and (4) employee skills are specific to the product market (and will remain so). In contrast, labor-market comparisons may be more important when (1) attracting and retaining qualified employees is difficult and (2) the costs (administrative, disruption, etc.) of recruiting replacements are high.

As this discussion suggests, knowing what other organizations are paying is only one part of the story. It is also necessary to know what those organizations are getting in return for their investment in employees. To find that out, some organizations examine ratios such as revenues/employees and revenues/labor cost. The first ratio includes the staffing component of employee cost but not the average cost per employee. The second ratio, however, includes both. Note that comparing these ratios across organizations requires caution. For example, different industries rely on different resources (e.g., labor and capital). So, comparing the ratio of revenues to labor costs of a petroleum company (capital intensive, high ratio) to a bank (labor intensive, low ratio) would be like comparing apples and oranges. But within industries, such comparisons can be useful. Besides revenues, other return-on-investment data might include product quality, customer satisfaction, and potential work force quality (e.g., average education levels). The "Competing by Meeting Stakeholders' Needs" box provides examples of how executive pay comparisons factor in product-market, labor-market, and business performance considerations.

RATE RANGES. As the preceding discussion suggests, obtaining a single "going rate" of market pay is a complex task that involves a number of subjective decisions—it is both an art and a science. Once a market rate has been chosen, how is it incorporated into the pay structure? Typically—especially for white-collar jobs—it is used for setting the midpoint of pay-rate ranges for either jobs or pay grades (discussed next). Market survey data are also often collected on minimum and maximum rates of pay as well. The use of ranges permits a company to recognize differences in employee performance, seniority, training, and so forth in setting individual pay (discussed in the next chapter).

Using Market Pay Data in Setting a Pay Strategy

Coca-Cola. The Company emphasizes total compensation opportunities and focuses less attention on the competitive posture of each component of compensation. The development of at-risk pay policies is driven more by Company strategy than by competitive practice. Over time, the level of the Company's competitiveness in compensation opportunities is based heavily on the Company's stock price performance relative to other large companies. In line with this principle, current total compensation competitiveness is targeted in the top quartile of the range of total compensation of a comparator group of companies described in the next section of this report. . . . The Company seeks talent from a broader group of companies than the Food, Beverage and Tobacco Groups against which performance is compared.

Total compensation comparators are selected by screening large public companies for such performance characteristics as profit growth and return on equity. Those companies exhibiting leadership in the performance measures over sustained periods are selected as benchmarks for the Company's total compensation standards.

Ford. The Compensation Committee wants the compensation of Ford executives to be competitive in the worldwide auto industry and with major U.S. companies. Each year, the Committee reviews a report from an outside consultant on Ford's compensation program for executives. The report discusses all aspects of compensation as well as how Ford's program compares with those of other large companies. Based on this report, its own review of various parts of the program, and its assessment of the skills, experience, and achievements of individual executives, the Committee decides the compensation of executives.

COMPETING BY MEETING STAKEHOLDERS' NEEDS

The consultant develops compensation data using a survey of several leading companies picked by the consultant and Ford. General Motors and Chrysler were included in the survey. Eighteen leading companies in other industries also were included because the job market for executives goes beyond the auto industry. Companies were picked based on size, reputation, and business complexity.

The Committee looks at the size and success of the companies and the types of jobs covered by the survey in determining executive compensation. One goal of Ford's compensation program is to approximate the survey group's average compensation, adjusted for company size and performance.

Procter & Gamble. When the company achieves solid earnings growth and stock price appreciation, executive compensation levels will be expected to equal or exceed the middle compensation range for a comparative group of companies. This group includes a combination of leading consumer products companies and other corporations of size and reputation comparable to Procter & Gamble (and with which Procter & Gamble must compete in hiring and retaining the employees it needs). The composition of this group is updated periodically in order to assure its continued relevance.

The Committee believes the compensation levels of the Company's executive officers are competitive and in line with those of comparable companies. This conclusion is derived in part from consultations with independent outside compensation consultants.

SOURCE: Excerpts from 1998 Coca-Cola, Ford, and Procter & Gamble proxy statements.

For some blue-collar jobs, however, particularly those covered by collective bargaining contracts, there may be a single rate of pay for all employees within the job.

KEY JOBS AND NONKEY JOBS. In using pay surveys, it is necessary to make a distinction between two general types of jobs: key jobs (or benchmark jobs) and nonkey jobs. **Key jobs** have relatively stable content and—perhaps most important—are common to many organizations. Therefore, it is possible to obtain market pay survey data on them. Note, however, that to avoid too much of an administrative burden, organizations may not gather market pay data on all such jobs. In contrast to key jobs, **nonkey jobs** are, to an important extent, unique to organizations; thus, by definition, they cannot be directly valued or compared through the use of market surveys. Therefore, they are treated differently in the pay-setting process.

DEVELOPING A JOB STRUCTURE

Although external comparisons of the sort we have been discussing are important, employees also evaluate their pay using internal comparisons. So, for example, a vice president of marketing may expect to be paid roughly the same amount as a vice president of information systems because they are at the same organizational level, with similar levels of responsibility and similar impacts on the organization's performance. A job structure can be defined as the relative worth of various jobs in the organization, based on these types of internal comparisons. We now turn to a discussion of how such decisions are made.

JOB EVALUATION. One typical way of measuring job worth is to perform an administrative procedure called **job evaluation.** A job evaluation system is composed of compensable factors and a weighting scheme based on the importance of each compensable factor to the organization. Simply stated, **compensable factors** are the characteristics of jobs that an organization values and chooses to pay for. These characteristics include job complexity, working conditions, required education, required experience, and responsibility. Most job evaluation systems use several compensable factors. Job analysis (discussed in Chapter 4) provides basic descriptive information on job attributes, and the job evaluation process assigns a value to these compensable factors.

Scores can be generated in a variety of ways, but they typically include input from a number of people. A job evaluation committee is commonly used to generate ratings. Although there are numerous ways to evaluate jobs, the most widely used is the point-factor system, which yields job evaluation points for each compensable factor.[8]

THE POINT-FACTOR SYSTEM. After generating scores for each compensable factor on each job, job evaluators often apply a weighting scheme to account for the differing importance of the compensable factors to the organization. Weights can be generated in two ways. First, a priori weights can be assigned, which means factors are weighted using expert judgments about the importance of each compensable factor. Second, weights can be derived empirically based on how important each factor seems to be in determining pay in the labor market. (Statistical methods such as multiple regression can be used for this purpose.) For the sake of simplicity, we assume in the following example that equal a priori weights are chosen, which means that the scores on the compensable factors can be simply summed.

Table 11.3 shows an example of a three-factor job evaluation system applied to three jobs. Note that the jobs differ in the levels of experience, education, and complexity required. Summing the scores on the three compensable factors provides an internally oriented assessment of relative job worth in the organization. In a sense, the computer programmer job is worth 41 percent (155/110 – 1) more than the computer operator job, and the systems analyst job is worth 91 percent (210/110 – 1) more than the computer operator job. Whatever pay level is chosen (based on benchmarking and competitive

TABLE 11.3 Example of a Three-Factor Job Evaluation System

	COMPENSABLE FACTORS			
JOB TITLE	EXPERIENCE	EDUCATION	COMPLEXITY	TOTAL
Computer operator	40	30	40	110
Computer programmer	40	50	65	155
Systems analyst	65	60	85	210

strategy), we would expect the pay differentials to be somewhat similar to these percentages. The internal job evaluation and external survey-based measures of worth can, however, diverge.

DEVELOPING A PAY STRUCTURE

In the example provided in Table 11.4, there are 15 jobs, 10 of which are key jobs. For these key jobs, both pay survey and job evaluation data are available. For the five nonkey jobs, by definition, no survey data are available, only job evaluation information. Note that, for simplicity's sake, we work with data from only two pay surveys and we use a weighted average that gives twice as much weight to survey 1. Also, our example works with a single structure. Many organizations have multiple structures that correspond to different job families (e.g., clerical, technical, professional) or product divisions.

How are the data in Table 11.4 combined to develop a pay structure? First, it is important to note that both internal and external comparisons must be considered in making compensation decisions. However, because the pay structures suggested by internal and external comparisons do not necessarily converge, employers must carefully balance them. Studies suggest that employers may differ significantly in the degree to which they place priority on internal- or external-comparison data in developing pay structures.[9]

At least three pay-setting approaches, which differ according to their relative emphasis on external or internal comparisons, can be identified.[10]

MARKET SURVEY DATA. The approach with the greatest emphasis on external comparisons (i.e., market survey data) is achieved by directly basing pay on market surveys that cover as many key jobs as possible. For example, the rate of pay for job A in Table 11.5 would be $1,919; for job B, $2,106; and for job C, $2,807. For nonkey jobs (jobs D, E, H, M, and O), however, pay survey information is not available, and we must

TABLE 11.4 Job Evaluation and Pay Survey Data

JOB	KEY JOB?	JOB TITLE	JOB EVALUATION	SURVEY 1 (S1)	SURVEY 2 (S2)	SURVEY COMPOSITE (2/3*S1 + 1/3*S2)
A	y	Computer operator	110	$2,012	$1,731	$1,919
B	y	Engineering tech I	115	2,206	1,908	2,106
C	y	Computer programmer	155	2,916	2,589	2,807
D	n	Engineering tech II	165	—	—	—
E	n	Compensation analyst	170	—	—	—
F	y	Accountant	190	3,613	3,099	3,442
G	y	Systems analyst	210	4,275	3,854	4,134
H	n	Computer programmer—senior	225	—	—	—
I	y	Director of personnel	245	4,982	4,506	4,823
J	y	Accountant—senior	255	5,205	4,270	4,893
K	y	Systems analyst—senior	270	5,868	5,652	5,796
L	y	Industrial engineer	275	5,496	4,794	5,262
M	n	Chief accountant	315	—	—	—
N	y	Senior engineer	320	7,026	6,572	6,875
O	n	Senior scientist	330	—	—	—

SOURCE: Adapted from S. Rynes, B. Gerhart, G.T. Milkovich, and J. Boudreau, *Current Compensation Professional Institute* (Scottsdale, AZ: American Compensation Association, 1988). Reprinted with permission.

TABLE 11.5 Pay Midpoints under Different Approaches

JOB	KEY JOB?	JOB TITLE	JOB EVALUATION	(1) SURVEY + POLICY	(2) PAY MIDPOINTS POLICY	(3) GRADES
A	y	Computer operator	110	$1,919	$1,835	$2,175
B	y	Engineering tech I	115	2,106	1,948	2,175
C	y	Computer programmer	155	2,807	2,856	3,310
D	n	Engineering tech II	165	3,083	3,083	3,310
E	n	Compensation analyst	170	3,196	3,196	3,310
F	y	Accountant	190	3,442	3,650	3,310
G	y	Systems analyst	210	4,134	4,104	4,444
H	n	Computer programmer—senior	225	4,444	4,444	4,444
I	y	Director of personnel	245	4,823	4,898	4,444
J	y	Accountant—senior	255	4,893	5,125	5,579
K	y	Systems analyst—senior	270	5,796	5,465	5,579
L	y	Industrial engineer	275	5,262	5,579	5,579
M	n	Chief accountant	315	6,486	6,486	6,713
N	y	Senior engineer	320	6,875	6,600	6,713
O	n	Senior scientist	330	6,826	6,826	6,713

SOURCE: Adapted from S. Rynes, B. Gerhart, G.T. Milkovich, and J. Boudreau, *Current Compensation Professional Institute* (Scottsdale, AZ: American Compensation Association, 1988). Reprinted with permission.

TABLE 11.6 Sample Pay Grade Structure

PAY GRADE	JOB EVALUATION POINTS RANGE		MONTHLY PAY RATE RANGE		
	MINIMUM	MAXIMUM	MINIMUM	MIDPOINT	MAXIMUM
1	100	150	$1,740	$2,175	$2,610
2	150	200	2,648	3,310	3,971
3	200	250	3,555	4,444	5,333
4	250	300	4,463	5,579	6,694
5	300	350	5,370	6,713	8,056

proceed differently. Basically, we develop a market **pay-policy line** based on the key jobs (for which there are both job evaluation and market pay survey data available). As Figure 11.1 shows, the data can be plotted with a line of best fit estimated. This line can be generated using a statistical procedure (regression analysis). Doing so yields the equation –$661 + $22.69 × Job-evaluation points. In other words, the predicted monthly salary (based on fitting a line to the key job data) is obtained by plugging the number of job evaluation points into this equation. Thus, for example, job D, a nonkey job, would have a predicted monthly salary of –$661 + $22.69 × 165 = $3,083.

As Figure 11.1 also indicates, it is not necessary to fit a straight line to the job evaluation and pay survey data. In some cases, a pay structure that provides increasing monetary rewards to higher-level jobs may be more consistent with the organization's goals or with the external market. For example, nonlinearity may be more appropriate if higher-level jobs are especially valuable to organizations and the talent to perform such jobs is rare. The curvilinear function in Figure 11.1 is described by the equation:

Natural logarithm of pay = $6.98 + .006 × Job evaluation points.

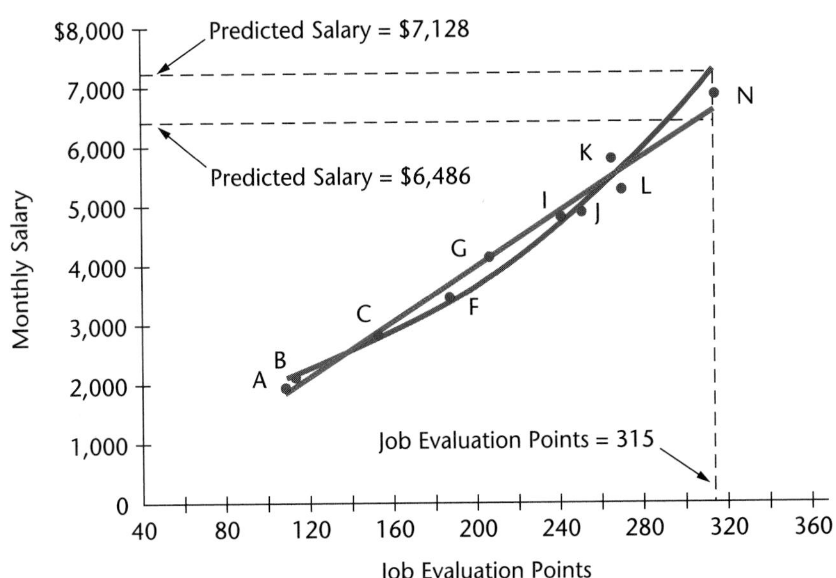

FIGURE 11.1 Pay Policy Lines, Linear and Natural Logarithmic Functions

PAY POLICY LINE. A second pay-setting approach that combines information from external and internal comparisons is to use the pay policy line to derive pay rates for both key and nonkey jobs. This approach differs from the first approach in that actual market rates are no longer used for key jobs. This introduces a greater degree of internal consistency into the structure because the pay of all the jobs is directly linked to the number of job evaluation points.

PAY GRADES. A third approach is to group jobs into a smaller number of pay classes or **pay grades.** Table 11.6 (see also Table 11.5, last column), for example, demonstrates one possibility: a five-grade structure. Each job within a grade would have the same rate range (i.e., be assigned the same midpoint, minimum, and maximum). The advantage of this approach is that the administrative burden of setting separate rates of pay for hundreds (even thousands) of different jobs is reduced. It also permits greater flexibility in moving employees from job to job without raising concerns about, for example, going from a job having 230 job evaluation points to a job with 215 job evaluation points. What might look like a demotion in a completely job-based system is often a nonissue in a grade-based system. Note that the **range spread** (the distance between the minimum and maximum) is larger at higher levels, in recognition of the fact that performance differences are likely to have more impact on the organization at higher job levels. (See Figure 11.2.)

The disadvantage of using grades is that some jobs will be underpaid and others overpaid. For example, job C and job F both fall within the same grade. The midpoint for job C under a grade system is $3,310 per month, or about $400 or so more than under the two alternative pay-setting approaches. Obviously, this will contribute to higher labor costs and potential difficulties in competing in the product market. Unless there is an expected return to this increased cost, the approach is questionable. Job F, on the other hand, is paid between $130 and $340 less per month under the grades system than it would be otherwise. Therefore, the company may find it more difficult to compete in the labor market.

STOP HERE

FIGURE 11.2
Sample Pay Grade Structure

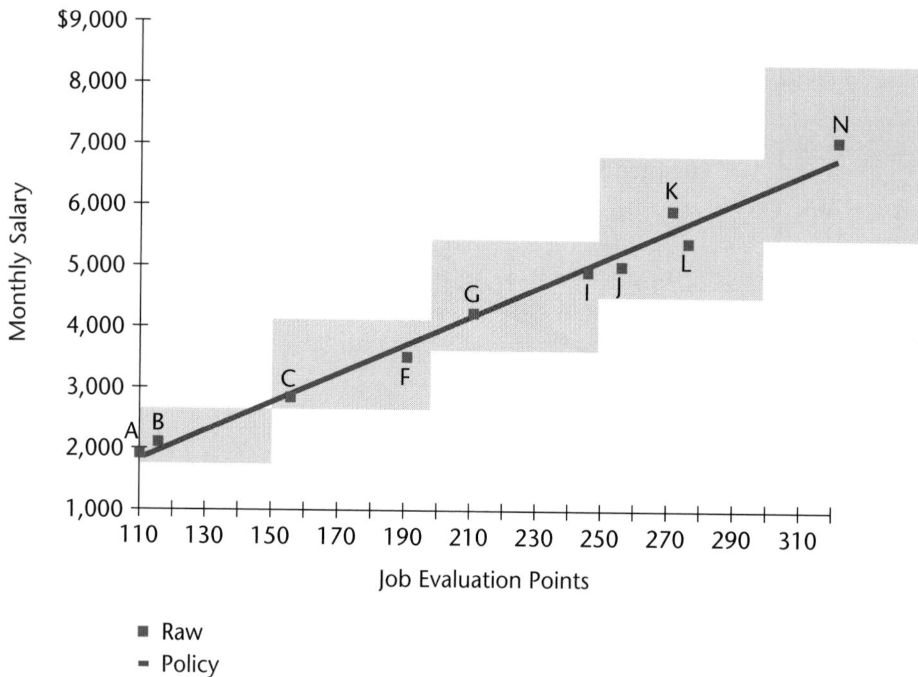

CONFLICTS BETWEEN MARKET PAY SURVEYS AND JOB EVALUATION

An examination of Table 11.5 suggests that the relative worth of jobs is quite similar overall, whether based on job evaluation or pay survey data. However, some inconsistencies typically arise, and these are usually indicated by jobs whose average survey pay is significantly below or above the pay policy line. The closest case in Table 11.5 is job L, for which the average pay falls significantly below the policy line. One possible explanation is that a relatively plentiful supply of people in the labor market are capable of performing this job, so the pay needed to attract and retain them is lower than would be expected given the job evaluation points. Another kind of inconsistency occurs when market surveys show that a job is paid higher than the policy line (e.g., job K). Again, this may be a reflection of relative supply and demand, in this case resulting in pay being driven higher.

How are conflicts between external and internal equity resolved, and what are the consequences? The example of the vice presidents of marketing and information processing may help illustrate the type of choice faced. The marketing VP job may receive the same number of job evaluation points, but market survey data may indicate that it typically pays less than the information-processing VP job, perhaps because of tighter supply for the latter. Does the organization pay based on the market survey (external comparison) or on the job evaluation points (internal comparison)?

Emphasizing the internal comparison would suggest paying the two VPs the same. In doing so, however, either the VP of marketing would be "overpaid" or the VP of information processing would be "underpaid." The former drives up labor costs (product-market problems); the latter may make it difficult to attract and retain a quality VP of information processing (labor-market problems).

Another consideration has to do with the strategy of the organization. In some organizations (e.g., Pepsi, Nike), the marketing function is critical to success. Thus, even though the market for marketing VPs is lower than that for information technology VPs, an organization may choose to be a pay leader for the marketing position (e.g., pay at the 90th percentile) but only meet the market for the information systems position (e.g., pay at the 50th percentile). In other words, designing a pay structure requires careful consideration of which positions are most central to dealing with critical environmental challenges and opportunities in reaching the organization's goals.[11]

What about emphasizing external comparisons? Two potential problems arise. First, the VP of marketing may be dissatisfied because he expects a job of similar rank and responsibility to that of the information technology VP to be paid similarly. Second, it becomes difficult to rotate people through different VP positions (e.g., as a training and development tool), because going to the marketing VP position might appear as a demotion to the VP of information processing.

There is no one right solution to such dilemmas. Each organization must decide which objectives are most essential and choose the appropriate strategy. However, there seems to be a growing sentiment that external comparisons deserve greater weight because organizations are finding it increasingly difficult to ignore market competitive pressures.[12]

MONITORING COMPENSATION COSTS

Pay structure influences compensation costs in a number of ways. Most obviously, the pay level at which the structure is pegged has an influence on these costs. However, this is only part of the story. The pay structure represents the organization's intended policy, but actual practice may not coincide with it. Take, for example, the pay grade structure presented earlier. The midpoint for grade 1 is $2,175, and the midpoint for grade 2 is $3,310. Now, consider the data on a group of individual employees in Table 11.7. One frequently used index of the correspondence between actual and intended pay is the **compa-ratio,** computed as follows:

Grade compa-ratio = Actual average pay for grade/Pay midpoint for grade

The compa-ratio provides a direct assessment of the degree to which actual pay is consistent with the pay policy. A compa-ratio less than 1.00 suggests that actual pay is lagging behind the policy, whereas a compa-ratio greater than 1.00 indicates that pay (and costs) exceeds that of the policy. Although there may be good reasons for compa-ratios to differ from 1.00, managers should also consider whether the pay structure is allowing costs to get out of control.

TABLE 11.7 Compa-Ratios for Two Grades

EMPLOYEE	JOB	PAY	MIDPOINT	EMPLOYEE COMPA-RATIOS
	Grade 1			
1	Engineering tech I	$2,306	$2,175	1.06
2	Computer programmer	2,066	2,175	.95
3	Engineering tech I	2,523	2,175	1.16
4	Engineering tech I	2,414	2,175	1.11
				1.07
	Grade 2			
5	Computer programmer	3,906	3,310	1.18
6	Accountant	3,773	3,310	1.14
7	Accountant	3,674	3,310	1.11
				1.15

GLOBALIZATION, GEOGRAPHIC REGION, AND PAY STRUCTURES

As Figure 11.3 shows, market pay structures can differ substantially across countries both in terms of their level and in terms of the relative worth of jobs. Compared with the labor market in Frankfurt, markets in Budapest and Bombay provide much lower levels of pay overall and much lower payoffs to skill, education, and advancement. These differences create a dilemma for global companies. For example, should a German engineer posted to Bombay be paid according to the standard in Frankfurt or Bombay? If Frankfurt, a sense of inequity is likely to exist among peers in Bombay. If the Bombay market standard is used, it may be all but impossible to find a German engineer willing to accept an assignment in Bombay. Typically, expatriate pay and benefits (e.g., housing allowance, tax equalization) continue to be linked more closely to the home country. However, this link appears to be slowly weakening and now depends more on the nature (e.g., developmental) and length of the assignment.[13]

Within the United States, Runzheimer International reports that 56 percent of companies have either a formal (30 percent) or informal (26 percent) policy that provides for pay differentials based on geographic location.[14] These differentials are intended to prevent inequitable treatment of employees who work in more expensive parts of the country. For example, the cost of living index for New York City is 22 percent higher than in the average metropolitan area, whereas it is 7 percent lower than average in Nashville. Therefore, an employee receiving annual pay of $50,000 in Nashville would require annual pay of $65,600 in New York City to retain the same purchasing power. The most common approach (74 percent of companies) is to move an employee higher in the pay structure to compensate for higher living costs. However, the drawback of this approach is that it may be difficult to adjust the salary downward if costs in that lo-

FIGURE 11.3
Earnings in Selected Occupations in Seven Cities

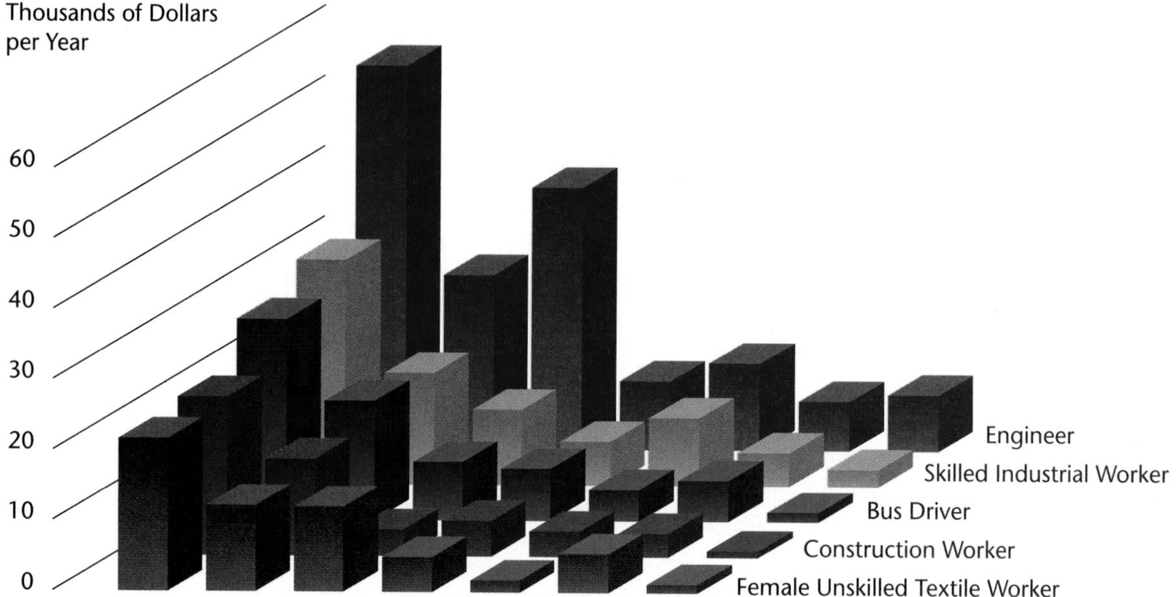

Earnings are adjusted to reflect purchasing power.
SOURCE: World Bank, *World Development Report 1995* (Oxford, England: Oxford University Press, 1995), p. 11. Reprinted with permission.

cation fall or the employee moves to a lower-cost area. Thus, 22 percent of the companies choose to pay an ongoing supplement that changes or disappears in the event of such changes.

The Importance of Process: Participation and Communications

Compensation management has been criticized for following the simplistic belief that "if the right technology can be developed, the right answers will be found."[15] In reality, however, any given pay decision is rarely obvious to the diverse groups that make up organizations, regardless of the decision's technical merit or basis in theory. Of course, it is important when changing pay practices to decide which program or combination of programs makes most sense, but it also matters how such decisions are made and how they are communicated.[16]

PARTICIPATION

Employee participation in compensation decision making can take many forms. For example, employees may serve on task forces charged with recommending and designing a pay program. They may also be asked to help communicate and explain its rationale. This is particularly true in the case of job evaluation as well as many of the programs discussed in the next chapter. To date, for what are perhaps obvious reasons, employee participation in pay level decisions remains fairly rare.

It is important to distinguish between participation by those affected by policies and those who must actually implement the policies. Managers are in the latter group (and often in the former group at the same time). As in other areas of human resource management, line managers are typically responsible for making policies work. Their intimate involvement in any change to existing pay practices is, of course, necessary.

COMMUNICATION

A dramatic example of the importance of communication was found in a study of how an organization communicated pay cuts to its employees and the effects on theft rates and perceived equity.[17] Two organization units received 15 percent across-the-board pay cuts. A third unit received no pay cut and served as a control group. The reasons for the pay cuts were communicated in different ways to the two pay-cut groups. In the "adequate explanation" pay-cut group, management provided a significant amount of information to explain its reasons for the pay cut and also expressed significant remorse. In contrast, the "inadequate explanation" group received much less information and no indication of remorse. The control group received no pay cut (and thus no explanation).

The control group and the two pay-cut groups began with the same theft rates and equity perceptions. After the pay cut, the theft rate was 54 percent higher in the "adequate explanation" group than in the control group. But in the "inadequate explanation" condition, the theft rate was 141 percent higher than in the control group. In this case, communication had a large, independent effect on employees' attitudes and behaviors.

Communication is likely to have other important effects. We know, for example, that not only actual pay but the comparison standard influences employee attitudes.[18] Under two-tier wage plans, employees doing the same jobs are paid two different rates, depending on when they were hired. Moreover, the lower-paid employees do not ordinarily move into the higher-paying tier. Common sense might suggest that the lower-paid employees would be less satisfied. Not necessarily. In fact, a study by Peter Capelli

Web Transforms the Art of Negotiating Raises

Thanks to the Internet, Holly Peckham negotiated herself a 21 percent pay increase when she switched public-relations firms earlier this year.

Unsure about her worth at the outset of her job search, she found a U.S. salary database on a Web site created by Marshall Consultants, a New York executive-search firm. It was a trove of salary information supplied by more than 16,000 communications professionals. Ms. Peckham's conclusion: She should be making about $37,000 a year as an account executive at a PR agency serving high-tech clients. That was about $9,000 more than she was earning as an assistant account executive at Schwartz Communications in Waltham, Massachusetts.

Chen PR Inc., also of Waltham, offered Ms. Peckham $32,000 and the desired promotion. She refused, citing her online research. "I told them the national average was between $36,000 and $38,000 and that I would be happy coming for between $34,000 and $36,000," she recollects. "My hands were shaking." She accepted $34,000.

In a world where information is power, salary negotiations have long been greatly imbalanced. But the Internet is changing that, as burgeoning numbers of Web sites offer salary surveys, job listings with specified pay levels, and even customized compensation analyses. Armed with this data, workers are finding their hands strengthened as they haggle over compensation for a new job—or try to improve their pay at a current one.

JobSmart, run by a regional public library agency in San Mateo, California, offers links to 150 free salary surveys on the Web that draw about 4,000 visitors a day. ExecU-Net, a for-profit job search network, divulges free information about the salary, bonus and stock options offered for about 650 upper-management positions entirely updated every two weeks. For a fee, users can get more specific information and contacts for those listings.

COMPETING THROUGH HIGH-PERFORMANCE WORK SYSTEMS

"I wouldn't be surprised if we see a lot more [applicants] coming in, having done online searches" for competitive salary information, says Barbara Ewen, a principal at Chen, the firm that hired Ms. Peckham. Ms. Peckham's research, plus her two years' experience, persuaded the firm to up the ante, Ms. Ewen says.

"The Internet has become the big level playing field for everyone" by exposing businesses that "are way below everyone else as far as pay is concerned," says Brian Krueger, a staffing and employee-development director for Keane Inc., a big information-technology consulting firm in Boston.

Mr. Krueger is already feeling the heat. Last spring, he tried to hire a new college graduate for Keane's software-maintenance training program. But the young man balked at Keane's proposed starting salary of about $35,000. Through Internet bulletin boards, the candidate located another potential Keane recruit who had rejected a higher offer.

The reason: Keane had pursued that applicant for its software-development program—where trainees typically earn several thousand dollars more than those in software maintenance, because they have programming experience. The contender ultimately accepted the original offer.

For most job seekers, cyberspace pay information merely represents a starting point. Free surveys posted online often provide pay information for a generic position but don't always take into account industry, company size, specific skills, geography—and demand. These Web sites only "can tell you if you are in the ballpark and can stop you from underbidding yourself," says Mary-Ellen Mort, project director of JobSmart.

Charles Wetzel, a 1998 graduate of Southern Methodist University in Dallas, says he figured out how much he should make in his first job by scrutinizing the salary levels of online vacancies posted by companies and help-wanted sites. One such site, CareerMosaic, claims to have 70,000 job listings, and roughly 20 percent of those listings contain salary information.

Based on his research, Mr. Wetzel

and Peter Sherer found that the lower-paid employees were more satisfied on average.[19] Apparently, those in the lower tier used different (lower) comparison standards than those in the higher tier. The lower-tier employees compared their jobs with unemployment or lower-paying jobs they had managed to avoid. As a result, they were more satisfied, despite being paid less money for the same work. This finding does not mean that two-tier wage plans are necessarily a good idea. Indeed, they seem to be diminishing in says he felt justified turning down a New Jersey transportation concern's offer of slightly more than $30,000 a year. "In my eyes," Mr. Wetzel says, "they fell $10,000 short." He took another pending offer—and became a management consultant in the Dallas office of Ernst & Young LLP. With the typical 1998 college graduate earning about $30,000, "I beat [that average] by over ten grand," the 22-year-old exults. "I didn't sell myself cheap."

Executive recruiter Korn/Ferry International unexpectedly got a firsthand lesson in the new rules of the game when it created an electronic job-search venture called Futurestep with *The Wall Street Journal*. To compile an internal database of possible applicants for midlevel managerial vacancies, Futurestep offers people a free analysis of their salary and bonus potential, among other things. It has completed more than 52,000 such analyses since June.

Unexpectedly, several Korn/Ferry recruiters signed up for Futurestep and "found out they were underpaid," says Man Jit Singh, the venture's chief executive.

The assessment revealed "that I was about 18 percent" below prevailing rates, says Peter Reed, a 28-year-old recruiter in Korn/Ferry's Chicago office. He says his Futurestep pay analysis will be "part of my action plan come review time" next spring. Korn/Ferry increased his base salary 10 percent in April. Company officials say Mr. Reed makes roughly $80,000 a year. Mr. Reed declined to comment on the figure.

"I'm sure we could have people in certain markets where, relative to a competitor, we might be under market," concedes Windle Priem, chief operating officer of Korn/Ferry, which is the nation's biggest search firm. With Futurestep, he frets, "we're certainly creating challenges for ourselves."

Indeed, three major corporations—including a toy maker that is a Korn/Ferry client—have complained to Mr. Singh because some of their managers used Futurestep to wrangle raises recently.

SOURCE: Joann S. Lublin, "Web Transforms Art of Negotiating Raises," *The Wall Street Journal* (September 22, 1998), p. B1.

SHOW ME THE MONEY

Some pay-data Web sites:

SPONSOR	INTERNET ADDRESS	WHAT IT PROVIDES	DOWNSIDE
JobSmart	Jobsmart.org	Links to 150 salary surveys available on the Web.	Some data are from 1996 or limited to California.
Wageweb	www.wageweb.com	Average salaries for more than 150 clerical, professional and managerial jobs.	Charges $100 for breakdowns by industry, geography, etc.
Exec-U-Net	www.execunet.com	Salary, bonus and options for about 650 management posts.	Charges an initial $125 for job details.
PinPoint Salary Service	members.aol.com/payraises	Individualized pay analyses, based on title, experience, desired industry, etc.	First job analysis costs $95.
Futurestep*	www.futurestep.com	Pay analyses for people eligible for managerial posts paying $50,000 to $200,000 a year.	Participants automatically subject to queries from Korn/Ferry recruiters.

*An alliance between recruiters Korn/Ferry International and *The Wall Street Journal.*

Source: WSJ reports

number. Rather, consistent with equity theory, it shows that the way employees compare their pay with other jobs matters, and managers need to take this into consideration. As the "Competing through High-Performance Work Systems" box shows, employees increasingly have access to salary survey information, which is likely to result in more comparisons and thus a greater need for effective communication.

Managers play the most crucial communication role because of their day-to-day interactions with their employees. Therefore, they must be prepared to explain why the pay structure is designed as it is and to judge whether employee concerns about the structure need to be addressed with changes to the structure. One common issue is deciding when a job needs to be reclassified because of substantial changes in its content. If an employee takes on more responsibility, she will often ask the manager for assistance in making the case for increased pay for the job.

Current Challenges

PROBLEMS WITH JOB-BASED PAY STRUCTURES

The approach taken in this chapter, that of defining pay structures in terms of jobs and their associated responsibilities, remains the most widely used in practice.[20] However, job-based pay structures have a number of potential limitations.[21] First, they may encourage bureaucracy. The job description sets out specific tasks and activities for which the incumbent is responsible and, by implication, those for which the incumbent is not responsible. Although this facilitates performance evaluation and control by the manager, it can also encourage a lack of flexibility and a lack of initiative on the part of employees: "Why should I do that? It's not in my job description." Second, the structure's hierarchical nature reinforces a top-down decision making and information flow as well as status differentials, which do not lend themselves to taking advantage of the skills and knowledge of those closest to production. Third, the bureaucracy required to generate and update job descriptions and job evaluations can become a barrier to change because wholesale changes to job descriptions can involve a tremendous amount of time and cost. Fourth, the job-based pay structure may not reward desired behaviors, particularly in a rapidly changing environment where the knowledge, skills, and abilities needed yesterday may not be very helpful today and tomorrow. Fifth, the emphasis on job levels and status differentials encourages promotion-seeking behavior but may discourage lateral employee movement because employees are reluctant to accept jobs that are not promotions or that appear to be steps down.

RESPONSES TO PROBLEMS WITH JOB-BASED PAY STRUCTURES

DELAYERING AND BANDING. In response to the problems caused by job-based pay structures, some organizations are **delayering,** or reducing the number of job levels to achieve more flexibility in job assignments and in assigning merit increases. Pratt and Whitney, for example, changed from 11 pay grades and 3,000 job descriptions for entry-level through middle-management positions to 6 pay grades and several hundred job descriptions.[22] These broader groupings of jobs are also known as broad bands. Table

TABLE 11.8 Example of Pay Bands

TRADITIONAL STRUCTURE		BANDED STRUCTURE	
GRADE	TITLE	BAND	TITLE
14	Senior accountant	6	Senior accountant
12	Accountant III		
10	Accountant II	5	Accountant
8	Accountant I		

SOURCE: P. LeBlanc, *Perspectives in Total Compensation* 3, no. 3 (March 1992), pp. 1–6. Used with permission of the National Practice Director, Sibson & Company, Inc.

FIGURE 11.4

IBM's New Job Evaluation Approach

Below is an abbreviated schematic illustration of the new—and simple—IBM job evaluation approach:

POSITION REFERENCE GUIDE

Band	Skills required	Leadership/Contribution	Scope/Impact
1			
2			
3			
4			
5			
6			
7			
8			
9			
10			

Factors: Leadership/Contribution
Band 06: Understand the mission of the professional group and vision in own area of competence.
Band 07: Understand the departmental mission and vision.
Band 08: Understand departmental/functional mission and vision.
Band 09: Has vision of functional or unit mission.
Band 10: Has vision of overall strategies.

Both the bands and the approach are global. In the U.S., bands 1–5 are nonexempt; bands 6–10 are exempt. Each cell in the table contains descriptive language about key job characteristics. Position descriptions are compared to the chart and assigned to bands on a "best fit" basis. There are no points or scoring mechanisms. Managers assign employees to bands by selecting a position description that most closely resembles the work being done by an employee using an online position description library.

That's it!

SOURCE: A.S. Richter, "Paying the People in Black at Big Blue," *Compensation and Benefits Review* (May-June 1998), pp. 51–59. Reprinted with permission.

11.8 shows how banding might work for a small sample of jobs. IBM's change to broadbands was accompanied by a change away from a point-factor job evaluation system to a more streamlined approach to evaluating jobs, as Figure 11.4 shows.

One possible consequence of delayering and banding is a reduced opportunity for promotion. Therefore, organizations need to consider what they will offer employees instead. In addition, to the extent that there are separate ranges within bands, the new structure may not represent as dramatic a change as it might appear. These distinctions can easily become just as entrenched as they were under the old system. Broadbands, with their greater spread between pay minimums and maximums, can also lead to weaker budgetary control and rising labor costs. Alternatively, the greater spread can permit managers to better recognize high performers with high pay. It can also permit the organization to reward employees for learning.

PAYING THE PERSON: PAY FOR SKILL, KNOWLEDGE, AND COMPETENCY. A second, related response to job-based pay structure problems has been to move away from linking pay to jobs and toward building structures based on individual characteristics such as skill or knowledge.[23] Competency-based pay is similar but usually refers to a plan that covers exempt employees (e.g., managers). The basic idea is that if you want employees to learn more skills and become more flexible in the jobs they perform, you should pay them to do it. (See Chapter 7 for a discussion of the implications of skill-based pay systems on training.) According to Gerald Ledford, however, it is "a fundamental departure" because employees are now "paid for the skills they are capable of using, not for the job they are performing at a particular point in time."[24]

Skill-based pay systems seem to fit well with the increased breadth and depth of skill that changing technology continues to bring.[25] For example, in a production environment, workers might be expected not only to operate machines but also to take responsibility for maintenance and troubleshooting, quality control, even modifying computer programs.[26] Toyota concluded years ago that "none of the specialists [e.g., quality inspectors, many managers, and foremen] beyond the assembly worker was actually adding any value to the car. What's more . . . assembly workers could probably do most of the functions of specialists much better because of their direct acquaintance with conditions on the line."[27]

In other words, an important potential advantage of skill-based pay is its contribution to increased worker flexibility, which in turn facilitates the decentralization of decision making to those who are most knowledgeable. It also provides the opportunity for leaner staffing levels because employee turnover or absenteeism can now be covered by current employees who are multiskilled.[28] In addition, multiskilled employees are important in cases where different products require different manufacturing processes or where supply shortages or other problems call for adaptive or flexible responses—characteristics typical, for example, of many newer so-called advanced manufacturing environments (e.g., flexible manufacturing, just-in-time systems).[29] More generally, it has been suggested that skill-based plans also contribute to a climate of learning and adaptability and give employees a broader view of how the organization functions. Both changes should contribute to better use of employees' know-how and ideas. Consistent with the advantages just noted, a field study found that a change to a skill-based plan led to better quality and lower labor costs in a manufacturing plant.[30]

Of course, skill-based and competency-based approaches also have potential disadvantages.[31] First, although the plan will likely enhance skill acquisition, the organization may find it a challenge to use the new skills effectively. If it has not been carefully planned, it may find itself with large new labor costs but little payoff. In other words, if skills change, work design must change as quickly to take full advantage. Second, if pay growth is based entirely on skills, problems may arise if employees "top out" by acquiring all the skills too quickly, leaving no room for further pay growth. (Of course, this problem can also afflict job-based systems.) Third, and somewhat ironically, skill-based plans may generate a large bureaucracy—usually a criticism of job-based systems. Training programs need to be developed. Skills must be described, measured, and assigned monetary values. Certification tests must be developed to determine whether an employee has acquired a certain skill. Finally, as if the challenges in obtaining market rates under a job-based system were not enough, there is almost no body of knowledge regarding how to price combinations of skills (versus jobs) in the marketplace. Obtaining comparison data from other organizations will be difficult until skill-based plans become more widely used.

CAN THE U.S. LABOR FORCE COMPETE?

We often hear that U.S. labor costs are simply too high to allow U.S. companies to compete effectively with companies in other countries. The average hourly labor costs (cash and benefits) for production workers in manufacturing in the United States and in other advanced industrialized and newly industrialized countries are given in the following table in U.S. dollars:[32]

	1985	1990	1995	1997
Industrialized				
United States	$13.01	$14.77	$17.19	$18.24
Germany	9.57	21.53	32.22	28.28
France	7.52	15.49	20.01	17.97
Japan	6.43	12.64	23.82	19.37
Newly industrialized				
Mexico	1.60	1.80	1.51	1.75
Hong Kong	1.73	3.20	4.82	5.42
Korea	1.25	3.82	7.29	7.22

Based solely on a cost approach, it would perhaps make sense to try to shift many types of production from Germany and Japan to the United States and from the United States to other countries, particularly the newly industrialized countries. Would this be a good idea? Not necessarily. There are several factors to consider.

INSTABILITY OF COUNTRY DIFFERENCE IN LABOR COSTS. First, note that relative labor costs are very unstable over time. For example, in 1985, U.S. labor costs were (13.01/9.57), or 36 percent greater than those of (West) Germany. But by 1990, the situation was reversed, with (West) German labor costs exceeding those of the United States by (21.53/14.77), or 46 percent, and remained higher. Did German employers suddenly become more generous, while U.S. employers clamped down on pay growth? Not exactly. Because all our figures are expressed in U.S. dollars, changes in currency exchange rates have an important influence on such comparisons, and these exchange rates often fluctuate significantly from year to year. For example, in 1985, when German labor costs were 74 percent of those in the United States, the U.S. dollar was worth 2.94 German marks. But in 1990, the U.S. dollar was worth 1.62 German marks. If the exchange rate in 1990 were still 1 to 2.94, the average German hourly wage in U.S. dollars would have been $11.80, or about 80 percent of the U.S. average. In any event, relative to countries like Germany, U.S. labor costs are now a bargain; this explains, in part, decisions by BMW and Mercedes–Benz to locate production facilities in South Carolina and Alabama, respectively, where labor costs are lower than Germany's by 30 percent or more.

SKILL LEVELS. Second, the quality and productivity of national labor forces can vary dramatically. This is an especially important consideration when comparisons are drawn between labor costs in industrialized countries like the United States and developing countries like Mexico. For example, the high school graduation rate in the United States is 75 percent versus 26 percent in Mexico.[33] Thus, lower labor costs may reflect the lower average skill level of the work force. As a consequence, certain types of skilled labor may be less available in low–labor-cost countries. On the other hand,

A New Breed of Manufacturing Plant?

GM has two truck assembly plants, one car assembly plant, and 29 parts plants in Mexico. With more than 70,000 workers, it's one of Mexico's largest employers. And it pays those workers an average $10 a day, compared to about $220 a day in wages and benefits for its U.S. workers.

GM considers the Silao plant, which has ranked No. 1 on its internal quality studies, its North American manufacturing showplace.

Silao, which began production in 1995, will manufacture about 146,000 pickups and sport utilities this year—119,000, or nearly 82 percent of them, for the USA or Canada—according to production tracker Monthly Autocast.

GM says the workers are paid six times Mexico's minimum wage. Benefits include subsidized housing, medical care, and food assistance worth 120 percent of their base salaries. There's also profit sharing and bonuses for quality.

In the past, American workers were able to overcome wage differences with foreign counterparts through greater efficiency and more sophisticated processes that cut overall costs. But GM's plant in Silao is typical of a new breed of global plant, the kind GM is building in markets

COMPETING THROUGH GLOBALIZATION

such as Poland, Hungary, Argentina, and Thailand.

Many of the ideas in place here come from New United Motor Manufacturing Inc., GM's joint venture with Toyota in Fremont, California. Instead of layers of management, workers are grouped in teams which make decisions on the way the work is done.

A governing rule is flexibility. Workers here aren't bound by the stiff work rules that increase costs in Detroit. Like Toyota workers, and those at Saturn in Spring Hill, Tennessee, Silao workers learn several jobs.

Globalization is on display with every new truck off the assembly line.

Drivers shuttle many to a parking lot where they are loaded aboard tractor-trailers headed deeper into the Mexican market to the south.

Meanwhile, railroad car carriers idling on sidings, bearing names like Conrail and Union Pacific are headed north into Texas or Arizona.

And at a roadside stand, a sticker on a medium-duty, dual–rear-wheeled truck without a bed, made in Silao, indicates that final assembly will be in Flint, Michigan.

SOURCE: C. Woodyard, "Global GM Plants at Strike's Center," *USA Today* (June 19, 1998), p. 3B. Reprinted with permission.

any given company needs only enough skilled employees for its own operations. As the "Competing through Globalization" box demonstrates, some companies have found that low labor costs do not necessarily preclude high quality.

PRODUCTIVITY. Third, and most directly relevant, are data on comparative productivity and unit labor costs, essentially meaning labor cost per hour divided by productivity per hour worked. One indicator of productivity is gross domestic product (or total output of the economy) per person, adjusted for differences in purchasing power. On this measure, the United States fares well. In 1996, these figures (in U.S. dollars) were:[34]

United States	$27,821
Japan	$23,235
Germany	$21,200
Korea	$13,580
France	$20,533
Mexico	$ 7,776

The combination of lower labor costs and higher productivity translates into lower unit labor costs in the United States than in Japan and Western Europe.[35]

NONLABOR CONSIDERATIONS. Fourth, any consideration of where to locate production cannot be based on labor considerations alone. For example, although the average hourly labor cost in Country A may be $15 versus $10 in Country B, if labor costs are 30 percent of total operating costs and nonlabor operating costs are roughly the same, then the total operating costs might be $65 (50 + 15) in Country A and $60 (50 + 10) in Country B. Thus, although labor costs in Country B are 33 percent less, total operating costs are only 7.7 percent less. This may not be enough to compensate for differences in skills and productivity, transportation costs, taxes, and so on. Further, the direct labor component of many products, particularly high-tech products (e.g., electronic components) may often be 5 percent or less. Thus, the effect on product price competitiveness may be insignificant.[36]

In fact, an increasing number of organizations have decided that it is more important to focus on nonlabor-related factors in deciding where to locate production.[37] Product development speed may be greater when manufacturing is physically close to the design group. Quick response to customers (e.g., making a custom replacement product) is difficult when production facilities are on the other side of the world. Inventory levels can be dramatically reduced through the use of manufacturing methods like just-in-time production. But suppliers need to be in close physical proximity.

EXECUTIVE PAY

The issue of executive pay has been given widespread attention in the press. On the one hand, the topic has received more coverage than it deserves because there are very few top executives and their compensation accounts for only a very small share of an organization's total labor costs. On the other hand, top executives have a disproportionate ability to influence organization performance, so decisions about their compensation are critical. Top executives also help set the tone or culture of the organization. If, for example, the top executive's pay seems unrelated to the organization's performance, staying high even when business is poor, employees may not understand why some of their pay should be at risk and depend on how the organization is performing.

How much do executives make? Table 11.9 provides some data. Note that long-term compensation, typically in the form of stock plans, is the major component of CEO pay in recent years because of the strong performance of the stock market.

Table 11.10 shows that some CEOs are paid well above the averages shown in Table 11.9. Additionally, in 1998, Michael Eisner of Disney received over $600 million in pay.

As Table 11.11 shows, U.S. top executives are also the highest paid in the world. (These figures are lower than those from *Business Week* because the latter pertain to larger companies.) The fact that the differential between top-executive pay and that of

TABLE 11.9 CEO Compensation
Business Week Survey ("365 of the Country's Largest Companies")

	SALARY PLUS BONUS	LONG-TERM COMPENSATION	TOTAL COMPENSATION	CHANGE IN PAY	CHANGE IN* S&P 500	CEO/WORKER**
1998	$2.1 million	$8.5 million	$10.6 million	36%	27%	419
1997	2.2 million	5.6 million	7.8 million	35	31	326
1996	2.3 million	3.2 million	5.8 million	54	23	209

SOURCE: "Executive Pay," *Business Week,* April 21, 1997, and April 20, 1998.
*Change in market value of the Standard & Poor's 500 group of companies
**Ratio of CEO pay to hourly employee pay

TABLE 11.10
Highest-Paid CEOs

	SALARY PLUS BONUS	LONG-TERM COMPENSATION	TOTAL COMPENSATION
Sanford Weill, Travelers Group	$7.4 million	$223.7 million	$230.7 million
Roberto Goizueta, Coca-Cola	4.1 million	107.8 million	111.8 million
Richard Scrushy, Healthsouth	13.4 million	93.4 million	106.8 million

SOURCE: "Executive Pay," *Business Week,* April 20, 1998.

TABLE 11.11 Total Remuneration of Chief Executive Officers in Selected Countries

COUNTRY	CEO TOTAL REMUNERATION[a]	CEO PURCHASING POWER (U.S. = 100)[b]	CEO/MANUFACTURING EMPLOYEE TOTAL REMUNERATION MULTIPLE[a]
United States	$871,000	100%	24
Brazil	597,000	66	41
France	586,000	40	16
Argentina	535,000	87	29
Germany	494,000	40	11
Japan	454,000	35	9
Mexico	350,000	71	44

[a]1996 data
[b]1997 data
SOURCE: Towers Perrin, "1997 Worldwide Total Remuneration," New York, 1997. Note: Data based on a company with $250 million in sales; total remuneration includes salary, bonus, company contributions, perquisites, and long-term incentives.

an average manufacturing worker is so much higher in the United States has been described as creating a "trust gap"—that is, in employees' minds, a "frame of mind that mistrusts senior management's intentions, doubts its competence, and resents its self-congratulatory pay." The issue becomes even more salient at a time when so many of the same companies with high executive pay are simultaneously engaging in layoffs or other forms of employment reduction. Employees might ask, "If the company needs to cut costs, why not cut executive pay rather than our jobs?"[38] The issue is one of perceived fairness in difficult economic times. One study, in fact, reported that business units with higher pay differentials between executives and rank-and-file employees had lower customer satisfaction, which was speculated to result from employees' perceptions of inequity coming through in customer relations.[39] Third, and perhaps more important than how much top executives are paid, is how they are paid. This is an issue we return to in the next chapter.

Government Regulation of Employee Compensation

EQUAL EMPLOYMENT OPPORTUNITY

Equal Employment Opportunity (EEO) regulation (e.g., Title VII, Civil Rights Act) prohibits sex- and race-based differences in employment outcomes such as pay, unless justified by business necessity (e.g., pay differences stemming from differences in job performance). In addition to regulatory pressures, organizations must be prepared to deal with changing labor-market and demographic realities. At least two trends are directly relevant in discussing EEO. First, the labor force participation rate of women has risen from 38 percent in 1960 to 59 percent in 1995. Second, between 1980 and 1990, the white population grew by 6.0 percent; the nonwhite population grew by 25.3 percent. The percentage of white males in organizations will probably continue to decline, making attention to EEO issues in compensation even more important.

Is there equality of treatment in pay determination? Typically, the popular press focuses on raw earnings ratios. For example, in 1997, among full-time workers, the ratio of female-to-male median earnings was .75, and the ratio of black-to-white earnings was .77.[40] These percentages have generally risen over the last two to three decades, but significant race and sex differences in pay clearly remain.[41]

The usefulness of raw percentages is limited, however, because some portion of earnings differences arises from differences in legitimate factors: education, labor-market experience, and occupation. Adjusting for such differences reduces earnings differences based on race and sex, but significant differences remain. With few exceptions, such adjustments rarely account for any more than one-half of the earnings differential.[42]

What aspects of pay determination are responsible for such differences? In the case of women, it is suggested that their work is undervalued. Another explanation rests on the "crowding" hypothesis, which argues that women were historically restricted to entering a small number of occupations. As a result, the supply of workers far exceeded demand, resulting in lower pay for such occupations. If so, market surveys would only perpetuate the situation.

Comparable worth (or pay equity) is a public policy that advocates remedies for any undervaluation of women's jobs. The idea is to obtain equal pay, not just for jobs of equal content (already mandated by the Equal Pay Act of 1963) but for jobs of equal value or worth. Typically, job evaluation is used to measure worth. Table 11.12, which is based on State of Washington data from one of the first comparable-worth cases, suggests that measures of worth based on internal comparisons (job evaluation) and external comparisons (market surveys) can be compared. In this case, many disagreements between the two measures appear. Internal comparisons suggest that women's jobs are underpaid, whereas external comparisons are less supportive of this argument. For example, although the licensed practical nurse job receives 173 job evaluation points and the truck driver position receives 97 points, the market rate (and thus the State of Washington employer rate) for the truck driver position is $1,493 per month versus only $1,030 per month for the nurse. The truck driver is paid nearly 127 percent more than the pay policy line would predict, whereas the nurse is paid only 75 percent of the pay policy line prediction.

One potential problem with using job evaluation to establish worth independent of the market is that job evaluation procedures were never designed for this purpose.[43] Rather, as demonstrated earlier, their major use is in helping to capture the market pay policy and then applying that to nonkey jobs for which market data are not available. In other words, job evaluation has typically been used to help apply the market pay policy, quite the opposite of replacing the market in pay setting.

As with any regulation, there are also concerns that EEO regulation obstructs market forces, which, according to economic theory, provide the most efficient means of pricing and allocating people to jobs. In theory, moving away from a reliance on market forces would result in some jobs being paid too much and others too little, leading to an oversupply of workers for the former and an undersupply for the latter. In addition, some empirical evidence suggests that a comparable-worth policy would not have much impact on the relative earnings of women in the private sector.[44] One limitation of such a policy is that it targets single employers, ignoring that men and women tend to work for different employers.[45] To the extent that segregation by employer contributes to pay differences between men and women, comparable worth would not be effective. In other words, to the extent that sex-based pay differences are the result of

TABLE 11.12 Job Evaluation Points, Monthly Prevailing Market Pay Rates, and Proportion of Incumbents in Job Who Are Female

BENCHMARK TITLE	MONTHLY EVALUATION POINTS	PREVAILING RATES[a]	PREVAILING RATE AS PERCENTAGE OF PREDICTED[b]	PERCENTAGE OF FEMALE INCUMBENTS
Warehouse worker	97	$1,286	109.1%	15.4%
Truck driver	97	1,493	126.6	13.6
Laundry worker	105	884	73.2	80.3
Telephone operator	118	887	71.6	95.7
Retail sales clerk	121	921	74.3	100.0
Data entry operator	125	1,017	82.1	96.5
Intermediate clerk typist	129	968	76.3	96.7
Highway engineering tech	133	1,401	110.4	11.1
Word processing equipment operator	138	1,082	83.2	98.3
Correctional officer	173	1,436	105.0	9.3
Licensed practical nurse	173	1,030	75.3	89.5
Automotive mechanic	175	1,646	120.4	0.0
Maintenance carpenter	197	1,707	118.9	2.3
Secretary	197	1,122	78.1	98.5
Administrative assistant	226	1,334	90.6	95.1
Chemist	277	1,885	116.0	20.0
Civil engineer	287	1,885	116.0	0.0
Highway engineer 3	345	1,980	110.4	3.0
Registered nurse	348	1,368	76.3	92.2
Librarian 3	353	1,625	90.6	84.6
Senior architect	362	2,240	121.8	16.7
Senior computer systems analyst	384	2,080	113.1	17.8
Personnel representative	410	1,956	101.2	45.6
Physician	861	3,857	128.0	13.6

[a]Prevailing market rate as of July 1, 1980. Midpoint of job range set equal to this amount.
[b]Predicted salary is based on regression of prevailing market rate on job evaluation points $2.43 × job evaluation points + 936.19, r = .77.
SOURCE: Reprinted with permission of *Public Personnel Management,* published by the International Personnel Management Association.

men and women working in different organizations with different pay levels, such policies will have little impact.

Perhaps most important, despite potential problems with market rates, the courts have consistently ruled that using the going market rates of pay is an acceptable defense in comparable-worth litigation suits.[46] The rationale is that organizations face competitive labor and product markets. Paying less or more than the market rate will put the organization at a competitive disadvantage. Thus, there is no comparable-worth legal mandate in the U.S. private sector. On the other hand, by the early 1990s, almost one-half of the states had begun or completed comparable-worth adjustments to public-sector employees' pay. In addition, in 1988 the Canadian province of Ontario mandated comparable worth in both the private and public sectors.

Another line of inquiry has focused on pinpointing where women's pay falls behind that of men. Some evidence indicates that women lose ground at the time they are hired and actually do better once they are employed for some time.[47] One interpretation is that when actual job performance (rather than the limited general qualification information available on applicants) is used in decisions, women may be less likely to encounter unequal treatment. If so, more attention needs to be devoted to ensuring fair treatment of applicants and new employees.[48] On the other hand, a "Glass Ceiling" is believed to exist in some organizations that allows women (and minorities) to come within sight of the top echelons of management, but not advance to them.

It is likely, however, that organizations will differ in terms of where women's earnings disadvantages arise. For example, advancement opportunities for women and other protected groups may be hindered by unequal access to the "old boy" or informal network. This, in turn, may be reflected in lower rates of pay. Mentoring programs have been suggested as one means of improving access. Indeed, one study found that mentoring was successful, having a significant positive effect on the pay of both men and women, with women receiving a greater payoff in percentage terms than men.[49]

MINIMUM WAGE, OVERTIME, AND PREVAILING WAGE LAWS

The 1938 **Fair Labor Standards Act (FLSA)** establishes a minimum wage for jobs that now stands at $5.15 per hour. State laws may specify higher minimum wages. The FLSA also permits a subminimum training wage that is approximately 85 percent of the **minimum wage,** which employers are permitted to pay most employees under the age of 20 for a period of up to 90 days.

The FLSA also requires that employees be paid at a rate of one and a half times their hourly rate for each hour of overtime worked beyond 40 hours in a week. The hourly rate includes not only the base wage but also other components such as bonuses and piece-rate payments. The FLSA requires overtime pay for any hours beyond 40 in a week that an employer "suffers or permits" the employee to perform, regardless of whether the work is done at the workplace or whether the employer explicitly asked or expected the employee to do it.[50] If the employer knows the employee is working overtime but neither moves to stop it nor pays time and a half, a violation of the FLSA may have occurred. A department store was the target of a lawsuit that claimed employees were "encouraged" to, among other things, write thank-you notes to customers outside of scheduled work hours but were not compensated for this work. Although the company denied encouraging this off-the-clock work, it reached an out-of-court settlement to pay between $15 million and $30 million in back pay (plus legal fees of $7.5 million) to approximately 85,000 sales representatives it employed between 1987 and 1990.[51]

Executive, professional, administrative, and outside sales occupations are **exempt** from FLSA coverage. *Nonexempt* occupations are covered and include most hourly jobs. One estimate is that just over 20 percent of employees fall into the exempt category.[52] Exempt status depends on job responsibilities and salary, and the standards can be fairly complicated. For example, seven criteria, including whether two or more people are supervised and whether there is authority to hire and fire, are used to determine whether an employee is an executive. The Wage and Hour Division, Employment Standards Administration, U.S. Department of Labor, and its local offices can provide further information on these definitions.

Two pieces of legislation—the 1931 Davis–Bacon Act and the 1936 Walsh–Healy Public Contracts Act—require federal contractors to pay employees no less than the prevailing wages in the area. Davis–Bacon covers construction contractors receiving federal money of more than $2,000. Typically, prevailing wages have been based on relevant union contracts, partly because only 30 percent of the local labor force is required to be used in establishing the prevailing rate. Walsh–Healy covers all government contractors receiving $10,000 or more in federal funds.

Finally, employers must take care in deciding whether a person working on its premises is classified as an employee or independent contractor. We address this issue in Chapter 13.

SUMMARY

In this chapter, we have discussed the nature of the pay structure and its component parts, the pay level, and the job structure. Equity theory suggests that social comparisons are an important influence on how employees evaluate their pay. Employees make external comparisons between their pay and the pay they believe is received by employees in other organizations. Such comparisons may have consequences for employee attitudes and retention. Employees also make internal comparisons between what they receive and what they perceive others within the organization are paid. These types of comparisons may have consequences for internal movement, cooperation, and attitudes (e.g., organization commitment). Such comparisons play an important role in the controversy over executive pay, as illustrated by the focus of critics on the ratio of executive pay to that of lower-paid workers.

Pay benchmarking surveys and job evaluation are two administrative tools widely used in managing the pay-level and job-structure components of the pay structure, which influence employee social comparisons. Pay surveys also permit organizations to benchmark their labor costs against other organizations'. Globalization is increasing the need for organizations to be competitive in both their labor costs and productivity.

The nature of pay structures is undergoing a fundamental change in many organizations. One change is the move to fewer pay levels to reduce labor costs and bureaucracy. Second, some employers are shifting from paying employees for narrow jobs to giving them broader responsibilities and paying them to learn the necessary skills.

Finally, a theme that runs through this chapter and the next is the importance of process in managing employee compensation. How a new program is designed, decided on, implemented, and communicated is perhaps just as important as its core characteristics.

DISCUSSION QUESTIONS

1. You have been asked to evaluate whether your organization's current pay structure makes sense in view of what competing organizations are paying. How would you determine what organizations to compare your organization with? Why might your organization's pay structure differ from those in competing organizations? What are the potential consequences of having a pay structure that is out of line relative to those of your competitors?
2. Top management has decided that the organization is too bureaucratic and has too many layers of jobs to compete effectively. You have been asked to suggest innovative alternatives to the traditional "job-based" approach to employee compensation and to list the advantages and disadvantages of these new approaches.
3. If major changes of the type mentioned in question 2 are to be made, what types of so-called process issues need to be considered? Of what relevance is equity theory in helping to understand how employees might react to changes in the pay structure?
4. Are executive pay levels unreasonable? Why or why not?
5. Your company plans to build a new manufacturing plant but is undecided where to locate it. What factors would you consider in choosing in which country (or state) to build the plant?
6. You have been asked to evaluate whether a company's pay structure is fair to women and minorities. How would you go about answering this question?

WEB EXERCISE

As shown in the "Competing through High Performance Work Systems" box (see pages 402 and 403), there are several web sites that provide salary surveys for clerical, professional, and managerial jobs. One of these sites is Job Smart.

Go to www.jobsmart.org. Click on "Salary Surveys." Click on "Profession-specific salary surveys." From the list of professions presented choose one that interests you. Review the information provided and answer the following questions.

1. What is the value of this web site for employers? For employees?
2. From an HRM perspective, what are the advantages of using web sites such as this one to establish salary ranges and adjust the current salary structure? What are the disadvantages?

MANAGING PEOPLE: FROM THE PAGES OF "BUSINESS WEEK"

BusinessWeek The CEO and the Board

It was, as always, an extravagantly festive event. On Aug. 10, some 500 guests of H.J. Heinz Chairman and Chief Executive Anthony J.F. O'Reilly gathered under chandeliers in a mammoth white pavilion set up at the swanky Leopardstown horse-racing track outside Dublin. More than half were flown in from around the world, put up at Ireland's finest hotels, and feted at a lavish three-day bash. Guests included H.J. Heinz Co. executives and directors, Wall Street analysts, and assorted politicians, tycoons, and friends. In recent years, Paul Newman, William Kennedy Smith, and the CEOs of PepsiCo, Sara Lee, and Clorox have joined in the fun.

A world-class salesman, bon vivant, and raconteur, O'Reilly has reigned as king of the $9.4 billion food powerhouse for the past 18 years. And perhaps nowhere is that truer than in the corporate boardroom at Heinz's Pittsburgh headquarters, where O'Reilly is first among equals on a board that includes many insiders, business associates, and even personal friends of the charismatic CEO. "Tony is larger than life, and he knows it," says Heinz director Donald R. Keough, 71, a former Coca-Cola Co. president and longtime friend.

In part, that's because he has performed: Through much of his tenure, shareholders have had little to complain about. He revived the company in the 1980s, becoming a Wall Street star. Even though growth is no longer red-hot, Heinz still does about as well as its average food-industry peer.

So why has Tony O'Reilly become the next target of activist investors leading the corporate governance movement?

The answer has as much to do with the evolution of corporate governance as it does with O'Reilly or Heinz. For despite O'Reilly's performance, unhappy shareholders such as Teachers Insurance & Annuity Assn.–College Retirement Equities Fund (TIAA–CREF) and California Public Employees' Retirement System (CalPERS) believe it is a textbook example of what a board should not be: a cozy club of loyalists headed by a powerful and charismatic chieftain. Now that view is being put to the test. Since late last year, TIAA–CREF—the $101 billion pension fund, which owns 2.7 million Heinz shares worth $113 million—has been waging a behind-the-scenes battle with O'Reilly over governance. Early next year, CalPERS is expected to push for board changes at Heinz. "The board is way too large, way too dominated by very old men, and it has not had enough turnover," says Kayla J. Gillan, CalPERS' general counsel.

For O'Reilly and the company he leads, the stakes are huge. Critics believe a stronger board would likely rein in his free-spending ways. O'Reilly's lavish bash was the 15th in a row, for example, even though Heinz is in the midst of laying off 2,500 employees. Heinz says the event, which also includes meetings with analysts and big customers, is an effective corporate marketing tool that is no more expensive than sponsoring a golf tournament.

A tougher board might also trim the generous options that have made O'Reilly one of America's highest-paid CEOs—even as his company's performance has slipped. And pressure on O'Reilly to pass the baton to his hard-charging no. 2, William R. Johnson, a move many on Wall Street would like, could grow. "I think Johnson is the right man for the times at Heinz," says Arthur B. Cecil, an analyst at T. Rowe Price Associates Inc., another big shareholder.

But the stakes go well beyond Heinz. The issues involved—what makes for an effective board or a good director—are at the core of a much broader debate about boardroom practices that is raging throughout Corporate America. After spending much of the past decade going after lackluster management, activist investors are turning a sterner eye on the job done by boards and directors, regardless of how a company or its stock are doing. If investors succeed in forcing tougher boardroom practices at Heinz, many other lackluster boards are likely to face similar pressure to shape up.

Such moves have gained momentum since November, when a National Association of Corporate Directors panel headed by governance guru Ira Millstein issued a sweeping set of guidelines that outlined "best practices" for boards. Early this year, TIAA–CREF began screening its corporate investments on 25 governance issues, from the ages of directors to their potential conflicts of interest with management. Where boards don't measure up, TIAA–CREF is prodding even well-run companies to strengthen the quality of their directors. CalPERS joined the fray in June by proposing its own strict board guidelines. Within months it, too, plans to target those that fail to make the grade. Even the Business Roundtable is getting into the act, in part to head off tougher measures by activists. It plans to publish its own set of principles on Sept. 10.

The list of best practices favored by the activists today is extensive. Since the aim is to ensure that directors ally themselves with shareholders, not management, the guiding principle is director independence. Governance experts believe boards should have no more than two or three inside directors, and key audit, nominating, and compensation committees should be composed entirely of outsiders. All director retainers should be paid in stock. Extras, such as pensions, which activists fear compromise independence, should be eliminated. No director should earn consulting, legal, or other fees from the company. Moreover, interlocking directorships—execs who serve on each others' boards—should be banned. Activists believe they encourage members to look out for each other.

Still, the new board standards have come in for some vociferous criticism. Many executives—and, indeed, many investors—remain skeptical. Although hundreds of companies are considering them, so far only a few—Ashland Inc. is one—have adopted them in any significant way. Citing such top companies as Walt Disney Co., which has also been criticized for weak boardroom practices, many directors dismiss the guidelines as rigid and academic. More to the point, they say they bear no correlation to performance. "I'm not for blanket rules," says John C. Bogle, chairman of mutual-fund giant Vanguard Group and a director of Mead Corp. "When you get into valuations of a stock, it's hard to know where one would put governance with fundamentals like dividend and earnings growth and financial strength."

If shareholders are doing well, O'Reilly and other skeptics ask, does the makeup of the board—or the rules under which it operates—really make a difference? In the past, the answers might well have been no. But governance experts now recognize it took years of decline and board inaction at such companies as American Express, GM, and Westinghouse Electric before a looming crisis forced reforms. So activists are focusing on avoiding a meltdown in the first place. "The key to good governance is to keep a well-performing corporation from becoming a poor-performing one," says B. Kenneth West, the exchairman of Harris Trust & Savings Bank who is a senior consultant for governance at TIAA–CREF.

That's what makes Heinz a near-perfect candidate for this fight. It's not like General Motors Corp. in 1992. In fact, Heinz isn't doing badly. Excluding a $420.9 million restructuring charge, the global food giant posted a 9.6 percent rise in net income, to $722.8 million, in fiscal 1997, ended on Apr. 30. Moreover, O'Reilly has made several moves long demanded by Wall Street during the past year. In mid-1996, he finally anointed William Johnson his heir apparent by naming him president and chief operating officer. In March, O'Reilly unveiled with much fanfare Project Millennia, a reorganization plan under which at least 25 plants will be closed or sold.

That's still far from O'Reilly's glory days. After taking the helm in 1979, he wowed investors by slashing expenses, stealing market share, and expanding globally. Profits and sales took off, as did Heinz stock. Total shareholder returns averaged 31 percent a year in the 1980s, nearly double the Standard & Poor's 500-stock index's 16.8 percent.

DUBIOUS DISTINCTION. But Heinz has offered up far more modest performance of late. Since the start of the decade, operating earnings have grown 43 percent; by contrast, rival Campbell Soup Co. has increased its income by 140 percent, to a projected $1.5 billion for fiscal 1997. And over the past five years, Heinz's annual shareholder returns of 13.9 percent have consistently underperformed the S&P, as well as the S&P food index. Only a runup since Johnson's appointment as president—the stock has gained 35 percent—has allowed Heinz to catch up with its food-industry rivals.

Nevertheless, the Heinz board continues to pay O'Reilly like a superstar. His total compensation of $182.9 million in the past six years ranks him among a handful of the best-paid CEOs. In five of those six years, he has won the dubious distinction of being among the five CEOs cited by *Business Week* as giving shareholders the least for their money. While much of that stems from gains on options granted early in his tenure, the hefty awards have continued even as performance has slipped. Indeed, the board has been so generous with O'Reilly's options that he is now Heinz's largest individual shareholder, with 1.6 percent of the stock.

A comparison with Campbell Soup Co. is telling. Last year alone, O'Reilly got a new options grant on 750,000 shares. That's more than the 646,800 shares Campbell Chairman David W. Johnson got in the past seven years combined. Still, O'Reilly defends his hefty options packet. "There could be no more honorable or fairer way [to be paid] in American capitalism," he insists.

That's not the only contrast between Heinz and Campbell that rankles shareholder activists. Once under duress itself from investors for being a lackluster, family-dominated sleeper, Campbell ousted the CEO in 1990 and hired outsider Johnson from Gerber Products Co. Since then, the company has become a pioneer in corporate governance: In 1992, Campbell became the first major company to publish board guidelines.

The shift appears to be paying off. Since 1992, Campbell's annual shareholder returns of 20.9 percent have far outdistanced those of Heinz. "You have to wonder how Campbell, with a model board, is outperforming Heinz," says Charles M. Elson, a law professor at Stetson University College of Law and a governance expert. "This is a captured and incestuous board. That may explain the difference."

The independence of the Heinz board is at the core of the dispute between O'Reilly and the governance crowd. For starters, Heinz' board remains loaded with insiders. Ten of the 19 board members are current or former Heinz employees. Governance experts believe that having so many insiders lends too much support for O'Reilly. "Why would an insider challenge the boss?" asks Elson. "That's a nice way to lose your job very quickly."

O'Reilly not only dismisses his critics, he argues vehemently that companies are better off with many inside directors. "If you have only one insider," he says, "the only person who talks to that board is the CEO, and every view is filtered through one mind to the board." Heinz President Johnson, a four-year board member who spoke on behalf of the inside directors, insists that they say what they think. "I' m sure there were times when Tony or a couple of other senior guys were rolling their eyes when someone said something he wished he hadn't heard," says Johnson.

Most of the outside directors who gather around the sierra chica granite table in Heinz's windowless boardroom are longtime colleagues or friends of O'Reilly, and not one outsider is a sitting CEO. Indeed, how the powerful executive maneuvered over the past 18 years is nothing less than a study in how to craft a board of directors.

As was common when O'Reilly became CEO in 1979, many board members had crossed paths elsewhere: Three outsiders also were directors of Mobil Corp., where O'Reilly had become a board member. Within a year, O'Reilly joined the Heinz board's nominating committee. By 1984, he took over as committee chairman and began to dominate the selection process.

To governance experts, that's a huge no-no. To foster independence, they believe board selection should remain in the hands of outside directors. They also frown on cross-directorships, since that can lead to a "you scratch my back, I'll scratch yours" mentality among directors who sit on boards together. But at nearly every turn, O'Reilly handpicked his new directors—almost always from boards he already sat on or from organizations affiliated with Heinz.

O'Reilly insists the shared experiences allow him to better evaluate potential directors. He defends his role as nominating committee chairman, claiming it allows him to get better talent. Adversaries counter that his role simply ensures he has virtually free rein to handpick his own directors. Complains Robert A.G. Monks, a principal in Lens Inc., an activist investment fund, "Everybody knows it's a matter of personal loyalty to the guy who put him or her there."

He and other experts also point to another troubling issue: O'Reilly has treated his board as generously as it has treated him. In three of his first four years as CEO, O'Reilly and directors hiked the pay of all outsiders and added lifelong director pensions. Later, O'Reilly added other raises and perks, including a $1 million donation to charity after a director's death. Along with annual retainers of $30,000 and yearly grants of 300 shares of stock, directors receive $1,500 for each meeting they attend. In all, it's pretty generous—about 20 percent above average for the nation's 100 largest companies, according to consultants Spencer Stuart.

SLOW MOVER. No less problematic is the fact that the board's executive committee, which has the authority to act when the board is not in session, is composed entirely of insiders. Chaired by O'Reilly, the committee regularly meets the day before the full board. Most companies restrict their purpose to emergency business. Not Heinz. In six of the past seven years, its executive committee has met more often than the board. By comparison, Campbell Soup's five-member executive committee has only one insider and has met once in three years. "O'Reilly has created two classes of directors: those that make the decisions and those that bless them," charges John M. Nash, president of the National Association of Corporate Directors. O'Reilly makes no apologies, arguing that the executive panel is more of a "reporting committee" that helps prepare for the full board.

Those who want Heinz to reform its board are in for a long fight. In the past, outside efforts to get Heinz to improve its governance practices have failed. While TIAA–CREF and CalPERS are stronger adversaries than Heinz has faced before, O'Reilly clearly has plenty of board support.

So far, that has added up to a stalemate. After a series of letters from TIAA–CREF and a meeting with West, asking O'Reilly to trim the insiders, he still refuses to budge—the only one of seven companies targeted by TIAA–CREF to do so. In fact, in June, O'Reilly added one more inside director—giving current and former executives a board majority. Meanwhile, activists want most of the old-timers to go, and some have asked that directors' pensions be eliminated and a larger share of directors' compensation be paid in stock.

Although O'Reilly says he might concede on the last two issues—if the board wants it—he insists he won't significantly reduce the number of insiders. "Outsiders are outsiders. They simply are not committed to the board in the same way as people who have their careers at stake here. Boards that listen to one man will be the prisoners of that man."

Perhaps. But many who have looked at the rarefied and privileged realm of Heinz's board, believe the company's inside and outside directors alike already are prisoners to one man: O'Reilly. If there are no board changes soon, the lobbying behind the scenes by TIAA–CREF could erupt into a public boardroom brawl. If it does, investors may finally get a chance to weigh in on whether they think boardroom practices really do matter.

QUESTIONS

1. Why has Heinz's corporate governance been criticized?
2. What, if any, changes would you recommend making to Heinz's corporate governance?
3. Is Anthony J.F. O'Reilly paid appropriately? Why or why not?

SOURCE: "The CEO and the Board," *Business Week*, September 15, 1997.

NOTES

1. J.S. Adams, "Inequity in Social Exchange," in *Advances in Experimental Social Psychology*, ed. L. Berkowitz (New York: Academic Press, 1965); P. S. Goodman, "An Examination of Referents Used in the Evaluation of Pay," *Organizational Behavior and Human Performance* 12 (1974), pp. 170–95.
2. J.B. Miner, *Theories of Organizational Behavior* (Hinsdale, IL: Dryden Press, 1980).
3. Steve Lohr, "Ford and Chrysler Outpace Japanese in Reducing Costs," *The New York Times*, June 18, 1992, p. D1.
4. B. Gerhart and G.T. Milkovich, "Organizational Differences in Managerial Compensation and Financial Performance," *Academy of Management Journal* 33 (1990), pp. 663–91; E.L. Groshen, "Why Do Wages Vary among Employers?" *Economic Review* 24 (1988), pp. 19–38.
5. G.A. Akerlof, "Gift Exchange and Efficiency-Wage Theory: Four Views," *American Economic Review* 74 (1984),

pp. 79–83; J.L. Yellen, "Efficiency Wage Models of Unemployment," *American Economic Review* 74 (1984), pp. 200–5.

6. S.L. Rynes and G.T. Milkovich, "Wage Surveys: Dispelling Some Myths about the 'Market Wage'," *Personnel Psychology* 39 (1986), pp. 71–90.
7. B. Gerhart and G.T. Milkovich, "Employee Compensation: Research and Practice," in *Handbook of Industrial and Organizational Psychology*, 2d ed., ed. M.D. Dunnette and L.M. Hough (Palo Alto, CA: Consulting Psychologists Press, 1992).
8. G.T. Milkovich and J. Newman, *Compensation* (Homewood, IL: BPI/Irwin, 1990).
9. B. Gerhart, G.T. Milkovich, and B. Murray, "Pay, Performance, and Participation," in *Research Frontiers in Industrial Relations and Human Resources*, ed. D. Lewin, O.S. Mitchell, and P.D. Sherer (Madison, WI: IRRA, 1992).
10. C.H. Fay, "External Pay Relationships," in *Compensation and Benefits*, ed. L.R. Gomez-Mejia (Washington, DC: Bureau of National Affairs, 1989).
11. J.P. Pfeffer and A. Davis-Blake, "Understanding Organizational Wage Structures: A Resource Dependence Approach," *Academy of Management Journal* 30 (1987), pp. 437–55.
12. H.Z. Levine, "The View from the Board: The State of Compensation and Benefits Today," *Compensation and Benefits Review* 24 (March 1992), p. 24.
13. C.M. Solomon, "Global Compensation: Learn the ABCs," *Personnel Journal* (July 1995), p. 70; R.A. Swaak, "Expatriate Management: The Search for Best Practices," *Compensation and Benefits Review* (March–April 1995), p. 21.
14. *1997–1998 Survey of Geographic Pay Differential Policies and Practices* (Rochester, WI: Runzeimer International).
15. E.E. Lawler III, *Pay and Organizational Development* (Reading, MA: Addison–Wesley, 1981).
16. R. Folger and M.A. Konovsky, "Effects of Procedural and Distributive Justice on Reactions to Pay Raise Decisions," *Academy of Management Journal* 32 (1989), pp. 115–30; Gerhart, Milkovich, and Murray, "Pay, Performance"; J. Greenberg, "Determinants of Perceived Fairness of Performance Evaluations," *Journal of Applied Psychology* 71 (1986), pp. 340–42; H.G. Heneman III, "Pay Satisfaction," *Research in Personnel and Human Resource Management* 3 (1985), pp. 115–39.
17. J. Greenberg, "Employee Theft as a Reaction to Underpayment of Inequity: The Hidden Cost of Pay Cuts," *Journal of Applied Psychology* 75 (1990), pp. 561–68.
18. Adams, "Inequity in Social Exchange"; C.J. Berger, C.A. Olson, and J.W. Boudreau, "The Effect of Unionism on Job Satisfaction: The Role of Work-Related Values and Perceived Rewards," *Organizational Behavior and Human Performance* 32 (1983), pp. 284–324; P. Capelli and P.D. Sherer, "Assessing Worker Attitudes under a Two-Tier Wage Plan," *Industrial and Labor Relations Review* 43 (1990), pp. 225–44; R.W. Rice, S.M. Phillips, and D.B. McFarlin, "Multiple Discrepancies and Pay Satisfaction," *Journal of Applied Psychology* 75 (1990), pp. 386–93.
19. Capelli and Sherer, "Assessing Worker Attitudes."
20. This section draws freely on B. Gerhart and R. D. Bretz, "Employee Compensation," in *Organization and Management of Advanced Manufacturing*, ed. W. Karwowski and G. Salvendy (New York: Wiley, 1994), pp. 81–101.
21. R. M. Kanter, *When Giants Learn to Dance* (New York: Simon & Schuster, 1989); E.E. Lawler III, *Strategic Pay* (San Francisco: Jossey–Bass, 1990); "Farewell, Fast Track," *Business Week* (December 10, 1990), pp. 192–200.
22. P.R. Eyers, "Realignment Ties Pay to Performance," *Personnel Journal* (January 1993), p. 74.
23. Lawler, *Strategic Pay*; G. Ledford, "3 Cases on Skill-Based Pay: An Overview," *Compensation and Benefits Review* (March–April 1991), pp. 11–23; G.E. Ledford, "Paying for the Skills, Knowledge, Competencies of Knowledge Workers," *Compensation and Benefits Review* (July–August 1995), p. 55.
24. Ledford, "3 Cases."
25. P.S. Adler, "Managing Flexible Automation," *California Management Review* 30, no. 3 (1988), pp. 34–56; T. Cummings and M. Blumberg, "Advanced Manufacturing Technology and Work Design," in *The Human Side of Advanced Manufacturing Technology*, ed. T.D. Wall, C.W. Clegg, and N.J. Kemp (Chichester, Great Britain: John Wiley & Sons, 1987); Y.P. Gupta, "Human Aspects of Flexible Manufacturing Systems," *Production and Inventory Management Journal* 30, no. 2 (1989), pp. 30–36; R.E. Walton and G. I. Susman, "People Policies for the New Machines," *Harvard Business Review* 87, no. 2 (1987), pp. 98–106; J.P. Womack, D.T. Jones, and D. Roos, *The Machine That Changed the World* (New York: Macmillan, 1990).
26. T.D. Wall, J.M. Corbett, R. Martin, C.W. Clegg, and P.R. Jackson, "Advanced Manufacturing Technology, Work Design, and Performance: A Change Study," *Journal of Applied Psychology* 75 (1990), pp. 691–97.
27. Womack et al., *The Machine That Changed the World*, p. 56.
28. Lawler, *Strategic Pay*.
29. Ibid.; Gerhart and Milkovich, "Employee Compensation."
30. B.C. Murray and B. Gerhart, "An Empirical Analysis of a Skill-Based Pay Program and Plant Performance Outcomes," *Academy of Management Journal* 41, no. 1 (1998), pp. 68–78.
31. Ibid.; N. Gupta, D. Jenkins, and W. Curington, "Paying for Knowledge: Myths and Realities," *National Productivity Review* (Spring 1986), pp. 107–23.

32. Data from U.S. Bureau of Labor Statistics website.
33. *Education at a Glance—OECD Indicators 1997* (Paris: OECD, 1997).
34. National Accounts (Paris: OECD, 1998); *Main Economic Indicators* (Paris: OECD, February 1998).
35. C. Sparks and M. Greiner, "U.S. and Foreign Productivity and Labor Costs," *Monthly Labor Review* (February 1997), pp. 26–35.
36. E. Faltermayer, "U.S. Companies Come Back Home," *Fortune*, December 30, 1991, pp. 106ff.
37. Ibid.
38. A. Farnham, "The Trust Gap," *Fortune*, December 4, 1989, pp. 56ff.
39. D.M. Cowherd and D.I. Levine, "Product Quality and Pay Equity between Lower-Level Employees and Top Management: An Investigation of Distributive Justice Theory," *Administrative Science Quarterly* 37 (1992), pp. 302–20.
40. Bureau of Labor Statistics, *Current Population Surveys* (website).
41. P. Ryscavage and P. Henle, "Earnings Inequality in the 1980s," *Monthly Labor Review* 113, no. 12 (1990), pp. 3–16; F. D. Blau and M. A. Beller, "Trends in Earnings Differentials by Gender, 1971–1981," *Industrial and Labor Relations Review* 41 (1988), pp. 513–29; L.A. Carlson and C. Swartz, "The Earnings of Women and Ethnic Minorities, 1959–1979," *Industrial and Labor Relations Review* 41 (1988), pp. 530–46; M.W. Horrigan and J.P. Markey, "Recent Gains in Women's Earnings: Better Pay or Longer Hours?" *Monthly Labor Review* 113, no. 7 (June 1990), pp. 11–17.
42. B. Gerhart, "Gender Differences in Current and Starting Salaries: The Role of Performance, College Major, and Job Title," *Industrial and Labor Relations Review* 43 (1990), pp. 418–33; G.G. Cain, "The Economic Analysis of Labor-Market Discrimination: A Survey," in *Handbook of Labor Economics*, ed. O. Ashenfelter and R. Layard (New York: North-Holland, 1986), pp. 694–785.
43. D.P. Schwab, "Job Evaluation and Pay-Setting: Concepts and Practices," in *Comparable Worth: Issues and Alternatives*, ed. E.R. Livernash (Washington, DC: Equal Employment Advisory Council, 1980).
44. B. Gerhart and N. El Cheikh, "Earnings and Percentage Female: A Longitudinal Study," *Industrial Relations* 30 (1991), pp. 62–78; R.S. Smith, "Comparable Worth: Limited Coverage and the Exacerbation of Inequality," *Industrial and Labor Relations Review* 61 (1988), pp. 227–39.
45. W.T. Bielby and J.N. Baron, "Men and Women at Work: Sex Segregation and Statistical Discrimination," *American Journal of Sociology* 91 (1986), pp. 759–99.
46. Rynes and Milkovich, "Wage Surveys"; G.T. Milkovich and J. Newman, *Compensation* (Homewood, IL: BPI/Irwin, 1993).
47. Gerhart, "Gender Differences in Current and Starting Salaries"; B. Gerhart and G.T. Milkovich, "Salaries, Salary Growth, and Promotions of Men and Women in a Large, Private Firm," in *Pay Equity: Empirical Inquiries*, ed. R. Michael, H. Hartmann, and B. O'Farrell (Washington, DC: National Academy Press, 1989).
48. Gerhart, "Gender Differences in Current and Starting Salaries"; B. Gerhart and S. Rynes, "Determinants and Consequences of Salary Negotiations by Graduating Male and Female MBAs," *Journal of Applied Psychology* 76 (1991), pp. 256–62.
49. D.J. Brass, "Men's and Women's Networks: A Study of Interaction Patterns and Influence in an Organization," *Academy of Management Journal* 28 (1985), pp. 327–43; B. Rosen, M. E. Templeton, and K. Kirchline, "First Few Years on the Job: Women in Management," *Business Horizons* 24, no. 12 (1981), pp. 26–29; K. Cannings and C. Montmarquette, "Managerial Momentum: A Simultaneous Model of the Career Progress of Male and Female Managers," *Industrial and Labor Relations Review* 44 (1991), pp. 212–28; R.A. Noe, "Women and Mentoring: A Review and Research Agenda," *Academy of Management Review* 13 (1988), pp. 65–78; G.F. Dreher and R.A. Ash, "A Comparative Study of Mentoring among Men and Women in Managerial, Professional, and Technical Positions," *Journal of Applied Psychology* 75 (1990), pp. 539–46.
50. A.W. Sherman Jr. and G. W. Bohlander, *Managing Human Resources* (Cincinnati: South-Western Publishing, 1992), p. 334.
51. G.A. Patterson, "Nordstrom Inc. Sets Back-Pay Accord on Suit Alleging 'Off-the-Clock' Work," *The Wall Street Journal*, January 12, 1993, p. A2.
52. R.I. Henderson, *Compensation Management: Rewarding Performance* (Englewood Cliffs, NJ: Prentice–Hall, 1989), p. 56.

Recognizing Employee Contributions with Pay

OBJECTIVES

After reading this chapter, you should be able to

1. Describe the fundamental pay programs for recognizing employees' contributions to the organization's success.
2. List the advantages and disadvantages of the pay programs.
3. List the major factors to consider in matching the pay strategy to the organization's strategy.
4. Explain the importance of process issues such as communication in compensation management.
5. Describe how U.S. pay practices compare with those of other countries.

Pitfalls in Paying for Performance

ENTER THE WORLD OF BUSINESS

In 1996 and 1997, Prudential Insurance took a total of $2.05 billion in pretax charges to cover the expected costs of a class-action settlement to compensate aggrieved customers. The settlement stems from a deceptive sales practice called churning, where customers with long-standing life insurance policies that had built up cash values were persuaded to take on new, larger policies with the assurance that the new policies would not cost any more. Agents earned substantial commissions by selling new policies. Sales managers and some executives also stood to gain because of bonuses linked to sales volume. Customers were allegedly tricked into signing authorization forms that permitted agents to cash in the old policies to pay the new, large premiums. When customers later needed to cash in their original policies to access the money they thought was there, it was gone. In other cases, when the cash value was drained by the premiums, customers were hit with large premium bills that they could not pay, thus losing coverage.

In suburban Nashville, bonus plan arrangements have been critical issues at Saturn, where the collective bargaining agreement with the United Auto Workers (UAW) specifies three components of pay. First is base pay that is approximately 12 percent less than what UAW workers at other General Motors (GM) plants receive. Second is a 12 percent at-risk component that depends on training (5 percent), quality (5 percent), and team skills (2 percent). If these goals are met, workers at Saturn earn the same as workers at other GM plants. Third, Saturn has a reward component that pays out depending on meeting schedule, productivity, and quality goals. In 1995 and 1996, bonuses at Saturn averaged roughly $10,000 per worker, resulting in Saturn workers earning several thousand dollars more than their GM counterparts. However, Saturn announced that 1997 bonuses would average $2,000, meaning that Saturn workers would earn about $4,000 less than their GM counterparts. Bonus payments were lower because of decreasing demand for Saturns and a resulting cutback in production.

As a consequence, Saturn workers voted to hold a referendum to decide whether to keep the unique Saturn–UAW collective bargaining contract (with its lower base pay) or change to the more traditional contract covering all other UAW members at GM. In March 1998, Saturn workers voted by a 2 to 1 margin to keep their unique contract. This margin was significantly closer than a similar vote held in 1992, which had a margin of 4 to 1. Further, one factor that helped to carry the vote was the UAW's ability to renegotiate the production goal (one criterion in determining bonus payout) down from 310,000 to 280,000 vehicles. The maximum bonus would be $5,000, less than the $10,000 of 1995 and 1996. Still, if the new goals were met, it would mean a larger payout than in 1997.

SOURCE: B. Gerhart, "Balancing Results and Behaviors in Pay for Performance Plans," *The Executive Handbook of Compensation*, ed. Charles Fay (Free Press, forthcoming). Reprinted with permission.

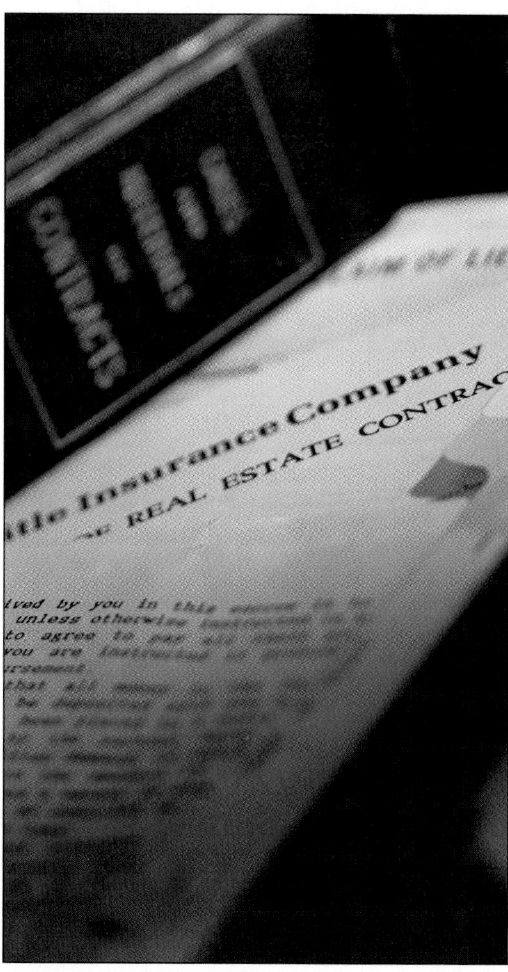

Introduction

The opening vignette illustrates some of the challenges in using the employee compensation system to motivate employee behavior. The problem is that the compensation system's power is sometimes misdirected, so it motivates the wrong behaviors. The pay system must encourage behaviors that both contribute to profits in the short run and build customer satisfaction for long-term success. In other situations, changing economic circumstances may lead to employee relations problems if employees believe they are being penalized for factors beyond their control.

In the preceding chapter, we focused on setting pay for jobs. In this chapter, we focus on using pay to recognize and reward employees' contributions to the organization's success. Employees' pay does not depend solely on the job they hold. Instead, differences in performance (individual, group, or organization), seniority, skills, and so forth are used as a basis for differentiating pay among employees.[1]

Several key questions arise in evaluating different pay programs for recognizing contributions. First, what are the costs of the program? Second, what is the expected return (e.g., in terms of influences on attitudes and behaviors) from such investments? Third, does the program fit with the organization's human resource strategy and its overall business strategy?

Organizations have a relatively large degree of discretion in deciding how to pay, especially compared with the pay level decisions discussed in the previous chapter. The same organizational pay level (or "compensation pie") can be distributed ("sliced") among employees in many ways. Whether each employee's share is based on individual performance, profits, seniority, or other factors, the size of the pie (and thus the cost to the organization) can remain the same.

Regardless of cost differences, different pay programs can have very different consequences for productivity and return on investment. Indeed, a study of how and how much 150 organizations paid found not only that the largest differences between organizations had to do with how they paid but that these differences resulted in different levels of profitability.[2]

How Does Pay Influence Individual Employees?

Pay plans are typically used to energize, direct, or control employee behavior. Equity theory, described in the previous chapter, is relevant here as well. Most employees compare their own pay with that of others, especially those in the same job. Perceptions of inequity may cause employees to take actions to restore equity. Unfortunately, some of these actions (e.g., quitting or lack of cooperation) may not be helpful to the organization.

Three additional theories also help explain compensation's effects: reinforcement, expectancy, and agency theories.

REINFORCEMENT THEORY. E. L. Thorndike's Law of Effect states that a response followed by a reward is more likely to recur in the future. The implication for compensation management is that high employee performance followed by a monetary reward will make future high performance more likely. By the same token, high performance not followed by a reward will make it less likely in the future. The theory emphasizes the importance of a person's actual experience of a reward.

EXPECTANCY THEORY. Although expectancy theory also focuses on the link between rewards and behaviors, it emphasizes expected (rather than experienced) rewards. In other words, it focuses on the effects of incentives. Behaviors (e.g., job performance) can be described as a function of ability and motivation. As described in Chapter 5, motivation is hypothesized to be a function of expectancy, instrumentality, and valence perceptions. Compensation systems differ according to their impact on these motivational components. Generally speaking, the main factor is instrumentality: the perceived link between behaviors and pay. Valence of pay outcomes should remain the same under different pay systems. Expectancy perceptions often have more to do with job design and training than pay systems. A possible exception would be skill-based pay, which directly influences employee training and thus expectancy perceptions.

Although expectancy theory implies that linking an increased amount of rewards to performance will increase motivation and performance, some authors have questioned this assumption, arguing that monetary rewards may increase extrinsic motivation but decrease intrinsic motivation. Extrinsic motivation depends on rewards (e.g., pay, benefits) controlled by an external source, whereas intrinsic motivation depends on rewards that flow naturally from work itself (e.g., performing interesting work).[3] In other words, paying a child to read books may diminish the child's natural interest in reading, and the child may in the future be less likely to read books unless there are monetary incentives. Although monetary incentives may reduce intrinsic motivation in some settings (e.g., education), the evidence suggests that such effects are small and isolated in work settings.[4] Therefore, while it is important to keep in mind that money is not the only effective way to motivate behavior and that monetary rewards will not always be the answer to motivation problems, it does not appear that monetary rewards run much risk of compromising intrinsic motivation in most work settings.

AGENCY THEORY. This theory focuses on the divergent interests and goals of the organization's stakeholders and the ways that employee compensation can be used to align these interests and goals. We cover agency theory in some depth because it provides especially relevant implications for compensation design.

An important characteristic of the modern corporation is the separation of ownership from management (or control). Unlike the early stages of capitalism, where owner and manager were often the same, today, with some exceptions (mostly smaller companies), most stockholders are far removed from the day-to-day operation of companies. Although this separation has important advantages (e.g., mobility of financial capital and diversification of investment risk), it also creates agency costs—the interests of the **principals** (i.e., owners) and their **agents** (i.e., managers) may no longer converge. What is best for the agent, or manager, may not be best for the owner.

Three types of agency costs arise in managerial compensation.[5] First, although shareholders seek to maximize their wealth, management may be spending money on things such as perquisites (e.g., "superfluous" corporate jets) or "empire building" (making acquisitions that do not add value to the company but may enhance the manager's prestige or pay). Second, managers and shareholders may differ in their attitudes toward risk. Shareholders can diversify their investments (and thus their risks) more easily than managers (whose only major source of income may be their job), so managers are typically more averse to risk. They may be less likely to pursue projects or acquisitions with high potential payoff. It also suggests a preference on the part of managers for relatively little risk in their pay (e.g., high emphasis on base salary, low emphasis on uncertain bonuses or incentives). Indeed, research shows that managerial compensation in manager-controlled firms is more often designed in this manner.[6] Third, decision making horizons may differ. For example, if managers change companies more than owners change ownership, managers may be more likely to maximize short-run performance (and pay), perhaps at the expense of long-term success.

Agency theory is also of value in the analysis and design of nonmanagers' compensation. In this case, the divergence of interests may exist between managers (now in the role of principals) and their employees (who take on the role of agents).

In designing either managerial or nonmanagerial compensation, the key question is, "How can such agency costs be minimized?" Agency theory says that the principal must choose a contracting scheme that helps align the interests of the agent with the principal's own interests (i.e., reduces agency costs). These contracts can be classified as either behavior-oriented (e.g., merit pay) or outcome-oriented (e.g., stock options, profit sharing, commissions).[7]

At first blush, outcome-oriented contracts seem to be the obvious solution. If profits are high, compensation goes up. If profits go down, compensation goes down. The interests of "the company" and employees are aligned. An important drawback, however, is that such contracts increase the agent's risk. And, because agents are averse to risk, they may require higher pay (a compensating wage differential) to make up for it.[8]

Behavior-based contracts, on the other hand, do not transfer risk to the agent and thus do not require a compensating wage differential. However, the principal must be able to monitor with little cost what the agent has done. Otherwise, the principal must either invest in monitoring and information or structure the contract so that pay is linked at least partly to outcomes.[9]

Which type of contract should an organization use? It depends partly on the following factors:[10]

Risk Aversion. Risk aversion among agents makes outcome-oriented contracts less likely.

Outcome Uncertainty. Profit is an example of an outcome. Agents are less willing to have their pay linked to profits to the extent that there is a risk of low profits. They would therefore prefer a behavior-oriented contract.

Job Programmability. As jobs become less programmable (i.e., less routine), outcome-oriented contracts become more likely because monitoring becomes more difficult.[11]

Measurable Job Outcomes. When outcomes are more measurable, outcome-oriented contracts are more likely.

Ability to Pay. Outcome-oriented contracts contribute to higher compensation costs because of the risk premium.

Tradition. A tradition or custom of using (or not using) outcome-oriented contracts will make such contracts more (or less) likely.

In summary, the reinforcement, expectancy, and agency theories all focus on the fact that behavior–reward contingencies can shape behaviors. However, agency theory is of particular value in compensation management because of its emphasis on the risk–reward trade-off, an issue that needs close attention when companies consider variable pay plans, which can carry significant risk.

How Does Pay Influence Labor Force Composition?

Traditionally, using pay to recognize employee contributions has been thought of as a way to influence the behaviors and attitudes of current employees, whereas pay level and benefits have been seen as a way to influence so-called membership behaviors:

Using Pay for Performance to Compete Globally

COMPETING THROUGH GLOBALIZATION

Globalization of markets and of companies requires a continuous search for ways to become more competitive. One response in countries where pay for performance has not been traditional is to move in that direction. For example, in Japan, Fujitsu Ltd. President Naoyuki Akikusa notes, "The pay of Japanese workers is among the highest in the world, but talented workers, who are in great demand in the international labor market, are not rewarded with salaries they deserve. An employer must offer a pay scale that rewards talent in order to keep good workers." Similarly, Hitachi Ltd. intends to reduce the portion of pay tied to seniority from 60 to 40 percent among its 30,000 white-collar employees over a three year period and increase the importance of performance. Matsushita, the electrical goods manufacturer, too plans to increase the use of merit-based pay. The financial sector is also preparing for the imminent "big bang" of deregulation. Japanese banks and brokerages that want to retain top performers realize that loyalty will not be enough when European and American rivals begin bidding for their services. Sanwa Bank, for example, will introduce an optional pay-for-performance system. Those who sign on will have the opportunity to earn 50 percent more than those who continue under the old system. If targets are not met, pay will be 30 percent lower than under the old system.

Other changes are in store for German workers of the former Daimler–Benz, who are now employed by Daimler–Chrysler. As Daimler–Benz's top executive, Jurgen Schrempp earned approximately $2 million per year. His counterpart at Chrysler, Robert Eaton, received around $16 million. It seems likely that Schrempp, who will eventually take over as chief at Daimler–Chrysler, will see a pay increase soon. In addition, Daimler–Chrysler has already announced that for its 1,600 upper-level managers, there will be a performance-based pay system unlike what Europeans are used to that will lower base pay but add stock options and other programs that link compensation to financial performance. Thus, the merger of the two automotive companies appears to be a catalyst for change that will help position Daimler–Chrysler to compete in the global product and labor markets.

SOURCE: "Labor Stands By as Companies Switch to Merit Pay," The *Nikkei Weekly* (August 10, 1998), p. 2; "Japan's Career Escalator Slows to a Halt: Performance-Related Pay Is Replacing Annual Increases and Jobs for Life," *The Financial Times* (February 27, 1998), p. 13; "A Secret Weapon for German Reform," *Business Week* (October 12, 1998), p. 138; "Chrysler Pay Draws Fire Overseas," *The Wall Street Journal* (May 26, 1998), p. B1. Reprinted with permission.

decisions about whether to join or remain with the organization. However, there is increasing recognition that individual pay programs may also affect the nature and composition of an organization's work force.[12] For example, it is possible that an organization that links pay to performance may attract more high performers than an organization that does not link the two. There may be a similar effect with respect to job retention.[13]

Continuing the analysis, different pay systems appear to attract people with different personality traits and values.[14] Organizations that link pay to individual performance may be more likely to attract individualistic employees, while organizations relying more heavily on team rewards are more likely to attract team-oriented employees. The implication is that the design of compensation programs needs to be carefully coordinated with the business and human resource strategy. Increasingly, both in the United States and abroad, employers are seeking to establish stronger links between pay and performance. (See the "Competing through Globalization" box.)

Programs

In compensating employees, an organization does not have to choose one program over another. Instead, a combination of programs is often the best solution. For example, one program may foster teamwork and cooperation but not enough individual initiative. Another may do the opposite. Used in conjunction, a balance may be attained.[15]

Table 12.1 provides an overview of the programs for recognizing employee contributions. Each program shares a focus on paying for performance. The programs differ according to four design features: (1) payment method, (2) frequency of payout, (3) ways of measuring performance, and (4) choice of which employees are covered. In a perhaps more speculative vein, the table also suggests the potential consequences of such programs for (1) performance motivation of employees, (2) attraction of employees, (3) or-

TABLE 12.1 Programs for Recognizing Individual Contributions

	MERIT PAY	INCENTIVE PAY	PROFIT SHARING	OWNERSHIP	GAIN-SHARING	SKILL-BASED
Design features						
Payment method	Changes in base pay	Bonus	Bonus	Equity changes	Bonus	Change in base pay
Frequency of payout	Annually	Weekly	Semiannually or annually	When stock sold	Monthly or quarterly	When skill or competency acquired
Performance measures	Supervisor's appraisal	Output, productivity, sales	Profit	Stock value	Production or controllable costs	Skill or competency acquisition
Coverage	All employees	Employees with direct influence on performance measures	Total organization	Total organization	Production or service unit	All employees
Consequences						
Performance motivation	Little relationship between pay and performance	Clear performance–reward connection	Little pay–performance relationship	Very little pay–performance relationship	Some impact in small units	Encourages learning
Attraction	Over time pays better performers more	Pays higher performers more	Helps with all employees	Can help lock in employees	Helps with all employees	Attracts learning-oriented employees
Culture	Competition within work groups	Encourages individual competition	Knowledge of business	Sense of ownership	Supports cooperation, problem solving	Learning and flexible organization
Costs	Requires well–developed performance appraisal system	Maintenance high	Relates costs to ability to pay	Cost not variable with performance	Ongoing maintenance needed; operating costs variable	Can be high
Contingencies						
Organization structure	Helped by measurable jobs and work units	Many independent jobs	Fits any company	Fits most companies	Fits small standalone work units	Fits most companies
Management style	Some participation desirable	Control	Works best with participation	Works best with participation	Fits participation	Works best with participation
Type of work	Individual unless group appraisals done	Stable, individual easily measurable	All types	All types	All types	

SOURCE: Adapted from E.E. Lawler III, "Pay for Performance: A Strategic Analysis," in *Compensation and Benefits,* ed. L.R. Gomez-Mejia (Washington, DC: Bureau of National Affairs, 1989). Reprinted with permission.

ganization culture, and (4) costs. Finally, there are three contingencies that may influence whether each pay program fits the situation: (1) organization structure, (2) management style, and (3) type of work. We now discuss the different programs and some of their potential consequences in more depth.

MERIT PAY

In merit pay programs, annual pay increases are usually linked to performance appraisal ratings. (See Chapter 8.) Some type of merit pay program exists in almost all organizations (although evidence on merit pay effectiveness is surprisingly scarce).[16] Indeed, given the pervasiveness of merit pay programs, we devote a good deal of attention to them here.

BASIC FEATURES. Many merit pay programs work off of a merit increase grid. As Table 12.2 indicates, the size and frequency of pay increases are determined by two factors. The first factor is the individual's performance rating (because better performers should receive higher pay). The second factor is position in range (i.e., an individual's compa-ratio). So, for example, an employee with a performance rating of EX and a compa-ratio of 120 would receive a pay increase of 9 to 11 percent. By comparison, an employee with a performance rating of EX and a compa-ratio of 85 would receive an increase of 13 to 15 percent. (Note that the general magnitude of increases in such a table is influenced by inflation rates. Thus, the percentage increases in such a grid would have been considerably lower in recent years.) One reason for factoring in the compa-ratio is to control compensation costs and maintain the integrity of the pay structure. If a person with a compa-ratio of 120 received a merit increase of 13 to 15 percent, she would soon exceed the pay range maximum. Not factoring in the compa-ratio would also result in uncontrolled growth of compensation costs for employees who continue to perform the same job year after year. Instead, some organizations think in terms of assessing where the employee's pay is now and where it should be, given a particular performance level. Consider Table 12.3. An employee who consistently performs at the EX level should be paid at 115 to 125 percent of the market (i.e., a compa-ratio of 115 to 125). To the extent that the employee is far from that pay level, larger and more frequent pay increases are necessary to move the employee to the correct position. On the other hand, if the employee is already at that pay level, smaller pay increases will be needed. The main objective in the latter case would be to provide pay increases that are sufficient to maintain the employee at the targeted compa-ratio.

In controlling compensation costs, another factor that requires close attention is the

TABLE 12.2 Example of Merit Increase Grid from Merck & Co., Inc.

	SUGGESTED MERIT INCREASE PERCENTAGE			
PERFORMANCE RATING	COMPA-RATIO 80.00–95.00	COMPA-RATIO 95.01–110.00	COMPA-RATIO 110.01–120.00	COMPA-RATIO 120.01–125.00
EX (Exceptional within Merck)	13–15%	12–14%	9–11%	To maximum of range
WD (Merck Standard with Distinction)	9–11	8–10	7–9	—
HS (High Merck Standard)	7–9	6–8	—	—
RI (Merck Standard Room for Improvement)	5–7	—	—	—
NA (Not Adequate for Merck)	—	—	—	—

SOURCE: K. J. Murphy, "Merck & Co., Inc., (B)" (Boston: Harvard Business School, case 491-006). Copyright © 1990 by the President & Fellows of Harvard College. Reprinted with permission.

TABLE 12.3
Performance Ratings and Compa-ratio Targets

PERFORMANCE RATING	COMPA-RATIO TARGET
EX (Exceptional within Merck)	115–125
WD (Merck Standard with Distinction)	100–120
HS (High Merck Standard)	90–110
RI (Merck Standard Room for Improvement)	80–95
NA (Not Adequate for Merck)	None

SOURCE: K.J. Murphy, "Merck & Co., Inc., (B)" (Boston: Harvard Business School, case 491-006).

distribution of performance ratings. (See Chapter 8.) In many organizations, 60 to 70 percent of employees fall into the top two (out of four to five) performance rating categories.[17] This means tremendous growth in compensation costs because most employees will eventually be above the midpoint of the pay range, resulting in compa-ratios well over 100. To avoid this, some organizations provide guidelines regarding the percentage of employees who should fall into each performance category, usually limiting the percentage that can be placed in the top two categories. These guidelines are enforced differently, ranging from true guidelines to strict forced-distribution requirements.

In general, merit pay programs have the following characteristics. First, there is a focus on identifying individual differences in performance. These are assumed to reflect differences in ability or motivation. By implication, system constraints on performance are not seen as significant. Second, the majority of information on individual performance is collected from the immediate supervisor. Peer and subordinate ratings are rare, and where they do exist, they tend to receive less weight than supervisory ratings.[18] Third, there is a policy of linking pay increases to performance appraisal results.[19] Fourth, the feedback under such systems tends to occur infrequently, often once per year at the formal performance review session. Fifth, the flow of feedback tends to be largely unidirectional, from supervisor to subordinate.

CRITICISMS OF TRADITIONAL MERIT PAY PROGRAMS. Criticisms of this process have been raised. For example, W. Edwards Deming, a leader of the total quality management movement, argued that it is unfair to rate individual performance because "apparent differences between people arise almost entirely from the system that they work in, not from the people themselves."[20] Examples of system factors include coworkers, the job, materials, equipment, customers, management, supervision, and environmental conditions. These are believed to be largely outside the worker's control, instead falling under management's responsibility. Deming argued that the performance rating is essentially "the result of a lottery."[21]

Deming also argued that the individual focus of merit pay discourages teamwork: "Everyone propels himself forward, or tries to, for his own good, on his own life preserver. The organization is the loser."[22] As an example, if people in the purchasing department are evaluated based on the number of contracts negotiated, they may have little interest in materials quality, even though manufacturing is having quality problems.

Deming's solution was to eliminate the link between individual performance and pay. This approach reflects a desire to move away from recognizing individual contributions. What are the consequences of such a move? It is possible that fewer employees with individual-achievement orientations would be attracted to and remain with the organization. One study of job retention found that the relationship between pay growth and individual performance over time was weaker at higher performance levels. As a consequence, the organization lost a disproportionate share of its top performers.[23]

In other words, too little emphasis on individual performance may leave the organization with average and poor performers.

Thus, although Deming's concerns about too much emphasis on individual performance are well taken, one must be careful not to replace one set of problems with another. Instead, there needs to be an appropriate balance between individual and group objectives. At the very least, ranking and forced-distribution performance-rating systems need to be considered with caution, lest they contribute to behavior that is too individualistic and competitive.

Another criticism of merit pay programs is the way they measure performance. If the performance measure is not perceived as being fair and accurate, the entire merit pay program can break down. One potential impediment to accuracy is the almost exclusive reliance on the supervisor for providing performance ratings, even though peers, subordinates, and customers (internal and external) often have information on a person's performance that is as good or better than that of the supervisor. A 360-degree performance feedback approach (discussed in Chapter 9) gathers feedback from each of these sources.

In general, process issues appear to be very important in administering merit pay. In any situation where rewards are distributed, employees appear to assess fairness along two dimensions: distributive (based on how much they receive) and procedural (what process was used to decide how much).[24] Some of the most important aspects of procedural fairness, or justice, appear in Table 12.4. These items suggest that employees desire clear and consistent performance standards, as well as opportunities to provide input, discuss their performance, and appeal any decision they believe to be incorrect.

Perhaps the most basic criticism is that merit pay does not really exist. High performers are not paid significantly more than mediocre or even poor performers in most cases.[25] For example, in the late 1980s and early 1990s, merit increase budgets often did not exceed 4 to 5 percent. Thus, high performers might receive 6 percent raises, versus 3.5 to 4 percent raises for average performers. On a salary of $40,000 per year, the difference in take-home pay would not be more than about $300 per year, or about $6 per

TABLE 12.4
Aspects of Procedural Justice in Pay Raise Decisions

Indicate the extent to which your supervisor did each of the following:

1. Was honest and ethical in dealing with you.
2. Gave you an opportunity to express your side.
3. Used consistent standards in evaluating your performance.
4. Considered your views regarding your performance.
5. Gave you feedback that helped you learn how well you were doing.
6. Was completely candid and frank with you.
7. Showed a real interest in trying to be fair.
8. Became thoroughly familiar with your performance.
9. Took into account factors beyond your control.
10. Got input from you before a recommendation.
11. Made clear what was expected of you.

Indicate how much of an opportunity existed, after the last raise decision, for you to do each of the following things:

12. Make an appeal about the size of a raise.
13. Express your feelings to your supervisor about the salary decision.
14. Discuss, with your supervisor, how your performance was evaluated.
15. Develop, with your supervisor, an action plan for future performance.

SOURCE: R. Folger and M.A. Konovsky, "Effects of Procedural and Distributive Justice on Reactions to Pay Raise Decisions," *Academy of Management Journal* 32 (1989), p. 115. Reprinted with permission.

FIGURE 12.1 Percentage of Employees Who Agreed That Better Performers Get Better Increases

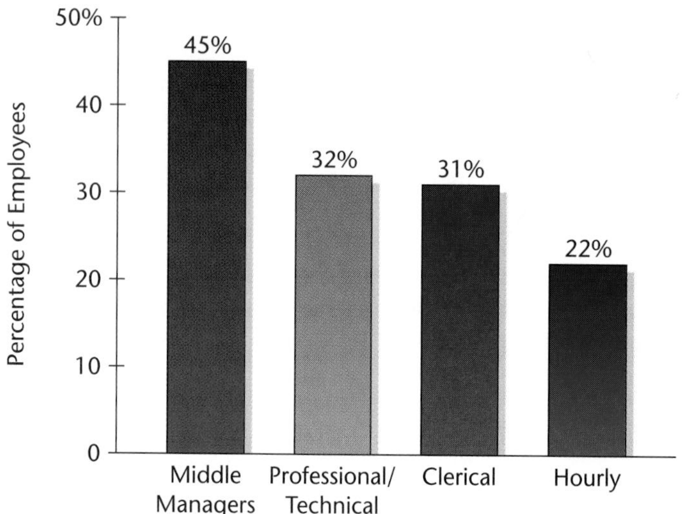

SOURCE: Hay Group, *The Hay Report: Compensation and Benefit Strategies for 1995 and Beyond* (Philadelphia: Hay Group, 1994). Reprinted with permission.

week. Critics of merit pay point out that this difference is probably not significant enough to influence employee behaviors or attitudes. Indeed, as Figure 12.1 indicates, many employees do not believe that there is any payoff to higher levels of performance.

Of course, small differences in pay can accumulate into large differences over time. The present value of the salary advantage would be $29,489 (based on a discount rate of 5 percent). For example, over the course of a 30-year career, an initial annual salary difference of $740 with equal merit increases thereafter of 7 percent would accumulate into a career salary advantage of $75,738.[26] Whether employees think in these terms is open to question, however. But even if they do not, nothing prevents an organization from developing a communication program that makes clear to employees that what may appear to be small differences in pay can add up to large differences over time. It should also be kept in mind that merit ratings are often closely linked to promotions, which in turn are closely linked to salary. Thus, even in merit pay settings where performance differences are not recognized in the short run, high performers are likely to have significantly higher career earnings.

Finally, the accumulation effect just described can also be seen as a drawback if it contributes to an entitlement mentality. Here, the concern is that a big merit increase given early in an employee's career remains part of base salary "forever." It does not have to be re-earned each year, and the cost to the organization grows over time, perhaps more than either the employee's performance or the organization's profitability would always warrant. Merit bonuses (payouts that do not become part of base salary), in lieu of traditional merit increases, are thus used by some organizations instead. Recent changes at Sears provide an example of an effort to reduce fixed costs and change from an entitlement mentality to a performance-driven mentality. (See the "Competing through High-Performance Work Systems" box.)

INDIVIDUAL INCENTIVES

Like merit pay, individual incentives reward individual performance, but with two important differences. First, payments are not rolled into base pay. They must be continuously earned and re-earned. Second, performance is usually measured as physical output (e.g., number of water faucets produced) rather than by subjective ratings.

Supporting Sears' Turnaround with Compensation

CEO Arthur Martinez describes Sears' strategic vision as being a compelling place to shop, work, and invest. The compensation system is used to reinforce the vision by linking pay not only to financial performance, but also to customer satisfaction and employee satisfaction. In addition, Martinez believes that an entitlement mentality must be avoided "at any cost." The compensation system that he found upon his arrival in 1992 paid Sears employees above the market, and annual increases were largely unrelated to how well the company performed. In contrast, Martinez believes that it is important to pay employees on the basis of performance and to make pay distinctions between employees—especially at higher levels. To energize people, incentive programs have been rolled out to broader groups of employees and the process is ongoing. For example, short-term, cash-based annual bonuses and stock options now cover approximately 15,000 salaried associates. In general, roughly 50 percent of the bonus depends on store performance and 50 percent on company performance. At the same time, base pay was reduced to a level more consistent with the market, the annual increase budget was cut to 1 percent, and individual compa-ratios were essentially limited to no more than approximately 110 percent. Just as interesting is what Sears has not done. It has not extended stock options to all of its employees. This is because the firm is not convinced that there is a sufficient line of sight for stock options to create value by changing behavior among this group of employees.

COMPETING THROUGH HIGH-PERFORMANCE WORK SYSTEMS

SOURCE: "Supporting Sears' Turnaround with Compensation: An Interview with Chairman and CEO Arthur C. Martinez," ACA *Journal* (Autumn 1997), pp. 8–17. Reprinted with permission.

Individual incentives have the potential to significantly increase performance. Locke and his colleagues found that monetary incentives increased production output by a median of 30 percent—more than any other motivational device studied.[27]

Nevertheless, individual incentives are relatively rare for a variety of reasons.[28] First, most jobs (e.g., those of managers and professionals) have no physical output measure. Instead, they involve what might be described as "knowledge work." Second, there are many potential administrative problems (e.g., setting and maintaining acceptable standards) that often prove intractable. Third, individual incentives may do such a good job of motivating employees that they do whatever they get paid for and nothing else. (See the Dilbert cartoon in Figure 12.2.) Fourth, as the name implies, individual incentives typically do not fit well with a team approach. Fifth, they may be inconsistent with the goals of acquiring multiple skills and proactive problem solving. Learning new skills often requires employees to slow or stop production. If the employees are paid based on production volume, they may not want to slow down or stop. Sixth, some incentive plans reward output volume at the expense of quality or customer service.

Therefore, although individual incentives carry potential advantages, they are not likely to contribute to a flexible, proactive, problem solving work force. In addition, such programs may not be particularly helpful in the pursuit of total quality management objectives.

PROFIT SHARING AND OWNERSHIP

PROFIT SHARING. At the other end of the individual–group continuum are profit sharing and stock ownership plans. Under **profit sharing,** payments are based on a measure of organization performance (profits), and the payments do not become part of the base salary. Profit sharing has two potential advantages. First, it may encourage em-

FIGURE 12.2
How Incentives Sometimes "Work"

SOURCE: DILBERT reprinted by permission of United Feature Syndicate, Inc.

ployees to think more like owners, taking a broad view of what needs to be done to make the organization more effective. Thus, the sort of narrow self-interest encouraged by individual incentive plans (and perhaps also by merit pay) is presumably less of an issue. Instead, increased cooperation and citizenship are expected. Second, because payments do not become part of base pay, labor costs are automatically reduced during difficult economic times, and wealth is shared during good times. Consequently, organizations may not need to rely on layoffs as much to reduce costs during tough times.[29]

Does profit sharing contribute to better organization performance? The evidence is not yet clear. Although there is consistent support for a correlation between profit sharing payments and profits, questions have been raised about the direction of causality.[30] For example, Ford, Chrysler, and GM all have profit sharing plans in their contracts with the United Auto Workers (UAW). The average profit sharing payment at Ford one year was $4,000 per worker versus an average of $550 per worker at GM and $8,000 at Chrysler. Given that the profit sharing plans are similar, it seems unlikely they caused Ford and Chrysler to be more profitable. Rather, it would appear that profits were higher at Ford for other reasons, resulting in higher profit sharing payments.

This example also helps illustrate the fundamental drawback of profit sharing. Why should automobile workers at GM receive profit sharing payments that are only 1/15th the size received by those doing the same type of work at Chrysler? Is it because Chrysler UAW members performed 15 times better than their counterparts at GM that year? Probably not. Rather, workers are likely to view top-management decisions regarding products, engineering, pricing, and marketing as more important. As a result, with the exception of top (and perhaps some middle) managers, most employees are unlikely to see a very strong connection between what they do and what they earn under profit sharing. This means that performance motivation is likely to change very little under profit sharing. Consistent with expectancy theory, motivation depends on a strong link between behaviors and valued consequences such as pay (instrumentality perceptions).

Another factor that reduces the motivational impact of profit sharing plans is that most plans are of the deferred type. Roughly 16 percent of full-time employees in medium-size and large private establishments participate in profit sharing plans, but only 1 percent of employees overall (i.e., about 6 percent of those in profit sharing plans) are in cash plans where profits were paid to employees during the current time period.[31]

Not only may profit sharing fail to increase performance motivation, but employees may also react very negatively when they learn that such plans do not pay out during business downturns.[32] First, they may not feel they are to blame because they have been performing their jobs well. Other factors are beyond their control, so why should they be penalized? Second, what seems like a "small" amount of risked pay for a manager earning $80,000 per year can be very painful to someone earning $15,000 or $20,000. The Saturn case in this chapter's opening vignette illustrates these points.

Consider also the case of the Du Pont Fibers Division, which had a plan that linked a portion of employees' pay to division profits.[33] After the plan's implementation, employees' base salary was about 4 percent lower than similar employees' in other divisions unless 100 percent of the profit goal (a 4 percent increase over the previous year's profits) was reached. Thus, there was what might be called downside risk. However, there was also considerable upside opportunity: If 100 percent of the profit goal was exceeded, employees would earn more than similar employees in other divisions. For example, if the division reached 150 percent of the profit goal (i.e., 6 percent growth in profits), employees would receive 12 percent more than comparable employees in other divisions.

How did the plan work? Initially, it worked fine. The profit goal was exceeded, and employees earned slightly more than employees in other divisions. In the following year, however, profits were down 26 percent, and the profit goal was not met. Employees received no profit sharing bonus. Instead, they earned 4 percent less than comparable employees in other divisions. Profit sharing was no longer seen as a very good idea. Du Pont management responded to employee concerns by eliminating the plan and returning to a system of fixed base salaries with no variable (or risk) component. This outcome is perhaps not surprising from an agency theory perspective, which suggests that employees must somehow be compensated before they will be willing to assume increased risk.

One solution some organizations choose is to design plans that have upside but not downside risk. In such cases, when a profit sharing plan is introduced, base pay is not reduced. Thus, when profits are high, employees share in the gain, but when profits are low, they are not penalized. Such plans largely eliminate what is purported to be a major advantage of profit sharing: reducing labor costs during business downturns. During business upturns, labor costs will increase. Given that the performance benefits of such plans are suspect, an organization runs the risk under such plans of increasing its labor costs with little return on its investment.

In summary, although profit sharing may be useful as one component of a compensation system (e.g., to enhance identification with broad organizational goals), it may need to be complemented with other pay programs that more closely link pay to outcomes that individuals or teams can control (or "own"). In addition, profit sharing runs the danger of contributing to employee resistance and higher labor costs, depending on how it is designed.

OWNERSHIP. Employee ownership is similar to profit sharing in some key respects, such as encouraging employees to focus on the success of the organization as a whole. In fact, with ownership, this focus may be even stronger. Also, like profit sharing, ownership may not result in motivation for very high individual performance. And, because employees may not realize any financial gain until they actually sell their stock (typically upon leaving the organization), the link between pay and performance may be even less obvious than under profit sharing. Thus, from a reinforcement theory standpoint (with its emphasis on actually experiencing rewards), performance motivation may be especially low.

One way of achieving employee ownership is through **stock options,** which give employees the opportunity to buy stock at a fixed price. Say that the employees receive options to purchase stock at $10 per share in 1995, and the stock price reaches $30 per share in 2000. They have the option of purchasing stock (i.e., "exercising" their stock options) at $10 per share in 2000, thus making a tidy return on investment if the shares are then sold. If the stock price goes down to $8 per share in the year 2000, however, there will be no financial gain. Therefore, employees are encouraged to act in ways that will benefit the organization.

Stock options have typically been reserved for executives. More recently, there seems to be a trend toward pushing eligibility farther down in the organization.[34] In fact, many companies, including PepsiCo, Merck, McDonald's, WalMart, and Procter & Gamble, now grant stock options to employees at all levels. Some studies suggest that organization performance is higher when a large percentage of top- and middle-level managers are eligible for long-term incentives such as stock options, which is consistent with agency theory's focus on the problem of encouraging managers to think like owners.[35] However, it is not clear whether these findings would hold up for lower-level employees, who may see much less opportunity to influence overall organization performance.

Employee stock ownership plans (ESOPs), under which employers provide employees with stock in the company, are the most common form of employee ownership, with the number of employees in such plans increasing from 4 million in 1980 to over 10 million in 1999 in the United States.[36] In Japan, 91 percent of companies listed on Japanese stock markets have an ESOP, and these companies appear to have higher average productivity than non-ESOP companies.[37] ESOPs raise a number of unique issues. On the negative side, they can carry significant risk for employees. An ESOP must, by law, invest at least 51 percent of assets in its company's stock, resulting in less diversification of investment risk (in some cases, no diversification). Consequently, when employees buy out companies in poor financial condition to save their jobs, or when the ESOP is used to fund pensions, employees risk serious financial difficulties if the company does poorly.[38] This is not just a concern for employees, because, as agency theory suggests, employees may require higher pay to offset increased risks of this sort.

ESOPs can be attractive to organizations because they have tax and financing advantages and can serve as a takeover defense (under the assumption that employee owners will be "friendly" to management). ESOPs give employees the right to vote their securities (if registered on a national exchange).[39] As such, some degree of participation in a select number of decisions is mandatory, but overall participation in decision making appears to vary significantly across organizations with ESOPs. Some studies suggest that the positive effects of ownership are larger in cases where employees have greater participation,[40] perhaps because the "employee–owner comes to psychologically experience his/her ownership in the organization."[41]

Finally, what are the monetary costs of ownership plans? In the case of options, a company does not realize an expense on its income statement until the option is exercised as long as the option price equals the market price at the time the option is issued. As such, companies may lose sight of their real cost. Briefly, one can compare the issuing of stock options to the government's printing money. The more money that is printed, the less valuable a dollar becomes. Similarly, if stock, in the form of either options or ESOPs, is distributed, but the real value of the company remains the same, then shareholder value is diluted.[42]

GAINSHARING, GROUP INCENTIVES, AND TEAM AWARDS

GAINSHARING. **Gainsharing** programs offer a means of sharing productivity gains with employees. Although sometimes confused with profit sharing plans, gainsharing differs in two key respects. First, instead of using an organization-level performance

TABLE 12.5
Example of Gainsharing (Scanlon Plan)
Single Ratio Scanlon Monthly Report

1. Sales	$1,100,000
2. Less sales returns, allowances, discounts	25,000
3. Net sales	1,075,000
4. Add: increase in inventory (at cost or selling price)	125,000
5. Value of production	1,200,000
6. Allowed payroll costs (20% of value of production)	240,000
7. Actual payroll costs	210,000
8. Bonus pool	30,000
9. Company share (50%)	15,000
Subtotal	15,000
10. Reserve for deficit months (25%)	3,750
11. Employee share—immediate distribution	11,250

SOURCE: Reprinted with permission, p. 57 from *Gainsharing: Plans for Improving Performance,* by Brian Graham-Moore and Timothy L. Ross. Copyright © 1990 by the Bureau of National Affairs, Inc., Washington, DC 20037.

measure (profits), the programs measure group or plant performance, which are likely to be seen as more controllable by employees. Second, payouts are distributed more frequently and not deferred. In a sense, gainsharing programs represent an effort to pull out the best features of organization-oriented plans like profit sharing and individual-oriented plans like merit pay and individual incentives. Like profit sharing, gainsharing encourages pursuit of broader goals than individual-oriented plans do. But, unlike profit sharing, gainsharing can motivate employees much as individual plans do because of the more controllable nature of the performance measure and the frequency of payouts. Indeed, studies indicate that gainsharing has a positive impact on performance.[43]

Table 12.5 shows the workings of one type of gainsharing, the Scanlon plan (developed in the 1930s by Joseph N. Scanlon, president of a local union at Empire Steel and Tin Plant in Mansfield, Ohio). The Scanlon plan provides a monetary bonus to employees (and the organization) if the ratio of labor costs to the sales value of production is kept below a certain standard, $240,000 (20 percent of $1.2 million) in this example. Because actual labor costs were $210,000, there is a savings of $30,000. The organization receives 50 percent of the savings, and the employees receive the other 50 percent, although part of the employees' share is set aside in the event that actual labor costs exceed the standard in upcoming months.

Gainsharing plans like the Scanlon plan and pay-for-performance plans in general often encompass more than just a monetary component. As Table 12.6 indicates, there is often a strong emphasis on taking advantage of employee know-how to improve the production process through teams and suggestion systems. In a related issue, a number of recommendations have been made about the organization conditions that should be in place for gainsharing to be successful. Commonly mentioned factors include (1) management commitment, (2) a need to change or a strong commitment to continuous improvement, (3) management's acceptance and encouragement of employee input, (4) high levels of cooperation and interaction, (5) employment security, (6) information sharing on productivity and costs, (7) goal setting, (8) commitment of all involved parties to the process of change and improvement, and (9) agreement on a performance standard and calculation that is understandable, seen as fair, and closely related to managerial objectives.[44]

TABLE 12.6 Employee Involvement Plans for Nonmanagement Employees

TYPE OF EMPLOYEE INVOLVEMENT PROGRAM	PERCENTAGE USING PROGRAM	MEDIAN PERCENTAGE OF EMPLOYEES PARTICIPATING	MEDIAN NUMBER OF HOURS SPENT PER PARTICIPATING EMPLOYEE PER YEAR
Individual suggestion plans	42%	20%	5
Ad hoc problem solving groups	44	20	22
Team group suggestion plans	28	25	10
Employee–management teams	19	15	40
Quality circles	26	16	50
Percentage of all plans using any type of employee involvement program	66		

SOURCE: J.L. McAdams, "Design, Implementation, and Results: Employee Involvement and Performance Reward Plans," *Compensation and Benefits Review* (March–April 1995), pp. 45–55. Reprinted with permission.

GROUP INCENTIVES AND TEAM AWARDS. Whereas gainsharing plans are often plantwide, group incentives and team awards typically pertain to a smaller work group.[45] Group incentives (like individual incentives) tend to measure performance in terms of physical output, whereas team award plans may use a broader range of performance measures (e.g., cost savings, successful completion of product design, meeting deadlines). As with individual incentive plans, these plans have a number of potential drawbacks. Competition between individuals may be reduced, but it may be replaced by competition between groups or teams. Also, as with any incentive plan, a standard-setting process must be developed that is seen as fair by employees, and these standards must not exclude important dimensions such as quality.

BALANCED SCORECARD

As the preceding discussion indicates, every pay program has advantages and disadvantages. Therefore, rather than choosing one program, some companies find it useful to design a mix of pay programs, one that has just the right chemistry for the situation at hand. Relying exclusively on merit pay or individual incentives may result in high levels of work motivation but unacceptable levels of individualistic and competitive behavior and too little concern for broader plant or organization goals. Relying too heavily on profit sharing and gainsharing plans may improve the degree of cooperation and concern for the welfare of the entire plant or organization, but it may reduce individual work motivation to unacceptable levels. However, a particular mix of merit pay, gainsharing, and profit sharing could contribute to acceptable performance on all these performance dimensions.

One approach that seeks to balance multiple objectives is the balanced scorecard (see Chapter 1), which Kaplan and Norton describe as a way for companies to "track financial results while simultaneously monitoring progress in building the capabilities and acquiring the intangible assets they would need for future growth."[46]

Table 12.7 shows how a mix of measures might be used by a manufacturing firm looking for a way to motivate improvements in a balanced set of key business drivers.

Managerial and Executive Pay

Because of their significant ability to influence organization performance, top managers and executives are a strategically important group whose compensation warrants special

TABLE 12.7 Illustration of Balanced Scorecard Incentive Concept

PERFORMANCE MEASURE	TARGET INCENTIVE	INCENTIVE SCHEDULE		ACTUAL PERFORMANCE	INCENTIVE EARNED
		PERFORMANCE	% TARGET		
Financial	$100	20%+	150%	18%	$100
• Return on capital employed		16–20%	100%		
		12–16%	50%		
		Below 12%	0%		
Customer	$40	1 in:	1	in 876	$ 20
• Product returns		1,000 +	150%		
		900–999	100%		
		800–899	50%		
		Below 800	0%		
Internal	$30	9%+	150%	11%	$ 45
• Cycle time reduction (%)		6–9%	100%		
		3–6%	50%		
		0–3%	0%		
Learning and growth	$30	Below 5%	150%	7%	$ 30
• Voluntary employee turnover		5–8%	100%		
		8–12%	50%		
Total	$200				$195

SOURCE: F.C. McKenzie and M.P. Shilling, "Avoiding Performance Traps: Ensuring Effective Incentive Design and Implementation," *Compensation and Benefits Review* (July-August 1998), pp. 57–65. Reprinted with permission.

attention. In the previous chapter, we discussed how much this group is paid. Here, we focus on the issue of how their pay is determined.

Each year, *Business Week* publishes a list of top executives who did the most for their pay and those who did the least. The latter group has been the impetus for much of the attention to executive pay. The problem seems to be that in some companies, top-executive pay is high every year, regardless of profitability or stock market performance. One study, for example, found that CEO pay changes by $3.25 for every $1,000 change in shareholder wealth. This relationship was interpreted to mean that "the compensation of top executives is virtually independent of corporate performance."[47]

How can executive pay be linked to organization performance? From an agency theory perspective, the goal of owners (shareholders) is to encourage the agents (managers and executives) to act in the best interests of the owners. This may mean less emphasis on noncontingent pay, such as base salary, and more emphasis on outcome-oriented "contracts" that make some portion of executive pay contingent on the organization's profitability or stock performance.[48] Among middle- and top-level managers, it is common to use both short-term bonus and long-term incentive plans to encourage the pursuit of both short- and long-term organization performance objectives. Indeed, in the *Business Week* survey discussed in Chapter 11, the average base salary plus short-term bonus of $2.2 million accounted for only 28 percent of average total executive compensation of $7.8 million. The remaining $5.6 million included stock options and other forms of long-term compensation.

To what extent do organizations use such pay-for-performance plans, and what are their consequences? A recent study suggests that organizations vary substantially in the extent to which they use both long-term and short-term incentive programs. The study further found that greater use of such plans among top- and middle-level managers was

TABLE 12.8
The Relationship between Managerial Pay and Organization Return on Assets

BONUS/BASE RATIO	LONG-TERM INCENTIVE ELIGIBILITY	PREDICTED RETURN ON ASSETS %	PREDICTED RETURN ON ASSETS $[a]
10%	28%	5.2%	$250 million
20	28	5.6	269 million
10	48	5.9	283 million
20	48	7.1	341 million

[a] Based on the assets of the average Fortune 500 company in 1990.
SOURCE: B. Gerhart and G.T. Milkovich, "Organizational Differences in Managerial Compensation and Financial Performance," *Academy of Management Journal* 33 (1990), pp. 663–91.

TABLE 12.9
Whirlpool's Three-Stakeholder Scorecard

STAKEHOLDER	MEASURES
Shareholder value	Economic value added
	Earnings per share
	Cash flow
	Total cost productivity
Customer value	Quality
	Market share
	Customer satisfaction
Employee value	High-performance culture index
	High-performance culture deployment
	Training and development diversity

SOURCE: E.L. Gubman, *The Talent Solution* (New York: McGraw–Hill, 1998).

associated with higher subsequent levels of profitability. As Table 12.8 indicates, greater reliance on short-term bonuses and long-term incentives (relative to base pay) resulted in substantial improvements in return on assets.[49]

Earlier, we saw how the balanced scorecard approach could be applied to paying manufacturing employees. It is also useful in designing executive pay. Table 12.9 shows how the choice of performance measures can be guided by a desire to balance shareholder- customer- and employee-related objectives. Arthur Martinez of Sears refers to financial results as a lagging indicator that tells the company how it has done in the past, whereas customer and employee satisfaction are leading indicators that tell the company how its financial results will be in the future. Thus, as noted in the chapter's earlier "Competing through High-Performance Work Systems" box, Sears ties compensation to each type of objective. Eastman Kodak follows a similar approach. In 1996, its CEO, George Fisher, had his annual bonus reduced by $290,000 from its 1995 level. Why? The bonus was based on three components: shareholder satisfaction, customer satisfaction, and employee satisfaction. Relative to 1995, only shareholder satisfaction was "strong." Therefore, the bonus was reduced. In 1997, Mr. Fisher agreed to a new contract that tied even more of his bonus to these criteria. So, Kodak does not reward only financial results. Nevertheless, George Fisher's total compensation for 1996 was still $5.5 million, the majority of which was based on stock plans. So, results continue to be the main driver of executive pay at Kodak.

Finally, there has been pressure from regulators and shareholders to better link pay and performance since 1992. The Securities and Exchange Commission (SEC) has re-

TABLE 12.10 Guidelines for Board of Directors Structure and Effective Governance

Interlocking boards	Top executives should not serve on each other's boards. Otherwise, there may be an incentive for executives to heed the Golden Rule too closely.
Outside versus inside directors	Inside directors are part of the management team and thus report to the top executive. Therefore, the number of inside directors should be kept to a minimum. Some committees, such as the nominating committee and the compensation committee, should be composed entirely of outside directors.
Outside directors meet without top executive	Such meetings permit directors to speak freely and consider actions that might be in the best interests of shareholders but unattractive to the top executive.
Director pensions	Directors with pensions may be reluctant to have conflicts with the top executive for fear of losing their directorship and thus their pension.
Director pay	Directors should be required to own a minimum amount of stock to align their interests with those of shareholders.

SOURCE: Adapted from J.A. Byrne, "The CEO and the Board," *Business Week* (September 15, 1997), p. 12.

quired companies to more clearly report executive compensation levels and the company's performance relative to that of competitors over a five-year period. The Omnibus Budget Reconciliation Act of 1993 eliminated the deductibility of executive pay that exceeds $1 million. However, most companies have been able to avoid the cap by taking advantage of an exemption for plans that link executive pay to company performance (e.g., using stock options).

Large retirement fund investors such as TIAA–CREF and CalPERS have proposed guidelines to better ensure that boards of directors act in shareholders' best interests when making executive pay decisions, rather than being beholden to management. Some of the governance practices believed to be related to director independence from management discussed in the case at the end of Chapter 11 are shown in Table 12.10. In addition, when a firm's future is at risk, the board may well need to demonstrate its independence from management by taking dramatic action, which may include removing the chief executive. The "Competing by Meeting Stakeholders' Needs" box on Columbia/HCA provides an example.

Process and Context Issues

In Chapter 11 we discussed the importance of process issues such as communication and employee participation. Significant differences in how such issues are handled can be found both across and within organizations, suggesting that organizations have considerable discretion in this aspect of compensation management.[50] As such, it represents another strategic opportunity to distinguish one's organization from the competition.

EMPLOYEE PARTICIPATION IN DECISION MAKING

Consider employee participation in decision making and its potential consequences. Involvement in the design and implementation of pay policies has been linked to higher pay satisfaction and job satisfaction, presumably because employees have a better understanding of and greater commitment to the policy when they are involved.[51]

What about the effects on productivity? Agency theory provides some insight. The

An Active Board Tries to Set Things Right at Columbia/HCA

At Columbia/HCA, like students with their report cards, hospitals received monthly score cards from headquarters telling them how they performed in admissions, earnings, supply costs, and several other financial categories. Purportedly missing from the scorecard was any measure of the quality of patient care. In addition, the score cards included something called "Case Mix Index," which showed the severity of the procedures billed to Medicare and thus the dollar level of reimbursement received from Medicare. For a hospital in Atlanta, the report card noted that the Case Mix Index was 1.01 versus a "budgeted" Case Mix Index of 1.15. How could the hospital reach its budgeted Case Mix Index? One suspicion is that hospitals in such cases may have chosen to "upcode" medical procedures to show additional medical problems to achieve their budgeted objective and thus obtain larger reimbursements from Medicare. Indeed, on May 30, 1997, *The Wall Street Journal* reported that at some Columbia/HCA hospitals, the percentage of Medicare cases having complications (which carry higher reimbursements than cases without complications) was 95 to 100 percent on an ongoing basis, whereas auditors claim that community hospitals typically have complication rates that are much lower (in the 40 to 60 percent range). As a result of such alleged improprieties under CEO Rick Scott's leadership, Columbia/HCA came under federal investigation, its stock price fell by 30 percent (while the broader market was moving upward), and shareholders sued.

The board of directors, led by Columbia/HCA's founder Dr. Thomas Frist, decided that the firm's reputation and shareholders' financial interests were increasingly being put at serious risk as the government's investigation of Columbial/HCA grew and that action needed to be taken. Therefore, they ousted CEO Scott and President David Vandewater. Dr. Frist took over as CEO and chairman of the board of directors. Dr. Frist is also a major shareholder (owning nearly 15 million shares) and at the time of the departure of Scott and Vandewater was vice chairman of the board of directors. One of Frist's first steps was to ban the use of compensation bonuses. Instead, managers were to receive straight salaries. At the same time, Frist said that he would work without a salary or bonus until the company was restructured. Also, to ensure that top executives would not leave during the difficult times to come and to align their interests with those of shareholders, Columbia/HCA made a special grant of 250,000 stock options to several top executives.

It remains to be seen whether Columbia/HCA can repair the damage its culture and incentive system did to its standing with customer, shareholder, and government stakeholders.

SOURCE: L. Lagnado, "Columbia/HCA Graded Its Hospitals on Severity of Their Medicare Cases," *The Wall Street Journal* (May 30, 1997), p. A6; L. Lagnado, "Columbia/HCA President, Three Aides Received 'Special' Stock Options to Stay," *The Wall Street Journal* (April 1, 1998), p. A4. Reprinted with permission.

delegation of decision making by a principal to an agent creates agency costs, because employees may not act in the best interests of top management. In addition, the more agents there are, the higher the monitoring costs.[52] Together, these suggest that delegation of decision making can be very costly.

On the other hand, agency theory suggests that monitoring would be less costly and more effective if performed by employees because they have knowledge about the workplace and behavior of fellow employees that managers do not have. As such, the right compensation system might encourage self-monitoring and peer monitoring.[53]

Researchers have suggested that two general factors are critical to encouraging such monitoring: monetary incentives (outcome-oriented contracts in agency theory) and an environment that fosters trust and cooperation. This environment, in turn, is a function of employment security, group cohesiveness, and individual rights for employees—in other words, respect for and commitment to employees.[54]

COMMUNICATION

Another important process issue is communication. Earlier, we spoke of its importance in the administration of merit pay, both from the perspective of procedural fairness and as a means of obtaining the maximum impact from a merit pay program. More generally, a change in any part of the compensation system is likely to give rise to employee concerns. Rumors and assumptions based on poor or incomplete information are always an issue in administering compensation, partly because of its importance to employee economic security and well-being. Therefore, in making any changes, it is crucial to determine how best to communicate reasons for the changes to employees. Some organizations now rely heavily on videotaped messages from the chief executive officer to communicate the rationale for major changes. Brochures that include scenarios for typical employees are also used, as are focus group sessions where small groups of employees are interviewed to obtain feedback about concerns that can be addressed in later communication programs.

PAY AND PROCESS: INTERTWINED EFFECTS

The preceding discussion treats process issues such as participation as factors that may facilitate the success of pay programs. At least one commentator, however, has described an even more important role for process factors in determining employee performance:

> Worker participation apparently helps make alternative compensation plans . . . work better—and also has beneficial effects of its own. . . . It appears that changing the way workers are treated may boost productivity more than changing the way they are paid.[55]

This suggestion raises a broader question: How important are pay decisions, per se, relative to other human resource practices? Although it may not be terribly useful to attempt to disentangle closely intertwined programs, it is important to reinforce the notion that human resource programs, even those as powerful as compensation systems, do not work alone.

Consider gainsharing programs. As described earlier, pay is often only one component of such programs. (See Table 12.6.) How important are the nonpay components?[56] On the one hand, there is ample evidence that gainsharing programs that rely almost exclusively on the monetary component can have substantial effects on productivity.[57] On the other hand, a study of an automotive parts plant found that adding a participation component (monthly meetings with management to discuss the gainsharing plan and ways to increase productivity) to a gainsharing pay incentive plan raised productivity. In a related study, employees were asked about the factors that motivated them to engage in active participation (e.g., suggestion systems). Employees reported that the desire to earn a monetary bonus was much less important than a number of nonpay factors, particularly the desire for influence and control in how their work was done.[58] A third study reported that productivity and profitability were both enhanced by the addition of employee participation in decisions, beyond the improvement derived from monetary incentives such as gainsharing.[59]

Organization Strategy and Compensation Strategy: A Question of Fit

Although much of our focus has been on the general, or average, effects of different pay programs, it is also useful to think in terms of matching pay strategies to organization strategies. To take an example from medicine, using the same medical treatment re-

TABLE 12.11 Matching Pay Strategy and Organization Strategy

PAY STRATEGY DIMENSIONS	ORGANIZATION STRATEGY	
	CONCENTRATION	GROWTH
Risk sharing (variable pay)	Low	High
Time orientation	Short-term	Long-term
Pay level (short run)	Above market	Below market
Pay level (long-run potential)	Below market	Above market
Benefits level	Above market	Below market
Centralization of pay decisions	Centralized	Decentralized
Pay unit of analysis	Job	Skills

SOURCE: Adapted from L.R. Gomez-Mejia and D.B. Balkin, *Compensation, Organizational Strategy, and Firm Performance* (Cincinnati: South-Western, 1992), Appendix 4b. Reprinted with permission.

gardless of the symptoms and diagnosis would be foolish. In choosing a pay strategy, one must consider how effectively it will further the organization's overall business strategy. Consider again the findings reported in Table 12.8. The average effect of moving from a pay strategy with below-average variability in pay to one with above-average variability is an increase in return on assets of almost two percentage points (from 5.2 percent to 7.1 percent). But in some organizations, the increase could be smaller. In fact, greater variability in pay could contribute to a lower return on assets in some organizations. In other organizations, greater variability in pay could contribute to increases in return on assets of greater than two percentage points. Obviously, being able to tell where variable pay works and where it does not could have substantial consequences.

In Chapter 2 we discussed directional business strategies, two of which were growth (internal or external) and concentration ("sticking to the knitting"). How should compensation strategies differ according to whether an organization follows a growth strategy or a concentration strategy? Table 12.11 provides some suggested matches. Basically, a growth strategy's emphasis on innovation, risk taking, and new markets is linked to a pay strategy that shares risk with employees but also provides them with the opportunity for high future earnings by having them share in whatever success the organization has. This means relatively low levels of fixed compensation in the short run but the use of bonuses and stock options, for example, that can pay off handsomely in the long run. Stock options have been described as the pay program "that built Silicon Valley," having been used by companies such as Apple, Sun Microsystems, and others.[60] When such companies become successful, everyone from top managers to secretaries can become millionaires if they own stock. Growth organizations are also thought to benefit from a less bureaucratic orientation, in the sense of having more decentralization and flexibility in pay decisions and in recognizing individual skills, rather than being constrained by job or grade classification systems. On the other hand, concentration-oriented organizations are thought to require a very different set of pay practices by virtue of their lower rate of growth, more stable work force, and greater need for consistency and standardization in pay decisions.

SUMMARY

Our focus in this chapter has been on the design and administration of programs that recognize employee contributions to the organization's success. These programs vary as to whether they link pay to individual, group, or organization performance. Often, it is not so much a choice of one program or the other as it is a choice between different combinations of programs that seek to balance individual, group, and organization objectives.

Wages, bonuses, and other types of pay have an important influence on an employee's standard of living. This carries at least two important implications. First, pay can be a powerful motivator. An effective pay strategy can have a substantial positive impact on an organization's success. Conversely, as the opening vignette to this chapter suggests, a poorly conceived pay strategy can have detrimental effects. Second, the importance of pay means that employees care a great deal about the fairness of the pay process. A recurring theme is that pay programs must be explained and administered in such a way that employees understand their underlying rationale and believe it is fair.

The fact that organizations differ in their business and human resource strategies suggests that the most effective compensation strategy may differ from one organization to another. Although benchmarking programs against the competition is informative, what is successful in some organizations may not be a good idea for others. The balanced scorecard suggests the need for organizations to decide what its key objectives are and use pay to support them.

DISCUSSION QUESTIONS

1. To compete more effectively, your organization is considering a profit sharing plan to increase employee effort and to encourage employees to think like owners. What are the potential advantages and disadvantages of such a plan? Would the profit sharing plan have the same impact on all types of employees? What alternative pay programs should be considered?
2. Gainsharing plans have often been used in manufacturing settings but can also be applied in service organizations. How could performance standards be developed for gainsharing plans in hospitals, banks, insurance companies, and so forth?
3. The opening vignette to the chapter described incentive plans that had unintended consequences. What could have been done to avoid such problems?
4. Your organization has two business units. One unit is a long-established manufacturer of a product that competes on price and has not been subject to many technological innovations. The other business unit is just being started. It has no products yet, but it is working on developing a new technology for testing the effects of drugs on people via simulation instead of through lengthy clinical trials. Would you recommend that the two business units have the same pay programs for recognizing individual contributions? Why?
5. Compare the U.S. and Japanese approaches to recognizing individual contributions with the pay system. Would any of the Japanese practices be of help in U.S. organizations? What cautions should be raised when considering importing practices from other countries?

WEB EXERCISE

The American Compensation Association (ACA) has information on compensation and benefits management, executive compensation, and international pay practices. Visit ACA's web site at www.acaonline.org. Click on the "Compensation Management" icon. This section of the web site has information related to recognizing individual contributions with pay including profit sharing, stock ownership plans, and group incentives. Click on "Information and News." Click on "Newsline." Review the current news as well as previous postings found on this page.

1. Find articles related to stock options. Read them.
2. What are some of the potential problems with using stock options to reward employees?

MANAGING PEOPLE: FROM THE PAGES OF "BUSINESS WEEK"

BusinessWeek At Northwest, An ESOP in Name Only

When Northwest Airlines Inc. staved off bankruptcy in 1993 by selling a third of the company to employees, both sides hailed the pact as the start of a new relationship between workers and managers. "Airline historians," predicted Northwest's top spokesman, "will probably record the events of the last year as the metamorphosis of a company and perhaps an industry."

Well, not quite. Today, Northwest's labor relations are the industry's worst. Its pilots struck on Aug. 29, and neither side seems in a hurry to settle. Even if they do soon, the unrest is likely to spread to the mechanics, who rejected a tentative pact on Aug. 19. Flight attendants may not be far behind.

Still, don't blame employee stock ownership plans for Northwest's woes. Northwest's experience shows, by conspicuous absence, what ESOPs need to be successful: genuine employee input into corporate decisions. Only by coupling a financial stake with worker involvement can employee ownership deliver on its promise. "An ESOP raises expectations that need to be met," says Corey Rosen, executive director at the National Center for Employee Ownership. Otherwise, "you can cause the company to perform worse because people feel manipulated."

SHORTCHANGED. Where did Northwest's ESOP go wrong? For starters, the stakes of many of its employees don't vary with the stock price. Northwest was a private company in 1993, and the $900 million that 39,000 employees gave in concessions was as much a loan as a true piece of the company. Only the pilots—whose large salaries allow them to take more risk—converted their take to common stock when Northwest went public in 1994. Most flight attendants and machinists didn't follow suit. They can still do so—but at a conversion rate 50 percent below the pilots'. The rest will be paid back their concessions in 2003. Their prospects remain the same whether Northwest stock trades at $60, as it did in March, or at today's $28.

Even the pilots feel shortchanged. Sure, they have sold 40 percent of their stock so far at a gain of $117 million. But that goes into their retirement accounts, while top Northwest executives were able to cash in millions of dollars worth of stock while it was near its peak. When the company then took out TV ads calling pilots greedy, many were outraged.

Northwest and its workers also failed to change how the company is run. Yes, three union representatives joined the board and the company asked them to stay on after the give-backs ended in 1996. But at the airport and in the sky, little changed. "We still have some of the employee committees," says pilot spokesman Paul Omodt, "but obviously they're not listening to us."

Compare that with UAL Corp.'s United Airlines Inc., whose employees bought 55 percent of the company in 1994. At United, the workers' share came in stock, and ticker-watching is now a daily ritual among employees. Moreover, the two sides set up procedures so that employees have a say in running the place; workers vetoed a proposed merger with U.S. Airways in 1995. The two sides also use mediation more often to resolve such issues as retiree benefits. United pilots hope to reach a new contract before the current one expires in April of 2000—a rare feat in the industry.

Of course, United has its own labor troubles, but even those reflect the holes in its ESOP. Last spring, the airline and the International Association of Machinists & Aerospace Workers traded angry words when the IAM tried to sign up ticket agents. The union succeeded, largely because agents felt excluded by the 1994 ESOP. Still, United's culture helped to prevent outright warfare. Says United CEO Gerald Greenwald, "To me, the test is whether we are able to talk our way through the tough issues."

That's a test Northwest and its unions have failed miserably. Pilots and executives are staring each other down while planes sit idle and other workers mull their own strikes. The question now is whether managers and employees can patch up their differences and get off the ground. If they wait too long, they risk a fate similar to that of Eastern Air Lines Inc. or Pan American Airways Inc.—carriers that set up ESOPs in the 1980s without really changing relations with employees. Just look in the corporate obituaries to see what happened to them.

QUESTIONS

1. Is money alone sufficient to make an ESOP effective?
2. How do the ESOPs at Northwest and United differ?
3. Would you suggest any changes be made to the Northwest ESOP?

SOURCE: David Leonhardt, "At Northwest, an ESOP in Name Only," *Business Week*, September 14, 1998, p. 63.

NOTES

1. We draw freely in this chapter on several literature reviews: B. Gerhart and G.T. Milkovich, "Employee Compensation: Research and Practice," in *Handbook of Industrial and Organizational Psychology*, vol. 3, 2d ed., ed. M.D. Dunnette and L.M. Hough (Palo Alto, CA: Consulting Psychologists Press, 1992); B. Gerhart, G.T. Milkovich, and B. Murray, "Pay, Performance, and Participation," in *Research Frontiers in Industrial Relations and Human Resources*, ed. D. Lewin, O.S. Mitchell, and P.D. Sherer (Madison, WI: Industrial Relations Research Association, 1992); B. Gerhart and R.D. Bretz, "Employee Compensation," in *Organization and Management of Advanced Manufacturing*, ed. W. Karwowski and G. Salvendy (New York: John Wiley & Sons, 1994).
2. B. Gerhart and G.T. Milkovich, "Organizational Differences in Managerial Compensation and Financial Performance," *Academy of Management Journal* 33 (1990), pp. 663–91.
3. E. Deci and R. Ryan, *Intrinsic Motivation and Self-Determination in Human Behavior* (New York: Plenum, 1985); A. Kohn, "Why Incentive Plans Cannot Work," *Harvard Business Review* (September-October 1993).
4. R. Eisenberger and J. Cameron "Detrimental Effects of Reward: Reality or Myth?" *American Psychologist* 51, no. 11 (1996), pp. 1153–66.
5. R.A. Lambert and D.F. Larcker, "Executive Compensation, Corporate Decision Making, and Shareholder Wealth," in *Executive Compensation*, ed. F. Foulkes (Boston: Harvard Business School Press, 1989), pp. 287–309.
6. L.R. Gomez-Mejia, H. Tosi, and T. Hinkin, "Managerial Control, Performance, and Executive Compensation,"

Academy of Management Journal 30 (1987), pp. 51–70; H.L. Tosi Jr. and L.R. Gomez-Mejia, "The Decoupling of CEO Pay and Performance: An Agency Theory Perspective," *Administrative Science Quarterly* 34 (1989), pp. 169–89.

7. K.M. Eisenhardt, "Agency Theory: An Assessment and Review," *Academy of Management Review* 14 (1989), pp. 57–74.
8. R.E. Hoskisson, M.A. Hitt, and C.W. L. Hill, "Managerial Incentives and Investment in R&D in Large Multiproduct Firms," *Organizational Science* 4 (1993), pp. 325–41.
9. Eisenhardt, "Agency Theory."
10. Ibid.; E.J. Conlon and J.M. Parks, "Effects of Monitoring and Tradition on Compensation Arrangements: An Experiment with Principal–Agent Dyads," *Academy of Management Journal* 33 (1990), pp. 603–22; K.M. Eisenhardt, "Agency- and Institutional-Theory Explanations: The Case of Retail Sales Compensation," *Academy of Management Journal* 31 (1988), pp. 488–511; Gerhart and Milkovich, "Employee Compensation."
11. G.T. Milkovich, J. Hannon, and B. Gerhart, "The Effects of Research and Development Intensity on Managerial Compensation in Large Organizations," *Journal of High Technology Management Research* 2 (1991), pp. 133–50.
12. G.T. Milkovich and A.K. Wigdor, *Pay for Performance* (Washington, DC: National Academy Press, 1991); Gerhart and Milkovich, "Employee Compensation."
13. C. Trevor, B. Gerhart, and J.W. Boudreau, "Voluntary Turnover and Job Performance: Curvilinearity and the Moderating Influences of Salary Growth and Promotions," *Journal of Applied Psychology* 82 (1997), pp. 44–61.
14. R.D. Bretz, R.A. Ash, and G.F. Dreher, "Do People Make the Place? An Examination of the Attraction–Selection–Attrition Hypothesis," *Personnel Psychology* 42 (1989), pp. 561–81; T.A. Judge and R.D. Bretz, "Effect of Values on Job Choice Decisions," *Journal of Applied Psychology* 77 (1992), pp. 261–71; D.M. Cable and T.A. Judge, "Pay Performances and Job Search Decisions: A Person–Organization Fit Perspective," *Personnel Psychology* 47 (1994), pp. 317–48.
15. A. Majchrzak, *The Human Side of Factory Automation* (San Francisco: Jossey-Bass, 1988); E.E. Lawler III, *Strategic Pay* (San Francisco: Jossey-Bass, 1990); Gerhart and Milkovich, "Employee Compensation."
16. R.D. Bretz, G.T. Milkovich, and W. Read, "The Current State of Performance Appraisal Research and Practice," *Journal of Management* 18 (1992), pp. 321–52; R.L. Heneman, "Merit Pay Research," *Research in Personnel and Human Resource Management* 8 (1990), pp. 203–63; Milkovich and Wigdor, *Pay for Performance*.
17. Bretz et al., "Current State of Performance Appraisal."
18. Ibid.
19. Ibid.
20. W.E. Deming, *Out of the Crisis* (Cambridge, MA: Center for Advanced Engineering Study, Massachusetts Institute of Technology, 1986), p. 110.
21. Ibid.
22. Ibid.
23. Trevor et al., "Voluntary Turnover."
24. R. Folger and M.A. Konovsky, "Effects of Procedural and Distributive Justice on Reactions to Pay Raise Decisions," *Academy of Management Journal* 32 (1989), pp. 115–30; J. Greenberg, "Determinants of Perceived Fairness of Performance Evaluations," *Journal of Applied Psychology* 71 (1986), pp. 340–42.
25. E.E. Lawler III, "Pay for Performance: A Strategic Analysis," in *Compensation and Benefits*, ed. L.R. Gomez-Mejia (Washington, DC: Bureau of National Affairs, 1989); A.M. Konrad and J. Pfeffer, "Do You Get What You Deserve? Factors Affecting the Relationship between Productivity and Pay," *Administrative Science Quarterly* 35 (1990), pp. 258–85; J.L. Medoff and K.G. Abraham, "Are Those Paid More Really More Productive? The Case of Experience," *Journal of Human Resources* 16 (1981), pp. 186–216; K.S. Teel, "Are Merit Raises Really Based on Merit?" *Personnel Journal* 65, no. 3 (1986), pp. 88–95.
26. B. Gerhart and S. Rynes, "Determinants and Consequences of Salary Negotiations by Graduating Male and Female MBAs," *Journal of Applied Psychology* (1991), pp. 256–62.
27. E.A. Locke, D.B. Feren, V.M. McCaleb, K.N. Shaw, and A.T. Denny, "The Relative Effectiveness of Four Methods of Motivating Employee Performance," in *Changes in Working Life*, ed. K.D. Duncan, M.M. Gruenberg, and D. Wallis (New York: Wiley, 1980), pp. 363–88.
28. Gerhart and Milkovich, "Employee Compensation."
29. This idea has been referred to as the "share economy." See M.L. Weitzman, "The Simple Macroeconomics of Profit Sharing," *American Economic Review* 75 (1985), pp. 937–53. For supportive empirical evidence, see the following studies: J. Chelius and R.S. Smith, "Profit Sharing and Employment Stability," *Industrial and Labor Relations Review* 43 (1990), pp. 256S–73S; B. Gerhart and L.O. Trevor, "Employment Stability under Different Managerial Compensation Systems," working paper 1995 (Cornell University: Center for Advanced Human Resource Studies); D.L. Kruse, "Profit Sharing and Employment Variability: Microeconomic Evidence on the Weitzman Theory," *Industrial and Labor Relations Review* 44 (1991), pp. 437–53.
30. Gerhart and Milkovich, "Employee Compensation"; M.L. Weitzman and D.L. Kruse, "Profit Sharing and Productivity," in *Paying for Productivity*, ed. A.S. Blinder (Washington, DC: Brookings Institution, 1990); D.L. Kruse, *Profit Sharing: Does It Make a Difference?* (Kalamazoo, MI: Upjohn Institute, 1993).

31. "GM/UAW: The Battle Goes On," Ward's Auto World (May 1995), p. 40; E.M. Coates III, "Profit Sharing Today: Plans and Provisions," *Monthly Labor Review* (April 1991), pp. 19–25.
32. American Management Association, *CompFlash*, April 1991, p. 3. General Motors' Saturn division has also scaled back its reliance on profit sharing because of lower-than-expected profits.
33. American Management Association, *CompFlash*, April 1991, p. 3.
34. "Executive Compensation: Taking Stock," *Personnel* 67 (December 1990), pp. 7–8; "Another Day, Another Dollar Needs Another Look," *Personnel* 68 (January 1991, pp. 9–13.
35. Gerhart and Milkovich, "Organizational Differences in Managerial Compensation."
36. *EBRI Databook on Employee Benefits* (Washington, DC: Employee Benefit Research Institute, 1995). www.nceo.org (National Center for Employee Ownership website).
37. D. Jones and T. Kato, "The Productivity Effects of Employee Stock Ownership Plans and Bonuses: Evidence from Japanese Panel Data," *American Economic Review* 185, no. 3 (June 1995), pp. 391–414.
38. "Employees Left Holding the Bag," *Fortune* (May 20, 1991), pp. 83–93; M.A. Conte and J. Svejnar, "The Performance Effects of Employee Ownership Plans," in *Paying for Productivity*, pp. 245–94.
39. Conte and Svejnar, "Performance Effects of Employee Ownership Plans."
40. Ibid.; T.H. Hammer, "New Developments in Profit Sharing, Gainsharing, and Employee Ownership," in *Productivity in Organizations*, ed. J.P. Campbell, R.J. Campbell and Associates (San Francisco: Jossey–Bass, 1988); K.J. Klein, "Employee Stock Ownership and Employee Attitudes: A Test of Three Models," *Journal of Applied Psychology* 72 (1987), pp. 319–32.
41. J.L. Pierce, S. Rubenfeld, and S. Morgan, "Employee Ownership: A Conceptual Model of Process and Effects," *Academy of Management Review* 16 (1991), pp. 121–44.
42. One study found that the value of shares was reduced annually by an amount roughly equal to 2.2 percent of pretax profits ("Unseen Apples and Small Carrots," *The Economist*, April 13, 1991, p. 75).
43. L. Hatcher and T.L. Ross, "From Individual Incentives to an Organization-wide Gainsharing Plan: Effects on Teamwork and Product Quality," *Journal of Organizational Behavior* 12 (1991), pp. 169–83; R.T. Kaufman, "The Effects of Improshare on Productivity," *Industrial and Labor Relations Review* 45 (1992), pp. 311–22; M.H. Schuster, "The Scanlon Plan: A Longitudinal Analysis," *Journal of Applied Behavioral Science* 20 (1984), pp. 23–28; J.A. Wagner III, P. Rubin, and T.J. Callahan, "Incentive Payment and Nonmanagerial Productivity: An Interrupted Time Series Analysis of Magnitude and Trend," *Organizational Behavior and Human Decision Processes* 42 (1988), pp. 47–74; M.M. Petty, B. Singleton, and D.W. Connell, "An Experimental Evaluation of an Organizational Incentive Plan in the Electric Utility Industry," *Journal of Applied Psychology* 77 (1992), pp. 427–36; J.L. McAdams, "Employee Involvement and Performance Reward Plans," *Compensation and Benefits Review* (March-April 1995), p. 45; W.N. Cooke, "Employee Participation Programs, Group-Based Incentives, and Company Performance: A Union–Nonunion Comparison," *Industrial and Labor Relations Review* 47 (1994), pp. 594–609.
44. T.L. Ross and R.A. Ross, "Gainsharing: Sharing Improved Performance," in *The Compensation Handbook*, 3d ed., ed. M.L. Rock and L.A. Berger (New York: McGraw–Hill, 1991).
45. T.M. Welbourne and L.R. Gomez-Mejia, "Team Incentives in the Workplace," in *The Compensation Handbook*, 3d ed.
46. R.S. Kaplan and D.P. Norton "Using the Balanced Scorecard as a Strategic Management System," *Harvard Business Review* (January-February 1996), pp. 75–85.
47. M.C. Jensen and K.J. Murphy, "Performance Pay and Top-Management Incentives," *Journal of Political Economy* 98 (1990), pp. 225–64.
48. M.C. Jensen and K.J. Murphy, "CEO Incentives—It's Not How Much You Pay, but How," *Harvard Business Review* 68 (May-June 1990), pp. 138–53.
49. Gerhart and Milkovich, "Organizational Differences in Managerial Compensation."
50. J. Cutcher-Gershenfeld, "The Impact on Economic Performance of a Transformation in Workplace Relations," *Industrial and Labor Relations Review* 44 (1991), pp. 241–60; Irene Goll, "Environment, Corporate Ideology, and Involvement Programs," *Industrial Relations* 30 (1991), pp. 138–49.
51. L.R. Gomez-Mejia and D.B. Balkin, *Compensation, Organizational Strategy, and Firm Performance* (Cincinnati: South-Western, 1992); G.D. Jenkins and E.E. Lawler III, "Impact of Employee Participation in Pay Plan Development," *Organizational Behavior and Human Performance* 28 (1981), pp. 111–28.
52. D.I. Levine and L.D. Tyson, "Participation, Productivity, and the Firm's Environment," in *Paying for Productivity*.
53. T. Welbourne, D. Balkin, and L. Gomez-Mejia, "Gainsharing and Mutual Monitoring: A Combined Agency–Organizational Justice Interpretation," *Academy of Management Journal* 38 (1995), pp. 881–99.
54. Ibid.
55. Blinder, *Paying for Productivity*.
56. Hammer, "New Developments in Profit Sharing"; Milkovich and Wigdor, *Pay for Performance*; D. J.B.

Mitchell, D. Lewin, and E.E. Lawler III, "Alternative Pay Systems, Firm Performance and Productivity," in *Paying for Productivity*.

57. Kaufman, "The Effects of Improshare on Productivity"; M.H. Schuster, "The Scanlon Plan: A Longitudinal Analysis," *Journal of Applied Behavioral Science* 20 (1984), pp. 23–28; J.A. Wagner III, P. Rubin, and T.J. Callahan, "Incentive Payment and Nonmanagerial Productivity: An Interrupted Time Series Analysis of Magnitude and Trend," *Organizational Behavior and Human Decision Processes* 42 (1988), pp. 47–74.
58. C.R. Gowen III and S.A. Jennings, "The Effects of Changes in Participation and Group Size on Gainsharing Success: A Case Study," *Journal of Organizational Behavior Management* 11 (1991), pp. 147–69.
59. L. Hatcher, T.L. Ross, and D. Collins, "Attributions for Participation and Nonparticipation in Gainsharing-Plan Involvement Systems," *Group and Organization Studies* 16 (1991), pp. 25–43; Mitchell et al., "Alternative Pay Systems."
60. A.J. Baker, "Stock Options—a Perk That Built Silicon Valley," *The Wall Street Journal* (June 23, 1993), p. A20.

13 CHAPTER

Employee Benefits

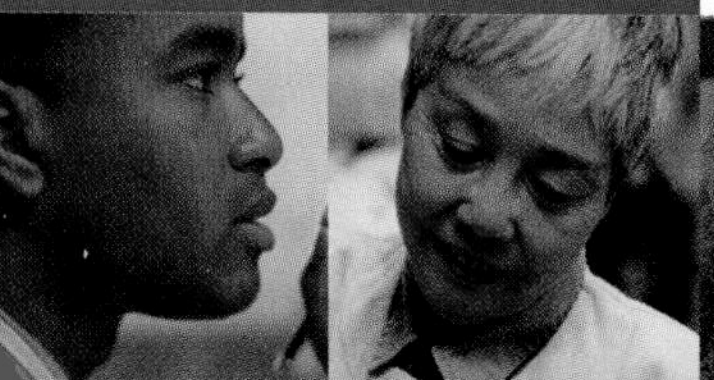

OBJECTIVES

After reading this chapter, you should be able to

1. Discuss the growth in benefits costs and the underlying reasons for that growth.
2. Explain the major provisions of employee benefits programs.
3. Describe the effects of benefits management on cost and work force quality.
4. Explain how employee benefits in the United States compare with those in other countries.
5. Explain the importance of effectively communicating the nature and value of benefits to employees.
6. Describe the regulatory constraints that affect the way employee benefits are designed and administered.

Aloft in a Career without Fetters

Dennis Gentry banks his plane above the pristine mansions and bland office buildings of America's new promised land, musing about wealth and freedom.

A friend of his is "working for the money, not because it's fun," he says buzzing over Silicon Valley. That may sound like an ordinary complaint, but

ENTER THE WORLD OF BUSINESS

not here. "He's making too much to stop," Mr. Gentry explains, shaking his head in bafflement at his buddy's high-technology trap.

After five years and several jobs in the Valley, Mr. Gentry and his friends seem to be living the Silicon Dream. At the age of 35, he is a senior software engineer with a six-figure income at interactive television company TiVo Inc. He and his pals—hardly tycoons, just ordinary smart engineers, accountants and marketers—have their pick of great jobs, at firms with stock option packages that promise bonanzas before they turn 40.

But what they prize the most—and guard most jealously—is unprecedented personal freedom.

Nobody cares if Mr. Gentry, an amiable giant of a man, hits the clouds during a workday afternoon—let alone how old he is or how many jobs he has held. In a tight labor market, he can quit his job and find a dozen more tomorrow. In a funky workplace culture he can pick his hours and dress as he pleases. In a booming industry he can auction his talents to the highest bidder, making more money than he knows what to do with.

It all flows from his aptitude for programming, work that is his idea of play and has been his chief passion for more than two decades.

"I don't really look for work," says Mr. Gentry, who grew up in rural Idaho. "I've always just walked into companies and told them I want to be there." He recently left a higher-paying position at Apple Computer Inc. for TiVo, exchanging more stock options for less job security. "Short-term, I'll have a little less free time, because it is a start-up company," he says. "But if it works, I'll have the option of retiring in four years, which is another level of freedom."

If it flops? "I could get another job that maintains my lifestyle in—maybe a day."

It certainly seems true. After all, even with storm clouds over the global economy and stock markets, headhunters still call computer companies cold, asking whoever answers the phone if they are interested in changing jobs. High-tech employment agencies rent billboards as far away as Lake Tahoe, a year-round playground four hours' drive from the Valley where its denizens head for weekend breaks.

Feverish demand for tech talent is redefining ordinary notions of a strategic career path, and frequent detours are commonplace. Mr. Gentry's brother Paul worked as a software engineer at Intuit Inc. before it went public. He made a pile of money in the IPO and now attends film school in New York. Then there is Don Surh, a freelance programmer who schedules jobs around his real love, making fine wine from grapes he buys in the Napa Valley.

There's a price for all the freedom: 80-hour workweeks when deadlines loom, stratospheric housing costs, and a grinding sameness in both the populace and the ugly strip-mall landscape. No wonder that escapism and rootlessness are rife.

"This place can be like one of those diamond mines, where people

come in past armed guards and can't leave the compound until they've finished their contracts," says Caron Lemay, a Canadian whose husband took a programming job in Cupertino, in the heart of the Valley. "People go to the mine thinking they will make a lot, but they work hard and blow their money on drinking and gambling. Here, it's rent, or vacations, or toys like fancy cars."

Certainly, few seem interested in hanging around forever. Mr. Gentry split the cost of his $80,000 private plane with a friend at work rather than invest in a home, so he could travel where he wants, when he wants. He lives in a standard-issue condo, where he keeps several ferrets as pets.

Others work relentlessly so they can later go on vacation for the rest of their lives. Or they compromise, like a couple of Mr. Gentry's friends who live in Hawaii and fly to the mainland for quick consulting stints when they need cash.

People here have changed the world, with products such as the personal computer, an Internet search engine, or cheap wireless telephones. But part of the bargain is grueling mental and physical stress. Ms. Benson wears stiff braces while she sleeps, the treatment for the tendinitis she picked up during long hours at the keyboard. "It's the Silicon Valley injury—this or carpal tunnel," she says blithely.

The sun is low in the sky as Mr. Gentry flies over Los Altos Hills, a neighborhood of newer money where piles of dirt abut freshly dug swimming pools. It is hot and nearly 6 P.M., but the sapphire pools are all empty. Almost everyone is still at work or stuck on the freeway as the weekend approaches.

Soaring above it all, Mr. Gentry surveys the Valley spread out before him, turning his craft as the mood strikes. From the air, San Jose's outskirts resemble a computer's guts: The car-clogged freeways are like cables snaking in and around low-slung factories shaped like semiconductor chips.

SOURCE: Quentin Hardy, "Aloft in a Career without Fetters," *The Wall Street Journal*, September 29, 1998, p. B1.

Introduction

If we think of benefits as a part of total employee compensation, many of the concepts discussed in the two previous chapters on employee compensation apply here as well. This means, for example, that both cost and behavioral objectives are important. The cost of benefits adds an average of 41 percent to every dollar of payroll, thus accounting for about 29 percent of the total employee compensation package. Controlling labor costs is not possible without controlling benefits costs. When Ford Motor Company pays over $500 in health care costs per car produced, its ability to sell automobiles at a competitive price is reduced.[1] On the behavioral side, benefits seem to influence whether potential employees come to work for a company, whether they stay, when they retire—perhaps even how they perform (although the empirical evidence, especially on the latter point, is surprisingly limited). And, as the opening vignette suggests, different employees look for different types of benefits. Employers need to regularly reexamine their benefits to see whether they fit the needs of today rather than yesterday.

Although it makes sense to think of benefits as part of total compensation, benefits have unique aspects. First, there is the question of legal compliance. Although direct compensation is subject to government regulation, the scope and impact of regulation on benefits is far greater. Some benefits, such as social security, are mandated by law. Others, although not mandated, are subject to significant regulation or must meet certain criteria to achieve the most favorable tax treatment; these include pensions and savings plans. The heavy involvement of government in benefits decisions reflects the central role benefits play in maintaining economic security.

A second unique aspect of benefits is that organizations so typically offer them that they have come to be institutionalized. Providing medical and retirement benefits of some sort has become almost obligatory for many employers. A large employer that did not offer such benefits to its full-time employees would be highly unusual, and the employer might well have trouble attracting and retaining a quality work force. However, the opening vignette provides an example of how the relationship between employers and employees is changing and how it may influence the types of benefits offered.

A third unique aspect of benefits, compared with other forms of compensation, is their complexity. It is relatively easy to understand the value of a dollar as part of a salary, but not as part of a benefits package. The advantages and disadvantages of different types of medical coverage, pension provisions, disability insurance, and so forth are often difficult to grasp, and their value (beyond a general sense that they are good to have) is rarely as clear as the value of one's salary. Most fundamentally, employees may not even be aware of the benefits available to them; and if they are aware, they may not understand how to use them. When employers spend large sums of money on benefits but employees do not understand the benefits or attach much value to them, the return on employers' benefits investment will be fairly dismal.[2] Thus, another reason for giving more responsibility to employees for retirement planning and other benefits is to increase their understanding of the value of such benefits.

Reasons for Benefits Growth

In thinking about benefits as part of total compensation, a basic question arises: Why do employers choose to channel a significant portion of the compensation dollar away from cash (wages and salaries) into benefits? Economic theory tells us that people prefer a dollar in cash over a dollar's worth of any specific commodity because the cash can be used to purchase the commodity or something else.[3] Thus, cash is less restrictive. Several factors, however, have contributed to less emphasis on cash and more on benefits in compensation. To understand these factors, it is useful to examine the growth in benefits over time and the underlying reasons for that growth.

Figure 13.1 gives an indication of the overall growth in benefits. Note that in 1929,

FIGURE 13.1 Growth of Employee Benefits, Percentage of Wages and Salaries, 1929–97

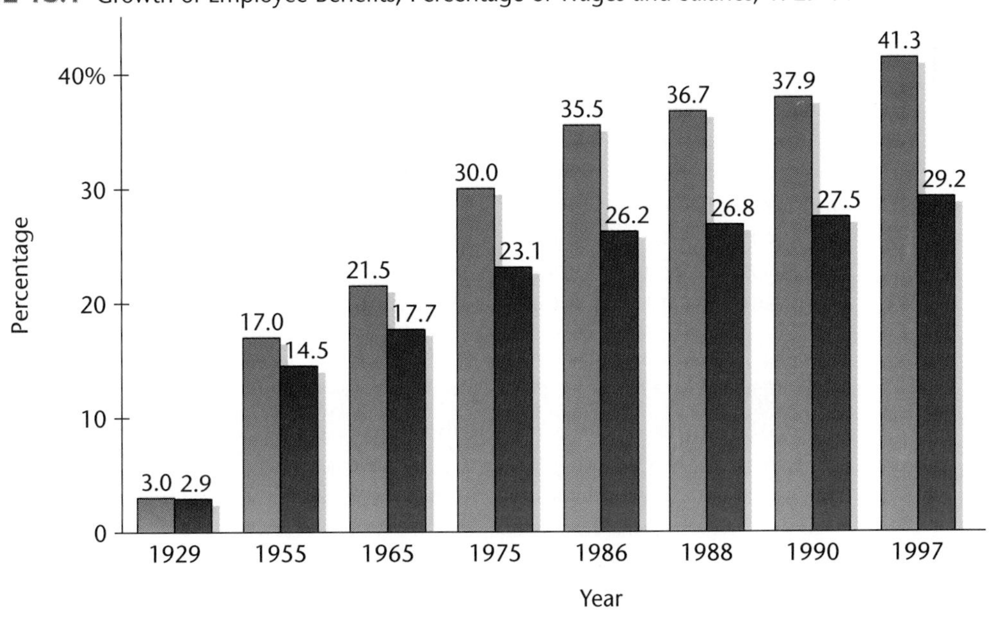

SOURCE: U.S. Chamber of Commerce Research Center, *Employee Benefits 1990, Employee Benefits 1997* (Washington, DC: U.S. Chamber of Commerce, 1991, and 1997).

on the eve of the Great Depression, benefits added an average of only 3 percent to every dollar of payroll. By 1955, this figure had grown to 17 percent, and it has continued to grow steadily, now accounting for about 41 percent on top of every payroll dollar.

Many factors contributed to this tremendous growth.[4] First, during the 1930s several laws were passed as part of Franklin Roosevelt's New Deal, a legislative program aimed at buffering people from the devastating effects of the Great Depression. The Social Security Act and other legislation established legally required benefits (such as the social security retirement system) and modified the tax structure in such a way as to effectively make other benefits—such as workers' compensation (for work-related injuries) and unemployment insurance—mandatory. Second, wage and price controls instituted during World War II, combined with labor-market shortages, forced employers to think of new ways to attract and retain employees. Because benefits were not covered by wage controls, employers channeled more resources in this direction. Once institutionalized, such benefits tended to remain even after wage and price controls were lifted.

Third, the tax treatment of benefits programs is often more favorable for employees than the tax treatment of wages and salaries, meaning that a dollar spent on benefits has the potential to generate more value for the employees than the same dollar spent on wages and salaries. The **marginal tax rate** is the percentage of additional earnings that goes to taxes. Consider the hypothetical employee in Table 13.1 and the effect on take-home pay of a $1,000 increase in salary. The total effective marginal tax rate is higher for higher-paid employees and also varies according to state and city. (New York State and New York City are among the highest.) A $1,000 annual raise for the employee earning $45,000 per year would increase net pay $560 ($1,000 × [1 – .44]). In contrast, an extra $1,000 put into benefits would lead to an increase of $1,000 in "take-home benefits."

Employers, too, realize tax advantages from certain types of benefits. Although both cash compensation and most benefits are deductible as operating expenses, employers (like employees) pay social security tax on salaries below a certain amount ($72,600 in 1999) and Medicare tax on the entire salary, as well as other taxes like workers' compensation and unemployment compensation. However, no such taxes are paid on most employee benefits. The bottom line is that the employer may be able to provide more value to employees by spending the extra $1,000 on benefits instead of salary.

The tax advantage of benefits also takes another form. Deferring compensation until retirement allows the employee to receive cash, but at a time (retirement) when the employee's tax rate is sometimes lower because of a lower income level. More important, perhaps, is that investment returns on the deferred money typically accumulate tax free, resulting in much faster growth of the investment.

A fourth factor that has influenced benefits growth is the cost advantage that groups

TABLE 13.1
Example of Marginal Tax Rates for an Employee Salary of $50,000

	NOMINAL TAX RATE	EFFECTIVE TAX RATE
Federal	28.0%	28.0%
State (New York)	6.8	4.9
City (New York)	4.2	3.0
Social security	6.2	6.2
Medicare	1.5	1.5
Total tax rate		43.6

NOTE: State and city taxes are deductible on the federal tax return, reducing their effective tax rate.

TABLE 13.2
Most Unusual Benefits

CMP Media	$30,000 total benefit for infertility treatments and adoption aid
Deloitte & Touche	$1,500 to $10,000 to employees who recommend a new hire
Fannie Mae	Ten paid hours a month for volunteer work
FedEx	Free ride in jump seat of company planes
Los Angeles Dodgers	Free Häagen–Dazs ice cream for staff whenever team is in first place and increases its lead
MOOG	35 extra vacation days in 10th year and every 5th year thereafter
J.P. Morgan	Free lunch every day for all employees at 60 Wall Street
SAS Institute	Child care for $200 for a month
Shell Oil	Automatic contribution of up to 10 percent of pay to every employee's savings account every year, no matter what employee contributes
Steelcase	1,200-acre camping and recreational area for employee use
Synovus	$50 to take annual physical, $200 reward if vital signs are OK
Xerox	Life Cycle account of $10,000 to help employees cross major thresholds such as buying a first house or financing college tuition

SOURCE: R. Levering and M. Moskowitz, "The 100 Best Companies to Work for in America," *Fortune* (January 12, 1998), p. 87.

typically realize over individuals. Organizations that represent large groups of employees can purchase insurance (or self-insure) at a lower rate because of economies of scale, which spread fixed costs over more employees to reduce the cost per person. Insurance risks can be more easily pooled in large groups, and large groups can also achieve greater bargaining power in dealing with insurance carriers or medical providers.

A fifth factor influencing the growth of benefits was the growth of organized labor from the 1930s through the 1950s. This growth was partly a result of another piece of New Deal legislation, the National Labor Relations Act, which greatly enhanced trade unions' ability to organize workers and negotiate contracts with employers. Benefits were often a key negotiation objective. (Indeed, they still are. It is estimated that more than half of workers who struck in the early 1990s did so over health care coverage issues.)[5] Unions were able to successfully pursue their members' interests in benefits, particularly when tax advantages provided an incentive for employers to shift money from cash to benefits. For unions, a new benefit such as medical coverage was a tangible success that could have more impact on prospective union members than a wage increase of equivalent value, which might have amounted to only a cent or two per hour. Also, many nonunion employers responded to the threat of unionization by implementing the same benefits for their own employees, thus contributing to benefits growth.

Finally, employers may also provide unique benefits as a means of differentiating themselves in the eyes of current or prospective employees. In this way, employers communicate key aspects of their culture that set them apart from the rest of the pack. Table 13.2 shows some examples.

Benefits Programs

Most benefits fall into one of the following categories: social insurance, private group insurance, retirement, pay for time not worked, and family-friendly policies.[6] Table 13.3, based on Bureau of Labor Statistics (BLS) data, provides an overview of the prevalence of specific benefits programs.

SOCIAL INSURANCE (LEGALLY REQUIRED)

SOCIAL SECURITY. Among the most important provisions of the Social Security Act of 1935 was the establishment of old-age insurance and unemployment insurance. The act was later amended to add survivors insurance (1939), disability insurance (1956), hospital insurance (Medicare, part A, 1965), and supplementary medical insurance (Medicare, part B, 1965) for the elderly. Together, these provisions constitute the federal Old Age, Survivors, Disability, and Health Insurance (OASDHI) program. Over 90 percent of U.S. employees are covered by the program, the main exceptions being railroad and federal, state, and local government employees, who often have their own plans. Note, however, that an individual employee must meet certain eligibility requirements to receive benefits. To be fully insured typically requires 40 quarters of covered employment and minimum earnings of roughly $600 per quarter. However, the eligibility rules for survivors and disability benefits are somewhat different.

Social security retirement (old-age insurance) benefits for fully insured workers begin at age 65 (full benefits) or age 62 (at a permanent reduction in benefits). Although the amount of the benefit depends on one's earnings history, benefits go up very little after a certain level; thus, high earners help subsidize benefit payments to low earners. Cost-of-living increases are provided each year that the consumer price index increases.

An important attribute of the social security retirement benefit is that it is free from state tax in about half of the states and entirely free from federal tax. However, the federal tax code has an earnings test for those who are still earning wages. In 1998, beneficiaries under age 65 were allowed to make $9,120; those between 65 and 69 were allowed to make $14,500. If these amounts are exceeded, the social security benefit is reduced $1 for every $2 in excess earnings for those under age 65 and $1 for every $3 for those 65 to 69. Those age 70 or older face no penalty. These provisions are important because of their effects on the work decisions of those between 62 and 70. The earnings test increases a person's incentive to retire (otherwise full social security benefits are not received), and if she continues to work, the incentive to work part-time rather than full-time increases.

How are retirement and other benefits financed? Both employers and employees are assessed a payroll tax. In 1999, each paid a tax of 7.65 percent (a total of 15.3 percent) on the first $72,600 of the employee's earnings. Of the 7.65 percent, 6.2 percent funds OASDHI, and 1.45 percent funds Medicare (part A). In addition, the 1.45 percent Medicare tax is assessed on all earnings.

What are the behavioral consequences of social security benefits? Because they are legally mandated, employers do not have discretion in designing this aspect of their benefits programs. However, social security does affect employees' retirement decisions. The eligibility age for benefits and the tax penalty for earnings above a certain level contribute to an outflow of employees once they reach their middle 60s. If, as some have suggested, pay rises with age more quickly than productivity does late in employees' careers, these retirements are a positive outcome for employers. Indeed, in recent years, many employers have relied heavily on early retirement incentives to reduce employment. On the other hand, when older employees leave, they take with them a great deal of experience and expertise.

UNEMPLOYMENT INSURANCE. Established by the 1935 Social Security Act, this program has four major objectives: (1) to offset lost income during involuntary unemployment, (2) to help unemployed workers find new jobs, (3) to provide an incentive for employers to stabilize employment, and (4) to preserve investments in worker skills by providing income during short-term layoffs (which allows them to return to their employer rather than start over with another employer).

The unemployment insurance program is financed largely through federal and state taxes on employers. Although, strictly speaking, the decision to establish the program is left to each state, the Social Security Act created a tax incentive structure that quickly led every state to establish a program. The federal tax rate is currently 0.8 percent. The state tax rate varies, the minimum being 5.4 percent on the first $7,000 of wages. Many states have a higher rate or impose the tax on a greater share of earnings. In 1997, Rhode Island employers incurred the highest costs, $707 per employee, whereas South Dakota was lowest at $91 per employee. The state average was $210, down from $224 in 1996.[7]

A very important feature of the unemployment insurance program is that no state imposes the same tax on every employer. Instead, the size of the tax depends on the employer's **experience rating.** Employers that have a history of laying off a large share of their work forces pay higher taxes than those who do not. In some states, an employer that has had very few layoffs may pay no state tax. In contrast, an employer with a poor experience rating could pay a tax as high as 5 to 10 percent, depending on the state.[8]

Unemployed workers are eligible for benefits if they (1) have a prior attachment to the work force (often 52 weeks or four quarters of work at a minimum level of pay), (2) are available for work, (3) are actively seeking work (including registering at the local unemployment office), and (4) were not discharged for cause (e.g., willful misconduct), did not quit voluntarily, and are not out of work because of a labor dispute.

Benefits also vary by state, but they are typically about 50 percent of a person's earnings and last for 26 weeks. Extended benefits for up to 13 weeks are also available in states with a sustained unemployment rate above 6.5 percent. Emergency extended benefits are also sometimes funded by Congress. All states have minimum and maximum weekly benefit levels. In contrast to social security retirement benefits, unemployment benefits are taxed as ordinary income.

Because unemployment insurance is, in effect, legally required, management's discretion is limited here, too. Management's main task is to keep its experience rating low by avoiding unnecessary work force reductions (by relying, for example, on the sorts of actions described in Chapter 5).

WORKERS' COMPENSATION. Prior to enactment of these laws, workers suffering work-related injuries or diseases could receive compensation only by suing for damages. Moreover, the common law (see Chapter 3) defenses available to employers meant that such lawsuits were not usually successful. In contrast, workers' compensation laws cover job-related injuries and death.[9] These laws operate under a principle of no-fault liability, meaning that an employee does not need to establish gross negligence by the employer. In return, employers receive immunity from lawsuits. (One exception is the employer who intentionally contributes to a dangerous workplace.) Employees are not covered when injuries are self-inflicted or stem from intoxication or "willful disregard of safety rules."[10] Approximately 90 percent of all U.S. workers are covered by state workers' compensation laws, although again there are differences among states, with coverage ranging from 70 percent to over 95 percent.

Workers' compensation benefits fall into four major categories: (1) disability income, (2) medical care, (3) death benefits, and (4) rehabilitative services.

Disability income is typically two-thirds of predisability earnings, although each state has its own minimum and maximum. In contrast to unemployment insurance benefits, disability benefits are tax free. The system is financed differently by different states, some having a single state fund, most allowing employers to purchase coverage from private insurance companies. Self-funding by employers is also permitted in most states. The cost to the employer is based on three factors. The first factor is the nature of the

TABLE 13.3 Percentage of Full-Time Workers Who Participate in Selected Benefit Programs

	MEDIUM-SIZE AND LARGE PRIVATE ESTABLISHMENTS, 1995	SMALL PRIVATE ESTABLISHMENTS, 1996
Medical care	77%	64%
Dental care	57	31
Short-term disability	53	29
Long-term disability insurance	42	22
Paid sick leave	58	50
All retirement	80	46
Defined benefit pension	52	15
Defined contribution	55	38
Life insurance	87	62
Paid leave		
Holidays	89	80
Vacation	96	86
Family leave	—[a]	—[a]

SOURCE: http://stats.bls.gov/ebshome.htm.
[a]Less than 0.5 percent.

occupations and the risk attached to each. Premiums for low-risk occupations may be less than 1 percent of payroll; the cost for some of the most hazardous occupations may be as high as 100 percent of payroll. The second factor is the state where work is located. For example, the loss of a leg may be worth $208,690 in Pennsylvania, but only $31,200 in Colorado.[11] The third factor is the employer's experience rating.

The cost of the workers' compensation system to U.S. employers has grown dramatically, leading to an increased focus on ways of controlling workers' compensation costs.[12] The experience rating system again provides an incentive for employers to make their workplaces safer. Dramatic injuries (e.g., losing a finger or hand) are less prevalent than minor ones, such as sprains and strains. Back strain is the most prevalent injury (31 percent of all injuries), costing an average of $24,000 per claim.[13] Many actions can be taken to reduce workplace injuries, such as work redesign and training.[14] Some changes can be fairly simple (e.g., permitting workers to sit instead of having them bend over). It is also important to hold managers accountable (e.g., in their performance evaluations) for making workplaces safer and getting employees back to work promptly following an injury. With the recent passage of the Americans with Disabilities Act, employers are under even greater pressure to deal effectively and fairly with workplace injuries. See the discussion in Chapter 4 on safety awareness programs for some of the ways employers and employees are striving to make the workplace safer.

PRIVATE GROUP INSURANCE

As we noted earlier, group insurance rates are typically lower than individual rates because of economies of scale, the ability to pool risks, and the greater bargaining power of a group. This cost advantage, together with tax considerations and a concern for employee security, helps explain the prevalence of employer-sponsored insurance plans. We discuss two major types: medical insurance, and disability insurance. Note that these programs are not legally required. Rather, they are offered at the discretion of employers.

MEDICAL INSURANCE. Not surprisingly, public opinion surveys indicate that medical benefits are by far the most important benefit to the average person.[15] As Table

13.3 indicates, most full-time employees, particularly in medium-size and large companies, are provided with such benefits by their employers. Three basic types of medical expenses are typically covered: hospital expenses, surgical expenses, and physicians' visits. Other benefits that employers may offer include dental care, vision care, birthing centers, and prescription drug programs. Perhaps the most important issue in benefits management is the challenge of providing quality medical benefits while controlling costs, a subject we return to in a later section.

The **Consolidated Omnibus Budget Reconciliation Act (COBRA)** of 1985 requires employers to permit employees to extend their health insurance coverage at group rates for up to 36 months following a "qualifying event" such as termination (except for gross misconduct), a reduction in hours that leads to the loss of health insurance, death, and other events. The beneficiary (whether the employee, spouse, or dependent) must have access to the same services as employees who have not lost their health insurance. Note that the beneficiaries do not receive the coverage for free. Rather, they receive the advantage of purchasing coverage at the group rather than the individual rate.

DISABILITY INSURANCE. Two basic types of disability coverage exist.[16] As Table 13.3 indicates, about 53 percent of employees in medium-size and large companies are covered by short-term disability plans and about 42 percent are covered by long-term disability plans. Short-term plans typically provide benefits for six months or less, at which point long-term plans take over, potentially covering the person for life. The salary replacement rate is typically between 50 and 70 percent, although short-term plans are sometimes higher. There are often caps on the amount that can be paid each month. Federal income taxation of disability benefits depends on the funding method. Where employee contributions completely fund the plan, there is no federal tax. Benefits based on employer contributions are taxed. Finally, disability benefits, especially long-term ones, need to be coordinated with other programs, such as social security disability benefits.

RETIREMENT

Earlier we discussed the old-age insurance part of social security, a legally required source of retirement income. Although this remains the largest single component of the elderly's overall retirement income (38 percent), the combination of private pensions (17 percent) and earnings from assets (i.e., savings and other investments like stock) account for an even larger share (25 percent). The remainder of the elderly's income comes from earnings (17 percent) and other (3 percent).[17]

Employers have no legal obligation to offer private retirement plans, but most do. As we note later, if a private retirement plan is provided, it must meet certain standards set forth by the Employee Retirement Income Security Act.

DEFINED BENEFIT. The most common type of retirement plan, defined benefit, guarantees ("defines") a specified retirement benefit level to employees based typically on a combination of years of service and age as well as on the employee's earnings level (usually the five highest earnings years). For instance, an organization might guarantee a monthly pension payment of $1,500 to an employee retiring at age 65 with 30 years of service and an average salary over the final 5 years of $40,000. As Table 13.3 indicates, 52 percent of full-time employees in large and medium-size companies and 15 percent in small companies were covered by such plans in 1995 and 1996, respectively. This translates into less than 30 percent of employees in all companies being covered by these plans, although most salaried employees in large (mostly Fortune 100) companies are covered under defined benefit plans. The replacement ratio (pension payment/final salary) ranges from about 21 percent for a worker aged 55 with 30 years of service who earned $35,000 in her last year to about 36 percent for a 65-year-old worker with 40 years of service who earned the same amount. With Social Security added in, the ratio for the 65-year-old worker increases to about 77 percent.[18]

Defined benefit plans insulate employees from investment risk, which is borne by the company. In the event of severe financial difficulties that force the company to terminate or reduce employee pension benefits, the **Pension Benefit Guaranty Corporation (PBGC)** provides some protection of benefits. Established by **the Employee Retirement Income Security Act (ERISA)** of 1974, the PBGC guarantees a basic benefit, not necessarily complete pension benefit replacement, for employees who were eligible for pensions at the time of termination. The maximum monthly benefit is limited to the lesser of 1/12 of an employee's annual gross income during a PBGC-defined period or roughly $2,500. The PBGC is funded by an annual contribution of $19 per plan participant, plus an additional variable rate premium for underfunded plans that can exceed $100 per participant.[19]

DEFINED CONTRIBUTION. Unlike defined benefit plans, defined contribution plans do not promise a specific benefit level for employees upon retirement. Rather, an individual account is set up for each employee with a guaranteed size of contribution. The advantage of such plans for employers is that they shift investment risk to employees and present fewer administrative challenges because there is no need to calculate payments based on age and service and no need to make payments to the PBGC.[20] As Table 13.3 indicates, 55 percent of medium-size and large companies and 38 percent of small companies have such plans. Note that in small companies defined contribution plans are actually more prevalent than defined benefit plans, perhaps because of employers' desire to avoid long-term obligations or perhaps because small companies, which tend to be younger, tend to adopt defined contribution plans. Many companies have both defined benefit and defined contribution plans.

There is a wide variety of defined contribution plans, a few of which are briefly described here. One of the simplest is a money purchase plan, under which an employer specifies a level of annual contribution (e.g., 10 percent of salary). At retirement age, the employee is entitled to the contributions plus the investment returns. The term "money purchase" stems from the fact that employees often use the money to purchase an annuity rather than taking it as a lump sum. Profit-sharing plans and employee stock ownership plans are also often used as retirement vehicles. Both permit contributions (cash and stock, respectively) to vary from year to year, thus allowing employers to avoid fixed obligations that may be burdensome in difficult financial times. Section 401(k) plans (named after the tax code section) permit employees to defer compensation on a pretax basis. Annual contributions in 1998 are limited to $10,000 and are typically adjusted each year according to the consumer price index.[21]

Defined contribution plans put the responsibility for wise investing squarely on the shoulders of the employee. These investment decisions will become more critical because 401(k) plans continue to grow rapidly, and by the year 2012 they alone are expected to provide as much as 50 percent of total retirement income (up from about 15 percent in 1992).[22] Several factors affect the amount of income that will be available to an employee upon retirement. First, the earlier the age at which investments are made, the longer the period returns can accumulate. As Figure 13.2 shows, an annual investment of $3,000 made between ages 21 and 29 will be worth much more at age 65 than a similar investment made between ages 31 and 39. Second, different investments have different historical rates of return. Between 1946 and 1990, the average annual return was 11.4 percent for stocks, 5.1 percent for bonds, and 5.3 percent for cash (e.g., bank savings accounts).[23] As Figure 13.2 shows, if historical rates of return were to continue,

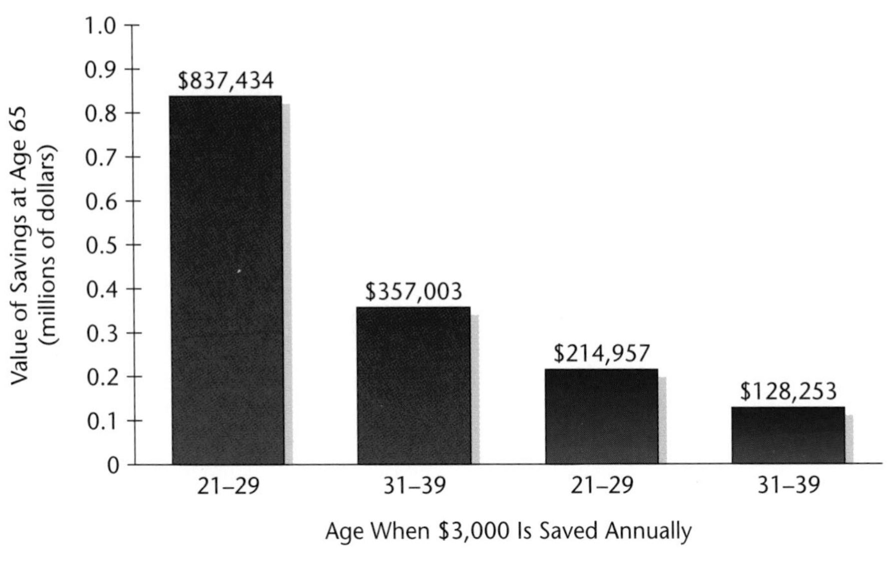

FIGURE 13.2
The Relationship of Retirement Savings to Age when Savings Begins and Type of Investment Portfolio

an investment in a mix of 60 percent stock, 30 percent bonds, and 10 percent cash between the ages of 21 and 29 would be worth almost four times as much at age 65 as would the same amount invested in a bank savings account. A third consideration is the need to counteract investment risk by diversification because stock and bond prices can be volatile in the short run. Thus, although stocks have the greatest rate of return, some investment advisors recommend a mix of stock, bonds, and cash, as shown in Figure 13.2, to reduce investment risk. Younger investors may wish to have more stock, while those closer to retirement age typically have less stock in their portfolios.

FUNDING, COMMUNICATION, AND VESTING REQUIREMENTS. ERISA does not require organizations to have pension plans, but those that are set up must meet certain requirements. In addition to the termination provisions discussed earlier, plans must meet certain guidelines on management and funding. For example, employers are required to make yearly contributions that are sufficient to cover future obligations. (As noted previously, underfunded plans require higher premiums.) ERISA also specifies a number of reporting and disclosure requirements involving the IRS, the Department of Labor, and employees.[24] Employees, for example, must receive within 90 days after entering a plan a **summary plan description (SPD)** that describes the plan's funding, eligibility requirements, risks, and so forth. Upon request, an employer must also make available to an employee an individual benefit statement, which describes the employee's vested and unvested benefits. Obviously, employers may wish to provide such information on a regular basis anyway as a means of increasing the understanding and value employees attach to their benefits.

ERISA guarantees employees that when they become participants in a pension plan and work a specified minimum number of years, they earn a right to a pension upon retirement. These are referred to as vesting rights.[25] A vested employee has the right to his pension at retirement age, regardless of whether he remains with the employer until that time. Employee contributions to their own plans are always completely vested. The vesting of employer-funded pension benefits must take place under one of two schedules. First, employers may choose to vest employees after five years. Until that time, employers can provide zero vesting if they choose. Second, employers may vest employees over a three-to-seven-year period, with at least 20 percent vesting in the third year and each year thereafter. These two schedules represent minimum requirements; employers are free to vest employees more quickly. These are the two choices relevant to the majority of employers. However, so-called "top-heavy" plans, where pension benefits for "key" employees (e.g., highly paid top managers) exceed a certain share of total pension benefits, require faster vesting for nonkey employees. On the other hand, multi-employer pension plans need not provide vesting until after 10 years of employment.

These requirements were put in place to prevent companies from terminating employees before they have reached retirement age or before they reach their length-of-service requirements in order to avoid paying pension benefits. It should also be noted that transferring employees or laying them off as a means of avoiding pension obligations is not legal either, even if such actions are motivated partly by business necessity.[26] On the other hand, employers are free to choose whichever of the two vesting schedules is most advantageous. For example, an employer that experiences high quit rates during the fourth and fifth years of employment may wish to choose five-year vesting as a way of minimizing pension costs.

The typical pension discourages employee turnover or delays it until the employer can recoup the training investment in employees.[27] Even if an employee's pension benefit is vested, it is usually smaller if the employee changes employers, mainly because the size of the benefit depends on earnings in the final years with an employer. Consider an employee who earns $30,000 after 20 years and $60,000 after 40 years.[28] The employer pays an annual retirement benefit equal to 1.5 percent of final earnings times the number of years of service. If the employee stays with the employer for 40 years, the annual benefit level upon retirement would be $36,000 (.015 × $60,000 × 40). If, instead, the employee changes employers after 20 years (and has the same earnings progression), the retirement benefit from the first employer would be $9,000 (.015 × $30,000 × 20). The annual benefit from the second employer would be $18,000 (.015 × $60,000 × 20). Therefore, staying with one employer for 40 years would yield an annual retirement benefit of $36,000, versus a combined annual retirement benefit of $27,000 ($9,000 + $18,000) if the employee changes employers once. It has also been suggested that pensions are designed to encourage long-service employees, whose earnings growth may eventually exceed their productivity growth, to retire. This is consistent with the fact that retirement benefits reach their maximum at retirement age.[29]

The fact that in recent years many employers have sought to reduce their work forces through early retirement programs is also consistent with the notion that pensions are used to retain certain employees, while encouraging others to leave. One early retirement program approach is to adjust years-of-service credit upward for employees willing to retire, resulting in a higher retirement benefit for them (and less monetary incentive to work). These work force reductions may also be one indication of a broader trend toward employees becoming less likely to spend their entire careers with a single employer. On one hand, if more mobility across employers becomes necessary or desirable, the current pension system's incentives against (or penalties for) mobility may require modification. On the other hand, perhaps increased employee mobility will reinforce the continued trend toward defined contribution plans [e.g., 401(k)s], which have greater portability (ease of transfer of funds) across employers.[30]

INTERNATIONAL COMPARISONS. About 45 percent of the U.S. private-sector labor force is covered by pension plans, compared with 100 percent in France, 92 percent in Switzerland, 42 percent in Germany, and 39 percent in Japan. Among those covered by pensions, U.S. workers are significantly less likely to be covered by defined benefit plans (28 percent) than Japanese workers (100 percent) or German workers (90 percent).

PAY FOR TIME NOT WORKED

At first blush, paid vacation, holidays, sick leave, and so forth may not seem to make economic sense. The employer pays the employee for time not spent working, receiving no tangible production value in return. Therefore, some employers may see little direct advantage. Perhaps for this reason, a minimum number of vacation days is mandated by law in Western Europe. As many as 30 days of vacation is not uncommon for relatively new employees in Europe. By contrast, there is no legal minimum in the United States, but 10 days is typical for large companies. U.S. workers must typically be with an employer for 20 to 25 years before they receive as much paid vacation as their Western European counterparts. In both the United States and Western Europe, around ten paid holidays is typical, regardless of length of service.[31]

Sick leave programs often provide full salary replacement for a limited period of time, usually not exceeding 26 weeks. The amount of sick leave is often based on length of service, accumulating with service (e.g., one day per month). Sick leave policies need to be carefully structured to avoid providing employees with the wrong incentives. For example, if sick leave days disappear at the end of the year (rather than accumulate), a "use it or lose it" mentality may develop among employees, contributing to greater absenteeism. Organizations have developed a number of measures to counter this.[32] Some allow sick days to accumulate, then pay employees for the number of sick days when they retire or resign. Employers may also attempt to communicate to their employees that accumulated sick leave is better saved to use as a bridge to long-term disability, because the replacement rate (i.e., the ratio of sick leave or disability payments to normal salary) for the former is typically higher. Sick leave payments may equal 100 percent of usual salary, whereas the replacement ratio for long-term disability might be 50 percent, so the more sick leave accumulated, the longer an employee can avoid dropping to 50 percent of usual pay when she is unable to work.

Although vacation and other paid leave programs help attract and retain employees, there is a cost to providing time off with pay, especially in a global economy. The fact that vacation and other paid leave practices differ across countries contributes to the differences in labor costs described in Chapter 10. Consider that, on average, in manufacturing, German workers work 245 hours less per year than U.S. workers (1,667 versus 1,912) and 413 hours less than Japanese workers (1,667 versus 2,080). (See Figure 13.3.) In other words, German workers are at work approximately 10 weeks less per year

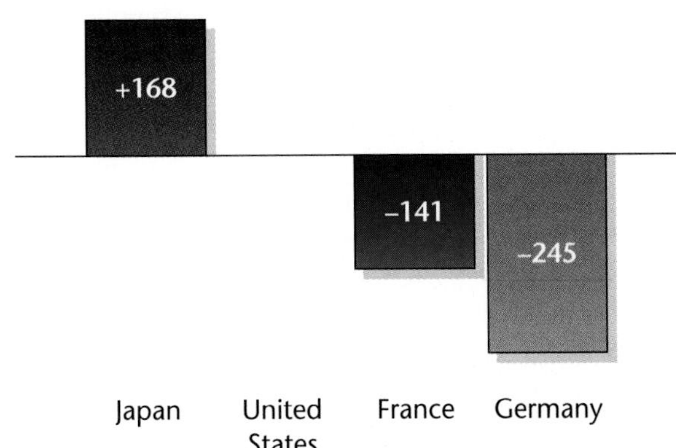

FIGURE 13.3 Normal Annual Hours Worked in Manufacturing Relative to United States

SOURCE: *World Report 1994* (Geneva, Switzerland: Labour Office, 1995), pp. 108–9.

than their Japanese counterparts. It is perhaps not surprising then that German manufacturers have looked outside Germany in many cases for alternative production sites.

FAMILY-FRIENDLY POLICIES

To ease employees' conflicts between work and nonwork, organizations may use *family-friendly policies* such as family-leave policies and child care. Although the programs discussed here would seem to be targeted to a particular group of employees, these programs often have "spillover effects" on other employees, who see them as symbolizing a general corporate concern for human resources, thus promoting loyalty even among employee groups that do not use the programs.[33]

Since 1993, the **Family and Medical Leave Act** requires organizations with 50 or more employees within a 75-mile radius to provide as much as 12 weeks of unpaid leave after childbirth or adoption; to care for a seriously ill child, spouse, or parent; or for an employee's own serious illness.[34] Employees are guaranteed the same or a comparable job on their return to work. Employees with less than one year of service or who work under 25 hours per week or who are among the 10 percent highest paid are not covered.

Many employers had already taken steps to deal with this issue, partly to help attract and retain key employees. As noted by one source, only "about 4 percent of American families fit the stereotypical image of a father who works outside the home and a mother who stays home and takes care of the children."[35]

The United States still offers significantly less unpaid leave than most Western European countries and Japan. Moreover, paid family leave remains rare in the United States (fewer than 5 percent are eligible for paid leave, despite some state laws), in even sharper contrast to Western Europe and Japan, where it is typically mandated by law.[36] Until the passage of the Americans with Disabilities Act, the only applicable law was the **Pregnancy Discrimination Act of 1978,** which requires employers that offer disability plans to treat pregnancy as they would any other disability.

Early experience with the Family and Medical Leave Act suggests that a majority of those opting for this benefit fail to take the full allotment of time. This is especially the case among female executives. Many of these executives find they do not enjoy maternity leave as much as they expected they would and miss the challenges associated with their careers. Others fear that their careers would be damaged in the long run by missing out on opportunities that might arise while they are out on leave.[37]

CHILD CARE. Over 4,000 U.S. companies currently provide some form of child care support to their employees, and this number is increasing yearly.[38] This support comes in several forms that vary in their degree of organizational involvement. The least level of involvement is when an organization merely supplies and helps employees collect information about the cost and quality of available child care. At the next level, organizations provide vouchers or discounts for employees to use at existing child care facilities. At the highest level, firms provide on-site child care directly to their employees. Toyota's Child Development Program (an extreme example of this) provides 24-hours-a-day care for children of workers at its Georgetown, Kentucky, plant. This facility is designed to meet the needs of employees working evening and night shifts who want their children to be on the same schedule as them. In this facility, the children are kept awake all night. At the end of the night shift, the parents pick up their children and the whole family goes home to bed.[39]

An organization's decision to staff its own child care facility should not be taken lightly. It is typically a costly venture with important liability concerns. Moreover, the results, in terms of reducing absenteeism and enhancing productivity, are often mixed.

One reason for this is that many organizations are "jumping on the day care bandwagon" without giving much thought to the best form of assistance for their specific employees.[40] Organizations that fail to do an adequate needs assessment (see Chapter 7) often wind up purchasing the wrong alternative. For example, one Fortune 500 company found that less than 2 percent of its work force used a flexible spending account that had been adopted as the chief company policy on child care. The waste and inefficiency of this practice could have been avoided had a more thorough needs analysis been conducted before the program was implemented.[41]

As an alternative example, Memphis-based First Tennessee Bank, which was losing 1,500 days of productivity a year because of child care problems, considered creating its own on-site day care center. Before acting, however, the company conducted a survey of its employees. This survey indicated that the only real problem with day care occurred when the parents' regular day care provisions fell through because of sickness on the part of the child or provider. Based on these findings, the bank opted to establish a sick-child care center, which was less costly and smaller in scope than a full-time center and yet still solved the employees' major problem. As a result, absenteeism dropped so dramatically that the program paid for itself in the first nine months of operation.[42]

Managing Benefits: Employer Objectives and Strategies

Although the regulatory environment places some important constraints on benefits decisions, employers retain significant discretion and need to evaluate the payoff of such decisions.[43] As discussed earlier, however, this evaluation needs to recognize that employees have come to expect certain things from employers. Employers who do not meet these expectations run the risk of violating what has been called an "implicit contract" between the employer and its workers. If employees believe their employers feel little commitment to their welfare, they can hardly be expected to commit themselves to the company's success.

Clearly, there is much room for progress in the evaluation of benefits decisions. Despite some of the obvious reasons for benefits—group discounts, regulation, and minimizing compensation-related taxes—organizations do not do as well as they could in spelling out what they want their benefits package to achieve and evaluating how well they are succeeding. Research suggests that most organizations do not have written benefits objectives.[44] Obviously, without clear objectives to measure progress, evaluation is difficult (and less likely to occur). Table 13.4 provides an example of one organization's written benefits objectives.

SURVEYS AND BENCHMARKING

As with cash compensation, an important element of benefits management is knowing what the competition is doing. Survey information on benefits packages is available from private consultants and, somewhat less regularly, the Bureau of Labor Statistics.[45] BLS data of the sort in Table 13.3 and the more detailed information on programs and provisions available from consultants are useful in designing competitive benefits packages. To compete effectively in the product market, cost information is also necessary. A widely used source is the annual survey conducted by the U.S. Chamber of Commerce, which provides information on benefits costs for specific categories as well as breakdowns by industry and organization size. Table 13.5 provides an excerpt of some of these data for 1996.

TABLE 13.4
One Company's Written Benefits Objectives

- To establish and maintain an employee benefit program that is based primarily on the employees' needs for leisure time and on protection against the risks of old age, loss of health, and loss of life.
- To establish and maintain an employee benefit program that complements the efforts of employees on their own behalf.
- To evaluate the employee benefit plan annually for its effect on employee morale and productivity, giving consideration to turnover, unfilled positions, attendance, employees' complaints, and employees' opinions.
- To compare the employee benefit plan annually with that of other leading companies in the same field and to maintain a benefit plan with an overall level of benefits based on cost per employee that falls within the second quintile of these companies.
- To maintain a level of benefits for nonunion employees that represents the same level of expenditures per employee as for union employees.
- To determine annually the costs of new, changed, and existing programs as percentages of salaries and wages and to maintain these percentages as much as possible.
- To self-fund benefits to the extent that a long-run cost savings can be expected for the firm and catastrophic losses can be avoided.
- To coordinate all benefits with social insurance programs to which the company makes payments.
- To provide benefits on a noncontributory basis, except for dependent coverage for which employees should pay a portion of the cost.
- To maintain continual communications with all employees concerning benefit programs.

SOURCE: *Employee Benefits,* 3d ed., Burton T. Beam, Jr., and John J. McFadden. Published by Dearborn Financial Publishing, Inc., Chicago.

TABLE 13.5
Employee Benefits by Category and Cost, 1996

	PERCENTAGE OF PAYROLL	COST IN DOLLARS
Legally required	8.8%	$3,014
Retirement and savings plans	6.3	2,144
Medical and other insurance	10.0	3,400
Paid rest periods	3.7	1,262
Payments for time not worked	10.2	3,476
Miscellaneous[a]	2.3	790
Totals	41.3	14,086

[a] Includes employee services and extra cash payment categories.
SOURCE: Adapted from the U.S. Chamber of Commerce Research Center, *Employee Benefits* (Washington, DC: U.S. Chamber of Commerce), 1997.

COST CONTROL

In thinking about cost control strategies, it is useful to consider several factors. First, the larger the cost of a benefit category, the greater the opportunity for savings. Second, the growth trajectory of the benefit category is also important. Even if costs are currently acceptable, the rate of growth may result in serious costs in the future. Third, cost containment efforts can only work to the extent that the employer has significant discretion in choosing how much to spend in a benefit category. Much of the cost of legally required benefits (e.g., social security) is relatively fixed, which constrains cost reduction efforts. Even with legally required benefits, however, employers can take actions to limit costs because of "experience ratings," which impose higher taxes on employers with high rates of unemployment or workers' compensation claims.

One benefit—medical and other insurance—stands out as a target for cost control for two reasons. First, its costs are substantial. They have, except for the past few years, been growing rapidly, and this growth is expected to resume. Second, employers have many options for attacking costs and improving quality.

HEALTH CARE: CONTROLLING COSTS AND IMPROVING QUALITY. As Table 13.6 indicates, the United States spends more on health care than any other country in the world. U.S. health care expenditures have gone from 5.3 percent of the gross national product ($27 billion) in 1960 to 14 percent (approximately $1 trillion) in 1996. Yet, the percentage of full-time workers receiving job-related health benefits has declined, with over 40 million Americans uninsured as of 1996.[46] The United States also compares poorly with Japan and Western Europe on measures of life expectancy and infant mortality. (See Table 13.6.)

Unlike workers in most Western European countries, who have nationalized health systems, the majority of Americans receiving health insurance get it through their (or a family member's) employers.[47] Consequently, health insurance, like pensions, discourages employee turnover because not all employers provide health insurance benefits.[48] Not surprisingly, the fact that many Americans receive coverage through their employers has meant that many efforts at controlling costs and increasing quality and coverage have been undertaken by employers. These efforts, broadly referred to as managed care, fall into six major categories: (1) plan design, (2) use of alternative providers, (3) use of alternative funding methods, (4) claims review, (5) education and prevention, and (6) external cost control systems.[49] Examples appear in Table 13.7.

One trend in plan design has been to shift costs to employees through the use of deductibles, co-insurance, exclusions and limitations, and maximum benefits.[50] These costs can be structured such that employees act on incentives to shift to less expensive plans.[51] Another trend has been to focus on reducing, rather than shifting, costs through such activities as preadmission testing and second surgical opinions. The use of alternative providers like **health maintenance organizations (HMOs)** and **preferred provider organizations (PPOs)** has also increased. HMOs differ from more traditional providers by focusing on preventive care and outpatient treatment, requiring employees to use only HMO services, and providing benefits on a prepaid basis. Many HMOs pay physicians and other health care workers on a flat salary basis instead of using the traditional fee-for-service system, under which a physician's pay may depend on the

TABLE 13.6 Health Care Costs and Outcomes in Various Countries, 1996

	LIFE EXPECTANCY MALE/FEMALE	INFANT MORTALITY RATE[a]	HEALTH EXPENDITURES PER CAPITA[b]	HEALTH EXPENDITURES AS A PERCENTAGE OF GDP	DOCTORS PER 1,000 PEOPLE	AVERAGE DAYS INPATIENT CARE
Japan	77/83	.38	$1,673	7.2%	1.8	45
Korea	70/76	.90	543	4.0	1.1	13
Canada	75/81	.60	2,065	9.6	2.1	12
United Kingdom	74/79	.62	1,297	6.9	1.6	10
France	74/82	.49	1,989	9.7	2.9	11
Germany	74/80	.50	2,233	10.5	3.4	14
Mexico	70/77	1.70	358	4.6	2.6	8
United States	73/79	.80	3,898	14.0	1.6	4

[a]Per 1,000 live births.
[b]Adjusted for purchasing power, U.S. dollars.
SOURCE: Organization for Economic Cooperation and Development, *OECD Health Data 98* (Paris: 1998).

TABLE 13.7
Ways Employers Use Managed Care to Control Health Care Costs

Plan design
Cost shifting to employees
- Deductibles
- Co-insurance
- Exclusions and limitations
- Maximum benefits

Cost reduction
- Preadmission testing
- Second surgical opinions
- Coordination of benefits
- Alternatives to hospital stays (e.g., home health care)

Alternative providers
Health maintenance organizations (HMOs)
Preferred provider organizations (PPOs)

Alternative funding methods
Self-funding

Claims review

Health education and preventive care
Wellness programs
Employee assistance programs (EAPs)

Encouragement of external control systems
National Council on Health Planning and Development
Employer coalitions

SOURCE: Adapted from B.T. Beam Jr. and J.J. McFadden, *Employee Benefits,* 3d ed. (Chicago: Dearborn Financial Publishing, 1992).

number of patients seen. Paying on a salary basis is intended to reduce incentives for physicians to schedule more patient visits or medical procedures than might be necessary. (Of course, there is the risk that incentives will be reduced too much, resulting in inadequate access to medical procedures and specialists.) PPOs are essentially groups of health care providers that contract with employers, insurance companies, and so forth to provide health care at a reduced fee. They differ from HMOs in that they do not provide benefits on a prepaid basis and employees often are not required to use the preferred providers. Instead, employers may provide incentives for employees to choose, for example, a physician who participates in the plan. In general, PPOs seem to be less expensive than traditional delivery systems but more expensive than HMOs.[52] Another trend in employers' attempts to control costs has been to vary required employee contributions based on the employee's health and risk factors rather than charging each employee the same premium.

Employee Wellness Programs. Employee wellness programs (EWPs) focus on changing behaviors both on and off work that could eventually lead to future health problems. EWPs are preventive in nature; they attempt to manage health care costs by decreasing employees' needs for services. Typically, these programs aim at specific health risks such as high blood pressure, high cholesterol levels, smoking, and obesity. They also try to promote positive health influences such as physical exercise and good nutrition.

EWPs are either passive or active. Passive programs use little or no outreach to individuals, nor do they provide ongoing support to motivate them to avail themselves of the resources. Active wellness centers assume that behavior change requires not only awareness and opportunity but support and reinforcement.

One example of a passive wellness program is a health education program. Health education programs have two central goals: raising awareness levels of health-related issues and informing people on health-related topics. In these kinds of programs, a health educator usually conducts classes or lunchtime lectures (or coordinates outside speakers). The program may also have various promotions (e.g., annual mile run or "smoke-outs") and include a newsletter that reports on current health issues. Health education programs are the most common form of employee wellness program.[53]

Another kind of passive employee wellness program is the fitness facility program. In this kind of program, the company sets up a center for physical fitness equipped with aerobic and muscle-building exercise machines and staffed with certified athletic trainers. The facility is publicized within the organization, and employees are free to use it on their own time. Aetna, for example, has created five state-of-the-art health clubs that serve over 7,500 workers.[54] Northwestern Mutual Life's fitness facilities are open 24 hours a day to its 3,300 employees.[55] Health education classes related to smoking cessation and weight loss may be offered in addition to the facilities.

Although fitness facility programs are usually more expensive than health education programs, both are classified as passive because they rely on individual employees to identify their problems and take corrective action. In contrast, active wellness centers assume that behavior change also requires encouragement and assistance. One kind of active wellness center is the outreach and follow-up model. This type of wellness center contains all the features of a passive model, but it also has counselors who handle one-on-one outreach and provide tailored, individualized programs for employees. Typically, tailored programs obtain baseline measures on various indicators (weight, blood pressure, lung capacity, etc.) and measure individuals' progress relative to these indicators over time. The programs set goals and provide small, symbolic rewards to individuals who meet their goals.

This encouragement needs to be particularly targeted to employees in high-risk categories (e.g., those who smoke, are overweight, or have high blood pressure) for two reasons. First, a small percentage of employees create a disproportionate amount of health-care costs; therefore, targeted interventions are more efficient. Second, research shows that those in high-risk categories are the most likely to perceive barriers to participating in company-sponsored fitness programs (e.g., family problems or work overload).[56] Thus, untargeted interventions are likely to miss the people that most need to be included.

Research on these different types of wellness centers leads to several conclusions.[57] First, the costs of health education programs are significantly less than those associated with either fitness facility programs or the follow-up model. Second, as indicated in Figure 13.4, all three models are effective in reducing the risk factors associated with cardiovascular disease (obesity, high blood pressure, smoking, and lack of exercise). However, the follow-up model is significantly better than the other two in reducing the risk factors.

Whether the added cost of follow-up programs compared with health education programs is warranted is a judgment that only employers, employees, and unions can make. However, employers like Sony and Quaker Oats believe that incentives are worth the extra cost and their employers can receive up to several hundred dollars for reducing their risk factors. There appears to be no such ambiguity associated with the fitness facility model, however. This type of wellness center costs as much or more than the follow-up model but only as effective as the health education model. Providing a fitness facility that does not include systematic outreach and routine long-term follow-up to assist people with risk factors is not cost-effective in reducing health risks. "Attendants may sit in the fitness center like the 'Maytag repairman' waiting for people to come."[58]

FIGURE 13.4
The Cost and Effectiveness of Three Different Types of Employee Wellness Designs

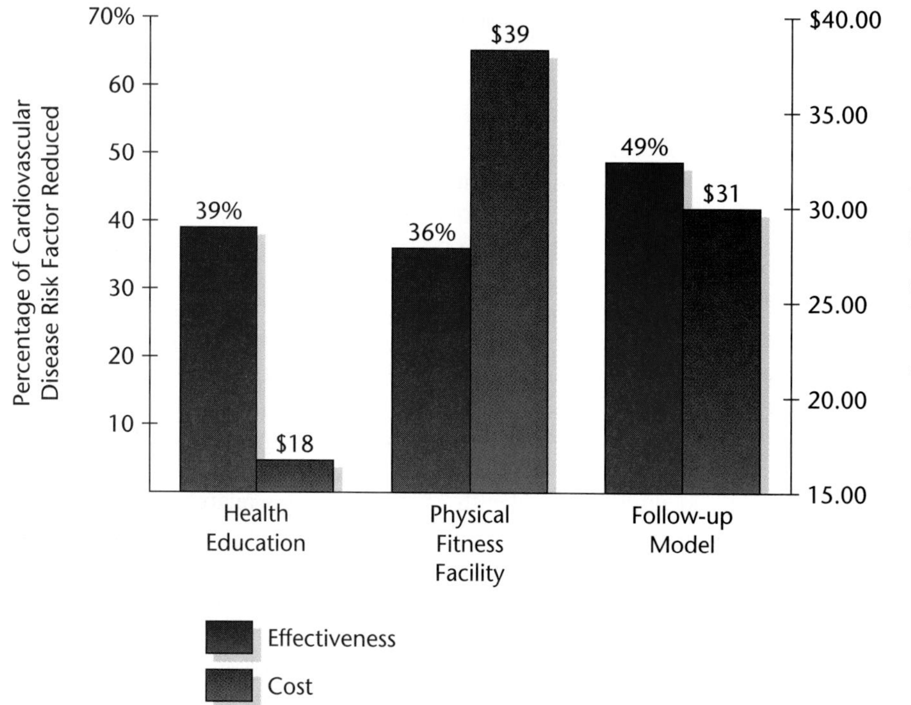

SOURCE: J.C. Erfurt, A. Foote, and M.A. Heirich, "The Cost Effectiveness of Worksite Wellness Programs for Hypertension Control, Weight Loss, Smoking Cessation and Exercise," *Personnel Psychology* 45 (1992), pp. 5–27. Used with permission.

Health Care Costs and Quality: Progress and Prospects. Efforts to control health care cost growth have borne fruit. Whereas from 1980 through 1993 there was double-digit annual growth in health care costs, between 1993 and 1996 employer expenditures on health care actually fell by nearly 20 percent. Time will tell whether such reductions are lasting or temporary. For example, a report by the Health Care Financing Administration projects that health care spending in the United States will double in the next 10 years. Why? Because 85 percent of working Americans with health care are already covered by managed care, so few additional savings can be obtained by further switches. Moreover, many managed care companies have existed on small profit margins, but this cannot continue indefinitely.

Two important phenomena are often encountered in cost-control efforts. First, piecemeal programs may not work well because steps to control one aspect (e.g., cost shifting of medical costs) may lead employees to "migrate" to other programs that provide medical treatment at no cost to them (e.g., workers' compensation). Second, there is often a so-called Pareto group, which refers to a small percentage (e.g., 20 percent) of employees being responsible for generating the majority (often 60 to 80 percent) of health care costs. Obviously, cost control efforts will be more successful to the extent that the costs generated by the Pareto group can be identified and managed effectively.[59]

Although cost control will continue to require a good deal of attention, there is a growing emphasis on monitoring health care quality, which has been described as "the next battlefield." A major focus will be on identifying best medical practices by measuring and monitoring the relative success of alternative treatment strategies using large-scale databases and research.[60] The "Competing by Meeting Stakeholders' Needs" box provides an example.

TABLE 13.8 Percentages of Firms Providing Benefits for Full-Time and Part-Time Employees

BENEFIT	PART-TIME (UNDER 20 HOURS PER WEEK)	FULL-TIME
Health	25%	100%
Sick leave	28	92
Vacation	47	100

SOURCE: Hewitt Associates, *Survey of Benefits for Part-Time Employees—1995* (Lincolnshire, IL: 1995).

STAFFING RESPONSES TO CONTROL BENEFIT COST GROWTH. Employers may change staffing practices to control benefits costs. First, because benefits costs are fixed (in that they do not usually go up with hours worked), the benefits cost per hour can be reduced by having employees work more hours. However, there are drawbacks to having employees work more hours. The Fair Labor Standards Act (FLSA) requires that nonexempt employees be paid time-and-a-half for hours in excess of 40 per week. Yet the decline in U.S. work hours tapered off in the late 1940s; work hours have actually gone up since then. It is estimated that Americans were working the equivalent of one month longer in 1987 than they were in 1969 and these higher levels continued into the 1990s.[61] Increased benefits were identified as one of the major reasons for this.

A second possible effect of FLSA regulations (though this is more speculative) is that organizations will try to have their employees classified as exempt whenever possible. The growth in the number of salaried workers (many of whom are exempt) may also reflect an effort by organizations to limit the benefits cost per hour without having to pay overtime. A third potential effect is the growth in part-time employment and the use of temporary workers, which may be a response to rising benefits costs.[62] As Table 13.8 indicates, part-time workers are much less likely to receive benefits than full-time workers. Benefits for temporary workers are also usually quite limited.

Third, employers may be more likely to classify workers as independent contractors rather than employees, which eliminates the employer's obligation to provide legally required employee benefits. However, the Internal Revenue Service scrutinizes such decisions carefully, as Microsoft and other companies have discovered. Microsoft was compelled to reclassify a group of workers as employees (rather than as independent contractors) and to grant them retroactive benefits.

NATURE OF THE WORK FORCE

Although general considerations such as cost control and "protection against the risks of old age, loss of health and life" (see Table 13.4) are important, employers must also consider the specific demographic composition and preferences of their current work forces in designing their benefits packages.

At a broad level, basic demographic factors such as age and sex can have important consequences for the types of benefits employees want. For example, an older work force is more likely to be concerned about (and use) medical coverage, life insurance, and pensions. A work force with a high percentage of women of child-bearing age may care more about disability leave. Young, unmarried men and women often have less interest in benefits generally, preferring higher wages and salaries.

Although some general conclusions about employee preferences can be drawn based on demographics, more finely tuned assessments of employee benefit preferences need to be done. One approach is to use marketing research methods to assess employees' preferences the same way consumers' demands for products and services are assessed.[63] Methods include personal interviews, focus groups, and questionnaires. Relevant questions might include

Employers Design Report Cards on HMOs Business Plan

Detroit's Big Three auto makers are fanatics about measuring the quality of suppliers of steel, rubber, and other car parts. Now, in collaboration with the United Auto Workers, they are applying some of the same zeal to rating the quality of health plans.

Dissatisfied with health-plan quality ratings available from consultants and other sources, representatives from General Motors Corp., Ford Motor Co., Chrysler Corp., and the UAW have been working for six months to develop a common report card for ranking the quality of health plans offered to Big Three employees. The new rating system will be included in handbooks that go to employees and retirees starting in mid-October.

The auto makers are among a small but growing number of big employers, including the federal government, that have responded to the confusion over how to measure health-plan quality by trying to design their own report cards, sometimes combining rating systems from two or more competing groups. The employers' goal is straightforward: They want to step up pressure on health maintenance organizations and other providers to treat patients better, cut costs, and generally shape up.

"Ranking health plans is only one step," says Woodrow Myers, director of health care management at Ford. Among the next steps: The auto makers want to rev up an existing program that gathers and publishes extensive information about costs and quality at hospitals in the Detroit area and use it as the basis for publishing data about hospitals around the country.

The Big Three are using data from three different surveys conducted by the National Committee for Quality Assurance, an independent nonprofit group in Washington, D.C. Among these is the Member Satisfaction Survey, which gauges whether consumers are happy with HMO service, including ease of getting an appointment and thoroughness of treatment.

The auto makers also want to put their health-plan scoring system and the methodology behind it on the Internet, so other employers can use it. Why? The more companies using the same rating system, the less money health plans waste filling out report-card forms.

"We'd rather have them focus resources on improving care," says Bruce Bradley, GM's director for managed care plans.

Already, federal employees (and anyone else) can use the World Wide Web to look up how dozens of health plans offered to federal workers around the country scored in patient-satisfaction surveys. The same Web pages also show whether a plan is accredited by the National Committee. (The address is http: //www.opm.gov/insure/98/html/plans.htm.)

Meanwhile, there's another big grading effort going on that health care industry officials and big employers are watching: The Health Care Financing Administration, the federal agency that runs Medicare, is developing a grading system for health plans as part of an effort to encourage more elderly beneficiaries to sign up for managed care programs.

Whatever HCFA does will have a powerful influence on health plans, and could set a pattern for private employers. But the Big Three, with combined annual health care budgets of more than $8 billion, will carry a lot of weight in the debate over what health care quality is and how to measure it.

"They really want the health care market to work, and they know it won't work until people have meaningful information," says David Lansky, president of the Foundation for Accountability, or Facct, in Portland,

- What benefits are most important to you?
- If you could choose one new benefit, what would it be?
- If you were given *x* dollars for benefits, how would you spend it?

As with surveys generally, care must be taken not to raise employee expectations regarding future changes. If the employer is not prepared to act on the employees' input, surveying may do more harm than good.

The preceding discussion may imply that the current makeup of the work force is a given, but such is not the case. As discussed earlier, the benefits package may have an important influence on the composition of the work force. For example, a benefits pack-

Oregon. The nonprofit group helped develop the Big Three/UAW report card.

As Big Three executives and their UAW counterparts discovered, producing consumer-friendly, comprehensive HMO scorecards isn't as straightforward as gauging deviations in the thickness of steel sheets.

"It's shocking how data are *not* available," says Nancy Rae, Chrysler's executive director for compensation and benefits. "Or you get data from four sources and it's not consistent."

Many UAW members already were getting inconsistent information from the car makers. GM, Ford, and Chrysler had previously published health plan ratings of their own, but these ranked many of the same plans differently. One aim of the new report card is to eliminate that kind of confusion.

Details of the report card are still being worked out, but those involved say the new scoring system will rank plans as "significantly below average," "average," or "significantly better than average" in four broad categories: consumer satisfaction, access and service, staying healthy (preventive care), and getting better/living with illness. Rankings will be represented by one, two, or three stars.

The auto makers and the union decided to develop their rankings by merging three sets of data supplied by the National Committee with a framework for reporting information in easy-to-grasp language developed by Facct. The industry group brought in experts from Rand Corp., a Santa Monica, California, think tank, to help reconcile the data and smooth out conflicts among the auto makers' previous rating systems.

The auto makers kept major HMOs informed about their new report card, and early reviews from health plan officials are mostly positive.

"I love the fact that there is collaboration in these reviews" because that limits the number of forms that need to be filled out, says Denise Christy, senior vice president for business development at Selectcare, a big Detroit HMO.

At Health Alliance Plan, another Detroit HMO with a large Big Three customer base, Associate Vice President Barbara Kopasz says the fact that HMOs are being monitored for quality will help them compete more effectively with the auto makers' traditional fee-for-service plans, which so far aren't being graded in the same way. (Auto industry officials say they want to extend the report-card approach to their indemnity plans.)

The problem, Ms. Kopasz concedes, is getting employees to take the rating system seriously. "People don't pay attention to it until they're forced to make health care decisions," she says.

Separately, the auto makers want to expand a survey that provides detailed information about quality and costs at hospitals in the seven counties around Detroit. The survey, published annually by the Southeast Michigan Employer and Purchaser Consortium, can tell a GM employee, for example, that the average cost of being treated for a heart attack at one Detroit area hospital is $15,118, and the hospital has a one-star rate of complications, or worse than the average rate for a large group of hospitals. By contrast, the average cost per case at another hospital in the region is $9,833 and the rate of complications is three stars, or better than the average of the comparison group.

This survey has prompted complaints from some hospital officials, who argue that the numbers don't account for differences in the severity of cases or the demographics of patients, says Ford's Dr. Myers. Still, he says, the Big Three, working with the American Hospital Association, are determined to expand the survey to hospitals in all locations where the auto makers have employees—in effect, almost everywhere in the country.

SOURCE: Joseph B. White, "Business Plan," *The Wall Street Journal,* Octoer 19, 1998, p. R18.

age that has strong medical benefits and pensions may be particularly attractive to older people or those with families. An attractive pension plan may be a way to attract workers who wish to make a long-term commitment to an organization. Where turnover costs are high, this type of strategy may have some appeal. On the other hand, a company that has very lucrative health care benefits may attract and retain people with high health care costs. Sick-leave provisions may also affect the composition of the work force. Organizations need to think about the signals their benefits packages send and the implications of these signals for the work force composition. In this vein, the benefits shown in Table 13.9 are designed to be attractive to a particular type of employee—those in the Silicon Valley information technology labor market.

TABLE 13.9
A Field Guide to High-Tech Perks

Sun Microsystems Inc.	Headquarters offers sun rooms with pool tables, basketball and volleyball courts, fitness equipment, and showers. "All the accouterments of a university," says spokesman Jeremy Barnish.
Yahoo! Inc.	Office attire for co-founder David Fil is typically "T-shirts, shorts, and bare feet," says Diane Hunt, director of corporate communications.
Excite Inc.	Internet firm is a round-the-clock, seven-day-a-week operation. Technical people "easily telecommute and work outside standard business hours—including East Coast hours," says spokeswoman Melissa Walia.
Qualcomm Inc.	Employees "go off on one-month junkets," says John Major, executive vice president, who adds, "I've never seen long pants on my chief engineer."
Adobe Systems Inc.	Employees get a three-week paid sabbatical every five years. And "a really neat benefit is everybody in the building has an office with a door," says Linda White, spokeswoman.

SOURCE: Q. Hardy, "Aloft in a Career without Fetters," *The Wall Street Journal* (September 29, 1998), p. B1.

COMMUNICATING WITH EMPLOYEES

Effective communication of benefits information to employees is critical if employers are to have any hope of realizing sufficient returns on their benefits investments. Research makes it clear that current employees and job applicants often have a very poor idea of what benefits provisions are already in place and the cost or market value of those benefits. One study asked employees to estimate both the amount contributed by the employer to their medical insurance and what it would cost the employees to provide their own health insurance. Table 13.10 shows that employees significantly underestimated both the cost and market value of their medical benefits. In the case of family coverage, employees estimated that the employer contributed $24, only 38 percent of the employer's actual contribution. This employer was receiving a very poor return on its benefits investment: $0.38 for every $1.00 spent.[64]

The situation with job applicants is no better. One study of MBA's found that 46 percent believed that benefits added 15 percent or less on top of direct payroll. Not surprisingly, perhaps, benefits was dead last on the applicants' priority list in making job choices.[65] A study of undergraduate business majors found similar results, with benefits ranked 15th (out of 18) in importance in evaluating jobs. These results must be interpreted with caution, however. Some research suggests that job attributes can be ranked low in importance, not because they are unimportant per se, but because all employers are perceived to be about the same on that attribute. If some employers offered noticeably poorer benefits, the importance of benefits could become much greater.

Organizations can take action to help remedy the problem of applicants' and employees' lack of knowledge about benefits. One study found that employees' awareness of benefits information was significantly increased through several media, including memoranda, question-and-answer meetings, and detailed brochures. The increased awareness, in turn, contributed to significant increases in benefits satisfaction. Another study suggests, however, that increased employee knowledge of benefits can have a positive or negative effect, depending on the nature of the benefits package. For example, there was a negative, or inverse, correlation between cost to the employee and benefits satisfaction overall, but the correlation was more strongly negative among employees with greater knowledge of their benefits.[66] The implication is that employees will be least satisfied with their benefits if their cost is high and they are well informed.

TABLE 13.10 Employee Perceptions versus Actual Cost and Market Value of Employer Contributions to Employee Medical Insurance

	EMPLOYER CONTRIBUTION			MARKET VALUE[a]		
COVERAGE	ACTUAL	EMPLOYEE PERCEPTION	RATIO	ACTUAL	EMPLOYEE PERCEPTION	RATIO
Individual	$34	$23	68%	$ 61	$37	61%
Family	64	24	38	138	43	31

Note: Dollar values in table represent means across three different insurance carriers for individual coverage and three different carriers for family coverage.
[a]Defined as the amount a nonemployee would have to pay to obtain same level of coverage.
SOURCE: Adapted from M. Wilson, G.B. Northcraft, and M.A. Neale, "The Perceived Value of Fringe Benefits," *Personnel Psychology* 38 (1985), pp. 309–20. Used with permission.

TABLE 13.11 Benefits Communication Techniques

Word of mouth	Booklets
Employee meetings	Computerized statements
Manuals	Letters to employees
Paycheck inserts	Posters
Annual reports	Check stubs
Personal counseling	Benefits fairs
Interactive computers	Annual benefits review
Television and video tapes	Slide presentations
Benefit quizzes	Telephone hot lines

SOURCE: "An Evaluation of Benefit Communication Strategy" by Michael C. Giallourakis and G. Stephen Taylor, which appeared in the 4th Quarter 1991 issue, was reprinted with permission from the *Employee Benefits Journal,* published by the International Foundation of Employee Benefit Plans, Brookfield, WI. Statements or opinions expressed in this article are those of the author and do not necessarily represent the views or positions of the International Foundation, its officers, directors, or staff.

One thing an employer should consider with respect to written benefits communication is that over 27 million employees in the United States may be functionally illiterate. Of course, there are many alternative ways to communicate benefits information. (See Table 13.11.) Nevertheless, most organizations spend less than $10 per year per employee to communicate information about benefits, and almost all of this is spent on written communication rather than on more personalized or "innovative" approaches such as benefits fairs, videos, and Web-based efforts. (See the "Competing through High-Performance Work Systems" box for a Web-based approach.) Considering that organizations spend an average of nearly $15,000 per worker per year on benefits, together with the complex nature of many benefits and the poor understanding of most employees, the typical communication effort seems woefully inadequate.[67] Organizations are spending less than $1 to communicate every $1,000 in benefits.

Rather than a single standard benefits package for all employees, flexible benefit plans (flex-plans, or cafeteria-style plans) permit employees to choose the types and amounts of benefits they want for themselves. The "Competing through Globalization" box gives an example. Plans vary according to such things as whether minimum levels of certain benefits (e.g., health care coverage) are prescribed and whether employees can receive money for having chosen a "light" benefits package (or have to pay extra for more benefits). One example is vacation, where some plans permit employees to give up vacation days for more salary or, alternatively, purchase extra vacation days through a salary reduction.

What are the potential advantages of such plans?[68] In the best case, almost all of the

Click and Shift: Workers Control Their Benefits Online

It's midnight, and you've got a lot on your mind. You want to enroll the family in a health maintenance organization, you need to arrange a loan from your 401(k) and change the mix of investments. And you'd really like to know what's happened to that claim from six weeks ago for your child's visit to the emergency room.

Getting all that done could mean several days of telephone tag and paper shuffling for most employees. But imagine being able to do it all with just a few clicks of the mouse on your home computer and still get a good night's sleep.

That's the future of corporate benefits, and the future is here today at a handful of U.S. companies that are putting their benefit plans online. New Jersey utility Public Service Electric & Gas Co., a unit of Public Service Enterprise Group, and computer maker Digital Equipment Corp. are among the pioneers in adopting interactive computer technology that allows workers to access benefit information, make changes, and conduct related business using personal computers.

By the turn of the century, interactive employee benefit systems are expected to be mainstream. "Everyone is working on it," says Barry Hall, a principal in the San Francisco office of Coopers & Lybrand LLP. He estimates that 80 percent to 90 percent of all companies are now either investigating or implementing this type of system.

Rooted in technology and driven by the corporate desire to cut costs, these new systems are expected to change fundamentally the way people deal with their benefits by giving them "more ownership, more control," says Steve McCormick of Watson Wyatt Worldwide, a management-consulting firm in Bethesda, Maryland. "It is a very, very significant change," says Mr. McCormick, who heads the firm's "virtual human resources" practice.

COMPETING THROUGH HIGH-PERFORMANCE WORK SYSTEMS

Part of the appeal is that employees will be able to get information on their own timetable. "You no longer need to call a person when an office is open to get a form or make an enrollment choice," explains Priscilla Craven, U.S. benefits communications and vendor manager at Digital.

An expanded computer system at the Maynard, Massachusetts, company began handling such benefits transactions in October, roughly the same time that PSE&G in Newark, New Jersey, started using its improved site on the Internet's World Wide Web for similar functions. At both companies, employees get into the system by entering an identification number and a password.

Once connected, they can get real-time information on company savings or 401(k) plans, and they can track historical performance updated daily over the past month, quarter, or even year-to-date, complete with graphs and charts. They can shift funds, taking advantage of asset-allocation models to make decisions.

They also can choose a health plan, researching their selection by viewing HMO report cards, and even select the doctor they wish to have.

"I have been in benefits for 36 years, and this is probably the most exciting time for the administrative side of it," says Dick Quinn, director of performance and rewards at PSE&G.

Technological advances have paved the way for these changes. Some companies first turned to computer networks a few years ago, using internal systems for annual open-enrollment periods. Recently, improved Internet security has made it

objectives discussed previously can be positively influenced. First, employees can gain a greater awareness and appreciation of what the employer provides them, particularly with plans that give employees a lump sum to allocate to benefits. Second, by permitting employee choice, there should be a better match between the benefits package and the employee's preferences. This, in turn, should improve employee attitudes and retention.[69] Third, employers may achieve overall cost reductions in their benefits programs. Cafeteria plans can be thought of as similar to defined contribution plans, whereas traditional plans are more like defined benefit plans. The employer can control the size of the contribution under the former, but not under the latter, because the cost and utilization of benefits is beyond the employer's control. Costs can also be controlled possible for corporate 401(k) providers to allow plan participants to make online transactions.

Now employers are going a step further, integrating their various programs online to create a kind of self-service benefits management.

"I think it is a logical extension of the increasing importance that both employees and employers place on the benefits packages," says Reggie Hall, principal and communications practice leader in the Dallas office of benefits consultants William M. Mercer Inc., New York.

The real growth, however, is expected because integrated online systems not only help employees but also cut costs significantly for employers. PSE&G says the cost of online enrollment is only half that of an automated voice system. And that is only the beginning.

"Our intent next year is to have completely eliminated the concept of annual open enrollment," says Mr. Quinn. This will eliminate all of the printing and communication costs associated with the annual sign-up period. When employees know they aren't locked into a health care choice for a full year, "it will make all of our managed care choices more attractive," he says.

Once an online system is up and running, it can be easy and inexpensive to add services that can make a big difference to employees. "We have been adding enhancements to the site almost weekly," says Mr. Quinn. The most recent change was a link to a state Web site that evaluates HMOs.

The ability to add to an existing benefits system is enabling some companies to take a building-block approach to the new technology. Philip Morris's Kraft Foods Inc., Northfield, Illinois, for instance, is building on the company's Intranet, or internal network, which was launched in February. It has limited links to the Internet—for locating primary care physicians, for example—and plans to add benefit enrollment next year.

GTE Corp., Stamford, Connecticut, this year expanded its Internet offerings by using a pilot group of employees to test online benefits enrollment.

Despite the promise, online systems aren't a "magic silver bullet," says Michael L. Trahan, who implements Internet operations for clients at Hewitt Associates, a Lincolnshire, Illinois, consulting firm. "It will still be one of several ways of getting access to information," he says, noting that voice-response telephone systems aren't likely to disappear soon.

One reason is that not every employee will have access to the Internet. At some manufacturing companies, for example, too few employees may have computers either at work or at home. "But if you have a company like Digital where 85 to 90 percent of the population has Internet access, this is a no-brainer," says Mr. Trahan.

Still, even this may not be a barrier for long, says Watson Wyatt's Mr. McCormick. "Where is it going to go? I can very confidently say it is going to the home," he says. Some combination of the telephone, television, and computer eventually will bring such functions into the family living room.

Other technologies also may come into play. Debit cards are now being developed for employee flexible-spending accounts, says Curtiss S. Butler, director of new media for Buck Consultants Inc., benefits-consulting unit of Mellon Bank Corp., Pittsburgh. Instead of a patient's having to file forms to be reimbursed for health care co-pays, he could have the amounts paid out of his account automatically by swiping a debit card through a card reader right in the doctor's office.

SOURCE: Lynn Asinof, "Click & Shift: Workers Control Their Benefits On-Line," *The Wall Street Journal*, November 21, 1997, pp. C1, C17.

by designing the choices so that employees have an incentive to choose more efficient options. For example, in the case of a medical flex-plan, employees who do not wish to take advantage of the (presumably more cost-effective) HMO have to pay significant deductibles and other costs under the alternative plans.

One drawback of cafeteria-style plans is their administrative cost, especially in the initial design and start-up stages. However, software packages and standardized flex-plans developed by consultants offer some help in this regard. Another possible drawback to these plans is adverse selection. Employees are most likely to choose benefits that they expect to need the most. Someone in need of dental work would choose as much dental coverage as possible. As a result, employer costs can increase signifi-

One Organization's Journey to International Flexible Remuneration

Preserving its company culture was an important aspect of Guinness Limited's efforts to move to an international flexible benefits plan.

Set in a land where heritage and culture are mainstays, even as the world moves closer to the 21st century, one international company is taking a giant leap toward a global flexible benefits plan. For Guinness Limited, this leap will occur in controlled, small steps to ensure its culture will be maintained into the next millennium.

Like other European organizations, Guinness is considering repackaging part, or all, of its employees' compensation and benefits packages to a style that is determined by the employee, not defined by the company. While this has been occurring in American-based businesses for quite some time, it is a relatively new occurrence across the Atlantic Ocean.

There are several reasons why Europeans are moving in this direction; but for some, the primary reason may not be what you think. In the United States, this movement occurred so employees could have a choice in their benefits; but most important, it helped reduce the benefits costs to an organization.

In Europe, cost control will be the result, but not the primary reason, to develop flex remuneration. Many European organizations realized that maintaining cultural values and demographic diversity were just as important, if not more important, than saving money.

COMPETING THROUGH GLOBALIZATION

At the 1998 European Compensation Conference in Brussels, Catherine Hearn, employee relations and policy director for Guinness Ltd., and Ginny Olds, principal at William M. Mercer Inc., detailed how the historic brewing company took a cautious, yet determined, step to implement "flex" benefits.

Olds said Guinness looked at flex remuneration as a means to an end. From the employer's perspective, the more-than-200-year-old company wanted to meet employee needs by increasing value delivery, improve communication and perceived values, and change the perception of compensation versus entitlement.

From the employer's viewpoint, Olds said the shift hopefully would reduce tax liabilities, acknowledge and maintain cultural and demographic diversity, support work force mobility, and manage costs.

It was a daunting task for the company and the consultant to look at making the change. Olds said there was poor employee awareness of what the company offered in total remuneration. Other constraints included

- High levels of mandatory benefits (in some countries).
- Vague or restrictive tax legislation.
- Cultural restraints such as status and paternalistic expectations.
- A lack of sophisticated service providers since the organization was headquartered outside North America.

Hearn said Guinness originally was an old-family company with strong roots in Ireland and the United Kingdom. "Generations had worked for Guinness. But we needed to update [our system] to accelerate

cantly as each employee chooses benefits based on their value to him. Another result of adverse selection is the difficulty in estimating what benefits costs will be under such a plan, especially in small companies. Adverse selection can be controlled, however, by placing limitations on coverage amounts, pricing benefits that are subject to adverse selection higher, or using a limited set of packaged options, which prevents employees from choosing too many benefits options that would be susceptible to adverse selection.

FLEXIBLE SPENDING ACCOUNTS. A flexible spending account permits pretax contributions to an employee account that can be drawn on to pay for uncovered health growth and go from paternalistic to more individual accountability."

Guinness enlisted the help of Mercer and underwent a three-stage feasibility study on introducing flexible benefits to Guinness worldwide. The first stage scoped which countries to include, the second stage detailed the organizational context, and the last stage presented a detailed study of the "flexibility" in select countries.

One of the world's largest brewers, Guinness brews its brands in nearly 50 countries and sells its beers in more than 150 nations. It employs more than 12,500 people worldwide.

After an in-depth study, Guinness selected three locations where company officials believed flexible benefits could work—Cruzcampo, Spain; the Republic of Ireland; and the mainland U.K. (excluding Northern Ireland). Each site had its advantages and disadvantages for implementing such a program.

Cruzcampo joined Guinness in the early 1900s. It has 2,400 employees in a highly regulated employment market. Hearn said there was a low awareness of the worth or value of the benefits among the employees. Here, it was decided to implement a three-year program, offering full flex benefits to the executive grades first, and gradually offer the benefits down throughout the company.

In Ireland, it was a totally different situation. An economic mainstay since its early days, Guinness is known as "the Celtic Tiger" in Ireland. Here, it is a highly unionized state with a decentralized employee administration.

"The company has offered such benefits as on-site medical facilities, a free lunch, and other items. There is a high cost to the benefits, but not necessarily something we want to withdraw from," Hearn said.

Guinness is looking at an integrated benefits strategy in Ireland that could use flexible benefits to

- Harmonize benefits across the various sites.
- Restructure provisions of certain benefits to ensure cost effectiveness.
- Create simple administration and an IT platform.
- Increase the level of employee understanding of the benefits package value.

Guinness is headquartered in the United Kingdom, where there are four divisions. Since flexible benefits have been a well-developed concept in the United Kingdom, Hearn said the recommended plan of action was simpler.

"We are looking at implementing a full flexible benefits plan for all employees on a voluntary basis; not looking to cut costs, but to do what is right in our culture," Hearn said.

This last point is important for Guinness as it moves forward in implementing flexible benefits companywide.

"Any change has to be in line with the desired Guinness culture. It is increasingly straightforward to implement, but the conditions have to be right," Hearn said.

"This is a global philosophy, not a global scheme. Three countries could develop flexible benefits. However, we will not implement a global scheme for everybody. Elsewhere we will implement greater flexibility where possible. We'll look in the future to see if the conditions become better."

SOURCE: Rodney K. Platt, "One Organization's Journey to International Flexible Remuneration," *ACA News* 41, no. 10 (November-December 1998), pp. 48–49.

care expenses (e.g., deductible or co-insurance payments). A separate account of up to \$5,000 per year is permitted for pretax contributions to cover dependent care expenses. The federal tax code requires that funds in the health care and dependent care accounts be earmarked in advance and spent during the plan year. Remaining funds revert to the employer.[70] Therefore, the accounts work best to the extent that employees have predictable expenses. The major advantage of such plans is the increase in take-home pay that results from pretax payment of health and dependent care expenses. Consider again the hypothetical employee with annual earnings of \$50,000 and an effective total marginal tax rate of 44 percent from Table 13.1. The take-home pay from an additional \$10,000 in salary with and without a flexible dependent care account is

	No Flexible Spending Care Account	*Flexible Spending Care Account*
Salary portion	$10,000	$10,000
Pretax dependent care contribution	–$ 0	–$ 5,000
Taxable salary	$10,000	$ 5,000
Tax (44 percent)	–$ 4,400	–$ 2,200
After-tax cost of dependent care	–$ 5,000	–$ 0
Take-home pay	$ 600	$ 2,800

Therefore, the use of a flexible spending account saves the employee $2,200 per year.

General Regulatory Issues

Although we have already discussed a number of regulatory issues, some additional ones require attention.

NONDISCRIMINATION RULES AND QUALIFIED PLANS

As a general rule, all benefits packages must meet certain rules to be classified as qualified plans.[71] What are the advantages of a qualified plan? Basically, it receives more favorable tax treatment than a nonqualified plan. In the case of a qualified retirement plan, for example, these tax advantages include (1) an immediate tax deduction for employers for their contributions to retirement funds, (2) no tax liability for the employee at the time of the employer deduction, and (3) investment returns (e.g., from stocks, bonds, money markets) on the retirement funds that accumulate tax free.[72]

What rules must be satisfied for a plan to obtain qualified status? Each benefit area has different rules. It would be impossible to describe the various rules here, but some general observations are possible. Taking pensions as an example again, vesting requirements must be met. More generally, qualified plans must meet so-called nondiscrimination rules. Basically, this means that a benefit cannot discriminate in favor of "highly compensated employees." One rationale behind such rules is that the tax benefits of qualified benefits plans (and the corresponding loss of tax revenues for the U.S. government) should not go disproportionately to the wealthy.[73] Rather, the favorable tax treatment is designed to encourage employers to provide important benefits to a broad spectrum of employees. The nondiscrimination rules discourage owners or top managers from adopting plans that benefit them exclusively.

SEX, AGE, AND DISABILITY

Beyond the Pregnancy Discrimination Act's requirements that were discussed earlier in the chapter, a second area of concern for employers in ensuring legal treatment of men and women in the benefits area has to do with pension benefits. Women tend to live longer than men, meaning that pension benefits for women are more costly, all else being equal. However, in its 1978 *Manhart* ruling, the Supreme Court declared it illegal for employers to require women to contribute more to a defined benefit plan than men: Title VII protects individuals, and not all women outlive all men.[74]

Two major age-related issues have received attention under the Age Discrimination in Employment Act (ADEA) and later amendments such as the Older Workers Benefit Protection Act (OWBPA). First, employers must take care not to discriminate against workers over age 40 in the provision of pay or benefits. As one example, employers cannot generally cease accrual (i.e., stop the growth) of retirement benefits at some age (e.g., 65) as a way of pressuring older employees to retire.[75] Second, early retirement incentive programs need to meet the following standards to avoid legal liability: (1) the employee is not coerced to accept the incentive and retire, (2) accurate information is provided regarding options, and (3) the employee is given adequate time (i.e., not pressured) to make a decision.

Employers also have to comply with the Americans with Disabilities Act (ADA), which went into effect in 1992. The ADA specifies that employees with disabilities must have "equal access to whatever health insurance coverage the employer provides other employees." However, the act also notes that the terms and conditions of health insurance can be based on risk factors as long as this is not a subterfuge for denying the benefit to those with disabilities. Employers with risk-based programs in place would be in a stronger position, however, than employers who make changes after hiring employees with disabilities.[76]

MONITORING FUTURE BENEFITS OBLIGATIONS

Financial Accounting Statement (FAS) 106, issued by the Financial Accounting Standards Board, became effective in 1993. This rule requires that any benefits (excluding pensions) provided after retirement (the major one being health care) can no longer be funded on a pay-as-you-go basis. Rather, they must be paid on an accrual basis, and companies must enter these future cost obligations on their financial statements.[77] The effect on financial statements can be substantial. For AT&T, a company with a large retiree population, the initial effect of adopting FAS 106 was a reduction in net income of between $5.5 billion and $7.5 billion. General Motors (GM) took a $20.8 billion reduction in net income, resulting in a total loss of $23.5 billion in 1992, the largest loss in corporate history.[78]

Increasing retiree health care costs (and the change in accounting standards) have led companies like GM to require its white-collar employees and retirees to pay insurance premiums for the first time in its history and to increase copayments and deductibles. Survey data indicate that some companies are ending retiree health care benefits altogether, while most have reduced benefits or increased retiree contributions. Obviously, such changes hit the elderly hard, especially those with relatively fixed incomes. Not surprisingly, legal challenges have arisen. The need to balance the interests of shareholders, current employees, and retirees in this area will be one of the most difficult challenges facing managers in the future.

Taken together, retiree medical care and pension liabilities (discussed earlier) can have a very large effect on a company's financial health. In fact, Standard & Poor's (S&P) reacted to GM's underfunded pension and massive retiree health care obligations by downgrading GM's debt from A-minus to BBB-plus. This was a warning to investors that GM had become a more risky company. As a result, GM's cost of raising capital increased. S&P warned that the cash needed by GM each year to cover its massive benefits obligations will be a substantial drain on the company's financial resources—and therefore a significant competitive disadvantage—for the foreseeable future.[79] Fortunately, by 1995, GM was able to make enough progress that its debt rating was increased.[80]

SUMMARY

Effective management of employee benefits is an important means by which organizations successfully compete. Benefits costs are substantial and continue to grow rapidly in some areas, most notably health care. Control of such costs is necessary to compete in the product market. At the same time, employers must offer a benefits package that permits them to compete in the labor market. Beyond investing more money in benefits, this attraction and retention of quality employees can be helped by better communication of the value of the benefits package and by allowing employees to tailor benefits to their own needs through flexible benefits plans.

Employers continue to be a major source of economic security for employees, often providing health insurance, retirement benefits, and so forth. Changes to benefits can have a tremendous impact on employees and retirees. Therefore, employers carry a significant social responsibility in making benefits decisions. At the same time, employees need to be aware that they will increasingly become responsible for their own economic security. Health care benefit design is changing to encourage employees to be more informed consumers, and retirement benefits will depend more and more on the financial investment decisions employees make on their own behalf.

DISCUSSION QUESTIONS

1. The opening vignette described how relationships between employers and employees are changing. What are the likely consequences of this change? Where does the social responsibility of employers end, and where does the need to operate more efficiently begin?
2. Your company, like many others, is experiencing double-digit percentage increases in health care costs. What suggestions can you offer that may reduce the rate of cost increases?
3. Why is communication so important in the employee benefits area? What sorts of programs can a company use to communicate more effectively? What are the potential positive consequences of more effective benefits communication?
4. What are the potential advantages of flexible benefits and flexible spending accounts? Are there any potential drawbacks?
5. Although benefits account for a large share of employee compensation, many feel there is little evidence on whether an employer receives an adequate return on the benefits investment. One suggestion has been to link benefits to individual, group, or organization performance. Explain why you would or would not recommend this strategy to an organization.

WEB EXERCISE

The Health Insurance Portability and Accountability Act (HIPAA) of 1996 is a major health care reform mandate that sets minimum standards to improve the access, portability, and renewability of health insurance coverage. Visit www.hcfa.gov/hipaq/hipaahm.htm (the Web site for HIPAA), which answers some commonly asked questions for small employers about the provisions of HIPAA.

1. What does *portability* mean?
2. What is a pre-existing condition? How does HIPPA affect how businesses can apply pre-existing condition exclusions to employees?
3. How does HIPPA benefit small employers?

MANAGING PEOPLE: FROM THE PAGES OF "BUSINESS WEEK"

BusinessWeek Commentary: The Health-Care Net Is Shrinking

For the past several years, no one has been complaining much about affordable health coverage or the plight of the uninsured—and for good reason. Medical costs have been so tame that companies and employees alike are paying less for health insurance, after inflation, than in the early 1990s. A record share of the population is working, giving more people access to employer plans. And wage hikes are beating inflation, so more families can afford co-payments.

Economic conditions have been nearly ideal—but how deep is their impact? Not very. True, the share of the population with employer coverage has stopped its downward spiral. But coverage hasn't recovered any lost ground either, leaving the ranks of the uninsured at high levels. The point was driven home on September 25, when the Census Bureau released 1997 health coverage statistics. In 1987, employers covered 69% of the nonelderly population. By 1993, the level was only 64%, where it has been stuck ever since, according to an analysis of Census data by Washington-based Employee Benefit Research Institute (EBRI).

This is bad news, since at least some of the current positive economic factors are sure to reverse course in the next year or two. Medical costs are starting to rise again, with premiums jumping 3.3% this year, according to KPMG Peat Marwick. If that continues, or if job growth or wage increases turn down, medical coverage is certain to slide more—landing more people suffering from more acute illnesses in emergency rooms of hospitals. Unfortunately, welfare reform will contribute to the problem, because former recipients usually find low-wage jobs that are the least likely to offer insurance. "It's only going to get worse," says Victoria Caldeira, a health care lobbyist for the National Federation of Independent Business, which represents small employers.

Nor is relief in sight. Since the flameout of Hillary Rodham Clinton's 1994 health care initiative, Democrats haven't had many new ideas for preventing the return of big cost increases, and neither have Republicans or business groups. Unless policymakers start to grapple with costs now or find new ways to help the uninsured, we may be caught flat-footed when the problem flares up again.

Still, there's no question that the past few years have helped alleviate the crisis of the early 1990s. The shift to managed care and lower overall inflation has worked wonders on expenses. After years of double-digit increases, premium hikes lagged the medical inflation rate from 1994 to 1997, according to annual surveys by KPMG. As a result, inflation-adjusted employer spending on employee health care has plunged by 22% since 1992, to $1.13 an hour, according to an analysis of Bureau of Labor Statistics data by the Economic Policy Institute, a Washington think tank.

Employers haven't shared much of the savings with their employees, though. Workers paid an average of $120 a month for family coverage last year. That's down just 5% from 1992, after adjusting for medical inflation, according to KPMG. Even though employers are offering health insurance plans to slightly more people than in 1989, three recent studies show, fewer employees are signing up because of the cost. "The main problem is affordable coverage," says Thomas H. Rice, a professor of public health at the University of California at Los Angeles who co-authored one of the studies.

If medical inflation returns in force, employers may again slash coverage or shift costs to workers, some of whom will drop their insurance coverage. Small employers are particularly vulnerable. Tugboat operator Thompson Marine Transportation Co., based in Morgan City, Louisiana, got hit with a 50% increase last month for the health insurance it offers its 25 workers. The company now shells out $6,200 a month to keep them covered, says owner Robert J. Thompson. "I wouldn't discontinue coverage if it goes up again, but I might have to ask my people to pay more," he says.

Not surprisingly, the pool of uninsured Americans climbed again in 1997, by about half a percentage point, to 18.3% of the nonelderly population, according to EBRI. Declining welfare rolls are a key reason. Although many low-wage workers remain eligible for Medicaid, they're not getting it. Health experts say part of the explanation may be that many states have done a poor job of providing the forms and assistance that these workers need to re-enroll after leaving welfare. In addition, many former welfare mothers may not realize that they're still eligible for Medicaid if they earn near-poverty incomes. Whatever the cause, Medicaid enrollment has declined by nearly two percentage points since 1993, to 11% of the population last year, according to EBRI. Since employer coverage is unchanged, more Americans are left uninsured.

Unfortunately, the problem is likely to get worse. Welfare reform's new time limits will probably force 1.5 million more recipients off the rolls in the next couple of years, according to studies. Many will land jobs with no insurance. And if unemployment edges back up, they'll probably be among the first to be left out in the cold.

Employer-based health insurance served the country well for half a century, ever since company plans proliferated in the 1940s. That model began to fray in the late 1980s. Given the high price of care today, it's not clear that small employers or those that pay rock-bottom wages can afford to remain in the game. Either we come up with a way to help them, or the system may soon break down even further.

QUESTIONS

1. What explains the drop in the percentage of people covered by health insurance?
2. How has the role of employers in providing health care coverage changed? What factors explain this change?
3. Have employers made similar changes in other benefits areas? If yes, are the reasons the same?

SOURCE: Aaron Bernstein, "Commentary: The Health-Care Net Is Shrinking," *Business Week*, October 12, 1998, p. 144+.

NOTES

1. K. Jackson, "Accounting Change Forces Ford to Post Loss in Billions," *Automotive News*, December 21, 1992, p. 6.
2. H.W. Hennessey, "Using Employee Benefits to Gain a Competitive Advantage," *Benefits Quarterly* 5, no. 1 (1989), pp. 51–57; B. Gerhart and G.T. Milkovich, "Employee Compensation: Research and Practice," in *Handbook of Industrial and Organizational Psychology*, vol. 3, 2d

ed., ed. M.D. Dunnette and L.M. Hough (Palo Alto, CA: Consulting Psychologists Press, 1992).

3. R. G. Ehrenberg and R.S. Smith, *Modern Labor Economics* (Glenview, IL: Scott, Foresman and Company, 1988).
4. B.T. Beam Jr. and J.J. McFadden, *Employee Benefits* (Chicago: Dearborn Financial Publishing, 1992).
5. Bureau of National Affairs, "Most Workers Who Struck in 1990 Did So over Health Coverage, AFL–CIO Says," *Daily Labor Report*, August 20, 1991, p. A12.
6. The organization and description in this section draws heavily on Beam and McFadden, *Employee Benefits*.
7. Bureau of National Affairs, *State Unemployment Insurance Funds* (October 2, 1997), pp. 316–17.
8. J.A. Penczak, "Unemployment Benefit Plans," in *Employee Benefits Handbook*, 3d ed., ed. J.D. Mamorsky (Boston: Warren, Gorham & Lamont, 1992).
9. J.V. Nackley, *Primer on Workers' Compensation* (Washington, DC: Bureau of National Affairs, 1989).
10. Beam and McFadden, *Employee Benefits*, p. 59.
11. Nackley, *Primer on Workers' Compensation*; P.M. Lencsis, *Workers Compensation* (Westport, CT: Quorum Books, 1998).
12. M.D. Fefer, "What to Do about Workers' Comp," *Fortune*, June 29, 1992, pp. 80ff.
13. Ibid.
14. J.R. Hollenbeck, D.R. Ilgen, and S.M. Crampton, "Lower Back Disability in Occupational Settings: A Review of the Literature from a Human Resource Management View," *Personnel Psychology* 45 (1992), pp. 247–78.
15. Gallup-collected data are summarized in Employee Benefit Research Institute, "Health-Care Reform: Trade-offs and Implications," EBRI Issue Brief, no. 125 (Washington, DC: Employee Benefit Research Institute, April 1992).
16. Beam and McFadden, *Employee Benefits*.
17. *Employee Benefits Notes*, July 1992, pp. 1–3. Original data from Susan Grad, *Income of the Population 55 or Older 1988*. U. S. Dept. of Health and Human Services, Social Security Administration, Publication 13-11871 (Washington, DC: Government Printing Office, 1988).
18. L.M. Dailey and J.A. Turner, "Private Pension Coverage in Nine Countries," *Monthly Labor Review*, May 1992, pp. 40–43; Hewitt Associates, *Salaried Employee Benefits Provided by Major Employers in 1990* (Lincolnshire, IL: Hewitt Associates, 1990); W. J. Wiatrowski, "New Survey Data on Pension Benefits," *Monthly Labor Review*, August 1991, pp. 8–21.
19. M. Slate, "The Retirement Protection Act," *Labor Law Journal* (April 1995), pp. 245–50.
20. R.M. McCaffery, "Employee Benefits and Services," in *Compensation and Benefits*, ed. L.R. Gomez-Mejia (Washington, DC: Bureau of National Affairs, 1989).
21. www.irs.gov
22. R.A. Ippolito, "Toward Explaining the Growth of Defined Contribution Plans," *Industrial Relations* 34 (1995), pp. 1–20.
23. J. Fierman, "How Secure Is Your Nest Egg?" *Fortune*, August 12, 1991, pp. 50–54.
24. Beam and McFadden, *Employee Benefits*.
25. B.J. Coleman, *Primer on Employee Retirement Income Security Act*, 3d ed. (Washington, DC: Bureau of National Affairs, 1989).
26. *Continental Can Company v. Gavalik*, summary in *Daily Labor Report* (December 8, 1987). Supreme Court lets stand Third Circuit ruling that pension avoidance scheme is ERISA violation. No. 234, p. A-14.
27. A.L. Gustman, O.S. Mitchell, and T.L. Steinmeier, "The Role of Pensions in the Labor Market: A Survey of the Literature," *Industrial and Labor Relations* 47 (1994), pp. 417–38.
28. D.A. DeCenzo and S.J. Holoviak, *Employee Benefits* (Englewood Cliffs, NJ: Prentice-Hall, 1990).
29. E.P. Lazear, "Why Is There Early Retirement?" *Journal of Political Economy* 87 (1979), pp. 1261–84; Gustman et al., "The Role of Pensions."
30. S. Dorsey, "Pension Portability and Labor Market Efficiency," *Industrial and Labor Relations* 48, no. 5 (1995), pp. 276–92.
31. U.S. data on paid holidays are from Hewitt Associates, *Salaried Employee Benefits Provided by Major U.S. Employers* (Lincolnshire, IL: Hewitt Associates, 1990); European data are from Commerce Clearing House, *Doing Business in Europe* (New York: Commerce Clearing House, 1990).
32. DeCenzo and Holoviak, *Employee Benefits*.
33. S.L. Grover and K.J. Crooker, "Who Appreciates Family Responsive Human Resource Policies: The Impact of Family-Friendly Policies on the Organizational Attachment of Parents and Non-parents," *Personnel Psychology* 48 (1995), pp. 271–88.
34. Employee Benefit Research Institute, "The Employer's Role in Helping Working Families," *Employee Benefit Notes* (November 1991), pp. 3–5; "Most Small Businesses Appear Prepared to Cope with New Family Leave Rules," *The Wall Street Journal*, February 8, 1993, pp. B1ff.
35. "The Employer's Role in Helping Working Families." For examples of child care arrangements in some well-known companies (e.g., AT&T, Apple, Exxon, IBM, Merck), see "A Look at Child-Care Benefits," *USA Today*, March 14, 1989, p. 4B.
36. Bureau of National Affairs, *101 Key Statistics on Work and Family for the 1990s* (Washington, DC: Bureau of National Affairs, 1989), p. 29.
37. P. Hardin, "Women Execs Should Feel at Ease about Taking Full Maternity Leave," *Personnel Journal* (September 1995), p. 19.

38. D.E. Friedman, "Addressing the Supply Problem: The Family Daycare Approach," in *Investing in People: A Strategy to Address America's Workforce Crisis* (Washington, DC: U.S. Department of Labor, 1989).
39. J. Fierman, "It's 2 A.M.: Let's Go to Work," *Fortune*, August 21, 1995, pp. 82–88.
40. E.E. Kossek, "Diversity in Child Care Assistance Needs: Employee Problems, Preferences, and Work-Related Outcomes," *Personnel Psychology* 43 (1990), pp. 769–91.
41. E. E. Kossek, *The Acceptance of Human Resource Innovation: Lessons from Management* (Westport, CT: Quorum, 1989).
42. G. Flynn, "Some of Your Best Ideas May be Working against You," *Personnel Journal* (October 1995), pp. 77–83.
43. R. Broderick and B. Gerhart, "Nonwage Compensation," in *The Human Resource Management Handbook,* ed. D. Lewin, D.J.B. Mitchell, and M.A. Zadi (San Francisco: JAI Press, 1996).
44. Hennessey, "Using Employee Benefits to Gain a Competitive Advantage."
45. For example, Hewitt Associates, *Salaried Employee Benefits;* Bureau of Labor Statistics, *Employee Benefits in State and Local Governments, 1990* (Washington, DC: U.S. Government Printing Office, 1992); Bureau of Labor Statistics, *Employee Benefits in Medium and Large Establishments, 1989* (Washington, DC: U.S. Government Printing Office, 1990); Bureau of Labor Statistics, *Employee Benefits in Small Private Establishments, 1990* (Washington, DC: U.S. Government Printing Office, 1991).
46. G. Koretz, "Bitter Medicine for Workers," *Business Week,* August 21, 1995, p. 20; Employee Benefit Research Institute, "Health Care Reform: Trade-offs and Implications," *EBRI Issue Brief* no. 125, April 1992; Employee Benefit Research Institute, "Employment-Based Health Care Benefits and Self-Funded Employment-Based Plans: An Overview" (September/October 1998).
47. Employee Benefit Research Institute, "Health Care Reform."
48. A.C. Monheit and P.F. Cooper, "Health Insurance and Job Mobility: The Effects of Public Policy on Job-Lock," *Industrial and Labor Relations Review* 48 (1994), pp. 86–102.
49. Beam and McFadden, *Employee Benefits.*
50. American Compensation Association, "Health Care Reform Strategies," *ACA NEWS* 37, no. 9 (1994), pp. 22–24.
51. M. Barringer and O.S. Mitchell, "Workers' Preferences among Company-Provided Health Insurance Plans," *Industrial and Labor Relations Review* 48 (1994), pp. 141–52.
52. Beam and McFadden, *Employee Benefits.*
53. J.E. Fielding and P.V. Pirerchia, "Frequency of Worksite Health Promotion Activities," *American Journal of Public Health* 79 (1989), pp. 16–20.
54. S. Tully, "America's Healthiest Companies," *Fortune*, June 12, 1995, pp. 98–106.
55. G. Flynn, "Companies Make Wellness Work," *Personnel Journal* (February 1995), pp. 63–66.
56. D.A. Harrison and L.Z. Liska, "Promoting Regular Exercise in Organizational Fitness Programs: Health-Related Differences in Motivational Building Blocks," *Personnel Psychology* 47 (1994), pp. 47–71.
57. J.C. Erfurt, A. Foote, and M.A. Heirich, "The Cost-Effectiveness of Worksite Wellness Programs for Hypertension Control, Weight Loss, Smoking Cessation and Exercise," *Personnel Psychology* 45 (1992), pp. 5–27.
58. Ibid.
59. H. Gardner, unpublished manuscript (Cheyenne, WY: Options & Choices, Inc., 1995).
60. H. B. Noble, "Quality Is Focus for Health Plans," *The New York Times*, July 3, 1995, p. A1; J.D. Klinke, "Medicine's Industrial Revolution," *The Wall Street Journal,* August 21, 1995, p. A8.
61. J. Schor, *The Overworked American: The Unexpected Decline of Leisure* (New York: Basic Books, 1991). U.S. Bureau of Labor Statistics, "Workers Are On the Job More Hours Over the Course of a Year," *Issues in Labor Statistics*, February 1997.
62. G. Mangum, D. Mayall, and K. Nelson, "The Temporary Help Industry: A Response to the Dual Internal Labor Market," *Industrial and Labor Relations Review* 38 (1985), pp. 599–611; M. Montgomery, "On the Determinants of Employer Demand for Part-Time Workers," *Review of Economics and Statistics* 70 (1988), pp. 112–17; F.A. Scott, M.C. Berger, and D.A. Black, "Effects of the Tax Treatment of Fringe Benefits on Labor-Market Segmentation," *Industrial and Labor Relations Review* 42 (1989), pp. 216–29. Some conflicting evidence on part-time workers, however, is provided by C. Tilly, "Reasons for the Continued Growth in Part Time Employment," *Monthly Labor Review* 114, no. 3 (1991), pp. 10–18.
63. Beam and McFadden, *Employee Benefits*.
64. M. Wilson, G.B. Northcraft, and M.A. Neale, "The Perceived Value of Fringe Benefits," *Personnel Psychology* 38 (1985), pp. 309–20. Similar results were found in other studies reviewed by H.W. Hennessey, P.L. Perrewe, and W.A. Hochwarter, "Impact of Benefit Awareness on Employee and Organizational Outcomes: A Longitudinal Field Experiment," *Benefits Quarterly* 8, no. 2 (1992), pp. 90–96.
65. R. Huseman, J. Hatfield, and R. Robinson, "The MBA and Fringe Benefits," *Personnel Administrator* 23, no. 7 (1978), pp. 57–60. See summary in H. W. Hennessey Jr., "Using Employee Benefits to Gain a Competitive Advantage," *Benefits Quarterly* 5, no. 1 (1989), pp. 51–57.
66. Hennessey et al., "Impact of Benefit Awareness." The same study found no impact of the increased awareness

and benefits satisfaction on overall job satisfaction; G.F. Dreher, R.A. Ash, and R.D. Bretz, "Benefit Coverage and Employee Cost: Critical Factors in Explaining Compensation Satisfaction," *Personnel Psychology* 41 (1988), pp. 237–54.

67. M.C. Giallourakis and G.S. Taylor, "An Evaluation of Benefit Communication Strategy," *Employee Benefits Journal* 15, no. 4 (1991), pp. 14–18; U.S. Chamber of Commerce, *Employee Benefits*.
68. Beam and McFadden, *Employee Benefits*.
69. For supportive evidence, see A.E. Barber, R.B. Dunham, and R.A. Formisano, "The Impact of Flexible Benefits on Employee Satisfaction: A Field Study," *Personnel Psychology* 45 (1992), pp. 55–75; E.E. Lawler, *Pay and Organizational Development* (Reading, MA: Addison-Wesley, 1981).
70. P. Biggins, "Flexible/Cafeteria Plans," in *Employee Benefits Handbook*, 3d ed.
71. For a description of these rules, see M.M. Sarli, "Nondiscrimination Rules for Qualified Plans: The General Test," *Compensation and Benefits Review* 23, no. 5 (September–October 1991), pp. 56–67.
72. Beam and McFadden, *Employee Benefits*, p. 359.
73. Ibid., p. 355.
74. *Los Angeles Dept. of Water & Power v. Manhart*, 435 US SCt 702 (1978), 16 EPD, 8250.
75. S.K. Hoffman, "Discrimination Litigation Relating to Employee Benefits," *Labor Law Journal* (June 1992), pp. 362–81.
76. Ibid., p. 375.
77. Ibid.
78. W.A. Reimert, "Accounting for Retiree Health Benefits," *Compensation and Benefits Review* 23, no. 5 (September–October, 1991), pp. 49–55; D.P. Levin, "20.8 Billion G.M. Charge for Benefits," *The New York Times*, February 2, 1993, p. D4.
79. J.B. White, "GM's Pension, Medical Cost Liabilities Cause S&P to Downgrade Firm's Debt," *The Wall Street Journal*, February 4, 1993, pp. A2ff.
80. N. Templin, "GM's Ratings on Senior Debt Raised a Notch," *The Wall Street Journal*, May 31, 1995, p. A5.

Perks and Fitness: No Longer a Nicety but A Necessity

VIDEO CASE

Employees today face longer hours, less job security, and the challenge of balancing work and nonwork. These are just a few factors that can raise employee's stress to unbearable and unhealthy levels. For example, at a Corning Inc. plant in Blacksburg, Virginia, it is not uncommon for employees to work more than 60 hours per week. Factories such as Corning Inc. prefer to pay overtime to hiring new employees for several reasons. Training new employees is a lengthy and costly process. Existing employees are constantly being taught new skills so it makes sense to fully utilize them. Using overtime fits the philosophy of flexibility to meet changes in customers' type and amount of orders. Liberal use of overtime provides workers with a degree of job security. Overtime can be cut before management has to lay off employees. While overtime provides extra money, it also has its costs. Employees have fewer hours for hobbies and other activities they use to relax. Employees on overtime spend less time with spouses, children, friends, and relatives. Employees who utilize overtime also have less time to spend doing day-to-day chores such as getting the car repaired, paying bills, or buying gifts. Excessive stress levels are caused not only by companies economic turmoil but also by opportunities that occur through entering global markets, developing new products and services, and mergers and acquisition of businesses (e.g., Daimler-Benz–Chrysler and First Chicago NBD–Banc One Corporation mergers.

Managers also feel the pressure to deal with stress. Managers know that stress is a barrier to motivating the workforce. They also recognize that stress can result in stress-related illnesses, such as high blood pressure, ulcers, and fatigue. These illnesses translate into higher benefits costs for the company as employees more frequently use health care benefits.

A number of companies use nontraditional benefits and perks to help employees cope with stress. S.C. Johnson Company in Racine, Wisconsin, encourages its employees and supervisors in the customer service department to alleviate pressure and stress through fun. It's not unusual for a supervisor and an employee to arm themselves with water pistols and fight it out to the drenching end! At each of its 20 buildings at its 200-acre campus in Raleigh, North Carolina, SAS Institute provides coffee break rooms stocked with free soda, fresh fruit, M&Ms and pastries. SAS employs a full-time ergonomics specialist to select office furniture that will reduce physical stress and strain. SAS provides a free health clinic as well as an eldercare program that helps employees locate nursing care facilities for aging parents.

Many companies provide benefits that help employees cope with the stresses and demands of balancing work and nonwork. Cigna Insurance Company offers employees the option of placing take-out meal orders with the company chef. Employees who don't have the energy to prepare meals after a long or difficult workday can take home a prepared meal. The company also offers an exercise physiologist to help employees suffering from stress. Andersen Consulting employs a concierge to run errands (such as shopping) for employees. Wilton-Connor Packaging Company employees can bring their laundry to work with them and have it done for $1 per load (ironing is 25 cents extra). The company also provides the services of a handyman to perform jobs such as painting at employees' homes. The only cost to the employee is the cost of the paint.

Companies are also offering wellness and exercise programs to help employees alleviate stress and enhance their health at the same time. Coca-Cola found that employees who participated in wellness and exercise programs used fewer sick days and tended to be more productive on their jobs. Home Depot found similar results and now provides exercise facilities and classes onsite for employees to help them stop smoking, eat healthy nutritious foods, and manage work-nonwork conflicts.

Are companies providing these services to look good to the community or because they are financially successful? Not really. It is shrewd business operations. For example, it is estimated that SAS Institute saves $50 million a year due to low turnover. SAS turnover rate is 4 percent per year compared to the industry norm of more than 20 percent per year. While the free health clinic costs $1 million to operate, it is $500,000 less than the costs the company would realize if employees were treated elsewhere.

DISCUSSION QUESTIONS

1. How might a company evaluate whether providing nontraditional benefits result in a financial payoff? What outcomes would they consider?
2. Do nontraditional benefits such as eldercare and concierge services help companies recruit and retain a more diverse workforce? Explain.
3. What other perks and benefits might companies consider to lower stress levels and improve productivity?

Source: Based on E.J. Pollock, "It's Getting Stressful!!! On the Job," *The Wall Street Journal*, October 20, 1998, pp. B1 & B4; T. Aeppel, "Living Overtime: A Factory Workaholic," *The Wall Street Journal*, October 13, 1998, pp. B1 & B18; T.D. Schellhardt, "An Idyllic Workplace under a Tycoon's Thumb," *The Wall Street Journal*, November 23, 1998, B1 & B4.

PART V

Special Topics in Human Resources

CHAPTER 14
Collective Bargaining and Labor Relations

CHAPTER 15
Managing Human Resources Globally

CHAPTER 16
Strategically Managing the HR Function

14 CHAPTER

Collective Bargaining and Labor Relations

OBJECTIVES

After reading this chapter, you should be able to

1. Describe what is meant by collective bargaining and labor relations.
2. Identify the labor relations goals of management, labor unions, and society.
3. Explain the legal environment's impact on labor relations.
4. Describe the major labor management interactions: organizing, contract negotiations, and contract administration.
5. Describe new, less adversarial approaches to labor management relations.
6. Explain how changes in competitive challenges (e.g., product-market competition and globalization) are influencing labor–management interactions.
7. Explain how labor relations in the public sector differ from labor relations in the private sector.

Labor Relations and the Bottom Line

ENTER THE WORLD OF BUSINESS

As in previous strikes during the 1990s, the main issue in the 54-day strike by the United Auto Workers (UAW) at two General Motors (GM) parts plants in Flint, Michigan, in 1998 was job security and whether GM would invest in plants in the United States or continue its effort to cut U.S. employment and shift production overseas to reduce its labor costs. The strike at the two parts plants shut down operations at virtually all of GM's North American vehicle assembly plants. As a result, GM was prevented from building 545,000 vehicles and its second- and third-quarter earnings were reduced by a total of $2.83 billion. Although GM hopes to make up for some of the lost production by running heavy overtime schedules at its plants, it still anticipates that annual earnings will be lower by $2 billion because of the strike. In addition, GM's market share dropped to a historic low of 20 percent. The labor relations dispute is the most recent in a long line of costly disputes between the UAW and GM during the 1990s. And, the future does not look rosy. GM plans to spin off its Delphi Automotive Systems parts unit in 1999. However, this move would eliminate 200,000 UAW workers from the GM payroll, something that may be unacceptable to the UAW. A similar plan had been in the works at Ford: to spin off its Visteon parts unit. However, Ford has put the idea on hold, according to some, because of UAW opposition. Ford has not had the same labor relations problems that GM has had and is interested in maintaining its good relationship with the UAW.

SOURCE: R.L. Simison, "GM Strike Reduced Its Earnings by $2.83 Billion in 2nd and 3rd Periods," *The Wall Street Journal,* August 17, 1998, p. A3; "GM: It'll Be a Long Road Back," *Business Week,* August 17, 1998, p. 38+.

Introduction

The events at GM illustrate both the important role of labor relations in running a business and the influence of competitive challenges on the nature of labor relations. Increased competition in the automobile market has forced GM to rethink the way its business is organized and managed, including its labor relations. To be more competitive, GM has decided it must become a smaller and more efficient producer of automobiles. It plans to substantially reduce its work force, which includes many UAW workers. GM is also attempting to shift its production to use less expensive labor. This includes setting up production facilities in places like Mexico and subcontracting work to nonunion U.S. facilities. However, the UAW will fight to protect its members' wages and employment. GM's and the UAW's conflicting objectives become readily apparent during a strike.

A strike (withholding labor) is a key union bargaining tool, and it is effective to the extent that is imposes costs on the company—in the example, lost sales. Strikes also impose costs on workers, however. In the short term, workers lose their income; in the longer term, they may be replaced by other workers, or their jobs may disappear altogether if the strike costs the company too many customers. Therefore, GM and the UAW realize that they also have mutual interests. Conflict must be balanced with cooperation if they are to survive.

The Labor Relations Framework

John Dunlop, former secretary of labor and a leading industrial relations scholar, suggested in the book *Industrial Relations Systems* (1958) that such a system consists of four elements: (1) an environmental context (technology, market pressures, and the legal framework, especially as it affects bargaining power); (2) participants, including employees and their unions, managements, and the government; (3) a "web of rules" (i.e., rules of the game) that describe the process by which labor and management interact and resolve disagreements (e.g., the steps followed in settling contract grievances); and (4) ideology.[1] For the industrial relations system to operate properly, the three participants must, to some degree, have a common ideology (e.g., acceptance of the capitalist system) and must accept the roles of the other participants. Acceptance does not translate into convergence of interests, however. To the contrary, some degree of worker–management conflict is inevitable because, although the interests of the two parties overlap, they also diverge in key respects (e.g., how to divide the economic profits).[2]

Therefore, according to Dunlop and other U.S. scholars of like mind, an effective industrial relations system does not eliminate conflict. Rather, it provides institutions (and a "web of rules") that resolve conflict in a way that minimizes its costs to management, employees, and society. The collective-bargaining system is one such institution, as are related mechanisms such as mediation, arbitration, and participation in decision making. These ideas formed the basis for the development in the 1940s of schools and departments of industrial and labor relations to train labor relations professionals who, working in both union and management positions, would have the skills to minimize costly forms of conflict such as strikes (which were reaching record levels at the time) and maximize integrative (win-win) solutions to such disagreements.[3]

A more recent industrial relations model, developed by Harry Katz and Thomas Kochan, is particularly helpful in laying out the types of decisions managements and unions make in their interactions and the consequences of such decisions for attainment of goals in areas such as wages and benefits, job security, and the rights and responsibilities of unions and managements.[4] According to Katz and Kochan, these choices occur at three levels.

First, at the strategic level, management makes basic choices such as whether to work with its union(s) or to devote its efforts to developing nonunion operations. Environmental factors (or competitive challenges) offer both constraints and opportunities in implementing strategies. For example, if public opinion toward labor unions becomes negative during a particular time period, some employers may see that as an opportunity to rid themselves of unions, whereas other employers may seek to develop a better working relationship with their unions. Similarly, increased competition may dictate the need to increase productivity or reduce labor costs, but whether this is accomplished by shifting work to nonunion facilities or by working with unions to become more competitive is a strategic choice that management faces.

Although management has often been the initiator of change in recent years, unions face a similar choice between fighting changes to the status quo and being open to new labor–management relationships (e.g., less adversarial forms of participation in decision making, such as labor–management teams).

Katz and Kochan suggest that labor and management choices at the strategic level in turn affect the labor–management interaction at a second level, the functional level, where contract negotiations and union organizing occur, and at the final, workplace level, the arena in which the contract is administered. In the opening vignette, GM's strategic-level choice to cut costs and increase productivity by moving production overseas, combined with the UAW's strategic choice to take a stand on the issue, contributed to conflict (a strike) at the workplace level over the administration of the contract. Although the relationships between labor and management at each of the three levels are somewhat interdependent, the relationship at the three levels may also differ. For example, while management may have a strategy of building an effective relationship with its unions at the strategic level, there may be significant day-to-day conflicts over work rules, grievances, and so forth at any given facility or bargaining unit.

The labor relations framework depicted in Figure 14.1 incorporates many of the ideas discussed so far, including the important role of the environment (i.e., the competitive challenges); union, management, and societal goals; and a separation of union–management interactions into categories (union organizing, contract negotiation, contract administration) that can have important influences on one another but may also be analyzed somewhat independently. The model also highlights the important role that relative bargaining power plays in influencing goals, union–management interactions, and the degree to which each party achieves its goals. Relative bargaining power, in turn, is significantly influenced by the competitive environment (i.e., legal, social, quality, high-performance work system, and globalization competitive challenges) and the size and depth of union membership.[5]

We now describe the components of this model in greater depth. The remainder of the chapter is organized into the following sections: the goals and strategies of society, management, and unions; union structure (including union administration and membership); the legal framework, perhaps the key aspect of the competitive environment for labor relations; union and management interactions (organizing, contract negotiation, contract administration); and goal attainment. Environmental factors (other than legal) and bargaining power are discussed in the context of these sections. In addition, two special topics, international comparisons and public sector labor relations, are discussed.

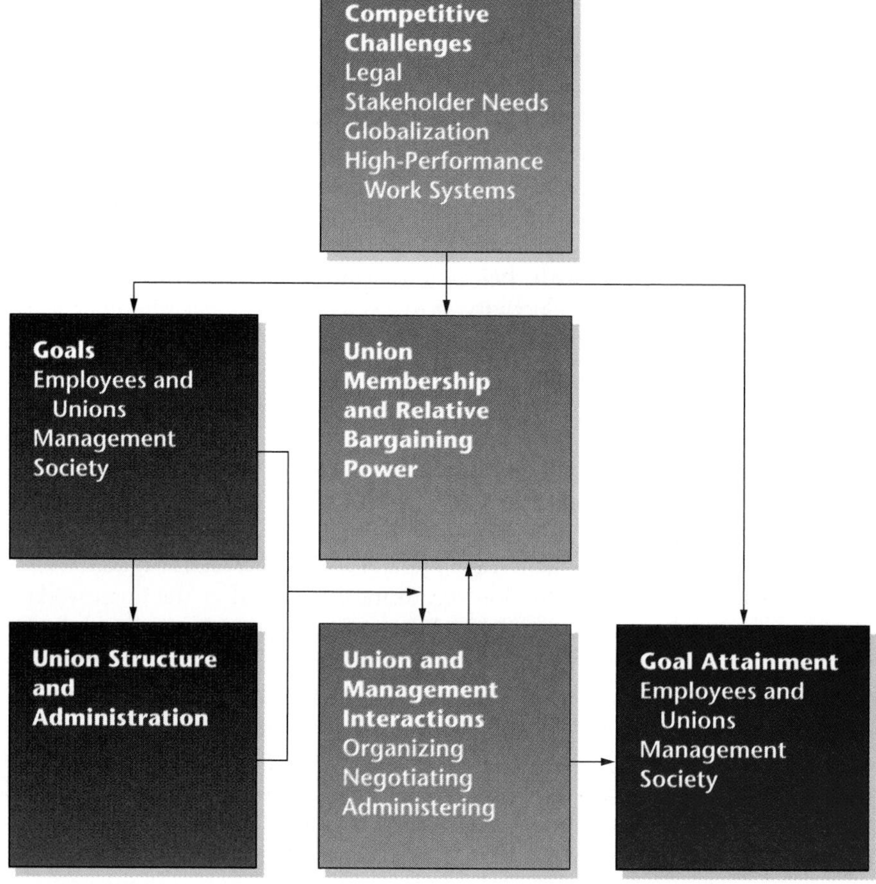

FIGURE 14.1
A Labor Relations Framework

Goals and Strategies

SOCIETY

In one sense, labor unions, with their emphasis on group action, do not fit well with the individualistic orientation of U.S. capitalism. However, industrial relations scholars such as Beatrice and Sidney Webb and John R. Commons argued in the late 1800s and early 1900s that individual workers' bargaining power was far smaller than that of employers, who were likely to have more financial resources and the ability to easily replace workers.[6] Effective institutions for worker representation (e.g., labor unions) were therefore seen as a way to make bargaining power more equal.

Labor unions' major benefit to society is the institutionalization of industrial conflict, which is therefore resolved in the least costly way. Thus, although disagreements between management and labor continue, it is better to resolve disputes through discussion (collective bargaining) than by battling in the streets. As an influential group of industrial relations scholars put it in describing the future of advanced industrial relations around the world: "Class warfare will be forgotten. The battles will be in the corridors instead of the streets, and memos will flow instead of blood."[7] In this sense, collective bargaining not only has the potential to reduce economic losses caused by strikes but may also contribute to societal stability. For this reason, industrial relations scholars have often viewed labor unions as an essential component of a democratic society.[8] These were some of the beliefs that contributed to the enactment of the National Labor Relations Act (NLRA) in 1935, which sought to provide an environment conducive to collective bargaining and has since regulated labor and management activities and interactions.

Even Senator Orrin Hatch, described by *Business Week* as "labor's archrival on Capitol Hill," has spoken of the need for unions:

> There are always going to be people who take advantage of workers. Unions even that out, to their credit. We need them to level the field between labor and management. If you didn't have unions, it would be very difficult for even enlightened employers not to take advantage of workers on wages and working conditions, because of [competition from] rivals. I'm among the first to say I believe in unions.[9]

Although an industrial relations system based on collective bargaining has drawbacks, so too do the alternatives. Unilateral control by management sacrifices workers' rights. Extensive involvement of government and the courts can result in conflict resolution that is expensive, slow, and imposed by someone (e.g., a judge) with much less firsthand knowledge of the circumstances than either labor or management.

MANAGEMENT

One of management's most basic decisions is whether to encourage or discourage the unionization of its employees. It may discourage unions because it fears higher wage and benefit costs, the disruptions caused by strikes, and an adversarial relationship with its employees or, more generally, greater constraints placed on its decision-making flexibility and discretion. Historically, management has used two basic strategies to avoid unionization.[10] It may seek to provide employment terms and conditions that employees will perceive as sufficiently attractive and equitable so that they see little gain from union representation. Or it may aggressively oppose union representation, even where there is significant employee interest. Use of the latter strategy has increased significantly during the last 20 to 30 years.

If management voluntarily recognizes a union or if employees are already represented by a union, the focus is shifted from dealing with employees as individuals to employees as a group. Still, certain basic management objectives remain: controlling labor costs and increasing productivity (by keeping wages and benefits in check) and maintaining management prerogatives in important areas such as staffing levels and work rules. Of course, management always has the option of trying to decertify a union (i.e., encourage employees to vote out the union in a decertification election) if it believes that the majority of employees no longer wish to be represented by the union.

LABOR UNIONS

Labor unions seek, through collective action, to give workers a formal and independent voice in setting the terms and conditions of their work. Table 14.1 shows typical provisions negotiated by unions in collective-bargaining contracts. Labor unions attempt to represent their members' interests in these decisions.

A major goal of labor unions is bargaining effectiveness, because with it comes the power and influence to make the employees' voices heard and to effect changes in the workplace.[11] As the opening to this chapter suggests, the right to strike is one important component of bargaining power. In turn, the success of a strike (actual or threatened) depends on the relative magnitude of the costs imposed on management versus

TABLE 14.1 Typical Provisions in Collective-Bargaining Contracts

Establishment and administration of the agreement	Job or income security	Paid and unpaid leave
Bargaining unit and plant supplements	Hiring and transfer arrangements	Vacations and holidays
Contract duration and reopening and renegotiation provisions	Employment and income guarantees	Sick leave
Union security and the checkoff	Reporting and call-in pay	Funeral and personal leave
Special bargaining committees	Supplemental unemployment benefit plans	Military leave and jury duty
Grievance procedures	Regulation of overtime, shift work, etc.	**Employee benefit plans**
Arbitration and mediation	Reduction of hours to forestall layoffs	Health and insurance plans
Strikes and lockouts	Layoff procedures; seniority; recall	Pension plans
Contract enforcement	Worksharing in lieu of layoff	Profit-sharing, stock purchase, and thrift plans
Functions, rights, and responsibilities	Attrition arrangements	Bonus plans
Management rights clauses	Promotion practices	**Special groups**
Plant removal	Training and retraining	Apprentices and learners
Subcontracting	Relocation allowances	Workers with disabilities and older workers
Union activities on company time and premises	Severance pay and layoff benefit plans	Women
Union–management cooperation	Special funds and study committees	Veterans
Regulation of technological change	**Plant operations**	Union representatives
Advance notice and consultation	Work and shop rules	Nondiscrimination clauses
Wage determination and administration	Rest periods and other in-plant time allowances	
General provisions	Safety and health	
Rate structure and wage differentials	Plant committees	
Allowances	Hours of work and premium pay practices	
Incentive systems and production bonus plans	Shift operations	
Production standards and time studies	Hazardous work	
Job classification and job evaluation	Discipline and discharge	
Individual wage adjustments		
General wage adjustments during the contract period		

SOURCE: T.A. Kochan, *Collective Bargaining and Industrial Relations* (Homewood, IL: Richard D. Irwin, 1980), p. 29. Original data from J.W. Bloch, "Union Contracts—A New Series of Studies," *Monthly Labor Review* 87 (October 1964), pp. 1184–85.

those imposed on the union. A critical factor is the size of union membership. More members translate into a greater ability to halt or disrupt production and also into greater financial resources for continuing a strike in the face of lost wages.

Union Structure, Administration, and Membership

A necessary step in discussing labor–management interactions is a basic knowledge of how labor and management are organized and how they function. Management has been described throughout this book. We now focus on labor unions.

NATIONAL AND INTERNATIONAL UNIONS

Most union members belong to a national or international union. Most national unions are composed of multiple local units, and most are affiliated with the American Federation of Labor and Congress of Industrial Organizations (AFL-CIO).

The largest AFL-CIO–affiliated national unions are listed in Table 14.2. (The National Education Association, with 2.3 million members, is not affiliated with the AFL-CIO.) An important characteristic of a union is whether it is a craft or industrial union. The electrical workers' and carpenters' unions are craft unions, meaning that the members all have a particular skill or occupation. Craft unions often are responsible for training their members (through apprenticeships) and for supplying craft workers to employers. Requests for carpenters, for example, would come to the union hiring hall, which would decide which carpenters to send out. Thus, craft workers may work for many employers over time, their constant link being to the union. A craft union's bargaining power depends greatly on the control it can exercise over the supply of its workers.

TABLE 14.2 Largest AFL–CIO–Affiliated Labor Unions

ORGANIZATION	NUMBER OF MEMBERS	
	1989	1997
Teamsters	1,161,000	1,271,000
State, County, Municipal (AFSCME)	1,090,000	1,236,000
Food and Commercial Workers (UFCW)	999,000	989,000
Automobile, Aerospace, and Agricultural (UAW)	917,000	766,000
Service Employees (SEIU)	762,000	1,081,000
Electrical Workers (IBEW)	744,000	654,000
Carpenters	613,000	324,000
Teachers (AFT)	544,000	694,000
Machinists and Aerospace	517,000	431,000
Communication Workers	492,000	504,000
Steelworkers	481,000	499,000
Needletrades, Industrial and Textile	333,000	225,000
Laborers	406,000	298,000
Operating Engineers	330,000	295,000
Hotel, Restaurant Employees	278,000	225,000
Plumbing and Pipefitting	220,000	220,000
Postal Workers	213,000	279,000
Paperworkers	210,000	226,000
Letter Carriers	201,000	210,000
Electronic, Electrical, and Salaried	171,000	128,000
Government Employees (AFGE)	156,000	170,000
Fire Fighters	142,000	156,000
Retail, Wholesale Department	137,000	71,000
Painters	128,000	80,000
Graphic Communications	124,000	90,000
Ironworkers	111,000	79,000
Sheet Metal Workers	108,000	93,000
Bakery, Confectionery, and Tobacco	103,000	95,000

SOURCE: Reprinted with permission from J.A. Fossum, *Labor Relations,* 5th ed. (Homewood, IL.: Richard D. Irwin, 1992). Recent data from *Directory of U.S. Labor Organizations,* 1998 ed. Copyright © 1998 by the Bureau of National Affairs, Inc., Washington, DC 20037.

In contrast, industrial unions are made up of members who are linked by their work in a particular industry (such as steelworkers and autoworkers). Typically they represent many different occupations. Membership in the union is a result of working for a particular employer in the industry. Changing employers is less common than it is among craft workers, and employees who change employers remain members of the same union only if they happen to move to other employers covered by that union. Whereas a craft union may restrict the number of, say, carpenters to maintain higher wages, industrial unions try to organize as many employees in as wide a range of skills as possible.

In the year 2000, three major unions (the United Auto Workers, the United Steelworkers, and the International Association of Machinists) will merge, a move that will create a union having more than 2 million members, which would make it the largest in the AFL-CIO. AFL-CIO leadership applauded the merger as an action that would contribute to better and more powerful representation of worker interests.[12] Organized labor hopes that mergers like this will reduce competition among unions and contribute to more success in organizing new members and achieving more bargaining power for current members.[13]

LOCAL UNIONS

Even when a national union plays the most critical role in negotiating terms of a collective-bargaining contract, negotiation occurs at the local level as well as over work rules and other issues that are locally determined. In addition, administration of the contract is largely carried out at the local union level. Consequently, the bulk of day-to-day interaction between labor and management takes place at the local union level.

The local of an industrial-based union may correspond to a single large facility or to a number of small facilities. In a craft-oriented union, the local may cover a city or a region. The local union typically elects officers (e.g., president, vice president, treasurer). Responsibility for contract negotiation may rest with the officers, or a bargaining committee may be formed for this purpose. Typically, the national union provides assistance, ranging from background data about other settlements and technical advice to sending a representative to lead the negotiations.

Individual members' participation in local union meetings includes the election of union officials and strike votes. However, most union contact is with the shop steward, who is responsible for ensuring that the terms of the collective-bargaining contract are enforced. The shop steward represents employees in contract grievances. Another union position, the business representative, performs some of the same functions, especially where the union deals with multiple employers, as is often the case with craft unions.

AMERICAN FEDERATION OF LABOR AND CONGRESS OF INDUSTRIAL ORGANIZATIONS (AFL–CIO)

The AFL-CIO is not a labor union but rather an association that seeks to advance the shared interests of its member unions at the national level, much like the Chamber of Commerce and the National Association of Manufacturers do for their member employers. As Figure 14.2 indicates, there are approximately 72 affiliated national and international unions and 60,000 locals. An important responsibility of the AFL-CIO is to represent labor's interests in public-policy issues such as civil rights, economic policy, safety, and occupational health. It also provides information and analysis that member unions can use in their activities: organizing new members, negotiating new contracts, and administering contracts.

FIGURE 14.2
Structure of the American Federation of Labor and Congress of Industrial Organizations (AFL-CIO)

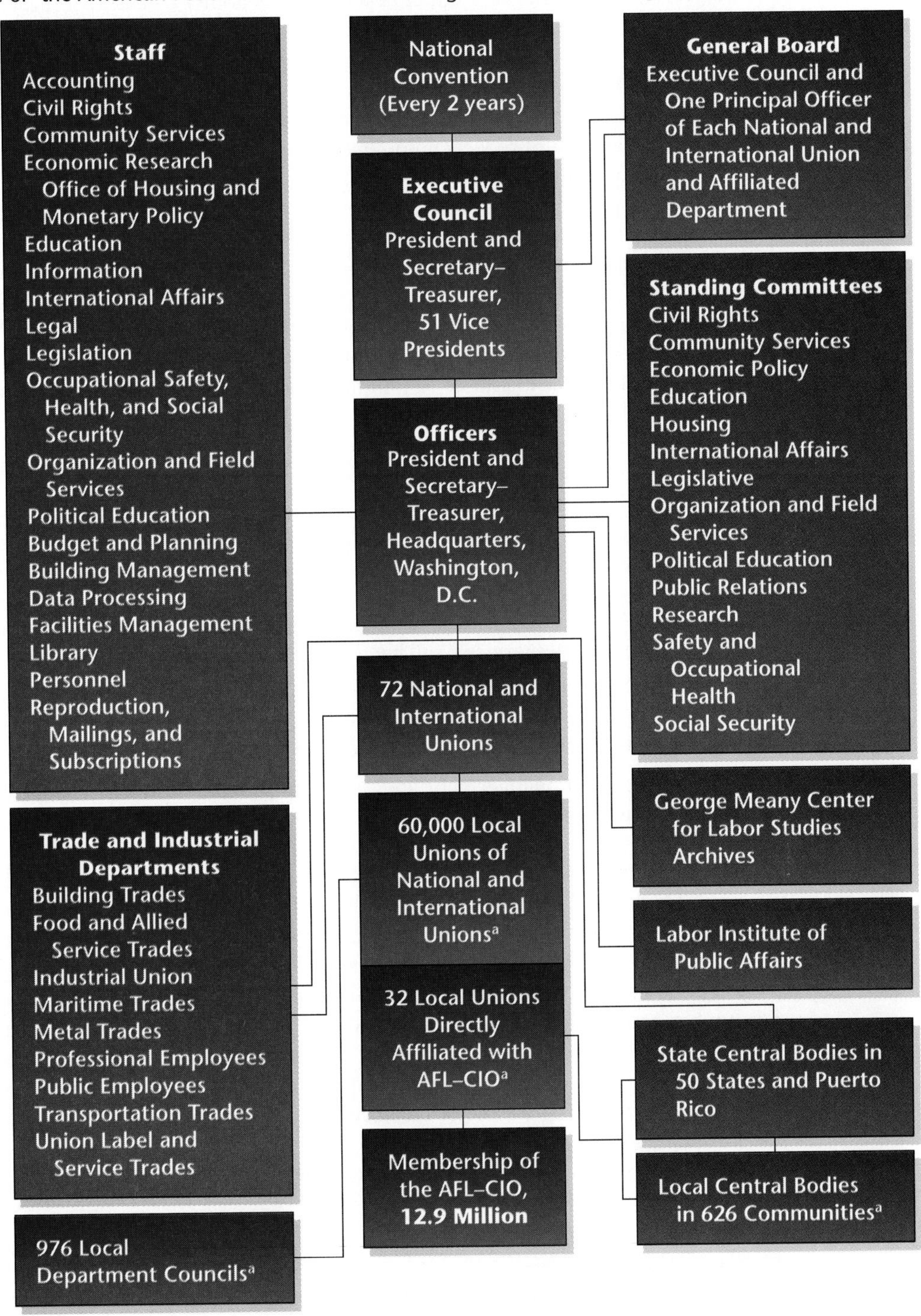

[a] 1989 data.
SOURCES: J.A. Fossum, *Labor Relations,* 5th ed. (Homewood, IL: Richard D. Irwin, 1992), p. 118. Updated with data from C. D. Gifford, *Directory of U.S. Labor Organizations,* 1998 (Washington, DC: Bureau of National Affairs, 1998).

UNION SECURITY

The survival and security of a union depends on its ability to ensure a regular flow of new members and member dues to support the services it provides. Therefore, unions typically place high priority on negotiating two contract provisions with an employer that are critical to a union's security or viability: checkoff provisions and union membership or contribution. First, under a **checkoff** provision, the employer, on behalf of the union, automatically deducts union dues from employees' paychecks.

A second union security provision focuses on the flow of new members (and their dues). The strongest union security arrangement is a **closed shop,** under which a person must be a union member (and thus pay dues) before being hired. A closed shop is, however, illegal under the NLRA. A **union shop** requires a person to join the union within a certain amount of time (30 days) after beginning employment. An **agency shop** is similar to a union shop but does not require union membership, only that dues be paid. **Maintenance of membership** rules do not require union membership but do require that employees who choose to join must remain members for a certain period of time (e.g., the length of the contract).

Under the 1947 Taft–Hartley Act (an amendment to the NLRA), states may pass so-called **right-to-work laws,** which make union shops, maintenance of membership, and agency shops illegal. The idea behind such laws is that compulsory union membership (or making employees pay union dues) infringes on the employee's right to freedom of association. From the union perspective, a big concern is "free riders," employees who benefit from union activities without belonging to a union. By law, all members of a bargaining unit, whether union members or not, must be represented by the union. If the union is required to offer service to all bargaining unit members, even those who are not union members, it may lose its financial viability.

UNION MEMBERSHIP AND BARGAINING POWER

At the strategic level, management and unions meet head-on over the issue of union organizing. Increasingly, employers are actively resisting unionization in an attempt to control costs and maintain their flexibility. Unions, on the other hand, must organize new members and hold on to their current members to have the kind of bargaining power and financial resources needed to achieve their goals in future organizing and to negotiate and administer contracts with management. For this reason we now discuss trends in union membership and possible explanations for those trends.

Since the 1950s, when union membership rose to 35 percent of employment, membership has consistently declined as a percentage of employment. It now stands at 14 percent of all employment and 10 percent of private-sector employment.[14] As Figure 14.3 indicates, this decline shows no indication of reversing (or even slowing down). If the trend continues, private-sector membership in unions may fall below 5 percent in the foreseeable future.[15]

What factors explain the decline in union membership? Several have been identified.[16]

STRUCTURAL CHANGES IN THE ECONOMY. At the risk of oversimplifying, we might say that unions have traditionally been strongest in urban workplaces (especially those outside the South) that employ middle-age workers in blue-collar jobs. However, much recent job growth has occurred among women and youth in the service sector of the economy. Although unionizing such groups is possible, unions have so far not had much success organizing these groups in the private sector. Despite the importance of structural changes in the economy, studies show that they account for no more than one-quarter of the overall union membership decline.[17] Also, Canada, which has been

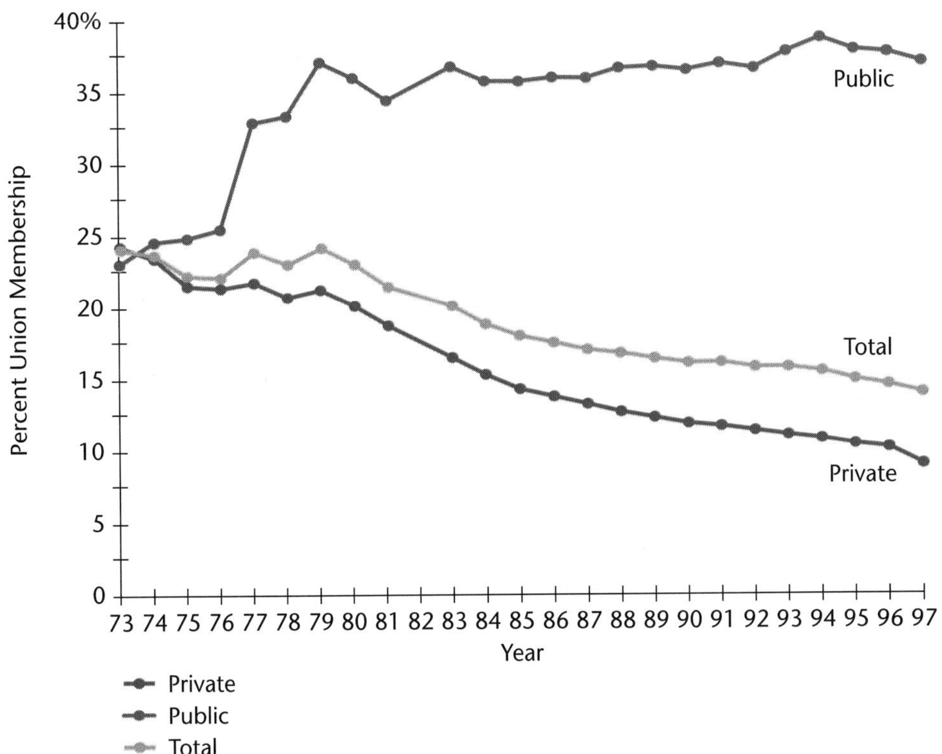

FIGURE 14.3 Union Membership Density among U.S. Wage and Salary Workers, 1973–1997

SOURCE: B.T. Hirsch and D.A. MacPherson, *Union Membership and Earnings Data Book 1994* (Washington, DC: Bureau of National Affairs, 1995).
DATA SOURCE: 1973–81, May Current Population Surveys (CPS); 1983–94, CPS Outgoing Rotation Group (ORG) Earnings Files. Values for 1982 are linearly interpolated from 1981 and 1983 values. Density is measured by the percentage of total, private-sector, and public-sector wage and salary workers who are union members. 1995–1997, http://stats/bls.gov/.

undergoing similar structural changes, has experienced growth in union membership since the early 1960s. Growth in union membership in Canada now stands at over 30 percent of employment, compared with 16 percent in the United States.

INCREASED EMPLOYER RESISTANCE. Almost one-half of large employers in a survey reported that their most important labor goal was to be union-free. This contrasts sharply with 30 years ago, when one observer wrote that "many tough bargainers [among employers] prefer the union to a situation where there is no union. Most of the employers in rubber, basic steel and the automobile industry fall in this category." The idea then was that an effective union could help assess and communicate the interests of employees to management, thus helping management make better decisions. But product-market pressures, such as foreign competition, have contributed to increasing employer resistance of unions. These changes in the competitive environment have contributed to a change in management's perspective and goals.[18]

Over 30 years ago, unions were often able to organize entire industries. For example, the UAW organized all four major producers in the automobile industry (GM, Ford, Chrysler, and American Motors). The UAW usually sought and achieved the same union–management contract at each company. As a consequence, a negotiated wage increase in the industry could be passed on to the consumer in the form of higher prices. No company was undercut by its competitors because the labor cost of all major producers in the industry was determined by the same union–management contract, and

Is Strong Labor Relations Good for Business?

Is it good business to deliberately cultivate a unionized work force? For Milwaukee-based Johnson Controls, the answer had always been no. That's why it endured strikes at its two seat-making factories by UAW workers who were trying to negotiate their first collective-bargaining contract with the company. The company had planned to continue to operate the plants by using managers and replacement workers to build seats for Ford Motor Company's hot-selling Expedition utility vehicle. However, Ford had a different idea. For years, it has considered its strong relationship with the UAW to be a competitive advantage. Thus, Ford's chief financial officer, John Devine, stated, "It is not in the best interests of our employees or Ford Motor Co. to accept seats made by replacement workers. . . . Our relationship with the union and respect we have with our team inside Ford are too important to us." The short-term cost to Ford was not trivial. On each of the five days it did not build Expeditions, it lost an estimated $5 million in net income. A short time later, Johnson Controls, with strong encouragement from Ford, agreed on a contract with the UAW at its two affected plants.

Although Ford has been accused of being too accommodating to the UAW, Ford believes it has saved billions by avoiding the smoldering resentment among UAW workers that it believes has adversely affected quality at General Motors. In addition, Ford has not had any major work stoppages in recent years, which cannot be said of GM, where a series of stoppages have cost it billions of dollars, as noted in the opening vignette of this chapter.

SOURCE: Robert L. Rose and Robert L. Simison, "Johnson Controls and UAW Reach Pact," *The Wall Street Journal*, February 21, 1997, p. A3; Robert L. Simison and Robert L. Rose, "In Backing the UAW, Ford Rankles Many of Its Parts Suppliers," *The Wall Street Journal*, February 13, 1997, p. A1.

the U.S. public had little option but to buy U.S.-made cars. However, the onset of foreign competition in the automobile market changed the competitive situation as well as the UAW's ability to organize the industry.[19] U.S. automakers were slow to recognize and respond to the competitive threat from foreign producers, resulting in a loss of market share and employment.

Competitive threats have contributed to increased employer resistance to union organizing and, in some cases, to an increased emphasis on ridding themselves of existing unions. (However, see the "Competing by Meeting Stakeholders' Needs" box.) Unionized workers receive, on average, 10 percent higher pay (excluding benefits) than their nonunion counterparts. Many employers have decided that they can no longer compete with these higher labor costs, and union membership has suffered as a result.[20] One measure of increased employer resistance is the dramatic increase in the late 1960s in the number of unfair employer labor practices (i.e., violations of sections of the NLRA such as section 8(a)(3), which prohibits firing employees for union organizing, as we discuss later) even though the number of elections held did not change much. (See Figure 14.4.) The use of remedies such as back pay for workers also grew, but the costs to employers of such penalties does not appear to have been sufficient to prevent the growth in employer unfair labor practices. Not surprisingly, the union victory rate in representation elections has decreased from almost 59 percent in 1960 to about 50 percent in recent years. Since 1980, the number of elections has declined by more than 50 percent. Moreover, decertification elections have gone from about 4 percent of elections in 1960 to about 14 percent of elections in 1996.[21]

At a personal level, some managers may face serious consequences if a union successfully organizes a new set of workers or mounts a serious organizing drive. One study indicated that 8 percent of the plant managers in companies with organizing drives were fired, and 10 percent of those in companies where the union was successful were

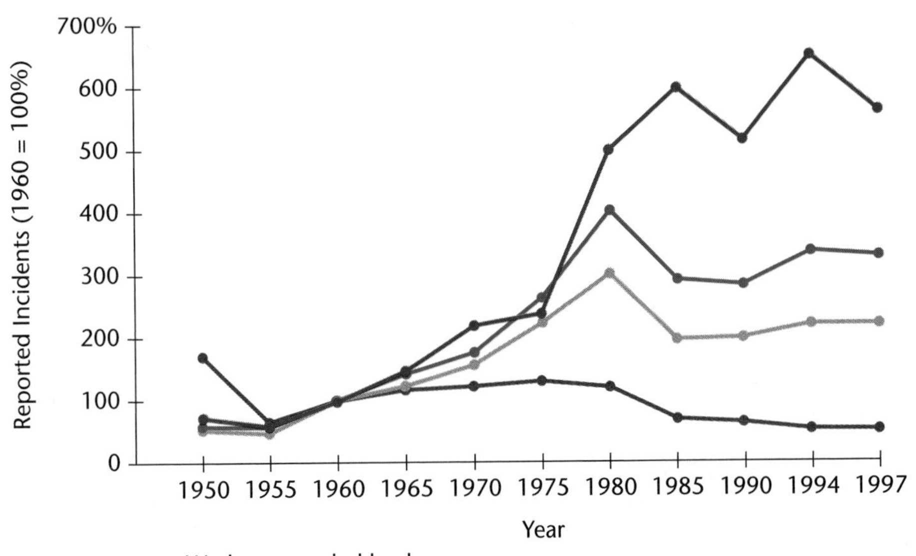

FIGURE 14.4 Employer Resistance to Union Organizing, 1950–97

NOTE: 8(a)(3) charges refer to the section of the NLRA that makes it an unfair employer labor practice to discriminate against (e.g., fire) employees who engage in union activities such as union organizing.
SOURCE: Adapted and updated from R.B. Freeman and J.L. Medoff, *What Do Unions Do?* (New York: Basic Books, 1984). Data for 1985, 1989, 1990, 1994 and 1997 from National Labor Relations Board annual reports.

fired (compared with 2 percent in a control group).[22] Furthermore, only 3 percent of the plant managers facing an organizing drive were promoted, and none of those ending up with a union contract were promoted (compared with 21 percent of the managers in the control group). Therefore, managers are often under intense pressure to oppose unionization attempts.

SUBSTITUTION WITH HRM. A major study of the human resource management strategies and practices among large, nonunion employers found that union avoidance was often an important employee relations objective.[23] Top management's values in such companies drive specific policies such as promotion from within, an influential personnel–human resource department, and above-average pay and benefits. These policies, in turn, contribute to a number of desirable outcomes such as flexibility, positive employee attitudes, and responsive and committed employees, which ultimately lead to higher productivity and better employee relations. In other words, employers attempt to remain nonunion by offering most of the things a union can offer, and then some, while still maintaining a productivity advantage over their competitors. (See the "Competing through Globalization" box.) Of course, one aspect of union representation that employers cannot duplicate is the independent employee voice that a union provides.

SUBSTITUTION BY GOVERNMENT REGULATION. Since the 1960s, regulation of many employment areas has increased, including equal employment opportunity, pensions, and worker displacement. Combined with existing regulations, this increase may result in fewer areas in which unions can provide worker rights or protection beyond those specified by law. Yet, Western European countries generally have more regulations and higher levels of union membership than the United States.[24]

UAW Concedes Defeat at Transplants—for Now

Workers at the Japanese-owned auto assembly plants in this country have turned their backs repeatedly on UAW organizers.

So now the UAW is virtually giving up on them, and turning its attention to trying to organize the two German-owned plants.

"We are working with the unions in Germany to try to organize the German plants here," says UAW President Steve Yokich. "It's hard to tell if that will bear fruit, but I don't think it will be as tough as it was with the Japanese plants."

Tough is an understatement in describing the UAW's quest to unionize the relatively young foreign-owned assembly plants.

The U.S. transplants now have about 44,000 workers in 16 auto and engine factories. Only three of those plants, with a total of 12,700 employees, have a UAW presence. And each of those three was opened with Big 3 assistance, and the understanding that workers would be represented by the UAW.

Meanwhile, transplant operations continue to grow in this country, and Big 3 employment continues to shrink. And the UAW, which depends heavily on the auto industry for its existence, has seen its membership slide from about 1.5 million in 1978 to 780,000 today. Workers at both the new auto assembly plants and the 300-plus new transplant supplier firms have shunned the union.

Yokich knows his job will not be easy. The transplants offer pay and benefits that are roughly equal to the Big 3 packages. And the social and political environments where the

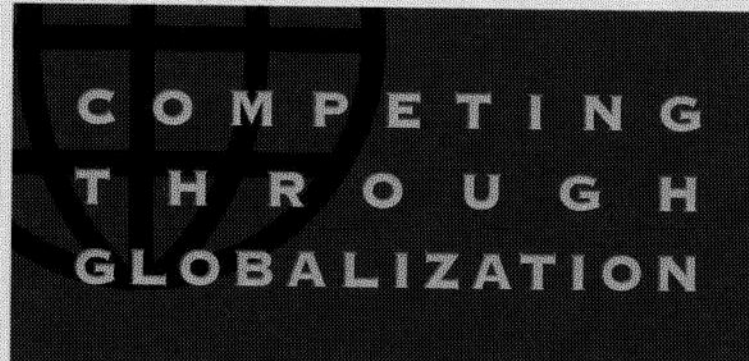

transplants are, particularly in the South, generally do not support union activity.

"Organizing is the toughest job in the UAW," the union chief says.

So for now, the UAW will give up on the Japanese transplants. In June, it plans to create a new vice president's position to concentrate solely on organizing efforts at the German plants and on independent suppliers.

"I told them to pull the plug on Nissan and Honda," Yokich says. "Quite frankly, in my view, that was an expenditure of 10 years, and we were no further along than we were when we started."

The union was soundly rejected during a 1989 vote at Nissan Motor Manufacturing Corp. U.S.A. in Smyrna, Tennessee. Since then, workers at Nissan, at Toyota's facilities in Kentucky, and at Honda's two plants in Ohio have shown little interest in the union.

Last summer, a second drive at Smyrna ended soon after it began, even after UAW-represented workers from nearby Saturn Corp. tried to pitch in on recruitment efforts.

So why would BMW and Mercedes–Benz be any more willing to work with the U.S. auto union? Yokich says he has two aces to play:

1. He says it is generally easier to organize during good economic times because workers do not fear for their jobs.
2. Workers sit on the boards of German automakers, and may be able to influence affairs in this country.

But organizing the Germans will not be a piece of cake.

Bobby Hitt, spokesman for BMW Manufacturing Corp. in Spartanburg County, South Carolina, says workers

WORKER VIEWS. Industrial relations scholars have long argued that the absence in the United States of a history of feudalism and of strong class distinctions found in Western Europe have contributed to a more pragmatic, business-oriented (versus class-conscious) unionism. Although this may help explain the somewhat lower level of union membership in the United States, its relevance in explaining the downward trend is not clear.

UNION ACTIONS. In some ways, unions have hurt their own cause. First, corruption in unions such as the Teamsters may have had a detrimental effect. Second, questions have been raised about how well unions have adapted to recent changes in the economic structure. Employee groups and economic sectors with the fastest growth rates tend to have the lowest rates of unionization.[25] Women are less likely to be in unions than men (12 percent versus 16 percent), and nonmanufacturing industries such as fithere receive competitive hourly wage rates of $18.25, not including benefits. He says workers also are eligible for annual bonuses and a car allowance. Big 3 workers earn $19 an hour, excluding benefits.

Most important, Hitt says the hourly workers make important decisions on the factory floor.

"Our process is a self-directed work team concept," Hitt says. "It does not easily attract a third party."

There are 1,500 hourly workers at the BMW plant, and the same number planned for the Mercedes factory in Vance, Alabama.

Yokich admits the pay and benefits are attractive to workers in the South. But he says UAW workers have a greater voice than their transplant counterparts in establishing employee programs, and he believes UAW workers are better trained.

However, the products from the transplant operations perennially end up on top of industry quality studies, like J.D. Power and Associates' Initial Quality Survey.

The union also must contend with plant expansions. During a plant expansion, employees often find themselves considering a job promotion or at least a move to a more appealing work slot. Workers on one shift may find an opportunity for moving to another shift. It is not traditionally the time when employees are clamoring for union representation.

BMW and Mercedes are expanding both their factories and their payrolls. BMW, which is expanding its Spartanburg plant, additionally said in recent months that it would hire 500 more workers in order to produce BMW's first "sport-activity vehicle" there.

Similarly, Mercedes is ramping up to full employment in Vance. On top of that, the company announced late last year that strong demand for its Alabama-built ML320 sport-utility is prompting it to spend $40 million and hire another 100 people.

The UAW also is not guaranteed that the power of Germany's auto workers union, IG Metall, will translate to power in South Carolina and Alabama. As is customary in German industry, the union holds a seat on the automaker's management board. Yet IG Metall tried to dissuade BMW from going to the United States in the first place. It failed. And while the Spartanburg project was under construction, IG Metall's complaints about nonunion construction labor led nowhere. The German union has vowed to assist the UAW since 1992.

Harley Shaiken, labor professor at the University of California in Berkeley, says the unionization of transplant factories is inevitable.

"I don't know when that will happen," Shaiken says, "but as the work force ages, as growth slows down, and as the Japanese try to cut corners in this competitive industry, this may lead to workers wanting representation."

But Jim Harbour, an auto industry consultant who studies productivity in plants, disagrees.

"They may have some luck with the Germans, but I doubt the day will ever come when the Japanese plants join the union," says Harbour, chairman of Harbour and Associates Inc. in Troy, Michigan.

"I think Yokich has lost it in there," Harbour says. "The more they stay without the union, the stronger they get."

But Yokich will not give up.

"The Japanese have quality, but they have a lot of injuries too," he says. "That's why the Japanese will come to us eventually."

SOURCE: *Automotive News*, April 27, 1998, pp. 8N-E to 8N-F.

nance, insurance, and real estate have a lower union representation (2 percent) than does manufacturing (16 percent). The South is also less heavily organized than the rest of the country, with, for example, South Carolina having a unionization rate of 4 percent, compared with 26 percent in New York State.[26]

Legal Framework

Although competitive challenges have a major impact on labor relations, the legal framework of collective bargaining is an especially critical determinant of union membership and relative bargaining power and, therefore, of the degree to which employers, employees, and society are successful in achieving their goals. The legal framework also constrains union structure and administration and the manner in which unions and employers interact. Perhaps the most dramatic example of labor laws' influence is the 1935 passage of the Wagner Act (also known as the National Labor Relations Act or NLRA), which actively supported collective bargaining rather than impeding it. As a result, union membership nearly tripled, from 3 million in 1933 (7.7 percent of all employment) to 8.8 million (19.2 percent of employment) by 1939.[27] With increased membership came greater union bargaining power and, consequently, more success in achieving union goals.

Before the 1930s, the legal system was generally hostile to unions. The courts generally viewed unions as coercive organizations that hindered free trade. Unions' focus on collective voice and collective action (e.g., strikes, boycotts) did not fit well with the U.S. emphasis on capitalism, individualism, freedom of contract, and property rights.[28]

The Great Depression of the 1930s, however, shifted public attitudes toward business and the free-enterprise system. Unemployment rates as high as 25 percent and a 30 percent drop in the gross national product between 1929 and 1933 focused attention on employee rights and on the shortcomings of the system as it existed then. The nation was in a crisis, and President Franklin Roosevelt responded with dramatic action, the New Deal. On the labor front, the 1935 NLRA ushered in a new era of public policy for labor unions, enshrining collective bargaining as the preferred mechanism for settling labor–management disputes.

The introduction to the NLRA states:

> It is in the national interest of the United States to maintain full production in its economy. Industrial strife among employees, employers, and labor organizations interferes with full production and is contrary to our national interest. Experience has shown that labor disputes can be lessened if the parties involved recognize the legitimate rights of each in their relations with one another. To establish these rights under the law, Congress enacted the National Labor Relations Act. Its purpose is to define and protect the rights of employees and employers, to encourage collective bargaining, and to eliminate certain practices on the part of labor and management that are harmful to the general welfare.[29]

The rights of employees are set out in Section 7 of the act, including the "right to self-organization, to form, join, or assist labor organizations, to bargain collectively through representatives of their own choosing, and to engage in other concerted activities for the purpose of collective bargaining. The act also gives employees the right to refrain from any or all of such activities except [in cases] requiring membership in a labor organization as a condition of employment."[30] Examples of protected activities include

- Union organizing.
- Joining a union, whether it is recognized by the employer or not.
- Going out on strike to secure better working conditions.
- Refraining from activity on behalf of the union.[31]

UNFAIR LABOR PRACTICES—EMPLOYERS

The NLRA prohibits certain activities by both employers and labor unions. Unfair labor practices by employers are listed in Section 8(a) of the NLRA. Section 8(a)(1) prohibits employers from interfering with, restraining, or coercing employees in exercising their rights to join or assist a labor organization or to refrain from such activities. Section 8(a)(2) prohibits employer domination of or interference with the formation or activities of a labor union. Section 8(a)(3) prohibits discrimination in any aspect of employment that attempts to encourage or discourage union-related activity. Section 8(a)(4) prohibits discrimination against employees for providing testimony relevant to enforcement of the NLRA. Section 8(a)(5) prohibits employers from refusing to bar-

TABLE 14.3 Examples of Employer Unfair Labor Practices

- Threatening employees with loss of their jobs or benefits if they join or vote for a union.
- Threatening to close down a plant if organized by a union.
- Questioning employees about their union membership or activities in a manner that restrains or coerces them.
- Spying or pretending to spy on union meetings.
- Granting wage increases that are timed to discourage employees from forming or joining a union.
- Taking an active part in organizing a union or committee to represent employees.
- Providing preferential treatment or aid to one of several unions trying to organize employees.
- Discharging employees for urging other employees to join a union or refusing to hire applicants because they are union members.
- Refusing to reinstate workers when job openings occur because the workers participated in a lawful strike.
- Ending operation at one plant and opening the same operation at another plant with new employees because employees at the first plant joined a union.
- Demoting or firing employees for filing an unfair labor practice or for testifying at an NLRB hearing.
- Refusing to meet with employees' representatives because the employees are on strike.
- Refusing to supply the employees' representative with cost and other data concerning a group insurance plan covering employees.
- Announcing a wage increase without consulting the employees' representative.
- Failing to bargain about the effects of a decision to close one of employer's plants.

SOURCE: National Labor Relations Board, *A Guide to Basic Law and Procedures under the National Labor Relations Act* (Washington, DC: U.S. Government Printing Office, 1991). See also www.nlrb.gov.

gain collectively with a labor organization that has standing under the act. Examples of employer unfair labor practices are listed in Table 14.3.

UNFAIR LABOR PRACTICES—LABOR UNIONS

Originally, the NLRA did not list any union unfair labor practices. These were added through the 1947 **Taft–Hartley Act.** The 1959 **Landrum–Griffin Act** further regulated unions' actions and their internal affairs (e.g., financial disclosure, conduct of elections). Section 8(b)(1)(a) of the NLRA states that a labor organization is not to "restrain or coerce employees in the exercise of the rights guaranteed in section 7" (described earlier). Table 14.4 provides examples of union unfair labor practices.

ENFORCEMENT

Enforcement of the NLRA rests with the National Labor Relations Board (NLRB), which is composed of a five-member board, the general counsel, and 33 regional offices. The basis for the NLRA is the commerce clause of the U.S. Constitution. Therefore, the NLRB's jurisdiction is limited to employers whose operations affect commerce generally and interstate commerce in particular. In practice, only purely local firms are likely to fall outside the NLRB's jurisdiction. Specific jurisdictional standards (nearly 20) that vary by industry are applied. Two examples of businesses that are covered (and the standards) are retail businesses that had more than $500,000 in annual business and newspapers that had more than $200,000 in annual business.

The NLRB's two major functions are to conduct and certify representation elections and prevent unfair labor practices. In both realms, it does not initiate action. Rather, it responds to requests for action. The NLRB's role in representation elections is discussed in the next section. Here, we discuss unfair labor practices.

Unfair labor practice cases begin with the filing of a charge, which is investigated by

TABLE 14.4 Examples of Union Unfair Labor Practices

- Mass picketing in such numbers that nonstriking employees are physically barred from entering the plant.
- Acts of force or violence on the picket line, or in connection with a strike.
- Threats to employees of bodily injury or that they will lose their jobs unless they support the union's activities.
- Fining or expelling members for crossing a picket line that is unlawful.
- Fining or expelling members for filing unfair labor practices or testifying before the NLRB.
- Insisting during contract negotiations that the employer agree to accept working conditions that will be determined by a group to which it does not belong.
- Fining or expelling union members for the way they apply the bargaining contract while carrying out their supervisory responsibilities.
- Causing an employer to discharge employees because they spoke out against a contract proposed by the union.
- Making a contract that requires an employer to hire only members of the union or employees "satisfactory" to the union.
- Insisting on the inclusion of illegal provisions in a contract.
- Terminating an existing contract and striking for a new one without notifying the employer, the Federal Mediation and Conciliation Service, and the state mediation service (where one exists).
- Attempting to compel a beer distributor to recognize a union, the union prevents the distributor from obtaining beer at a brewery by inducing the brewery's employees to refuse to fill the distributor's orders.
- Picketing an employer to force it to stop doing business with another employer who has refused to recognize the union (a "secondary boycott").

SOURCE: National Labor Relations Board, *A Guide to Basic Law and Procedures under the National Labor Relations Act* (Washington, DC: U.S. Government Printing Office, 1991). See also www.nlrb.gov.

a regional office. A charge must be filed within six months of the alleged unfair practice, and copies must be served on all parties. (Registered mail is recommended.) If the NLRB finds the charge to have merit and issues a complaint, there are two possible actions. It may defer to a grievance procedure agreed on by the employer and union. Otherwise, a hearing is held before an administrative law judge. The judge makes a recommendation, which can be appealed by either party. The NLRB has the authority to issue cease-and-desist orders to halt unfair labor practices. It can also order reinstatement of employees, with or without back pay. Note, however, that the NLRA is not a criminal statute, and punitive damages are not available. If an employer or union refuses to comply with an NLRB order, the board has the authority to petition the U.S. Court of Appeals. The court can choose to enforce the order, remand it to the NLRB for modification, change it, or set it aside altogether.

Union and Management Interactions: Organizing

To this point, we have discussed macro trends in union membership. Here, we shift our focus to the more micro questions of why individual employees join unions and how the organizing process works at the workplace level.

WHY DO EMPLOYEES JOIN UNIONS?

Virtually every model of the decision to join a union focuses on two questions.[32] First, is there a gap between the pay, benefits, and other conditions of employment that employees actually receive versus what they believe they should receive? Second, if such a gap exists and is sufficiently large to motivate employees to try to remedy the situation, is union membership seen as the most effective or instrumental means of change? The outcome of an election campaign hinges on how the majority of employees answer these two questions.

THE PROCESS AND LEGAL FRAMEWORK OF ORGANIZING

The NLRB is responsible for ensuring that the organizing process follows certain steps. At the most general level, the NLRB holds a union representation election if at least 30 percent of employees in the bargaining unit sign authorization cards, which indicate their interest in holding an election. If over 50 percent of the employees sign authorization cards, the union may request that the employer voluntarily recognize it. If fewer than 50 percent of the employees sign, or if the employer refuses to recognize the union voluntarily, the NLRB conducts a secret-ballot election. The union is certified by the NLRB as the exclusive representative of employees if over 50 percent of employees vote for the union. If more than one union appears on the ballot and neither gains a simple majority, a runoff election is held. Once a union has been certified as the exclusive representative of a group of employees, no additional elections are permitted for one year. After the negotiation of a contract, an election cannot be held for the contract's duration or for three years, whichever comes first. The parties to the contract may agree not to hold an election for longer than three years, but an outside party cannot be barred for more than three years.

As mentioned previously, union members' right to be represented by leaders of their own choosing was expanded under the Taft–Hartley Act to include the right to vote an existing union out—that is, to decertify it. The process follows the same steps as a representation election. A decertification election is not permitted when a contract is in effect. Research indicates that when decertification elections are held, unions typically do not fare well, losing about 70 percent of the time during the mid 1990s. Moreover, the number of such elections has increased from roughly 5 percent of all elections in the 1950s and 1960s to about 14 percent in the mid-1990s.[33]

The NLRB also is responsible for determining the appropriate bargaining unit and the employees who are eligible to participate in organizing activities. A unit may cover employees in one facility or multiple facilities within a single employer, or the unit may cover multiple employers. In general, employees on the payroll just prior to the ordering of an election are eligible to vote, although this rule is modified in some cases where, for example, employment in the industry is irregular. Most employees who are on strike and who have been replaced by other employees are eligible to vote in an election (e.g., a decertification election) that occurs within 12 months of the onset of the strike.

The following types of employees cannot be included in bargaining units: agricultural laborers, independent contractors, supervisors, and managers. Beyond this, the NLRB attempts to group together employees who have a community of interest in their wages, hours, and working conditions. In many cases, this grouping will be sharply contested, with management and the union jockeying to include or exclude certain employee subgroups in the hope of influencing the outcome of the election.

ORGANIZING CAMPAIGNS: MANAGEMENT AND UNION STRATEGIES AND TACTICS. Tables 14.5 and 14.6 list common issues that arise during most campaigns. Unions attempt to persuade employees that their wages, benefits, treatment by employers, and opportunity to influence workplace decisions are not sufficient and that the union will be effective in obtaining improvements. Management emphasizes that it has provided a good package of wages, benefits, and so on. It also argues that, whereas a union is unlikely to provide improvements in such areas, it will likely lead to certain costs for employees, such as union dues and the income loss resulting from strikes.

As Table 14.7 indicates, employers use a variety of methods to oppose unions in organizing campaigns, some of which may go beyond what the law permits, especially in the eyes of union organizers. This perception is supported by our earlier discussion,

TABLE 14.5 Prevalence of Certain Union Issues in Campaigns

UNION ISSUES	PERCENTAGE OF CAMPAIGNS
Union will prevent unfairness and will set up a grievance procedure and seniority system.	82%
Union will improve unsatisfactory wages.	79
Union strength will provide employees with voice in wages, working conditions.	79
Union, not outsider, bargains for what employees want.	73
Union has obtained gains elsewhere.	70
Union will improve unsatisfactory sick leave and insurance.	64
Dues and initiation fees are reasonable.	64
Union will improve unsatisfactory vacations and holidays.	61
Union will improve unsatisfactory pensions.	61
Employer promises and good treatment may not be continued without union.	61
Employees choose union leaders.	55
Employer will seek to persuade or frighten employees to vote against union.	55
No strike without vote.	55
Union will improve unsatisfactory working conditions.	52
Employees have legal right to engage in union activity.	52

SOURCE: J.A. Fossum, *Labor Relations,* 5th ed. (Homewood, IL: Richard D. Irwin, 1992), p. 149. Original data adapted from J.G. Getman, S.B. Goldberg, and J.B. Herman, *Union Representation Elections: Law and Reality* (New York: Russell Sage Foundation, 1976), Table 4–3.

TABLE 14.6 Prevalence of Certain Management Issues in Campaigns

MANAGEMENT ISSUES	PERCENTAGE OF CAMPAIGNS
Improvements not dependent on unionization.	85%
Wages good, equal to, or better than under union contract.	82
Financial costs of union dues outweigh gains.	79
Union is outsider.	79
Get facts before deciding; employer will provide facts and accept employee decision.	76
If union wins, strike may follow.	70
Loss of benefits may follow union win.	67
Strikers will lose wages; lose more than gain.	67
Unions not concerned with employee welfare.	67
Strike may lead to loss of jobs.	64
Employer has treated employees fairly and/or well.	60
Employees should be certain to vote.	54

SOURCES: J.A. Fossum, *Labor Relations,* 5th ed. (Homewood, IL: Richard D. Irwin, 1992), p. 149. Original data adapted from J.G. Getman, S.B. Goldberg and J.B. Herman, *Union Representation Elections: Law and Reality* (New York: Russell Sage Foundation, 1976), Table 4–2.

which noted a significant increase in employer unfair labor practices since the late 1960s. (See Figure 14.4.)

Why would employers increasingly break the law? Fossum suggests that the consequences (e.g., back pay and reinstatement of workers) of doing so are "slight."[34] His review of various studies suggests that discrimination against employees involved in union organizing decreases union organizing success significantly and that the cost of

TABLE 14.7
Percentage of Firms Using Various Methods to Oppose Union Organizing Campaigns

Survey of employers	
Consultants used	41%
Unfair labor practice charges filed against employer	24
Survey of union organizers	
Consultants and/or lawyers used	70
Unfair labor practices by employer	
Charges filed	36
Discharges or discriminatory layoffs	42[a]
Company leaflets	80
Company letters	91
Captive audience speech	91[b]
Supervisor meetings with small groups of employees	92
Supervisor intensity in opposing union	
Low	14
Moderate	34
High	51

[a] This percentage is larger than the figure for charges filed because it includes cases in which no unfair labor practice charge was actually filed against the employer.
[b] Refers to management's requiring employees to attend a session on company time at which the disadvantages of union membership are emphasized.
SOURCE: R.B. Freeman and M.M. Kleiner, "Employer Behavior in the Face of Union Organizing Drives," *Industrial and Labor Relations Review* 43, no. 4 (April 1990), pp. 351–65. © Cornell University.

back pay to union activists reinstated in their jobs is far smaller than the costs that would be incurred if the union managed to organize and gain better wages, benefits, and so forth.

Still, the NLRB attempts to maintain a noncoercive atmosphere under which employees feel they can exercise free choice. It will set aside an election if it believes that either the union or the employer has created "an atmosphere of confusion or fear of reprisals."[35] Examples of conduct that may lead to an election result being set aside include

- Threats of loss of jobs or benefits by an employer or union to influence votes or organizing activities.
- A grant of benefits or a promise of benefits as a means of influencing votes or organizing activities.
- An employer or union making campaign speeches to assembled groups of employees on company time less than 24 hours before an election.
- The actual use or threat of physical force or violence to influence votes or organizing activities.[36]

Supervisors have the most direct contact with employees. Thus, as Exhibit 14.1 indicates, it is critical that they be proactive in establishing good relationships with employees if the company wishes to avoid union organizing attempts. It is also important for supervisors to know what not to do should a drive take place.

In response to organizing difficulties, the union movement has tried alternative approaches. **Associate union membership** is not linked to an employee's workplace and does not provide representation in collective bargaining. Instead, the union provides other services, such as discounts on health and life insurance or credit cards.[37] In return, the union receives membership dues and a broader base of support for its activities. As-

EXHIBIT 14.1
What Supervisors Should and Should Not Do to Stay Union-Free

WHAT TO DO:

Report any direct or indirect signs of union activity to a core management group.

Deal with employees by carefully stating the company's response to pro-union arguments. These responses should be coordinated by the company to maintain consistency and to avoid threats or promises.

Take away union issues by following effective management practice all the time. This includes

- Deliver recognition and appreciation.
- Solve employee problems.
- Protect employees from harassment or humiliation.
- Provide business-related information.
- Be consistent in treatment of different employees.
- Accommodate special circumstances where appropriate.
- Ensure due process in performance management.
- Treat all employees with dignity and respect.

WHAT TO AVOID:

Threatening employees with harsher terms and conditions of employment or employment loss if they engage in union activity.

Interrogating employees about pro-union or anti-union sentiments that they or others may have or reviewing union authorization cards or pro-union petitions.

Promising employees that they will receive favorable terms or conditions of employment if they forgo union activity

Spying on employees known to be, or suspected of being, engaged in pro-union activities.

SOURCE: J.A. Segal "Unshackle Your Supervisors to Stay Union Free," *HRMagazine*, June 1998, pp. 177–84.

sociate membership may be attractive to employees who wish to join a union but cannot because their workplace is not organized by a union.

Corporate campaigns seek to bring public, financial, or political pressure on employers during the organizing (and negotiating) process.[38] For example, the Building and Construction Trades Department of the AFL-CIO successfully lobbied Congress to eliminate $100 million in tax breaks for a Toyota truck plant in Kentucky until Toyota agreed to use union construction workers and pay union wages.[39] The Amalgamated Clothing and Textile Workers Union (ACTWU) corporate campaign against J.P. Stevens during the late 1970s was one of the first and best known. The ACTWU organized a boycott of J.P. Stevens products and threatened to withdraw its pension funds from financial institutions where J.P. Stevens officers acted as directors. J.P. Stevens subsequently agreed to a contract with the ACTWU.[40]

Unions also hope to use their financial assets to influence companies. As of 1997, union retirement funds held $1.4 trillion in corporate stock, about 14 percent of all outstanding shares. Although unions share control of these assets with company-appointed trustees, the AFL-CIO hopes to leverage these assets to influence company policies.[41]

Union and Management Interactions: Contract Negotiation

The majority of contract negotiations take place between unions and employers that have been through the process before. In most cases, management has come to accept the union as an organization that it must work with. But when the union has just been

TABLE 14.8 Types and Examples of Bargaining Structures

MULTIEMPLOYER (CENTRALIZED)	SINGLE EMPLOYER —MULTIPLANT	SINGLE EMPLOYER —SINGLE PLANT (DECENTRALIZED)
Craft union (narrow)		
Construction trades	Airline	Craft union in small manufacturing plant
Longshoring	Teachers	Hospital
Hospital association	Police	
	Firefighters	
	Railroad	
Industrial or multiskill union (broad)		
Coal mining (underground)	Automobiles	Industrial union in small manufacturing plant
Basic steel (pre-1986)	Steel (post-1986)	
Hotel association	Farm equipment	
	State government	
	Textile	

SOURCE: H.C. Katz and T.A. Kochan, *An Introduction to Collective Bargaining and Industrial Relations* (New York: McGraw-Hill, 1992). © 1992 McGraw-Hill. Used with permission of the McGraw-Hill Companies.

certified and is negotiating its first contract, the situation can be very different. In fact, unions are unable to negotiate a first contract in 27 to 37 percent of the cases.[42]

Labor–management contracts differ in their bargaining structures—that is, the range of employees and employers that are covered. As Table 14.8 indicates, the contracts differ, first, according to whether narrow (craft) or broad (industrial) employee interests are covered. Second, they differ according to whether they cover multiple employers or multiple plants within a single employer. (A single employer may have multiple plants—some union and some nonunion.) Different structures have different implications for bargaining power and the number of interests that must be incorporated in reaching an agreement.

THE NEGOTIATION PROCESS

Richard Walton and Robert McKersie suggested that labor–management negotiations could be broken into four subprocesses: distributive bargaining, integrative bargaining, attitudinal structuring, and intraorganizational bargaining.[43] **Distributive bargaining** focuses on dividing a fixed economic "pie" between the two sides. A wage increase, for example, means that the union gets a larger share of the pie, management a smaller share. It is a win-lose situation. **Integrative bargaining** has a win-win focus; it seeks solutions beneficial to both sides. So, if management needs to reduce labor costs, it could reach an agreement with the union to avoid layoffs in return for the union agreeing to changes in work rules that might enhance productivity.

Attitudinal structuring refers to the relationship and trust between labor and management negotiators. Where the relationship is poor, it may be difficult for the two sides to engage in integrative bargaining because there is little trust that the other side will carry out its part of the deal. For example, the union may be reluctant to agree to productivity-enhancing work-rule changes to enhance job security if, in the past, it has made similar concessions but believes that management did not stick to its assurance of greater job security. Thus, the long-term relationship between the two parties can have a very important impact on negotiations and their outcomes.

Intraorganizational bargaining reminds us that labor–management negotiations involve more than just two parties. Within management, and to an even greater extent within the union, different factions can have conflicting objectives. High-seniority workers, who are least likely to be laid off, may be more willing to accept a contract that has layoffs (especially if there is also a significant pay increase for those whose jobs are not at risk). Less-senior workers would likely feel very differently. Thus, negotiators and union leaders must simultaneously satisfy both the management side and their own internal constituencies. If they do not, they risk the union membership's rejecting the contract, or they risk being voted out of office in the next election. Management, too, is unlikely to be of one mind about how to approach negotiations. Some will focus more on long-term employee relations, others will focus on cost control, and still others will focus on what effect the contract will have on stockholders.

MANAGEMENT'S PREPARATION FOR NEGOTIATIONS

Clearly, the outcome of contract negotiations can have important consequences for labor costs and labor productivity and, therefore, for the company's ability to compete in the product market. Adapting Fossum's discussion, we can divide management preparation into the following seven areas, most of which have counterparts on the union side.[44]

1. *Establishing interdepartment contract objectives*—The employer's industrial relations department needs to meet with the accounting, finance, production, marketing, and other departments and set contract goals that will permit each department to meet its responsibilities. As an example, finance may suggest a cost figure above which a contract settlement would seriously damage the company's financial health. The bargaining team needs to be constructed to take these various interests into account.
2. *Reviewing the old contract*—This step focuses on identifying provisions of the contract that might cause difficulties by hindering the company's productivity or flexibility or by leading to significant disagreements between management and the union.
3. *Preparing and analyzing data*—Information on labor costs and the productivity of competitors, as well as data the union may emphasize, needs to be prepared and analyzed. The union data might include cost-of-living changes and agreements reached by other unions that could serve as a target. Data on employee demographics and seniority are relevant for establishing the costs of such benefits as pensions, health insurance, and paid vacations. Finally, management needs to know how much it would be hurt by a strike. How long will its inventory allow it to keep meeting customer orders? To what extent are other companies positioned to step in and offer replacement products? How difficult would it be to find replacement workers if the company decided to continue operations during a strike?
4. *Anticipating union demands*—Recalling grievances over the previous contract, having ongoing discussions with union leaders, and becoming aware of settlements at other companies are ways of anticipating likely union demands and developing potential counterproposals.
5. *Establishing the cost of possible contract provisions*—Wages have not only a direct influence on labor costs but often an indirect effect on benefit costs (e.g., social security, paid vacation). Recall that benefits add 35 to 40 cents to every dollar's worth of wages. Also, wage or benefit increases that seem manageable in the first year of a contract can accumulate to less manageable levels over time.
6. *Preparing for a strike*—If management intends to operate during a strike, it may need to line up replacement workers, increase its security, and figure out how to deal with incidents on the picket line and elsewhere. If management does not intend to operate during a strike (or if the company will not be operating at normal levels), it needs

to alert suppliers and customers and consider possible ways to avoid the loss of their business. This could even entail purchasing a competitor's product in order to have something to sell to customers.

7. *Determining strategy and logistics*—Decisions must be made about the amount of authority the negotiating team will have. What concessions can it make on its own, and which ones require it to check with top management? On which issues can it compromise, and on which can it not? Decisions regarding meeting places and times must also be made.

NEGOTIATION STAGES AND TACTICS

Negotiations go through various stages.[45] In the early stages, many more people are often present than in later stages. On the union side, this may give all the various internal interest groups a chance to participate and voice their goals. This, in turn, helps send a message to management about what the union feels it must do to satisfy its members, and it may also help the union achieve greater solidarity. Union negotiators often present an extensive list of proposals at this stage, partly to satisfy their constituents and partly to provide themselves with issues on which they can show flexibility later in the process. Management may or may not present proposals of its own; sometimes it prefers to react to the union's proposals.

During the middle stages, each side must make a series of decisions, even though the outcome is uncertain. How important is each issue to the other side? How likely is it that disagreement on particular issues will result in a strike? When and to what extent should one side signal its willingness to compromise on its position?

In the final stage, pressure for an agreement increases as the deadline for a strike approaches. Public negotiations may be only part of the process. Negotiators from each side may have one-on-one meetings or small-group meetings where public-relations pressures are reduced. In addition, a neutral third party may become involved, someone who can act as a go-between or facilitator. In some cases, the only way for the parties to convince each other of their resolve (or to convince their own constituents of the other party's resolve) is to allow an impasse to occur.

Various books suggest how to avoid impasses by using mutual gains or integrative bargaining tactics. For example, *Getting to Yes* (New York: Penguin Books, 1991), by Roger Fisher and William Ury, describes four basic principles:

1. Separate the people from the problem.
2. Focus on interests, not positions.
3. Generate a variety of possibilities before deciding what to do.
4. Insist that the results be based on some objective standard.

BARGAINING POWER, IMPASSES, AND IMPASSE RESOLUTION

Employers' and unions' conflicting goals are resolved through the negotiation process just described. An important determinant of the outcome of this process is the relative bargaining power of each party, which can be defined as the "ability of one party to achieve its goals when faced with opposition from some other party to the bargaining process."[46] In collective bargaining, an important element of power is the relative ability of each party to withstand a strike. Although strikes are rare, the threat of a strike often looms large in labor–management negotiations. The relative ability to take a strike, whether one occurs or not, is an important determinant of bargaining power and, therefore, of bargaining outcomes.

MANAGEMENT'S WILLINGNESS TO TAKE A STRIKE

Management's willingness to take a strike comes down to two questions:

1. *Can the company remain profitable over the long run if it agrees to the union's demands?* The answer is more likely to be yes to the extent that higher labor costs can be passed on to consumers without losing business. This, in turn, is most likely when (1) the price increase is small because labor costs are a small fraction of total costs or (2) there is little price competition in the industry. Low price competition can result from regulated prices, from competition based on quality (rather than price), or from the union's organizing all or most of the employers in the industry, which eliminates labor costs as a price factor.

Unions share part of management's concern with long-term competitiveness because a decline in competitiveness can translate into a decline in employment levels. On the other hand, the majority of union members may prefer to have higher wages, despite employment declines, particularly if a minority of the members (those with low seniority) suffer more employment loss and the majority keep their employment with higher wages.

2. *Can the company continue to operate in the short run despite a strike?* Although "hanging tough" on its bargaining goals may pay off for management in the long run, the short-run concern is the loss of revenues and profits from production being disrupted. In the example that opened this chapter, GM knew it needed to reduce labor costs in the long run in order to be competitive, but the short-run cost was a strike that disrupted the sales of what may have been its hottest seller, the Saturn. The cost to strikers is a loss of wages and possibly a permanent loss of jobs.

Under what conditions is management most able to take a strike? The following factors are important:[47]

1. *Product demand*—Management is less able to afford a strike when the demand for its product is strong because that is when more revenue and profits are lost.
2. *Product perishability*—A strike by certain kinds of employees (e.g., farm workers at harvest time, truckers transporting perishable food, airline employees at peak travel periods) will result in permanent losses of revenue, thus increasing the cost of the strike to management.
3. *Technology*—An organization that is capital intensive (versus labor intensive) is less dependent on its employees and more likely to be able to use supervisors or others as replacements. Telephone companies are typically able to operate through strikes, even though installing new equipment or services and repair work may take significantly longer than usual.
4. *Availability of replacement workers*—When jobs are scarce, replacement workers are more available and perhaps more willing to cross picket lines. Using replacement workers to operate during a strike raises the stakes considerably for strikers who may be permanently replaced. Most strikers are not entitled to reinstatement until there are job openings for which they qualify. If replacements were hired, such openings may not occur for some time (if at all).
5. *Multiple production sites and staggered contracts*—Multiple sites and staggered contracts permit employers to shift production from the struck facility to facilities that, even if unionized, have contracts that expire at different times (so they are not able to strike at the same time).
6. *Integrated facilities*—When one facility produces something that other facilities need for their products, the employer is less able to take a strike because the disruption to production goes beyond that single facility. The UAW strike at the Lordstown plant, which completely shut down production at Saturn, is a good example. The just-in-time

production system, which provides very little stockpiling of parts, further weakens management's ability to take a strike.

7. *Lack of substitutes for the product*—A strike is more costly to the employer if customers have a readily available alternative source from which to purchase the goods or services the company provides.

Bargaining outcomes also depend on the nature of the bargaining process and relationship, which includes the types of tactics used and the history of labor relations. The vast majority of labor–management negotiations do not result in a strike, because a strike is typically not in the best interests of either party. Furthermore, both the union and management usually realize that if they wish to interact effectively in the future, the experience of a strike can be difficult to overcome. When strikes do occur, the conduct of each party during the strike can also have a lasting effect on labor–management relations. Violence by either side or threats of job loss by hiring replacements can make future relations difficult.

IMPASSE-RESOLUTION PROCEDURES: ALTERNATIVES TO STRIKES

Given the substantial costs of strikes to both parties, procedures that resolve conflicts without strikes have arisen in both the private and public sectors. Because many public-sector employees do not have the right to strike, alternatives are particularly important in that arena.

Three often-used impasse-resolution procedures are mediation, fact finding, and arbitration. All of them rely on the intervention of a neutral third party, most typically provided by the Federal Mediation and Conciliation Service (FMCS), which must be notified 30 days prior to a planned change in contract terms (including a strike). **Mediation** is the least formal but most widely used of the procedures (in both the public and private sectors). One survey found it was used by nearly 40 percent of all large private-sector bargaining units.[48] A mediator has no formal authority but, rather, acts as a facilitator and go-between in negotiations.

A **fact finder,** most commonly used in the public sector, typically reports on the reasons for the dispute, the views and arguments of both sides, and (in some cases) a recommended settlement, which the parties are free to decline. That these recommendations are made public may give rise to public pressure for a settlement. Even if a fact finder's settlement is not accepted, the hope is that he will identify or frame issues in such a way as to facilitate an agreement. Sometimes, for the simple reason that fact finding takes time, the parties reach a settlement during the interim.

The most formal type of outside intervention is **arbitration,** under which a solution is actually chosen by an arbitrator (or arbitration board). In some instances, the arbitrator can fashion her own solution (conventional arbitration). In other cases, the arbitrator must choose either the management's or union's final offer (final offer arbitration) on either the contract as a whole or on an issue-by-issue basis. Traditionally, arbitrating the enforcement or interpretation of contract terms (rights arbitration) has been widely accepted, whereas arbitrating the actual writing or setting of contract terms (interest arbitration, our focus here) has been reserved for special circumstances. These include some public-sector negotiations, where strikes may be especially costly (e.g., police, firefighters) and a very few private-sector situations, where strikes have been especially debilitating to both sides (e.g., the steel industry in the 1970s).[49] One reason for avoiding greater use of interest arbitration is a strong belief that the parties closest to the situation (unions and management, not an arbitrator) are in the best position to effectively resolve their conflicts.

Union and Management Interactions: Contract Administration

GRIEVANCE PROCEDURE

Although the negotiation process (and the occasional resulting strike) receive the most publicity, the negotiation process typically occurs only about every three years, whereas contract administration goes on day after day, year after year. The two processes—negotiation and administration—are linked, of course. Vague or incomplete contract language developed in the negotiation process can make administration of the contract difficult. Such difficulties can, in turn, create conflict that can spill over into the next negotiation process.[50] Furthermore, events during the negotiation process—strikes, the use of replacement workers, or violence by either side—can lead to management and labor difficulties in working successfully under a contract.

A key influence on successful contract administration is the grievance procedure for resolving labor–management disputes over the interpretation and execution of the contract. During World War II, the War Labor Board helped institutionalize the use of arbitration as an alternative to strikes to settle disputes that arose during the term of the contract. The soon-to-follow Taft-Hartley Act further reinforced this preference. Today, the great majority of grievance procedures have binding arbitration as a final step, and only a minority of strikes occur during the term of a contract. (Most occur during the negotiation stage.) Strikes during the term of a contract can be especially disruptive because they are more unpredictable than strikes during the negotiation phase, which occur only at regular intervals.

Beyond its ability to reduce strikes, a grievance procedure can be judged using three criteria.[51] First, how well are day-to-day contract questions resolved? Time delays and heavy use of the procedure may indicate problems. Second, how well does the grievance procedure adapt to changing circumstances? For example, if the company's business turns downward and the company needs to cut costs, how clear are the provisions relating to subcontracting of work, layoffs, and so forth? Third, in multiunit contracts, how well does the grievance procedure permit local contract issues (e.g., work rules) to be included and resolved?

From the employees' perspective, the grievance procedure is the key to fair treatment in the workplace, and its effectiveness rests both on the degree to which employees feel they can use it without fear of recrimination and whether they believe their case will be carried forward strongly enough by their union representative. The **duty of fair representation** is mandated by the NLRA and requires that all bargaining-unit members, whether union members or not, have equal access to and representation by the union in the grievance procedure. Too many grievances may indicate a problem, but so may too few. A very low grievance rate may suggest a fear of filing a grievance, a belief that the system is not effective, or a belief that representation is not adequate.

As Table 14.9 suggests, most grievance procedures have several steps prior to arbitration. Moreover, the majority of grievances are settled during the earlier steps of the process, which is desirable both to reduce time delays and to avoid the costs of arbitration. If the grievance does reach arbitration, the arbitrator makes the final ruling in the matter. A series of Supreme Court decisions in 1960, commonly known as the Steelworkers' Trilogy, established that the courts should essentially refrain from reviewing the merits of arbitrators' decisions and, instead, limit judicial review to the question of whether the issue was subject to arbitration under the contract.[52] Furthermore, unless the contract explicitly states that an issue is not subject to arbitration, it will be assumed that arbitration is an appropriate means of deciding the issue. Giving further strength to the role of arbitration is the NLRB's general policy of deferring to arbitration.

TABLE 14.9
Steps in a Typical Grievance Procedure

Employee-initiated grievance

Step 1

a. Employee discusses grievance or problem orally with supervisor.
b. Union steward and employee may discuss problem orally with supervisor.
c. Union steward and employee decide (1) whether problem has been resolved or (2) if not resolved, whether a contract violation has occurred.

Step 2

a. Grievance is put in writing and submitted to production superintendent or other designated line manager.
b. Steward and management representative meet and discuss grievance. Management's response is put in writing. A member of the industrial relations staff may be consulted at this stage.

Step 3

a. Grievance is appealed to top line management and industrial relations staff representatives. Additional local or international union officers may become involved in discussions. Decision is put in writing.

Step 4

a. Union decides on whether to appeal unresolved grievance to arbitration according to procedures specified in its constitution and/or bylaws.
b. Grievance is appealed to arbitration for binding decision.

Discharge grievance

a. Procedure may begin at step 2 or step 3.
b. Time limits between steps may be shorter to expedite the process.

Union or group grievance

a. Union representative initiates grievance at step 1 or step 2 on behalf of affected class of workers or union representatives.

SOURCE: T.A. Kochan, *Collective Bargaining and Industrial Relations* (Homewood, IL: Richard D. Irwin, 1980), p. 395.

What types of issues most commonly reach arbitration? Data from the FMCS on a total of 3,460 grievances in 1997 show that discharge and disciplinary issues topped the list with 1,941 cases.[53] Other frequent issues include the use of seniority in promotion, layoffs, transfers, work assignments and scheduling (684 cases); distribution of overtime or use of compulsory overtime (105 cases); and subcontracting (79 cases).

What criteria do arbitrators use to reach a decision? In the most common case—discharge or discipline—the following due process questions are important:[54]

1. *Did the employee know what the rule or expectation was and what the consequences of not adhering to it were?*
2. *Was the rule applied in a consistent and predictable way?* In other words, are all employees treated the same?
3. *Are facts collected in a fair and systematic manner?* An important element of this principle is detailed record keeping. Both employee actions (e.g., tardiness) and management's response (verbal or written warnings) should be carefully documented.
4. *Does the employee have the right to question the facts and present a defense?* An example in a union setting is a hearing with a shop steward present.
5. *Does the employee have the right to appeal a decision?* An example is recourse to an impartial third party, such as an arbitrator.
6. *Is there progressive discipline?* Except perhaps for severe cases, an arbitrator will typically look for evidence that an employee was alerted as early as possible that his be-

Look Who's Pushing Productivity

David W. Groetsch has brought in plenty of consultants over the years to his 500-worker unit of Aluminum Co. of America, which makes equipment for the packaging industry. As the division president, he has tried all the trends, from quality to teams. But the union as consultant? That was a new one. The International Association of Machinists (IAM), which represents 170 of his workers at a Denver plant, came knocking in 1994, asking to help create a high-performance work system.

Groetsch agreed to give it a whirl. He sent three managers from Denver to join local IAM leaders in a week-long course at the union's school in Maryland. There, they learned how to set up a labor–management partnership and spur productivity—and in the process protect jobs. Then, as any consultant would do, the IAM sent experts—free of charge—to Denver to help union leaders and managers from manufacturing to marketing create team systems and joint decision-making councils. Relations on the shop floor have already improved, says Groetsch, although he doesn't yet have hard data on efficiency gains. "If someone from Andersen Consulting had said: 'We can improve product delivery, customer satisfaction, and profitability—hire me,' I would have yawned," says Groetsch. "But when the union walked in and said all that, it got my attention."

The IAM is at the forefront of a revolutionary change in the way unions view cooperation with management. After decades of suspicion and hostility toward company-sponsored teams, some unions now are actively embracing partnerships with employers, even pushing the trend. The goal: to protect workers' jobs and pay by making their employers more competitive. Unions also want to win employees more say over their work and how their companies are run. "The days of 1950s-style table-banging aren't gone yet, but that's the easy way for union leaders," says Laborers' President Arthur A. Coia, whose union is active in such ventures. "It's a lot harder to ask: 'What does the employer need to stay competitive' with union wages, and then help them to achieve it."

COMPETING THROUGH HIGH-PERFORMANCE WORK SYSTEMS

Labor's new attitude marks a shift experts have been urging for years. By developing expertise in new work systems, unions have a chance to make themselves valuable to employers battling today's intense global and domestic competition. Partnerships also could help to dilute the antagonism many executives feel toward unions. In Las Vegas, for instance, the Hotel Employees & Restaurant Employees Union has forged cooperative relations with once hostile big hotels by wiping out cumbersome work rules. Managers now have flexibility to schedule extra room cleanings when many customers show up at once, for example. "They typify what the labor leaders of tomorrow will be," says Arthur M. Goldberg, the head of Hilton Hotels Corp.'s gaming unit, which owns three Vegas casinos. "They'll tell us some of our problems before we even realize them and work to solve them."

Still, even the most willing unions continue to battle over traditional issues such as wages. Consider the United Steelworkers (USW), which has an extensive partnership with Wheeling–Pittsburgh Steel Corp.

havior was inappropriate and the employee was given a chance to change prior to some form of severe discipline, such as discharge.

7. *Are there unique mitigating circumstances?* Although discipline must be consistent, individuals differ in terms of their prior service, performance, and discipline record. All of these factors may need to be considered.

NEW LABOR–MANAGEMENT STRATEGIES

Jack Barbash has described the nature of the traditional relationship between labor and management (during both the negotiation and administration phases) as follows:

> Bargaining is a love-hate, cooperation-conflict relationship. The parties have a common interest in maximizing the total revenue which finances their respective returns. But they take on adversarial postures in debating how the revenue shall be divided as between wages and profits. It is the adversarial posture which has historically set the tone of the relationship.[55]

that includes a board seat. Despite the ties, it has been on strike since October over pensions. "It's perfectly logical for labor and management to cooperate to enlarge the pie and fight over how to split it up," says former Labor Secretary Ray Marshall, who is the USW's representative on USX Corp.'s board.

The USW made the first national push for partnerships in 1993, when it demanded that major steelmakers designate a union board seat and set up management–union councils at all levels of the company. Steelmakers were suspicious, and USX vowed not to give up a board seat. In the end, all but Allegheny Teledyne Inc. gave in. Last year, the union won similar pacts in aluminum and is pursuing the idea wherever it can. "This is the model we want for the whole union," says Roy Murray, the USW's collective-bargaining director.

Today, cooperation in steel is advancing but far from complete. After years of enmity, some managers aren't keen to share decision-making. Others don't feel the need if business is thriving. At USX's Fairfield (Alabama) plant, the unit making tubular steel faces stiff competition, so managers nurture the partnership, hoping to spur efficiency and quality gains. But on the flat-rolled side, where demand is strong, managers are less committed, union officials say. USX declined to comment.

The IAM has opted for a soft-sell approach, marketing itself as a resource for employers. Three experts at its school in Hollywood, Maryland, scour the country for IAM locals and companies willing to sign on to high-performance training. Interested parties, such as those at the Alcoa plant, take a weeklong course at the school, where plant manager and local union officers study side by side, learning everything from the history of high-performance systems to new accounting methods to measure them.

The Laborers takes a different tack, supplying skilled workers to companies as they need them. Several years ago, it set up a foundation jointly with contractors to provide bid specifications on construction projects nationwide. The foundation, staffed equally by union and industry officials, also offers to supply trained union workers. Contractors pay union wages for those workers but use the service only when they wish; even nonunion companies are eligible. This is a huge shift for construction unions, which typically consider nonunion contractors the enemy. The payoff: The union gets more jobs for its members even if it can't win election battles against nonunion contractors.

The program has paid off for contractors, too. Radian International, an environmental cleanup joint venture between Dow Chemical and Hartford Steam Boiler Inspection & Insurance, was having a difficult time finding workers with the extensive training required for a new contract to clean up lead on an Environmental Protection Agency Superfund site in Missouri. They finally hired through the Laborers' foundation. "We can't always find qualified people in this field, so the union acts like a temp service," says Timothy J. Mains, a Radian lawyer.

AFL-CIO President John J. Sweeney is prodding unions into more aggressive recruitment, triggering clashes with employers. Labor's new stance on cooperation will not change that. But employers might feel better knowing that competitiveness is also on labor's agenda.

SOURCE: Aaron Bernstein, "Look Who's Pushing Productivity," *Business Week*, April 7, 1997.

Although there have always been exceptions to the adversarial approach, there are signs of a more general transformation to less adversarial workplace relations (at least where the union's role is accepted by management).[56] This transformation has two basic objectives: (1) to increase the involvement of individuals and work groups in overcoming adversarial relations and increasing employee commitment, motivation, and problem solving and (2) to reorganize work so that work rules are minimized and flexibility in managing people is maximized. These objectives are especially important for companies that need to be able to shift production quickly in response to changes in markets and customer demands (e.g., steel minimills). The specific programs aimed at achieving these objectives include employee involvement in decision making, self-managing employee teams, labor–management problem-solving teams, broadly defined jobs, and sharing of financial gains and business information with employees.[57] The "Competing through High-Performance Work Systems" box describes this new cooperative approach.

Union resistance to such programs has often been substantial, precisely because the programs seek to change the nature of workplace relations and the role that unions play. Without the union's support, these programs are less likely to survive and less likely to be effective if they do survive.[58] Union leaders have often feared that such programs will weaken unions' role as an independent representative of employee interests. Indeed, according to the NLRA, to "dominate or interfere with the formation or administration of any labor organization or contribute financial or other support to it" is an unfair labor practice. An example of a prohibited practice is "taking an active part in organizing a union or committee to represent employees."[59]

One case that has received much attention is that of Electromation, a small electrical parts manufacturer. In 1992 the NLRB ruled that the company had violated Section 8(a)(2) of the NLRA by setting up worker–management committees (typically about six workers and one or two managers) to solve problems having to do with absenteeism and pay scales.[60] The original complaint was filed by the Teamsters union, which was trying to organize the (nonunion) company and felt that the committees were, in effect, illegally competing with them to be workers' representatives. Similarly, Polaroid recently dissolved an employee committee that had been in existence for over 40 years in response to the U.S. Department of Labor's claim that it violated the NLRA. The primary functions of the employee committee had been to represent employees in grievances and to advise senior management on issues such as pay and company rules and regulations. In a third case, the NLRB ruled in 1993 that seven worker–management safety committees at DuPont Co. were illegal under the NLRB because they were dominated by management. The committee members were chosen by management and their decisions were subject to the approval of the management members of the committees. Finally, the committees made decisions about issues that were mandatory subjects of bargaining with the employees' elected representative—the chemical workers union.[61] The impact of such cases will be felt both in nonunion companies as union organizers move to fill the worker-representation vacuum and in unionized companies as managements find they must deal more directly and effectively with their unions.

In late 1994, the Commission on the Future of Worker–Management Relations (also referred to as the Dunlop Commission, after its chair, former secretary of labor John Dunlop) recommended that Congress clarify Section 8(a)(2) and give employers more freedom to use employee involvement programs without risking legal challenges. In 1996, the U.S. Congress passed the Teamwork for Employees and Managers Act, which supporters said would remove legal roadblocks to greater employee involvement. Critics claimed the act went too far and would bring back employer-dominated labor organizations, which existed prior to the passage of the NLRA in 1935. The Clinton Administration vetoed the bill, meaning that employers will continue to face some uncertainty about legal issues. Table 14.10 provides some guidance on when the use of teams might be illegal.

Although there are legal concerns to address, some evidence suggests that these new approaches to labor relations—incorporating greater employee participation in decisions, using employee teams, multiskilling, rotating jobs, and sharing financial gains—can contribute significantly to an organization's effectiveness.[62] One study, for example, compared the features of traditional and transformational approaches to labor relations at Xerox.[63] As Table 14.11 indicates, the transformational approach was characterized by better conflict resolution, more shop-floor cooperation, and greater worker autonomy and feedback in decision making. Furthermore, compared with the traditional approach, transformational labor relations were found to be associated with lower costs, better product quality, and higher productivity. The Commission on the Future of Worker–Management Relations concluded that the evidence is "overwhelming that

TABLE 14.10
When Teams Are Illegal

Primary factors to look for that could mean a team violates national labor law:	
Representation	Does the team address issues affecting nonteam employees? (i.e., does it represent other workers?)
Subject matter	Do these issues involve matters such as wages, grievances, hours of work, and working conditions?
Management involvement	Does the team deal with any supervisors, managers, or executives on any issue?
Employer domination	Did the company create the team or decide what it would do and how it would function?

SOURCE: T. Kochan and P. Osterman, *The Mutual Gains Enterprise* (Boston: Harvard Business School Press, 1994), p. 202, originally from A. Bernstein, "Making Teamwork Work—And Appeasing Uncle Sam," *Business Week,* January 25, 1993, p. 101.

TABLE 14.11
Patterns in Labor–Management Relations Using Traditional and Transformational Approaches

	PATTERN	
DIMENSION	TRADITIONAL	TRANSFORMATIONAL
Conflict resolution		
Frequency of conflicts	High	Low
Speed of conflict resolution	Slow	Fast
Informal resolution of grievances	Low	High
Third- and fourth-step grievances	High	Low
Shop-floor cooperation		
Formal problem-solving groups (e.g., quality, reducing scrap, employment security)	Low	High
Informal problem-solving activity	Low	High
Worker autonomy and feedback		
Formal autonomous work groups	Low	High
Informal worker autonomous activity	Low	High
Worker-initiated changes in work design	Low	High
Feedback on cost, quality, and schedule	Low	High

SOURCE: Adapted from J. Cutcher-Gershenfeld, "The Impact of Economic Performance of a Transformation in Workplace Relations," *Industrial and Labor Relations Review* 44 (1991), pp. 241–60.

employee participation and labor–management partnerships are good for workers, firms, and the national economy." National survey data also indicate that most employees want more influence in workplace decisions and believe that such influence leads to more effective organizations.[64]

Labor Relations Outcomes

The effectiveness of labor relations can be evaluated from management, labor, and societal perspectives. Management seeks to control costs and enhance productivity and quality. Labor unions seek to raise wages and benefits and exercise control over how employees spend their time at work (e.g., through work rules). Each of the three parties typically seeks to avoid forms of conflict (e.g., strikes) that impose significant costs on everyone. In this section, we examine several outcomes.

TABLE 14.12 Work Stoppages Involving 1,000 or More Workers

YEAR	STOPPAGES	NUMBER OF WORKERS (THOUSANDS)	PERCENTAGE OF TOTAL WORKING TIME
1950	424	1698	0.26%
1955	363	2055	0.16
1960	222	896	0.09
1965	268	999	0.10
1970	381	2468	0.29
1975	235	965	0.09
1980	187	795	0.09
1985	54	324	0.03
1990	44	185	0.02
1995	31	192	0.02
1996	37	273	0.02
1997	29	339	0.01

SOURCE: http://stats.bls.gov.

STRIKES

Table 14.12 presents data on strikes in the United States that involved 1,000 or more employees. Because strikes are more likely in large units, the lack of data on smaller units is probably not a major concern, although such data would, of course, raise the figure on the estimated time lost to strikes. For example, for the 1960s, this estimate is .12 percent using data on strikes involving 1,000 or more employees versus .17 percent for all strikes. Although strikes impose significant costs on union members, employers, and society, it is clear from Table 14.12 that strikes are the exception rather than the rule. Very little working time is lost to strikes in the United States, and their frequency today is quite low by historical standards. Does this mean that the industrial relations system is working well? Not necessarily. Some would view the low number of strikes as another sign of labor's weakness.

WAGES AND BENEFITS

In 1997, full-time, private-sector unionized workers received, on average, wages 28 percent higher than their nonunion counterparts.[65] Total compensation was 35 percent higher for union-covered employees because of an even larger effect of unions on benefits.[66] However, these are raw differences. To assess the net effect of unions on wages more accurately, adjustments must be made. We now briefly highlight a few of these.

The union wage effect is likely to be overestimated to the extent that unions can more easily organize workers who are already highly paid or who are more productive. The gap is likely to be underestimated to the extent that nonunion employers raise wages and benefits in response to the perceived "union threat" in the hope that their employees will then have less interest in union representation. When these and other factors are taken into account, the net union advantage in wages, though still substantial, is reduced to about 10 percent. The union benefits advantage is also reduced, but it remains larger than the union wage effect, and the union effect on total compensation is therefore larger than the wage effect alone.[67]

Beyond differences in pay and benefits, unions typically influence the way pay and promotions are determined. Whereas management often seeks to deal with employees as individuals, emphasizing performance differences in pay and promotion decisions, unions seek to build group solidarity and avoid the possibly arbitrary treatment of employees. To do so, unions focus on equal pay for equal work. Any differences among employees in pay or promotions, they say, should be based on seniority (an objective measure) rather than on performance (a subjective measure susceptible to favoritism). It is very common in union settings for there to be a single rate of pay for all employees in a particular job classification.

PRODUCTIVITY

There has been much debate regarding the effects of unions on productivity.[68] Unions are believed to decrease productivity in at least three ways: (1) the union pay advantage causes employers to use less labor and more capital per worker than they would otherwise, which reduces efficiency across society; (2) union contract provisions may limit permissible work loads, restrict the tasks that particular workers are allowed to perform, and require employers to use more employees for certain jobs than they otherwise would; and (3) strikes, slowdowns, and working-to-rule (i.e., slowing down production by following every workplace rule to an extreme) result in lost production.[69]

On the other hand, unions can have positive effects on productivity.[70] Employees, whether members of a union or not, communicate to management regarding how good a job it is doing by either the "exit" or "voice" mechanisms. "Exit" refers to simply leaving the company to work for a better employer. "Voice" refers to communicating one's concerns to management without necessarily leaving the employer. Unions are believed to increase the operation and effectiveness of the voice mechanism.[71] This, in turn, is likely to reduce employee turnover and its associated costs. More broadly, voice can be seen as including the union's contribution to the success of labor–management cooperation programs that make use of employee suggestions and increased involvement in decisions. A second way that unions can increase productivity is (perhaps ironically) through their emphasis on the use of seniority in pay, promotion, and layoff decisions. Although management typically prefers to rely more heavily on performance in such decisions, using seniority has a potentially important advantage—namely, it reduces competition among workers. As a result, workers may be less reluctant to share their knowledge with less-senior workers because they do not have to worry about less-senior workers taking their jobs. Finally, the introduction of a union may have a "shock effect" on management, pressuring it into tightening standards and accountability and paying greater heed to employee input in the design and management of production.[72]

Although there is evidence that unions have both positive and negative effects on productivity, most studies have found that union workers are more productive than nonunion workers. Nevertheless, it is generally recognized that most of the findings on this issue are open to a number of alternative explanations, making any clear conclusions difficult. For example, if unions raise productivity, why has union representation of employees declined over time, even within industries?[73] A related concern is that unionized establishments are more likely to survive where there is some inherent productivity advantage unrelated to unionism that actually offsets a negative impact of unionism. If so, these establishments would be overrepresented, whereas establishments that did not survive the negative impact of unions would be underrepresented. Consequently, any negative impact of unions on productivity would be underestimated.

PROFITS AND STOCK PERFORMANCE

Even if unions do raise productivity, a company's profits and stock performance may still suffer if unions raise costs (e.g., wages) or decrease investment by a greater amount. Recent studies find that unions have a "large" negative effect on profits and that union coverage tends to decline more quickly in firms experiencing lower shareholder returns, suggesting that some firms become more competitive partly by reducing union strength.[74] Similarly, one study finds that each dollar of unexpected increase in collectively bargained labor costs results in a dollar reduction in shareholder wealth. Other research suggests that investment in research and development is lower in unionized firms.[75] Strikes, although infrequent, lower shareholder returns in both the struck companies and companies (e.g., suppliers) linked to those companies.[76] These research findings describe the average effects of unions. The consequences of more innovative union–management relationships for profits and stock performance are less clear.

The International Context

Except for China, Russia, and the Ukraine, the United States has more union members than any other country. Yet, as Table 14.13 indicates, aside from France and Korea, the United States has the lowest unionization rate (union density) of any country in the table. Even more striking are differences in union coverage, the percentage of employees whose terms and conditions of employment are governed by a union contract. (See Table 14.13.) In Western Europe, it is common to have coverage rates of 80 to 90 percent, meaning that the influence of labor unions far outstrips what would be implied by their membership levels.[77] Why are the unionization rate and coverage comparatively low? One explanation is that the United States does not have as strong a history of deep class-based divisions in society as other countries do. For example, labor and social democratic political parties are commonplace in Western Europe, and they are major players in the political process. Furthermore, the labor movement in Western Europe is broader than that in the United States. It extends not just to the workplace but—through its own or closely related political parties—directly into the national political process.

TABLE 14.13 Union Membership and Union Coverage, Selected Countries, 1995

	MEMBERSHIP		COVERAGE
COUNTRY	NUMBER (THOUSANDS)	PERCENTAGE OF EMPLOYMENT (DENSITY)	PERCENTAGE OF EMPLOYMENT
United States	16,360	14	12
Canada	4,128[a]	37	37[b]
Japan	12,410[b]	24	25
Korea	1,615	13	—
Germany	9,300	29	90[b]
France	1,758	9	90
United Kingdom	7,280	33	37
Sweden	3,180[c]	91	85
Mexico	7,000[d]	43	—
Argentina	3,200	39	73
Brazil	15,205	44[d]	—

[a]1993.
[b]1996.
[c]1994.
[d]1991.
SOURCE: International Labour Office, *World Labour Report, 1997–98* (Geneva, Switzerland).

What is the trend in union membership rates and coverage? In the United States, we have seen earlier that the trend is clearly downward, at least in the private sector. Although there have also been declines in membership rates in many other countries, coverage rates have stayed high in many of these countries. In the United States, deregulation and competition from foreign-owned companies have forced companies to become more efficient. Combined with the fact that the union wage premium in the United States is substantially larger than in other advanced industrialized countries, it is not surprising that management opposition would be higher in the United States than elsewhere.[78] This, in turn, may help explain why the decline in union influence has been especially steep in the United States.

It seems likely that—with the growing globalization of markets—labor costs and productivity will continue to be key challenges. The European Community's movement toward a common market and the North American Free Trade Agreement among the United States, Canada, and Mexico both suggest that goods, services, and production will continue to move more freely across international borders. Where vast differences in wages, benefits, and other costs of doing business (e.g., regulation) exist, there will be a tendency to move to areas that are less costly, unless skills are unavailable or productivity is significantly lower there. Unless labor unions can increase their productivity sufficiently or organize new production facilities, union influence is likely to decline.

In addition to membership and coverage, the United States differs from Western Europe in the degree of formal worker participation in decision making. Works' councils (joint labor–management decision-making institutions at the enterprise level) and worker representation on supervisory boards of directors (codetermination) are mandated by law in countries such as Germany. The Scandinavian countries, Austria, and Luxembourg have similar legislation. German works' councils make decisions about changes in work or the work environment, discipline, pay systems, safety, and other human resource issues. The degree of codetermination on supervisory boards depends on the size and industry of the company. For example, in German organizations having more than 2,000 employees, half of the board members must be worker representatives. (However, the chairman of the board, a management representative, can cast a tie-breaking vote.) In contrast, worker representation on boards of directors in the United States is still rare.[79] Thus, the recent merger of Daimler–Benz and Chrysler means that former Chrysler managers will need to adapt to Germany's system of worker representation.

The works' councils exist in part because collective bargaining agreements in countries such as Germany tend to be oriented toward industrywide or regional issues, with less emphasis on local issues. However, competitive forces have led employers to increasingly opt out of centralized bargaining, even in the countries best known for centralized bargaining, like Sweden and Germany.[80]

The Public Sector

Unlike the private sector, union membership in the public sector grew in the 1960s and 1970s and remained fairly stable through the 1980s. As of 1997, 37 percent of government employees were union members, and 42 percent of all government employees were covered by a collective-bargaining contract.[81] Like the NLRA in the private sector, changes in the legal framework contributed significantly to union growth in the public sector. One early step was the enactment in Wisconsin of collective-bargaining legislation in 1959 for its state employees.[82] Executive Order 10988 provided collective-bargaining rights for federal employees in 1962. By the end of the 1960s, most states had passed similar laws. The Civil Service Reform Act of 1978, Title VII, later established the Federal Labor Relations Authority (modeled after the NLRB). Many states have similar administrative agencies to administer their own laws.

An interesting aspect of public-sector union growth is that much of it has occurred in the service industry and among white-collar employees—groups that have traditionally been viewed as difficult to organize. The American Federation of State, County, and Municipal Employees (AFSCME) with 1.3 million members, has had about 325,000 members in health care, 325,000 in clerical jobs, and over 400,000 in all white-collar occupations.[83]

In contrast to the private sector, strikes are illegal at the federal level of the public sector and in most states. At the local level, all states prohibit strikes by police (Hawaii being a partial exception) and firefighters (Idaho being the exception). Teachers and state employees are somewhat more likely to have the right to strike, depending on the state. Legal or not, strikes nonetheless do occur in the public sector. In 1997, of the 29 strikes involving 1,000 or more workers, 3 were in the public sector.

SUMMARY

Labor unions seek to represent the interests of their members in the workplace. Although this may further the cause of industrial democracy, management often finds that unions increase labor costs while setting limits on the company's flexibility and discretion in decision making. As a result, the company may witness a diminished ability to compete effectively in a global economy. Not surprisingly, management in nonunion companies often feels compelled to actively resist the unionization of its employees. This, together with a host of economic, legal, and other factors, has contributed to union losses in membership and bargaining power in the private sector. There are some indications, however, that managements and unions are seeking new, more effective ways of working together to enhance competitiveness while giving employees a voice in how workplace decisions are made.

DISCUSSION QUESTIONS

1. Why do employees join unions?
2. What has been the trend in union membership in the United States, and what are the underlying reasons for the trend?
3. What are the consequences for management and owners of having a union represent employees?
4. What are the general provisions of the National Labor Relations Act, and how does it affect labor–management interactions?
5. What are the features of traditional and nontraditional labor relations? What are the potential advantages of the "new" nontraditional approaches to labor relations?
6. How does the U.S. industrial and labor relations system compare with systems in other countries, such as those in Western Europe?

WEB EXERCISE

Many unions are merging with other U.S. as well as international unions. Visit www.uaw.com, the web site for the United Auto Workers. This site discusses recent mergers the UAW has participated in as well as includes UAW news releases (for example, click on "Creating a Strong New Union").

1. From the union's standpoint, what are the advantages of merging with other national unions? With international unions?
2. What are the disadvantages of these mergers from the company's perspective? Are there any advantages that a company might realize?

MANAGING PEOPLE: FROM THE PAGES OF "BUSINESS WEEK"

BusinessWeek A Floor Under Foreign Factories?

The global economic crisis has turned up the heat on companies that use cheap overseas labor. Nike Inc. announced in mid-October that it would lift wages for its entry-level factory workers in Indonesia by 22 percent to offset that country's devalued currency. Other companies have been thrashing out ways to address such problems without being undercut by rivals.

Now, nearly a year behind schedule, a long-divided presidential task force on sweatshops is finally poised to agree on a factory monitoring system. The task force was spurred into action by a rival effort by the American Apparel Manufacturers Assn (AAMA). Both programs set guideline for companies to police their factories and suppliers.

Neither plan addresses the central issue of what wage levels should be in poor countries. And participants say only the code that can attract the most companies will survive. So the AAMA's less stringent version may prevail if the task force falters at the last moment.

Still, the efforts, plus another launched earlier this year by the Council on Economic Priorities, a New York public interest group, represent a potentially major step toward global labor standards. The International Labor Organization has had workplace standards on the books for decades. But they have done little, since governments don't enforce them. The new efforts, by contrast, are attempts by companies to self-regulate in the face of negative publicity about sweatshops. If they succeed, a floor of basic working conditions could begin to evolve around the globe.

The new programs are off to a shaky start, however. Back in 1996, the presidential task force—with 18 garment makers and labor and human-rights groups—set out a new code of conduct for factories that would set minimum working hours and health and safety conditions. Ever since, the group has been battling over a monitoring system to ensure compliance.

This summer, the task force deadlocked over minimum wage levels and unionization rights, but a rump of four human-rights groups and Nike, Liz Claiborne, Phillips Van Heusen, and Reebok continued to meet. The group, with White House prodding, held an 11-hour meeting on October 19 and planned to wrap up a final agreement in principle on October 23.

The plan is to establish the Fair Labor Assn. (FLA), a private entity to be controlled 50–50 by corporate and human-rights or labor representatives. The FLA would accredit auditors, such as accounting firms, to certify companies as complying with the code of conduct. It would inspect about a fifth of a company's factories for certification, and perhaps 5 percent a year after it's certified. Audits would be confidential, though auditors must work with local human-rights or labor groups.

Critics, though, say the plan will achieve little unless it addresses wages and unionization rights. The 1996 code requires companies to pay the local minimum wage or the prevailing industry wage and to recognize employee rights to form unions. But the Union of Needletrades, Industrial & Textile Employees and a human-rights group want a study of apparel workers' basic needs, on the assumption that many earn less than a "living wage." The FLA, they say, should apply the results to the code. Dissidents also want companies in countries such as China to pull out if unionization efforts are thwarted, as currently occurs. The task force refused, though members say the FLA still can examine wages absent a formal requirement to do so.

Corporate task force members fear that few other companies would sign on to the dissidents' stiff monitoring plan. As proof, they point to the AAMA, whose members, including Sara Lee, Jockey International, and VF, make 85 percent of the $100 billion of wholesale clothes sold in the U.S. annually. That group has approved a similar code of conduct, only less strict. It requires companies to pay only the existing minimum wage, not the prevailing industry one, which often is higher.

What's more, the AAMA effort began in part to avoid involvement with the union members of the White House group, says AAMA President Larry K. Martin. The AAMA plans to set up an independent association and intends to approach human-rights groups and universities about joining. It also has worked with Elliot Schrage, a Columbia University business professor who's active in antisweatshop activities. But "I doubt if we'll have unions involved, since we're management folks," says Martin.

The two efforts pose a dilemma for companies that want to deal with sweatshops. Human-rights groups are sure to continue efforts to expose bad factories. Companies that sign on to either plan could allay some criticism. But they also may become bigger targets if their factories don't pass muster or are certified but critics find violations anyway. These "strict standards create risk for any company that joins, but we think the risk is even greater for those that [don't] address these problems," says Roberta S. Karp, Liz Claiborne Inc.'s general counsel and task force co-chair.

Both groups hope to win over companies to their anti-sweatshop codes. Already, Wal-Mart Stores Inc., which has been accused of selling clothes made in sweatshops, has expressed interest in the AAMA plan, a spokesperson says. Indeed, as the Asian crises batter developing countries, sweatshop abuses are likely to grow—and companies will want more than ever to curb them.

QUESTIONS

1. From labor's point of view, what challenges does the "mobility of capital" create for protecting workers' rights?
2. Should companies be obligated to pay a "living wage" to workers? What would the likely consequences be for workers?
3. If international labor standards are to be enforced, what is the best means? Should enforcement take the form of self-regulation by industry groups or should national governments cooperate in enforcing such standards?
4. As a consumer, do the conditions under which people work matter to you in choosing a product to buy?

SOURCE: Aaron Bernstein "A Floor Under Foreign Factories?" *Business Week*, November 2, 1998, pp. 126–27.

NOTES

1. J.T. Dunlop, *Industrial Relations Systems* (New York: Holt, 1958).
2. C. Kerr, "Industrial Conflict and Its Mediation," *American Journal of Sociology* 60 (1954), pp. 230–45.
3. In 1946, roughly 1.5 percent of working time was lost to strikes. This compares with 0.3 percent of working time lost in the period 1950–79. See A.M. Glassman and T.G. Cummings, *Industrial Relations: A Multidimensional View* (Glenview, IL: Scott, Foresman, 1985), p. 64; W.H. Holley Jr. and K.M. Jennings, *The Labor Relations Process* (Chicago: Dryden Press, 1984), p. 207.
4. T.A. Kochan, *Collective Bargaining and Industrial Relations* (Homewood, IL: Richard D. Irwin, 1980), p. 25; H.C. Katz and T.A. Kochan, *An Introduction to Collective Bargaining and Industrial Relations* (New York: McGraw–Hill, 1992), p. 10.
5. Katz and Kochan, *An Introduction to Collective Bargaining*.
6. S. Webb and B. Webb, *Industrial Democracy* (London: Longmans, Green, 1987); J. R. Commons, *Institutional Economics* (New York: Macmillan, 1934).
7. C. Kerr, J.T. Dunlop, F. Harbison, and C. Myers, "Industrialism and World Society," *Harvard Business Review* (February 1961), pp. 113–26.
8. T.A. Kochan and K.R. Wever, "American Unions and the Future of Worker Representation," in *The State of the Unions*, ed. G. Strauss et al. (Madison, WI: Industrial Relations Research Association, 1991).
9. "Why America Needs Unions, but Not the Kind It Has Now," *Business Week*, May 23, 1994, p. 70.
10. Katz and Kochan, *An Introduction to Collective Bargaining*.
11. J. Barbash, *The Elements of Industrial Relations (Madison,* WI: University of Wisconsin Press, 1984).
12. "Auto, Steel, Machinists Unions Announce Accord to Merge by 2000," *Daily Labor Report*, July 28, 1995, p. AA-1.
13. Ibid.; A.Q. Nomani, "Struggling to Survive, Unions Battle Unions to Build Memberships," *The New York Times*, October 28, 1995, p. A1.
14. Bureau of National Affairs, "Proportion of Union Members Declines to Low of 15.8 Percent," *Daily Labor Report*, February 9, 1993, pp. B3–B7.
15. B.T. Hirsch, *Labor Unions and the Economic Performance of Firms* (Kalamazoo, MI: W.E. Upjohn Institute, 1991); R.B. Freeman, "Contraction and Expansion: The Divergence of Private Sector and Public Sector Unionism in the United States," *Journal of Economic Perspectives* 2 (1988), pp. 63–88; G.N. Chaison and D.G. Dhavale, "A Note on the Severity of the Decline in Union Organizing Activity," *Industrial and Labor Relations Review* 43 (1990), pp. 366–73.
16. Katz and Kochan, *An Introduction to Collective Bargaining*. Katz and Kochan in turn build on work by J. Fiorito and C. L. Maranto, "The Contemporary Decline of Union Strength," *Contemporary Policy Issues* 3 (1987), pp. 12–27.
17. G. N. Chaison and J. Rose, "The Macrodeterminants of Union Growth and Decline," in *The State of the Unions*.
18. T.A. Kochan, R.B. McKersie, and J. Chalykoff, "The Effects of Corporate Strategy and Workplace Innovations in Union Representation," *Industrial and Labor Relations Review* 39 (1986), pp. 487–501; Chaison and Rose, "The Macrodeterminants of Union Growth"; J. Barbash, *Practice of Unionism* (New York: Harper, 1956), p. 210; W.N. Cooke and D.G. Meyer, "Structural and Market Predictors of Corporate Labor Relations Strategies," *Industrial and Labor Relations Review* 43 (1990), pp. 280–93; T.A. Kochan and P. Capelli, "The Transformation of the Industrial Relations and Personnel Function," in *Internal Labor Markets*, ed. P. Osterman (Cambridge, MA: MIT Press, 1984).
19. Kochan and Capelli, "The Transformation of the Industrial Relations and Personnel Function."
20. S.B. Jarrell and T.D. Stanley, "A Meta-analysis of the Union–Nonunion Wage Gap," *Industrial and Labor Relations Review* 44 (1990), pp. 54–67; P.D. Lineneman, M.L. Wachter, and W.H. Carter, "Evaluating the Evidence on Union Employment and Wages," *Industrial and Labor Relations Review* 44 (1990), pp. 34–53.
21. National Labor Relations Board annual reports.
22. R.B. Freeman and M.M. Kleiner, "Employer Behavior in the Face of Union Organizing Drives," *Industrial and Labor Relations Review* 43 (1990), pp. 351–65.
23. F.K. Foulkes, "Large Nonunionized Employers," in *U.S. Industrial Relations 1950–1980: A Critical Assessment*,

eds. J. Steiber et al. (Madison, WI: Industrial Relations Research Association, 1981).

24. Katz and Kochan, *An Introduction to Collective Bargaining.*
25. E.E. Herman, J.L. Schwarz, and A. Kuhn, *Collective Bargaining and Labor Relations* (Englewood Cliffs, NJ: Prentice–Hall, 1992), p. 32. Note that the percentage of employed workers increased less quickly because employment grew 18 percent during the same period.
26. BLS Website; AFL–CIO website.
27. Herman et al., *Collective Bargaining*, p. 33.
28. Kochan, *Collective Bargaining and Industrial Relations*, p. 61.
29. National Labor Relations Board, *A Guide to Basic Law and Procedures under the National Labor Relations Act* (Washington, DC: U.S. Government Printing Office, 1991).
30. Ibid.
31. Ibid.
32. H.N. Wheeler and J.A. McClendon, "The Individual Decision to Unionize," in *The State of the Unions.*
33. National Labor Relations Board annual reports.
34. J.A. Fossum, *Labor Relations*, 5th ed. (Homewood, IL: Richard D. Irwin, 1992), p. 149.
35. National Labor Relations Board, *A Guide to Basic Law*, p. 17.
36. Ibid.
37. Herman et al., *Collective Bargaining;* P. Jarley and J. Fiorito, "Associate Membership: Unionism or Consumerism?" *Industrial and Labor Relations Review* 43 (1990), pp. 209–24.
38. Katz and Kochan, *An Introduction to Collective Bargaining;* R.L. Rose, "Unions Hit Corporate Campaign Trail," *The Wall Street Journal*, March 8, 1993, p. B1.
39. P. Jarley and C.L. Maranto, "Union Corporate Campaigns: An Assessment," *Industrial and Labor Relations Review* 44 (1990), pp. 505–24.
40. Katz and Kochan, *An Introduction to Collective Bargaining.*
41. A. Bernstein, "Working Capital: Labor's New Weapon?" *Business Week*, September 27, 1997.
42. Chaison and Rose, "The Macrodeterminants of Union Growth."
43. R.E. Walton and R.B. McKersie, *A Behavioral Theory of Negotiations* (New York: McGraw–Hill, 1965).
44. Fossum, *Labor Relations*, p. 262; see also C.S. Loughran, *Negotiating a Labor Contract: A Management Handbook*, 2d ed. (Washington, DC: Bureau of National Affairs, 1990).
45. C.M. Steven, *Strategy and Collective Bargaining Negotiations* (New York: McGraw-Hill, 1963); Katz and Kochan, *An Introduction to Collective Bargaining.*
46. Kochan, *Collective Bargaining and Industrial Relations.*
47. Fossum, Labor Relations, pp. 183–84.
48. Kochan, *Collective Bargaining and Industrial Relations*, p. 272.
49. Herman et al., *Collective Bargaining.*
50. Katz and Kochan, *An Introduction to Collective Bargaining.*
51. Kochan, *Collective Bargaining and Industrial Relations*, p. 386.
52. *United Steelworkers v. American Manufacturing Co.*, 363 U.S. 564 (1960); *United Steelworkers v. Warrior Gulf and Navigation Co.*, 363 U.S. 574 (1960); *United Steelworkers v. Enterprise Wheel and Car Corp.*, 363 U.S. 593 (1960).
53. Original data from U.S. Federal Mediation and Conciliation Service, *Fiftieth Annual Report, Fiscal Year 1997* (Washington, DC: U.S. Government Printing Office, 1997). www.fmcs.gov.
54. J.R. Redecker, *Employee Discipline: Policies and Practices* (Washington, DC: Bureau of National Affairs, 1989).
55. Barbash, *The Elements of Industrial Relations*, p. 6.
56. T.A. Kochan, H.C. Katz, and R.B. McKersie, *The Transformation of American Industrial Relations* (New York: Basic Books, 1986), chap. 6.
57. J.B. Arthur, "The Link between Business Strategy and Industrial Relations Systems in American Steel Minimills," *Industrial and Labor Relations Review* 45 (1992), pp. 488–506; M. Schuster, "Union Management Cooperation," in *Employee and Labor Relations*, ed. J.A. Fossum (Washington, DC: Bureau of National Affairs, 1990); E. Cohen-Rosenthal and C. Burton, *Mutual Gains: A Guide to Union–Management Cooperation*, 2d ed. (Ithaca, NY: ILR Press, 1993); T.A. Kochan and P. Osterman, *The Mutual Gains Enterprise* (Boston: Harvard Business School Press, 1994); E. Applebaum and R. Batt, *The New American Workplace* (Ithaca, NY: ILR Press, 1994).
58. A.E. Eaton, "Factors Contributing to the Survival of Employee Participation Programs in Unionized Settings," *Industrial and Labor Relations Review* 47, no. 3 (1994), pp. 371–89.
59. National Labor Relations Board, *A Guide to Basic Law.*
60. A. Bernstein, "Putting a Damper on That Old Team Spirit," *Business Week*, May 4, 1992, p. 60.
61. Bureau of National Affairs, "Polaroid Dissolves Employee Committee in Response to Labor Department Ruling," *Daily Labor Report*, June 23, 1992, p. A-3; K. G. Salwen, "DuPont Is Told It Must Disband Nonunion Panels," *The Wall Street Journal*, June 7, 1993, p. A-2.
62. Kochan and Osterman, *Mutual Gains;* J.P. MacDuffie, "Human Resource Bundles and Manufacturing Performance: Organizational Logic and Flexible Production Systems in the World Auto Industry," *Industrial and Labor Relations Review* 48, no. 2 (1995), pp. 197–221; W.N. Cooke, "Employee Participation Programs, Group-Based Incentives, and Company Performance: A Union–Nonunion Comparison," *Industrial and Labor Relations Review* 47, no. 4 (1994), pp. 594–609; C. Doucouliagos, "Worker Participation and Productivity in Labor-Managed and Participatory Capitalist Firms: A Meta-

Analysis," *Industrial and Labor Relations Review* 49, no. 1 (1995), pp. 58–77.

63. J. Cutcher-Gershenfeld, "The Impact of Economic Performance of a Transformation in Workplace Relations," *Industrial and Labor Relations Review* 44 (1991), pp. 241–60.
64. R.B. Freeman and J. Rogers, *Proceedings of the Industrial Relations Research Association*, 1995.
65. http://stats.bls.gov.
66. Herman et al., *Collective Bargaining*, pp. 274–75. In the union sector, total compensation was $18.25 ($12.11 in wages, $6.14 in benefits). In the nonunion sector, total compensation was $13.48 ($10.03 in wages, $3.45 in benefits).
67. Jarrell and Stanley, "A Meta-Analysis"; R.B. Freeman and J. Medoff, *What Do Unions Do?* (New York: Basic Books, 1984).
68. J.T. Addison and B.T. Hirsch, "Union Effects on Productivity, Profits, and Growth: Has the Long Run Arrived?" *Journal of Labor Economics* 7 (1989), pp. 72–105.
69. R.B. Freeman and JL. Medoff, "The Two Faces of Unionism," *Public Interest* 57 (Fall 1979), pp. 69–93.
70. L. Mishel and P. Voos, *Unions and Economic Competitiveness* (Armonk, NY: M. E. Sharpe, 1991).
71. Freeman and Medoff, "Two Faces."
72. S. Slichter, J. Healy, and E.R. Livernash, *The Impact of Collective Bargaining on Management* (Washington, DC: Brookings Institution, 1960); Freeman and Medoff, "Two Faces."
73. Freeman and Medoff, "What Do Unions Do?"; Herman et al., *Collective Bargaining;* Addison and Hirsch, "Union Effects on Productivity"; Katz and Kochan, *An Introduction to Collective Bargaining;* Lineneman et al., "Evaluating the Evidence."
74. B.E. Becker and C.A. Olson, "Unions and Firm Profits," *Industrial Relations* 31, no. 3 (1992), pp. 395–415; B.T. Hirsch and B.A. Morgan, "Shareholder Risks and Returns in Union and Nonunion Firms," *Industrial and Labor Relations Review* 47, no. 2 (1994), pp. 302–18.
75. Addison and Hirsch, "Union Effects on Productivity." See also B.T. Hirsch, *Labor Unions and the Economic Performance of Firms* (Kalamazoo, MI: W.E. Upjohn Institute, 1991); J. M. Abowd, "The Effect of Wage Bargains on the Stock Market Value of the Firm," *American Economic Review* 79 (1989), pp. 774–800; Hirsch, *Labor Unions*.
76. B.E. Becker, and C.A. Olson, "The Impact of Strikes on Shareholder Equity," *Industrial and Labor Relations Review* 39, no. 3 (1986), pp. 425–38; O. Persons, "The Effects of Automobile Strikes on the Stock Value of Steel Suppliers," *Industrial and Labor Relations Review* 49, no. 1 (1995), pp. 78–87.
77. C. Brewster, "Levels of Analysis in Strategic HRM: Questions Raised by Comparative Research," Conference on Research and Theory in HRM, Cornell University, October 1997.
78. C. Chang and C. Sorrentino, "Union Membership in 12 Countries," *Monthly Labor Review* 114, no. 12 (1991), pp. 46–53; D.G. Blanchflower and R.B. Freeman, "Going Different Ways: Unionism in the U.S. and Other Advanced O.E.C.D. Countries" (Symposium on the Future Role of Unions, Industry, and Government in Industrial Relations. University of Minnesota), cited in Chaison and Rose, "The Macrodeterminants of Union Growth," p. 23.
79. J.P. Begin and E.F. Beal, *The Practice of Collective Bargaining* (Homewood, IL: Richard D. Irwin, 1989); T.H. Hammer, S.C. Currall, and R.N. Stern, "Worker Representation on Boards of Directors: A Study of Competing Roles," *Industrial and Labor Relations Review* 44 (1991), pp. 661–80; Katz and Kochan, *An Introduction to Collective Bargaining;* H. Gunter and G. Leminsky, "The Federal Republic of Germany," in *Labor in the Twentieth Century*, ed. J.T. Dunlop and W. Galenson (New York: Academic Press, 1978), pp. 149–96.
80. "Adapt or Die," *The Economist*, July 1, 1995, p. 54; G. Steinmetz, "German Firms Sour on Stem That Keeps Peace with Workers: Centralized Bargaining, a Key to Postwar Gains, Inflates Costs, Companies Fear," *The Wall Street Journal*, October 17, 1995, p. A1.
81. Herman et al., *Collective Bargaining*, p. 348; B.T. Hirsch and D.A. MacPherson, *Union Membership and Earnings Data Book 1994* (Washington, DC: Bureau of National Affairs, 1995).
82. J.F. Burton and T. Thomason, "The Extent of Collective Bargaining in the Public Sector," in *Public Sector Bargaining*, ed. B. Aaron, J.M. Najita, and J.L. Stern (Washington, DC: Bureau of National Affairs, 1988).
83. www.afscme.org.

15 CHAPTER

Managing Human Resources Globally

OBJECTIVES

After reading this chapter, you should be able to

1. Identify the recent changes that have caused companies to expand into international markets.
2. Discuss the four factors that most strongly influence HRM in international markets.
3. List the different categories of international employees.
4. Identify the four levels of global participation and the HRM issues faced within each level.
5. Discuss the ways companies attempt to select, train, compensate, and reintegrate expatriate managers.

Doubling the Trouble in China

ENTER THE WORLD OF BUSINESS

China has become a growth market for U.S. businesses, and one in which they scramble to compete without a good idea of the rules of competition. Currently, about 200 million of the potential 1.2 billion Chinese citizens live in cities where Western goods—from Hewlett-Packard computers to Combos salty snacks—are available. However, doing business in China is far from similar to doing business in the United States.

Wm. Wrigley Jr. Co., maker of such brands as Doublemint gum, hoped to sell 400 million sticks of gum in China during 1995. However, the firm finds getting the gum from the production line to the customer presents an unusual challenge. China has poor roads, jammed rivers, and clogged railways, which make distribution quite difficult. In addition, corruption and low motivation add to the headaches of getting products to market.

The first challenge is to find reliable distributors. Because most distributors are state-owned, they have little entrepreneurial incentive and no experience in how to position a brand. But distribution is critical: Wrigley's gum either dries out or the sugar bleeds through the packaging after about eight months; thus, the firm wants it consumed within eight months of manufacture. After manufacturing the gum in Guangzhou, just north of Hong Kong, it is shipped by freighter to Shanghai. However, off the coast the freighters are often stopped by patrol boats to determine whether the freighters are also carrying smuggled goods. If so, the freight might be impounded and it may take two months to get the gum back into the distribution system. Then, when the gum is loaded onto trucks in port, the trucks are often stopped by bandits or provincial gendarmes demanding exorbitant fees. Finally, once the gum arrives in Shanghai it is out of Wrigley's control and the full responsibility of the distributors. Many of these distributors are former units of state-owned trading companies. Few see the need to deliver the gum to customers; rather, they operate under former rules and wait for customers to get the gum from the warehouse.

To help build demand and get its product in customer hands, Wrigley employs teams of sales representatives who walk the streets handing out free Wrigley posters and displays. These reps visit small kiosks (sometimes plywood stands) on the street and help stock the gum for them.

Wrigley has discovered that doing business in China presents a host of human resource issues it would never dream of having to face in the United States.

SOURCE: C. Smith, "Doublemint in China: Distribution Isn't Double the Fun," *The Wall Street Journal*, December 5, 1995, pp. B1, B3.

Introduction

The environment in which business competes is rapidly becoming globalized. More and more companies are entering international markets by exporting their products overseas, building plants in other countries, and entering into alliances with foreign companies. Of the world's largest organizations, 23 have their headquarters outside the United States. Of the top 100 organizations, 59 have their headquarters in the United States, followed by Europe with 38. Japan is currently home to 11 of the 50 largest banks in the world, whereas the United States is home to only 6.[1]

A survey of 12,000 managers from 25 different countries indicates how common international expansion has become, both in the United States and in other countries.[2] Of the U.S. managers surveyed, 26 percent indicated that their companies had recently expanded internationally. Among the larger companies (10,000 or more employees), 45 percent had expanded internationally during the previous two years. Currently, exports account for 11 percent of the gross domestic product in the United States, and they have been growing at a rate of 12 percent a year since 1987.[3]

Indeed, most organizations now function in the global economy. Thus, U.S. businesses are entering international markets at the same time foreign companies are entering the U.S. market.

What is behind the trend toward expansion into global markets? Companies are attempting to gain a competitive advantage, which can be provided by international expansion in a number of ways. First, these countries are new markets with large numbers of potential customers. For companies that are producing below their capacity, they provide a means of increasing sales and profits. Second, many companies are building production facilities in other countries as a means of capitalizing on those countries' lower labor costs for relatively unskilled jobs. For example, many of the *maquiladora* plants (foreign-owned plants located in Mexico that employ Mexican laborers) provide low-skilled labor at considerably lower cost than in the United States. In 1996, the average manufacturing hourly wage in Mexico was $1.50.[4]

According to a survey of almost 3,000 line executives and HR executives from 12 countries, international competition is the number one factor affecting HRM. Those surveyed indicated they expect it to remain the most important factor in the year 2000. The globalization of business structures and globalization of the economy ranked fourth and fifth, respectively.[5] Deciding whether to enter foreign markets and whether to develop plants or other facilities in other countries, however, is no simple matter, and many human resource issues surface.

This chapter discusses the human resource issues that must be addressed to gain competitive advantage in a world of global competition. This is not a chapter on international human resource management (i.e., the specific HRM policies and programs companies use to manage human resources across international boundaries).[6] The chapter focuses instead on the key factors that must be addressed to strategically manage human resources in an international context. We discuss some of the important events that have increased the global nature of business over the past few years. We then identify some of the factors that are most important to HRM in global environments. Finally, we examine particular issues related to managing expatriate managers. These issues present unique opportunities for firms to gain competitive advantage.

Current Global Changes

Several recent social and political changes have accelerated the movement toward international competition. The effects of these changes have been profound and far-reaching. Many are still evolving. In this section, we discuss the major developments that have accentuated the need for organizations to gain a competitive advantage through effectively managing human resources in a global economy.

EUROPEAN ECONOMIC COMMUNITY

European countries have managed their economies individually for years. Because of the countries' close geographic proximity, their economies have become intertwined. This created a number of problems for international businesses; for example, the regulations of one country, such as France, might be completely different from those of another country, such as Germany. In response, most of the European countries agreed to participate in the European Economic Community, which began in 1992. The EEC is a confederation of most of the European nations that agree to engage in free trade with one another, with commerce regulated by an overseeing body called the European Commission (EC). Under the EEC, legal regulation in the participating countries has become more, although not completely, uniform. Assuming the EEC's trend toward free trade among members continues, Europe has become one of the largest free markets in the world. In addition, as of 1999, all of the members of the European Economic Community share a common currency, the euro. This ties the members' economic fates even more closely with one another.

NORTH AMERICAN FREE TRADE AGREEMENT (NAFTA)

NAFTA is an agreement among Canada, the United States, and Mexico that has created a free market even larger than the European Economic Community. The United States and Canada already had a free trade agreement since 1989, but NAFTA brought Mexico into the consortium. The agreement has been prompted by Mexico's increasing willingness to open its markets and facilities in an effort to promote economic growth.[7] As previously discussed, the *maquiladora* plants exemplify this trend. In addition, some efforts have been made to expand the membership of NAFTA to other Latin American countries, such as Chile.

NAFTA has increased U.S. investment in Mexico because of Mexico's substantially lower labor costs for low-skilled employees. This has had two effects on employment in the United States. First, many low-skilled jobs went south, decreasing employment opportunities for U.S. citizens who lack higher-level skills. Second, it has increased employment opportunities for Americans with higher-level skills beyond those already being observed.[8]

THE GROWTH OF ASIA

An additional global market that is of economic consequence to many firms lies in Asia. While Japan has been a dominant economic force for over 20 years, recently countries such as Singapore, Hong Kong, and Malaysia have become significant economic forces. In addition, China, with its population of over 1 billion and trend toward opening its markets to foreign investors, presents a tremendous potential market for goods. In fact, a consortium of Singaporean companies and governmental agencies has jointly developed with China a huge industrial township in eastern China's Suzhou city that will consist of ready-made factories for sale to foreign companies.[9] While Asia has recently been the victim of a large-scale economic recession termed the Asian flu, it is fully expected to regain its stature as an attractive market for products and investment over the next few years.

GENERAL AGREEMENT ON TARIFFS AND TRADE (GATT)

GATT is an international framework of rules and principles for reducing trade barriers across countries around the world. It currently consists of over 100 member nations. The most recent round of GATT negotiations resulted in an agreement to cut tariffs (taxes on imports) by 40 percent, to reduce government subsidies to businesses, expand protection of intellectual property such as copyrights and patents, and establish rules for investing and trading in services. It also established the World Trade Organization (WTO) to resolve disputes among GATT members.

These changes—the European Economic Community, NAFTA, the growth of Asia, and GATT—all exemplify events that are pushing companies to compete in a global economy. These developments are opening new markets and new sources of technology and labor in a way that has never been seen in history. However, this era of increasing international competition accentuates the need to manage human resources effectively to gain competitive advantage in a global marketplace. This requires understanding the effects of some of the factors that can determine the effectiveness of various HRM practices and approaches.

Factors Affecting HRM in Global Markets

Companies that enter global markets must recognize that these markets are not simply mirror images of their home country. Countries differ along a number of dimensions that influence the attractiveness of direct foreign investment in each country. These differences determine the economic viability of building an operation in a foreign location, and they have a particularly strong impact on HRM in that operation. Researchers in international management have identified a number of factors that can affect HRM in global markets, and we focus on four factors, as depicted in Figure 15.1: culture, education–human capital, the political–legal system, and the economic system.[10]

FIGURE 15.1 Factors Affecting Human Resource Management in International Markets

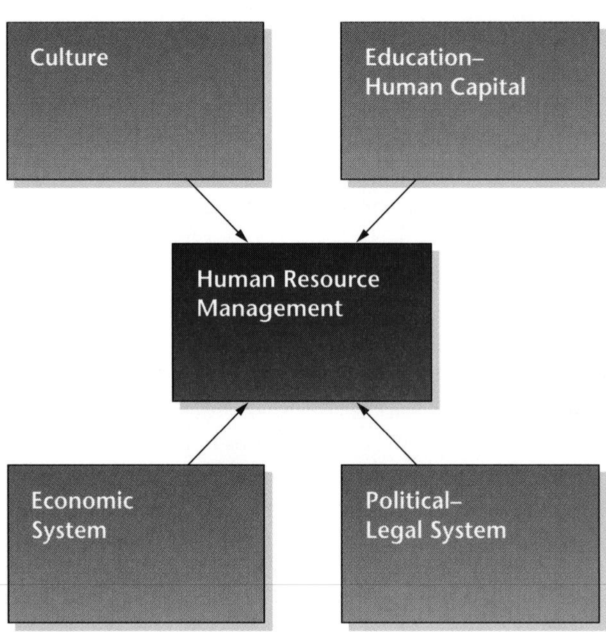

Treating Employees as Customers in Asia

Prior to the meltdown of the Asian economy, skilled workers were in such short supply that it forced HR to truly view employees as customers. Even in the midst of this economic crisis, such a mindset enables HR to focus on creating competitive advantage through people.

Most of Asia is characterized by a shortage of skilled talent. In addition, given the large number of multinational firms entering or growing their businesses in the region, the labor market has become very competitive. Thus, retention of skilled employees is a major goal of firms doing business in Asia.

First, employers must treat potential employees like customers, in fact selling them on the value of working for their company. "We have to sell our jobs," states C.H. Lee, VP of HR and demand flow manufacturing at American Standard Companies in Shanghai. "We have to differentiate our jobs from our competitors'. We have to show why the future is brightest with us."

Second, firms must offer significant training opportunities as a benefit of employment. For example, the Gillette Company offers an International Training Program where promising executives are sent to the corporate office in Boston for 18 months. This program costs between $40,000 and $55,000 depending upon whether the employee is single or married.

Finally, firms must be sensitive to the culture and try to work within it rather than against it. For example, McDonald's emphasizes the cultural similarities through seeking out individuals who already share the company's values. The firm then takes its overall philosophy and integrates it into the local culture or market. Thus, a company value such as merit-based pay increases was implemented in Korea (a culture that emphasizes equality of treatment), such that people were paid differently, but the differences were minor in terms of overall compensation. "It was a first step, allowing us to introduce the concept," says Bob Wilner, home office director of international HR. McDonald's has achieved an admirable record on retention through good salaries, benefits, and training, but most importantly, it creates a sense of family. "We want our company to be part of our workers' families and lives," he says. "When we open a restaurant, we invite the families of our workers to eat there first—even before the local dignitaries. People really get a sense of pride, and it pays off."

SOURCE. R. Grossman, "HR in Asia," *HRMagazine* 42, no. 7 (July 1997), pp. 105–10.

CULTURE

By far the most important factor influencing international HRM is the culture of the country in which a facility is located. *Culture* is defined as "the set of important assumptions (often unstated) that members of a community share."[11] These assumptions consist of beliefs about the world and how it works and the ideals that are worth striving for.[12]

Culture is important to HRM for two reasons. First, it often determines the other three factors. Culture can greatly affect a country's laws, in that laws are often the codification of right and wrong as defined by the culture. Culture also affects human capital, because if education is greatly valued by the culture, then members of the community try to increase their human capital. Finally, as we will discuss later, cultures and economic systems are closely intertwined.[13]

However, the most important reason that culture is important to HRM is that it often determines the effectiveness of various HRM practices. Practices found to be effective in the United States may not be effective in a culture that has different beliefs and values.[14] (See the "Competing by Meeting Stakeholders' Needs" box.) For example, U.S. companies rely heavily on individual performance appraisal, and rewards are tied to individual performance. In Japan, however, individuals are expected to subordinate their wishes and desires to those of the larger group. Thus, individual-based evaluation and incentives are not nearly as effective there and, in fact, are seldom observed among Japanese organizations.[15]

In this section we will examine a model that attempts to characterize different cultures. This model illustrates why culture can have a profound influence on HRM.

HOFSTEDE'S CULTURAL DIMENSIONS. In a classic study of culture, Geert Hofstede identified four dimensions on which various cultures could be classified.[16] In a later study, he added a fifth dimension that aids in characterizing cultures.[17] The relative scores for 10 major countries are provided in Table 15.1. **Individualism/collectivism** describes the strength of the relation between an individual and other individuals in the society—that is, the degree to which people act as individuals rather than as members of a group. In individualist cultures, such as the United States, Great Britain, and the Netherlands, people are expected to look after their own interests and the interests of their immediate families. The individual is expected to stand on her own two feet rather than be protected by the group. In collectivist cultures, such as Colombia, Pakistan, and Taiwan, people are expected to look after the interest of the larger community, which is expected to protect people when they are in trouble.

The second dimension, **power distance,** concerns how a culture deals with hierarchical power relationships—particularly, the unequal distribution of power. It describes the degree of inequality among people that is considered to be normal. Cultures with small power distance, such as those of Denmark and Israel, seek to eliminate inequalities in power and wealth as much as possible, whereas countries with large power distances, such as India and the Philippines, seek to maintain those differences.

Differences in power distance often result in miscommunication and conflicts between people from different cultures. For example, in Mexico and Japan, individuals are always addressed by their titles (e.g., Señor Smith or Smith-san, respectively). Individuals from the United States, however, often believe in minimizing power distances by using first names. Although this is perfectly normal, and possibly even advisable in the United States, it can be offensive and a sign of disrespect in other cultures.

The third dimension, **uncertainty avoidance,** describes how cultures seek to deal

TABLE 15.1 Cultural Dimension Scores for 10 Countries

	PD[a]	ID	MA	UA	LT
United States	40 L[b]	91 H	62 H	46 L	29 L
Germany	35 L	67 H	66 H	65 M	31 M
Japan	54 M	45 M	95 H	92 H	80 H
France	68 H	71 H	43 M	86 H	30[c] L
Netherlands	38 L	80 H	14 L	53 M	44 M
Hong Kong	68 H	25 L	57 H	29 L	96 H
Indonesia	78 H	14 L	46 M	48 L	25[c] L
West Africa	77 H	20 L	46 M	54 M	16 L
Russia	95[c] H	50[c] M	40[c] L	90[c] H	10[c] L
China	80[c] H	20[c] L	50[c] M	60[c] M	118 H

[a] PD = power distance; ID = individualism; MA = masculinity; UA = uncertainty avoidance; LT = long-term orientation.
[b] H = top third; M = medium third; L = bottom third (among 53 countries and regions for the first four dimensions; among 23 countries for the fifth).
[c] Estimated.
SOURCE: Reprinted with permission of G. Hofstede, "Cultural Constraints in Management Theories," *Academy of Management Executive 7* (1993), p. 91.

with the fact that the future is not perfectly predictable. It is defined as the degree to which people in a culture prefer structured over unstructured situations. Some cultures, such as those of Singapore and Jamaica, have weak uncertainty avoidance. They socialize individuals to accept this uncertainty and take each day as it comes. People from these cultures tend to be rather easygoing and flexible regarding different views. Other cultures, such as those of Greece and Portugal, socialize their people to seek security through technology, law, and religion. Thus, these cultures provide clear rules as to how one should behave.

Fourth, the **masculinity–femininity** dimension describes the division of roles between the sexes within a society. In "masculine" cultures, such as those of Germany and Japan, what are considered traditionally masculine values—showing off, achieving something visible, and making money—permeate the society. These societies stress assertiveness, performance, success, and competition. "Feminine" cultures, such as those of Sweden and Norway, promote values that have been traditionally regarded as feminine, such as putting relationships before money, helping others, and preserving the environment. These cultures stress service, care for the weak, and solidarity.

Finally, the fifth dimension comes from the philosophy of the Far East and is referred to as the **long-term–short-term orientation.** Cultures high on the long-term orientation focus on the future and hold values in the present that will not necessarily provide an immediate benefit, such as thrift (saving) and persistence. Hofstede found that many Far Eastern countries such as Japan and China have a long-term orientation. Short-term orientations, on the other hand, are found in the United States, Russia, and West Africa. These cultures are oriented toward the past and present and promote respect for tradition and for fulfilling social obligations.

The current Japanese criticism of management practices in the United States illustrates the differences in long/short-term orientation. Japanese managers, traditionally exhibiting a long-term orientation, engage in 5- to 10-year planning. This leads them to criticize U.S. managers, who are traditionally much more short-term in orientation because their planning often consists of quarterly to yearly time horizons.

These five dimensions help us understand the potential problems of managing employees from different cultures. Later in this chapter we will explore how these cultural dimensions affect the acceptability and utility of various HRM practices. However, it is important to note that these differences can have a profound influence on whether a company chooses to enter a given country. One interesting finding of Hofstede's research was the impact of culture on a country's economic health. He found that countries with individualist cultures were more wealthy. Collectivist cultures with high power distance were all poor.[18] Cultures seem to affect a country's economy through their promotion of individual work ethics and incentives for individuals to increase their human capital. Figure 15.2 maps the countries Hofstede studied on the two characteristics of individualism/collectivism and economic success.

IMPLICATIONS OF CULTURE FOR HRM. Cultures have an important impact on approaches to managing people. As we discuss later, the culture can strongly affect the education–human capital of a country, the political–legal system, and the economic system. As Hofstede found, culture also has a profound impact on a country's economic health by promoting certain values that either aid or inhibit economic growth.

More important to this discussion, however, is that cultural characteristics influence the ways managers behave in relation to subordinates, as well as the perceptions of the appropriateness of various HRM practices. First, cultures differ strongly on such things as how subordinates expect leaders to lead, how decisions are handled within the hierarchy, and (most important) what motivates individuals. For example, in Germany, managers achieve their status by demonstrating technical skills, so employees look to

FIGURE 15.2
The Position of the Studied Countries on Their Individualism Index (IDV) versus Their 1970 National Wealth

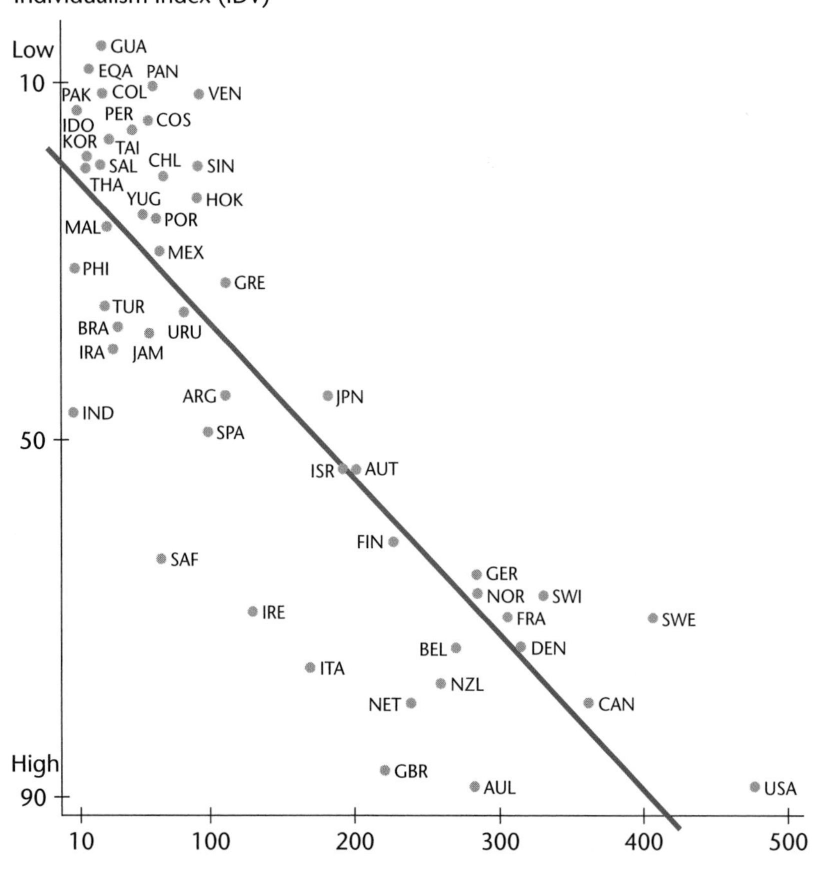

National Wealth in 1970 (GNP/capita) in 10$
IDV.GNP = .84

ARA	Arab countries (Egypt, Lebanon, Lybia, Kuwait, Iraq, Saudi Arabia, U.A.E.)
ARG	Argentina
AUL	Australia
AUT	Austria
BEL	Belgium
BRA	Brazil
CAN	Canada
CHL	Chile
COL	Colombia
COS	Costa Rica
DEN	Denmark
EAF	East Africa (Kenya, Ethiopia, Zambia)
EQA	Equador
FIN	Finland
FRA	France
GBR	Great Britain
GER	Germany
GRE	Greece
GUA	Guatemala
HOK	Hong Kong
IDO	Indonesia
IND	India
IRA	Iran
IRE	Ireland
ISR	Israel
ITA	Italy
JAM	Jamaica
JPN	Japan
KOR	South Korea
MAL	Malaysia
MEX	Mexico
NET	Netherlands
NOR	Norway
NZL	New Zealand
PAK	Pakistan
PAN	Panama
PER	Peru
PHI	Philippines
POR	Portugal
SAF	South Africa
SAL	El Salvador
SIN	Singapore
SPA	Spain
SWE	Sweden
SWI	Switzerland
TAI	Taiwan
THA	Thailand
TUR	Turkey
URU	Uruguay
USA	United States
VEN	Venezuela
WAF	West Africa (Nigeria, Ghana, Sierra Leone)
YUG	Yugoslavia

SOURCE: Geert Hofstede, "The Cultural Relativity of Organizational Practices and Theories," *Journal of International Business Studies* 14, no. 2 (Fall 1983), p. 89.

them to assign their tasks and resolve technical problems. In the Netherlands, on the other hand, managers focus on seeking consensus among all parties and must engage in an open-ended exchange of views and balancing of interests.[19] Clearly, these methods have different implications for selecting and training managers in the different countries.

Second, cultures strongly influence the appropriateness of HRM practices. For example, as previously discussed, the extent to which a culture promotes an individualistic versus a collectivist orientation will impact the effectiveness of individually oriented human resource systems. In the United States, companies often focus selection systems on assessing an individual's technical skill and, to a lesser extent, social skills. In collectivist cultures, on the other hand, companies focus more on assessing how well an individual will perform as a member of the work group.

Similarly, cultures can influence compensation systems. Individualistic cultures such as those found in the United States often exhibit great differences between the highest- and lowest-paid individuals in an organization, with the highest-paid individual often receiving 200 times the salary of the lowest. Collectivist cultures, on the other hand, tend to have much flatter salary structures, with the top-paid individual receiving only about 20 times the overall pay of the lowest-paid one.

Cultural differences can affect the communication and coordination processes in organizations. Collectivist cultures, as well as those with less of an authoritarian orientation, value group decision making and participative management practices more highly than do individualistic cultures. When a person raised in an individualistic culture must work closely with those from a collectivist culture, communication problems and conflicts often appear. Much of the emphasis on "cultural diversity" programs in organizations focuses on understanding the cultures of others in order to better communicate with them. An example of how important cultural differences can be is provided in the "Competing through High-Performance Work Systems" box.

EDUCATION–HUMAN CAPITAL

A company's potential to find and maintain a qualified work force is an important consideration in any decision to expand into a foreign market. Thus, a country's human capital resources can be an important HR issue. Human capital refers to the productive capabilities of individuals—that is, the knowledge, skills, and experience that have economic value.[20]

Countries differ in their levels of human capital. For example, as discussed in Chapter 1, the United States suffers from a human capital shortage because the jobs being created require skills beyond those of most new entrants into the work force.[21] In former East Germany, there is an excess of human capital in terms of technical knowledge and skill because of that country's large investment in education. However, East Germany's business schools did not teach management development, so there is a human capital shortage for managerial jobs.[22] Similarly, companies in what used to be West Germany have shifted toward types of production and service that require high-skilled workers; this is creating a human capital shortage for high-skill jobs, yet the unemployment rate remains high because of a large number of low-skilled workers.[23] However, the high skills and low wages of workers in many countries make their labor forces quite attractive.

A country's human capital is determined by a number of variables. A major variable is the educational opportunities available to the labor force. In the Netherlands, for instance, government funding of school systems allows students to go all the way through

Managing in Russia

Managing employees from different cultures always presents unique problems. This is exemplified among firms trying to do business in Russia. First, many natives matured in their work habits under a communist system that was devoid of any recognition of the customer—a system in which decisions were all made by the general director. Thus, these employees, while having technical skills, are prepared neither to see the value in customer service nor to take on any decision making authority. This presents a myriad of problems for firms seeking to develop high-performance work systems that emphasize employee involvement in decision making as a means of creating competitive advantage in the marketplace.

Second, Russia's cultural norms simply result in very different day-to-day behaviors. Take phone skills, for example. In the United States any time you call a major company (as well as just about any small business), you are likely to have your phone call answered within only a few rings and then be greeted by a friendly voice saying something like "Good morning, XYZ Corporation. Where may I direct your call?" On the other hand, in Russia individuals never identify themselves or their organizations when answering the phone, and some may simply answer it by shouting "Yes?" In addition, some expatriate managers say that they have attended meetings where a phone rang repeatedly without anyone answering it. Finally, someone picked up the phone, hung it right back up without speaking to the caller, and then left it off the hook for the rest of the meeting. They reasoned that if the phone call was important, the person would call back.

COMPETING THROUGH HIGH-PERFORMANCE WORK SYSTEMS

This highlights the need for extensive training for Russian employees working for U.S. companies. Firms that hope to compete need to invest in training employees in such broad topics as economics (understanding how markets work) all the way down to such basic skills as answering the phone. For example, Pepsi International Bottlers provides its high-performing leaders with customized training based on evaluations of their personal strengths and weaknesses. Potential training areas are negotiation, customer focus, and business writing. This training costs roughly $3,000 per person. Clearly, the lesson is that firms that fail to upgrade Russian employees' skills and help them adapt to Western business practices will not survive for long.

SOURCE: M. Cooley, "HR in Russia: Training for Long Term Success," *HRMagazine* 42, no. 12 (December 1997), pp. 98–106.

graduate school without paying.[24] Similarly, the free education provided to citizens in the former Soviet bloc resulted in high levels of human capital, in spite of the poor infrastructure and economy that resulted from the socialist economic systems. In contrast, some Third World countries, such as Nicaragua and Haiti, have relatively low levels of human capital because of a lack of investment in education.

A country's human capital may profoundly affect a foreign company's desire to locate there or enter that country's market. Countries with low human capital attract facilities that require low skills and low wage levels. This explains why U.S. companies desire to locate their currently unionized low-skill–high-wage manufacturing and assembly jobs to Mexico, where they can obtain low-skilled workers for substantially lower wages. Similarly, Japan ships its messy, low-skill work to neighboring countries while maintaining its high-skill work at home.[25] Countries like Mexico, with relatively low levels of human capital, might not be as attractive for operations that consist of more high-skill jobs.

Countries with high human capital are attractive sites for direct foreign investment that creates high-skill jobs. In Ireland, for example, over 25 percent of 18-year-olds attend college, a rate much higher than other European countries. In addition, Ireland's economy supports only 1.1 million jobs for a population of 3.5 million. The combination of high education levels, a strong work ethic, and high unemployment makes the country attractive for foreign firms because of the resulting high productivity and low turnover. The Met Life insurance company set up a facility for Irish workers to analyze medical insurance claims. It has found the high levels of human capital and the high work ethic to provide such a competitive advantage that the company is currently looking for other work performed in the United States to be shipped to Ireland. Similarly, for this reason, many believe that NAFTA will result in a loss of low-skill jobs in the United States but also in an increased number of high-skill jobs in the United States. The increase in high-skill jobs would result from increased commerce between the two nations combined with the higher levels of human capital available in the United States versus Mexico.[26]

POLITICAL–LEGAL SYSTEM

The regulations imposed by a country's legal system can strongly affect HRM. The political–legal system often dictates the requirements of certain HRM practices, such as training, compensation, hiring, firing, and layoffs. In large part, the legal system is an outgrowth of the culture in which it exists. Thus, the laws of a particular country often reflect societal norms about what constitutes legitimate behavior.[27]

For example, the United States has led the world in eliminating discrimination in the workplace. Because of the importance this has in our culture, we also have legal safeguards such as equal employment opportunity laws (discussed in Chapter 3) that strongly affect the hiring and firing practices of firms. As a society, we also have strong beliefs regarding the equity of pay systems; thus, the Fair Labor Standards Act (discussed in Chapter 15), among other laws and regulations, sets the minimum wage for a variety of jobs. We have regulations that dictate much of the process for negotiation between unions and management. These regulations profoundly affect the ways human resources are managed in the United States.

Similarly, the legal regulations regarding HRM in other countries reflect their societal norms. For example, in Germany, employees have a legal right to "codetermination" at the company, plant, and individual levels. At the company level, a firm's employees have direct influence on the important decisions that affect them, such as large investments or new strategies. This is brought about through having employee representatives on the supervisory council (*Aufsichtsrat*). At the plant level, codetermination exists through works councils. These councils have no rights in the economic management of the company, but they can influence HRM policies on such issues as working hours, payment methods, hirings, and transfers. Finally, at the individual level, employees have contractual rights, such as the right to read their personnel files and the right to be informed about how their pay is calculated.[28]

The EEC provides another example of the effects of the political–legal system on HRM. The EEC's Community Charter of December 9, 1989, provides for the fundamental social rights of workers. These rights include freedom of movement, freedom to choose one's occupation and be fairly compensated, guarantee of social protection via social security benefits, freedom of association and collective bargaining, equal treatment for men and women, and a safe and healthy work environment, among others.

ECONOMIC SYSTEM

A country's economic system influences HRM in a number of ways. As previously discussed, a country's culture is integrally tied to its economic system, and these systems provide many of the incentives for developing their human capital. In socialist economic systems, there are ample opportunities for developing human capital because the education system is free. However, under these systems, there is little economic incentive to develop human capital because there are no monetary rewards for increasing human capital. In addition, in former Soviet bloc countries, an individual's investment in human capital did not always result in a promotion. Rather, it was investment in the Socialist Party that led to career advancements.

In capitalist systems, the opposite situation exists. There is less opportunity to develop human capital without higher costs. (You have probably observed tuition increases at U.S. universities.) However, those who do invest in their individual human capital, particularly through education, are more able to reap monetary rewards, thus providing more incentive for such investment. In the United States, individuals' salaries usually reflect differences in human capital (i.e., high-skill workers receive higher compensation than low-skill workers). In fact, research estimates that an individual's wages increase by between 10 and 16 percent for each additional year of schooling.[29]

In addition to the effects of an economic system on HRM, the health of the system can have an important impact. For example, we referred earlier to lower labor costs in Mexico. In developed countries with a high level of wealth, labor costs tend to be quite high relative to those in developing countries. While labor costs are related to the human capital of a country, they are not perfectly related, as shown by Table 15.2. This table provides a good example of the different hourly labor costs for manufacturing jobs in various countries.

An economic system also affects HRM directly through its taxes on compensation packages. Thus, the differential labor costs shown in Table 15.2 do not always reflect the actual take-home pay of employees. Socialist systems are characterized by tax systems that redistribute wealth by taking a higher percentage of a person's income as she moves up the economic ladder. Capitalist systems attempt to reward individuals for their efforts by allowing them to keep more of their earnings. Table 15.3 shows that a manager being paid $100,000 would take home vastly different amounts in different countries because of the varying tax rates. Companies that do business in other countries have to present compensation packages to expatriate managers that are competitive in take-home, rather than gross, pay. HRM responses to these issues affecting expatriate managers will be discussed in more detail later in this chapter.

In conclusion, every country varies in terms of its culture, human capital, legal system, and economic systems. These variations directly influence the types of HRM sys-

TABLE 15.2
Gross Hourly Compensation in Several Countries

Country	Compensation
Germany	$28.28
Switzerland	24.19
Sweden	22.24
Austria	21.92
Netherlands	20.61
Japan	19.37
United States	18.24
France	17.94
Italy	16.74
Britain	15.47
Greece	9.59[a]
Portugal	5.29
Mexico	1.75
Sri Lanka	.48[a]

SOURCE: U.S. Department of Labor, *International Comparisons of Hourly Compensation Costs for Production Workers in Manufacturing,* 1997; Bureau of Labor Statistics, 1998.
[a] 1996 data.

TABLE 15.3
Maximum Marginal Federal Tax Rates

COUNTRY	INCOME TAX HIGHEST PERSONAL NATIONAL RATE
United States	40%
Germany	56%
France	54%
Britain	40%
Netherlands	60%
Sweden	55%
Italy	46%
Japan	50%
South Korea	44%

SOURCE: "America vs. the New Europe: By the Numbers," *Fortune,* December 21, 1998.

tems that must be developed to accommodate the particular situation. The extent to which these differences affect a company depends on how involved the company is in global markets. In the next sections we discuss important concepts of global business and various levels of global participation, particularly noting how these factors come into play.

Managing Employees in a Global Context

TYPES OF INTERNATIONAL EMPLOYEES

Before discussing the levels of global participation, we need to distinguish between parent countries, host countries, and third countries. A **parent country** is the country in which the company's corporate headquarters is located. For example, the United States is the parent country of General Motors. A **host country** is the country in which the parent country organization seeks to locate (or has already located) a facility. Thus, Great Britain is a host country for General Motors because GM has operations there. A **third country** is a country other than the host country or parent country, and a company may or may not have a facility there.

There are also different categories of employees. **Expatriate** is the term generally used for employees sent by a company in one country to manage operations in a different country. With the increasing globalization of business, it is now important to distinguish among different types of expatriates. **Parent-country nationals (PCNs)** are employees who were born and live in the parent country. **Host-country nationals (HCNs)** are those employees who were born and raised in the host, as opposed to the parent, country. Finally, **third-country nationals (TCNs)** are employees born in a country other than the parent country and host country but who work in the host country. Thus, a manager born and raised in Brazil employed by an organization located in the United States and assigned to manage an operation in Thailand would be considered a TCN.

Research shows that countries differ in their use of various types of international employees. One study revealed that Japanese multinational firms have more ethnocentric HRM policies and practices (e.g., they tend to use Japanese expatriate managers more than local host-country nationals) than either European or U.S. firms. This study also found that the use of ethnocentric HRM practices is associated with more HRM problems.[30]

FIGURE 15.3
Levels of Global Participation

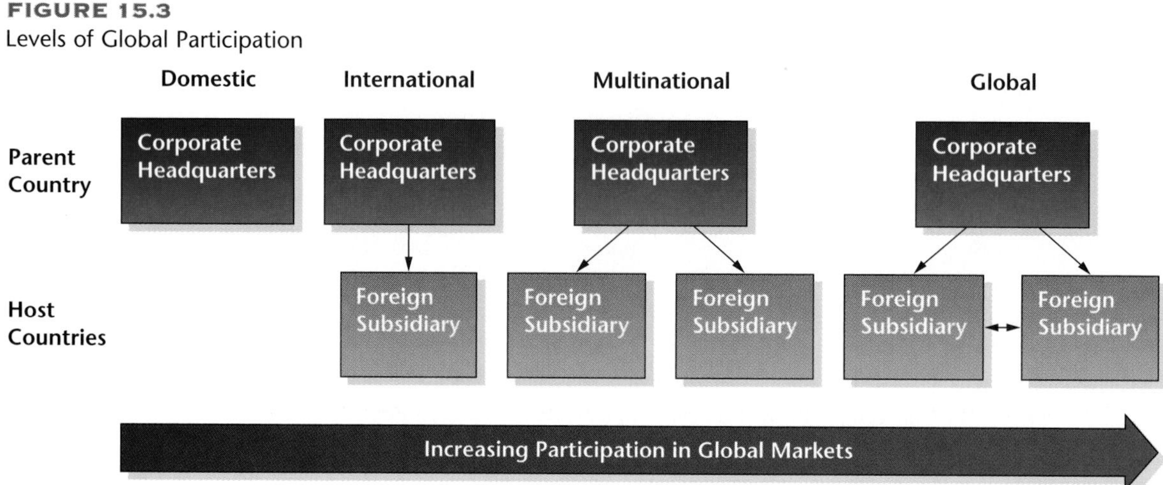

LEVELS OF GLOBAL PARTICIPATION

We often hear companies referred to as "multinational" or "international." However, it is important to understand the different levels of participation in international markets. This is especially important because as a company becomes more involved in international trade, different types of HRM problems arise. In this section, we examine Nancy Adler's categorization of the various levels of international participation from which a company may choose.[31] Figure 15.3 depicts these levels of involvement.

DOMESTIC. Most companies begin by operating within a domestic marketplace. For example, an entrepreneur may have an idea for a product that meets a need in the U.S. marketplace. This individual then obtains capital to build a facility that allows the product or service to be produced in a quantity that meets the needs of a small market niche. This requires recruiting, hiring, training, and compensating a number of individuals who will be involved in the production process, and these individuals are usually drawn from the local labor market. The focus of the selection and training programs is often on the employees' technical competence to perform job-related duties and to some extent on interpersonal skills. In addition, because the company is usually involved in only one labor market, determining the market rate of pay for various jobs is relatively easy.

As the product grows in popularity, the owner might choose to build additional facilities in different parts of the country to reduce the costs of transporting the product over large distances. In deciding where to locate these facilities, the owner must consider the attractiveness of the local labor markets. Various parts of the country may have different cultures that make those areas more or less attractive according to the work ethics of the potential employees. Similarly, the human capital in the different areas may vary greatly because of differences in educational systems. Finally, local pay rates may differ. It is for these reasons that the U.S. economy in the past 10 years has experienced a movement of jobs from northern states, which are characterized by strong unions and high labor costs, to the Sunbelt states, which have lower labor costs and are less unionized.

Incidentally, even domestic companies face problems with cultural diversity. In the United States, for example, the representation of women and minorities is increasing within the work force. These groups come to the workplace with worldviews that differ from those of the traditional white male. Thus, we are seeing more and more emphasis on developing systems for managing cultural diversity within single-country organizations, even though the diversity might be on a somewhat smaller scale than the diversity of cultures across national boundaries.[32]

It is important to note that companies functioning at the domestic level face an environment with very similar cultural, human capital, political–legal, and economic situations, although some variation might be observed across states and geographic areas.

INTERNATIONAL. As more competitors enter the domestic market, companies face the possibility of losing market share; thus, they often seek other markets for their products. This usually requires entering international markets, initially by exporting products but ultimately by building production facilities in other countries. The decision to participate in international competition raises a host of human resource issues. All the problems regarding locating facilities are magnified. One must consider whether a particular location provides an environment where human resources can be successfully acquired and managed.

Now the company faces an entirely different situation with regard to culture, human capital, the political–legal system, and the economic system. For example, the availability of human capital is of utmost importance, and there is a substantially greater variability in human capital between the United States and other countries than there is among the various states in the United States.

A country's legal system may also present HR problems. For example, France has a relatively high minimum wage, which drives labor costs up. In Germany, companies are legally required to offer employees influence in the management of the firm. Companies that develop facilities in other countries have to adapt their HR practices to conform to the host country's laws. This requires the company to gain expertise in the country's HRM legal requirements and knowledge about how to deal with the country's legal system, and it often requires the company to hire one or more HCNs. In fact, some countries legally require companies to hire a certain percentage of HCNs for any foreign-owned subsidiary.

Finally, cultures have to be considered. To the extent that the country's culture is vastly different from that of the parent organization, conflicts, communication problems, and morale problems may occur. Expatriate managers must be trained to identify these cultural differences, and they must be flexible enough to adapt their styles to those of their host country. This requires an extensive selection effort to identify individuals who are capable of adapting to new environments and an extensive training program to ensure that the culture shock is not devastating. The "Competing through Globalization" box illustrates just how different the environment can be in different countries.

MULTINATIONAL. Whereas international companies build one or a few facilities in another country, they become multinational when they build facilities in a number of different countries, attempting to capitalize on lower production and distribution costs in different locations. The lower production costs are gained by shifting production from higher-cost locations to lower-cost locations. For example, some of the major U.S. automakers have plants all over the world. They continue to shift their production from the United States, where labor unions have gained high wages for their members, to *maquiladora* facilities in Mexico, where the wages are substantially lower. Similarly, these companies minimize distribution costs by locating facilities in Europe for manufacturing and assembling automobiles to sell in the European market. They are also now expanding into some of the former Soviet bloc countries to produce automobiles for the European market.

The HRM problems multinational companies face are similar to those international companies face, only magnified. Instead of having to consider only one country's or two countries' cultural, human capital, legal, and economic systems, the multinational com-

Colombia, SA, Sure Isn't Columbia, SC

Many executives at U.S. companies assume that competing in different countries will require some minor modifications in business processes and practices due to legal, political, and cultural differences, but few understand how different the business environment can truly be. Selling soft drinks in Colombia, South America, exemplifies the divergence from a traditional U.S.-based approach to selling them.

Carlos Manuel Acevedo manages a soft-drink bottling plant for Postobon—formally Gaseosas Posada Tobon, SA—in Barrancabermeja, Colombia. Soon after he arrived, the local leader of a guerrilla group known as the National Liberation Army visited and announced that he needed 50 cases of beer and 20 cases of soda. Two guerrilla groups compete for power in the local area, moving freely about the region. These guerrillas, financed by extorting Colombian and foreign-owned companies and protecting drug producers, mostly simply force the government to meet certain demands such as agrarian reform, rather than seeking to overthrow the government. Given that his predecessor had been gunned down by the guerrilla group in front of the plant, Mr. Acevedo quickly decided to provide the beverages at a 10 percent discount.

To minimize the risk of kidnapping, Mr. Acevedo changes the timing and site of monthly management meetings. He avoids visiting the local army bases. He denies making protection payments to the guerrillas to avoid problems, but many companies secretly do. Highjackings or torchings of delivery trucks are not common, but do occur occasionally.

In addition, competition for customers is fierce, and sales techniques differ slightly from those in the United States. For example, one salesman for Postobon sought to make a sale with a vocational school by offering complimentary five-gallon water bottles, \$600 in cash, a new kiosk, and 80 free cases of soda. The competing salesman at Coca-Cola made a similar offer though Coca-Cola officials state that they do not normally pay cash for contracts. However, Postobon won the contract by also offering uniforms for the soccer team and newly painted lines on the school's soccer field.

SOURCE: T. Vogel, "Business Marches On in Colombia, despite Constant Rebel Influence," *The Wall Street Journal*, interactive edition, March 13, 1998.

pany must address these differences for a large number of countries. This accentuates the need to select managers capable of functioning in a variety of settings, provide them with necessary training, and provide for flexible compensation systems that take into account the different market pay rates, tax systems, and costs of living.

Multinational companies now employ many "inpatriates"—managers from different countries who become part of the corporate headquarters staff. This creates a need to integrate managers from different cultures into the culture of the parent company. In addition, multinational companies now take more expatriates from countries other than the parent country and place them in facilities of other countries. For example, a manager from Scotland, working for a U.S. company, might be assigned to run an operation in South Africa. This practice accentuates the need for cross-cultural training to provide managerial skills for interaction with individuals from different cultures.

GLOBAL. Many researchers now propose a fourth level of integration: global organizations. Global organizations compete on state-of-the-art, top-quality products and services and do so with the lowest costs possible. Whereas multinational companies attempt to develop identical products distributed worldwide, global companies increasingly emphasize flexibility and mass customization of products to meet the needs of particular clients. Multinational companies are usually driven to locate facilities in a country as a means of reaching that country's market or lowering production costs, and the company must deal with the differences across the countries. Global firms, on the other hand, choose to locate a facility based on the ability to effectively, efficiently, and flexibly produce a product or service and attempt to create synergy through the cultural differences.

This creates the need for HRM systems that encourage flexible production (thus presenting a host of HRM issues). These companies proactively consider the cultures, human capital, political–legal systems, and economic systems to determine where production facilities can be located to provide a competitive advantage. Global companies have multiple headquarters spread across the globe, resulting in less hierarchically structured organizations that emphasize decentralized decision making. This results in the need for human resource systems that recruit, develop, retain, and use managers and executives who are competent transnationally.

A transnational HR system is characterized by three attributes.[33] **Transnational scope** refers to the fact that HR decisions must be made from a global rather than a national or regional perspective. This creates the need to make decisions that balance the need for uniformity (to ensure fair treatment of all employees) with the need for flexibility (to meet the needs of employees in different countries). **Transnational representation** reflects the multinational composition of a company's managers. Global participation does not necessarily ensure that each country is providing managers to the company's ranks. This is a prerequisite if the company is to achieve the next attribute. **Transnational process** refers to the extent to which the company's planning and decision-making processes include representatives and ideas from a variety of cultures. This attribute allows for diverse viewpoints and knowledge associated with different cultures, increasing the quality of decision making.

These three characteristics are necessary for global companies to achieve cultural synergy. Rather than simply integrating foreigners into the domestic organization, a successful transnational company needs managers who will treat managers from other cultures as equals. This synergy can be accomplished only by combining selection, training, appraisal, and compensation systems in such a way that managers have a transnational rather than a parochial orientation. However, a survey of 50 companies in the United States and Canada found that global companies' HR systems are far less transnational in scope, representation, and process than the companies' strategic planning systems and organizational structures.[34]

In conclusion, entry into international markets creates a host of HRM issues that must be addressed if a company is to gain competitive advantage. Once the choice has been made to compete in a global arena, companies must seek to manage employees who are sent to foreign countries (expatriates and third-country nationals). This causes the need to shift from focusing only on the culture, human capital, political–legal, and economic influences of the host country to examining the ways to manage the expatriate managers who must be located there. Selection systems must be developed that allow the company to identify managers capable of functioning in a new culture. These managers must be trained to identify the important aspects of the new culture in which they will live as well as the relevant legal–political and economic systems. Finally, these managers must be compensated to offset the costs of uprooting themselves and their families to move to a new situation vastly different from their previous lives. In the next section, we address the issues regarding the management of expatriates.

MANAGING EXPATRIATES IN GLOBAL MARKETS

We have outlined the major macrolevel factors that influence HR in global markets. These factors can affect a company's decision whether to build facilities in a given country. In addition, if a company does develop such facilities, these factors strongly affect the HR practices used. However, one important issue that has been recognized over the past few years is the set of problems inherent in selecting, training, compensating, and reintegrating expatriate managers.

The importance to the company's profitability of making the right expatriate assignments should not be underestimated. Expatriate managers' average compensation package is approximately $250,000,[35] and the cost of an unsuccessful expatriate assignment (i.e., one who returns early) is approximately $100,000.[36] In spite of the importance of these assignments, U.S. organizations have been astoundingly unsuccessful in their use of expatriates. Between 16 and 40 percent of all U.S. employees sent on expatriate assignments overseas return early, a rate almost two to three times that of foreign nationals.[37] In addition, of those expatriates who remain on assignment, many are ineffective, resulting in a loss of productivity. In fact, 30 to 50 percent of U.S. expatriates are evaluated by their firms as either ineffective or marginally effective in their performance.[38]

In this final section of the chapter, we discuss the major issues relevant to the management of expatriate managers. These issues cover the selection, training, compensation, and reacculturation of expatriates.

SELECTION OF EXPATRIATE MANAGERS. One of the major problems in managing expatriate managers is determining which individuals in the organization are most capable of handling an assignment in a different culture. Expatriate managers must have technical competence in the area of operations; otherwise, they will be unable to earn the respect of subordinates. However, technical competence has been almost the sole variable used in deciding whom to send on overseas assignments, despite the fact that multiple skills are necessary for successful performance in these assignments.[39]

A successful expatriate manager must be sensitive to the country's cultural norms, flexible enough to adapt to those norms, and strong enough to make it through the inevitable culture shock. In addition, the manager's family must be similarly capable of adapting to the new culture. These adaptive skills have been categorized into three dimensions:[40] (1) the self dimension (the skills that enable a manager to maintain a positive self-image and psychological well-being); (2) the relationship dimension (the skills required to foster relationships with the host-country nationals); and (3) the perception dimension (those skills that enable a manager to accurately perceive and evaluate the host environment). One study of international assignees found that they considered the following five factors to be important in descending order of importance: family situation, flexibility and adaptability, job knowledge and motivation, relational skills, and extracultural openness.[41] Table 15.4 presents a series of considerations and questions to ask potential expatriate managers to assess their ability to adapt to a new cultural environment.

Little evidence suggests that U.S. companies have invested much effort in attempting to make correct expatriate selections. One researcher found that only 5 percent of the firms she surveyed administered any tests to determine the degree to which expatriate candidates possessed cross-cultural skills.[42] More recent research reveals that only 35 percent of firms choose expatriates from multiple candidates and that those firms emphasize only technical job-related experience and skills in making these decisions.[43] These findings glaringly demonstrate that U.S. organizations need to improve their success rate in overseas assignments. As discussed in Chapter 6, the technology for assessing individuals' knowledge, skills, and abilities has advanced. The potential for selection testing to decrease the failure rate and productivity problems of U.S. expatriate managers seems promising.

A final issue with regard to expatriate selection is the use of women in expatriate assignments. For a long time U.S. firms believed that women would not be successful

TABLE 15.4 Interview Worksheet for International Candidates

Motivation
- Investigate reasons and degree of interest in wanting to be considered.
- Determine desire to work abroad, verified by previous concerns such as personal travel, language training, reading, and association with foreign employees or students.
- Determine whether the candidate has a realistic understanding of what working and living abroad requires.
- Determine the basic attitudes of the spouse toward an overseas assignment.

Health
- Determine whether any medical problems of the candidate or his or her family might be critical to the success of the assignment.
- Determine whether she is in good physical and mental health, without any foreseeable change.

Language ability
- Determine potential for learning a new language.
- Determine any previous language(s) studied or oral ability (judge against language needed on the overseas assignment).
- Determine the ability of the spouse to meet the language requirements.

Family considerations
- How many moves has the family made in the past among different cities or parts of the United States?
- What problems were encountered?
- How recent was the last move?
- What is the spouse's goal in this move?
- What are the number of children and the ages of each?
- Has divorce or its potential, death of a family member weakened family solidarity?
- Will all the children move? Why or why not?
- What are the location, health, and living arrangements of grandparents and the number of trips normally made to their home each year?
- Are there any special adjustment problems that you would expect?
- How is each member of the family reacting to this possible move?
- Do special educational problems exist within the family?

Resourcefulness and initiative
- Is the candidate independent; can he make and stand by his decisions and judgments?
- Does she have the intellectual capacity to deal with several dimensions simultaneously?
- Is he able to reach objectives and produce results with whatever personnel and facilities are available, regardless of the limitations and barriers that might arise?
- Can the candidate operate without a clear definition of responsibility and authority on a foreign assignment?
- Will the candidate be able to explain the aims and company philosophy to the local managers and workers?
- Does she possess sufficient self-discipline and self-confidence to overcome difficulties or handle complex problems?
- Can the candidate work without supervision?
- Can the candidate operate effectively in a foreign environment without normal communications and supporting services?

Adaptability
- Is the candidate sensitive to others, open to the opinions of others, cooperative, and able to compromise?
- What are his reactions to new situations, and efforts to understand and appreciate differences?
- Is she culturally sensitive, aware, and able to relate across the culture?
- Does the candidate understand his own culturally derived values?
- How does the candidate react to criticism?
- What is her understanding of the U.S. government system?

continued on page 552

TABLE 15.4 Interview Worksheet for International Candidates *continued*

Adaptability *continued*

- Will he be able to make and develop contacts with his or her peers in the foreign country?
- Does she have patience when dealing with problems?
- Is he resilient; can he bounce back after setbacks?

Career planning

- Does the candidate consider the assignment anything other than a temporary overseas trip?
- Is the move consistent with her progression and that planned by the company?
- Is his career planning realistic?
- What is the candidate's basic attitude toward the company?
- Is there any history or indication of interpersonal problems with this employee?

Financial

- Are there any current financial and/or legal considerations that might affect the assignment, e.g., house purchase, children and college expenses, car purchases?
- Are financial considerations negative factors, will undue pressures be brought to bear on the employee or her family as a result of the assignment?

SOURCE: Reprinted with permission, pp. 55–57 from *Multinational People Management,* by D.M. Noer. Copyright © 1989 by the Bureau of National Affairs, Inc., Washington, DC 20037.

managers in countries where women have not traditionally been promoted to management positions (e.g., in Japan and other Asian countries). However, recent evidence indicates that this is not true. Robin Abrams, an expatriate manager for Apple Computer's Hong Kong office, states that nobody cares whether "you are wearing trousers or a skirt if you have demonstrated core competencies." In fact, some women believe that the novelty of their presence among a group of men increases their credibility with locals. Thus, the number of female expatriates doubled to 12 percent from 1990 to 1995 and is expected to increase to 20 percent by the year 2000, according to one survey.[44]

TRAINING AND DEVELOPMENT OF EXPATRIATES. Once an expatriate manager has been selected, it is necessary to prepare that manager for the upcoming assignment. Because these individuals already have job-related skills, some firms have focused development efforts on cross-cultural training. A review of the cross-cultural training literature found support for the belief that cross-cultural training has an impact on effectiveness.[45] However, in spite of this, cross-cultural training is hardly universal. According to one 1995 survey, nearly 40 percent of the respondents offered no cross-cultural preparation to expatriates.[46]

What exactly is emphasized in cross-cultural training programs? The details regarding these programs was discussed in Chapter 7. However, for now, it is important to know that most attempt to create an appreciation of the host country's culture so that expatriates can behave appropriately.[47] This entails emphasizing a few aspects of cultural sensitivity. First, expatriates must be clear about their own cultural background, particularly as it is perceived by the host nationals. With an accurate cultural self-awareness, managers can modify their behavior to accentuate the effective characteristics while minimizing those that are dysfunctional.[48] Table 15.5 displays the ways Americans tend to be perceived by those in other countries.

Second, expatriates must understand the particular aspects of culture in the new work environment. Although culture is an elusive, almost invisible phenomenon, as-

TABLE 15.5
Americans as Others See Them

People from other countries are often puzzled and intrigued by the intricacies and enigmas of U.S. culture. Here is a selection of actual observations by foreigners visiting the United States. As you read them, ask yourself in each case whether the observer is accurate and how you would explain the trait in question.

India

"Americans seem to be in a perpetual hurry. Just watch the way they walk down the street. They never allow themselves the leisure to enjoy life; there are too many things to do."

Kenya

"Americans appear to us rather distant. They are not really as close to other people—even fellow Americans—as Americans overseas tend to portray. It's almost as if an American says, 'I won't let you get too close to me.' It's like building a wall."

Turkey

"Once we were out in a rural area in the middle of nowhere and saw an American come to a stop sign. Though he could see in both directions for miles and no traffic was coming, he still stopped!"

Colombia

"The tendency in the United States to think that life is only work hits you in the face. Work seems to be the one type of motivation."

Indonesia

"In the United States everything has to be talked about and analyzed. Even the littlest thing has to be 'Why, Why, Why?' I get a headache from such persistent questions."

Ethiopia

"The American is very explicit; he wants a 'yes' or 'no.' If someone tries to speak figuratively, the American is confused."

Iran

"The first time . . . my [American] professor told me, 'I don't know the answer, I will have to look it up,' I was shocked. I asked myself, 'Why is he teaching me?' In my country, a professor would give the wrong answer rather than admit ignorance."

SOURCE: J. Feig and G. Blair, *There Is a Difference,* 2d ed. (Washington, DC: Meridian House International, 1980). As cited in Nancy Adler, *International Dimensions of Organizational Behavior,* 2d ed. (Boston: PWS-Kent, 1991).

tute expatriate managers must perceive the culture and adapt their behavior to it. This entails identifying the types of behaviors and interpersonal styles that are considered acceptable in both business meetings and social gatherings. For example, Germans value promptness for meetings to a much greater extent than do Latin Americans.

Finally, expatriates must learn to communicate accurately in the new culture. Some firms attempt to use expatriates who speak the language of the host country, and a few provide language training. However, most companies simply assume that the host-country nationals all speak the parent-country's language. Although this assumption might be true, seldom do these nationals speak the parent-country language fluently. Thus, expatriate managers must be trained to communicate with others when language barriers exist. Table 15.6 offers some tips for communicating across language barriers.

Effective cross-cultural training helps ease an expatriate's transition to the new work environment. It can also help avoid costly mistakes, such as the expatriate who attempted to bring two bottles of brandy into the Muslim country of Qatar. The brandy was discovered by customs; not only was the expatriate deported, the company was also "disinvited" from the country.[49]

TABLE 15.6
Communicating across Language Barriers

Verbal behavior
- *Clear, slow speech.* Enunciate each word. Do not use colloquial expressions.
- *Repetition.* Repeat each important idea using different words to explain the same concept.
- *Simple sentences.* Avoid compound, long sentences.
- *Active verbs.* Avoid passive verbs.

Nonverbal behavior
- *Visual restatements.* Use as many visual restatements as possible, such as pictures, graphs, tables, and slides.
- *Gestures.* Use more facial and hand gestures to emphasize the meaning of words.
- *Demonstration.* Act out as many themes as possible.
- *Pauses.* Pause more frequently.
- *Summaries.* Hand out written summaries of your verbal presentation.

Attribution
- *Silence.* When there is a silence, wait. Do not jump in to fill the silence. The other person is probably just thinking more slowly in the non-native language or translating.
- *Intelligence.* Do not equate poor grammar and mispronunciation with lack of intelligence; it is usually a sign of second-language use.
- *Differences.* If unsure, assume difference, not similarity.

Comprehension
- *Understanding.* Do not just assume that they understand; assume that they do not understand.
- *Checking comprehension.* Have colleagues repeat their understanding of the material back to you. Do not simply ask whether they understand or not. Let them explain what they understand to you.

Design
- *Breaks.* Take more frequent breaks. Second-language comprehension is exhausting.
- *Small modules.* Divide the material into smaller modules.
- *Longer time frame.* Allocate more time for each module than usual in a monolingual program.

Motivation
- *Encouragement.* Verbally and nonverbally encourage and reinforce speaking by non-native language participants.
- *Drawing out.* Explicitly draw out marginal and passive participants.
- *Reinforcement.* Do not embarrass novice speakers.

SOURCE: Used with permission of N. Adler, *International Dimensions of Organizational Behavior,* 2d ed. (Boston: PWS-Kent, 1991).

COMPENSATION OF EXPATRIATES. One of the more troublesome aspects of managing expatriates is determining the compensation package. As previously discussed, these packages average $250,000, but it is necessary to examine the exact breakdown of these packages. Most use a balance sheet approach to determine the total package level. This approach entails developing a total compensation package that equalizes the purchasing power of the expatriate manager with that of employees in similar positions in the home country and provides incentives to offset the inconveniences incurred in the location. Purchasing power includes all of the expenses associated with the expatriate assignment. Expenses include goods and services (e.g., food, personal care, clothing, recreation, and transportation), housing (for a principal residence), income taxes (paid to federal and local governments), reserve (e.g., savings, payments for benefits, pension contributions), and shipment and storage (costs associated with moving and/or storing personal belongings). A typical balance sheet is shown in Figure 15.4.

As you can see from this figure, the employee starts with a set of costs for taxes, housing, goods and services, and reserve. However, in the host country, these costs are significantly higher. Thus, the company must make up the difference between costs in the home and those in the host country, and then provide a premium and/or incentive for the employee to go through the trouble of living in a different environment. Table 15.7 provides an idea of just how much these add-ons can cost for an expatriate. As we see, these benefits combined amount to a 114 percent increase in compensation cost above the base pay.

Total pay packages have four components. First, there is the base salary. Determining the base salary is not a simple matter, however. Fluctuating exchange rates between countries may make an offered salary a raise some of the time, a pay cut at other times. In addition, the base salary may be based on comparable pay in the parent country or it may be based on the prevailing market rates for the job in the host country. Expatriates are often offered a salary premium beyond that of their present salary as an inducement to accept the expatriate assignment.

Tax equalization allowances are a second component. They are necessary because of countries' different taxation systems in high-tax countries. For example, a senior executive earning $100,000 in Belgium (with a maximum marginal tax rate of 70.8 percent) could cost a company almost $1 million in taxes over five to seven years.[50] Under most

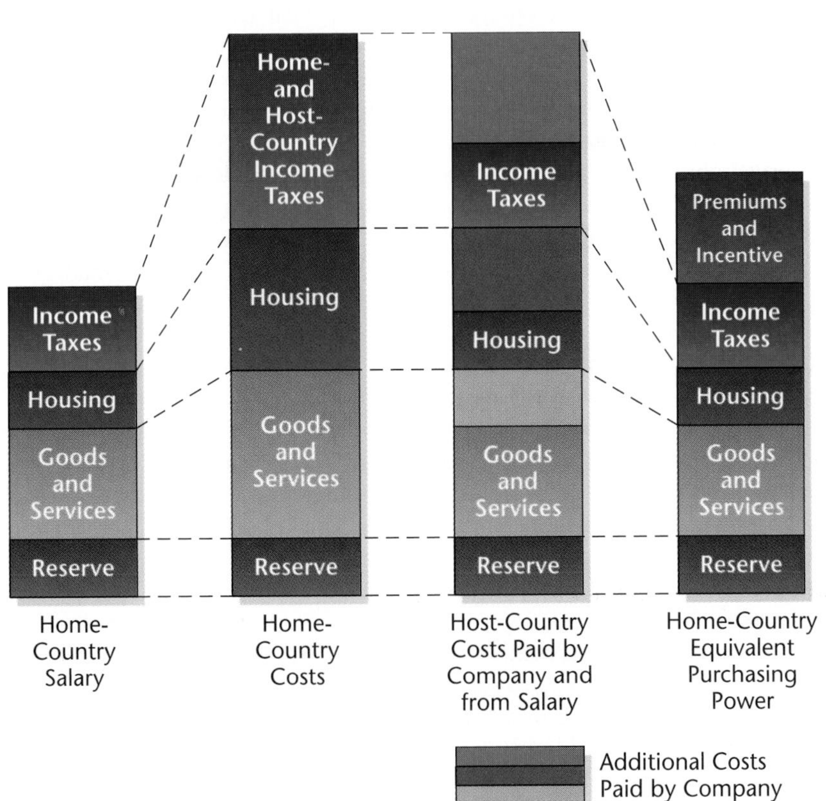

FIGURE 15.4 The Balance Sheet for Determining Expatriate Compensation

SOURCE: C. Reynolds, "Compensation of Overseas Personnel," in *Handbook of Human Resource Administration*, 2d. ed., J.J. Famularo (New York: McGraw-Hill, 1986), p. 51. Reprinted with permission.

TABLE 15.7
Average Amount of Allowance as a Percentage of Base Pay

Housing (purchase)	38%
Goods and services (cost of living)	24
Education	22
Position	17
Hardship	13

SOURCE: Foster Higgins, "Survey on Expatriate Compensation and Benefits, 1996," cited in B. Fitzgerald-Turner, "Myths of Expatriate Life," *HRMagazine* 42, no. 6 (June 1997), pp. 65–74.

tax equalization plans, the company withholds the amount of tax to be paid in the home country, then pays all of the taxes accrued in the host country.

A third component, benefits, presents additional compensation problems. Most of the problems have to do with the transportability of the benefits. For example, if an expatriate contributing to a pension plan in the United States is moved to a different country, does the individual have a new pension in the host country, or should the individual be allowed to contribute to the existing pension in her home country? What about health care systems located in the United States? How does the company ensure that expatriate employees have equal health care coverage? For example, in one company, the different health care plans available resulted in situations where it might cost significantly less to have the employee fly to the United States to have a procedure performed rather than to have it done in the host country. However, the health plans did not allow this alternative.

Finally, allowances are often offered to make the expatriate assignment less unattractive. Cost-of-living allowances are payments that offset the differences in expenditures on day-to-day necessities between the host country and the parent country. Housing allowances ensure that the expatriate can maintain the same home-country living standard. Education allowances reimburse expatriates for the expense of placing their children in private English-speaking schools. Relocation allowances cover all the expenses of making the actual move to a new country, including transportation to and from the new location, temporary living expenses, and shipping and/or storage of personal possessions. Figure 15.5 illustrates a typical summary sheet for an expatriate manager's compensation package.

REACCULTURATION OF EXPATRIATES. A final issue of importance to managing expatriates is dealing with the reacculturation process when the managers reenter their home country. Reentry is no simple feat. Culture shock takes place in reverse. The individual has changed, the company has changed, and the culture has changed while the expatriate was overseas. According to one source, 60 to 70 percent of expatriates did not know what their position would be upon their return, and 46 percent ended up with jobs that gave them reduced autonomy and authority.[51] Twenty percent of workers want to leave the company when they return from an overseas assignment, and this presents potentially serious morale and productivity problems.[52] In fact, the most recent estimates are that 25 percent of expatriate managers leave the company within one year of returning from their expatriate assignments.[53] If these repatriates leave, the company has virtually no way to recoup its substantial investment in human capital.[54]

Companies are increasingly making efforts to help expatriates ease through this transition. Two characteristics help in this transition process: communication and validation.[55] Communication refers to the extent to which the expatriate receives information and recognizes changes while abroad. The closer the contact with the home

FIGURE 15.5
International Assignment Allowance Form

John H. Doe **Name**		1 October 1999 **Effective Date**	
Singapore **Location of Assignment**		Manager, SLS./Serv. AP/ME **Title**	
Houston, Texas **Home Base**	1234 **Emp. No.**	202 **LCA Code**	202 **Tax Code**

Reason for Change: International Assignment

	Old	New
Monthly Base Salary		$5,000.00
Living Cost Allowance		$1,291.00
Foreign Service Premium		$ 750.00
Area Allowance		- 0 -
Gross Monthly Salary		$7,041.00
Housing Deduction		$ 500.00
Hypothetical Tax		$ 570.00
Other		
Net Monthly Salary		$5,971.00

Prepared by ____________ **Date** ____________

Vice President, Human Resources ____________ **Date** ____________

organization while abroad, the more proactive, effective, and satisfied the expatriate will be upon reentry. Validation refers to the amount of recognition received by the expatriate upon return home. Expatriates who receive recognition from their peers and their bosses for their foreign work and their future potential contribution to the company have fewer troubles with reentry compared with those who are treated as if they were "out of the loop."

Finally, one research study noted the role of an expatriate manager's expectations about the expatriate assignment in determining repatriation adjustment and job performance. This study found that managers whose job expectations (constraints and demands in terms of volume and performance standards) and nonwork expectations (living and housing conditions) were met exhibited a greater degree of repatriation adjustment and higher levels of job performance.[56] Monsanto has an extensive repatriation program that begins long before the expatriate returns. The program entails providing extensive information regarding the potential culture shock of repatriation and information on how family members, friends, and the office environment might have changed. Then, a few months after returning, expatriate managers hold "debriefing" sessions with several colleagues to help work through difficulties. Monsanto believes that this program provides them with a source of competitive advantage in international assignments.[57]

SUMMARY

Today's organizations are more involved in international commerce than ever before, and the trend will continue. Recent historic events such as the development of the EEC, NAFTA, the growth of Asia, and GATT have accelerated the movement toward a global market. Companies competing in the global marketplace require top-quality people to compete successfully. This requires that managers be aware of the many factors that significantly affect HRM in a global environment, such as the culture, human capital, political–legal system, and economic system, and that they understand how these factors come into play in the various levels of global participation. Finally, it requires that they be adept at developing HR systems that maximize the effectiveness of all human resources, particularly with regard to expatriate managers. Managers cannot overestimate the importance of effectively managing human resources to gain competitive advantage in today's global marketplace.

DISCUSSION QUESTIONS

1. What current trends and/or events (besides those mentioned at the outset of the chapter) are responsible for the increased internationalization of the marketplace?
2. According to Hofstede (in Table 15.1), the United States is low on power distance, high on individuality, high on masculinity, low on uncertainty avoidance, and low on long-term orientation. Russia, on the other hand, is high on power distance, moderate on individuality, low on masculinity, high on uncertainty avoidance, and low on long-term orientation. Many U.S. managers are transplanting their own HRM practices into Russia while companies seek to develop operations there. How acceptable and effective do you think the following practices will be and why: (a) Extensive assessments of individual abilities for selection? (b) Individually based appraisal systems? (c) Suggestion systems? (d) Self-managing work teams?
3. The chapter notes that political–legal and economic systems can reflect a country's culture. The former Eastern bloc countries seem to be changing their political–legal and economic systems. Is this change brought on by their cultures, or will culture have an impact on the ability to change these systems? Why?
4. Think of the different levels of global participation. What companies that you are familiar with exhibit the different levels of participation?
5. Think of a time when you had to function in another culture (e.g., on a vacation or job). What were the major obstacles you faced, and how did you deal with them? Was this a stressful experience? Why? How can companies help expatriate employees deal with the stress?
6. What types of skills do you need to be able to manage in today's global marketplace? Where do you expect to get those skills? What classes and/or experiences will you need?

WEB EXERCISE

The introduction of a single currency, the euro, for countries who are part of the European Economic Community, has important implications for multinational companies. Germany, France, Spain, Italy, Ireland, The Netherlands, Austria, Belgium, Finland, Portugal, and Luxembourg are the first members of the European Economic Community to adopt the Euro. Go to www.shrmglobal.org. This is the web site for the Society for Human Resource Management Global Forum. As you review the web site notice that it includes both publications on topics related to the global management of human resources as well as links to other web sites that address global issues and provide country-specific information.

Under "Publications" click on the "Expatriate Newsletter." This is a newsletter written by Arthur Andersen. Current and back issues of the newsletter are available. To learn more about the euro and its implications for HRM click on "Expatriate Newsletter, 4th Quarter 1998."

1. Why is the introduction of the euro a significant world economic event?
2. What HR issues does the introduction of the euro present to multinational companies?

MANAGING PEOPLE: FROM THE PAGES OF "BUSINESS WEEK"

BusinessWeek Top of the World, MA

It's easy to see why AT&T Chairman and CEO C. Michael Armstrong has had a tough time convincing Wall Street that he can turn the telecom giant into a growth company. Revenues inched up a meager 1.5% in 1997, to $51.3 billion, and are forecast to increase 2% to 3% this year. The reason is simple: Virtually all of the company's revenues are coming from the highly competitive and increasingly less profitable long-distance business. The ultimate insult came in early December when archrival MCI WorldCom Inc. surpassed AT&T in market captialization, largely because investors think that MCI WorldCom is better positioned in the fast-growing data and international markets.

On Dec. 8, Armstong's plan to break out of the slow-growth box became clearer: AT&T will acquire IBM's Global Network for $5 billion. When the deal is completed—probably in mid-1999—the new business will give an immediate $2.5 billion bump to AT&T's top line.

More important, the deal will give AT&T an international data network and 5,000 employees skilled in managing a vast array of network technologies. That should help AT&T attract telecom business from multinationals and win new outsourcing contracts for managing data networks. "We are now a global player," said Armstrong in an interview after the announcement. "We have redefined ourselves from a domestic long-distance company into a global communications provider."

The Global Network acquisition caps a remarkable year in which Armstrong has struck several major deals to get a troubled AT&T back on track. In January, he agreed to buy Teleport Communications Group Inc. for $11 billion to get into local service for the U.S. business market. In June, he said he was buying cable provider Tele-Communications Inc. for $33 billion to get into the residential local-calling market. Although Armstrong has won plaudits for his bold steps, he is still far from proving that the deals will succeed.

The latest acquisition dovetails neatly with a planned joint venture with British Telecom PLC. AT&T and BT had said they would spend $5 billion to build a high-capacity network in 100 cities; IBM's Global Network already has facilities in 93 of them. AT&T and BT still plan upgrades, but the IBM net will speed up its ability to attract customers. The market AT&T and BT are targeting is tantalizing: $20 billion to $30 billion a year and growing 10% to 15% annually, estimates the Gartner Group Inc. And the IBM Global Network "clearly positions us as the market leader in network operations," says Rick Roscitt, CEO of AT&T's outsourcing unit.

The benefits didn't come cheap. AT&T paid about $1 billion more for the network, which is burdened by old technologies, than analysts thought it should fetch. "Five billion dollars for a 1980s network is pretty expensive," snipes CEO Michael J. Mahoney of rival Viatel Inc., which is building a new network in Europe.

But Armstrong is stressing the growth opportunity, not the cost. And the Street is listening: News of the deal pushed AT&T's stock to 67, putting its market cap back ahead of MCI WorldCom's.

QUESTIONS

1. AT&T's movement into the global leagues came mainly from its acquisition of Global Network from IBM. Previously, the firm had been largely domestic. What issues do you see AT&T will have in trying to manage a global workforce?
2. What are the issues that HR needs to be concerned with in managing this acquisition?

SOURCE: Peter Elstroom, "Top of the World, Ma," *Business Week*, December 21, 1998.

NOTES

1. P.J. Dowling, "Human Resource Issues in International Business," *Syracuse Journal of International Law and Commerce* 13, no. 2 (1986), pp. 255–71.
2. R.M. Kanter, "Transcending Business Boundaries: 12,000 World Managers View Change," *Harvard Business Review*, May–June 1991, pp. 151–64.

3. R. Norton, "Will a Global Slump Hurt the U.S.?" *Fortune*, February 22, 1993, pp. 63–64.
4. U.S. Department of Labor, "International Comparisons of Hourly Compensation Costs for Production Workers in Manufacturing, 1975–1996," Bureau of Labor Statistics news release, USDL 98–38, February 9, 1998.
5. Towers Perrin, *Priorities for Competitive Advantage: A Worldwide Human Resource Study* (Valhalla, NY: Towers Perrin, 1991).
6. R. Schuler, "An Integrative Framework of Strategic International Human Resource Management," *Journal of Management* (1993), pp. 419–60.
7. L. Rubio, "The Rationale for NAFTA: Mexico's New 'Outward Looking' Strategy," *Business Economics* (1991), pp. 12–16.
8. H. Cooper, "Economic Impact of NAFTA: It's a Wash, Experts Say," *The Wall Street Journal*, Interactive Edition, June 17, 1997.
9. J. Mark, "Suzhou Factories Are Nearly Ready," *Asian Wall Street Journal*, August 14, 1995, p. 8.
10. R. Peiper, *Human Resource Management: An International Comparison* (Berlin: Walter de Gruyter, 1990).
11. V. Sathe, *Culture and Related Corporate Realities* (Homewood, IL: Richard D. Irwin, 1985).
12. M. Rokeach, *Beliefs, Attitudes, and Values* (San Francisco: Jossey-Bass, 1968).
13. L. Harrison, *Who Prospers? How Cultural Values Shape Economic and Political Success* (New York: Free Press, 1992).
14. N. Adler, *International Dimensions of Organizational Behavior*, 2d ed. (Boston: PWS-Kent, 1991).
15. R. Yates, "Japanese Managers Say They're Adopting Some U.S. Ways," *Chicago Tribune*, February 29, 1992, p. B1.
16. G. Hofstede, "Dimensions of National Cultures in Fifty Countries and Three Regions," in *Expectations in Cross-Cultural Psychology*, eds. J. Deregowski, S. Dziurawiec, and R.C. Annis (Lisse, Netherlands: Swets and Zeitlinger, 1983).
17. G. Hofstede, "Cultural Constraints in Management Theories," *Academy of Management Executive* 7 (1993), pp. 81–90.
18. G. Hofstede, "The Cultural Relativity of Organizational Theories," *Journal of International Business Studies* 14 (1983), pp. 75–90.
19. G. Hofstede, "Cultural Constraints in Management Theories."
20. S. Snell and J. Dean, "Integrated Manufacturing and Human Resource Management: A Human Capital Perspective," *Academy of Management Journal* 35 (1992), pp. 467–504.
21. W. Johnston and A. Packer, *Workforce 2000: Work and Workers for the Twenty-first Century* (Indianapolis, IN: Hudson Institute, 1988).
22. H. Meyer, "Human Resource Management in the German Democratic Republic: Problems of Availability and the Use of Manpower Potential in the Sphere of the High-Qualification Spectrum in a Retrospective View," in *Human Resource Management: An International Comparison*, ed. R. Peiper (Berlin: Walter de Gruyter, 1990).
23. P. Conrad and R. Peiper, "Human Resource Management in the Federal Republic of Germany," in Ibid.
24. N. Adler and S. Bartholomew, "Managing Globally Competent People," *The Executive* 6 (1992), pp. 52–65.
25. B. O'Reilly, "Your New Global Workforce," *Fortune*, December 14, 1992, pp. 52–66.
26. Ibid.
27. J. Ledvinka and V. Scardello, *Federal Employment Regulation in Human Resource Management* (Boston: PWS-Kent, 1991).
28. Conrad and Peiper, "Human Resource Management in the Federal Republic of Germany."
29. R. Solow, "Growth with Equity through Investment in Human Capital," The George Seltzer Distinguished Lecture, University of Minnesota.
30. R. Kopp, "International Human Resource Policies and Practices in Japanese, European, and United States Multinationals," *Human Resource Management* 33 (1994), pp. 581–99.
31. Adler, *International Dimensions of Organizational Behavior*.
32. S. Jackson & Associates, *Diversity in the Workplace: Human Resource Initiatives* (New York: The Guilford Press, 1991).
33. Adler and Bartholomew, "Managing Globally Competent People."
34. Ibid.
35. L. Copeland and L. Griggs, *Going International* (New York: Random House, 1985).
36. K.F. Misa and J.M. Fabriacatore, "Return on Investments of Overseas Personnel," *Financial Executive* 47 (April 1979), pp. 42–46.
37. R. Tung, "Selection and Training Procedures of U.S., European, and Japanese Multinational Corporations," *California Management Review* 25, no. 1 (1982), pp. 57–71.
38. Copeland and Griggs, *Going International*.
39. M. Mendenhall, E. Dunbar, and G.R. Oddou, "Expatriate Selection, Training, and Career-Pathing: A Review and Critique," *Human Resource Management* 26 (1987), pp. 331–45.
40. M. Mendenhall and G. Oddou, "The Dimensions of Expatriate Acculturation," *Academy of Management Review* 10 (1985), pp. 39–47.
41. W. Arthur and W. Bennett, "The International Assignee: The Relative Importance of Factors Perceived to Contribute to Success," *Personnel Psychology* 48 (1995), pp. 99–114.
42. R. Tung, "Selecting and Training of Personnel for Over-

seas Assignments," *Columbia Journal of World Business* 16, no. 2 (1981), pp. 68–78.

43. Moran, Stahl, & Boyer, Inc., *International Human Resource Management* (Boulder, CO: Moran, Stahl, & Boyer, Inc., 1987).
44. "Work Week," *The Wall Street Journal*, September 5, 1995, p. A1.
45. J.S. Black and M. Mendenhall, "Cross-Cultural Training Effectiveness: A Review and Theoretical Framework for Future Research," *Academy of Management Review* 15 (1990), pp. 113–36.
46. B. Fitzgerald-Turner, "Myths of Expatriate Life," *HRMagazine* 42, no. 6 (June 1997), pp. 65–74.
47. P. Dowling and R. Schuler, *International Dimensions of Human Resource Management* (Boston: PWS-Kent, 1990).
48. Adler, *International Dimensions of Organizational Behavior*.
49. Dowling and Schuler, *International Dimensions of Human Resource Management*.
50. R. Schuler and P. Dowling, *Survey of ASPA/I Members* (New York: Stern School of Business, New York University, 1988).
51. C. Solomon, "Repatriation: Up, Down, or Out," *Personnel Journal* (1995), pp. 28–37.
52. "Workers Sent Overseas Have Adjustment Problems, a New Study Shows," *The Wall Street Journal*, June 19, 1984, p. 1.
53. J.S. Black, "Repatriation: A Comparison of Japanese and American Practices and Results," *Proceedings of the Eastern Academy of Management Bi-annual International Conference* (Hong Kong, 1989), pp. 45–49.
54. J.S. Black, "Coming Home: The Relationship of Expatriate Expectations with Repatriation Adjustment and Job Performance," *Human Relations* 45 (1992), pp. 177–92.
55. Adler, *International Dimensions of Organizational Behavior*.
56. Black, "Coming Home."
57. C. Solomon, "Repatriation: Up, Down, or Out?"

16 CHAPTER Strategically Managing the HR Function

OBJECTIVES

After reading this chapter you should be able to

1. Describe the roles that HR plays in firms today and the categories of HR activities.
2. Discuss how the HR function can define its mission and market.
3. Explain the approaches to evaluating the effectiveness of HR practices.
4. Describe the new structures for the HR function.
5. Relate how process reengineering is used to review and redesign HR practices.
6. Discuss the types of new technologies that can improve the efficiency and effectiveness of HR.
7. Describe how outsourcing HR activities can improve service delivery efficiency and effectiveness.

Blowing Up HR

ENTER THE WORLD OF BUSINESS

Fortune columnist Thomas A. Stewart wrote, "Nestling warm and sleepy in your company, like the asp in Cleopatra's bosom, is a department whose employees spend 80 percent of their time on routine administrative tasks. Nearly every function of this department can be performed more expertly for less by others. Chances are its leaders are unable to describe their contribution to value added except in trendy, unquantifiable, and wannabe terms—yet, like a serpent unaffected by its own venom, the department frequently dispenses to others advice on how to eliminate work that does not add value. It is also an organization where the average advertised salary for professional staffers increased 30 percent last year.

I am describing, of course, your human resources department, and have a modest proposal: Why not blow it up?"

SOURCE: T. Stewart, "Taking on the Last Bureaucracy," *Fortune*, January 15, 1996, p. 105.

Introduction

Throughout this book we have emphasized how human resource practices can help companies gain a competitive advantage. We identified specific practices related to managing the internal and external environment; designing work and measuring work outcomes; and acquiring, developing, and compensating human resources. We have also discussed the best of current research and practice to show how they may contribute to a company's competitive advantage.

As Chapter 1 said, the role of the HR function has been evolving over time. As we see in the opening vignette, it has now reached a crossroads. Although it began as a purely administrative function, most HR executives now see the function's major role as being much more strategic. However, this evolution has resulted in a misalignment between the skills and capabilities of members of the function and the new requirements placed on it. Virtually every HR function in top companies is going through a transformation process to create a function that can play this new strategic role while successfully fulfilling its other roles. Managing this process is the subject of this chapter. First, we will discuss the various roles and activities of the HR function. Then we will examine how to develop a market- or customer-oriented HR function. We will then describe the current structure of most HR functions. Finally, we will explore measurement approaches for assessing the effectiveness of the function.

Roles and Activities of the HR Function

Many authors have posited the various roles of the HR function. However, recently a consensus has developed around four major roles for the HR function. Dave Ulrich of the University of Michigan proposes two dimensions to exploring the role of HR as noted in Figure 16.1. The vertical dimension represents the *focus* of a future/strategic orientation versus a day-to-day/operational orientation. The *activities* are depicted as people versus process along the horizontal dimension.[1] This categorization argues for HR functions playing roles (with their associated metaphors) in the management of strategic human resources (strategic partner), the management of firm infrastructure (administrative expert), the management of transformation and change (change agent), and the management of employee contribution (employee advocate). These roles are discussed next.

FIGURE 16.1
HR Roles in Building a Competitive Organization

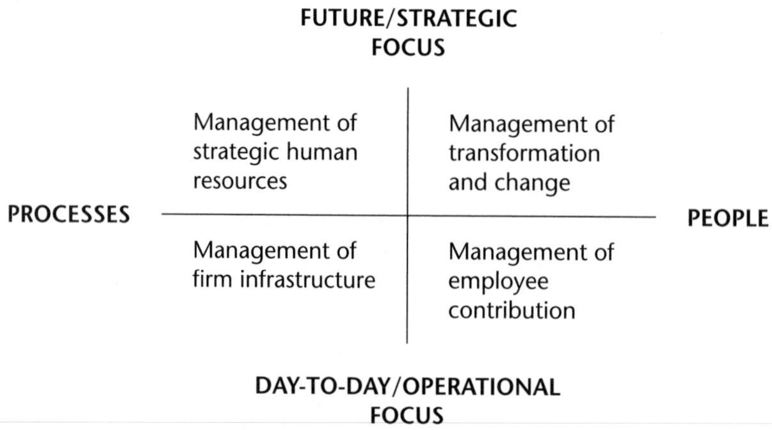

FUTURE/STRATEGIC FOCUS

PROCESSES			PEOPLE
	Management of strategic human resources	Management of transformation and change	
	Management of firm infrastructure	Management of employee contribution	

DAY-TO-DAY/OPERATIONAL FOCUS

SOURCE: D. Ulrich, *Human Resource Champions* (Boston: Harvard Business School Press, 1998).

ROLES OF HR

STRATEGIC PARTNER. One of the most important roles that HR can play today is that of a strategic partner. As Ulrich notes, this role focuses on providing strategy execution as the deliverable. Strategy execution stems from aligning HR strategies to business strategies.[2]

For example, when Continental Airlines began its turnaround, Gordon Bethune proposed a four-pronged strategy of Fly to Win (achieve the top quartile in industry margins), Fund the Future (reduce debt), Make Reliability a Reality (have an industry-leading product), and Working Together (have a company where employees enjoy coming to work every day). Ken Carrig, VP of HR at Continental, helped to lead the HR function to develop systems and plans that would ensure the execution of strategy. For example, with regard to pay, they kept the base pay low relative to competitors (to create a labor cost advantage), but then heavily leveraged the variable pay to create an opportunity for employees to earn above the industry average if company performance improved. This variable pay consisted of (1) an on-time bonus where all employees received a $65 bonus check in any month in which Continental was in the top three in the industry in on-time arrivals and (2) a profit-sharing plan which paid out if Continental returned to profitability. These incentives played a critical role in moving Continental to the top of the industry in on-time performance as well as profitability.[3]

ADMINISTRATIVE EXPERT. Playing the role of administrative expert requires designing and delivering efficient and effective HR systems, processes, and practices.[4] These include systems for selection, training, developing, appraising, and rewarding employees as we have discussed in previous chapters.

Continental also exemplifies this efficient delivery of HR systems. As part of its effort to turn the airline around, the HR function examined its delivery of HR systems and found a number of inefficiencies. Through outsourcing and streamlining of its processes, it achieved HR operating ratios (e.g., HR FTEs to total FTEs; HR expense to total expense) far below the industry average. In fact, this efficiency saved the company $4.5 million per year.[5]

EMPLOYEE ADVOCATE. The employee advocate role entails managing the commitment and contributions of employees.[6] No matter how skilled a work force may be, if they are alienated or angry, they will not contribute their efforts to the firm's success, nor will they stay with the firm for very long. Thus, the role of employee advocate is of great importance for firms seeking to gain competitive advantage through people.

For example, with regard to its role as employee advocate within Continental, the HR function developed a number of communication mechanisms both for informing employees of company developments and plans, and for informing company officers of employee concerns. One such mechanism was the town meeting, where CEO Bethune would meet with large groups of employees to let them ask questions and air their grievances. Employees' commitment and trust grew as they saw their concerns being taken seriously by the leadership of the company.[7]

CHANGE AGENT. The final role, change agent, requires that HR play a role in transforming organizations to meet the new competitive conditions. In today's fast-changing competitive world, firms need to both constantly change and develop a capacity for change. HR members must help in identifying and managing processes for change.[8]

Continental's turnaround required both massive changes in operating performance and large-scale change in the culture of the organization. To increase operating performance required developing more realistic schedules as well as getting employees committed to meeting those schedules. Realistic schedules were created and reviewed by employee committees, and their participation and the on-time incentive increased their commitment to meeting the schedules. The culture of antagonism and mistrust had to be replaced by one of cooperation and trust. The profit sharing plans, revamping of top management team (36 of 48 officers were fired), burning of the 800-page employee manual, and town meetings all contributed to changing the culture at Continental.[9]

ACTIVITIES OF HR

In addition to the roles that HR plays, one must also understand the activities in which HR engages in terms of their strategic value. One way of classifying these activities is depicted in Figure 16.2. Transactional activities (the day-to-day transactions such as benefits administration, record keeping, and employee services) are low in their strategic value. Traditional activities such as performance management, training, recruiting, selection, compensation, and employee relations are the nuts and bolts of HR. These activities have moderate strategic value, since they often form the practices and systems to ensure strategy execution. Transformational activities create long-term capability and adaptability for the firm. These activities include knowledge management, management development, cultural change, and strategic redirection and renewal. Obviously, these activities comprise the greatest strategic value for the firm.

FIGURE 16.2
Categories of HR Activities and Percentages of Time Spent on Them

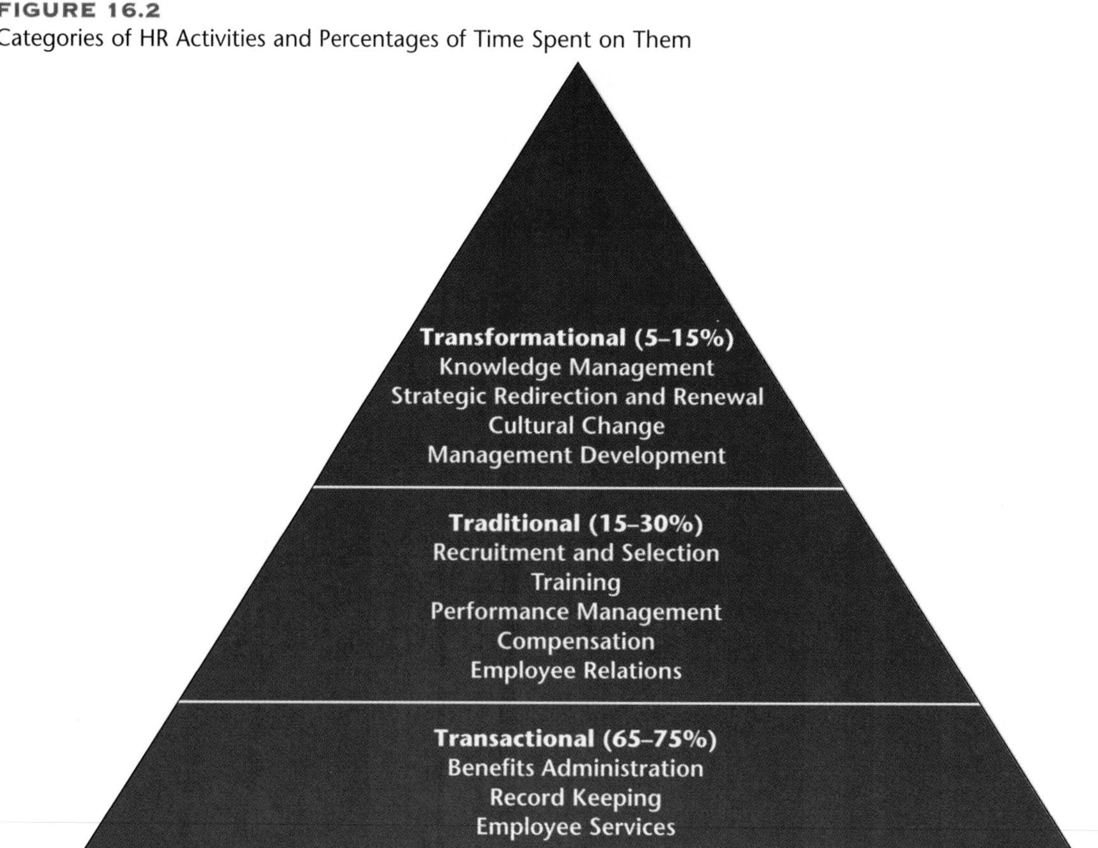

SOURCE: P. Wright, G. McMahan, S. Snell, and B. Gerhart, *Strategic Human Resource Management: Building Human Capital and Organizational Capability.* Technical report. Cornell University, 1998.

Human Resource Departments Become Business Partners

The human resource function has lately taken on a new role at many organizations: business partner. "It's a role that has been talked about for 15 years, and now it's becoming a reality," notes David Ulrich, professor of business at the University of Michigan's School of Business. "Companies now are finding that the HR issues are, in fact, center stage to business competitiveness."

To become a full-fledged partner in business, the human resource department must evaluate its role, practices, and effectiveness. At Clorox, human resource managers learned through a survey that their department simply was not adding value to the company's operations. So they developed a new strategy, including a reorganization of the department so that the department structure matched the overall business structure. Six senior human resource managers, called "client managers," now understand and support the needs of each of the functional areas across the company's six divisions. Using technology, Clorox set up a call center for answering basic questions about payroll and benefits. The new shared-services center takes care of the three main areas of human resources: compensation and benefits, human resources management systems, and individual and organizational effectiveness. And because HR managers now attend regular business meetings, they know what issues are important to the company and the people who work for it. Thus, "we deploy HR programs like lightning now," says Janet M. Brady, vice president of human resources.

At Matthew Bender & Co. Inc., a legal publisher with employees located in New York and California, E. Lynne Pou, former vice president of human resources, launched an initiative called Primary Partners. "We had believed for some time that we ought to get out of the transaction business and into adding higher value to the groups that we worked with." Pou decided that the best way to evaluate human resource's role and learn how to add value was to find out firsthand how each department worked. "One of the things that you have to do to a legitimate business partner is to actually get in there and learn the business," says Pou. By doing so, human resource managers could determine whether the right people were doing the right jobs.

COMPETING THROUGH HIGH-PERFORMANCE WORK SYSTEMS

Ultimately, through Primary Partners, each human resource director became a business partner (and contact) for a department. For instance, Mark Howe is the primary partner for the company's operations department, which in turn is responsible for customer service, credit, and fulfillment. Howe spent three months studying who Matthew Bender's customers are, what they needed, and how those needs were being met. In his investigation, Howe learned that customer service employees' performance was assessed on mechanical factors such as attendance or number of calls received. These factors didn't improve customer service, so they shouldn't have been part of performance evaluation. Howe recommended a revamping of performance expectations and a system that reflected actual customer service.

Line managers at Matthew Bender now view the HR department as a valuable resource and partner. Linda Reiss, vice president of operations, says that through the Primary Partners initiative, HR managers now have a more balanced view of the business, so they can better match business needs with employee needs.

These two companies illustrate how evaluating the existing human resource role and moving toward a view of the human resource function as a business partner adds value that enhances the organization's competitiveness. "It's like the tortoise and the hare," says Clorox's Janet Brady. "Maybe we were late in starting, but we're right out in front because we're not just talking about it, we're actually doing it."

SOURCE: Jennifer J. Laabs, "Put Your Job on the Line," *Personnel Journal*, June 1995, pp. 74–88.

As we see in the figure, most HR functions spend the vast majority of their time on transactional activities, with substantially less on traditional ones and very little on transformational activities. However, virtually all HR functions, in order to add value to the firm, must increase their efforts in the traditional and transformational activities. (See the "Competing through High-Performance Work Systems" box.) To do this, however, requires that HR executives (1) develop a strategy for the HR function, (2) assess the current effectiveness of the HR function, and (3) redesign, reengineer, or outsource

HR processes to improve efficiency and effectiveness. These issues will be discussed in the following sections.

Strategic Management of the HR Function

In light of the various roles and activities of the HR function, we can easily see that it is highly unlikely that any function can (or should) effectively deliver on all roles and all activities. While this is a laudable goal, resource constraints in terms of time, money, and head count require that the HR executive make strategic choices about where and how to allocate these resources for maximum value to the firm.

Chapter 2 focused on explaining the strategic management process that takes place at the organization level and discussing the role of HRM in this process. HRM has been seen as a strategic partner that has input into the formulation of the company's strategy and develops and aligns HR programs to help implement the strategy. However, for the HR function to become truly strategic in its orientation, it must view itself as being a separate business entity and engage in strategic management in an effort to effectively serve the various internal customers.

In this respect, one recent trend within the field of HRM, consistent with the total quality management philosophy, is for the HR executive to take a customer-oriented approach to implementing the function. In other words, the strategic planning process that takes place at the level of the business can also be performed with the HR function. HR executives in more progressive U.S. companies have begun to view the HR function as a strategic business unit and have tried to define that business in terms of their customer base, their customers' needs, and the technologies required to satisfy customers' needs (Figure 16.3). For example, Weyerhauser Corporation's human resources department identified 11 characteristics that would describe a quality human resource organization; these are presented in Table 16.1.

FIGURE 16.3 Customer-Oriented Perspective of the HR Function

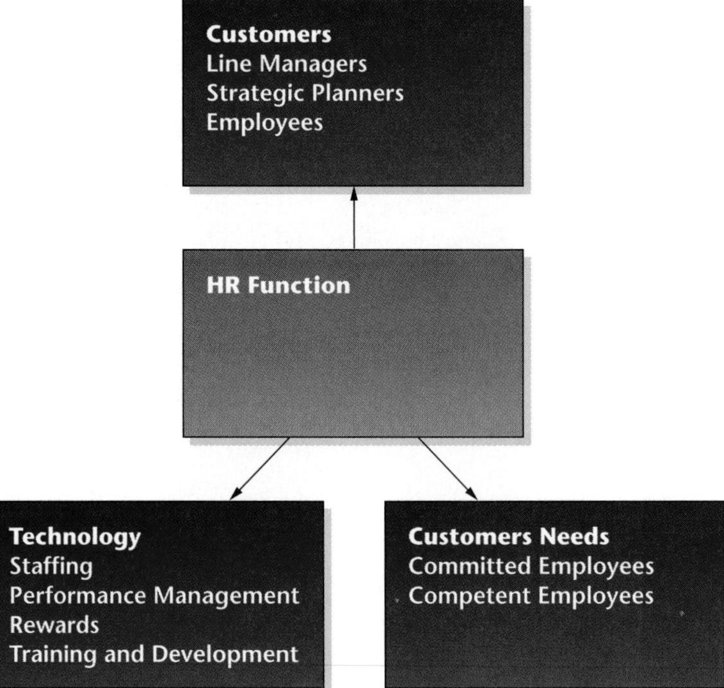

TABLE 16.1
Characteristics of HR Quality at Weyerhauser Corporation

- Human resources products and service are linked to customer requirements.
- Customer requirements are translated into internal service applications.
- Processes for producing products and services are documented with cost/value relationships understood.
- Reliable methods and standardized processes are in place.
- Waste and inefficiency are eliminated.
- Problem solving and decision making are based on facts and data.
- Critical success variables are tracked, displayed, and maintained.
- Human resources employees are trained and educated in total quality tools and principles.
- Human resource systems have been aligned to total quality implementation strategies.
- Human resource managers provide leadership and support to organizations on large-scale organizational change.
- Human resource professionals function as "strategic partners" in managing the business and implementing total quality principles.

A customer orientation is one of the most important changes in the HR function's attempts to become strategic. It entails first identifying customers. The most obvious example of HR customers are the line managers who require HR services. In addition, the strategic planning team is a customer in the sense that it requires the identification, analysis, and recommendations regarding people-oriented business problems. Employees are also HR customers because the rewards they receive from the employment relationship are determined and/or administered by the HR department.

In addition, the products of the HR department must be identified. Line managers want to have high-quality employees committed to the organization. The strategic planning team requires information and recommendations for the planning process as well as programs that support the strategic plan once it has been identified. Employees want compensation and benefit programs that are consistent, adequate, and equitable, and they want fair promotion decisions. At Southwest Airlines, the "People" department administers customer surveys to all clients as they leave the department to measure how well their needs have been satisfied.

Finally, the technologies through which HR meets customer needs vary depending on the need being satisfied. Selection systems ensure that applicants selected for employment have the necessary knowledge, skills, and abilities to provide value to the organization. Training and development systems meet the needs of both line managers and employees by providing employees with development opportunities to ensure they are constantly increasing their human capital and, thus, providing increased value to the company. Performance management systems make clear to employees what is expected of them and ensure line managers and strategic planners that employee behavior will be in line with the company's goals. Finally, reward systems similarly benefit all customers (line managers, strategic planners, and employees). These systems ensure line managers that employees will use their skills for organizational benefit, and they provide strategic planners with ways to ensure that all employees are acting in ways that will support the strategic plan. Obviously, reward systems provide employees with an equitable return for their investment of skills and effort.

For example, Whirlpool Corporation's HR managers go through a formalized process of identifying their customer, the need/value they satisfy, and the technology used to satisfy the customer. As Whirlpool planned for start-up of a centralized service supercenter, the plan called for hiring between 100 and 150 employees to serve as call takers who receive service requests from Whirlpool appliance owners and set up service appointments from these calls. The HR manager in charge of developing a selection system for hiring these call takers identified the operations manager in charge of phone service as the HR department's customer, the delivery of qualified phone call takers as the need satisfied, and the use of a structured interview and paper-and-pencil tests as the technologies employed. This customer service orientation may be the trend of the future. It provides a means for the HR function to specifically identify who its customers are, what customers' needs are being met, and how well those needs are being met.

Measuring HR Effectiveness

The strategic decision making process for the HR function requires that decision makers have a good sense of the effectiveness of the current HR function. This information provides the foundation for decisions regarding which processes, systems, and skills of HR employees need improvement. Often, HR functions that have been heavily involved in transactional activities for a long time tend to lack systems, processes, and skills for delivering state-of-the-art traditional activities and are thoroughly unable to contribute in the transformational arena. Thus, diagnosis of the effectiveness of the HR function provides critical information for its strategic management.

In addition, having good measures of the function's effectiveness provides the following benefits:[10]

- *Marketing the function:* Evaluation is a sign to other managers that the HR function really cares about the organization as a whole and is trying to support operations, production, marketing, and other functions of the company. Information regarding cost savings and benefits is useful to prove to internal customers that HR practices contribute to the bottom line. Such information is also useful for gaining additional business for the HR function.
- *Providing accountability:* Evaluation helps determine whether the HR function is meeting its objectives and effectively using its budget.

APPROACHES FOR EVALUATING EFFECTIVENESS

There are two commonly used approaches for evaluating the effectiveness of HR practices: the audit approach and the analytic approach.

AUDIT APPROACH. The **audit approach** focuses on reviewing the various outcomes of the HR functional areas. Both key indicators and customer satisfaction measures are typically collected. Table 16.2 lists examples of key indicators and customer satisfaction measures for staffing, equal employment opportunity, compensation, benefits, training, performance management, safety, labor relations, and succession planning. The development of electronic employee databases and information systems has made it much easier to collect, store, and analyze the functional key indicators (more on this later in the chapter) than in the past, when information was kept in file folders.

We previously discussed how HR functions can become much more customer-oriented as part of the strategic management process. If, in fact, the function desires to be more customer-focused, then one important source of effectiveness data can be the customers. Just as firms often survey their customers to determine how effectively the customers feel they are being served, the HR function can survey its internal customers.

One important internal customer is the employees of the firm. Employees often have both direct contact with the HR function (through activities such as benefits adminis-

TABLE 16.2 Examples of Key Indicators and Customer Satisfaction Measures for HR Functions

KEY INDICATORS	CUSTOMER SATISFACTION MEASURES
Staffing	
Average days taken to fill open requisitions Ratio of acceptances to offers made Ratio of minority/women applicants to representation in local labor market Per capita requirement costs Average years of experience/education of hires per job family	Anticipation of personnel needs Timeliness of referring qualified workers to line supervisors Treatment of applicants Skill in handling terminations Adaptability to changing labor market conditions
Equal employment opportunity	
Ratio of EEO grievances to employee population Minority representation by EEO categories Minority turnover rate	Resolution of EEO grievances Day-to-day assistance provided by personnel department in implementing affirmative action plan Aggressive recruitment to identify qualified women and minority applicants
Compensation	
Per capita (average) merit increases Ratio of recommendations for reclassification to number of employees Percentage of overtime hours to straight time Ratio of average salary offers to average salary in community	Fairness of existing job evaluation system in assigning grades and salaries Competitiveness in local labor market Relationship between pay and performance Employee satisfaction with pay
Benefits	
Average unemployment compensation payment (UCP) Average workers' compensation payment (WCP) Benefit cost per payroll dollar Percentage of sick leave to total pay	Promptness in handling claims Fairness and consistency in the application of benefit policies Communication of benefits to employees Assistance provided to line managers in reducing potential for unnecessary claims
Training	
Percentage of employees participating in training programs per job family Percentage of employees receiving tuition refunds Training dollars per employee	Extent to which training programs meet the needs of employees and the company Communication to employees about available training opportunities Quality of introduction/orientation programs
Employee appraisal and development	
Distribution of performance appraisal ratings Appropriate psychometic properties of appraisal forms	Assistance in identifying management potential Organizational development activities provided by HR department
Succession planning	
Ratio of promotions to number of employees Ratio of open requisitions filled internally to those filled externally	Extent to which promotions are made from within Assistance/counseling provided to employees in career planning
Safety	
Frequency/severity ratio of accidents Safety-related expenses per $1,000 of payroll Plant security losses per square foot (e.g., fires, burglaries)	Assistance to line managers in organizing safety programs Assistance to line managers in identifying potential safety hazards Assistance to line managers in providing a good working environment (lighting, cleanliness, heating, etc.)

continued on page 572

TABLE 16.2 Examples of Key Indicators and Customer Satisfaction Measures for HR Functions *continued*

KEY INDICATORS	CUSTOMER SATISFACTION MEASURES
Labor relations	
Ratio of grievances by pay plan to number of employees	Assistance provided to line managers in handling grievances
Frequency and duration of work stoppages	Efforts to promote a spirit of cooperation in plant
Percentage of grievances settled	Efforts to monitor the employee relations climate in plant
Overall effectiveness	
Ratio of personnel staff to employee population	Accuracy and clarity of information provided to managers and employees
Turnover rate	Competence and expertise of staff
Absenteeism rate	Working relationship between organizations and HR department
Ratio of per capita revenues to per capita cost	
Net income per employee	

SOURCE: Reprinted with permission excerpts from Chapter 1.5, "Evaluating Human Resource Effectiveness," pp. 187–227, by Anne S. Tsui and Luis R. Gomez-Mejia, from *Human Resource Management: Evolving Roles and Responsibilities;* edited by Lee Dyer. Copyright © 1988 by The Bureau of National Affairs, Inc., Washington DC 20037.

tration and payroll) and indirect contact with the function through their involvement in activities such as receiving performance appraisals, pay raises, and training programs. Many organizations such as AT&T, Motorola, and General Electric use their regular employee attitude survey as a way to assess the employees as users–customers of the HR programs and practices.[11] However, the problem with assessing effectiveness only from the employees' perspective is that often they are responding not from the standpoint of the good of the firm, but, rather, from their own individual perspective. For example, employees notoriously and consistently express dissatisfaction with pay level (who doesn't want more money?), but to simply ratchet up pay across the board would put the firm at a serious labor cost disadvantage.

Thus, many firms have gone to surveys of top-line executives as a better means of assessing the effectiveness of the HR function. The top-level line executives can see how the systems and practices are impacting both employees and the overall effectiveness of the firm from a strategic standpoint. This can also be useful for determining how well HR employees' perceptions of their function's effectiveness align with the views of their line colleagues. For example, a study of 14 firms revealed that HR executives and line executives agreed on the relative effectiveness of HR's delivery of services such as staffing and training systems (i.e., which were most and least effectively delivered) but not on the absolute level of effectiveness. As Figure 16.4 shows, HR ratings of their effectiveness in different roles also diverged significantly from line executives. In addition, line executives viewed HR as being significantly less effective with regard to HR's actual contributions to the firm's overall effectiveness, as we see in Figure 16.5.[12]

THE ANALYTIC APPROACH. The **analytic approach** focuses on either (1) determining whether the introduction of a program or practice (e.g., training program or a new compensation system) has the intended effect or (2) estimating the financial costs and benefits resulting from an HR practice. For example, in Chapter 7, we discussed how companies can determine a training program's impact on learning, behavior, and results. Evaluating a training program is one strategy for determining whether the pro-

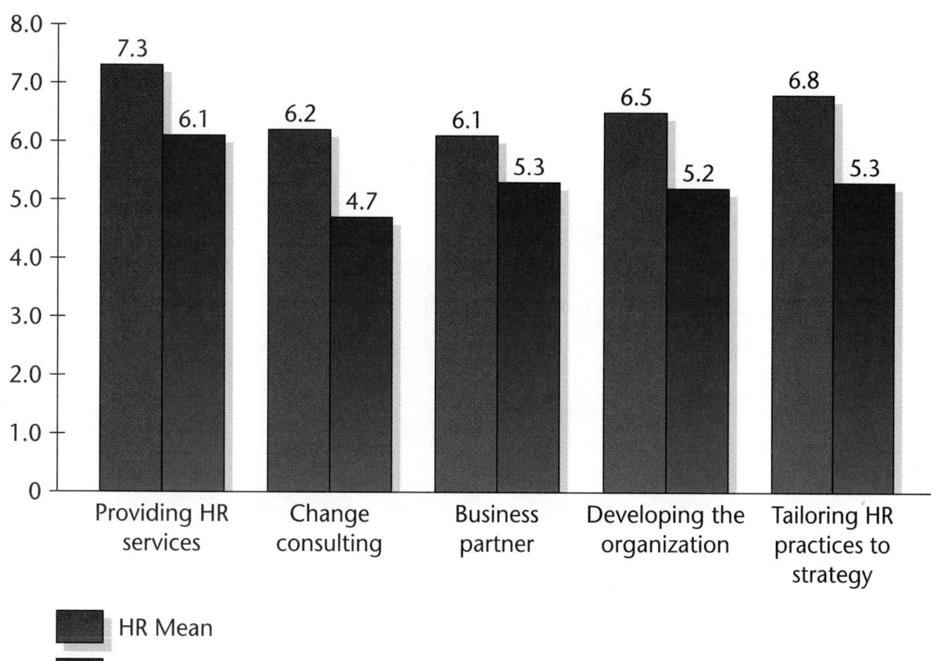

FIGURE 16.4 Comparing HR and Line Executives' Evaluations of the Effectiveness of HR Roles

SOURCE: P. Wright, G. McMahan, S. Snell, and B. Gerhart. "Comparing Line and HR Executives' Perceptions of HR Effectiveness: Services, Roles, and Contributions." CAHRS (Center for Advanced Human Resource Studies) working paper 98–29, School of ILR, Cornell University, Ithaca, NY.

gram works. Typically, in an overall evaluation of effectiveness, we are interested in determining the degree of change associated with the program.

The second strategy involves determining the dollar value of the training program, taking into account all the costs associated with the program. Using this strategy, we are not concerned with how much change occurred but rather with the dollar value (costs versus benefits) of the program. Table 16.3 lists the various types of cost–benefit analyses that are done. The human resource accounting approach attempts to place a dollar value on human resources as if they were physical resources (e.g., plant and equipment) or financial resources (e.g., cash). Utility analysis attempts to estimate the financial impact of employee behaviors (e.g., absenteeism, turnover, job performance, and substance abuse).

For example, wellness programs are a popular HR program for reducing health care costs through reducing employees' risk of heart disease and cancer. In Chapter 5, we summarized the results of a study of four different types of wellness programs. Part of the evaluation involved determining the costs and benefits associated with the four programs over a three-year period.[13] A different type of wellness program was implemented at each site. Site A instituted a program involving raising employees' awareness of health risks (distributing news articles, blood pressure testing, health education classes). Site B set up a physical fitness facility for employees. Site C raised awareness of health risks and followed up with employees who had identified health risks. Site D provided health education and follow-up counseling and promoted physical competition and health-related events. Table 16.4 shows the effectiveness and cost-effectiveness of the Site C and Site D wellness models.

FIGURE 16.5
Comparing HR and Line Executives' Evaluations of the Effectiveness of HR Contributions

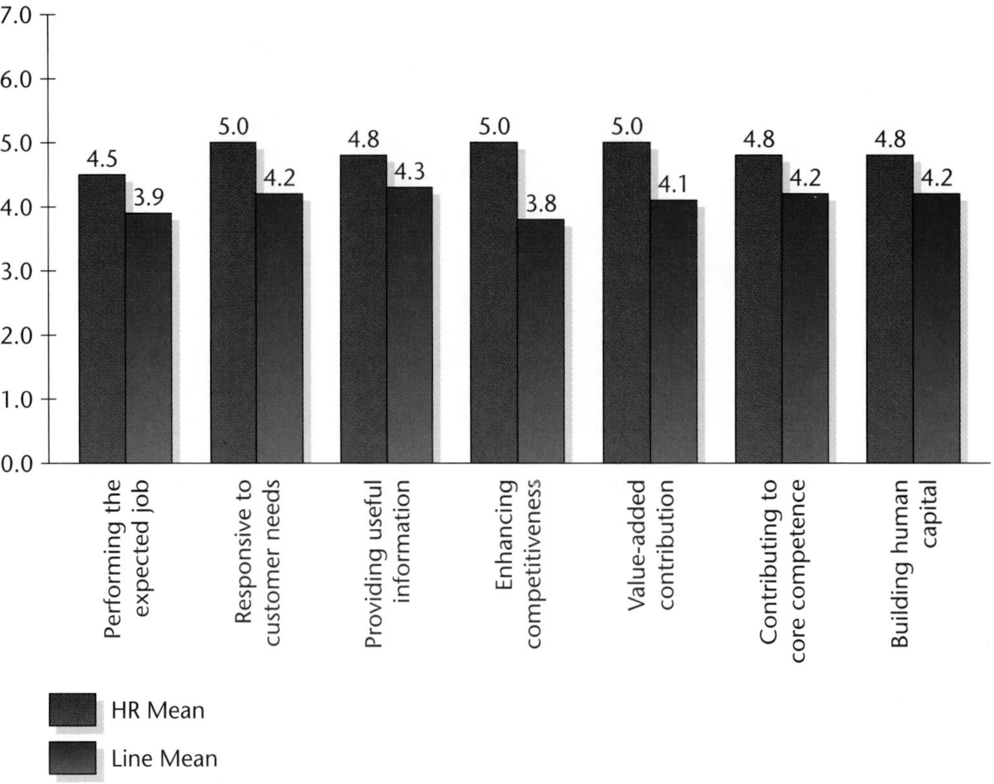

SOURCE: P. Wright, G. McMahan, S. Snell, and B. Gerhart. "Comparing Line and HR Executives' Perceptions of HR Effectiveness: Services, Roles, and Contributions." CAHRS (Center for Advanced Human Resource Studies) working paper 98–29, School of ILR, Cornell University, Ithaca, NY.

The analytic approach is more demanding than the audit approach because it requires the detailed use of statistics and finance. A good example of the level of sophistication that can be required for cost–benefit analysis is shown in Table 16.5. This table shows the types of information needed to determine the dollar value of a new selection test for entry-level computer programmers.

Improving HR Effectiveness

Once a strategic direction has been established and HR's effectiveness evaluated, leaders of the HR function can explore how to improve its effectiveness in contributing to the firm's competitiveness. Returning briefly to Figure 16.1, which depicted the different activities of the HR function, often the improvement focuses on two aspects of the pyramid. First, within each activity, HR needs to improve both the efficiency and effectiveness in performing each of the activities. Second, often there is a push to eliminate as much of the transactional work as possible (and some of the traditional work) to free up time and resources to focus more on the higher–value-added transformational work. Redesign of the structure (reporting relationships) and processes (through outsourcing and information technology) enables the function to achieve these goals simultaneously. Figure 16.6 depicts this process. The "Competing by Meeting Stakeholders' Needs" box describes one company's efforts.

TABLE 16.3
Types of Cost–Benefit Analysis

Human resource accounting
- Capitalization of salary
- Net present value of expected wage payments
- Returns on human assets and human investments

Utility analysis
- Turnover costs
- Absenteeism and sick leave costs
- Gains from selection programs
- Impact of positive employee attitudes
- Financial gains of training programs

SOURCE: Based on A.S. Tsui and L.R. Gomez-Mejia, "Evaluating HR Effectiveness," in *Human Resource Management: Evolving Roles and Responsibilities,* ed. L. Dyer (Washington, DC: Bureau of National Affairs, 1988), pp. 1–196.

TABLE 16.4
Effectiveness and Cost-Effectiveness of Two Wellness Programs for Four Cardiovascular Disease Risk Factors

	SITE C	SITE D
Annual direct program costs, per employee per year	$30.96	$38.57
Percentage of cardiovascular disease risks[a] for which risk was moderately reduced or relapse prevented	48%	51%
Percentage of preceding entry per annual $1 spent per employee	1.55%	1.32%
Amount spent per 1% of risks reduced or relapse prevented	$.65	$.76

[a] High blood pressure, overweight, smoking, and lack of exercise.
SOURCE: J.C. Erfurt, A. Foote, and M.A. Heirich, "The Cost-Effectiveness of Worksite Wellness Programs," *Personnel Psychology* 45 (1992), p. 22.

RESTRUCTURING TO IMPROVE HR EFFECTIVENESS

Traditional HR functions were structured around the basic HR subfunctions such as staffing, training, compensation, appraisal, and labor relations. Each of these areas had a director who reported to the VP of HR, who often reported to a VP of finance and administration. However, for the HR function to truly contribute strategically to firm effectiveness, the senior HR person must be part of the top management team (reporting directly to the chief executive officer), and there must be a different structural arrangement within the function itself.

A recent generic structure for the HR function is depicted in Figure 16.7. As we see, the HR function effectively is divided into three divisions: the Centers for Expertise, the field generalists, and the Service Center.[14] The Centers for Expertise usually consist of the functional specialists in the traditional areas of HR such as recruitment, selection, training, and compensation. These individuals ideally act as consultants in the development of state-of-the-art systems and processes for use in the organization. The field generalists consist of the HR generalists who are assigned to a business unit within the firm. These individuals usually have dual reporting relationships to both the head of the line business and the head of HR (although the line business tends to take priority). They ideally take responsibility for helping the line executives in their business strategically address people issues, and they ensure that the HR systems enable the business to execute its strategy. Finally, the Service Center consists of individuals who ensure that the transactional activities are delivered throughout the organization. These ser-

TABLE 16.5
Example of Analysis Needed to Determine the Dollar Value of a Selection Test

Cost-benefit information	
Current employment	4,404
Number separating	618
Number selected	618
Average tenure	9.69 years
Test information	
Number of applicants	1,236
Testing cost per applicant	$10
Total test cost	$12,360
Average test score	.80 SD
Test validity	.76
SD_y (per year)[a]	$10,413

Computation

Quantity = Average tenure × Applicants selected
= 9.69 years × 618 applicants
= 5,988 person-years

Quality = Average test score × Test validity × SD_y
= .80 × .76 × $10,413
= $6,331 per year

Utility = (Quantity × Quality) – Costs
= (5,988 person-year × $6,331 per year) – $12,360
= $37.9 million

[a] SD_y = Dollar value of a one standard difference in job performance. Approximately 40% of average salary.

SOURCE: From J.W. Boudreau, "Utility Analysis," in *Human Resource Management: Evolving Roles and Responsibilities,* ed. L. Dyer (Washington, DC: Bureau of National Affairs, 1988), p. 150; F.L. Schmidt, J.E. Hunter, R.C. McKenzie, and T.W. Muldrow, "Impact of Valid Selection Procedures on Work-Force Productivity," *Journal of Applied Psychology* 64 (1979), pp. 609–26.

vice centers often leverage information technology to efficiently deliver employee services. For example, organizations such as Chevron have created call-in service centers where employees can dial a central number where service center employees are available to answer their questions and process their requests and transactions.

Such structural arrangements improve service delivery through specialization. Center for Expertise employees can develop current functional skills without being distracted by transactional activities, and generalists can focus on learning the business environment without having to maintain expertise in functional specializations. Finally, Service Center employees can focus on efficient delivery of basic services across business units.

OUTSOURCING TO IMPROVE HR EFFECTIVENESS

Restructuring the internal HR function and redesigning the processes represent internal approaches to improving the effectiveness of the HR function. However, increasingly HR executives are seeking to improve the effectiveness of the systems, processes, and services the function delivers through outsourcing. Outsourcing entails contracting with an outside vendor to provide a product or service to the firm, as opposed to producing the product using employees within the firm.

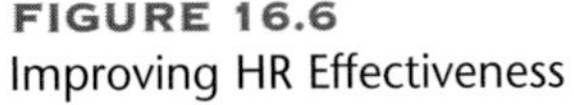

FIGURE 16.6
Improving HR Effectiveness

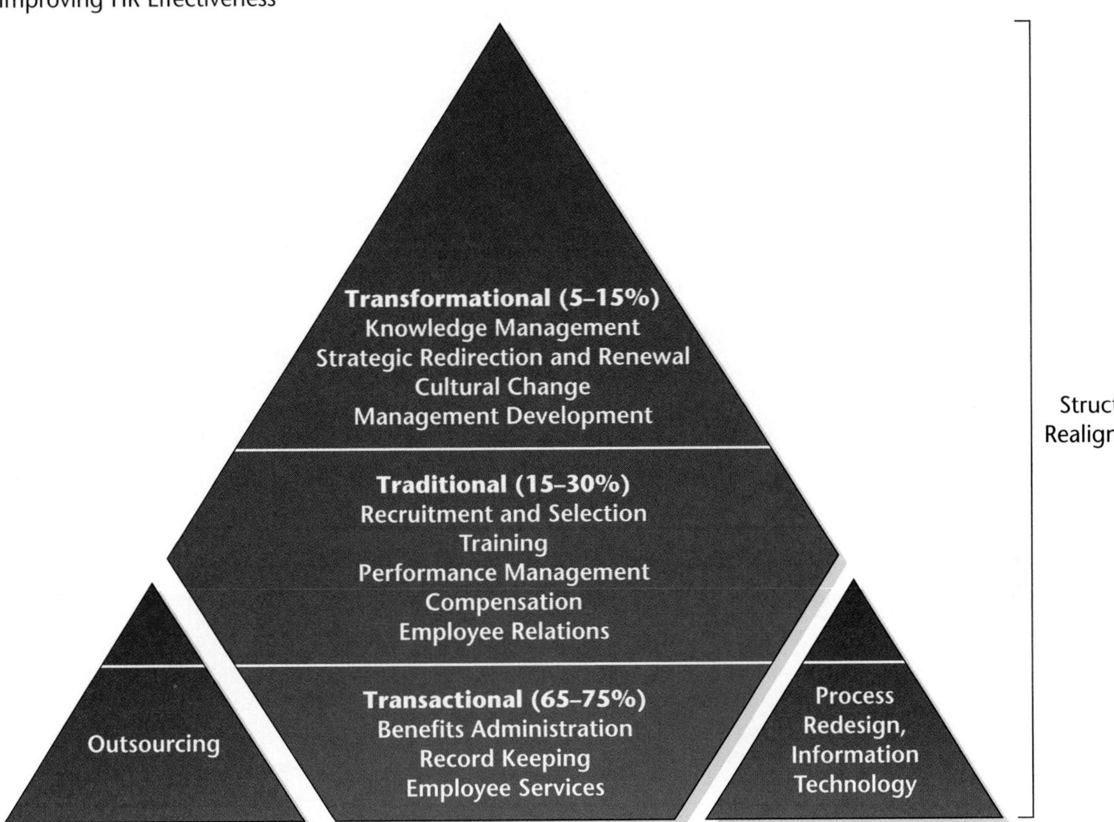

Why would a firm outsource an HR activity or service? Usually this is done for one of two reasons: Either the outsourcing partner can provide the service more cheaply than it would cost to do it internally, or the partner can provide it more effectively than it can be performed internally. Early on, firms resorted to outsourcing for efficiency reasons. Why would using an outsourced provider be more efficient than having internal employees provide a service? Usually it is because outsourced providers are specialists who are able to develop extensive expertise that can be leveraged across a number of companies.

For example, consider a relatively small firm that seeks to develop a pension system for employees. To provide this service to employees, the HR function would need to learn all of the basics of pension law. Then it would need to hire a person with specific expertise in administering a pension system in terms of making sure that employee contributions are withheld and that the correct payouts are made to retired employees. Then the company would have to hire someone with expertise in investing pension funds. If the firm is small, requirements of the pension fund might not fill the time (80 hours per week) of these two new hires. Assume that it only takes 20 total hours a week for these people to do their job. The firm would be wasting 60 hours of employee time each week. However, a firm that specializes in providing pension administration services to multiple firms could provide the 20 hours of required time to that firm and three other firms for the same cost as had the firm performed this activity internally. Thus, the

Wake County Automates to Improve HR Service

The Wake County Personnel Department in Raleigh, North Carolina, was buried under paper. In the staff's recruiting efforts alone, papers authorizing the department to hire new employees passed through so many hands that code numbers and other critical information were often incorrect. Job applications piled up, and by the time staffers responded to applicants, positions were often filled. (Sometimes applicants were actually offered jobs that were no longer available.) In payroll, pay stubs informing employees of vacation time were often outdated. "It was always a matter of having to play catch-up," says Laura Andrew, the payroll manager. In benefits, staffers had to wade through files for current forms. (The division receives bills from 30 different vendors for short-term disability, life insurance, and three different flexible benefit plans.) "The whole situation was a manual nightmare," says Brenda Martin, systems administrator.

It was obvious to nearly everyone that something had to be done. When the department requested a new computer system from upper management, it got immediate approval. The department formed a cross-functional team to research the options thoroughly, making sure the system would do exactly what was needed. Staff agreed that the new system had to be organized according to job position, help cut down paperwork and other manual labor, integrate functions so that all divisions had access to the same information, and be flexible for future modification.

The new system tracks a position from the time it is open until someone is hired, and then adds information continually from each division (payroll, benefits, etc.) to create up-to-date files. It is also user-friendly. Like the best technology, not only does the system save time, it improves accuracy. Employees know exactly how much leave they have, and there are no under- or overpayments. Benefits staff can quickly manipulate data to serve the current work force as well as retirees. In recruitment, all correspondence is automated and information is current; applicants no longer have to wait weeks just to find out a job has already been filled. "Automation has given us access to data immediately and improves our flexibility to respond to applicants and to departments in a short period of time," says Deborah Gyant, recruitment supervisor.

With the freedom and flexibility automation has given the personnel department, staff can focus on larger HR issues and better serve the whole organization. "Now we can move on, we can provide a different level of customer service for our departments and do some of the things we never had time to do," says Gyant.

SOURCE: G. Flynn, "A New HRIS in Wake County Streamlines HR," *Personnel Journal*, May 1994, pp. 137–42.

specialist firm could charge the focal firm 50 percent of what it would cost the small firm to do the pensions internally. Of that 50 percent, 25 percent (20 hours) would go to paying direct salaries and the other 25 percent would be profit. Here the focal firm would save 50 percent of its expenses while the provider would make money.

Now consider the aspect of effectiveness. Because the outsourced provider works for a number of firms and specializes in pensions, its employees develop state-of-the-art knowledge of running pension plans. They can learn unique innovations from one company and transfer that learning to a new company. In addition, employees can be more easily and efficiently trained because all of them will be trained in the same processes and procedures. Finally, due to the experience in providing pension services on a constant basis, the firm is able to develop a capability to perform these services that could never be developed by two individuals working 25 percent of the time on these services.

What kind of services are being outsourced? Firms primarily outsource transactional activities and services of HR such as pension and benefits administration as well as payroll. However, a number of traditional and some transformational activities have been

FIGURE 16.7
Old and New Structures for the HR Organization

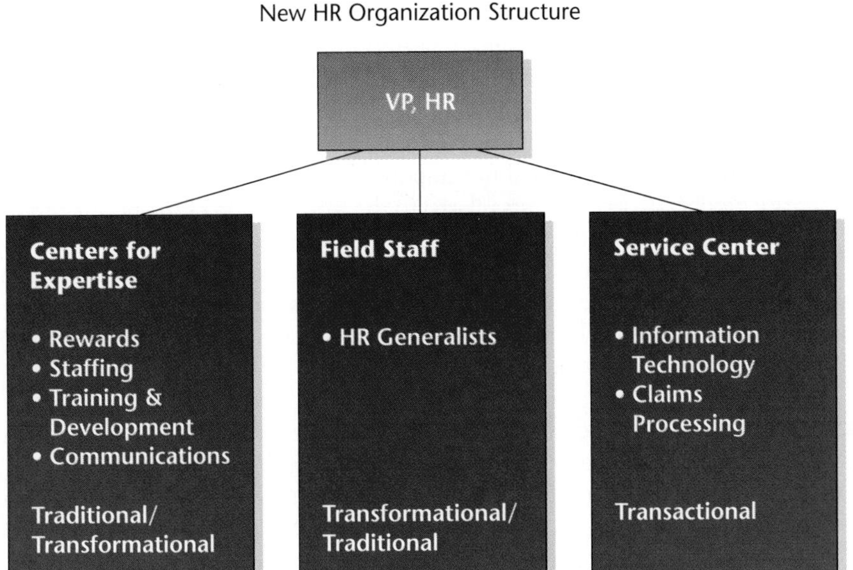

SOURCE: P. Wright, G. McMahan, S. Snell, and B. Gerhart, *Strategic Human Resource Management: Building Human Capital and Organizational Capability.* Technical report. Cornell University, 1998.

outsourced as well. For example, Compaq Computer outsourced a large portion of its staffing activities. The firm contracted with a company to conduct all of the interviewing of its hourly crew and some managerial employees. Compaq found that while the cost was higher than it might have been if the work had been done internally, it provided more flexibility to quickly and efficiently react (not having to lay off employees) if its hiring needs decreased.

IMPROVING HR EFFECTIVENESS THROUGH PROCESS REDESIGN

In addition to structural arrangements, process redesign enables the HR function to more efficiently and effectively deliver HR services. Process redesign often uses information technology, but information technology applications are not a requirement. Thus, we will discuss the general issue of process reengineering and then explore information technology applications that have aided HR in process redesign.

FIGURE 16.8
The Reengineering Process

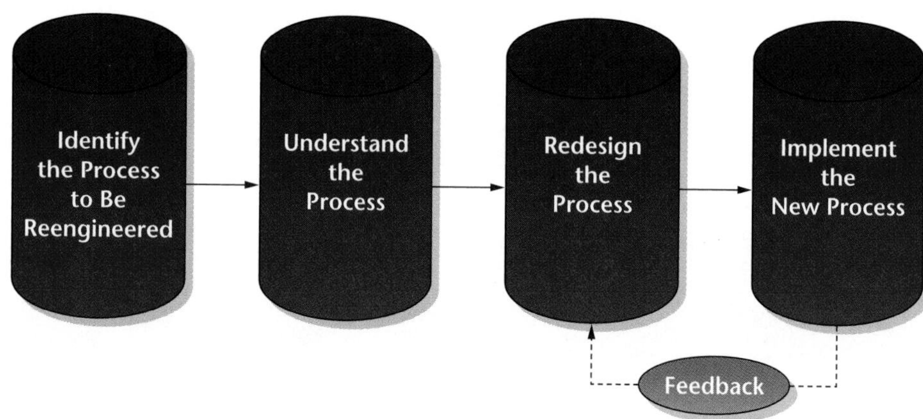

Reengineering is a complete review of critical work processes and redesign to make them more efficient and able to deliver higher quality. Reengineering is especially critical to ensuring that the benefits of new technology can be realized. Applying new technology to an inefficient process will not improve efficiency or effectiveness. Instead, it will increase product or service costs related to the introduction of the new technology.

Reengineering can be used to review the HR department functions and processes, or it can be used to review specific HR practices such as work design or the performance management system. The reengineering process involves the four steps shown in Figure 16.8: Identify the process to be reengineered, understand the process, redesign the process, and implement the new process.[15]

IDENTIFYING THE PROCESS. Managers who control the process or are responsible for functions within the process (sometimes called "process owners") should be identified and asked to be part of the reengineering team. Team members should include employees involved in the process (to provide expertise) and those outside the process, as well as internal or external customers who see the outcome of the process.

UNDERSTANDING THE PROCESS. Several things need to be considered when evaluating a process:

- Can jobs be combined?
- Can employees be provided with more autonomy? Can decision making and control be built into the process through streamlining it?
- Are all the steps in the process necessary?
- Are data redundancy, unnecessary checks, and controls built into the process?
- How many special cases and exceptions have to be dealt with?
- Are the steps in the process arranged in their natural order?
- What is the desired outcome? Are all of the tasks necessary? What is the value of the process?

Various techniques are used to understand processes. **Data-flow diagrams** are useful to show the flow of data among departments. Figure 16.9 shows a data-flow diagram for payroll data. This figure shows the steps in producing a paycheck. Information about the employee and department are sent to the general account. The payroll check is issued based on a payment voucher that is generated from the general accounting ledger. *Data-entity relationship diagrams* show the types of data used within a business function and the

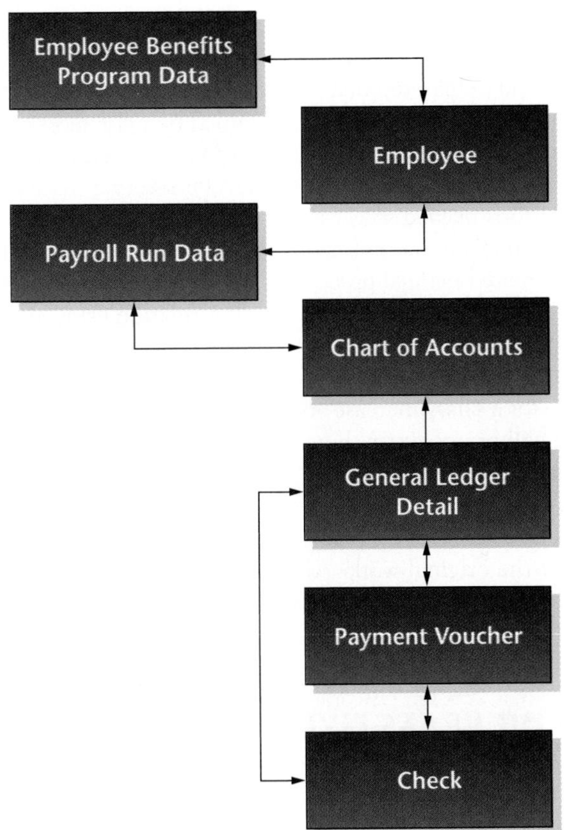

FIGURE 16.9 A Data-Flow Diagram for Payroll Data

relationship among the different types of data. In *scenario analysis*, simulations of real-world issues are presented to data end users. The end users are asked to indicate how an information system could help address their particular situations and what data should be maintained to deal with those situations. *Surveys* and *focus groups* collect information about the data collected, used, and stored in a functional area, as well as information about time and information-processing requirements. Users may be asked to evaluate the importance, frequency, and criticality of automating specific tasks within a functional area. For example, how critical is it to have an applicant tracking system that maintains data on applicants' previous work experience? *Cost-benefit analyses* compare the costs of completing tasks with and without an automated system or software application. For example, the analysis should include the costs in terms of people, time, materials, and dollars; the anticipated costs of software and hardware; and labor, time, and material expenses.[16]

REDESIGNING THE PROCESS. During the redesign phase, the team develops models, tests them, chooses a prototype, and determines how to integrate the prototype into the organization.

IMPLEMENTING THE PROCESS. The company tries out the process by testing it in a limited, controlled setting before expanding companywide. For example, J.M. Huber Corporation, a New Jersey–based conglomerate that has several operating divisions scattered throughout the United States, used reengineering to avoid installing new software onto inefficient processes.[17] HR staff began by documenting and studying the existing work flow and creating a strategy for improving efficiency. Top management, midlevel managers, and human resources staff worked together to identify the processes that they most wanted to improve. They determined that the most critical issue was to develop a client-server system that could access data more easily than the mainframe computer they were currently using. Also, the client-server system could eliminate many of the requisitions needed to get access to data, which slowed down work. The HR department's efforts have streamlined record-keeping functions, eliminated redundant steps, and automated manual processes. The fully automated client-server system allows employees to sign up and change benefits information using an interactive voice-response system that is connected to the company's database. In addition, managers have easier access to employee's salary history, job descriptions, and other data. If an employee is eligible for a salary increase and the manager requests a change and it is approved, the system will process it (without entry by a clerical worker), and the changes will be seen on the employee's paycheck. Results of the reengineering effort are impressive. The redesigned processes have reduced the number of problems that HR has to give to other departments by 42 percent, cut work steps by 26 percent, and eliminated 20 percent of the original work. Although the company is spending upwards of $1 million to make the technology work, it estimates that the investment should pay for itself in five years.

IMPROVING HR EFFECTIVENESS THROUGH USING NEW TECHNOLOGIES

Several new and emerging technologies can help improve the effectiveness of the HR function. **New technologies** are current applications of knowledge, procedures, and equipment that have not been used previously. New technology usually involves automation—that is, replacing human labor with equipment, information processing, or some combination of the two.

In HRM, technology has already been used for three broad functions: transaction processing, reporting, and tracking; decision support systems; and expert systems.[18] **Transaction processing** refers to computations and calculations used to review and document HR decisions and practices. This includes documenting relocation, training expenses, and course enrollments and filling out government reporting requirements (such as EEO-1 reports, which require companies to report information to the government regarding employees' race and gender by job category). **Decision support systems** are designed to help managers solve problems. They usually include a "what if" feature that allows users to see how outcomes change when assumptions or data change. These systems are useful, for example, for helping companies determine the number of new hires needed based on different turnover rates or the availability of employees with a certain skill in the labor market. **Expert systems** are computer systems incorporating the decision rules of people deemed to have expertise in a certain area. The system recommends actions that the user can take based on the information provided by the user. The recommended actions are those that a human expert would take in a similar situation (e.g., a manager's interviewing a job candidate). We discuss expert systems in more detail later in this chapter.

The newest technologies being applied to HRM include interactive voice technology, the Internet, client-server architecture, relational databases, imaging, development of specialized software, CD-ROM, and laser disc technology. These technologies improve effectiveness through increasing access to information, improving communica-

FIGURE 16.10 The Competitive Advantage of Technology

SOURCE: DILBERT reprinted by permission of United Feature Syndicate, Inc.

tions, improving the speed with which HR transactions and information can be gathered, and reducing the costs and making it easier to administer HR functions such as recruiting, training, and performance management. Technology enables

- Employees to gain complete control over their training and benefits enrollments (more self-service).
- The creation of a paperless employment office.
- Streamlining the HR department's work.
- Knowledge-based decision support technology, which allows employees and managers to access knowledge on an as-needed basis.
- Employees and managers to select the type of media they want to use to send and receive information.
- Work to be completed at any time, any place, day or night.
- Closer monitoring of employees' work.[19]

As Dilbert shows in Figure 16.10, managers who cannot use or fail to use new technologies will be at a competitive disadvantage.

There is evidence that new technology is related to improvements in productivity. Improvements in productivity have been credited largely to downsizing, restructuring, and reengineering. But technology is also responsible because new technology has allowed companies to find leaner, more flexible ways of operating.[20] A study of companies in a variety of industries found that investments in computers provided a better return than investments in other kinds of capital.[21] Technology requires companies to have appropriately skilled and motivated people and streamlined work processes. In some cases technology is replacing human capital.[22] For example, Statewide, the regional telephone unit of Pacific Telesis Group, used to dispatch about 20,000 trucks a day to fix customers' lines. New technology has enabled the company to find broken lines using computer signals. As a result, now fewer truck dispatches (and fewer drivers) are necessary.

INTERACTIVE VOICE TECHNOLOGY. Interactive voice technology uses a conventional personal computer to create an automated phone-response system. This technology is especially useful for benefits administration. For example, at Hannaford Brothers, a supermarket chain spread through the Northeastern United States, the HR department installed an interactive voice-response system that allows employees to get information on their retirement accounts, stock purchases, and benefits plans by using the touchtone buttons on their phone.[23] Employees can also directly enroll in programs and speak to an HR representative if they have questions. As a result of the technology, the company was able to reduce the size of the HR staff and more quickly serve employees' benefits needs.

THE INTERNET. The **Internet** is a widely used tool for communications, a method for sending and receiving communications quickly and inexpensively, and a way to locate and gather resources, such as software and reports.[24] According to one survey, 11 percent of the North American population over age 16 are on the Internet, and 17.6 million people use the World Wide Web (which we discuss later).[25] To gain access to the Internet, you need a personal computer with a direct connection via an existing network or a modem to dial into the Internet. Educational institutions, government agencies, and commercial service providers such as Prodigy, CompuServe, and America Online provide access to the Internet.

Managers can communicate with other managers at their location or across the globe, leave messages or documents, and get access to *rooms* that are designated for conversation on certain topics (the Americans with Disabilities Act, for example). Various *newsgroups* exist, which are bulletin boards dedicated to areas of interest, where you can read, post, and respond to messages and articles. Internet sites can have *home pages*—mailboxes that identify the person or company and contain text, images, sounds, and even moving pictures.

The **World Wide Web** is a user-friendly service on the Internet. It provides browser software that enables the user to explore its items (e.g., *Mosaic* and *Netscape*). Every home page on the Web has an address, or "uniform resources locator" (URL). Many organizations are creating Web sites to provide financial information to investors, advertise products and services, give the latest news releases about the company, and post position openings.[26] The Internet is a valuable source of information on a wide range of HR topics available from professional societies, schools, and government agencies. Table 16.6 provides Internet and Web site addresses related to HR topics. (In Chapter 5, we provided World Wide Web sites for recruiting sources.)

One manager at Hydro Quebec, a large Canadian utility, used the Internet to research topics related to TQM and business process reengineering. When the company wanted information on diversity and women's issues, the manager logged into a Cornell University Web site and quickly downloaded two dozen reports dealing with the topic. When the company needed to develop a satisfaction survey, the manager used the Internet to identify similar-sized companies that had conducted comprehensive surveys. Within one day, 30 HR professionals, including managers at Federal Express and United Parcel Service, responded. The manager has also networked with HR managers at Motorola, IBM, and other companies.[27]

NETWORKS AND CLIENT-SERVER ARCHITECTURE. Traditionally, different computer systems (with separate databases) are used for payroll, recruiting, and other human resource functions. A **network** is a combination of desktop computers, computer terminals, and mainframes or minicomputers that share access to databases and a means to transmit information throughout the system. A common form of network involves client-server architecture. **Client-server architecture** provides the means of consolidating data and applications into a single system (the client).[28] The data can be accessed by multiple users. Also, software applications can be stored on the server and "borrowed" by other users. Client-server architecture allows easier access to data, faster response time, and maximum use of the computing power of the personal computer.

For example, a pharmaceutical company with 50,000 employees worldwide has used client-server technology to create an employee information system that integrates data

TABLE 16.6
Sample of Online Resources Related to HR Topics

ADDRESS	DESCRIPTION
listserv@psuum.psu.edu	Training and development
mailbase@mailbase.ac.uk	Business process reengineering
listserv@mizzoul.missouri.edu	Human resource development
listserv@cornell.edu	General HR topics
http://www.shrm.org	Society of Human Resource Management
http://www.hrhq.com	HR Headquarters (products and services)
http://www.ilr.cornell.edu/	Cornell University (databases; government and academic reports)
http://www.fedworld.gov/#top/	FedWorld (labor information and government agency news)
http://www.osha.gov	Occupational Safety and Health Administration
http://www.fed.org/fed/uscompanies/labor	Office of the American Workplace Best Practices Clearinghouse
http://www.fed.org/fed/	Foundation for Enterprise Development (information on motivation and compensation issues and other subjects)
http://www.asqc.org	American Society for Quality Control
http://matrix.casti.com:com/qc/	Quality resource

SOURCE: *Personnel Journal* 24-hour business center, July 1995; Internet World Wide Web Sites; B.A. Rubin, "The Internet: Where Few Trainers Have Gone Before," *Training and Development,* August 1994, pp. 25–30; A. Doran, "The Internet," *The Review,* August-September 1995, p. 35; M.I. Finney, "It's All in Knowing How," *HR Magazine,* July 1995, pp. 36–43.

from six databases.[29] The available data includes financial, operational, and human resource information. A manager at a European location can compare her plant's human resource costs with those for the entire company or a plant in Ohio, and at the same time senior management can use the same data to compare the productivity of the Ohio plant with a plant in Maine.

RELATIONAL DATABASES. **Databases** contain several data files (topics), which are made up of employee information (records) containing data fields. A data field is an element or type of information such as employee name, social security number, or job classification.

In a **relational database,** information is stored in separate files, which look like tables. These files can be linked by common elements (fields) such as name, identification number, or location. This contrasts with the traditional file structure, in which all data associated with an employee was kept in one file. In the relational database shown in Figure 16.11, employees' personal information is located in one file and salary information in another, but both topics of information can be accessed via the employees' social security numbers.

Users of relational databases have the ability to file and retrieve information according to any field or multiple fields across different tables or databases. They provide an easy way to organize data. Also, the number of data fields that can be kept for any employee using a relational database is limitless. The ability to join or merge data from several different tables or to view only a subset of data is especially useful in human resource management. Databases that have been developed to track employee benefit costs, training courses, and compensation, for example, contain separate pieces of em-

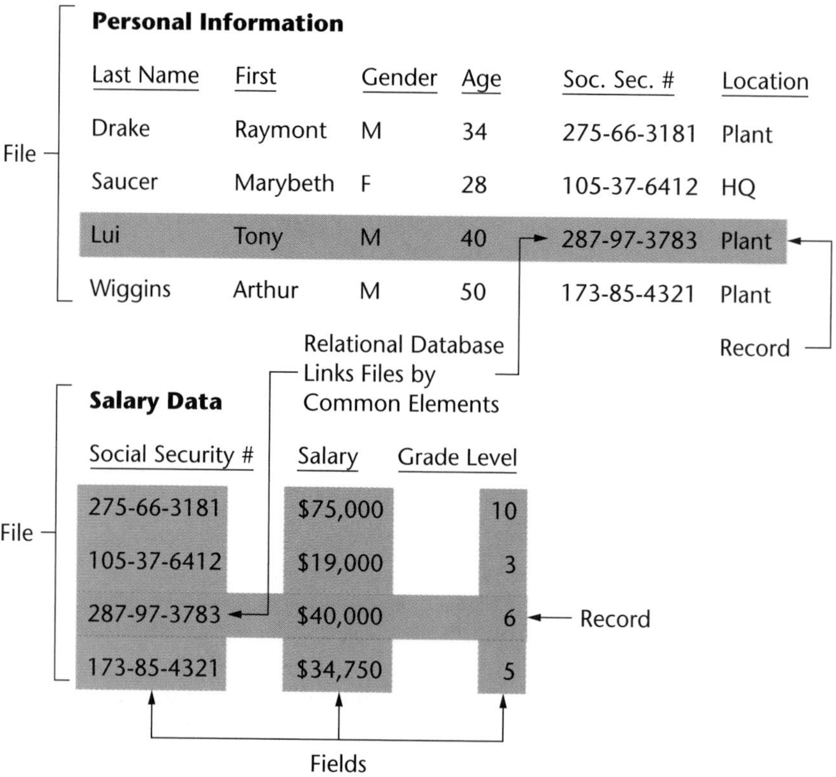

FIGURE 16.11
Example of a Relational Database

ployee information that can be accessed and merged as desired by the user. Relational technology also allows databases to be established in several different locations. Users in one plant or division location can access data from any other company location. Consider an oil company. Human resources data—such as the names, salaries, and skills of employees working on an oil rig in the Gulf of Mexico—can be stored at company headquarters. Databases at the oil-rig site itself might contain employee name, safety equipment issued, and appropriate skill certification. Headquarters and oil-rig managers can access information on each database as needed.

IMAGING. **Imaging** refers to scanning documents, storing them electronically, and retrieving them.[30] Imaging is particularly useful because paper files take a large volume of space and are difficult to access. Imaging has been used in applicant tracking and in benefits management. Applicants' resumés can be scanned and stored in a database so they will be available for access at a later date. Some software applications (such as *Resumix*) allow the user to scan the resumé based on key items such as job history, education, or experience. At Warner-Lambert, the compensation and benefits department provides HR-related services for over 15,000 retirees.[31] Eight employees retire and die each month; approximately 100 employees terminate each month. This "exit" activity created a tremendous volume of paper for each employee, as well as requests for data from analysts in the department. It was very time-consuming and inefficient to locate the data and refile them. Using imaging, the compensation and benefits department was able to better serve its customers by reducing the time needed to locate a file or handle a phone inquiry from a retiree, providing the ability for sharing files among analysts simultaneously, eliminating the need to refile, and reducing the physical space needed to store the files.

CD-ROM AND LASER DISC TECHNOLOGY. Both CD-ROM and laser disc technology have revolutionized training. Using a personal computer, animation, video clips, and graphics can be integrated into a training session. Also, the user can interact with the training material through a joystick or touch-screen monitor. **CD-ROM** uses a laser to read text, graphics, audio, and video from an aluminum disc. **Laser disc** technology uses a laser to provide high-quality video and sound. Laser disc technology can be used individually (as a source of video on a computer screen) or as part of computer instruction in a classroom setting.

At Pilgrim Nuclear Power Plant in Plymouth, Massachusetts, a newly hired security guard learns the layout of the facility by using a computer, television, monitor, joystick, and video disc.[32] The new hire can tour the trash-compaction facility, examine the components on a panel of electrical controls, ride up elevators, and listen to colleagues discuss machinery, equipment, and high-radiation areas he should be aware of. There are more than 77,000 individual photos on the laser disc, and explorers can travel at a normal walking speed, look upward or downward, quickly change locations, and store images for future reference.

As mentioned in Chapter 7, use of the computer in training provides a safe environment for learning how to operate potentially dangerous equipment or tasks in which an error might have grave consequences (such as a heart transplant). Use of the computer also allows employees to learn at their own pace, skip material and review material, and learn when and where material is available. (They do not have to wait for a class to be scheduled, they only need access to the equipment.)

EXPERT SYSTEMS. As we discussed earlier, expert systems are technologies that mimic a human expert. Expert systems have three elements:

- A knowledge base that contains facts, figures, and rules about a specific subject.
- A decision making capability that draws conclusions from those facts and figures to solve problems and answer questions.
- A user interface that gathers and gives information to the person using the system.

The use of expert systems in HRM is relatively new. Some companies use expert systems to help employees decide how to allocate their monies for benefits, help managers schedule the labor requirements for projects, and assist managers in conducting selection interviews. Pic 'n Pay stores (a chain of shoe stores) uses an expert system for the initial job interview. Candidates call a toll-free phone number. The candidates then respond to 100 questions, and the computer records the responses and scores them. At headquarters, a team of trained interviewers evaluates the responses and designs a list of follow-up questions, which are administered by the hiring manager. The expert system resulted in reducing employee turnover by 50 percent and reducing losses due to theft by 39 percent. Also, hiring of minorities has risen 8 percent, implying that decision biases may be less significant using the expert system.[33]

A large international food processor uses an expert system called *Performer,* designed to provide training and support to its plant operators. One of the problems the company was facing was determining why potato chips were being scorched in the fryer operation. An operator solved the problem using *Performer*. He selected the "troubleshooting" menu, then "product texture/flavor," then "off oil flavor." The program listed probable causes, beginning with high oxidation during frying. The operator chose that cause, and the system recommended adjusting the cooking line's oil flush, providing detailed steps for that procedure. Following those steps resolved the problem.[34]

Expert systems can deliver both high quality and lower costs. By using the decision processes of experts, the system enables many people to arrive at decisions that reflect the expert's knowledge. An expert system helps avoid the errors that can result from fatigue and decision biases. The efficiencies of an expert system can be realized if it can be operated by fewer employees or less-skilled (and likely less costly) employees than the company would otherwise require.

GROUPWARE. **Groupware** (or electronic meeting software) is a software application that enables multiple users to track, share, and organize information and to work on the same document simultaneously.[35] A groupware system combines such elements as electronic mail, document management, and an electronic bulletin board. The most popular brand of groupware is *Lotus Notes*.

Companies have been using groupware to improve business processes such as sales and account management, to improve meeting effectiveness, and to identify and share knowledge in the organization. (See our earlier discussion of creating a learning organization in Chapter 7.) Monsanto uses *Lotus Notes* to link salespeople, account managers, and competitor-intelligence analysts.[36] The database contains updated news on competitors and customers, information from public news sources, salespeople's reports, an in-house directory of experts, and attendees' notes from conventions and conferences. Many companies are also creating their own "intranet," a private company network that competes with groupware programs such as *Lotus Notes*. Intranets are cheaper and simpler to use than groupware programs but pose potential security problems because of the difficulty of keeping people out of the network.[37]

Software Applications for HRM

Today, nearly 1,000 personal-computer–based human resource applications are available.[38] Because of the wide variety, several publications that deal exclusively with human resource management (e.g., *HR Magazine*, *Personnel Journal*) devote one issue a year to reviewing software applications. In the following sections we review the software applications available in the areas of staffing, human resource planning, training and career development, performance management, and compensation and benefits.

STAFFING APPLICATIONS

Common software applications used in the area of staffing include applicant tracking, recruitment practices tracking, help in meeting equal employment opportunity reporting requirements, and aid in maintaining databases of employee information.

APPLICANT RECRUITING AND TRACKING. Applicant tracking helps a company maintain its information on job candidates and identify suitable candidates for particular positions. An effective applicant tracking system does the following:

1. Retrieves applications by name, social security number, or other identifiers.
2. Tracks all the events in the application process (e.g., interviews, tests).
3. Allows the user to determine how long an application has remained active.
4. Contains the information needed to meet equal employment opportunity reporting requirements, such as name, gender, race, and date of application.
5. Tracks data entry (allows for entry of only essential applicant information).

6. Simplifies the recruiter's function (provides basic data needed to schedule interviews, generate reports, and reduce the list of job candidates).
7. Allows an evaluation of recruiting strategy to be made (e.g., by identifying which sources of advertising bring in the best candidates or the cost-effectiveness of visiting various college campuses).
8. Permits customization (allows additional types of data to be added to the file, such as test results or job offers).
9. Increases the applicant pool (potential job candidates can be identified and tracked earlier; qualified candidates can be tracked after a position is filled).
10. Increases selection criteria by allowing simultaneous searches based on several types of criteria, such as skills, work history, and educational background.[39]

EQUAL EMPLOYMENT OPPORTUNITY AND AFFIRMATIVE ACTION REPORTING REQUIREMENTS. To comply with equal employment opportunity requirements, companies have to provide reports to the federal government. The most common is the EEO-1 report, which shows the number of employees by race and gender within nine job categories (e.g., professional, office and clerical, craft workers). A section of an EEO report is shown in Figure 16.12. The EEO-1 report is usually submitted annually to the Equal Employment Opportunity Commission. All government contractors and any employers who have been found to engage in illegal hiring practices are also required to file affirmative action reports. To complete either kind of report, employers need to

1. Describe the work force by job category and job classification.
2. Evaluate the adverse impact of employment practices on representatives of protected classes (e.g., women and minorities) in the work force.
3. Determine the availability of jobs for qualified members of protected classes.
4. Evaluate the company's utilization of qualified protected class members.
5. Describe the company's goals and timetables for implementing equal employment opportunity or affirmative action initiatives.
6. Monitor those initiatives.[40]

Because of EEO and affirmative action reporting requirements, employers need to keep track of job candidates' and employees' race and gender and the percentages of women and minorities in the internal and external work force by job category. Collecting this information into databases makes it easier to track affirmative action and EEO-related statistics. Many software packages are available that generate the necessary EEO and affirmative action reports (one of the most popular being *ABRA 2000 Human Resource System*).

DEVELOPING A MASTER EMPLOYEE DATABASE. Companies usually keep data about employees in one large file. Information in the master employee database can be used for many purposes: administering payroll, tracking compensation and benefit costs, human resource planning, and meeting EEO reporting requirements. The master employee database usually includes information such as the employee's name, social security number, job status (full- or part-time), hiring date, position, title, rate of pay, citizenship status, job history, job location, mailing address, birth date, and emergency contacts.

USING STAFFING APPLICATIONS FOR DECISION MAKING. Information related to applicant recruiting and tracking can help managers make recruiting practices

FIGURE 16.12

Section D—Employment Data of EEO-1 Report

Number of Employees				Male							Female					
			Overall Total	White	Black	Hispanic	Asian	American Indian			White	Black	Hispanic	Asian	American Indian	
			A	B	C	D	E	F		A	B	C	D	E	F	G
Officials and Managers		1														
Professionals		2														
Technicians		3														
Sales Workers		4														
Office and Clerical		5														
Craft Workers (Skilled)		6														
Operatives (Semiskilled)		7														
Laborers (Unskilled)		8														
Service Workers		9														
Total		10														
Total employment reported in previous EEO-1 report		11														
Formal on-the-Job Training	White Collar	12														
	Production	13														

SOURCE: Adapted from V.R. Ceriello, *Human Resource Management* (New York: Lexington Books, 1991), p. 420.

more efficient and productive. For example, managers can evaluate the yield of recruiting sources. Those sources that produce the greatest number of applicants who are offered and accept positions are targeted for subsequent recruiting efforts, and low-yield sources are abandoned. Managers can also determine which recruiters are providing the most successful employees. EEO reporting and adverse-impact analyses can help managers evaluate the extent to which women and minority employees are gaining access to managerial and other highly compensated and valued positions in the company.

At Nike, recruitment has become less costly and time-consuming because the company uses an applicant tracking system.[41] Before the automated system was implemented, job applicants had to submit a separate resumé for each job they were interested in. The old system also lacked the capability to process and store data from unsolicited job applications. Most of the 35,000 unsolicited applications Nike received were thrown away. Using *Resumix*, the applicant tracking program mentioned earlier, the company uses imaging technology to quickly enter every resumé it receives into the system. *Resumix* also gives managers the ability to cross-reference resumés. Using *Resumix*, Nike has lowered the time and cost of employee recruitment. The company is running fewer newspaper ads, and the ads are more general, generating a greater variety of candidates. *Resumix* has also reduced the time needed to fill positions.

HUMAN RESOURCE PLANNING APPLICATIONS

Two principal computer applications are related to human resource planning: succession planning and forecasting.[42] Succession planning ensures that the company has employees who are prepared to move into positions that become available because of retirement, promotion, transfers, terminations, or expansion of the business. Forecasting includes predicting the number of employees who have certain skills and the number of qualified individuals in the labor market.

Because human resource planning involves company-specific calculations involved in determining future employee turnover, growth rates, and promotion patterns, human resource planning applications usually require more customization than applications for other human resource functions. They usually contain several data files, including a starting-population file, exit-rate file, growth-rate file, and promotion patterns. The starting-population file lists employees by job classification within each job family. These file lists usually include all active, regular, full-time employees. However, starting-population files may include only specific populations of employees. Starting-population data that may be used include job grade, gender, race or ethnicity, age, service, training, and experience information. Starting-population lists that are limited to specific populations of employees are used to identify the mobility patterns of these employee groups. Exit-rate data include promotion patterns, training completion rates, turnover rates, and hiring rates. Growth-rate data include the percentage increase in the number of employees within the job or demographic characteristic (e.g., females) of interest. Promotion patterns include the rate of movement into and out of each position.

Information regarding starting population and exit and growth rates is useful for conducting work-force profile analysis and work-force dynamics analysis.[43]

WORK-FORCE PROFILE ANALYSIS. To determine future labor supply and demand, it is necessary to identify the characteristics of the current work force, a process known as a work-force profile review. The software can be used to generate reports that provide information regarding employee demographics (such as age), the number of employees in each job classification, and the interaction between demographics and company characteristics (e.g., the average age of employees within each job classification or division of the company).

WORK-FORCE DYNAMICS ANALYSIS. A work-force dynamics analysis involves analyzing employee movement over time. Promotion, demotion, transfer, and turnover data are used. Employee movement data can also be used to forecast the effects of layoffs or hiring on the future work force. Work-force dynamics analysis provides the following kinds of information:

1. Number of new hires, transfers, and promotions by job classification or department.
2. The total number of promotions, or the number of promotions from a specific job to another job or from one division to another division.
3. The number of employees the company will need in the future.
4. The number of employees who will be available to fill future job openings.

USING HUMAN RESOURCE PLANNING APPLICATIONS FOR DECISION MAKING. The work-force profile review provides managers with information regarding

1. Divisions or departments that have the greatest concentration of employees who are nearing retirement age.
2. Job classifications in which there are too few employees who are ready for promotion.
3. Job classifications in which there are few women or minorities.
4. Job classifications or departments that have large groups of employees who lack basic skills.

An example of a human resource planning application is Cyborg Systems' *Workforce Planning* module.[44] This application, which can be run on either a mainframe or a personal computer, retains data on employees' skills and work experience, education, job history, and termination and separation. It permits integration with payroll applications so that data can be shared between the databases. It reports on the number of people hired, terminated, transferred, and promoted by pay class. It also reports on the net change and percentage change in hiring, termination, or transfers during each business cycle, month, or other time frame chosen by the user.

Managers can use information about employee movement, skills, and job openings to make decisions about where employees should be deployed to help the company successfully execute its business strategy.

PERFORMANCE MANAGEMENT APPLICATIONS

Employees' performance ratings, disciplinary actions, and work-rule violations can be stored in electronic databases. Personal computers are also increasingly being used for monitoring the actual performance and productivity of service employees.[45] For example, at a General Electric customer service center, agents answer over 14,000 telephone inquiries per day. The agents' calls are recorded and reviewed to help the agent improve customer service. American Airlines also monitors the telephone calls that come into its reservation centers. Managers can hear what the agents tell customers and see what agents enter on their personal computer screens. One of the disadvantages of monitoring is that employees sometimes find it demoralizing, degrading, and stressful. To avoid the potential negative effect of performance monitoring, managers must communicate why employees are being monitored. Nonmanagement employees also need to be involved in monitoring and coaching less-experienced employees. Legislation regarding computer monitoring may occur in the future. Both the U.S. House and Senate have considered legislation designed to protect employees' rights from being violated by computer monitoring (the Privacy for Consumers and Workers Act).

USING PERFORMANCE MANAGEMENT APPLICATIONS FOR DECISION MAKING. Performance management applications are available to help managers tailor performance rating systems to jobs and assist the manager in identifying solutions to performance problems.[46] Software is available to help the manager customize performance rating forms for each job. The manager determines the performance standard for each job and rates each employee according to the appropriate standards. The manager receives a report summarizing the employees' strengths and weaknesses. The report also provides information regarding how different an employee's performance was from the established standard.

Performance diagnosis applications ask the manager for information about performance problems (e.g., Has the employee been trained in the skills that caused the performance problem?) and the work environment (e.g., Does the employee work under time pressure?). The software analyzes the information and provides the manager with solutions to consider in dealing with the performance problem.

TRAINING AND CAREER DEVELOPMENT APPLICATIONS

Training applications have been used primarily to track information related to training administration (e.g., course enrollments, tuition reimbursement summaries, and training costs), employee skills, and employees' training activities. Important database elements for training administration include training courses completed, certified skills, and educational experience. Georgia Power, a utility company, uses a database system that tracks internal training classes, available classroom space, instructor availability, costs, and the salaries of training class members.[47] Figure 16.13 illustrates a screen showing training costs for an accounting department. Cost information can be used by managers to determine which departments are exceeding their training budgets. This information can be used to reallocate training dollars during the next budget period. Databases are also available that provide professional employees, such as engineers and lawyers, with access to summaries of journal articles, legal cases, and books to help these employees keep up to date.[48]

Career development applications assess the employees' career interests, work values, and career goals. The computer provides employees with information about positions in the company that meet their interests and values. Company information systems may also have career development plans for each employee. These may include information such as skill strengths, projected training and development needs, target positions, and ratings of readiness for managerial or other positions.

USING TRAINING AND CAREER DEVELOPMENT APPLICATIONS FOR DECISION MAKING. Managers can use skills inventories to ensure that they are getting the maximum benefit out of their training budget. Using skills inventories, managers can determine which employees need training and can suggest training programs that are appropriate for their job and skill levels. Skill inventories are also useful for identifying employees who are qualified for promotions and transfers. Finally, they can also be useful for

FIGURE 16.13 Example of a Training Budget Screen

Cost Center: Accounting

Total Budget: 4500

	Budget	Expenditure	Variance
Course	3500	1000	2500
Accommodation	600	00	600
Meals	300	00	300
Travel	100	00	100
Total	4500	1000	3500

SOURCE: Adapted from Spectrum Human Resource Systems Corporation, "TD/2000: Training and Development System: Sample Screens and Reports" (Denver, CO).

helping managers to quickly build employee teams with the necessary skills to respond to customer needs, product changes, international assignments, or work problems.

Career development applications can help managers improve the effectiveness of their career development discussions with employees. They also help employees determine their interests, goals, and work values, which is often a difficult and uncomfortable task for managers. By having employees complete a self-assessment of interests, goals, and values, managers and employees can have a more efficient and effective career development discussion that focuses on developing career plans and helping employees progress toward their career goals.

Career development applications also can help managers advise employees on available development opportunities (e.g., new jobs). For example, 3M has an internal-search system that helps managers identify qualified internal candidates for job openings and a job-information system that provides employees with access to information about internal job openings and the opportunity to nominate themselves for openings.[49]

COMPENSATION AND BENEFITS APPLICATIONS

Applications in compensation and benefits include payroll, job evaluation, salary surveys, salary-planning, international compensation, and benefits management.

PAYROLL. Meeting a payroll involves calculating and reporting federal, state, and local taxes; computing gross pay, deductions, and net pay for each pay period; arranging for transfer of monies into appropriate accounts; distributing payments and records to employees; and reporting dollars allocated to payroll and benefits to the accounting function. Several issues have to be considered in designing or choosing a payroll system. The company must decide whether payroll will be administered in-house or by a service bureau. The company must also decide the extent of integration between payroll and other human resource information systems.

In many companies, payroll is done by a service bureau, a company that provides payroll services to other organizations. One of the advantages of a service bureau is that it ensures that the company's payroll meets federal, state, and local laws. It also provides a level of computer expertise that may be unavailable within the company. Many service bureaus have developed other human resource applications that integrate with their payroll systems. A problem arises when a company wants to use human resource applications that have not been developed by the service bureau. The service bureau may be unable or unwilling to integrate its payroll system with other applications.

Besides deciding whether to have its payroll done by a service bureau, managers have to decide whether payroll will be integrated with other human resource data systems. In an integrated payroll system, the information in the payroll system is shared with other databases. In most companies, payroll is not linked to other human resource information systems. However, the trend is toward integrated systems because of the reduced costs resulting from sharing databases. Another advantage of an integrated payroll is that it cuts down on the storage of redundant information, thus speeding up the computer's computing time. Tesseract Corporation's payroll system is completely integrated with both its human resource manager and its benefits systems. Information needed for salary planning and compliance with government regulations can be shared between the systems. The integration of payroll with other systems raises important security issues because access to payroll data needs to be restricted to certain employees.

JOB EVALUATION. Job evaluation involves determining the worth of each job and establishing pay rates. In computerized job evaluation, jobs are given points, and the relative worth of each job is determined by the total number of points.[50] Managers and employees complete surveys that ask them to rate their jobs' level of problem solving, interaction with customers, and other important compensable factors. The survey data are entered into the computer. A summary of the survey responses is generated and checked for accuracy (e.g., jobs high in complexity should also have high ratings of required job knowledge). The computer calculates a point value to assign each job to a salary grade.

SALARY SURVEYS. Salary surveys are sent to competing companies to gain information about compensation rates, pay levels, or pay structures. The information gathered may include salary ranges, average salary of job incumbents, and total compensation of job incumbents. Software designed specifically for this purpose collects, records, analyzes, and generates reports comparing company salary ranges with those of competitors.

SALARY PLANNING. Salary planning anticipates changes in employees' salaries because of seniority or performance. Salary planning applications calculate merit-increase budgets and allocate salary increases based on merit or seniority. They also allow users to see what effect changes in the amount of money devoted to merit, seniority, or cost-of-living wage increases would have on compensation budgets.

Home Box Office (HBO) has a proactive approach toward compensation.[51] The company believes that all employees should understand their salary, why it was assigned, and what type of merit increase they can expect. Merit increases are based on performance ratings. The information service staff helps the human resource department administer the performance reviews by providing an evaluation report for each employee. The report includes the employee's current salary and performance evaluations from previous years. The information systems staff also assists in the bonus-administration program, converting each employee's performance ratings into a bonus rating, developing calculation worksheets, entering data, and providing a wide range of reports that are needed to determine the amount of money available for merit raises. One of the software products related to the bonus system is a report that estimates and calculates bonuses for employees and confirms the approved bonus.

INTERNATIONAL COMPENSATION. Software applications also perform U.S. and foreign tax calculations necessary to determine the costs of international assignments. Many international compensation applications can also calculate salary levels and cost-of-living differentials between U.S. and foreign cities.

BENEFITS MANAGEMENT. Benefits can be classified into three types: time benefits (e.g., sick leave, parental leave), risk benefits (various forms of health and long-term disability insurance that help employees and their families in case of injury or death), and security benefits (retirement and savings programs).[52] Benefits management includes tracking coverage for employees and former employees, producing reports on changes in benefits coverage, and determining employee eligibility for benefit plans. Software is available to help administer flexible benefits programs, pensions, retirement planning, and defined benefit and defined contribution plans. These applications can track the employee's enrollment in each part of the benefit plan, track claims, communicate premium costs to employees, calculate taxes, and determine employee eligibility for coverage. Siemens Corporation uses a flexible benefit software application that allows employees from all 40 Siemens companies to enroll in and inquire about their benefits plans by using a touchtone telephone.[53] Benefits software applications can reduce the time it takes to process changes in employees' benefit plans. They also allow employers to track current benefit expenses and project future benefits costs.

Benefits software applications can also help companies comply with federal legislation regarding benefits. For example, the Comprehensive Omnibus Budget Reconciliation Act (COBRA) requires companies to offer health benefits to terminated and retired employees. The company must ensure that all eligible former employees and their dependents have been notified of their option of continuing health care benefits; it must also track who accepts and who declines coverage and determine when COBRA coverage has expired.[54] Software is available that automates the record-keeping and reporting requirements necessary to comply with COBRA.

USING COMPENSATION AND BENEFITS APPLICATIONS FOR DECISION MAKING. The software applications mentioned provide graphic depictions of pay ranges and salary lines. They allow managers to quickly see the effects of changes in compensation rates and policies. Compensation and benefit applications can be useful for determining the impact of different percentages of pay increases on total compensation costs. Managers can use job-evaluation data to determine which jobs are over- or underpaid in comparison with other jobs in the company. Hypothetical pay ranges can be constructed based on different compensation strategies. For example, the costs of a "lead the market" strategy can be determined before the company decides on this compensation approach.

Managers can also use compensation information to make adjustments in an individual employee's compensation. For example, managers can determine whether employee performance ratings are related to merit increases and can identify the employee's position within the pay range.

Benefits applications are useful for evaluating the costs of changes in benefits availability and how changes in the characteristics of the employee population (such as age or gender) may affect benefits costs. The implications of different types of early retirement programs on benefits costs can also be considered before a program is offered.

SUMMARY

The roles required of the HR function have changed as people have become recognized as a true source of competitive advantage. This has required a transformation of the HR function from focusing solely on transactional activities to an increasing involvement in strategic activities. In fact, according to a recent study, 64 percent of HR executives said that their HR function is in a process of transformation.[55] It is the strategic management of the HR function that will determine whether HR will transform itself to a true strategic partner or simply be blown up.

In this chapter we have explored the various changing roles of the HR function. HR today must play roles as an administrative expert, employee advocate, change agent, and strategic partner. The function must also deliver transactional, traditional, and transformational services and activities to the firm, and it must be both efficient and effective. HR executives must strategically manage the HR function just as the firm must be strategically managed. This requires that HR develop measures of the function's performance through customer surveys and analytical methods. These measures can form the basis for planning ways to improve performance. HR performance can increase through new structures for the function, through using reengineering and information technology, and through outsourcing.

DISCUSSION QUESTIONS

1. Tom Stewart, in the opening vignette, suggested that HR be blown up. Do you agree? Why or why not? Which parts should be blown up and how?
2. Why have the roles and activities of the HR function changed over the past 20 to 30 years? What has been driving this change? How effectively do you think HR has responded?
3. How can the processes for strategic management discussed in Chapter 2 be transplanted to manage the HR function?
4. Why do you think that few companies take the time to determine the effectiveness of HR practices? Should a company be concerned about evaluating HR practices? Why? What might people working in the HR function gain by evaluating the function?
5. How might imaging technology be useful for recruitment? For training? For benefits administration? For performance management?
6. Employees in your company currently choose and enroll in benefits programs after reading communications brochures, completing enrollment forms, and sending them to their HR rep. A temporary staff has to be hired to process the large amount of paperwork that is generated. Enrollment forms need to be checked, sorted, batched, sent to data entry, keypunched, returned, and filed. The process is slow and prone to errors. How could you use process reengineering to make benefit enrollment more efficient and effective?
7. Some argue that outsourcing an activity is bad because the activity is no longer a means of distinguishing the firm from competitors. (All competitors can buy the same service from the same provider, so it cannot be a source of competitive advantage.) Is this true? If so, why would a firm outsource any activity?

WEB EXERCISE

Hewlett–Packard (HP) is one of the world's largest computer companies and producer of test and measurement instruments. HP is well known for its printers that set the standard for technology, performance, and reliability. HP also manufactures medical electronic equipment, instruments and systems for chemical analysis, hand-held calculators, and electronic components. With 125,000 employees worldwide, HP is headquartered in Palo Alto, California. HP is consistently recognized as one of the best companies to work for. Visit its web site at www.hp.com. Click on "Company Information" and "About HP." Review HP's corporate objectives (click on "Corporate Objectives and the HP Way") and the company's commitment to diversity and work life (click on "Diversity and Work Life").

1. What are HP's corporate objectives?
2. What human resource practices help HP reach its corporate objectives?

MANAGING PEOPLE: FROM THE PAGES OF "BUSINESS WEEK"

BusinessWeek Andersen vs. Andersen: Next Stop, Splitsville: What a Divorce Will Cost Andersen Consulting

George T. Shaheen, CEO of Andersen Consulting, stands behind a podium at the University of Chicago, fielding questions from MBA candidates. Most of the queries come from Andersen Consulting wannabes—students eager to impress the leader of one of the nation's largest, most successful, and highest-paying consulting firms. Then up stands a renegade: a woman, hired by Andersen Consulting out of Princeton University, who left to attend business school. She plans to return to the industry—but not necessarily with Shaheen's firm, in part because of concerns about Andersen Consulting's nasty separation battle from sister company Arthur Andersen & Co. "Wait a minute," Shaheen says, sensing a challenge. "You don't want to come back to AC?" When the woman shakes her head, Shaheen can't resist teasing her with an insult: "No wonder you went to Princeton."

That sort of cocky attitude has helped propel Shaheen and his army of 64,000 to the top of the consulting world. Hired out as experts on projects as diverse as managing purchasing systems for Texas Instruments Inc. and installing finance software for the DuPont Co., they have racked up 20% average annual revenue gains over the past five years. In calendar 1988, revenues exceeded $8 billion.

But now Andersen faces its toughest challenge yet: negotiating an ugly divorce from auditors Arthur Andersen in the coming months. The consultants have clashed with the auditors almost from the moment they became a separate division of Andersen Worldwide in 1989. But the squabbling boiled over 13 months ago, when Shaheen asked an arbitrator to decide how the two sides should proceed—as one bickering unit or two independent firms.

Shaheen wants independence, which could be expensive. The contract with parent Andersen Worldwide calls for exiting partners to pay 1.5 times annual revenue, or as much as $10 billion based on 1997 revenues. So far, Arthur Andersen has not demanded that payment. The consultants, meanwhile, are requesting the return of $500 million they've paid the auditing firm since 1994. They're arguing that Arthur Andersen broke the contract when it began its own consulting business. But Shaheen is running a risk: If Andersen Consulting is forced to pay anywhere close to $10 billion for its freedom, it would sap capital just as his firm is making a push into a hot new growth area: outsourcing the job of operating a corporation's computer systems and technology networks.

Like so many failed marriages, this one fell apart over money. The power of the Andersen name—an asset the consultants may be forced to give up in the split—opened doors for the consultants early on. But as the consulting practice exploded, the Andersen Consulting partners chafed at the stratospheric yearly payments they, as the more profitable division, had to pay to balance the firm's income and expenses. For 1998, they are scheduled to kick in some $200 million. Andersen Consulting expects the arbitration to be resolved by the end of the year, though it could drag out longer since Arthur Andersen has contested the arbitrator's jurisdiction.

Meanwhile, both sides are proceeding as if they were already on their own. "We have to be ready," says Arthur Andersen's worldwide managing partner, Jim Wadia. For his firm, that means expanding new businesses, including information-technology consulting. Though Arthur Andersen generally targets smaller clients than Andersen Consulting, this is already causing problems for the consulting firm. "We're experiencing more and more marketplace confusion and competition, which is frustrating and detrimental to our future," says Shaheen.

The confusion comes just as Andersen Consulting is moving into new areas of business and placing its biggest bet yet on its new outsourcing practice. DuPont was one of the first big clients to sign an outsourcing contract with the firm. Andersen employs about 400 people that manage DuPont's order-processing and finance systems under a 10-year contract. When the partnership dispute erupted, DuPont Chief Information Officer Robert R. Ridout worried that it would distract Andersen Consulting's employees and drain its finances. "Had we, in essence, picked a partner that could look at the long term, or could they only focus on the short term?" he recalls thinking. It took face-to-face meetings with Shaheen to calm Ridout's concerns. Still, DuPont has a clause in its contract to provide the option of pulling out of the deal.

Outsourcing is brutally competitive—especially in the area of electronic services. Unlike Andersen, computer-servicing giants Electronic Data Systems (EDS) and IBM can actually buy and install very expensive hardware. And hordes of entrepreneurial outfits can offer narrowly targeted expertise. But Andersen Consulting's strength is its combination of technology know-how and international reach—it has offices in 46 countries—plus a deep pool of talent. Sprint PCS, the Kansas City (Mo.) cellular-telephone carrier, uses about 150 Andersen consultants to run its internal help desk and other back-office departments. "They can really bring on the armies," says Sherry L. Browne, chief information officer for Sprint Corp. But it's expensive. Sprint pays up to 40% more for Andersen consultants than it would for technical workers hired off the street. So management plans to take back the business as soon as the expertise can be transferred in-house.

Outsourcing contracts now generate $1 billion a year for Andersen Consulting, or more than 10% of revenues. Shaheen hopes to increase that to 40% within five years. Although profit margins on outsourcing projects run about 15%, half the level made on traditional consulting jobs, it's a fast-growing area.

Shaheen, 54, is no stranger to risk. He pushed Andersen Consulting to its quasi-independent role under the Andersen Worldwide umbrella 10 years ago and followed in 1992 with a shift beyond the firm's traditional expertise in technology systems into business strategy and work force issues. In late 1996, he reorganized the firm around worldwide industry groups such as financial services and communications, rather than geographical regions. Now, he's leading an E-commerce initiative. "It's the same thing Bill Gates did," he says of his switch. "The Internet will drive change that is fundamental to the way we do business."

Andersen sees a broader system of commerce shaping up in Internet-based telecommunications networks. More and more businesses—from car dealers to health maintenance organizations—will provide services and information over the Net. "So you need a whole modification of business processes," says Shaheen. "Many will be designed and built by businesses like ours."

Shaheen has clearly staked a lot on his firm's technology consulting practice. But as Andersen expands that franchise it will have to wrestle with some fundamental limitations. Rivals such as EDS and IBM are, respectively, about 3 times and 10 times as big as Andersen Consulting. And unlike Andersen, they have the capital to supply hardware as well as advice. One obvious answer would be an initial public offering, but Shaheen says that is not in the cards. He disdains the notion of being accountable to shareholders and is confident Andersen won't need the capital.

Being a partnership also limits Andersen's ability to attract talent. It can't offer stock options to employees below partner—a prized asset for tech workers. Andersen consultants don't have ownership until they become partners, a cutthroat 12- to 15-year haul most young hires are unwilling to undertake. At other firms, associates are given authority earlier. "The market has changed, and they haven't figured that out yet," says an analyst who left for a job at a small public firm that included stock options. "The world is our oyster."

To address consultant concerns, Andersen has launched programs to reduce travel time and improve communication with partners, but the battle with Arthur Andersen also has taken a toll. Andersen Consulting's churn rate—the percentage of employees leaving each year—has edged up from 16% in 1996 to nearly 18% in 1998. The acrimony helped persuade one four-year consultant to jump ship to Arthur Andersen only weeks ago. "There's a whole lot of turmoil inside," the executive said, arguing that the auditing firm had remained better focused. "[Andersen Consulting] took their eye off the people side." What the firm needs now is a good divorce settlement—and to move on.

QUESTIONS

1. What are the issues that exist between Andersen Consulting and Arthur Andersen? If you were the head of HR for the larger organization, how might you try to manage these issues without breaking the firm up into two separate firms?
2. In what ways are the competitive environments different for an auditing/accounting firm versus a consulting firm? What are the implications of these with regard to people?
3. Assume you are the head of HR at Andersen Consulting. What are the implications of this split for the role your HR function plays in organizational effectiveness?
4. What changes will you need to make in your HR function to contribute in these new roles?

SOURCE: Roger O. Crockett, "Andersen vs. Andersen: Next Stop, Splitsville," *Business Week*, January 18, 1999.

NOTES

1. D. Ulrich, *Human Resource Champions* (Boston: Harvard Business School Press, 1998).
2. Ibid.
3. K. Carrig, "Reshaping Human Resources for the Next Century: Lessons from a High-Flying Airline," *Human Resource Management* 36, no. 2 (1997), pp. 277–89.
4. Ulrich, *Human Resource Champions*.
5. Carrig, "Reshaping."
6. Ulrich, *Human Resource Champions*.
7. Carrig, "Reshaping."
8. Ulrich, *Human Resource Champions*.
9. Carrig, "Reshaping."
10. A.S. Tsui and L.R. Gomez-Mejia, "Evaluating HR Effectiveness," in *Human Resource Management: Evolving Roles and Responsibilities*, ed. L. Dyer (Washington, DC: Bureau of National Affairs, 1988), pp. 1-187–1-227.
11. D. Ulrich, "Measuring Human Resources: An Overview of Practice and a Prescription for Results," *Human Resource Management* 36, no. 3 (1997), pp. 303–20.
12. P. Wright, G. McMahan, S. Snell, and B. Gerhart, "Comparing Line and HR Executives' Perceptions of HR Effectiveness: Services, Roles, and Contributions," CAHRS (Center for Advanced Human Resource Studies) working paper 98–29, School of ILR, Cornell Uni-

versity, Ithaca, NY.
13. J.C. Erfurt, A. Foote, and M.A. Heirich, "The Cost-Effectiveness of Worksite Wellness Programs," *Personnel Psychology* 15 (1992), p. 22.
14. P. Wright, G. McMahan, S. Snell, and B. Gerhart, *Strategic HRM: Building Human Capital and Organizational Capability*, Technical report. Cornell University, Ithaca, NY, 1998.
15. T.B. Kinni, "A Reengineering Primer," *Quality Digest* (January 1994), pp. 26–30; "Reengineering Is Helping Health of Hospitals and Its Patients," *Total Quality Newsletter* (February 1994), p. 5; R. Recardo, "Process Reengineering in a Finance Division," *Journal for Quality and Participation* (June 1994), pp. 70–73.
16. L. Quillen, "Human Resource Computerization: A Dollar and Cents Approach," *Personnel Journal* (July 1989), pp. 74–77.
17. S. Greengard, "New Technology Is HR's Route to Reengineering," *Personnel Journal* (July 1994), pp. 32c–32o.
18. R. Broderick and J.W. Boudreau, "Human Resource Management, Information Technology, and the Competitive Edge," *Academy of Management Executive* 6 (1992), pp. 7–17.
19. S.E. O'Connell, "New Technologies Bring New Tools, New Rules," *HR Magazine* (December 1995), pp. 43–48; S.F. O'Connell, "The Virtual Workplace Moves at Warp Speed," *HR Magazine* (March 1996), pp. 51–57.
20. E. Brynjolfsson and L. Hitt, "The Productivity Paradox of Information Technology," *Communications of the ACM* (December 1993), pp. 66–77.
21. "Seven Critical Success Factors for Using Information Technology," *Total Quality Newsletter* (February 1994), p. 6.
22. J.E. Rigdon, "Technological Gains Are Cutting Costs in Jobs and Services," *The Wall Street Journal*, February 24, 1995, pp. A1, A5, A6.
23. S. Greengard, "How Technology Is Advancing HR," *Personnel Journal* (September 1993), pp. 80–90.
24. S. Greengard, "Catch the Wave as HR Goes Online," *Personnel Journal* (July 1995), pp. 54–68; M.I. Finney, "It's All in the Knowing How," *HR Magazine* (July 1995), pp. 36–43; "A Survey of the Internet," *The Economist* (special section), July 1, 1995, pp. 3–18; A. Doran, "The Internet: The New Tool for the HR Professional," *The Review* (August-September 1995), pp. 32–35; A.L. Sprout, "The Internet Inside Your Company," *Fortune*, November 27, 1995, pp. 161–68.
25. J. Sandberg, "On-Line Population Reaches 24 Million in North America," *The Wall Street Journal*, October 30, 1995, p. B2.
26. S. Greengard, "Home, Home on the Web," *Personnel Journal* (March 1996), pp. 26–33.
27. S. Greengard, "Catch the Wave."
28. T.L. Hunter, "How Client/Server Is Reshaping the HRIS," *Personnel Journal* (July 1992), pp. 38–46; B. Busbin, "The Hidden Costs of Client/Server," *The Review* (August-September 1995), pp. 21–24.
29. D. Drechsel, "Principles for Client/Server Success," *The Review* (August-September 1995), pp. 26–29.
30. A.L. Lederer, "Emerging Technology and the Buy–Wait Dilemma: Sorting Fact from Fantasy," *The Review* (June-July 1993), pp. 16–19.
31. D.L. Fowler, "Imaging in HR: A Case Study," *The Review* (October-November 1994), pp. 29–33.
32. S. Greengard, "How Technology Is Advancing HR."
33. "Dial a Job Interview," *Chain Store Age Executive* (July 1994), pp. 35–36.
34. P.A. Galagan, "Think Performance: A Conversation with Gloria Gery," *Training and Development* (March 1994), pp. 47–51.
35. J. Clark and R. Koonce, "Meetings Go High-Tech," *Training and Development* (November 1995), pp. 32–38; A.M. Townsend, M.E. Whitman, and A.R. Hendrickson, "Computer Support Adds Power to Group Processes," *HR Magazine* (September 1995), pp. 87–91.
36. T.A. Stewart, "Getting Real about Brainpower," *Fortune*, November 27, 1994, pp. 201–3.
37. B. Ziegler, "Internet Software Poses Big Threat to Notes, IBM's Stake in Lotus," *The Wall Street Journal*, November 7, 1995, pp. A1, A8.
38. R.B. Frantzreb, ed., *The 1993 P5 Personnel Software Census* (Roseville, CA: Advanced Personnel Systems, 1993).
39. P. Anthony, "Track Applicants, Track Costs," *Personnel Journal* (April 1990), pp. 75–81; L. Stevens, "Resume Scanning Simplifies Tracking," *Personnel Journal* (April 1993), pp. 77–79.
40. V.R. Ceriello and C. Freeman, *Human Resource Management Systems* (Lexington, MA: Lexington Books, 1991).
41. J. Cohan, "Nike Uses *Resumix* to Stay Ahead in the Recruitment Game," *Personnel Journal* (November 1992), p. 9 (supplement).
42. S.E. Forrer and Z.B. Leibowitz, *Using Computers in Human Resources* (San Francisco: Jossey–Bass, 1991); Ceriello and Freeman, *Human Resource Management Systems*.
43. M.J. Kavanaugh, H.G. Guental, and S.I. Tannenbaum, *Human Resource Information Systems* (Boston: PWS–Kent, 1990).
44. Cyborg Systems Inc., advertising brochure titled "The Solution Series," 1992.
45. G. Bylinsky, "How Companies Spy on Employees," *Fortune*, November 4, 1991, pp. 131–40.
46. Forrer and Leibowitz, *Using Computers in Human Resources*.
47. Ibid.
48. L. Granick, A.Y. Dessaint, and G.R. VandenBos, "How

Information Systems Can Help Build Professional Competence," in *Maintaining Professional Competence*, ed. S.L. Willis and S.S. Dubin (San Francisco: Jossey–Bass, 1990), pp. 278–305.

49. Personal communication, Susan Runkel, *Career Resources*, April 18, 1992.
50. F.H. Wagner, "The Nuts and Bolts of Computer-Assisted Job Evaluation," *The Review* (October-November 1991), pp. 16–22.
51. M. Coleman-Carlone, "HBO's Program for Merit Pay," *Personnel Journal* (May 1990), pp. 86–90.
52. Ceriello and Freeman, *Human Resource Management Systems*.
53. H. Glatzer, "Top Secret—Maybe," *Human Resource Executive* 7 (1993), pp. 26–29.
54. Kavanaugh et al., *Human Resource Information Systems*.
55. S. Csoka and B. Hackett, *Transforming the HR Function for Global Business Success*, Report 1209-19RR, New York: The Conference Board, 1998.

Saturn Corporation and the UAW: A Test of Labor's Partnership with Management

A BRIEF HISTORY OF SATURN'S DEVELOPMENT

Like the other members of the Big Three in the U.S. auto industry, since the late 1970s, General Motors had been losing ground steadily to high-quality small Japanese imports. Although the U.S. auto industry had been working to improve product quality and design, the companies

found it virtually impossible to gain market share on the Japanese, who maintained a rapid pace of design and quality improvements.

By 1984, Roger Smith, the chairman of GM, was well into a search for an innovative strategic move. A team of 99 GM managers and UAW officials, chosen from across the United States, was given the mission to study GM divisions and other top-performing, internationally successful corporations to create a new type of organization—one that would build a successful small car. The goal was to produce a vehicle better than Honda's Accord or Toyota's Camry.

The "Group of 99" was insistent that Saturn Corporation be formed as a separate subsidiary so that it would have the freedom not only to create a culture of its own but also to break any and all rules that constrained its parent company. To help GM's finances substantially, Saturn had to slash costs, boost quality, and improve the relationships that traditionally existed among workers, their union, and management. Although 1985 marked the formal start-up of Saturn, production did not begin until 1990. In the interim, a joint committee of managers and union officials shared equal responsibility for site selection, organizational design, product decisions, and hiring. As part of this process, a "living" agreement (one with no expiration date that is intended to be modified when needed) was bargained by the union and management. Among other things, it reduced work classifications (therefore increasing the flexibility to deploy workers) and guaranteed job security. Saturn would have one classification for production workers and five for skilled trades. Additionally, everyone would be put on salary, part of which eventually would be determined by productivity and quality level.

By early 1988, as the production and assembly plants were being constructed in Spring Hill, Tennessee, Saturn representatives began visiting GM plants and UAW local halls searching for workers. Under the partnership agreement, all Saturn employees were to be selected from current UAW members drawn from 136 different locations in 34 states. The Saturn recruiters told current and laid-off workers that were interested to be prepared to shed old habits and to work as a team. All blue-collar and white-collar applicants had to be approved by a Saturn panel drawn from both union members and management.

For most Saturn managers, the joint recruitment and selection process was the first time UAW local leadership had real input into a "management" process. It was a new experience for most workers, too. Eric Smith came to Saturn from the Oldsmobile plant in Lansing, Michigan. "I like the idea of working with my brain, not just my hands," said the line worker. For Delbert Arkin, Saturn offered a way of escaping restrictive work rules that prevented him from making simple repairs to the machine he ran 40 to 60 hours a week. The decision to go to Saturn was not always easy, however, because employees gave up their former plant seniority when they transferred to the Spring Hill plant.

SATURN'S PERFORMANCE

In June 1990, with start-up costs of roughly \$3.5 billion, full production of the Saturn automobile began. Early reports were that customers were delighted with their new cars; however, some quality problems arose, including a worse than average defect rate. Additionally, two recalls occurred. As Saturn moved into a new model year, improvements were made to correct problems, and quality improved markedly. However, from the start, production seriously lagged behind expectation.

In the 1991 model year, Saturn built just 50,000 cars, one-third the original projection and well below capacity of 240,000. However, in the same year, Saturn sold, on the average, more cars per dealer than any other manufacturer, including Honda, which had been the leader for two years. The 1992 results were similar. A 1992 J.D. Power survey showed that Saturn owners recommended their car to people more often than owners of any other car. Even when productivity hit 90 percent of capacity at the end of that year, the low level of production kept Saturn from breaking even, and the pressure for improved production affected the labor relations in Saturn facilities.

In 1993, Saturn's results reached a new height when total monthly sales for February surpassed those of the Honda Accord. By the spring of 1995, when the 1 millionth Saturn rolled off the Spring Hill assembly line, GM had yet to recoup their original investment, now more than $5 billion. The factory produced 305,000 vehicles that year; its 333 U.S. Saturn dealers maintained a low inventory—only a 42 day supply—as the company looked for ways to increase capacity. Two years earlier, the company hired 1,000 new employees for a third shift, hoping to boost production and eliminate some of the stress for the work force. But the move had not improved production figures sufficiently. Also in 1993, Saturn executives failed to get a second plant built to boost capacity to 500,000 vehicles a year. Without an additional plant, Saturn could not generate its own production capital and would continue losing money. Without investment for a redesign, Saturn would not be able to maintain its momentum—especially in the face of competition, such as Chrysler's Neon. But other GM divisions with greater profit potential demanded the company's investment.

THE LABOR–MANAGEMENT RELATIONSHIP

Obviously, from its inception, Saturn has been designed and run as a radical experiment. The company is managed under a unique union–management partnership agreement which gives workers a voice in all planning and operating decisions. The President of UAW Local 1853 participates in all decisions, including pricing, capital expenditures, and dealer operations. "It's as different as it could be," says R. Timothy Epps, vice-president of people systems at Saturn, as he compares the Saturn experience to his years in other organizations. "We're committed to an entirely different set of beliefs. One is to have UAW involvement in all aspects of the business. The other crucial principle is that we believe that those people affected by a decision should be involved in the decision."

Cooperation between organized labor and management is not a new concept, but few firms have pushed it as far as Saturn has. At each managerial level—from the president to team line managers—and within all staff functions, a UAW counterpart shares decision making equally with Saturn managers. The top decision-making group, the Strategic Action Committee (SAC), does long-range planning and makes the policy and product decisions. This committee includes the president of Saturn, his union counterpart, several vice-presidents, and a representative of the international office of the UAW.

At the shop floor level, labor-management relations differ substantially from those found in a traditional auto plant. Because Saturn uses a semiautonomous work team approach, there are no supervisors, and each team has a jointly appointed work team counselor. Above this level, people called *work-unit module advisers* serve as troubleshooters for the teams within each business unit. Although the union continues to play a strong role, it is a decision-making role, not just a reactive, adversarial role activated only when conflict occurs.

The history of Saturn and the partnership agreement only sound utopian, however. As both management and union officials readily admit, they have found it difficult to eliminate the familiar confrontational approach in favor of a spirit of constructive cooperation. It took a long time for the union to develop the trust in management that was necessary to continue to make the system work. Early on, both parties tested the other to see how power sharing would really work.

CURRENT STATE OF AFFAIRS AT SATURN

GM has changed its definition of what Saturn stands for, and the company's unique character has become "General Motorized." In an effort to make money on Saturn and capitalize on its marketing triumphs, GM recently placed Saturn under its corporate organizational umbrella. It began considering bigger Saturns designed by the global GM machine (including a clone of GM's Opel Vectra made in Germany). The cars would be built in GM's Wilmington, Delaware plant beginning around the year 2000 and use more GM parts than in the past. In addition, GM decided that Saturn will market the corporation's electric vehicles and will serve as GM's flag bearer for a planned assault on the Japanese market.

In 1998, the unique labor agreement expired. As contract talks progressed, the union overwhelmingly voted to give union representatives authorization to strike if they failed to reach an agreement with General Motors. The union was unhappy with a number of issues. First, the union was upset with the outsourcing of parts to nonunion suppliers. Second, the union was unhappy with bonus cuts despite maintaining productivity and exceeding quality levels. Third, the union believed that GM had cut them out of important decisions such as the plan to build new vehicles at the Delaware plant—vehicles that could be produced at Saturn. After months of talks, the two sides reached an agreement that satisfied the union's concerns about job security, input on management decisions, and pay.

At the same time the unique labor agreement was being renegotiated, Saturn CEO Skip LaFauve's responsibilities were changed as he was appointed to head GM's small-car group. This was an important development because LaFauve's leadership was critical for maintaining the integrity of labor agreement. Conflict is part of labor and management relations. But under LaFauve's leadership conflict was managed through finding better solutions or options rather than in an adversarial manner.

Saturn continues to struggle to reach profitability. A slump in the demand for small cars cut yearly output at the plant to 240,000 from a possible 315,000 cars. Demand for 1999 models is off five percent compared to 1998 levels.

Because of the need to improve profits and reduce production costs, GM is threatening to replace the innovative labor agreement with a standard GM contract. For example, Saturn's contract provisions dealing guaranteed job security for most of the labor force and pay-based on performance are being reconsidered. Also, GM directors approval to build a sports-utility vehicle (SUV) at Saturn is contingent on the union agreeing to work rule changes and job cuts designed to improve profits. For example, GM wants the union to reduce the number of labor hours it takes to build the SUV to 17 hours of labor (down from the 22 hours it now takes to build a car). As a result of the reduced demand for small cars, Saturn is faced with the need to reduce as many as 1000 jobs from Saturn's 7000-employee labor force. A significant signal that the cooperative labor-management agreement has eroded is that Mike Bennett and almost the entire local UAW leadership were voted out after 13 years they were replaced with union leaders who favor less close ties with management.

Saturn is at a critical point. Whether the UAW and Saturn can continue to work together in the spirit that first united them is seriously challenged. New Saturn president Cynthia Trudell vows, "There will be change. If we are to stay in business we have to be more fully productive." Saturn worker Rick Arnett remains uncertain about the future: "I don't think things will get better. I think they gradually will get worse. . . . I don't think management trusts us. They still think we are trying to get away with something." New UAW Local 1853 president Ron Hankins will lead delicate talks over work rule changes and possible job changes needed to cut costs and secure the new SUV for Saturn.

DISCUSSION QUESTIONS

1. Describe the elements of the human resource and labor relations system at Saturn Corporation that provide a competitive advantage. (The basic principles of the Saturn-UAW agreement can be found at www.erols.com/core/company/philosophy.html).
2. What is the role of a union in an organization such as Saturn Corporation? If in fact decision making is truly shared, is a union needed?
3. What arguments exist against an arrangement such as Saturn's partnership? Is such a system in the best interests of the employees? List arguments for and against a shared partnership arrangement.
4. What skills would managers and union leaders need to develop to successfully make such a cooperative, shared system work? Would these skills be needed on the shop floor, too?
5. What effect will bringing Saturn inside the GM corporate organization have on labor–management relations within Saturn? Within GM?
6. Do you think Saturn Corporation will survive? Explain your answer.

SOURCES: Cabriella Stern and Rebecca Blumenstein, "GM Is Expected to Back Proposal for Midsize Version of Saturn Car," *The Wall Street Journal*, May 24, 1996, B4; "GM Saturn Unit Trumpets Profit Turned in 1993," *The Wall Street Journal*, January 5, 1993; "Saturn Experiment Is Deemed Successful Enough to Expand," *The Wall Street Journal*, April 18, 1995, B1–B2; "Saturn's Mystique Is Endangered as GM Changes the Car and the Organization," *The Wall Street Journal*, July 27, 1995, B1; L. Armstrong, "Here Comes GM's Saturn," *Business Week*, April 9, 1990, 56–62; B. Geber, "Saturn's Grand Experiment," *Training*, June 1992, 27–35; C.M. Solomon, "Behind the Wheel at Saturn," *Personnel Journal*, June 1991, 72–74; N. Templin, "Union Election at GM's Saturn to Test Labor's Partnership with Management," *The Wall Street Journal*, March 24, 1993; A4; O. Suris, "Recall by Saturn Could Tarnish Its Reputation," *The Wall Street Journal*, August 11, 1993, A3, A7, K. Miller, "Saturn and Union Agree to Keep Unique Contract," September 5, 1998 www.detnews.com, D. Phillips, "Saturn Needs Union to Help Cut Costs," February 26, 1999, www.detnews.com. For more information about Saturn Corporation, including new cars and the company's history and recent news, visit World Wide Web sites at http://www.saturn.com and http://www.erols.com/core/whats.new.html.

Glossary

Acceptability The extent to which a performance measure is deemed to be satisfactory or adequate by those who use it.

Action plan A written document that includes the steps that the trainee and manager will take to ensure that training transfers to the job.

Action steps The part of a written affirmative plan that specifies what an employer plans to do to reduce underutilization of protected groups.

Adventure learning Learning focused on the development of teamwork and leadership skills using structured outdoor activities.

Affective outcomes Outcomes such as attitudes and motivation.

Agency shop A union security provision that requires an employee to pay union membership dues but not to join the union.

Agent In agency theory, a manager, or one who acts on behalf of an owner (principal); in human resources management, may refer to an employee.

Alternative dispute resolution (ADR) A method of resolving disputes that does not rely on the legal system. Often proceeds through the four stages of open door policy, peer review, mediation, and arbitration.

Americans with Disabilities Act (ADA) A 1990 act prohibiting individuals with disabilities from being discriminated against in the workplace.

Analytic approach Type of assessment of HR effectiveness that involves determining the impact of, or the financial costs and benefits of, a program or practice.

Anticipatory socialization Socialization that occurs before an individual joins a company. Includes expectations about the company, job, working conditions, and interpersonal relationships.

Appraisal politics A situation in which evaluators purposefully distort a rating to achieve personal or company goals.

Apprenticeship A work-study training method with both on-the-job and classroom training.

Arbitration A procedure for resolving collective-bargaining impasses by which an arbitrator chooses a solution to the dispute.

Assessment Collecting information and providing feedback to employees about their behavior, communication style, or skills.

Assessment center A process in which multiple raters evaluate employees' performance on a number of exercises.

Associate union membership A form of union membership by which the union receives dues in exchange for services (e.g., health insurance, credit cards) but does not provide representation in collective bargaining.

Attitude awareness and change program Program focusing on increasing employees' awareness of differences in cultural and ethnic backgrounds, physical characteristics, and personal characteristics that influence behavior toward others.

Attitudinal structuring The aspect of the labor–management negotiation process that refers to the relationship and level of trust between the negotiators.

Audiovisual instruction Overheads, slides, and video.

Audit approach Type of assessment of HR effectiveness that involves review of customer satisfaction or key indicators (e.g., turnover rate, average days to fill a position) related to an HR functional area (e.g., recruiting, training).

Balanced scorecard A means of performance measurement that gives managers a chance to look at their company from the perspectives of internal and external customers, employees, and shareholders.

Basic skills Reading, writing, and communication skills needed to understand the content of a training program.

Behavior-based program A program focusing on changing the organizational policies and individual behaviors that inhibit employees' personal growth and productivity.

Benchmarks© An instrument designed to measure the factors that are important to success.

Benefits In reference to training evaluation, refers to what of value the company gains from a training program.

Bona fide occupational qualification (BFOQ) A job qualification based on race, sex, religion, and so on that an employer asserts is a necessary qualification for the job.

Career The pattern of work-related experiences that span the course of a person's life.

Career management system A system to retain and motivate employees by identifying and meeting their development needs (also called *development planning systems*).

Career support Coaching, protection, sponsorship, and providing challenging assignments, exposure, and visibility.

CD-ROM Technology that uses a laser to read text, graphics, audio, and video from an aluminum disc.

Centralization Degree to which decision-making authority resides at the top of the organizational chart.

Checkoff A union contract provision that requires an employer to deduct union dues from employees' paychecks.

Client-server architecture Computer design that provides a method to consolidate data and applications into a single host system (the client).

Climate for transfer Trainees' perceptions of characteristics of the work environment (social support and situational constraints) that can either facilitate or inhibit use of trained skills or behavior.

Closed shop A union security provision requiring a person to be a union member before being hired.

Coach A peer or manager who works with an employee to motivate her, help her develop skills, and provide reinforcement and feedback.

Cognitive ability Includes three dimensions: verbal comprehension, quantitative ability, and reasoning ability.

Cognitive outcomes Outcomes used to determine the degree to which trainees are familiar with principles, facts, techniques, procedures, or processes emphasized in a training program.

Community of practice A group of employees who work together, learn from each other, and develop a common understanding of how to get work accomplished.

Compa-ratio An index of the correspondence between actual and intended pay.

Compensable factors The characteristics of jobs that an organization values and chooses to pay for.

Competitive advantage A company's ability to make products or offer services that are valued by customers more than those of competing firms.

Competitiveness A company's ability to maintain and gain market share in its industry.

Compliance officer Specially trained agent of the U.S. Department of Labor responsible for ensuring that employers meet OSHA requirements.

Concentration strategy A strategy focusing on increasing market share, reducing costs, or creating and maintaining a market niche for products and services.

Concurrent validation A criterion-related validity study in which a test is administered to all the people currently in a job and then incumbents' scores are correlated with existing measures of their performance on the job.

Consequences The incentives that employees receive for performing well.

Consolidated Omnibus Budget Reconciliation Act (COBRA) The 1985 act that requires employers to permit employees to extend their health insurance coverage at group rates for up to 36 months following a qualifying event, such as layoff.

Content validation A test-validation strategy performed by demonstrating that the items, questions, or problems posed by a test are a representative sample of the kinds of situations or problems that occur on the job.

Contingent work force Temporary, part-time, and self-employed workers who are not considered full-time employees.

Continuous learning The requirement that employees understand the relationships among their jobs, their work units, and the company and that they acquire skills and knowledge needed for self-improvement and for improving the company's products and services.

Coordination training Training a team in how to share information and decision-making responsibilities to maximize team performance.

Copyright A legal protection of the expression of an idea (e.g., a training manual for a software program) but not the ideas that the material contains (e.g., the use of help windows in the program).

Corporate campaigns Union activities designed to exert public, financial, or political pressure on employers during the union-organizing process.

Correlation coefficient A statistic that measures the degree to which two sets of numbers are related to each other.

Cost-benefit analysis The process of determining the economic benefits of a training program using accounting methods.

Criterion-related validity A method of establishing the validity of a personnel selection method by showing a substantial correlation between test scores and job-performance scores.

Cross-cultural preparation The process of educating employees (and their families) who are given an assignment in a foreign country.

Cross-training Training in which team members understand and practice each other's skills so that members are prepared to step in and take another member's place should he or she temporarily or permanently leave the team.

Data flow diagram A diagram showing the flow of data among departments.

Database The set of topics on which a human resource information system collects and maintains information.

Decentralization Degree to which decision-making authority is distributed throughout the lower levels of the organizational chart.

Decision support systems Problem-solving systems that usually include a "what-if" feature that allows users to see how outcomes change when assumptions or data change.

Delayering Reducing the number of job levels within an organization.

Development The acquisition of knowledge, skills, and behaviors that improve an employee's ability to meet changes in job requirements and in client and customer demands.

Development planning system A system to retain and motivate employees by identifying and meeting their development needs (also called *career management system*).

Direct applicants People who apply for a job vacancy without prompting from the organization.

Direct costs Training costs including salaries and benefits for all employees involved in training; program material and supplies, equipment or classroom rentals or purchases; and travel costs.

Disinvestment strategy An emphasis on liquidation and divestiture of businesses.

Disparate impact A theory of discrimination based on facially neutral employment practices that disproportionately exclude a protected group from employment opportunities.

Disparate treatment A theory of discrimination based on different treatment given to individuals because of their race, color, religion, sex, national origin, age, or disability status.

Distributed work Work done outside of the traditional work environment, including at home, while traveling, and anywhere an employee can interact with managers, peers, customers, products, or processes using technology.

Distributive bargaining The part of the labor–management negotiation process that focuses on dividing a fixed economic "pie."

Diversity training Training designed to change employee attitudes about diversity and/or develop skills needed to work with a diverse work force.

Downsizing The planned elimination of large numbers of personnel designed to enhance organizational effectiveness.

Downward move A job change involving a reduction in an employee's level of responsibility and authority.

Due process Policies by which a company formally lays out the steps an employee can take to appeal a termination decision.

Duty of fair representation The National Labor Relations Act requirement that all bargaining-unit members have equal access to and representation by the union in contract negotiation and administration (e.g., grievance procedures).

Efficiency wage theory A theory according to which a paid wage influences the productivity of a worker.

Electronic performance support system (EPSS) Computer applications that can provide, as requested, skills training, information access, and expert advice.

Employee assistance programs (EAPs) Employer programs that attempt to ameliorate problems encountered by workers who are drug dependent, alcoholic, or psychologically troubled.

Employee Retirement Income Security Act (ERISA) The 1974 act that increased the fiduciary responsibilities of pension plan trustees, established vesting rights and portability provisions, and established the Pension Benefit Guaranty Corporation (PBGC).

Employee stock ownership plan (ESOP) An employee ownership plan that provides employers certain tax and financial advantages when stock is granted to employees.

Employee survey research A process of monitoring employees job satisfaction and organizational and other important job attitudes using questionnaires, interviews, or focus groups.

Employee wellness programs (EWPs) Preventive programs that attempt to promote good health among employees who are not necessarily having current health problems.

Employment-at-will doctrine The doctrine that, in the absence of a specific contract, either an employer or employee could sever an employment relationship at any time.

Encounter phase The phase when an employee begins a new job.

Equal employment opportunity (EEO) The government's attempt to ensure that all individuals have an equal opportunity for employment, regardless of race, color, religion, sex, or national origin.

Ergonomics The interface between individuals' physiological characteristics and the physical work environment.

Euro A single currency initially including 11 European Union nations.

Exempt Employees who are not covered by the Fair Labor Standards Act. Exempt employees are not eligible for overtime pay.

Expatriate Employee sent by his or her company in one country to manage operations in a different country.

Expectancy theory The theory that says that the attractiveness of any job is a function of valence, instrumentality, and expectancy.

Experience rating A rating that determines the size of an employer's unemployment and workers' compensation taxes, based on that employer's history of laying off employees and its injury rates.

Expert systems Computer systems incorporating the decision rules of people recognized as experts in a certain area.

External analysis Examining the organization's operating environment to identify strategic opportunities and threats.

External growth strategy An emphasis on acquiring vendors and suppliers or buying businesses that allow a company to expand into new markets.

External labor market Persons outside the firm who are actively seeking employment.

Fact finder A person who reports on the reasons for a labor–management dispute, the views and arguments of both sides, and a nonbinding recommendation for settling the dispute.

Fair Labor Standards Act (FLSA) The 1938 law that established the minimum wage and overtime pay.

Family and Medical Leave Act The 1993 act that requires employers with 50 or more employees to provide up to 12 weeks of unpaid leave after childbirth or adoption; to care for a seriously ill child, spouse, or parent; or for an employee's own serious illness.

Feedback Information that employees receive while they are performing concerning how well they are meeting objectives.

Financial Accounting Statement (FAS) 106 The rule issued by the Financial Accounting Standards Board in 1993 requiring companies to fund benefits provided after retirement on an accrual rather than a pay-as-you-go basis and to enter these future cost obligations on their financial statements.

Forecasting The attempts to determine the supply of and demand for various types of human resources to predict areas within the organization where there will be future labor shortages or surpluses.

Formal education programs Employee development programs, including short courses offered by consultants or universities, executive M.B.A. programs, and university programs.

Four-fifths rule A rule that states that an employment test has disparate impact if the hiring rate for a minority group is less than four-fifths, or 80 percent, of the hiring rate for the majority group.

Frame of reference A standard point that serves as a comparison for other points and thus provides meaning.

Gainsharing A form of group compensation based on group or plant performance (rather than organizationwide profits) that does not become part of the employee's base salary.

General duty clause The provision of the Occupational Health and Safety Act that states that an employer has an overall obligation to furnish employees with a place of employment free from recognized hazards.

Generalizability The degree to which the validity of a selection method established in one context extends to other contexts.

Glass ceiling A barrier to advancement to higher-level jobs in the company that adversely affects women and minorities. The barrier may be due to lack of access to training programs, development experiences, or relationships (e.g., mentoring).

Goals What an organization hopes to achieve in the medium to long-term future.

Goals and timetables The part of a written affirmative action plan that specifies the percentage of women and minorities that an employer seeks to have in each job group and the date by which that percentage is to be attained.

Group-building methods Training methods that help trainees share ideas and experiences, build group identity, understand the dynamics of interpersonal relationships, and get to know their own strengths and weaknesses and those of their coworkers.

Group mentoring program A program pairing a successful senior employee with a group of four to six less-experienced protégés.

Groupware Software application that enables multiple users to track, share, and organize information and to work on the same database or document simultaneously.

Hands-on methods Training methods that require the trainee to be actively involved in learning.

Health maintenance organization (HMO) A health-care plan that provides benefits on a prepaid basis for employees who are required to use only HMO medical service providers.

High-leverage training Training practice that links training to strategic business goals, has top management support, relies on an instructional design model, and is benchmarked to programs in other organizations.

High-performance work systems Work systems that maximize the fit between the company's social system and technology.

Host country The country in which the parent-country organization seeks to locate or has already located a facility.

Host-country nationals (HCNs) Employees born and raised in a host country.

Human resource information system (HRIS) A system to acquire, store, manipulate, analyze, retrieve, and distribute information related to a company's human resources.

Human resource management The policies, practices, and systems that influence employees' behavior, attitudes, and performances.

Hyperlinks Links that allow a Web user to easily move from one Web page to another.

Imaging A process for scanning documents, storing them electronically, and retrieving them.

In-basket A simulation of the administrative tasks of a manager's job.

Indirect costs Costs not directly related to the design, development, or delivery of the training program.

Individualism/collectivism One of Hofstede's cultural dimensions; describes the strength of the relation between an individual and other individuals in a society.

Input Instructions that tell employees what, how, and when to perform; also the support they are given to help them perform.

Instructional design process A systematic approach for developing training programs.

Integrative bargaining The part of the labor–management negotiation process that seeks solutions beneficial to both sides.

Interactional justice A concept of justice referring to the interpersonal nature of how the outcomes were implemented.

Internal analysis The process of examining an organization's strengths and weaknesses.

Internal growth strategy A focus on new market and product development, innovation, and joint ventures.

Internal labor force Labor force of current employees.

Internet A tool used for communications and to locate and gather resources such as software and reports.

Interview Situation in which people may be asked questions about their work and personal experiences, strengths and weaknesses, and career plans.

Intraorganizational bargaining The part of the labor–management negotiation process that focuses on the conflicting objectives of factions within labor and management.

Involuntary turnover Turnover initiated by the organization (often among people who would prefer to stay).

ISO 9000 A series of quality assurance standards developed by the International Organization for Standardization in Switzerland. ISO 9000 certification is a requirement for doing business in many countries, including the European Community, Austria, Finland, Iceland, Liechtenstein, Norway, Sweden, Switzerland, Australia, Japan, South America, and Africa.

Job analysis The process of getting detailed information about jobs.

Job description A list of the tasks, duties, and responsibilities that a job entails.

Job design The process of defining the way work will be performed and the tasks that will be required in a given job.

Job enlargement Adding challenges or new responsibilities to an employee's current job.

Job enrichment Ways to add complexity and meaningfulness to a person's work.

Job evaluation An administrative procedure used to measure job worth.

Job experiences The relationships, problems, demands, tasks, and other features that employees face in their jobs.

Job involvement The degree to which people identify themselves with their jobs.

Job rotation The process of systematically moving a single individual from one job to another over the course of time. The job assignments may be in various functional areas of the company or movement between jobs in a single functional area or department.

Job satisfaction A pleasurable feeling that results from the perception that one's job fulfills or allows for the fulfillment of one's important job values.

Job specification A list of the knowledge, skills, abilities, and other characteristics that an individual must have to perform a job.

Job structure The relative pay of jobs in an organization.

Joint union—management training program Program providing a wide range of services designed to help employees learn skills that are directly related to their job and also develop skills that are valuable in other companies or industries.

Key jobs Benchmark jobs, used in pay surveys, that have relatively stable content and are common to many organizations.

Landrum-Griffin Act The 1959 act that regulated unions' actions and their internal affairs (e.g., financial disclosure and conduct of elections).

Laser disc technology Technology that uses a laser to provide high-quality video and sound.

Leaderless group discussion A team of five to seven employees assigned a problem to solve together within a certain time period.

Leading indicator An objective measure that accurately predicts future labor demand.

Learning organization An organization whose employees are continuously attempting to learn new things and apply what they learn to improve product or service quality.

Long-term–short-term orientation One of Hofstede's cultural dimensions; describes how a culture balances immediate benefits with future rewards.

Maintenance of membership Union rules requiring members to remain members for a certain period of time (e.g., the length of the union contract).

Malcolm Baldrige National Quality Award An award established in 1987 to promote quality awareness, to recognize quality achievements of U.S. companies, and to publicize successful quality strategies.

Managing diversity The process of creating an environment that allows all employees to contribute to organizational goals and experience personal growth.

Marginal employee An employee performing at a barely acceptable level due to lack of ability and/or motivation to perform well. Performance is not due to poor work conditions.

Marginal tax rate The percentage of an additional dollar of earnings that goes to taxes.

Masculinity-femininity One of Hofstede's cultural dimensions; describes the division of roles between the sexes within a society.

Mediation A procedure for resolving collective-bargaining impasses by which a mediator with no formal authority acts as a facilitator and go-between in the negotiations.

Mentor An experienced, productive senior employee who helps develop a less-experienced employee.

Merit increase grid A grid that combines an employee's performance rating with that employee's position in a pay range to determine the size and frequency of his or her pay increases.

Minimum wage The lowest amount that employers are legally allowed to pay; the 1990 amendment of the Fair Labor Standards Act permits a subminimum wage to workers under the age of 20 for a period of up to 90 days.

Motivation to learn The desire of the trainee to learn the content of a training program.

Myers-Briggs Type Indicator (MBTI) A psychological test used for team building and leadership development that identifies employees' preferences for energy, information gathering, decision making, and life-style.

Needs assessment The process used to determine if training is necessary.

Negative affectivity A dispositional dimension that reflects pervasive individual differences in satisfaction with any and all aspects of life.

Network A combination of desktop computers, computer terminals, and mainframes or minicomputers that share access to databases and a method to transmit information throughout the system.

New technologies Current applications of knowledge, procedures, and equipment that have not been previously used. Usually involves replacing human labor with equipment, information processing, or some combination of the two.

Nonkey jobs Jobs that are unique to organizations and that cannot be directly valued or compared through the use of market surveys.

Occupational Safety and Health Act of 1970 (OSHA) The law that authorizes the federal government to establish and enforce occupational safety and health standards for all places of employment affecting interstate commerce.

Opportunity to perform The extent to which the trainee is provided with or actively seeks experience with newly learned knowledge; opportunity to use learned capabilities.

Organizational analysis A process for determining the appropriateness of training.

Organizational commitment The degree to which an employee identifies with the organization and is willing to put forth effort on its behalf.

Organizational socialization The process by which new employees are transformed into effective members of a company.

Outcome fairness The judgment that people make with respect to the outcomes received relative to the outcomes received by other people with whom they identity.

Outplacement counseling Counseling to help displaced employees manage the transition from one job to another.

Output A job's performance standards.

Outsourcing An organization's use of an outside organization for a broad set of services.

Overlearning The continuation of practice even after trainees have been able to perform the objective several times.

Parent country The country in which a company's corporate headquarters is located.

Parent-country nationals (PCNs) Employees who were born and live in a parent country.

Pay grade Jobs of similar worth or content grouped together for pay administration purposes.

Pay level The average pay, including wages, salaries, and bonuses, of jobs in an organization.

Pay-policy line A mathematical expression that describes the relationship between a job's pay and its job evaluation points.

Pay structure The relative pay of different jobs (job structure) and how much they are paid (pay level).

Pension Benefit Guaranty Corporation (PBGC) The agency that guarantees to pay employees a basic retirement benefit in the event that financial difficulties force a company to terminate or reduce employee pension benefits.

Performance appraisal The process through which an organization gets information on how well an employee is doing his or her job.

Performance feedback The process of providing employees with information regarding their performance effectiveness.

Performance management The means through which managers ensure that employees' activities and outputs are congruent with the organization's goals.

Performance planning and evaluation (PPE) Any system that seeks to tie the formal performance appraisal process to the company's strategies by specifying at the beginning of the evaluation period the types and level of performance that must be accomplished in order to achieve the strategy.

Person analysis A process for determining whether employees need training, who needs training, and whether employees are ready for training.

Person characteristics An employee's knowledge, skills, ability, and attitudes.

Personnel selection The process by which companies decide who will or will not be allowed into their organization.

Power distance One of Hofstede's cultural dimensions; concerns how a culture deals with hierarchical power relationships and the unequal distribution of power.

Predictive validation A criterion-related validity study that seeks to establish an empirical relationship between applicants' test scores and their eventual performance on the job.

Preferred provider organization (PPO) A group of health-care providers who contract with employers, insurance companies, and so forth to provide health care at a reduced fee.

Pregnancy Discrimination Act of 1978 The law that requires employers that offer disability plans to treat pregnancy as they would any other disability.

Presentation methods Training methods in which trainees are passive recipients of information.

Principal In agency theory, the owner of a business; in human resource management, may refer to a manager.

Procedural justice A concept of justice focusing on the methods used to determine the outcomes received.

Profit sharing A group compensation plan in which payments are based on a measure of organization performance (profits) and do not become part of the employees' base salary.

Progression of withdrawal A set of behaviors that dissatisfied individuals enact to avoid the work situation.

Promotion Advances into positions with greater challenge, more responsibility, and more authority than the employee's previous job.

Protean career A career that is frequently changing due to both changes in the person's interests, abilities, and values and changes in the work environment.

Psychological contract The expectations that employers and employees have about each other.

Psychological success The feeling of pride and accomplishment that comes from achieving life goals.

Psychological support Serving as a friend and role model, providing positive regard and acceptance, and creating an outlet for a protégé to talk about anxieties and fears.

Quantitative ability Concerns the speed and accuracy with which one can solve arithmetic problems of all kinds.

Range spread The distance between the minimum and maximum amounts in a pay grade.

Reaction outcomes Trainees' perceptions of a training program including the facilities, trainers, and content.

Readability The difficulty level of written materials.

Readiness for training The extent to which (1) employees have the personal characteristics necessary to learn program content and apply it on the job and (2) the work environment will facilitate learning and not interfere with performance

Realistic job preview Accurate information about the attractive and unattractive aspects of a job, working conditions, company, and location to ensure that potential employees develop appropriate expectations.

Reasonable accommodation Making facilities readily accessible to and usable by individuals with disabilities.

Reasoning ability Refers to a person's capacity to invent solutions to many diverse problems.

Recruitment The process of seeking applicants for potential employment.

Reengineering Review and redesign of work processes to make them more efficient and improve the quality of the end product or service.

Referrals People who are prompted to apply for a job by someone within the organization.

Relational database A database structure that stores information in separate files that can be linked by common elements.

Reliability The consistency of a performance measure; the degree to which a performance measure is free from random error.

Repatriation The preparation of expatriates for return to the parent company and country from a foreign assignment.

Repurposing Directly translating a training program that uses a traditional training method onto the Web.

Request for proposal (RFP) A document that outlines for potential vendors and consultants the type of service the company is seeking, the type and number of references needed, the number of employees who need to be trained, funding for the project, the follow-up process used to determine level of satisfaction and service, expected date of completion of the project, and the date when proposals must be received by the company.

Results Measurements used to determine a training program's payoff for a company.

Return on investment (ROI) A measure comparing a training program's monetary benefits with its cost.

Right-to-work laws State laws that make union shops, maintenance of membership, and agency shops illegal.

Role ambiguity Uncertainty about what an organization expects from an employee in terms of what to do and how to do it.

Role analysis technique A method that enables a role occupant and other members of the role occupant's role set to specify and examine their expectations for the role occupant.

Role behaviors Behaviors that are required of an individual in his or her role as a job holder in a social work environment.

Role conflict Recognition of incompatible or contradictory demands by the person occupying the role.

Role overload A state in which too many expectations or demands are placed on a person.

Role play A participant taking the part or role of a manager or other employee.

Role underload A state in which too few expectations or demands are placed on a person.

Sabbatical A leave of absence from the company to renew or develop skills.

Safety awareness programs Employer programs that attempt to instill symbolic and substantive changes in the organization's emphasis on safety.

School-to-work Programs including basic-skills training and joint training ventures with universities, community colleges, and high schools.

Selection The process by which an organization attempts to identify applicants with the necessary knowledge, skills, abilities, and other characteristics that will help it achieve its goals.

Self-directed learning A program in which employees take responsibility for all aspects of learning.

Self-efficacy The employees' belief that they can successfully learn the content of a training program.

Self-service Giving employees control of HR transactions.

Situational interview An interview procedure where applicants are confronted with specific issues, questions, or problems that are likely to arise on the job.

Skill-based outcomes Outcomes used to assess the level of technical or motor skills and behaviors.

Skill-based pay Pay based on the skills employees acquire and are capable of using.

Specificity The extent to which a performance measure gives detailed guidance to employees about what is expected of them and how they can meet these expectations.

Standard deviation rule A rule used to analyze employment tests to determine disparate impact; it uses the difference between the expected representation for minority groups and the actual representation to determine whether the difference between the two is greater than would occur by chance.

Stock option An employee ownership plan that gives employees the opportunity to buy the company's stock at a previously fixed price.

Strategic choice The organization's strategy; the ways an organization will attempt to fulfill its mission and achieve its long-term goals.

Strategic congruence The extent to which the performance management system elicits job performance that is consistent with the organization's strategy, goals, and culture.

Strategic human resource management (SHRM) A pattern of planned human resource deployments and activities intended to enable an organization to achieve its goals.

Strategy formulation The process of deciding on a strategic direction by defining a company's mission and goals, its external opportunities and threats, and its internal strengths and weaknesses.

Strategy implementation The process of devising structures and allocating resources to enact the strategy a company has chosen.

Succession planning The identification and tracking of high-potential employees capable of filling higher-level managerial positions.

Summary plan description A reporting requirement of the Employee Retirement Income Security Act (ERISA) that obligates employers to describe the plan's funding, eligibility requirements, risks, and so forth within 90 days after an employee has entered the plan.

Support network A group of two or more trainees who agree to meet and discuss their progress in using learned capabilities on the job

System-level learning Learning that an organization is able to preserve over time.

Taft-Hartley Act The 1947 act that outlined unfair union labor practices.

Task analysis The process of identifying the tasks, knowledge, skills, and behaviors that need to be emphasized in training.

Team leader training Training of the team manager or facilitator.

Technic of Operations Review (TOR) Method of determining safety problems via an analysis of past accidents.

Third country A country other than a host or parent country.

Third-country nationals (TCNs) Employees born in a country other than a parent or host country.

360-degree feedback process A performance appraisal process for managers that includes evaluations from a wide range of persons who interact with the manager. The process includes self-evaluations as well as evaluations from the manager's boss, subordinates, peers, and customers.

Total quality management (TQM) A cooperative form of doing business that relies on the talents and capabilities of both labor and management to continually improve quality and productivity.

Training A planned effort to facilitate the learning of job-related knowledge, skills, and behavior by employees.

Training administration Coordinating activities before, during, and after a training program.

Training outcomes A way to evaluate the effectiveness of a training program based on cognitive, skill-based, affective, and results outcomes.

Transaction processing Computations and calculations used to review and document HR decisions and practices.

Transfer The movement of an employee to a different job assignment in a different area of the company.

Transfer of training The use of knowledge, skills, and behaviors learned in training on the job.

Transitional matrices Matrices showing the proportion or number of employees in different job categories at different times.

Transnational process The extent to which a company's planning and decision-making processes include representatives and ideas from a variety of cultures.

Transnational representation Reflects the multinational composition of a company's managers.

Transnational scope A company's ability to make HR decisions from an international perspective.

Uncertainty avoidance One of Hofstede's cultural dimensions; describes how cultures seek to deal with an unpredictable future.

Union shop A union security provision that requires a person to join the union within a certain amount of time after being hired.

Upward feedback A performance appraisal process for managers that includes subordinates' evaluations.

Utility The degree to which the information provided by selection methods enhances the effectiveness of selecting personnel in real organizations.

Utility analysis An assessment of the dollar value of training based on the difference in job performance between trained and untrained employees, the number of individuals trained, the length of time training is expected to influence performance, and the variability in job performance among untrained employees.

Validity The extent to which a performance measure assesses all the relevant—and only the relevant—aspects of job performance.

Verbal comprehension Refers to a person's capacity to understand and use written and spoken language.

Virtual reality Computer-based technology that provides trainees with a three-dimensional learning experience. Trainees operate in a simulated environment that responds to their behaviors and reactions.

Voicing A formal opportunity to complain about one's work situation

Voluntary turnover Turnover initiated by employees.

Web-based training Training delivered on public (Internet) or private computer networks (intranets) and displayed by a Web browser.

Whistle-blowing Making grievances public by going to the media or government.

Work-force utilization review A comparison of the proportion of workers in protected subgroups with the proportion that each subgroup represents in the relevant labor market.

World Wide Web Service on the Internet that provides browser software allowing the user to explore the items (home pages) on the Web.

Name and Company Index

Subject Index